Your fully reengineered Microsoft Study Guide.

The all-new learning format of your Microsoft study guide delivers in-depth prep [...] tive-by-objective review—along with great new study tools to help prepare you for the j [...]

- Relevant exam objectives highlighted at the start of each chapter

- "Why This Chapter Matters" and "Real World" sidebars on how you can apply learning concepts to the job

- Case scenario exercises where you work through a multi-step, real-world solution

- Troubleshooting labs on a simulated operating system for practical field experience

D0099744

3 User Accounts

Exam Objectives in this Chapter:

- Create and manage user accounts.
  - Create and modify user accounts by using the Active Directory Users and Computers MMC snap-in.
  - Create and modify user accounts by using automation.
  - Import user accounts.
- Manage local, roaming, and mandatory user profiles.
- Troubleshoot user accounts.
  - Diagnose and resolve account lockouts.
  - Diagnose and resolve issues related to user account properties.
- Troubleshoot user authentication issues.

Why This Chapter Matters

Before individuals in your enterprise can begin to access resources they require, you must enable authentication of those individuals. Of course, the primary component of that authentication is the user's identity, maintained as an account in Active Directory. In this chapter, you will review and enhance your knowledge related to the creation, maintenance, and troubleshooting of user accounts and authentication.

Each enterprise, and each day, brings with it a unique set of challenges related to user management. The properties you configure for a standard user account are likely to be different from those you apply to the account of a Help Desk team member, which are different still from those configured on the built-in Administrator account. Skills that are effective to create or modify a single user account become clumsy and inefficient when you are working with masses of accounts, for example when managing the accounts for a number of new hires.

To effectively address a diverse sampling of account management scenarios, we will examine a variety of user management skills and tools including the Active Directory Users & Computers snap-in and powerful command-line utilities.

3-1

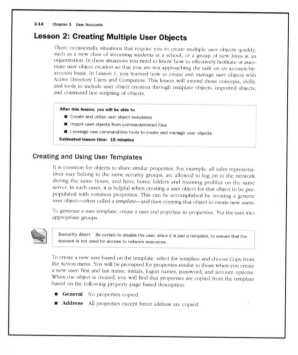

Lesson 2: Creating Multiple User Objects

There occasionally situations that require you to create multiple user objects quickly, such as a new class of incoming students at a school, or a group of new hires at an organization. In these situations you need to know how to effectively facilitate or automate user object creation so that you are not approaching the task on an account-by-account basis. In Lesson 1, you learned how to create and manage user objects with Active Directory Users and Computers. This lesson will extend those concepts, skills, and tools to include user object creation through template objects, imported objects, and command line scripting of objects.

After this lesson, you will be able to

- Create and utilize user object templates
- Import user objects from comma-delimited files
- Leverage new command-line tools to create and manage user objects

Estimated lesson time: 15 minutes

Creating and Using User Templates

It is common for objects to share similar properties. For example, all sales representatives may belong to the same security groups, are allowed to log on to the network during the same hours, and have home folders and roaming profiles on the same server. In such cases, it is helpful when creating a user object for that object to be pre-populated with common properties. This can be accomplished by creating a generic user object—often called a *template*—and then copying that object to create new users.

To generate a user template, create a user and populate its properties. Put the user into appropriate groups.

> **Security Alert** Be certain to disable the user, since it is just a template, to ensure that the account is not used for access to network resources.

To create a new user based on the template, select the template and choose Copy from the Action menu. You will be prompted for properties similar to those when you create a new user: first and last name, initials, logon names, password, and account options. When the object is created, you will find that properties are copied from the template based on the following property-page based description:

- **General** No properties copied.
- **Address** All properties except Street address are copied.

- "Off the Record" sidebars bridge the gap between how things *should* work and how they *do* work

- Security Alerts and Planning Tips you can apply in the real world

- Complete objective-by-objective review section

- Exam highlights—key points and terms you should know

- Exam tips written by industry insiders

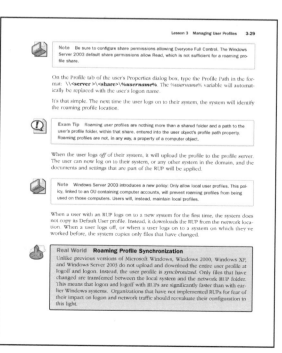

> **Note** Be sure to configure share permissions allowing Everyone Full Control. The Windows Server 2003 default share permissions allow Read, which is not sufficient for a roaming profile share.

On the Profile tab of the user's Properties dialog box, type the Profile Path in the format: \\<server>\<share>\%username%. The %username% variable will automatically be replaced with the user's logon name.

It's that simple. The next time the user logs on to their system, the system will identify the roaming profile location.

> **Exam Tip** Roaming user profiles are nothing more than a shared folder and a path to the user's profile folder, within that share, entered into the user object's profile path property. Roaming profiles are not, in any way, a property of a computer object.

When the user logs *off* of their system, it will upload the profile to the profile server. The user can now log on to their system, or any other system in the domain, and the documents and settings that are part of the RUP will be applied.

> **Note** Windows Server 2003 introduces a new policy: Only allow local user profiles. This policy, linked to an OU containing computer accounts, will prevent roaming profiles from being used on those computers. Users will, instead, maintain local profiles.

When a user with an RUP logs on to a new system for the first time, the system does not copy its Default User profile. Instead, it downloads the RUP from the network location. When a user logs off, or when a user logs on to a system on which they've worked before, the system copies only files that have changed.

> **Real World**   **Roaming Profile Synchronization**
>
> Unlike previous versions of Microsoft Windows, Windows 2000, Windows XP, and Windows Server 2003 do not upload and download the entire user profile at logoff and logon. Instead, the user profile is *synchronized*. Only files that have changed are transferred between the local system and the network RUP folder. This means that logon and logoff with RUPs are significantly faster than with earlier Windows systems. Organizations that have not implemented RUPs for fear of their impact on logon and network traffic should re-evaluate their configuration in this light.

MCSA/MCSE

Exam 70-291

Implementing, Managing, and
Maintaining a Microsoft®

WINDOWS
SERVER 2003
NETWORK
INFRASTRUCTURE

J.C. Mackin and Ian McLean

Self-Paced

Training Kit

PUBLISHED BY
Microsoft Press
A Division of Microsoft Corporation
One Microsoft Way
Redmond, Washington 98052-6399

Library of Congress Cataloging-in-Publication Data
Mackin, J. C.
     MCSA/MCSE self-paced training kit (exam 70-291): implementing, managing, and maintaining a Microsoft Windows Server 2003 network infrastructure / J. C. Mackin, Ian McLean.
          p. cm.
     ISBN 0-7356-1439-3
     1. Electronic data processing personnel--Certification.   2. Microsoft software--Examinations--study guides.   3. Microsoft Windows server.
A. II. Title.

     QA76.3.M3225   2003
     005.7'13769--dc21   2003054026

Printed and bound in the United States of America.

3 4 5 6 7 8 9   QWT   8 7 6 5

Distributed in Canada by H.B. Fenn and Company Ltd.

A CIP catalogue record for this book is available from the British Library.

Microsoft Press books are available through booksellers and distributors worldwide. For further information about international editions, contact your local Microsoft Corporation office or contact Microsoft Press International directly at fax (425) 936-7329. Visit our Web site at www.microsoft.com/mspress. Send comments to *tkinput@microsoft.com*.

Acquisitions Editor: Kathy Harding
Project Editors: Valerie Woolley and Jean Trenary
Technical Editor: Tony Northrup

Body Part No. X08-16603

J.C. Mackin

J.C. Mackin (MCSA, MCSE, MCT) is a writer, editor, consultant, and trainer whose books include the Internet Security and Acceleration Server 2000 Training Kit. He holds a Master's degree in Telecommunications and Network Management.

Ian McLean

Ian McLean (MCSE, MCDBA, MCT) has over 35 years experience in industry, commerce and education. He started his career as an electronics engineer before going into distance learning and then education as a university professor, and currently runs his own consultancy company. Ian has written 14 books plus many papers and technical articles. He has been working with networks since the early 1980s and with Microsoft network operating systems since 1997.

Contents at a Glance

Part 1 Learn at Your Own Pace

1 Understanding Windows Server 2003 Networks .1-1
2 Understanding TCP/IP 2-1
3 Monitoring and Troubleshooting TCP/IP Connections 3-1
4 Configuring DNS Servers and Clients 4-1
5 Implementing a DNS Infrastructure 5-1
6 Monitoring and Troubleshooting DNS 6-1
7 Configuring DHCP Servers and Clients 7-1
8 Monitoring and Troubleshooting DHCP 8-1
9 Routing with Windows Server 2003 9-1
10 Configuring and Managing Remote Access .10-1
11 Managing Network Security 11-1
12 Maintaining a Network Infrastructure 12-1

Part 2 Prepare for the Exam

13 Implementing, Managing, and Maintaining IP Addressing (1.0) 13-1
14 Implementing, Managing, and Maintaining Name Resolution (2.0) . . .14-1
15 Implementing, Managing, and Maintaining Network Security (3.0) . . .15-1
16 Implementing, Managing, and Maintaining Routing
    And Remote Access (4.0) 16-1
17 Maintaining a Network Infrastructure (5.0) .17-1

Practices

Working with Octet Notations 2-18

Working with Subnet Masks and Subnets 2-37

Configuring TCP/IP Addresses 2-47

Using Network Monitor 3-13

Running Network Diagnostics and Netdiag 3-26

Capturing Name Resolution Traffic. 4-8

Installing a DNS Server 4-38

Configuring a Primary DNS Suffix. 4-55

Configuring a DNS Server to Perform Recursion .4-56

Comparing NetBIOS and DNS Name Resolution Traffic. 5-12

Verifying SRV Resource Records for Active Directory DNS 5-14

Deploying a Secondary DNS Server 5-37

Creating a Zone Delegation 5-59

Deploying a Stub Zone 5-71

Using DNS Troubleshooting Tools 6-12

Installing and Configuring a DHCP Server 7-15

Performing a Manual Backup of the DHCP Server. 7-37

Creating a New Superscope 7-37

Analyzing DHCP Messages 8-14

Enabling and Configuring Routing And Remote Access. 9-25

Configuring Demand-Dial Routing. 9-38

Installing and Configuring NAT 9-48

Creating a Dial-Up Access Server 10-19

Deploying Remote Access. 10-43

Configuring a VPN 10-61

Deploying a RADIUS Server. 10-78

Creating and Using the Security Configuration And Analysis Console 11-14

Using Network Security Protocols. 11-51

Troubleshoot IPSec with IPSec Monitor 11-74

Troubleshoot Logon Issues with Network Monitor 11-77

Use Event Logs for Troubleshooting 11-78

Sampling Performance 12-17

Verifying the Configuration of DNS Forwarding. 12-28

Configuring Services 12-38

Tables

Table 1-1: Management and Monitoring Tools Subcomponents 1-26

Table 1-2: Networking Service Subcomponents. 1-27

Table 1-3: Other Network File And Print Services Subcomponents. 1-28

Table 1-4: Certificate Services Subcomponents 1-28

Table 2-1: Private Address Ranges 2-8

Table 2-2: Potential Values in a Binary Octet 2-11

Table 2-3: IP Address Classes 2-15

Table 2-4: Subnet Masks.. 2-17

Table 2-5: Class C Subnet Mask Options (Static) 2-35

Table 2-6: VLSM Subnet IDs 2-36

Table 3-1: Network Monitor Versions... 3-4

Table 3-2: Network Monitor Capture Window 3-7

Table 3-3: Netdiag Tests 3-23

Table 4-1: Computer Names and Name Suffixes 4-4

Table 4-2: Comparisons of NetBIOS and DNS Names......................... 4-5

Table 4-3: Typical Resource Record Fields 4-33

Table 4-4: FQDNs of a Multihomed Host..................................... 4-48

Table 5-1: Zone Replication Options 5-24

Table 5-2: Default DNS Installation Settings.................................. 5-44

Table 5-3: Name Checking Methods 5-50

Table 6-1: Command-Line Options Available with Set.......................... 6-6

Table 6-2: DNS Performance Counters 6-26

Table 8-1: DHCP Header Fields 8-6

Table 8-2: DHCP Server Log Fields 8-22

Table 8-3: Log Event Codes 50 and Above 8-23

Table 8-4: DHCP Database Corruption Errors 8-37

Table 9-1: Comparing Static and Dynamic Routing............................ 9-18

Table 9-2: Comparison of Translated Connections Features.................... 9-47

Table 10-1: Authentication Protocol Features................................. 10-11

Table 10-2: Authentication Protocol Support 10-12

Table 10-3: Encryption Types.. 10-32

Table 11-1: Network Security Protocols 11-4

Table 11-2: Security Template Sections 11-6

Table 11-3: Security Templates 11-7

Table 11-4: Secedit Syntax 11-10

Table 11-5: Security Options for Improving Network Security.................. 11-12

Table 11-6: Netsh IPSec (Dynamic|Static) Show Commands................... 11-33

Table 11-7: IPSec Main Mode Statistics 11-35

Table 11-8: IPSec Quick Mode Statistics..................................... 11-36

Table 11-9: Netcap Syntax.. 11-38

Table 12-1: Helpful Counters.. 12-6

Table 12-2: Repair Actions 12-25

Troubleshooting Labs

Chapter 4 4-61
Chapter 5 5-76
Chapter 6 6-30
Chapter 7 7-48
Chapter 8 8-40
Chapter 9 9-76
Chapter 10 10-83
Chapter 11 11-82

Case Scenarios Exercises

Chapter 1 1-30
Chapter 2 2-51
Chapter 3 3-31
Chapter 4 4-60
Chapter 5 5-74
Chapter 6 6-29
Chapter 7 7-46
Chapter 8 8-38
Chapter 9 9-77
Chapter 10 10-82
Chapter 12 12-40

Contents

About This Book xxi
   Intended Audience xxi
   Prerequisites xxi
   About the CD-ROM. xxi
   Features of This Book xxiii
      Informational Notes. xxiv
      Notational Conventions xxv
      Keyboard Conventions xxvi
   Getting Started xxvi
      Hardware Requirements. xxvi
      Software Requirements xxvii
      Setup Instructions. xxvii
   The Microsoft Certified Professional Program xviii
      Certifications xxix
      Requirements for Becoming a Microsoft Certified Professional xxx
   Technical Support xxx
   Evaluation Edition Software Support xxxi

Part 1   Learn at Your Own Pace

1   Understanding Windows Server 2003 Networks   1-1
   Before You Begin. 1-1
   Lesson 1: Understanding Network Infrastructures. .1-3
      Defining a Network Infrastructure 1-3
      Analyzing Windows Server 2003 Networks 1-6
      Lesson Review 1-11
      Lesson Summary 1-12
   Lesson 2: Networking with Default Components in Windows Server 2003 1-13
      Viewing Network Connections. 1-13
      Default Networking and Workgroups 1-20
      Routing and Windows Server 2003 Network Infrastructure 1-20
      Lesson Review 1-21
      Lesson Summary 1-22
   Lesson 3: Extending a Windows Server 2003 Network Infrastructure 1-23
      Adding Components to a Connection 1-23
      Installing Windows Networking Components 1-25
      Adding Active Directory to a Windows Infrastructure. 1-28
      Lesson Review 1-28

Lesson Summary 1-29

Case Scenario Exercise 1-30

Exam Highlights 1-31

Key Points 1-31

Key Terms. 1-32

Questions and Answers 1-35

2 Understanding TCP/IP   2-1

Before You Begin. 2-1

Lesson 1: Understanding TCP/IP. 2-2

Exploring the Layers of the TCP/IP Model 2-2

Lesson Review 2-5

Lesson Summary 2-6

Lesson 2: Understanding IP Addressing 2-7

Using Public IP Addresses 2-7

Using Private IP Addresses 2-7

Examining IP Addressing Methods 2-8

Understanding the Structure of IP Addresses 2-9

Subnet Masks 2-16

Understanding Default Gateways 2-18

Practice: Working with Octet Notations 2-18

Lesson Review 2-19

Lesson Summary 2-20

Lesson 3: Subnetting and Supernetting IP Networks 2-22

Understanding Subnetting 2-22

Estimating Subnet Address Ranges 2-32

Summarizing Routes Through Supernetting 2-32

Using Classless Interdomain Routing 2-33

Using Variable-Length Subnet Masks 2-34

Practice: Working with Subnet Masks and Subnets 2-37

Lesson Review 2-40

Lesson Summary 2-41

Lesson 4: Installing and Configuring TCP/IP 2-42

Installing TCP/IP 2-42

Examining TCP/IP Configuration Methods 2-43

Practice: Configuring TCP/IP Addresses 2-47

Lesson Review 2-50

Lesson Summary 2-50

Case Scenario Exercise 2-51

Exam Highlights 2-54

    Key Points 2-54

    Key Terms. 2-55

Questions and Answers 2-56

3   Monitoring and Troubleshooting TCP/IP Connections   3-1

Before You Begin. 3-2

Lesson 1: Analyzing Traffic Using Network Monitor .3-3

    Understanding Network Monitor 3-3

    Exploring Network Monitor Components 3-4

    How Network Monitor Works 3-6

    Adding Parsers to Network Monitor. 3-12

    Practice: Using Network Monitor. 3-13

    Lesson Review 3-16

    Lesson Summary 3-17

Lesson 2: Troubleshooting TCP/IP Connections 3-19

    Faulty TCP/IP Configuration 3-19

    Network Diagnostics 3-20

    Troubleshooting Connections Using Ping and PathPing 3-23

    Troubleshooting with Tracert. 3-25

    Troubleshooting Using the ARP Tool 3-26

    Practice: Running Network Diagnostics and Netdiag. 3-26

    Lesson Review 3-30

    Lesson Summary 3-31

Case Scenario Exercise 3-31

Exam Highlights 3-34

    Key Points 3-34

    Key Terms. 3-35

Questions and Answers 3-36

4   Configuring DNS Servers and Clients   4-1

Before You Begin. 4-2

Lesson 1: Understanding Name Resolution in Windows Server 2003 4-3

    Comparing DNS and NetBIOS. 4-3

    Disabling NetBIOS. 4-7

    Practice: Capturing Name Resolution Traffic 4-8

    Lesson Review 4-10

    Lesson Summary 4-10

Lesson 2: Understanding DNS in Windows Server 2003 Networks 4-12

   Exploring DNS 4-12

   DNS Components 4-14

   Understanding How a DNS Query Works 4-16

   Understanding How Caching Works 4-22

   Lesson Review 4-24

   Lesson Summary 4-25

Lesson 3: Deploying DNS Servers 4-26

   Installing the DNS Server Service 4-26

   Configuring a DNS Server 4-27

   Understanding Server Types 4-29

   Creating Resource Records 4-31

   Viewing and Clearing the DNS Server Cache 4-37

   Practice: Installing a DNS Server 4-38

   Lesson Review 4-42

   Lesson Summary 4-43

Lesson 4: Configuring DNS Clients 4-44

   Configuring Client Settings 4-44

   Configuring Dynamic Update Options 4-51

   Default Client Update Behavior 4-52

   Configuring TCP/IP Settings for DNS Clients 4-53

   Viewing and Clearing the DNS Resolver Cache 4-54

   Practice 1: Configuring a Primary DNS Suffix 4-55

   Practice 2: Configuring a DNS Server to Perform Recursion 4-56

   Lesson Review 4-59

   Lesson Summary 4-59

Case Scenario Exercise 4-60

Troubleshooting Lab 4-61

Exam Highlights 4-63

   Key Points 4-63

   Key Terms 4-64

Questions and Answers 4-65

5   Implementing a DNS Infrastructure   5-1

   Before You Begin 5-2

Lesson 1: Configuring DNS Server Properties 5-3

   Exploring DNS Server Properties Tabs 5-3

   Practice 1: Comparing NetBIOS and DNS Name Resolution Traffic 5-12

   Practice 2: Verifying SRV Resource Records for Active Directory in DNS 5-14

Lesson Review 5-18
Lesson Summary 5-19
Lesson 2: Configuring Zone Properties and Transfers 5-20
Exploring DNS Zone Properties. 5-20
Practice: Deploying a Secondary DNS Server. .5-37
Lesson Review 5-40
Lesson Summary 5-42
Lesson 3: Configuring Advanced DNS Server Properties 5-43
Tuning Advanced Server Options. 5-43
Lesson Review 5-52
Lesson Summary 5-55
Lesson 4: Creating Zone Delegations. 5-56
Delegating Zones 5-56
Creating a Zone Delegation 5-59
Practice: Creating a Zone Delegation 5-59
Lesson Review 5-62
Lesson Summary 5-64
Lesson 5: Deploying Stub Zones 5-65
Understanding Stub Zones. 5-65
Benefits of Stub Zones 5-66
When to Use Stub Zones. 5-66
Stub Zone Updates 5-70
Practice: Deploying a Stub Zone 5-71
Lesson Review 5-72
Lesson Summary 5-73
Case Scenario Exercise 5-74
Troubleshooting Lab 5-76
Exam Highlights 5-78
Key Points 5-78
Key Terms. 5-79
Questions and Answers. 5-80

6   **Monitoring and Troubleshooting DNS**   **6-1**
Before You Begin. 6-1
Lesson 1: Using DNS Troubleshooting Tools 6-3
Querying DNS with Nslookup 6-3
Viewing the DNS Events Log 6-9
DNS Debug Log. 6-11
Practice: Using DNS Troubleshooting Tools 6-12

Lesson Review 6-18

Lesson Summary 6-19

Lesson 2: Using DNS Monitoring Tools. 6-20

Using Replication Monitor 6-20

Monitoring DNS Performance with System Monitor. 6-24

Lesson Review 6-27

Lesson Summary 6-28

Case Scenario Exercise 6-29

Troubleshooting Lab 6-30

Exam Highlights 6-32

Key Points 6-32

Key Terms. 6-33

Questions and Answers 6-34

7   Configuring DHCP Servers and Clients   7-1

Before You Begin. 7-2

Lesson 1: Configuring the DHCP Server 7-3

Benefits of DHCP 7-3

Installing the DHCP Server Service 7-4

Authorizing the Server 7-5

Configuring Scopes 7-6

Assigning DHCP Options 7-11

Activating a Scope. 7-13

Configuring the Client 7-13

Verifying the Configuration 7-15

Practice: Installing and Configuring a DHCP Server. 7-15

Lesson Review 7-20

Lesson Summary 7-21

Lesson 2: Managing DHCP in Windows Networks 7-22

Changing DCHP Server Status 7-22

Managing DHCP from a Command Line. .7-24

Connecting Clients to Remote DHCP Servers. 7-26

Using Superscopes 7-26

Changing the Addressing of a Subnet 7-30

Backing Up the DHCP Server Database. .7-31

Manually Compacting a DHCP Server 7-33

Using Options Classes 7-34

Practice 1: Performing a Manual Backup of the DHCP Server 7-37

Practice 2: Creating a New Superscope. 7-37

Lesson Review 7-39

Lesson Summary 7-40

Lesson 3: Configuring DHCP Servers to Perform DNS Updates. 7-41

Configuring Dynamic Updates with DHCP. 7-41

Lesson Review 7-45

Lesson Summary 7-46

Case Scenario Exercise 7-46

Troubleshooting Lab 7-48

Exam Highlights 7-50

Key Points 7-50

Key Terms. 7-50

Questions and Answers 7-51

8   Monitoring and Troubleshooting DHCP   8-1

Before You Begin. 8-2

Lesson 1: Analyzing DHCP Traffic. 8-3

Understanding How Clients Obtain Configuration .8-3

Practice: Analyzing DHCP Messages 8-14

Lesson Review 8-18

Lesson Summary 8-19

Lesson 2: Monitoring DHCP Through Audit Logging .8-20

Exploring DHCP Audit Logging. 8-20

Understanding DHCP Server Log File Format 8-22

Lesson Review 8-25

Lesson Summary 8-26

Lesson 3: Troubleshooting DHCP. 8-27

Verifying the Client Configuration 8-27

Verifying the Server Configuration 8-32

Reconciling the DHCP Database 8-34

Checking Event Viewer. 8-35

Lesson Review 8-37

Lesson Summary 8-38

Case Scenario Exercise 8-38

Troubleshooting Lab 8-40

Exam Highlights 8-41

Key Points 8-41

Key Terms. 8-42

Questions and Answers 8-43

9   Routing with Windows Server 2003   9-1

Before You Begin. 9-2
Lesson 1: Configuring Windows Server 2003 for LAN Routing 9-3
    Understanding Routing 9-3
    Using Routing And Remote Access 9-4
    Using the Routing And Remote Access Console. 9-5
    Configuring Routing And Remote Access Service Properties 9-7
    Managing General IP Routing Properties 9-12
    Working with Routing Tables. 9-14
    Exploring LAN Routing Scenarios 9-18
    Understanding Static Routes 9-20
    Static Routing Design Considerations 9-25
    Practice: Enabling and Configuring Routing And Remote Access 9-25
    Lesson Review 9-26
    Lesson Summary 9-27
Lesson 2: Configuring Demand-Dial Routing 9-28
    Configuring Demand-Dial Interfaces 9-28
    Deploying a Demand-Dial Router-to-Router Configuration 9-36
    Troubleshooting Demand-Dial Routing. 9-37
    Practice: Configuring Demand-Dial Routing 9-38
    Lesson Review 9-43
    Lesson Summary 9-44
Lesson 3: Configuring NAT 9-45
    Understanding NAT 9-45
    Troubleshooting NAT 9-48
    Practice: Installing and Configuring NAT. 9-48
    Lesson Review 9-54
    Lesson Summary 9-56
Lesson 4: Configuring and Managing Routing Protocols. 9-57
    Understanding Routing Protocols 9-57
    Configuring RIP 9-58
    OSPF Overview 9-61
    Understanding DHCP Relay Agent. 9-63
    Lesson Review 9-67
    Lesson Summary 9-67
Lesson 5: Configuring Packet Filters 9-68
    Understanding Packet Filters 9-68
    Lesson Review 9-73
    Lesson Summary 9-74

Exam Highlights 9-78
  Key Topics 9-78
  Key Terms. 9-79
Questions and Answers 9-80

10   Configuring and Managing Remote Access   10-1
Before You Begin. 10-2
Lesson 1: Configuring Remote Access Connections 10-3
  Using Dial-Up Networking. 10-3
  Using Remote Access Client Addressing 10-4
  Configuring Remote Access Authentication .10-7
  Practice: Creating a Dial-Up Access Server 10-19
  Lesson Review 10-22
  Lesson Summary 10-23
Lesson 2: Authorizing Remote Access Connections. 10-24
  Configuring Dial-In Properties of the User Account 10-24
  Understanding Remote Access Policies. 10-27
  Exploring Remote Access Authorization Scenarios 10-34
  Troubleshooting Dial-Up Remote Access Connections. 10-39
  Configuring Access Beyond the Remote Access Server. 10-40
  Managing Remote Access Clients. 10-42
  Practice: Deploying Remote Access 10-43
  Lesson Review 10-47
  Lesson Summary 10-48
Lesson 3: Implementing VPNs. 10-49
  Understanding Virtual Private Networks 10-49
  Troubleshooting Remote Access VPNs 10-55
  Troubleshooting Router-to-Router VPNs 10-55
  Configuring VPN Types 10-56
  Practice: Configuring a VPN 10-61
  Lesson Review 10-67
  Lesson Summary 10-68
Lesson 4: Deploying the Internet Authentication Service 10-69
  Exploring RADIUS Server Scenarios 10-69
  Exploring RADIUS Proxy Scenarios 10-72
  Deploying IAS as a RADIUS Server 10-74
  Practice: Deploying a RADIUS Server 10-78
  Lesson Review 10-81
  Lesson Summary 10-81
Case Scenario Exercise 10-82

Troubleshooting Lab 10-83

Exam Highlights 10-84

    Key Topics 10-85

    Key Terms. 10-85

Questions and Answers 10-86

11   Managing Network Security   11-1

Before You Begin. 11-2

Lesson 1: Implementing Secure Network Administration Procedures 11-3

    Introducing Network Security Protocols 11-3

    Using Security Templates to Administer Network Security. 11-4

    Understanding Security Template Settings That
    Affect Network Security 11-12

    Applying the Principle of Least Privilege. 11-13

    Practice: Creating and Using the Security Configuration
    And Analysis Console 11-14

    Lesson Review 11-22

    Lesson Summary 11-23

Lesson 2: Monitoring Network Protocol Security .11-24

    Understanding IPSec. 11-24

    Negotiation Configuration. 11-27

    Negotiation Process 11-28

    Understanding Kerberos 11-39

    Practice: Using Network Security Protocols 11-51

    Lesson Review 11-69

    Lesson Summary 11-70

Lesson 3: Troubleshooting Network Protocol Security 11-71

    Problem 1: Making Your IPSec Policy Work 11-72

    Problem 2: Determining Whether Your IPSec
    Blocking Rules Are Working 11-73

    Problem 3: Determining Whether Kerberos Is Being
    Used for Authentication 11-74

    Practice 1: Troubleshoot IPSec with IPSec Monitor. 11-74

    Practice 2: Troubleshoot Logon Issues with Network Monitor 11-77

    Practice 3: Use Event Logs for Troubleshooting 11-78

    Lesson Review 11-79

    Lesson Summary 11-81

Troubleshooting Lab 11-82

Exam Highlights 11-87

    Key Points 11-87

    Key Terms. 11-88

Questions and Answers 11-89

12   Maintaining a Network Infrastructure   **12-1**
   Before You Begin. 12-2
   Lesson 1: Monitoring Network Performance 12-3
      Using the Networking Tab in Task Manager 12-3
      Performance Console Differences. 12-7
      Monitoring Network Traffic with Netstat 12-13
      Windows Server 2003 "Lite" and "Full" Network Monitor Tools. 12-16
      Practice: Sampling Performance 12-17
      Lesson Review 12-19
      Lesson Summary 12-20
   Lesson 2: Troubleshooting Internet Connectivity 12-21
      Identifying the Specific Networking Issue 12-21
      Verifying the Computer's Network Settings 12-24
      Bridging Multiple Networks. 12-26
      Practice: Verifying the Configuration of DNS Forwarding 12-28
      Lesson Review 12-28
      Lesson Summary 12-30
   Lesson 3: Troubleshooting Server Services 12-31
      Diagnosing and Resolving Issues Related to Service Dependency. 12-31
      Using Service Recovery Options to Diagnose and
      Resolve Service-Related Issues 12-33
      Practice: Configuring Services 12-38
      Lesson Review 12-39
      Lesson Summary 12-40
   Case Scenario Exercise 12-40
   Exam Highlights 12-42
      Key Points 12-42
      Key Terms. 12-43
   Questions and Answers 12-44

Part 2   Prepare for the Exam

13   Implementing, Managing, and Maintaining IP Addressing (1.0)   **13-1**
   Tested Skills and Suggested Practices 13-2
   Further Reading 13-4
   Objective 1.1: Configure TCP/IP Addressing on a Server Computer 13-6
   Objective 1.2: Manage DHCP 13-15
   Objective 1.3: Troubleshoot TCP/IP Addressing 13-27
   Objective 1.4: Troubleshoot DHCP 13-35

14   Implementing, Managing, and Maintaining Name Resolution (2.0)   14-1

Tested Skills and Suggested Practices 14-2

Further Reading 14-3

Objective 2.1: Install and Configure the DNS Server Service. 14-5

Objective 2.2: Manage DNS. 14-17

Objective 2.3: Monitor DNS 14-28

15   Implementing, Managing, and Maintaining Network Security (3.0)   15-1

Tested Skills and Suggested Practices 15-2

Further Reading 15-4

Objective 3.1: Implement Secure Network Administration Procedures 15-5

Objective 3.2: Install and Configure Software Update Infrastructure 15-16

Objective 3.3: Monitor Network Protocol Security. .15-20

Objective 3.4: Troubleshoot Network Protocol Security 15-29

**16   Implementing, Managing, and Maintaining Routing
And Remote Access (4.0)   16-1**

Tested Skills and Suggested Practices 16-2

Further Reading 16-4

Objective 4.1: Configure Routing And Remote Access User Authentication. 16-7

Objective 4.2: Manage Remote Access. 16-19

Objective 4.3: Manage TCP/IP Routing 16-26

Objective 4.4: Provide Secure Access Between Private Networks 16-33

Objective 4.5: Troubleshoot Client Access to Remote Access Services 16-38

Objective 4.6: Troubleshoot Routing and Remote Access Routing 16-44

17   Maintaining a Network Infrastructure (5.0)   17-1

Tested Skills and Suggested Practices 17-1

Further Reading 17-3

Objective 5.1: Monitor Network Traffic. 17-4

Objective 5.2: Troubleshoot Connectivity to the Internet 17-11

Objective 5.3: Troubleshoot Server Services 17-16

Glossary. G-1

Index I-1

About This Book

Welcome to *MCSA/MCSE Self-Paced Training Kit (Exam 70-291): Implementing, Managing, and Maintaining a Microsoft Windows Server 2003 Network Infrastructure*. This book prepares you for the 70-291 exam by teaching you how to configure, manage, and troubleshoot various aspects of a Microsoft Windows Server 2003 network infrastructure. Each chapter walks you through the hands-on deployment and management of these various aspects, including the network addressing, name resolution, routing, remote access, and security. After you read this book, answer the associated questions, and perform all of the exercises included, you will have gained a thorough understanding of the essential components supporting Windows Server 2003 networks.

 See Also For more information about becoming a Microsoft Certified Professional (MCM), see the section entitled "The Microsoft Certified Professional Program" later in this introduction.

Intended Audience

This book was developed for information technology (IT) professionals who plan to take the related Microsoft Certified Professional exam 70-291, as well as IT professionals who implement, administer, and support Windows Server 2003 networks.

 Note Exam skills are subject to change without prior notice and at the sole discretion of Microsoft.

Prerequisites

This training kit requires that students meet the following prerequisites:

- 18 months professional experience working with Windows networks
- Familiarity with networking concepts equivalent to that of a CompTIA Network+ certification

About the CD-ROM

This book includes a Supplemental CD-ROM. This CD-ROM contains a variety of informational aids to complement the book content:

- An electronic version of this book (eBook). For information about using the eBook, see the section "The eBooks" later in this introduction.

- The Microsoft Press Readiness Review Suite, powered by Measure Up. This suite of practice tests and objective reviews contains questions of varying degrees of complexity and offers multiple testing modes. You can assess your understanging of the concepts presented in this book and use the results to develop a learning plan that meets your needs.

- A Macromedia Flash introduction to Software Update Services (SUS).

- An eBook of the *Microsoft Encyclopedia of Networking, Second Edition*, and of the *Microsoft Encyclopedia of Security* provide complete and up-to-date reference materials for networking and security.

- Sample chapters from the following book titles give you additional information and introduce you to other resources that are available from Microsoft Press:

  ❑ *Microsoft Windows Server 2003 Administrator's Companion* by Charlie Russel, Sharon Crawford, and Jason Gerend

  ❑ *Microsoft Windows Server 2003 Deployment Kit: A Microsoft Resource Kit*

  ❑ *Microsoft Windows Security Resource Kit*

- A 22-page white paper published June 2002, entitled "Software Update Services Overview." This paper provides a good introduction to SUS but does not cover issues specific to Windows Server 2003.

- A 95-page white paper published January 2003, entitled "Deploying Microsoft Software Update Services." This paper provides in-depth information about implementing SUS on both Windows 2000 and Windows Server 2003 networks.

> **Important**   Although deploying SUS is not listed among the objectives for exam 70-291, you may nevertheless see questions related to this topic on MCSE exams. It is therefore highly recommended that you review these papers and practice deploying SUS on a test network before taking exam 70-291.

- SUS Server 1.0 with Service Pack 1 (SP1).

- Automatic Updates client (SUS Server 1.0 with Service Pack 1 (SP1).)

- SUS Server with SP1 Release Notes and Installation Instructions.

A second CD-ROM contains a 180-day evaluation edition of Microsoft Windows Server 2003, Enterprise Edition.

> **Important**   The 180-day evaluation edition provided with this training kit is not the full retail product and is provided only for the purposes of training and evaluation. Microsoft Technical Support does not support this evaluation edition.

For additional support information regarding this book and the supplemental CD-ROM (including answers to commonly asked questions about installation and use), visit the Microsoft Press Technical Support Web site at *http://www.microsoft.com/mspress/support/*. You can also e-mail tkinput@microsoft.com or send a letter to Microsoft Press, Attn: Microsoft Press Technical Support, One Microsoft Way, Redmond, WA 98052-6399.

Features of This Book

This book is divided into two parts. Use Part 1 to learn at your own pace and practice what you've learned with practical exercises. Part 2 contains questions and answers that you can use to test yourself on what you've learned.

Part 1: Learn at Your Own Pace

Each chapter in Part 1 identifies the exam objectives that are covered within the chapter, provides an overview of why the topics matter by identifying how the information applies in the real world, and lists any prerequisites that must be met to complete the lessons presented in the chapter.

The chapters are divided into lessons. Lessons contain practices made up of one or more hands-on exercises. These exercises give you an opportunity to use the skills being presented or explore the part of the application being described. Each lesson also has a set of review questions to test your knowledge of the material covered in the lesson. The answers to the questions are found in the Questions and Answers section at the end of each chapter.

After the lessons, you are given an opportunity to apply what you've learned in a case scenario exercise. In this exercise, you work through a multistep solution for a realistic case scenario. You are also given an opportunity to work through a troubleshooting lab that explores difficulties you might encounter when applying what you've learned in this book on the job.

Each chapter ends with a summary of key concepts, as well as a short section listing key topics and terms you need to know before taking the exam, summarizing the key learnings with a focus on the exam.

Real World: Helpful Information

You will find sidebars like this one that contain related information you might find helpful. "Real World" sidebars contain specific information gained through the experience of IT professionals like you.

Part 2: Prepare for the Exam

Part 2 helps to familiarize you with the types of questions that you will encounter on the MCP exam. By reviewing the objectives and the sample questions you can focus on the specific skills that you need to improve before taking the exam.

> **See Also**   For a complete list of MCP exams and their related objectives, go to *http://www.microsoft.com/traincert/mcp*.

Part 2 is organized by the exam's objectives. Each chapter covers one of the primary groups of objectives, called *Objective Domains*. Each chapter lists the tested skills you need to master to answer the exam questions and includes a list of further readings to help you improve your ability to perform the tasks or skills specified by the objectives.

Within each Objective Domain, you will find the related objectives that are covered on the exam. Each objective provides you with several practice exam questions. The answers are accompanied by explanations of each correct and incorrect answer.

> **Note**   These questions are also available on the companion CD-ROM as a practice test.

Informational Notes

The following types of reader aids appear throughout the training kit:

> **Tip**   Contains methods of performing a task more quickly or in a not-so-obvious way.

> **Important**   Contains information that is essential to completing a task.

> **Note**   Contains supplemental information.

> **Caution**   Contains valuable information about possible loss of data; be sure to read this information carefully.

> **Warning**   Contains critical information about possible physical injury; be sure to read this information carefully.

Planning Contains hints and useful information that should help you plan an implementation.

 Security Alert Highlights information you need to know to maximize security in your work environment.

 Exam Tip Flags information you should know before taking the certification exam.

 Off the Record Contains practical advice about the real-world implications of information presented in the lesson.

Notational Conventions

The following conventions are used throughout this book.

- Characters or commands that you type appear in **bold** type.

- *Italic* in syntax statements indicates placeholders for variable information. Italic is also used for book titles, URLs, and key words and terms when they are first introduced.

- Names of files and folders appear in Title caps, except when you are to type them directly. Unless otherwise indicated, you can use all lowercase letters when you type a filename in a dialog box or at a command prompt.

- Filename extensions appear in all lowercase.

- Acronyms appear in all uppercase.

- Monospace type represents code samples, examples of screen text, or entries that you might type at a command prompt or in initialization files.

- Square brackets [ ] are used in syntax statements to enclose optional items. For example, [*filename*] in command syntax indicates that you can choose to type a filename with the command. Type only the information within the brackets, not the brackets themselves.

- Braces { } are used in syntax statements to enclose required items. Type only the information within the braces, not the braces themselves.

Keyboard Conventions

- A plus sign (+) between two key names means that you must press those keys at the same time. For example, "Press Alt+Tab" means that you hold down Alt while you press Tab.

- A comma (,) between two or more key names means that you must press each of the keys consecutively, not together. For example, "Press Alt, F, X" means that you press and release each key in sequence. "Press Alt+W, L" means that you first press Alt and W at the same time, and then release them and press L.

Getting Started

This training kit contains hands-on exercises to help you learn about deploying, managing, and troubleshooting a network infrastructure. Use this section to prepare your self-paced training environment.

To complete some of these procedures, you must have two networked computers and a means of connecting both computers to the Internet. Both computers must also be capable of running Windows Server 2003.

> **Caution**   Many of these exercises require you to configure settings that will affect addressing and other features your network. For this reason, it is not recommended that you perform these exercises on computers that are connected to a larger network.

Hardware Requirements

Each computer must have the following minimum configuration. All hardware should be on the Microsoft Windows Server 2003 Hardware Compatibility List.

- Minimum 133 MHz in the Intel Pentium/Celeron family or the AMD K6/Athlon/Duron family

- 128 MB memory

- 2 GB available hard disk space

- Display monitor capable of 800 x 600 resolution or higher.

- CD-ROM or DVD-ROM drive

- Microsoft Mouse or compatible pointing device

Software Requirements

The following software is required to complete the procedures in this training kit.

- Windows Server 2003, Enterprise Edition (A 180-day evaluation edition of Windows Server 2003, Enterprise Edition is included on the CD-ROM.)

> **Caution**   The 180-day evaluation edition provided with this training kit is not the full retail product and is provided only for the purposes of training and evaluation. Microsoft Technical Support does not support this evaluation edition. For additional support information regarding this book and the CD-ROMs (including answers to commonly asked questions about installation and use), visit the Microsoft Press Technical Support Web site at *http://mspress.microsoft.com /mspress/support/*. You can also e-mail tkinput@microsoft.com or send a letter to Microsoft Press, Attn: Microsoft Press Technical Support, One Microsoft Way, Redmond, WA 98052-6399.

Setup Instructions

Set up your computer according to the manufacturer's instructions.

For the exercises that require networked computers, you need to make sure the computers can communicate with each other. Once the computers are physically networked, install Windows Server 2003 on each computer. Use the following table during installation to help you configure each computer when the Windows Setup Wizard is run:

Windows Setup Wizard Page	Setting for First Computer	Setting for Second Computer
Regional And Language Options	Default (English).	Default (English).
Personalize Your Software	Type your name and organization.	Type your name and organization.
Your Product Key	Type the product key provided with the Windows Server 2003 CD-ROM.	Type the product key provided with the Windows Server 2003 CD-ROM.
Licensing Modes	Default.	Default.
Computer Name And Administrator Password	Computer Name: Computer1 Administrator Password: [Type a strong password of your choice.]	Computer Name: Computer2 Administrator Password: [Type a strong password of your choice, preferably distinct from that of the first computer.]

Windows Setup Wizard Page	Setting for First Computer	Setting for Second Computer
Modem Dialing Information	Default.	Default.
Date And Time Settings	Your date, time, and time zone.	Your date, time, and time zone.
Networking Settings	Default (Typical Settings).	Default (Typical Settings).
Workgroup Or Computer Domain	Default (workgroup named WORKGROUP).	Default (workgroup named WORKGROUP).

Caution   In general, you should not perform these configurations on computers that are part of a larger network. However, if you do, you *must* verify with your network administrator that the addresses, computer names, domain name, and other settings used do not conflict with network operations.

The Microsoft Press Readiness Review Suite

The CD-ROM includes a practice test made up of 300 sample exam questions and an objective review with an additional 125 questions. Use the practice test to reinforce your learning and identify areas in which you need to gain more experience before taking the exam.

▶   **To install the practice test and object review, complete the following steps:**

1. Insert the Supplemental CD-ROM into your CD-ROM drive.

Note   If AutoRun is disabled on your machine, refer to the Readme.txt file on the CD-ROM.

2. Click Readiness Review Suite on the User Interface menu and follow the prompts.

The eBooks

The CD-ROM includes an electronic version of this training kit, as well as eBooks for both the *Microsoft Encyclopedia of Security* and the *Microsoft Encyclopedia of Networking, Second Edition*. The eBooks are in portable document format (PDF) and can be viewed using Adobe Acrobat Reader. For more information, see the Readme.txt file included in the root folder of the Supplemental CD-ROM.

The Microsoft Certified Professional Program

The Microsoft Certified Professional (MCP) program provides the best method to prove your command of current Microsoft products and technologies. The exams and corresponding certifications are developed to validate your mastery of critical competencies as you design and develop, or implement and support, solutions with Microsoft products and technologies. Computer professionals who become Microsoft certified are recognized as experts and are sought after industrywide. Certification brings a variety of benefits to the individual and to employers and organizations.

> **See Also**   For a full list of MCP benefits, go to *http://www.Microsoft.com/traincert/start /itpro.asp.*

Certifications

The Microsoft Certified Professional program offers multiple certifications based on specific areas of technical expertise:

- ***Microsoft Certified Professional (MCP).***   Individuals with demonstrated in-depth knowledge of at least one Microsoft Windows operating system or architecturally significant platform. An MCP is qualified to implement a Microsoft product or technology as part of a business solution for an organization.

- ***Microsoft Certified Solution Developer (MCSD).***   Professional developers qualified to analyze, design, and develop enterprise business solutions with Microsoft development tools and technologies, including the Microsoft .NET Framework.

- ***Microsoft Certified Application Developer (MCAD).***   Professional developers qualified to develop, test, deploy, and maintain powerful applications using Microsoft tools and technologies, including Microsoft Visual Studio .NET and XML Web services.

- ***Microsoft Certified Systems Engineer (MCSE).***   Individuals qualified to analyze business requirements and design and implement the infrastructure for business solutions based on the Microsoft Windows and Microsoft Windows Server 2003 operating systems.

- ***Microsoft Certified Systems Administrator (MCSA).***   Individuals with the skills to manage and troubleshoot existing network and system environments based on the Microsoft Windows and Microsoft Windows Server 2003 operating systems.

- ***Microsoft Certified Database Administrator (MCDBA).***   Individuals qualified to design, implement, and administer Microsoft SQL Server databases.

- ***Microsoft Certified Trainer (MCT).***   Individuals who are instructionally and technically qualified to deliver Microsoft Official Curriculum through a Microsoft Certified Technical Education Center (CTEC).

Requirements for Becoming a Microsoft Certified Professional

The certification requirements differ for each certification and are specific to the products and job functions addressed by the certification.

To become a Microsoft Certified Professional, you must pass rigorous certification exams that provide a valid and reliable measure of technical proficiency and expertise. These exams are designed to test your expertise and ability to perform a role or task with a product, and are developed with the input of professionals in the industry. Questions on the exams reflect how Microsoft products are used in actual organizations, giving them real-world relevance.

- Microsoft Certified Product (MCP) candidates are required to pass one current Microsoft certification exam. Candidates can pass additional Microsoft certification exams to further qualify their skills with other Microsoft products, development tools, or desktop applications.

- Microsoft Certified Solution Developers (MCSDs) are required to pass three core exams and one elective exam. (MCSDs for Microsoft .NET candidates are required to pass four core exams and one elective.)

- Microsoft Certified Application Developers (MCADs) are required to pass two core exams and one elective exam in an area of specialization.

- Microsoft Certified Systems Engineers (MCSEs) are required to pass five core exams and two elective exams.

- Microsoft Certified Systems Administrators (MCSAs) are required to pass three core exams and one elective exam that provide a valid and reliable measure of technical proficiency and expertise.

- Microsoft Certified Database Administrators (MCDBAs) are required to pass three core exams and one elective exam that provide a valid and reliable measure of technical proficiency and expertise.

- Microsoft Certified Trainers (MCTs) are required to meet instructional and technical requirements specific to each Microsoft Official Curriculum course they are certified to deliver. The MCT program requires ongoing training to meet the requirements for the annual renewal of certification. For more information about becoming a Microsoft Certified Trainer, visit *http://www.microsoft.com/traincert /mcp/mct* or contact a regional service center near you.

Technical Support

Every effort has been made to ensure the accuracy of this book and the contents of the companion CD-ROM. If you have comments, questions, or ideas regarding this book or the companion CD-ROM, please send them to Microsoft Press using either of the following methods:

E-mail:	tkinput@microsoft.com
Postal mail:	Microsoft Press
	Attn: MCSE Self-Paced Training Kit (Exam 70-291): Series Editor
	One Microsoft Way
	Redmond, WA 98052-6399

For additional support information regarding this book and the CD-ROM (including answers to commonly asked questions about installation and use), visit the Microsoft Press Technical Support Web site at *http://www.microsoft.com/mspress/support/*. To connect directly to the Microsoft Press Knowledge Base and enter a query, visit *http://www.microsoft.com/mspress/support/search.asp*. For support information regarding Microsoft software, please connect to *http://support.microsoft.com*.

Evaluation Edition Software Support

The 180-day evaluation edition provided with this training kit is not the full retail product and is provided only for the purposes of training and evaluation. Microsoft Technical Support does not support this evaluation edition.

> **Caution**　The evaluation edition of Microsoft Windows Server 2003, Enterprise Edition included with this book should not be used on a primary work computer. The evaluation edition is unsupported. For online support information relating to the full version of Microsoft Windows Server 2003, Enterprise Edition that *might* also apply to the evaluation edition, you can connect to *http://support.microsoft.com*.

Information about any issues relating to the use of this evaluation edition with this training kit is posted to the Support section of the Microsoft Press Web site (*http://www.microsoft.com/mspress/support/*). For information about ordering the full version of any Microsoft software, please call Microsoft Sales at (800) 426-9400 or visit *http://www.microsoft.com*.

Part 1
Learn at Your Own Pace

1 Understanding Windows Server 2003 Networks

Exam Objectives in this Chapter:

- Diagnose and resolve issues related to Automatic Private IP Addressing (APIPA)

Why This Chapter Matters

Familiarity with the components of a network infrastructure is an essential prerequisite for working as a system administrator. Because the network infrastructure elements presented in this chapter are likely to mirror those in any office network; it is therefore imperative that you understand these components, how they interoperate, and the contexts in which they are used.

Examples abound. First, without properly understanding the name resolution differences between Windows NT and Windows Server 2003 domains, you won't be able to troubleshoot related problems efficiently in a mixed network environment. You also need to understand how addressing relates to network infrastructure; for example, if you notice an APIPA address on a computer, you need to understand the implications of this address for your physical topology and then be able to troubleshoot accordingly. Finally, this chapter matters because, as a network administrator, you need to know how to add services, protocols, and clients to network connections; to change the binding order of connections, protocols, and network providers; and to recognize low-level differences between workgroups and domains.

Lessons in this Chapter:

- Lesson 1: Understanding Network Infrastructures 1-3
- Lesson 2: Networking with Default Components in Windows Server 2003 . . .1-13
- Lesson 3: Extending a Windows Server 2003 Network Infrastructure 1-23

Before You Begin

To complete this chapter, you must have

- Physically networked two computers.

- Performed a Windows Server 2003 installation with default settings on both computers. The computers should be named Computer1 and Computer2. (See the

About This Book section for specific instructions on how to perform a default installation by using the Windows Setup Wizard.)

■ Assigned the local Administrator account on both computers a strong password of your choosing.

■ Created a private user account, with your name, that has not been granted Administrator privileges. Use this account for all computer activity outside the exercises in this book.

Security Alert   In general, you should stay logged on as Administrator only briefly to perform administrative functions. Alternatively, you can use the Runas command-line command or the Run As shortcut menu command to invoke Administrator privileges when necessary from a Domain User account. Leaving a computer logged on as Administrator can be dangerous when you are connected to the Internet. To protect against malicious network intrusions and damaging computer viruses, be sure to log off Administrator or shut down your computer after you finish exercises in this book.

Lesson 1: Understanding Network Infrastructures

A network infrastructure consists of many interrelated technologies and systems. Network administrators must become proficient in these technologies to maintain, support, and troubleshoot network functioning.

> **Note**   Throughout this training kit, Windows Server 2003 and Windows Server 2003 family refer to the following family of products: Microsoft Windows Server 2003, Standard Edition; Microsoft Windows Server 2003, Enterprise Edition; and Microsoft Windows Server 2003, Datacenter Edition. Specific editions of the Windows Server 2003 family will be called out as appropriate. (Although Microsoft Windows Server 2003, Web Edition is also part of the Windows Server 2003 family, Web Edition does not necessarily support the features discussed in this training kit.)

> **After this lesson, you will be able to**
> - Describe the difference between a physical and logical network infrastructure
> - Describe several elements of a Windows Server 2003 network infrastructure
>
> **Estimated lesson time: 20 minutes**

Defining a Network Infrastructure

A *network infrastructure* is a set of physical and logical components that provide the basis for connectivity, security, routing, management, access, and other integral features on a network.

Most frequently, a network infrastructure is both inherited and designed. If a network connects to the Internet, for example, certain aspects of the network, such as the Transmission Control Protocol/Internet Protocol (TCP/IP) protocol suite, are inherited from the Internet. Other network aspects, such as the physical layout of basic network elements, can be designed when the network is first created and are then inherited by later versions of the network.

Physical Infrastructure

A network's *physical infrastructure* is its *topology*—the physical design of the network—along with hardware components such as cabling, routers, switches, bridges, hubs, servers, and hosts. The physical infrastructure also includes technologies such as Ethernet, 802.11b wireless, Public Switched Telephone Network (PSTN), and Asynchronous Transfer Mode (ATM), all of which define methods of communication over certain types of physical connections. Familiarity with the physical infrastructure of a network is considered prerequisite knowledge for the 70-291 exam, and as such, this topic is beyond the scope of this training kit.

Figure 1-1 shows an example physical infrastructure.

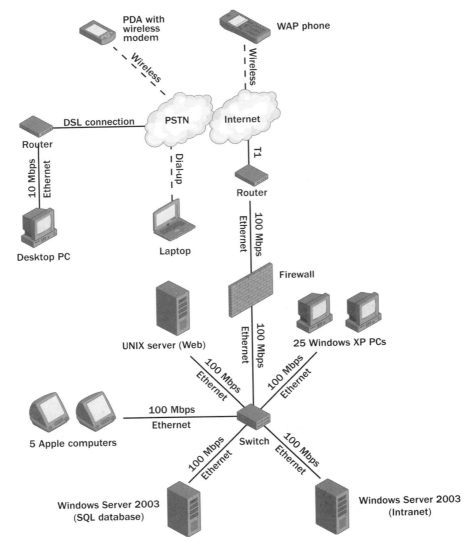

Figure 1-1   Physical infrastructure of a network

Logical Infrastructure

The *logical infrastructure* of a network is composed of the many software elements that connect, manage, and secure hosts on the network. The logical infrastructure allows for communication between computers over the pathways that are described in the physical topology. Example elements of the logical infrastructure include network components such as Domain Name System (DNS), network protocols such as TCP/IP, network client software such as Client Service For NetWare, and network services such as the Quality of Service (QoS) Packet Scheduler.

Once a network has been designed, the maintenance, administration, and management of its logical infrastructure requires intimate familiarity with many aspects of the network's technologies. For example, the network administrator of even a small organization needs to know how to create various types of network connections; how to install and configure network protocols required for various network needs; how to configure manual and automatic addressing methods appropriate to network needs; how to configure name resolution methods; and how to troubleshoot network problems related to connectivity, addressing, access, security, and name resolution.

In medium and large networks, network administrators must routinely perform more complex tasks, such as configuring remote access through dial-up connections and virtual private networks (VPNs); creating, modifying, and troubleshooting routing interfaces and routing tables; creating, supporting, and troubleshooting security based on public key cryptography; and making maintenance decisions for heterogeneous networks that include operating systems such as Microsoft Windows, UNIX, and Novell NetWare.

Figure 1-2 illustrates an example logical infrastructure.

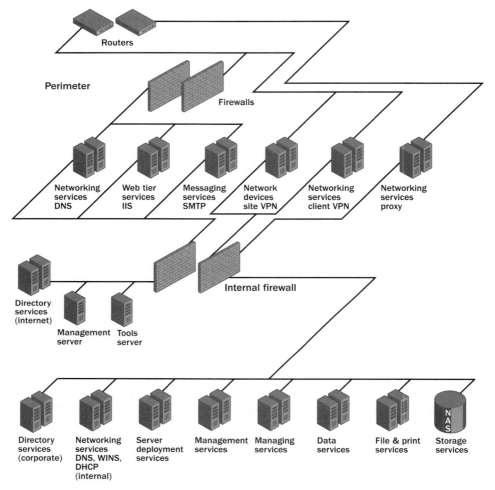

Figure 1-2   Logical infrastructure of a network

Analyzing Windows Server 2003 Networks

The following sections describe many of the logical elements of Windows Server 2003 networks.

Network Connections

In Microsoft Windows, *network connections* are logical interfaces between software (such as protocols) and hardware (such as modems or network adapters). Network connections can be seen in the Network Connections window, shown in Figure 1-3. Connections are prioritized and are normally configured with various types of protocols, services, and client software.

Figure 1-3   Network Connections window

Network Protocols   *Network protocols* are network languages used for computer-to-computer communication. For example, Windows networks, UNIX networks, and the Internet all rely on the TCP/IP network protocol for basic communication.

In Windows, connections can communicate with foreign hosts only by using network protocols that are installed on the local computer and bound to that connection. TCP/IP (version 4) is installed and bound by default to every connection. However, the NWLink protocol must be manually installed, configured, and bound to connections requiring compatibility with Novell NetWare networks that do not use TCP/IP. (NWLink is the Microsoft implementation of the Internetwork Packet Exchange/Sequenced Packet Exchange [IPX/SPX] protocol, which is native to NetWare.) In addition, the AppleTalk protocol must be manually installed and bound to connections requiring compatibility with Apple networks that do not use TCP/IP.

> **Note**   TCP/IP is actually a group of protocols referred to as a *stack* or *suite*. This protocol stack includes Address Resolution Protocol (ARP), Internet Protocol (IP), Transmission Control Protocol (TCP), User Datagram Protocol (UDP), Domain Name System (DNS), Hypertext Transfer Protocol (HTTP), and many others.

Figure 1-4 shows the full list of protocols that can be readily installed and bound to particular connections. If your network relies on a protocol not listed, you must supply this protocol independently.

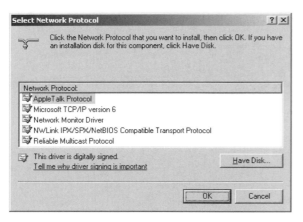

Figure 1-4   Readily installable protocols

Network Services   *Network services* are programs that provide features, such as quality of service, to hosts or protocols on a network. Figure 1-5 shows network services that can be readily installed and bound to network connections. Additional services can be installed from the Windows Server 2003 Setup disk or from a third-party source.

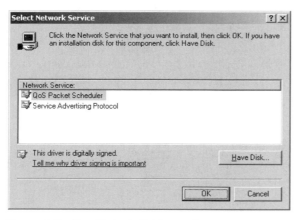

Figure 1-5   Readily installable services

Network Clients   In Windows, *network clients* are programs that allow a computer to connect to a network operating system. For example, by installing Client Service For NetWare and binding the service to a particular connection, you can connect to Net-Ware networks.

Addressing

Addressing is the practice of maintaining a coherent system of addresses within your network so that all computers can communicate.

In a network, each host normally distinguishes itself by using a specific network address. For example, IP version 4 provides a method for computers with 4-byte addresses to communicate with each other. Addresses must be configured so that the first part of the address (the network ID) matches that of the other computers on the local network, or *subnet*. To allow such computers to communicate with hosts on different subnets, you must connect the subnets by using routers (such as the Routing And Remote Access service of Windows Server 2003).

Addresses can be configured manually, distributed automatically through the use of a DHCP server, or self-configured.

Name Resolution

Most networks use a naming system so that people can refer to computers by name instead of by address. *Name resolution* is the process of translating a computer name into an address, and vice versa.

Because Windows can use two different naming systems, NetBIOS and DNS, Windows networks support two name resolution systems. NetBIOS is native to older Microsoft networks, and today it is used primarily for compatibility with legacy features and systems. DNS is the native naming system of the Internet and all Windows operating systems released since Microsoft Windows 2000.

To resolve NetBIOS names, Microsoft networks can send broadcast queries to all systems on the same network segment or send requests to a WINS server. To resolve DNS (host) names, Microsoft networks rely on the DNS protocol and DNS servers.

To function properly, both of these name resolution services must be configured and supported by a knowledgeable network administrator.

Network Computer Groups

In Windows, computers can be grouped into workgroups or domains.

- A *workgroup* is a simple grouping of resources intended to help users find such resources as printers and shared folders. By default, computers in Windows workgroups use the NetBIOS naming system to name computers and resolve those names. NetBIOS is used with associated protocols, such as Common Internet File System (CIFS)—an extension of the Server Message Block (SMB) protocol—to provide file sharing, security for network shares, and network browsing features. However, no centralized security or management features are available.

- A *domain* is a collection of computers, defined by a network administrator, that share a common directory, security policies, and relationships with other domains. Security and directory information are stored in domain controllers within each domain.

Active Directory

In Windows Server 2003 networks, domains are created in and supported by Microsoft Active Directory directory service. *Active Directory* is a distributed database and directory service that is replicated among all domain controllers on the network. The Active Directory database stores information about network objects including domains, computers, users, and other objects. The distributed nature of Active Directory gives network users access to permitted resources anywhere on the network by using a single logon process. It also provides a single point of administration for all network objects.

The term *domains* is used to refer both to groupings of computers in Active Directory and to hierarchical name suffixes such as microsoft.com in DNS. Remember that Active Directory domains and DNS domains are separate entities governed by separate systems. However, to simplify administration, Active Directory domains and their member computers are normally assigned names that match DNS names. In this way, the Active Directory namespace and the DNS namespace overlap.

Figure 1-6 illustrates the overlapping Active Directory and DNS namespaces.

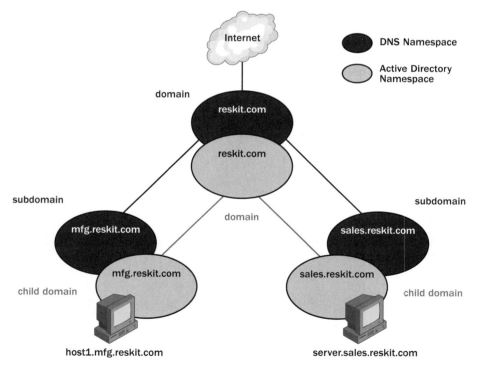

Figure 1-6   DNS and Active Directory namespaces

Remote Access

Remote access connections must be configured for users who connect to a Windows network from a nonlocal site. The two basic methods for remote access include direct dial-up to a network computer and virtual private networks. For dial-up access, you must not only configure a server to answer incoming calls, but you must also configure authentication, access permissions, and encryption requirements. VPNs enable private connections to cross a public network such as the Internet. These network connections require a different set of configuration procedures for authentication, encryption, and security.

Network Address Translation

Network Address Translation (NAT) is a method of allowing computers internal to your network that have been given nonpublic addresses to communicate with computers on the Internet. When you configure NAT to be used with your network infrastructure, this setup affects the addressing scheme of your network. *Internet Connection Sharing* (ICS) is a simple implementation of NAT included with recent Windows operating systems.

Certificate Infrastructure

Certificates are used for public key cryptography, which is an important security element in Windows Server 2003 networks. Certificates and public key cryptography are used in many Windows features, such as the Secure Sockets Layer (SSL), the Internet Protocol Security (IPSec) protocol (which encrypts IP communications), smart cards, and the Encrypting File System (EFS, which secures files on a network). The certificate infrastructure supported in Windows Server 2003 networks integrates with the *Public Key Infrastructure* (PKI) system: a system of digital certificates, certification authorities, and other registration authorities that authenticate each party involved in an electronic transaction.

Lesson Review

The following questions are intended to reinforce key information presented in this lesson. If you are unable to answer a question, review the lesson materials and try the question again. You can find answers to the questions in the "Questions and Answers" section at the end of this chapter.

1. You are the administrator for your company's network, which includes computers running Windows Server 2003, computers running Microsoft Windows XP Professional, and a server running Novell NetWare. The Novell NetWare server has only the IPX/SPX network protocol configured. You want every network computer to be able to access features in the NetWare network operating system, the Windows Server 2003 network operating system, and the Internet. Which protocols must be installed on your network computers?

2. Which of the following does not rely on certificates and public key cryptography?

 a. SSL

 b. EFS

 c. IPSec

 d. Workgroup security

3. Which protocol provides names and name resolution for workgroups in Windows?

 a. NetBIOS

 b. CIFS

 c. DNS

 d. Kerberos

Lesson Summary

- A network's physical infrastructure is its topology—the physical design of the network—along with hardware components such as cabling, routers, switches, bridges, hubs, servers, and hosts. The physical infrastructure also includes technologies that define methods of communication over specific types of physical connections.

- A network's logical infrastructure is made up of the many software elements that connect, manage, and secure hosts on the network.

- In Windows, network connections are logical interfaces between software (such as protocols) and hardware (such as modems or network adapters). Connections are prioritized and are normally configured with various types of protocols, services, and client software.

- Protocols are network languages used for computer-to-computer communication.

- Addressing is the practice of maintaining a system of addresses within your network so that all computers can identify each other.

- Most networks use a naming system so that people can refer to computers by name instead of by address. Name resolution is the process of translating these names into addresses, and vice versa.

Lesson 2: Networking with Default Components in Windows Server 2003

If computers running Windows Server 2003 (or any versions of Windows since Microsoft Windows 98) are physically connected to each other through network adapters, you do not need to configure any settings on these computers to begin networking. Windows Server 2003 automatically detects local area network (LAN) connections and allows for basic communication among all Windows hosts. You can also configure new network connections, such as dial-up connections, without installing any additional components.

After this lesson, you will be able to

■ Describe the networking features of a default Windows Server 2003 installation

Estimated lesson time: 20 minutes

Viewing Network Connections

In a Windows network, a *connection* is a logically configured interface between a physical network and a network adapter or modem. You can view the connections currently configured on your computer by using the Network Connections tool in Control Panel.

Configuring Connections

Windows Server 2003 automatically detects and configures connections associated with network adapters installed on the local computer. These connections are then displayed in the Network Connections menu, along with any manually configured connections and the New Connection Wizard. The New Connection Wizard allows you to configure additional network connections, such as dial-up connections.

Viewing Default Components of Network Connections

Connections by themselves do not allow network hosts to communicate. Instead, the network clients, services, and protocols associated with (or bound to) the connection provide connectivity through any particular connection. The General tab of a connection's properties dialog box shows the network components used by the connection. These components consist of network clients, services, and protocols.

Figure 1-7 shows the default components associated with a network connection. The check box next to each component indicates whether that component is bound to the connection. In this example, the Network Load Balancing service is installed on the local computer but is not bound to the connection.

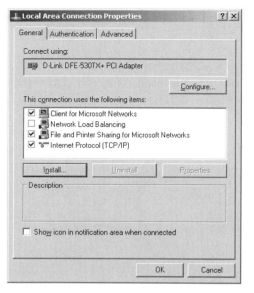

Figure 1-7   Default components for a connection

Network clients are software components, such as Client Service For NetWare and Client For Microsoft Networks, that allow the local computer to connect with a destination network operating system. By default, Client For Microsoft Networks is bound to all local area connections. Client For Microsoft Networks allows Windows client computers to perform CIFS-related networking tasks, such as connecting to shared folders.

Network services are software components, such as File And Printer Sharing For Microsoft Networks, Network Load Balancing, and QoS Packet Scheduler, that provide additional features for network connections. File And Printer Sharing For Microsoft Networks, which allows the local computer to share folders for network access, is installed and bound to local area connections by default.

Network protocols are basic software components such as TCP/IP and AppleTalk that allow a computer to communicate with other computers. Network clients and services are built on top of network protocols. By default, the TCP/IP protocol is bound to all connections.

Viewing Advanced Connection Settings

To view advanced connection settings, open the Network Connections window and select Advanced Settings from the Advanced menu.

The Advanced Settings dialog box, shown in Figure 1-8, displays the order (priority) of each connection. By adjusting the order of the connections, you can configure the computer to attempt network communication through various available connections in the order you define. You can also adjust the binding order of the services used for each connection.

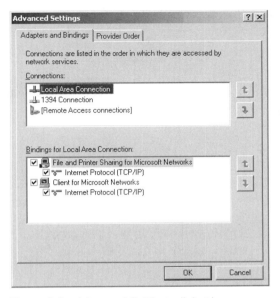

Figure 1-8   Advanced Settings dialog box

Provider Order Tab   The Provider Order tab of the Advanced Settings dialog box, shown in Figure 1-9, displays the order in which various network providers, such as a NetWare Network, Microsoft Windows Network, or Microsoft Terminal Services, will be attempted. Note that network provider order is not attached to specific connections. If a computer is configured to bind to NetWare before Windows networks, the computer will do so for every connection.

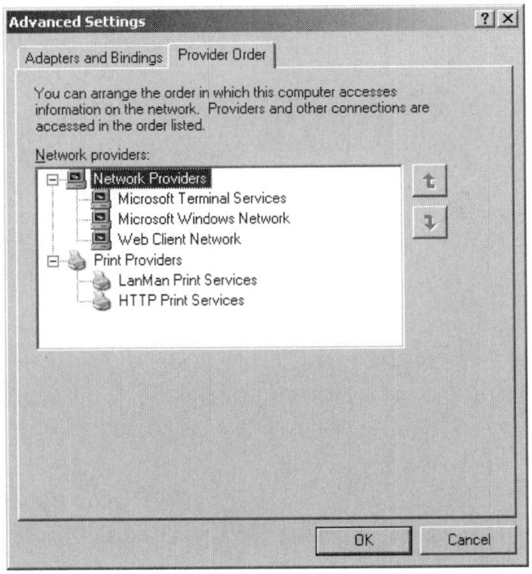

Figure 1-9   Provider Order tab

In a default installation, Microsoft Terminal Services is given priority over the Microsoft Windows Network because Microsoft Terminal Services, when used, is intended to be used in place of other connections. Also by default, a connection to a Web Client Network is attempted only when the first two providers fail to respond.

The Provider Order tab also displays the order for print providers. According to default settings, LanMan Print Services (the print provider used in typical Windows networks) is given priority over HTTP Print Services.

Default TCP/IP Settings

You can view TCP/IP settings configured for any connection by opening the Internet Protocol (TCP/IP) Properties dialog box. To open this dialog box, open a connection's properties dialog box, select Internet Protocol (TCP/IP) from the list of network components, and click Properties. Figure 1-10 shows the Internet Protocol (TCP/IP) Properties dialog box associated with the default LAN connection.

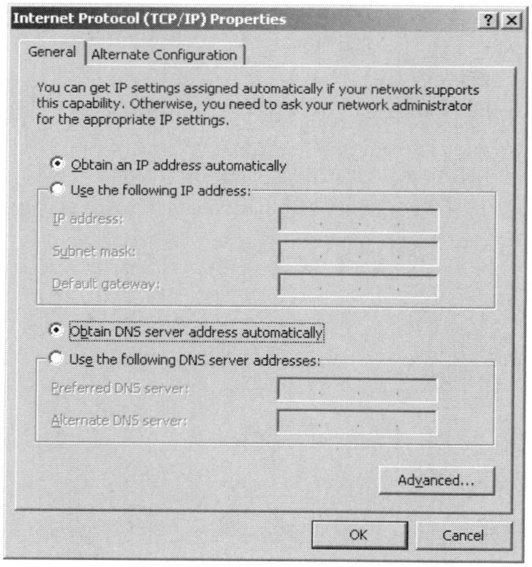

Figure 1-10   Default TCP/IP settings

As shown in Figure 1-10, the IP address of a computer is assigned automatically in a default Windows installation. For a new computer on a network, or for a network on which no DHCP server has been configured, the computer assigns itself an IP address in the range of 169.254.0.1–169.254.255.254. This address is available through a feature called Automatic Private IP Addressing (APIPA).

Automatic Private IP Addressing

APIPA is an addressing feature for simple networks that consist of a single network segment. Whenever a computer running Windows Server 2003 has been configured to obtain an IP address automatically, and when no DHCP server or alternate configuration is available, the computer uses APIPA to assign itself a private IP address in the range of 169.254.0.1–169.254.255.254.

To determine whether Automatic Private IP Addressing is currently enabled and active, enter **ipconfig /all** at a command prompt. The resulting text identifies your IP address and other information. If the Autoconfiguration Enabled line reads Yes and the IP address is in the 169.254.0.1–169.254.255.254 range, Automatic Private IP Addressing is active.

This automatic addressing feature works only for computers on a network segment that cannot obtain an IP address through other means. If a DHCP server later becomes available to a host that has assigned itself an APIPA address, the computer changes its IP address to one obtained from the DHCP server. Computers using APIPA addresses can communicate only with other computers using APIPA addresses on the same network segment; they are not directly reachable from the Internet. Note also that through APIPA, you cannot configure a computer with a DNS server address, a default gateway address, or a WINS server address. If you want a computer to obtain an address automatically and also want to specify a default gateway, DNS server, or WINS server when no DHCP server is available, you can do so by using an alternate configuration.

APIPA is available on any computer running Windows 98, Microsoft Windows Millennium Edition (Me), Windows 2000, Windows XP, or Windows Server 2003.

Disabling APIPA   If you want to ensure that APIPA will not be used, you can either configure an alternate address in the connection's IP properties, or disable the automatic addressing feature by editing the Registry. Note that to disable APIPA for one adapter and to disable APIPA for all adapters requires you to edit different Registry keys.

To disable APIPA on a single adapter by editing the Registry, complete the following steps:

1. Use the Registry Editor Regedit.exe to add the Registry entry **IPAutoconfigurationEnabled** with a value of **0** (REG_DWORD data type) in the following subkey:

   HKEY_LOCAL_MACHINE\SYSTEM\CurrentControlSet\Services\Tcpip\Parameters\Interfaces*interface*

2. Restart the computer.

To disable APIPA for multiple adapters by editing the Registry, complete the following steps:

1. Set the value of the IPAutoconfigurationEnabled entry to **0** (REG_DWORD data type) in the following Registry subkey:

   HKEY_LOCAL_MACHINE\SYSTEM\CurrentControlSet\Services\Tcpip\Parameters

2. Restart the computer.

> **Exam Tip**   Be sure to memorize the APIPA-related Registry keys for the exam.

Troubleshooting APIPA   For computers running any version of Windows since Windows 98, APIPA addresses are default addresses. That is, they are assigned to connected hosts whose network configuration has not been altered since the operating system was installed. In certain small networks, you might want to leave the computers with these default APIPA addresses so as to simplify network communication and administration. If so, you can run the Ipconfig /all command on networked computers to determine whether the address assigned to each computer's local area connection falls within the APIPA range of 169.254.0.1–169.254.255.254.

If the Ipconfig /all command does not reveal an APIPA address, the output instead reveals one of three scenarios: no address with or without an error message, an all-zeros address, or a nonzero IP address outside of APIPA range.

When no IP address has been assigned to a host, an error message might provide the specific cause. For example, the Ipconfig /all output might inform you that the media (in other words, the network cable) has been disconnected. At this point, you can check the network cable attachments and then run the Ipconfig /renew command to obtain a new IP address through the APIPA feature. Should this strategy fail to provide the host with a new IP address, you should then proceed to diagnose hardware problems such as faulty cables, hubs, and switches.

Sometimes the Ipconfig /all command output does not provide an explicit cause for the computer's failure to obtain an IP address. If so, suspect problems with the network adapter. Verify that the computer in question has a network adapter properly installed, along with the most recent version of the appropriate driver. Then run the Ipconfig /renew command to attempt to obtain an IP address again. If problems persist, you should proceed to diagnose hardware issues.

> **Real World   Troubleshooting Without Tools**
>
> As a sysadmin, you are ideally supposed to break out hard-core paraphernalia like oscilloscopes and multimeters at the first sign of a network hardware disturbance. In real life, however, many sysadmins (especially those in small companies) don't know how to use such tools and thus find ways to troubleshoot without them. For example, when traffic on the network has stopped, you can begin troubleshooting simply by restarting the hub or switch. If that solution doesn't fix the problem, try vacuuming out the ports on your hubs and adapters, as well as the connector ends on your network cables. Dust can often be the culprit in disrupted connectivity.
>
> Even after you rule out problems that can be easily remedied, you can still often determine without the use of high-tech gadgets the cause of the connectivity problem. For the connection unable to receive an APIPA address, simply replace the cable with another one you know to be functioning. If the computer is then able to obtain an APIPA address after you run the Ipconfig /renew command, you can attribute the network disruption to the faulty cable you just replaced.
>
> If the problem persists, you can use a special *crossover* cable to avoid the hub and connect the stranded computer directly to another. If in this configuration both computers obtain APIPA addresses, you can determine that the hub was the cause of the network disruption. If either of the computers still cannot obtain an APIPA address, replace the network card on the stranded computer.

Other APIPA errors do not generate error messages in the Ipconfig output. For example, if the Ipconfig /all command merely reveals an all-zeros IP address, the IP address might have been released by the Ipconfig /release command and never renewed. In this case, run the Ipconfig /renew command to obtain a new address. If the all-zeros address persists, check the appropriate Registry entries to make sure APIPA has not been disabled.

If, by running the Ipconfig /all command, you see that your computer has obtained a nonzero IP address that is outside the APIPA range, you should run the Ipconfig /renew command to see whether this address is simply held from a previous (and recent) configuration. If a non-APIPA address persists when you want an APIPA address, check the IP properties for the connection and verify that the computer has been configured to obtain an address automatically. Then click the Alternate Configuration tab and verify that the Automatic Private IP Address option is selected, as shown in Figure 1-11.

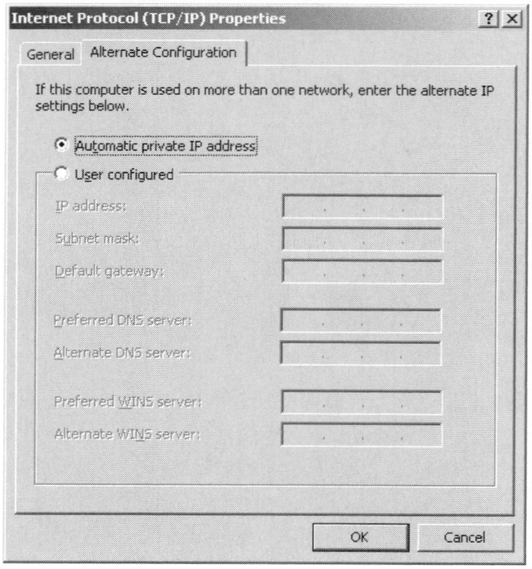

Figure 1-11 Configuring an APIPA client

Off the Record In reality, an APIPA address is just a temporary address that allows computers to communicate before you can assign them a "real" one. You are probably never going to see a company network based on APIPA addresses because such addresses are incompatible with shared Internet connections, subnetting, and centralized administration. If you want to combine automatic addressing with Internet connectivity, subnets, or address administration, use a DHCP server.

Default Networking and Workgroups

Physically connected computers running Windows Server 2003 are grouped by default in a single workgroup named WORKGROUP. Computer names are NetBIOS names, resolved using NetBT broadcasts to the local network segment. The workgroup itself merely serves as a name for a group of computers and offers no centralized security or management features. File sharing, network security, browsing, and printing within the workgroup are handled on each local computer by the CIFS protocol. Neither Active Directory nor DNS is available.

Routing and Windows Server 2003 Network Infrastructure

Although a default Windows Server 2003 installation does not include routing capabilities, the Windows Setup Wizard for Windows Server 2003 does install the Routing And Remote Access service in a disabled state. By using the Routing And Remote Access console, you can enable this service and configure many routing-type features, such as remote access, LAN routing, and NAT.

Note that you can configure a computer running Windows Server 2003 to perform routing functions only when that computer is configured with more than one network adapter. Computers such as these are said to be *multihomed*. Multihomed servers can act as routers when each network adapter connects to a separate network.

Lesson Review

The following questions are intended to reinforce key information presented in this lesson. If you are unable to answer a question, review the lesson materials and try the question again. You can find answers to the questions in the "Questions and Answers" section at the end of this chapter.

1. You have installed Windows Server 2003 on a multihomed computer named Server001. Network Adapter A is connected to a large network in which 80 percent of the servers run NetWare and 20 percent run Windows Server 2003. Network Adapter B is connected to a large network in which 80 percent of the servers run Windows Server 2003 and 20 percent run NetWare. According to server logs, Network Adapter B sends and receives more traffic than Network Adapter A does. How should you specify the order of network providers for Server001 in general and the binding order of services for Network Adapter A and Network Adapter B, respectively?

    _____

    _____

    _____

    _____

2. Which of the following are automatically configured in Windows Server 2003?

    a. Local area connections

    b. Dial-up networking

    c. Routing tables

3. Which of the following components are automatically assigned to connections?

    a. Client Service For NetWare

    b. Network Monitor Driver

    c. Client For Microsoft Networks

4. Which of the following features is not configurable through the Routing And Remote Access console?

    a. Dial-up networking

    b. Packet filtering

    c. Internet Connection Sharing

    d. Active Directory

5. Which of the following is a requirement for networking on a Windows Server 2003 network?

    a. DHCP

    b. Network protocol

    c. WINS

Lesson Summary

■ A default installation of Windows computers allows you to begin networking immediately, provided that your network consists of a single network segment of physically connected computers running any versions of Windows since Windows 98.

■ By default, and in the absence of a DHCP server, Windows Server 2003 assigns detected connections with an IP address in the range of 169.254.0.1–169.254.255.254.

■ You can view connections currently configured on your computer by using the Network Connections window or menu. If you want to configure additional network connections, such as dial-up connections, use the New Connection Wizard.

■ To view the network components bound to any particular connection, open the properties dialog box associated with that connection. By default, Client For Microsoft Networks, File And Printer Sharing For Microsoft Networks, and the Internet Protocol are bound to each connection.

■ The Advanced Settings dialog box, accessible through the Network Connections window, shows the binding order of network protocols, network services, network providers, and print providers, all of which can be modified.

Lesson 3: Extending a Windows Server 2003 Network Infrastructure

Although Windows Server 2003 provides a simple network infrastructure with every default installation, you can greatly extend this infrastructure by installing and configuring additional network components. If you have Administrator privileges on a local computer, for example, you can install new clients, services, and protocols to be used by particular network connections. In addition, you can configure your computer running Windows Server 2003 to perform additional network functions by installing Windows components or adding server roles. Examples of these functions include centralized addressing (DHCP) and name resolution (WINS, DNS) services for your network.

After this lesson, you will be able to

- Locate and install Windows networking components as needed
- Describe the function of various Windows networking subcomponents

Estimated lesson time: 15 minutes

Adding Components to a Connection

The default Windows Server 2003 network infrastructure consists of IP addressing in the 169.254.0.1–169.254.255.254 range and a single workgroup of other Windows-based computers. Name resolution is handled in the network by NetBT broadcasts to the network segment. File sharing, security, browsing, and printing within the workgroup are handled by the CIFS protocol. Network connections are automatically configured with Client For Microsoft Networks, File And Printer Sharing For Microsoft Networks, and TCP/IP.

You can bind additional clients, services, and protocols to a local area connection by opening the properties dialog box associated with the connection and clicking Install. This process opens the Select Network Component Type dialog box, shown in Figure 1-12.

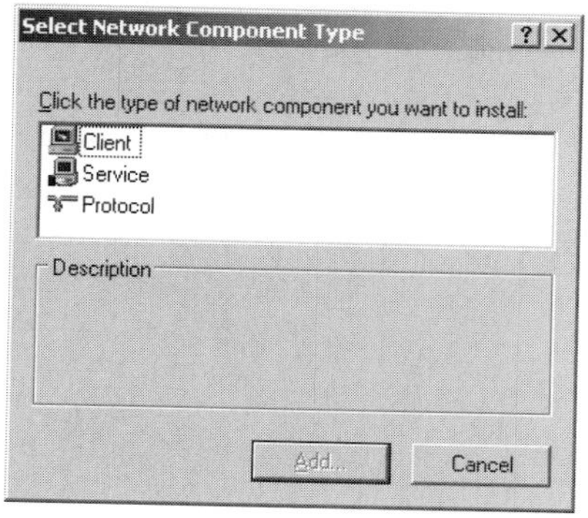

Figure 1-12   Binding a network component to a connection

Before binding new network components to a connection, be sure the network component is actually needed. Network performance is enhanced and network traffic is reduced when only the required protocols and clients are installed; excessive services can hinder performance on your local computer.

To add a network component, complete the following steps:

1. Open Network Connections.

2. Right-click the connection to which you want to add a network component, and then click Properties. Do one of the following:

   ❑ If this is a local area connection, click Install.

   ❑ If this is a dial-up, VPN, or incoming connection, select the Networking tab, and then click Install.

3. In the Select Network Component Type dialog box, select either Client, Service, or Protocol, and then click Add. Do one of the following:

   ❑ If you do not need a separate installation disk for the component, select the appropriate client, service, or protocol, and then click OK.

   ❑ If you have an installation disk for the component, click Have Disk, insert the installation disk into the selected drive, and then click OK.

Installing Client Service For NetWare

To install Client Service For NetWare, open a connection, click Install, select Client, select Client Service For NetWare, and then click OK. If necessary, reboot the computer. Besides installing the actual network client service in question, this procedure also automatically installs the NWLink (IPX) protocol, which is required in order to communicate with NetWare networks. After you install the client, the client is bound to all network adapters and should be unbound from network adapters that do not require it.

Frame Types and the NWLink (IPX) Protocol

The IPX frame type describes the method of encapsulating data in an IPX packet. Although you can usually accept the default Auto Detect mode for frame type settings with the NWLink protocol, the Auto Detect feature cannot properly resolve situations in which multiple frame types exist. This situation can happen, for example, if both Novell NetWare 3.11 (frame type 802.3) and later (frame type 802.2) versions of NetWare servers exist on your network. In such a case, you must edit the Registry to allow for the different frame types.

Installing Windows Networking Components

By using the Add Or Remove Programs tool in Control Panel to add and remove Windows components, you can extend the networking functionality of Windows Server 2003. To access these additional Windows components, open Add Or Remove Programs in Control Panel, and then click Add/Remove Windows Components.

This process opens the Windows Components Wizard. Figure 1-13 shows the Windows Components page of this wizard.

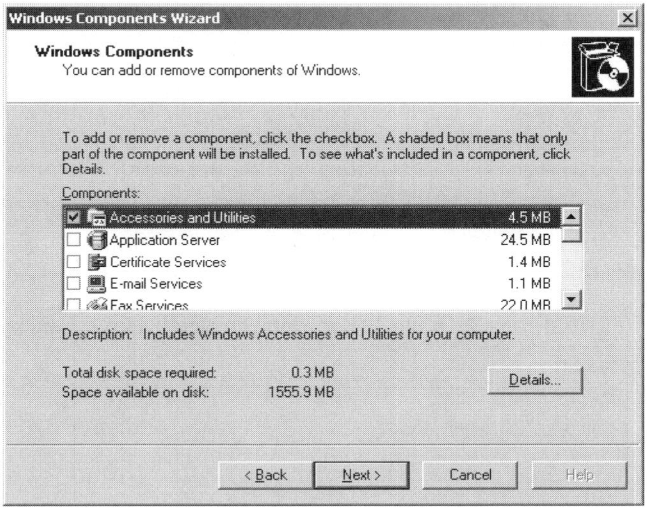

Figure 1-13   Windows Components Wizard

The Windows Components page shows all installable Windows Server 2003 components. These components are the same ones that can be chosen in the Windows Setup Wizard during Windows Server 2003 installation.

> **Note**   Windows Server 2003 provides a simplified way of adding new components through the Manage Your Server window. This window, which you can access through the Start Menu, allows you to add server roles such as print server, mail server, DNS server, or DHCP server. Adding a server role automatically installs any Windows components required for that role.

Of the Windows components not installed by default in Windows Server 2003, four contain subcomponents related to the network infrastructure: Management And Monitoring Tools, Networking Services, Other Network File And Print Services, and Certificate Services.

> **Tip**   You can quickly access the Windows networking components by opening Network Connections and selecting Optional Networking Components from the Advanced menu. This process opens the Windows Optional Networking Components Wizard, which includes three components: Management And Monitoring Tools, Networking Services, and Other Network File And Print Services. Certificate Services cannot be installed through this shortcut.

Management And Monitoring Tools Component

The Management And Monitoring Tools component provides tools for the administration, monitoring, and management of network communications. Among these tools are Network Monitor, which allows you to capture and analyze frames on a network, and Simple Network Management Protocol (SNMP), which allows you to manage and monitor devices on TCP/IP networks. Table 1-1 describes all the subcomponents available in the Management And Monitoring Tools component of Windows Server 2003.

Table 1-1   Management And Monitoring Tools Subcomponents

Subcomponent	Description
Connection Manager Administration Kit	Installs a tool for the creation of customized remote access connections that you can distribute to your users.
Connection Point Services	Installs Phone Book Service, which enables the distribution of phone books for a Connection Manager profile. Requires Internet Information Services (IIS).
Network Monitor Tools	Analyzes packets of data transferred over a network.
Simple Network Management Protocol	Includes agents that monitor the activity in network devices and that report to the network console workstation.
WMI SNMP Provider	Allows client applications to access static and dynamic SNMP information through Windows Management Instrumentation (WMI).

Networking Services Component

This component provides essential support for networking, including a variety of specialized, network-related services and protocols. Table 1-2 lists and describes the subcomponents available in the Networking Services component of Windows Server 2003.

Table 1-2   Networking Services Subcomponents

Subcomponent	Description
Domain Name System (DNS)	Sets up a DNS server that answers query and update requests for DNS names.
Dynamic Host Configuration Protocol (DHCP)	Sets up a DHCP server that automatically assigns temporary IP addresses to client computers on the same network.
Internet Authentication Service	Enables authentication, authorization, and accounting of dial-up and VPN users. Supports the RADIUS protocol.
RPC over HTTP Proxy	Enables Remote Procedure Call (RPC)/Distributed Component Object Model (DCOM) to travel over the Hypertext Transfer Protocol (HTTP) via IIS.
Simple TCP/IP Services	Supports the following TCP/IP services: Character Generator, Daytime, Discard, Echo, and Quote Of The Day.
Windows Internet Name Service (WINS)	Sets up a WINS server that registers and resolves NetBIOS names for clients.

Other Network File And Print Services Component

This component provides file and print services for the Macintosh operating system, as well as print services for UNIX. Table 1-3 lists and describes the subcomponents available in Other Network File And Print Services.

Table 1-3   Other Network File And Print Services Subcomponents

Subcomponent	Description
File Services For Macintosh	Enables Macintosh users to both store files and gain access to files on a server running Microsoft Windows.
Print Services For Macintosh	Enables Macintosh users to send jobs to a print spooler on a server running Microsoft Windows.
Print Services For UNIX	Enables UNIX clients to print to any printer available to the local computer.

Exam Tip   Be sure to know the functions of the Network File And Print Services subcomponents for the exam.

Certificate Services Component

This Windows component provides services for issuing and managing certificates that are used in software security systems employing public key technologies. Among other functions, certificates are used to verify the contents of e-mail, validate the sender and recipient of messages, authenticate Web clients and servers, identify smart cards, and encrypt files. Table 1-4 lists and describes the subcomponents included in this Windows Server 2003 component.

Table 1-4   Certificate Services Subcomponents

Subcomponent	Description
Certificate Services CA	Sets up a certificate authority (CA) that issues and manages digital certificates.
Certificate Services Web Enrollment Support	Allows you to publish Web pages on your server to submit requests and retrieve certificates from a CA.

Adding Active Directory to a Windows Infrastructure

To install Active Directory on your network, simply promote a computer to the status of domain controller by adding the Domain Controller role in the Manage Your Server window.

Adding Active Directory dramatically changes the logical infrastructure of a Windows network. For example, if no DNS server has previously been configured, the name resolution method on the network switches from NetBIOS to DNS. Network-level security and authentication based on the Kerberos protocol are also introduced. Finally, adding Active Directory introduces many features associated with the directory service itself, including a global catalog that contains information about every object in the directory and a replication service that distributes directory data across the network.

Lesson Review

The following questions are intended to reinforce key information presented in this lesson. If you are unable to answer a question, review the lesson materials and try the question again. You can find answers to the questions in the "Questions and Answers" section at the end of this chapter.

1. Which Windows subcomponent should you install to allow Macintosh users to store and access folders in a Windows Server 2003 network?

   _____

2. Which Windows component should you install if you want to set up DHCP, DNS, and WINS?

   a. Management And Monitoring Tools

   b. Networking Services

   c. Other File And Print Services

3. You want your computer running Windows Server 2003 to interoperate with a NetWare network that contains servers running both NetWare 3.11 and NetWare 4.1. How should you configure the NWLink protocol to handle this situation?

    a. Leave the protocol in Auto Detect mode.

    b. Configure the frame type as 802.2.

    c. Configure the frame type as 802.3.

    d. Configure the Registry to allow both 802.2 and 802.3 frame types.

4. Which of the following network features does not rely on a Public Key Infrastructure?

    a. IPSec

    b. File sharing

    c. SSL

5. How is name resolution normally performed in Windows Server 2003 and Windows 2000 native domains?

_____

6. Which Windows subcomponent includes agents that allow you to monitor and control Windows servers, UNIX servers, and network devices?

_____

Lesson Summary

- You can bind additional clients, services, and protocols to a network connection by opening the properties dialog box associated with a connection and clicking Install.

- By installing and configuring various Windows components, you can add services to your network such as centralized addressing (DHCP) and name resolution (WINS, DNS).

- Although you can usually accept the default Auto Detect mode for frame type settings with the NWLink protocol, the Auto Detect feature cannot properly resolve situations in which multiple frame types exist.

- To install Active Directory on your network, simply promote a computer to the status of domain controller by adding the Domain Controller role. The introduction of Windows Server 2003 Active Directory domains dramatically changes the logical infrastructure of a Windows network.

Case Scenario Exercise

After physically connecting the 15 computers in Contoso's small company network, you run the Ipconfig /all command on each computer. Most hosts reveal an APIPA address, but some exceptions exist.

CS-7 shows the following output:

```
C:\Documents and Settings\Administrator>ipconfig /all

Windows IP Configuration

        Host Name . . . . . . . . . . . . : CS-7
        Primary Dns Suffix  . . . . . . . :
        Node Type . . . . . . . . . . . . : Mixed
        IP Routing Enabled. . . . . . . . : No
        WINS Proxy Enabled. . . . . . . . : No

Ethernet adapter Local Area Connection:

        Media State . . . . . . . . . . . : Media disconnected
        Description . . . . . . . . . . . : Intel(R) PRO/100 P Mobile Combo Adapter
        Physical Address. . . . . . . . . : 00-D0-59-80-B7-F6
```

1. In attempting to fix the problem, what should be your first step?

   _____

   _____

2. Host CS-8 shows no output at all from the Ipconfig /all command. You have verified that a network adapter is physically installed. What should be your next step?

   _____

   _____

3. Host CS-10 reveals an IP address of 0.0.0.0. You run the Ipconfig /renew command, but the address stays the same. If you want the computer to adopt an APIPA address, what should be your next step?

   _____

   _____

   _____

   _____

   _____

Chapter Summary

- By default, networked computers are grouped in a single workgroup named WORKGROUP. The underlying protocol for the network is the TCP/IP suite. Computer names are NetBIOS names, and names are resolved only by using NetBT broadcasts to the local network segment. Security is configured locally at each computer; no centralized security exists.

- When no DHCP server is present, the computers assign themselves APIPA addresses in the range of 169.254.0.1–169.254.255.254. This default addressing feature provides basic connectivity but does not allow for shared Internet connections, subnetting, or any centralized administration of addresses.

- You can greatly extend the default infrastructure of a Windows Server 2003 network by installing and configuring additional network components or adding server roles.

- You can add centralized addressing (DHCP) and name resolution (WINS, DNS) services for your network.

- If you have Administrator privileges on a local computer, you can install new clients, services, and protocols to be used by particular network connections.

- You can configure various services, such as the Routing And Remote Access service or Certificate Services, to run on the server computer and provide a service for other network hosts.

Exam Highlights

Before taking the exam, review the key points and terms that are presented below to help you identify topics you need to review. Return to the lessons for additional practice, and review the "Further Reading" sections in Part 2 for pointers to more information about topics covering the exam objectives.

Key Points

- Be familiar with APIPA address ranges. Specifically, in test questions you might have to recognize an APIPA address as a sign that a DHCP server is not reachable or is malfunctioning.

- When a computer fails to obtain an APIPA address (in the absence of a DHCP server), this issue usually signals hardware problems.

- Memorize the Registry keys necessary to disable APIPA on either all adapters or a specific adapter.

- Be familiar with NetWare frame types. Know when Auto Detect mode will lead to errors.

- Be familiar with the installable Windows components and subcomponents that relate to networking, such as File Services For Macintosh, Print Services For Macintosh, and Print Services For UNIX.

Key Terms

APIPA   A TCP/IP feature in Windows XP and products in the Windows Server 2003 family that automatically configures a unique IP address when the TCP/IP protocol is configured for dynamic addressing and a DHCP server is not available. IP addresses are chosen randomly from the range 169.254.0.1 through 169.254.255.254, and assigned a subnet mask of 255.255.0.0. The APIPA range of IP addresses is reserved by the Internet Assigned Numbers Authority (IANA), and IP addresses within this range are not used on the Internet.

NetBT   An abbreviation for NetBIOS over TCP/IP, a protocol which provides a foundation for higher-layer Microsoft network communications, including SMB and CIFS.

CIFS   An extension of the SMB protocol that provides the basis for file sharing and other functions on Microsoft networks. Among the enhancements of CIFS over SMB is the ability of CIFS to operate directly over DNS without NetBIOS.

NWLink   The Microsoft implementation of the IPX/SPX protocol used on NetWare networks. NWLink allows connectivity between Windows-based computers and NetWare networks running IPX/SPX.

Questions and Answers

Page
1-13
Lesson Review Questions

1. You are the administrator for your company's network, which includes computers running Windows Server 2003, computers running Microsoft Windows XP Professional, and a server running Novell NetWare. The Novell NetWare server has only the IPX/SPX network protocol configured. You want every network computer to be able to access features in the NetWare network operating system, the Windows Server 2003 network operating system, and the Internet. Which protocols must be installed on your network computers?

   NWLink and TCP/IP

2. Which of the following does not rely on certificates and public key cryptography?

   a. SSL

   b. EFS

   c. IPSec

   d. Workgroup security

   d

3. Which protocol provides names and name resolution for workgroups in Windows?

   a. NetBIOS

   b. CIFS

   c. DNS

   d. Kerberos

   a

Page
1-23
Lesson Review Questions

1. You have installed Windows Server 2003 on a multihomed computer named Server001. Network Adapter A is connected to a large network in which 80 percent of the servers run NetWare and 20 percent run Windows Server 2003. Network Adapter B is connected to a large network in which 80 percent of the servers run Windows Server 2003 and 20 percent run NetWare. According to server logs, Network Adapter B sends and receives more traffic than Network Adapter A does.

How should you specify the order of network providers for Server001 in general and the binding order of services for Network Adapter A and Network Adapter B, respectively?

The network provider order should specify Microsoft Windows Network ahead of NetWare. For the connection to Network Adapter A, you should specify Client Service For NetWare ahead of Client For Microsoft Networks. For the connection to Network Adapter B, you should specify Client For Microsoft Networks ahead of Client Service For NetWare.

2. Which of the following are automatically configured in Windows Server 2003?

   a. Local area connections

   b. Dial-up networking

   c. Routing tables

   a

3. Which of the following components are automatically assigned to connections?

   a. Client Service For NetWare

   b. Network Monitor Driver

   c. Client For Microsoft Networks

   c

4. Which of the following features is not configurable through the Routing And Remote Access console?

   a. Dial-up networking

   b. Packet filtering

   c. Internet Connection Sharing

   d. Active Directory

   d

5. Which of the following is a requirement for networking on a Windows Server 2003 network?

   a. DHCP

   b. Network protocol

   c. WINS

   b

Page
1-30
Lesson Review Questions

1. Which Windows subcomponent should you install to allow Macintosh users to store and access folders in a Windows Server 2003 network?

   File Services For Macintosh

2. Which Windows component should you install if you want to set up DHCP, DNS, and WINS?

   a. Management And Monitoring Tools

   b. Networking Services

   c. Other File And Print Services

   b

3. You want your computer running Windows Server 2003 to interoperate with a NetWare network that contains servers running both NetWare 3.11 and NetWare 4.1. How should you configure the NWLink protocol to handle this situation?

   a. Leave the protocol in Auto Detect mode.

   b. Configure the frame type as 802.2.

   c. Configure the frame type as 802.3.

   d. Configure the Registry to allow both 802.2 and 802.3 frame types.

   d

4. Which of the following network features does not rely on a Public Key Infrastructure?

   a. IPSec

   b. File sharing

   c. SSL

   b

5. How is name resolution normally performed in Active Directory Domains?

   Through the DNS protocol

6. Which Windows subcomponent includes agents that allow you to monitor and control Windows servers, UNIX servers, and network devices?

   Simple Network Management Protocol

Page
1-32

Case Scenario

1. In attempting to fix the problem, what should be your first step?

Verify that the Ethernet cable is properly connected to the network adapter on one end and to the Ethernet hub or switch at the other end.

2. Host CS-8 shows no output at all from the Ipconfig /all command. You have verified that a network adapter is physically installed. What should be your next step?

Use Device Manager to verify that the most recent version of the network adapter driver is installed and that the device is working properly.

3. Host CS-10 reveals an IP address of 0.0.0.0. You run the Ipconfig /renew command, but the address stays the same. What should be your next step?

Delete the following Registry keys, if they exist:

HKEY_LOCAL_MACHINE\SYSTEM\CurrentControlSet\Services\Tcpip\Parameters\IPAutocon-figurationEnabled

HKEY_LOCAL_MACHINE\SYSTEM\CurrentControlSet\Services\Tcpip\Parameters\Inter-faces*interface*\IPAutoconfigurationEnabled

Network Interface Layer

The *network interface layer* is the step in the communication process that describes standards for physical media and electrical signaling. Examples of standards defined at the network interface layer include Ethernet, Token Ring, Fiber Distributed Data Interface (FDDI), X.25, Frame Relay, RS-232, and V.35.

Internet Layer

The *internet layer* of the TCP/IP model is the step in the communication process during which information is packaged, addressed, and routed to network destinations. ARP, IP, and ICMP are examples of internet-layer protocols within the TCP/IP suite.

- **ARP**   Whereas IP routes packets to logical addresses that might be dozens of network segments away, ARP finds the physical computers for which IP packets are destined within each network segment. After using ARP to look up hardware addresses, TCP/IP hosts store known IP-to-MAC address mappings in a local ARP cache. You can view this cache with arp –a command or clear it with the arp –d command.

> **Off the Record**   In the MCSE exam world, the arp –d command supposedly saves your day whenever you cannot connect to a computer, located in broadcast range, whose network card has just been changed. Here's what you're supposed to see: the new adapter has furnished the seemingly-stranded computer with a fresh hardware address, thus rendering obsolete your currently stored IP-to-MAC address mapping for that remote host. Until you clear your local ARP cache, your computer will keep trying to reach the remote one by calling out a defunct hardware address. So goes the theory.
>
> In reality, virtually all ARP entries are dynamic, which means they are automatically added and aged out of the cache as needed. Dynamic ARP entries have a life span of only 2 minutes if they are not renewed. So, if your computer happens to cache the IP-to-MAC address mapping of another host, immediately after which someone shuts down that remote box, opens it up, replaces its network card, and miraculously gets it back online before all of 120 seconds have elapsed, and if, despite this feat, you are still too impatient to wait out the intervening moments before you can ping same address, then the arp –d command really may save your day. Otherwise, you needn't worry about it.

- **IP**   IP is primarily responsible for addressing and routing packets between hosts. An IP packet can be lost, delivered out of sequence, duplicated, or delayed, as can information in any other protocol. However, IP itself does not attempt to recover from these types of errors. The acknowledgment of packets delivered, the sequencing of packets, and the recovery of lost packets are the responsibility of a higher-layer protocol, such as TCP.

- **ICMP**   With ICMP, hosts and routers that use IP can report errors and exchange limited control and status information. You can use the Ping command to send ICMP echo request messages and record the receipt of ICMP echo reply messages. With these messages, you can detect communication failures and troubleshoot common TCP/IP connectivity problems.

> **Real World   ICMP and Firewalls**
>
> As a network administrator, you typically need to concern yourself with ICMP message types when you are configuring firewalls that face the public Internet. Most firewalls, including the including the Basic Firewall (also known as Internet Connection Firewall) included in Windows Server 2003, allow you to specify the ICMP message requests to which the firewall responds. For example, if you want to be able to ping the firewall, you need to configure the firewall to respond to incoming echo requests.

Transport Layer

The *transport layer* of the TCP/IP model is the step in the communication process during which the standards of data transport are determined. TCP and UDP are examples of transport-layer protocols within the TCP/IP suite.

- **TCP**   TCP receives data from the application layer and processes the data as a stream of bytes. These bytes are grouped into segments that TCP then numbers and sequences for delivery to a network host. When TCP receives a stream of data from a network host, it sends the data to the intended application.

  TCP ports enable different applications and programs to use TCP services on a single host, as shown in Figure 2-2. Each program that uses TCP ports listens for messages arriving on its associated port number. Data sent to a specific TCP port is thus received by the application listening at that port.

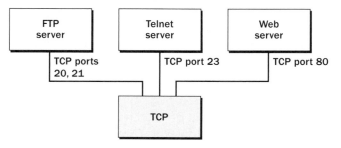

Figure 2-2   TCP ports

> **Exam Tip**   By using packet filtering at a router, you can block or allow TCP or UDP traffic based on port number. Some exam questions require you to know which ports you must leave open to allow the following protocols to pass through to your network: File Transfer Protocol (FTP; TCP ports 20 and 21), Hypertext Transfer Protocol (HTTP; TCP port 80), Hypertext Transfer Protocol Secure/Secure Sockets Layer (HTTPS/SSL; TCP port 443), Point-to-Point Tunneling Protocol (PPTP; TCP port 1723), and L2TP/IPSec (UDP ports 500, 1701, and 4500). Be sure to memorize these port numbers before taking the exam!

- **UDP**   Many network services (such as DNS) rely on UDP instead of TCP as a transport protocol. UDP enables fast transport of datagrams by eliminating the reliability features of TCP such as delivery guarantees and sequence verification. Unlike TCP, UDP is a *connectionless* service that provides only best-effort datagram delivery to network hosts. A source host that needs reliable communication must use either TCP or a program that provides its own sequencing and acknowledgment services.

> **Exam Tip**   For the exam, you need to know that connectionless services in TCP/IP networks rely on UDP as a transport.

Application Layer

The *application layer* of the TCP/IP model is the step in the communication process during which end-user data is manipulated, packaged, and sent to and from transport-layer ports. Application-layer protocols often describe a user-friendly method of presenting, naming, sending, or receiving data over TCP/IP. Common examples of application-layer protocols native to the TCP/IP suite include HTTP, Telnet, FTP, Trivial File Transfer Protocol (TFTP), Simple Network Management Protocol (SNMP), Domain Name System (DNS), Post Office Protocol 3 (POP3), Simple Mail Transfer Protocol (SMTP), and Network News Transfer Protocol (NNTP).

Lesson Review

The following questions are intended to reinforce key information presented in this lesson. If you are unable to answer a question, review the lesson materials and try the question again. You can find answers to the questions in the "Questions and Answers" section at the end of this chapter.

1. Which is the only layer of the TCP/IP reference model that does not contain any TCP/IP protocols?

   a. The network interface layer

   b. The internet layer

   c. The transport layer

   d. The application layer

2. Which of the following TCP/IP protocols does not function at the internet layer?

   a. IP

   b. ARP

   c. TCP

   d. ICMP

3. Which of the following is a transport-layer protocol?

   a. IGMP

   b. UDP

   c. DNS

   d. Ethernet

4. Which of the following services connect to UDP ports? (Choose all that apply.)

   a. NetBIOS

   b. DNS

   c. Ethernet

   d. Telnet

Lesson Summary

- The TCP/IP protocol stack is based on a four-layer reference model, including the network interface, internet, transport, and application layers.

- Whereas IP routes packets to logical addresses that might be dozens of network segments away, ARP finds the physical computers for which IP packets are destined within each network segment.

- TCP is a required TCP/IP standard that provides reliable, connection-oriented packet delivery service. UDP provides a connectionless datagram service that, unlike TCP, does not guarantee delivery or verify sequencing for any datagrams. Both TCP and UDP provide ports at which applications can connect to transport-layer services.

Lesson 2: Understanding IP Addressing

To be able to communicate on a private TCP/IP network or on the public Internet, each host on the network must be identified by a 32-bit IP address. These IP addresses can be grouped into two categories: public IP addresses and private IP addresses. *Public addresses* are the globally unique addresses that are connected to the Internet. *Private addresses* are confined to specific ranges that can be used by any private network but that cannot be seen on the public Internet.

Administering a Windows Server 2003 network requires that you understand the nature of IP addressing, including public and private addressing mechanisms, decimal and binary notations, address classes, subnet masks, and default gateways.

After this lesson, you will be able to

- Describe the various IP addressing types available in Windows Server 2003
- Convert IP addresses between dotted-decimal and binary notation
- Distinguish between the default network ID and host ID for any IP address
- Explain the function of subnet masks and default gateways

Estimated lesson time: 45 minutes

Using Public IP Addresses

Every IP address on the public Internet is unique. To allow networks to obtain unique addresses for the Internet, the Internet Assigned Numbers Authority (IANA) divides up the nonreserved portion of the IP address space and delegates responsibility for address allocation to a number of regional registries throughout the world. These registries include Asia-Pacific Network Information Center (APNIC), American Registry for Internet Numbers (ARIN), and Réseaux IP Européens (RIPE NCC). The regional registries allocate blocks of addresses to a small number of large Internet service providers (ISPs) that then assign smaller blocks to customers and smaller ISPs.

Typically, your ISP assigns you one public IP address for each of your computers that is directly connected to the ISP. This IP address can be assigned dynamically to each computer when the computer connects, or it can be reserved statically for your dedicated line or dial-up account.

Using Private IP Addresses

The IANA has reserved a certain number of IP addresses that are never used on the global Internet. These private IP addresses are used for hosts that require IP connectivity but that do not need to be seen on the public network. For example, a user connecting computers in a home TCP/IP network does not need to assign a public IP address to each host. The user instead can take advantage of the address ranges shown in Table 2-1 to provide addresses for hosts on the network.

Table 2-1   Private Address Ranges

Starting Address	Ending Address
10.0.0.0	10.255.255.254
172.16.0.0	172.31.255.254
192.168.0.0	192.168.255.254

Hosts addressed with a private IP address can connect to the Internet through the use of a proxy server or a computer running Windows Server 2003 configured as a Network Address Translation (NAT) server. Windows Server 2003 also includes the Internet Connection Sharing (ICS) feature that provides simplified NAT services to clients in a private network.

Examining IP Addressing Methods

IP addresses can be provided manually, dynamically by a DHCP server, or automatically by using Automatic Private IP Addressing (APIPA).

Manual IP Addressing

Occasionally, you need to assign addresses manually. For example, manual configuration is required in a network with multiple network segments and in which no DHCP server is present. In addition, if you want to set up a computer to be a DHCP server in a network, you should plan to assign its IP address manually. Finally, if you want a computer to serve as an essential network server, such as a DNS server, WINS server, or domain controller, you should plan to assign the servers a static IP address. Although you can assign static IP addresses by using DHCP address reservations, many administrators prefer to keep essential servers free of DHCP dependence and therefore assign addresses to these servers manually.

In other cases, however, manual configurations are recommended only when DHCP is not available or feasible. Administering manually assigned IP addresses can be time-consuming and confusing, especially in medium to large networks.

Dynamic Host Configuration Protocol

A DHCP server automatically provides IP addresses to DHCP clients from the range or ranges of available addresses you determine. You can also configure a DHCP server to

2 Understanding TCP/IP

Exam Objectives in this Chapter:

- Configure TCP/IP addressing on a server computer
- Troubleshoot TCP/IP addressing
  - ❏ Diagnose and resolve issues related to incorrect configuration

Why This Chapter Matters

> As a network administrator, you will be working with TCP/IP every day. Among your responsibilities will be, no doubt, assigning configurations to TCP/IP hosts on the one hand and then troubleshooting configuration errors on the other. To even begin to fulfill this duty, you will need a thorough understanding of the concepts behind IP addressing. This chapter will explain these concepts and enable you to diagnose problems related to the incorrect configuration of IP subnets, default gateways, subnet masks, or addresses. It will also enable you to verify an address space configuration by teaching you how to determine the number bits to reserve for a subnet ID and host ID. Finally, this chapter will teach you how and when to implement manual, automatic, and alternate IP configurations in your network.

Lessons in this Chapter:

- Lesson 1: Understanding TCP/IP 2-2
- Lesson 2: Understanding IP Addressing 2-7
- Lesson 3: Subnetting and Supernetting IP Networks 2-22
- Lesson 4: Installing and Configuring TCP/IP 2-42

Before You Begin

To complete this chapter, you must have

- Physically networked two computers.
- Performed a Windows Server 2003 installation with default settings on both computers. The computers should be named Computer1 and Computer2. (See the About This Book section for specific instructions on how to perform a default installation by using the Windows Setup Wizard.)
- Assigned the local Administrator account on both computers a strong password.
- Created a private user account, with your name, that has not been granted Administrator privileges. Use this account for all computer activity outside the exercises and procedures in this book.

Lesson 1: Understanding TCP/IP

TCP/IP is a suite of protocols that provides the foundation for Windows networks and the Internet. The TCP/IP protocol stack is based on a four-layer reference model, including the network interface, internet, transport, and application layers.

The core of TCP/IP services exists at the internet and transport layers. In particular, Address Resolution Protocol (ARP), IP, TCP, User Datagram Protocol (UDP), and Internet Control Message Protocol (ICMP) are used in all TCP/IP installations.

After this lesson, you will be able to

- Describe the four layers of the TCP/IP model
- Give examples of the protocols that exist at each layer of the TCP/IP protocol stack
- Describe the basic functions of ARP, IP, ICMP, TCP, and UDP

Estimated lesson time: 10 minutes

Exploring the Layers of the TCP/IP Model

End-to-end communication through TCP/IP is based on four conceptual steps, or layers. Figure 2-1 shows these four layers of the TCP/IP model.

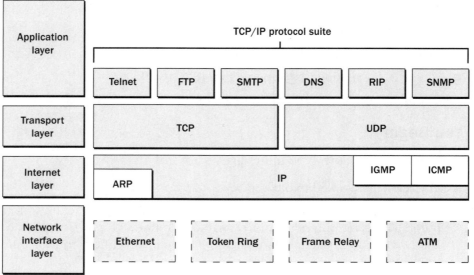

Figure 2-1   Four-layer TCP/IP model and protocol stack

assign clients automatically with other options, such as the addresses of DNS and WINS servers, gateway addresses, and other parameters.

DHCP is covered in more detail in Chapter 7, "Configuring DHCP Servers and Clients," and Chapter 8, "Monitoring and Troubleshooting DHCP."

Automatic Private IP Addressing

APIPA is an automatic addressing feature used for simple networks lacking a DHCP server and consisting of a single network segment. APIPA is discussed in more detail in Chapter 1, "Understanding Windows Server 2003 Networks."

Alternate Configuration

Like APIPA, an alternate configuration provides an IP address for computers unable to find a DHCP server. However, when you specify an alternate configuration on a given computer, that computer defaults (in the absence of a DHCP server) to the manually configured alternate address instead of an APIPA address.

This feature is useful when the computer is used on more than one network and when one of the networks does not have a DHCP server. For example, suppose you use your laptop computer both at the office and at home. The same network adapter is used for both networks, and you configure the local area connection to obtain an IP address automatically. With this simple configuration, the laptop acquires a DHCP-allocated TCP/IP configuration at the office. At home, where you have no DHCP server, the laptop adopts the alternate configuration you have defined, including an IP address, subnet mask, and default gateway appropriate for the home network.

Understanding the Structure of IP Addresses

People usually recognize IP addresses by their distinctive sequence of four numbers separated by dots, such as 192.168.100.22. However, this version of an IP address is really just a transcription—called *dotted-decimal notation*—that people use to remember the address easily. Whereas decimal notation is the 10-digit numbering system that most people use every day, computer processing is based on binary notation, which uses only the digits 1 and 0 to represent all values. The native form of an IP address is thus binary.

The logic behind IP addressing is revealed when you look at this native binary version of IP addresses. To be able to configure, manage, and troubleshoot IP addressing, therefore, you must be able to understand and work with the binary form of IP addresses, as well as translate between binary and decimal notations.

> ### Real World   Manually Converting Binary and Decimal Notations
>
> In the age of computers and scientific calculators, making manual conversions between binary and decimal notation might seem like an outmoded and unnecessarily tedious means of solving an arithmetic problem. Truth be told, network administrators on the job rarely need to make such conversions, and when they do, administrators are far more likely to rush to a calculator for help than to a pencil and paper. Even during the certification exam, you can avoid performing manual conversions because at many test centers a scientific calculator is built into the exam interface. (All test centers include at least a non-scientific calculator.)
>
> So, you might ask, why not simply rely on calculators to perform decimal–binary conversions and avoid performing these operations by hand? The short answer is that by learning to perform these calculations by hand, you will visualize IP addresses more clearly and therefore be able to spot and repair IP configuration problems more easily. This skill is especially important for subnetted networks, in which IP address schemes can appear confusing.
>
> Regardless of this practical benefit, performing manual conversions between the dotted-decimal and binary notation of an IP address is simply a skill expected of a good network administrator, the same way a modern accountant who relies on accounting software for everyday calculations is still expected to be able to perform long division. If that analogy doesn't provide ample motivation, just think that learning to perform these operations by hand gives you a backup method of performing conversions when a scientific calculator is unavailable, as well as an always-available means to flaunt esoteric knowledge and impress your coworkers.

Converting Between Binary and Decimal Notation

Accustomed to decimal systems, people naturally prefer to express decimal values over their binary equivalents. With dotted-decimal notation, each 32-bit address value of an IP address is viewed as four base-10 groupings ranging from 0 to 255, as in the example "192.168.0.225." These values represent the four 8-bit values that make up the 32-bit address. In both binary and decimal notations, each of the four groupings is referred to as an *octet*. However, only in binary form is it possible to see the value of each individual bit. For example, the IP address 192.168.0.225 is expressed in binary notation in the following manner:

```
11000000 10101000 00000000 11100001
```

For any 32-bit IP address, octets and bit places are numbered from left to right. Consequently, the first octet refers to the leftmost octet, and bit places 1 through 8 refer to the eight leftmost bit places, beginning on the far left. The second octet refers to the next eight bits (bit places 9–16), followed by the third octet (bit places 17–24), and the fourth octet (bit places 25–32). Periods are used to separate the four octets in dotted-decimal notation, and spaces are used to separate them in binary notation.

Table 2-2 shows the scientific and decimal notations associated with each bit place within a binary octet. Notice that as you move from left to right and begin with the first bit's value of 128, each successive bit represents half the potential value of the previous bit. In reverse direction, as you move from right to left and begin with the eighth bit's value of 1, each successive bit represents double the potential value of the previous bit. This pattern allows you to easily recall the potential value of each bit place within an octet.

Table 2-2   Potential Values in a Binary Octet

Octet	First Bit	Second Bit	Third Bit	Fourth Bit	Fifth Bit	Sixth Bit	Seventh Bit	Eighth Bit
Scientific notation	2^7	2^6	2^5	2^4	2^3	2^2	2^1	2^0
Decimal notation	128	64	32	16	8	4	2	1
Example	1	0	1	0	1	1	0	0

Note that these bit places represent values held only when a given bit place contains a 1. When an octet contains a 0 in any bit place, the value of the bit is 0. For example, if the first bit place is filled with a bit value of 1, the equivalent decimal value is 128. Where the bit value is 0, the equivalent decimal value is 0 as well. If all the bit places in an octet are filled with 1s, the equivalent decimal value is 255. If all the bit places are filled with 0s, the equivalent decimal value is 0.

Binary-to-Decimal Conversion Example   The following binary string shows a possible first octet in an IP address:

```
10101100
```

In this eight-digit binary number the first, third, fifth, and sixth bit places contain 1. All other bit places are filled with 0. To understand the decimal value of this binary octet, you can easily draw a conversion table, such as the one shown here, in which to enter the potential bit values of the octet:

128	64	32	16	8	4	2	1
1	0	1	0	1	1	0	0

Using this table as a reference, you can perform simple addition of each bit place's decimal equivalent value to find the decimal sum for this octet string, as follows:

first bit (128) + third bit (32) + fifth bit (8) + sixth bit (4) = octet total (172)

Because the sum is 172, the first octet of the example IP address is expressed as 172 in decimal form.

Next, suppose that the following four octets represent the complete IP address:

```
10101100 00010001 00000111 00011011
```

After using this method on the other octets, you can determine that the complete dotted-decimal equivalent of the IP address is 172.17.7.27.

Decimal-to-Binary Conversion Example   You convert an octet from decimal to binary form by adding a 1-bit or 0-bit in the octet's bit places from left to right until the desired target decimal value is achieved. If adding a 1-bit in a given bit place causes your total to exceed the target decimal value, simply add a 0-bit instead and move to the next bit place.

For example, suppose you want to convert the IP address 172.31.230.218 into binary form. First write out the sequence of potential bit values in a table, as shown here:

128	64	32	16	8	4	2	1

You can begin by considering the potential value of the first bit place (128). Because 128 does not exceed the target value of 172, write a 1 in the first bit place and note 128 as your running subtotal. Next, look at the potential value of the second bit place (64). Because 128 + 64 overshoots your target of 172, write a 0 in this second bit place. After this, move to the third bit, whose potential value is 32. Because the sum of 128 and 32 does not exceed the target value of 172, write a 1 in this third bit place. The running subtotal of the first 3 bits is therefore 128 + 0 + 32, or 160. Now move to the fourth bit place, whose potential value is 16. The sum of 160 and 16 overshoots the target value of 172, so you must write a 0 in this bit place.

Next, consider that the potential value of the fifth bit place is 8. The sum of 160 and 8 does not exceed the target value of 172; consequently, you should write a 1 in this fifth bit place. The running subtotal of the first 5 bits is now 128 + 0 + 32 + 0 + 8 = 168. Finally, note that the potential value of the sixth bit is 4. The sum of 168 and 4 yields the target value of 172, so you should write a 1 in the sixth bit place and a 0 in both the seventh and eighth bit places.

The first octet is therefore written as follows in binary notation:

```
10101100
```

To convert the entire address 172.31.230.218 from decimal to binary, simply complete the same process with the remaining three octets. The result is the following binary notation:

```
10101100 00011111 11100110 11011010
```

Using Calculator to Perform Notation Conversion   Although being able to perform manual conversions between binary and decimal notation is a useful skill, you can also use Microsoft Calculator to compute these conversions quickly. Once you open Calculator, the functions necessary for notation conversion appear when you select Scientific from the View menu. Once the tool is in Scientific view, select either Dec or Bin to enter the desired value in the source notation. For example, if you want to convert 11001100 to decimal notation, first select Bin. Next, enter the binary value, as shown in Figure 2-3. (Whenever possible, use the Copy and Paste functions to perform this last step.)

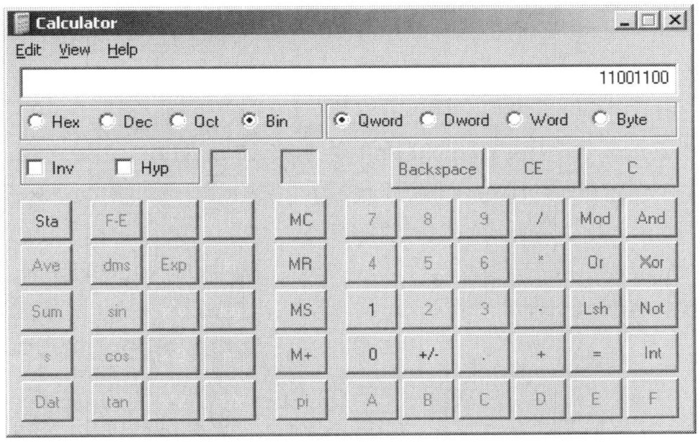

Figure 2-3   Entering binary values in Calculator

Once you have entered the value, simply select the Dec option to view the value in the target notation.

Note   As with common decimal notation, leftmost 0s in binary are not registered by Calculator. Therefore, an IP octet of 00001110 is expressed as 1110 in the utility. For this reason, you should always count the number of bits shown in Calculator so that you do not incorrectly note the value. For example, you could easily mistake the binary value 1100001 (decimal value 97) for an IP octet of 11000001 (decimal value 193). If fewer than 8 bits are shown, you should always add 0s to the left side of the bit string when you want to represent the value as an IP octet. You can also use the digit grouping feature to avoid making similar errors. (Digit grouping, however, is unfortunately not available on the exam.)

Network ID and Host ID

The routers that direct packets of data between TCP/IP networks do not usually need to know the exact host for which an IP packet is destined. Instead, routers need to read from an IP packet only the destination network address of which the particular destination host is a member. The routers then use information stored in their routing tables to determine how to move the packet toward the network of the destination host. Only after the packet is delivered to the destination's network segment is the precise location of the destination host determined.

To assist in this routing process, an IP address is divided into two components:

■ The first part of an IP address, the *network ID*, identifies a particular network within a larger TCP/IP internetwork (such as the Internet).

■ The last part of an IP address, the *host ID*, identifies a TCP/IP host (a workstation, server, router, or other TCP/IP device) specific to the network defined by the network ID.

Figure 2-4 shows a sample view of an IP address (131.107.16.200) as it is divided into network ID and host ID sections. In this example, the network ID portion (131.107) is indicated by the first two numbers of the IP address. The host ID portion (16.200) is indicated by the last two numbers of the IP address.

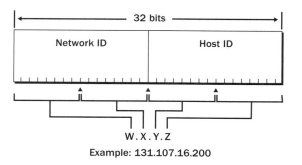

Figure 2-4   Network and host IDs

You should follow several general guidelines when assigning network IDs and host IDs:

■ The network ID and host ID bits cannot be all 1s. If all bits are set to 1, the address is interpreted as a broadcast rather than a host ID.

- The network ID and host ID bits cannot be all 0s. If all bits are set to 0, the address is interpreted to mean "this network only."

- The host ID must be unique to the local network ID.

IP Address Classes

The *class* of an address, which is determined by the value of the first octet, designates which of its 32 bits represent the default network ID. The address class also defines, for each network ID, how many hosts that network can support. The Internet community has defined five address classes. Only Class A, B, and C addresses are used for assignment to TCP/IP nodes.

Table 2-3 uses *w.x.y.z* to designate the four octet values in any given IP address. The table is used to show the following:

- How the value of the first octet (*w*) of any given IP address effectively indicates the class of address

- How the octets in an address are divided into network ID and host ID

- The number of possible networks and hosts per network available for each class

Table 2-3   IP Address Classes

Class	Value of *w*	Value of First Bits	Network ID	Host ID	Number of Networks within Class	Number of Hosts per Network (Default)
A	1–126	0	*w*	*x.y.z*	126	16,777,214
B	128–191	10	*w.x*	*y.z*	16,384	65,534
C	192–223	110	*w.x.y*	*z*	2,097,152	254
D	224–239	1110	Reserved for multicast addressing	N/A	N/A	N/A
E	240–254	1111	Reserved for experimental use	N/A	N/A	N/A

Figure 2-5 illustrates the differences among Class A, B, and C addresses.

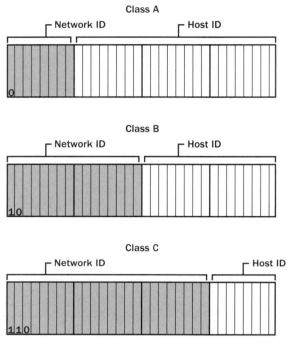

Figure 2-5   IP address classes

Subnet Masks

Another setting whose proper configuration is required for TCP/IP to function is the *subnet mask*. This value is used by a host to determine whether the destination of a packet is on the local network or on a remote network. Each subnet mask is a 32-bit address that uses a string of 1-bits to block, or *mask*, the network ID of a packet's destination address and to distinguish this network ID from the host ID. Every host on a TCP/IP network requires a subnet mask—either a default subnet mask, which is used when a network has not been subnetted (and therefore consists of a single subnet), or a custom subnet mask, which is typically used when a network is divided into multiple subnets.

For example, the following 32-bit number represents the default subnet mask used by hosts configured with a Class B address (such as 172.20.16.200):

```
11111111 11111111 00000000 00000000 (255.255.0.0)
```

If a TCP/IP host with the address 172.20.16.200 sends a packet to the address 172.21.17.201, the host first performs a bitwise AND operation between the local address and the locally configured subnet mask. Because ANDing two numbers results in a figure with 0s in all bit places except those where both original binary numbers have 1-bits, the result of ANDing 172.20.16.200 and 255.255.0.0 is 172.20.0.0. The host then performs a bitwise AND operation between the destination address and this same subnet mask, which results in the binary equivalent of 172.21.0.0. TCP/IP then compares the values resulting from these two bitwise AND operations. If the two values are identical, the TCP/IP host concludes that the destination is on the local subnet. If the two values differ, the host determines that the destination is remote.

Network Prefix Length Representation of Subnet Masks

Because the network ID bits must always be chosen in a contiguous fashion from the high-order (leftmost) bits, a shorthand way of expressing a subnet mask is to denote the number of bits that define the network ID as a *network prefix*. The subnet mask can then be expressed using network prefix notation: *IP address /network prefix*. For example, the IP address 131.107.16.200 and subnet mask 255.255.0.0 can be designated more simply by the notation 131.107.16.200/16. The 16 after the slash represents the number of 1-bits used in this particular subnet mask. Similarly, /24 designates a subnet mask of 255.255.255.0 for a Class C address such as 206.73.118.23/24.

 Note   Network prefix notation is also known as *classless interdomain routing* (CIDR; pronounced "cider") notation.

Table 2-4 displays default subnet masks for the Internet address classes.

Table 2-4   Subnet Masks

Address Class	Default Subnet Mask in Binary	Network Prefix with Decimal Equivalent
Class A	11111111 00000000 00000000 00000000	/8 = 255.0.0.0
Class B	11111111 11111111 00000000 00000000	/16 = 255.255.0.0
Class C	11111111 11111111 11111111 00000000	/24 = 255.255.255.0

Understanding Default Gateways

If a TCP/IP host needs to communicate with a host on another network, it usually does so through a router. Routers contain multiple interfaces connected to separate networks, and *routing* is the process of receiving IP packets at one interface and sending these packets out another interface toward a final destination. For a given host on a TCP/IP network, the *default gateway* is the IP address of a router, within broadcast range, that is configured to forward IP traffic to other networks.

When a computer attempts to communicate with another host on an IP network, the computer uses the subnet mask to determine whether the destination host is local or remote. If the destination is a host on the local network segment, the computer simply sends the packet on the local network by means of a broadcast. If, however, the destination is a remote host, the computer forwards the packet to the default gateway defined in its TCP/IP properties. The router specified at the default gateway address is then responsible for forwarding the packet to the correct network.

Practice: Working with Octet Notations

In this practice, you manually convert decimal notation to binary notation, and binary notation to decimal notation. You also practice converting subnet masks.

Exercise 1: Manually Convert Numbers from Decimal to Binary Notation

Convert the number given at the top of each table. Use the table to work out your answer, then perform the same conversion in Calculator to see if you obtain the same result.

Decimal notation: 159

128	64	32	16	8	4	2	1

Binary notation: _____

Decimal notation: 65

128	64	32	16	8	4	2	1

Binary notation: _____

Binary notation: 1001010

128	64	32	16	8	4	2	1

Decimal notation: __

Binary notation: 01110011

128	64	32	16	8	4	2	1

Decimal notation: ___

Exercise 2: Convert Between Dotted-Decimal and Network Prefix Subnet Masks

In this practice, you convert nondefault subnet masks from dotted-decimal to network prefix, and from network prefix to dotted-decimal. Note that these values represent nondefault subnet masks, which are explained in Lesson 3 of this chapter.

Use Calculator and Table 2-4 to help you convert between the two ways of expressing a subnet mask.

1. 255.255.255.192
2. 255.255.252.0
3. /27
4. /21

Lesson Review

The following questions are intended to reinforce key information presented in this lesson. If you are unable to answer a question, review the lesson materials and try the question again. You can find answers to the questions in the "Questions and Answers" section at the end of this chapter.

1. What does the local host use to determine the destination network ID of a particular packet?

   a. The IP header

   b. The subnet mask

   c. The address class

2. A host determines that the destination network ID of a packet is the same as its own network ID. What does the host do with the packet?

   a. It broadcasts an ARP request to determine the Media Access Control (MAC) address of the destination host and transmits the packet on the local network.

   b. It sends the packet to the server, which broadcasts the packet on the local network.

   c. It sends the packet to the default gateway for delivery.

3. Which of the following is the dotted-decimal notation equivalent of the binary address 11001100 00001010 11001000 00000100? To answer the question, first perform notation conversion manually, and then verify your answer with Calculator.

   a. 204.18.200.3

   b. 204.34.202.4

   c. 204.10.200.4

   d. 202.10.200.4

4. Which of the following is the binary equivalent of the dotted-decimal address 207.209.68.100? To answer the question, first perform notation conversion manually, and then verify your answer with Calculator.

   a. 11001111 11010001 01000100 01100100

   b. 11000111 11010001 01000100 01100100

   c. 11001111 11010001 01000100 01101100

   d. 11001111 11010001 11001101 01100100

5. Determine the dotted-decimal equivalent of the following address. Use CIDR notation to designate the default subnet mask. First perform this notation conversion manually, and then verify your answer with Calculator.

   10010010 01101011 00100111 10001001

Lesson Summary

■ Public IP addresses are the globally unique addresses that are connected to the Internet. Private IP addresses are confined to specific ranges and can be used by any private network.

■ An alternate configuration enables an automatically configured computer to use a manually specified IP address configuration instead of APIPA in the absence of a DHCP server.

■ In TCP/IP, the default gateway is the router that connects the host's subnet to other networks.

- The subnet mask of the local host is used to compare the network ID of the local host to the network ID of every IP packet it sends on the network. If the network ID of the host matches the destination network ID of the IP packet, the packet is transmitted on the local network. If the destination network ID of the packet is different from that of the host, the packet is sent to the local default gateway.

- The address class of an IP address determines its default subnet mask.

Lesson 3: Subnetting and Supernetting IP Networks

By manipulating subnet masks, you can customize address space to suit your network needs. Using subnetting, you can subdivide networks into distinct and separate groups. Using supernetting and CIDR, you can combine separate networks into a single address space.

After this lesson, you will be able to

- Manipulate subnet masks to configure subnets for a variety of network restrictions and needs
- Given any network address and subnet mask, determine the number of subnets and hosts available
- Determine the range of IP addresses for each subnet implied by a given network address and subnet mask
- Manipulate subnet masks to configure a supernetted address space
- Configure variable-length subnet masks to meet network requirements for subnets of varying sizes

Estimated lesson time: 70 minutes

Understanding Subnetting

Subnet masks are used by hosts to determine which portion of an IP address is considered the network ID of that address. Class A, B, and C addresses use default subnet masks that cover the first 8, 16, and 24 bits, respectively, of a 32-bit address. The logical network that is defined by a subnet mask is known as a *subnet*.

Default subnet mask values are acceptable for networks that do not need to be subdivided. For example, on a network with 100 computers connected only through Gigabit Ethernet cards, cables, and switches, all hosts can communicate with each other by using the local network. Routers are not needed within the network to shield excessive broadcasts or to connect hosts on separate physical segments. For such simple requirements, a single Class C network ID is sufficient. Figure 2-6 illustrates a single-subnet network such as this.

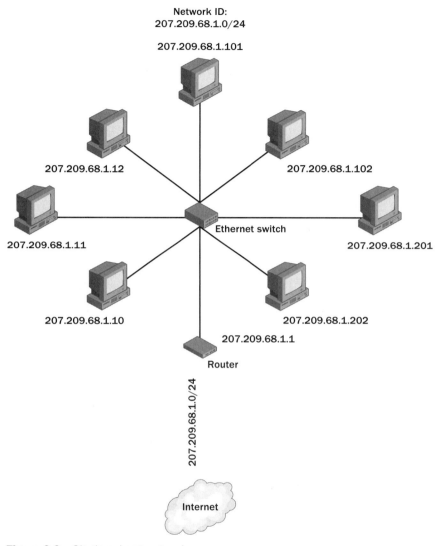

Figure 2-6   Single-subnet network

What Is Subnetting?

Subnetting refers to the practice of logically subdividing a network address space by extending the string of 1-bits used in the subnet mask of a network. This extension enables you to create multiple subnets within the original network address space.

For example, when the default subnet mask of 255.255.0.0 is used for hosts within the Class B network of 131.107.0.0, the IP addresses 131.107.1.11 and 131.107.2.11 are found on the same subnet, and these hosts communicate with each other by means of a broadcast. However, when the subnet mask is extended to 255.255.255.0, the addresses 131.107.1.11 and 131.107.2.11 are found on different subnets. To communicate with each other, hosts with addresses 131.107.1.11/24 and 131.107.2.11/24 send IP packets to the default gateway, which is then responsible for routing the datagram toward the destination subnet. Hosts external to the network continue to use the default subnet mask to communicate with hosts within the network. Figure 2-7 and Figure 2-8 illustrate the two versions of this network.

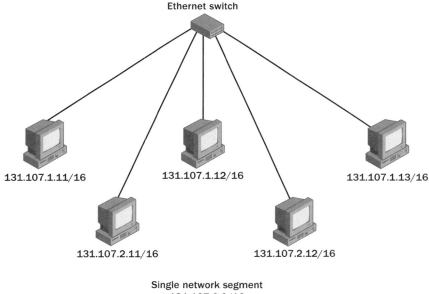

Ethernet switch

131.107.1.11/16   131.107.1.12/16   131.107.1.13/16

131.107.2.11/16   131.107.2.12/16

Single network segment
131.107.0.0/16

Figure 2-7   Class B address space not subnetted

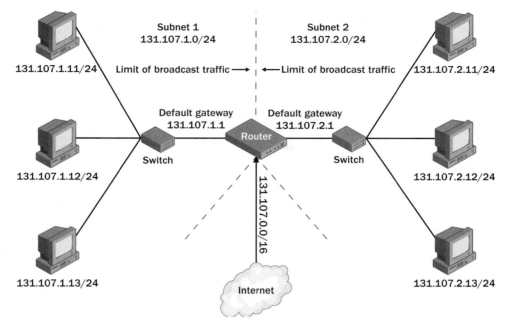

Figure 2-8   Subnetted Class B address space

Whereas the original Class B network address space in Figure 2-7 consisted of a single subnet of up to 65,534 hosts, the new subnet mask configured in Figure 2-8 allows you to subdivide this original space into 256 subnets with as many as 254 hosts each.

Advantages of Subnetting

Subnetting is often used to accommodate a divided physical topology or to restrict broadcast traffic on a network. Other advantages of subnetting include improved security (by restricting unauthorized traffic behind routers) and simplified administration (by delegating control of subnets to other departments or administrators).

Accommodating Physical Topology   Suppose you are designing a campus network with 200 hosts spread over four buildings—Voter Hall, Twilight Hall, Monroe Hall, and Sunderland Hall. You want each of these four buildings to include 50 hosts. If your ISP has allocated to you the Class C network 208.147.66.0, you can use the addresses 208.147.66.1–208.147.66.254 for your 200 hosts. However, because these hosts are distributed among four physically separate locations, these hosts are not all able to communicate with each other by means of a local network broadcast. By extending the subnet mask and borrowing 2 bits from the host ID portion of your address space, you can divide the network into four logical subnets. You can then use a router to connect the four physical networks. Figure 2-9 illustrates this scenario.

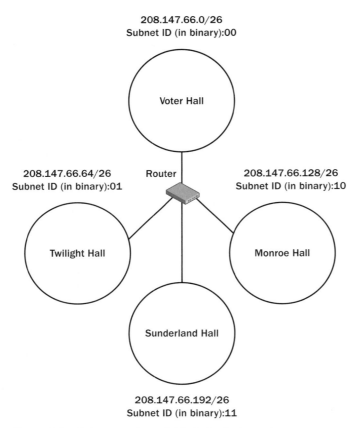

208.147.66.0/26
Subnet ID (in binary):00

Voter Hall

208.147.66.64/26   Router   **208.147.66.128/26**
Subnet ID (in binary):01   **Subnet ID (in binary):10**

Twilight Hall   Monroe Hall

Sunderland Hall

208.147.66.192/26
Subnet ID (in binary):11

Figure 2-9   Subnetting in a divided physical topology

Restricting Broadcast Traffic   A *broadcast* is a network message sent from a single computer and distributed to all other devices on the same physical network segment. Broadcasts are resource-intensive because they use up network bandwidth and request the attention of every network adapter and processor on the local network segment.

Routers block broadcasts and protect networks from becoming overburdened with unnecessary traffic. Because routers also define the logical limits of subnets, subnetting a network indirectly allows you to limit the propagation of broadcast traffic in that network.

Determining Host Capacity for Networks

For any specific network address, you can determine the quantity of host addresses available within that network by raising 2 to the power of the number of bits in the host ID, and then subtracting 2. For instance, the network address 192.168.0.0/24 reserves 8 bits for the host ID. Therefore, you can determine the number of hosts by calculating $2^8 - 2$, which equals 254.

> **Tip**   Using Calculator, you can easily compute the value of 2 to any power with the x^y button. This function appears only in Scientific view.

Excluding All-0s and All-1s Host IDs   The value 2^x yields the total number of distinct bit value combinations for a binary number of x bits, including the combinations of all 0s and all 1s. For example, the value 2^3 yields 8, which is the number of distinct bit value combinations for 3 bits. The list of these eight possible combinations is as follows:

- 000 = 0 (decimal)
- 001 = 1 (decimal)
- 010 = 2 (decimal)
- 011 = 3 (decimal)
- 100 = 4 (decimal)
- 101 = 5 (decimal)
- 110 = 6 (decimal)
- 111 = 7 (decimal)

However, combinations of all 0s and all 1s (0 and 7 in the preceding list) cannot be assigned to hosts because these addresses are reserved for other purposes. Specifically, the all-0s host ID is invalid because it is used to specify a network without specifying a host. The all-1s host ID cannot be assigned to a particular host because it is used by IP to broadcast a message to every host on a network. Because these values cannot be assigned to hosts, you must account for these nonusable host IDs by subtracting 2 from 2^x when determining the host capacity of your network.

Determining Subnet Capacity

When the string of 1-bits in the subnet mask is extended beyond its default to create multiple subnets within any address space, the host ID is shortened, and a new address space for the subnet IDs is created, as shown in Figure 2-10 and Figure 2-11.

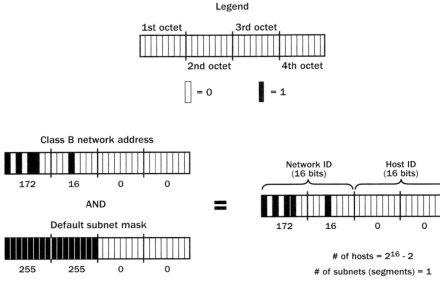

Figure 2-10   Default Class B address space

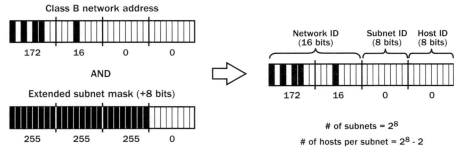

Figure 2-11   Address space with subnet ID

To determine the number of subnets available within an address space, simply calculate the value of 2^y, where y equals the number of bits in the subnet ID. For example, when the network address space 172.16.0.0/16 is subnetted to /24, 8 bits are reserved for the subnet ID. Therefore, the number of available subnets is 2^8, or 256. You do not usually need to subtract 2 from this total because most modern routers (including the Routing And Remote Access service in Microsoft Windows NT Server, Microsoft Windows 2000 Server, and Windows Server 2003) can accept a subnet ID made up of all 1s or all 0s.

When you are configuring an address space and subnet mask to suit your network needs, be sure to assign a number of bits to the subnet ID that will accommodate all the subnets you now use and plan to use in the future. Remember, when determining this figure, that each physical network counts as a subnet.

> **Tip**   Using Calculator, you can quickly determine the number of bits you need to assign to the subnet ID. Simply subtract 1 from the number of subnets that your network requires in decimal format, switch to binary, and count the bit places. For example, if you need to accommodate 31 subnets, enter **30** and select Bin. The result is 11110. Therefore, you need to reserve 5 bits for the subnet ID.

Hosts per Subnet   Calculating the number of host IDs per subnet is the same as calculating the number of host IDs per network. When your network address space has been subnetted, the value $2^x - 2$ (where x equals the number of bits in the host ID) yields the number of hosts per subnet. For example, because the address space 172.16.0.0/24 reserves 8 bits for the host ID, the number of available hosts per subnet is equal to $2^8 - 2$, or 254. To calculate the number of hosts available for your entire subnetted network, simply multiply this figure by the number of available subnets. In this example, the address space 172.16.0.0/24 yields 254 × 256, or 65,024 total hosts.

When you are configuring a network address space and subnet mask to suit your network needs, be sure to assign a number of bits to the host ID that will accommodate both the number of hosts you now use per subnet and plan to use per subnet in the future.

> **Tip**   Using Calculator, you can quickly determine the number of bits you need to assign to the host ID. Simply add 1 to the number of hosts you need to accommodate per subnet, enter this number in decimal format, convert to binary, and count the bit places. For example, if you need to accommodate 33 hosts per subnet, enter **34** in Calculator, and then select Bin. The result is 100010, which means that to accommodate your network needs, you must reserve 6 bits for the host ID.

Subnet Examples

In the preceding example, the original address space 172.16.0.0/16 was subnetted by extending the string of 1-bits within the subnet mask a full octet to 255.255.255.0. In practice, the string of 1-bits within subnet masks can be extended any number of bits, not just full octets.

For example, Figure 2-12 shows the address space for 10.0.0.0/12. Because this address is a Class A address, the default number of 1-bits in the subnet mask is 8; the mask has been extended 4 bits. Thus, 4 bits remain for the subnet ID and 20 bits remain for the host ID. On such a network, the range of addresses on the first subnet (ID 000) is 10.0.0.1–10.15.255.254.

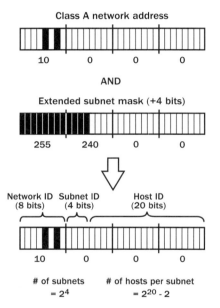

Figure 2-12   Subnetted Class A address space

In Figure 2-13, a Class B address of 172.20.0.0 has been given a custom subnet mask of 255.255.248.0, which extends the default subnet mask by 5 bits. On such a network, the range of addresses on the first subnet (ID 00000) is 172.20.0.1–172.20.7.254.

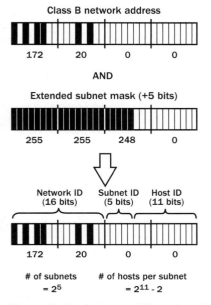

Figure 2-13 Subnetted Class B address space

Figure 2-14 shows a Class C address of 192.168.0.0/26. In this example, 2 bits have been reserved for the subnet ID and 6 have been reserved for the host ID. On such a network, the range of addresses on the first subnet (ID 00) is 192.168.0.1–192.168.0.62.

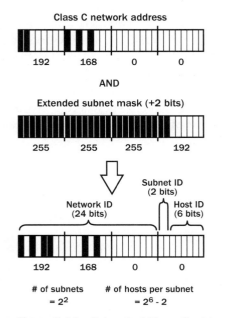

Figure 2-14 Subnetted Class C address space

Estimating Subnet Address Ranges

By using the dotted-decimal form of the subnet mask, you can estimate the ranges of IP addresses in each subnet simply by subtracting from 256 the value of the relevant octet in the subnet mask. For example, for a Class C network such as 207.209.68.0 with a subnet mask of 255.255.255.192, subtracting 192 from 256 results in the value 64. As a result, the network's subnet address ranges are grouped in 64: 207.209.68.0–207.209.68.63, 207.209.68.64–207.209.68.127, etc. For a Class B network such as 131.107.0.0 with a subnet mask of 255.255.240.0, subtracting 240 from 256 yields 16. Therefore, the subnet address ranges reveal groupings of 16 in the third and relevant octet, whereas the fourth octet ranges from 0–255: 131.107.0.0–131.107.15.255, 131.107.16.0–131.107.31.255, and so on.

Remember that hosts cannot be assigned an all-1s or all-0s host ID, so the first and last address of every subnet range cannot be assigned to hosts.

Summarizing Routes Through Supernetting

To prevent the depletion of higher-class network IDs, the Internet authorities devised a scheme called *supernetting*, which allows many networks (routes) to be grouped together (or summarized) in a single larger network. Supernetting offers the advantage of more efficient allocation of network address space.

For example, suppose an organization needs to accommodate 2000 hosts. This number is too large for a single Class C network ID, which can accommodate only 254 hosts. Although a Class B network can accommodate as many as 65,534 hosts, only 16,383 Class B network IDs exist, and the number of unused Class B networks is rapidly decreasing. It therefore does not make sense for an ISP to assign a valuable Class B network (if the ISP even has one to assign) to an organization that plans to use only 3 percent of that space. By using supernetting, an ISP can assign an organization a block of Class C addresses that can be treated as a single network somewhere between a Class C and a Class B address. In this example, a block of 8 Class C network IDs could meet the organization's needs by accommodating 2032 hosts.

How Supernetting Works

Supernetting differs from subnetting in that supernetting borrows bits from the network ID and masks them as the host ID. For example, suppose your ISP has assigned you a block of 8 network addresses ranging from 207.46.168.0 through 207.46.175.0. Assigning a /21 subnet mask (instead of the default /24) to routers at your ISP and to all hosts within your organization results in all your networks being seen as a single network because, thanks to the shortened network ID stemming from the /21 subnet mask, the network ID portion of each of these 8 addresses is now seen as identical. Figure 2-15 illustrates this scenario.

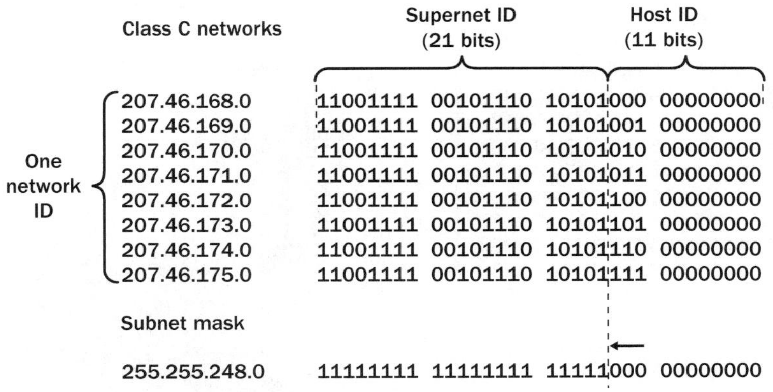

Class C networks	Supernet ID (21 bits)			Host ID (11 bits)
	207.46.168.0	11001111	00101110	10101000 00000000
	207.46.169.0	11001111	00101110	10101001 00000000
One network ID	207.46.170.0	11001111	00101110	10101010 00000000
	207.46.171.0	11001111	00101110	10101011 00000000
	207.46.172.0	11001111	00101110	10101100 00000000
	207.46.173.0	11001111	00101110	10101101 00000000
	207.46.174.0	11001111	00101110	10101110 00000000
	207.46.175.0	11001111	00101110	10101111 00000000

Subnet mask

255.255.248.0   11111111 11111111 11111000 00000000

Figure 2-15   Supernetted block of Class C addresses

Using Classless Interdomain Routing

CIDR is an efficient method of accounting for supernets within route tables. Were it not for CIDR, route tables would need a separate entry to handle every original network in the supernet. CIDR allows the entire supernet to be handled with a single entry, as shown in Figure 2-16.

Note   Blocks of supernetted addresses assigned by Internet regional registries or by ISPs are often called *CIDR blocks*, and the term *CIDR* is commonly used to refer to supernetting in general.

Note   CIDR is not compatible with Routing Information Protocol (RIP) version 1, a legacy protocol used in some older routers. CIDR requires that routers use classless routing protocols such as RIP version 2 or the Open Shortest Path First (OSPF) routing protocol. For more information on routing protocols, see Lesson 4 in Chapter 9, "Routing with Windows Server 2003."

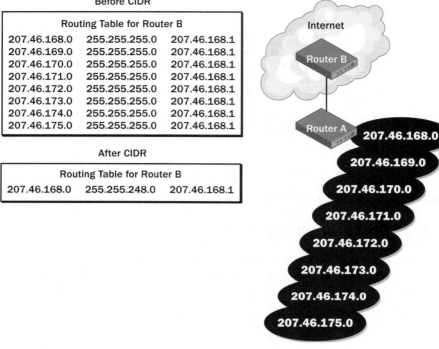

Figure 2-16   Using CIDR for efficient supernetting

Address Space Perspective

The use of CIDR to allocate addresses promotes a new perspective on IP network IDs. In the preceding example, the CIDR block (207.46.168.0, 255.255.248.0) can be thought of in two ways:

- A block of 8 Class C network IDs

- An address space in which 21 bits are fixed and 11 bits are assignable

In the latter perspective, network IDs lose their class-based heritage and become part of a classless IP address space. Each network ID, regardless of length, is an address space in which the network ID bits are fixed and the host bits are variable. The host bits are assignable as host IDs, or, using subnetting techniques, can be used in whatever manner best suits the needs of the organization.

Using Variable-Length Subnet Masks

Traditionally, a single subnet mask is shared by every host and router within an organization. When a single subnet mask is used throughout an entire network, the network can be broken down into subnets, each of which includes the same number of available host IDs.

However, with *variable-length subnet masks* (VLSMs), routers within an organization can handle different subnet masks. Most commonly, VLSMs are used to allow subnets themselves to be subnetted. For example, a large organization may own the address space 131.107.0.0 /16; in this scenario, routers external to the organization use the first 16 bits of the address to determine the network ID and route traffic appropriately. Once data is received from the Internet, the organization's front routers may use a /22 subnet mask to route traffic to any of the internal organization's 64 regional offices. Next, once data is received from the front routers, the field routers at regional offices may use a /25 subnet mask to route traffic to any of 8 office departments.

> **Note**   As with CIDR, VLSMs rely on classless routing protocols such as RIP version 2 and OSPF. VLSMs are not compatible with older routing protocols such as RIP version 1.

Using VLSMs to Accommodate Varying Subnet Sizes

You can also use VLSMs within a single hierarchy level to divide a network into subnets of different sizes. This can allow you to use your network address space more efficiently.

For example, if your network needs one subnet to accommodate 100 computers, a second subnet to accommodate 50 computers, and a third subnet to accommodate 20 computers, this arrangement cannot be designed with traditional default mask options for a single Class C network ID. As Table 2-5 shows, any single default mask fails to accommodate either enough subnets or enough hosts per subnet to meet all of your network needs.

Table 2-5   Class C Subnet Mask Options (Static)

Network Address	Subnets	Hosts per Subnet
208.147.66.0/24	1	254
208.147.66.0/25	2	126
208.147.66.0/26	4	62
208.147.66.0/27	8	30

In situations such as these, you can use VLSMs to accommodate your specific network needs without having to acquire new address space from your ISP.

When using VLSMs to divide your network into subnets of varying sizes, a specific pattern of subnet IDs with trailing 0s must be used, up to a maximum of seven subnets for a Class C network. These trailing 0s prevent the subnet address spaces from overlapping with each other. When the subnet IDs with VLSMs are fixed in the specific pattern shown in Table 2-6, subnets do not overlap, and addresses are interpreted unambiguously.

Table 2-6 VLSM Subnet IDs

Subnet Number	Subnet ID (Binary)	Subnet Mask	Hosts per Subnet	Example Subnet Address
1	0	255.255.255.128	126	208.147.66.0.0/25
2	10	255.255.255.192	62	208.147.66.0.128/26
3	110	255.255.255.224	30	208.147.66.0.192/27
4	1110	255.255.255.240	14	208.147.66.0.224/28
5	11110	255.255.255.248	6	208.147.66.0.240/29
6	111110	255.255.255.252	2	208.147.66.0.248/30
7	111111	255.255.255.252	2	208.147.66.0.252/30

Figure 2-17 illustrates how you can use VLSMs to accommodate 3 subnets of 100, 50, and 20 hosts, respectively.

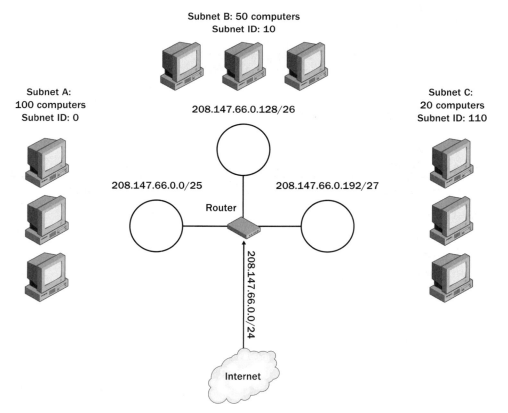

Figure 2-17 Using VLSMs for flexible subnetting

Maximizing Available Host IDs with VLSMs   In Table 2-6, notice that the seventh and final subnet listed is the same size as the sixth and is distinguished by an all-1s subnet ID instead of by the trailing 0 used with the other subnet IDs. As an alternative to using the maximum 7 subnets presented, you could define the all-1s subnet ID at any level in the table to replace all of the subnets listed below that subnet. For example, you could define a subnet ID of 1111 to replace subnets 5 through 7 listed in the table. Doing so would give you a second subnet of 14 hosts, instead of 3 subnets accommodating a total of 10 hosts. This technique thus allows you to maximize the number of hosts your 5-subnet network can accommodate.

Tip   If your Class C network contains 3, 5, 6, or 7 subnets, you can maximize the number of available host IDs in your network by using VLSMs.

Practice: Working with Subnet Masks and Subnets

In this practice, you use Calculator and the tips on pages 2-27 and 2-29 to determine the missing subnet information.

Exercise 1: Calculate Subnet Masks

Assume your ISP has allocated you the network address 206.73.118.0/24. Using the requirement shown at the top of the table, complete the table by determining the number of bits required for the subnet ID or host ID, the number of bits left for the host ID or subnet ID, the network prefix version of the subnet mask, and then the dotted-decimal version of the subnet mask.

Example: Requirement = 6 subnets

Number of bits required for subnet ID	(Answer: 3)
Number of bits left for host ID	(Answer: 5)
Network prefix version of subnet mask	(Answer: /27)
Dotted-decimal version of subnet mask	(Answer: 255.255.255.224)

Requirement = 9 subnets

Number of bits required for subnet ID	
Number of bits left for host ID	
Network prefix version of subnet mask	
Dotted-decimal version of subnet mask	

Requirement = 3 subnets

Number of bits required for subnet ID

Number of bits left for host ID

Network prefix version of subnet mask

Dotted-decimal version of subnet mask

Requirement = 20 hosts per subnet

Number of bits required for host ID

Number of bits left for subnet ID

Network prefix version of subnet mask

Dotted-decimal version of subnet mask

Exercise 2: Calculate Various Subnet Information

Determine the network class and default subnet mask for each network ID in the following table. Then use Calculator to determine the actual subnet mask configured for the address, the number of available subnets, and the number of available hosts per subnet.

Network ID	Network Class	Default Subnet Mask	Configured Subnet Mask (Dotted-Decimal)	Number of Available Subnets	Number of Available Hosts per Subnet
207.209.68.0 /27					
131.107.0.0 /20					
10.0.0.0 /13					
208.147.66.0/25					

Off the Record   Although you need to know how to perform these calculations for the exam, most sysadmins avoid doing so on the job. Administrators who need to determine subnet-related information typically use what is called a *subnet calculator* or *network calculator*. Many of these utilities can be downloaded for free, and some even operate directly from Web pages. Typically, subnet calculators allow you to enter some addressing requirements, such as a network address and number of hosts per subnet, and then automatically calculate the rest of the addressing information for you. This information can include the appropriate subnet mask, the number of subnets, the binary form of the address, and the subnet broadcast address.

Exercise 3: Estimate Subnet Address Ranges

In this exercise, you estimate subnet address ranges by determining the ranges of the first three subnets within a subnetted network. For each network address and subnet mask given in column A, subtract from 256 the value of the relevant octet in the subnet mask. List this value as the grouping value in column B. Then, beginning with 0, list the first four multiples of this same value in column C. Use these values to complete columns D and E, as shown in the example given.

(A) Network Address and Subnet Mask	(B) Grouping Value	(C) First Four Multiples of B (Including 0)	(D) Beginning Address of First Three Subnet Ranges	(E) Ending Address of First Three Subnet Ranges
10.0.0.0 255.240.0.0	256 − 240 = 16	0, 16, 32, 48	10.0.0.0, 10.16.0.0, 10.32.0.0	10.15.255.255, 10.31.255.255, 10.47.255.255
172.16.0.0 255.255.224.0				
172.18.0.0 255.255.248.0				
192.168.1.0 255.255.255.192				

Exercise 4: Determine Whether Two Addresses Are on the Same Subnet

By using the AND function available in Calculator, you can determine whether two addresses in a subnetted network are located on the same logical subnet. Simply perform two AND operations between the relevant octet in the subnet mask of the network and the corresponding octet of each IP address in question. If the result of these operations is the same, the two addresses are on the same logical subnet.

For example, if the subnet mask of the network is 255.255.255.240 and the IP addresses in question are 192.168.0.220 and 192.168.0.190, calculate 240 AND 220 and then write down your result (208). Then calculate 240 AND 190 and write down your result (176). Because the results are different, the two addresses are on separate logical subnets.

Using the method just described, complete the following table.

Subnet Mask	Address #1	AND Result #1	Address #2	AND Result #2	Same Subnet?
255.255.255.192	192.168.1.116		192.168.1.124		
255.255.255.224	192.168.0.180		192.168.0.192		
255.255.252.0	172.16.100.234		172.16.98.234		
255.255.240.0	172.16.64.10		172.16.72.200		

Lesson Review

The following questions are intended to reinforce key information presented in this lesson. If you are unable to answer a question, review the lesson materials and try the question again. You can find answers to the questions in the "Questions and Answers" section at the end of this chapter.

1. You are the network administrator for the Philadelphia branch office of a large company. The IT department at company headquarters in New York has assigned you the network address space 172.16.0.0/21 to accommodate the entire Philadelphia branch network. This network consists of 4 subnets with 40 hosts each, to which you have already assigned the network addresses 172.16.0.0/24, 172.16.1.0/24, 172.16.2.0/24, and 172.16.3.0/24. All routers within the organization support both CIDR and VLSMs.

   Using your current addressing scheme and without changing the subnet mask you have configured for your network, how many more subnets will you be able to accommodate in the Philadelphia branch office?

2. You are the network administrator for a large company. Your company network has been assigned the network address 131.107.0.0/16. Which subnet mask should you configure for the network if you want to accommodate 25 subnets with up to 2000 hosts per subnet? Give the answer in both CIDR (network prefix) and dotted-decimal notations.

3. Your ISP has assigned you 2 Class C network addresses, 131.107.10.0 and 131.107.11.0, to accommodate your network's 400 hosts. Which network address and subnet mask (expressed as a network prefix) can you assign to this address space so that your routers and hosts view these 2 networks as a single network?

   a. 131.107.10.0/23

   b. 131.107.11.0/24

   c. 131.107.10.0/22

   d. 131.107.11.0/22

4. You are the administrator for your company network, which has the address 131.107.0.0/24. You have not yet subnetted the network, but you want to isolate the eight hosts in the Art department on a single subnet. Using VLSMs, how can you configure the network so that within the limitations of this network requirement, the network in general can accommodate the maximum number of hosts? Use the following table to supply your answers. Use only as many rows as necessary to account for all subnets you need.

Subnet Number	Subnet ID (Binary)	Subnet Mask (Decimal)	Number of Host IDs per Subnet	Network Address (with Network Prefix)
1				
2				
3				
4				
5				
6				
7				

Lesson Summary

- Multiple subnets of a network can be created when you extend the string of 1-bits in the network's default subnet mask. This extension enables you to create new logical networks within the original, single-subnet address space.

- Subnetting is often used to accommodate a divided physical topology or to restrict broadcast traffic on a network. Other advantages of subnetting include improved security (by restricting unauthorized traffic behind routers) and simplified administration (by limiting the size of network segments).

- For any specific network address, you can determine the quantity of host addresses available within that network by calculating $2^x - 2$, where x equals the number of bits in the host ID. To determine the number of subnets available within an address space, calculate the value of 2^y, where y equals the number of bits in the subnet ID.

- Supernetting differs from subnetting in that supernetting borrows bits from the network ID and masks them as the host ID. Thus, you can group different networks together as a single network. CIDR is an efficient method of accounting for supernets within route tables.

- With VLSMs, routers within an organization can handle different subnet masks. VLSMs are most commonly used to allow subnets themselves to be subnetted. You can also use VLSMs within a single hierarchy level to divide a network into subnets of different sizes. This technique allows your network to make more efficient use of address space.

Lesson 4: Installing and Configuring TCP/IP

By default, TCP/IP is installed and configured for automatic addressing when Windows 2003 Server Setup is run. Regardless of the networking options selected and configured during the setup program, you can always install and configure TCP/IP after Windows Server 2003 installation is complete.

After this lesson, you will be able to

- Install TCP/IP on a computer running Windows Server 2003
- Configure Windows Server 2003 with an automatically assigned address
- Configure Windows Server 2003 with an alternate static address
- Configure a Windows Server 2003 host with a manual static address
- Use the Ipconfig and Ping commands to verify the status of TCP/IP hosts

Estimated lesson time: 30 minutes

Installing TCP/IP

As part of the Typical Settings setup option, TCP/IP is installed by default during installation of Windows Server 2003. For this reason, you do not usually need to install TCP/IP once the Windows Server 2003 Setup program has been performed. However, if TCP/IP has been uninstalled from a computer, or if the protocol was cleared during the Windows Server 2003 Setup program, you need to install the protocol if you want to connect the computer to a TCP/IP network.

To install TCP/IP, complete the following steps:

> **Note**   You must be logged on as a member of the Administrators group to complete this procedure. If your computer is connected to a network, network policy settings might also prevent you from completing this procedure.

1. In the Network Connections window, right-click the network connection for which you want to install and enable TCP/IP, and then select Properties.

2. In the General tab (for a local area connection) or the Networking tab (all other connections), if Internet Protocol (TCP/IP) is not in the list of installed components, do the following:

   a. Click Install.

   b. Click Protocol, and then click Add.

   c. In the Select Network Protocol dialog box, click Internet Protocol (TCP/IP), and then click OK.

3. Verify that the Internet Protocol (TCP/IP) check box is selected, and then click Close.

Examining TCP/IP Configuration Methods

If you have already installed TCP/IP, you can configure IP addressing and other TCP/IP features by using the Internet Protocol (TCP/IP) Properties dialog box. To access this dialog box, open Network Connections, right-click the appropriate network connection, and then select Properties. In the properties dialog box that opens, select Internet Protocol (TCP/IP) from the list of components, and click Properties.

When configuring IP addressing, you must first decide whether to let the address be configured automatically (the default setting in a Windows Server 2003 installation) or to configure the address manually. Figures 2-18 and 2-19 show the General tab of the Internet Protocol (TCP/IP) Properties dialog box, where this decision is made. Notice that when the Obtain An IP Address Automatically option is selected, a new Alternate Configuration tab appears.

Note   To configure TCP/IP properties on any computer, you must be logged on as a member of the Administrators group.

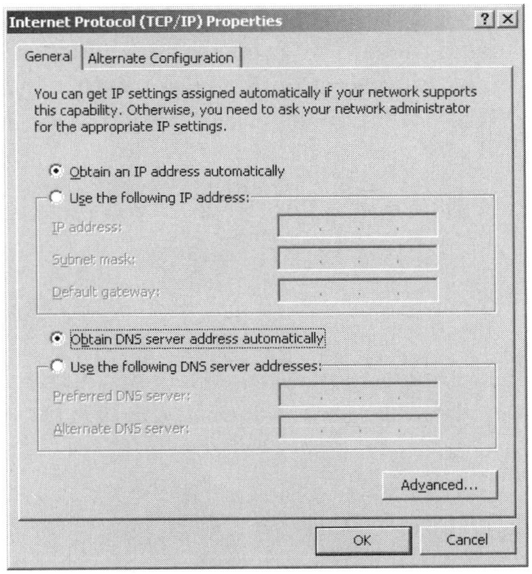

Figure 2-18   Automatically configuring an IP address

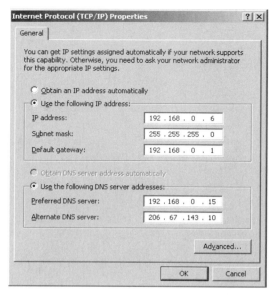

Figure 2-19   Manually configuring an IP address

Automatic Configuration

Leaving the default automatic configuration in the TCP/IP Properties dialog box, as shown in Figure 2-18, results in a DHCP-assigned address if a DHCP server is available. If no DHCP server is available, this setting results in an alternate manual (static) configuration, if one has been entered in the Alternate Configuration tab. If no static alternate configuration has been defined, this setting results in an APIPA-assigned address when no DHCP server is available.

To configure TCP/IP for dynamic addressing from a DHCP server, complete the following steps:

1. Open Network Connections, right-click the appropriate network connection, and then select Properties.

2. In the General tab (for a local area connection) or the Networking tab (all other connections), select the Internet Protocol (TCP/IP) component, and then click Properties.

3. Select Obtain An IP Address Automatically, and then click OK.

Note   This procedure assumes that a DHCP server is available to the host on which the procedure is performed.

Alternate Configuration Tab   The settings in the Alternate Configuration tab of the Internet Protocol (TCP/IP) Properties dialog box determine a host's IP address when the host has been configured for automatic addressing and when no DHCP server can be found. As shown in Figure 2-20 and Figure 2-21, the two basic choices in this tab are to give the host an APIPA address or to configure an alternate address manually.

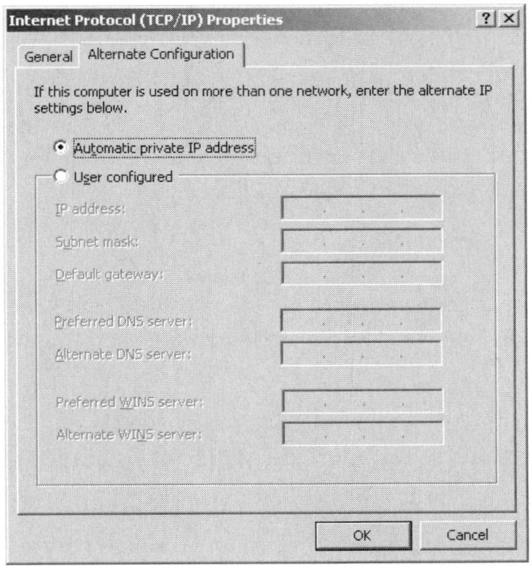

Figure 2-20   Configuring an alternate APIPA address

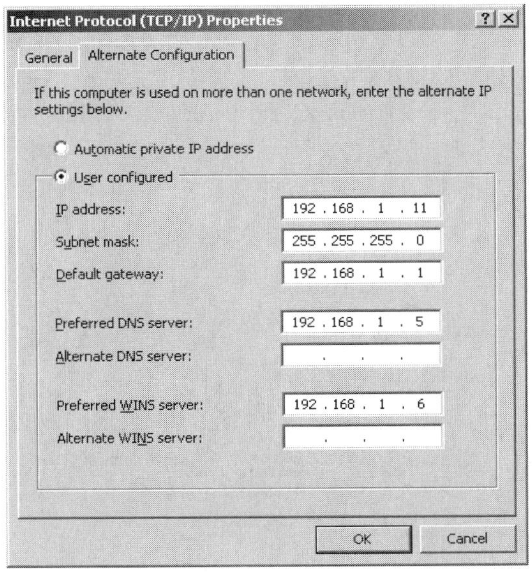

Figure 2-21   Configuring an alternate static address

To configure a local TCP/IP connection for APIPA, complete the following steps:

1. Open Network Connections, right-click the appropriate network connection, and then select Properties.

2. In the General tab, select the Internet Protocol (TCP/IP) component, and then click Properties. The Internet Protocol (TCP/IP) Properties dialog box appears.

3. In the General tab, select Obtain An IP Address Automatically.

4. In the Alternate Configuration tab, select Automatic Private IP Address. Click OK.

> **Note**   This procedure assumes that a DHCP server is not available to the host. You cannot configure a host to bypass a DHCP-assigned address for an APIPA address.

> **Note**   APIPA does not provide automatic configuration of a default gateway, DNS server, or WINS server. It is designed for networks that consist of a single network segment and that are not connected to the Internet.

To configure a local TCP/IP connection for an alternate static configuration, complete the following steps:

1. Open Network Connections, right-click the appropriate network connection, and then select Properties.

2. In the General tab, select the Internet Protocol (TCP/IP) component, and then click Properties. The Internet Protocol (TCP/IP) Properties dialog box appears.

3. In the General tab, select Obtain An IP Address Automatically.

4. In the Alternate Configuration tab, select User Configured, and then type appropriate values in the following boxes:

   ❏ IP Address

   ❏ Subnet Mask

   ❏ Default Gateway (optional)

   ❏ Preferred DNS Server (optional)

   ❏ Alternate DNS Server (optional)

   ❏ Preferred WINS Server (optional)

   ❏ Alternate WINS Server (optional)

Manual Configuration

By manually configuring the properties of the TCP/IP protocol through the properties of a network connection, you can statically assign an IP address, subnet mask, default gateway, DNS servers, and WINS servers. You can also configure manual settings in the Windows Server 2003 Setup Wizard by selecting Custom Settings (as opposed to Typical Settings) in the Networking Settings dialog box.

To configure a TCP/IP connection manually for static addressing, complete the following steps:

1. Open Network Connections, right-click the appropriate network connection, and then select Properties.

2. In the General tab (for a local area connection) or the Networking tab (all other connections), select the Internet Protocol (TCP/IP) component, and then click Properties.

3. In the Internet Protocol (TCP/IP) Properties dialog box, select Use The Following IP Address, and then do one of the following:

   ❑ For a local area connection, assign the IP address, subnet mask, and default gateway.

   ❑ For all other connections, assign the IP address.

4. (Optional) In the Preferred DNS Server text box and the Alternate DNS Server text box, type the primary and secondary DNS server addresses.

5. (Optional) To configure a WINS server, click Advanced, click the WINS tab, and click Add to add the address of an available WINS server.

Practice: Configuring TCP/IP Addresses

In this practice, you configure a static IP address for Computer1 and an alternate address for Computer2. Until now, your computers have been assigned APIPA addresses.

> **Note**   This practice assumes that you have completed a default installation of Windows Server 2003 on both Computer1 and Computer2, and that the two computers are physically networked. It also assumes that you have no other computers on your network.

Exercise 1: Verifying Your Current IP Address

In this exercise, you review the current IP configuration on Computer1.

1. Log on to Computer1 as Administrator.

2. Click the Start button, and then select Command Prompt.

3. At the command prompt, type **ipconfig** and then press Enter. This command is used to show your IP address configuration. The output that is produced shows your network connections.

   Next to Autoconfiguration IP Address, you will see your current address of 169.254.y.z, where y and z refer to the host ID currently assigned to Computer1 by the APIPA feature. The subnet mask is the default of 255.255.0.0. By default, Computer1 has been assigned an APIPA address because a default Windows Server 2003 installation specifies that the IP address of the host is assigned automatically. In the absence of a DHCP server, the host uses an APIPA address.

Exercise 2: Configuring a Manual Address

In this exercise, you assign a static IP address to Computer1. A static IP address is needed for computers that will later host important network services such as DNS or DHCP.

1. While you are still logged on to Computer1 as Administrator, open Network Connections, right-click Local Area Connection, and then select Properties.

2. In the This Connection Uses The Following Items area of the Local Area Connection Properties dialog box, select Internet Protocol (TCP/IP).

3. Click Properties.

4. In the General tab of the Internet Protocol (TCP/IP) Properties dialog box, select Use The Following IP Address.

5. In the IP Address text box, type **192.168.0.1**.

6. Click the Subnet Mask text box to place your cursor inside it. The subnet mask 255.255.255.0 appears in the Subnet Mask text box. Click OK.

7. In the Local Area Connection Properties dialog box, click Close.

8. Log off Computer1.

Exercise 3: Configuring an Alternate Static Address

In this exercise, you alter the IP configuration on Computer2 so that in the absence of a DHCP server, Computer2 assigns itself an IP address that you specify.

1. Log on to Computer2 as Administrator, open Network Connections, right-click Local Area Connection, and then select Properties.

   In the This Connection Uses The Following Items area, you will see that Client For Microsoft Networks, File And Printer Sharing For Microsoft Networks, and Internet Protocol (TCP/IP) are used by the local area network (LAN) connection.

2. In the Local Area Connection Properties dialog box, in the This Connection Uses The Following Items area, select Internet Protocol (TCP/IP).

3. Click Properties.

In the General tab of the Internet Protocol (TCP/IP) Properties dialog box, notice that Obtain An IP Address Automatically and Obtain DNS Server Address Automatically are selected.

4. Click the Alternate Configuration tab.

Automatic Private IP Address is selected. Because no DHCP server is available, the APIPA feature is activated for Computer2.

5. Select User Configured.

6. In the IP Address text box, type **192.168.0.2**.

7. Click the Subnet Mask text box to place the cursor inside it. The default subnet mask of 255.255.255.0 appears in the Subnet Mask text box. Leave this entry as the default subnet mask.

You have just defined an alternate IP address configuration of 192.168.0.2/24 for Computer2. This configuration can be used until you configure a DHCP server for your network.

8. Click OK.

9. In the Local Area Connection Properties dialog box, click Close.

Exercise 4: Verifying the Connection

In this exercise, you verify that the new IP addresses have taken effect and that the two computers are communicating.

1. While you are logged on to Computer2 as Administrator, open a command prompt.

2. At the command prompt, type **ipconfig** and press Enter.

The Ipconfig output appears. Next to IP Address, you will see the new alternate address that you have configured, 192.168.0.2.

3. At the command prompt, type **ping computer1**. This command is used to verify a TCP/IP connection between two hosts.

The output confirms not only that Computer1 and Computer2 are communicating through TCP/IP, but also that the IP address of Computer1 has been successfully changed to 192.168.0.1.

4. Log off Computer2.

Lesson Review

The following questions are intended to reinforce key information presented in this lesson. If you are unable to answer a question, review the lesson materials and try the question again. You can find answers to the questions in the "Questions and Answers" section at the end of this chapter.

1. Which of the following is most likely true for a computer with an IP address of 169.254.130.13?

   a. The address has been configured manually.

   b. The subnet mask of the address is 255.255.255.0.

   c. No DHCP server is on the network.

2. You have configured an alternate static IP address for a computer as 192.168.0.1. However, when you run the Ipconfig utility, you see that the computer is reporting a different address. What is the most likely cause of this?

   a. A DHCP server is assigning the computer an address.

   b. Another manually configured address is taking precedence over the alternate address.

   c. The computer has been assigned an APIPA address.

3. If you have performed a default installation of Windows Server 2003, how is the specific IP address of the local host determined?

4. What differences exist between the TCP/IP address configuration options for a local area connection and those for other connection types, such as a dial-up connection?

Lesson Summary

- TCP/IP addresses can be configured automatically or manually. Automatic addressing is the default selection and designates that a host be assigned an address by a DHCP server.

- When no DHCP server is available, automatic addressing assigns the host any alternate address you have configured in the Alternate Configuration tab of the TCP/IP Properties dialog box.

- If no DHCP server is available and you have not configured a static alternate address, automatic addressing assigns your host an APIPA address in the range from 169.254.0.1 through 169.254.255.254.

- Manual addressing can be performed during Windows Server 2003 Setup or afterward. Manual IP addressing allows you to designate a static IP address and subnet mask for a local host, along with the addresses of any default gateways, DNS servers, or WINS servers you want to specify.

Case Scenario Exercise

You work as a network consultant, and you have been hired by three companies to solve problems related to network connectivity. While visiting each company, you draw sections of the relevant portions of the network. Use the following drawings to determine the IP configuration error that has led to a disruption of network connectivity at each company.

1. What is the configuration error?

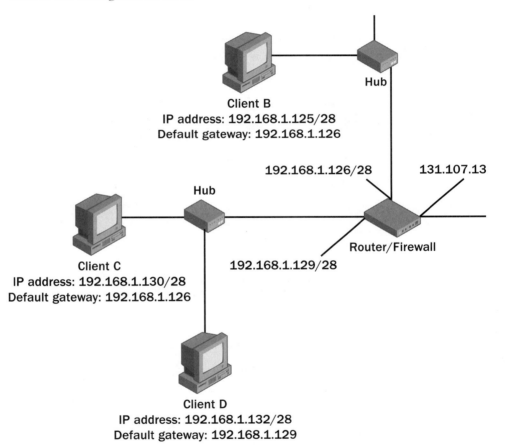

Client B
IP address: 192.168.1.125/28
Default gateway: 192.168.1.126

Hub

192.168.1.126/28   131.107.13

Hub

Router/Firewall

Client C
IP address: 192.168.1.130/28
Default gateway: 192.168.1.126

192.168.1.129/28

Client D
IP address: 192.168.1.132/28
Default gateway: 192.168.1.129

2. What is the configuration error?

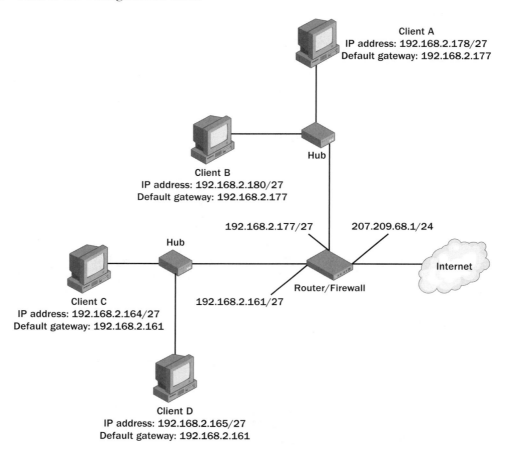

Client A
IP address: 192.168.2.178/27
Default gateway: 192.168.2.177

Hub

Client B
IP address: 192.168.2.180/27
Default gateway: 192.168.2.177

192.168.2.177/27   207.209.68.1/24

Hub

Internet

Client C
IP address: 192.168.2.164/27
Default gateway: 192.168.2.161

Router/Firewall

192.168.2.161/27

Client D
IP address: 192.168.2.165/27
Default gateway: 192.168.2.161

Chapter 2   Understanding TCP/IP   **2-53**

3. What is the configuration error?

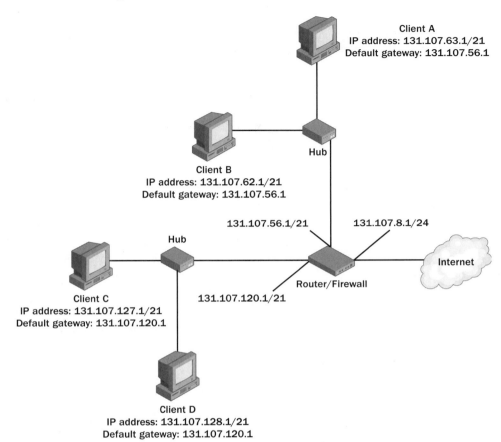

Client A
IP address: 131.107.63.1/21
Default gateway: 131.107.56.1

Hub

Client B
IP address: 131.107.62.1/21
Default gateway: 131.107.56.1

Hub

131.107.56.1/21   131.107.8.1/24

Internet

Client C
IP address: 131.107.127.1/21
Default gateway: 131.107.120.1

Router/Firewall

131.107.120.1/21

Client D
IP address: 131.107.128.1/21
Default gateway: 131.107.120.1

Chapter Summary

- TCP/IP provides the networking foundation for Windows networks and for the Internet. TCP includes the internet-layer protocols ARP, IP, and ICMP, and the transport-layer protocols TCP and UDP.

- Host IP addresses need to be unique on every IP network.

- The first part of an IP address is always used as a network address or network ID, and the last part is used as a host address or host ID.

- The subnet mask of the local host is a 32-bit address used to compare the network ID of the local host to the network ID of every IP packet the host sends on the network.

- If the network ID of the host matches the destination network ID of the IP packet, the packet is transmitted on the local network.

- If the destination network ID of the packet is different from that of the host, the packet is sent to the local default gateway.

- Multiple logical subnets of a network can be created when the string of 1-bits in the network's default subnet mask is extended.

- When no DHCP server is available, automatic addressing assigns the host any alternate address you have configured in the Alternate Configuration tab of the TCP/IP Properties dialog box.

- If no DHCP server is available and you have not configured a static alternate address, automatic addressing assigns your host an APIPA address in the range from 169.254.0.1 through 169.254.255.254.

Exam Highlights

Before taking the exam, review the key points and terms that are presented below to help you identify topics you need to review. Return to the lessons for additional practice, and review the "Further Reading" sections in Part 2 for pointers to more information about topics covering the exam objectives.

Key Points

- Be able to determine which octets are used by a given IP address to distinguish its network ID and host ID.

- Be comfortable using Calculator to perform the following tasks:

  ❑ Converting between decimal and binary forms of an address

  ❑ Converting between the network prefix and dotted-decimal versions of a subnet mask

  ❑ Using the AND operation to determine whether two addresses are configured on the same logical subnet

  ❑ Determining how many bits to allocate to a subnet ID and host ID, given your network needs, and then translating those requirements into a subnet mask

- Be able to estimate the subnet address ranges of a network by looking at the dotted-decimal form of its subnet mask.

- Understand the concept of CIDR blocks so that you will recognize and understand them on exam questions.

■ Be able to spot configuration errors such as an incorrect default gateway or an incompatible IP address.

Key Terms

■ **Address Resolution Protocol (ARP)**   In TCP/IP, a protocol that uses broadcast traffic on the local network to resolve a logically assigned IP address to its physical hardware or MAC layer address.

■ **Internet Control Message Protocol (ICMP)**   A required maintenance protocol in the TCP/IP suite that reports errors and allows simple connectivity. The Ping utility uses ICMP to perform TCP/IP troubleshooting.

■ **classless interdomain routing (CIDR)**   An IP address and routing management method that allocates IP addresses in a way that reduces the number of routes stored on any individual router, while also increasing the number of available IP addresses.

■ **variable-length subnet masks (VLSMs)**   Subnet masks that vary from router to router within a network. VLSMs allow greater flexibility in subnet address ranges than static subnet masks do.

Questions and Answers

Page 2-6 **Lesson 1 Review**

1. Which is the only layer of the TCP/IP reference model that does not contain any TCP/IP protocols?

    a. The network interface layer

    b. The internet layer

    c. The transport layer

    d. The application layer

    a

2. Which of the following TCP/IP protocols does not function at the internet layer?

    a. IP

    b. ARP

    c. TCP

    d. ICMP

    c

3. Which of the following is a transport-layer protocol?

    a. IGMP

    b. UDP

    c. DNS

    d. Ethernet

    b

4. Which of the following services connect to UDP ports? (Choose all that apply.)

    a. NetBIOS

    b. DNS

    c. Ethernet

    d. Telnet

    a, b

Page 2-18 **Exercise 1: Manually Convert Numbers from Decimal to Binary Notation**

Convert the number given at the top of each table. Use the table to work out your answer, then perform the same conversion in Calculator to see if you obtain the same result.

Decimal notation: 159

128	64	32	16	8	4	2	1

Binary notation: **10011111**

Decimal notation: 65

128	64	32	16	8	4	2	1

Binary notation: **01000001**

Binary notation: 1001010

128	64	32	16	8	4	2	1

Decimal notation: **74**

Binary notation: 01110011

128	64	32	16	8	4	2	1

Decimal notation: **115**

Page
2-19
Exercise 2: Convert Between Dotted-Decimal and Network Prefix Subnet Masks

1. 255.255.255.192

   /26

2. 255.255.252.0

   /22

3. /27

   255.255.255.224

4. /21

   255.255.248.0

Lesson 2 Review

1. What does the local host use to determine the destination network ID of a particular packet?

   a. The IP header

   b. The subnet mask

   c. The address class

   b

2. A host determines that the destination network ID of a packet is the same as its
own network ID. What does the host do with the packet?

   a. It broadcasts an ARP request to determine the Media Access Control (MAC)
   address of the destination host and transmits the packet on the local network.

   b. It sends the packet to the server, which broadcasts the packet on the local
   network.

   c. It sends the packet to the default gateway for delivery.

   a

3. Which of the following is the dotted-decimal notation equivalent of the binary
address 11001100 00001010 11001000 00000100? To answer the question, first perform notation conversion manually, and then verify your answer with Calculator.

   a. 204.18.200.3

   b. 204.34.202.4

   c. 204.10.200.4

   d. 202.10.200.4

   c

4. Which of the following is the binary equivalent of the dotted-decimal address
207.209.68.100? To answer the question, first perform notation conversion manually, and then verify your answer with Calculator.

   a. 11001111 11010001 01000100 01100100

   b. 11000111 11010001 01000100 01100100

   c. 11001111 11010001 01000100 01101100

   d. 11001111 11010001 11001101 01100100

   a

5. Determine the dotted-decimal equivalent of the following address. Use CIDR notation to designate the default subnet mask. First perform this notation conversion manually, and then verify your answer with Calculator.

`10010010 01101011 00100111 10001001`

146.107.39.137/16

Page
2-37

Exercise 1: Calculate Subnet Masks

Example Requirement = 6 subnets

Number of bits required for subnet ID	(Answer: 3)
Number of bits left for host ID	(Answer: 5)
Network prefix version of subnet mask	(Answer: /27)
Dotted-decimal version of subnet mask	(Answer: 255.255.255.224)

Requirement = 9 subnets

Number of bits required for subnet ID	**4**
Number of bits left for host ID	**4**
Network prefix version of subnet mask	**/28**
Dotted-decimal version of subnet mask	**255.255.255.240**

Requirement = 3 subnets

Number of bits required for subnet ID	**2**
Number of bits left for host ID	**6**
Network prefix version of subnet mask	**/26**
Dotted-decimal version of subnet mask	**255.255.255.192**

Requirement = 20 hosts per subnet

Number of bits required for host ID	**5**
Number of bits left for subnet ID	**3**
Network prefix version of subnet mask	**/27**
Dotted-decimal version of subnet mask	**255.255.255.224**

Exercise 2: Calculate Various Subnet Information

Network ID	Network Class	Default Subnet Mask	Configured Subnet Mask (Dotted-Decimal)	Number of Available Subnets	Number of Available Hosts per Subnet
207.209.68.0 /27	C	/24 or 255.255.255.0	255.255.255.224	8	30
131.107.0.0 /20	B	/16 or 255.255.0.0	255.255.240.0	16	4094
10.0.0.0 /13	A	/8 or 255.0.0.0	255.248.0.0	32	524,286
208.147.66.0/25	C	/24 or 255.255.255.0	255.255.255.128	2	126

Exercise 3: Estimate Subnet Address Ranges

(A) Network Address and Subnet Mask	(B) Grouping Value	(C) First Four Multiples of B (Including 0)	(D) Beginning Address of First Three Subnet Ranges	(E) Ending Address of First Three Subnet Ranges
10.0.0.0 255.240.0.0	256 – 240 = 16	0, 16, 32, 48	10.0.0.0, 10.16.0.0, 10.32.0.0	10.15.255.255, 10.31.255.255, 10.47.255.255
172.16.0.0 255.255.224.0	256 – 224 = 32	0, 32, 64, 96	172.16.0.0, 172.16.32.0, 172.16.64.0	172.16.31.255, 172.16.63.255, 172.16.95.255
172.18.0.0 255.255.248.0	256 – 248 = 8	0, 8, 16, 24	172.18.0.0, 172.18.8.0, 172.18.16.0	172.18.7.255, 172.18.15.255, 172.18.23.255
192.168.1.0 255.255.255.192	256 – 192 = 64	0, 64, 128, 192	192.168.1.0, 192.168.1.64, 192.168.1.128	192.168.1.63, 192.168.1.127, 192.168.1.191

Exercise 4: Determine Whether Two Addresses are on the Same Subnet

Subnet Mask	Address #1	AND Result #1	Address #2	AND Result #2	Same Subnet?
255.255.255.192	192.168.1.116	64	192.168.1.124	64	Yes
255.255.255.224	192.168.0.180	160	192.168.0.192	192	No
255.255.252.0	172.16.100.234	100	172.16.98.234	96	No
255.255.240.0	172.16.64.10	64	172.16.72.200	64	Yes

Page
2-40

Lesson 3 Review

1. You are the network administrator for the Philadelphia branch office of a large company. The IT department at company headquarters in New York has assigned you the network address space 172.16.0.0/21 to accommodate the entire Philadelphia branch network. This network consists of 4 subnets with 40 hosts each, to which you have already assigned the network addresses 172.16.0.0/24, 172.16.1.0/24, 172.16.2.0/24, and 172.16.3.0/24. All routers within the organization support both CIDR and VLSMs.

   Using your current addressing scheme and without changing the subnet mask you have configured for your network, how many more subnets will you be able to accommodate in the Philadelphia branch office?

   4

2. You are the network administrator for a large company. Your company network has been assigned the network address 131.107.0.0/16. Which subnet mask should you configure for the network if you want to accommodate 25 subnets with up to 2000 hosts per subnet? Give the answer in both CIDR (network prefix) and dotted-decimal notations.

   /21 or 255.255.248.0

3. Your ISP has assigned you 2 Class C network addresses, 131.107.10.0 and 131.107.11.0, to accommodate your network's 400 hosts. Which network address and subnet mask (expressed as a network prefix) can you assign to this address space so that your routers and hosts view these 2 networks as a single network?

   a. 131.107.10.0/23

   b. 131.107.11.0/24

   c. 131.107.10.0/22

   d. 131.107.11.0/22

   a

4. You are the administrator for your company network, which has the address 131.107.0.0/24. You have not yet subnetted the network, but you want to isolate the eight hosts in the Art department on a single subnet. Using VLSMs, how can you configure the network so that within the limitations of this network requirement, the network in general can accommodate the maximum number of hosts? Use the following table to supply your answers. Use only as many rows as necessary to account for all subnets you need.

Subnet Number	Subnet ID (Binary)	Subnet Mask (Decimal)	Number of Host IDs per Subnet	Network Address (with Network Prefix)
1	0	255.255.255.128	126	131.107.0.0/25
2	10	255.255.255.192	62	131.107.0.128/26
3	110	255.255.255.224	30	131.107.0.192/27
4	1110	255.255.255.240	14	131.107.0.224/28
5	1111	255.255.255.240	14	131.107.0.240/28
6				
7				

Page
2-50

Lesson 4 Review

1. Which of the following is most likely true for a computer with an IP address of 169.254.130.13?

    a. The address has been configured manually.

    b. The subnet mask of the address is 255.255.255.0.

    c. No DHCP server is on the network.

    c

2. You have configured an alternate static IP address for a computer as 192.168.0.1. However, when you run the Ipconfig utility, you see that the computer is reporting a different address. What is the most likely cause of this?

    a. A DHCP server is assigning the computer an address.

    b. Another manually configured address is taking precedence over the alternate address.

    c. The computer has been assigned an APIPA address.

    a

3. If you have performed a default installation of Windows Server 2003, how is the specific IP address of the local host determined?

    After a default installation of Windows Server 2003, the IP address of the local host is assigned by a DHCP server, if one is available. If no DHCP server is available, the local host is assigned any alternate address you have configured in the Alternate Configuration tab of the TCP/IP Properties dialog box. If no DHCP server is available and you have not configured a static alternate address, the host is assigned an APIPA address in the range from 169.254.0.1 through 169.254.255.254.

4. What differences exist between the TCP/IP address configuration options for a local area connection and those for other connection types, such as a dial-up connection?

    For nonlocal-area connections, you cannot configure an alternate static IP address or an APIPA address.

Page
2-51

Case Scenario Exercise

1. What is the configuration error?

    Client C has an incorrectly configured default gateway. The default gateway should be set to 192.168.1.129.

2. What is the configuration error?

    The subnet mask is improperly connected for the network. It should be set to 255.255.255.240 or /28.

3. What is the configuration error?

    Client D's IP address is configured in the wrong logical subnet. The third octet must be in the range from 120 through 127.

3 Monitoring and Troubleshooting TCP/IP Connections

Exam Objectives in this Chapter:

- Troubleshoot TCP/IP addressing
  - ❏ Diagnose and resolve issues related to incorrect configuration
- Monitor network traffic
- Troubleshoot connectivity to the Internet

Why This Chapter Matters

This chapter introduces you to the range of tools used most often in troubleshooting Internet Protocol (IP) networks. Lesson 1 introduces you to Network Monitor, a protocol analyzer used to perform frame-by-frame analysis of network traffic. Network administrators can use protocol analyzers to determine, for example, why name resolution fails or why connections to network resources are unreliable. Simply put, without a protocol analyzer such as Network Monitor, you would not be able to determine firsthand what is really happening on your network.

In Lesson 2, you are introduced to the tools used most often in troubleshooting network connectivity. Sysadmins use some of these tools (such as Ipconfig and Ping) every day if not hourly. Other tools, such as Network Diagnostics, provide administrators with a simple means to troubleshoot connectivity problems in a more comprehensive manner.

Lessons in this Chapter:

- Lesson 1: Analyzing Traffic Using Network Monitor 3-3
- Lesson 2: Troubleshooting TCP/IP Connections 3-19

Before You Begin

To complete this chapter, you must have

■ Physically networked two computers.

■ Performed a Microsoft Windows Server 2003 installation with default settings on both computers. The computers should be named Computer1 and Computer2.

■ Assigned Computer1 a static address of 192.168.0.1/24.

■ Configured Computer2 to obtain an address automatically.

■ Assigned Computer2 an alternate configuration address of 192.168.0.2/24.

Lesson 1: Analyzing Traffic Using Network Monitor

To analyze network traffic, you need to use a protocol analyzer such as Network Monitor. You can install Network Monitor by using the Windows Components Wizard. This wizard is available through the Welcome To Microsoft Windows Server 2003 screen or through the Add Or Remove Programs tool in Control Panel.

> **After this lesson, you will be able to**
> - Use Network Monitor to capture, view, and save data
>
> **Estimated lesson time: 30 minutes**

Understanding Network Monitor

Network Monitor is a software-based traffic analysis tool that allows a user to perform these tasks:

- Capture frames directly from the network
- Display and filter captured frames, immediately after capture or at a later time
- Edit captured frames and transmit them on the network (full version only)
- Capture frames from a remote computer (full version only)

For example, as a network administrator, you might use Network Monitor to diagnose hardware and software problems when the server computer cannot communicate with other computers. Frames captured by Network Monitor can be saved to a file and reviewed for later analysis. Network application developers can also use Network Monitor to monitor and debug network applications as they are developed.

> **Note**   A *frame* is an encapsulation of layer 2, or network interface–layer, data. To say that Network Monitor captures frames is to say that it reads and displays encapsulations that include both network interface–layer data (such as Ethernet data) and higher-layer data from protocols such as Address Resolution Protocol (ARP), IP, Transmission Control Protocol (TCP), and Domain Name System (DNS). Technically speaking, a frame is distinct from a packet in that a *packet* is an encapsulation of layer 3, or internet-layer, data. However, these terms are often used interchangeably.

Two versions of Network Monitor are available. The basic version is shipped with Windows Server 2003, and the full version is shipped with Microsoft Systems Management Server. Table 3-1 summarizes the differences between these two versions of the Network Monitor tool.

Off the Record   In theory, there's a huge difference between the two versions of Network Monitor: in the basic version, you can capture only the local computer's communication exchanges, and in the full version, you can capture traffic exchanges among any computers on the entire network segment. Sadly, however, this distinction really holds only for networks that use hubs instead of switches to connect hosts. In reality, most modern networks use switches, which forward frames only to the recipient computer. Switches effectively limit the functionality of protocol analyzers such as Network Monitor by screening out all traffic that is not originating from or destined for the computer on which the protocol analyzer is running. So if, like most others, your network is using switches instead of hubs, you unfortunately won't be able to experience the supposedly enormous benefit of the full version.

Table 3-1   Network Monitor Versions

Function	Network Monitor (Basic)	Network Monitor (Full)
Local capturing	To and from only the computer running Network Monitor	All devices on the entire network segment
Remote capturing	Not available	Yes
Determining top user of network bandwidth	Not available	Yes
Determining which protocol consumes the most bandwidth	Not available	Yes
Determining which devices are routers	Not available	Yes
Resolving a device name into a Media Access Control (MAC) address	Not available	Yes
Editing and retransmitting network traffic	Not available	Yes

Exploring Network Monitor Components

Network Monitor is composed of an administrative tool called Network Monitor and an agent called the Network Monitor Driver. Both components must be installed for you to capture, display, and analyze network frames.

Using the Network Monitor Administrative Tool

You use Network Monitor to display the frames that a computer running Windows Server 2003 sends or receives.

To install Network Monitor, complete the following steps:

1. Open Add Or Remove Programs in Control Panel.

2. In Add Or Remove Programs, click Add/Remove Windows Components to launch the Windows Components Wizard.

3. On the first page of the Windows Components Wizard, select Management And Monitoring Tools, and then click Details. (Do not select the Management And Monitoring Tools check box.)

4. In the Management And Monitoring Tools window, select the Network Monitor Tools check box, and then click OK.

5. In the Windows Components Wizard, click Next. If you are prompted for additional files, insert your Windows Server 2003 CD, or type a path to the location of the files on the network.

6. Click Finish when installation has completed.

Installing the Network Monitor Driver

When you install Network Monitor, the Network Monitor Driver is installed automatically on the same computer. However, sometimes you need to install the Network Monitor Driver without installing the Network Monitor tool itself. For example, if a user of the full version of Network Monitor wants to capture traffic from a remote Windows XP Professional computer, he or she must install the Network Monitor Driver on that remote computer. You can install the Network Monitor Driver only on computers running Windows Server 2003, Microsoft Windows XP Professional, or Microsoft Windows 2000.

You must be logged on as Administrator or be a member of the Administrators group to complete this procedure. If your computer is connected to a network, network policy settings might also prevent you from completing this procedure.

To install the Network Monitor Driver, complete the following steps:

1. Open Network Connections.

2. In the Network Connections window, right-click the network connection for which you want to install and enable the Network Monitor Driver, and then click Properties.

3. In the Local Area Connection Properties dialog box, click Install.

4. In the Select Network Component Type dialog box, click Protocol, and then click Add.

5. In the Select Network Protocol dialog box, select Network Monitor Driver, and then click OK.

6. If prompted for additional files, insert your Windows Server 2003 CD, or type a path to the network location of the files.

How Network Monitor Works

Network Monitor tracks the network *data stream*, which consists of all of the information transferred over a network at any given time. Before transmission, the networking software divides this information into smaller segments (frames), each of which contains the following information:

- The source address of the computer that sent the message
- The destination address of the computer that received the frame
- Header information of each protocol used to send the frame
- The data (or a portion of it) being sent to the destination computer

The Windows Server 2003 version of Network Monitor can copy to a buffer the frames originating from or sent to the local computer. The process by which Network Monitor copies frames is referred to as *data capture*.

The amount of information that Network Monitor can capture is limited only by the amount of memory available on your system. However, you usually need to capture only a small subset of the frames traveling on your network. To isolate a subset of frames you can design a capture filter, which functions like a database query, to isolate the information that you specify. You can filter frames on the basis of source and destination addresses, network interface–layer protocols, internet-layer protocols, transport-layer protocols, protocol properties, and pattern offset.

Examining the Network Monitor Interface

When you launch Network Monitor for the first time after installation, the Select A Network window opens, as shown in Figure 3-1, and prompts you to choose a particular network adapter through which Network Monitor should analyze traffic. The network you choose becomes the default listening network for Network Monitor whenever you open the tool. You can later access this window in Network Monitor by opening the Capture menu and selecting Networks. This allows you to switch listening networks after the first use.

Figure 3-1   Select A Network window

After you select a network from the Select A Network window, this window closes, and the Capture window appears. The Capture window, which is the main window of Network Monitor, provides different types of useful statistical data for analyzing overall network performance. This window includes a graph pane, a session statistics pane, a station statistics pane, and a total statistics pane, as shown in Figure 3-2.

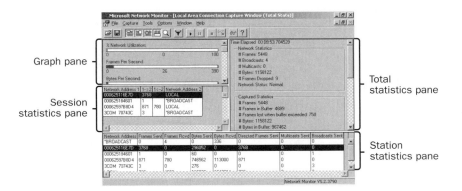

Figure 3-2   Capture window

Table 3-2 describes the type of data summarized in each of these four panes.

Table 3-2   Network Monitor Capture Window

Pane	Description
Graph	Displays the current activity as a set of bar charts indicating the following status information: % Of Network Utilization, Frames Per Second, Bytes Per Second, Broadcasts Per Second, and Multicasts Per Second during the capture process
Session statistics	Displays a summary of the conversations between two hosts, and indicates which host is initiating broadcasts and multicasts
Station statistics	Displays a summary of the total number of frames initiated by a host, the number of frames and bytes sent and received, and the number of broadcast and multicast frames initiated

Table 3-2   Network Monitor Capture Window

Pane	Description
Total statistics	Displays statistics for the traffic detected on the network as a whole, the statistics for the frames captured, per second utilization statistics, and network adapter card statistics

Capturing Data in Network Monitor

To begin capturing data in Network Monitor, from the Capture menu, select Start. Alternatively, to start a capture you can also press F10 or click the Start Capture button on the toolbar. The Start Capture button is designated by the play symbol shown in Figure 3-3.

When packets are being captured, you will see new data being registered in the panes of the Capture window. To stop the capture, from the Capture menu, select Stop. Alternatively, to stop a capture you can also press F11 or click the Stop Capture button on the toolbar. The Stop Capture button is designated by the stop symbol shown in Figure 3-3.

To view a capture, from the Capture menu, select Display Captured Data. Alternatively, to view a capture you can also press F12 or click the Display Captured Data button on the toolbar, which is designated by the eyeglasses symbol shown in Figure 3-3.

You can also stop and view the data in one step. To perform this task, from the Capture menu, you can select Stop And View while the data is being captured. Alternatively, to stop the capture and view the results immediately, you can also press Shift+F11 or click the Stop And View Capture button on the toolbar. The Stop And View Capture button is designated by a combination of the stop symbol and the eyeglasses symbol shown in Figure 3-3.

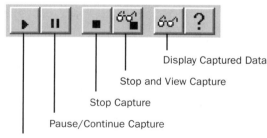

Figure 3-3   Network Monitor toolbar functions

Exam Tip   You can use Network Monitor to find out certain details—such as the MAC address of a network interface card (NIC), the globally unique identifier (GUID) of a client computer, or the port used by a protocol—that might have been lost with documentation.

Analyzing Captured Data

When you choose to view a capture, the Frame Viewer window appears, displaying the summary pane. The summary pane displays all of the captured frames in sequence, as shown in Figure 3-4.

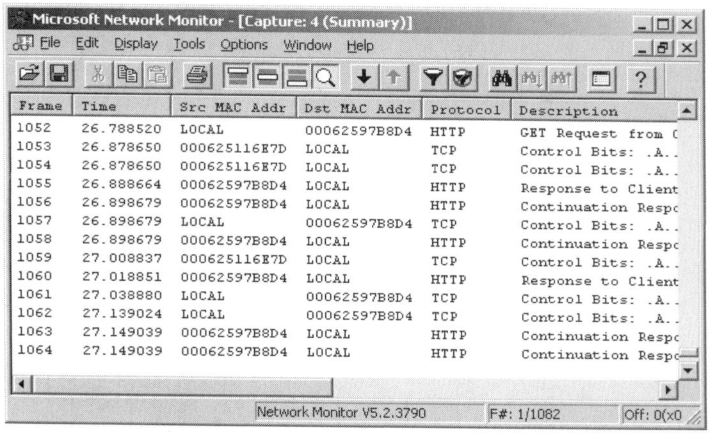

Figure 3-4   Summary pane of the Frame Viewer window

By double-clicking any frame in the summary pane, you can toggle between the original summary pane view and the three-pane view, which includes the summary pane, the details pane, and the hexadecimal (hex) pane. Figure 3-5 shows the three-pane view of the Frame Viewer window.

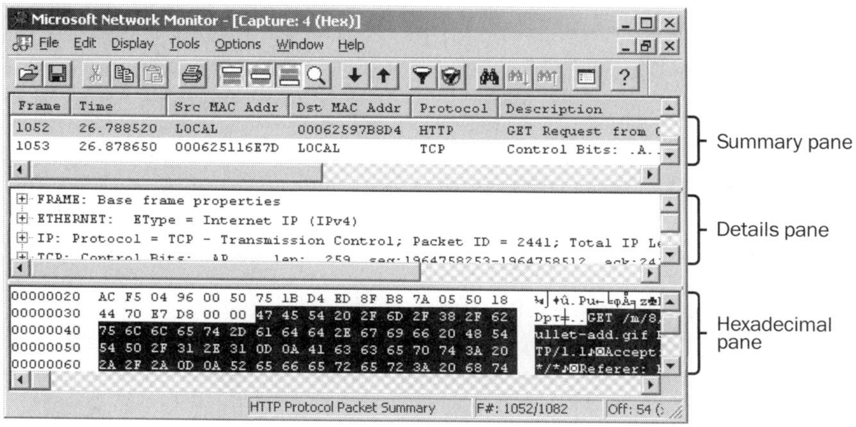

Figure 3-5   Three panes of the Frame Viewer window

The following sections describe the function of these three panes.

Summary Pane   The summary pane lists all frames that are included in the current view of the captured data. When a frame is highlighted in the summary pane, Network Monitor displays the frame's contents in the details pane and hex pane.

You can sort (by clicking the mouse), move, and resize the following nine columns in the summary pane:

- **Frame**   All frames captured during one capture session are numbered in the order of capture time. The frame number, beginning with 1, appears in this column. Remember that frames can be received in a different order than they are sent.

- **Time**   This column displays the frame's capture time relative to the beginning of the capture process. It can be configured to display the time of day when the frame was captured, or time elapsed since the previous frame capture.

- **Src MAC Addr (source MAC address)**   This column displays the hardware address of the computer that sent the frame or the router that forwarded it.

- **Dst MAC Addr (destination MAC address)**   This column displays the hardware address of the target computer.

- **Protocol**   This column lists the highest protocol that Network Monitor recognizes within the frame.

- **Description**   This column contains a summary of the frame's contents. The summary information can show the first protocol used in that frame, the last protocol used in that frame, or an automatic selection.

- **Src Other Addr (source other address)**   This column displays an additional identifying address for the originator of the frame, other than the MAC address. This address might be an IP or Internetwork Packet Exchange (IPX) address.

- **Dst Other Addr (destination other address)**   This column is the same as Src Other Addr, except it gives the destination of the frame instead of the source of the frame.

- **Type Other Addr (type other address)**   This column specifies which type of address is displayed in the previous two columns (for example, if the Src Other Addr and Dst Other Addr fields are displaying IP or IPX addresses).

Details Pane   The details pane displays protocol information for the frame currently highlighted in the summary pane. When a frame contains several protocol layers, the details pane displays the outermost level first. When you select a protocol in the details pane, the associated hexadecimal strings are highlighted in the hex pane.

Hexadecimal Pane   The hex pane displays in hexadecimal format the content of the selected frame. When information is selected in the details pane, the corresponding hexadecimal data appears highlighted in the hex pane. This area can be useful, for example, to developers who need to determine precise information about a network application protocol.

Looking Within Frames

The Frame Viewer window details pane shows the various protocols contained within a frame. In terms of networking models, the protocols are presented with the lowest layers (such as the network interface layer protocol Ethernet) appearing highest, and the highest layers (such as the application layer protocol DNS) appearing lowest. This pattern occurs because Network Monitor presents all data in the order in which it is received on the wire.

The following example represents a frame captured from the Computer Browser service, viewed in the Frame Viewer window details pane:

```
+ Frame: Base frame properties
+ ETHERNET: EType = Internet IP (IPv4)
+ IP: Protocol = UDP - User Datagram; Packet ID = 1576;
    Total IP Length = 236; Options = No Options
+ UDP: Src Port: NETBIOS Datagram Service (138);
    Dst Port: NETBIOS Datagram Service (138); Length = 216 (0xD8)
+ NBT: DS: Type = 17 (DIRECT GROUP)
+ SMB: C transact, File = \MAILSLOT\BROWSE
+ Browser: Workgroup Announcement [0x0c] WORKGROUP
```

Each protocol is presented here in collapsed or summary form. You can expand the complete protocol information by clicking on any plus symbol. The first layer, frame, is added by Network Monitor to describe the frame. This description includes data such as total frame length and time change from previous frame. The next layer, Ethernet, is the outermost protocol of the captured frame and corresponds to the network interface layer of the TCP/IP model. The internet layer follows with the IP protocol. Within this particular protocol stack, the User Datagram Protocol (UDP) is used as the TCP/IP transport-layer protocol.

Network Monitor and the OSI Model   The final three protocols shown in the previous frame example are Microsoft network protocols that are not part of the standard TCP/IP stack. Because these protocols were not originally built on TCP/IP, they are sometimes referred to by their position within the older, more general Open Systems Interconnection (OSI) networking model. The OSI and TCP/IP networking models are compared in Figure 3-6.

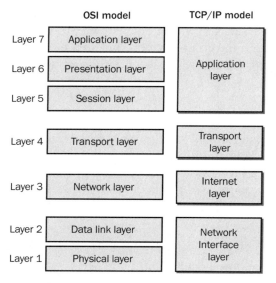

Figure 3-6   OSI networking model

An example of a protocol described most often by its position within the OSI model occurs with the next protocol listed in the sample frame, the session-layer interface NetBT. NetBIOS over TCP/IP (NetBT), represented as NBT in Network Monitor, was designed to connect the transport-layer protocols of TCP/IP—TCP and UDP—to the higher NetBIOS network programs, such as Client for Microsoft Networks, used by Microsoft network protocols.

> **Exam Tip**   For the exam, remember that NetBT is an example of a *session-layer interface*.

The next protocol in the frame, Server Message Block (SMB), traditionally runs on Net-BIOS and allows files and folders to be shared over a Microsoft network. (Although this protocol has been extended and officially renamed Common Internet File System [CIFS], it is still recognized in Network Monitor as SMB.) Finally, the last protocol in the frame is referred to as Browser. It represents the Computer Browser service, which runs on top of SMB and allows users to browse network elements in Windows.

Adding Parsers to Network Monitor

The process of reading, analyzing, and describing the contents of frames is known as *parsing*. In Network Monitor, parsers are .dll files that are responsible for breaking down and reading messages from various protocols. By default, Network Monitor includes more than 20 parsers that are responsible for parsing over 90 protocols.

You can extend the functionality of Network Monitor by adding new parsers. For example, if your organization uses a proprietary protocol, the development team can provide a .dll that Network Monitor can use to parse the new protocol. To perform this task, you must first add the .dll to the WINDOWS\System32\Netmon\Parsers folder, which is where all parsers for Network Monitor are stored. In addition, you must then add an entry for the new parser and protocol in the Parser.ini file. This file, which includes entries for all parsers and protocols used by Network Monitor, is stored in the WINDOWS\System32\Netmon folder.

Off the Record   Adding an entry to the Parser.ini file looks intimidating until you realize that the syntax for every entry is exactly the same. First, in the [parsers] section, merely add the following without the quotations, substituting the name of your parser and protocol as appropriate: "***parser_name***.dll = 0: ***protocol_name***"

Then, lower in the file you will find a section corresponding to each protocol. Simply copy and paste one of these areas and substitute the name and description of your protocol, as appropriate.

Exam Tip   On the exam, you will need to remember the two steps necessary for adding a new parser to Network Monitor. In addition, you will need to know the precise names and locations of both the Parser.ini file and the Parsers folder. Remember, the Parser.ini file is in the \System32\Netmon folder, which is the parent folder of the Parsers folder.

Practice: Using Network Monitor

In this practice, you install Network Monitor, perform a sample network capture, and save captured data.

Exercise 1: Installing Network Monitor

In this exercise, you install the Windows components necessary to run the Network Monitor tool.

1. Log on to Computer1 as Administrator.

2. Insert the Windows Server 2003 installation CD into a local CD-ROM drive.

3. In Control Panel, open Add Or Remove Programs.

4. In the left column of the Add Or Remove Programs window, click Add/Remove Windows Components. The Windows Components page of the Windows Components Wizard appears.

5. In the Components area, select the Management And Monitoring Tools component. Do not select the Management And Monitoring Tools check box.

6. Click Details. The Management And Monitoring Tools dialog box appears.

7. In the Subcomponents Of Management And Monitoring Tools area, select the Network Monitor Tools check box.

8. Click OK.

9. On the Windows Components page of the Windows Components Wizard, click Next. The Configuring Components page appears while the Network Monitor Tools component is installing. When installation is complete, the Completing The Windows Components Wizard page appears.

10. Click Finish.

11. Close the Add Or Remove Programs window.

Exercise 2: Creating a Network Capture in Network Monitor

In this exercise, you capture and view traffic using the Network Monitor tool.

1. While you are logged on to Computer1 as Administrator, open Network Monitor by clicking Start, selecting Administrative Tools, and then clicking Network Monitor.

   The Microsoft Network Monitor dialog box appears, indicating that you should specify a network on which to capture data.

2. Click OK.

   The Select A Network window appears.

3. In the Select A Network window, expand the Local Computer icon in the left pane.

   The network adapters and modems available on your local computer are displayed. The modem connection is named Dial-up Connection Or VPN.

4. Select the network named Local Area Connection, and then click OK.

   The Microsoft Network Monitor tool opens, displaying the Capture window associated with the network adapter you have just selected.

5. In the Capture window, click the Start Capture button on the toolbar.

6. Open a command prompt.

7. At the command prompt, type **ping computer2** and then press Enter. This command is used to test network connections.

   You will see four lines of output resembling those shown in Figure 3-7. This output demonstrates that Computer1 and Computer2 are communicating on the network segment.

Figure 3-7   Ping output

8. After the output has completed, switch to Network Monitor and click the Stop And View Capture button on the toolbar. Alternatively, to perform this step you can press Shift+F11.

   The Frame Viewer window opens, named Capture: 1. The word *Summary* also appears in parentheses, indicating that the summary pane, which is the only visible pane, is the active pane in the window. The purpose of the summary pane is to list in order all of the frames you have just captured.

9. Double-click any one of the frames listed in the summary pane.

   The Frame Viewer window opens two additional panes: the details and hexadecimal panes. These panes provide more information about the frame you have just double-clicked.

10. Double-click again any one of the frames listed in the summary pane.

   The details and hexadecimal panes disappear. You can toggle between the one-pane view and the three-pane view by double-clicking a frame in the summary pane.

11. From the File menu, select Save As.

   The Save As dialog box appears.

12. In the File Name text box, type **Ping Capture**, and then click Save.

   The Ping Capture.cap file is saved in the \Desktop\My Documents\My Captures folder.

13. From the File menu, select Close.

   The Frame Viewer window closes, revealing the Capture window again in Network Monitor.

Exercise 3: Saving a Frame to a Text File

In this exercise, you copy the contents of a packet into a text file. Perform the exercise in Network Monitor while you are logged on to Computer1 as Administrator.

1. From the File menu, select Open.

   The Open dialog box appears, displaying the Ping Capture.cap file in the My Captures folder.

2. Select the Ping Capture file, and click Open.

   The Ping Capture.cap file appears in the Frame Viewer window.

3. In the summary pane, find a frame that lists ICMP under the Protocol heading.

4. Select this ICMP frame.

5. Press Ctrl+C to copy the frame.

6. Open the Notepad utility in Windows.

   The Untitled – Notepad window opens.

7. In the Untitled – Notepad window, press Ctrl+V to paste the frame into the new text file.

   The complete data contents of the copied frame are pasted into the window. Notice how the first line contains all of the fields, in sequence, of the summary pane in the Frame Viewer window. Next, the bulk of the pasted output, about 40 lines, corresponds to the information from the details pane in the Frame Viewer window. Here, all of the details pane information is expanded, and none of the protocol headers are collapsed into a summary form. Finally, the last group of lines of the pasted output represents the hex data from the hexadecimal pane of the Frame Viewer window.

8. In Notepad, press Ctrl+S to save the file.

   The Save As dialog box appears.

9. Using the navigation buttons and folder icons available within the dialog box, adjust the target folder so that the file will be saved in \Desktop\My Documents\My Captures. Do not save the file yet.

10. In the Encoding drop-down list box, select Unicode.

11. In the File Name text box, replace *.txt by typing **ICMP frame**, and then click Save.

12. Close the ICMP Frame.txt – Notepad window.

13. In Network Monitor, from the File menu, select Exit to quit Network Monitor. If you are prompted to save entries in your address database, click No.

14. Log off Computer1.

Lesson Review

The following questions are intended to reinforce key information presented in this lesson. If you are unable to answer a question, review the lesson materials and try the question again. You can find answers to the questions in the "Questions and Answers" section at the end of this chapter.

1. Which of the following is not required to capture frames from a network adapter on a remote computer?

   a. Install the Network Monitor Driver on the remote computer.

   b. Install the Network Monitor Driver on the local computer.

   c. Install the full version of Network Monitor on the local computer.

   d. Install the full version of Network Monitor on the remote computer.

2. Which session-layer interface is used to connect Client for Microsoft Networks to the TCP/IP protocol?

   a. SMB

   b. NetBIOS

   c. NetBT

   d. Browser

3. You are the network administrator of a large company with headquarters in Boston and five branch offices throughout North America. The company has recently deployed a new network application that uses a distinct protocol called XTXA developed by your organization. The application package includes an Xtxa.dll file that enables Network Monitor to parse this proprietary protocol. You want to take advantage of this function so that you can troubleshoot and solve problems related to the application. Which steps must you perform so that you can capture and analyze XTXA traffic in Network Monitor? (Choose two.)

   a. Copy the Xtxa.dll file to the \System32\Netmon folder.

   b. Copy the Xtxa.dll file to the \System32\Netmon\Parsers folder.

   c. Add an entry for the Xtxa.dll file to the \System32\Netmon\Parser.ini file.

   d. Add an entry for the Xtxa.dll file to the \System32\Netmon\Parsers\Parser.ini file.

Lesson Summary

■ Network Monitor is a protocol analyzer that allows you to capture and analyze network traffic.

■ The Network Monitor tool is a subcomponent of the Management And Monitoring Tools component of Windows Server 2003. When you install Network Monitor, the Network Monitor Driver protocol is installed automatically on the same computer.

■ Two versions of Network Monitor exist. The basic version is included with Windows Server 2003, and the full version is included with Systems Management Server. The basic version allows you to capture frames only on the local computer. The full version allows you to capture frames from across the network.

■ By default, Network Monitor can parse over 90 protocols. To extend this functionality by adding a parser for use with Network Monitor, you must first add the .dll to the WINDOWS\System32\Netmon\Parsers folder, which is where all parsers for Network Monitor are stored. In addition, you must then add an entry for the new parser and protocol in the Parser.ini file.

Lesson 2: Troubleshooting TCP/IP Connections

The basic strategy for troubleshooting network connectivity is first to pinpoint the location of a problem, and then to begin verifying functionality at the lower networking layers.

If you have a faulty network connection from a specific host, you can begin by checking your basic IP configuration for errors. If no errors exist in your IP address, subnet mask, gateway, or other IP configuration parameters, you can use various utilities to determine whether the problem exists at, above, or below the TCP/IP internet layer.

After this lesson, you will be able to

- Use the Ipconfig, Network Diagnostics, and Netdiag utilities to troubleshoot a network configuration
- Use the Ping, PathPing, Tracert, and Arp utilities to troubleshoot faulty connections

Estimated lesson time: 45 minutes

Faulty TCP/IP Configuration

When troubleshooting a TCP/IP networking problem, begin by checking the TCP/IP configuration on the computer experiencing the problem.

Ipconfig   Use the Ipconfig command to get basic host computer configuration information, including the IP address, subnet mask, and default gateway. When Ipconfig is used with the /all switch, it produces a more detailed configuration report for all network interfaces.

After executing the Ipconfig command, you can review the Ipconfig output for configuration errors. For example, if a computer has been configured with an IP address that is a duplicate of an existing IP address on the network, the subnet mask appears as 0.0.0.0.

Figure 3-8 gives an example output from an Ipconfig /all command.

Figure 3-8   Output of Ipconfig /all

Network Diagnostics

Network Diagnostics is a graphical troubleshooting tool, built into the Windows Server 2003 interface, that provides detailed information about the local computer's networking configuration. To access the tool, first launch Help And Support from the Start menu. From the Help And Support Center window, click Tools in the Support Tasks area. Finally, expand Help And Support Center Tools from the Tools list, and then select Network Diagnostics. The Network Diagnostics window appears in the right pane of Help And Support Center, as shown in Figure 3-9.

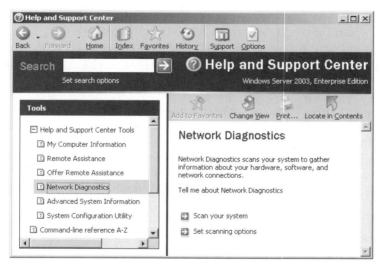

Figure 3-9   Network Diagnostics

When you click Scan Your System, Network Diagnostics runs a series of tests that gathers information about the local computer's environment, as shown in Figure 3-10.

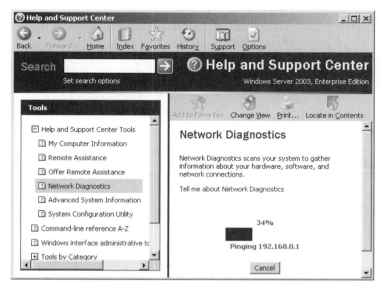

Figure 3-10   Network Diagnostics gathering network data

Information gathered is reported in a series of categories. Each category contains condensed trees of data that you can expand by clicking the associated plus symbol.

By default, Network Diagnostics collects information about only three categories: the Internet Service category, which includes information about Microsoft Outlook Express Mail, Microsoft Outlook Express News, and Internet Explorer Web Proxy configuration; the Computer Information category, which includes Registry parameter settings for the computer system, operating system, and operating system version; and the Modems And Network Adapters category, which includes Registry parameter settings for modems, network adapters, and network clients.

However, by clicking the Set Scanning Options button in the Network Diagnostics window, you can add and remove categories of data to be collected. You can also alter the diagnostic actions performed for each category, as shown in Figure 3-11.

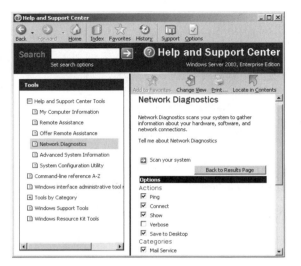

Figure 3-11   Network Diagnostics options

> **Real World   Using the Save To File Feature**
>
> In general, diagnosing and troubleshooting client computers from over the network is more efficient than doing so locally. But this task is not always possible—sometimes the network problem experienced at the client computer precludes establishing a connection across which to run diagnostic tools. When the problem is both serious and remote—such as when an employee in your organization calls you from a different city and requests assistance in connecting to the network—you typically have to talk the employee through elaborate procedures to gather enough information to solve the problem.
>
> The Network Diagnostics tool includes the Save To File feature, which gives you another way to help diagnose remote clients to which you cannot connect directly. Instead of talking users through Ipconfig, Ping, and other utilities run from the command prompt, you can simply have them run the Network Diagnostics tool from the graphical user interface (GUI), save the file to a floppy disk, and then e-mail you the file from another computer.

Netdiag

Netdiag is a command-line utility that you must install manually from the Windows Server 2003 installation CD. The utility is included in the group of tools called the Windows Support Tools. You can install this group of tools by browsing the CD to the \Support\Tools folder and double-clicking Suptools.msi. After the setup program is complete, you can run Netdiag from the installation directory you selected during the setup process.

Like Network Diagnostics, Netdiag runs a series of tests on the local computer and then displays the results of those tests. To troubleshoot network problems, scan the Netdiag output for error messages.

Table 3-3 shows a small selection of the default tests run by Netdiag.

Table 3-3   Netdiag Tests

Test Name	Details
Netcard Queries Test	Lists the network adapter configuration details, including the adapter name, IP address, and default gateway. If this test shows an unresponsive network adapter, the remaining tests are aborted.
Domain Membership Test	Checks to confirm details of the primary domain, including computer role, domain name, and domain GUID. Checks to see whether Netlogon service is started, adds the primary domain to the domain list, and queries the primary domain security identifier (SID).
NetBT Name Test	Checks that the workstation service name <00> is equal to the computer name. Also checks that the messenger service name <03> and server service name <20> are present on all interfaces and that none of these names are in conflict. Similar to the nbtstat –n command.
WINS Service Test	Sends NetBT name queries to all the configured WINS servers.
DNS Test	Checks whether DNS cache service is running, and whether this computer is correctly registered on the configured DNS servers. If the computer is a domain controller (DC), DNS test checks whether all the DNS entries in Netlogon.dns are registered on the DNS server. If the entries are incorrect and the /fix option is on, try to re-register the domain controller record on a DNS server.
Bindings Test	Lists all bindings, including interface name, lower module name, upper module name, whether the binding is currently enabled, and the owner of the binding.
WAN Configuration Test	Displays the settings and status of current active remote access connections.
IP Security Test	Tests whether IP security is enabled and displays a list of active Internet Protocol Security (IPSec) policies.

If the results of these tests do not clarify the source of your network problem, a next possible step is to pinpoint breaks of connectivity on your TCP/IP network.

Troubleshooting Connections Using Ping and PathPing

Ping is a tool that helps to verify IP-level connectivity; PathPing is a tool that detects packet loss over multiple-hop trips. When troubleshooting, the Ping command is used to send an Internet Control Message Protocol (ICMP) echo request to a target host name or IP address. Use Ping whenever you want to verify that a host computer can send IP packets to a destination host. You can also use the Ping tool to locate remote hardware problems and incompatible configurations.

When troubleshooting network connectivity, use the Ping command to perform the following sequence of tasks.

> **Note**   The first two steps of the following sequence are already performed by the Ipconfig /all command and Netdiag. (Network Diagnostics automatically performs only the second step. If Network Diagnostics reports that this self-ping test has failed, you can perform the first step manually.)

1. Ping the loopback address to verify that TCP/IP is installed and configured correctly on the local computer. To perform this step, enter **ping 127.0.0.1** at a command prompt.

   If the loopback step fails, the IP stack is not responding. This problem might be occurring because the TCP drivers are corrupted, the network adapter might not be working, or another service might be interfering with IP.

2. Ping the IP address of the local computer to verify that an address has been added correctly. To perform this step, enter **ping *<IP address of local host>*** at a command prompt.

3. Ping the IP address of the default gateway. This step verifies that the default gateway is reachable and that the local host can communicate with another host on the network. To perform this step, enter **ping *<IP address of default gateway>*** at a command prompt.

4. Ping the IP address of a remote host located beyond the default gateway. This step verifies that you can communicate with hosts outside your local network segment. To perform this step, enter **ping *<IP address of remote host>*** at a command prompt.

5. Ping the host name of a remote host to verify that you can resolve remote host names. To perform this step, enter ping <host name of remote host> at a command prompt.

6. Run a PathPing analysis to a remote host to determine which (if any) routers on the way to the destination are malfunctioning. To perform this step, enter pathping <IP address of remote host> at a command prompt.

Note   To perform this last step more quickly, you can substitute the Tracert utility for the PathPing utility. Tracert reveals breaks in connectivity but does not provide statistics about router performance. Tracert is described in more detail in the following section.

Ping uses host name resolution to resolve a computer name to an IP address, so if pinging succeeds by address, but fails by name, the problem lies in host name resolution, not network connectivity.

If you cannot ping successfully at any point, check to make sure the following are true:

- The local computer's IP address and subnet mask are correctly configured.

- A default gateway is configured and the link between the host and the default gateway is operational. For troubleshooting purposes, make sure only one default gateway is configured.

Note   If the remote system being pinged is across a high-delay link such as a satellite link, responses might take longer to be returned. You can use the –w switch to specify a longer time-out. For example, the command *ping –w 2000 172.16.48.10* waits 2 seconds before timing out. (The default setting is 1 second, expressed as 1000 milliseconds.)

Troubleshooting with Tracert

Tracert is a route-tracing utility that allows you to track the path of a forwarded packet from router to router for up to 30 hops. Tracert works by sending ICMP echo requests to an IP address, while incrementing the Time to Live (TTL) field in the IP header, starting at 1, and analyzing the ICMP errors that are returned. Tracert prints out an ordered list of the routers in the path that returned these error messages. In the following example, Tracert is used to trace the path from the local computer to a remote computer named www.contoso.com:

```
C:\>tracert www.contoso.com
Tracing route to www.contoso.com [10.102.252.1]
over a maximum of 30 hops:
  1 300 ms 281 ms 280 ms roto.contoso.com [10.181.164.100]
  2 300 ms 301 ms 310 ms sl-stk-1-S12-T1.contoso.com [10.228.192.65]
  3 300 ms 311 ms 320 ms sl-stk-5-F0/0.contoso.com [10.228.40.5]
  4 380 ms 311 ms 340 ms icm-fix-w-H2/0-T3.contoso.com [10.228.10.22]
  5 310 ms 301 ms 320 ms arc-nas-gw.arc.contoso.com [10.203.230.3]
  6 300 ms 321 ms 320 ms n254-ed-cisco7010.contoso.com [10.102.64.254]
  7 360 ms 361 ms 371 ms www.contoso.com [10.102.252.1]
```

Exam Tip   You need to know the difference between Tracert and PathPing on the exam. Use Tracert to quickly determine where a break occurs in the path of connectivity to a remote location. PathPing is more useful when you have connectivity to a site but are experiencing erratic packet loss or high delay. In these cases, PathPing tells you exactly where packet loss is occurring.

Troubleshooting Using the ARP Tool

Network traffic sometimes fails because a router's proxy ARP request returns the wrong address. If you can ping both the loopback address and your own IP address, but you cannot ping a computer on the local subnet, the next step is to check the ARP cache for errors.

The ARP command is useful for viewing the ARP cache. If two hosts on the same subnet cannot ping each other successfully, try running the ARP command with the –a switch on each computer to see whether the computers have the correct MAC addresses listed for each other. To determine a host's MAC address, you can use the Ipconfig /all command or the Getmac command. Then use the ARP command with the -d switch to delete any entry that might be incorrect. Add entries by using ARP with the –s switch.

If you cannot ping a computer on a local subnet by IP address, and the ARP –a command reveals no errors in hardware address mappings, you should investigate for errors in the physical media, such as LAN cards, hubs, and cables.

Practice: Running Network Diagnostics and Netdiag

In this practice, you run both Network Diagnostics and the Netdiag utility. You then save the output of these tests to files.

Exercise 1: Running Network Diagnostics

In this exercise, you save the output from the Network Diagnostics tool to an HTML file.

1. Log on to Computer1 as Administrator.

2. Click Start, and then click Help And Support.

   The Help And Support Center window opens.

3. Under the Support Tasks list on the right side of the Help And Support Center window, click Tools.

4. In the Tools list on the left side of the Help And Support Center window, expand Help And Support Center Tools, and then click Network Diagnostics.

   The Network Diagnostics tool appears on the right side of the Help And Support Center window.

5. Click the Scan Your System button.

   Information loads for a few seconds, and then three headings of status information are displayed: Internet Service, Computer Information, and Modems And Network Adapters.

6. Expand all of the categories by clicking the plus symbols under them.

   All of the information trees under each heading expand, revealing the full results of the tests just run.

7. Take a few moments to browse the information available in the expanded trees.

8. In the Network Diagnostics window, click the Set Scanning Options button.

   Below the Options heading, the Actions area and the Categories area are shown.

9. Under the Actions area, select the Verbose check box.

10. In the Categories area, clear the following check boxes: Mail Service, News Service, Internet Proxy Server, Computer Information, Operating System, and Windows Version.

    Only Modems, Network Clients, and Adapters should now be selected.

11. In the Network Diagnostics window, click the Scan Your System button to begin gathering information.

    When the tests have completed, the Network Diagnostics window reveals three sets of information under a single heading: Modems And Network Adapters.

12. In the Network Diagnostics window, click the Save To File button to save to a file the results of the test just run.

    A message indicates that the file just created has been saved to the desktop and to another specified location.

13. Click OK to close the message.

14. Next to the Save To File button in the Network Diagnostics window, click Show Saved Files.

    A folder opens revealing one location of the new file.

15. On the Windows Quick Launch toolbar, click Show Desktop.

    Another copy of the Hypertext Markup Language (HTML) file created by Network Diagnostics is visible on the desktop.

16. Cut and paste this document to the My Documents folder.

17. Close any remaining open windows.

Exercise 2: Installing Windows Support Tools

Before beginning this exercise, insert the Windows Server 2003 installation CD-ROM into the CD-ROM drive on Computer1.

1. While you are logged on to Computer1 as Administrator, browse the Windows Server 2003 CD to the \Support\Tools folder.

2. In the Tools folder, double-click Suptools.msi.

The Windows Support Tools Setup Wizard opens.

3. Click Next.

The End User License Agreement page appears.

4. Click the I Agree option, and then click Next.

The User Information page appears.

5. In the Name text box and the Organization text box, enter your name and organization, and click Next.

The Destination Directory page appears.

6. Leave the default install path, and click Install Now.

After installation is complete, the Completing The Windows Support Tools Setup Wizard page appears.

7. Click Finish to exit the wizard.

Exercise 3: Running Netdiag from Across the Network

In this exercise, you use the Telnet utility to connect to Computer1. You then run the Netdiag utility from the Telnet prompt.

1. While you are logged on to Computer1 as Administrator, open the Services console by clicking the Start button, selecting Administrative Tools, and then clicking Services.

The Services console opens.

2. In the right pane of the Services console, select Telnet from the list of services.

Note that the Status field is blank for Telnet service.

3. Start the Telnet service. One way to accomplish this task is to double-click the Telnet icon, select Manual from the Startup Type drop-down list box, click Apply, click Start, and then click OK.

The Service Control status box appears while the Telnet service is starting. It disappears when the service has started successfully. In the Services console, the Status field for the Telnet service now contains the word *Started*.

4. Close the Services console.

5. Log on to Computer2 as Administrator.

6. On Computer2, open a command prompt and enter **telnet computer1**.

You will be warned about sending your password to a remote computer.

7. Press y, and then press Enter.

If you have assigned the Administrator account the same password on Computer2 as on Computer1, you will receive a Welcome message and a command prompt from Telnet Server. If you have assigned the two Administrator accounts separate passwords, you must enter the Administrator credentials for Computer1 before you receive this message and command prompt.

8. After you have received the Welcome message, type **netdiag** at the Telnet command prompt, and then press Enter.

Information gathers for a few moments, and then the output of the Netdiag utility appears at the command prompt. This utility has been run on Computer1.

9. Briefly review the Netdiag output.

10. At the Telnet command prompt, type **cd my documents**, and then press Enter.

The directory on Computer1 from which you are executing commands changes.

11. At the Telnet prompt, type **netdiag >NetdiagOutput.txt**, and then press Enter.

A copy of the Netdiag output is saved to the My Documents folder on Computer1.

12. At the Telnet prompt, type **netdiag /v >VerboseNetdiagOutput.txt**, and then press Enter.

A copy of the verbose Netdiag output is saved to the My Documents folder on Computer1.

13. Switch back to Computer1 and open the My Documents folder.

14. Open NetdiagOutput.txt, and then open VerboseNetdiagOutput.txt.

15. Take a minute to compare the output from these two modes of the Netdiag utility.

16. In the My Documents folder, use the shortcut to the NetDiag folder to open the HTML file that you created and saved through Network Diagnostics.

17. Take a minute to compare the information in this file with the information in the two files generated from the Netdiag utility.

18. Close all open windows on Computer1 and Computer2.

19. Log off Computer1 and Computer2.

Lesson Review

The following questions are intended to reinforce key information presented in this lesson. If you are unable to answer a question, review the lesson materials and try the question again. You can find answers to the questions in the "Questions and Answers" section at the end of this chapter.

1. You cannot ping a computer on a local subnet, even after you reboot the computer. What should you do next?

   a. Check for hardware errors.

   b. Run Ipconfig with the /all switch.

   c. Run Network Diagnostics in verbose mode.

2. After changing the network card of a certain computer, you find that you can no longer ping that computer from another computer on the local subnet. You have checked the TCP/IP configuration on both computers and have found no errors. Both computers can also ping themselves successfully. Finally, you have also verified that the most recent version of the new NIC driver is installed and that Device Manager reports the device is working correctly. What should be your next step?

   a. Check for errors in the ARP cache.

   b. Perform a Network Monitor trace from the nearest router.

   c. Run Ipconfig with the /all switch.

3. From a host named C1, you cannot ping another host named C2 that is located on the same subnet. You have examined the IP properties of both computers and have determined that neither computer contains TCP/IP configuration errors. Both computers can ping themselves, but only C2 can ping other computers. You have also verified that no errors exist in either computer's IP-to-hardware address mappings. What should be your next step?

   a. Check for hardware errors on C1.

   b. Run Network Diagnostics.

   c. Check for errors in the ARP cache.

   d. Check for hardware errors on C2.

4. You are experiencing a delay when you connect to a remote Web site. Which tool allows you to determine which particular routers are responsible for the delay?

   a. Netdiag

   b. Network Diagnostics

   c. Tracert

   d. PathPing

Lesson Summary

- Use the Ipconfig command to get basic host computer configuration information, including the IP address, subnet mask, and default gateway. The /all switch adds more detailed information for each network adapter.

- Network Diagnostics is a graphical troubleshooting tool that provides detailed information about a local computer's networking configuration. You can access the tool through Help And Support.

- Like Network Diagnostics, the Netdiag command-line utility runs a series of tests on the local computer and then displays the results of those tests.

- Ping is a tool that helps to verify IP-level connectivity; the PathPing tool detects packet loss over multiple-hop trips.

- When troubleshooting a connection, first ping the loopback address, then the local IP address, then the default gateway, then a remote host by IP address, and then a remote host by host name. If you are troubleshooting delays to a remote host, use PathPing.

- Tracert is a route-tracing utility that allows you to track the path of a forwarded packet from router to router for up to 30 hops. Use Tracert when you have no connectivity to a site under investigation because it tells you where connectivity stops.

- If you can ping the loopback address, your own IP address, and the default gateway, but you cannot ping a computer on the local subnet, the next step is to check the ARP cache for errors.

- If you cannot ping a computer on a local subnet by IP address, and the ARP –a command reveals no errors in hardware address mappings, you should investigate physical media such as LAN cards, hubs, and cables for errors.

Case Scenario Exercise

You are the network administrator for a company employing 300 people and consisting of one headquarters and two branch offices in neighboring cities. The IT department is located at the headquarters, whose network consists of three subnets behind a firewall. Each of the branch offices consists of a single subnet behind a firewall. The three offices communicate with each other over the Internet.

Figure 3-12 shows a map of the company network.

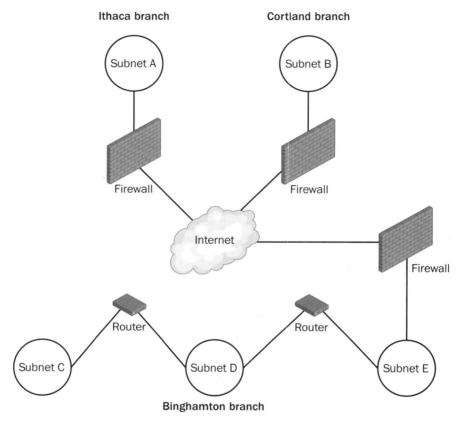

Figure 3-12   The company network map

As part of your responsibilities, you must field calls from employees in all three offices. Typically, workers describe a problem they are experiencing, and you must decide which diagnostic tool is most appropriate to use in solving the problem.

The problems from six different callers are described next. For each case, determine whether the situation can best be resolved by using Network Monitor, Ping, Tracert, PathPing, Netdiag, or Network Diagnostics. Provide a reason to justify each of your choices. Write your answers in the space provided.

1. A user on your local subnet (Subnet E) cannot connect to any network resources.

_____

_____

2. A user on Subnet C cannot connect to resources on Subnet E.

_____

_____

3. A user on Subnet C can connect to resources on the company extranet in both branch offices, but connectivity to the Cortland branch is slow. Images often do not appear on extranet pages hosted at the Cortland branch.

_____

_____

4. A user on Subnet C reports that sometimes when she tries to specify a network resource by name, a connection cannot be established. The user knows her IP address, and you have configured all client computers on her subnet to run the Telnet service.

_____

_____

5. A user at the Ithaca branch reports erratic network service. He does not know his IP address, and you have not enabled the Telnet service on client computers at the Ithaca office.

_____

_____

6. Management has asked a staff member to deploy a messaging application for use across all three branch offices. The staff member calls you and reports that although the messaging software seems to work within each branch, it does not seem to work across branches. He also does not know the TCP port number used by the messaging application.

_____

_____

Chapter Summary

- Network Monitor is a protocol analyzer that allows you to capture and analyze network traffic. By default, Network Monitor can parse over 90 protocols.

- To extend this functionality and add a parser for use with Network Monitor, you must first copy the .dll to the WINDOWS\System32\Netmon\Parsers folder, which is where all parsers for Network Monitor are stored. You must then add an entry for the new parser and protocol in the Parser.ini file.

- Use the Ipconfig command to get basic host computer configuration information, including the IP address, subnet mask, and default gateway. The /all switch adds more detailed information for each network adapter.

- When troubleshooting a connection, first ping the loopback address, then the local IP address, then the default gateway, then a remote host by IP address, and then a remote host by host name. If you are troubleshooting delays to a remote host, use PathPing.

- Tracert is a route-tracing utility that allows you to track the path of a forwarded packet from router to router for up to 30 hops. Use Tracert when you have no connectivity to a remote site because it tells you where connectivity stops.

- Network Diagnostics is a graphical troubleshooting tool, built into the Windows Server 2003 interface, that provides detailed information about a local computer's networking configuration. The tool is accessed through Help And Support Center. Like Network Diagnostics, the Netdiag utility runs a series of tests on the local computer and then displays the results of those tests.

Exam Highlights

Before taking the exam, review the key points and terms that are presented below to help you identify topics you need to review. Return to the lessons for additional practice, and review the "Further Reading" sections in Part 2 for pointers to more information about topics covering the exam objectives.

Key Points

- You can use Network Monitor to find certain details—such as the MAC address of a host, the GUID of a client computer, or the port used by a protocol—that might have been lost with documentation.

- Remember the steps necessary to allow Network Monitor to parse a new protocol, such as a protocol used by an application specific to your organization.

- Remember that to troubleshoot a connection, you must ping a distinct sequence of hosts: the loopback address, the local IP address, the default gateway, a remote host by IP address, and finally, a remote host by host name.

- Know the difference between Tracert and PathPing. Use Tracert when you are troubleshooting lack of connectivity to a remote host. If you are troubleshooting delays to a remote host, use PathPing.

Key Terms

parser   A dynamic link library (DLL) that reads and analyzes messages of a particular protocol captured from the network.

PathPing   A command-line tool that detects packet loss over multiple-hop trips.

Network Diagnostics   A graphical troubleshooting tool in Windows Server 2003 that provides detailed information about the local computer's networking configuration.

Netdiag   A command-line troubleshooting tool, included in the Windows Support Tools package on the Windows Server 2003 CD, that provides detailed information about a local computer's networking configuration.

Globally Unique Identifier (GUID)   A 16-byte value generated from the unique identifier on a device, the current date and time, and a sequence number. A GUID is used to identify a particular device or component.

Questions and Answers

Page
3-17 **Lesson 1 Review**

1. Which of the following is not a requirement to capture frames from a network adapter on a remote computer?

    a. Install the Network Monitor Driver on the remote computer.

    b. Install the Network Monitor Driver on the local computer.

    c. Install the full version of Network Monitor on the local computer.

    d. Install the full version of Network Monitor on the remote computer.

    d

2. Which session-layer interface is used to connect Client for Microsoft Networks to the TCP/IP protocol?

    a. SMB

    b. NetBIOS

    c. NetBT

    d. Browser

    c

3. You are the network administrator of a large company with headquarters in Boston and five branch offices throughout North America. The company has recently deployed a new network application that uses a distinct protocol called XTXA developed by your organization. The application package includes an Xtxa.dll file that enables Network Monitor to parse this proprietary protocol. You want to take advantage of this function so that you can troubleshoot and solve problems related to the application. Which steps must you perform so that you can capture and analyze XTXA traffic in Network Monitor? (Choose two.)

    a. Copy the Xtxa.dll file to the \System32\Netmon folder.

    b. Copy the Xtxa.dll file to the \System32\Netmon\Parsers folder.

    c. Add an entry for the Xtxa.dll file to the \System32\Netmon\Parser.ini file.

    d. Add an entry for the Xtxa.dll file to the \System32\Netmon\Parsers\Parser.ini file.

b, c

Lesson 2 Review

Page
3-30

1. You cannot ping to a computer on a local subnet, even after you reboot the computer. What should you do next?

    a. Check for hardware errors.

    b. Run Ipconfig with the /all switch.

    c. Run Network Diagnostics in verbose mode.

b

2. After changing the network card of a certain computer, you have found that you can no longer ping that computer from another computer on the local subnet. You have checked the TCP/IP configuration on both computers and find no errors. Both computers can also ping themselves successfully. Finally, you have also verified that the most recent version of the new NIC driver is installed and that Device Manager reports the device is working correctly. What should be your next step?

    a. Check for errors in the ARP cache.

    b. Perform a Network Monitor trace from the nearest router.

    c. Run Ipconfig with the /all switch.

a

3. From a host named C1, you cannot ping another host named C2 that is located on the same subnet. You have examined the IP properties of both computers and have determined that neither computer contains TCP/IP configuration errors. Both computers can ping themselves, but only C2 can ping other computers. You have also verified that no errors exist in either computer's IP-to-hardware address mappings. What should be your next step?

    a. Check for hardware errors on C1.

    b. Run Network Diagnostics.

    c. Check for errors in the ARP cache.

    d. Check for hardware errors on C2.

a

4. You are experiencing a delay when you connect to a remote Web site. Which tool allows you to determine whether particular routers are responsible for the delay?

    a. Netdiag

    b. Network Diagnostics

    c. Tracert

    d. PathPing

d

Case Scenario

Page
3-33

1. A user on your local subnet (Subnet E) cannot connect to any network resources.

Ping is best used because you need to perform basic troubleshooting and the computer is local.

2. A user on Subnet C cannot connect to resources on Subnet E.

Tracert is best used to begin troubleshooting this problem because in this case, two routers separate the subnets. This utility enables you to determine at which subnet or router the problem occurs.

3. A user on Subnet C can connect to resources on the company extranet in both branch offices, but connectivity to the Cortland branch is slow. Images often do not appear on extranet pages hosted at the Cortland branch.

PathPing is best used in this case because connectivity is erratic and slow. This tool enables you to determine whether erratic packet loss is occurring at the Cortland branch firewall or at another router.

4. A user on Subnet C reports that sometimes when she tries to specify a network resource by name, a connection cannot be established. The user knows her IP address, and you have configured all client computers on her subnet to run the Telnet service.

In this case, you can use Telnet to access the IP address in question and run Netdiag from across the network. This strategy provides you a full range of IP configuration information, including the client's configured name servers.

5. A user at the Ithaca branch reports erratic network service. He does not know his IP address, and you have not enabled the Telnet service on client computers at the Ithaca office.

In this case, you can talk the user through the process of using the Network Diagnostics tool. He can then save the output to a file and e-mail you the results. Because the network problems he is experiencing are erratic, to resolve the problem you will probably need to view a wide variety of IP configuration information (such as that provided by this tool).

6. Management has asked a staff member to deploy a messaging application for use across all three branch offices. The staff member calls you and reports that although the messaging software seems to work within each branch, it does not seem to work across branches. He also does not know the TCP port number used by the messaging application.

You can use Network Monitor to determine the port number used by the application. Then you can configure the firewalls at each branch to allow traffic through that port.

4 Configuring DNS Servers and Clients

Exam Objectives in this Chapter:

- Troubleshoot TCP/IP addressing
- Install and configure the DNS Server service
- Manage DNS record settings

Why This Chapter Matters

Name resolution is a complex topic that can appear difficult to understand, but mastering its concepts is nonetheless essential if you want to become a Windows Server 2003 networking expert. Because the Active Directory directory service depends on the Domain Name System (DNS) for its most basic functioning, without a clear understanding of how DNS works, you will not be able to effectively troubleshoot networks running Microsoft Windows Server 2003.

This chapter introduces foundational concepts related to name resolution in Windows Server 2003 networks and, in particular, DNS. The chapter then describes the process of configuring DNS servers and DNS clients in a Windows Server 2003 network. Along the way, you are introduced to essential troubleshooting tools such as Nbtstat and Ipconfig /flushdns to help you solve name resolution problems in your network.

Lessons in this Chapter:

- Lesson 1: Understanding Name Resolution in Windows Server 2003 4-3
- Lesson 2: Understanding DNS in Windows Server 2003 Networks 4-12
- Lesson 3: Deploying DNS Servers. 4-26
- Lesson 4: Configuring DNS Clients 4-44

Before You Begin

To complete this chapter, you must have

- Networked two computers, named Computer1 and Computer2, each running Windows Server 2003. Computer1 should be assigned a static address of 192.168.0.1/24, and Computer2 should be assigned an alternate address of 192.168.0.2/24. Computer2 should also be configured to obtain an IP address automatically.

- A phone line and dial-up Internet service provider (ISP) account. (Although you can substitute a dedicated Internet connection for this requirement, you will have to make appropriate adjustments to lesson exercises.)

- Installed the Network Monitor Tools subcomponent of the Management And Monitoring Tools Windows component on Computer1.

- Installed Windows Support Tools on Computer1.

Lesson 1: Understanding Name Resolution in Windows Server 2003

Virtually every network requires a mechanism to resolve computer names to Internet Protocol (IP) addresses. This requirement arises because people and applications tend to connect to network computers by specifying a name, whereas lower-level services generally use addresses to identify hosts. For historical reasons, two computer naming systems coexist in Windows Server 2003 networks: NetBIOS and DNS. Because these naming systems are not related, they require separate mechanisms to resolve their names to IP addresses.

After this lesson, you will be able to

- Describe name resolution methods in Windows Server 2003 networks
- Compare and contrast NetBIOS names and DNS names
- Describe name resolution procedures for NetBIOS and DNS
- Use the Nbtstat command to view and flush the NetBIOS name cache
- Disable NetBIOS on a network

Estimated lesson time: 30 minutes

Comparing DNS and NetBIOS

DNS is the preferred naming system in the Windows Server 2003 family and, compared to NetBIOS, offers superior scalability, security, and compatibility with the Internet. Although DNS requires configuration before it can function, it is still an essential element in Active Directory domains and is therefore used in most Windows Server 2003 networks. However, NetBIOS is still often used as a backup name resolution method, particularly because it can provide, without configuration, name resolution for computers located on the same network segment. In addition, NetBIOS is used for compatibility with older Windows features, such as browsing the Microsoft Windows Network through My Network Places or connecting to shares through Universal Naming Convention (UNC) addresses such as \\computer1\share1.

Note   NetBIOS is not actually a naming system but an application programming interface (API), used in older Microsoft networks, that allows computers to connect and communicate. Naming and name resolution are two of the many services NetBIOS offers.

In Windows Server 2003 networks, DNS name resolution takes priority over NetBIOS name resolution. This prioritization is handled by the DNS Client service, which is responsible for directing name resolution. The DNS Client service first attempts name resolution through DNS; if this fails, the DNS Client service then submits the name to NetBIOS.

> **Note** The DNS Client service is also known as the *resolver*.

Comparing Computer Names

When you install Windows Server 2003 on a computer, you must assign the computer a name. This name, which you can modify in the System Properties dialog box, forms the basis both for its DNS host name and its NetBIOS name. Specifically, an individual label such as "server1" assigned to a computer is known as a *host name* in DNS. Provided that it does not exceed 15 characters, the same name is then also used as the NetBIOS name.

Despite this similarity, DNS is distinct from NetBIOS in that the DNS namespace is hierarchical. Each DNS host name is merely a part of a full name, known as a *fully qualified domain name* (FQDN), that specifies both the host name and its domain. An example of an FQDN is www.lucernepublishing.com. NetBIOS includes no such hierarchy; as a result, every NetBIOS name must be unique on the network.

Table 4-1 summarizes the various name types and name components used in Windows Server 2003 networks.

Table 4-1   Computer Names and Name Suffixes

Name Type	Description
NetBIOS name	A NetBIOS name is used to uniquely identify a NetBIOS service listening on the first IP address that is bound to an adapter. This unique NetBIOS name is resolved to the IP address of the server through broadcast, the Windows Internet Name Service (WINS), or the Lmhosts file. NetBIOS computer names are 15 characters, whereas NetBIOS service names are 16 characters. By default, the first 15 characters of the NetBIOS service name are the same as the host name, padded with zeros. The sixteenth character is used to identify the specific NetBIOS service.
Host name	The term host name typically refers to the first label of an FQDN. For example, the first label of the FQDN client1.lucernepublishing.com is client1. A host name is also often referred to as *computer name*.

Table 4-1   Computer Names and Name Suffixes

Name Type	Description
Primary DNS suffix	Every computer in a Windows Server 2003 network can be assigned a primary DNS suffix to be used in name resolution and name registration. The primary DNS suffix is specified on the Computer Name tab of the properties dialog box in My Computer. The primary DNS suffix is also known as the *primary domain name* and the *domain name*. For example, the FQDN c1.lucernepublishing.com has the primary DNS suffix lucernepublishing.com.
Connection-specific DNS suffix	The connection-specific DNS suffix is a DNS suffix that is assigned to an adapter. The connection-specific DNS suffix is also known as an *adapter DNS suffix*. For example, a connection-specific DNS suffix might be subnet2.lucernepublishing.com.
FQDN	The FQDN is a DNS name that uniquely identifies the computer on the network. Typically, it is a concatenation of the host name, the primary DNS suffix, and a period. For example, an FQDN might be client1.lucernepublishing.com.
Full computer name	The full computer name is a type of FQDN. The same computer can be identified by more than one FQDN, but only the FQDN that concatenates the host name and the primary DNS suffix represents the full computer name.

Table 4-2 compares the general features of NetBIOS computer names and DNS host names.

Table 4-2   Comparison of NetBIOS and DNS Names

	NetBIOS Computer Name	DNS Computer Name
Type	Flat	Hierarchical
Character restrictions	Unicode characters, numbers, white space, symbols: ! @ # $ % ^ & ') (. - _ { } ~	A–Z, a–z, 0–9, and the hyphen (-); period (.) has special reserved meaning
Maximum length	15 characters	63 bytes per label; 255 bytes per FQDN
Name service	WINS NetBIOS broadcast Lmhosts file	DNS Hosts file

Comparing Name Resolution Procedures

Within each of the two general categories of name resolution—DNS and NetBIOS—Windows Server 2003 networks provide a set of methods to resolve computer names.

For DNS, these name resolution methods include the following:

- Name lookup in the local DNS client cache. Names can be cached from previous queries or loaded from the Hosts file found in the WINDOWS\System32\Drivers\Etc folder.

- DNS server query.

For NetBIOS name resolution, these methods include the following:

- Name lookup in the local NetBIOS name cache

- WINS server query

- Query of local network through NetBIOS broadcasts

- Name lookup in the Lmhosts file, found in the WINDOWS\System32\Drivers\Etc folder

> **Exam Tip**   Remember the following NetBIOS-related commands for the exam:
>
> - Nbtstat –c (Lists the names in the local NetBIOS name cache)
> - Nbtstat –R (Purges the local NetBIOS name cache)

Determining When DNS Is Required

In general, DNS is required for networks under the circumstances described in the following sections.

Networks Using Microsoft Windows 2000 or Windows Server 2003 Domains   When computers are members of a Windows 2000 or Windows Server 2003 domain, DNS must be configured. Active Directory is tightly integrated with DNS, and DNS is used by Active Directory as its locator service. (A *locator service* assists clients in a Windows Server 2003 or Windows 2000 domain to find hosts and services with an unknown location within a given domain.)

DNS for Internet or Intranet Access   You must use DNS if you need to connect to computers on your network or the Internet by specifying DNS host names.

Determining When NetBIOS Is Required

Windows Server 2003 networks support NetBIOS over TCP/IP (NetBT) for backward compatibility with earlier versions of Windows and for compatibility with NetBIOS applications. Microsoft Windows NT domains—as well all workgroups using Microsoft Windows 95, Microsoft Windows 98, Microsoft Windows Millennium Edition (Me), and Windows NT—use NetBIOS names and the NetBIOS protocol.

NetBIOS name resolution is also necessary for network clients using applications or services that require NetBIOS name resolution. An example of such a service is the Computer Browser service, which enables network browsing through the Microsoft Windows Network icon in Windows Explorer.

Finally, NetBIOS name resolution is required in networks for which DNS has not yet been fully configured. An example is a computer workgroup in which no DNS server has been installed. In this case, NetBIOS broadcasts are required to resolve computer names.

> ### Real World   Browsing without NetBIOS
>
> Although no solution besides NetBIOS can provide broadcast-based name reso-lution, some secure alternatives for network browsing are available. First, if you have added network shares to the Active Directory global catalog, users can locate and connect to these shares through Windows Explorer. Alternatively, you can use Distributed File System (DFS) to build an easily browsed structure for all the shared folders on your network. After users connect to the root DFS share, they can browse shared resources regardless of the server that hosts the share. Finally, don't forget that although network *browsing* is not available without Net-BIOS, you can still *connect* to network resources through My Network Places as long as you specify those resources by name.

Disabling NetBIOS

NetBIOS is enabled by default for all local area connections in Windows Server 2003. However, if you have implemented DNS on your network and do not need to provide compatibility with versions of Windows earlier than Windows 2000, you have the option of disabling NetBIOS for any or all network connections.

The main advantage of disabling NetBIOS is improved network security. NetBIOS as a service stores information about network resources that can be collected by any host through broadcast-based queries. Feasibly, this information could be exploited by a malicious intruder. Another advantage of disabling NetBIOS is that doing so can sim-plify administration by reducing the number of naming infrastructures that you must configure, maintain, and support.

The most obvious disadvantage of disabling NetBIOS is that it renders inoperable net-work browsing through the Microsoft Windows Network icon. (You access this icon in Windows Explorer by expanding My Network Places and by then double-clicking the Entire Network icon.) Network browsing is made possible by the availability of browse lists compiled by the Computer Browser service; the Computer Browser service relies on NetBIOS and the NetBT protocol. Another disadvantage of disabling NetBIOS is that it decreases fault tolerance. If DNS is improperly configured, name resolution fails. Finally, some networks use third-party applications that require NetBIOS. Before disabling NetBIOS on your network, be sure to set up a test network to see whether all needed applications function properly.

To disable WINS/NetBIOS name resolution, complete the following steps:

1. Open the Network Connections window.

2. Right-click Local Area Connection, and then click Properties.

   The Local Area Connection Properties dialog box opens.

3. In the list of components, click Internet Protocol (TCP/IP), and then click Properties.

   The Internet Protocol (TCP/IP) Properties dialog box opens.

4. Click Advanced.

   The Advanced TCP/IP Settings dialog box opens.

5. Click the WINS tab.

6. Click the Disable NetBIOS Over TCP/IP option.

7. Click OK twice, and then click Close.

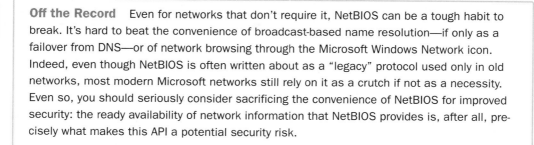

Off the Record   Even for networks that don't require it, NetBIOS can be a tough habit to break. It's hard to beat the convenience of broadcast-based name resolution—if only as a failover from DNS—or of network browsing through the Microsoft Windows Network icon. Indeed, even though NetBIOS is often written about as a "legacy" protocol used only in old networks, most modern Microsoft networks still rely on it as a crutch if not as a necessity. Even so, you should seriously consider sacrificing the convenience of NetBIOS for improved security: the ready availability of network information that NetBIOS provides is, after all, precisely what makes this API a potential security risk.

Practice: Capturing Name Resolution Traffic

In this practice, you create a network capture of name resolution in progress.

Exercise 1: Capturing Name Resolution Traffic

In this exercise, you clear both name caches on Computer1. You then ping Computer2 by name and review a Network Monitor capture of this process.

1. Log on to Computer1 as Administrator.

2. Open a command prompt.

3. At the prompt, type **ipconfig /flushdns**, and then press Enter.

   This purges the DNS Client service cache on the local computer.

4. At the prompt, type **nbtstat –R**, and then press Enter.

   This purges the NetBIOS name cache on the local computer.

5. Open Network Monitor.

6. From the Capture menu, select Networks.

7. In the Select A Network window, configure Network Monitor to capture traffic on the local area network (LAN) and not the dial-up connection.

8. In Network Monitor, start a new capture.

9. Switch back to the command prompt, type **ping computer2**, and press Enter.

10. After you receive four replies from Computer2, switch back to Network Monitor, and click the Stop And View Capture button on the toolbar to stop and view the capture.

    The Capture window opens, displaying the frames you have just captured.

11. Look at the protocols listed in the new network capture.

    In Network Monitor, NBT represents NetBT, and DNS represents Domain Name System. Based on the protocol you see in this capture and on the description provided for given frames, determine whether NetBIOS name resolution or DNS name resolution has been used to resolve the computer name Computer2. Why has this method been used and not the other method? Write your answer in the space provided.

    _____

    _____

    _____

    _____

    _____

12. Save the capture to the My Documents\My Captures folder as Name Resolution 1.

13. Exit Network Monitor and close the command prompt window.

14. Log off Computer1.

Lesson Review

The following questions are intended to reinforce key information presented in this lesson. If you are unable to answer a question, review the lesson materials and try the question again. You can find answers to the questions in the "Questions and Answers" section at the end of this chapter.

1. The network you administer includes 10 computers running Windows Server 2003 and 200 computers running Microsoft Windows XP Professional. In the network, you have deployed a DNS server named DNS1 to host the zone lucernepublishing.com. You have also configured the zone to allow dynamic updates. A DHCP server is responsible for the IP configuration of all computers running Windows XP Professional. One of these computers, c1.lucernepublishing.com, can be contacted only by IP address and not by name. Which of the following actions can you take to reregister this computer in DNS? (Choose all that apply.)

    a. Execute the Nbtstat –R command.

    b. Execute the Ipconfig /registerdns command.

    c. Shut down and restart c1.lucernepublishing.com.

    d. Execute the Nbtstat /registerdns command.

2. Which of the following is a legal NetBIOS computer name?

    a. host1.microsoft.com

    b. host1_local

    c. host10_microsoft

    d. host1-microsoft

3. Which command can you use to purge the local NetBIOS name cache?

Lesson Summary

- Two types of computer names usually exist in Windows Server 2003 networks: DNS names and NetBIOS names. Each name type requires its own mechanism for being resolved to IP addresses.

- NetBIOS names and the NetBIOS protocol are required for Windows NT domains, for pre-Windows 2000 workgroups, and for compatibility with certain network services, such as the Computer Browser service.

- DNS names and the DNS protocol are required for Active Directory domains and for compatibility with the Internet or intranets.

- To resolve computer names, the DNS Client service in Windows Server 2003 always attempts DNS name resolution before NetBIOS name resolution.

- Both NetBIOS names and DNS names are based on the name you assign a computer in the System Properties dialog box. If you assign a computer name longer than 15 characters, NetBIOS uses a version of the name that is truncated to 15 characters.

Lesson 2: Understanding DNS in Windows Server 2003 Networks

DNS enables you to locate computers and other resources by name on an IP internetwork. Before DNS, host names in IP networks were organized in a flat namespace and resolved with static Hosts files. By providing a hierarchical structure and an automated method of caching and resolving host names, DNS resolves many of the administrative and structural difficulties associated with naming hosts on the Internet.

After this lesson, you will be able to

- Describe the structure of DNS namespaces
- Describe how the Internet namespace is organized and governed
- Describe components of DNS networks such as DNS servers, DNS clients, resolvers, forwarders, zones, roots, and resource records
- Describe how name queries are handled by DNS clients and servers
- Describe the function of the root hints file

Estimated lesson time: 50 minutes

Exploring DNS

DNS allows people and programs to connect to IP hosts by specifying a name such as ftp.lucernepublishing.com. In doing so, DNS provides a standard both for naming hosts and for locating IP hosts specified by name.

DNS Namespace

The naming system on which DNS is based is a hierarchical and logical tree structure called the *DNS namespace*. The DNS namespace has a unique root that can have any number of subdomains. In turn, each subdomain can have more subdomains. For example, the root "" (empty string) in the Internet namespace has many top-level domain names, one of which is com. The domain com can, for example, have a subdomain for the Lucerne Publishing company, lucernepublishing.com, which in turn can have a further subdomain for manufacturing, called mfg.lucernepublishing.com. Organizations can also create private networks and use their own private DNS namespaces that are not visible on the Internet.

Domain Names

Every node in the DNS domain tree can be identified by an FQDN. The FQDN is a DNS domain name that has been stated unambiguously to indicate its location relative to the root of the DNS domain tree. For example, the FQDN for the manufacturing server in the lucernepublishing.com domain is constructed as mfgserver.lucernepublishing.com., which is the concatenation of the host name (mfgserver) with the primary DNS suffix (lucernepublishing.com), and the trailing dot (.). The trailing dot is a standard separator between the top-level domain label and the empty string label corresponding to the root. (In everyday usage, the trailing dot is usually dropped, but it is added by the DNS Client service during actual queries.)

Internet Domain Namespace

The DNS root (the topmost level) of the Internet domain namespace is managed by the Internet Corporation for Assigned Names and Numbers (ICANN). ICANN coordinates the assignment of identifiers that must be globally unique for the Internet to function, including Internet domain names, IP address numbers, and protocol parameter and port numbers.

Beneath the root DNS domain lie the top-level domains, also managed by ICANN. Three types of top-level domains exist:

- **Organizational domains**   These domains are named using a three-character code that indicates the primary function or activity of the organizations contained within the DNS domain. Some organizational domains can be used globally, although others are used only for organizations within the United States. Most organizations located in the United States are contained within one of these organizational domains.

- **Geographical domains**   These domains are named using the two-character country and region codes established by the International Organization for Standardization (ISO) 3166, such as uk (United Kingdom) or it (Italy). These domains are generally used by organizations outside the United States, but this is not a requirement.

- **Reverse domains**   These are special domains, named in-addr.arpa, that are used for IP-address-to-name mappings (referred to as reverse lookups).

In November 2000, ICANN announced seven additional top-level domains:

- .aero
- .biz
- .coop
- .info
- .museum
- .name
- .pro

> **Important** For the most up-to-date information about these new top-level domains, consult *http://www.icann.org/tlds*.

Beneath the top-level domains, ICANN and other Internet naming authorities, such as Network Solutions or Nominet (in the United Kingdom), delegate domains to various organizations such as Microsoft (microsoft.com) or Carnegie Mellon University (cmu.edu). These organizations connect to the Internet, assign names to hosts within their domains, and use DNS servers to manage the name-to-IP-address mappings within their portion of the namespace. These organizations can also delegate subdomains to other users or customers. ISPs, for example, receive a delegation from ICANN and can delegate subdomains to their customers.

Private Domain Namespace

In addition to the top-level domains on the Internet, organizations can also have a *private namespace*: a DNS namespace based on a private set of root servers independent of the Internet's DNS namespace. Within a private namespace, you can name and create your own root server or servers and any subdomains as needed. Private names cannot be seen or resolved on the Internet. An example of a private domain name is mycompany.local.

DNS Components

DNS relies on the proper configuration of DNS servers, zones, resolvers, and resource records.

DNS Servers

A *DNS server* is a computer that runs a DNS server program, such as the DNS Server service or Berkeley Internet Name Domain (BIND). DNS servers contain DNS database information about some portion of the DNS domain tree structure and resolve name resolution queries issued by DNS clients. When queried, DNS servers can provide the requested information, provide a pointer to another server that can help resolve the query, or respond that the information is unavailable or does not exist.

A DNS server is authoritative for a zone if it hosts the zone, either as a primary or secondary DNS server. A server is authoritative for a domain when that server relies on locally configured resource records, as opposed to cached information, to answer queries about hosts within that domain. Such servers define their portion of the DNS namespace.

Servers can be authoritative for one or more levels of the domain hierarchy. For example, the root DNS servers on the Internet are authoritative only for the top-level domain names such as .com and not for subdomains such as lucernepublishing.com. The servers authoritative for .com are authoritative only for names such as lucernepublishing.com, and not for third-level domains such as example.lucernepublishing.com. However, within the Lucerne Publishing namespace, the server or servers authoritative for example.lucernepublishing.com can also be authoritative for widgets.example.lucernepublishing.com.

DNS Zones

A *DNS zone* is a contiguous portion of a namespace for which a server is authoritative. A server can be authoritative for one or more zones, and a zone can contain one or more contiguous domains. For example, one server can be authoritative for both microsoft.com and lucernepublishing.com zones, and each of these zones can include two or more domains.

Contiguous domains such as .com, lucernepublishing.com, and example.lucernepublishing.com can become separate zones through the process of delegation, by which the responsibility for a subdomain within the DNS namespace is assigned to a separate entity.

Zone files contain resource records for the zones for which a server is authoritative. In many DNS server implementations, zone data is stored in text files; however, DNS servers running on Windows 2000 or Windows Server 2003 domain controllers can also store zone information in Active Directory.

DNS Resolvers

A *DNS resolver* is a service that uses the DNS protocol to query for information from DNS servers. DNS resolvers communicate with either remote DNS servers or the DNS server program running on the local computer. In Windows Server 2003, the function of the DNS resolver is performed by the DNS Client service. Besides acting as a DNS resolver, the DNS Client service provides the added function of caching DNS mappings.

Resource Records

Resource records are DNS database entries that are used to answer DNS client queries. Each DNS server contains the resource records it needs to answer queries for its portion of the DNS namespace. Resource records are each described as a specific record type, such as host address (A), alias (CNAME), and mail exchanger (MX). (See the "Creating Resource Records" section in Lesson 3 for more information on specific record types.)

Understanding How a DNS Query Works

When a DNS client needs to look up a name used by an application, it queries DNS servers to resolve the name. Each query message the client sends contains the following three pieces of information:

- A DNS domain name, stated as an FQDN. (The DNS Client service adds the suffixes necessary to generate an FQDN if they are not provided by the original client program.)

- A specified query type, which can specify either a resource record by type or a specialized type of query operation.

- A specified class for the DNS domain name. (For the DNS Client service, this class is always specified as the Internet [IN] class.)

For example, the name could be specified as the FQDN for a particular host computer, such as host-a.example.microsoft.com., and the query type could be specified as a search for an A resource record by that name. You can think of a DNS query as a client asking a server a two-part question, such as, "Do you have any A resource records for a computer named hostname.example.microsoft.com?" When the client receives an answer from the server, the client reads the received A resource record and learns the IP address of the computer name originally queried for.

DNS Resolution Methods

DNS queries resolve in a number of different ways. In a basic scenario, the DNS client contacts a DNS server, which then uses its own database of resource records to answer a query. However, by referring to its cache first, a DNS client can sometimes answer a query without contacting a server at all. Another way that DNS queries are often resolved is through recursion. (See the section "Understanding Recursion" later in this lesson for more information.) Using this process, a DNS server can query other DNS servers on behalf of the requesting client in order to resolve the FQDN. When the DNS server receives the answer to the query, it then sends an answer back to the client. A final method by which DNS queries are resolved is through iteration (also explained in more detail in the "Understanding Recursion" section). Through this process, the client itself attempts to contact additional DNS servers to resolve a name. When a client does so, it uses separate and additional queries based on referral answers from DNS servers.

DNS Query Steps

In general, the DNS query process occurs in two parts:

- A name query begins at a client computer and is passed to the DNS Client service for resolution.

■ When the query cannot be resolved locally, DNS servers can be queried as needed to resolve the name.

Both of these processes are explained in more detail in the following sections.

Part 1: The Local Resolver   Figure 4-1 presents an overview of the default DNS query process, in which a client is configured to make recursive queries to a server. In this scenario, if the DNS Client service cannot resolve the query from locally cached information, the client makes only a single query to a DNS server, which is then responsible for answering the query on behalf of the client.

In the figure, queries and answers are represented by Qs and As, respectively. The higher numbered queries are made only when the previous query is unsuccessful. For example, Q2 is performed only when Q1 is unsuccessful.

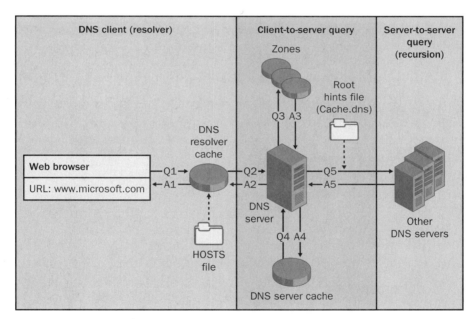

Figure 4-1   The local resolver

The query process begins when a DNS domain name is used in a program on the local computer. In the example shown in Figure 4-1, a Web browser calls the FQDN www.microsoft.com. The request is then passed to the DNS Client service (the DNS resolver cache) to resolve this name by using locally cached information. If the queried name can be resolved, the query is answered and the process is completed.

The local resolver cache can include name information obtained from two possible sources:

- If a Hosts file is configured locally, any host-name-to-address mappings from that file are loaded into the cache when the DNS Client service is started and after the Hosts file is updated.

- Resource records obtained in answered responses from previous DNS queries are added to the cache and kept for a period of time.

If the query does not match an entry in the cache, the resolution process continues with the client querying a DNS server to resolve the name.

Part 2: Querying a DNS Server   The DNS Client service uses a server search list ordered by preference. This list includes all preferred and alternate DNS servers configured for each of the active network connections on the system. The client first queries the DNS server specified as the preferred DNS server in the connection's Internet Protocol (TCP/IP) Properties dialog box. If no preferred DNS servers are available, alternate DNS servers are used. Figure 4-2 shows a sample list of preferred and alternate DNS servers, as configured in Windows Server 2003.

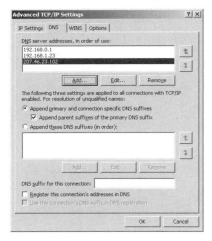

Figure 4-2   Preferred and alternate servers

When a DNS server receives a query, it first checks to see whether it can answer the query authoritatively—that is, on the basis of information contained in a locally configured zone on the server. If the queried name matches a corresponding resource record in local zone information, the server answers authoritatively, using this information to resolve the queried name.

If no zone information exists for the queried name, the server then checks to see whether it can resolve the name by using locally cached information from previous queries. If a match is found here, the server answers with this information. Again, if the preferred server can answer with a positive matched response from its cache to the requesting client, the query is completed.

Understanding Recursion

If the queried name does not find a matched answer at its preferred server—either from its cache or zone information—the query process continues in a manner dependent on the DNS server configuration. In the default configuration, the DNS server performs recursion to resolve the name. In general, *recursion* in DNS refers to the process of a DNS server querying other DNS servers on behalf of an original querying client. This process, in effect, turns the original DNS server into a DNS client.

If recursion is disabled on the DNS server, the client performs iterative queries by using root hint referrals from the DNS server. *Iteration* refers to the process of a DNS client making repeated queries to different DNS servers.

Exam Tip   On the exam, you should understand the term *recursion* to mean simply that a DNS server is contacting other servers when it cannot by itself answer a query. You will not be asked about iteration on the exam.

Root Hints

To perform recursion properly, the DNS server first needs to know where to begin searching for names in the DNS domain namespace. This information is provided in the form of *root hints*, a list of preliminary resource records used by the DNS service to locate servers authoritative for the root of the DNS domain namespace tree.

By default, DNS servers running Windows Server 2003 use a preconfigured root hints file, Cache.dns, that is stored in the WINDOWS\System32\Dns folder on the server computer. The contents of this file are preloaded into server memory when the service is started and contain pointer information to root servers for the DNS namespace. Figure 4-3 shows the default root hints file.

```
cache.dns - Notepad                                                    _ □ ×
File  Edit  Format  View  Help

;   Root Name Server Hints File:

;       These entries enable the DNS server to locate the root name servers
;       (the DNS servers authoritative for the root zone).
;       For historical reasons this is known often referred to as the
;       "Cache File"

@                           NS         d.root-servers.net.
d.root-servers.net          A          128.8.10.90
@                           NS         a.root-servers.net.
a.root-servers.net          A          198.41.0.4
@                           NS         h.root-servers.net.
h.root-servers.net          A          128.63.2.53
@                           NS         c.root-servers.net.
c.root-servers.net          A          192.33.4.12
@                           NS         g.root-servers.net.
g.root-servers.net          A          192.112.36.4
@                           NS         f.root-servers.net.
f.root-servers.net          A          192.5.5.241
@                           NS         b.root-servers.net.
b.root-servers.net          A          128.9.0.107
@                           NS         j.root-servers.net.
j.root-servers.net          A          192.58.128.30
@                           NS         k.root-servers.net.
k.root-servers.net          A          193.0.14.129
@                           NS         l.root-servers.net.
l.root-servers.net          A          198.32.64.12
@                           NS         m.root-servers.net.
m.root-servers.net          A          202.12.27.33
@                           NS         i.root-servers.net.
i.root-servers.net          A          192.36.148.17
@                           NS         e.root-servers.net.
e.root-servers.net          A          192.203.230.10
```

Figure 4-3 Root hints file

In Windows Server 2003, the root hints file already contains addresses of root servers
in the Internet DNS namespace. Therefore, if you are using the DNS Server service in
Windows Server 2003 to resolve Internet-based DNS names, the root hints file needs no
manual configuration. If, however, you are using the DNS service on a private network,
you can edit or replace this file with similar records that point to your own internal root
DNS servers. Furthermore, for a computer that is hosting a root DNS server, you should
not use root hints at all. In this scenario, Windows Server 2003 automatically deletes
the Cache.dns file used for root hints.

Query Example

The following example illustrates default DNS query behavior. In the example, the client queries its preferred DNS server, which then performs recursion by querying hierarchically superior DNS servers. In the example, the DNS client and all DNS servers are
assumed to have empty caches.

In the example shown in Figure 4-4, a client somewhere on the Internet needs to
resolve the name example.lucernepublishing.com to an IP address.

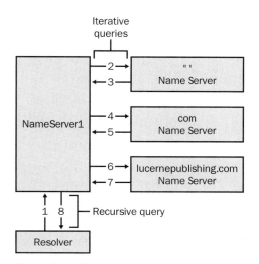

Figure 4-4   Illustration of recursion

When the DNS Client service on the client computer begins the query process, the following events take place:

1. The client contacts NameServer1 with a query for example.lucernepublishing.com.

2. NameServer1 checks its cache and zones for the answer but does not find it, so it contacts a server authoritative for the Internet (that is, a root server) with a query for example.lucernepublishing.com.

3. The server at the root of the Internet does not know the answer, so it responds with a referral to a server authoritative for the .com domain.

4. NameServer1 contacts a server authoritative for the .com domain with a query for example.lucernepublishing.com.

5. The server authoritative for the .com domain does not know the exact answer, so it responds with a referral to a server authoritative for the lucernepublishing.com domain.

6. NameServer1 contacts the server authoritative for the lucernepublishing.com domain with a query for example.lucernepublishing.com.

7. The server authoritative for the lucernepublishing.com domain does know the answer. It responds with the requested IP address.

8. NameServer1 responds to the client query with the IP address for example.lucernepublishing.com.

Query Response Types

Queries can return a variety of answers to the client, including these, which are the most common:

- An authoritative answer
- A positive answer
- A referral answer
- A negative answer

An *authoritative answer* is a positive answer returned to the client and delivered with the authority bit set in the DNS message. This authority bit indicates that the answer was obtained from a server with direct authority for the queried name.

A *positive answer* contains the queried resource record matching the queried name and record type specified in the original query message.

A *referral answer* contains additional resource records not specified by name or type in the query. This type of answer is returned to the client if the recursion process is not supported by the DNS server. These records are meant to act as helpful reference answers that the client can use to continue the query by using iteration. For example, if the queried host name is "www" and no A resource record but only a CNAME resource record for this name is found in the zone, the DNS server can include this CNAME information when responding to the client. If the client is able to perform iteration, it can make additional queries using this referral information in an attempt to fully resolve the name for itself.

A *negative answer* from the server can indicate that one of two possible results was encountered while the server attempted to process and recursively resolve the query fully and authoritatively:

- An authoritative server reported that the queried name does not exist in the DNS namespace.
- An authoritative server reported that the queried name exists but no records of the specified type exist for that name.

After the response is made to the query, the resolver passes the results of the query, in the form of either a positive or negative response, back to the requesting program and caches the response.

Understanding How Caching Works

Both the DNS Client service and the DNS Server service maintain caches. Caching provides a way to improve DNS performance and to substantially reduce DNS-related query traffic on the network.

DNS Client Cache

The DNS client cache is also called the DNS resolver cache. Whenever the DNS Client service starts, all host-name-to-IP-address mappings contained in a static file named Hosts are preloaded into the DNS resolver cache. The Hosts file can be found in WINDOWS \System32\Drivers\Etc.

> **Tip**   Whenever you add an entry to the Hosts file, that entry is immediately loaded into the DNS resolver cache.

In addition to the entries in the Hosts file, the DNS resolver cache also includes entries the client has received in response to a query from DNS servers. The DNS resolver cache is emptied whenever the DNS Client service is stopped.

DNS Server Cache

As DNS servers make recursive queries on behalf of clients, they temporarily cache resource records. These cached records contain information acquired in the process of answering queries on behalf of a client. Later, when other clients place new queries that request information matching cached resource records, the DNS server can use the cached information to answer these queries.

The DNS server cache is cleared whenever the DNS Server service is stopped. In addition, you can clear the DNS server cache manually in the DNS console—the administrative tool used for DNS administration—by right-clicking the server icon in the console tree and then clicking Clear Cache. Finally, if you have installed Windows Support Tools, you can clear the server cache at the command line by entering the command **Dnscmd /clearcache** at a command prompt.

Time to Live Values   A Time to Live (TTL) value applies to all cached resource records, whether in the DNS resolver cache or the DNS server cache. As long as the TTL for a cached resource record does not expire, a DNS resolver or server can continue to use that record to answer queries. By default, the TTL is 3600 seconds (1 hour), but this parameter can be adjusted at both the zone and record level.

> **Note**   DNS uses multiple levels of caching to improve efficiency and performance. The downside is that, when queries are resolved by means of cached information, clients will not see the effects of a change in DNS immediately. On the public Internet, it can take as long as four hours for users to have access to the new information—regardless of how the TTL is configured.

Lesson Review

The following questions are intended to reinforce key information presented in this lesson. If you are unable to answer a question, review the lesson materials and try the question again. You can find answers to the questions in the "Questions and Answers" section at the end of this chapter.

1. On the network you administer, you maintain a primary DNS server authoritative for the zone lucernepublishing.com. You have also deployed two caching-only servers that forward all requests to the primary server. If most of the name queries directed toward the caching-only servers are for names within the lucernepublishing.com domain, which parameter can you modify on the primary server to decrease DNS query traffic between the caching-only servers and the primary server?

   _____

2. What is the root domain of a namespace containing the FQDN first.domain1.local.?

   a. None; the namespace has no root domain.

   b. domain1.

   c. local.

   d. "" (empty string).

3. Which step does the resolver first perform to resolve a DNS name?

   a. It checks its local cache.

   b. It reads from the Hosts file.

   c. It broadcasts the local subnet.

   d. It queries the local DNS server.

4. Your network computers are turned on for the first time after a power outage. When a DNS client first submits a recursive query to a local DNS server to resolve an Internet name for which the server is not authoritative, which step takes place first?

   a. The DNS client resolves the name from its cache.

   b. The DNS server resolves the name from its cache.

   c. The DNS server forwards the recursive query to an upstream DNS server.

   d. The DNS server contacts root servers configured in the Cache.dns file.

Lesson Summary

- The DNS namespace is hierarchical and is based on a unique root that can have any number of subdomains. An FQDN is a name of a DNS host in this namespace that indicates the host's location relative to the root of the DNS domain tree. An example of an FQDN is host1.subdomain.microsoft.com.

- A DNS zone is a contiguous portion of a namespace for which a server is authoritative. A server can be authoritative for one or more zones, and a zone can contain one or more contiguous domains. A DNS server is authoritative for a zone if it hosts the zone, either as a primary or secondary DNS server. Each DNS zone contains the resource records it needs to answer queries for its portion of the DNS namespace.

- The DNS Client service (or resolver) first attempts to resolve computer names using locally cached information, which includes the contents of the Hosts file. If the name cannot be found in the cache, the resolver queries a DNS server. If the DNS server cannot resolve the name through its authoritative records or through its local cache, the DNS server by default performs recursion to resolve the name on behalf of the client.

- Recursion is the process of a DNS server querying other servers on behalf of a DNS client. For the DNS server to perform recursion properly, the server needs to know where to begin searching for names in the DNS domain namespace. This information is provided by the root hints file, Cache.dns, that is stored on the server computer.

- A TTL value applies to all cached resource records. As long as the TTL for a cached resource record does not expire, a DNS server can continue to use that record to answer queries.

Lesson 3: Deploying DNS Servers

Within private networks, DNS servers enable clients to resolve computer names defined within the private namespace. However, when DNS servers are properly configured and connected to the Internet, they can also allow clients to resolve Internet-based names without querying external name servers directly.

After this lesson, you will be able to

- Install and configure a DNS server
- Create DNS zones and resource records
- Describe the difference between primary, secondary, caching-only, and stub servers
- Create a caching-only server
- Describe several of the most common types of resource records
- View and clear the DNS server cache

Estimated lesson time: 60 minutes

Installing the DNS Server Service

By default, all computers running Windows Server 2003 and Windows XP have the DNS Client service installed and running. However, the DNS Server service is not installed by default in any Windows operating system. To install the DNS Server service on a computer running Windows Server 2003, you first need to add the DNS server role through the Manage Your Server page.

Once you have added this role, the DNS console appears in the Administrative Tools program group. The DNS console is the main tool for configuring and monitoring DNS servers, zones, domains, and resource records.

> **Note**   As an alternative to adding the DNS server role, you can install the DNS Server service through Add Or Remove Programs in Control Panel. Select Add/Remove Windows Components, and use the Windows Components Wizard to install the Domain Name System (DNS) subcomponent within the Networking Services Windows component.

To install a DNS server, complete the following steps:

1. Insert the Windows Server 2003 installation CD-ROM into the computer on which you want to install a DNS server.

2. Verify that you have assigned the computer a static address.

3. Click Start and then click Manage Your Server to open the Manage Your Server page.

4. Click Add Or Remove A Role.

5. On the Preliminary Steps page of the Configure Your Server Wizard, follow the instructions, and then click Next.

6. On the Configuration Options page, select the Custom Configuration option, and click Next.

7. On the Server Role page, select DNS Server in the Server Role list, and then click Next.

8. In the Summary Of Selections page, click Next.

   When the DNS server component has finished installing, the Configure A DNS Server Wizard appears.

9. To configure the DNS server you have just installed, follow the prompts and accept all default settings to complete the Configure A DNS Server Wizard.

Configuring a DNS Server

To simplify the customization of DNS server settings and the creation of new zones, you can run the Configure A DNS Server Wizard. This wizard is invoked automatically when you add the DNS server role. After the wizard is run, you can refine your DNS server configuration later through the DNS console. (You can access this console through Administrative Tools on the Start menu.) You can also configure your DNS server completely through the server properties dialog box in the DNS console without ever running the Configure A DNS Server Wizard.

To run or rerun the Configure A DNS Server Wizard after the DNS Server service is installed, right-click the server you want to configure in the DNS console tree, and then select Configure A DNS Server. This process is shown in Figure 4-5.

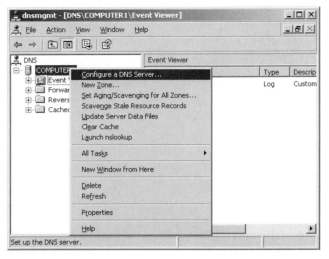

Figure 4-5 Launching the Configure A DNS Server Wizard

Creating Zones

Zones are created in one of two categories: forward lookup and reverse lookup. In forward lookup zones, DNS servers map FQDNs to IP addresses. In reverse lookup zones, DNS servers map IP addresses to FQDNs. Forward lookup zones thus answer queries to resolve FQDNs to IP addresses, and reverse lookup zones answer queries to resolve IP addresses to FQDNs.

> **Note** You can create a root server in a DNS namespace by naming a zone with a single dot, "." When you perform this task, you cannot configure the server to forward queries to another name server.

To create forward and reverse lookup zones, you can use the Configure A DNS Server Wizard. You can also create new zones at any time by using the DNS console. To do so, right-click either the Forward Lookup Zones folder or the Reverse Lookup Zones folder, and then select New Zone, as shown in Figure 4-6. This process launches the New Zone Wizard.

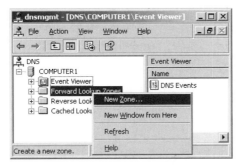

Figure 4-6   Creating a new zone

Zone Types

The New Zone Wizard allows you to configure the server's role in each of its zones. These roles include the following:

- **Primary**   In this kind of zone, the zone data provides the original source data for all domains in the zone. Zone data can be backed up from this zone to a secondary zone.

- **Secondary**   This kind of zone is an authoritative backup zone for the primary zone or for other secondary zones.

- **Stub**   This server hosts a stub zone, which is a copy of a zone containing only those resource records necessary to identify the authoritative DNS servers for the master zone.

Understanding Server Types

The DNS *server type* refers to the type of zone the server is hosting—or, in the case of caching-only servers, whether it is hosting a zone at all. The following sections describe some of the essential features of the various server types.

Primary Servers

A primary server is created when a primary zone is added, either through the New Zone Wizard, the Configure A DNS Server Wizard, or command-line tools.

The primary server for a zone acts as the zone's central point of update. Newly created zones are always this type. With Windows Server 2003, you can deploy primary zones in one of two ways: as standard primary zones or primary zones integrated with Active Directory.

Standard Primary Zones   For standard primary zones, only a single server can host and load the master copy of the zone. If you create a zone and keep it as a standard primary zone, no additional primary servers for the zone are permitted.

The standard primary model implies a single point of failure. For example, if the primary server for a zone is unavailable to the network, no changes to the zone can be made. Note that queries for names in the zone are not affected and can continue uninterrupted, as long as secondary servers for the zone are available to answer them.

Active Directory–Integrated Zones   When you deploy an Active Directory–integrated zone, zone data is stored and replicated in Active Directory. Using an Active Directory–integrated zone increases fault tolerance and (by default) turns every domain controller in the domain running a DNS server into a primary server. To configure a primary zone as an Active Directory–integrated zone, the original DNS server on which the zone is created must be an Active Directory domain controller. The process of deploying Active Directory–integrated zones is discussed in Chapter 5, "Implementing a DNS Infrastructure."

Secondary Servers

DNS design specifications recommend that at least two DNS servers be used to host each zone. For standard primary zones, a secondary server is required to allow the zone to appear to other DNS servers in the network.

Secondary servers provide a means to offload DNS query traffic in areas of the network where a zone is heavily queried and used. Additionally, if a primary server is down, a secondary server provides name resolution in the zone until the primary server is available.

The servers from which secondary servers acquire zone information are called *masters*. A master can be the primary server or another secondary server. You specify the secondary server's master servers when the server's secondary zone is created, through either the New Zone Wizard, the Configure A DNS Server Wizard, or command-line tools.

> **Tip**   Secondary servers are best placed as close as possible to clients that have a high demand for names used in the zone. Also, you should consider placing secondary servers across a router, either on other subnets or across wide area network (WAN) links. This setup provides efficient use of a secondary server as a backup in cases where an intermediate network link becomes the point of failure between DNS servers and clients that use the zone.

Stub Servers

Stub DNS servers host *stub zones*: abbreviated copies of a zone that contain only a list of the authoritative name servers for its master zone. A DNS server hosting a stub zone attempts to resolve queries for computer names in the master zone by querying these name servers listed. Stub zones are most frequently used to enable a parent zone to keep an updated list of the name servers available in a child zone.

Caching-Only Servers

Caching-only servers do not host any zones and are not authoritative for any particular domain. The information they contain is limited to what has been cached while resolving queries.

In determining when to use this kind of server, note that when it is initially started, it has no cached information. The information is obtained over time as client requests are serviced. However, if you are dealing with a slow WAN link between sites, this option might be ideal because once the cache is built, traffic across the WAN link decreases. DNS queries are also resolved faster, improving the performance of network applications. In addition, the caching-only server does not perform zone transfers, which can also be network-intensive in WAN environments. Finally, a caching-only DNS server can be valuable at a site where DNS functionality is needed locally, but administering domains or zones is not desirable for that location.

> **Exam Tip**   When you need to minimize name resolution traffic across WAN links without increasing zone transfer traffic, install a caching-only server.

By default, the DNS Server service acts as a caching-only server. Caching-only servers thus require little or no configuration.

To install a caching-only DNS server, complete the following steps:

1. Install the DNS server role on the server computer.
2. Do not configure the DNS server (as you might normally) to load any zones.
3. Verify that server root hints are configured or updated correctly.

Creating Resource Records

New zones contain only two resource records: the start-of-authority (SOA) record corresponding to the zone and a name server (NS) record corresponding to the local DNS server created for the zone. After you create a zone, you must add additional resource records to it. Although some records might be added automatically, others (such as MX and CNAME records) need to be added manually.

To add a resource record for a zone manually, right-click the zone icon in the DNS console and from the shortcut menu, select the appropriate resource record you want to create, as shown in Figure 4-7.

Figure 4-7   Creating resource records

To add a resource record to a zone, complete the following steps:

1. Open the DNS console.

2. In the console tree, right-click the applicable zone and select Other New Records.

   The Resource Record Type dialog box appears.

3. In the Select A Resource Record Type list box, select the type of resource record you want to add.

4. Click Create Record.

5. In the New Resource Record dialog box, enter the information needed to complete the resource record.

6. After you specify all of the necessary information for the resource record, click OK to add the new record to the zone.

7. Click Done to return to the DNS console.

Resource Record Format

Resource records appear in varying formats, depending on the context in which they are used. For example, when lookups and responses are made using DNS, resource records are represented in binary form in packets. In the DNS console, resource records are represented graphically so that they can be viewed and modified easily. However, at the source—in the zone database files—resource records are represented as text entries. In fact, by creating resource records in the DNS console, you are automatically adding text entries to the corresponding zone's database file.

In these zone files, resource records have the following syntax:

```
Owner TTL Class Type RDATA
```

Table 4-3 describes each of these fields.

Table 4-3   Typical Resource Record Fields

Name	Description
Owner	The name of the host or the DNS domain to which this resource record belongs.
Time To Live	A 32-bit integer that represents, in seconds, the length of time that a DNS server or client should cache this entry before it is discarded. This field is optional, and if it is not specified, the client uses the minimum TTL in the SOA record.
Class	The field that defines the protocol family in use. For Windows DNS servers, the resource record is always of the class Internet, abbreviated IN. This field is optional and is not automatically generated.
Type	The field that identifies the type of resource record, such as A or SRV.
RDATA	The resource record data. It is a variable-length field that represents the information being described by the resource record type. For example, in an A resource record, this is the 32-bit IP address that represents the host identified by the owner.

Most resource records are represented as single-line text entries. If an entry is going to span more than one line, parentheses can encapsulate the information. In many implementations of DNS, only the SOA resource record can contain multiple lines. For readability, blank lines and comments ignored by the DNS server are often inserted in the zone files. Comments always start with a semicolon (;) and end with a carriage return.

Record Types

The most common resource records you need to create manually include the following:

- Host (A)
- Alias (CNAME)
- Mail exchanger (MX)
- Pointer (PTR)
- Service location (SRV)

Host (A) Resource Records   Host (A) resource records make up the majority of resource records in a zone database. These records are used in a zone to associate DNS domain names of computers (or hosts) to their IP addresses. They can be added to a zone in different ways:

- You can manually create an A resource record for a static TCP/IP client computer by using the DNS console or the Dnscmd support tool at the command line.

- Computers running Windows 2000, Windows XP, or Windows Server 2003 use the DHCP Client service to dynamically register and update their own A resource records in DNS when an IP configuration change occurs.

- Dynamic Host Configuration Protocol (DHCP)–enabled client computers running earlier versions of Microsoft operating systems can have their A resource records registered and updated by proxy if they obtain their IP lease from a qualified DHCP server. (Only the DHCP service provided with Windows Server 2003 currently supports this feature.)

Once created in the DNS console, an A resource record that maps the host name server1.lucernepublishing.com to the IP address 172.16.48.1 is represented textually within the lucernepublishing.com.dns zone file as follows:

```
server1          A       172.16.48.1
```

> **Exam Tip**   If you can ping a computer by IP address but not by name, the computer is missing an A resource record in DNS. You can attempt to remedy this situation by executing the Ipconfig /registerdns command at that computer—but only if the client computer is running a version of Windows 2000, Windows XP, or Windows Server 2003.

Alias (CNAME) Resource Records   Alias (CNAME) resource records are also sometimes called *canonical names*. These records allow you to use more than one name to point to a single host. For example, the well-known server names (ftp, www) are typically registered using CNAME resource records. These records map the host name specific to a given service (such as ftp.lucernepublishing.com) to the actual A resource record of the computer hosting the service (such as server-boston.lucernepublishing.com).

CNAME resource records are also recommended for use in the following scenarios:

- When a host specified in an A resource record in the same zone needs to be renamed

- When a generic name for a well-known server such as www needs to resolve to a group of individual computers (each with individual A resource records) that provide the same service (for example, a group of redundant Web servers)

Once created in the DNS console, a CNAME resource record that maps the alias ftp.lucernepublishing.com to the host name ftp1.lucernepublishing.com would be represented textually within the lucernepublishing.com.dns zone file as follows:

```
ftp              CNAME     ftp1.lucernepublishing.com.
```

MX Resource Records   The mail exchanger (MX) resource record is used by e-mail applications to locate a mail server within a zone. It allows a domain name such as lucernepublishing.com, specified in an e-mail address such as joe@lucernepublishing.com, to be mapped to the A resource record of a computer hosting the mail server for the domain. This type of record thus allows a DNS server to handle e-mail addresses in which no particular mail server is specified.

Often, multiple MX records are created to provide fault tolerance and failover to another mail server when the preferred server listed is not available. Multiple servers are given a server preference value, with the lower values representing higher preference. Once created in the DNS console, such MX resource records would be represented textually within the lucernepublishing.com.dns zone file as follows:

```
@        MX     1      mailserver1.lucernepublishing.com.
@        MX     10      mailserver2.lucernepublishing.com.
@        MX     20      mailserver3.lucernepublishing.com.
```

Note   In this example, the @ symbol represents the local domain name contained in an e-mail address.

PTR Resource Records   The pointer (PTR) resource record is used only in reverse lookup zones to support reverse lookups, which perform queries to resolve IP addresses to host names or FQDNs. Reverse lookups are performed in zones rooted in the in-addr.arpa domain. PTR resource records are added to zones by the same manual and automatic methods used to add A resource records.

Once created in the DNS console, a PTR resource record that maps the IP address 172.16.48.1 to the host name server1.lucernepublishing.com would be represented textually within a zone file as follows:

```
1              PTR      server1.lucernepublishing.com.
```

Note   In this example, the 1 represents the name assigned to the host within the 172.16.48.in-addr.arpa domain. This domain, which is also the name of the hosting zone, corresponds to the 172.16.48.0 subnet.

SRV Resource Records   Service location (SRV) resource records are used to specify the location of specific services in a domain. Client applications that are SRV-aware can use DNS to retrieve the SRV resource records for given application servers.

Windows Server 2003 Active Directory is an example of an SRV-aware application. The Netlogon service uses SRV records to locate domain controllers in a domain by searching the domain for the Lightweight Directory Access Protocol (LDAP) service.

> **Tip**   All of the SRV records required for an Active Directory domain controller can be found in a file named Netlogon.dns, located in the WINDOWS\System32\Config folder. If SRV records are missing in your DNS zone, you can reload them automatically by running the Netdiag /fix command at a command prompt. (The Netdiag command is available after you install Windows Support Tools from the Windows Server 2003 CD-ROM.)

If a computer needs to locate a domain controller in the lucernepublishing.com domain, the DNS client sends an SRV query for the name:

```
_ldap._tcp.lucernepublishing.com.
```

The DNS server then responds to the client with all records matching the query.

Although most SRV resource records are created automatically, you might need to create them through the DNS console to add fault tolerance or troubleshoot network services. The following example shows the textual representation of two SRV records that have been configured manually in the DNS console:

```
_ldap._tcp   SRV     0  0 389     dc1.lucernepublishing.com.
             SRV    10  0 389     dc2.lucernepublishing.com.
```

In the example, an LDAP server (domain controller) with a priority of 0 (highest) is mapped to port 389 at the host dc1.lucernepublishing.com. A second domain controller with a lower priority of 10 is mapped to port 389 at the host dc2.lucernepublishing.com. Both entries have a 0 value in the weight field, which means no load balancing has been configured among servers with equal priority.

> **Exam Tip**   On the exam as well as real life, you can deploy Active Directory with the "least amount of administrative effort" by installing your network's first DNS domains, along with its first Active Directory domains, on computers running Windows 2000 Server or Windows Server 2003. This news is hardly surprising because only in Windows environments are the many SRV records required for Active Directory created automatically. If you want to deploy DNS on a UNIX server and integrate the UNIX server into an Active Directory infrastructure, configure the UNIX server as a secondary DNS server.

Viewing and Clearing the DNS Server Cache

The contents of the DNS server cache can be viewed only in the DNS console. To view the cache contents, from the View menu select Advanced, as shown in Figure 4-8.

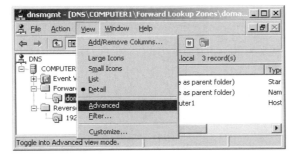

Figure 4-8   DNS console Advanced view

Once the DNS console View mode is set to Advanced, a new folder appears in the DNS console tree, Cached Lookups. This folder displays the DNS server cache in a hierarchical format. Figure 4-9 shows sample contents of the Cached Lookups folder.

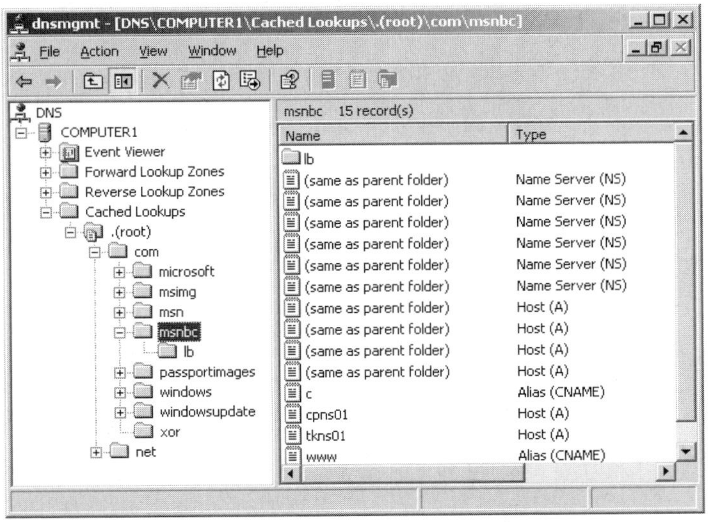

Figure 4-9   DNS server cache

To clear the DNS server cache, you can right-click the DNS Server icon in the DNS console and select Clear Cache, as shown in Figure 4-10. Alternatively, you can restart the DNS Server service or use the Dnscmd /clearcache command.

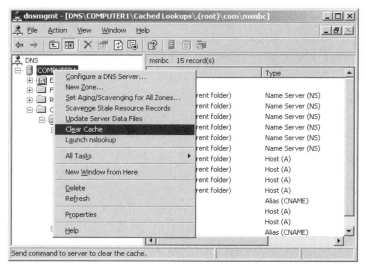

Figure 4-10   Clearing the DNS server cache

Practice: Installing a DNS Server

In this practice, you install and configure a DNS server on Computer1.

Exercise 1: Installing the DNS Windows Component

To complete this exercise, you must have the Windows Server 2003 installation CD-ROM loaded in Computer1.

1. Log on to Computer1 as Administrator.

2. Open Control Panel, and then click Add Or Remove Programs.

   The Add Or Remove Programs window opens.

3. Click Add/Remove Windows Components.

   The Windows Components page of the Windows Components Wizard opens.

4. In the Components area, highlight the Networking Services component. Be sure not to select the Networking Services check box.

5. Click Details.

   The Networking Services window opens.

6. In the Subcomponents Of Networking Services area, select the Domain Name System (DNS) check box.

7. Click OK.

   In the Windows Components Wizard, the Networking Services check box should now be gray.

8. Click Next.

   The Configuring Components page appears while the new component is being installed. After installation is complete, the Completing The Windows Components Wizard page appears.

9. Click Finish.

10. Click Close to close the Add Or Remove Programs window.

Exercise 2: Creating a Dial-Up Connection

In this exercise, you create a dial-up connection to the Internet. If Computer1 already has an Internet connection available through a dedicated line, you can skip this exercise, but be sure to rename the Internet connection "MyISP."

1. While you are logged on to Computer1 as Administrator, open the Network Connections window.

2. From the File menu, select New Connection.

   The New Connection Wizard opens.

3. Click Next.

4. Click Next on the Network Connection Type page to accept the default selection, Connect To The Internet.

5. Click Next on the Internet Connection page to accept the default selection, Connect Using A Dial-Up Modem.

6. On the Connection Name page, type **MyISP** in the ISP Name text box, and then click Next.

7. On the Phone Number To Dial page, type the telephone number of your ISP in the Phone Number text box, and then click Next.

8. Click Next on the Connection Availability page to accept the default selection, Anyone's Use.

9. On the Internet Account Information page, type your ISP account information in the User Name, Password, and Confirm Password text boxes.

10. Click Next.

    The Completing The New Connection Wizard page appears.

11. Click Finish.

    The Connect MyISP page appears.

12. Click the Properties button.

    The MyISP Properties dialog box appears.

13. Click the Options tab.

14. Clear the Prompt For Name And Password, Certificate, Etc. check box.

15. Clear the Prompt For Phone Number check box.

16. Click OK.

    The Connecting MyISP message box appears while your computer dials in to your ISP through your newly configured connection. When you have connected, you will receive a confirmation message in the system tray portion of your taskbar.

    You are now connected to the Internet.

Exercise 3: Configuring the New DNS Server

In this exercise, you use the Configure A DNS Server Wizard to create a simple DNS server installation. After the wizard is complete, your DNS server will be configured to answer forward and reverse lookup queries for the domain1.local domain and to handle recursive queries from internal clients. To complete successfully, the Configure A DNS Server Wizard requires an Internet connection.

1. While you are logged on to Computer1 as Administrator, verify that you are connected to the Internet through the MyISP connection.

2. Open the DNS console by clicking Start, selecting Administrative Tools, and then selecting DNS.

    The DNS console opens.

3. Expand the COMPUTER1 icon in the console tree.

4. Right-click COMPUTER1 in the console tree and select Configure A DNS Server from the shortcut menu.

    The Configure A DNS Server Wizard launches.

5. Click Next.

    The Select Configuration Action page appears.

6. Select the Create A Forward And Reverse Lookup Zones option, and then click Next.

    The Forward Lookup Zone page appears.

7. Click Next to accept the default selection, Yes.

    The Zone Type page appears.

8. Click Next to accept the default selection, Primary Zone.

   The Zone Name page appears.

9. In the Zone Name text box, type **domain1.local**, and then click Next.

   The Zone File page appears.

10. Click Next to accept the default selection, Create A New File With This File Name.

    The Dynamic Update page appears.

11. Click Next to accept the default selection, Do Not Allow Dynamic Updates.

    The Reverse Lookup Zone page appears.

12. Click Next to accept the default selection, Yes.

    The Zone Type page appears.

13. Click Next to accept the default selection, Primary Zone.

    The Reverse Lookup Zone page appears.

14. In the Network ID text box, type **192.168.0**.

    The reverse lookup zone name is automatically configured in the Reverse Lookup Zone Name text box.

15. Click Next.

    The Zone File page appears.

16. Click Next to accept the default selection, Create A New File With This File Name.

    The Dynamic Update page appears.

17. Click Next to accept the default selection, Do Not Allow Dynamic Updates.

    The Forwarders page appears.

18. Click Next to accept the default selection, No.

    The Completing The Configure A DNS Server Wizard page appears.

19. Click Finish.

20. In the DNS console, expand the console tree in the left pane so you can see the new zone domain1.local listed in the Forward Lookup Zones folder. You can also see the new zone 192.168.0.x Subnet listed in the Reverse Lookup Zones folder.

Exercise 4: Testing the DNS Server

Windows Server 2003 allows you to verify your DNS server configuration with two tests on the DNS server computer. These two tests are included on the Monitoring tab of the server properties dialog box, available through the DNS console.

1. While you are logged on to Computer1 as Administrator, make sure you are connected to the Internet through the MyISP connection.

2. In the console tree within the DNS console, right-click COMPUTER1 and select Properties.

   The COMPUTER1 Properties dialog box opens.

3. Click the Monitoring tab.

4. Select the A Simple Query Against This DNS Server check box and the A Recursive Query To Other DNS Servers check box.

5. Click Test Now.

   The Test Results area shows the successful results of the tests you have just performed.

6. Click OK to close the Computer1 Properties dialog box.

7. Log off Computer1.

> **Exam Tip** You need to understand the DNS server tests for the exam. First, know that the simple test is based on a reverse lookup of the loopback address 127.0.0.1. Therefore, if the simple test fails, you should verify that a record named 1 is found in the reverse lookup zone named 0.0.127.in-addr.arpa (visible only in the DNS console Advanced view). Next, the recursive test verifies that the DNS server can communicate with other DNS servers and that the root hints are correctly configured.

Lesson Review

The following questions are intended to reinforce key information presented in this lesson. If you are unable to answer a question, review the lesson materials and try the question again. You can find answers to the questions in the "Questions and Answers" section at the end of this chapter.

1. You have just updated a host resource record. What other associated resource record might now need to be updated?

   _____

2. Your DNS server has failed the recursive test. Assuming that the server can otherwise communicate with other DNS servers, name two potential causes of this scenario.

   _____

   _____

3. Which resource record is used to resolve domain names specified in e-mail addresses to the IP address of the mail server associated with the domain?

   a. PTR

   b. MX

   c. A

   d. CNAME

4. On a new DNS server, you create a zone "" and then create subdomains from that root domain. Which function will the new server be able or unable to perform?

   a. The server will be unable to cache names.

   b. The server will be able to function only as a forwarding server.

   c. The server will be unable to resolve Internet names.

   d. The server will be unable to connect to the Internet.

Lesson Summary

- DNS servers are authoritative for the zones they host. Forward lookup zones answer queries for IP addresses, and reverse lookup zones answer queries for FQDNs.

- A DNS server that hosts a primary zone is said to act as a primary DNS server. Primary DNS servers store original source data for zones. With Windows Server 2003, you can implement primary zones in one of two ways: as standard primary zones, in which zone data is stored in a text file, or as an Active Directory–integrated zone, in which zone data is stored in the Active Directory database.

- A DNS server that hosts a secondary zone is said to act as a secondary DNS server. Secondary DNS servers are authoritative backup servers for the primary server. The servers from which secondary servers acquire zone information are called masters. A master can be the primary server or another secondary server.

- A caching-only server forwards all requests to other DNS servers and hosts no zones. However, caching-only servers cache responses received from other DNS servers and can therefore improve name resolution for a network that does not host a zone.

- New zones contain only two resource records: the SOA record corresponding to the zone, and an NS record corresponding to the local DNS server created for the zone. After you create a zone, additional resource records need to be added to it. The most common resource records to be added are host (A), alias (CNAME), MX, SRV, and PTR.

Lesson 4: Configuring DNS Clients

Configuring DNS clients generally entails configuring client computer names, specifying DNS suffixes for these computer names, determining DNS servers for the DNS clients to query, and customizing query behavior for these DNS clients. In addition, you can configure how DNS clients update their records in DNS.

After this lesson, you will be able to

- Configure computer names that conform to DNS standards
- Configure a primary DNS suffix for a computer
- Configure a connection-specific suffix for an adapter
- Configure a DNS server list for network connections
- Configure a DNS suffix search list for network connections
- Configure a DNS client to request dynamic DNS updates
- View and clear the DNS client cache

Estimated lesson time: 60 minutes

Configuring Client Settings

To configure DNS client computers in Windows Server 2003 networks, you need to perform the following tasks at a minimum:

- Set a DNS computer or host name for each computer. For example, in the FQDN client1.example.microsoft.com., the DNS computer name is the leftmost label, client1.

- Set a primary DNS suffix for the computer. This suffix, when added to the host name, forms the full computer name. In the previous example, the primary DNS suffix is example.microsoft.com.

- Set a list of DNS servers for the client to use when resolving DNS names. This list includes a preferred DNS server and can also include alternate DNS servers to use if the preferred server is unavailable.

In addition, given the needs of the DNS clients you want to configure, you might also need to perform any or all of the following tasks.

- Set the DNS suffix search list or search method to be used by the client when it performs DNS query searches for short, unqualified domain names.

- Set a connection-specific DNS suffix for each particular adapter on a DNS client computer. For example, if the host named host1.lucernepublishing.com is connected to two subnets through different network adapters, the computer can be seen on one subnet as host1.subnet1.microsoft.com and on another as host1.subnet2.microsoft.com.

- Modify dynamic DNS update behavior.

The following sections describe these tasks in more detail.

Setting Computer Names

When setting names for DNS, think of the computer or host name as the leftmost portion of an FQDN. For example, in wkstn1.example.microsoft.com., *wkstn1* is the computer name. You can modify this computer name by using the Computer Name tab of the System Properties dialog box.

> **Note**   You can access the System Properties dialog box by right-clicking My Computer and selecting Properties, or by double-clicking System in Control Panel.

The computer name you assign must conform to the restrictions of DNS-supported characters defined in Request for Comments (RFC) 1123. According to these restrictions, the name you assign must not exceed 63 bytes, and it can only include the following characters:

- Uppercase letters, A through Z
- Lowercase letters, a through z
- Numbers, 0 through 9
- Hyphens (-)

> **Note**   In practice, DNS names are not case-sensitive.

Accommodating NetBIOS Names

If you are supporting both NetBIOS and DNS namespaces on your network, you can assign to computers a separate computer name for each namespace, but this practice is not advisable. Names you assign to computers running Windows 2000, Windows XP, and Windows Server 2003 must conform to the DNS specifications described previously, but you should also try to accommodate NetBIOS in this host name selection. To accommodate NetBIOS, assign names that are only 15 or fewer characters long.

Setting the Primary DNS Suffix

You can specify or modify a computer's primary DNS suffix in the DNS Suffix And Net-BIOS Computer Name dialog box, as shown in Figure 4-11.

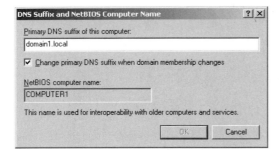

Figure 4-11   Specifying a primary DNS suffix

To access this dialog box, in the System Properties dialog box, click the Computer Name tab, and then click Change to change the computer name. In the Computer Name Changes dialog box, click More.

By default, the primary DNS suffix is the same as the name of the Active Directory domain to which the computer belongs. If the computer does not belong to a domain, no primary DNS suffix is specified by default.

Setting Connection-Specific DNS Suffixes

By clicking the Advanced button in a connection's Internet Protocol (IP) Properties dialog box, you can open the connection's Advanced TCP/IP Settings dialog box. On the DNS tab of this dialog box, as shown in Figure 4-12, you can create a DNS suffix to be used specifically by this connection. This suffix is known as a *connection-specific DNS suffix*.

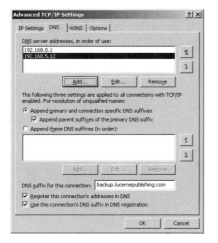

Figure 4-12   Configuring a connection-specific suffix

When the connection-specific DNS suffix is added to a DNS computer or host name, an FQDN is assigned to a specific adapter on the computer.

For example, as shown in Figure 4-13, a multihomed server computer named host-a can be named according to both its primary and connection-specific DNS domain names.

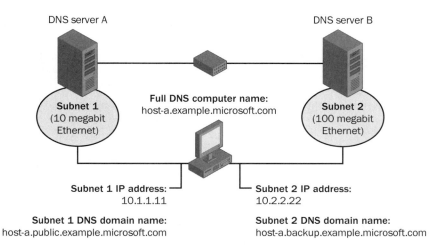

Figure 4-13   Using connection-specific suffixes

In this example, the server computer host-a attaches to two separate subnets— Subnet 1 and Subnet 2—that are also linked at redundant points by using two routers for additional paths between each subnet. Given this configuration, host-a provides access as follows through its separately named LAN connections:

■ The name host-a.public.example.microsoft.com provides access using LAN connection 1 over Subnet 1, a lower speed (10-Mb) Ethernet LAN, for normal access to users who have typical file and print service needs.

■ The name host-a.backup.example.microsoft.com provides access using LAN connection 2 over Subnet 2, a higher speed (100-Mb) Ethernet LAN, for reserved access by server applications and administrators who have special needs, such as troubleshooting server networking problems, performing network-based backup, or replicating zone data between servers.

The computer can also be accessed in a manner that does not specify a particular LAN connection. To connect to the computer through either LAN connection, clients specify the computer's full computer name, host-a.example.microsoft.com.

When configured as shown in Figure 4-13, a DNS client running Windows 2000, Windows XP, or Windows Server 2003 can register resource records in DNS according to its three distinct names and sets of IP addresses, as shown in Table 4-4.

Table 4-4   FQDNs of a Multihomed Host

DNS Name	IP Addresses	Description
host-a.example.microsoft.com	10.1.1.11, 10.2.2.22	The full computer name. The computer registers A and PTR resource records for all configured IP addresses under this name in the example.microsoft.com zone.
host-a.public.example.microsoft.com	10.1.1.11	The connection-specific DNS name for LAN connection 1, which registers A and PTR resource records for IP address 10.1.1.11 in the public.example.microsoft.com zone.
host-a.backup.example.microsoft.com	10.2.2.22	The connection-specific DNS name for LAN connection 2, which registers A and PTR resource records for IP address 10.2.2.22 in the backup.example.microsoft.com zone.

Configuring a DNS Servers List

After consulting its cache, the DNS Client service next attempts name resolution through its preferred connection, which is the first connection listed in the output of the Ipconfig command. Through this connection, the resolver (DNS client) queries the address designated as that connection's preferred DNS server. Although each network adapter can be configured with a unique list of DNS servers, it's perfectly valid to configure each network adapter identically to make DNS resolution more predictable.

To help DNS clients resolve names when initial query attempts fail, each connection configured on the DNS client computer can contain a list of DNS servers to contact. As shown in Figure 4-14, you can configure a preferred server and a single alternate server for any connection in that connection's Internet Protocol (TCP/IP) Properties dialog box.

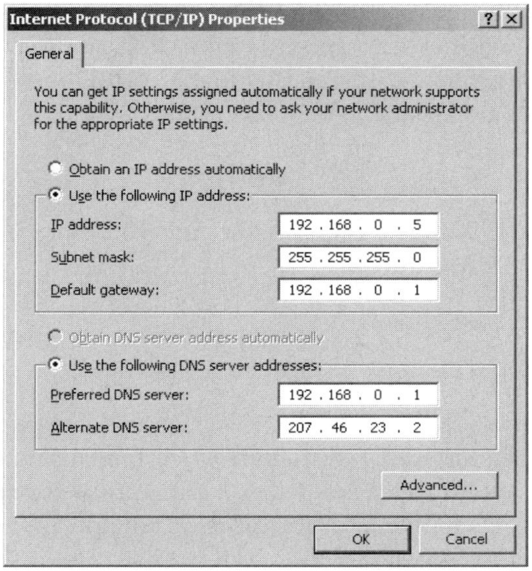

Figure 4-14   Specifying DNS servers

However, for a given connection, you can create a DNS server list of any length in the connection's Advanced TCP/IP Settings dialog box. In this list, the first entry is treated as the preferred server and the remaining alternate servers are queried together.

When resolving names, the DNS Client service queries the DNS servers in the following order:

1. The DNS Client service sends the query to the first server on the preferred adapter's list of DNS servers and waits 1 second for a response.

2. If the DNS Client service does not receive a response from the first server within 1 second, it sends the query to the first DNS servers on all adapters that are still under consideration and waits 2 seconds for a response.

3. If the DNS Client service does not receive a response from any server within 2 seconds, the resolver sends the query to all DNS servers on all adapters that are still under consideration and waits another 2 seconds for a response.

4. If the DNS Client service still does not receive a response from any server, it sends the query to all DNS servers on all adapters that are still under consideration and waits 4 seconds for a response.

5. If it still does not receive a response from any server, the resolver sends the query to all DNS servers on all adapters that are still under consideration and waits 8 seconds for a response.

If the DNS Client service receives a positive response, it stops querying for the name, adds the response to the cache, and returns the response to the client. If the DNS Client service has not received a response from any server by the end of the 8-second time period, the resolver responds with a time-out.

DNS Suffix Search Lists

The DNS Client service attaches DNS suffixes to any name that you enter in a query when either of the following conditions is true:

- The name is a single-label unqualified name.

- The name is a multiple-label unqualified name, and the DNS Client service did not resolve it as an FQDN.

Default DNS Suffix Searches   By default, the DNS Client service first attaches the primary domain suffix of the local computer to the unqualified name. If the query fails to resolve this name, the DNS Client service then adds any connection-specific suffix that you have assigned to a network adapter. Finally, if these queries are also unsuccessful, the DNS Client service adds the parent suffix of the primary DNS suffix.

For example, suppose the full computer name of a multihomed computer is computer1.domain1.microsoft.com. The network adapters on Computer1 have been assigned the connection-specific suffixes subnet1.domain1.microsoft.com and subnet2.domain1.microsoft.com, respectively. If on this same computer you type **computer2** into the Address text box in Internet Explorer and then press Enter, the local DNS Client service first tries to resolve the name Computer2 by performing a query for the name computer2.domain1.microsoft.com. If this query is unsuccessful, the DNS Client service queries for the names computer2.subnet1.domain1.microsoft.com and computer2.subnet2.domain1.microsoft.com. If this query does not succeed in resolving the name, the DNS Client service queries for the name computer2.microsoft.com.

Custom DNS Suffix Search Lists   You can customize suffix searches by creating a DNS suffix search list in the Advanced TCP/IP Settings dialog box, as shown in Figure 4-15.

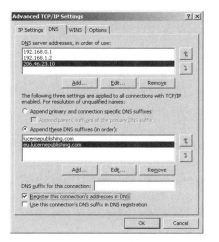

Figure 4-15   Adding suffixes to DNS queries

The Append These DNS Suffixes option lets you specify a list of DNS suffixes to add to unqualified names. If you enter a DNS suffix search list, the DNS Client service adds those DNS suffixes in order and does not try any other domain names. For example, if the suffixes appearing in the search list in Figure 4-15 are configured and you submit the unqualified, single-label query "coffee," the DNS Client service first queries for coffee.lucernepublishing.com and then for coffee.eu.lucernepublishing.com.

Configuring Dynamic Update Options

When configured to do so, DNS servers running on Windows 2000 or Windows Server 2003 can accept dynamic updates of A and PTR resource records. The updates themselves must be performed either by a DNS client running Windows 2000, Windows XP, or Windows Server 2003, or by a DHCP server (on behalf of a DNS client) running Windows 2000 or Windows Server 2003.

Exam Tip   For the exam, remember that UNIX-based DNS servers running Berkeley Internet Name Domain (BIND) 8.1.2 or later can accept dynamic updates.

Dynamic updates can occur only when clients are configured with a domain suffix that matches the zone name hosted by the preferred DNS server. In other words, for the record of a computer named Client1 to be dynamically updated in the lucernepublishing. com zone, the FQDN of that computer must be client1.lucernepublishing.com., and the client must specify as its DNS server the IP address of the DNS server hosting lucernepublishing.com.

Default Client Update Behavior

By default, DNS clients that are configured with a static IP address and an appropriate domain suffix attempt to register and update both A and PTR resource records with the preferred DNS server. However, DNS clients that obtain their address from a DHCP server attempt to register and update only their A resource records with the preferred DNS server. In this case, the PTR resource record is updated by the DHCP server when the lease is assigned. Windows clients that are not capable of performing dynamic updates—such as DNS clients running Windows Me or Windows NT 4—can have both A and PTR resource records updated on their behalf by a specially configured DHCP server.

To configure a DNS client to attempt dynamic updates in DNS, make sure the Register This Connection's Addresses In DNS check box is selected on the DNS tab of the Advanced TCP/IP Settings dialog box, as shown in Figure 4-15. (It is selected by default.) This configures the DNS client to attempt to register and update the computer's full computer name (primary domain name). When you clear this check box, the DNS client no longer attempts dynamic updates. If you configure a DNS suffix for the connection, you can also specify that the DNS client attempt to dynamically register and update an FQDN based on this connection-specific suffix. To do so, click the Use This Connection's DNS Suffix In DNS Registration check box. (It is not selected by default.)

To force a DNS client to attempt dynamic registration of its A and PTR resource records, type **ipconfig /registerdns** at a command prompt.

> **Note**   For Internet Connection Sharing (ICS) clients, Dynamic DNS updates are configured in a distinct manner. When DNS clients running Windows 2000, Windows XP, or Windows Server 2003 obtain their IP configuration from a computer running ICS, those clients can update their records in DNS only when the Use This Connection's DNS Suffix In DNS Registration is selected. You do not need to specify a connection-specific suffix. Instead, the primary DNS suffix forms the FQDN.

Configuring TCP/IP Settings for DNS Clients

The following procedure summarizes the steps necessary to enable clients to use DNS.

To configure TCP/IP settings for DNS clients, complete the following steps:

1. Open the Network Connections window.

2. Right-click the network connection you want to configure, and then select Properties.

   The connection's properties dialog box appears.

3. On the General tab (for a local area connection) or the Networking tab (all other connections), select the Internet Protocol (TCP/IP) component, and then click Properties.

   The Internet Protocol (IP) Properties dialog box appears.

4. If you want to obtain DNS server addresses from a DHCP server, select Obtain DNS Server Address Automatically.

5. If you want to manually configure DNS server addresses, select Use The Following DNS Server Addresses, and in the Preferred DNS Server text box and Alternate DNS Server text box, type the preferred DNS server and alternate DNS server IP addresses.

6. To configure advanced DNS properties, click Advanced, select the DNS tab, and do one or more of the following:

   a. To configure an additional DNS server IP address, click the topmost Add button and specify a DNS server IP address.

   b. To modify the resolution behavior for unqualified DNS names, do the following:

   ❑ To configure the client to resolve an unqualified name by adding the primary DNS suffix and the DNS suffix of each connection (if configured), select Append Primary And Connection Specific DNS Suffixes. If you also want to search the parent suffixes of the primary DNS suffix up to the second-level domain, select the Append Parent Suffixes Of The Primary DNS Suffix check box.

   ❑ To configure the client to resolve an unqualified name by adding the suffixes from a list of configured suffixes, select Append These DNS Suffixes, and then click Add to add suffixes to the list.

   c. To configure a connection-specific DNS suffix, type the DNS suffix in the DNS Suffix For This Connection text box.

d. To modify DNS dynamic update behavior, do the following:

❏ To configure the client to register the connection's IP address with the local computer's full computer name in DNS, select the Register This Connection's Addresses In DNS check box. This option is enabled by default. This option requires that the primary DNS suffix of the computer match a domain hosted by the preferred DNS server.

❏ To configure the client to register the connection's IP address with a connection-specific FQDN, select the Use This Connection's DNS Suffix In DNS Registration check box. This option is disabled by default.

❏ To completely disable DNS dynamic updates for all names on the computer, clear the Register This Connection's Addresses In DNS check box for all connections in Network Connections.

Viewing and Clearing the DNS Resolver Cache

The *DNS resolver cache*, also known as the DNS client cache, is maintained separately from the DNS server cache. This resolver cache is checked first by DNS clients before they attempt to query a DNS server. New entries are added to the resolver cache whenever a DNS client receives a query response from a DNS server.

To view the DNS client cache, enter **ipconfig /displaydns** at a command prompt. The output of this command includes entries loaded from the local Hosts file, as well as any recently obtained resource records for name queries resolved by the system.

To clear the DNS resolver cache, you can enter **ipconfig /flushdns** at the command prompt. Alternatively, you can restart the DNS Client service by using the Services console, an administrative tool accessible through the Start menu.

> **Exam Tip**   Remember the following DNS-related commands for the exam:
>
> **1.** Ipconfig /displaydns. Displays the contents of the DNS client cache
>
> **2.** Ipconfig /flushdns. Purges the contents of the DNS client cache
>
> **3.** Ipconfig /registerdns. Refreshes all DHCP leases and reregisters DNS names with DNS zones configured to accept dynamic updates
>
> Know also that the Ipconfig /registerdns command can be used only on clients running Windows 2000, Windows XP, and Windows Server 2003.

Exam Tip   For the exam, remember that you sometimes need to run Ipconfig /flushdns on your computer before you can see the benefit of having fixed a DNS problem elsewhere on the network. For example, suppose you are unable to ping a UNIX computer by name from a Windows client. You manually create a host (A) resource record for the UNIX computer to remedy the situation, but when you again try to ping the UNIX computer by name, you still receive an error response. This problem occurs because the Windows client has cached a negative response to the earlier query for the UNIX computer name. To fix the problem, flush the DNS client cache by executing Ipconfig /flushdns on the Windows computer. This command forces the Windows client to attempt from scratch to resolve the UNIX computer name instead of just responding with the cached negative response.

Practice 1: Configuring a Primary DNS Suffix

In this practice, you configure a primary DNS suffix for Computer1 and Computer2 and then observe changes resulting from this procedure in the DNS console.

Exercise 1: Adding Suffix Names to Computers

In this exercise, you configure a primary DNS suffix for Computer1 and Computer2.

1. Log on to Computer1 as Administrator.
2. In Control Panel, open the System tool.

    The System Properties dialog box opens.
3. Click the Computer Name tab.
4. Click the Change button.

    The Computer Name Changes dialog box opens.
5. Click More.

    The DNS Suffix And NetBIOS Computer Name dialog box opens.
6. In the Primary DNS Suffix Of This Computer text box, type **domain1.local**.
7. Click OK.
8. In the Computer Name Changes dialog box, click OK.

    The Computer Name Changes message box appears, indicating that you need to restart the computer for the changes to take effect.

9. Click OK.

10. In the System Properties dialog box, click OK.

The System Settings Change dialog box opens, which asks you whether you want to restart your computer now.

11. Click Yes.

12. While Computer1 is restarting, perform this same procedure on Computer2, assigning the primary DNS suffix of domain1.local, and then choosing to restart the computer.

Exercise 2: Verifying Changes in DNS

In this exercise, you verify the changes you made in Exercise 1, "Adding Suffix Names to Computers."

1. Log on to Computer1 as Administrator.

2. Open a command prompt and type **ping computer1**.

3. Answer the following question in the space provided:

How is the suffix change apparent in the output of the Ping command?

_____

_____

_____

4. Log off Computer1.

Practice 2: Configuring a DNS Server to Perform Recursion

In this practice, you configure the DNS server on Computer1 to answer recursive queries for Internet-based DNS names from Computer2. You then initiate a recursive query from Computer2 and monitor the results.

Because Computer2 is assigned a private address, it can communicate with the Internet only by means of an address translation service such as Network Address Translation (NAT) or ICS. As a result, the first step in this practice is to configure ICS on Computer1.

Exercise 1: Enabling ICS

In this exercise, you enable ICS on Computer1. This feature performs address translation for all computers on the network segment and enables them to communicate with Internet hosts. ICS also provides addresses for DHCP clients on the local segment and configures these clients to use the ICS computer as a DNS server. After ICS is enabled, the DNS server on the ICS server performs recursion to answer the DNS queries from local clients.

1. Log on to Computer1 as Administrator.

2. Open the Network Connections window.

3. If the MyISP connection is active in the Network Connections window, right-click MyISP and select Disconnect.

4. After the dial-up connection has finished disconnecting, right-click MyISP and select Properties.

   The MyISP Properties dialog box opens.

5. Click the Advanced tab.

6. In the Internet Connection Sharing area, select the Allow Other Network Users To Connect Through This Computer's Internet Connection check box.

7. Click OK.

   The Network Connections dialog box opens.

8. Read the text in the box, and then click Yes.

   At this point, the local computer is assigned an IP address of 192.168.0.1. You might temporarily lose network connectivity while these changes are being made.

9. Log on to Computer2 as Administrator.

10. Restart Computer2.

Exercise 2: Performing Recursive Queries

In this exercise, you use Network Monitor to capture a DNS query from Computer2. After Computer1 performs recursion to answer the query, you explore the capture and verify that new entries corresponding to the query have been loaded into the DNS Server cache.

1. Connect Computer1 to the Internet through the MyISP connection.

2. Log on to Computer2 as Administrator and open a command prompt.

3. At the command prompt, type **ipconfig /all**, and then press Enter.

   Because ICS has been enabled on the network, Computer2 now specifies 192.168.0.1, the address of Computer1, as its DNS server. Computer2 therefore resolves DNS queries through Computer1.

4. At the command prompt, type **ipconfig /flushdns**, and then press Enter.

   The resolver cache clears, which forces Computer2 to contact a DNS server to resolve all DNS names.

5. Switch to Computer1, open Network Monitor, and begin a Network Monitor capture.

6. Switch back to Computer2, and then open Internet Explorer. If you receive a message box informing you that an enhanced security configuration is currently enabled, select the check box to prevent this message from appearing again, and then click OK.

7. In the Address text box in Internet Explorer, type **http://www.windowsupdate.com**, and then press Enter.

   The connection is successful.

8. Switch back to Computer1 and in Network Monitor, click the Stop And View Capture button.

9. In the Capture: 1 (Summary) window, locate and double-click the first DNS frame in the capture. Note that the FQDN queried for in the first line is www.windowsupdate.com.

10. Within the expanded DNS frame in the details (center) pane, expand the section named DNS Flags.

    A set of flagged messages appear. These messages are true when the corresponding flag is set to 1.

11. Answer the following question: Which of the DNS flags is set to 1 and not 0?

    Recursive Query Desired

    This flag serves as a request that the DNS server perform recursion to answer the query if necessary.

12. Close Network Monitor. Do not save the capture or choose to save any entries to the database.

13. Open the DNS console. (If the DNS console is already open, close the console and reopen it.)

14. In the console tree, select the COMPUTER1 icon.

15. From the View menu, select Advanced.

    A new folder named Cached Lookups appears in the console tree.

16. Expand the Cached Lookups folder, and then expand the .(root) folder.

    Within the .(root) folder, browse the subfolders to locate the CNAME record www.windowsupdate.com.

    Computer1 has performed recursion to answer Computer2's recursive query. The DNS Server service has then cached the records returned in the response to the query.

17. Log off Computer1 and Computer2.

Lesson Review

The following questions are intended to reinforce key information presented in this lesson. If you are unable to answer a question, review the lesson materials and try the question again. You can find answers to the questions in the "Questions and Answers" section at the end of this chapter.

1. From your computer client1, you discover that you cannot ping another computer named client2.lucernepublishing.com by name, but you can ping it by IP address. You determine that no A resource record exists for client2.lucernepublishing.com in the DNS server zone files, so you create one manually. What must you do before you can successfully ping client2.lucernepublishing.com by name from client1?

_____

_____

2. How can you configure a stand-alone server named Bing1 to dynamically register an A resource record in the humongousinsurance.com zone without assigning a primary DNS suffix to the computer? (Assume that the humongousinsurance.com zone is configured to accept dynamic updates.)

_____

_____

_____

_____

_____

Lesson Summary

- The primary DNS suffix is the suffix that, when added to the client host name, forms the full computer name.

- When a connection-specific DNS suffix is added to a DNS computer or host name, an FQDN is assigned to a specific adapter on the computer. This suffix can be configured on the DNS tab of the Advanced TCP/IP Settings dialog box.

- When queries are submitted for unqualified names, the DNS Client service by default first adds the primary DNS suffix to the unqualified name and then submits a query for this name. If that strategy does not work, the DNS Client service then adds any connection-specific suffixes to the name and submits this new query. If that strategy does not work, the DNS Client service then adds the parent suffix of the primary DNS suffix to the name and submits this final query.

- By default, DNS clients running Windows 2000, Windows XP, and Windows Server 2003 attempt to dynamically register and update their resource records in DNS. Clients assigned a static IP address attempt to update both A and PTR resource records. Clients assigned an IP address through DHCP attempt to update only A resource records, and the PTR resource record update is performed by the DHCP server. To force a DNS client to attempt dynamic registration, use the Ipconfig /registerdns command (or restart the computer).

- To view the DNS client cache, enter **ipconfig /displaydns** at a command prompt. To flush the DNS client cache, enter **ipconfig /flushdns** at a command prompt.

Case Scenario Exercise

You have been hired as a consultant by Northwind Traders, whose main office is in Burlington, Vermont. Northwind Traders has merged with Adventure Works, whose office is in Caribou, Maine. Each of these company offices has a network that hosts an Active Directory–integrated zone. The two networks are connected by means of a dedicated 128 Kbps line.

Figure 4-16 presents the relevant portion of the internetwork.

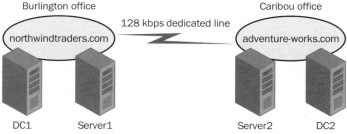

Figure 4-16   The Northwind and Adventure Works networks

1. Of the servers shown in Figure 4-16, which ones can you infer are acting as DNS servers, and why?

   _____

   _____

2. Users in each office report that they cannot resolve DNS names of computers in the other office. What kind of DNS server can you deploy at each location to remedy this situation?

   _____

   _____

3. Northwind Traders wants to open a satellite office in Burlington, but it does not want this new office to host any zones. The satellite office users are expected to use the Internet heavily for marketing and research. What can you do to improve DNS name resolution for users in this satellite office?

Troubleshooting Lab

In the following lab, you troubleshoot name resolution on Computer1 and Computer2.

1. Log on to Computer1 as Administrator.

2. Open a command prompt and enter the command **nbtstat –R**.

3. At the command prompt, enter the command **ping computer2**.

   The ping attempt is successful.

4. Use the procedure named "To disable WINS/NetBIOS name resolution" in Lesson 1 to disable NetBIOS for the local area connection on Computer1.

5. Open a command prompt and type the command **nbtstat –R**.

6. At the command prompt, enter **ping computer2**.

   The ping attempt is not successful.

7. At the command prompt, enter **ping computer2.domain1.local**.

   The ping attempt is not successful.

8. Answer the following question: Given that the DNS server is configured on Computer1, why are you unable to ping computer2.domain1.local?

9. Open a new command prompt by clicking Start, pointing to All Programs, pointing to Windows Support Tools, and clicking Command Prompt. At the Support Tools command prompt, enter **dnscmd . /Config ..AllZones /AllowUpdate 1**.

   This command enables dynamic updates on all zones hosted by the local DNS server.

10. Log on to Computer2 as Administrator.

11. On Computer2, on the DNS tab in the Advanced TCP/IP Settings dialog box for the local area connection, select the Use This Connection's DNS Suffix In DNS Registration check box. Click OK twice, and then click Close.

12. Open a new command prompt on Computer2 and enter **ipconfig /registerdns**.

13. Switch back to Computer1, open a new command prompt, and enter **ping computer2**.

The ping is still unsuccessful. Because the local DNS Client service has cached the negative response from the previous query, you must clear the cache before you see the successful results of the ping.

14. At the command prompt on Computer1, type **ipconfig /flushdns**.

15. At the command prompt on Computer1, type **ping computer2**.

The ping is successful.

16. Reenable NetBIOS for the local area connection on Computer1.

17. Log off Computer1 and Computer2.

Chapter Summary

- Two types of computer naming systems exist in Windows Server 2003 networks: DNS and NetBIOS. To resolve computer names, the DNS Client service in Windows Server 2003 always attempts DNS name resolution before NetBIOS name resolution.

- DNS names and the DNS protocol are required for Active Directory domains and for compatibility with the Internet or intranets. DNS host names cannot exceed 63 bytes.

- The DNS namespace is hierarchical and is based on a unique root that can have any number of subdomains. An FQDN is a name of a DNS host in this namespace that indicates the host's location relative to the root of the DNS domain tree. An example of an FQDN is host1.subdomain.microsoft.com.

- A DNS zone is a contiguous portion of a namespace for which a server is authoritative. A server can be authoritative for one or more zones, and a zone can contain one or more contiguous domains. A DNS server is authoritative for a zone if it hosts the zone, either as a primary or secondary DNS server. Each DNS zone contains the resource records it needs to answer queries for its portion of the DNS namespace.

- The DNS Client service (or resolver) first attempts to resolve computer names by using locally cached information. If this process is unsuccessful, the resolver queries a DNS server. If the DNS server cannot resolve the name through its authoritative records or through its local cache, the DNS server performs recursion to resolve the name on behalf of the client.

- Recursion is the process of a DNS server querying other servers on behalf of a DNS client. For the DNS server to perform recursion properly, the server needs to know where to begin searching for names in the DNS domain namespace. This information is provided by the root hints file, Cache.dns, that is stored on the server computer.

- A caching-only server forwards all requests to other DNS servers and hosts no zones. However, caching-only servers cache responses received from other DNS servers and can therefore improve name resolution for a network that does not host a zone.

- New zones contain only two resource records: the SOA record corresponding to the zone, and an NS record corresponding to the local DNS server created for the zone. After you create a zone, additional resource records need to be added to it. The most common resource records to be added are host (A), alias (CNAME), MX, SRV, and PTR.

- By default, DNS clients running Windows 2000, Windows XP, and Windows Server 2003 attempt to dynamically register and update their resource records in DNS. Clients assigned a static IP address attempt to update both A and PTR resource records. Clients assigned an IP address through DHCP attempt to update only A resource records, and the PTR resource record update is performed by the DHCP server. To force a DNS client to attempt dynamic registration, use the Ipconfig /registerdns command (or restart the computer).

- To view the DNS client cache, type **ipconfig /displaydns** at a command prompt. To flush the DNS client cache, type **ipconfig /flushdns** at a command prompt.

Exam Highlights

Before taking the exam, review the key points and terms that are presented in this chapter.

Key Points

- Know the complete sequence of steps taken when the DNS Client service attempts to resolve a name. Understand how the DNS client cache, the DNS server cache, and recursion fit into this process.

- Understand the function of A, PTR, CNAME, MX, and SRV resource records.

- Know the difference between primary, secondary, and stub zones.

- Understand the function of the Cache.dns file.

- Know when to use Nbtstat –c, Nbtstat –R, Ipconfig /displaydns, Ipconfig /flushdns, and Ipconfig /registerdns.

- Understand the benefit of caching-only servers.

- Understand which DNS clients can attempt dynamic updates in DNS. Understand the different records that DHCP and non-DHCP clients attempt to update by default. Finally, know which settings in the Advanced TCP/IP Settings dialog box affect dynamic update behavior.

Key Terms

NetBIOS   An API used in older Microsoft networks that allows computers to connect and communicate. Naming and name resolution are two of the many services NetBIOS offers.

FQDN   Fully qualified domain name. A DNS name that uniquely identifies a computer on the network. For example, an FQDN might be client1.microsoft.com.

recursion   The process of a DNS server querying other DNS servers to resolve a name on behalf of a DNS client.

recursive query   A client query that requests recursion from the server.

stub zone   A copy of a zone containing only those resource records necessary to identify the authoritative DNS servers for the master zone.

Questions and Answers

Lesson 1, Practice

Page
4-9
1. Look at the protocols listed in the new network capture.

In Network Monitor, NBT represents NetBT, and DNS represents Domain Name System. Based on the protocol you see in this capture and on the description provided for given frames, determine whether NetBIOS name resolution or DNS name resolution has been used to resolve the computer name Computer2. Why has this method been used and not the other method? Write your answer in the space provided.

NetBIOS name resolution has been used because, although Windows Server 2003 networks use DNS name resolution when this service is available, no DNS server has been configured yet on this network. In such cases, Windows Server 2003 networks use the NetBT protocol and NetBIOS name resolution to resolve computer names to IP addresses.

Lesson 1 Review

Page
4-10
1. The network you administer includes 10 computers running Windows Server 2003 and 200 computers running Microsoft Windows XP Professional. In the network, you have deployed a DNS server named DNS1 to host the zone lucernepublishing. com. You have also configured the zone to allow dynamic updates. A DHCP server is responsible for the IP configuration of all computers running Windows XP Professional. One of these computers, c1.lucernepublishing.com, can be contacted only by IP address and not by name. Which of the following actions can you take to reregister this computer in DNS? Choose all that apply.

  a. Execute the Nbtstat –R command.

  b. Execute the Ipconfig /registerdns command.

  c. Shut down and restart c1.lucernepublishing.com.

  d. Execute the Nbtstat /registerdns command.

  b, c

2. Which of the following is a legal NetBIOS computer name?

  a. host1.microsoft.com

  b. host1_local

  c. host10_microsoft

  d. host1-microsoft

  b

3. Which command can you use to purge the local NetBIOS name cache?

Nbtstat –R

Lesson 2 Review

Page
4-24

1. On the network you administer, you maintain a primary DNS server authoritative for the zone lucernepublishing.com. You have also deployed two caching-only servers that forward all requests to the primary server. If most of the name queries directed toward the caching-only servers are for names within the lucernepublishing.com domain, which parameter can you modify on the primary server to decrease DNS query traffic between the caching-only servers and the primary server?

You can increase the TTL value of resource records at the zone level.

2. What is the root domain of a namespace containing the FQDN first.domain1.local.?

a. None. The namespace has no root domain.

b. domain1.

c. local.

d. "" (empty string).

d

3. Which step does the resolver first perform to resolve a DNS name?

a. It checks its local cache.

b. It reads from the Hosts file.

c. It broadcasts the local subnet.

d. It queries the local DNS server.

a

4. Your network computers are turned on for the first time after a power outage. When a DNS client first submits a recursive query to a local DNS server to resolve an Internet name for which the server is not authoritative, which step takes place first?

a. The DNS client resolves the name from its cache.

b. The DNS server resolves the name from its cache.

c. The DNS server forwards the recursive query to an upstream DNS server.

d. The DNS server contacts root servers configured in the Cache.dns file.

d

Lesson 3 Review

Page
4-42

1. You have just updated a host resource record. What other associated resource record might now need to be updated?

The PTR record associated with the same host

2. Your DNS server has failed the recursive test. Assuming that the server can otherwise communicate with other DNS servers, name two potential causes of this scenario.

The DNS server has been configured as a root server, or the root hints file is improperly configured.

3. Which resource record is used to resolve domain names specified in e-mail addresses to the IP address of the mail server associated with the domain?

    a. PTR

    b. MX

    c. A

    d. CNAME

b

4. On a new DNS server, you create a zone "" and then create subdomains from that root domain. Which function will the new server be able or unable to perform?

    a. The server will be unable to cache names.

    b. The server will be able to function only as a forwarding server.

    c. The server will be unable to resolve Internet names.

    d. The server will be unable to connect to the Internet.

c

Lesson 4, Practice 1, Exercise 2

Page
4-56

1. Answer the following question in the space provided:

How is the suffix change apparent in the output of the Ping command?

Before the responses to the Internet Control Message Protocol (ICMP) echo requests are received, the Ping output reads, "Pinging computer1. domain1.local [192.168.0.1] with 32 bytes of data:"

Lesson 4 Review

Page
4-59

1. From your computer client1, you discover that you cannot ping another computer named client2.lucernepublishing.com by name, but you can ping it by IP address. You determine that no A resource record exists for client2.lucernepublishing.com in the DNS server zone files, so you create one manually. What must you do before you can successfully ping client2.lucernepublishing.com by name from client1?

Run the Ipconfig /flushdns command on client1 to clear the negative response from the cache.

2. How can you configure a stand-alone server named Bing1 to dynamically register an A resource record in the humongousinsurance.com zone without assigning a primary DNS suffix to the computer? (Assume that the humongousinsurance.com zone is configured to accept dynamic updates.)

In the Advanced TCP/IP Settings dialog box, configure a connection-specific DNS suffix of humongousinsurance.com, and then select the option to use the connection's suffix in DNS registration. Finally, specify the IP address of the primary DNS server hosting the humongous-insurance.com zone as the preferred DNS server for Bing1.

Case scenario

Page
4-60

1. Of the servers shown in Figure 4-16, which ones can you infer are acting as DNS servers, and why?

DC1 and DC2. Active Directory–integrated zones must be hosted on domain controllers.

2. Users in each office report that they cannot resolve DNS names of computers in the other office. What kind of DNS server can you deploy at each location to remedy this situation?

You can deploy a secondary server at each location that holds authoritative information for the remote Active Directory–integrated zone.

3. Northwind Traders wants to open a satellite office in Burlington, but it does not want this new office to host any zones. The satellite office users are expected to use the Internet heavily for marketing and research. What can you do to improve DNS name resolution for users in this satellite office?

You can deploy a caching-only server to improve DNS name resolution efficiency.

Troubleshooting lab

Page
4-61

1. Answer the following question: Given that the DNS server is configured on Computer1, why are you unable to ping computer2.domain1.local?

No A resource record exists for Computer2 in the zone domain1.local.

5 Implementing a DNS Infrastructure

Exam Objectives in this Chapter:

- Configure a DNS server
- Configure DNS zone options
- Configure DNS forwarding
- Manage DNS zone settings
- Manage DNS server options

Why This Chapter Matters

The Domain Name System (DNS) is too vital an element in a network infrastructure to be merely deployed and forgotten on a single server. For medium-sized and large organizations, DNS must be distributed throughout the network and kept up to date. Network administrators are tasked with the responsibility of maintaining this infrastructure, a job which requires understanding the nuances of features such as zone transfers, delegations, stub zones, round robin, and netmask ordering. Because of its importance, this chapter is one of the most heavily tested sections on the 70-291 exam.

This chapter introduces you to the main configuration options available for DNS servers and zones, many of which are available in the server properties and zone properties dialog boxes. In addition, this chapter teaches you how and why to implement delegations and stub zones in your Windows Server 2003 networks.

Lessons in this Chapter:

- Lesson 1: Configuring DNS Server Properties 5-3
- Lesson 2: Configuring Zone Properties and Transfers 5-20
- Lesson 3: Configuring Advanced DNS Server Properties 5-43
- Lesson 4: Creating Zone Delegations 5-56
- Lesson 5: Deploying Stub Zones 5-65

Before You Begin

To complete this chapter, you must have

- Networked two computers, named Computer1 and Computer2, each running Windows Server 2003. Computer1 should be assigned a static address of 192.168.0.1/24, and Computer2 should be configured to obtain an address automatically. Computer2 should have an alternate configuration address of 192.168.0.2/24. Both Computer1 and Computer2 should have a configured primary DNS suffix of domain1.local.

- A phone line and dial-up Internet service provider (ISP) account. (If you choose to substitute a dedicated Internet connection for this requirement, you should rename this Internet connection "MyISP." You may also need to make other minor adjustments to the lesson exercises.)

- Installed the Network Monitor Tools subcomponent of the Management And Monitoring Tools Windows component on Computer1. A Network Monitor capture file named Name Resolution 1 should be saved to the My Captures folder in My Documents on Computer1. This capture, created before DNS is deployed on the network, shows the traffic exchanged on the network after the Ping computer2 command is executed on Computer1.

- Installed the Domain Name System (DNS) subcomponent of the Networking Services. Once installed, the DNS server should host a primary forward lookup zone named domain1.local and a primary reverse lookup zone corresponding to the 192.168.0.0/24 address space. Both zones are configured to accept secure and nonsecure updates. A host (A) resource record for both Computer1 and Computer2 should exist in the domain1.local zone.

- Installed Windows Support Tools on Computer1.

- Created a dial-up connection to the Internet named MyISP on Computer1 that you have shared through Internet Connection Sharing (ICS). Computer2 should receive a fresh Internet Protocol (IP) configuration from Computer1 after ICS is enabled. (If you are using a dedicated Internet connection instead of a dial-up account, you should apply this requirement to the dedicated connection.)

- Selected the Use This Connection's DNS Suffix In DNS Registration option on the DNS tab in the Advanced TCP/IP Settings dialog box for the Local Area Connection on Computer2.

Lesson 1: Configuring DNS Server Properties

Once you have installed a DNS server, you might need to modify its default settings to suit your network needs. In this lesson, you learn the various settings that you can configure through the server properties dialog box in the DNS console. The settings you configure in this properties dialog box do not apply to a particular zone but to the server in general.

After this lesson, you will be able to

- Configure a DNS server to listen for queries on selected network adapters
- Configure a DNS server to forward all or select DNS queries to an upstream DNS server
- Determine when it is necessary to modify root hints

Estimated lesson time: 45 minutes

Exploring DNS Server Properties Tabs

The DNS server properties dialog box allows you to configure settings that apply to the DNS server and all its hosted zones. You can access this dialog box in the DNS console tree by right-clicking the DNS server you want to configure and then selecting Properties, as shown in Figure 5-1.

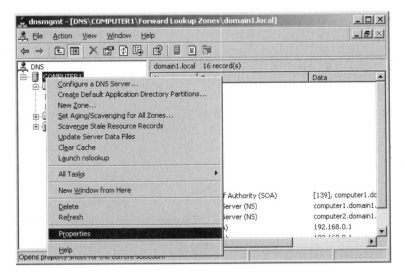

Figure 5-1   Accessing the DNS server properties dialog box

The DNS server properties dialog box contains eight tabs, which are introduced next.

Interfaces Tab

The Interfaces tab allows you to specify which of the local computer's IP addresses the DNS server should listen to for DNS requests. For example, if your server is multi-homed and has one IP address for the local network and another IP address connected to the Internet, you can prevent the DNS server from servicing DNS queries from outside the local network. To perform this task, specify that the DNS server listen only on the computer's internal IP address, as shown in Figure 5-2.

By default, the setting on this tab specifies that the DNS server listens on all IP addresses associated with the local computer.

Figure 5-2   Interfaces tab

Forwarders Tab

The Forwarders tab allows you to forward DNS queries received by the local DNS server to upstream DNS servers, called *forwarders*. Using this tab, you can specify the IP addresses of the upstream forwarders, and you can specify the domain names of queries that should be forwarded. For example, in Figure 5-3, all queries received for the domain lucernepublishing.com will be forwarded to the DNS server 207.46.132.23. When, after receiving and forwarding a query from an internal client, the local forwarding server receives a query response back from 207.46.132.23, the local forwarding server then passes this query response back to the original querying client. The process of forwarding selected queries in this way is known as *conditional forwarding*.

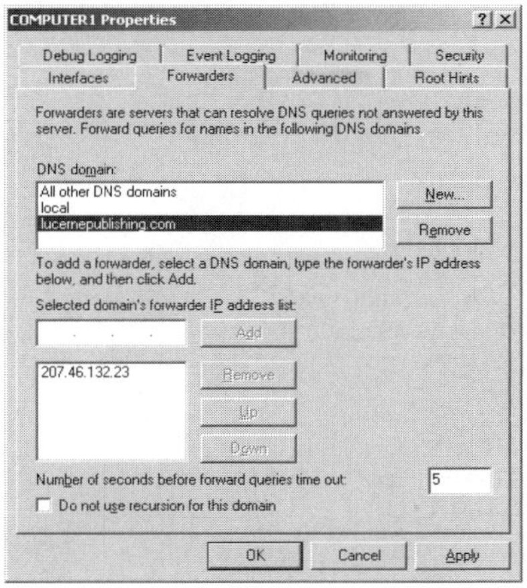

Figure 5-3   Forwarders tab

In all cases, a DNS server configured for forwarding uses forwarders only after it has determined that it cannot resolve a query using its authoritative data (primary or secondary zone data) or cached data.

> **Tip**   To specify how long the forwarding server should wait for a response from a forwarder before timing out, on the Forwarders tab, enter a value in the Number Of Seconds Before Forward Queries Time Out text box. The default setting is 5.

When to Use Forwarders   In some cases, network administrators might not want DNS servers to communicate directly with external servers. For example, if your organization is connected to the Internet by means of a slow wide area link, you can optimize name resolution performance by channeling all DNS queries through one forwarder, as shown in Figure 5-4. Through this method, the server cache of the DNS forwarder has the maximum potential to grow and reduce the need for external queries.

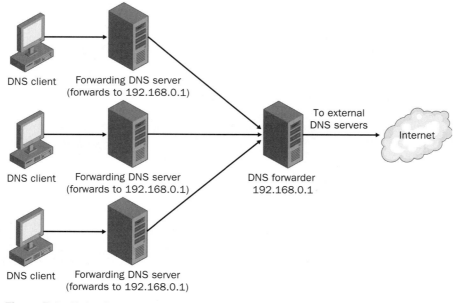

Figure 5-4   Using forwarding to consolidate caching

Another common use of forwarding is to allow DNS clients and servers inside a firewall to resolve external names securely. When an internal DNS server or client communicates with external DNS servers by making iterative queries, normally the ports used for DNS communication with all external servers must be left open to the outside world through the firewall. However, by configuring a DNS server inside a firewall to forward external queries to a single DNS forwarder outside your firewall, and by then opening ports only to this one forwarder, you can resolve names without exposing your network to outside servers. Figure 5-5 illustrates this arrangement.

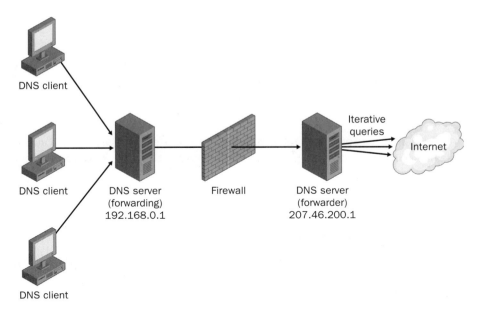

Figure 5-5   Secure iteration with forwarders

Disabling Recursion   The Forwarders tab allows you to disable recursion on any queries, specified by domain, that have been configured to be forwarded to an upstream server. When recursion is not disabled (the default), the local DNS server attempts to resolve a fully qualified domain name (FQDN) after a forwarder has failed to do so. This condition is preferable if you want to optimize settings for fault tolerance: if the upstream forwarder is down, name resolution can fall back to the local DNS server.

However, when under this default setting the forwarder receives the forwarded query and still fails to resolve it, the subsequent fallback recursion that occurs at the local DNS server is usually redundant and delays an inevitable query failure message response. Disabling recursion on queries for which forwarding has been configured thus optimizes the speed of negative query responses at the expense of fault tolerance.

When forwarders are configured this way in combination with disabling recursion, the local DNS server is known as a *slave server* because in these cases, it is completely dependent on the forwarder for queries that it cannot resolve locally.

Note   Do not confuse the use of the term *slave server* with the term *slave zone*, which is used in some implementations of DNS. In some non-Microsoft DNS servers, such as Berkeley Internet Name Domain (BIND), primary zones are called *master zones* and secondary zones are called *slave zones*.

Advanced Tab

The Advanced tab, shown in Figure 5-6, allows you to enable, disable, and configure certain DNS server options and features such as recursion, round robin, automatic scavenging, and netmask ordering. To learn more about the features configurable on this tab, see Lesson 3, "Configuring Advanced DNS Server Properties," in this chapter.

> **Note** Whereas the Forwarders tab allows you to disable recursion on selected queries for domains used with forwarders, the Advanced tab allows you to disable recursion for all queries received by the local DNS server.

> **Note** If you disable recursion on a DNS server using the Advanced tab, you cannot use forwarders on the same server, and the Forwarders tab becomes inactive.

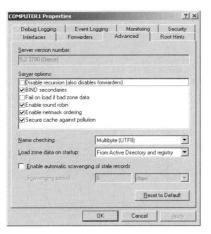

Figure 5-6 Advanced tab

Root Hints Tab

The Root Hints tab contains a copy of the information found in the WINDOWS\System32\Dns\Cache.dns file. For DNS servers answering queries for Internet names, this information does not need to be modified. However, when you are configuring a root DNS server (named ".") for a private network, you should delete the entire Cache.dns file. (When your DNS server is hosting a root server, the Root Hints tab itself is unavailable.)

In addition, if you are configuring a DNS server within a large private namespace, you can use this tab to delete the Internet root servers and specify the root servers in your network instead.

> **Note**   Every few years, the list of root servers on the Internet is slightly modified. Because the Cache.dns file already contains so many possible root servers to contact, it is not necessary to modify the root hints file as soon as these changes occur. However, if you do learn of the availability of new root servers, you can choose to modify your root hints accordingly. As of this writing, the last update to the root servers list was made on November 5, 2002. You can download the latest version of the named cache file from InterNIC at *ftp://rs.internic.net /domain/named.cache*.

Figure 5-7 shows the Root Hints tab.

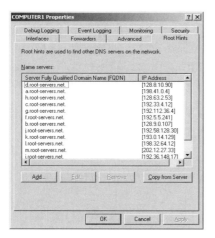

Figure 5-7   Root Hints tab

Debug Logging Tab

The Debug Logging tab allows you to troubleshoot the DNS server by logging the packets it sends and receives. Because logging all packets is resource-intensive, this tab allows you to restrict which packets to log, as specified by transport protocol, source IP address, packet direction, packet type, and packet contents. For more information on this feature, see Lesson 1 of Chapter 6, "Monitoring and Troubleshooting DNS."

Figure 5-8 shows the Debug Logging tab.

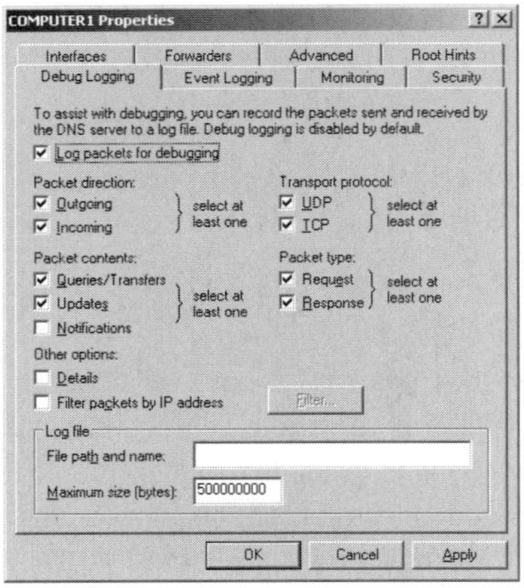

Figure 5-8   Debug Logging tab

Event Logging Tab

You can access the DNS Events log through the Event Viewer node in the DNS console.

The Event Logging tab, shown in Figure 5-9, allows you to restrict the events written to the DNS Events log file to only errors or to only errors and warnings. It also allows you to disable DNS logging. For more powerful features related to the filtering of DNS events, use the Filtering tab of the DNS Events Properties dialog box. You can open this dialog box by selecting Event Viewer in the left pane of the DNS console, right-clicking DNS Events in the right pane, and selecting Properties.

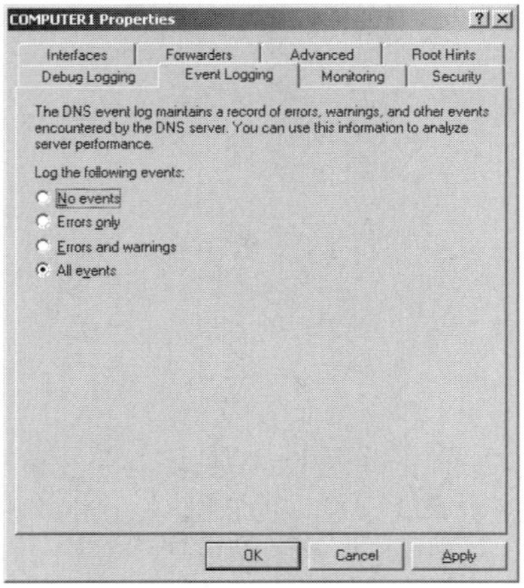

Figure 5-9   Event Logging tab

Monitoring Tab

The Monitoring tab allows you to test basic DNS functionality with two simple tests. The first test is a simple query against the local DNS server. To perform the first test successfully, the server must be able to answer forward and reverse queries targeted at itself.

The second test is a recursive query to the root DNS servers. To perform this second test successfully, the DNS server computer must be able to connect to the root servers specified on the Root Hints tab.

The Monitoring tab, shown in Figure 5-10, also allows you to schedule these tests to be conducted at regular intervals. The results of the tests, whether performed manually or automatically, are shown in the Test Results area of the tab.

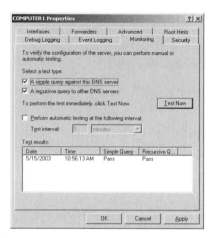

Figure 5-10   Monitoring tab

Security Tab

The Security tab is available only when the DNS server is also a domain controller. This tab allows you to control which users are granted permissions to view, configure, and modify the DNS server and its zones. By clicking the Advanced button, you can further refine settings related to DNS server permissions.

Figure 5-11 shows the Security tab.

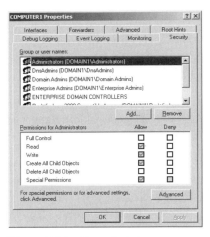

Figure 5-11   Security tab

Practice 1: Comparing NetBIOS and DNS Name Resolution Traffic

In this practice, you perform a capture of name resolution traffic and compare the result to a similar capture that was performed in Lesson 1 of Chapter 4, "Configuring DNS Servers and Clients."

Exercise 1: Capturing Name Resolution Traffic

In this exercise, you perform a Network Monitor capture of name resolution traffic from Computer2 and then compare this capture to one already saved on Computer1.

1. Log on to Computer2 as Administrator.

2. Install Network Monitor on Computer2, as explained in Lesson 1 of Chapter 3, "Monitoring and Troubleshooting TCP/IP Connections."

3. On Computer2, open Network Monitor.

4. If a message box appears requesting that you specify a network on which to capture data, click OK.

   The Select A Network window opens.

5. Select the adapter associated with your internal local area network (LAN), and then click OK.

6. Click the Start Capture button to begin a network trace.

7. Open a command prompt.

   The next two steps force Computer2 to contact Computer1 during the name resolution process.

8. At the prompt, type **nbtstat –R**, and then press Enter. This step clears the cache of any NetBIOS name mappings.

9. At the prompt, type **ipconfig /flushdns**, and then press Enter. This step clears the cache of host (DNS) name mappings.

10. At the command prompt, type **ping computer1**, and then press Enter.

    The ping is successful. Notice how in this output, domain1.local has been appended to "computer1" in the original query.

11. After the Ping output has completed, switch back to Network Monitor, and click Stop And View Capture. The Frame Viewer window opens in Network Monitor, displaying the frames just captured.

12. From the File menu, select Save As to open the Save As dialog box.

13. In the File Name text box, type **Name Resolution 2**.

14. On Computer2, save the file to the My Captures folder.

15. Compare the traffic in the Name Resolution 2 file to the traffic in the Name Resolution 1 file saved in the My Captures folder on Computer1. Then answer the following questions in the spaces provided.

    What is the essential difference between the two captures?

    _____

    _____

    _____

    _____

    _____

    What accounts for the difference in name resolution methods?

    _____

    _____

    _____

16. Close all open windows on Computer1 and Computer2. If prompted to save any open files, click No.

17. Log off Computer1 and Computer2.

Practice 2: Verifying SRV Resource Records for Active Directory in DNS

After you first install the Active Directory directory service, you must verify that the installation has created the proper service location (SRV) resource records in DNS. In this practice, you install an Active Directory domain by promoting Computer1 to the status of domain controller. You then examine the DNS console to verify that the SRV resource records required for the new domain1.local Active Directory domain have been created. Finally, you join Computer2 to the new domain.

Exercise 1: Installing Active Directory

In this exercise, you install Active Directory and promote Computer1 to the status of domain controller in a new domain.

1. Log on to Computer1 as Administrator.

2. Verify that Computer1 is disconnected from the Internet.

3. Click Start, and then click Manage Your Server.

   The Manage Your Server page appears.

4. On the Manage Your Server page, click the Add Or Remove A Role option.

   The Preliminary Steps page of the Configure Your Server Wizard appears.

5. Read the text on the page, and then click Next.

   The Server Role page appears.

6. In the Server Role list, select Domain Controller (Active Directory), and then click Next.

   The Summary Of Selections page appears.

7. Read the text on the page, and then click Next.

   The Welcome page of the Active Directory Installation Wizard appears.

8. Click Next.

   The Operating System Compatibility page appears.

9. Read all of the text on this page, and then answer the following question in the space provided.

   What is the restriction that applies to clients running Microsoft Windows 95 and Microsoft Windows NT 4 SP3 or earlier?

   _____

   _____

10. Click Next.

   The Domain Controller Type page appears.

11. Click Next to accept the default selection, Domain Controller For A New Domain.

   The Create New Domain page appears.

12. Click Next to accept the default selection, Domain In A New Forest.

   The New Domain Name page appears.

13. In the Full DNS Name For New Domain text box, type **domain1.local**, and click Next.

   The NetBIOS Domain Name page appears.

14. Click Next to accept the default selection of DOMAIN1 in the Domain NetBIOS Name text box.

   The Database And Log Folders page appears.

15. Click Next to accept the default selections in the Database Folder text box and the Log Folder text box.

   The Shared System Volume page appears.

16. Click Next to accept the default selection in the Folder Location text box.

   The DNS Registration Diagnostics page appears.

17. Read the diagnostic results, and then click Next.

   The Permissions page appears.

18. Click Next to accept the default selection, Permissions Compatible Only With Windows 2000 Or Windows Server 2003 Operating Systems.

> **Exam Tip**   If you want to continue to use Windows NT 4 RAS on your Active Directory network, you must select the option Permissions Compatible With Pre-Windows 2000 Operating Systems. Otherwise, domain users connecting through RAS cannot be authenticated. To adjust this setting after running the Active Directory Installation Wizard, add the Everyone group to the Pre-Windows 2000 Compatible Access domain local security group. (This adjustment allows the Everyone group read access on all users and groups in the domain.) For the exam, know that to perform this step at a command prompt, you must type the command **net localgroup "pre-windows 2000 compatible access" everyone /add**.

The Directory Services Restore Mode Administrator Password page appears.

19. In the Restore Mode Password text box and the Confirm Password text box, type a strong password.

   This setting specifies that the password you have just entered must be used whenever you log on as Administrator in Directory Services Restore mode.

20. Click Next.

   The Summary page appears.

21. Read the text on the page, and then click Next.

   The Active Directory Installation Wizard window appears while Active Directory is being installed. When installation is complete, the Completing The Active Directory Installation Wizard page appears.

22. Click Finish.

   The Active Directory Installation Wizard dialog box appears, indicating that Windows must be restarted before the changes will take effect.

23. Click Restart Now.

Exercise 2: Verifying SRV Resource Records in DNS

In this exercise, you verify that new SRV resource records have been added to the domain1.local zone.

1. From Computer1, log on to Domain1 as Administrator. Use the same password that you originally assigned to the Computer1 Administrator account.

2. If you see the final page in the Configure Your Server Wizard, indicating that the server is now a domain controller, click Finish.

3. Open the DNS console. Expand the COMPUTER1, Forward Lookup Zones, and the Domain1.local nodes.

   Six subdomains are now listed under Domain1.local. They have been created by the installation of Active Directory.

4. In the DNS console tree, browse to locate an SRV resource record named _ldap._tcp.dc._msdcs.domain1.local. To perform this task, read each label in the name of the resource record from right to left, starting with the Domain1.local node. For example, once you have opened the _msdcs.domain1.local node, open the Dc node, and finally the _tcp node. You see the _ldap service location (SRV) resource record in the details pane when the _tcp node is selected, as shown in Figure 5-12.

Figure 5-12   SRV resource records for a domain controller

This resource record is used to locate domain controllers for the domain1.local domain. It is the most important record to check after you have installed Active Directory.

5. In the DNS console tree, browse to locate an SRV resource record named _ldap._tcp.gc._msdcs.domain1.local.

   This resource record is used to locate Active Directory global catalogs for the domain1.local domain. The records have been created successfully.

6. Log off Computer1.

Exercise 3: Joining a Computer to the New Domain

In this exercise, you join Computer2 to the new domain.

1. Log on to Computer2 as Administrator.

2. In Control Panel, double-click System.

   The System Properties dialog box opens.

3. On the Computer Name tab, click the Change button.

   The Computer Name Changes dialog box opens.

4. In the Member Of area, select Domain.

5. In the Domain text box, type **domain1.local,** and then click OK.

   The Computer Name Changes dialog box opens, prompting you for an account name and password with the permissions to add Computer2 to Domain1.

6. In the User Name text box, type **administrator**.

7. In the Password text box, type the password that you originally assigned to the Administrator account for Computer1. (This password is now the password for the Administrator account in Domain1.)

8. Click OK.

The Computer Name Changes message box appears, welcoming you to the domain1.local domain.

9. Click OK.

A message box indicates that you need to restart the computer for the changes to take effect.

10. Click OK, and then click OK in the System Properties dialog box.

The System Settings Change message box appears, asking whether you want to restart the computer now.

11. Click Yes to restart the computer.

Computer2 restarts.

Lesson Review

The following questions are intended to reinforce key information presented in this lesson. If you are unable to answer a question, review the lesson materials and try the question again. You can find answers to the questions in the "Questions and Answers" section at the end of this chapter.

1. How can you use forwarding to increase security of DNS queries?

_____

_____

_____

_____

_____

_____

2. Using the DNS server properties dialog box, how can you prevent a multihomed DNS server from answering DNS queries received through specific network cards?

_____

_____

3. You administer a network that consists of a single domain. On this network, you have configured a new DNS server named DNS1 to answer queries for Internet names from the local domain. However, although DNS1 is connected to the Internet, it continues to fail its recursive test on the Monitoring tab of the server properties dialog box. Which of the following could be the potential cause for the failure?

   a. You have configured DNS1 in front of a firewall.

   b. DNS1 hosts a zone named "."

   c. Your root hints have not been modified from the defaults.

   d. You have not configured DNS1 to forward any queries to upstream servers.

4. Which of the following events could serve as a legitimate reason to modify (but not delete) the default root hints on the Root Hints tab of a DNS server properties dialog box? (Choose all that apply.)

   a. The Internet root servers have changed.

   b. The server will not be used as a root server.

   c. You have disabled recursion on the server.

   d. Your server is not used to resolve Internet names.

Lesson Summary

■ The Interfaces tab of the DNS server properties dialog box allows you to specify which of the local computer's IP addresses the DNS server should listen to for DNS requests.

■ The Forwarders tab of the DNS server properties dialog box allows you to forward DNS queries received by the local DNS server to upstream DNS servers, called forwarders. This tab also allows you to disable recursion for select queries (as specified by domain).

■ By configuring a DNS server inside a firewall to forward external queries to a single DNS forwarder outside your firewall, and by then opening ports through the firewall only to this one forwarder, you can resolve DNS names without exposing your network to outside servers.

■ The Root Hints tab provides a simple way to modify the contents in the Cache.dns file. If you are using your DNS server to resolve Internet names, you do not normally need to modify these entries. However, if you are using your DNS server only to answer queries for hosts in a separate and private DNS namespace, you should alter these root hints to point to the root servers in your network. Finally, if your DNS server computer is itself the root server (named ".") of your private namespace, you should delete the Cache.dns file.

■ The Monitoring tab of the DNS server properties dialog box allows you to check basic DNS functionality with two simple tests: a simple query against the local DNS server, and a recursive query to the root DNS servers.

Lesson 2: Configuring Zone Properties and Transfers

You can perform many essential tasks related to administering and managing a DNS infrastructure through the properties dialog boxes of your network's hosted zones. These tasks include configuring and managing zone transfers, enabling dynamic updates, and modifying zone types.

After this lesson, you will be able to

- Configure a DNS zone for dynamic updates
- Change the DNS zone type
- Store zone data in the Active Directory database
- Add name server (NS) resource records to a zone
- Configure zone transfers from secondary zones
- Describe the events that can trigger a zone transfer
- Describe the process of a zone transfer

Estimated lesson time: 70 minutes

Exploring DNS Zone Properties

The primary means to configure zone settings is through the zone properties dialog box, which is accessible through the DNS console. Each properties dialog box for a standard zone has five tabs: General, Start Of Authority (SOA), Name Servers, WINS, and Zone Transfers. Properties dialog boxes for Active Directory–integrated zones include a sixth tab, Security, that allows you to configure access permissions for the zone.

To open a properties dialog box for a particular zone, right-click the node of the zone you want to configure in the DNS console, and then select Properties, as shown in Figure 5-13.

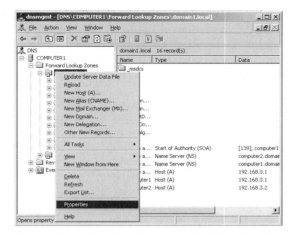

Figure 5-13   Opening the properties dialog box for a zone

General Tab

The General tab, shown in Figure 5-14, allows you to temporarily suspend name resolution and to configure four basic features: zone type (including Active Directory integration), zone file name, dynamic updates, and aging.

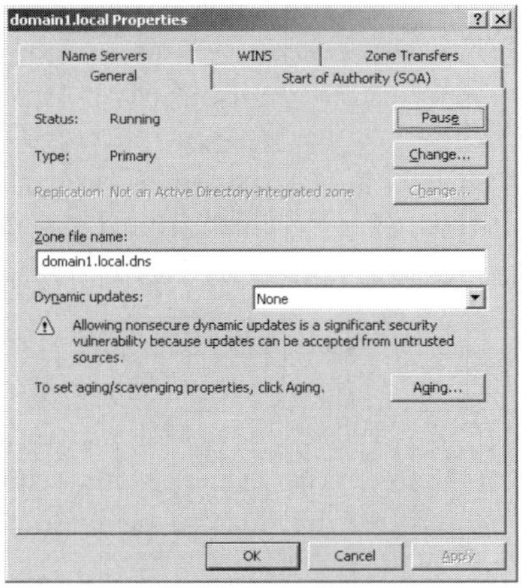

Figure 5-14   General tab

Zone Status   The Pause button allows you to pause and resume name resolution for the zone. Note that this feature does not allow you to pause or resume the DNS Server service.

Zone Type   Clicking Change opens the Change Zone Type dialog box, as shown in Figure 5-15.

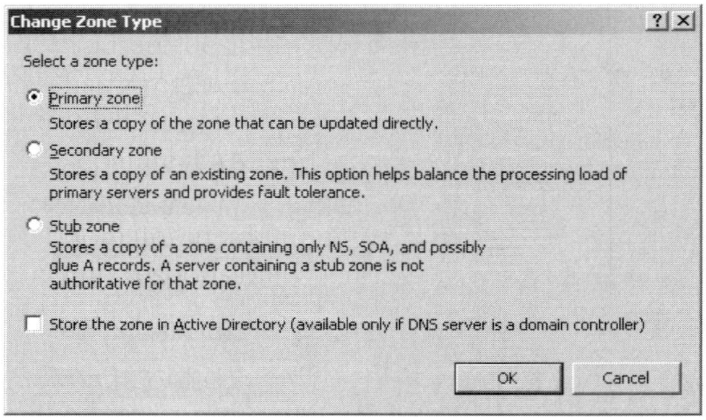

Figure 5-15   Change Zone Type dialog box

The Change Zone Type dialog box allows you to reconfigure the zone as a primary, secondary, or stub zone. A *primary zone* stores the most current records and settings for the zone. For each standard zone that is not Active Directory–integrated, only one primary DNS server is allowed, and this server contains the only read/write version of the zone database. A *secondary zone* is a read-only copy of the primary zone used to improve performance and fault tolerance. A *stub zone* is a copy of a zone that contains only those resource records necessary to identify the actual authoritative DNS servers for that zone. (Stub zones are discussed in more detail in Lesson 5 of this chapter.)

Active Directory Service Integration   Selecting the Store The Zone In Active Directory check box in the Change Zone Type dialog box allows you to store the primary zone information in the Active Directory database instead of in the WINDOWS\System32\Dns folder. In Active Directory–integrated zones, zone data is replicated through Active Directory. In most cases, this eliminates the need to configure zone transfers to secondary servers.

> **Exam Tip**   To migrate a standard primary server, configure a secondary server, transfer the zone to the secondary server, and then promote the secondary server to a primary server. After the secondary server has been promoted, you can delete the original primary server.

There are several advantages to integrating your DNS zone with Active Directory. First, because Active Directory performs zone replication, you do not need to configure a separate mechanism for DNS zone transfers. Fault tolerance, along with improved performance from the availability of multiple read/write primary servers, is automatically supplied by the presence of multimaster replication on your network. Second, Active Directory allows for single properties of resource records to be updated and replicated among DNS servers. Avoiding the transfer of many and complete resource records decreases the load on network resources during zone transfers. Finally, Active Directory integration allows you to configure access security for stored records, which prevents unauthorized updates.

Planning   If you can deploy an Active Directory–integrated zone, do. It reduces administrative headache, improves security, and minimizes zone transfer traffic. Because of these advantages, you should plan to use a standard primary or secondary zone only when you want to deploy a DNS server on a computer that is not an Active Directory domain controller.

Zone Replication   When you opt to store zone information in the Active Directory database, the associated Change button becomes enabled, as shown in Figure 5-16. This button allows you to configure replication parameters for the Active Directory–integrated zone.

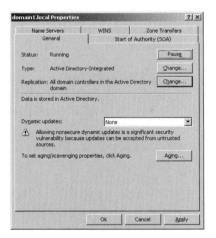

Figure 5-16   Change button for zone replication

Clicking the Change button opens the Change Zone Replication Scope dialog box, shown in Figure 5-17. This dialog box allows you to determine among which servers in the Active Directory forest the zone data should be replicated.

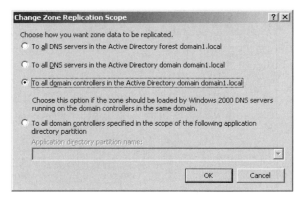

Figure 5-17   Setting the zone replication scope

Table 5-1 describes the four options available in this dialog box.

Table 5-1   Zone Replication Options

Options	Description
To All DNS Servers In The Active Directory Forest	Replicates zone data to all DNS servers running on domain controllers in the Active Directory forest. Usually, this option provides the broadest scope of replication.
To All DNS Servers In The Active Directory Domain	Replicates zone data to all DNS servers running on domain controllers in the Active Directory domain.
To All Domain Controllers In The Active Directory Domain	Replicates zone data to all domain controllers in the Active Directory domain. If you want Microsoft Windows 2000 DNS servers to load an Active Directory zone, you must select this setting for that zone.
To All Domain Controllers Specified In The Scope Of The Following Application Directory Partition	Replicates zone data according to the replication scope of the specified application directory partition. For a zone to be stored in the specified application directory partition, the DNS server hosting the zone must be enlisted in the specified application directory partition.

When deciding which replication option to choose, consider that the broader the replication scope, the greater the network traffic caused by replication. For example, if you choose to have Active Directory–integrated DNS zone data replicated to all DNS servers in the forest, this setting produces greater network traffic than does replicating the DNS zone data to all DNS servers in a single Active Directory domain in that forest. On the other hand, replicating zone data to all DNS servers in a forest can improve forestwide name resolution performance and increase fault tolerance.

Application Directory Partitions and DNS Replication   An *application directory partition* is a directory partition that is replicated among a specified subset of domain controllers running Windows Server 2003.

- Built-in application directory partitions

    For DNS, two built-in application directory partitions exist for each Active Directory domain: DomainDnsZones and ForestDnsZones. The DomainDnsZones application directory partition is replicated among all DNS servers that are also domain controllers in an Active Directory domain. The ForestDnsZones application directory partition is replicated among all DNS servers that are also domain controllers in an Active Directory forest. Each of these application directory partitions is designated by a DNS subdomain and an FQDN. For example, in an Active Directory domain named bern.lucernepublishing.com whose root domain in the Active Directory forest is lucernepublishing.com, the built-in DNS application partition directories are specified by these FQDNs: DomainDnsZones.bern.lucernepublishing.com and ForestDnsZones.lucernepublishing.com.

    When you select the To All DNS Servers In The Active Directory Forest option in the Change Zone Replication Scope dialog box, you are in fact choosing to store DNS zone data in the ForestDnsZones application directory partition. When you select the To All DNS Servers In The Active Directory Domain option, you are choosing to store DNS zone data in the DomainDnsZones application directory partition.

> **Note**   If either of these application directory partitions is deleted or damaged, you can recreate them in the DNS console by right-clicking the server node and selecting Create Default Application Directory Partitions.

- Creating custom application directory partitions

    You can also create your own custom application directory partitions for use with DNS and enlist chosen domain controllers in your network to host replicas of this partition.

    To accomplish this task, first create the partition by typing the following command:

    dnscmd [*servername*] /createdirectorypartition *FQDN*

    Then enlist other DNS servers in the partition by typing the following command:

    dnscmd *servername* /enlistdirectorypartition *FQDN*

    For example, to create an application directory partition named SpecialDns on a computer named Server1 in the Active Directory domain contoso.com, type the following command:

    dnscmd server1 /createdirectorypartition SpecialDns.contoso.com

To enlist a computer named Server2 in the application directory partition, type the following command:

dnscmd server2 /enlistdirectorypartition SpecialDns.contoso.com

> **Note** You must be a member of the Enterprise Admins group to create an application directory partition.

To store DNS data in a custom application directory partition, select the fourth (bottom) option in the Change Zone Replication Scope dialog box, and specify the custom application directory partition in the drop-down list box. This option—To All Domain Controllers Specified In The Scope Of The Following Application Directory Partition—is available only if custom application directory partitions are available for DNS on your network.

- Replication with Windows 2000 servers

  Because application directory partitions are not available on Windows 2000 domain controllers, you must select the third option in the Change Zone Replication Scope dialog box if you want the zone data to be read by Windows 2000 DNS servers. With this option—To All Domain Controllers In the Active Directory Domain—data is not replicated merely among all DNS server domain controllers, but among all domain controllers regardless of whether they are also DNS servers.

> **Exam Tip** Expect to be tested on application directory partition concepts and commands, as well as the options in the Change Zone Replication Scope dialog box.

Zone File Name For standard zones not stored in Active Directory, the default zone filename is created by adding a .dns extension to the zone name. The Zone File Name text box on the General tab allows you to change the default name of this file.

Dynamic Updates The General tab also allows you to configure a zone with dynamic updates in resource records. As shown in Figure 5-18, three dynamic update settings are available for Active Directory–integrated DNS zones: None, Nonsecure And Secure, and Secure Only. For standard zones, only two settings are available: None and Nonsecure And Secure.

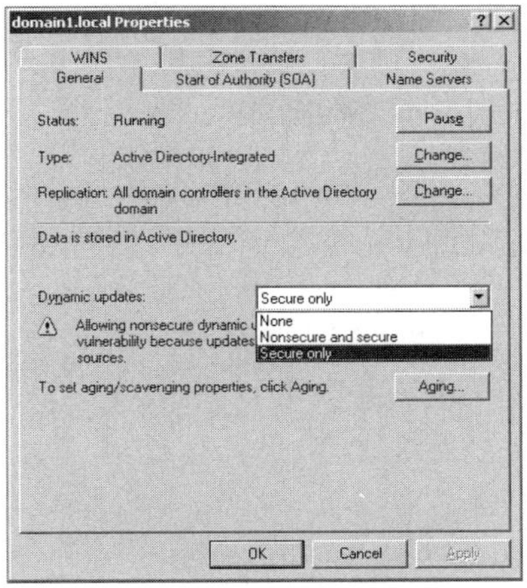

Figure 5-18   Zone settings for dynamic updates

When you select the None setting in the properties for a zone, you must manually per-form registrations and updates to zone records. However, when you enable either the Nonsecure And Secure setting or the Secure Only setting, client computers can auto-matically create or update their own resource records. This functionality greatly reduces the need for manual administration of zone records, especially for DHCP cli-ents and roaming clients.

Figure 5-19 shows a typical dynamic update process.

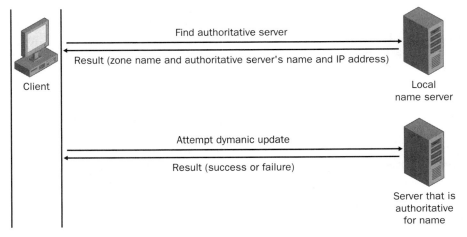

Figure 5-19   Dynamic update process

Whenever a triggering event occurs on a DNS client computer, the DHCP Client service, not the DNS Client service, attempts to perform a dynamic update of the A resource record with the DNS server. This update process is designed so that if a change to the IP address information occurs because of DHCP, this update is immediately sent to the DNS server. The DHCP Client service attempts to perform this dynamic update function for all network connections used on the system, including those not configured to use DHCP. Whether this attempt at a dynamic update is successful depends first and foremost on whether the zone has been configured to allow dynamic updates.

Dynamic Update Triggers   The following events trigger the DHCP Client service to send a dynamic update to the DNS server:

- An IP address is added, removed, or modified in the Transmission Control Protocol/Internet Protocol (TCP/IP) properties configuration for any one of the local computer's installed network connections.

- An IP address lease changes or renews with the DHCP server for any one of the local computer's installed network connections—for example, when the computer is started or if the Ipconfig /renew command is used.

- The Ipconfig /registerdns command is used on a DNS client computer to manually force a refresh of the client name registration in DNS.

- The DNS client computer is turned on.

- A member server within the zone is promoted to a domain controller.

Secure Dynamic Updates   Secure dynamic updates can be performed only in Active Directory–integrated zones. For standard zones, the Secure Only option does not appear in the Dynamic Updates drop-down list box. These updates use the secure Kerberos authentication protocol to create a secure context and ensure that the client updating the resource record is the owner of that record.

> **Note**   Only clients running a version of Windows 2000, Microsoft Windows XP, or Windows Server 2003 can attempt to send dynamic updates to a DNS server. Dynamic updates are not available for any version of Windows NT, Windows 95, Microsoft Windows 98, or Microsoft Windows Millennium Edition (Me). However, a DNS client computer (such as a DHCP server) can perform dynamic updates on behalf of other clients if the server is configured to do so.

- Secure Dynamic Updates and the DnsUpdateProxy group

    When only secure dynamic updates are allowed in a zone, only the owner of a record can update that record. (The owner of a record is the computer that originally registers the record.) This restriction can cause problems in situations where a DHCP server is being used to register host (A) resource records on behalf of client computers that cannot perform dynamic updates. In such cases, the DHCP server becomes the owner of the record, not the computers themselves. If the downlevel client computer is later upgraded to Windows 2000 or some other operating system that is capable of performing dynamic updates, the computer will not be recognized as the owner and will consequently be unable to update its own records. A similar problem might arise if a DHCP server fails that has registered records on behalf of downlevel clients: none of the clients will be able to have their records updated by a backup DHCP server.

To avoid such problems, add to the DnsUpdateProxy security group DHCP servers that register records on behalf of other computers. Members of this group are prevented from recording ownership on the resource records they update in DNS. This procedure consequently loosens security for these records until they can be registered by the real owner.

> **Exam Tip**   Expect to be tested on DnsUpdateProxy on the exam.

Aging   By clicking Aging on the General tab, you can open the Zone Aging/Scavenging Properties dialog box, shown in Figure 5-20. These properties provide a means of finding and clearing outdated records from the zone database.

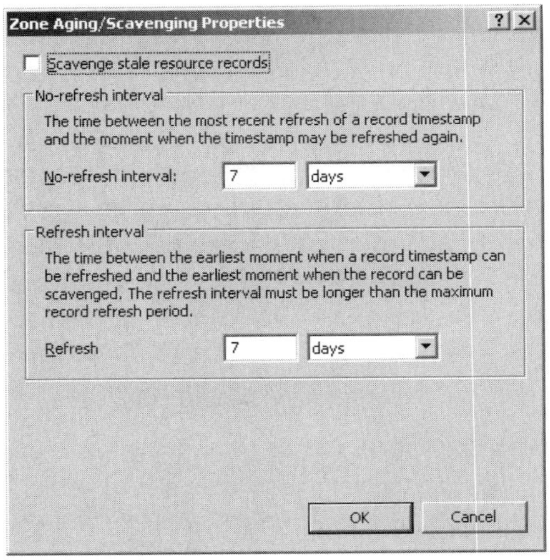

Zone Aging/Scavenging Properties   ? X

☐ Scavenge stale resource records

No-refresh interval

The time between the most recent refresh of a record timestamp and the moment when the timestamp may be refreshed again.

No-refresh interval: [7]   [days ▼]

Refresh interval

The time between the earliest moment when a record timestamp can be refreshed and the earliest moment when the record can be scavenged. The refresh interval must be longer than the maximum record refresh period.

Refresh   [7]   [days ▼]

[OK]   [Cancel]

Figure 5-20   Zone Aging/Scavenging Properties dialog box

Enabling Aging   *Aging* in DNS refers to the process of placing a timestamp on a dynamically registered resource record and then tracking the age of this record. *Scavenging* refers to the process of deleting outdated resource records on which timestamps have been placed. Scavenging can occur only when aging is enabled. Both aging and scavenging are disabled by default.

To enable aging for a particular zone, you have to enable this feature both at the zone level and at the server level. To enable aging at the zone level, in the Zone Aging/Scavenging Properties dialog box, select the Scavenge Stale Resource Records check box. To enable aging at the server level, first open the Server Aging/Scavenging Properties dialog box by right-clicking the server icon in the DNS console and then clicking Set Aging/Scavenging For All Zones. Then, in the Server Aging/Scavenging Properties dialog box, select the Scavenge Stale Resource Records check box.

After aging is enabled, a timestamp based on the current server time is placed on all dynamically registered records in the zone. When the DHCP Client service or DHCP server later performs a dynamic update of the records, a timestamp refresh is attempted. Manually created resource records are assigned a timestamp of 0; this value indicates that they will not be aged.

> **Note**   When aging and scavenging are enabled for a zone, zone files cannot be read by pre-Windows 2000 DNS servers.

Modifying no-refresh intervals   The *no-refresh interval* is the period after a timestamp during which a zone or server rejects a timestamp refresh. The no-refresh feature prevents unnecessary refreshes from being processed by the server and reduces unnecessary zone transfer traffic. The default no-refresh interval is seven days.

Modifying refresh intervals   The *refresh interval* is the time after the no-refresh interval during which timestamp refreshes are accepted and resource records are not scavenged. After the no-refresh and refresh intervals expire, records can be scavenged from the zone. The default refresh interval is 7 days. Consequently, when aging is enabled, dynamically registered resource records can be scavenged after 14 days by default.

> **Tip**   If you modify the no-refresh or refresh interval, be sure to follow the guideline that the refresh interval should be equal to or greater than the no-refresh interval.

Performing Scavenging   Scavenging in a zone is performed either automatically or manually. For scavenging to be performed automatically, you must enable automatic scavenging of stale resource records on the Advanced tab of DNS server properties. When this feature is not enabled, you can perform manual scavenging in a zone by right-clicking the server icon in the DNS console tree and then selecting Scavenge Stale Resource Records from the shortcut menu.

Start Of Authority (SOA) Tab

The Start Of Authority (SOA) tab, shown in Figure 5-21, allows you to configure the SOA resource record for the zone. When a DNS server loads a zone, it uses the SOA resource record to determine basic, authoritative information about the zone. These settings also determine how often zone transfers are performed between primary and secondary servers.

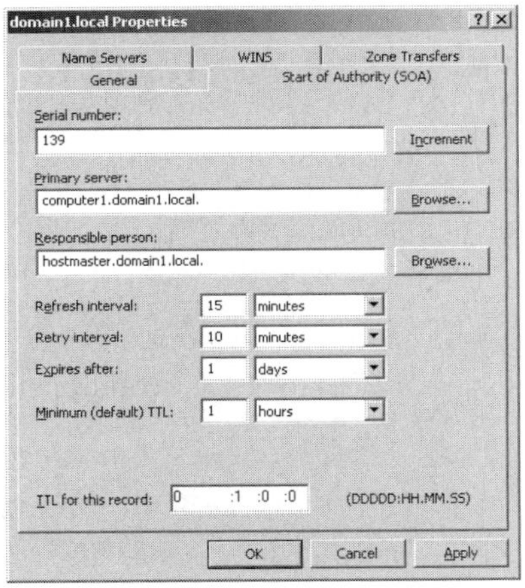

Figure 5-21   Start Of Authority (SOA) tab

Serial Number   The Serial Number text box on the Start Of Authority (SOA) tab contains the revision number of the zone file. This number increases each time a resource record changes in the zone or when the value is manually incremented on this tab by clicking Increment.

When zones are configured to perform zone transfers, the master server is intermittently queried for the serial number of the zone. This query is called the *SOA query*. If, through the SOA query, the serial number of the master zone is determined to be equivalent to the local serial number, no transfer is made. However, if the serial number for the zone at the master server is greater than that at the requesting secondary server, the secondary server initiates a transfer.

Primary Server   The Primary Server text box on the Start Of Authority (SOA) tab contains the full computer name for the primary DNS server of the zone. This name must end with a period.

Responsible Person   When this text box is configured, it contains a responsible person (RP) resource record of the person responsible for administering the zone. An RP resource record specifies a domain mailbox name for the responsible person. The name of the record entered into this field should always end with a period.

Refresh Interval   The value you configure in the Refresh Interval field determines how long a secondary DNS server waits before querying the master server for a zone renewal. When the refresh interval expires, the secondary DNS server requests a copy of the current SOA resource record for the zone from its master server source, which then answers this SOA query. The secondary DNS server then compares the serial number of the source server's current SOA resource record (as indicated in the master's response) with the serial number of its own local SOA resource record. If they are different, the secondary DNS server requests a zone transfer from the primary DNS server. The default value for this setting is 15 minutes.

> **Exam Tip**   Increasing the refresh interval decreases zone transfer traffic.

Retry Interval   The value you configure in the Retry Interval box determines how long a secondary server waits before retrying a failed zone transfer. Normally, this time is less than the refresh interval. The default value is 10 minutes.

Expires After   The value you configure in the Expires After box determines the length of time that a secondary server, without any contact with its master server, continues to answer queries from DNS clients. After this time elapses, the data is considered unreliable. The default value is 1 day.

Minimum (Default) TTL   The value you configure in the Minimum (Default) TTL box determines the default Time to Live (TTL) that is applied to all resource records in the zone. The default value is 1 hour.

TTL values are not relevant for resource records within their authoritative zones. Instead, the TTL refers to the cache life of a resource record in nonauthoritative servers. A DNS server that has cached a resource record from a previous query discards the record when that record's TTL has expired.

> **Exam Tip**   If you have deployed caching-only servers in your network in addition to a primary server, increasing the minimum TTL can decrease name resolution traffic between the caching-only servers and the primary server.

TTL For This Record   The value you configure in this text box determines the TTL of the present SOA resource record. This value overrides the default value setting in the preceding field.

Once configured in the DNS console, an SOA resource record is represented textually in the zone file, as shown in this example:

```
@IN SOA computer1.domain1.local. hostmaster.domain1.local. (
  5099    ; serial number
  3600    ; refresh (1 hour)
  600     ; retry (10 mins)
  86400   ; expire (1 day)
  60   )  ; minimum TTL (1 min)
```

Name Servers Tab

The Name Servers tab, shown in Figure 5-22, allows you to configure NS resource records for a zone. These records cannot be created elsewhere in the DNS console.

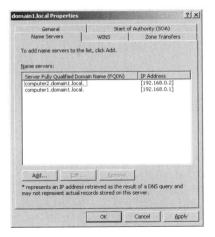

Figure 5-22   Name Servers tab

You use NS resource records to specify the authoritative name servers for a given zone. The NS resource record of the first primary server of a zone is configured automatically.

Note   Every zone must contain at least one NS resource record at the zone root.

The following line is an example NS record taken from the database file for the lucernepublishing.com zone:

```
@ NS  dns1.lucernepublishing.com.
```

In this record, the "@" symbol represents the zone defined by the SOA record in the same zone file. The complete entry, then, effectively maps the lucernepublishing.com domain to a DNS server hosted on a computer named dns1.lucernepublishing.com.

> **Exam Tip** In primary zones, zone transfers by default are allowed only to servers specified on the Name Servers tab. This restriction is new to Windows Server 2003.

WINS Tab

You use the WINS tab, shown in Figure 5-23—or the WINS-R tab in reverse lookup zones—to configure Windows Internet Name Service (WINS) servers to aid in name resolution for a given zone after DNS servers have failed to resolve a queried name.

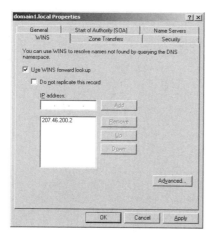

Figure 5-23 WINS tab

> **Exam Tip** When you configure WINS lookup for a forward lookup zone, a WINS resource record pointing to the WINS server you specify on the WINS tab is added to the zone database. When you configure WINS-R lookup for a reverse lookup zone, a corresponding WINS-R resource record is added to the zone database.

Zone Transfers Tab

The Zone Transfers tab, shown in Figure 5-24, allows you to restrict zone transfers from the local master server. For primary zones, zone transfers to secondary servers by default are either completely disabled or limited to name servers configured on the Name Servers tab. The former restriction applies when the DNS server has been added by using the Manage Your Server window; the latter, when it has been added by using the Windows Components Wizard. As an alternative to these default restrictions, you can customize zone transfer restrictions by selecting the Only To The Following Servers option and then specifying the IP addresses of allowed secondary servers in the list below this option.

Secondary zones by default do not allow zone transfers to other secondary zones, but you can enable this feature simply by selecting the Allow Zone Transfers check box.

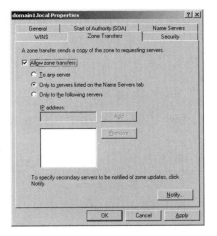

Figure 5-24   Zone Transfers tab

Off the Record   In Windows 2000, the default setting on the Zone Transfers tab for primary zones was to allow transfers to any server, but this feature created an unnecessary security hole. Think about it: why would you want to enable anyone who can access your DNS server to set up a secondary server and peruse your network's resource records? Restricting zone transfers by default is a lot smarter—it allows you to prevent unauthorized copying of zone data.

Notification   The Zone Transfers tab also allows you to configure notification to secondary servers. To perform this task, click Notify on the Zone Transfers tab when zone transfers are enabled. This action opens the Notify dialog box, as shown in Figure 5-25, in which you can specify secondary servers that should be notified whenever a zone update occurs at the local master server. By default, when zone transfers are enabled, all servers listed on the Name Servers tab are automatically notified of zone changes.

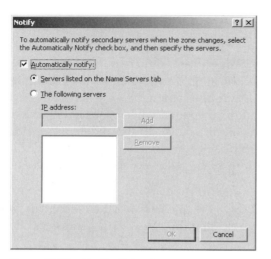

Figure 5-25   Notify dialog box

Notification and Zone Transfer Initiation   Zone transfers in standard zones can be triggered by any of three events:

- They can be triggered when the refresh interval of the primary zone's SOA resource record expires.

- They can be triggered when a secondary server boots up.

  In these first two cases, the secondary server initiates an SOA query to find out whether any updates in the zone have occurred. Transfers occur only if the zone database has been revised.

- They are triggered when a change occurs in the configuration of the primary server and this server has specified particular secondary DNS servers to be notified of zone updates.

When a zone transfer initiates, the secondary server performs either an incremental zone transfer (IXFR) query or an all zone transfer (AXFR) query to the master server. Computers running Windows 2000 Server and Windows Server 2003 perform IXFR queries by default. Through IXFR queries, only the newly modified data is transferred across the network. Computers running Windows NT Server do not support IXFR queries and can perform only AXFR queries. Through AXFR queries, the entire zone database is transferred to the secondary server.

Primary DNS servers running Windows Server 2003 support both IXFR and AXFR zone transfers.

Figure 5-26 illustrates the transfer query process between secondary and master servers.

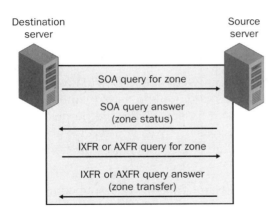

Figure 5-26   Zone transfer negotiations

Note   You do not need to configure zone transfers or notification among domain controllers or DNS servers in Active Directory–integrated zones. For the servers within these zones, transfers are conducted automatically.

Practice: Deploying a Secondary DNS Server

In this practice, you create a secondary zone and then configure zone transfers between the two zones.

Exercise 1: Configuring a Secondary Zone

In this exercise, you install a DNS server on Computer2 and then configure the new DNS server to host a secondary zone.

Important   The following exercise assumes that you have installed the DNS server on Computer1 by using the Windows Components Wizard (as described in Chapter 4, Lesson 3). In this case, zone transfers from the Domain1.local zone are enabled by default but restricted to authoritative name servers. If instead you have installed the DNS server on Computer1 by using the Manage Your Server window to add the DNS server role, zone transfers for all locally hosted zones are disabled by default. In this case, before beginning this exercise, be sure to enable zone transfers for the Domain1.local zone and restrict zone transfers to servers listed on the Name Servers tab.

1. From Computer2, log on to Domain1 as Administrator. Remember to specify the password you originally assigned to the Administrator account on Computer1.

2. On Computer2, install the Windows Support Tools, as explained in Lesson 2 of Chapter 3, "Monitoring and Troubleshooting TCP/IP Connections."

Windows Support Tools includes the Dnscmd command-line utility.

3. On Computer2, install the Domain Name System (DNS) Windows subcomponent of the Networking Services Windows component, as explained in Lesson 3 of Chapter 4, "Configuring DNS Servers and Clients." For the purposes of this exercise, you can safely dismiss any messages or errors you receive about Computer2 having a dynamically assigned IP address. Do not change the address configuration on Computer2.

4. Once the installation of the Domain Name System (DNS) subcomponent is complete, open a command prompt.

5. At the command prompt, enter the following command: **dnscmd computer1 /recordadd domain1.local @ ns computer2.domain1.local**.

This command adds an NS record in domain1.local for Computer2, which makes Computer2 an authoritative server in the zone. By default, when a DNS server has been installed by using the Windows Components Wizard, zone transfers are allowed only to authoritative servers.

6. On Computer2, open the DNS console.

7. In the DNS console tree, right-click Forward Lookup Zones and select New Zone.

8. In the New Zone Wizard, click Next.

9. On the Zone Type page, select the Secondary Zone option, and then click Next.

10. On the Zone Name page, in the Zone Name text box, type **domain1.local** and then click Next.

11. In the Master DNS Server page, in the IP Address text box, type **192.168.0.1**, click Add, and then click Next.

12. On the Completing The New Zone Wizard page, click Finish.

13. In the DNS console tree, expand Forward Lookup Zones and select the Domain1.local node.

14. Right-click the Domain1.local node, and then select Transfer From Master.

15. If the zone fails to load, wait 1 minute and then try again. Repeat this step until the zone loads successfully.

16. When a copy of the domain1.local zone appears in the DNS console on Computer2, take a few moments to browse the zone properties dialog box and the items on the zone's Action (shortcut) menu.

17. Right-click the DNS node in the DNS console, and then click Connect To DNS Server.

The Connect To DNS Server dialog box opens.

18. Select the option The Following Computer, and then type **COMPUTER1** in the associated text box.

19. Click OK. The COMPUTER1 node now appears above the COMPUTER2 node in the DNS console. Use both server nodes in the DNS console on Computer2 to answer the following questions in the spaces provided.

    Which functions on the Action menu are available for the domain1.local zone through the COMPUTER2 node that are not available on the Action menu for the same zone through the COMPUTER1 node?

    _____

    Can you create or configure resource records for domain1.local through the COMPUTER2 node in the DNS console?

    _____

    _____

Exercise 2: Reviewing Notification Settings

In this exercise, you review the default configuration for zone transfer notification.

1. From Computer2, while you are logged on to Domain1 as Administrator, expand the COMPUTER1 icon in the DNS console, and then open the Domain1.local Properties dialog box associated with this primary zone.

2. Click the Name Servers tab.

    Computer2 has been added as a result of adding an NS command in Exercise 1, "Configuring a Secondary Zone."

3. On the Zone Transfers tab, click Notify. The Notify dialog box opens.

    By default, the primary zone automatically notifies the servers listed on the Name Servers tab of zone changes.

    Because Computer2 is now configured on the Name Servers tab, the secondary server is notified of any zone changes. When Computer2 receives notification from the primary server, this secondary DNS server normally initiates an IXFR query for an incremental zone transfer.

4. Click Cancel.

5. In the Domain1.local Properties dialog box, click the Start Of Authority (SOA) tab. Using the settings configured on this tab, answer the following questions in the spaces provided.

According to the settings on the Start Of Authority (SOA) tab, if Computer2 loses contact with Computer1, how long will the DNS server on Computer2 continue to answer queries from DNS clients?

_____

How often is Computer2 configured to query Computer1 to find out whether any changes have been made to the zone?

_____

If Computer2 discovers it cannot contact Computer1 when it initiates an SOA query, how long does it wait before trying again?

_____

If another primary DNS server named dns.domain2.local successfully queries Computer1 for the IP address of Computer2, how long does Computer2's A resource record stay alive in the cache of dns.domain2.local?

_____

6. Click OK to close the Domain1.local Properties dialog box.

7. In the DNS Console, right-click the Computer1 icon, and then click Delete.

   A DNS message box appears asking you to confirm the deletion.

8. In the DNS message box, click Yes.

   Computer1 is removed from the DNS console on Computer2, but the server settings remain intact in the DNS console on Computer1.

9. Log off Computer2.

Lesson Review

The following questions are intended to reinforce key information presented in this lesson. If you are unable to answer a question, review the lesson materials and try the question again. You can find answers to the questions in the "Questions and Answers" section at the end of this chapter.

1. Describe the process by which secondary servers determine whether a zone transfer should be initiated.

   _____

   _____

   _____

   _____

2. What is the difference between IXFR and AXFR queries?

_____

_____

_____

_____

3. You have multiple DHCP servers on your network, some of which are configured to register DNS records on behalf of pre-Windows 2000 clients. You have configured DNS to allow only secure updates. However, you find that some DNS records are not being updated properly. How can you solve this problem?

_____

4. You oversee administration for a wide area network (WAN) belonging to the Proseware company, which has one central office in Rochester and two branch offices in Buffalo and Syracuse. The network, which consists of one domain, has one primary DNS zone running on a Windows Server 2003 computer at the central office, and one secondary DNS zone at each branch. Network users are complaining that they often cannot connect to sites at remote branches. Administrators have determined that network bandwidth between the central office and branches has become saturated with zone transfers, and that zone transfers are being initiated before they can complete. Which of the following steps would help resolve the problem with the least effort?

    a. Install Active Directory on the network, and promote the servers hosting the secondary DNS zones to domain controllers.

    b. Increase the network bandwidth by establishing a fiber-optic connection between the two sites.

    c. Increase the refresh interval on the primary DNS server.

    d. Increase the refresh interval on the secondary DNS servers.

5. You discover that an administrator has adjusted the default TTL value for your company's primary DNS zone to 5 minutes. Which of the following is the most likely effect of this change?

    a. Resource records cached on the primary DNS server expire after 5 minutes.

    b. DNS clients have to query the server more frequently to resolve names for which the server is authoritative.

    c. Secondary servers initiate a zone transfer every 5 minutes.

    d. DNS hosts reregister their records more frequently.

6. Which of the following is not a benefit of storing DNS zones in the Active Directory database?

   a. Less frequent transfers

   b. Decreased need for administration

   c. Less saturation of network bandwidth

   d. Secure dynamic updates

Lesson Summary

- When you deploy a DNS server on a domain controller, you can choose to store the zone data in the Active Directory database. Active Directory–integrated zones minimize zone transfer traffic, improve security, decrease administrative overhead, and improve fault tolerance. Zone data can be configured to be replicated among all DNS servers in the Active Directory forest, among all DNS servers in the Active Directory domain, among all domain controllers in the Active Directory domain, or among all servers enlisted in a custom application directory partition.

- When a DNS zone allows dynamic updates, certain DNS client computers can register and update their resource records with a DNS server. When secure dynamic updates are required in the zone, only the owner of the record can update the record. Secure dynamic updates can be required only on Active Directory–integrated zones. Client computers running Windows 2000, Windows XP, and Windows Server 2003 can perform dynamic updates.

- The DnsUpdateProxy group is typically used for DHCP servers performing dynamic DNS updates on behalf of other computers. Members of this group do not record ownership on the resource records they register in DNS. This behavior restriction prevents problems from arising in zones that allow only secure dynamic updates.

- The Start Of Authority (SOA) tab allows you to configure the zone's SOA resource record and several parameters that affect zone transfers, such as Refresh Interval, Retry Interval, Expires After, and Minimum (Default) TTL.

- The Zone Transfers tab allows you to control transfers from the current zone. By default, zone transfers are either completely disabled or limited to servers specified on the Name Servers tab. The nature of this restriction depends on the zone type and the manner in which the DNS server has been installed.

Lesson 3: Configuring Advanced DNS Server Properties

Advanced DNS server properties refer to the nine settings that can be configured on the Advanced tab of the DNS server properties dialog box. These properties relate to server-specific features such recursion, round robin, and netmask ordering.

After this lesson, you will be able to

- ■ Describe the function and purpose of all of the options available for configuration on the Advanced tab of the DNS server properties dialog box
- ■ Reset all advanced server settings to defaults

Estimated lesson time: 50 minutes

Tuning Advanced Server Options

When initialized for service, DNS servers running on Windows Server 2003 apply installation settings taken either from the boot information file, the Registry, or the Active Directory database. You can modify these settings on the Advanced tab of the server properties dialog box in the DNS console, as shown in Figure 5-27.

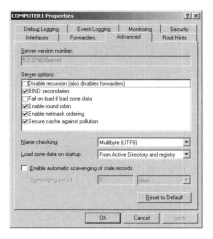

Figure 5-27   DNS server properties Advanced tab

The server installation settings include six server options, which are either on or off, and three other server features with various selections for configuration. Table 5-2 shows the default settings for all nine features.

Table 5-2   Default DNS Installation Settings

Property	Setting
Disable Recursion	Off
BIND Secondaries	On
Fail On Load If Bad Zone Data	Off
Enable Round Robin	On
Enable Netmask Ordering	On
Secure Cache Against Pollution	On
Name Checking	Multibyte (UTF8)
Load Zone Data On Startup	From Active Directory And Registry
Enable Automatic Scavenging Of Stale Records	Off (requires configuration when enabled)

In most situations, these installation defaults are acceptable and do not require modification. However, when needed, you can use the DNS console to tune these advanced parameters and accommodate special deployment needs and situations.

> **Exam Tip**   These options are heavily tested on the 70-291 exam. Be especially familiar with Disable Recursion, BIND Secondaries, Enable Round Robin, and Enable Netmask Ordering.

You can restore these default settings at any time using the Advanced tab by clicking Reset To Default.

To restore DNS server default preferences, complete the following steps:

1. Open the DNS console.
2. In the console tree, right-click the applicable DNS server, and then select Properties.
3. In the server properties dialog box, click the Advanced tab.
4. Click Reset To Default, and then click OK.

The following sections describe the available installation options in more detail.

Disable Recursion

The Disable Recursion server option is disabled by default. Consequently, the DNS server performs recursion to resolve client queries unless a special client configuration overrides this default behavior. Through recursion, the DNS server queries other servers on behalf of the requesting client and attempts to fully resolve an FQDN. Queries continue through iteration until the server receives an authoritative answer for the queried name. The server then forwards this answer back to the original requesting client.

When the Disable Recursion option is enabled, however, the DNS Server service does not answer the query for the client but instead provides the client with *referrals*, which are resource records that allow a DNS client to perform iterative queries to resolve an FQDN. This option might be appropriate, for example, when clients need to resolve Internet names but the local DNS server contains resource records only for the private namespace. Another case in which recursion might be disabled is when, because of its configuration or placement within a local network, a DNS server is incapable of resolving DNS names external to the local network.

> **Warning**   If you disable recursion on a DNS server using the Advanced tab, you will not be able to use forwarders on the same server, and the Forwarders tab becomes inactive.

BIND Secondaries

The BIND Secondaries option is enabled by default. As a result, DNS servers running on Windows Server 2003 do not use fast transfer format when performing a zone transfer to secondary DNS servers based on BIND. This restriction allows for zone transfer compatibility with older versions of BIND.

> **Note**   BIND is a common implementation of DNS written and ported to most available versions of the UNIX operating system.

Fast transfer format is an efficient means of transferring zone data that provides data compression and allows multiple records to be transferred per individual Transmission Control Protocol (TCP) message. Fast zone transfer is always used among Windows-based DNS servers, so the BIND Secondaries option does not affect communications among Windows servers. However, only BIND versions 4.9.4 and later can handle these fast zone transfers.

If you know your DNS server will be performing zone transfers with DNS servers using BIND version 4.9.4 or later, you should disable this option to allow fast zone transfers to occur.

> **Note**   As of this writing, the most current version of BIND is 9.2.2.

To enable or disable fast transfer format during zone transfers, complete the following steps:

1. Open the DNS console.

2. In the console tree, select the applicable DNS server.

3. From the Action menu, select Properties.

   The server properties dialog box opens.

4. Click the Advanced tab.

5. In the Server Options list, select or clear the BIND Secondaries check box, and then click OK. (This option is enabled by default.)

Fail On Load If Bad Zone Data

By default, the Fail On Load If Bad Zone Data option is disabled. As a result, a DNS server running on Windows Server 2003 loads a zone even when it determines that errors exist in the zone's database file. Errors are logged, but the zone load still proceeds. After the zone loads, the DNS server can attempt to answer queries for the zone in question.

When you enable this option, however, the DNS server does not load a zone when the server determines that errors exist in the zone's database file.

Enable Netmask Ordering

The Enable Netmask Ordering option is selected by default. This default setting ensures that, in response to a request to resolve a single computer name matching multiple host (A) resource records, DNS servers in Windows Server 2003 first return to the client any IP address that is in the same subnet as the client.

Note   Multihomed computers typically have registered multiple host (A) resource records for the same host name. When a client attempts to resolve the host name of a multihomed computer by contacting a DNS server, the DNS server returns to the client a *response list* or *answer list* containing all the resource records matching the client query. Upon receiving the response list from the DNS server, a DNS client attempts to contact the target host with the first IP address in the response list. If this attempt fails, the client then attempts to contact the second IP address, and so on. The Enable Netmask Ordering option and the Enable Round Robin option are both used to change the order of resource records returned in this response list.

Simple Example: Local Network Priority   A multihomed computer, server1.lucerne-publishing.com, has three A resource records for each of its three IP addresses in the lucernepublishing.com zone. These three records appear in the following order in the zone, either in the zone file or in Active Directory:

```
server1   IN   A   192.168.1.27
server1   IN   A   10.0.0.14
server1   IN   A   172.16.20.4
```

When a DNS client resolver at IP address 10.4.3.2 queries the server for the IP addresses of the host server1.lucernepublishing.com, the DNS Server service notes that the originating IP network address (10.0.0.0) of the client matches the network (class A) ID of the 10.0.0.14 address in the answer list of resource records. The DNS Server service then reorders the addresses in the response list, as follows:

```
server1   IN   A   10.0.0.14
server1   IN   A   192.168.1.27
server1   IN   A   172.16.20.4
```

If the IP address of the requesting client has no local network match with any of the resource records in the answer list, the list is not prioritized in this manner.

Complex Example: Local Subnet Priority   In a network that uses IP subnetting (nondefault subnet masks), a DNS server first returns any IP addresses that match both the client's network ID and subnet ID before returning any IP addresses that match only the client's network ID.

For example, a multihomed computer, server1.lucernepublishing.com, has four A resource records corresponding to each of its four IP addresses in the lucernepublishing.com zone. Two of these IP addresses are for distinct and separate networks. The other two IP addresses share a common IP network address, but because custom netmasks of 255.255.248.0 are used, the IP addresses are located in different subnets. These example resource records appear in the following order in the zone, either in the zone file or in Active Directory:

```
server1   IN   A   192.168.1.27
server1   IN   A   172.16.22.4
server1   IN   A   10.0.0.14
server1   IN   A   172.16.31.5
```

If the IP address of the requesting client is 172.16.22.8, both of the IP addresses that match the same IP network as the client, the 172.16.0.0 network, are returned at the top of the response list to the client. However, in this example, the 172.16.22.4 address is placed ahead of the 172.16.31.5 address because it matches the client IP address down through the 172.16.20.0 subnet address.

The reordered answer list returned by the DNS service follows:

```
server1   IN  A  172.16.22.4
server1   IN  A  172.16.31.5
server1   IN  A  192.168.1.27
server1   IN  A  10.0.0.14
```

To disable local subnet prioritization for multihomed names, complete the following steps:

1. Open the DNS console and select the applicable DNS server.

2. From the Action menu, select Properties.

3. In the server properties dialog box, click the Advanced tab.

4. In the Server Options list, clear the Enable Netmask Ordering check box, and then click OK.

> **Exam Tip**   Netmask ordering is often referred to as the LocalNetPriority setting on MCSE exams. This name originates from the corresponding LocalNetPriority option used with the Dnscmd command-line utility.

Enable Round Robin

The Enable Round Robin option is selected by default. This setting ensures that, in response to a request to resolve the name of a multihomed computer, DNS servers in Windows Server 2003 rotate the order of matching A resource records in the response list returned to subsequent clients. This feature provides a simple way to balance the network load for frequently queried multihomed computers among all the computer's network adapters. This feature is also commonly used to balance requests among multiple servers that offer identical network services, such as an array of Web servers providing content for a single Web site.

> **Note**   Local subnet priority supersedes the use of round robin rotation for multihomed computers. When enabled, however, round robin is used as a secondary method to sort multiple records returned in a response list.

Round Robin Example   The Web server named server1.lucernepublishing.com has three network adapters and three distinct IP addresses. In the stored zone (either in a database file or in Active Directory), the three A resource records mapping the host name to each of its IP addresses appear in this fixed order:

```
server1   IN   A   10.0.0.1
server1   IN   A   10.0.0.2
server1   IN   A   10.0.0.3
```

The first DNS client—Client1—that queries the server to resolve this host's name receives the list in this default order. However, when a second client—Client2—sends a subsequent query to resolve this name, the list is rotated as follows:

```
server1   IN   A   10.0.0.2
server1   IN   A   10.0.0.3
server1   IN   A   10.0.0.1
```

Disabling Round Robin   When you clear the Enable Round Robin check box, round robin is disabled for the DNS server. In this case, when clients query the DNS server to resolve the host name of a multihomed computer, the server always returns the matching A resource records in the order in which those records appear in the zone.

Secure Cache Against Pollution

By default, the Secure Cache Against Pollution option is enabled. This setting allows the DNS server to protect its cache against referrals that are potentially polluting or nonsecure. When the setting is enabled, the server caches only those records with a name that corresponds to the domain for which the original queried name was made. Any referrals received from another DNS server along with a query response are simply discarded.

For example, if a query is originally made for example.microsoft.com, and a referral answer provides a record for a name outside the microsoft.com domain name tree (such as msn.com), that name is discarded if the Secure Cache Against Pollution option is enabled. This setting helps prevent unauthorized computers from impersonating another network server.

When this option is disabled, however, the server caches all the records received in response to DNS queries—even when the records do not correspond to the queried-for domain name.

Name Checking

By default, the Name Checking drop-down list box on the Advanced tab of the DNS server properties dialog box is set to Multibyte (UTF8). Thus, the DNS service by default verifies that all domain names handled by the DNS service conform to the Uni-code Transformation Format (UTF). *Unicode* is a 2-byte encoding scheme, compatible with the traditional 1-byte US-ASCII format, that allows for binary representation of most languages.

Figure 5-28 shows the four name-checking methods you can select from the Name Checking drop-down list box, and each is described in Table 5-3.

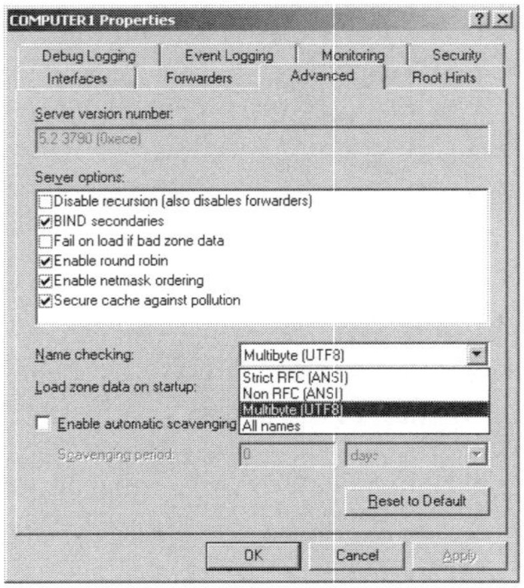

Figure 5-28   Name-checking methods

Table 5-3   Name-Checking Methods

Method	Description
Strict RFC (ANSI)	Uses strict checking of names. These restrictions, set in Request for Comments (RFC) 1123, include limiting names to uppercase and lowercase letters (A–Z, a–z), numbers (0–9), and hyphens (-). The first character of the DNS name can be a number.
Non RFC (ANSI)	Permits names that are nonstandard and that do not follow RFC 1123 Internet host naming specifications.
Multibyte (UTF8)	Permits recognition of characters other than ASCII, including Unicode, which is normally encoded as more than one octet (8 bits) in length. With this option, multibyte characters can be transformed and represented using UTF-8 support, which is provided with Windows Server 2003. Names encoded in UTF-8 format must not exceed the size limits clarified in RFC 2181, which specifies a maximum of 63 octets per label and 255 octets per name. Character count is insufficient to determine size because some UTF-8 characters exceed one octet in length. This option allows for domain names using non-English alphabets.
All Names	Permits any naming conventions.

Despite the flexibility of the UTF-8 name-checking method, you should consider changing the Name Checking option to Strict RFC when your DNS servers perform zone transfers to non-Windows servers that are not UTF-8–aware. Although DNS server implementations that are not UTF-8–aware might be able to accept the transfer of a zone containing UTF-8 encoded names, these servers might not be able to write back those names to a zone file or reload those names from a zone file.

You should use the other two Name Checking options, Non RFC and All Names, only when a specific application requires them.

Load Zone Data On Startup

By default, the Load Zone Data On Startup drop-down list box is set to the From Active Directory And Registry option. Thus, by default DNS servers in Windows Server 2003 initialize with the settings specified in the Active Directory database and the server Registry.

However, this setting includes two other options, From Registry and From File, as shown in Figure 5-29.

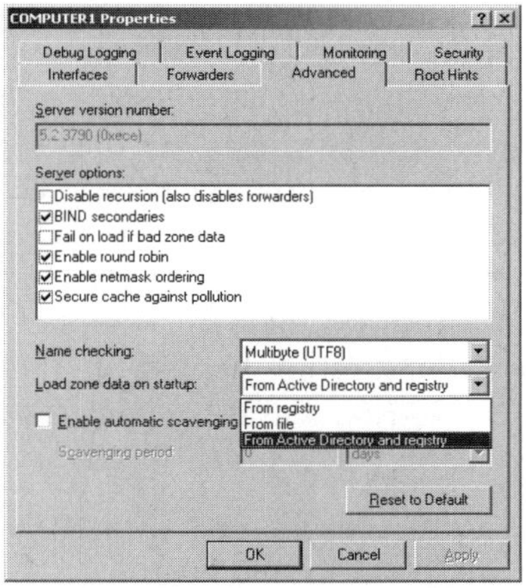

Figure 5-29   Server initialization options

When you select the From Registry option for the Load Zone Data On Startup setting, the DNS server is initialized by reading parameters stored in the Windows Registry. When you select the From File option, the DNS server is initialized by reading parameters stored in a boot file, such as those used by BIND servers.

To use such a file, you should supply a copy of a boot file from a BIND-based DNS server. On BIND-based DNS servers, this file is typically called the Named.boot file. The format of this file must be the older BIND 4 format, not the more recent BIND 8 boot file format. When a boot file is used, settings in the file are applied to the server, overriding the settings stored in the Registry on the DNS server. However, for any parameters not configurable using boot file directives, Registry defaults (or stored reconfigured server settings) are applied by the DNS Server service.

Enable Automatic Scavenging Of Stale Records

By default, the Enable Automatic Scavenging Of Stale Records option is cleared on the Advanced tab. According to this setting, DNS servers in Windows Server 2003 by default do not automatically delete stale or outdated resource records from a zone for which Aging has been enabled.

When this setting is enabled, scavenging of stale resource records is performed automatically at the interval configured in the Scavenging Period.

Lesson Review

The following questions are intended to reinforce key information presented in this lesson. If you are unable to answer a question, review the lesson materials and try the question again. You can find answers to the questions in the "Questions and Answers" section at the end of this chapter.

1. You are the network administrator for Lucerne Publishing. The Lucerne Publishing network consists of a single domain, lucernepublishing.com, that is protected from the Internet by a firewall. The firewall runs on a computer named NS1 that is directly connected to the Internet. NS1 also runs the DNS Server service, and its firewall allows DNS traffic to pass between the Internet and the DNS Server service on NS1 but not between the Internet and the internal network. The DNS Server service on NS1 is configured to use round robin. Behind the firewall, two computers are running Windows Server 2003—NS2 and NS3—which DNS a primary and secondary DNS server, respectively, for the lucernepublishing.com zone.

    Users on the company network report that, although they use host names to connect to computers on the local private network, they cannot use host names to connect to Internet destinations such as www.microsoft.com.

    Which of the following actions requires the least amount of administrative effort to enable network users to connect to Internet host names?

    a. Disable recursion on NS2 and NS3.

    b. Enable netmask ordering on NS1.

    c. Configure NS2 and NS3 to use NS1 as a forwarder.

    d. Disable round robin on NS1.

2. You are the administrator for a large network consisting of 10 domains. You have configured a standard primary zone for the mfg.lucernepublishing.com domain on a DNS server computer named Server1. You have also configured a UNIX server, named Server2, to host a secondary zone for the same domain. The UNIX server is running BIND 8.2.1.

You notice that zone transfers between the primary and secondary servers seem to generate more traffic than expected, putting a strain on network resources.

What can you do to decrease the network burden of zone transfers between the primary and secondary servers?

  a. Clear the BIND Secondaries check box on Server1.

  b. Configure a boot file on Server1 to initialize BIND-compatible settings.

  c. Select the BIND Secondaries check box on Server1.

  d. Configure a boot file on Server2 to enable fast zone transfers.

3. What is the function of round robin? Which feature takes priority, round robin or netmask ordering?

  _____

  _____

  _____

  _____

  _____

  _____

4. You are the chief network administrator for the Proseware company network, which has four branch offices. Each branch office has its own LAN, which is connected to the Internet using a T1 line. Through virtual private network (VPN) connectivity over the Internet, a single intranet is maintained and replicated over Web servers at each branch office. The four Web servers have unique IP addresses but share a single FQDN, intranet.proseware.com, as shown in Figure 5-30.

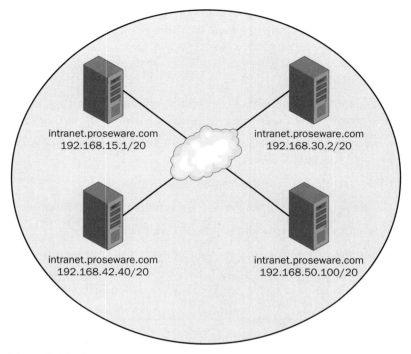

Figure 5-30 Proseware intranet servers

Within the Proseware network, a DNS client computer with the IP address 192.168.33.5 submits a query to a DNS server for the name intranet.proseware.com. Assuming that the Netmask Ordering option is enabled on the DNS server, which IP address is returned to the DNS client? (Hint: Determine which of the four Web servers shares the same subnet ID as that of the querying client computer.)

Lesson Summary

- The Advanced tab of the DNS server properties dialog box allows you to configure nine installation settings.

- The Disable Recursion server option is disabled by default, so recursion is enabled for the DNS server, and the server performs queries for its clients unless a special client configuration overrides this behavior.

- The BIND Secondaries option is enabled by default. Thus, DNS servers in Windows Server 2003 do not use fast transfer format when performing a zone transfer to BIND-based DNS servers. This feature allows for zone transfer compatibility with older versions of BIND.

- The Enable Netmask Ordering option is selected by default. As a result, in response to a request to resolve the name of a multihomed computer (a computer with more than one IP address), DNS servers in Windows Server 2003 by default first return to the client any IP address that is in the same subnet as the client's.

- The Enable Round Robin option is selected by default. Thus, in response to a request to resolve a name hosted at multiple addresses, and in cases where subnet prioritization does not apply, DNS servers in Windows Server 2003 by default rotate the order of matching A resource records in the response list returned to different clients.

Lesson 4: Creating Zone Delegations

Managing a large namespace such as that of the Internet would be impossible were it not for the potential to delegate the administration of domains. Through the delegation process, a new zone is created when the responsibility for a subdomain within a DNS namespace is assigned to a separate entity. This separate entity can be an autonomous organization or a branch within your company.

You can create a zone delegation in the DNS console by running the New Delegation Wizard.

After this lesson, you will be able to

- Create a delegated zone within a DNS namespace
- Explain the benefits of zone delegations

Estimated lesson time: 30 minutes

Delegating Zones

To delegate a zone means to assign authority over portions of your DNS namespace to subdomains within this namespace. A zone delegation occurs when the responsibility for the resource records of a subdomain is passed from the owner of the parent domain to the owner of the subdomain. For example, in Figure 5-31, the management of the microsoft.com domain is delegated across two zones: microsoft.com and mydomain.microsoft.com. In the example, the administrator of the mydomain.microsoft.com zone controls the resource records for that subdomain.

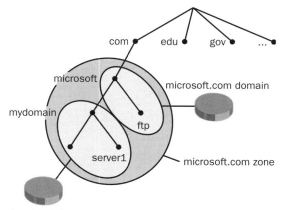

mydomain.microsoft.com zone

Figure 5-31   Zone delegation example

When to Delegate Zones

You should consider delegating a zone within your network whenever any of the following conditions are present:

- You need to delegate management of a DNS domain to a branch or department within your organization.
- You need to distribute the load of maintaining one large DNS database among multiple name servers to improve name resolution performance and fault tolerance.
- You need hosts and host names to be structured according to branch or departmental affiliation within your organization.

When choosing how to structure zones, you should use a plan that reflects the structure of your organization.

How Delegations Work

For a delegation to be implemented, the parent zone must contain both an A resource record and an NS resource record pointing to the authoritative server of the newly delegated domain. These records are necessary both to transfer authority to the new name servers and to provide referrals to clients performing iterative queries. In this section, you walk through an example of delegating a subdomain to a new zone.

> **Note**   These records are automatically created by the DNS console when you create a new delegation.

In Figure 5-32, an authoritative DNS server computer for the newly delegated example.microsoft.com subdomain is given a name based on a derivative subdomain included in the new zone (ns1.us.example.microsoft.com). To make this server known to others outside the newly delegated zone, two resource records are needed in the microsoft.com zone to complete delegation to the new zone. These records are automatically created when you run the New Delegation Wizard in the DNS console.

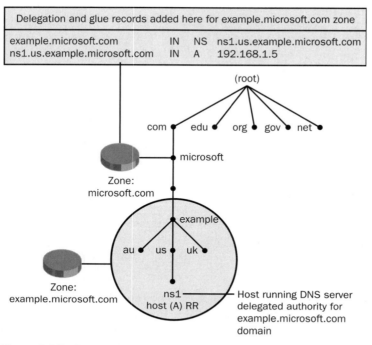

Figure 5-32   Resource records for delegation

These records include the following:

■ An NS record (also known as a *delegation record*) to create the actual delegation. This record is used to advertise to querying clients that the computer named ns1.us.example.microsoft.com is an authoritative server for the delegated subdomain.

■ An A resource record (also known as a *glue record*) to resolve the name of the server specified in the NS record to its IP address. Glue records are necessary when the name server authoritative for the delegated zone is also a member of the delegated domain. The process of resolving the host name in this record to the delegated DNS server in the NS record is sometimes referred to as *glue chasing*.

Note   After you have created a delegation through the DNS console, a glue record appears automatically in the zone data. However, this record is hidden from view in the DNS console.

Suppose an external DNS server (acting as a client) wants to resolve the FQDN box.example.microsoft.com. When this computer queries a name server authoritative for the microsoft.com domain, this name server responds with the glue record, informing the querying client that a name server authoritative for the example.microsoft.com domain is ns1.us.example.microsoft.com, with an IP address of 192.168.1.5. The querying computer then performs another iterative query to the name server ns1.us.example.microsoft.com. This latter name server finally responds to the querying computer with the IP address of the host box.example.microsoft.com, for which the name server is authoritative.

> **Note**   Delegations take precedence over forwarding. If, in the preceding example, the server authoritative for the microsoft.com domain were configured to forward to all queries that it could not answer, the server would still answer a query for the name box.example.microsoft.com by contacting ns1.us.example.microsoft.com, not by contacting the forwarder specified on the Forwarders tab.

Creating a Zone Delegation

To create a zone delegation, first create the domain to be delegated on the server that will be hosting the delegated zone. Then run the New Delegation Wizard on the server hosting the parent zone by right-clicking the parent zone node in the DNS console and selecting New Delegation.

To complete the New Delegation Wizard, you need to specify the name of the delegated subdomain and the name of at least one name server that will be authoritative for the new zone. After you run the wizard, a node appears in the DNS console tree representing the newly delegated subdomain, and this node contains the delegation (NS) resource record of the authoritative server you have just specified. The glue record appears in the zone data but not in the DNS console.

To create a zone delegation, complete the following steps:

1. Open the DNS console.
2. In the console tree, right-click the applicable domain and select New Delegation.

   The New Delegation Wizard launches.
3. Follow the instructions provided in the New Delegation Wizard to finish creating the newly delegated domain.

Practice: Creating a Zone Delegation

In this practice, you create a new zone on Computer2 that becomes a delegated subdomain of the domain1.local domain. You then create a delegation on Computer1 that is linked to this new zone on Computer2. Finally, you verify the new configuration.

Exercise 1: Creating a Zone to Be Delegated

In this exercise, you create a new zone on Computer2.

1. From Computer2, log on to Domain1 as Administrator.

2. Open the DNS console.

3. In the DNS console tree, right-click the Forward Lookup Zones node, and select New Zone.

    The New Zone Wizard launches.

4. Click Next.

    The Zone Type page appears.

5. Click Next to accept the default selection, Primary Zone.

    The Zone Name page appears.

6. In the Name text box, type **sub.domain1.local** and click Next.

    The Zone File page appears.

7. Click Next to accept the default selection, Create A New File With This File Name.

    The Dynamic Update page appears.

8. Select Allow Both Nonsecure And Secure Dynamic Updates, and click Next.

    The Completing The New Zone Wizard page appears.

9. Click Finish.

Exercise 2: Adding Host (A) Resource Records to the Zone

In this exercise, you add records to the new zone that you will later use to verify the zone delegation.

1. From Computer2, while you are logged on to Domain1 as Administrator, open the DNS console if it is not already open.

2. In the DNS console tree, select the Sub.domain1.local node. Next, right-click the Sub.domain1.local node and select New Host (A).

    The New Host dialog box appears.

3. In the Name text box, type **computer1**.

4. In the IP Address text box, type **192.168.0.1** (the IP address currently assigned to Computer1), and then click Add Host.

    A message box indicates that the host record was successfully created.

5. Click OK. The New Host dialog box remains open, with the Name text box and IP Address text box now empty.

6. In the Name text box, type **computer2**.

7. In the IP Address text box, type the IP address currently assigned to Computer2.

8. Click Add Host.

    A message box indicates that the host record was successfully created.

9. Click OK and then click Done.

10. Log off Computer2.

Exercise 3: Creating a Delegation

In this exercise, you create a delegation on Computer1 that connects to the zone sub.domain1.local on Computer2.

1. From Computer1, log on to Domain1 as Administrator.

2. Open the DNS console.

3. In the DNS console tree, select the Domain1.local node. Next, right-click the Domain1.local node and select New Delegation

    The New Delegation Wizard launches.

4. Click Next.

    The Delegated Domain Name page appears.

5. In the Delegated Domain text box, type **sub**, and then click Next.

    The Name Servers page appears.

6. Click Add.

    The New Resource Record dialog box appears.

7. In the Server Fully Qualified Domain Name text box, type **computer2.sub. domain1.local**.

8. In the IP Address text box, type the IP address currently assigned to Computer2.

9. Click Add and then click OK.

10. On the Name Servers page of the New Delegation Wizard, click Next.

    The Completing The New Delegation Wizard page appears.

11. Click Finish.

    In the DNS console tree, you will now see the Sub delegation node under the domain1.local zone.

12. Use the DNS console to answer the following question: how many host (A) resource records does Computer1 hold for the sub.domain1.local domain?

Exercise 4: Testing the Configuration

In this exercise, you ping the hosts in the newly delegated domain. You perform this exercise on Computer1, which uses the local DNS server for name resolution.

1. If you have not already done so, from Computer1, log on to Domain1 as Administrator.

2. Open a command prompt and type **ping computer1.sub.domain1.local**. Then press Enter.

   An output indicates that the host computer1.sub.domain1.local is responding from the IP address 192.168.0.1. If the ping is unsuccessful, at the command prompt type **ipconfig /flushdns**, wait 2 minutes, and then press Enter.

3. After the Ping output has completed, at the command prompt type **ping computer2.sub.domain1.local**, and then press Enter.

   An output indicates that computer2.sub.domain1.local is responding from the IP address 192.168.0.2. If the ping is unsuccessful, at the command prompt type **ipconfig /flushdns**, wait 2 minutes, and then press Enter.

   The new computer names are being resolved to IP addresses even though the local computer, Computer1, conducts name resolution through the local DNS server, which contains no host records for the sub.domain1.local domain. The local DNS server is correctly forwarding queries for hosts within the sub.domain1.local subdomain to the name server authoritative for that domain, which is Computer2.

4. Log off Computer1.

Lesson Review

The following questions are intended to reinforce key information presented in this lesson. If you are unable to answer a question, review the lesson materials and try the question again. You can find answers to the questions in the "Questions and Answers" section at the end of this chapter.

1. You are designing the DNS namespace for a company named Proseware, which has a registered domain name of proseware.com. Proseware has a central office in Rochester and one branch office each in Buffalo and Syracuse. Each office has a separate LAN and network administrator. You want to configure a single DNS server at each location, and you want the central office to host the proseware.com domain. In addition, you want the administrators in Buffalo and Syracuse to maintain responsibility for DNS names and name resolution within their networks.

Which of the following steps should you take?

a. Configure a standard primary server in Rochester to host the proseware.com zone. Delegate a subdomain to each of the branch offices. Configure a secondary server in both Buffalo and Syracuse to host each of the delegated subdomains.

b. Configure a standard primary server in Rochester to host the proseware.com zone. Configure a secondary server in both Buffalo and Syracuse to improve performance and fault tolerance to the zone.

c. Configure the DNS server in Rochester to host a standard primary zone for the proseware.com domain. Configure the DNS servers in both Buffalo and Syracuse to each host a standard primary zone for a subdomain of proseware.com. Create a delegation from the DNS server in Rochester to each of these subdomains.

d. Configure the DNS server in Rochester to host a standard primary zone for the proseware.com domain. Configure the DNS servers in both Buffalo and Syracuse to host a standard primary zone for a subdomain of proseware.com. Add secondary zones on each DNS server to pull transfers from the primary zones hosted on the other two DNS servers.

2. You are the administrator for your company's network, which consists of a central office LAN and three branch office LANs, all in different cities. You have decided to design a new DNS infrastructure while deploying Active Directory on your network. Your goals for the network are first to implement a single Active Directory forest across all four locations, and second to minimize response times for users connecting to resources anywhere on the network. Assume that all branch offices have domain controllers running DNS servers.

Which of the following actions best meets these goals?

a. Configure a single Active Directory domain for all four locations and configure a single Active Directory–integrated DNS zone that replicates through the entire domain.

b. Configure a single Active Directory domain for all four locations, and configure a standard primary zone at the central office with zone transfers to secondary zones at each branch office.

c. Configure an Active Directory domain and a DNS domain for the central office, delegate a DNS subdomain to each branch office, and configure an Active Directory–integrated zone in each location that replicates through the entire forest.

d. Configure an Active Directory domain and a DNS domain for the central office, delegate a DNS subdomain to each branch office, and configure an

Active Directory–integrated zone in each location that replicates through the entire domain.

3. Which resource records are added to a parent zone to delegate a given subdomain? What are the specific functions of these records?

_____

_____

_____

_____

_____

4. The DNS server NS1 hosts the zone lucernepublishing.com and is configured to forward all queries for which the server is not authoritative. NS1 receives a query for sub.lucernepublishing.com, a delegated subdomain. Where will the query be directed?

_____

_____

Lesson Summary

- To delegate a zone means to assign authority over portions of your DNS namespace to subdomains within this namespace. A zone delegation occurs when the responsibility for the resource records of a subdomain is passed from the owner of the parent domain to the owner of the subdomain.

- You should consider delegating a zone within your network when you need to delegate management of a DNS domain to a branch or department within your organization; when you need to distribute the load of maintaining one large DNS database among multiple name servers to improve name resolution performance and fault tolerance; or when you need hosts and host names to be structured according to branch or departmental affiliation within your organization.

- For a delegation to be implemented, the parent zone must contain both an A resource record and an NS resource record pointing to the authoritative server of the newly delegated domain. These records are necessary to both transfer authority to the new name servers and provide referrals to clients performing iterative queries. These records are automatically created by the DNS console when you create a new delegation.

- To create a zone delegation, first create the domain to be delegated on the server that will be hosting the delegated zone. Then run the New Delegation Wizard on the server hosting the parent zone by right-clicking the parent zone node in the DNS console and selecting New Delegation.

Lesson 5: Deploying Stub Zones

A *stub zone* is an abbreviated copy of a zone, updated regularly, that contains only the NS records belonging to a master zone. A server hosting a stub zone does not answer a query directly for the zone, but instead directs these queries to any of the name servers specified in the stub zone's NS resource records.

After this lesson, you will be able to

- Create a stub zone
- Describe the benefits and limitations of stub zones

Estimated lesson time: 30 minutes

Understanding Stub Zones

When you configure a new zone using the New Zone Wizard, you have the option of creating the new zone as a primary, secondary, or stub zone, as shown in Figure 5-33. When you create a stub zone, a zone is configured that maintains only those records—NS resource records—needed to locate the name servers of the master zone specified by the name of the stub zone.

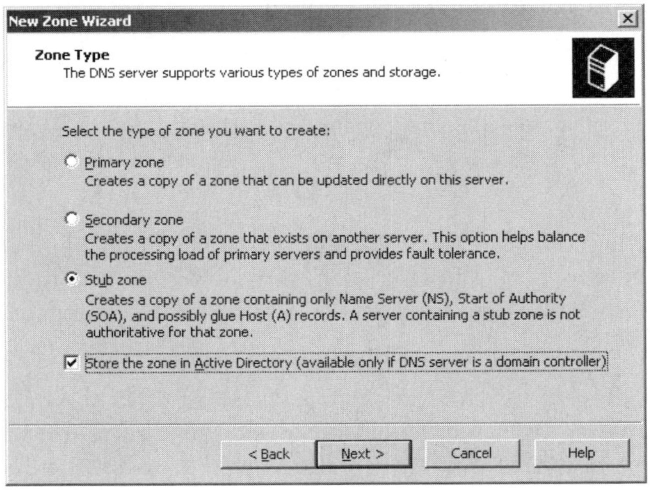

Figure 5-33   Creating a stub zone

Stub zones are used to keep all the NS resource records from a master zone current. To configure a stub zone, you need to specify at least one name server, the master, whose IP address doesn't change. Any new name servers that you add to the master zone later are updated to the stub zone automatically through zone transfers.

You cannot modify a stub zone's resource records. Any changes you want to make to these records in a stub zone must be made in the original primary zone from which the stub zone is derived.

To add a stub zone, complete the following steps:

1. Open the DNS console.

2. In the console tree, right-click a DNS server, and then select New Zone to open the New Zone Wizard.

3. Follow the instructions to create a new stub zone.

Benefits of Stub Zones

Stub zones allow you to achieve the following benefits:

- **Improve name resolution** Stub zones enable a DNS server to perform recursion by using the stub zone's list of name servers without querying the root server.

- **Keep foreign zone information current** By updating the stub zone regularly, the DNS server hosting the stub zone maintains a current list of name servers for a different zone, such as a delegated zone on a different DNS server.

- **Simplify DNS administration** By using stub zones throughout your DNS infrastructure, you can distribute zone information without using secondary zones.

> **Important** Stub zones do not serve the same purpose as secondary zones and are not an alternative when planning for fault tolerance, redundancy, or load sharing.

When to Use Stub Zones

Stub zones are most frequently used to keep track of the name servers authoritative for delegated zones. Most often, stub zones are hosted on the parent DNS servers of those delegated zones.

A DNS server that has delegated a child zone to a different DNS server is usually informed of new authoritative DNS servers added to the child zone only when the resource records for these new DNS servers are added to the parent zone manually. With stub zones, a DNS server can host a stub zone for one of its delegated (child) zones and obtain updates of that zone's authoritative servers whenever additional name servers are added to the master zone. This functionality is explained in the following example, illustrated in Figure 5-34.

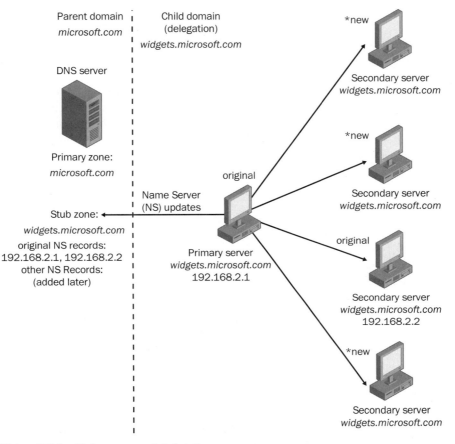

Figure 5-34   Stub zones and delegations

> **Exam Tip**   Expect to be tested on stub zones on the 70-291 exam. First and foremost, you need to be able to recognize scenarios in which deploying a stub zone is appropriate.

Stub Zone Example

A DNS server authoritative for the parent zone microsoft.com delegated a child zone, widgets.microsoft.com, to separate DNS servers. When the delegation for the child zone widgets.microsoft.com was originally performed, it contained only two NS resource records for the widgets.microsoft.com zone's authoritative DNS servers. Later, administrators of this zone configured additional DNS servers as authoritative for the zone but did not notify the administrators of the parent zone, microsoft.com. As a result, the DNS server hosting the parent zone is not informed of the new DNS servers authoritative for its child zone, widgets.microsoft.com, and continues to query the only two authoritative DNS servers that exist in the stub zone.

You can remedy this situation by configuring the DNS server authoritative for the parent zone, microsoft.com, to host a stub zone for its child zone, widgets.microsoft.com. When the administrator of the authoritative DNS server for microsoft.com updates the resource records for its stub zone, it queries the master server for widgets.microsoft.com to obtain that zone's authoritative DNS server records. Consequently, the DNS server authoritative for the parent zone learns about the new name servers authoritative for the widgets.microsoft.com child zone and is able to perform recursion to all of the child zone's authoritative DNS servers.

Other Uses for Stub Zones

You can also use stub zones to facilitate name resolution across domains in a manner that avoids searching the DNS namespace for a common parent server. Stub zones can thus replace secondary zones in cases where achieving DNS connectivity across domains is important but providing data redundancy for the master zone is not. Also note that stub zones improve name resolution and eliminate the burden to network resources that would otherwise result from large zone transfers.

Figure 5-35 illustrates using stub zones to facilitate name resolution in this way. In the example, a query for the host name ns.mgmt.ldn.microsoft.com is submitted to two different name servers. In the first case, the server authoritative for the mfg.wa.microsoft.com domain accepts the query. Many other name servers must then be contacted before the destination name server authoritative for the appropriate domain (mgmt.ldn.microsoft.com) receives the query. In the second case, the DNS server authoritative for the actg.wa.microsoft.com domain receives a query for the same name, ns.mgmt.ldn.microsoft.com. Because this second server also hosts a stub zone for the destination mgmt.ldn.microsoft.com, the server already knows the address of the server authoritative for ns.mgmt.ldn.microsoft.com, and it sends a recursive query directly to the authoritative server.

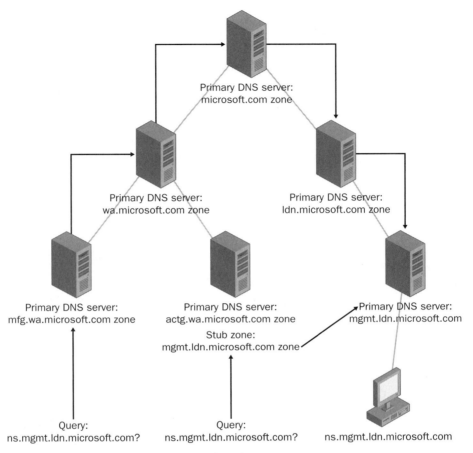

Figure 5-35   Using stub zones across domains

Stub Zone Resource Records

A stub zone contains SOA, NS, and A glue resource records for authoritative DNS servers in a zone. The SOA type identifies the primary DNS server for the actual zone (master server) and other zone property information. The NS resource record type contains a list of authoritative DNS servers for a zone (primary and secondary servers). The A glue resource records hold the IP addresses of the DNS servers authoritative for the zone.

> **Note**   As with delegations, stub zones contain glue records in the zone data, but these glue records are not visible in the DNS console.

Stub Zone Resolution

When a DNS client performs a recursive query operation on a DNS server hosting a stub zone, the DNS server uses the stub zone's resource records to resolve the query.

The DNS server then queries the authoritative servers specified in the stub zone's NS resource records. If the DNS server cannot find any of the authoritative name servers listed in its stub zone, it attempts standard recursion.

The DNS server stores the resource records it receives from a stub zone's authoritative servers in its cache and not in the stub zone itself; only the SOA, NS, and A resource records returned in response to the query are stored in the stub zone. The resource records stored in the cache are cached according to the Time to Live (TTL) value in each resource record. The SOA, NS, and A resource records, which are not written to the cache, expire according to the interval specified in the stub zone's SOA resource record, which is created during the creation of the stub zone and updated during transfers to the stub zone from the original primary zone.

When a DNS server receives a query for which recursion has been disabled, the DNS server returns a referral pointing to the servers specified in the stub zone.

Stub Zone Updates

When a DNS server loads a stub zone, it queries the zone's master server for the SOA resource record, NS resource records at the zone's root, and A resource records. During updates to the stub zone, the master server is queried by the DNS server hosting the stub zone for the same resource record types requested during the loading of the stub zone. The SOA resource record's refresh interval determines when the DNS server hosting the stub zone attempts a zone transfer (update). Should an update fail, the SOA resource record's retry interval determines when the update is retried. Once the retry interval has expired without a successful update, the expiration time as specified in the SOA resource record's Expires field determines when the DNS server stops using the stub zone data.

You can use the DNS console to perform the following stub zone update operations:

- **Reload**   This operation reloads the stub zone from the local storage of the DNS server hosting it.

- **Transfer From Master**   The DNS server hosting the stub zone determines whether the serial number in the stub zone's SOA resource record has expired and then performs a zone transfer from the stub zone's master server.

- **Reload From Master**   This operation performs a zone transfer from the stub zone's master server regardless of the serial number in the stub zone's SOA resource record.

Exam Tip   For the 70-291 exam, you need to understand the differences among these three operations, which can apply to secondary zones as well as stub zones.

Practice: Deploying a Stub Zone

In this practice, you create a stub zone on Computer1 that pulls transfers from the delegated subdomain sub.domain1.local.

Exercise 1: Creating a Stub Zone

In this exercise, you run the New Zone Wizard on Computer1 to create a stub zone.

> **Important**   The following exercise assumes that you have installed the DNS server on Computer2 by using the Windows Components Wizard (as described in Chapter2, Lesson 3). In this case, zone transfers from the Sub.domain1.local zone are enabled by default but restricted to authoritative name servers. If instead you have installed the DNS server on Computer2 by using the Manage Your Server window to add the DNS server role, zone transfers for all locally hosted zones are disabled by default. In this case, before beginning this exercise, be sure to enable zone transfers for the Sub.domain1.local zone and restrict zone transfers to servers listed on the Name Servers tab.

1. From Computer1, log on to Domain1 as Administrator.
2. At a command prompt, type the following command: **dnscmd computer2 /recordadd sub.domain1.local @ ns computer1.domain1.local**.

    This command adds Computer1 to the Name Servers tab in the Sub.domain1.local Properties dialog box in the DNS console on Computer2.
3. Open the DNS console, right-click the Forward Lookup Zones node, and select New Zone.

    The New Zone Wizard launches.
4. Click Next.

    The Zone Type page appears.
5. Select Stub Zone, clear the Store The Zone In Active Directory check box, and click Next.

    The Zone Name page appears.
6. In the Zone Name text box, type **sub.domain1.local**, and then click Next.

    The Zone File page appears.
7. Click Next to accept the default selection, Create A New File With This File Name.

    The Master DNS Servers page appears.

8. In the IP Address text box, type the IP address currently assigned to Computer2, click Add, and then click Next.

   The Completing The New Zone Wizard page appears.

9. Click Finish.

   The sub.domain1.local zone now appears in the DNS console tree under the Forward Lookup Zones node.

10. Right-click the Sub.domain1.local node in the console tree (not the details pane), and then select Transfer From Master.

> **Tip**   If you receive an error message, wait 10 seconds and try step 15 again.

11. When the zone loads successfully, the node shows only three resource records: the SOA resource record for the zone and the NS resource records pointing to Computer2 and Computer1.

12. Log off Computer1.

Lesson Review

The following questions are intended to reinforce key information presented in this lesson. If you are unable to answer a question, review the lesson materials and try the question again. You can find answers to the questions in the "Questions and Answers" section at the end of this chapter.

1. What is the most common use of a stub zone?

   _____

   _____

2. Which of the following is *not* a benefit of using a stub zone?

   a. Improving name resolution performance

   b. Keeping foreign zone information current

   c. Simplifying DNS administration

   d. Increasing fault tolerance for DNS servers

3. When would you choose to implement a stub zone over a secondary zone? When would you choose to implement a secondary zone over a stub zone?

_____

_____

_____

_____

_____

_____

_____

_____

_____

Lesson Summary

- A stub zone is an abbreviated copy of a zone, updated regularly, that contains only the NS records belonging to a master zone. Stub zones are most frequently used to keep track of the name servers authoritative for delegated zones and are most frequently hosted on the parent DNS servers of those delegated zones.

- Stub zones can also be used to facilitate name resolution across domains in a manner that avoids searching the DNS namespace for a common parent server.

- To create a stub zone, you open the New Zone Wizard by right-clicking the DNS server icon in the DNS console and selecting New Zone. In the New Zone Wizard, you select the stub zone type and then follow the wizard's instructions.

- To configure a stub zone, you need to specify at least one name server, the master, with an IP address that doesn't change. Any new name servers that you add to the master zone are later updated to the stub zone automatically through zone transfers.

- Stub zones do not serve the same purpose as secondary zones and are not an alternative when planning for fault tolerance, redundancy, or load sharing.

Case Scenario Exercise

You have been hired as a consultant by Lucerne Publishing, which is in the process of redeploying its DNS server infrastructure on Windows Server 2003. Lucerne Publishing's in-house network designer, Klaus, has requested your services for your expertise in Windows Server 2003.

Lucerne Publishing has its headquarters in Lucerne and has two branch offices in Bern and Geneva. The Lucerne branch hosts the parent domain, lucernepublishing.com. The Bern and Geneva offices each host subdomains and contain their own domain controllers.

Figure 5-36 presents the relevant portion of the network.

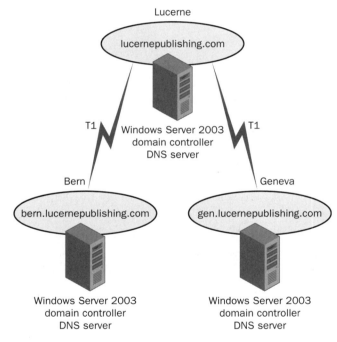

Figure 5-36   Lucerne Publishing's network

Klaus wants to achieve four goals in his network:

  A. Minimize name resolution traffic across WAN links

  B. Minimize DNS replication traffic across WAN links

  C. Secure DNS replication traffic across WAN links

  D. Optimize name resolution traffic for client computers

1. Which of these goals are met by deploying an Active Directory–integrated zone with the default replication scope on domain controllers in all three locations throughout the network?

2. If an Active Directory–integrated zone is deployed for the lucernepublishing.com domain, which option should you recommend be configured in the Change Zone Replication Scope dialog box shown in Figure 5-37? Assume that improving name resolution response time is more important than minimizing network traffic.

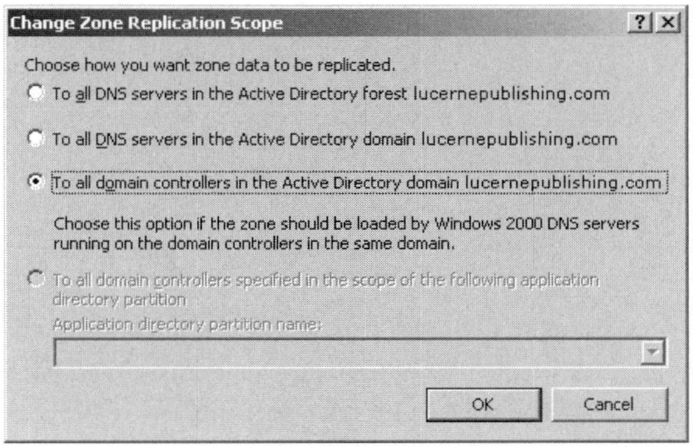

Figure 5-37   Zone replication scope settings for the lucernepublishing.com domain

3. The Bern branch office has 200 employees, and you want to deploy DNS in a way that minimizes the administrative load for network managers at the Lucerne office. However, you also want DNS servers in headquarters to be updated on any new authoritative servers deployed in the Bern office. How can you achieve these goals?

4. Klaus has informed you that his network administrators have unsuccessfully attempted to deploy a test secondary DNS server in one of the branch offices. He says the administrators specified the correct IP address of a primary DNS server running Windows Server 2003 in the Lucerne office, yet the secondary server was unable to transfer data from the primary zone. Given that this test network was successfully deployed on Windows 2000 a few years ago, what is the most likely cause of the problem?

_____

_____

_____

_____

_____

Troubleshooting Lab

In the following exercise, you fix a faulty Active Directory installation on Computer1 by automatically recreating missing SRV resource records with the Netdiag utility. You then configure the domain1.local zone to allow only secure dynamic updates. This strategy can be useful in troubleshooting fake networked computers, in which malicious intruders assume DNS registrations owned by domain computers.

1. From Computer1, log on to Domain1 as Administrator.

2. Open the DNS console.

3. Delete the following two SRV resource records: _kerberos._tcp.dc._msdcs. domain1.local, and _ldap._tcp.dc._msdcs.domain1.local.

4. Close the DNS console.

   Make sure Computer1 is not connected to the Internet when you perform the following step.

5. At a command prompt, type **netdiag /fix**.

6. The utility runs for a few moments. After it has completed, browse the output. You will see that some tests have failed and some fixes have been applied.

7. Open the DNS console and browse to the _tcp.dc._msdcs.domain1.local domain.

   In the details pane, you can see that the two records you deleted have been recreated.

8. Close the DNS console.

9. Open a command prompt and enter **dnscmd /zoneresettype domain1.local /dsprimary**.

   This command changes the domain1.local zone to an Active Directory–integrated zone. This type of zone allows you to require secure dynamic updates.

10. At the command prompt, type **dnscmd . /config domain1.local /allowupdate 2**.

   This command configures domain1.local to allow only secure updates. When secure updates are required, only the computer that first created a resource record is allowed to update that record.

11. Open the DNS console, and then open the Domain1.local Properties dialog box. On the General tab, you can see that the zone is now described as Active Directory–Integrated and that it allows only secure dynamic updates.

12. Close the DNS console, and then log off Computer1.

Chapter Summary

- The Forwarders tab of the DNS server properties dialog box allows you to forward DNS queries received by the local DNS server to upstream DNS servers, called forwarders. This tab also allows you to disable recursion for select queries (as specified by domain).

- The Root Hints tab of the DNS server properties dialog box provides a simple way to modify the contents in the Cache.dns file. If you are using your DNS server to resolve Internet names, you do not normally need to modify these entries. However, if you are using your DNS server only to answer queries for hosts in a separate and private DNS namespace, you should alter these root hints to point to the root servers in your network. Finally, if your DNS server computer is itself the root server (named ".") of your private namespace, you should delete the Cache.dns file.

- When you deploy a DNS server on a domain controller, you can choose to store the zone data in the Active Directory database. Active Directory–integrated zones minimize zone transfer traffic, improve security, decrease administrative overhead, and improve fault tolerance. You can configure zone data to be replicated among all DNS servers in the Active Directory forest, among all DNS servers in the Active Directory domain, among all domain controllers in the Active Directory domain, or among all servers enlisted in a custom application directory partition.

- The SOA resource record includes several parameters that affect zone transfers, such as Refresh Interval, Retry Interval, Expires After, and Minimum (Default) TTL.

- When nonsecure dynamic updates are allowed in a zone, any computer can update a resource record in a DNS zone. When only secure dynamic updates are allowed, only the owner of a record can update it. Secure dynamic updates can be required only on Active Directory–integrated zones.

■ The DnsUpdateProxy group is typically used for DHCP servers performing dynamic DNS updates on behalf of other computers. Members of this group do not record ownership on the resource records they register in DNS. This behavior prevents problems from arising in zones that allow only secure dynamic updates.

■ The Zone Transfers tab allows you to restrict transfers from the current zone. By default, zone transfers from primary servers are either completely disabled or limited to servers specified on the Name Servers tab. The nature of this restriction depends upon the manner in which the DNS server has been installed.

■ Through netmask ordering, an IP address whose subnet matches that of the querying DNS client is placed at the top of the response list.

■ Through round robin, the order of all matching A resource records is rotated in the response list returned to successive querying clients. This feature provides a simple way to balance the network load for frequently accessed network services among all the servers hosting that service.

■ To delegate a zone means to assign authority over portions of your DNS namespace to subdomains within this namespace. A zone delegation occurs when the responsibility for the resource records of a subdomain is passed from the owner of the parent domain to the owner of the subdomain.

■ A stub zone is an abbreviated copy of a zone, updated regularly, that contains only the SOA and NS resource records belonging to the master zone. Stub zones are most frequently used to keep track of the name servers authoritative for delegated zones and are most frequently hosted on the parent DNS servers of those delegated zones.

Exam Highlights

Before taking the exam, review the key points and terms that are presented in this chapter.

Key Points

■ Understand the various zone replication scope options available for Active Directory–integrated zones.

■ Understand the scenarios in which forwarding is likely to be deployed.

■ Understand the implications of enabling or disabling round robin, netmask ordering, BIND secondaries, and recursion.

■ Understand the difference between secure and nonsecure dynamic updates.

■ Understand the function of the DnsUpdateProxy group.

- Understand the implications of increasing or decreasing the Refresh Interval, Retry Interval, Expires After, and Minimum (Default) TTL parameters in the SOA resource record.

- Understand the scenarios in which primaries, secondaries, stub zones, and Active Directory–integrated zones are likely to be deployed.

- Understand the scenarios in which delegations are likely to be configured.

Key Terms

application directory partition   A partition of data replicated in the Active Directory database on a subset of domain controllers. Application directory partitions contain information for use by a particular application or service, such as DNS.

iteration (iterative queries)   The process of querying different DNS servers in succession to resolve a computer name to an IP address.

Questions and Answers

Lesson 1, Practice 1, Exercise 1

Page 5-13

15. Compare the traffic in the Name Resolution 2 file to the traffic in the Name Resolution 1 file saved in the My Captures folder on Computer1. Then answer the following questions in the spaces provided.

What is the essential difference between the two captures?

In Name Resolution 2, the first two frames are a DNS query and DNS response for the name computer1.domain1.local. In Name Resolution 1, the NetBIOS over TCP/IP (NetBT) protocol was used to resolve the name Computer2 on the LAN. This difference shows that DNS has replaced NetBIOS as the name resolution method on the network.

What accounts for the difference in name resolution methods?

In Windows Server 2003 networks, DNS name resolution is attempted before NetBIOS name resolution. NetBIOS resolution was performed in the first example because DNS was not fully configured on the network.

Lesson 1, Practice 2, Exercise 1

Page 5-14

9. What is the restriction that applies to clients running Microsoft Windows 95 and Microsoft Windows NT 4 SP3 or earlier?

By default, these clients will not be able to log on to a domain through a domain controller running Windows Server 2003.

Lesson 1 Review

Page 5-18

1. How can you use forwarding to increase security of DNS queries?

When an internal DNS server performs iterative queries on the Internet to resolve names, this process requires your internal network to be exposed to outside servers. Through forwarding, you can restrict cross-firewall DNS traffic to only two computers—the internal forwarding DNS server and the DNS forwarder outside a firewall. With this arrangement, the external forwarder can perform iterative queries on behalf of internal servers without exposing the network.

2. Using the DNS server properties dialog box, how can you prevent a multihomed DNS server from answering DNS queries received through specific network cards?

On the Interfaces tab, you can configure the server to listen for DNS queries through only one IP address.

3. You administer a network that consists of a single domain. On this network, you have configured a new DNS server named DNS1 to answer queries for Internet names from the local domain. However, although DNS1 is connected to the Internet, it continues to fail its recursive test on the Monitoring tab of the server properties dialog box. Which of the following could be the potential cause for the failure?

   a. You have configured DNS1 in front of a firewall.

   b. DNS1 hosts a zone named "."

   c. Your root hints have not been modified from the defaults.

   d. You have not configured DNS1 to forward any queries to upstream servers.

   b

4. Which of the following events could serve as a legitimate reason to modify (but not delete) the default root hints on the Root Hints tab of a DNS server properties dialog box? (Choose all that apply.)

   a. The Internet root servers have changed.

   b. The server will not be used as a root server.

   c. You have disabled recursion on the server.

   d. Your server is not used to resolve Internet names.

   a, d

Lesson 2, Practice, Exercise 1

Page 5-39

19. Which functions on the Action menu are available for the domain1.local zone through the COMPUTER2 node that are not available on the Action menu for the same zone through the COMPUTER1 node?

   New functions are Transfer From Master and Reload From Master.

   Can you create or configure resource records for domain1.local through the COMPUTER2 node in the DNS console?

   No, you cannot create or configure resource records for domain1.local through the COMPUTER2 node.

Lesson 2, Practice, Exercise 2

Page
5-39

5. In the Domain1.local Properties dialog box, click the Start Of Authority (SOA) tab. Using the settings configured on this tab, answer the following questions in the spaces provided.

According to the settings on the Start Of Authority (SOA) tab, if Computer2 loses contact with Computer1, how long will the DNS server on Computer2 continue to answer queries from DNS clients?

One day

How often is Computer2 configured to query Computer1 to find out whether any changes have been made to the zone?

Every 15 minutes

If Computer2 discovers it cannot contact Computer1 when it initiates an SOA query, how long does it wait before trying again?

10 minutes

If another primary DNS server named dns.domain2.local successfully queries Computer1 for the IP address of Computer2, how long does Computer2's A resource record stay alive in the cache of dns.domain2.local?

1 hour

Lesson 2 Review

Page
5-40

1. Describe the process by which secondary servers determine whether a zone transfer should be initiated.

The secondary server conducts an SOA query, in which the serial number value in the primary zone's SOA resource record is compared to the serial number value in the secondary server's own version of the zone database. If the secondary server determines that the master zone has a higher serial number, a transfer is initiated.

2. What is the difference between IXFR and AXFR queries?

IXFR queries initiate an incremental zone transfer. In these transfers, only the updated information is transferred across the network. AXFR queries initiate an all zone transfer. In these transfers, the complete zone database is transferred across the network.

3. You have multiple DHCP servers on your network, some of which are configured to register DNS records on behalf of pre-Windows 2000 clients. You have configured DNS to allow only secure updates. However, you find that some DNS records are not being updated properly. How can you solve this problem?

Add the DHCP servers to the DnsUpdateProxy built-in security group.

4. You oversee administration for a wide area network (WAN) belonging to the Proseware company, which has one central office in Rochester and two branch offices in Buffalo and Syracuse. The network, which consists of one domain, has one primary DNS zone running on a Windows Server 2003 computer at the central office, and one secondary DNS zone at each branch. Network users are complaining that they often cannot connect to sites at remote branches. Administrators have determined that network bandwidth between the central office and branches has become saturated with zone transfers, and that zone transfers are being initiated before they can complete. Which of the following steps would help resolve the problem with the least effort?

   a. Install Active Directory on the network, and promote the servers hosting the secondary DNS zones to domain controllers.

   b. Increase the network bandwidth by establishing a fiber-optic connection between the two sites.

   c. Increase the refresh interval on the primary DNS server.

   d. Increase the refresh interval on the secondary DNS servers.

   c

5. You discover that an administrator has adjusted the default TTL value for your company's primary DNS zone to 5 minutes. Which of the following is the most likely effect of this change?

   a. Resource records cached on the primary DNS server expire after 5 minutes.

   b. DNS clients have to query the server more frequently to resolve names for which the server is authoritative.

   c. Secondary servers initiate a zone transfer every 5 minutes.

   d. DNS hosts reregister their records more frequently.

   b

6. Which of the following is not a benefit of storing DNS zones in the Active Directory database?

   a. Less frequent transfers

   b. Decreased need for administration

   c. Less saturation of network bandwidth

   d. Secure dynamic updates

   a

Lesson 3 Review

Page
5-52

1. You are the network administrator for Lucerne Publishing. The Lucerne Publishing network consists of a single domain, lucernepublishing.com, that is protected from the Internet by a firewall. The firewall runs on a computer named NS1 that is directly connected to the Internet. NS1 also runs the DNS Server service, and its firewall allows DNS traffic to pass between the Internet and the DNS Server service on NS1 but not between the Internet and the internal network. The DNS Server service on NS1 is configured to use round robin. Behind the firewall, two computers are running Windows Server 2003—NS2 and NS3—which host a primary and secondary DNS server, respectively, for the lucernepublishing.com zone.

   Users on the company network report that, although they use host names to connect to computers on the local private network, they cannot use host names to connect to Internet destinations such as www.microsoft.com.

   Which of the following actions requires the least amount of administrative effort to enable network users to connect to Internet host names?

   a. Disable recursion on NS2 and NS3.

   b. Enable netmask ordering on NS1.

   c. Configure NS2 and NS3 to use NS1 as a forwarder.

   d. Disable round robin on NS1.

   c

2. You are the administrator for a large network consisting of 10 domains. You have configured a standard primary zone for the mfg.lucernepublishing.com domain on a DNS server computer named Server1. You have also configured a UNIX server, named Server2, to host a secondary zone for the same domain. The UNIX server is running BIND 8.2.1.

   You notice that zone transfers between the primary and secondary servers seem to generate more traffic than expected, putting a strain on network resources.

   What can you do to decrease the network burden of zone transfers between the primary and secondary servers?

   a. Clear the BIND Secondaries check box on Server1.

   b. Configure a boot file on Server1 to initialize BIND-compatible settings.

   c. Select the BIND Secondaries check box on Server1.

   d. Configure a boot file on Server2 to enable fast zone transfers.

   a

3. What is the function of round robin? Which feature takes priority, round robin or netmask ordering?

Round robin rotates the order of matching resource records in the response list returned to DNS clients. Each successive DNS client that queries for a multihomed name gets a different resource record at the top of the list. Round robin is secondary to subnet prioritization. When the Enable Netmask Ordering check box is also selected, round robin is used as a secondary means to order returned resource records for multihomed names.

4. You are the chief network administrator for the Proseware company network, which has four branch offices. Each branch office has its own LAN, which is connected to the Internet using a T1 line. Through virtual private network (VPN) connectivity over the Internet, a single intranet is maintained and replicated over Web servers at each branch office. The four Web servers have unique IP addresses but share a single FQDN, intranet.proseware.com, as shown in Figure 5-38.

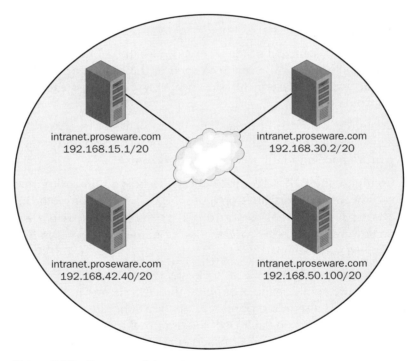

Figure 5-38   Proseware intranet servers

Within the Proseware network, a DNS client computer with the IP address 192.168.33.5 submits a query to a DNS server for the name intranet.proseware.com. Assuming that the Netmask Ordering option is enabled on the DNS server, which IP address is returned to the DNS client? (Hint: Determine which of the four Web servers shares the same subnet ID as that of the querying client computer.)

192.168.42.40

Lesson 4, Practice, Exercise 3

Page
5-61
12. Use the DNS console to answer the following question: how many host (A) resource records does Computer1 hold for the sub.domain1.local domain?

None

Lesson 4 Review

Page
5-62
1. You are designing the DNS namespace for a company named Proseware, which has a registered domain name of proseware.com. Proseware has a central office in Rochester and one branch office each in Buffalo and Syracuse. Each office has a separate LAN and network administrator. You want to configure a single DNS server at each location, and you want the central office to host the proseware.com domain. In addition, you want the administrators in Buffalo and Syracuse to maintain responsibility for DNS names and name resolution within their networks.

Which of the following steps should you take?

a. Configure a standard primary server in Rochester to host the proseware.com zone. Delegate a subdomain to each of the branch offices. Configure a secondary server in both Buffalo and Syracuse to host each of the delegated subdomains.

b. Configure a standard primary server in Rochester to host the proseware.com zone. Configure a secondary server in both Buffalo and Syracuse to improve performance and fault tolerance to the zone.

c. Configure the DNS server in Rochester to host a standard primary zone for the proseware.com domain. Configure the DNS servers in both Buffalo and Syracuse to each host a standard primary zone for a subdomain of proseware.com. Create a delegation from the DNS server in Rochester to each of these subdomains.

d. Configure the DNS server in Rochester to host a standard primary zone for the proseware.com domain. Configure the DNS servers in both Buffalo and Syracuse to host a standard primary zone for a subdomain of proseware.com. Add secondary zones on each DNS server to pull transfers from the primary zones hosted on the other two DNS servers.

c

2. You are the administrator for your company's network, which consists of a central office LAN and three branch office LANs, all in different cities. You have decided to design a new DNS infrastructure while deploying Active Directory on your network. Your goals for the network are first to implement a single Active Directory forest across all four locations and second to minimize response times for users connecting to resources anywhere on the network. Assume that all branch offices have domain controllers running DNS servers.

    Which of the following actions best meets these goals?

    a. Configure a single Active Directory domain for all four locations and configure a single Active Directory–integrated DNS zone that replicates through the entire domain.

    b. Configure a single Active Directory domain for all four locations, and configure a standard primary zone at the central office with zone transfers to secondary zones at each branch office.

    c. Configure an Active Directory domain and a DNS domain for the central office, delegate a DNS subdomain to each branch office, and configure an Active Directory–integrated zone in each location that replicates through the entire forest.

    d. Configure an Active Directory domain and a DNS domain for the central office, delegate a DNS subdomain to each branch office, and configure an Active Directory–integrated zone in each location that replicates through the entire domain.

    a

3. Which resource records are added to a parent zone to delegate a given subdomain? What are the specific functions of these records?

    An NS resource record and an A resource record are created in the delegated subdomain on the parent zone. The NS resource record directs queries to the DNS server, specified by name, that is authoritative for the delegated zone. The A resource record, called a glue record, allows the computer name specified in the NS resource record to be mapped to an IP address.

4. The DNS server NS1 hosts the zone lucernepublishing.com and is configured to forward all queries for which the server is not authoritative. NS1 receives a query for sub.lucernepublishing.com, a delegated subdomain. Where will the query be directed?

    The query will be directed to the server authoritative for the sub.lucernepublishing.com zone, not to the configured forwarder.

Lesson 5 Review

Page
5-72

1. What is the most common use of a stub zone?

Stub zones are most frequently used by a parent zone to keep an updated list of NS resource records for delegated subdomains.

2. Which of the following is *not* a benefit of using a stub zone?

　a. Improving name resolution performance

　b. Keeping foreign zone information current

　c. Simplifying DNS administration

　d. Increasing fault tolerance for DNS servers

d

3. When would you choose to implement a stub zone over a secondary zone? When would you choose to implement a secondary zone over a stub zone?

A stub zone is useful when you have delegated a subdomain and want to keep your records of the NS resource records for that delegation updated. Stub zones are also useful when you need to improve name resolution by providing links to authoritative DNS servers across domains. In both cases, a stub zone is preferable to a secondary server when you want to avoid the storage demands of a full secondary zone or the network resource demands associated with zone transfers. You should implement a secondary zone instead of a stub zone when you need to provide data redundancy for your master zone and when improving query response times is more important than minimizing the use of network resources.

Case Scenario Exercise

Page
5-74

1. Which of these goals are met by deploying an Active Directory–integrated zone on domain controllers in all three locations throughout the network?

All four goals are met by this solution.

2. If an Active Directory–integrated zone is deployed for the lucernepublishing.com domain, which option should you recommend be configured in the Change Zone Replication Scope dialog box shown in Figure 5-39? Assume that improving name resolution response time is more important than minimizing network traffic.

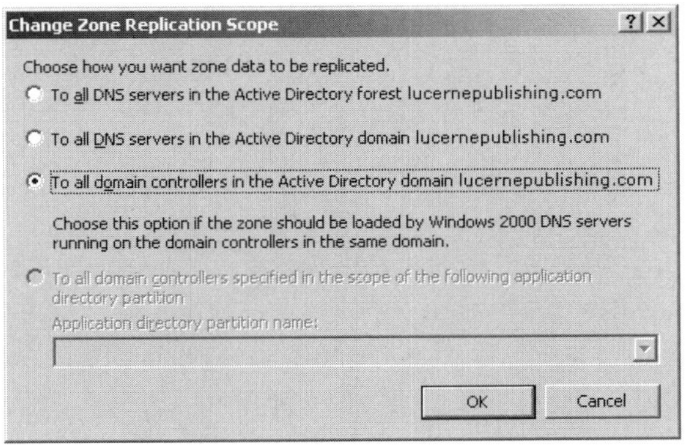

Figure 5-39   Zone replication scope settings for the lucernepublishing.com domain

To All DNS Servers In The Active Directory Forest Lucernepublishing.com

3. The Bern branch office has 200 employees, and you want to deploy DNS in a way that minimizes the administrative load for network managers at the Lucerne office. However, you also want DNS servers in headquarters to be updated on any new authoritative servers deployed in the Bern office. How can you achieve these goals?

Create a delegation for the bern.lucernepublishing.com domain, and then deploy a stub zone at headquarters that transfers NS records from the primary server of the bern.lucernepublishing.com.

4. Klaus has informed you that his network administrators have unsuccessfully attempted to deploy a test secondary DNS server in one of the branch offices. He says the administrators specified the correct IP address of a primary DNS server running Windows Server 2003 in the Lucerne office, yet the secondary server was unable to transfer data from the primary zone. Given that this test network was successfully deployed on Windows 2000 a few years ago, what is the most likely cause of the problem?

In Windows Server 2003, zone transfers from primary servers by default are either completely disabled or restricted to servers specified on the Name Servers tab. The nature of this default restriction depends on the manner in which the DNS server has been installed. By selecting the Allow Zone Transfers check box in the zone properties dialog box, selecting Only To Servers Listed On The Name Servers Tab, and then specifying the secondary server on the Name Servers tab in zone properties, you create the necessary NS resource record and allow zone transfers.

6 Monitoring and Troubleshooting DNS

Exam Objectives in this Chapter:

- Monitor DNS

Why This Chapter Matters

Domain Name System (DNS) is the single most important service in Microsoft Windows Server 2003 networks. When DNS breaks, so does the Active Directory directory service and most Internet connectivity. Because of its importance, you need to be able to monitor, diagnose, and repair DNS to ensure its proper functioning on your network.

This chapter introduces you to the tools and procedures necessary to monitor and troubleshoot DNS name resolution. These tools include the Nslookup utility, the DNS Events log, Replication Monitor, and the DNS log.

Lessons in this Chapter:

- Lesson 1: Using DNS Troubleshooting Tools. 6-3
- Lesson 2: Using DNS Monitoring Tools. 6-20

Before You Begin

To complete this chapter, you must have

- Networked two computers, named Computer1 and Computer2, each running Windows Server 2003. Computer1 should be assigned a static address of 192.168.0.1/24, and Computer2 should be configured to obtain an address automatically. Computer2 should have an alternate configuration address of 192.168.0.2/24. Both Computer1 and Computer2 should have a configured primary DNS suffix of domain1.local.

- A phone line and dial-up ISP account. (If you choose to substitute a dedicated Internet connection for this requirement, you should rename this Internet connection "MyISP." You may also need to make other minor adjustments to lesson exercises.)

- Installed the Domain Name System (DNS) subcomponent of the Networking Services Windows component on Computer1. Once installed, the DNS server should host a primary forward lookup zone named domain1.local that is configured to accept dynamic updates. A host (A) resource record for both Computer1 and Computer2 should exist in the domain1.local zone.

- Promoted Computer1 to a domain controller (DC) in a new Active Directory domain and forest named domain1.local. Computer2 should be a member of the domain. After Active Directory is installed, the DNS zone domain1.local should be configured as an Active Directory–integrated zone, and the zone should be configured to accept only secure dynamic updates.

- Created a dial-up connection to the Internet named MyISP on Computer1 that you have shared through Internet Connection Sharing (ICS). Computer2 should be receiving its Internet Protocol (IP) configuration from ICS. (If you are using a dedicated Internet connection instead of a dial-up account, you should apply this requirement to the dedicated line.)

- Installed Windows Support Tools on Computer1 and Computer2.

- Selected the Use This Connection's DNS Suffix In DNS Registration option on the DNS tab in the Advanced TCP/IP Settings dialog box for the Local Area Connection on Computer2 (Required for dynamic updates with ICS).

Lesson 1: Using DNS Troubleshooting Tools

The most common tools used for troubleshooting DNS include Nslookup, the DNS Events log, and the DNS log. *Nslookup* is used to query DNS servers directly and to determine the contents of zones. The *DNS Events log* is a file accessible through Event Viewer to which errors and other events related to the DNS Server service are written. The *DNS log*, which is also called the DNS debug log or the DNS server log, is a separate log maintained by the DNS server and configured on the Debug Logging tab of the DNS server properties dialog box. You can configure this log file to capture all DNS messages sent or received by the DNS server.

After this lesson, you will be able to

- Use the Nslookup utility to perform queries, to set and view options, and to view zone data
- Use the DNS Events log to review DNS errors and events
- Configure the DNS server to capture all packets to the Dns.log file
- Locate and open the Dns.log file

Estimated lesson time: 45 minutes

Querying DNS with Nslookup

Nslookup is a command-line tool provided in most operating systems, including the Windows Server 2003 family. It offers the ability to perform query testing of DNS servers and to obtain detailed responses at the command prompt. This information can be useful for diagnosing and solving name resolution problems, for verifying that resource records are added or updated correctly in a zone, and for debugging other server-related problems.

Nslookup can be run either as a simple command executed once (noninteractive mode) or as a program that accepts serial commands and queries (interactive mode).

Performing Simple Queries

You can use Nslookup in noninteractive mode to determine the IP address(es) associated with a single host name. For example, the following command executed at the command prompt returns the IP addresses associated with the fully qualified domain name (FQDN) www.microsoft.com:

```
C:\>nslookup www.microsoft.com
```

The following sample output is generated from this command:

```
C:\>nslookup www.microsoft.com

Server:  localhost
Address:  127.0.0.1

Non-authoritative answer:
Name:    www.microsoft.akadns.net
Addresses:  207.46.230.220, 207.46.197.102, 207.46.197.100, 207.46.230.218
Aliases:  www.microsoft.com
```

To resolve the query, the Nslookup utility submits the name to the DNS server specified for the primary connection on the local client computer. This DNS server can then answer the query from its cache or through recursion.

If you would like to troubleshoot a specific DNS server instead of the one specified for the primary connection on the local client computer, you can specify that DNS server in the Nslookup command. For example, the following command executed at the command prompt queries the DNS server at 207.46.123.2 for the name www.microsoft.com:

```
C:\>nslookup www.microsoft.com 207.46.138.20
```

You can also use Nslookup to resolve IP addresses to host names. For example, the following command executed at the command prompt returns the FQDN associated with the address 207.46.230.220, as shown in this output:

```
C:\>nslookup 207.46.249.222
Server:  localhost
Address:  127.0.0.1

Name:    www.microsoft.com
Address:  207.46.249.222
```

> **Note**   Reverse lookups rely on pointer (PTR) resource records configured in reverse lookup domains. Reverse lookup domains are not available for all Internet hosts.

Using Interactive Mode

If you need to resolve more than a single host name or IP address, or if you want to troubleshoot DNS by performing various functions, you can use Nslookup as an interactive program. To enter interactive mode, simply type **nslookup** at the command prompt and press Enter.

In interactive mode, Nslookup accepts commands that allow the program to perform a variety of functions, such as displaying the specific contents of messages included in DNS exchanges, simulating a zone transfer, or searching for any or all records of a specific type at a given server. These commands can be displayed by entering the Help or ? command, as shown in Figure 6-1.

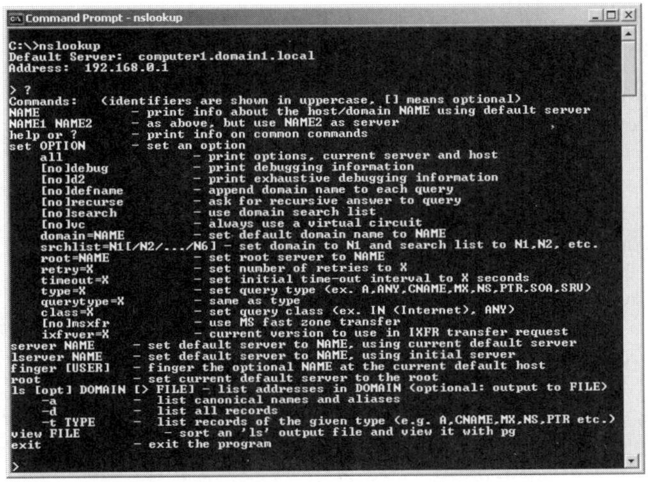

Figure 6-1   Nslookup commands

Exploring Nslookup Options

When in interactive mode, you can also use the Set command to configure Nslookup options that determine how the resolver carries out queries. For example, Nslookup can be set to Debug or Nodebug. By default, the Nodebug option is enabled, but when you enable the Debug option by using the Set Debug command, Nslookup enters Debug mode. In Debug mode, Nslookup displays the DNS response messages communicated from the DNS server.

> **Important**   Commands entered in Nslookup interactive mode are case-sensitive and must be typed in lowercase.

You can view the options currently configured for Nslookup by running the Set All command, as shown in Figure 6-2.

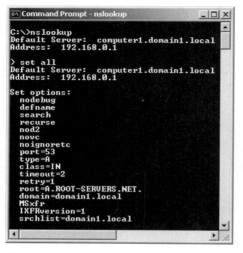

Figure 6-2 Displaying Nslookup options

Table 6-1 describes the most common options configured with the Set command.

Table 6-1 Command-Line Options Available with Set

Option	Purpose
set all	Shows the configuration status of all options.
set [no]debug	Puts Nslookup in Debug mode. With Debug mode turned on, more information is printed about the packet sent to the server and the resulting answer.
set [no]d2	Puts Nslookup in Verbose Debug mode so you can examine the query and response packets between the resolver and the server.
set domain=*<domain name>*	Tells the resolver which domain name to append for unqualified queries, including all queried names not followed by a trailing dot.
set timeout=*<time-out value>*	Tells the resolver which time-out value to use, in seconds. This option is useful for slow links where queries frequently time out and the wait time must be lengthened.
set type=*<record type>* or set querytype=*<record type>* or set q=*<record type>*	Tells the resolver which type of resource records to search for (for example, A, PTR, or SRV). If you want the resolver to query for all types of resource records, type **set type=all**.

The next section describes how to perform common tasks by using Nslookup in interactive mode.

Looking Up Different Data Types

By default, names queried for in Nslookup return only matching host address (A) resource records. To look up different data types within the domain namespace, use the Set Type or Set Querytype (Set Q) command at the command prompt. For example, to query for mail exchanger (MX) resource records only instead of A resource records, type **set q=mx**, as shown here:

```
C:\>nslookup
Default Server:  localhost
Address:  127.0.0.1

set q=mx
> microsoft.com
Server:  localhost
Address:  127.0.0.1

Non-authoritative answer:
microsoft.com    MX preference = 10, mail exchanger = mailc.microsoft.com
microsoft.com    MX preference = 10, mail exchanger = maila.microsoft.com
microsoft.com    MX preference = 10, mail exchanger = mailb.microsoft.com

microsoft.com     nameserver = dns1.cp.msft.net
microsoft.com     nameserver = dns1.tk.msft.net
microsoft.com     nameserver = dns3.uk.msft.net
microsoft.com     nameserver = dns1.dc.msft.net
microsoft.com     nameserver = dns1.sj.msft.net
mailc.microsoft.com      internet address = 131.107.3.121
mailc.microsoft.com      internet address = 131.107.3.126
maila.microsoft.com      internet address = 131.107.3.124
maila.microsoft.com      internet address = 131.107.3.125
mailb.microsoft.com      internet address = 131.107.3.122
mailb.microsoft.com      internet address = 131.107.3.123
dns1.cp.msft.net         internet address = 207.46.138.20
dns1.tk.msft.net         internet address = 207.46.245.230
dns3.uk.msft.net         internet address = 213.199.144.151
dns1.dc.msft.net         internet address = 64.4.25.30
dns1.sj.msft.net         internet address = 65.54.248.222>
```

 Tip   To query for a record of any type, execute the Nslookup command Set q=any.

The first time a query is made for a remote name, the answer is authoritative, but subsequent queries are nonauthoritative. This pattern appears for the following reason: The first time a remote host is queried, the local DNS server contacts the DNS server that is authoritative for that domain. The local DNS server then caches that information so that subsequent queries are answered nonauthoritatively out of the local server's cache.

Querying Another Name Server Directly

To query another name server directly, use the Server or Lserver commands to switch to that name server. The Lserver command uses the local server to get the address of the server to switch to, whereas the Server command uses the current default server to get the address.

After you execute either of these commands, all subsequent lookups in the current Nslookup session are performed at the specified server until you switch servers again. The following lines illustrate such a server switch:

```
C:\> nslookup
Default Server:  nameserver1.lucernepublishing.com
Address:  10.0.0.1

server nameserver2

Default Server:  nameserver2.lucernepublishing.com
Address:  10.0.0.2
>
```

Using Nslookup to View Zone Data

You can use Nslookup to simulate a zone transfer using the Ls command, which is useful to see all the hosts within a remote domain. The syntax for the Ls command is as follows:

```
ls [- a | d | t type] domain [> filename]
```

Using Ls with no switches returns a list of all address and name server data. The –a switch returns alias and canonical names, –d returns all data, and –t filters by type. The following lines present an example Ls output when this command is used without switches:

```
>ls contoso.com
[nameserver1.contoso.com]
nameserver1.contoso.com.    NS     server = ns1.contoso.com
nameserver2.contoso.com           NS      server = ns2.contoso.com
nameserver1                       A       10.0.0.1
nameserver2                       A       10.0.0.2
>
```

Zone transfers can be blocked at the DNS server so that only authorized addresses or networks can perform this function. The following error is returned if zone transfer security has been set:

```
*** Can't list domain <example>.: Query refused
```

Exam Tip   For the exam, you need to remember that the Ls command simulates a zone transfer, and that zone transfers are restricted by default in Windows Server 2003. To query a Windows Server 2003 DNS server with the Ls command, be sure to allow zone transfers to the computer on which you are running Nslookup.

Viewing the DNS Events Log

You can view the DNS Events log by using the Event Viewer node in the DNS console, as shown in Figure 6-3. You can also view this same log in the Event Viewer console, where it is named the DNS Server log.

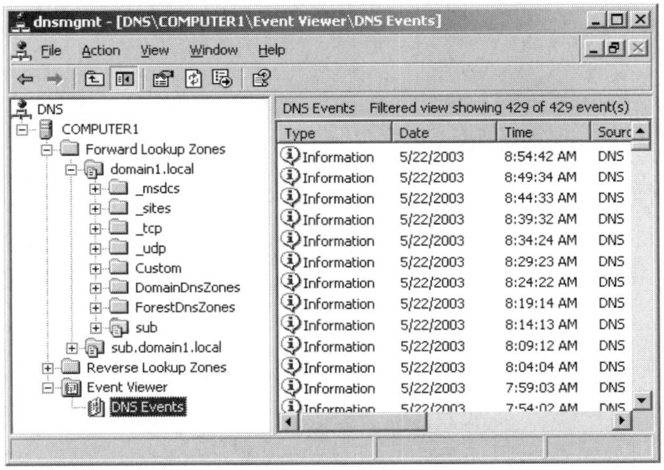

Figure 6-3   Viewing the DNS Events log

The DNS Events log records DNS server errors. If you are having problems with DNS, you can check Event Viewer for DNS-related events.

Configuring the DNS Events Log

By default, the DNS Events log records all DNS events. However, you can restrict the type of events written to the log either through the Event Logging tab of the DNS server properties dialog box or through the properties dialog box of the DNS Events log itself. The DNS Events Properties dialog box allows greater management control and filtering features.

To open the DNS Events Properties dialog box, right-click the DNS Events log in the DNS console, and then select Properties. The DNS Events Properties dialog box contains a General tab and a Filter tab. The General tab, shown in Figure 6-4, allows you to configure the log filename, log file location, log file maximum size, and expiration date of logged events.

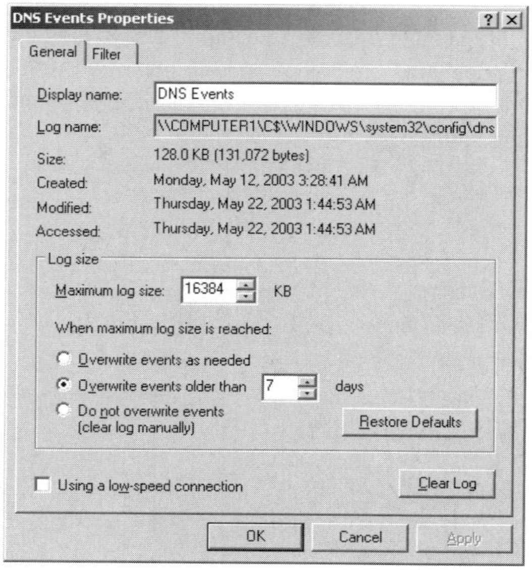

Figure 6-4   DNS Events Properties dialog box General tab

The Filter tab, shown in Figure 6-5, allows you to restrict events written to the DNS Events log by event type, event source, event ID, date, and other parameters.

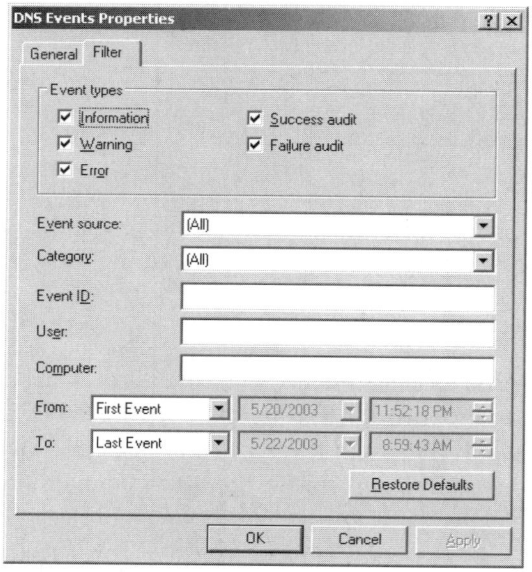

Figure 6-5   Filtering DNS event logging

DNS Debug Log

In addition to the DNS Events log, the DNS Server service also maintains a separate log used for debugging. This DNS debug log is a file named Dns.log that is stored in the WINDOWS\System32\Dns\ folder. Because the Dns.log file is actively used by the DNS Server service, you can view this file only after the DNS Server service has been stopped. In addition, because the native format of the Dns.log file is Rich Text Format (RTF), you should use WordPad to view all of its contents properly.

By default, the DNS debug log contains only DNS errors. However, you can also use it to capture all DNS packets sent or received by the local DNS server. To enable DNS packet logging, open the DNS server properties dialog box and click the Debug Logging tab. By default, the Log Packets For Debugging check box is cleared and the rest of the tab is unavailable.

However, after you have selected the Log Packets For Debugging check box, as shown in Figure 6-6, you can configure which DNS packets you want captured to the DNS log.

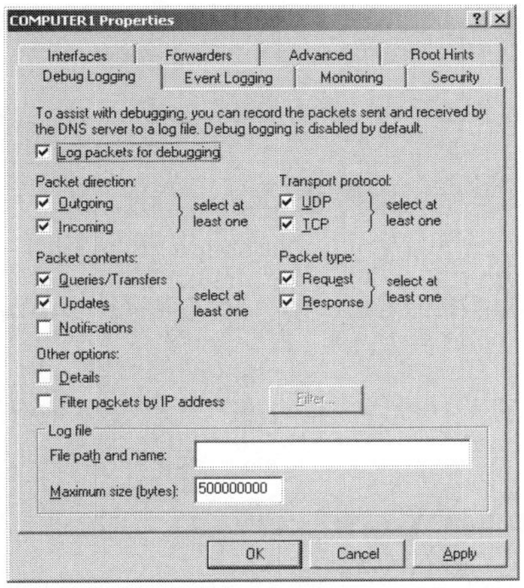

Figure 6-6   Debug logging enabled

Using the Debug Logging tab, you can configure the DNS log file to record the following types of events:

- Queries
- Notification messages from other servers
- Dynamic updates
- Content of the question section for DNS query messages
- Content of the answer section for DNS query messages
- Number of queries this server sends

- Number of queries this server has received

- Number of DNS requests received over a User Datagram Protocol (UDP) port

- Number of DNS requests received over a Transmission Control Protocol (TCP) port

- Number of full packets sent by the server

- Number of packets written through by the server and back to the zone

> **Caution** Do not leave DNS debug logging enabled during normal operation because it consumes both processing and hard disk resources. Enable it only when diagnosing and solving DNS problems.

Practice: Using DNS Troubleshooting Tools

In this practice, you use Nslookup to perform basic DNS troubleshooting functions. You then configure the DNS log to capture packets and view the results.

Exercise 1: Using Nslookup in Noninteractive Mode

In this exercise, you use Nslookup to perform forward and reverse lookups.

1. From Computer1, log on to Domain1 as Administrator.

2. Connect Computer1 to the Internet if it is not already connected.

3. Open a command prompt and type **netsh interface ip set dns "local area connection" static 192.168.0.1**.

   This command ensures that the local DNS server is queried before a remote DNS server.

4. At the command prompt, type **nslookup www.msn.com.**, and press Enter.

5. If you receive a time-out response, type the command again. You should receive an output similar to the following:

```
Server:  computer1.domain1.local
Address:  192.168.0.1

Name:    www.msn.com
Addresses:  207.68.171.254, 207.68.172.253, 207.68.172.254, 207.68.173.253
            207.68.173.254, 207.68.171.253
```

These IP addresses are associated with the FQDN www.msn.com.

6. At the command prompt, type **nslookup 207.68.173.253**, and then press Enter.

    If you receive a time-out response, type the command again. You will most likely receive an output similar to this:

    ```
    Server:  computer1.domain1.local
    Address:  192.168.0.1

    Name:    feeds2.msn.com
    Address:  207.68.173.253
    ```

Exercise 2: Using Nslookup in Interactive Mode

In this exercise, you use Nslookup in interactive mode to compare the outputs of look-ups in Nodebug, D2, and Debug modes. You then perform specialized queries within the default zone.

1. If you have not already done so, from Computer1, log on to Domain1 as Administrator.

2. At a command prompt, type **dnscmd /zoneresetsecondaries domain1.local /nonsecure**.

    This command enables zone transfers to any server, which allows you to view the full contents of the domain1.local zone by using Nslookup.

3. At a command prompt, type **nslookup** and then press Enter.

    An output appears similar to the one shown here. This output indicates that you have entered interactive mode. The angle bracket (>) symbol designates the Nslookup prompt.

    ```
    Default Server:  computer1.domain1.local
    Address:  192.168.0.1
    >
    ```

4. At the Nslookup prompt, type **set all** and then press Enter.

    An output appears similar to the one here, which shows all of the options currently selected for Nslookup:

    ```
    Default Server:  computer1.domain1.local
    Address:  192.168.0.1

    Set options:
      nodebug
      defname
      search
      recurse
    ```

```
nod2
 novc
noignoretc
 port=53
 type=A
 class=IN
 timeout=2
 retry=1
 root=A.ROOT-SERVERS.NET.
 domain=domain1.local
 MSxfr
 IXFRversion=1
 srchlist=domain1.local
>
```

Notice that the first option listed is nodebug. When this option is active, Nslookup output is concise.

5. At the Nslookup prompt, type **www.msnbc.com.**, and press Enter.

    If you receive a time-out response, type the command again. An output displays the computer name associated with the alias www.msnbc.com, the IP address or addresses resolved from this FQDN, and the alias www.msnbc.com.

6. At the Nslookup prompt, type **set d2** and then press Enter.

    Nslookup enters Verbose Debug mode.

7. At the Nslookup prompt, type **set all** and then press Enter. Use the output from this command to answer the following question in the space provided.

    What are two differences between the list of options now and when you first ran the Set All command in step 4?

    _____

8. At the Nslookup prompt, type **www.msnbc.com.**, and then press Enter. Be sure to include the trailing dot (.) after the name.

    You receive a detailed response that includes three sections: a SendRequest() section, a Got Answer section, and a Non-Authoritative Answer section.

9. Locate all three of these sections, and then answer the following questions in the spaces provided.

    What do each of the first two sections represent?

    _____

    _____

Why have these sections now appeared in the output of this query?

_____

Why is the answer section considered nonauthoritative?

_____

_____

_____

10. At the command prompt, type **set nod2** and then press Enter.

    A message indicates that D2 mode is disabled and that Nslookup is still in Debug mode.

11. At the command prompt, type **www.msnbc.com.**, and then press Enter. Be sure to include the trailing dot (.).

    Nslookup produces an output.

12. Compare the resulting output to the output that resulted from the same query in step 7, when Nslookup was in D2 mode. Answer the following question in the space provided.

    What is the specific difference between D2 mode and the current Debug mode?

    _____

    _____

13. At the command prompt, type **set nodebug** and then press Enter.

    Nslookup is now no longer in Debug mode.

14. At the command prompt, type **ls domain1.local** and then press Enter.

    An output lists every A and name server (NS) resource record configured in the domain1.local domain. Because Nslookup is no longer in Debug mode, the full contents of these resource records are not shown.

15. At the command prompt, type **set q=srv** and then press Enter.

    This command restricts subsequent queries to only service (SRV) resource records in the domain.

16. At the command prompt, type **ls –t domain1.local** and then press Enter.

    An output lists every SRV resource record configured in the domain1.local domain.

> **Tip**   If you simply want to view a list of all SRV resource records in a domain and do not need to make subsequent queries, you can perform steps 15 and 16 as one step by typing the command **ls –t srv domain1.local** at the Nslookup prompt.

17. At the command prompt, type **_ldap._tcp** and then press Enter.

    An output appears similar to the one here, which shows the full contents of the SRV resource record named _ldap._tcp:

    ```
    Server:  computer1.domain1.local
    Address:  192.168.0.1

    _ldap._tcp.domain1.local        SRV service location:
            priority      = 0
            weight        = 100
            port          = 389
            svr hostname  = computer1.domain1.local
    computer1.domain1.local internet address = 192.168.0.1
    computer1.domain1.local internet address = 207.46.252.233
    >
    ```

18. At the Nslookup prompt, type **exit** and then press Enter.

    The Nslookup program quits.

19. At a command prompt, type **dnscmd /zoneresetsecondaries domain1.local /securens**.

    This command restores the zone transfer settings of the zone so that zone transfers are allowed only to servers configured with an NS record in the zone data.

20. Close the command prompt window.

Exercise 3: Using the DNS Log for Debugging

In this exercise, you enable debug logging for the DNS Server service. You then perform queries to generate log entries, stop the DNS Server service, and view the captured DNS messages in the Dns.log file using WordPad.

1. If you have not already done so, from Computer1, log on to Domain1 as Administrator.

2. Open the DNS console.

3. In the DNS console tree, right-click COMPUTER1, and then select Properties.

    The COMPUTER1 Properties dialog box opens.

4. Click the Debug Logging tab.

5. Select the Log Packets For Debugging check box.

   The options on the tab become configurable.

6. Take a moment to look at which DNS packets are configured to be logged according to the default settings, and then click OK.

7. Verify that Computer1 is connected to the Internet, and then open a command prompt.

8. Type **nslookup www.technet.com.** Then press Enter. Don't forget to include the trailing dot after the FQDN.

9. If you receive a time-out error, perform step 8 again.

10. Open the Services console by clicking Start, pointing to Administrative Tools, and then selecting Services.

11. In the Services console, locate the DNS Server service in the list of services in the details pane.

12. Stop the service by right-clicking the DNS Server list entry and selecting Stop.

13. Launch Windows Explorer and open the WINDOWS\System32\Dns folder.

14. Right-click the Dns.log file, and then select Open With.

    The Open With dialog box opens.

15. Select WordPad from the list of programs, and then click OK.

    The Dns.log file opens in WordPad.

16. In the log, locate the captured series of DNS query and response messages used to resolve the name www.technet.com. The exchange resembles the following:

```
13:49:42 848 PACKET   UDP Rcv 192.168.0.1        0003   Q [0001   D   NOERROR] (3)w
www(7)technet(3)com(0)

13:49:42 848 PACKET   UDP Snd 192.168.0.1        36f6   Q [0000       NOERROR] (3)w
www(7)technet(3)com(0)

13:49:42 848 PACKET   UDP Rcv 207.68.112.30   36f6 R Q [0080       NOERROR] (3)www
(7)technet(3)com(0)

13:49:42 848 PACKET   UDP Snd 207.68.144.151 36f6   Q [0000       NOERROR] (3)www(
7)technet(3)com(0)

13:49:43 848 PACKET   UDP Rcv 207.68.144.151 36f6 R Q [0084 A     NOERROR] (3)www(
7)technet(3)com(0)
```

17. Answer the following question in the space provided.

Why is the first message referring to www.technet.com captured by the log labeled UDP? Why is it labeled Rcv, or Receive?

_____

_____

_____

_____

_____

_____

18. Close the Dns.log file.

19. In the Services console, start the DNS Server service.

20. On the Debug Logging tab of the COMPUTER1 Properties dialog box, clear the Log Packets For Debugging check box.

21. Click OK to close the COMPUTER1 Properties dialog box.

22. Log off Computer1.

Lesson Review

The following questions are intended to reinforce key information presented in this lesson. If you are unable to answer a question, review the lesson materials and try the question again. You can find answers to the questions in the "Questions and Answers" section at the end of this chapter.

1. Which command should you execute at the command prompt to perform a reverse lookup for the IP address 207.46.230.218?

_____

2. Which command should you execute at the Nslookup prompt to view all contents of the zone contoso.com?

   a. ls –d contoso.com

   b. ls –t contoso.com

   c. ls –a contoso.com

   d. ls –any contoso.com

3. Which command should you execute at the Nslookup prompt to view a list of all SRV resource records in a domain?

    a. set q=srv

    b. set q=srv <*domain name*>

    c. ls –t srv <*domain name*>

    d. ls –d srv <*domain name*>

4. What are two ways that you can limit the DNS Events log to record only errors and warnings?

    _____

    _____

    _____

    _____

    _____

5. You enable packet logging in the properties dialog box of your DNS server. What must you do to be able to view the log contents, properly formatted?

    _____

    _____

Lesson Summary

- Nslookup offers the ability to perform query testing of DNS servers and to obtain detailed responses at the command prompt.

- The DNS Events log records errors with the DNS Server service component of the Windows Server 2003 operating system. If you are having problems with DNS, you can check Event Viewer for DNS-related events.

- The DNS Server service maintains a separate log used for debugging. This DNS debug log is a file named Dns.log that is stored in the WINDOWS\System32\Dns\ folder.

- To enable DNS packet logging to the Dns.log file, select the Log Packets For Debugging check box on the Debug Logging tab in the DNS server properties dialog box.

Lesson 2: Using DNS Monitoring Tools

Replication Monitor and System Monitor can both be used to monitor DNS functionality. Replication Monitor performs the important function of monitoring DNS replication in Active Directory–integrated zones, whereas System Monitor enables you to track any of some 62 real-time performance measurements related to DNS.

After this lesson, you will be able to

- Use Replication Monitor to monitor replication or DNS zone data
- Use System Monitor counters to monitor DNS performance

Estimated lesson time: 30 minutes

Using Replication Monitor

Replication Monitor (replmon.exe) is a graphical tool, included in Windows Support Tools, that allows you to monitor and troubleshoot Active Directory replication. This feature is essential in monitoring DNS data transfer for Active Directory–integrated zones.

You can use Replication Monitor to perform the following functions:

- Force replication of DNS data throughout various replication scopes.

- See when a replication partner fails.

- Display replication topology.

- Poll replication partners and generate individual histories of successful and failed replication events.

- Display changes that have not yet replicated from a given replication partner.

- Monitor replication status of domain controllers from multiple forests.

After you have installed Windows Support Tools, you can launch Replication Monitor by typing **replmon** at a command prompt (or in the Run dialog box) and then pressing Enter. This procedure opens the Replication Monitor, shown in Figure 6-7.

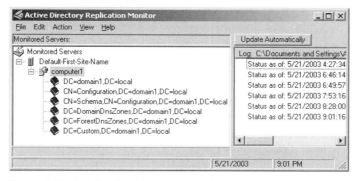

Figure 6-7   Replication Monitor console

Replication Monitor allows you to monitor Active Directory replication through specific domain controllers on your network. However, no domain controllers are included in the console tree by default. To add a domain controller to the Replication Monitor console tree, right-click the Monitored Servers icon and then click Add Monitored Server. Once you have added all the servers you intend to monitor, you can save this console configuration as an .ini file and open the file from within Replication Monitor on subsequent uses.

Directory Partitions and Active Directory–Integrated Zones

For each server listed in the console tree, you can display the Active Directory partitions installed on that server by expanding the associated server icon. Domain controllers that are DNS servers and that host a single Active Directory–integrated zone include a replica of five such partitions by default.

The following list describes these five partitions for an Active Directory domain and DNS zone named contoso.com:

- **DC=contoso,DC=com**   The domain partition, which contains objects (such as users and computers) associated with the local domain. Each domain controller stores a full replica of the domain partition for its local domain. In addition, in this partition DNS data is stored for compatibility with Microsoft Windows 2000 DNS servers. To store DNS zone data in the domain partition, set the zone replication scope in the DNS console to All Domain Controllers In The Domain. (This is the default setting.)

- **CN=Configuration,DC=contoso,DC=com**   The configuration partition, which contains replication topology and other configuration information that must be replicated throughout the forest. Each DC in the forest has a replica of the same configuration partition. However, this partition does not include DNS zone data.

- **CN=Schema,DC=contoso,DC=com**   The schema partition, which contains the classSchema and attributeSchema objects that define the types of objects that can exist in the Active Directory forest. Every DC in the forest has a replica of the same schema partition. However, this partition does not include DNS zone data.

- **DC=DomainDnsZones,DC=contoso,DC=com**   The built-in application directory partition named DomainDnsZones, which is replicated among all Windows Server 2003 domain controllers that are also DNS servers in a particular Active Directory domain. To store DNS zone data in the DomainDnsZones partition, set the zone replication scope in the DNS console to All DNS Servers In The Active Directory Domain.

- **DC=ForestDnsZones,DC=contoso,DC=com**   The built-in application directory partition named ForestDnsZones, which is replicated among all Windows Server 2003 domain controllers that are also DNS servers in an Active Directory forest. To store DNS zone data in the ForestDnsZones partition, set the zone replication scope in the DNS console to All DNS Servers In The Active Directory Forest.

You can also create custom application directory partitions and enlist the domain controllers you choose to store a replica of that partition. In Figure 6-7, Replication Monitor displays such an application directory partition, named Custom. To store DNS zone data in a custom application directory partition, set the zone replication scope in the DNS console to All Domain Controllers Specified In The Scope Of The Following Application Directory Partition. Then select the desired application directory partition from the drop-down list.

To find out which Active Directory partition is used to store data for a particular DNS zone, you can either check the DNS zone properties in the DNS console or use the Dnscmd /zoneinfo command.

Real World   Dnscmd Switches for DNS Replication

The Dnscmd utility might not be heavily tested on the exam, but this command-line tool can still help you by making your job easier. For example, instead of clicking through endless dialog boxes, you can use Dnscmd both to determine and to change the zone replication scope. To determine the zone replication scope for a domain named domain1.local, simply type the following command at a command prompt: dnscmd /zoneinfo domain1.local. Then look for an entry named directory partition in the output. To change zone replication scope, use the /zonechangedirectorypartition switch followed by any of the following switches, as appropriate: /domain (for all DNS servers in the domain), /forest (for all DNS servers in the forest), and /legacy (for all domain controllers in the domain). For example, to set the replication scope of a zone named domain1.local to all DNS servers in the domain, type the following command: dnscmd /zonechangedirectorypartition domain1.local /domain.

If you have proper credentials, you can even perform these commands remotely. In this case, simply specify the server name after *dnscmd*.

Forcing Active Directory–Integrated Zone Replication

Once you know the directory partition in which DNS zone information is stored, you can force replication for that zone in Replication Monitor. This procedure can help resolve name resolution problems caused by outdated zone data.

To force Active Directory–integrated zone replication, right-click the appropriate partition in the Replication Monitor console tree and select Synchronize This Partition With All Servers.

This procedure opens the dialog box shown in Figure 6-8.

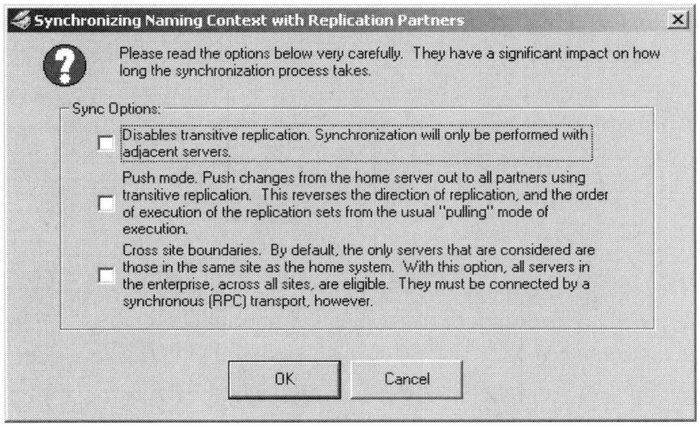

Figure 6-8   Forcing replication

When forcing a replication, you can use this dialog box to replicate only to neighboring servers, to replicate out to all servers on the local site, or to replicate to all servers across sites.

Searching for Replication Errors

DNS errors in Active Directory–integrated zones can result from faulty zone replication. You can use Replication Monitor to search the domain for such replication errors. To do so, from the Action menu select Domain, and then select Search Domain Controllers For Replication Errors, as shown in Figure 6-9.

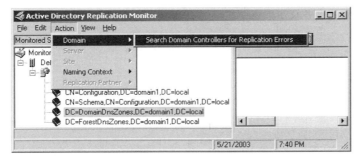

Figure 6-9 Searching for replication errors

As an alternative, you can configure Replication Monitor to send an e-mail to an administrator after a specified number of replication failures. To perform this task, from the View menu select Options. In the Active Directory Replication Monitor Options dialog box, select the Notify When Replication Fails After This Number Of Attempts option, and then specify the number of failures that you want to trigger an e-mail. Finally, select the Send Mail To check box and specify an e-mail address in the associated text box.

Exam Tip Replication Monitor provides a general means to monitor Active Directory replication and spot replication errors. To perform detailed analysis and troubleshooting of Active Directory replication, use the Repadmin command-line utility, also included in Windows Support Tools.

Monitoring DNS Performance with System Monitor

System Monitor is a tool located in the Performance console tree that allows you to select any of hundreds of system-related measurements for real-time monitoring. Each particular measurement, such as % Processor Time or Avg. Disk Queue Length, is known as a *counter*. Counters related to similar network subsystems are grouped into performance *objects*.

When you select and add counters to System Monitor, the tool displays graphs that track real-time measurements specified by those counters, as shown in Figure 6-10.

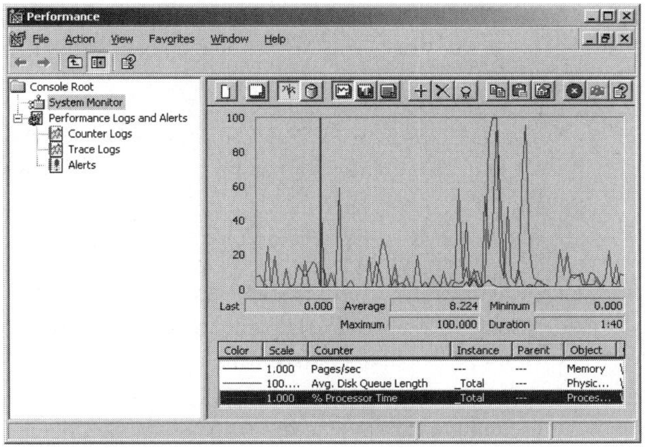

Figure 6-10   System Monitor graphs

To access System Monitor, open the Performance console by clicking Start, selecting Administrative Tools, and then clicking Performance. (Alternatively, you can type **perfmon** at a command prompt or in the Run dialog box and then press Enter.) In the Performance console, select the System Monitor node in the console tree.

> **See Also**   For more information on how to use System Monitor and the Performance console, see Chapter 12, "Maintaining a Network Infrastructure."

DNS Server Performance Counters

The DNS performance object in System Monitor includes 62 counters. You can use these counters to measure and monitor various aspects of server activity, such as the following:

- Overall DNS server performance statistics, such as the number of overall queries and responses processed by a DNS server

- UDP or TCP counters, for measuring DNS queries and responses that are processed using either of these transport protocols

- Dynamic update and secure dynamic update counters, for measuring registration and update activity generated by dynamic clients

- Memory usage counters, for measuring system memory use and memory allocation patterns created by operating the server computer as a DNS server running Windows Server 2003

- Recursive lookup counters, for measuring queries and responses when the DNS Server service uses recursion to look up and fully resolve DNS names on behalf of requesting clients

- Windows Internet Name Service (WINS) lookup counters, for measuring queries and responses made to WINS servers when the WINS lookup integration features of the DNS Server service are used

- Zone transfer counters, including specific counters for measuring the following: all zone transfer (AXFR), incremental zone transfer (IXFR), and DNS zone update notification activity

> **Off the Record**   Most performance counters in System Monitor are used only rarely. Despite this, there is a running joke among network administrators that System Monitor is the most essential of all administrative tools. This is because, when left running with its real-time graphs prominently displayed for all to see, it never fails to give your boss the impression that you are busy at work.

Table 6-2 presents some of the most useful DNS performance counters. These counters allow you to determine how often a specified DNS server is queried and how often errors are generated.

Table 6-2   DNS Performance Counters

Counter	Description
Caching Memory	The total amount of system memory in use by the DNS Server service for caching. Monitor this counter to determine whether the cache use is optimizing the use of available memory.
Dynamic Update Received	The total number of dynamic update requests received by the DNS server. Monitor this counter after enabling dynamic updates to determine whether DNS clients are attempting to update their DNS addresses.
Dynamic Update Rejected	The total number of dynamic updates rejected by the DNS server. Monitor this counter to compare the value against Dynamic Update Received and to determine how many systems are experiencing problems updating DNS addresses.
Dynamic Update Written To Database	The total number of dynamic updates written to the database by the DNS server. Monitor this counter to compare the value against Dynamic Update Received and to determine how many systems are successfully updating records in DNS.
Secure Update Failure	The total number of secure updates failed on the DNS server. Monitor this counter to determine whether any clients cannot perform secure dynamic updates. Monitor this counter to compare the value against Secure Update Received and to determine how many systems fail to perform secure updates in DNS.

Table 6-2   DNS Performance Counters

Counter	Description
Secure Update Received	The total number of secure update requests received by the DNS server. Monitor this counter to compare the value against Secure Update Failure and to determine how many systems are successfully performing secure updates in DNS.
Total Query Received	The total number of queries received by the DNS server. Monitor this counter to create baselines of server usage.
Total Query Received/Sec	The average number of queries received by the DNS server in each second. Monitor this counter to create baselines of server use in high-use networks.
Total Response Sent	The total number of responses sent by the DNS server. Monitor this counter to create baselines of server use.
Total Response Sent/Sec	The average number of responses sent by the DNS server in each second. Monitor this counter to create baselines of server use in high-use networks.
Zone Transfer Failure	The total number of failed zone transfers of the master DNS server. Monitor this counter to troubleshoot name resolution failures.
Zone Transfer Request Received	The total number of zone transfer requests received by the master DNS server. Monitor this counter to compare the value against Zone Transfer Failure and Zone Transfer Success.
Zone Transfer Success	The total number of successful zone transfers of the master DNS server. Monitor this counter to troubleshoot name resolution failures.

Security Alert   Use the Performance Log Users and the Performance Monitor Users local security groups to ensure that only trusted users can access and manipulate sensitive performance data. These security groups are new in Windows Server 2003.

Lesson Review

The following questions are intended to reinforce key information presented in this lesson. If you are unable to answer a question, review the lesson materials and try the question again. You can find answers to the questions in the "Questions and Answers" section at the end of this chapter.

1. Users in the main office of your company report that they cannot reliably connect to resources at a branch office. The two offices belong to a single Active Directory domain, contoso.com, that includes both Windows Server 2003 and Windows 2000 DNS servers. You have configured the DNS domain for contoso.com as an Active Directory–integrated zone. How can you force replication to ensure that the most current DNS data is immediately updated across the wide area network (WAN) link?

   _____

   _____

2. Which performance counters should you track if you want to determine the percentage of secure dynamic update requests that have failed?

   _____

3. Zone data for adatum.com is stored in the DomainDnsZones application directory partition. How can you force replication for this zone throughout the entire forest?

   _____

   _____

   _____

Lesson Summary

- Replication Monitor is a graphical tool that allows you to monitor and troubleshoot Active Directory replication. This feature is essential in monitoring and troubleshooting DNS zone transfers for Active Directory–integrated zones.

- Replication Monitor displays the Active Directory partitions installed on each server in the tool's console tree. Domain controllers that are DNS servers and that host a single Active Directory–integrated zone include a replica of five such partitions by default.

- To find out which Active Directory partition is used to store data for a particular DNS zone, you can either check the DNS zone properties in the DNS console or use the Dnscmd /zoneinfo command. Once you know the directory partition in which DNS zone information is stored, you can force replication for that zone in Replication Monitor. This procedure helps resolve name resolution problems caused by outdated zone data.

- DNS errors in Active Directory–integrated zones can result from faulty zone replication. You can use Replication Monitor to search the domain for such replication errors.

- System Monitor is a tool located in the Performance console tree that allows you to select any of hundreds of system-related measurements for real-time monitoring. The DNS performance object in System Monitor includes 62 counters.

Case Scenario Exercise

You are a network administrator for Trey Research, a company specializing in the development of wind-powered generators and other renewable energy sources. Trey research is based in Monterey, California, and it has a single branch office in Syracuse, New York. After you return from a week-long vacation, you have to face a number of technical issues, including the following:

1. In your unread e-mail, you find an urgent message from the administrator at the Syracuse branch. In the e-mail, the administrator informs you that users at the Syracuse office cannot reliably resolve computer names in the Monterey office over the virtual private network (VPN) connection. The administrator includes the following information, which has been copied and pasted from the DNS Events log on the Syracuse DNS server computer, ns5.treyresearch.net.

   ❑ A zone transfer request for the secondary zone treyresearch.net was refused by the master DNS server at 192.168.0.15. Check the zone at the master server 192.168.0.15 to verify that zone transfer is enabled to this server. To do so, use the DNS console, and select master server 192.168.0.15 as the applicable server, then in secondary zone treyresearch.net Properties, view the settings on the Zone Transfers tab. Based on the settings you choose, make any configuration adjustments there (or possibly in the Name Servers tab) so that a zone transfer can be made to this server.

   If the DNS server at the Monterey office has been installed by using the Windows Components Wizard, which of the following actions should you perform to enable name resolution for clients at the Syracuse branch? Assume that you want to keep or restore the default security settings for zone transfers.

   a. Configure ns5.treyresearch.net to be notified of zone updates.

   b. Add an A resource record to the treyresearch.net zone pointing to the computer ns5.treyresearch.net.

   c. Configure the treyresearch.net zone to allow zone transfers to any server.

   d. Add an NS resource record to the treyresearch.net zone pointing to the computer ns5.treyresearch.net.

2. Sometime after fixing this problem, you decide to create a delegation named syr.treyresearch.net for the Syracuse office. However, you find that users at the Monterey office cannot resolve computer names at the branch office. Using the Nslookup utility to troubleshoot the problem on a Monterey DNS server, ns1.treyresearch.net, you receive the following output:

```
C:\>nslookup
Default Server:  ns1.treyresearch.net
```

```
Address:  192.168.0.15

ls treyresearch.net
  [ns1.treyresearch.net]
treyresearch.net.          A    192.168.0.15
treyresearch.net.          NS   server = ns1.treyresearch.net
treyresearch.net.          NS   server = ns5.treyresearch.net
gc._msdcs                  A    192.168.0.15
ns1                        A    192.168.0.15
ns5                        A    192.168.1.2
DomainDnsZones             A    192.168.0.15
ForestDnsZones             A    192.168.0.15
syr                        NS   server = ns1.treyresearch.net
>
```

> **Exam Tip**   Windows Support Tools includes a command-line utility called DNSLint whose
> main function is to help resolve faulty delegations such as this. DNSLint can also be used to
> verify DNS records used for Active Directory replication and to search for various record types
> on multiple DNS servers.

What error is causing the problem in name resolution?

_____

_____

_____

3. The syr.treyresearch.net domain is configured as an Active Directory–integrated
   zone at the Syracuse branch office. The zone replication scope has been set to All
   DNS Servers In The Active Directory Forest. Which partition in Replication Monitor
   should you use to force replication of the zone data for the syr.treyresearch.net
   domain?

   a. DC=treyresearch,DC=net

   b. DC=ForestDnsZones,DC=treyresearch,DC=net

   c. DC=ForestDnsZones,DC=syr,DC=treyresearch,DC=net

   d. DC=DomainDnsZones,DC=syr,DC=treyresearch,DC=net

Troubleshooting Lab

In this lab, you troubleshoot a problem related to name resolution.

1. From Computer1, log on to Domain1 as Administrator. Verify that the DNS Management console has not been started.

2. Verify that Computer1 is connected to the Internet through the MyISP connection.

3. From Computer2, log on to Domain1 as Administrator.

4. Verify that you can connect to the Internet on Computer2 by browsing to an external Web site such as *http://www.msn.com*. You can safely dismiss any warnings you receive about the Web site being blocked by the Microsoft Internet Explorer Enhanced Security Configuration.

5. On Computer2, insert the Supplemental Course Materials CD-ROM.

6. Locate and double-click the following batch file: \70-291\labs\Chapter06\ ch6a.bat.

   The batch file executes.

7. On Computer2, attempt again to connect to the Internet by browsing to a different Web site such as *http://www.windowsupdate.com*.

   The attempt is unsuccessful.

8. On Computer 2, open a command prompt and type **dnscmd computer1 /clearcache**.

   This command clears the DNS server cache on Computer1.

 Exam Tip   Know this command for the exam.

9. At the command prompt, type **nslookup www.msn.com.**

   Name resolution is unsuccessful.

10. Use the Nslookup utility in D2 mode to capture the query and accompanying response message for the external FQDN www.msn.com. (Do not forget to include the trailing dot.) This process is described in Exercise 2, "Using Nslookup in Interactive Mode," in Lesson 1 of this chapter.

11. After you receive the desired output from Nslookup, compare the Rcode values shown in the SendRequest and Got Answer sections, and then answer the following questions in the space provided.

    Does the current problem with name resolution stem from an error at the DNS client or the DNS server? How do you know?

    _____

12. Type **exit** and then press Enter to exit the Nslookup utility.

13. At a new command prompt on Computer2, type **dnscmd computer1 /info**, and then press Enter.

    An output appears that provides a configuration summary of the DNS server on Computer1.

14. In the output, locate the Configuration Flags column. In this column, the properties that are set to 0 are disabled, and those that are set to 1 are enabled. Answer the following question in the space provided.

Which of the currently enabled properties on the Computer1 DNS server could potentially prevent users on Computer2 from resolving Internet names?

_____

15. Locate and double-click the following file on the Supplemental Course Materials CD-ROM: \70-291\Labs\Chapter06\Ch6b.bat.

The batch file is executed, restoring the correct DNS settings. (The batch file will not alter the correct DNS settings if they are already configured.)

16. Using Internet Explorer, verify that you can once again connect to Internet resources specified by DNS name.

17. Log off both Computer1 and Computer2.

Chapter Summary

- Nslookup is a command-line tool that allows you to query and troubleshoot DNS servers.

- The DNS Events log records errors with the DNS Server service component of the Windows Server 2003 operating system.

- The DNS Server service maintains a debug log in a file named Dns.log that is stored in the \WINDOWS\System32\Dns\ folder.

- Replication Monitor is a graphical tool that allows you to monitor and troubleshoot Active Directory replication. You can use Replication Monitor to force Active Directory–integrated zone replication and to search the domain for replication errors.

- System Monitor allows you to monitor real-time performance statistics. The DNS performance object in System Monitor includes 62 counters.

Exam Highlights

Before taking the exam, review the key points and terms that are presented in this chapter.

Key Points

- Know the basic commands and switches used with the Nslookup utility.

- Be comfortable reading DNS Events log messages.

- Know how to force replication and check for replication errors in Active Directory–integrated zones.

- Know by name the various partitions in which Active Directory–integrated zone data can be stored.

Key Terms

replica   A copy of an Active Directory partition stored on a domain controller.

schema   The set of definitions for the universe of objects that can be stored in a directory. For each object class, the schema defines which attributes an instance of the class must have, which additional attributes it can have, and which other object classes can be its parent object class.

classSchema   An object used to define classes in the schema. A classSchema object provides the template for building directory objects of that class. Examples of classSchema include User and Server.

attributeSchema   An object used to define attributes in the schema. An attribute-Schema object determines the allowable contents and syntax for instances of that attribute in the directory. Examples of attributeSchema include User-Principal-Name and Telex-Number.

recursive query   A query that asks a DNS server to perform recursion.

Questions and Answers

Lesson 1, Practice, Exercise 2

Page
6-14
7. At the Nslookup prompt, type **set all** and then press Enter. Use the output from this command to answer the following question in the space provided.

What are two differences between the list of options now and when you first ran the Set All command in step 4?

Debug has replaced nodebug, and d2 has replaced nod2.

9. Locate all three of these sections, and then answer the following questions in the spaces provided.

What do each of the first two sections represent?

The first two sections correspond to the query and response messages sent between the resolver and the server.

Why have these sections now appeared in the output of this query?

These sections now appear because the d2 option has been enabled.

Why is the answer section considered nonauthoritative?

The answer section is nonauthoritative because the answer has been cached by a nonauthoritative server in a previous query. A nonauthoritative server was thus able to resolve the query.

12. Compare the resulting output to the output that resulted from the same query in step 7, when Nslookup was in D2 mode. Answer the following question in the space provided.

What is the specific difference between D2 mode and the current Debug mode?

D2 mode, or Verbose Debug mode, shows both query and answer messages. Debug mode shows just answer messages.

Lesson 1, Practice, Exercise 3

Page
6-18
17. Answer the following question in the space provided.

Why is the first message referring to www.technet.com captured by the log labeled UDP? Why is it labeled Rcv, or Receive?

The Nslookup www.technet.com command was essentially a DNS query. DNS queries are carried by the UDP transport protocol, and the log has been configured to capture both DNS queries and all DNS traffic carried by UDP. The first packet is labeled Receive because the DNS query originated at the DNS resolver, not at the server logging traffic. The DNS server first received the query for www.technet.com from the DNS resolver.

Lesson 1 Review

Page
6-18

1. Which command should you execute at the command prompt to perform a reverse lookup for the IP address 207.46.230.218?

   nslookup 207.46.230.218

2. Which command should you execute at the Nslookup prompt to view all contents of the zone contoso.com?

   a. ls –d contoso.com

   b. ls –t contoso.com

   c. ls –a contoso.com

   d. ls –any contoso.com

   a

3. Which command should you execute at the Nslookup prompt to view a list of all SRV resource records in a domain?

   a. set q=srv

   b. set q=srv *<domain name>*

   c. ls –t srv *<domain name>*

   d. ls –d srv *<domain name>*

   c

4. What are two ways that you can limit the DNS Events log to record only errors and warnings?

   In the DNS console, open the DNS server properties dialog box and click the Event Logging tab. Then select the Errors And Warnings option. Alternatively, in the DNS console, open the DNS Events Properties dialog box and click the Filter tab. Then clear the Information check box, the Success Audit check box, and the Failure Audit check box.

5. You enable packet logging in the properties dialog box of your DNS server. What must you do to be able to view the log contents, properly formatted?

   You must stop the DNS Server service and open the WINDOWS\System32\Dns\Dns.log file in an RTF editor such as WordPad.

Lesson 2 Review

Page
6-27
1. Users in the main office of your company report that they cannot reliably connect to resources at a branch office. The two offices belong to a single Active Directory domain, contoso.com, that includes both Windows Server 2003 and Windows 2000 DNS servers. You have configured the DNS domain for contoso.com as an Active Directory–integrated zone. How can you force replication to ensure that the most current DNS data is immediately updated across the wide area network (WAN) link?

   In Replication Monitor, force replication on the domain partition. Select the synchronization option to cross-site boundaries.

2. Which performance counters should you track if you want to determine the percentage of secure dynamic update requests that have failed?

   Secure Update Received and Secure Update Failure

3. Zone data for adatum.com is stored in the DomainDnsZones application directory partition. How can you force replication for this zone throughout the entire forest?

   Change the zone replication scope option to All DNS Servers In The Adatum.com Active Directory Forest. Then force replication of the ForestDnsZones application directory partition in Replication Monitor.

Case Scenario Exercise

Page
6-29
1. Which of the following actions should you perform to enable name resolution for clients at the Syracuse branch? Assume that you want to keep or restore the default security settings for zone transfers.

   a. Configure ns5.treyresearch.net to be notified of zone updates.

   b. Add an A resource record to the treyresearch.net zone pointing to the computer ns5.treyresearch.net.

   c. Configure the treyresearch.net zone to allow zone transfers to any server.

   d. Add an NS resource record to the treyresearch.net zone pointing to the computer ns5.treyresearch.net.

   d

2. Sometime after fixing this problem, you decide to create a delegation named syr.treyresearch.net for the Syracuse office. However, you find that users at the Monterey office cannot resolve computer names at the branch office. Using the Nslookup utility to troubleshoot the problem on a Monterey DNS server, ns1.treyresearch.net, you receive the following output:

```
C:\>nslookup
Default Server:  ns1.treyresearch.net
Address:  192.168.0.15

ls treyresearch.net
 [ns1.treyresearch.net]
treyresearch.net.              A       192.168.0.15
treyresearch.net.              NS      server = ns1.treyresearch.net
treyresearch.net.              NS      server = ns5.treyresearch.net
gc._msdcs                      A       192.168.0.15
ns1                            A       192.168.0.15
ns5                            A       192.168.1.2
DomainDnsZones                 A       192.168.0.15
ForestDnsZones                 A       192.168.0.15
syr                            NS      server = ns1.treyresearch.net
>
```

What error is causing the problem in name resolution?

The syr.treyresearch.net domain has been improperly delegated to the server ns1.treyresearch.net, which is the DNS server in the Monterey office. The server specified should be located at the Syracuse branch.

3. The syr.treyresearch.net domain is configured as an Active Directory–integrated zone at the Syracuse branch office. The zone replication scope has been set to All DNS Servers In The Active Directory Forest. Which partition in Replication Monitor should you use to force replication of the zone data for the syr.treyresearch.net domain?

a. DC=treyresearch,DC=net

b. DC=ForestDnsZones,DC=treyresearch,DC=net

c. DC=ForestDnsZones,DC=syr,DC=treyresearch,DC=net

d. DC=DomainDnsZones,DC=syr,DC=treyresearch,DC=net

b

Troubleshooting Lab

Page
6-31

11. Does the current problem with name resolution stem from an error at the DNS client or the DNS server? How do you know?

The DNS server. The Got Answer section reveals an Rcode value of SERVFAIL.

14. In the output, locate the Configuration Flags column. In this column, the properties that are set to 0 are disabled, and those that are set to 1 are enabled. Answer the following question in the space provided.

Which of the currently enabled properties on the Computer1 DNS server could potentially prevent users on Computer2 from resolving Internet names?

NoRecursion

7 Configuring DHCP Servers and Clients

Exam Objectives in this Chapter:

- Manage DHCP
    - Manage DHCP clients and leases
    - Manage DHCP databases
    - Manage DHCP scope options
    - Manage reservations and reserved clients

Why This Chapter Matters

Together with Domain Name System (DNS), the Dynamic Host Configuration Protocol (DHCP) serves as a basic foundation of a Microsoft Windows Server 2003 network infrastructure. In all but the smallest networks, DHCP provides hosts with an Internet Protocol (IP) configuration needed to communicate with other computers on the network. This configuration includes—at a minimum—an IP address and subnet mask, but it typically also includes a primary domain suffix, a default gateway, preferred and alternate DNS servers, WINS servers, and several other options. Without being able to provide clients with a reliable and automatic means of adopting such a configuration, you would quickly be overburdened as an administrator with the task of managing these configurations manually.

DHCP is an IP standard designed to reduce the complexity of administering these address configurations. By issuing leases from a central database, DHCP automatically manages address assignment and configures other essential settings for your network clients.

Lessons in this Chapter:

- Lesson 1: Configuring the DHCP Server 7-3
- Lesson 2: Managing DHCP in Windows Networks. 7-22
- Lesson 3: Configuring DHCP Servers to Perform DNS Updates 7-41

Before You Begin

To complete this chapter, you must have

- Networked two computers, named Computer1 and Computer2, each running a member of the Windows Server 2003 family. Computer1 should be assigned a static address of 192.168.0.1/24 with a statically assigned preferred DNS server address of 192.168.0.1. Computer2 should be configured to obtain an address automatically. Computer2 should have an alternate configuration address of 192.168.0.2/24. Both Computer1 and Computer2 should have a configured primary DNS suffix of domain1.local.

- Installed the Domain Name System (DNS) subcomponent of the Networking Services Windows component on Computer1. Once installed, the DNS server should host a primary forward lookup zone named domain1.local that is configured to accept dynamic updates. A host (A) resource record for both Computer1 and Computer2 should exist in the domain1.local zone.

- Promoted Computer1 to a domain controller in a new Active Directory domain and forest named domain1.local. Computer2 should be a member of the domain. After the Active Directory directory service is installed, the DNS zone domain1.local should be configured as an Active Directory–integrated zone, and the zone should be configured to accept only secure dynamic updates.

- Created a dial-up connection to the Internet named MyISP on Computer1 that you have shared through Internet Connection Sharing (ICS). Computer2 should be receiving its IP configuration from ICS. (You can substitute another type of Internet connection for this requirement, but you will have to make appropriate adjustments to lesson exercises.)

- Installed Windows Support Tools on Computer1 and Computer2.

- Selected the Use This Connection's DNS Suffix In DNS Registration option on the DNS tab in the Advanced TCP/IP Settings dialog box for the Local Area Connection on Computer2.

Lesson 1: Configuring the DHCP Server

DHCP allows you to automatically assign IP addresses, subnet masks, and other configuration information to client computers on the local network. When a DHCP server is available, computers that are configured to obtain an IP address automatically request and receive their IP configuration from that DHCP server upon booting. When a DHCP server is unavailable, such clients automatically adopt an alternate configuration or an Automatic Private IP Addressing (APIPA) address.

Implementing a basic DHCP server requires installing the server; authorizing the server; configuring scopes, exclusions, reservations, and options; activating the scopes; and finally, verifying the configuration.

After this lesson, you will be able to

- Install a DHCP server
- Authorize a DHCP server
- Create and configure a DHCP scope, including address ranges, exclusions, reservations, and commonly used options
- Describe and implement the 80/20 rule for DHCP servers and scopes
- Activate a scope
- Configure a client to obtain an address from a DHCP server
- Use the Ipconfig /renew command to renew a client lease

Estimated lesson time: 70 minutes

Benefits of DHCP

With a DHCP server installed and configured on your network, DHCP-enabled clients can obtain IP addresses and related configuration parameters each time they start and join your network. DHCP servers provide this configuration in the form of an address lease offer to requesting clients.

One main advantage of using DHCP is that DHCP servers greatly reduce the time required to configure and reconfigure computers on your network. DHCP simplifies administration not only by supplying clients with IP addresses, but also (optionally) with the addresses of the default gateway, DNS servers, WINS servers, and other servers useful to the client. Another advantage of DHCP is that by assigning IP addresses automatically, it allows you to avoid configuration errors resulting from entering IP address information manually at every host. For example, DHCP helps prevent address conflicts caused when the same IP address is mistakenly assigned to two hosts.

Installing the DHCP Server Service

To set up a DHCP server, you must first install the DHCP Server role. This role is not installed by the Windows Server Setup Wizard by default and can be added either through the Windows Components Wizard or through the Manage Your Server window.

To install a DHCP server through the Manage Your Server window, from the Start menu select Manage Your Server, click Add Or Remove A Role, and then select the DHCP Server role. Click Next to begin the installation process.

To launch the Windows Components Wizard, open Control Panel and double-click Add Or Remove Programs. Then, in the Add Or Remove Programs window, click Add/ Remove Windows Components. The Dynamic Host Configuration Protocol (DHCP) component, like the DNS component, is a subcomponent of the Networking Services component in the Windows Components Wizard.

Note   You must be logged on as an administrator—for example, a member of the domain local security group DHCP Administrators or of the global group Domain Admins—to install and manage a Windows component such as DHCP.

Tip   Assign a static IP address to the computer on which you install the DHCP server.

After the installation wizard has completed, you can verify that the DHCP Server service has been installed on your computer by opening the DHCP console administrative tool. To access the DHCP console, click Start, select Administrative Tools, and then select DHCP.

The DHCP console, shown in Figure 7-1, is the interface from which you can configure and manage virtually all features related to your DHCP server, including scopes, exclusions, reservations, and options.

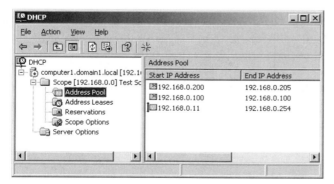

Figure 7-1   DHCP console

Authorizing the Server

DHCP servers must be authorized if they are to be integrated in Active Directory networks. Only domain controllers and domain member servers participate in Active Directory, and only these server types can become authorized. When your network includes Active Directory domains, the first DHCP server you install on the network must be an authorized DHCP server.

Stand-alone or workgroup DHCP servers running Microsoft Windows 2000 Server or Windows Server 2003 cannot become authorized in Active Directory networks, but they can coexist with these networks as long as they are not deployed on a subnet with any authorized DHCP servers. (Note, however, that this configuration is not recommended.)

Stand-alone DHCP servers implemented together with authorized servers are known as *rogue servers*. When a rogue DHCP server running Windows Server 2003 or Windows 2000 Server detects an authorized server on the same subnet, the stand-alone server automatically stops its own DHCP Server service and stops leasing IP addresses to DHCP clients.

When the DHCP Server service is installed on a domain controller, you can perform the authorization procedure simply by right-clicking the server node in the DHCP console and selecting Authorize. You can use the following procedure, however, to authorize DHCP servers hosted on both domain controllers and member servers.

Caution   Although you can install a DHCP server on a domain controller, this practice is not recommended for reasons discussed in the Security Concerns section in this chapter.

Note   To have the necessary permissions to authorize or deauthorize a DHCP server, you must be a member of the global security group Enterprise Admins.

To authorize a DHCP server in Active Directory, complete the following steps:

1. Open the DHCP console.
2. In the console tree, select DHCP.
3. From the Action menu, select Manage Authorized Servers.

   The Manage Authorized Servers dialog box opens.
4. Click Authorize.
5. When prompted, type the name or IP address of the DHCP server to be authorized, and then click OK.
6. When the Confirm Authorization dialog box appears, click OK again. Click Close in the Managed Authorized Servers dialog box to return to the DHCP console.

Configuring Scopes

A DHCP *scope* is a pool of IP addresses within a logical subnet, such as 192.168.0.11 through 192.168.0.254, that the DHCP server can assign to clients. Scopes provide the essential means for the server to manage distribution and assignment of IP addresses and of any related configuration parameters to clients on the network.

> **Exam Tip**   When a DHCP server uses a given scope to assign addresses to clients on the local network, the server itself needs to be assigned an address that is compatible with that scope. For example, if a scope distributes addresses within the 192.168.1.0/24 range to the local network segment, the DHCP server interface facing that segment must be assigned a static address within the same 192.168.1.0/24 range.

An IP address within a defined scope that is offered to a DHCP client is known as a *lease*. When a lease is made to a client, the lease is *active*. Each lease has a specified duration, and the client must periodically renew the lease if the client is going to continue to use the address. The default lease duration value is eight days.

Leases can be renewed for a variety a reasons. First, a client automatically attempts to renew its lease after 50 percent of the client lease time elapses. A client also attempts to renew a lease upon restarting. When a DHCP client shuts down and restarts, it typically obtains a fresh lease for the same IP address it had prior to the shutdown. Finally, leases are refreshed when you execute the Ipconfig /renew command from a DHCP client computer.

You create scopes in DHCP by using the New Scope Wizard, which you can launch by right-clicking the DHCP server node in the DHCP console and then selecting New Scope from the Action menu.

The pages of the New Scope Wizard listed next allow you to configure the corresponding scope features:

- **Scope Name page**   This page allows you to assign a name for the scope.

- **IP Address Range page**   This page allows you to specify the starting and ending IP addresses that define the range of the scope, along with the subnet mask you want to assign to the distributed addresses.

- **Add Exclusions page**   This page allows you to specify the IP addresses within the defined range that you do not want to lease to DHCP clients.

- **Lease Duration page**   This page allows you to define the lease duration values. These lease durations are then assigned to DHCP clients.

- **Configure DHCP Options page**   This page allows you to determine whether to configure DHCP options for the scope through subsequent pages in the New Scope Wizard or later (after the wizard has completed) through the DHCP console.

> **Important**   If you select the option to configure DHCP options later, the wizard does not give you an opportunity to activate the scope. You must activate the scope manually before it can begin leasing addresses.

- **Router (Default Gateway) page (optional)**   This page allows you to specify which default gateway (and alternates) should be assigned to DHCP clients.

- **Domain Name And DNS Servers page (optional)**   This page allows you to specify both the parent domain to be assigned to client computers and the addresses of DNS servers to be assigned to the client.

- **WINS Servers page (optional)**   This page allows you to specify the addresses of WINS servers to be assigned to the client. Clients use WINS servers to convert NetBIOS names to IP addresses.

- **Activate Scope page (optional)**   This page allows you to determine whether the scope should be activated after the wizard has completed.

You can modify these features later through the DHCP console.

IP Address Range

When defining the IP address range of a scope, you should use the consecutive addresses that make up the subnet for which you are enabling the DHCP service. However, you should also be sure to exclude from this defined range any addresses of statically configured computers already existing on your network. To exclude predefined addresses, you can simply choose to limit the scope range so that it does not include any statically assigned addresses. Alternatively, you can configure a scope that makes up the entire subnet and then immediately define *exclusion ranges* (see the next section) for all of the subnet's statically addressed computers.

One common method for handling the need for both static and dynamically assigned addresses within an address range is to reserve the first 10 addresses within any subnet for statically addressed servers and to begin the DHCP scope with the eleventh address. For example, in the subnet 192.168.1.0, you can keep the addresses 192.168.1.1 through 192.168.1.10 for your statically addressed servers, such as your DHCP server, your DNS server, your WINS server, and other servers with addresses that should not change. You can then define the addresses 192.168.1.11 through 192.168.1.254 as the range for the subnet's DHCP scope. (In another common implementation, the first 20 addresses are reserved for statically addressed servers.)

If servers on your network have already been configured with static addresses in the middle of the subnet range, such as 192.168.1.110 and 192.168.1.46, you should use exclusion ranges to keep these addresses from being assigned to other computers. Otherwise, because each subnet can use only a single range of IP addresses for its scope, you need to severely restrict the number of addresses available for lease.

Exclusion Ranges

An *exclusion range* is a set of one or more IP addresses, included within the range of a defined scope, that you do not want to lease to DHCP clients. Exclusion ranges assure that the server does not offer to DHCP clients on your network any addresses in these ranges. For example, Figure 7-2 shows two exclusion ranges being configured for a new scope, one of which consist of only one IP address. By setting an exclusion for these addresses, you specify that DHCP clients are never offered these addresses when they request a lease from the server.

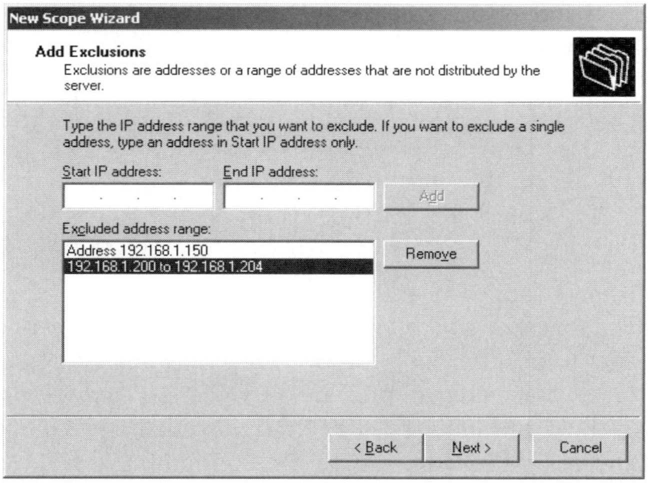

Figure 7-2   Configuring an exclusion range

You can also use exclusion ranges at the edges of ranges. For example, you can define a scope's range as 192.168.1.1 through 192.168.1.254 and then define an exclusion range of 192.168.1.1 through 192.168.1.10 to accommodate the servers within the subnet that have IP addresses that are configured manually (statically).

Tip   Because Windows Server 2003 recommends that a computer running the DHCP service have its IP address statically configured, be sure the server computer has its IP address either outside of, or excluded from, the range of the scope.

After you define a DHCP scope and apply exclusion ranges, the remaining addresses form the available *address pool* within the scope. Pooled addresses are eligible for dynamic assignment by the server to DHCP clients on your network.

Using the 80/20 Rule for Servers and Scopes

To provide fault tolerance for the DHCP service within a given subnet, you might want to configure two DHCP servers to assign addresses for the same subnet. With two DHCP servers deployed, if one server is unavailable, the other server can take its place and continue to lease new addresses or renew existing clients.

For balancing DHCP server use in this case, a good practice is to use the 80/20 rule to divide the scope addresses between the two DHCP servers. If Server 1 is configured to make available most (approximately 80 percent) of the addresses, Server 2 can be configured to make the other addresses (approximately 20 percent) available to clients.

For example, in a typical subnet with the address 192.168.1.0, the first 10 addresses are reserved for static addresses, and the IP address range for the DHCP scope defined on the subnet is 192.168.1.11 through 192.168.1.254. To comply with the 80/20 rule, both Server 1 and Server 2 define the same range for the scope, but the exclusions configured on each server differ. On Server 1, the exclusion range is configured as the final 20 percent of the scope, or 192.168.1.205 through 192.168.1.254; this range allows the server to lease addresses to the first 80 percent of the scope's range. On Server 2, the exclusion range for the scope is configured as the first 80 percent of the scope, or 192.168.1.11 through 192.168.1.204. This range allows Server 2 to lease addresses to the final 20 percent of the scope's range.

Figure 7-3 illustrates this example of the 80/20 rule.

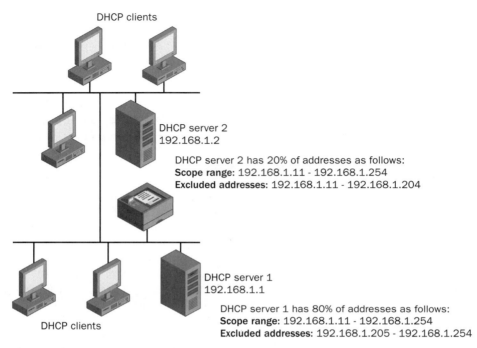

Figure 7-3   80/20 rule for DHCP subnets

Creating Reservations

You use a *reservation* to create a permanent address lease assignment by the DHCP server. Reservations assure that a specified hardware device on the subnet can always use the same IP address. For example, if you have defined the range 192.168.1.11 through 192.168.1.254 as your DHCP scope, you can then reserve the IP address 192.168.1.100 within that scope for the network adapter whose hardware address is 00-b0-d0-01-18-86. Every time the computer hosting this adapter boots, the server recognizes the adapter's Media Access Control (MAC) hardware address and leases the same address 192.168.1.100.

To create a reservation within the DHCP console, open the scope in which you want to create a reservation, right-click Reservations, and then select New Reservation. This procedure opens the New Reservation dialog box, shown in Figure 7-4. To configure a reservation, you must type appropriate values into the Reservation Name, IP Address, and MAC Address text boxes.

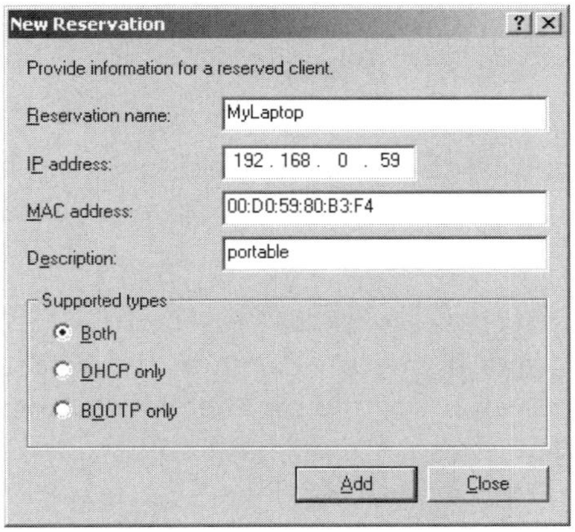

Figure 7-4   New Reservation dialog box

Reservations cannot be used interchangeably with manual (static) configurations. Certain computers, such as those hosting a DNS server or a DHCP server, require their IP addresses to be configured manually and not automatically by means of a DHCP server. In such cases, reservations are not a valid alternative to static configurations.

However, you can use a reservation when you want to assign a specific address to a non-essential computer. Through this method, you can dedicate an address while still enjoying the other benefits of DHCP, including centralized management, address conflict prevention, and scope option assignment. For example, you might find that a print server's specific IP address configuration is more easily managed through a centrally configured reservation, which is continually renewed, than through a manual configuration locally at the server. Finally, you should remember that reservations can be made only to DHCP clients. In other words, a DHCP server can lease a reservation only to clients that have been configured to obtain an IP address automatically.

> **Exam Tip**   Look for questions in which a particular address is simultaneously reserved and excluded. In such cases, the reservation can't work.

Assigning DHCP Options

DHCP options provide clients with additional configuration data, such as specific server addresses, along with an address lease. For example, when the Transmission Control Protocol/Internet Protocol (TCP/IP) properties of a client computer have been configured to obtain a DNS server address automatically, that computer is relying on DHCP options configured at the DHCP server to acquire a DNS server address (or set of addresses).

You can configure options at the reservation level, scope level, or server level. Options set at the reservation level override all others, and scope-level options override server-level options.

To configure options for a reservation, select the particular reservation's icon in the DHCP console tree, and then from the Action or shortcut menu, select Configure Options. To configure options for a scope (after completing the New Scope Wizard), select the Scope Options folder in the DHCP console tree, and then from the Action or shortcut menu, select Configure Options. To configure options for a server, select the Server Options folder in the DHCP console tree, and then from the Action or shortcut menu, select Configure Options. The dialog box that opens after each of these procedures is virtually the same. The Scope Options dialog box is shown as an example in Figure 7-5.

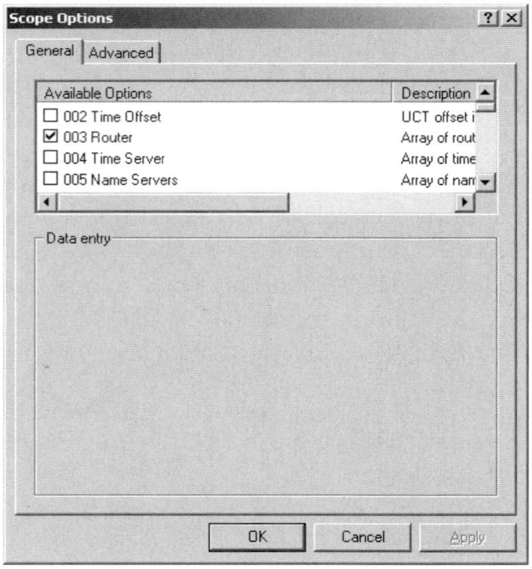

Figure 7-5   Configuring DHCP options

More than 60 standard DHCP options are available. The most common of these include the following:

■ **003 Router**   A preferred list of IP addresses for routers on the same subnet as DHCP clients. The client can then contact these routers as needed to forward IP packets destined for remote hosts.

- **006 DNS Servers**   The IP addresses for DNS name servers that DHCP clients can contact and use to resolve a domain host name query.

- **015 DNS Domain Name**   An option that specifies the domain name that DHCP clients should use when resolving unqualified names during DNS domain name resolution. This option also allows clients to perform dynamic DNS updates.

- **044 WINS/NBNS Servers**   The IP addresses of primary and secondary WINS servers for the DHCP client to use.

- **046 WINS/NBT Node Type**   A preferred NetBIOS name resolution method for the DHCP client to use—such as b-node (0x1) for broadcast only or h-node (0x8) for a hybrid of point-to-point and broadcast methods.

- **051 Lease**   An option that assigns a special lease duration only to remote access clients. This option relies on user class information advertised by this client type. (User classes are discussed in more detail in Lesson 2 of this chapter.)

Activating a Scope

After you define and configure a scope, the scope must be *activated* before the DHCP server can begin providing service to clients. However, you should not activate a new scope until you have specified the DHCP options for it.

To activate a scope, complete the following steps:

1. Open the DHCP console.

2. In the console tree, select the applicable scope.

3. From the Action menu, select Activate.

> **Note**   The Action menu command changes to Deactivate when the selected scope is currently activated. In production environments, you should not deactivate a scope unless you are retiring it permanently from use on your network.

> **Exam Tip**   Expect to see a question in which DHCP is not functioning because either the scope has not been activated or the server has not been authorized.

Configuring the Client

To configure a client to receive its IP address information from a DHCP server, open the Internet Protocol (TCP/IP) Properties dialog box for the appropriate network connection. By selecting the Obtain An IP Address Automatically option, you enable the client to obtain from the DHCP server an IP address, subnet mask, and all DHCP options except for DNS options. To configure the client to receive DNS options from the DHCP server, select the Obtain DNS Server Address Automatically option.

If you are migrating the client from a statically assigned address, you can apply the new configuration simply by closing the open dialog boxes.

Migrating from APIPA or Alternate Configurations

If a client has already been configured to obtain an IP address and DNS server address automatically, and the network is *not* using ICS, you merely need to renew the IP configuration to apply the settings from the newly configured DHCP server.

To renew a configuration, enter the **ipconfig /renew** command at the command prompt. Alternatively, you can restart the client computer, and the new IP configuration is applied as the computer reboots.

Migrating from an ICS Connection

ICS is a shared dial-up connection on a server that provides Internet access to network clients and automatically configures client computers with an address in the 192.168.0.*x* subnet range. Because this service competes with the DHCP Server service, you should delete any shared (ICS-enabled) dial-up connections on the server and restart the server computer before installing the DHCP Windows component or adding the DHCP Server role.

> **Real World   Migrating ICS Clients**
>
> ICS clients are already configured to obtain an IP address automatically, so in theory, they require no reconfiguration beyond a simple reboot if you want to migrate to DHCP. However, you might find that in practice, ICS clients stubbornly cling to their ICS addresses even after DHCP is deployed. To prevent such complications, you can first apply a manual (static) address to the client computers after the ICS connection is deleted; this procedure breaks the ICS connection. Then restart the client computers. After the clients restart, they will migrate cleanly to DHCP as soon as you reconfigure them to obtain an address automatically.

After the DHCP server is installed and configured, you can apply the new automatic configuration to the client as you would to any statically configured client—by selecting the Obtain An IP Address Automatically option and (optionally) the Obtain DNS Server Address Automatically option in the Internet Protocol (TCP/IP) Properties dialog box.

Verifying the Configuration

After you configure your DHCP server, and after you have authorized the server and activated the scope, you need to verify that the service is working on your client computers. Restart your DHCP client computers (or use Ipconfig /renew) and then enter the **ipconfig /all** command at the command prompt. With the /all switch, the Ipconfig command displays all of the parameters you have configured for the lease, including DHCP options.

> **Tip** You can assign users to the domain local security group DHCP Users if you want to allow them to read DHCP information without being able to manage or modify this data.

Practice: Installing and Configuring a DHCP Server

In this practice, you install and configure a new DHCP server. Because the two-computer configuration currently uses ICS, which uses its own version of DHCP, you must first delete the shared dial-up connection and restart both computers before proceeding with the DHCP server installation. This precaution prevents the two services from conflicting with one another.

> **Important** This practice assumes that you have deployed ICS through a dial-up connection. If instead you are using another type of Internet connection, you will need to make whatever adjustments are required to deploy a DHCP server on your test network.

Exercise 1: Deleting the ICS-Enabled Connection

ICS provides its own addressing service that conflicts with the addressing service provided by a DHCP server. In this exercise, you delete ICS to prepare for the installation of a DHCP server.

1. From Computer1, log on to Domain1 as Administrator.

2. Open the Network Connections window and disconnect the MyISP connection if it is not already disconnected.

3. Right-click MyISP, and then select Delete.

   The Confirm Connection Delete message box opens, asking you to confirm the deletion.

4. Click Yes.

5. Restart Computer1.

6. Switch to Computer2 and log on to Domain1 as Administrator.

7. Open a command prompt and type the following command:

   netsh interface ip set address local static 192.168.0.2 255.255.255.0.

   This command sets the Local Area Connection to a static address of 192.168.0.2/24.

8. After the command has executed, type the following command:

   netsh interface ip set dns local static 192.168.0.1.

   This command sets the preferred DNS server of the Local Area Connection to the address 192.168.0.1.

   The static address and preferred DNS server configuration is used temporarily until the new DHCP server is configured. This step is recommended only because you are switching from one dynamic addressing service (ICS) to another.

9. After the command has executed, restart Computer2.

Exercise 2: Adding a DHCP Server Role

In this exercise, you install and add a DCHP server role on Computer1. During this process, you configure and activate a new scope. Following this, you authorize the new DHCP server.

Before you begin this exercise, on Computer1, insert the Windows Server 2003 installation CD-ROM.

1. From Computer1, log on to Domain1 as Administrator.

2. At a command prompt, type the following command:

   netsh interface ip set address local static 192.168.0.1 255.255.255.0.

   This command ensures that the address shown is assigned statically to the Local Area Connection. Even if you originally assigned a static address to Computer1, ICS overrides this setting and replaces it by assigning the address 192.168.0.1 dynamically—not statically—to the local computer. DHCP servers and other essential network servers, however, normally require static addresses.

3. After the command has completed, close the command prompt.

4. From the Start menu, select Manage Your Server.

   The Manage Your Server window opens.

5. Click the Add Or Remove A Role option.

   The Preliminary Steps page of the Configure Your Server Wizard appears.

6. On the Preliminary Steps page, click Next.

   The Server Role page appears.

7. From the Server Role list, select DHCP Server and then click Next.

   The Summary Of Selections page appears.

8. Click Next.

   The Configuring Components page appears while the DHCP server is installing. After installation of the DHCP server is complete, the Welcome page of the New Scope Wizard appears.

9. On the Welcome page, click Next.

   The Scope Name page appears.

10. In the Name text box, type **Test Scope**.

11. Leave the Description text box empty, and click Next.

    The IP Address Range page appears.

12. In the Start IP Address text box, type **192.168.0.11**.

13. In the End IP Address text box, type **192.168.0.254**.

14. Verify that the subnet mask value reads 255.255.255.0, and click Next.

    The Add Exclusions page appears.

15. In the Start IP Address text box, type **192.168.0.100**, and then click Add.

    The address moves into the Excluded Address Range window.

16. In the Start IP Address text box, type **192.168.0.200**.

17. In the End IP Address text box, type **192.168.0.205**.

18. Click Add.

    The new IP address range is added to the Excluded Address Range window.

19. Click Next.

    The Lease Duration page appears.

20. Read all of the text on this page.

21. Click Next to accept the default setting of 8 days.

    The Configure DHCP Options page appears.

22. Click Next to accept the default selection of Yes.

    The Router (Default Gateway) page appears.

23. In the IP Address text box type **192.168.0.1**, and then click Add.

    The address moves into the lower window.

24. Click Next.

The Domain Name And DNS Servers page appears.

25. In the Parent Domain text box, type **domain1.local**.

26. In the IP Address text box type **192.168.0.1**, and then click Add.

27. Click Next.

The WINS Servers page appears.

28. Click Next.

The Activate Scope page appears.

29. Click Next to accept the default selection to activate the scope.

The Completing The New Scope Wizard page appears.

30. Click Finish.

The Configure Your Server Wizard indicates that the server is now a DHCP server.

31. In the Configure Your Server Wizard, click Finish.

32. Open the DHCP console by clicking Start, selecting Administrative Tools, and then clicking DHCP.

The DHCP console opens.

33. In the DHCP console tree, expand the Computer1.domain1.local node.

The Scope folder and Server Options folder appear under the server node. Next to the server node, a red arrow points downward, indicating that the DHCP server has not yet been authorized.

34. Right-click the server icon and select Authorize.

35. Press F5 to refresh the console.

The red arrow pointing downward becomes a green arrow pointing upward, indicating that the server is now authorized. (If necessary, repeat step 35 until the green arrow appears.)

36. Close the DHCP console.

Exercise 3: Configuring a DHCP Client

In this exercise, you configure Computer2 to obtain an address automatically. This procedure allows the computer to lease an address from the newly configured DHCP server.

1. From Computer1, while you are logged on to Domain1 as Administrator, open the DNS console.

2. Delete any A and PTR resource records for Computer2 in the domain1.local and 192.168.0.*x* subnet zones.

   This step ensures that a DNS record corresponding to the new DHCP scope will be properly created and updated.

3. Close the DNS console.

4. Switch to Computer2 and log on to Domain1 as Administrator.

5. Open the Local Area Connection Properties dialog box, and then open the Internet Protocol (TCP/IP) Properties dialog box.

6. On the General tab, select the Obtain An IP Address Automatically option.

7. Select the Obtain DNS Server Address Automatically option.

8. Click OK.

9. In the Local Area Connection Properties dialog box, click Close.

   The new configuration is applied by the time the dialog box closes.

10. At a command prompt type **ipconfig /registerdns**, and then press Enter.

Exercise 4: Testing the Configuration

In this exercise, you verify the configuration on both the client and the server.

1. From Computer2, while you are still logged on to Domain1 as Administrator, open a command prompt.

2. At the command prompt type **ipconfig /all**, and then press Enter.

   The new IP configuration obtained through DHCP is displayed, including the address of 192.168.0.11. The Default Gateway, DHCP Server, and DNS Server parameters are all set to 192.168.0.1.

3. Switch to Computer1.

4. If you have not already done so, from Computer1, log on to Domain1 as Administrator.

5. Open the DHCP console.

6. In the console tree, expand the Scope node, and select the Address Leases folder.

7. Right-click the Address Leases folder, and then select Refresh.

8. Answer the following question in the space provided.

   How many active address leases now appear in the details pane of the DHCP console when the Address Leases folder is selected? To which computer is this address assigned?

   _____

9. Close the DHCP console.

10. Open the DNS console and verify that a new A resource record has been created for Computer2.

11. Log off Computer1 and Computer2.

Lesson Review

The following questions are intended to reinforce key information presented in this lesson. If you are unable to answer a question, review the lesson materials and try the question again. You can find answers to the questions in the "Questions and Answers" section at the end of this chapter.

1. You have configured a scope with an address range of 192.168.0.11 through 192.168.0.254. However, your DNS server on the same subnet has already been assigned a static address of 192.168.0.200. With the least administrative effort, how can you allow for compatibility between the DNS server's address and DHCP service on the subnet?

   _____

   _____

   _____

2. Which of the following servers are eligible to be the first DHCP server on your network? (Choose all that apply.)

   a. A Windows Server 2003 domain controller in an Active Directory network

   b. A Windows 2000 Server workgroup server in a network with no domains

   c. A Windows Server 2003 workgroup server in an Active Directory network

   d. A Windows 2000 Server member server in an Active Directory network

3. A DHCP scope has been configured with the 003 Router option, which provides clients with the address of a default gateway. However, after running the Ipconfig/renew command and then the Ipconfig /all command at a computer named Client1, you find that this client is being assigned an IP address within the defined scope but not the address of a default gateway. Which of the following answers could explain this behavior?

   a. Client1 has become disconnected from the network.

   b. Client1's IP address is acquired by means of a reservation at the DHCP server.

   c. No scope options have been defined at the server level.

   d. The scope has not been activated.

4. Besides Administrators, name two security groups that have the authority to manage DHCP servers.

5. While running the New Scope Wizard, you select the option not to configure any DHCP options. Afterward, you find that the DHCP server is not assigning addresses within the defined scope. Which is the most likely reason that DHCP address assignment is not functioning?

Lesson Summary

- When a DHCP server is available, computers that have been configured to obtain an IP address automatically, on booting, request and receive their IP configuration from that DHCP server.

- DHCP servers must be authorized if they are to be made available in Active Directory networks.

- A DHCP scope is a continuous range of IP addresses, defined within a single logical subnet, that the DHCP server can assign to clients. After you define and configure a scope, the scope must be activated before the DHCP server can begin providing service to clients.

- An exclusion range is a set of one or more IP addresses, included within the range of a defined scope, that you do not want to lease to DHCP clients. You use a reservation to create a permanent address lease assignment by the DHCP server.

- DHCP options provide clients with additional configuration data, such as the addresses of a client's default gateway or DNS server, along with an address lease.

Lesson 2: Managing DHCP in Windows Networks

In an enterprise environment, managing DHCP service requires you to perform a broad range of functions, from changing the status of a DHCP server, to backing up the server, to using command-line tools to configure a DHCP server from over wide area network (WAN) links. In addition, enterprise networks often include various topology restrictions or other practical limitations requiring situational design adjustments in DHCP service. Effective DHCP administrators need to be able to handle these adjustments, such as providing DHCP service through routers or configuring more than one logical subnet on a single physical network segment.

After this lesson, you will be able to

- Start, stop, restart, pause, and resume the DHCP Server service by means of the DHCP console, the command-line interface, and the Services console
- Disable the DHCP Server service
- Use the Netshell (Netsh) command-line environment to administer the DHCP Server service
- Configure superscopes to provide DHCP service for more than one logical subnet on a single physical subnet
- Change the addressing of a subnet for which the DHCP Server service is configured
- Back up and restore the DHCP server database
- Move a DHCP server
- Manually compact a DHCP server database
- Use options classes to configure a subset of DHCP clients with specific options

Estimated lesson time: 70 minutes

Changing DCHP Server Status

You can use various tools to start or stop the DHCP Server service: the DHCP console, the command-line interface, and the Services console.

DHCP Console

Within the DHCP console, the Action menu that appears when the server icon is selected contains an All Tasks submenu that includes the options Start, Stop, Pause, Resume, and Restart. This same Action menu and All Tasks submenu also appear in the DHCP console when you right-click the DHCP server icon.

To start or stop a DHCP server, complete the following steps:

1. Open the DHCP console.

2. In the console tree, select the applicable DHCP server.

3. On the Action menu, point to All Tasks and then select one of the following:

   ❑ To start the service, select Start.

   ❑ To stop the service, select Stop.

   ❑ To interrupt the service, select Pause.

   ❑ To continue a service after it has been paused, select Resume.

   ❑ To stop and then automatically restart the service, select Restart.

Command-Line Interface

You can also start, stop, pause, and resume the DHCP Server service by executing the following commands, respectively, at the command prompt.

■ Net Start Dhcpserver

■ Net Stop Dhcpserver

■ Net Pause Dhcpserver

■ Net Continue Dhcpserver

Services Console

The Services console is a graphical administration tool that you can open by clicking Start, selecting Administrative Tools, and then clicking Services. To access controls for the DCHP Server service, double-click the DHCP server node in the list of services in the details pane. This procedure opens the DHCP Server Properties dialog box, shown in Figure 7-6.

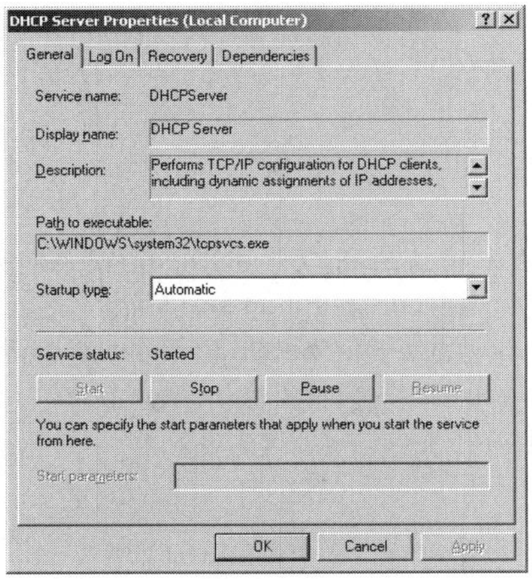

Figure 7-6   DHCP Server Properties dialog box

The Services console offers an important addition to the Start, Stop, Pause, and Resume controls available in both the DHCP console and the command-line interface. In the Startup Type drop-down list, you can select the Disabled option. When this option is selected, the service cannot be started until the setting is changed. This setting is useful, for example, when you need to move a DHCP database to another computer and you want to ensure that the old server remains stopped even after you perform the migration.

> **Note**   If the service is running when you select the Disabled option, the setting applies after the next shutdown.

Managing DHCP from a Command Line

Windows Server 2003 includes the Netshell (Netsh) command-line environment, which provides an interface from which you can manage many functions and features of your server. The Netsh commands for DHCP make up a fully equivalent alternative to console-based management. Using this command-line tool can be useful in the following situations:

- When managing DHCP servers in WANs, you can use commands at the Netsh command prompt to perform administrative tasks across slow-speed network links.

- When managing a large number of DHCP servers, you can use commands in Batch mode to automate recurring administrative tasks that need to be performed for all DHCP servers.

To enter the Netsh command-line environment, you simply execute the Netsh command at a command prompt. This procedure opens the Netsh> prompt. To access the DHCP administration interface, execute the DHCP command at the Netsh> prompt to enter the dhcp context. This process is illustrated here:

```
C:\>netsh
netsh>dhcp
netsh dhcp>
```

> **Note**   You do not need to step gradually into the various levels of Netsh prompts to execute a Netsh command. For example, to view a DHCP server configuration summary, you can simply open a command prompt and type the following in one line: **netsh dhcp server show all**. However, entering each context separately allows you—through the use of the Help, List, or ? commands—to view a list of commands available within each context.

Although the Netsh dhcp> prompt allows you to add, delete, and view DHCP servers on your network, many more DHCP management controls are accessible through the

Netsh dhcp server> prompt and the Netsh dhcp server scope> prompt. To access the Netsh dhcp server> prompt, simply execute the Server command at the Netsh dhcp> prompt. To access a Netsh dhcp server scope> prompt, enter the Scope <*scope IP address*> command at the Netsh dhcp server> prompt. This process is illustrated here:

```
netsh>dhcp
netsh dhcp>server
netsh dhcp server>scope 192.168.0.0

Changed the current scope context to 192.168.0.0 scope.
netsh dhcp server scope>
```

At any given prompt, you should use the Help, List, or ? command to view the full list of commands available within each context. To learn about usage associated with any particular command, you can use the Help, List, or ? command after any given command. For example, to learn about the options available with the Set command, you can enter **set help** at a prompt within any Netsh context.

You can also use Windows Server 2003 online help to learn more about the Netsh utility.

> **Note**   To manage a DHCP server by using the Netsh command line, you must be logged on as a member of either the local Administrators group or the local DHCP Administrators group on the applicable server computer.

To use DHCP commands interactively at the command prompt, complete the following steps:

1. Open a command prompt.

2. Enter **netsh**.

3. At the Netsh> command prompt, enter **dhcp**.

4. At the Netsh dhcp> command prompt, enter either **server <*servername*>** or **server <*ip_address*>** for the server you want to manage. To manage the local server, simply type **server**.

5. Once connected, you can use any supported Netshell command for DHCP.

   Type **/?** or **help** to display the immediate DHCP subcommand menu, or enter **list** to list all Netshell subcommands available for use with DHCP.

> **Note**   See the "Troubleshooting Lab" section at the end of this and other chapters for example applications of the Netsh utility.

Connecting Clients to Remote DHCP Servers

Through the use of network broadcasts, DHCP allows client computers to locate DHCP servers on the local subnet and to obtain an IP address from that local server. However, routers by default prevent broadcasts from crossing into other subnets. Consequently, without some other added functionality, every physical subnet would need to contain a DHCP server for clients to receive DHCP service.

This added functionality can be provided in the form of RFC 1542–compliant routers, which can be configured not to block DHCP broadcasts, or DHCP relay agents, which can be configured to intercept broadcasted DHCP messages and transport them across the network to the IP address of a DHCP server.

Before passing a DHCP message on to a DHCP server, both RFC 1542–compliant routers and DHCP relay agents write their own address inside a certain field (named Giaddr) within that message. This address recorded within the DHCP message informs the DHCP server of the subnet ID of the originating subnet of the DHCP request and, consequently, of the proper scope from which to issue addresses to that subnet.

DHCP relay agents and RFC 1542–compatible routers are discussed in more detail in Lesson 4 of Chapter 9, "Routing with Windows Server 2003." The Giaddr field is discussed in more detail in Lesson 3 of Chapter 8, "Monitoring and Troubleshooting DHCP."

Using Superscopes

A *superscope* is an administrative grouping of scopes that is used to support *multinets*, or multiple logical subnets on a single network segment. Multinetting commonly occurs when the number of hosts on a physical segment grows beyond the capacity of the original address space. By creating a logically distinct second scope (such as 207.46.150.0) to add to an original scope (such as 207.46.9.0), and then grouping these two scopes into a single superscope, you can double your physical segment's capacity for addresses. (In multinet scenarios, routing is also required to connect the logical subnets.) In this way, the DHCP server can provide clients on a single physical network with leases from more than one scope.

 Note   Superscopes contain only a list of member scopes or child scopes that can be activated together; they are not used to configure other details about scope use.

To create a superscope, you must create a scope first. After you have created a scope, you can create a superscope by right-clicking the DHCP server icon in the DHCP console tree and then selecting New Superscope. This procedure launches the New Superscope Wizard. In the wizard, select the scope or scopes that you would like to add as members. You can also add new scopes to the superscope later.

To create a superscope, complete the following steps:

1. Open the DHCP console.

2. In the console tree, select the applicable DHCP server.

3. From the Action menu, select New Superscope.

   This menu command appears only if at least one scope that is not currently part of a superscope has been created at the server.

4. Follow the instructions in the New Superscope Wizard.

Superscope Configurations for Multinets

The next section shows how a simple DHCP network consisting originally of one physical network segment and one DHCP server can be extended by means of superscopes to support multinet configurations.

Superscope Supporting Local Multinets   Figure 7-7 illustrates multinetting on a single physical network (Subnet A) with a single DHCP server.

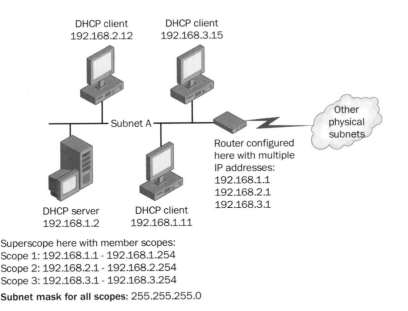

Figure 7-7   Multinetting on a single network segment

To support this scenario, you can configure a superscope that includes as members the original scope (Scope 1) and the additional scopes for the logical multinets you need to support (Scopes 2 and 3).

> **Note**   When you are supporting two logical subnets on one physical segment, use a router to connect traffic from one subnet to another.

Superscope Supporting Remote Multinets   Figure 7-8 illustrates a configuration used to support multinets on a physical network (Subnet B) that is separated from the DHCP server. In this scenario, a superscope defined on the DHCP server joins the two multinets on a remote segment beyond the router. Because DHCP traffic is normally restricted to the local subnet, a DHCP relay agent is used to support clients on the remote segment.

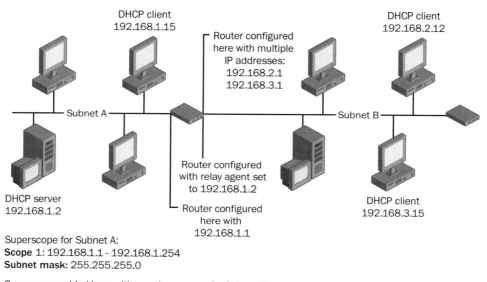

Superscope for Subnet A:
Scope 1: 192.168.1.1 - 192.168.1.254
Subnet mask: 255.255.255.0

Superscope added here with member scopes for Subnet B:
Scope 2: 192.168.2.1 - 192.168.2.254
Scope 3: 192.168.3.1 - 192.168.3.254
Subnet mask: 255.255.255.0

Figure 7-8   Routed multinetting

Superscopes Supporting Two Local DHCP Servers   Without superscopes, two DHCP server computers issuing leases on a single segment would create address conflicts. Figure 7-9 illustrates such a scenario.

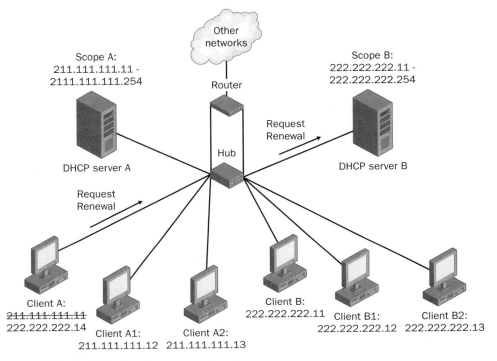

Figure 7-9   Conflicts in a two-server subnet

In this configuration, DHCP Server A manages a different scope of addresses from that of DHCP Server B, and neither has any information about addresses managed by the other. A problem arises when a client that has previously registered with Server A, for example, releases its name during a proper shutdown and later reconnects to the network.

When the client (Client A) reboots, it tries to renew its address lease. However, if Server B responds to Client A's request before Server A does, Server B rejects the foreign address renewal request with a *negative acknowledgment* (NACK). As a result of this process, Client A's address resets, and Client A is forced to seek a new IP address. In the process of obtaining a new address lease, Client A might be offered an address that places it on an incorrect logical subnet.

Figure 7-10 shows how, using superscopes on both DHCP servers, you can avoid these problems and manage two scopes predictably and effectively. In this configuration, both servers are still located on the same physical subnet. A superscope included on both Server A and Server B includes as members both scopes defined on the physical subnet. To prevent the servers from issuing leases in each other's scopes, each server excludes the full scope range belonging to the other server.

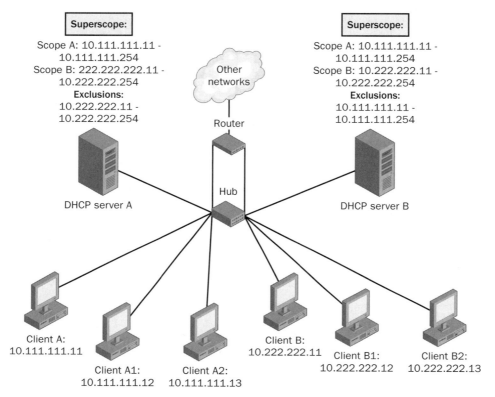

Figure 7-10   Two servers using a superscope

In this example, Server B is configured to exclude the scope managed by Server A, and vice versa. This configuration prevents the servers from sending negative acknowledgments to DHCP clients attempting to renew IP addresses from the excluded logical range of addresses. Because each server is informed of the scope managed by the other server, each server simply ignores requests from clients originating from the other server's scope.

Changing the Addressing of a Subnet

In the course of DHCP administration, you might find it necessary to modify or completely change a subnet's addressing.

If you merely need to modify the range of a current scope, you can achieve this task by changing the address range or exclusion ranges of the subnet's defined DHCP scope.

> **Important**   Change scope properties with care so as not to exclude active leases, and so as not to include within the reconfigured scope any addresses on the subnet that have been manually assigned to other computers.

If you need to migrate to a completely new scope, however, you must first add a new scope to the DHCP server and then migrate to that new scope. To perform such a migration, first create and activate the new scope, and then deactivate the old scope. Do not delete the deactivated scope until the clients have migrated to the new scope. To migrate clients, either wait for the clients to automatically renew their leases (after 50 percent of the configured scope lease time has elapsed) or manually renew clients by executing the Ipconfig /release command followed by the Ipconfig /renew command on the client computers. Once all clients have been moved or forced to seek leases in another scope, you can safely delete the inactive scope.

> **Exam Tip**   You can enable conflict detection on the Advanced tab of the DHCP server properties dialog box. This feature allows you to specify the number of times the DHCP server will ping a given address on the network before assigning that address to a client. If the ping receives a reply, the address will not be assigned. This feature is useful, for example, if you need to deploy a new DHCP server to replace one that has recently failed. In this case, without the aid of an up-to-date DHCP server database, conflict detection can ensure that currently active leases are not assigned to other clients.

Backing Up the DHCP Server Database

Maintaining a backup of the DHCP database protects you from data loss if the DHCP database is lost (for example, due to hard disk failure) or becomes corrupted.

The two backup methods supported by the DHCP server are synchronous (automatic) backups that occur automatically every 60 minutes and asynchronous (manual) backups, performed using the Backup command in the DHCP console. Only manual backups can be used to perform manual database restorations. Automatic backups are used to restore the database only when the DHCP service detects database corruption.

When a backup occurs, the entire DHCP database is saved, including the following:

- All scopes, including superscopes and multicast scopes
- Reservations

- Leases

- All options, including server options, scope options, reservation options, and class options

However, some DHCP data is not saved in any type of backup. For example, credentials specified for DNS dynamic update are not backed up with a manual or automatic backup. (You can configure these credentials through the Advanced tab of DHCP server properties.)

Performing a Manual Backup

To perform a manual backup of the DHCP database, right-click the DHCP server icon in the DHCP console, and then select Backup. To restore the DHCP database, right-click the DHCP server icon in the DHCP console, and then select Restore.

Backup Locations   The default DHCP database manual backup path is \WINDOWS\ System32\Dhcp\Backup. You can change the database backup folder by selecting a different local folder during a manual backup or by changing the backup folder location in the DHCP server properties dialog box.

When planning your backup strategy, keep the following in mind:

- When you perform manual backups, you don't need to stop the DHCP service unless you're moving your database to a new server.

- The backup folder location must be a local path.

Migrating a DHCP Server   Migrating a DHCP server from one server to another requires you to move the DHCP database to the new server. To move the DHCP database, simply back it up and then restore it to another location, as explained in the following procedures.

To back up the DHCP database (at the source server), complete the following steps:

1. Open the DHCP console.

2. In the console tree, select the applicable DHCP server.

3. From the Action menu, select Backup.

   The Browse For Folder dialog box opens.

4. Select the folder that will contain the backup DHCP database, and then click OK.

   You must choose a local drive for the DHCP database backup folder.

5. Stop the DHCP server.

   This step prevents the server from assigning new address leases to clients after the database has been backed up.

6. In the Services console, disable the DHCP Server service in the list of services.

    To perform this task, launch the Services console and double-click DHCP Server. In the DHCP Server Properties dialog box, from the Startup Type drop-down list, select Disabled and click OK. This setting prevents the DHCP server from starting after the database has been transferred.

7. Copy the folder that contains the backup DHCP database to the destination DHCP server.

To restore the DHCP database (at the destination server), complete the following steps:

1. If you have not already installed the DHCP Server role, do so.

2. Open the DHCP console.

3. In the console tree, select the applicable DHCP server.

4. From the Action menu, select Restore.

    The Browse For Folder dialog box opens.

5. In the Browse For Folder dialog box, select the folder that contains the backup DHCP database, and then click OK. If prompted to stop and restart the service, click Yes.

    The database you are restoring must have been created manually using the Backup command on the DHCP console Action menu. Backups created automatically by the DHCP service cannot be used to perform manual database restorations.

Manually Compacting a DHCP Server

To support the offline compaction and repair of Jet databases, such as the DHCP database and the Windows Internet Name Service (WINS) database, Windows Server 2003 includes the Jetpack.exe tool.

The DHCP Server service performs dynamic Jet compaction of the DHCP database while the server is online—which reduces the need to use Jetpack.exe for offline compaction. However, offline compaction is a more efficient means of defragmenting the DHCP database than is dynamic compaction.

You should plan to use Jetpack.exe to compact a Jet database periodically whenever the database grows beyond 30 MB. In addition, performing offline compaction is recommended if you receive error messages indicating that the DHCP database has become corrupted.

To manually compact or repair the DHCP database, complete the following steps:

1. On a DHCP server computer, open a command prompt.

2. Use the Jetpack.exe tool to perform offline compaction.

The correct syntax for Jetpack.exe is as follows:

```
jetpack database_name temporary_database_name
```

The following are example commands to compact the DHCP database:

```
cd WINDOWS\system32\dhcp
net stop dhcpserver
jetpack dhcp.mdb tmp.mdb
net start dhcpserver
```

Using Options Classes

An *options class* is a way for the server to manage options provided to clients within a scope. When an options class is added to the server, clients of that class can be provided class-specific option types for their configuration. Options classes can be of two types:

- Vendor classes are used to assign vendor-specific options to clients identified as sharing a commonly defined vendor type.

- User classes are used to assign options to clients identified as sharing a common need for similar DHCP options configuration.

You can view the available options classes by selecting Define User Classes, Define Vendor Classes, or Set Predefined Options from the server node shortcut menu. By default, the options you can configure for a reservation, scope, or server are those that belong to the DHCP Standard Options vendor class and to the Default User Class user class.

> **Exam Tip**   In Windows Server 2003, the DHCP server includes a predefined user class named Default Routing And Remote Access class. Options within this class apply only to clients that request an address configuration while connecting to Routing And Remote Access. One such option that you are likely to see on the exam is 051 Lease. By configuring this option, you can assign shorter lease durations to your remote access clients than to your other DHCP clients.

Implementing User Classes

User classes allow you to apply a particular configuration of DHCP options to any subset of DHCP clients you define. To implement a user class, you first define the class at the DHCP server by assigning an ID and set of options for the class. Then you assign selected client computers to the class by using the Ipconfig /setclassid command. When these clients subsequently communicate with DHCP servers, they announce their class ID and inherit the options of that class.

A custom user class is helpful when you need to assign distinct options to distinct sets of client computers. For example, your network might require that clients with the security clearance to bypass the company firewall be assigned a unique default gate-way. In this example, you could configure options to distribute the unique default gateway to the security-exempt class.

To create a custom or new user class, right-click the DHCP server icon in the DHCP console and select Define User Classes, as shown in Figure 7-11.

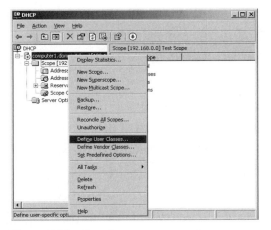

Figure 7-11   Creating a new user class

You then need to set an ID string for the class. You designate this class ID string when you first create the class in the DHCP console, as shown in Figure 7-12. After defining a new class and specifying an ID string for that class, you can then set desired options for that class.

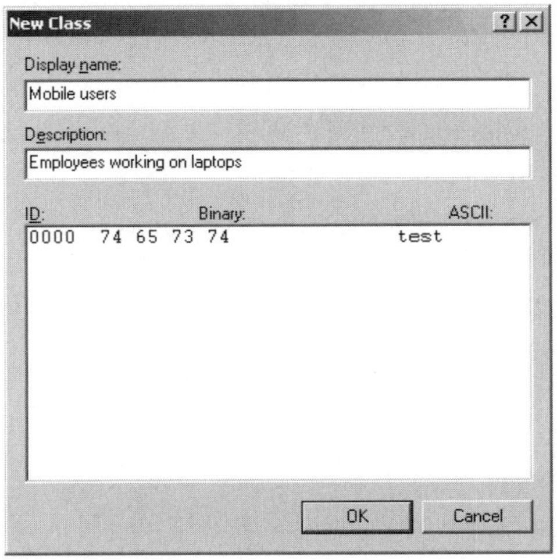

Figure 7-12   Designating a new class ID

Finally, for the desired computers to inherit the options of the new class, you need to set the class ID of appropriate client computers to match the ID you have defined for that class at the DHCP server. You can achieve this task by executing the Ipconfig /setclassid command at a command prompt at each client computer. The user class option permits only one class ID to be used for identifying clients. In other words, each client computer can be identified as a member of only a single user class at the DHCP server.

To create a new user or vendor class, complete the following steps:

1. Open the DHCP console.

2. In the console tree, select the applicable DHCP server.

3. From the Action menu, select one of the following:

    ❑ To create a new user class, select Define User Classes.

    ❑ To create a new vendor class, select Define Vendor Classes.

4. Click Add.

    The New Class dialog box opens.

5. In the Display Name text box, provide a friendly name for the class. Optionally, fill in the Description text box.

6. In the ID text box, set the same binary or ASCII string that matches the DHCP class ID string that is either implemented or set at member clients.

7. Click OK and then Close to return to the DHCP console.

To set DHCP class ID information at a client computer, complete the following steps:

1. At a DHCP-enabled client computer running Windows 2000, Microsoft Windows XP, or Windows Server 2003, open a command prompt.

2. Use the Ipconfig /setclassid command to set the DHCP class ID the client uses when obtaining its lease from the DHCP server.

    You can use the Ipconfig /setclassid command as demonstrated in the following example command, which sets an ASCII string (MyNewClassId) as the DHCP class ID string for the local area network (LAN) connection in use at the client computer:

    ```
    C:\>ipconfig /setclassid "Local Area Connection" MyNewClassId

    Windows IP Configuration

    Successfully set the class id for adapter Local Area Connection.
    ```

Note You can use the Ipconfig /showclassid *<adapter number>* command to display all the DHCP class IDs allowed by the DHCP server for any network adapter installed on your computer.

Practice 1: Performing a Manual Backup of the DHCP Server

In this practice, you back up the DHCP database.

Exercise 1: Backing Up the DHCP Database

In this exercise, you back up the DHCP database and then verify that the backup has been performed.

1. From Computer1, log on to Domain1 as Administrator.
2. Open the DHCP console.
3. In the console tree, right-click the DHCP server node (named Computer1.domain1.local), and then select Backup.

   The Browse For Folder dialog box opens. The default folder in which to save the backed-up database is WINDOWS\System32\Dhcp\Backup.
4. Click OK to accept the default selection.
5. In Windows Explorer, browse to WINDOWS\System32\Dhcp\Backup.

   In this folder, you will see a file named DhcpCfg. This file contains a backed-up copy of the DHCP database.
6. Right-click the file named DhcpCfg and select Properties.

   The DhcpCfg Properties dialog box opens.

   According to the date and time listed next to Modified, the file has been modified just recently. The backup was successful.
7. Click OK to close the DhcpCfg Properties dialog box.

Practice 2: Creating a New Superscope

In this practice, you create a test superscope.

Exercise 1: Creating a Superscope and Member Scopes

In this exercise, you create a superscope that includes the existing scope Test Scope. You then add a second scope to the superscope.

1. If you have not already done so, from Computer1, log on to Domain1 as Administrator.
2. Open the DHCP console.
3. In the DHCP console tree, right-click the Computer1.domain1.local icon, and then select New Superscope.

   The New Superscope Wizard launches.

4. Click Next.

   The Superscope Name page appears.

5. In the Name text box, type **Super1**, and then click Next.

   The Select Scopes page appears.

6. In the Available Scopes area, select the only scope listed: [192.168.0.0] Test Scope.

7. Click Next.

   The Completing The New Superscope Wizard page appears.

8. Click Finish.

   In the DHCP console, a new superscope named Super1 appears. This new super-scope includes the scope named Test Scope.

9. Expand the Superscope Super1 folder.

10. Right-click the Superscope Super1 folder and select New Scope.

    The New Scope Wizard launches.

11. Use the settings specified in the following table to complete the New Scope Wizard. Leave the defaults for all unspecified settings.

New Scope Wizard Page	Setting
Scope Name	Name: Test Scope 2
IP Address Range	Start IP Address: 192.168.1.11 End IP Address: 192.168.1.254
Subnet Mask	255.255.255.0 Length = 24
Add Exclusions	[defaults]
Lease Duration	[defaults]
Configure DHCP Options	[default]
Router (Default Gateway)	[default]
Domain Name And DNS Servers	[defaults]
WINS Servers	[default]
Activate Scope	[default]

After you complete the New Scope Wizard, two scopes should now be listed under the superscope Super1: Test Scope and Test Scope 2.

12. Take a minute to browse the new settings in the DHCP console.

    If this configuration were in a production environment, a router would be needed to allow the 192.168.0.0 subnet to communicate with the 192.168.1.0 subnet.

Because this testing configuration does not include a router and cannot be used, the new superscope Super1 and new scope Test Scope 2 should both be deleted.

> **Important**   A superscope must always be deleted before you can delete any of its member scopes.

13. Right-click the Superscope Super1 folder and then select Delete.

    A message box appears indicating that only the superscope and not the child scopes will be deleted.

14. Click Yes.

15. In the DHCP console, right-click the Scope [192.168.1.0] Test Scope 2 folder, and then select Delete.

    A message box appears asking you to confirm the deletion.

16. Click Yes.

17. Close the DHCP console.

18. Log off Computer1.

Lesson Review

The following questions are intended to reinforce key information presented in this lesson. If you are unable to answer a question, review the lesson materials and try the question again. You can find answers to the questions in the "Questions and Answers" section at the end of this chapter.

1. Within your only subnet, you want 10 specific DHCP clients (out of 150 total on the network) to use a test DNS server that is not assigned to any other computers through DHCP. How can you best achieve this objective?

   _____

   _____

   _____

   _____

2. You want to migrate a subnet to a new scope. You create a new scope and then deactivate the old scope. Which of the following is an appropriate next step?

   a. Run the Ipconfig /release command and then the Ipconfig /renew command on every client computer.

   b. Restart the DHCP Server service.

    c. Delete the old scope.

    d. Authorize the DHCP server.

3. Name three steps necessary to move a DHCP database to another server.

_____

_____

4. You have only one physical network segment, but you have run out of addresses within your current scope of 207.46.159.0/24 to accommodate all your DHCP clients. Using only one DHCP server, what can you do to introduce new addresses on your subnet while preserving the addresses of the existing clients?

_____

_____

_____

_____

_____

Lesson Summary

- A superscope is an administrative grouping of scopes that is used to support multi-nets, or multiple logical subnets, on a single physical subnet.

- If you need to migrate to a completely new scope, first create and activate the new scope, and then deactivate the old scope. Before removing a scope, however, be sure to deactivate the scope long enough to migrate clients to the new scope.

- To perform a backup of the DHCP database, right-click the DHCP server icon in the DHCP console, and then select Backup. To restore the DHCP database from a previously backed-up copy, right-click the DHCP server icon in the DHCP console, and then select Restore. To move the DHCP database, back it up and then restore it to another location.

- Use the Jetpack.exe tool to perform an offline compaction of the DHCP database.

- When an options class is added to the server, clients of that class can be provided class-specific DHCP options for their configuration. When you create a class, you create an ID for that class. To make a DHCP client a member of a class, use the Ipconfig /setclassid command.

Lesson 3: Configuring DHCP Servers to Perform DNS Updates

By default, DHCP servers interact with DNS servers by performing dynamic updates of pointer (PTR) resource records on behalf of DHCP clients that are also DNS clients. You can modify this default behavior in various ways by changing the settings on both the DHCP-DNS client and on the DHCP server.

After this lesson, you will be able to

- Describe the default DHCP settings for DNS clients on both DNS clients and DHCP servers
- Configure DNS dynamic update behavior for DNS clients
- Configure DNS dynamic update behavior for DHCP servers
- Explain the purpose, benefits, and disadvantages of the DnsUpdateProxy security group

Estimated lesson time: 25 minutes

Configuring Dynamic Updates with DHCP

By default, post-Windows 2000 DHCP clients attempt to perform dynamic updates of their host (A) resource records in DNS whenever an address event (such as an address renewal) occurs. However, these same clients do not attempt to perform dynamic updates of their PTR resource records; instead, post-Windows 2000 DHCP clients request that the DHCP server attempt to update their PTR resource records in DNS on behalf of the client.

Default DNS Update Settings for DHCP Servers

By default, a DHCP server registers records on behalf of a DHCP client only according to client request. That is, because the DHCP client by default requests that the server update only the client's PTR resource records, the DHCP server attempts only this type of update. However, a server can also be configured to attempt an update of both A and PTR resource records, regardless of the client request. This behavior is determined by the settings on the DNS tab of the DHCP server properties dialog box, shown in Figure 7-13.

> **Note**   These settings can also be configured in the scope properties dialog box or the reservation properties dialog box.

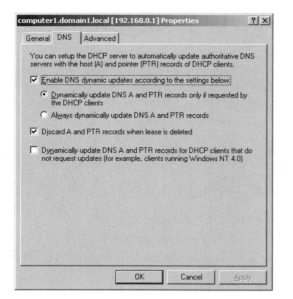

Figure 7-13   Default DNS client settings for DHCP servers

When the Enable DNS Dynamic Updates According To The Settings Below check box is selected, which is the default, dynamic update is enabled for the DHCP server. When it is enabled, either of two options is specified. If the first option, the default, is selected (shown in Figure 7-13), the DHCP server attempts to update resource records only according to the client's request. When you select the second option, the DHCP server always attempts to update the client's A and PTR resource records after an address event, regardless of the client request. However, this setting is significant only for DHCP clients capable of requesting dynamic updates, including computers running Windows 2000, Windows XP, or Windows Server 2003.

When you clear the Enable DNS Dynamic Updates According To The Settings Below check box, the DHCP server never attempts dynamic updates on behalf of Windows 2000, Windows XP, or Windows Server 2003 clients.

Another setting you can configure on the DNS tab of the DHCP server properties dialog box is the Discard A And PTR Records When Lease Is Deleted check box. By default, this check box is selected, which means that the DHCP server removes clients' resource records from DNS when their DHCP address leases are deleted. However, by clearing this check box, you can configure the DHCP server to leave client records in DNS even when a client's DHCP address lease is deleted.

The final dynamic update setting you can configure on this tab determines whether the DHCP server should provide dynamic DNS update service on behalf of DHCP clients not capable of performing dynamic updates, such as computers running Microsoft Windows NT 4. By default, Windows Server 2003 DHCP servers do not attempt to perform dynamic updates on behalf of these clients. To modify this default behavior, select the appropriate (lowest) check box on the DNS tab of the server properties dialog box (shown in Figure 7-13).

Using the DnsUpdateProxy Security Group

As previously described, you can configure a Windows Server 2003 DHCP server so that it dynamically registers both A and PTR resource records on behalf of DHCP clients. In this configuration, the use of secure dynamic updates with Windows Server 2003 DNS servers can occasionally lead to stale resource records. Because secure dynamic updates require that the owner of a resource record update that record, resource records are not updated if your configuration ever changes.

For example, suppose the following sequence of events occurs:

1. A Windows Server 2003 DHCP server (DHCP1) performs a secure dynamic update on behalf of one of its clients for a specific DNS domain name.

2. Because DHCP1 successfully created the name, DHCP1 becomes the owner of the name.

3. Once DHCP1 becomes the owner of the client name and associated resource records, only DHCP1 can update the name or its IP address.

In some circumstances, this situation might cause problems. For instance, suppose DHCP1 later fails. If a second backup DHCP server (DHCP2) comes online, DHCP2 is unable to update the client's resource record because DHCP2 is not the owner of the record.

In a similar example, suppose DHCP1 has registered the name host.example.microsoft.com on behalf of a client running a version of Windows earlier than Windows 2000. Then the administrator upgrades that client computer to Windows XP Professional. Because the DHCP server (DHCP1) is the owner of this name, the client cannot update its DNS records once the computer is upgraded.

To solve these kinds of problems, Windows Server 2003 Active Directory provides a built-in security group called DnsUpdateProxy. Any object created by the members of this group has no security settings. As a result, initially, the object has no owner, and it can therefore be updated by a DHCP server or client that did not create it, even in zones requiring secure updates. However, as soon as the first DHCP server or client that is not a member of the DnsUpdateProxy group modifies such a record, that server or client then becomes its owner. After that point, only the owner can update the record in zones requiring secure updates. Thus, if every DHCP server registering resource records for older clients is a member of this group, and the clients themselves are not members of the group, the problems discussed earlier are eliminated.

Adding Members to the DnsUpdateProxy Group   You can configure the DnsUpdate-Proxy global security group through the Active Directory Users And Computers console, as shown in Figure 7-14.

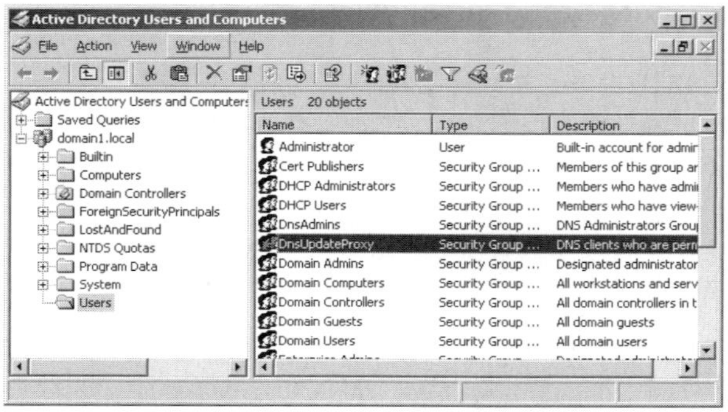

Figure 7-14   Configuring DnsUpdateProxy

> **Important**   If you are using multiple DHCP servers for fault tolerance, and secure DNS dynamic updates are required on zones serviced by these DHCP servers, be sure to add each of the computers operating a Windows Server 2003 DHCP server to the DnsUpdateProxy global security group.

Security Concerns   Although adding all DHCP servers to this special built-in group helps resolve some concerns about maintaining secure DNS updates, this solution also introduces some additional security risks.

For example, any DNS domain names registered by the computer running the DHCP server are not secure. The A resource record for the DHCP server itself is an example of such a record. To protect against this risk, you can manually specify a different owner for any DNS records associated with the DHCP server itself.

However, a more significant issue arises if the DHCP server (which is a member of the DnsUpdateProxy group) is installed on a domain controller. In this case, all service location (SRV), host (A), or alias (CNAME) resource records registered by the Netlogon service for the domain controller are not secure. To minimize this problem, you should not install a DHCP server on a domain controller when using dynamic updates.

> **Caution**   For Windows Server 2003, the use of secure dynamic updates can be compromised by running a DHCP server on a domain controller when the Windows Server 2003 DHCP service is configured to perform registration of DNS records on behalf of DHCP clients. To avoid this problem, deploy DHCP servers and domain controllers on separate computers.

Lesson Review

The following questions are intended to reinforce key information presented in this lesson. If you are unable to answer a question, review the lesson materials and try the question again. You can find answers to the questions in the "Questions and Answers" section at the end of this chapter.

1. Which action needs to be taken if you want to configure a DHCP server to update both A resource records and PTR resource records on behalf of a Windows NT 4 client?

   a. No action is required.

   b. On the DNS tab of the DHCP server properties dialog box, select Dynamically Update DNS A And PTR Records For DHCP Clients That Do Not Request Updates.

   c. On the DNS tab of the DHCP server properties dialog box, select Always Dynamically Update DNS A And PTR Records.

   d. Register the client as a dynamic host with the DHCP server.

2. You have not modified the default settings for DNS on the DHCP client or server. Which of the following client record or records will be updated in DNS by the DHCP server? (Assume that the clients are running Windows XP.)

   a. The PTR resource record

   b. The A resource record

   c. Both the PTR and A resource records

   d. Neither the PTR nor the A resource record

3. For a zone in which only secure dynamic updates are allowed, you have configured your DHCP server to perform dynamic updates on behalf of Windows NT clients. All other dynamic DNS settings on the DHCP server have the default settings. After you migrate the clients to Windows XP, you find that their A resource records are no longer being updated. What is the most likely explanation for this problem?

   _____

4. Under what conditions is it not considered secure to host a DHCP server on a domain controller? Why is this setup not secure?

   _____

   _____

   _____

Lesson Summary

- By default, a DHCP server updates the PTR record of a DHCP client running Windows 2000, Windows XP, or Windows Server 2003. This behavior is the equivalent of performing dynamic updates according to client request.

- You can modify dynamic update behavior for a DHCP server on the DNS tab of the DHCP server properties dialog box. Optional settings include always performing updates (regardless of client request), never performing updates, performing updates for clients running versions of Windows earlier than Windows 2000, and removing client records in DNS when an address lease is deleted.

- When a DNS zone accepts only secure dynamic updates, a configuration in which DHCP servers perform dynamic updates on behalf of clients can occasionally lead to stale resource records. Because secure dynamic updates require that the owner of a resource record update that record, resource records are not updated if your configuration ever changes.

- Any resource record registered or updated by the members of the DnsUpdateProxy group has no security settings. Therefore, initially, the record has no owner, and it can therefore be updated by a DHCP server or client that did not create it, even in zones requiring secure updates.

- When the first DHCP server or client that is not a member of the DnsUpdateProxy group modifies or updates a resource record, that server or client then becomes its owner. After that point, only that owner can update the record in zones requiring secure updates.

Case Scenario Exercise

You are a network administrator for Proseware, Inc., a book publishing company that operates out of a single building in Kansas City, Missouri. Proseware employs 200 full-time workers, all of whom work on desktop computers, and 100 part-time workers, all of whom work on personal laptops. The part-time employees change docking stations frequently and work on various floors throughout the company building. Part-time employees work in the office at least one day per week.

You are responsible for solving the following network problems. Answer the following questions by recommending the best course of action.

1. The address space used by your organization is 207.46.1.21–207.46.1.254. This space is not large enough to accommodate all 300 workers at once; as a result, your network frequently runs out of DHCP leases. Nevertheless, no more than 30 part-time employees work in the office on any given day. How can you make

more efficient use of your current address space and provide enough leases for all workers?

    a. Assign all laptops an alternate configuration address within a compatible address space.

    b. Create a user class for part-time employees and adjust the lease duration in this user class to 1 day.

    c. Increase conflict detection attempts on the DHCP server to prevent address conflicts.

    d. Assign part-time employees addresses within one of the private address ranges.

2. Your DHCP server crashes and cannot be brought back online. Your last backup is four days old. How can you best preserve the current address space without restarting all company computers?

    a. Deploy a new DHCP server with the same address scope, and raise conflict detection attempts to 3.

    b. Deploy a new DHCP server with the same address scope, and increase the new lease duration to 15 days.

    c. Restore the previous DHCP database from a backup.

    d. Run the Ipconfig /renew command on all computers.

3. The DNS domain proseware.local is an Active Directory–integrated domain that requires secure dynamic updates. Your DHCP server is configured to register DNS records for downlevel clients, and it is not a member of the DnsUpdateProxy group. Fifty client computers have recently been upgraded to Windows XP Professional from Windows NT 4. After the upgrade, users start reporting that they can no longer access some network resources. Which of the following solutions enables you to fix the problem with the least amount of administrative effort?

    a. Shut down and restart the upgraded client computers.

    b. Run Ipconfig /renew, and then Ipconfig /registerdns on all client computers.

    c. Enable aging and scavenging in the proseware.local zone, and then decrease the no-refresh and refresh intervals in aging/scavenging properties.

    d. Add the DHCP server to the DnsUpdateProxy Windows security group.

Troubleshooting Lab

In this lab, you troubleshoot a problem related to name resolution.

1. From Computer2, log on to Domain1 as Administrator.

2. Insert the Supplemental Course Materials CD-ROM into the disk drive.

3. Locate and double-click the following batch file: \70-291\labs\Chapter07\Ch7a.bat.

4. Open a command prompt and enter the following command: **ipconfig /renew**.

   After several moments, you will receive a timeout error. The error indicates either that the server cannot be contacted or that access is denied.

5. Use the Ipconfig command to determine the IP address currently assigned to Computer2. If Computer2 has assigned itself the alternate configuration address of 192.168.0.2, proceed to step 6. If not, enter the Ipconfig /renew command again, verify that the alternate address of 192.168.0.2 has successfully been assigned, and then proceed to step 6.

6. Enter the following command: **netsh dhcp server 192.168.0.1 show all**.

   An output describes the server configuration and status.

7. Review this output and then answer the following question.

   Does this output suggest that the DHCP Server service is running or inactive?

   _____

8. Enter the following command: **netsh dhcp server 192.168.0.1 show scope**.

   An output describes the features of the server's only configured scope.

9. Answer the following questions: How is the state of the scope described? Why is Computer2 unable to obtain an address lease from the DHCP server?

   _____

   _____

10. At the command prompt, enter the following command:

    netsh dhcp server 192.168.0.1 scope 192.168.0.0 set state 1.

11. At the command prompt, enter the following command:

    netsh dhcp server 192.168.0.1 show scope.

    The scope is now described as Active.

12. At the command prompt, enter the following command: **ipconfig /renew**.

    The address configuration is successfully renewed.

13. Log off Computer2.

Chapter Summary

- DHCP servers must be authorized if they are to be made available in Active Directory networks.

- A DHCP scope is a continuous range of IP addresses, defined within a single logical subnet, that a DHCP server can assign to clients. After you define and configure a scope, the scope must be activated before the DHCP server can begin providing service to clients.

- An exclusion range is a set of one or more IP addresses, included within the range of a defined scope, that you do not want to lease to DHCP clients. You use a reservation to create a permanent address lease assignment by the DHCP server.

- DHCP options are used to provide clients with additional configuration data, such as the addresses of a client's default gateway or DNS server, along with an address lease.

- A superscope is an administrative grouping of scopes that is used to support multinets, or multiple logical subnets, on a single physical subnet.

- When an options class is added to the server, clients of that class can be provided class-specific DHCP options for their configuration. When you create a class, you create an ID for that class. To make a DHCP client a member of a class, use the Ipconfig /setclassid command.

- By default, a DHCP server updates the PTR record of a DHCP client running Windows 2000, Windows XP, or Windows Server 2003. This is the equivalent of performing dynamic updates according to client request. You can configure a DHCP server to update both A and PTR resource records by selecting the option (on the DNS tab of DHCP server properties) to always dynamically update records.

- Any resource record registered or updated by the members of the DnsUpdateProxy group has no security settings. Consequently, initially, the record has no owner, and it can therefore be updated by a DHCP server or client that did not create it, even in zones requiring secure updates.

Exam Highlights

Before taking the exam, review the key points and terms that are presented in this chapter.

Key Points

- Understand DHCP scopes, exclusions, and reservations.
- Understand DHCP leases and associated commands for releasing and renewing.
- Understand the function of superscopes.
- Understand the function of options classes.
- Understand how DHCP servers can be configured to perform DNS updates.

Key Terms

multinets   Multiple logical subnets configured on a single network segment. Multinets communicate with each other through a router.

Jetpack   A command-line utility used to compact databases.

rogue server   A stand-alone DHCP server implemented on an Active Directory network.

Questions and Answers

Lesson 1, Practice, Exercise 4

Page
7-19

8. Answer the following questions in the spaces provided.

How many active address leases now appear in the details pane of the DHCP console when the Address Leases folder is selected? To which computer is this address assigned?

One. It is assigned to computer2.domain1.local.

Lesson 1 Review

Page
7-20

1. You have configured a scope with an address range of 192.168.0.11 through 192.168.0.254. However, your DNS server on the same subnet has already been assigned a static address of 192.168.0.200. With the least administrative effort, how can you allow for compatibility between the DNS server's address and DHCP service on the subnet?

By configuring an exclusion for the address 192.168.0.200, you can most easily allow for compatibility between the DNS server and the currently configured DHCP scope.

2. Which of the following servers are eligible to be the first DHCP server on your network? (Choose all that apply.)

   a. A Windows Server 2003 domain controller in an Active Directory network

   b. A Windows 2000 Server workgroup server in a network with no domains

   c. A Windows Server 2003 workgroup server in an Active Directory network

   d. A Windows 2000 Server member server in an Active Directory network

   a, b, d

3. A DHCP scope has been configured with the 003 Router option, which provides clients with the address of a default gateway. However, after running the Ipconfig /renew command and then the Ipconfig /all command at a computer named Client1, you find that this client is being assigned an IP address within the defined scope but not the address of a default gateway. Which of the following answers could explain this behavior?

   a. Client1 has become disconnected from the network.

   b. Client1's IP address is acquired by means of a reservation at the DHCP server.

   c. No scope options have been defined at the server level.

   d. The scope has not been activated.

   b

4. Besides Administrators, name two security groups that have the authority to manage DHCP servers.

Enterprise Admins and DHCP Administrators

5. While running the New Scope Wizard, you select the option not to configure any DHCP options. Afterward, you find that the DHCP server is not assigning addresses within the defined scope. Which is the most likely reason that DHCP address assignment is not functioning?

The scope has not been activated.

Lesson 2 Review

Page
7-39

1. Within your only subnet, you want 10 specific DHCP clients (out of 150 total on the network) to use a test DNS server that is not assigned to any other computers through DHCP. How can you best achieve this objective?

The best way to achieve this objective is to create a new user class, configure for this class a 006 DNS Servers option that specifies the IP address of the test DNS server, and then set the class of the 10 DHCP clients by running the Ipconfig /setclassid command.

2. You want to migrate a subnet to a new scope. You create a new scope and then deactivate the old scope. Which of the following is an appropriate next step?

   a. Run the Ipconfig /release command and then the Ipconfig /renew command on every client computer.

   b. Restart the DHCP Server service.

   c. Delete the old scope.

   d. Authorize the DHCP server.

   a

3. Name three steps necessary to move a DHCP database to another server.

Back up the database; copy the backed up database to the new server; restore the backed up copy of the database to the new server.

4. You have only one physical network segment, but you have run out of addresses within your current scope of 207.46.159.0/24 to accommodate all your DHCP clients. Using only one DHCP server, what can you do to introduce new addresses on your subnet while preserving the addresses of the existing clients?

Create and activate a superscope that includes the currently active scope as a member. Obtain a second network ID from your ISP. Create, configure, and activate an additional scope that defines a range for the new logical subnet. Add this new scope to the superscope. Use a router to connect the two logical subnets on the physical subnet.

For the same reason, in a DNS zone that accepts both nonsecure and secure updates, hosting a DHCP server on a domain controller is never secure.

Lesson 3 Review

Page
7-45 The following questions are intended to reinforce key information presented in this lesson. If you are unable to answer a question, review the lesson materials and try the question again.

1. Which action needs to be taken if you want to configure a DHCP server to update both A resource records and PTR resource records on behalf of a Windows NT 4 client?

    a. No action is required.

    b. On the DNS tab of the DHCP server properties dialog box, select Dynamically Update DNS A And PTR Records For DHCP Clients That Do Not Request Updates.

    c. On the DNS tab of the DHCP server properties dialog box, select Always Dynamically Update DNS A And PTR Records.

    d. Register the client as a dynamic host with the DHCP server.

    b

2. You have not modified the default settings for DNS on the DHCP client or server. Which of the following client record or records will be updated in DNS by the DHCP server? (Assume that the clients are running Windows XP.)

    a. The PTR resource record

    b. The A resource record

    c. Both the PTR and A resource records

    d. Neither the PTR nor the A resource record

    a

3. For a zone in which only secure dynamic updates are allowed, you have configured your DHCP server to perform dynamic updates on behalf of Windows NT clients. All other dynamic DNS settings on the DHCP server have the default settings. After you migrate the clients to Windows XP, you find that their A resource records are no longer being updated. What is the most likely explanation for this problem?

    The DHCP server is not a member of the DnsUpdateProxy security group.

4. Under what conditions is it not considered secure to host a DHCP server on a domain controller? Why is this setup not secure?

    If a DNS zone that accepts only secure dynamic updates, hosting a DHCP server on a domain controller is not secure when the server is a member of the security group DnsUpdateProxy. In this case, all of the resource records created by the Netlogon service for the domain controller lack security.

    For the same reason, in a DNS zone that accepts both nonsecure and secure updates, hosting a DHCP server on a domain controller is never secure.

Case Scenario Exercise

Page
7-46 You are a network administrator for Proseware, Inc., a book publishing company that operates out of a single building in Kansas City, Missouri. Proseware employs 200 full-time workers, all of whom work on desktop computers, and 100 part-time workers, all of whom work on personal laptops. The part-time employees change docking stations frequently and work on various floors throughout the company building. Part-time employees work in the office at least one day per week.

You are responsible for solving the following network problems. Answer the following questions by recommending the best course of action.

1. The address space used by your organization is 207.46.1.21–207.46.1.254. This space is not large enough to accommodate all 300 workers at once; as a result, your network frequently runs out of DHCP leases. Nevertheless, no more than 30 part-time employees work in the office on any given day. How can you make more efficient use of your current address space and provide enough leases for all workers?

   a. Assign all laptops an alternate configuration address within a compatible address space.

   b. Create a user class for part-time employees and adjust the lease duration in this user class to 1 day.

   c. Increase conflict detection attempts on the DHCP server so as to prevent address conflicts.

   d. Assign part-time employees addresses within one of the private address ranges.

   b

2. Your DHCP server crashes and cannot be brought back online. Your last backup is four days old. How can you best preserve the current address space without restarting all company computers?

   a. Deploy a new DHCP server with the same address scope, and raise conflict detection attempts to 3.

   b. Deploy a new DHCP server with the same address scope, and increase the new lease duration to 15 days.

   c. Restore the previous DHCP database from a backup.

   d. Run the Ipconfig /renew command on all computers.

   a

3. The DNS domain proseware.local is an Active Directory–integrated domain that requires secure dynamic updates. Your DHCP server is configured to register DNS records for downlevel clients, and is not a member of the DnsUpdateProxy group. Fifty client computers have recently been upgraded to Windows XP Professional from Windows NT 4. After the upgrade, users start reporting that they can no longer access some network resources. Which of the following solutions enables you to fix the problem with the least amount of administrative effort?

   a. Shut down and restart the upgraded client computers.

   b. Run Ipconfig /renew, and then Ipconfig /registerdns on all client computers.

   c. Enable aging and scavenging in the proseware.local zone, and then decrease the no-refresh and refresh intervals in aging/scavenging properties.

   d. Add the DHCP server to the DnsUpdateProxy Windows security group.

   c

Troubleshooting Lab

Page
7-48
7. Review this output and then answer the following question.

   Does this output suggest that the DHCP Server service is running or inactive?

   Running

9. Answer the following question: How is the state of the scope described?

   Disabled

8 Monitoring and Troubleshooting DHCP

Exam Objectives in this Chapter:

- Troubleshoot DHCP
    - Diagnose and resolve issues related to DHCP authorization
    - Verify DHCP reservation configuration
    - Check the system event log and DHCP audit log files for related events
    - Diagnose and resolve issues related to configuration of DHCP server and scope options
    - Verify database integrity

Why This Chapter Matters

When a DHCP server crashes, it can eventually take down most other services on a network. This problem occurs because in a typical network, client computers depend on DHCP servers to locate essential servers such as DNS servers and default gateways. In addition, when DHCP leases expire after a DHCP failure, computers typically lose their ability to communicate with each other. DHCP servers are thus a central point of failure, and it is essential that you be able to diagnose and repair problems that appear when DHCP service stops functioning properly.

To diagnose and repair problems related to Dynamic Host Configuration Protocol (DHCP), you need to understand the nature of DHCP communication. This chapter assists in this effort by first describing the pattern of DHCP message exchanges so that they can be analyzed in a Network Monitor capture. The chapter then introduces the format and contents of DHCP server log entries. Finally, the chapter provides basic troubleshooting procedures that allow you to find and repair DHCP problems on your network.

Lessons in this Chapter:

- Lesson 1: Analyzing DHCP Traffic 8-3
- Lesson 2: Monitoring DHCP Through Audit Logging 8-20
- Lesson 3: Troubleshooting DHCP. 8-27

Before You Begin

To complete this chapter, you must have

- Networked two computers, named Computer1 and Computer2, each running Microsoft Windows Server 2003. Computer1 should be assigned a static address of 192.168.0.1/24 with a statically assigned preferred DNS server address of 192.168.0.1. Computer2 should be configured to obtain an address automatically and have an alternate configuration address of 192.168.0.2/24. It should also be configured to obtain a DNS server address automatically.

- Installed a DNS server on Computer1. Once installed, the DNS server should host a primary forward lookup zone named domain1.local that is configured to accept dynamic updates.

- Promoted Computer1 to a domain controller in a new Active Directory domain and forest named domain1.local. Computer2 should be a member of the domain. After the Active Directory directory service is installed, the DNS zone domain1.local should be configured as an Active Directory–integrated zone, and the zone should be configured to accept only secure dynamic updates.

- Deleted any dial-up connection previously installed on Computer1.

- Installed a DHCP server on Computer1. The DHCP server should host a scope named Test Scope whose Internet Protocol (IP) address range is 192.168.0.11/24–192.168.0.254/24. The scope should have the 003 Router and 006 DNS Servers options configured, each specifying the IP address of 192.168.0.1. The 015 DNS Domain Name option should also be configured at the scope level and should specify the primary DNS suffix of domain1.local. Computer2 should receive its IP configuration from the DHCP server, and Computer2's A resource record in the domain1.local zone should reflect the IP address assigned by the DHCP server.

- Installed Windows Support Tools on Computer1 and Computer2.

- Installed Network Monitor Tools on Computer1 and Computer2. Network Monitor should be configured to listen on the local area network (LAN) connection.

Lesson 1: Analyzing DHCP Traffic

To troubleshoot DHCP problems effectively, you need to be able to analyze DHCP traffic captured on the network. This analysis entails being able to read and understand the various messages that are communicated between DHCP clients and servers during various stages of the leasing process.

After this lesson, you will be able to

■ Describe the stages of a DHCP leasing process

■ Recognize and read various DHCP messages in a Network Monitor trace

Estimated lesson time: 60 minutes

Understanding How Clients Obtain Configuration

DHCP clients use two different processes to communicate with DHCP servers and obtain a configuration. The initialization process occurs when a client computer first starts and attempts to join the network. The renewal process occurs after a client has a lease but needs to renew that lease with the server.

Initial Lease Process

The first time a DHCP-enabled client starts, it automatically engages the following initialization process to obtain a lease from a DHCP server:

1. The DHCP client broadcasts a DHCP Discover message to the local subnet.

2. A DHCP server can respond with a DHCP Offer message that contains an offered IP address for lease to the client.

3. If no DHCP servers respond to the client discovery request, the client can proceed in either of two ways:

   ❑ If the client is running Microsoft Windows 2000, the client configures itself with an Automatic Private IP Addressing (APIPA) address.

   ❑ If the client is running Microsoft Windows XP or a member of the Windows Server 2003 family, the client configures itself with an alternate address (if provided). If no static alternate address has been provided, the client configures itself with an APIPA address.

If the client is running a version of Windows earlier than Windows 2000, or if no static alternate address has been provided and IP autoconfiguration has been disabled, the client fails to initialize. If left running, it continues to resend DHCP Discover messages (4 times every 5 minutes) until it receives a DHCP Offer message from a server.

4. As soon as a DHCP Offer message is received, the client selects the offered address by replying to the server with a DHCP Request message.

   Typically, the offering server sends a DHCP Acknowledgment (DHCP ACK) message approving the lease. (DHCP options information is included in the acknowledgment.)

5. Once the client receives acknowledgment, it configures its Transmission Control Protocol/Internet Protocol (TCP/IP) properties using the information in the reply and joins the network.

Figure 8-1 illustrates the lease process just described between the DHCP server and client.

DHCP client   DHCP servers

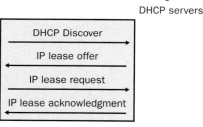

DHCP Discover

IP lease offer

IP lease request

IP lease acknowledgment

Figure 8-1   DHCP lease process

Lease Renewal Process

When a DHCP client shuts down and restarts, it typically obtains a lease for the same IP address it had prior to the shutdown. Leases are also renewed after 50 percent (four days by default) of the client lease time elapses and when the Ipconfig /renew command is executed on the client.

When the Ipconfig /renew command is executed, the client tries to renew its lease with the DHCP server as follows:

1. The client sends a DHCP Request message directly to the server that leased it, to renew and extend its current address lease.

2. If the server is reachable, it typically sends a DHCP ACK to the client, which renews the current lease.

   Also, as in the initial lease process, other DHCP options information is included in this reply. If any options information has changed since the client first obtained its lease, the client updates its configuration accordingly.

3. If the client is unable to communicate with its original DHCP server, the client waits until it reaches a *rebinding state*. By default, this state occurs seven days after the last lease renewal. When the client reaches this state, it attempts to renew its current lease with any available DHCP server.

4. If a server responds with a DHCP Offer message to update the current client lease, the client can renew its lease based on the offering server and continue operation.

5. If the lease expires and no server has been contacted, the client must immediately discontinue using its leased IP address.

6. The client then follows the same process used during its initial startup operation to obtain a new IP address lease.

> **Note**   In some cases, a DHCP server can return a DHCP Negative Acknowledgment (DHCP NACK) message to the client instead of the ACK in step 2.
>
> The NACK message is sent to a client to indicate that the IP address that the client has requested cannot be provided by the DHCP server. This situation can occur when a client requests an invalid or duplicate address for the network. If a client receives a negative acknowledgment, the lease renewal fails. In this case, the client begins a new lease initialization process.

Analyzing DHCP Messages

The DHCP messages exchanged in the various stages of a lease process can be seen and analyzed in Network Monitor captures. This section describes the structure of individual DHCP messages so that they can be recognized within a larger pattern of exchanges between DHCP clients and servers.

Figure 8-2 illustrates the general structure of a DHCP frame. As shown in the figure, the header is made up of 15 sections, including a variable-length Options section. The DHCP message type is distinguished by Option 53, which is required for use in all DHCP messages.

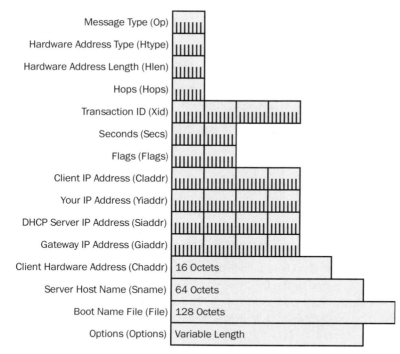

Figure 8-2   DHCP frame structure

Table 8-1 shows the values of each of these fields.

Table 8-1   DHCP Header Fields

Field	Description
Message Type (Op)	The message type.
Hardware Address Type (Htype)	The hardware address type, as defined in the Address Resolution Protocol (ARP) section of Request for Comments (RFC) 1700 (for example, 0x1 means 10 MB Ethernet).
Hardware Address Length (Hlen)	The hardware address length, in octets (for example, 0x6 for a traditional 6-byte Ethernet address).
Hops (Hops)	The signal that determines whether the message has originated on a remote subnet. Incremented by DHCP relay agents and RFC 1542–compliant routers.
Transaction ID (Xid)	A random number used to denote a conversation between a DHCP client and a DHCP server (for example, a lease acquisition).
Seconds (Secs)	The number of seconds elapsed since the DHCP Client service commenced the address acquisition process. Filled in by the DHCP client.

Table 8-1 DHCP Header Fields

Field	Description
Flags (Flags)	The flags set by the client. In RFC 2131, the Broadcast flag is the only flag defined. A DHCP client that can't receive unicast IP datagrams until it has been configured with an IP address sets this Broadcast flag.
Client IP Address (Ciaddr)	The DHCP client address. Zero, unless the client already has an IP address and can respond to ARP requests.
Your IP Address (Yiaddr)	The address given by the DHCP server to the DHCP client.
DHCP Server IP Address (Siaddr)	The IP address of the DHCP server that's offering a lease (returned by DHCP Offer).
Relay (Gateway) IP Address (Giaddr)	The DHCP relay agent or RFC 1542–compliant router IP address, used when booting using a DHCP relay agent or RFC 1542–compliant router.
Client Hardware Address (Chaddr)	The client hardware address.
Server Host Name (Sname)	A 64-byte field reserved for the server host name. Not used in Windows XP or Windows Server 2003.
Boot File Name (File)	The name of the file containing a boot image for a Boot Protocol (BOOTP) client.
Options (Options)	A variable-length set of fields containing DHCP options. Option 53 is required in every DHCP message and describes the message type. Other commonly used options include Lease Renewal Time and Lease Rebinding Time.

DHCP Discover The following listing is an excerpt from a Network Monitor capture showing the IP and DHCP portions of a DHCP Discover packet. In the IP section, you can see the destination address is 255.255.255.255 (broadcast) and the source address is 0.0.0.0. The DHCP section identifies the packet as a Discover message and identifies the client in two places by using the physical address of the network card. Note that the values in the DHCP: Client Ethernet Address (Chaddr) field and the DHCP: Client Identifier field are identical.

```
IP: ID = 0x0; Proto = UDP; Len: 328
   IP: Version = 4 (0x4)
   IP: Header Length = 20 (0x14)
   IP: Service Type = 0 (0x0)
       IP: Precedence = Routine
       IP: ...0.... = Normal Delay
       IP: ....0... = Normal Throughput
       IP: .....0.. = Normal Reliability
   IP: Total Length = 328 (0x148)
   IP: Identification = 0 (0x0)
   IP: Flags Summary = 0 (0x0)
       IP: .......0 = Last fragment in datagram
```

```
     IP: ......0. = May fragment datagram if necessary
  IP: Fragment Offset = 0 (0x0) bytes
  IP: Time to Live = 128 (0x80)
  IP: Protocol = UDP - User Datagram
  IP: Checksum = 0x39A6
  IP: Source Address = 0.0.0.0
  IP: Destination Address = 255.255.255.255
  IP: Data: Number of data bytes remaining = 308 (0x0134)

DHCP: Discover           (xid=21274A1D)
   DHCP: Op Code          (op)     = 1 (0x1)
   DHCP: Hardware Type     (htype)  = 1 (0x1) 10Mb Ethernet
   DHCP: Hardware Address Length (hlen) = 6 (0x6)
   DHCP: Hops             (hops)   = 0 (0x0)
   DHCP: Transaction ID    (xid)    = 556223005 (0x21274A1D)
   DHCP: Seconds          (secs)   = 0 (0x0)
   DHCP: Flags            (flags)  = 0 (0x0)
       DHCP: 0.............. = No Broadcast
   DHCP: Client IP Address (ciaddr) = 0.0.0.0
   DHCP: Your   IP Address (yiaddr) = 0.0.0.0
   DHCP: Server IP Address (siaddr) = 0.0.0.0
   DHCP: Relay  IP Address (giaddr) = 0.0.0.0
   DHCP: Client Ethernet Address (chaddr) = 08002B2ED85E
   DHCP: Server Host Name  (sname)  = <Blank>
   DHCP: Boot File Name    (file)   = <Blank>
   DHCP: Magic Cookie = [OK]
   DHCP: Option Field      (options)
       DHCP: DHCP Message Type     = DHCP Discover
       DHCP: Client-identifier     = (Type: 1) 08 00 2b 2e d8 5e
       DHCP: Host Name             = CLIENT1
       DHCP: Parameter Request List = (Length: 7) 01 0f 03 2c 2e 2f 06
       DHCP: End of this option field
```

DHCP Offer   In the IP section of the following capture excerpt, the source address is now the DHCP server IP address, and the destination address is the broadcast address 255.255.255.255. The DHCP section identifies the packet as an offer. The DHCP: Your IP Address (Yiaddr) field contains the IP address the server is offering to the client. Note that the DHCP: Client Ethernet Address (Chaddr) field still contains the physical address of the requesting client. Also, the DHCP Option Field section shows the various options being sent by the server along with the IP address. In this case, the server is sending the subnet mask, default gateway (router), lease time, WINS server address (NetBIOS Name Service), and the NetBIOS node type.

```
IP: ID = 0x3C30; Proto = UDP; Len: 328
  IP: Version = 4 (0x4)
  IP: Header Length = 20 (0x14)
  IP: Service Type = 0 (0x0)
      IP: Precedence = Routine
      IP: ...0.... = Normal Delay
      IP: ....0... = Normal Throughput
      IP: .....0.. = Normal Reliability
  IP: Total Length = 328 (0x148)
  IP: Identification = 15408 (0x3C30)
```

```
IP: Flags Summary = 0 (0x0)
    IP: .......0 = Last fragment in datagram
    IP: ......0. = May fragment datagram if necessary
IP: Fragment Offset = 0 (0x0) bytes
IP: Time to Live = 128 (0x80)
IP: Protocol = UDP - User Datagram
IP: Checksum = 0x2FA8
IP: Source Address = 10.54.48.151
IP: Destination Address = 255.255.255.255
IP: Data: Number of data bytes remaining = 308 (0x0134)

DHCP: Offer                   (xid=21274A1D)
    DHCP: Op Code            (op)    = 2 (0x2)
    DHCP: Hardware Type      (htype) = 1 (0x1) 10Mb Ethernet
    DHCP: Hardware Address Length (hlen) = 6 (0x6)
    DHCP: Hops               (hops)  = 0 (0x0)
    DHCP: Transaction ID     (xid)   = 556223005 (0x21274A1D)
    DHCP: Seconds            (secs)  = 0 (0x0)
    DHCP: Flags              (flags) = 0 (0x0)
        DHCP: 0.............. = No Broadcast
    DHCP: Client IP Address (ciaddr) = 0.0.0.0
    DHCP: Your   IP Address (yiaddr) = 10.54.50.5
    DHCP: Server IP Address (siaddr) = 0.0.0.0
    DHCP: Relay  IP Address (giaddr) = 0.0.0.0
    DHCP: Client Ethernet Address (chaddr) = 08002B2ED85E
    DHCP: Server Host Name  (sname)  = <Blank>
    DHCP: Boot File Name    (file)   = <Blank>
    DHCP: Magic Cookie = [OK]
    DHCP: Option Field      (options)
        DHCP: DHCP Message Type    = DHCP Offer
        DHCP: Subnet Mask          = 255.255.240.0
        DHCP: Renewal Time Value (T1) = 8 Days,  0:00:00
        DHCP: Rebinding Time Value (T2) = 14 Days,  0:00:00
        DHCP: IP Address Lease Time = 16 Days,  0:00:00
        DHCP: Server Identifier    = 10.54.48.151
        DHCP: Router               = 10.54.48.1
        DHCP: NetBIOS Name Service = 10.54.16.154
        DHCP: NetBIOS Node Type    = (Length: 1) 04
        DHCP: End of this option field
```

DHCP Request   The client responds to the DHCP Offer packet by sending a DHCP Request message. In the IP section of the following capture, the source address of the client is still 0.0.0.0 and the destination for the packet is still 255.255.255.255. The client retains 0.0.0.0 because the client hasn't received approval from the server to start using the address offered. The destination is still broadcast because more than one DHCP server might have responded and might be holding a reservation for an offer made to the client.

Broadcasting one particular requested address lets those other DHCP servers know that they can release their offered addresses and return them to their available pools. The DHCP section identifies the packet as a request and verifies the offered address by using the DHCP: Requested Address field. The DHCP: Server Identifier field in the DHCP: Option Field section shows the IP address of the DHCP server offering the lease.

```
IP: ID = 0x100; Proto = UDP; Len: 328
   IP: Version = 4 (0x4)
   IP: Header Length = 20 (0x14)
   IP: Service Type = 0 (0x0)
      IP: Precedence = Routine
      IP: ...0.... = Normal Delay
      IP: ....0... = Normal Throughput
      IP: .....0.. = Normal Reliability
   IP: Total Length = 328 (0x148)
   IP: Identification = 256 (0x100)
   IP: Flags Summary = 0 (0x0)
      IP: .......0 = Last fragment in datagram
      IP: ......0. = May fragment datagram if necessary
   IP: Fragment Offset = 0 (0x0) bytes
   IP: Time to Live = 128 (0x80)
   IP: Protocol = UDP - User Datagram
   IP: Checksum = 0x38A6
   IP: Source Address = 0.0.0.0
   IP: Destination Address = 255.255.255.255
   IP: Data: Number of data bytes remaining = 308 (0x0134)

DHCP: Request              (xid=21274A1D)
   DHCP: Op Code           (op)     = 1 (0x1)
   DHCP: Hardware Type      (htype)  = 1 (0x1) 10Mb Ethernet
   DHCP: Hardware Address Length (hlen) = 6 (0x6)
   DHCP: Hops              (hops)   = 0 (0x0)
   DHCP: Transaction ID    (xid)    = 556223005 (0x21274A1D)
   DHCP: Seconds           (secs)   = 0 (0x0)
   DHCP: Flags             (flags)  = 0 (0x0)
       DHCP: 0.............. = No Broadcast
   DHCP: Client IP Address (ciaddr) = 0.0.0.0
   DHCP: Your   IP Address (yiaddr) = 0.0.0.0
   DHCP: Server IP Address (siaddr) = 0.0.0.0
   DHCP: Relay  IP Address (giaddr) = 0.0.0.0
   DHCP: Client Ethernet Address (chaddr) = 08002B2ED85E
   DHCP: Server Host Name  (sname)  = <Blank>
   DHCP: Boot File Name     (file)   = <Blank>
   DHCP: Magic Cookie = [OK]
   DHCP: Option Field      (options)
      DHCP: DHCP Message Type   = DHCP Request
      DHCP: Client Identifier   = (Type: 1) 08 00 2b 2e d8 5e
      DHCP: Requested Address   = 10.54.50.5
      DHCP: Server Identifier   = 10.54.48.151
      DHCP: Host Name           = CLIENT1
      DHCP: Dynamic DNS updates = (Length: 26) 00 00 00 63 6f 6d ...
      DHCP: Client Class information = (Length: 8) 4d 53 46 54 20 35 2e 30
      DHCP: Parameter Request List = (Length: 7) 01 0f 03 2c 2e 2f 06
      DHCP: End of this option field
```

If the client has previously had a DHCP-assigned IP address, and the client is restarted, the client specifically requests this previously leased IP address in the DHCP Request packet. Microsoft clients populate DHCP Option Field DHCP: Requested Address with the previously assigned address. Strictly RFC-compliant clients populate the DHCP: Client IP Address (Ciaddr) field with the address requested. The DHCP server accepts either. If the server determines that the client can still use the address, it either remains silent or sends an ACK of the DHCP Request message. If the server determines that the client cannot have the address, it sends a NACK.

> **Exam Tip**   The *DHCP Request message* is the message that requests dynamic updates from the DHCP server. Typically, the Request message supplies the fully qualified domain name (FQDN) of the client so that the DHCP server can then update the client's PTR resource record accordingly. One way to remember this point is to think of the setting in the DHCP server properties dialog box: Update According To Client Request. Well, here is the "Request."

DHCP ACK   The DHCP server normally responds to the DHCP Request message with a DHCP ACK, thus completing the initialization cycle. This message contains a committed IP address for the client to use for a stated period of time, along with other optional client parameters.

The source address in the following capture is the DHCP server IP address, and the destination address is still 255.255.255.255. The DHCP section identifies the packet as an ACK. The DHCP: Your IP Address (Yiaddr) field contains the client's address, and the DHCP: Client Ethernet Address (Chaddr) field contains the physical address of the network card in the requesting client.

```
IP: ID = 0x3D30; Proto = UDP; Len: 328
   IP: Version = 4 (0x4)
   IP: Header Length = 20 (0x14)
   IP: Service Type = 0 (0x0)
      IP: Precedence = Routine
      IP: ...0.... = Normal Delay
      IP: ....0... = Normal Throughput
      IP: .....0.. = Normal Reliability
   IP: Total Length = 328 (0x148)
   IP: Identification = 15664 (0x3D30)
   IP: Flags Summary = 0 (0x0)
      IP: .......0 = Last fragment in datagram
      IP: ......0. = May fragment datagram if necessary
   IP: Fragment Offset = 0 (0x0) bytes
   IP: Time to Live = 128 (0x80)
   IP: Protocol = UDP - User Datagram
   IP: Checksum = 0x2EA8
   IP: Source Address = 10.54.48.151
   IP: Destination Address = 255.255.255.255
   IP: Data: Number of data bytes remaining = 308 (0x0134)

DHCP: ACK                   (xid=21274A1D)
   DHCP: Op Code            (op)     = 2 (0x2)
```

```
DHCP: Hardware Type        (htype) = 1 (0x1) 10Mb Ethernet
DHCP: Hardware Address Length (hlen) = 6 (0x6)
DHCP: Hops                 (hops)  = 0 (0x0)
DHCP: Transaction ID       (xid)   = 556223005 (0x21274A1D)
DHCP: Seconds              (secs)  = 0 (0x0)
DHCP: Flags                (flags) = 0 (0x0)
    DHCP: 0.............. = No Broadcast
DHCP: Client IP Address (ciaddr) = 0.0.0.0
DHCP: Your   IP Address (yiaddr) = 10.54.50.5
DHCP: Server IP Address (siaddr) = 0.0.0.0
DHCP: Relay  IP Address (giaddr) = 0.0.0.0
DHCP: Client Ethernet Address (chaddr) = 08002B2ED85E
DHCP: Server Host Name  (sname)  = <Blank>
DHCP: Boot File Name    (file)   = <Blank>
DHCP: Magic Cookie = [OK]
DHCP: Option Field     (options)
    DHCP: DHCP Message Type     = DHCP ACK
    DHCP: Renewal Time Value (T1) = 8 Days,  0:00:00
    DHCP: Rebinding Time Value (T2) = 14 Days,  0:00:00
    DHCP: IP Address Lease Time = 16 Days,  0:00:00
    DHCP: Server Identifier     = 10.54.48.151
    DHCP: Subnet Mask           = 255.255.240.0
    DHCP: Router                = 10.54.48.1
    DHCP: NetBIOS Name Service  = 10.54.16.154
    DHCP: NetBIOS Node Type     = (Length: 1) 04
    DHCP: End of this option field
```

DHCP NACK   DHCP NACK messages are most often used when the client computer has been moved to a new location. However, the message can also indicate that the client's lease with the server has expired. The following capture provides an example.

```
IP: ID = 0x3F1A; Proto = UDP; Len: 328
  IP: Version = 4 (0x4)
  IP: Header Length = 20 (0x14)
  IP: Service Type = 0 (0x0)
    IP: Precedence = Routine
    IP: ...0.... = Normal Delay
    IP: ....0... = Normal Throughput
    IP: .....0.. = Normal Reliability
  IP: Total Length = 328 (0x148)
  IP: Identification = 16154 (0x3F1A)
  IP: Flags Summary = 0 (0x0)
    IP: .......0 = Last fragment in datagram
    IP: ......0. = May fragment datagram if necessary
  IP: Fragment Offset = 0 (0x0) bytes
  IP: Time to Live = 128 (0x80)
  IP: Protocol = UDP - User Datagram
  IP: Checksum = 0x2CBE
  IP: Source Address = 10.54.48.151
  IP: Destination Address = 255.255.255.255
  IP: Data: Number of data bytes remaining = 308 (0x0134)

DHCP: NACK              (xid=74A005CE)
  DHCP: Op Code         (op)   = 2 (0x2)
```

```
DHCP: Hardware Type       (htype)  = 1 (0x1) 10Mb Ethernet
DHCP: Hardware Address Length (hlen) = 6 (0x6)
DHCP: Hops                (hops)   = 0 (0x0)
DHCP: Transaction ID      (xid)    = 1956644302 (0x74A005CE)
DHCP: Seconds             (secs)   = 0 (0x0)
DHCP: Flags               (flags)  = 0 (0x0)
    DHCP: 0.............. = No Broadcast
DHCP: Client IP Address (ciaddr) = 0.0.0.0
DHCP: Your   IP Address (yiaddr) = 0.0.0.0
DHCP: Server IP Address (siaddr) = 0.0.0.0
DHCP: Relay  IP Address (giaddr) = 0.0.0.0
DHCP: Client Ethernet Address (chaddr) = 08002B2ED85E
DHCP: Server Host Name  (sname)  = <Blank>
DHCP: Boot File Name    (file)   = <Blank>
DHCP: Magic Cookie = [OK]
DHCP: Option Field      (options)
    DHCP: DHCP Message Type    = DHCP NACK
    DHCP: Server Identifier    = 10.54.48.151
    DHCP: End of this option field
```

After receiving the NACK, the client then begins the discover process again. However, this time, the DHCP Discover packet attempts to lease the same address for which the client has just received the NACK. This process can be seen in the DHCP: Requested Address field within the following DHCP Discover message. The DHCP Offer message that follows this DHCP Discover message includes an offer that might or might not correspond to this requested address.

```
DHCP: Discover            (xid=3ED14752)
    DHCP: Op Code         (op)     = 1 (0x1)
    DHCP: Hardware Type   (htype)  = 1 (0x1) 10Mb Ethernet
    DHCP: Hardware Address Length (hlen) = 6 (0x6)
    DHCP: Hops            (hops)   = 0 (0x0)
    DHCP: Transaction ID  (xid)    = 1053902674 (0x3ED14752)
    DHCP: Seconds         (secs)   = 0 (0x0)
    DHCP: Flags           (flags)  = 0 (0x0)
        DHCP: 0.............. = No Broadcast
    DHCP: Client IP Address (ciaddr) = 0.0.0.0
    DHCP: Your   IP Address (yiaddr) = 0.0.0.0
    DHCP: Server IP Address (siaddr) = 0.0.0.0
    DHCP: Relay  IP Address (giaddr) = 0.0.0.0
    DHCP: Client Ethernet Address (chaddr) = 08002B2ED85E
    DHCP: Server Host Name  (sname)  = <Blank>
    DHCP: Boot File Name    (file)   = <Blank>
    DHCP: Magic Cookie = [OK]
    DHCP: Option Field      (options)
        DHCP: DHCP Message Type    = DHCP Discover
        DHCP: Client Identifier    = (Type: 1) 08 00 2b 2e d8 5e
        DHCP: Requested Address    = 10.54.51.5
        DHCP: Host Name            = CLIENT1
        DHCP: Parameter Request List = (Length: 7) 01 0f 03 2c 2e 2f 06
        DHCP: End of this option field
```

Practice: Analyzing DHCP Messages

In this practice, you analyze traffic for both a DHCP lease initialization and a DHCP lease renewal.

Exercise 1: Capturing DHCP Lease Initialization Traffic

In this exercise, you release and then renew the IP configuration on Computer2 while Network Monitor is capturing traffic. You then stop, filter, and view the capture.

1. From Computer1, log on to Domain1 as Administrator.

2. Open Network Monitor.

3. Begin a capture in Network Monitor by clicking Start Capture.

4. From Computer2, log on to Domain1 as Administrator.

5. Open a command prompt.

6. At the command prompt, type **ipconfig /release**, and then press Enter.

   After a moment, an output indicates that the IP address of the computer is now 0.0.0.0. Computer2 is no longer communicating on the network.

7. At the command prompt, type **ipconfig /renew**, and then press Enter.

8. When the command produces an output, switch to Computer1.

9. On Computer1, stop the network capture in Network Monitor by clicking Stop And View Capture.

10. From the Display menu in Network Monitor, select Filter.

    The Display Filter dialog box opens.

11. Double-click the expression Protocol = = Any.

    The Expression dialog box opens.

12. Click Disable All.

    All of the protocols move to the Disabled Protocols area.

13. In the Disabled Protocols area, find and double-click the DHCP protocol.

    The DHCP protocol moves to the Enabled Protocols area.

14. Click OK.

15. In the Display Filter dialog box, click OK.

The Frame Viewer window of Network Monitor should now display only five DHCP frames.

16. Save the capture to the My Captures folder with the filename DHCP Lease Initialization. Before saving, be sure to select the Filtered check box in the Save As dialog box.

17. Close Network Monitor. Do not save the capture again.

Exercise 2: Analyzing the Lease Initialization Capture

In this exercise, you analyze the five DHCP frames captured in the DHCP Lease Initialization file.

1. From Computer1, while you are logged on to Domain1 as Administrator, double-click the DHCP Lease Initialization file in the My Captures folder.

The capture opens in Network Monitor.

2. Answer the following questions in the spaces provided:

a. What are the names of the five DHCP messages? Write them in sequence, as indicated by the contents of the description field for each frame.

_____

b. Which is the only message that is not a broadcast? Why is this so?

_____

_____

_____

_____

_____

c. Which DHCP messages make up the client lease initialization process?

_____

d. Look at the Options field in each DHCP message. Which two DHCP messages include client configurations for the Domain Name, Router, and Domain Name Server options?

_____

e. Which User Datagram Protocol (UDP) port is used as the source port when sending information from the DHCP client and as the destination port when sending information to the DHCP client?

_____

     f. Which UDP port is used as the source port when sending information from the DHCP server and as the destination port when sending information to the DHCP server?

---

     g. Which of the five DHCP messages is the only one to contain a Dynamic DNS Updates section within the DHCP Options field?

---

  3. Select the Dynamic DNS Updates section within this message. (This section should be visible in the details or center pane when the DHCP Options field is expanded.)

    The data corresponding to the Dynamic DNS Updates section is highlighted in the hexadecimal (bottom) pane.

  4. Answer the following questions: What information is contained in the Dynamic DNS Updates section? Which resource record will the DHCP server update with this information?

---

  5. Close Network Monitor.

Exercise 3: Capturing DHCP Lease Renewal Traffic

In this exercise, you capture traffic from a DHCP lease renewal.

  1. If you have not already done so, from Computer1, log on to Domain1 as Administrator.

  2. Open Network Monitor.

  3. Start a capture by clicking Start Capture.

  4. Switch to Computer2. Unlock Computer2 if necessary by re-entering the DOMAIN1\administrator credentials

  5. At a command prompt, type **ipconfig /renew**, and then press Enter.

    After a few moments, an output displays the newly refreshed IP configuration.

  6. Switch to Computer1.

  7. In Network Monitor, stop the capture by clicking Stop And View Capture.

  8. Using the process described in Exercise 1, "Capturing DHCP Lease Initialization Traffic," filter the capture to display only DHCP frames.

9. Save the capture to the My Captures folder with the filename DHCP Lease Renewal. When saving, be sure to select the Filtered check box in the Save As dialog box.

10. Close Network Monitor. Do not save the capture again.

Exercise 4: Analyzing the Lease Renewal Capture

In this exercise, you analyze the frames captured in the DHCP Lease Renewal file.

1. From Computer1, while you are logged on to Domain1 as Administrator, double-click the DHCP Lease Renewal file in the My Captures folder.

   The capture opens in Network Monitor.

2. Answer the following questions in the spaces provided:

   a. How many messages make up a DHCP lease renewal?

   _____

   b. What are the names of the captured DHCP messages? Write them in sequence, as indicated by the contents of the description field for each frame.

   _____

   c. What is the difference in the method by which these messages have been communicated, as opposed to the corresponding messages captured in the DHCP lease initialization?

   _____

   _____

3. Locate the DHCP fields named Client IP Address and Your IP Address in both captured frames, and then answer the following questions:

   a. In a lease renewal, does the DHCP client request a renewal of a specific IP address?

   _____

   b. Which particular DHCP message field renews the client's configuration of DHCP options?

   _____

4. Close Network Monitor.

Lesson Review

The following questions are intended to reinforce key information presented in this lesson. If you are unable to answer a question, review the lesson materials and try the question again. You can find answers to the questions in the "Questions and Answers" section at the end of this chapter.

1. You have configured a subnet with two DHCP servers, DHCP1 and DHCP2. DHCP1 provides addresses within the first 80 percent of the subnet's scope range, and DHCP2 provides addresses for the remaining 20 percent of the scope range. Computer ClientA obtains a fresh address from DHCP1, after which you immediately take DHCP1 off the network. How long will it take before ClientA attempts to obtain a new address from DHCP2?

   a. Four days

   b. Five days

   c. Seven days

   d. Eight days

2. Which of the following messages is not exchanged as part of a DHCP lease initialization?

   a. Renew

   b. Request

   c. ACK

   d. Discover

3. Which two messages are exchanged in a DHCP lease renewal?

   _____

4. What is the default period of time after which a DHCP client attempts to renew its IP address lease?

   _____

Lesson Summary

- The DHCP client initialization process occurs when a client computer first starts and attempts to join the network. The initialization process consists of an exchange of four broadcast messages.

- A DHCP client first attempts to locate a DHCP server on the local network by broadcasting a DHCP Discover message.

- If a DHCP server hears the Discover message, it normally responds by broadcasting a DHCP Offer message that contains an IP address offer to the client.

- The DHCP client responds to the DHCP Offer message with a DHCP Request message that requests the offered IP address.

- Finally, the offering server broadcasts a DHCP ACK message that approves the lease and assigns DHCP options to the client.

Lesson 2: Monitoring DHCP Through Audit Logging

By default, all DHCP server activity is recorded and written daily to a text file. This DHCP logging feature, known as *audit logging*, allows you to monitor and troubleshoot DHCP server performance.

After this lesson, you will be able to

- Locate and analyze DHCP audit logs in Windows Server 2003
- Diagnose and resolve issues related to DHCP authorization

Estimated lesson time: 20 minutes

Exploring DHCP Audit Logging

By default, the DHCP Server service writes daily audit logs to the folder WINDOWS\ System32\Dhcp. These audit log files are text files named after the day of the week. For example, DhcpSrvLog-Mon is the log file that records all DHCP server activity between midnight and 11:59 P.M. on Monday, and DhcpSrvLog-Tue is the log file that records all DHCP server activity between midnight and 11:59 P.M. on Tuesday. Audit log files are typically overwritten after seven days, at which time a new log file of the same name is created. For example, the audit log file named DhcpSrvLog-Tue that is created at midnight on January 5 is replaced by a new file of the same name that is created at midnight on January 12.

You can modify the location of these log files on the Advanced tab of the DHCP server properties dialog box, shown in Figure 8-3. To do so, adjust the value in the Audit Log File Path text box.

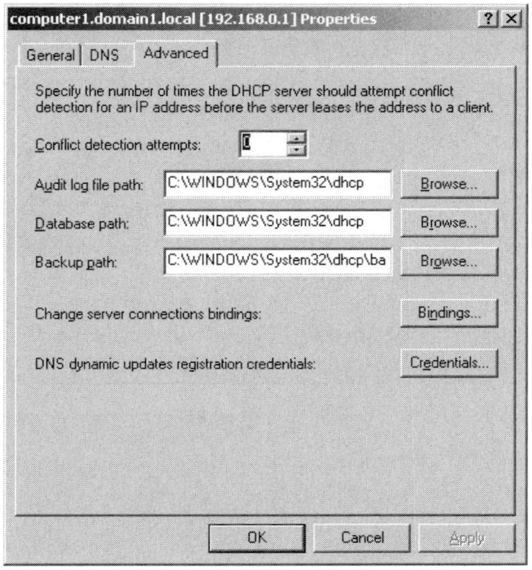

Figure 8-3   Modifying the audit log file location

The DHCP console also allows you to disable audit logging completely on the General tab of the DHCP server properties dialog box, shown in Figure 8-4. To perform this task, clear the Enable DHCP Audit Logging check box. (Audit Logging is enabled by default.)

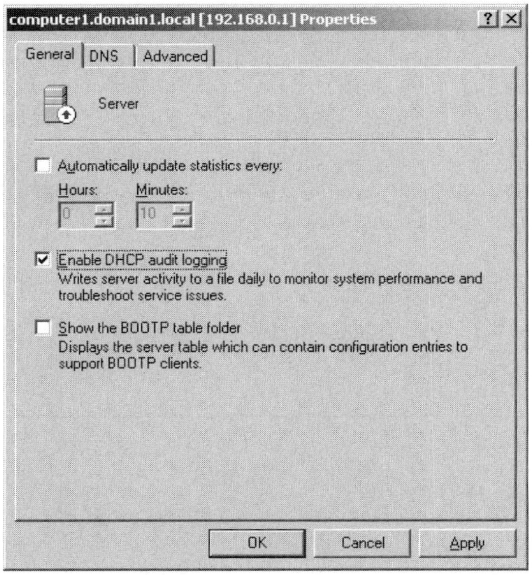

Figure 8-4   Disabling audit logging

Assuming the default is set, the largest size that the current audit log file can reach is 1 MB. Also by default, if the amount of disk space remaining on the server disk falls below 20 MB, audit logging is halted. When sufficient space again becomes available, DHCP audit logging resumes.

Understanding DHCP Server Log File Format

DHCP server logs are comma-delimited text files with each log entry representing a single line of text. Figure 8-5 shows a sample audit log file.

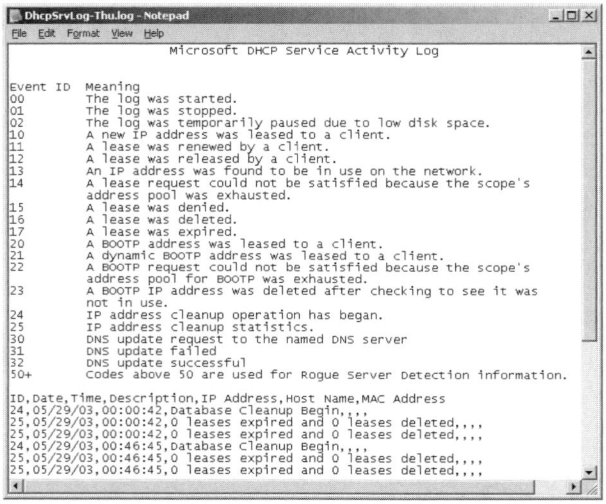


```
                Microsoft DHCP Service Activity Log

Event ID  Meaning
00        The log was started.
01        The log was stopped.
02        The log was temporarily paused due to low disk space.
10        A new IP address was leased to a client.
11        A lease was renewed by a client.
12        A lease was released by a client.
13        An IP address was found to be in use on the network.
14        A lease request could not be satisfied because the scope's
          address pool was exhausted.
15        A lease was denied.
16        A lease was deleted.
17        A lease was expired.
20        A BOOTP address was leased to a client.
21        A dynamic BOOTP address was leased to a client.
22        A BOOTP request could not be satisfied because the scope's
          address pool for BOOTP was exhausted.
23        A BOOTP IP address was deleted after checking to see it was
          not in use.
24        IP address cleanup operation has began.
25        IP address cleanup statistics.
30        DNS update request to the named DNS server
31        DNS update failed
32        DNS update successful
50+       Codes above 50 are used for Rogue Server Detection information.

ID,Date,Time,Description,IP Address,Host Name,MAC Address
24,05/29/03,00:00:42,Database Cleanup Begin,,,,
25,05/29/03,00:00:42,0 leases expired and 0 leases deleted,,,,
25,05/29/03,00:00:42,0 leases expired and 0 leases deleted,,,,
24,05/29/03,00:46:45,Database Cleanup Begin,,,,
25,05/29/03,00:46:45,0 leases expired and 0 leases deleted,,,,
25,05/29/03,00:46:45,0 leases expired and 0 leases deleted,,,,
```

Figure 8-5 Sample DHCP audit log file

A log file entry contains the fields of ID, Date, Time, Description, IP Address, Host Name, and MAC Address. A comma is used to separate each field, even when a field is empty. For example, in the following log entry, two commas in a row indicate that both the IP Address and MAC Address fields are empty:

```
55,06/03/03,09:08:57,Authorized(servicing),,domain1.local,,
```

Table 8-2 describes the values of DHCP server log fields.

Table 8-2 DHCP Server Log Fields

Field	Description
ID	A DHCP server event ID code
Date	The date on which this entry was logged on the DHCP server
Time	The time at which this entry was logged on the DHCP server
Description	A description of this DHCP server event

Table 8-2   DHCP Server Log Fields

Field	Description
IP Address	The IP address of the DHCP client
Host Name	The host name of the DHCP client
MAC Address	The Media Access Control (MAC) address used by the network adapter hardware of the client

Common Event Codes

DHCP server audit log files use reserved event ID codes to provide information about the type of server event or activity logged. Event IDs lower than 50 are described in the log file itself and therefore do not need to be memorized.

Server Authorization Events

Table 8-3 presents additional server log event ID codes and descriptions. These codes pertain to the Active Directory authorization status of the DHCP server. Unlike the preceding events, these events are not described in the log file. Therefore, you should become familiar with these codes or use Windows Server 2003 Help to assist you when you need to determine what a code represents.

Table 8-3   Log Event Codes 50 and Above

Event ID	Description
50	Unreachable domain The DHCP server could not locate the applicable domain for its configured Active Directory installation.
51	Authorization succeeded The DHCP server was authorized to start on the network.
52	Upgraded to a Windows Server 2003 operating system The DHCP server was recently upgraded to Windows Server 2003, Standard Edition; therefore, the unauthorized DHCP server detection feature (used to determine whether the server has been authorized in Active Directory) was disabled.
53	Cached authorization The DHCP server was authorized to start using previously cached information. Active Directory was not visible at the time the server was started on the network.
54	Authorization failed The DHCP server was not authorized to start on the network. When this event occurs, it is likely followed by the server being stopped.
55	Authorization (servicing) The DHCP server was successfully authorized to start on the network.

Table 8-3   Log Event Codes 50 and Above

Event ID	Description
56	Authorization failure, stopped servicing The DHCP server was not authorized to start on the network and was shut down by Windows Server 2003. You must first authorize the server in the directory before starting it again.
57	Server found in domain Another DHCP server exists and is authorized for service in the same Active Directory domain.
58	Server could not find domain The DHCP server could not locate the specified Active Directory domain.
59	Network failure A network-related failure prevented the server from determining whether it is authorized.
60	No DC is DS-enabled No Active Directory domain controller (DC) was located. For detecting whether the server is authorized, a domain controller that is enabled for Active Directory is needed.
61	Server found that belongs to DS domain Another DHCP server that belongs to the Active Directory domain was found on the network.
62	Another server found Another DHCP server was found on the network.
63	Restarting rogue detection The DHCP server is trying once more to determine whether it is authorized to start and provide service on the network.
64	No DHCP-enabled interfaces The DHCP server has its service bindings or network connections configured so that it is not enabled to provide service. This configuration usually means one of the following: ■ The network connections of the server are either not installed or not actively connected to a network. ■ The server has not been configured with at least one static IP address for one of its installed and active network connections. ■ All of the statically configured network connections for the server are disabled.

Excerpts from a Sample DHCP Server Audit Log

The following excerpt shows a normal start and authorization of a DHCP server with no errors. The first two events correspond to the successful authorization at startup. The last two events correspond to the periodic DHCP database cleanup that occurs every 60 minutes.

```
ID,Date,Time,Description,IP Address,Host Name,MAC Address
00,06/03/03,09:08:57,Started,,,,
55,06/03/03,09:08:57,Authorized(servicing),,domain2.local,,
11,06/03/03,09:48:25,Renew,192.168.0.11,server2.domain2.local,0003FFBC3B46,
24,06/03/03,10:08:58,Database Cleanup Begin,,,,
25,06/03/03,10:08:58,0 leases expired and 0 leases deleted,,,,
```

In the following excerpt, the DHCP server is found not to be authorized when it is started. This situation can happen, for example, when a new server is installed. In this example, the DHCP server is authorized in Active Directory 10 minutes after startup, after which the server is able to begin servicing clients.

```
ID,Date,Time,Description,IP Address,Host Name,MAC Address
00,06/08/03,22:35:10,Started,,,,
56,06/08/03,22:35:10,Authorization failure, stopped servicing,,domain1.local,,
55,06/08/03,22:45:38,Authorized(servicing),,domain1.local,,
```

 Tip When a DHCP server stops providing leases to clients, you should always check the DHCP log to determine whether an authorization failure has occurred.

Lesson Review

The following questions are intended to reinforce key information presented in this lesson. If you are unable to answer a question, review the lesson materials and try the question again. You can find answers to the questions in the "Questions and Answers" section at the end of this chapter.

1. Beginning on Monday, you find that you can no longer ping some of your network clients. When you consult Monday's DHCP server log file, you find the following event:

   ```
   54,6/09/03,06:47:29,Authorization failed,,domain1.local,,
   ```

   What action most likely accounts for the network problems? Who has performed this action? (Assume that the log file indicates that the DHCP server was functioning properly before the authorization failure.)

   _____

   _____

2. What most likely accounts for the error shown in the following DHCP audit log?

   ```
   00,5/24/03,08:21:57,Started,,,,
   54,5/24/03,08:21:58,Authorization failed,,domain1.local,,
   ```

   a. The server has been started for the first time.

   b. The server cannot communicate on the network.

    c. The server has been unauthorized by a senior network manager.

    d. The server is not running Windows Server 2003.

3. By default, how long do logged events last in DHCP server logs?

    a. One day

    b. One week

    c. One month

    d. Until the log grows beyond 1 MB

Lesson Summary

- Through a feature known as audit logging, all daily DHCP server activity is recorded in comma-delimited text files. By default, DHCP server log files can be found in the folder WINDOWS\System32\Dhcp.

- DHCP server log files have names such as DhcpSrvLog-Mon and DhcpSrvLog-Tue that correspond to the day of the week on which the DHCP activity is recorded. Files are overwritten every week.

- Events in DHCP server log files are specified by event ID. Event IDs below 50 are described in each log file and do not need to be memorized. Events over 50 pertain to Active Directory authorization status. You can either learn these events or consult a reference when you need to determine their meaning.

- When a DHCP server stops providing leases to clients, you should always check the DHCP log to determine whether an authorization failure or some other error has occurred.

Lesson 3: Troubleshooting DHCP

This lesson presents a procedural guide that you can use to troubleshoot DHCP failures. As with most such guides, you should modify the order of recommended troubleshooting procedures to suit the needs of your particular situation. The following pages nonetheless provide a schematic overview that will help you to organize DHCP troubleshooting in the future.

After this lesson, you will be able to

- Diagnose DHCP configuration errors
- Resolve issues related to DHCP authorization
- Resolve issues related to an incorrect scope configuration

Estimated lesson time: 45 minutes

Verifying the Client Configuration

One of the first signals of a DHCP failure appears either when a client loses connectivity to network resources or when a new client cannot establish such connectivity in the first place. In these cases, you need to determine whether the problem originates on the client or elsewhere.

Begin by using the Ipconfig command to determine whether the DHCP client has received an address lease from the DHCP server. If so, the Ipconfig /all output shows that DHCP is enabled, and the IP address is described as an "IP Address" and not an "Autoconfiguration IP Address." Alternatively, you can check the address type listed on the Support tab of the status dialog box for the connection. You open this dialog box, shown in Figure 8-6, by double-clicking the relevant connection in the Network Connections window. When the IP address has been assigned by a DHCP server, the address type is described on the Support tab as Assigned By DHCP.

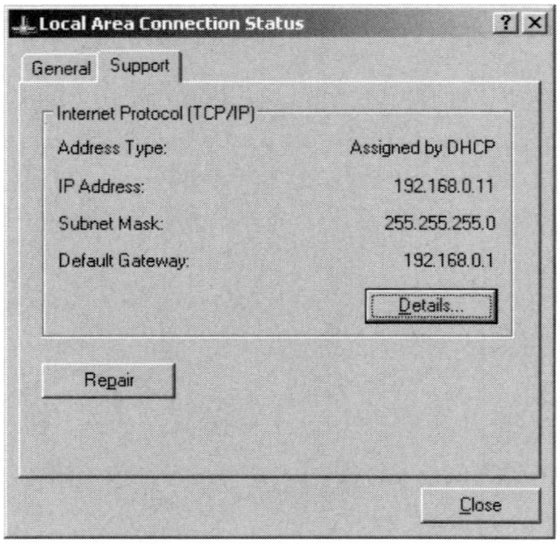

Figure 8-6   Verifying address type

If the client has been assigned by DHCP an address that is compatible with the rest of the network, and no warning messages have appeared about address conflicts, you can assume that the network problem does not result from an addressing error on the local client.

Address Conflicts

If a client computer has been assigned an address in use by another computer on the network, a warning message informing you of this conflict appears in the system tray. You can also learn about such address conflicts in the System log, which you can access through Event Viewer. Figure 8-7 shows this type of warning message.

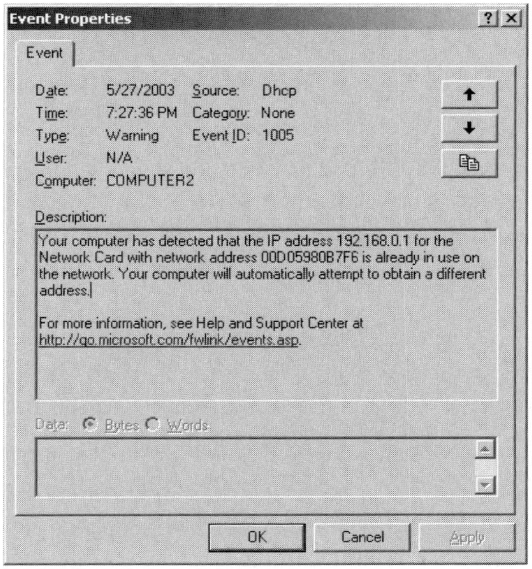

Event Properties ? X

Event

Date: 5/27/2003   Source: Dhcp
Time: 7:27:36 PM Category: None
Type: Warning   Event ID: 1005
User: N/A
Computer: COMPUTER2

Description:

Your computer has detected that the IP address 192.168.0.1 for the
Network Card with network address 00D05980B7F6 is already in use on
the network. Your computer will automatically attempt to obtain a different
address.

For more information, see Help and Support Center at
http://go.microsoft.com/fwlink/events.asp.

Data: ⦿ Bytes ○ Words

[OK]   [Cancel]   [Apply]

Figure 8-7   Address conflict warning message in Event Viewer

When you receive a warning message about an address conflict, and when you can verify that the client has received its IP configuration from a DHCP server, this conflict can be a sign of competing DHCP servers or of a sudden DHCP scope redeployment.

To check for competing DHCP servers, you can use the Dhcploc.exe utility (included in Windows Support Tools) to locate rogue DHCP servers on the network. After removing rogue servers as needed, verify that no two remaining DHCP servers can issue address leases from the same address range.

To recover gracefully from a scope redeployment, first increase the conflict detection attempts on the server and then renew client leases. To renew a client lease, use either the Ipconfig /renew command or the Repair button in the relevant connection's status dialog box. If you need to renew many leases, you can use the Shutdown /i command to restart multiple remote computers.

Note   The Shutdown /i command opens a graphical tool that allows you to select a number of remote computers to shut down.

Using the Repair Button

Clicking the Repair button on the Support tab of a connection's status dialog box (shown in Figure 8-6) performs the following six functions in sequence:

1. Broadcast a DHCP Request message to renew the currently assigned client IP address. (This step is performed only if the client is a DHCP client.) This function is similar to the one provided by the Ipconfig /renew command, but in the case of the Ipconfig /renew command, the request to renew the currently active IP address is sent by unicast, not broadcast, to the DHCP server that assigned the address. If no address (0.0.0.0) is currently assigned to the client, the first step performed by the Repair button (as with the Ipconfig /renew command) is to broadcast a DHCP Discover packet to the network.

2. Flush the ARP cache. This step is the functional equivalent of entering **arp –d** * at a command prompt.

3. Flush the NetBIOS cache. This step is the functional equivalent of entering the **nbtstat –R** command at a command prompt.

4. Flush the DNS cache. This step is the functional equivalent of entering the **ipconfig /flushdns** command at a command prompt.

5. Reregister the client's NetBIOS name and IP address with a WINS server. This step is the functional equivalent of entering the **nbtstat –RR** command at a command prompt.

6. Reregister the client's computer name and IP address with DNS. This step is the functional equivalent of entering the **ipconfig /registerdns** command at a command prompt.

Exam Tip For the exam, know the operations performed by the Repair button and their command-line equivalents.

Failure to Obtain a DHCP Address

When the Ipconfig /all command output or the connection status dialog box reveals that the client address is assigned by APIPA or by an alternate configuration, you can first attempt to refresh the IP configuration by using either the Ipconfig /renew command or the Repair button in the connection's status dialog box.

If the problem persists, this situation can signal either the absence of a DHCP server or relay agent deployed within broadcast range, a break in the physical connection, or an error at the DHCP server or scope. If you can verify that a DHCP server or relay agent is deployed within broadcast range, verify next that the physical connection to the

DHCP server or relay agent is functioning properly. Note that to ping the DHCP server or relay agent successfully, you might need to assign a temporary manual address that places the client on the same logical subnet as its default gateway.

> **Tip**   If you do not know the location, address, or name of a DHCP server on your network, enter **netsh dhcp show server** at a command prompt. This command provides you with the names and addresses of all servers authorized in Active Directory.

Once you can rule out problems in physical connectivity, and if you can rule out problems in the configuration or status of the DHCP relay agent (if deployed), you can move on to troubleshoot the DHCP server and scope. When troubleshooting the DHCP server for the client's failure to obtain an IP address, verify that the server is fully installed, configured, and authorized. When troubleshooting the scope for the client's failure to obtain an IP address, verify that the scope is active and that the available leases have not all been assigned to other clients. (See the "Verifying the Server Configuration" section later in this lesson for more information on troubleshooting these problems at the server and scope.)

Address Obtained from Incorrect Scope

If the Ipconfig /all command output or the connection's status dialog box reveals that the client has obtained an address from a DHCP server, and you determine that this address belongs to an incorrect scope, first verify that no competing servers exist on the network. To assist in this task, you can use the Dhcploc.exe utility to determine whether rogue servers are distributing IP addresses. If no rogue servers exist, verify that all DHCP servers authorized on the network are leasing from distinct address ranges. No overlap in leasable address space should exist among active DHCP servers.

The correct DHCP server might also have supplied an address from an incorrect scope. Multiple scopes can be active on a single DHCP server; scopes not native to the server's own subnet are used for remote clients. However, the DHCP server can match remote clients to the proper scope only when the RFC 1542–compliant router or DHCP relay agent through which the client communicates is properly addressed. In this scenario, when a remote client is assigned an incorrect address by the DHCP server, verify that the DHCP relay agent or router forwarding DHCP messages is itself correctly addressed.

> **Note**   DHCP Request messages contain a certain field named Giaddr that informs the DHCP server of the originating subnet of the request. When the field is empty, the client is assigned an address from the local scope. When the Giaddr field contains an address, as in the following case, the DHCP server assigns the client an address from a scope compatible with this address.
>
> ```
> DHCP: Relay  IP Address (giaddr) = 192.168.2.1
> ```

Verifying the Server Configuration

When verifying the DHCP server configuration, you can begin with the DHCP server address. To provide leases for clients on the local subnet, the DHCP server computer must be assigned an address whose network ID is common to that logical subnet. In addition, the DHCP Server service must be bound to the connection to that subnet. To verify a DHCP server's network bindings, select the Advanced tab in server properties and click the Bindings button. This procedure opens the Bindings dialog box, shown in Figure 8-8.

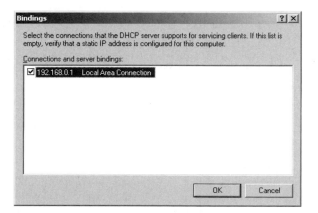

Figure 8-8   DHCP server bindings

After you have verified that the DHCP server is properly addressed and bound, verify that the DHCP server is authorized in Active Directory. You can determine that a server is not authorized when a red arrow pointing down marks the server icon in the DHCP console tree. When the server is authorized, the server icon is marked by a green arrow pointing up.

Verifying the Scope Configuration

To verify the scope configuration, begin by verifying that the scope is activated. Active and inactive scopes are designated by the same up and down arrows that are used to designate authorized and unauthorized servers.

Once you have verified that the scope has been activated, make sure the address range for the scope has been properly configured. For a scope that provides addresses to computers on the local network segment and logical subnet, make sure the network ID of the scope matches that of the DHCP server computer. This matter is simple when you are using default subnet masks, but when the local network or scope uses a mask other than /8, /16, or /24, you should use the AND function in Calculator to verify that the server address and scope addresses contain the same network ID.

Once the address range has been verified, make sure the available leases within the scope have not all been assigned. If you need to increase the number of available leases, you can achieve this task in a number of ways. First, you might try simply to increase the scope's address range if room is available. Second, you can recreate the scope with a shortened subnet mask (such as /23 instead of /24) and then change the subnet mask on all computers on the local network. Finally, you might prefer to deploy multinets with multiple scopes and a router.

As an alternative, you can attempt to accommodate more computers within your current available address space simply by decreasing the lease duration in the scope properties. When the lease duration is shortened, computers that are shut down or temporarily removed from the network do not keep their addresses for long. These addresses are then made available for use by other computers.

> **Exam Tip**   Look for questions in which you need to shorten the lease duration within a scope to accommodate many users within an address space. Typically, these scenarios involve many users on laptops or telecommuters dialing in from remote locations.

As you continue to verify the scope configuration, check the exclusions defined in the address pool. Are all of the statically assigned addresses on the network being excluded if they lie within the scope range? Are any addresses being excluded unnecessarily?

Next, move to the configured reservations. If clients with reserved addresses are not properly obtaining address leases, verify that the reserved addresses are not simultaneously being excluded. Also verify that the reserved addresses lie within the scope's defined address range. Finally, verify that the MAC addresses have been properly registered for each address reservation.

Next, for DHCP servers that have deployed multiple scopes for use with remote subnets, verify that each scope is properly defined. For a scope to serve a remote subnet, the scope's configured address range must match the network ID of the DHCP relay agent or RFC 1542–compatible router deployed on that subnet.

Finally, for networks on which multiple DHCP servers are deployed within a given broadcast range, verify that superscopes are configured and that the address ranges leased by each server are excluded by the other DHCP servers.

Real World   Obtaining and Verifying MAC Addresses for Reservations

To configure an address reservation, you need to know the hardware address of the computer whose address you want to reserve. The basic graphical user interface (GUI) way to get the hardware address of a local computer—or of a remote computer over a Remote Desktop connection—is through the Local Area Connection Status dialog box. In the dialog box, select the Support tab and then click the Details button. This procedure opens the Network Connection Details dialog box, which includes summary information such as the computer's MAC address, its IP address, its DHCP server address, its DNS server address, and other useful nuggets. The Ipconfig /all output also includes the MAC address of the local computer.

These methods are nice, but there is actually a much faster way to obtain MAC addresses of local and remote computers. Windows Support Tools includes a utility called Getmac, which, when used with the /s switch, allows you to obtain the physical address of any computer on the network—even those on a remote subnet. By piping the Getmac output into the clipboard, you can paste the MAC address of the remote computer into the New Reservation dialog box.

For example, type the following command at a command prompt:

getmac /s computer2 | clip

Then open Notepad and press Ctrl+V. This operation pastes the output from the previous Getmac operation. From Notepad, you can then copy Computer2's hardware address and paste it into the New Reservation dialog box.

Reconciling the DHCP Database

If you detect that DHCP database information is missing or inconsistent, you can attempt to resolve the problem by reconciling DHCP data for any or all scopes.

Scope IP address lease information is stored in two forms by the DHCP Server service:

- Detailed IP address lease information, stored in the DHCP database
- Summary IP address lease information, stored in the DHCP database

When reconciling scopes, the detail and summary entries are compared to find inconsistencies.

If you choose to repair inconsistencies found in this process, the DHCP server either returns the addresses in question to their original owners or creates a temporary reservation for these address. These reservations are valid for the lease time assigned to the scope. When the lease time expires, the addresses are recovered for future use.

To reconcile the DHCP database, complete the following steps:

1. Open the DHCP console.

2. In the console tree, click the applicable DHCP server.

3. On the Action menu, click Reconcile All Scopes.

4. In the Reconcile All Scopes dialog box, click Verify.

   Inconsistencies found are reported in the status window.

5. If the database is found to be consistent, click OK.

   If the database is not consistent, click the displayed addresses that need to be reconciled, and click Reconcile to repair inconsistencies.

To reconcile an individual scope, complete the following steps:

1. Open the DHCP console.

2. In the console tree, click the applicable scope.

3. On the Action menu, click Reconcile.

4. In the Reconcile dialog box, click Verify.

   Inconsistencies found are reported in the status window.

5. If the scope is found to be consistent, click OK.

   If the scope is not consistent, select the displayed addresses that need to be reconciled, and click Reconcile to repair inconsistencies.

Checking Event Viewer

When you experience a DHCP-related error on the network, you can use errors registered in the event log to help guide your troubleshooting efforts. You can search for these errors by opening Event Viewer and then selecting the System log in the console tree. On DHCP server computers, DHCP messages written to the log are designated by a source description of DHCPServer, as shown in Figure 8-9.

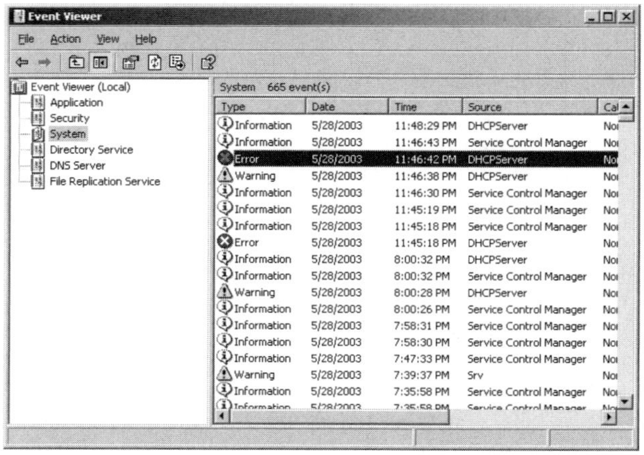

Figure 8-9   DHCP server errors

To diagnose DHCP server errors, double-click the DHCPServer events to read the associated message. The following text provides an example of a DHCP server error message registered in the event log:

```
The DHCP/BINL service on the local machine, belonging to the
Windows Administrative domain domain1.local, has determined that it is
not authorized to start. It has stopped servicing clients. The following
are some possible reasons for this:

This machine is part of a directory service enterprise and is
not authorized in the same domain. (See help on the DHCP Service
Management Tool for additional information.)

This machine cannot reach its directory service enterprise
and it has encountered another DHCP service on the network
belonging to a directory service enterprise on which the local machine
is not authorized.

Some unexpected network error occurred.
```

You can also use the System log in Event Viewer to search for errors on DHCP clients. On DHCP clients, DHCP events written to the log are designated by a source description of *Dhcp*.

The following text provides an example of a DHCP client error registered in the event log:

```
The IP address lease 192.168.0.11 for the Network Card with network
address 00D05380B7F6 has been denied by the DHCP server 192.168.0.1 (The DHCP Server
sent a DHCPNACK message).
```

> **Note**   If you need more information about DHCP server behavior than the event log provides, consult the server audit log, as described in Lesson 2 of this chapter.

Detecting DHCP Jet Data Corruption in Event Viewer

The following DHCP service messages, shown in Table 8-4, can appear in the System event log when the DHCP server database becomes corrupted.

Table 8-4   DHCP Database Corruption Errors

Event ID	Source	Description
1014	DhcpServer	The JET database returned the following Error: -510.
1014	DhcpServer	The JET database returned the following Error: -1022.
1014	DhcpServer	The JET database returned the following Error: -1850.

When you detect these errors in Event Viewer, you can use the Jetpack utility to perform a manual offline compaction of the DHCP database. In cases where Jetpack.exe fails to repair the database, you should restore the DHCP server database by using the DHCP console. (These procedures are both described in Lesson 2 of Chapter 7, "Configuring DHCP Servers and Clients.") Another way to recover the DHCP server database is to enter **netsh dhcp server set databaserestoreflag 1** at a command prompt. This procedure sets the restore flag, which permits the DHCP Server service to load a copy of the DHCP database in its default backup directory when the service is reinitialized.

Lesson Review

The following questions are intended to reinforce key information presented in this lesson. If you are unable to answer a question, review the lesson materials and try the question again. You can find answers to the questions in the "Questions and Answers" section at the end of this chapter.

1. You are responsible for implementing DHCP according to your company's official network plan. On one subnet, the network design specifications require that the DHCP server be assigned an address of 207.46.47.150 and that this server lease addresses to the local network segment through the scope of 207.46.48.0. However, the network designer has neglected to provide you with an appropriate subnet mask to assign the server and scope. Which subnet mask can you assign to the server and scope that will place the DHCP server and clients on the same logical subnet and reserve the fewest number of bits possible for the host ID?

2. Your company needs to provide leases for 280 users, but it has enough addresses for only 254. Of the 280 employees, 50 connect to the office network only biweekly through a VPN connection. What can you do to provide enough addresses for all users?

3. When do you need to increase conflict detection attempts on the DHCP server?

Lesson Summary

■ When troubleshooting DHCP, first determine whether the error is on the client, in the physical network, or on the server.

■ Use the connection status dialog box or the output from the Ipconfig /all command to determine whether a client address has been properly obtained from a DHCP server.

■ Verify that each client lies within broadcast range of a configured DHCP server, DHCP relay agent, or RFC 1542–compatible router.

■ To verify a DHCP server configuration, verify that the server has been properly installed, authorized, and bound.

■ To verify a scope configuration, verify that the scope is activated, and check the settings for the address range, subnet mask, exclusions, reservations, and superscopes.

Case Scenario Exercise

You are a network administrator for Fourth Coffee, a company based in Rutland, Vermont. Your company recently purchased 60 new client computers and plans to add them to the 245 already deployed on the network. This network consists of a single segment that includes a single DHCP server. Before the new computers are deployed, your DHCP server issues address leases through a single scope of 10.0.0.0/24.

You are responsible for deploying the 60 new computers and resolving any problems that arise after the changes. Answer the following questions by recommending the best course of action in response to each problem presented.

1. With the least administrative effort, how can you best provide enough addresses for the 290 clients that require dynamic addressing and still allow for connectivity among all networked computers? (Choose only one answer.)

   a. Create a new superscope and then add the 10.0.0.0/24 and 10.0.1.0/24 scopes to the new superscope.

   b. Reconfigure the scope as 10.0.0.0/23 and set conflict detection attempts to 3. Restart all computers by using the Shutdown /i command.

   c. Add a second DHCP server on the network segment to distribute address leases through the 10.0.1.0/24 scope.

   d. Add a second DHCP server on the network segment to distribute address leases through the 10.0.0.0/24 scope. Restart all computers by using the Shutdown /i command.

2. Your boss wants to reserve 20 computers in a special subnet within the 192.168.0.0/24 range and place these computers on the same network segment as the other computers. To achieve this task, you deploy a new DHCP server to issue leases in the 192.168.0.0/24 address range and create 20 lease reservations for the new set of computers. However, after the new DHCP server is deployed, the scope does not issue any new leases even though it is activated. Which of the following would most likely cause this scenario?

   a. You have not reconciled the scopes on the new DHCP server.

   b. You have not verified the database consistency.

   c. You have not excluded the range of addresses issued by the original DHCP computer.

   d. You have not assigned the new DHCP server an address within the 192.168.0.0/24 range.

3. After you enable the new scopes to issue addresses, some users begin to complain that they can no longer access network resources. Checking the DHCP server audit logs, you find several NACK messages. What steps should you take to resolve this problem? (Choose all that apply.)

   a. Create a superscope on each DHCP server consisting of the active scopes deployed on the network segment.

   b. Create client reservations for all appropriate clients on the original DHCP server.

   c. On the original DHCP server, exclude the full range of addresses within the special 192.168.0.0/24 subnet.

   d. On the new DHCP server, exclude the full range of addresses issued by the original DHCP server.

Troubleshooting Lab

In this lab, you troubleshoot a DHCP failure.

1. From Computer2, log on to Domain1 as Administrator.

2. Insert the Supplemental Course Materials CD-ROM into the Computer2 disk drive.

3. Locate and double-click the following batch file: \70-291\labs\Chapter08\Ch8a.bat.

4. Open a command prompt on Computer2 and enter the following: **ipconfig /renew**.

   The address fails to renew.

5. Take a few minutes to troubleshoot the connection on both computers. Using either Netsh commands or the DHCP console, verify that the server has been authorized, that the scope is active, and that the DHCP server has been given an appropriate address. Next, verify that the scope's features—such as exclusion ranges, reservations, options, and address ranges—have been properly defined.

6. After you have completed the tasks in step 5, answer the following question: Why is the DHCP server not leasing addresses?

   _____

7. After you have discovered the error, use the Ipconfig command to verify that Computer2 has adopted its alternate address of 192.168.0.2. If the address is listed as 0.0.0.0, enter **ipconfig /renew**.

8. When you can verify that Computer2 has adopted the alternate configuration address of 192.168.0.2, locate and double-click the following batch file on the Supplemental Course Materials CD: \70-291\labs\Chapter08\Ch8b.bat.

   The proper settings for the DHCP server are restored. The settings are not altered if they are already correctly configured.

9. On Computer2, at a command prompt type the following command: **ipconfig /renew**.

   Computer2 receives a fresh IP configuration from the DHCP server.

10. Log off Computer1 and Computer2.

Chapter Summary

■ The DHCP client initialization process occurs when a client computer first starts and attempts to join the network. The initialization process consists of an exchange of four broadcast messages: Discover, Offer, Request, and ACK.

■ Through a feature known as audit logging, all daily DHCP server activity is recorded in comma-delimited text files. By default, DHCP server log files can be found in the folder WINDOWS\System32\Dhcp.

■ Events in DHCP server log files are specified by event ID. Event IDs below 50 are described in each log file and do not need to be memorized. Events over 50 pertain to rogue server detection (Active Directory authorization status). You can either learn these events or consult a reference when you need to determine their meaning.

■ When a DHCP server stops providing leases to clients, you should always check the DHCP log to determine whether an authorization failure has occurred.

■ When troubleshooting DHCP, first determine whether the error is on the client, in the physical network, or on the server.

■ To verify a DHCP server configuration, verify that the server has been properly installed, authorized, and bound.

■ To verify a scope configuration, verify that the scope is activated, and check the settings for the address range, subnet mask, exclusions, reservations, and superscopes.

Exam Highlights

Before taking the exam, review the key points and terms that are presented in this chapter.

Key Points

■ Understand the various types of DHCP messages and the functions they serve.

■ Know the various ways to renew and refresh an address lease: Ipconfig /renew, the Repair button, and restarting the client computer.

■ Understand the distinct function of the DHCP audit log, and be able to read audit log messages.

■ Understand the benefits of raising conflict detection on the DHCP server.

■ Understand the benefits and disadvantages of long and short lease durations.

■ Be able to spot configuration errors in a DHCP server and scope.

Key Terms

DHCP Discover   A DHCP message broadcast by a DHCP client that allows the client to find a DHCP server.

DHCP NACK   A message sent by a DHCP server to a client to indicate that the IP address that the client requested is not correct for the local IP network served by the DHCP server.

Giaddr   A field in a DHCP message that records the address of a relay agent or RFC 1542–compatible router. This field allows a DHCP server to assign appropriate addresses to clients on remote subnets.

database restore flag   A setting that indicates whether the DHCP Server service loads a copy of the DHCP database in its default backup directory when the service is reinitialized. By default, the flag is set to 0, and the backup is not loaded when the service starts. When the flag is set to 1, the backup is loaded when the service starts.

Lesson 1, Practice, Exercise 2

Page
8-15
2. Answer the following questions in the spaces provided:

    a. What are the names of the five DHCP messages? Write them in sequence, as indicated by the contents of the description field for each frame.

Release, Discover, Offer, Request, ACK

    b. Which is the only message that is not a broadcast? Why is this so?

Release. The message is not a broadcast because the server's location is known at this point, and to complete the release, the client does not need to communicate with any other DHCP servers that might exist on the network. The server's location is known because the client had already discovered the server when obtaining the same lease that is being released by the message.

    c. Which DHCP messages make up the client lease initialization process?

Discover, Offer, Request, ACK

    d. Look at the Options field in each DHCP message. Which two DHCP messages include client configurations for the Domain Name, Router, and Domain Name Server options?

Offer and ACK

    e. Which User Datagram Protocol (UDP) port is used as the source port when sending information from the DHCP client, and the destination port when sending information to the DHCP client?

68

    f. Which UDP port is used as the source port when sending information from the DHCP server, and the destination port when sending information to the DHCP server?

67

    g. Which of the five DHCP messages is the only one to contain a Dynamic DNS Updates section within the DHCP Options field?

DHCP Request

4. Answer the following questions: What information is contained in the Dynamic DNS Updates section? Which resource record will the DHCP server update with this information?

The section contains the full computer name (host name and domain name) of the DHCP client. The DHCP server updates the PTR resource record with this information.

Lesson 1, Practice, Exercise 4

Page
8-17

2. Answer the following questions in the spaces provided:

   a. How many messages make up a DHCP lease renewal?

   2

   b. What are the names of the captured DHCP messages? Write them in sequence, as indicated by the contents of the description field for each frame.

   Request, ACK

   c. What is the difference in the method by which these messages have been communicated, as opposed to the corresponding messages captured in the DHCP lease initialization?

   These messages have not been broadcast but have been sent directly to the DHCP server or client.

3. Locate the DHCP fields named Client IP Address and Your IP Address in both captured frames, and then answer the following questions:

   a. In a lease renewal, does the DHCP client request a renewal of a specific IP address?

   Yes

   b. Which particular DHCP message field renews the client's configuration of DHCP options?

   The Option field in the ACK message

Lesson 1 Review

Page
8-18

1. You have configured a subnet with two DHCP servers, DHCP1 and DHCP2. DHCP1 provides addresses within the first 80 percent of the subnet's scope range, and DHCP2 provides addresses for the remaining 20 percent of the scope range. Computer ClientA obtains a fresh address from DHCP1, after which you immediately take DHCP1 off the network. How long will it take before ClientA attempts to obtain a new address from DHCP2?

   a. Four days

   b. Five days

   c. Seven days

   d. Eight days

    c

2. Which of the following messages is not exchanged as part of a DHCP lease initialization?

   a. Renew

   b. Request

   c. ACK

   d. Discover

   a

3. Which two messages are exchanged in a DHCP lease renewal?

   Request and ACK

4. What is the default period of time after which a DHCP client attempts to renew its IP address lease?

   Four days

Lesson 2 Review

Page
8-25

1. Beginning on Monday, you find that you can no longer ping some of your network clients. When you consult Monday's DHCP server log file, you find the following event:

   ```
   54,6/09/03,06:47:29,Authorization failed,,domain1.local,,
   ```

   What action most likely accounts for the network problems? Who has performed this action?

   The server has become unauthorized within Active Directory. This action can be performed only by a member of the Enterprise Admins group.

2. What most likely accounts for the errors shown in the following DHCP audit log?

   ```
   00,5/24/03,08:21:57,Started,,,,
   54,5/24/03,08:21:58,Authorization failed,,domain1.local,,
   ```

   a. The server has been started for the first time.

   b. The server cannot communicate on the network.

   c. The server has been unauthorized by a senior network manager.

   d. The server is not running Windows Server 2003.

   a

3. By default, how long do logged events last in DHCP server logs?

   a. One day

   b. One week

   c. One month

   d. Until the log grows beyond 1 MB

   b

Lesson 3 Review

Page
8-37

1. You are responsible for implementing DHCP according to your company's official network plan. On one subnet, the network design specifications require that the DHCP server be assigned an address of 207.46.47.150 and that this server lease addresses to the local network segment through the scope of 207.46.48.0. However, the network designer has neglected to provide you with an appropriate subnet mask to assign the server and scope. Which subnet mask can you assign to the server and scope that will place the DHCP server and clients on the same logical subnet and reserve the fewest number of bits possible for the host ID?

   255.255.224.0

2. Your company needs to provide leases for 280 users, but it has enough addresses for only 254. Of the 280 employees, 50 connect to the office network only biweekly through a VPN connection. What can you do to provide enough addresses for all users?

   Decrease the lease duration.

3. When do you need to increase conflict detection attempts on the DHCP server?

   When a scope is redeployed and leases are in use by computers on the network

Case Scenario Exercise

Page
8-38

1. With the least amount of administrative effort, how can you best provide enough addresses for the 290 clients that require dynamic addressing and still allow for connectivity among all networked computers? (Choose only one answer.)

   a. Create a new superscope and then add the 10.0.0.0/24 and 10.0.1.0/24 scopes to the new superscope.

   b. Reconfigure the scope as 10.0.0.0/23 and set conflict detection attempts to 3. Restart all computers by using the Shutdown /i command.

c. Add a second DHCP server on the network segment to distribute address leases through the 10.0.1.0/24 scope.

d. Add a second DHCP server on the network segment to distribute address leases through the 10.0.0.0/24 scope. Restart all computers by using the Shutdown /i command.

b

2. Your boss wants to reserve 20 computers in a special subnet within the 192.168.0.0/24 range and place these computers on the same network segment as the other computers. To achieve this task, you deploy a new DHCP server to issue leases in the 192.168.0.0/24 address range and create 20 lease reservations for the new set of computers. However, after the new DHCP server is deployed, the scope does not issue any new leases even though it is activated. Which of the following would most likely cause this scenario?

a. You have not reconciled the scopes on the new DHCP server.

b. You have not verified the database consistency.

c. You have not excluded the range of addresses issued by the original DHCP computer.

d. You have not assigned the new DHCP server an address within the 192.168.0.0/24 range.

d

3. After you enable the new scopes to issue addresses, some users begin to complain that they can no longer access network resources. Checking the DHCP server audit logs, you find several NACK messages. What steps should you take to resolve this problem? (Choose all that apply.)

a. Create a superscope on each DHCP server consisting of the active scopes deployed on the network segment.

b. Create client reservations for all appropriate clients on the original DHCP server.

c. On the original DHCP server, exclude the full range of addresses within the special 192.168.0.0/24 subnet.

d. On the new DHCP server, exclude the full range of addresses issued by the original DHCP server.

a, c, d

Troubleshooting Lab

Page
8-40

1. After you have completed the tasks in step 5, answer the following question: Why is the DHCP server not leasing addresses?

The scope on the DHCP server has no defined range of addresses.

9 Routing with Windows Server 2003

Exam Objectives in this Chapter:

- Manage Routing And Remote Access routing interfaces
- Manage packet filters
- Manage TCP/IP routing
    - Manage routing protocols
    - Manage routing tables
    - Manage routing ports
- Troubleshoot demand-dial routing
- Troubleshoot connectivity to the Internet
- Verify that the DHCP relay agent is working correctly

Why This Chapter Matters

Routing provides the basis for the Internet and for most network communication. Though routing is an essential aspect of most networks, configuring and supporting routers is rarely a simple matter. Routing through dial-up lines, for example, requires knowledge about authentication, static routes, and address assignment that is specific to routing scenarios. Routing over dedicated lines, meanwhile, presents its own specific set of challenges. To function effectively in their jobs, network administrators must be able to manage the many complex elements of routed networks that require support and configuration, such as routing protocols and routing tables.

Microsoft Windows Server 2003 can be configured as a network router. When feasible, deploying Windows Server 2003 routers allows for some distinct advantages over dedicated hardware routers, including lower cost, ease of management, and integration with Windows security and group policies. This chapter describes how to configure and manage the many routing features associated with the Routing And Remote Access service in Windows Server 2003, including network address translation, demand-dial routing, and packet filters.

Lessons in this Chapter:

■ Lesson 1: Configuring Windows Server 2003 for LAN Routing 9-3

■ Lesson 2: Configuring Demand-Dial Routing 9-28

■ Lesson 3: Configuring NAT 9-45

■ Lesson 4: Configuring and Managing Routing Protocols 9-57

■ Lesson 5: Configuring Packet Filters 9-68

Before You Begin

To complete this chapter, you must have

■ Two networked computers, named Computer1 and Computer2, each running Windows Server 2003. Computer1 should be assigned a static address of 192.168.0.1/24, and Computer2 should be configured to obtain an address automatically. Computer2 should also have an alternate configuration address of 192.168.0.2/24.

■ Connected each computer's modem to a separate phone line (highly recommended).

■ Installed a DNS server on both computers. Computer1 hosts an Active Directory–integrated primary zone named domain1.local, which accepts only secure dynamic updates. Computer2 hosts a standard secondary zone of domain1.local and the delegated subdomain of sub.domain1.local as a standard primary zone. Computer1 hosts a standard stub zone of sub.domain1.local.

■ Configured Computer1 as a domain controller in the domain1.local domain and Computer2 as a member of the domain. The domain functional level is Windows 2000 mixed mode.

■ Installed a DHCP server on Computer1. The DHCP server is authorized in the domain and includes the scope Test Scope whose IP address range is 192.168.0.11–192.168.0.254. Through DHCP options, the scope assigns a router (gateway) of 192.168.0.1, a DNS server of 192.168.0.1, and a DNS domain name of domain1.local.

■ Installed Windows Support Tools on both computers.

■ Installed Network Monitor on both computers.

■ Deleted any dial-up connections configured on either computer.

Lesson 1: Configuring Windows Server 2003 for LAN Routing

Routing features in Windows Server 2003 are provided by the Routing And Remote Access service, which is installed in a disabled state. *Routing And Remote Access* is essentially a software router that can be configured to connect separate network segments.

After this lesson, you will be able to

- Configure Windows Server 2003 as a network router
- Configure and manage routing features in Routing And Remote Access
- View and maintain routing tables
- Configure and maintain static routes

Estimated lesson time: 90 minutes

Understanding Routing

Routing is the process of transferring data across an internetwork from one local area network (LAN) to another. Whereas a *bridge* connects network segments and shares traffic as necessary according to hardware addresses, a router receives and forwards traffic along appropriate pathways according to software addresses. Consequently, bridges, operating at the second, or data link layer of the Open Systems Interconnect (OSI) networking model, are sometimes called "layer 2" devices. Routers, which operate at the third, or network layer of the OSI model, are known as "layer 3" devices.

In IP networks, routing is performed according to IP routing tables. All IP hosts use routing tables to forward IP traffic; IP routers are distinctive from hosts in that they can use these routing tables to forward traffic that has been received from another router or host.

Figure 9-1 illustrates the role of routers in connecting networks.

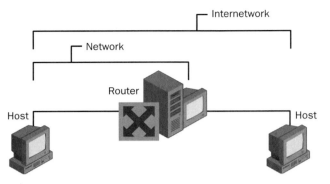

Figure 9-1 Local area networks connected by a router

Using Routing And Remote Access

The Routing And Remote Access service in Windows Server 2003 is a multiprotocol software router that can be readily integrated with Windows features such as security accounts and group policies. The service can be configured for LAN-to-LAN, LAN-to-WAN, virtual private network (VPN), and Network Address Translation (NAT) routing through IP networks. In addition, the service can be configured for routing features such as IP multicasting, demand-dial routing, DHCP relay, and packet filtering. Finally, it offers built-in support for the dynamic routing protocols Routing Information Protocol (RIP) version 2 and Open Shortest Path First (OSPF).

> **Note** Windows Server 2003 also supports AppleTalk routing. However, whereas Internetwork Packet Exchange (IPX) routing is supported in Microsoft Windows 2000, computers running Windows Server 2003 cannot function as IPX routers.

Hardware routers include many built-in ports, each of which typically connects to a distinct network segment. The hardware router can route traffic from any one port to another. For Routing And Remote Access, however, the number of network segments among which traffic can be routed is limited by the number of network interfaces installed on the Windows Server 2003 computer running the service. For example, if you have configured your Windows Server 2003 computer with two network cards and a modem, the Routing And Remote Access service can route traffic among three networks.

Figure 9-2 illustrates an example of a Windows Server 2003 computer running the Routing And Remote Access service and configured with four network adapters. In this scenario, the Routing And Remote Access service is routing IP traffic among four LANs.

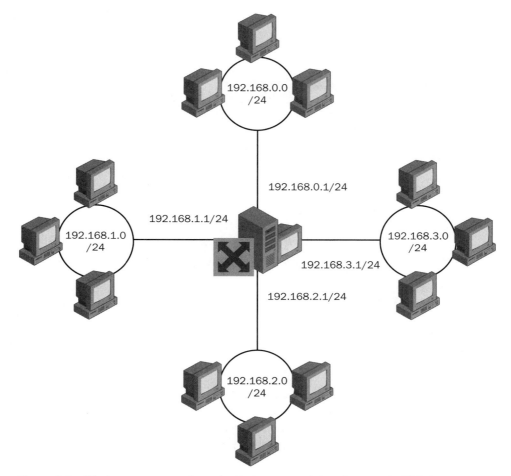

Figure 9-2   Windows router configured with four network interface cards (NICs)

Enabling Routing And Remote Access

The Routing And Remote Access service is installed by Windows Server 2003 Setup in a disabled state. You can enable and configure the service by running the Routing And Remote Access Server Setup Wizard. Note that if the server on which you want to configure the Routing And Remote Access service is a member server of an Active Directory domain, you must add the server's computer account to the RAS And IAS Servers domain local security group before the router can function. If the server is already a domain local controller, it will be automatically added to this security group.

Using the Routing And Remote Access Console

The Routing And Remote Access console is the graphical user interface (GUI) tool used to configure routing in Windows Server 2003. In a basic installation in which Routing

And Remote Access has been configured only for LAN routing, the Routing And Remote Access console includes two main nodes for each server node: the Network Interfaces node and the IP Routing node. Figure 9-3 shows these nodes.

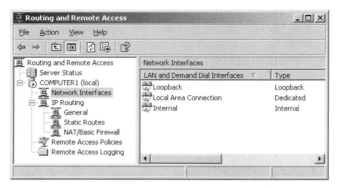

Figure 9-3   Routing And Remote Access console

Adding Interfaces

In the Routing And Remote Access console, a *network interface* is a software component that connects to a physical device such as a modem or a network card. To configure routing through Routing And Remote Access, you must first verify that all software interfaces through which you want to route traffic are listed in the Network Interfaces node.

The server running Routing And Remote Access usually detects all network adapters when the Routing And Remote Access Server Setup Wizard is run. Network interfaces corresponding to these adapters are then listed in the Network Interfaces node and are immediately available for configuration in the Routing And Remote Access console.

However, preconfigured dial-up connections are not available in Routing And Remote Access. If you want to configure routing through an on-demand or persistent dial-up connection, a VPN connection, or a Point-to-Point Protocol over Ethernet (PPPoE) connection, you must add this connection type manually through the Network Interfaces node in the Routing And Remote Access console. All three of these connection types are known collectively as *demand-dial interfaces*. Once your demand-dial interface is added, you can then apply to it Routing And Remote Access routing features such as NAT, static routes, or DHCP relay.

> **Note**   Remember that a demand-dial interface does not necessarily refer to a dial-up connection. It can also refer to a VPN or PPPoE connection over a dedicated line.

To add a dial-up connection, VPN connection, or PPPoE connection, complete the following steps:

1. Open the Routing And Remote Access console.

2. In the console tree, click Network Interfaces.

3. Right-click Network Interfaces, and then click New Demand-Dial Interface.

4. Follow the instructions in the Demand Dial Interface Wizard.

The only other occasion when you need to add an interface manually in the Routing And Remote Access console is when you add a new network adapter after you have configured and enabled Routing And Remote Access. To perform this task, use the Interfaces node within the IP Routing node, as described in the next procedure.

To add a routing interface, complete the following steps:

1. Open Routing And Remote Access.

2. In the console tree, click General.

3. Right-click General, and then click New Interface.

4. In Interfaces, click the interface you want to add, and then click OK.

5. If applicable, complete any configuration dialog boxes for the interface.

Using the IP Routing Node

In the Routing And Remote Access console, the IP Routing node allows you to configure basic features of IP routing. As shown in Figure 9-3, this node by default includes three subnodes: General, Static Routes, and NAT/Basic Firewall.

Configuring Routing And Remote Access Service Properties

You configure the Routing And Remote Access service properties in the properties dialog box of the server node in the Routing And Remote Access console. These properties include routing, demand-dial, and remote access enabling; authentication configuration; client address assignment; Point-to-Point Protocol (PPP) options; and logging features.

General Tab

The General tab, shown in Figure 9-4, allows you to configure the Routing And Remote Access service as a LAN router, demand-dial router, remote access server, or all three. For example, if you have selected the Local Area Network (LAN) Routing Only option and have not selected the Remote Access Server check box, neither demand-dial routing nor remote access will be available. Before you can even create any demand-dial interfaces, you must enable Routing And Remote Access for demand-dial routing by selecting the LAN And Demand-Dial Routing option. Similarly, to allow remote clients to connect to the local server, the Remote Access Server check box must be selected.

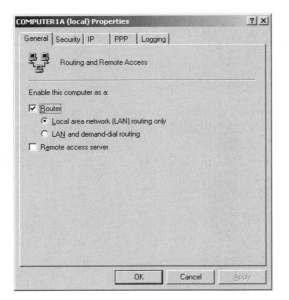

Figure 9-4   Router security properties

Security Tab

The Security tab, shown in Figure 9-5, allows you to configure authentication methods, connection request logging, and preshared keys for Internet Protocol Security (IPSec). These security options are applied to remote access clients as well as to demand-dial routers.

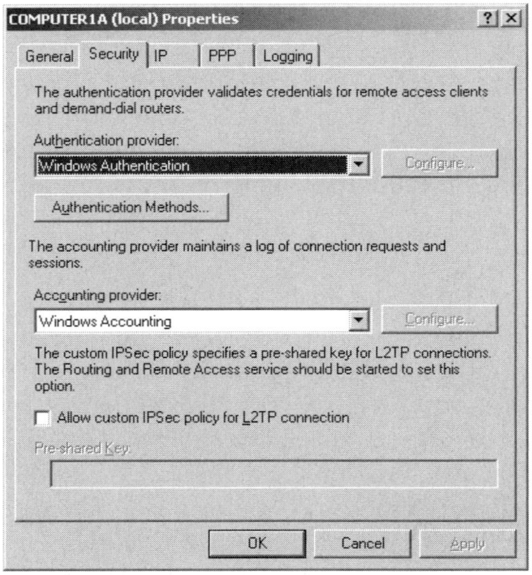

Figure 9-5   Security tab of the Routing And Remote Access service properties

IP Tab

The IP tab is shown in Figure 9-6. This tab allows you to configure the Routing And Remote Access service to route IP packets over LAN, remote access, or demand-dial connections. Whereas options on the General tab apply to routing, demand-dial, and remote access service in general, the function of the IP tab is to enable specifically IP traffic to pass through the various connection types. Consequently, to configure IP routing and remote access successfully, you must select appropriate options on both the General tab and the IP tab.

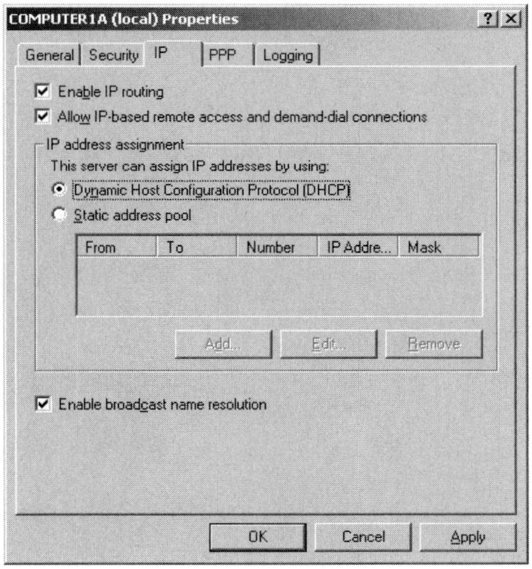

Figure 9-6   Router IP properties

In the IP Address Assignment area of the IP tab, you can configure how the server assigns IP addresses to remote access clients. When selected, the Dynamic Host Configuration Protocol (DHCP) option indicates that the remote access clients will be assigned addresses from a DHCP server. This DHCP server, if not configured on the Routing And Remote Access service itself, must be connected to the remote access interface through a DHCP relay agent.

Alternatively, when the Static Address Pool option is selected, Routing And Remote Access acts as its own DHCP-type server. In this case, you must manually specify a range of addresses from which the Routing And Remote Access service assigns addresses to clients.

Finally, the IP tab also includes an Enable Broadcast Name Resolution check box. Selecting this option enables a remote access client to resolve computer names on all network segments connected directly to the Routing And Remote Access computer, even when no DNS or WINS server is available. Essentially, this option, which is enabled by default, allows the router to pass NetBIOS over TCP/IP (NetBT) broadcasts from the remote access client to all of the network segments connected to the router. Figure 9-7 illustrates a network in which this feature has been enabled.

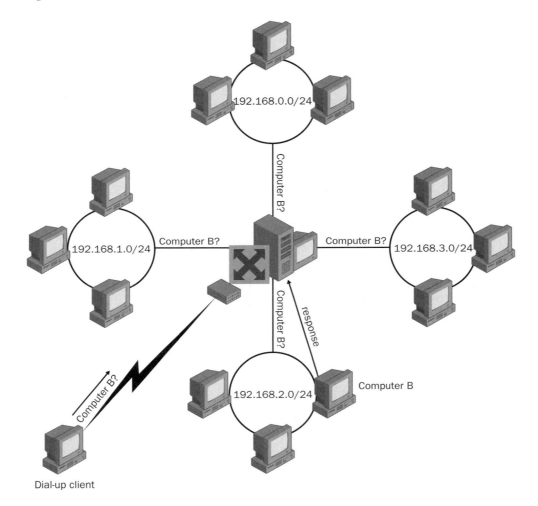

Figure 9-7 Routing And Remote Access broadcast name resolution enabled

PPP Tab

You use the PPP tab to negotiate and authenticate dial-up connections. The configuration options available on this tab, shown in Figure 9-8, allow you to enable and disable four PPP-related options: Multilink Connections, Dynamic Bandwidth Control Using

BAP Or BACP, Link Control Protocol (LCP) Extensions, and Software Compression. All four of these options are enabled by default.

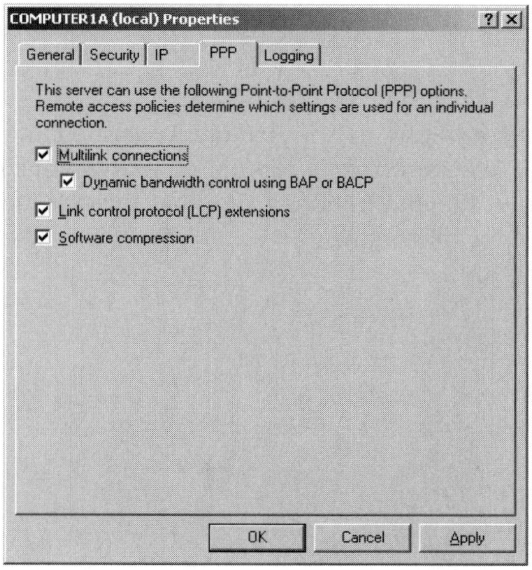

Figure 9-8   PPP properties for Routing And Remote Access

Multilink Connections   When the Multilink Connections check box is selected, the Routing And Remote Access service allows Multilink connections from remote access clients. With Multilink, multiple physical links operate as a single logical link over which data is sent and received. Thus, PPP clients can increase their bandwidth by fusing separate connections to the remote access server. (Multilink requires additional configuration at the client.)

Dynamic Bandwidth Control Using BAP Or BACP   When the Dynamic Bandwidth Control Using BAP Or BACP check box is selected, Multilink connections add or drop additional PPP connections to accommodate a rise or fall in available bandwidth. Bandwidth Allocation Protocol (BAP) and Bandwidth Allocation Control Protocol (BACP) work together to provide this service, which is known as bandwidth on demand (BOD).

Link Control Protocol (LCP) Extensions   The Link Control Protocol (LCP) Extensions check box must be selected to support certain advanced PPP features such as callback. Leave this option enabled unless clients cannot successfully connect through PPP. Disabling this check box might resolve problems with older clients that do not support these extensions.

Software Compression   The Software Compression check box enables Routing And Remote Access to perform compression of PPP data at the software level. Leave this option enabled unless the modem connecting to the PPP client is capable of compressing PPP data at the hardware level.

Logging Tab

The Logging tab allows you to configure Routing And Remote Access logging options. By default, the Routing And Remote Access service is configured to log only errors and warnings. Figure 9-9 shows the other logging options. Note that this tab includes an option to log additional information for debugging.

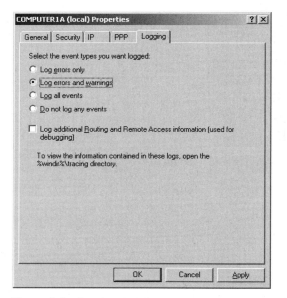

Figure 9-9   Routing And Remote Access logging options

Managing General IP Routing Properties

Certain features provided by the Routing And Remote Access service relate to IP routing in general. You can manage these features only in the General Properties dialog box associated with the General subnode within the IP Routing node in the Routing And Remote Access console.

To open the General Properties dialog box, right-click the General node within IP Routing and then click Properties. The General Properties dialog box contains three tabs: Logging, Preference Levels, and Multicast Scopes. (Because multicasting is not covered on the 70-291 exam, only the first two of these tabs are discussed here.)

Logging Tab

Figure 9-10 shows the Logging tab. This tab allows you to configure which IP routing events are written to the Event Log. By default, only errors are written to the Event Log, but you can select two higher logging levels: Log Errors And Warnings, and Log The Maximum Amount Of Information. In addition, you can disable logging in IP routing when you select the Disable Event Logging option.

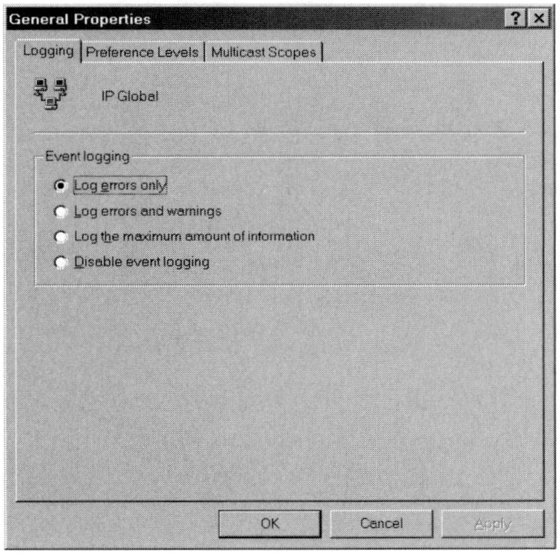

Figure 9-10   IP Routing log configuration

Preference Levels Tab

Figure 9-11 shows the Preference Levels tab. IP routing decisions are performed according to routing tables, and this feature allows you to arrange the priority of routes collected from various sources. When two sources provide a conflict in routes, only the route with the higher preference level is added to the routing table. These preference levels therefore supersede any metrics assigned to routes.

Preference levels are listed in order. The first (top) route source has the highest priority and the lowest rank number (1). The lowest route source has the lowest priority and the highest rank number (120). You can adjust the rank of a route source by clicking a source on the list and using the Move Up button and Move Down button as needed.

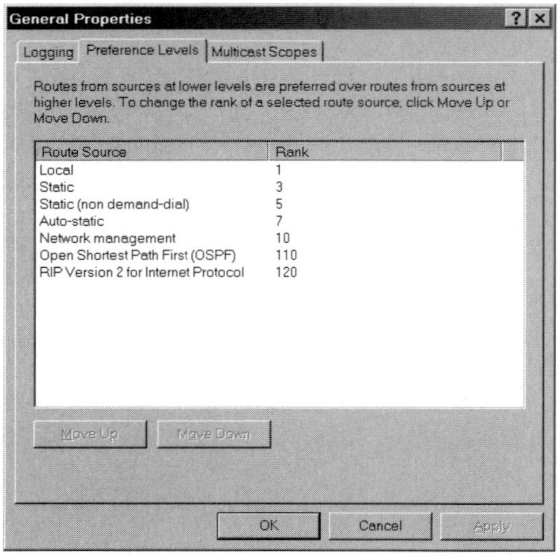

Figure 9-11 IP Routing preference levels

Working with Routing Tables

Routers read the destination addresses of received packets and then route those packets according to directions provided by routing tables. Figure 9-12 shows a routing table used by an IP router.

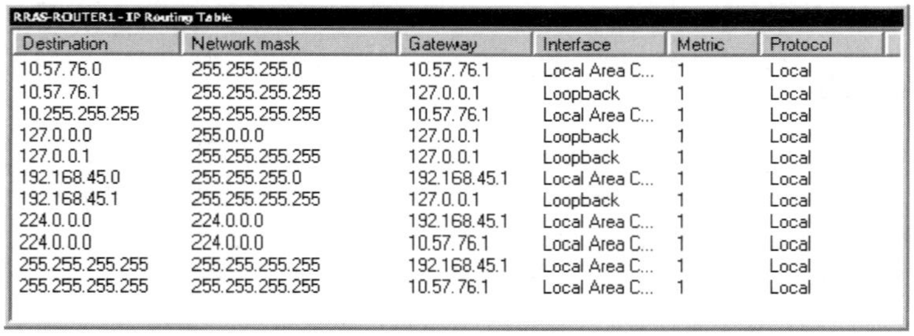
RRAS-ROUTER1 - IP Routing Table

Destination	Network mask	Gateway	Interface	Metric	Protocol
10.57.76.0	255.255.255.0	10.57.76.1	Local Area C...	1	Local
10.57.76.1	255.255.255.255	127.0.0.1	Loopback	1	Local
10.255.255.255	255.255.255.255	10.57.76.1	Local Area C...	1	Local
127.0.0.0	255.0.0.0	127.0.0.1	Loopback	1	Local
127.0.0.1	255.255.255.255	127.0.0.1	Loopback	1	Local
192.168.45.0	255.255.255.0	192.168.45.1	Local Area C...	1	Local
192.168.45.1	255.255.255.255	127.0.0.1	Loopback	1	Local
224.0.0.0	224.0.0.0	192.168.45.1	Local Area C...	1	Local
224.0.0.0	224.0.0.0	10.57.76.1	Local Area C...	1	Local
255.255.255.255	255.255.255.255	192.168.45.1	Local Area C...	1	Local
255.255.255.255	255.255.255.255	10.57.76.1	Local Area C...	1	Local

Figure 9-12 IP Routing table

The routing table contains entries called *routes* that provide directions toward destination networks or hosts. Three types of routes exist:

- **Host route** This type of route provides a route to a specific destination host or to a broadcast address. In IP routing tables, host routes are distinguished by a 255.255.255.255 network mask.
- **Network route** This type of route provides a route to a specific destination network. In IP routing tables, network routes can be distinguished by any subnet mask between 0.0.0.0 and 255.255.255.255.

■ **Default route**   Routing tables contain a single default route. This route is used to forward all packets whose destination address does not match any address listed in the routing table. In IP routing tables, the default route is defined by the 0.0.0.0 address and 0.0.0.0 network mask.

Viewing the IP Routing Table

You can view the IP routing table through the Routing And Remote Access console or through a command prompt.

In the Routing And Remote Access console, expand the IP Routing node, right-click the Static Routes node, and then click Show IP Routing Table. (Figure 9-12 shows an example output from this operation.)

To view the routing table from a command line, type **route print** and press Enter. Figure 9-13 shows an example output.

```
C:\Documents and Settings\Administrator.COMPUTER1>route print

IPv4 Route Table
===========================================================================
Interface List
0x1 ........................... MS TCP Loopback interface
0x2 ...00 50 ba 40 5c 73 ...... D-Link DFE-530TX+ PCI Adapter
0x10003 ...00 53 45 00 00 00 ...... WAN (PPP/SLIP) Interface
0x20004 ...00 53 45 00 00 00 ...... WAN (PPP/SLIP) Interface
===========================================================================
===========================================================================
Active Routes:
Network Destination        Netmask          Gateway       Interface  Metric
          0.0.0.0          0.0.0.0     207.46.252.3   207.46.252.88      1
        127.0.0.0        255.0.0.0        127.0.0.1       127.0.0.1      1
      192.168.1.0    255.255.255.0      192.168.1.1     192.168.1.1      1
      192.168.1.1  255.255.255.255        127.0.0.1       127.0.0.1      1
     192.168.1.31  255.255.255.255        127.0.0.1       127.0.0.1     50
    192.168.1.255  255.255.255.255      192.168.1.1     192.168.1.1      1
     207.46.252.3  255.255.255.255   207.46.252.88   207.46.252.88      1
    207.46.252.88  255.255.255.255        127.0.0.1       127.0.0.1     50
   207.46.252.255  255.255.255.255   207.46.252.88   207.46.252.88     50
        224.0.0.0        240.0.0.0      192.168.1.1     192.168.1.1      1
        224.0.0.0        240.0.0.0   207.46.252.88   207.46.252.88     50
  255.255.255.255  255.255.255.255      192.168.1.1     192.168.1.1      1
Default Gateway:       207.46.252.3
===========================================================================
Persistent Routes:
  None

C:\Documents and Settings\Administrator.COMPUTER1>
```

Figure 9-13   Routing table viewed from a command prompt

Reading the IP Routing Table

Routers use routing tables to determine where to send packets. When IP packets are sent to an IP router, the router reads the destination address of the packet and compares that destination address to the entries in the routing table. One of these entries is used to determine which interface to use to send the packet and to which *hop* (gateway) the packet will be sent next.

To assist in this process, each routing table entry includes the five columns described in the following sections, as shown in Figure 9-13.

Network Destination   This column provides entries that the router compares to the destination address of every received IP packet. A few of these entries are common to most routing tables. For example, the entry 0.0.0.0 represents the *default route*, used when no other matches are found in the routing table. The entry 127.0.0.0 points to the *loopback address* of 127.0.0.1, which corresponds to the local machine. Each entry of 224.0.0.0, furthermore, refers to a separate multicast route. Finally, entries with a final octet value of 255 represent a broadcast address. Broadcast addresses include specific subnet broadcast addresses, such as 192.168.1.255, and the *limited broadcast address* 255.255.255.255, which is general for all networks and routers.

Netmask   The value in this column determines which part of the IP packet's destination address is compared to the entries in the Network Destination column. This information is important because the largest match determines the route or table entry that is applied to the packet.

For instance, suppose the router whose routing table is shown in Figure 9-13 receives two packets, the first destined for the address 192.168.1.1 and the second destined for the address 192.168.1.2. Both packets match the third routing table entry because the netmask value of 255.255.255.0 signifies that the first three octets (plus a 0 for the fourth octet) are compared to the table's network destination value of 192.168.1.0.

However, only the first packet matches the fourth entry because the netmask of 255.255.255.255 signals that all four octets are compared to the table's network destination value of 192.168.1.1. The fourth entry is thus applied to the first packet because this entry represents the largest match in the routing table. In this manner, the third entry is applied to the second packet because that entry represents the packet's only match in the routing table aside from the default route.

Gateway   When a particular route or table entry is applied to a packet, the gateway value determines the next address or hop for which that packet is destined. For example, according to the routing table shown in Figure 9-13, an IP packet with a destination such as 206.73.118.5 (which matches only the default route of 0.0.0.0) would next be forwarded to the gateway address of 207.46.252.3. Note that the gateway value for the default route is the same as the default gateway address configured in TCP/IP properties.

A basic concept to understand for the gateway value is that this address should be distinct from that of the network destination listed in the same routing table entry, even when the network destination itself is within broadcast range of the router. For example, in Figure 9-13, the sixth entry provides directions to the 207.46.252.0/24 destination—one of two subnets to which the router is directly connected. (The other subnet is 192.168.1.0/24.)

Even though the router is directly connected to the 207.46.252.0/24 subnet, the router receives packets destined for this subnet only through its 192.168.1.1 interface. (Packets originating from the 207.46.252.0/24 subnet do not need the router to reach the same subnet.) From this perspective, you can see that the next hop for packets originating from one of the router's local subnets is the opposite interface of the router. Therefore, the routing table specifies as the gateway the router's interface on that destination subnet (207.46.252.88).

> **Tip** Another way to understand the necessary distinction between the gateway address and the network destination address is to think of each routing table entry as providing directions (an interface and gateway) to a given destination. With this analogy in mind, it makes sense that these entries wouldn't provide directions merely by repeating the destination queried for. (How do you get to 192.168.1.5? Just go there!) Consequently, when the network destination is within a router's broadcast range, the router's routing table provides directions to this destination by pointing not to the destination itself but to the router's own local address that faces the destination. This gateway value will thus be the same as the interface value. Similarly, even in cases where the destination is one of the router's own addresses, the routing table specifies a distinct address—the loopback address of 127.0.0.1—as the interface and gateway.

Interface When a particular route (table entry) is applied to a packet, the interface value specified in that route determines which local network interface is used to forward the packet to the next hop. For example, in Figure 9-13, an IP packet with a destination of 131.107.23.101 matches only the default route. According to the routing table, such a packet is sent through the interface 207.46.252.88 toward the default gateway address.

Metric This column indicates the cost of using a route. If separate routes (entries) match an IP packet's destination address equally, the metric is used to determine which route is applied. Lower metrics have precedence over higher metrics.

For the routing protocol RIP, the metric is determined by the number of hops before the network destination. However, you can use any algorithm to determine the metric if you are configuring a route manually.

Static and Dynamic Routing

For every host and router, IP automatically builds a simple routing table that includes only the essential network destinations. These addresses can occur in eight types and include the default address, the loopback address, the default gateway address, locally configured addresses, local subnet addresses, local subnet broadcast addresses, the limited broadcast address, and multicast addresses for each adapter.

All of these eight routing table entry types describe routes that are connected directly to the IP host or router. This default arrangement might work for simple routing situations, but in a complex network, a router needs to be told which among its many interfaces to use to send packets destined for unknown (non-neighboring) networks.

To allow routing tables to properly forward traffic to hosts that are outside broadcast range, you must choose between one of two alternatives. First, you can add routes to these destinations manually by using the Route Add command or by using the Routing And Remote Access console. This process defines *static routing*. Second, you can configure a dynamic routing protocol such as RIP or OSPF to allow routers to share routing table information with each other. This process defines *dynamic routing*.

Table 9-1 compares some of the basic differences between static and dynamic routing.

Table 9-1   Comparing Static and Dynamic Routing

Static Routing	Dynamic Routing
A feature of IP.	A feature of routing protocols such as RIP or OSPF.
Routers do not share routing information.	Routers share routing information automatically.
Routing tables are built and sustained manually.	Routing tables are built and sustained dynamically.

Exploring LAN Routing Scenarios

You can use routers in many different topologies and network configurations. When you configure a server running Routing And Remote Access as a router, you can specify the following:

- The protocols to be routed (IP or AppleTalk) by the router
- Routing protocols (RIP or OSPF) for each protocol to be routed
- LAN or wide area network (WAN) media (network adapters, modems, or other dial-up equipment)

Simple Routing Scenario

Figure 9-14 shows a simple network configuration with a server running Routing And Remote Access and connecting two LAN segments (Network A and Network B). In this configuration, routing protocols are not necessary, and static routes need not be added manually because the router is directly connected to all the networks to which it needs to route packets.

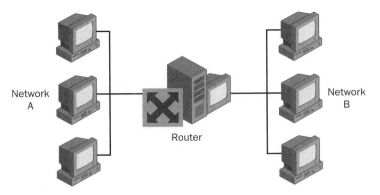

Figure 9-14   Local routing without routing protocols or static routes

Multiple-Router Scenario

Figure 9-15 shows a more complex router configuration. In this scenario, three networks (Networks A, B, and C) are connected by two routers (Routers 1 and 2). Router 1 is directly connected to Networks A and B, and Router 2 is directly connected to Networks B and C. Router 1 must notify Router 2 that Network A can be reached through Router 1, and Router 2 must notify Router 1 that Network C can be reached through Router 2. This information is automatically communicated by means of routing protocols such as RIP or OSPF. When a user on Network A wants to communicate with a user on Network C, the user's computer on Network A forwards the packet to Router 1. Router 1 then forwards the packet to Router 2. Router 2 then forwards the packet to the user's computer on Network C.

Without the use of routing protocols, a network administrator has to enter static routes into the routing tables of Router 1 and Router 2. Although static routes work in simple networks, they are difficult to implement on a large scale. In addition, static routes do not automatically adapt to changes in the internetwork topology.

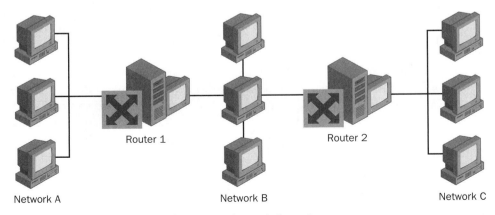

Figure 9-15   Routing with routing protocols or static routes

Understanding Static Routes

Static routed networks do not use routing protocols such as RIP or OSPF to communicate routing information between routers. A static routed IP environment is best suited to small, single-path, static IP internetworks. For best results, the internetwork should be limited to fewer than 10 subnets. In addition, these subnets should be arranged consecutively (in a straight line) so that traffic pathways are predictable. A final guideline for static routing is that the topology for internetworks relying on static routing should not change over time. Figure 9-16 illustrates such a network.

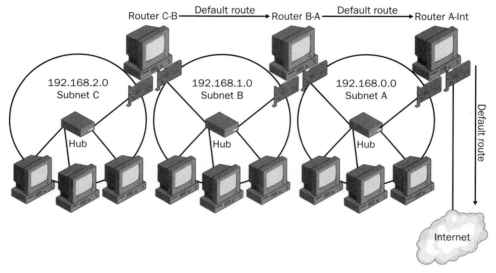

Figure 9-16 Candidate network for static routing

In the example provided in Figure 9-16, Router C-B can see all computers on Subnets C and B. When Router C-B receives a packet destined for an address outside Subnet C or B, it forwards this packet along the default route to Router B-A. Because all computers outside Subnets B or C lie in the direction of the default route, static routes need not be added to the routing table on Router C-B.

However, for Router B-A, which sees all computers on Subnets B and A, the computers on Subnet C do not lie in the direction of the default route. If Router B-A receives a packet destined for Subnet C, it incorrectly forwards the packet to Router A-Int unless instructed to do otherwise. Adding a static route to the routing table on Router B-A, as shown in Figure 9-17, allows Router B-A to properly direct traffic destined for Subnet C toward Router C-B.

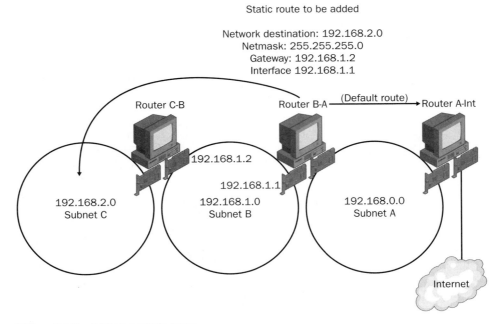

Static route to be added

Network destination: 192.168.2.0
Netmask: 255.255.255.0
Gateway: 192.168.1.2
Interface 192.168.1.1

Router C-B

Router B-A —— (Default route) → Router A-Int

192.168.1.2

192.168.1.1

192.168.2.0
Subnet C

192.168.1.0
Subnet B

192.168.0.0
Subnet A

Internet

Figure 9-17   Adding a static route

Router A-Int, meanwhile, can see the computers only on Subnet A and the computer connected upstream at the Internet service provider (ISP). Because the default route directs traffic toward the Internet, traffic destined for Subnets C and B is improperly forwarded to the Internet without static routes instructing Router A-Int to handle this traffic differently. Figure 9-18 illustrates these routes. Note that the static route for Subnet C can point toward only the neighboring router, Router B-A, which itself does not see Subnet C. This static route, then, relies on the static route configured on router B-A that in turn directs appropriate traffic to Router C-B.

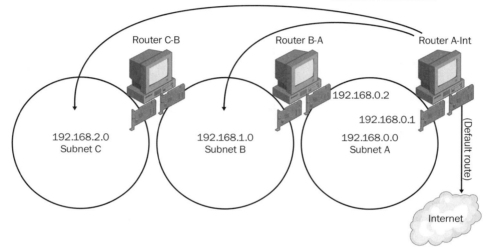

Static routes to be added

Network destination: 192.168.2.0
Netmask: 255.255.255.0
Gateway: 192.168.0.2
Interface: 192.168.0.1

Network destination: 192.168.1.0
Netmask: 255.255.255.0
Gateway: 192.168.0.2
Interface: 192.168.0.1

Figure 9-18 Adding more static routes

Adding Static Routes

You can add static routes through either the Routing And Remote Access console or a command prompt.

To add a static route in Routing And Remote Access, complete the following steps:

1. Open Routing And Remote Access.
2. In the console tree, right-click Static Routes.
3. Click New Static Route.
4. In the Static Route dialog box, specify the Interface, Destination, Network Mask, Gateway, and Metric settings.

Note Static routes added by means of the Routing And Remote Access console are *persistent*: they remain active even after the routing computer is restarted.

To add a static IP route at a command prompt, open a command prompt and type the following:

route add *destination* **mask** *netmask gateway* **metric** *costmetric* **if** *interface*

Specifying the metric is optional, and the interface is chosen automatically if you do not include it. For example, to add a static route to the 10.0.0.0 network that uses a netmask of 255.0.0.0 and a gateway of 192.168.0.1, you need only type the following at a command prompt: **route add 10.0.0.0 mask 255.0.0.0 192.168.0.1**.

Also note the following when using the Route command:

■   Static routes added with the Route command are not persistent unless the –p switch is used.

As in the following example, use the –p switch with the Route command if you want the static route to remain in effect even after the routing computer is rebooted:

route add –p 10.0.0.0 mask 255.0.0.0 192.168.0.1

■   Use the Route Delete command to delete a route that you have added. After route delete, you need only type as much as is necessary to distinguish the route:

route delete 10.0.0.0

■   Static routes that you add by means of the Route command are not listed as static routes in the Routing And Remote Access console. However, you can view them along with other routes when you use the Routing And Remote Access console to view the routing table.

■   Interfaces in the Route command are designated by a hexadecimal number, not by the interface address. You can view the number assigned to each interface in the Interface List section of the Route Print output:

```
C:\>route print

IPv4 Route Table
===========================================================================
Interface List
0x1 .......................... MS TCP Loopback interface
0x2 ...00 50 ba 40 5c 73 ...... D-Link DFE-530TX+ PCI Adapter
0x10003 ...00 53 45 00 00 00 ...... WAN (PPP/SLIP) Interface
0x20004 ...00 53 45 00 00 00 ...... WAN (PPP/SLIP) Interface
```

To refer to one of these interfaces, you can either type the hexadecimal number as shown (including the "0x" prefix), or convert the hexadecimal number to a decimal value. Note also that hexadecimal values 0x1–0x9 are equivalent to 1–9 in decimal.

As a result, the following two routes are equivalent:

```
route add 192.168.2.0 mask 255.255.255.0 192.168.1.2 IF 0x2
route add 192.168.2.0 mask 255.255.255.0 192.168.1.2 IF 2
```

The following two routes are also equivalent, given that the hexadecimal value 0x10003 is equivalent to the decimal value of 65539:

```
route add 207.46.2.0 mask 255.255.255.0 207.46.1.2 IF 0x10003
route add 207.46.2.0 mask 255.255.255.0 207.46.1.2 IF 65539
```

Advantages of Static Routing

Static routing is advantageous in small networks for which configuring a few static routes is simpler than configuring a dynamic routing protocol.

Besides this ease of deployment, another advantage of static routing is that static routes are less resource-intensive than are dynamic routing protocols. They do not require communication among routers, and this feature makes static routes preferable to dynamic routing protocols for low-bandwidth WAN links.

A final advantage of static routing is that, unlike dynamic routing protocols, static routes provide support for *unnumbered connections*: connections in which one or both of the connecting logical interfaces (usually in a demand-dial connection) fail to obtain an IP address. Typically, demand-dial routing operates through numbered connections, which means that both the calling and answering router obtain an IP address from each other and assign these IP addresses to the logical endpoints of the point-to-point connection.

When this process fails in Windows Server 2003, the connecting logical interfaces are normally assigned Automatic Private IP Addressing (APIPA) addresses. Unnumbered connections thus occur only when either router does not support APIPA.

Disadvantages of Static Routing

The main disadvantage of static routing is that it is a feasible means of maintaining only small routed networks. As a network grows, the administrative cost of maintaining static routes quickly outweighs the cost of implementing and maintaining a dynamic routing protocol.

A second disadvantage of static routing is the lack of fault tolerance. If a route is improperly configured, connectivity is disrupted until the problem is diagnosed and fixed.

> **Off the Record**   On the exam, you might see static routes being used in a corporate LAN scenario, but in the real world they are used only when no other option is feasible. Maintaining static routes for real networks would just be too tedious and time-consuming. Not only would you have to spend time creating the static routes, but you would also need to perform all updates and troubleshooting manually.
>
> In comparison, the RIP dynamic routing protocol, which essentially performs the same function as static routes, is easy to install and requires almost no maintenance. For larger networks requiring the OSPF dynamic routing protocol, static routing is not even an option.
>
> Basically, the only time you should use static routes instead of RIP or OSPF is when a connection to a remote router is intermittent. In these cases, dynamic routing protocols cannot be used because they require routers to communicate every few seconds (30 for RIP, 10 for OSPF).

Static Routing Design Considerations

To prevent problems, you should consider the following design issues before you implement static routing.

Peripheral Router Configuration

Peripheral routers by definition have only one neighboring router. Found at the periphery of networks, they connect the outer subnets of an organization to its network backbone. To simplify configuration, you should normally configure a peripheral router with a default route that points to its neighboring router. In Figure 9-16 shown earlier, Router C-B is a peripheral router. Its default route should therefore point to the neighboring router, Router B-A.

Default Routes and Routing Loops

You should avoid configuring two neighboring routers with default routes that point to each other. A default route passes all traffic that is not on a directly connected network to a specified router. Two routers that have default routes pointing to each other will produce a routing loop for traffic with an unreachable destination.

Practice: Enabling and Configuring Routing And Remote Access

In this practice, you use the Routing And Remote Access Server Setup Wizard on Computer1 to configure the Routing And Remote Access service for LAN routing.

Exercise: Running the Routing And Remote Access Server Setup Wizard

In this exercise, you configure and enable the Routing And Remote Access service on Computer1.

1. From Computer1, log on to Domain1 as Administrator.

2. Open the Routing And Remote Access console by clicking Start, selecting Administrative Tools, and then clicking Routing And Remote Access.

   The Routing And Remote Access console opens.

3. In the console tree, right-click the COMPUTER1 (Local) node, and then click Configure And Enable Routing And Remote Access.

   The Routing And Remote Access Server Setup Wizard launches.

4. Click Next.

   The Configuration page appears.

5. Read all of the options available on this page.

6. Select the Custom Configuration option, and then click Next.

7. The Custom Configuration page appears.

8. Read all of the options available on this page, and then answer the following question:

   How many basic routing functions can be configured through this wizard?

   _____

9. Select the LAN Routing check box, and then click Next.

   The Completing The Routing And Remote Access Server Setup Wizard page appears.

10. Click Finish.

    A message box indicates that Routing And Remote Access has been installed and asks you whether you want to start the service.

11. Click Yes.

    The Routing And Remote Access service starts.

12. Log off Computer1.

Lesson Review

The following questions are intended to reinforce key information presented in this lesson. If you are unable to answer a question, review the lesson materials and try the question again. You can find answers to the questions in the "Questions and Answers" section at the end of this chapter.

1. Your department connects to the Internet through a Digital Subscriber Line (DSL) that it shares with the rest of the organization. However, you have just obtained a faster T1 connection to the Internet that you want to reserve for the IT department's use. A DHCP server provides all of your users with an IP configuration, but IT staff computers are interspersed throughout the same subnets as those of other staff members. How can you allow only IT staff members to use the new T1 line to connect to the Internet? You want to configure this setup only once and make the changes permanent.

2. You are unable to connect to any computers outside your local subnet. You run the Route Print command and note the line below. What is most likely the cause of the problem?

```
Network Destination        Netmask          Gateway         Interface
        0.0.0.0           0.0.0.0        192.168.1.1      192.168.1.1
```

3. You attempt to add a persistent static route through the Route command, but it does not appear in the Route Print output of the local machine. You have assigned the route a metric of 1. Assuming that you have entered the command successfully, what could be the cause of the problem?

4. Which protocols are used to allow Multilink connections to add and drop dial-up lines as needed?

Lesson Summary

- The Routing And Remote Access service in Windows Server 2003 is a multiprotocol software router that can be readily integrated with Windows features such as security accounts and group policies. The Routing And Remote Access console is the principal tool used for configuring and managing this service.

- Routers read the destination addresses of received packets and then route those packets according to directions provided by routing tables. In Windows Server 2003, you can view the IP routing table through the Routing And Remote Access console or through the Route Print command.

- You can assign preference levels to route sources by using the General Properties dialog box, which you can access through the General subnode within the IP Routing node. These preferences determine which routes take precedence when two or more sources provide overlapping routes.

- Without dynamic routing protocols, a router requires static routes to connect to non-neighboring subnets when those subnets do not lie in the same direction as the default route.

- You can add static routes by using the Routing And Remote Access console or by using the Route Add command. Adding the –p switch to the Route Add command makes the static route persistent, which means it remains even after the router is rebooted.

Lesson 2: Configuring Demand-Dial Routing

You can use demand-dial interfaces to build connections between remote routers in a configuration known as *demand-dial routing*. Demand-dial routing is used most often when the expense of providing a dedicated link between two remote routers is prohibitive, or when the connection is not used frequently enough to justify the expense of a dedicated line.

After this lesson, you will be able to

- Configure demand-dial routing
- Manage demand-dial interfaces
- Troubleshoot demand-dial routing

Estimated lesson time: 60 minutes

Configuring Demand-Dial Interfaces

The first step in deploying demand-dial routing is to configure a demand-dial interface on each computer you want to function as a demand-dial router. You can configure these interfaces by using the Demand-Dial Interface Wizard. You can run this wizard as an extension of the Routing And Remote Access Server Setup Wizard, or as an option after the Routing And Remote Access service has already been configured and enabled.

If you have previously configured and enabled the Routing And Remote Access service without demand-dial functionality, you must enable this functionality before you create any demand-dial interfaces. You achieve this task by selecting the LAN And Demand-Dial Routing option on the General tab of the Routing And Remote Access service properties dialog box, as shown in Figure 9-19.

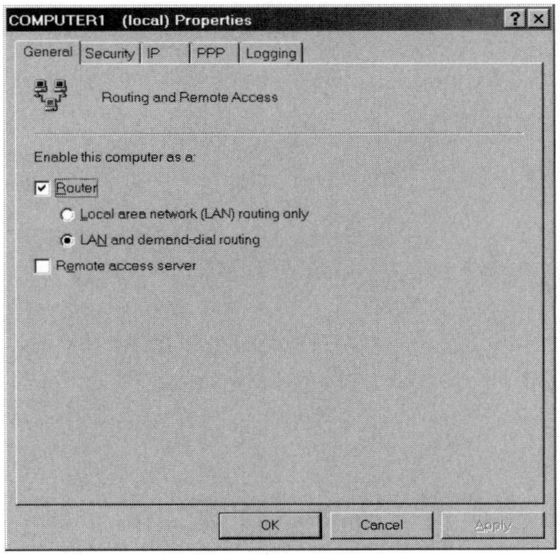

Figure 9-19   Enabling demand-dial routing

Once you have enabled demand-dial routing, you can launch the Demand-Dial Interface Wizard by right-clicking the Network Interfaces node in the Routing And Remote Access console tree and then clicking New Demand-Dial Interface. The wizard allows you to configure the basic features of the interface.

After the basic demand-dial interface has been created, you can configure and manage its properties in a more detailed way in the Routing And Remote Access console. Demand-dial interface management in the Routing And Remote Access console can be divided into four areas: shortcut menu commands, network interface properties, port and device properties, and IP routing interface features.

Shortcut Menu Commands

The shortcut menu commands for each demand-dial interface are those that appear when you right-click the interface in the details pane of the Routing And Remote Access console. The interfaces themselves appear in the details pane when you select the Network Interfaces node in the Routing And Remote Access console tree. (See Figure 9-20.) Note that in addition to the management features listed below, this shortcut menu allows you to connect/disconnect and enable/disable the demand-dial interface.

Figure 9-20   Shortcut menu management features

The following list describes the four commands that are unique to the demand-dial interface shortcut menu:

- **Set Credentials**   Allows you to configure the user name and password that the interface uses when it connects to a remote router.

- **Unreachability Reason**   Explains why the last connection attempt was unsuccessful.

- **Set IP Demand-Dial Filters**   Allows you to limit the type of traffic that initiates a demand-dial connection through this interface. Connections can be limited (filtered) by source address, destination address, and protocol.

- **Dial-Out Hours**   Allows you to restrict the number of hours that the demand-dial interface can be used.

Network Interface Properties

When the Network Interfaces node is selected, you can configure these settings in the properties dialog box of the demand-dial interface. The dialog box consists of the four tabs described in the following sections.

General Tab   This tab allows you to adjust modem features and to set the primary phone number associated with the demand-dial interface. You can use the Alternates button when editing the properties of a dial-up connection to configure a list of alternate phone numbers for the interface to call in case one is unreachable. You can also choose to adjust the alternate list automatically so that numbers successfully reached are given higher priority.

Options Tab   This tab is shown in Figure 9-21.

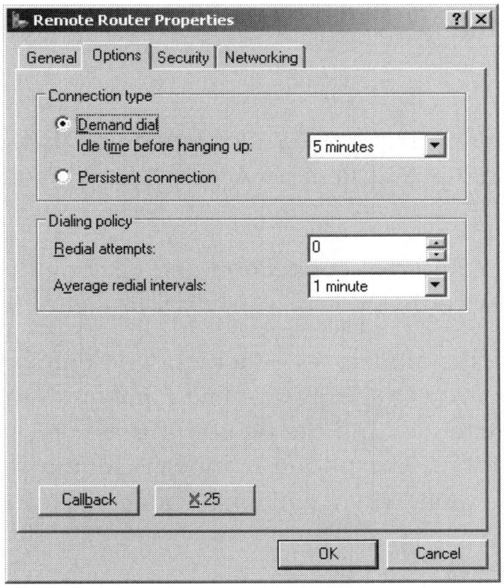

Figure 9-21   Demand-dial interface options

In the Connection Type area, this tab allows you to configure the interface as Demand Dial or Persistent Connection. Demand-dial interfaces dial on demand, and persistent interfaces redial whenever the connection is lost. Also note that when you configure the interface as Demand Dial, this tab allows you to specify the amount of time the connection should stay idle before it disconnects.

The Dialing Policy area allows you to configure the number of redial attempts and the time interval between redials.

The Callback button allows you to configure the callback feature. This feature requires the interface, when it receives a call, to disconnect the call and immediately call back to a predetermined number, thus ensuring that only authorized parties establish a connection.

The X.25 button allows you to configure the interface for use over X.25 networks.

Security Tab   This tab allows you to require password and/or data encryption for the demand-dial connection. Advanced settings allow you to specify a set of allowable authentication protocols over which the interface can submit and receive user credentials. By default, Challenge Handshake Authentication Protocol (CHAP), Microsoft CHAP (MS-CHAP), and Microsoft CHAP version 2 (MS-CHAP v2) are selected as the authentication protocols. (Chapter 10, "Configuring and Managing Remote Access," discusses authentication protocols and encryption in more detail.) Finally, this tab also allows you to specify a logon script for use with the demand-dial interface.

Networking Tab   This tab allows you to bind and configure typical elements of a network connection, such as Internet Protocol, File And Printer Sharing For Microsoft Networks, and Client For Microsoft Networks.

Port and Device Properties

The Ports Properties dialog box is shown in Figure 9-22. You open this dialog box by right-clicking the Ports node in the Routing And Remote Access console and clicking Properties.

By selecting the modem used in the demand-dial connection and clicking the Configure button, you open the Configure Device dialog box, as shown in Figure 9-23.

This dialog box enables you to configure the modem for either inbound only or inbound and outbound connections. It also allows you to specify a phone number for the device. This number can be read by the calling interface and can be used for remote access policies that use the Called-Station-Id attribute. The phone number is required for BAP-enabled connections and is dialed by the client when additional connections are created.

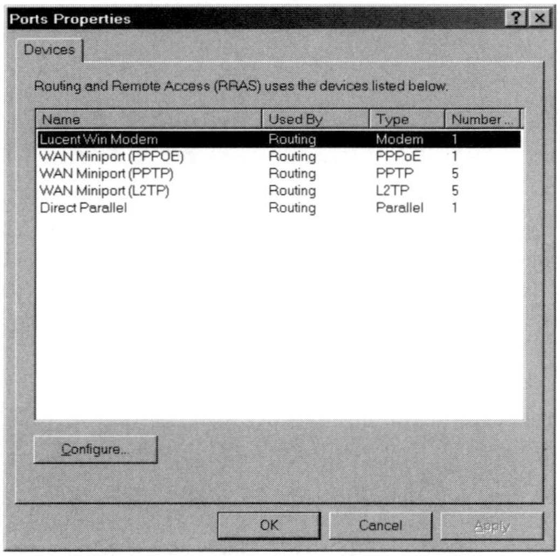

Figure 9-22   Ports properties

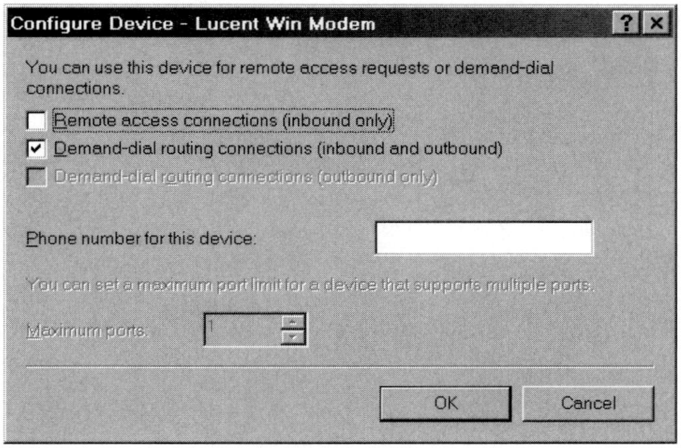

Configure Device - Lucent Win Modem   ? X

You can use this device for remote access requests or demand-dial connections.

☐ Remote access connections (inbound only)

☑ Demand-dial routing connections (inbound and outbound)

☐ Demand-dial routing connections (outbound only)

Phone number for this device: _____

You can set a maximum port limit for a device that supports multiple ports.

Maximum ports: ____

OK   Cancel

Figure 9-23   Demand-dial device configuration

A final management feature associated with the Ports node is the Port Status dialog box. When you select the Ports node in the Routing And Remote Access console, the list of connection ports is listed in the details pane. This list includes the available modem device or devices. You can view details about the status of a modem by double-clicking the modem device and opening the Port Status dialog box. This dialog box presents statistics about a modem (when active) and allows you to reset the modem connection.

IP Routing Interface Features

These management features are accessible through the IP Routing node of the Routing And Remote Access console. When you select the General node within the IP Routing node, the interfaces configured for your server appear in the details pane. Right-clicking a demand-dial interface reveals various demand-dial management and troubleshooting commands, as shown in Figure 9-24.

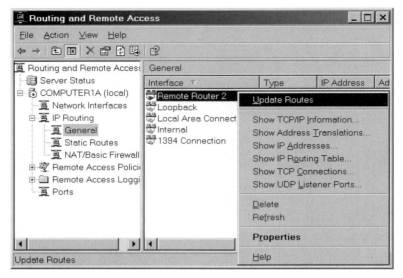

Figure 9-24   IP Routing demand-dial interface commands

Update Routes   This command appears on the shortcut menu of the IP Routing demand-dial interface. When the RIP routing protocol is installed and this feature is enabled, selecting the Update Routes command automatically updates the static routes across the demand-dial interface. Static routes updated with this command require no further configuration and are thus known as *autostatic* routes. Because of the intermittent nature of dial-on-demand connections, autostatic routes for these connections are used in place of normal router-to-router communication through RIP. Note also that you can update autostatic routes automatically by using a script scheduled to run periodically by the Task Scheduler service.

TCP/IP Statistics   The next group of features available on this shortcut menu allows you to view current TCP/IP information such as that available with the command-line commands Ipconfig, Route Print, and Netstat. You can use this information, which includes details about active TCP and User Datagram Protocol (UDP) connections, bytes sent, and assigned IP addresses, to verify and troubleshoot network connectivity.

IP Routing Interface Properties   Finally, the demand-dial interface shortcut menu allows you to open the demand-dial interface properties dialog box, shown in Figure 9-25. This dialog box is distinct from the demand-dial interface properties dialog box available when the Network Interfaces node is selected. This dialog box contains three tabs: General, Multicast Boundaries, and Multicast Heartbeat. Because multicasting is not covered on the 70-291 exam, only the General tab configuration options are discussed here.

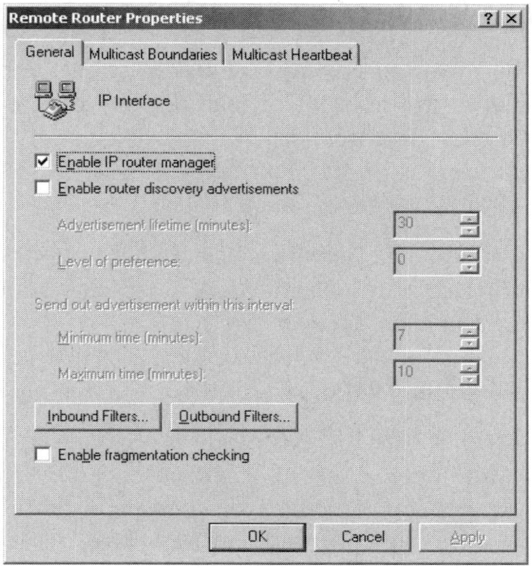

Figure 9-25 IP Routing interface properties

On the General tab, the Enable IP Router Manager check box is enabled by default. IP Router Manager is a component of the Routing And Remote Access service that is responsible for many routing features, including packet filtering, network address translation, and dynamic routing. You can clear the check box to temporarily disable IP routing and change the Administrative Status of the interface to Down.

The Enable Router Discovery Advertisements check box is cleared by default. This check box refers to a feature called *router discovery* that requires configuration at the host in addition to the router. Through this feature, network hosts send out router *solicitations* to discover routers. Routers then respond to these solicitations through periodic *advertisements*. Through these advertisements, hosts can then determine when these routers are down. Router discovery solicitations and advertisements work through Internet Control Message Protocol (ICMP) messages.

The Input Filters button and Output Filters button refer to a feature called *packet filtering*. Through this feature, which is described in more detail in Lesson 5 of this chapter, you can configure Routing And Remote Access to allow or deny traffic on the basis of source, destination, or protocol type (TCP or UDP port).

The Enable Fragmentation Checking check box, cleared by default, refers to a feature of packet filtering. If you have blocked packets from a given source address, this option ensures that fragments of packets originating from the same address are blocked as well.

Deploying a Demand-Dial Router-to-Router Configuration

Although the concept of demand-dial routing is simple, implementing demand-dial routing is relatively complex because of the number of features requiring configuration. The following sections describe these features.

Connection Endpoint Addressing

The connection must be made over public data networks, such as the public switched telephone network (PSTN). The endpoint of the connection must be identified by a phone number or other endpoint identifier.

Authenticating and Authorizing the Calling Router

Demand-dial routing in Windows Server 2003 networks requires a calling router and a called router, each running Routing And Remote Access. Each router can be configured to act as both a calling and called router, but during every connection attempt, the router acting as the calling router must be authenticated and authorized.

Authentication is based on the calling router's set of credentials that are passed during the connection establishment process. The credentials that are passed must correspond to a user account. Authorization is granted based on the dial-in permission of the user account and remote access policies. You can configure authentication and authorization by using the Routing And Remote Access Wizard.

Differentiating Between Remote Access Clients and Routers

Both routing and remote access services coexist on the same server running Routing And Remote Access. Both remote access clients and routers can call the same phone number. The server running Routing And Remote Access that answers the call must be able to distinguish a remote access client from a router that is calling to create a demand-dial connection.

To differentiate a remote access client from a demand-dial router, the user name in the authentication credentials sent by the calling router must exactly match the name of a demand-dial interface on the answering router. Otherwise, the incoming connection is assumed to be a remote access connection.

Configuring Both Ends of the Connection

You must configure both ends of the connection even if only one end of the connection is initiating a demand-dial connection. Configuring only one side of the connection allows packets to be routed in only one direction; normal communication, however, requires that information travel in both directions.

Configuring Static Routes

Although you can use dynamic routing protocols with persistent dial-up connections, you cannot use them effectively over temporary dial-on-demand connections. For these connections, routes to network IDs that require the use of the demand-dial interface must be added to the routing table as static routes.

Also note that you must choose one static route to initiate the dial-on-demand connection. To achieve this task, verify that the Use This Route To Initiate Demand-Dial Connections check box is selected in the properties of the appropriate static route, as shown in Figure 9-26.

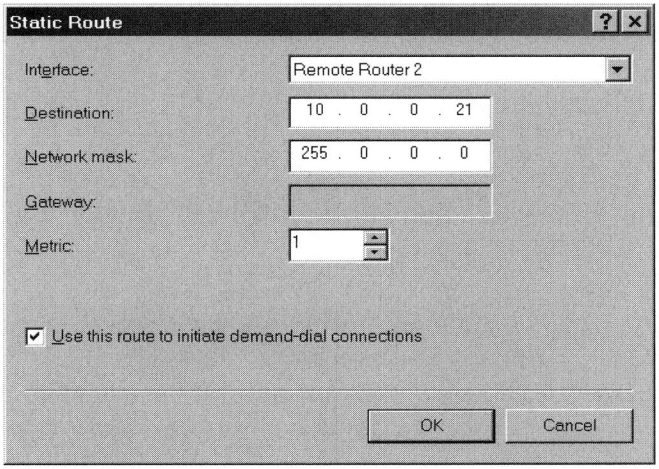

Figure 9-26   Linking a static route to a dial-on-demand connection

Troubleshooting Demand-Dial Routing

The following list provides a conceptual summary of the configuration requirements for a demand-dial routing deployment and of the associated potential points of failure. Review this summary and refer back to it as needed to help you troubleshoot routing through demand-dial interfaces.

1. A number of basic features must be enabled on both ends of the connection for demand-dial routing to function. First, verify that Routing And Remote Access is configured and enabled on both servers. Second, make sure both servers have been enabled for LAN and demand-dial routing in the Routing And Remote Access console. Next, make sure IP routing is enabled. Finally, verify that the necessary demand-dial interfaces are not in a disabled state.

2. Demand-dial routing requires that static routes be configured for both ends of the demand-dial connection. Verify that these routes are correctly configured. For dial-on-demand routing, verify that the Use This Route To Initiate Demand-Dial Connections check box is selected.

3. For the connection to function as a link in a routed network, the demand-dial connection must not be interpreted as a remote access connection. To ensure that the connection is interpreted correctly, verify that the user name of the calling router's credentials match the name of a demand-dial interface configured on the answering router. Verify that the calling router's credentials consisting of user name, password, and domain name are correct and can be validated by the answering router.

4. Answering routers must be authorized to function in Active Directory domains. For an answering router that is a member of an Active Directory domain, verify that the computer account of the answering router computer is a member of the RAS And IAS Servers security group.

5. Routed connections are both authenticated and encrypted. (This topic is discussed in more detail in Chapter 10.) To ensure that a demand-dial routed connection can be established, verify that in conjunction with a remote access policy, the calling router and the answering router are enabled to use at least one common authentication method and one common encryption method.

6. Restrictions can be configured for each demand-dial interface in the form of dial-out hours and demand-dial filters. For each interface, verify that the dial-out hours or demand-dial filters for the demand-dial interface on the calling router are not preventing the connection attempt.

7. Demand-dial interfaces communicate through ports, which can be disabled in the Routing And Remote Access console for inbound or outbound traffic. If a connection fails to be established at either end of a demand-dial routing connection, verify that the dial-up ports being used are configured to allow demand-dial routing (inbound and outbound).

8. Packet filters can block access beyond a connection endpoint. If you cannot connect to resources beyond the answering router, verify that no packet filters on either demand-dial interface are preventing the flow of wanted traffic. Each demand-dial interface can be configured with IP input and output filters that allow you to control the exact nature of TCP/IP traffic allowed into and out of the demand-dial interface. (Packet filtering is discussed in more detail in Lesson 5 of this chapter.)

Practice: Configuring Demand-Dial Routing

Although true routing cannot be demonstrated with only two computers, Exercise 1, "Installing Internet Information Services on Computer2," shows you how to configure two routers to establish a TCP/IP connection through the PSTN. This process requires you to create the necessary demand-dial interfaces, the appropriate user accounts to be authenticated, and the static routes necessary for the connection—the process of configuring demand-dial routing. Finally, you verify the connection by opening a Web page hosted on the remote computer.

Exercise 1: Installing Internet Information Services on Computer2

In this exercise, you install Internet Information Services (IIS) on Computer2 and create a default Web page for the Web site. Before you perform this exercise, make sure you have inserted the Windows Server 2003 Setup CD-ROM into Computer2.

1. From Computer2, log on to Domain1 as Administrator.
2. In Control Panel, open Add Or Remove Programs.

   The Add Or Remove Programs window opens.
3. Click the Add/Remove Windows Components button.

   The Windows Components page of the Windows Components Wizard appears.
4. In the Components area, select the Application Server component without clicking its check box.
5. Click the Details button.

   The Application Server window appears.
6. In the Subcomponents Of Application Server area, click the Internet Information Services (IIS) check box.

   The Internet Information Services (IIS) check box is selected along with the Enable Network COM+ Access check box.
7. Click OK.
8. On the Windows Components page, click Next.

   The Configuring Components page appears while the new Windows component is installed. After installation is complete, the Completing The Windows Components Wizard page appears.
9. Click Finish.
10. Copy the following contents into a Notepad file:

    ```
    <html>
    <head>
    <title>Welcome</title>
    </head>
    <h1>Sample Web Page</h1>
    <body>
    Welcome to the Web page on Computer 2
    </body>
    </html>
    ```
11. Save the file as Default.htm in the C:\Inetpub\Wwwroot directory.

Exercise 2: Configuring Routing And Remote Access for Demand-Dial Routing

In this exercise, you use the Routing And Remote Access Server Setup Wizard and the Demand-Dial Interface Wizard to configure Computer1 for demand-dial routing. This exercise requires that both Computer1 and Computer2 be connected by modem to two separate phone lines.

1. Log on to Computer1 as Administrator.

2. Open the Routing And Remote Access console.

3. In the console tree, right-click the COMPUTER1 node, and then click Disable Routing And Remote Access. When a message box appears asking you to confirm, click Yes.

   The Routing And Remote Access Server Setup Wizard can be run only when the service is in a disabled state.

4. After the service has stopped, right-click the COMPUTER1 node, and then click Configure And Enable Routing And Remote Access.

   The Routing And Remote Access Server Setup Wizard opens.

5. Click Next. The Configuration page appears.

6. Select the Secure Connection Between Two Private Networks option, and then click Next.

   The Demand-Dial Connections page appears.

7. Click Next to accept the default selection of Yes.

   The IP Address Assignment page appears.

8. Click the From A Specified Range Of Addresses option, and then click Next.

   The Address Range Assignment page appears.

9. Click the New button.

   The New Address Range dialog box opens.

10. Type **10.0.0.11** into the Start IP Address text box and **10.0.0.20** into the End IP Address text box.

11. Click OK.

12. On the Address Range Assignment page, click Next.

    The Completing The Routing And Remote Access Server Setup Wizard page appears.

13. Click Finish.

    A message indicates that the Routing And Remote Access service is starting. Then the Demand-Dial Interface Wizard appears.

14. Click Next.

    The Interface Name page appears.

15. Leave the default name of Remote Router, and click Next.

    The Connection Type page appears.

16. Leave the default selection of Connect Using A Modem, ISDN Adapter, Or Other Physical Device, and click Next.

    The Select A Device page appears.

17. Ensure that your modem is selected, and then click Next.

    The Phone Number page appears.

18. In the Phone Number Or Address text box, type the phone number of the line that is connected to the other computer, and then click Next.

    The Protocols And Security page appears.

19. Select the Add A User Account So A Remote Router Can Dial In check box. Leave the Route IP Packets On This Interface check box selected.

20. Click Next. The Static Routes For Remote Networks page appears.

21. Click the Add button.

    The Static Route dialog box opens.

22. Type **10.0.0.0** in the Destination text box and **255.0.0.0** in the Network Mask check box. Leave the Metric setting as 1.

23. Click OK.

24. On the Static Routes For Remote Networks page, click Next.

    The Dial In Credentials page appears.

25. Read the text on this page. In the Password text box and the Confirm Password text box, type the same password you have assigned to the Domain1\Administrator account, and then click Next.

    The Dial Out Credentials page appears.

26. In the User Name text box, type **remote router**.

27. Leave the Domain text box blank.

28. In the Password text box and the Confirm Password text box, type the password you have assigned to the Domain1\Administrator account.

29. Click Next.

    The Completing The Demand-Dial Interface Wizard page appears.

30. Click Finish.

31. Perform steps 4–30 on Computer2 but specify an address range assignment of 10.0.0.21–10.0.0.30 in step 10.

Exercise 3: Testing the Configuration

In this exercise, you verify that the connection is able to pass traffic from one router to another.

1. If you have not already done so, from Computer1 log on to Domain1 as Administrator.

2. In the Routing And Remote Access console tree, select the Network Interfaces node.

3. In the details pane, right-click the Remote Router interface and then click Connect.

   The Interface Connection message box appears while the router is connecting. Computer2 answers the phone after two rings.

4. When the Connection State appears as Connected in the Routing And Remote Access console, switch to Computer2 and log on as Administrator.

5. On Computer2, at a command prompt type **ipconfig /all**, and then press Enter.

6. In the following space, write the address assigned to the interface named PPP Adapter RAS Server (Dial In) Interface:

   _____

7. Switch to Computer1.

8. Open an Internet Explorer window.

9. In Internet Explorer, type **http://*ip_address*** into the Address box, where *ip_address* is the address you wrote down in step 6 earlier. For example, if the address you wrote down was 10.0.0.21, type **http://10.0.0.21** in the Address box.

10. Press Enter.

    Close any warnings that Internet Explorer displays. The Welcome To The Web Page On Computer 2 message displays. The demand-dial interface from Computer1 has successfully connected to the Web site on Computer2 through the demand-dial interface on Computer2.

11. In the Routing And Remote Access console of Computer1, right-click the local server node, and then click Disable Routing And Remote Access.

    A message box asks you to confirm the decision.

12. Click Yes.

13. On Computer2, repeat steps 11–12.

14. Reboot both computers.

Lesson Review

The following questions are intended to reinforce key information presented in this lesson. If you are unable to answer a question, review the lesson materials and try the question again. You can find answers to the questions in the "Questions and Answers" section at the end of this chapter.

1. Using Routing And Remote Access, you have configured demand-dial routing to join a branch office to your corporate LAN. However, even though you are using the RIP protocol, routes are not being updated across the WAN link. Why is this happening, and how can you allow the routes to be updated?

   _____

   _____

   _____

2. You are connected to a branch office over a demand-dial connection. How can you best prevent your users from connecting to the branch office during lunch hours?

   _____

3. You have a branch office connected to your main office through a dial-on-demand Integrated Services Digital Network (ISDN) connection. You want to stop Hypertext Transfer Protocol (HTTP) requests from initiating the connection. How can you achieve this goal?

   _____

   _____

4. Your main office is connected to a branch office through demand-dial routing. Either router is configured to call or answer the call of the other router as needed. However, the Finance Department has asked you to ensure that telephone connection charges between demand-dial routers be predominantly incurred by the main office. How can you achieve this goal?

   _____

   _____

Lesson Summary

- Demand-dial routing is the process of sending traffic from one router to another over a dial-up connection. This dial-up connection can be enabled as needed in a dial-on-demand scenario or remain connected as a persistent link.

- During every demand-dial connection attempt, the router acting as the calling router must be authenticated and authorized by the called router. Authentication is based on the calling router's set of credentials that are passed during the connection establishment process. The credentials that are passed must correspond to a user account. Authorization is granted based on the dial-in permission of the user account and remote access policies.

- To differentiate a remote access client from a demand-dial router, the user name in the authentication credentials sent by the calling router must exactly match the name of a demand-dial interface on the answering router. Otherwise, the incoming connection is assumed to be a remote access connection.

- To implement demand-dial routing, you must designate a static route to initiate the dial-on-demand connection.

- You can configure demand-dial routing for various features through Routing And Remote Access. These features include callback, demand-dial filters, packet filters, and dial-out hours.

Lesson 3: Configuring NAT

With the Network Address Translation (NAT) component of the Windows Server 2003 Routing And Remote Access service, IP packets exchanged between the local network and Internet are both routed and re-addressed. This re-addressing allows multiple client computers to connect to the Internet by sharing a single public address or pool of public addresses. With NAT, you can assign all your internal clients private addresses; only the external interface of the NAT computer requires a public address.

After this lesson, you will be able to

- Configure NAT on a Windows Server 2003 network
- Describe the difference between Internet Connection Sharing (ICS) and NAT
- Troubleshoot NAT-related problems

Estimated lesson time: 45 minutes

Understanding NAT

NAT is a service built into a router that modifies the header information in IP datagrams before sending them on to their destinations. This functionality allows host computers to connect to the Internet by sharing one or more publicly registered IP addresses on the computer running the NAT service. The computer on which NAT is configured can act as a network address translator, a simplified DHCP server, a DNS proxy, and a Windows Internet Name Service (WINS) proxy. Figure 9-27 illustrates this service.

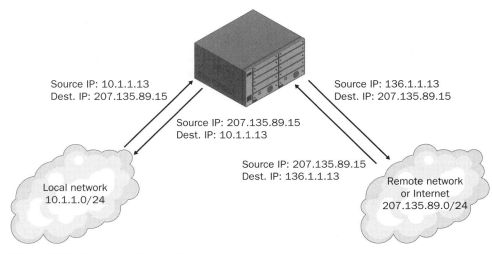

Figure 9-27 Network Address Translation

You can configure NAT through a demand-dial interface or through a persistent connection. A demand-dial interface connects only when a client requests the connection. A persistent connection can be either a dedicated line such as a DSL or T1 line or a dial-up interface that automatically redials when the line is dropped.

Difference Between NAT and ICS

Like NAT, the ICS feature built into Windows provides Internet connectivity to hosts through a single interface—a dial-up or permanent connection—on a Windows computer. Like NAT, ICS also allows internal clients to preserve private IP addresses while these clients connect to public external addresses. Finally, NAT includes a component called Basic Firewall that blocks all but response traffic from entering the internal network. This component corresponds to the Internet Connection Firewall service, which provides the identical function for ICS.

The main difference between NAT and ICS is configurability. ICS is preconfigured and automatically sets the internal address of the computer hosting the shared connection to 192.168.0.1. All internal clients exist on one physical subnet and are assigned addresses within the 192.168.0.0/24 range. These internal clients point to the ICS computer for DNS resolution. The external, shared interface is configured with a single public address.

With NAT, you can choose any private IP address as the internal address of the NAT computer, and you have the option of disabling the DHCP server and DNS proxy capabilities. For example, if you already have the DHCP or DNS service configured for your network, you can disable these functions when you configure NAT. If you do configure NAT to provide DHCP service for internal clients, you can choose any address scope you want NAT clients to use. In addition, unlike with ICS, you can configure NAT to work with multiple internal interfaces (although the addresses assigned to internal clients through these interfaces must all belong to a single logical subnet).

A final difference between ICS and NAT is that with NAT, you can configure the external, shared interface with either a single public address or multiple public addresses. Multiple public addresses can be useful, for example, when you want to map various public IP addresses to specific internal servers.

> **Exam Tip**   When assigning IP addresses, ICS does not check for conflicts with static addresses already owned by computers on the network. For this reason, you should not deploy ICS on a network whose essential servers are pre-configured with static addresses near the beginning of the 192.168.0.0/24 range. Note also that if essential servers are pre-configured with static addresses in a different logical address space (such as 192.168.1.0/24), deploying ICS might render those essential servers inaccessible. Consequently, if in a scenario on the exam, any essential network services stop functioning after ICS is installed, look for an option to replace ICS with NAT.

Table 9-2 summarizes the features and capabilities of ICS and the NAT routing protocol in Windows Server 2003.

Table 9-2   Comparison of Translated Connections Features

Internet Connection Sharing	Network Address Translation
Single check box configuration	Manual configuration
Single public IP address	Single or multiple public IP addresses
Fixed address range (192.168.0.0/24) for internal hosts	Configurable address range for internal hosts
Single internal interface connecting to a single logical subnet	Single or multiple internal interfaces connecting to a single logical subnet
Installed using Network And Dial-Up Connections	Installed using Routing And Remote Access console
Microsoft Windows 98 Second Edition or later	Windows 2000 Server or Windows Server 2003
Internet Connection Firewall	Basic Firewall

Real World   Incoming Calls and NAT

ICS has one nice feature that NAT does not: when configured on a dial-up connection, ICS does not answer incoming calls. In contrast, if you configure NAT through a demand-dial interface, that interface instructs the modem to answer incoming calls after only two rings. This limitation can be annoying, particularly if you use one phone line for both a shared Internet connection and voice calls. In this case, if you do not pick up after only one ring, the modem is likely to screech just as you start talking to your caller and destroy any possibility of a pleasant chat.

If you cannot use ICS but still want to use the same phone line for the Internet connection as for voice calls, you can edit the Registry to pick up the phone after a high number of rings. To perform this task, open the Registry Editor and add a REG_DWORD value called NumberOfRings to the following Registry key:

HKEY_LOCAL_MACHINE\SYSTEM\CurrentControlSet\Services\RasMan\Parameters

You can set this value anywhere between 0 and 20. In a future service pack, the 0 value might stop the modem from answering at all, but for now, it produces the same behavior as the 2 value does. If you want to stop the modem from intercepting voice calls, the best you can do is set the NumberOfRings value to 20. It's not a perfect solution, but then again, any caller rude enough to let your phone ring 20 times without hanging up probably deserves to be screeched at.

Troubleshooting NAT

The following list provides a conceptual summary of the configuration requirements for a deployment of NAT and of the associated potential points of failure. Review this summary and refer back to it as needed to help you troubleshoot NAT.

1. NAT requires that the appropriate external (public) and internal (private) interfaces be added to the NAT protocol in the Routing And Remote Access console. Typically, the internal interface is created by default, but the external interface might need to be created manually before it can be added. Once both interfaces are added, verify that the public interface (named Remote Router by default for demand-dial connections) is designated as the public interface in its properties dialog box within the NAT/Basic Firewall node. Similarly, the private interface should be designated as the private interface in its properties dialog box within the NAT/Basic Firewall node.

2. NAT requires that a default static route be added in the Routing And Remote Access console. For this static route, the destination and network mask should be configured as 0.0.0.0, the gateway should be set to None, and the interface should be set to the public (external) interface connected to the Internet.

3. NAT requires that a DHCP service be properly configured for internal clients. If you have not configured a DHCP server, verify that the DHCP allocator is enabled on the Address Assignment tab of the NAT/Basic Firewall Properties dialog box.

4. For NAT to be used in conjunction with DNS name resolution, a DNS server must either be configured on the NAT computer or specified through the DNS proxy in NAT. If you have not configured a DNS server on the NAT computer, verify that DNS Proxy is enabled on the Name Resolution tab in the NAT/Basic Firewall Properties dialog box.

5. Certain NAT features require more complex configuration. If you have assigned an address pool to the external interface, verify that the addresses and mask have been configured correctly. For special ports, verify the configuration of the public address and port and the private address and port.

Practice: Installing and Configuring NAT

In this practice, you deploy NAT through a new demand-dial interface. You then tour management features associated with NAT.

 Security Alert   To complete some of the following exercises, you must connect to an external Web site while logged on as Administrator. In a production environment, however, you should avoid exposing your computer to the Internet as much as possible while logged on as Administrator. As an alternative, you can perform administrative tasks by using the Runas command while you are logged on as a user who does not have administrative privileges.

Exercise 1: Configuring NAT Through a Demand-Dial Interface

In this practice, you configure NAT through a demand-dial interface.

▶ **To install NAT on Computer1**

1. Log on to Domain1 from Computer1 as Administrator.

2. Open the Routing And Remote Access console.

3. In the console tree, right click the COMPUTER1 (Local) node and from the short-cut menu, select Configure And Enable Routing And Remote Access.

   The Routing And Remote Access Server Wizard launches.

4. Select Network Address Translation (NAT) and click Next.

   The NAT Internet Connection page appears.

5. Select Create A New Demand-Dial Interface To The Internet, and then click Next.

   The Network Selection page appears.

6. Verify that Local Area Connection is selected in the Network Interfaces area, and then click Next.

   The Ready To Apply Selection page appears.

7. Click Next.

   The Demand-Dial Interface Wizard launches.

8. Click Next. The Interface Name page appears.

   The default name provided is Remote Router.

9. Click Next to accept the default name.

   The Connection Type page appears. The default selection is Connect Using A Modem, ISDN Adapter, Or Other Physical Device.

10. Click Next to accept the default selection.

    The Select A Modem page appears. Your modem should be highlighted.

11. Verify that the modem to be connected to the Internet is selected, and click Next.

    The Phone Number page appears.

12. In the Phone Number Or Address text box, type the phone number that corresponds to your ISP's dial-in line, and then click Next.

    The Protocols And Security page appears.

13. Leave the Route IP Packets On This Interface check box selected, and then click Next.

    The Dial Out Credentials page appears.

14. Type the user name and password for your ISP in the appropriate text boxes. Be sure to type the password in both the Password text box and the Confirm Password text box. Note that for most ISPs, the Domain text box should be left blank.

15. Click Next.

The Completing The Demand-Dial Interface Wizard page appears.

16. Click Finish.

The Completing The Routing And Remote Access Server Wizard page appears.

Read the summary provided on this page. Note that NAT and Basic Firewall have been configured for the new demand-dial interface. Also note that the wizard has detected the DNS and DHCP servers on the local computer, so NAT has automatically been configured to rely on these external services. If no such servers had been detected, you would have been given an opportunity to configure the DHCP allocator and DNS proxy services through NAT.

17. Click Finish.

▶ **To test the new NAT configuration**

1. Log on to Domain1 from Computer2 as Administrator.

2. On Computer2, open Internet Explorer and type **http://www.windowsup-date.com** in the Address box. Close any warnings that appear.

> **Note**   On Computer2, Internet Explorer might time out before the demand-dial interface on Computer1 finishes connecting to your ISP. If you receive a message in Internet Explorer indicating that the page cannot be displayed, click the Refresh button to try again.

If it has not already done so, the demand-dial interface on Computer1 named Remote Router dials in to your ISP.

After this connection is established, and because of the NAT service running on Computer1, Internet Explorer is able to connect to the Web from Computer2.

3. On Computer1, right-click the NAT/Basic Firewall icon in the scope pane of the Routing And Remote Access console.

A shortcut menu appears, allowing you to add another interface for NAT, to view DHCP allocator information, and to view DNS proxy information.

4. From the shortcut menu, select Properties.

The NAT/Basic Firewall Properties dialog box opens.

5. Click the Address Assignment tab.

6. Answer the following question: Which NAT service can be configured on this tab?

_____

7. Click the Name Resolution tab.

8. Answer the following question: Which NAT function can be configured on this tab?

_____

9. Click Cancel to close the NAT/Basic Firewall Properties dialog box.

Exercise 2: Viewing and Configuring NAT Features

In this exercise, you view the various functions and configuration options available for NAT. These include configuring the default static route, reviewing address mappings, configuring packet filters, configuring address pools, configuring special ports, and configuring ICMP filters.

▶ **To view the default route required for NAT**

1. If you have not already done so, From Computer1, log on to Domain1 as Administrator, and then open the Routing And Remote Access console.

2. In the Routing And Remote Access console tree, expand the COMPUTER1 (Local) node, and then expand the IP Routing node.

3. Select the Static Routes node. One static route—the default route—is listed in the details pane. For NAT to function, this default route must be configured.

> **Important**   You must add this default static route manually if you have configured NAT without the help of the Routing And Remote Access Server Wizard.

4. The default route is defined by a particular destination address and net mask. Write this address and net mask in the space provided:

_____

▶ **To review NAT mappings**

1. If you have not already done so, log on to Domain1 from Computer2 as Administrator.

2. On Computer2, at a command prompt type **ipconfig** to determine the IP address assigned to the local area connection. Write this address in the space provided:

_____

3. Open Internet Explorer and browse to an external Web site such as *http://www.windowsupdate.com*.

4. On Computer1, in the scope pane of the Routing And Remote Access console, select the NAT/Basic Firewall node.

5. In the details pane, right-click the Remote Router icon, and then click Show Mappings.

   The COMPUTER1 – Network Address Translation Session Mapping Table opens.

6. From the list of mappings in the table, select an entry whose private address corresponds to Computer2's address and whose remote port corresponds to the port used for Web traffic (80).

7. Write down the public address listed for this session mapping in the space provided:

   _____

8. Answer the following question: Which physical interface owns the public address that the NAT service has mapped to the private address of Computer2?

   _____

9. Close the COMPUTER1 – Network Address Translation Session Mapping Table.

 **To review NAT features**

1. On Computer1, while you are still logged on to Domain1 as Administrator, and while the NAT/Basic Firewall node is still selected in the Routing And Remote Access console, right-click the Remote Router icon in the details pane and then click Properties.

   The Remote Router Properties dialog box opens with the NAT/Basic Firewall tab displayed. Note that this tab is where you enable and disable the NAT and Basic Firewall functions.

2. In the Static Packet Filters area, read the one-sentence description of packet filtering. Packet filters are described in more detail in Lesson 5 of this chapter.

3. Click the Address Pool tab. If you have acquired a public address range from your ISP, you can use this tab to assign those addresses to your external interface.

4. Click the Add button.

   The Add Address Pool dialog box opens, which contains a Start Address text box, a Mask text box, and an End Address text box.

5. Answer the following questions:

   a. Do these configuration parameters require that the deployable address pool you assign to the external interface be a contiguous address space?

   _____

   b. Using Calculator, determine which subnet mask you must assign to the address pool 207.46.200.0–207.46.207.255.

   _____

   c. What is the maximum number of addresses contained within a pool assigned a subnet mask of 255.255.255.248?

   _____

6. Click Cancel to close the Add Address Pool dialog box.

7. In the Reserve Public Addresses area of the Address Pool tab, read the description of the reservations function.

8. Answer the following question: When would you use the Reservations button in configuring NAT properties?

   _____

9. Click the Services And Ports tab. At the top of the tab, read the description of the available functions.

10. In the Services area, click FTP Server. The Edit Service dialog box appears.

11. At the top of the dialog box, read the description of this configuration feature.

    If you had external users connecting to an internal FTP server, you could use this dialog box to configure the NAT service to forward FTP requests to the appropriate internal server. Figure 9-28 shows such a scenario.

> **Exam Tip** For the 70-291 exam, you need to know that the functionality provided by the Services And Ports tab and illustrated in Figure 9-28 is known as configuring *special ports*. To configure a special port means to map an internal service (such as a Web, Telnet, or FTP server) to the external interface of the NAT computer. This feature allows external requests for internal services to be forwarded to the proper computer.

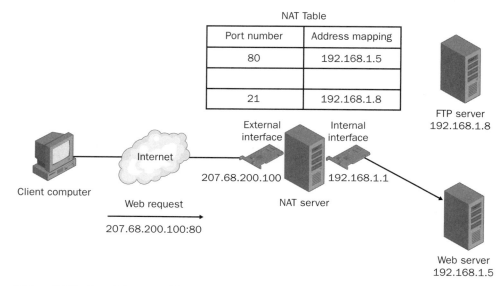

NAT Table

Port number	Address mapping
80	192.168.1.5
21	192.168.1.8

Figure 9-28   Special ports with NAT

12. Click Cancel to close the Edit Services dialog box.

13. In the Remote Router Properties dialog box, select the ICMP tab and read the description at the top.

This tab allows you to restrict various types of ICMP messages. These messages are used for various network functions, such as the PING command or ICMP router discovery.

14. Answer the following questions: By default, does your router block outsiders from pinging your external interface? By default, does your router block insiders from pinging your external interface?

---

15. Click Cancel to close the Remote Router Properties dialog box.

16. Log off Computer1 and Computer2.

Lesson Review

The following questions are intended to reinforce key information presented in this lesson. If you are unable to answer a question, review the lesson materials and try the question again. You can find answers to the questions in the "Questions and Answers" section at the end of this chapter.

1. You add a new computer to provide Internet connectivity to your network, which consists of a single subnet of client computers with static addresses ranging between 192.168.0.1 through 192.168.0.65 and critical servers with static addresses ranging between 192.168.0.100 through 192.168.0.120. After configuring ICS on the new computer, still none of the computers can connect to the Internet. What is the simplest way to solve the problem?

   _____

   _____

2. Your network has 11 critical servers assigned various static addresses in the range 192.168.0.1–192.168.0.20. After you configure ICS on your network, users can no longer log on to the network, and network computers can no longer locate domain controllers or connect to network objects specified by name. Assuming that you cannot change the addresses of the critical servers, how can you best solve the problem?

   _____

   _____

   _____

3. Your network has critical servers assigned static addresses in the range 10.0.0.1–10.0.0.20. Client computers have been assigned static addresses in the range 10.0.0.21–10.0.0.100. None of the currently assigned network addresses should be changed. You configure a NAT server to distribute IP addresses in the same IP subnet as the current computers and to provide Internet connectivity. However, the computers on your network still cannot connect to the Internet. What is the most likely cause of the problem?

   _____

   _____

4. Your NAT server uses a DSL connection. From your ISP, you have obtained a block of eight addresses to be mapped to the external interface of the NAT computer. How can you configure this?

   _____

   _____

Lesson Summary

- NAT is a service built into a router that modifies the source address of IP datagrams before sending them on to their destinations. This functionality allows NAT clients to connect to the Internet by sharing one or more publicly registered IP addresses on the computer running the NAT service.

- In Routing And Remote Access, NAT can also be configured to function as a DHCP allocator, a DNS proxy, or a WINS proxy.

- NAT can be understood as a fully configurable version of ICS.

- To function, NAT requires that a default route be configured with no gateway specified.

- NAT clients on the same subnet as the NAT server must be configured to use the NAT server as a default gateway.

Lesson 4: Configuring and Managing Routing Protocols

The dynamic routing protocols RIP and OSPF allow routers to determine appropriate paths along which to send traffic. The service DHCP Relay Agent is also considered a routing protocol in Routing And Remote Access; this service allows a DHCP server to provide an IP configuration to computers on remote subnets.

After this lesson, you will be able to

■ Deploy RIP routing

■ Determine whether RIP or OSPF is best suited for your network

■ Deploy DHCP Relay Agent

Estimated lesson time: 40 minutes

Understanding Routing Protocols

In Routing And Remote Access, *routing protocols* provide communication between routers. Windows Server 2003 includes four routing protocols that can be added to the Routing And Remote Access service: the dynamic routing protocols RIP and OSPF, the multicast routing protocol IGMP Router And Proxy, and DHCP Relay Agent.

Adding and Configuring Routing Protocols

To configure a routing protocol, you must first add the routing protocol to the Routing And Remote Access console. You perform this task by right-clicking the General node within IP Routing in the Routing And Remote Access console and clicking New Routing Protocol, as shown in Figure 9-29.

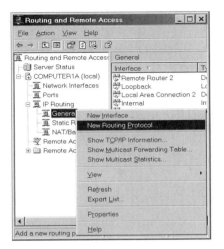

Figure 9-29   Making a routing protocol available for configuration

Once the routing protocol is available for configuration in the Routing And Remote Access console, you must enable the protocol on the appropriate network interfaces. You perform this task by right-clicking the new protocol in the console tree and then clicking New Interface on the shortcut menu. After the protocol has been enabled on the appropriate interfaces, you can configure the routing protocol through the protocol properties or the interface properties.

Configuring RIP

RIP is a dynamic routing protocol that helps routers determine the best path through which to send given data. Routes to destinations are chosen according to lowest cost. By default, this cost is determined by the number of hops or routers between endpoints; however, you can manually adjust the cost of any route as needed.

Importantly, RIP discards routes that are determined to have a cost higher than 15. This feature effectively limits the size of the network in which RIP can operate. Another important feature of RIP is that RIP-enabled routers advertise their entire routing tables to each other every 30 seconds. The service therefore generates a substantial amount of network traffic.

RIP Environment

A RIP routed environment is best suited to a small-to-medium-sized, multipath, dynamic IP internetwork:

- A *small-to-medium-sized internetwork* is defined as 10 to 50 networks. In addition, the diameter of a RIP network cannot exceed 15 routers.

- *Multipath* means that multiple paths are available for packets to travel between any two endpoints on the internetwork.

- *Dynamic* means that the topology of the internetwork changes over time.

Advantages and Disadvantages of RIP

The main advantage of RIP is that it is easy to deploy. You can implement it on your network simply by enabling the protocol on each router. However, RIP does not scale well to large networks because of the 15-hop limitation. Other disadvantages of RIP include its high convergence times in medium-sized networks and its inability to factor costs other than hops (such as bandwidth) into the route cost metric.

Managing RIP Security

RIP includes a number of configurable security features, including authentication, peer filtering, route filters, and neighbors.

Exam Tip   You need to be familiar with these RIP security features for the exam.

RIP Authentication   To prevent the corruption of RIP routes by an unauthorized RIP router or a malicious attacker, you can configure RIP router interfaces to use simple password authentication. Received RIP announcements that do not match the configured password are discarded. Note, however, that the password is sent in plaintext. Any user with a network sniffer such as Network Monitor can capture the RIP announcements and view the password.

You configure RIP authentication by selecting the Activate Authentication check box and specifying a password on the General tab of the RIP interface properties dialog box, as shown in Figure 9-30.

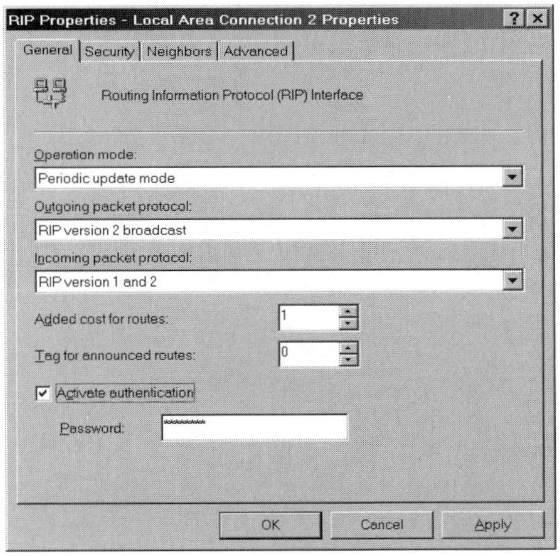

Figure 9-30   Activating RIP authentication

Peer Filtering   You can configure each RIP router with a list of routers (designated by IP address) from which RIP announcements are accepted. By default, RIP announcements from all sources are accepted. By configuring a list of RIP peers, RIP announcements from unauthorized RIP routers are discarded.

You configure RIP peer filtering on the Security tab of the global RIP Properties dialog box, as shown in Figure 9-31.

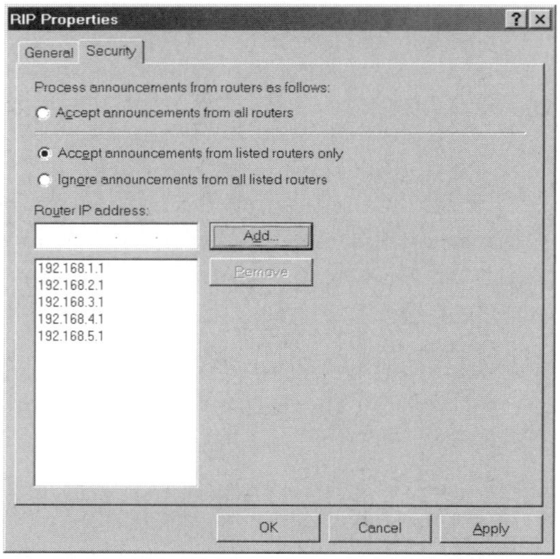

Figure 9-31   Peer filtering in RIP

Route Filters   You can configure route filters on each RIP interface so that the only routes considered for addition to the routing table are those that reflect reachable network IDs within the internetwork. For example, if an organization is using subnets of the private network ID 10.0.0.0, route filtering can be used so that the RIP routers discard all routes except those within the 10.0.0.0 network ID.

You configure route filters on the Security tab of the RIP Properties dialog box, as shown in Figure 9-32.

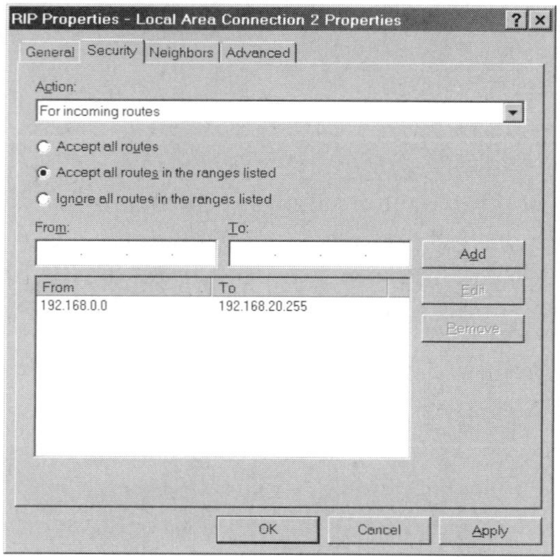

Figure 9-32   Route filtering in RIP

Neighbors   By default, RIP either broadcasts (RIP version 1 or RIP version 2) or multicasts (RIP version 2 only) announcements. To prevent RIP traffic from being received by any node except neighboring RIP routers, the server running Routing And Remote Access can unicast RIP announcements.

You configure RIP neighbors on the Neighbors tab of the RIP Properties dialog box, as shown in Figure 9-33.

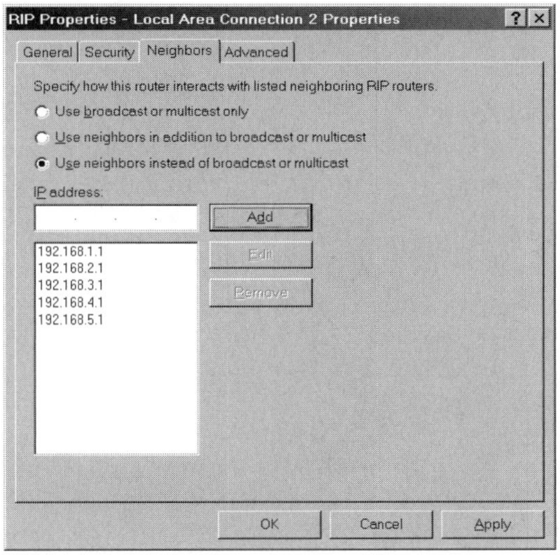

Figure 9-33   Configuring RIP unicast message recipients, or neighbors

OSPF Overview

OSPF is designed for exchanging routing information within a large or very large internetwork.

The biggest advantage of OSPF is that it is efficient; OSPF requires little network overhead even in very large internetworks. The biggest disadvantage of OSPF is its complexity; it requires proper planning and is difficult to configure and administer.

OSPF uses a Shortest Path First (SPF) algorithm to compute routes in the routing table. The SPF algorithm computes the shortest (least cost) path between the router and all the networks of the internetwork. SPF-calculated routes are always loopfree.

Instead of exchanging routing table entries like RIP routers, OSPF routers maintain a map of the internetwork that is updated after any change to the network topology. This map, called the *link state database*, is synchronized between all the OSPF routers and is used to compute the routes in the routing table. Neighboring OSPF routers form an *adjacency*, which is a logical relationship between routers to synchronize the link state database.

Changes to internetwork topology are efficiently flooded across the entire internetwork to ensure that the link state database on each router is synchronized and accurate at all times. Upon receiving changes to the link state database, the routing table is recalculated.

As the size of the link state database increases, memory requirements and route computation times increase. To address this scaling problem, OSPF divides the internetwork into *areas* (collections of contiguous networks) that are connected to each other through a backbone area. Each router keeps a link state database for only those areas that are connected to the router. Area border routers (ABRs) connect the backbone area to other areas.

To further reduce the amount of routing information flooded into areas, OSPF allows the use of stub areas. A *stub area* can contain a single entry and exit point (a single ABR), or multiple ABRs when any of the ABRs can be used to reach external route destinations.

Figure 9-34 shows a diagram of an OSPF internetwork.

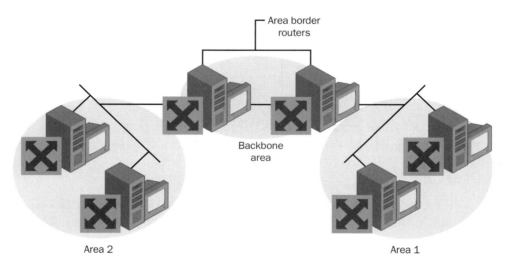

Figure 9-34   A sample OSPF topology

OSPF vs. RIP

OSPF has the following advantages over RIP:

- OSPF can scale to large or very large internetworks.
- OSPF has no hop limit.

- OSPF has faster convergence times.

- OSPF uses less network bandwidth.

- OSPF-calculated routes are always loopfree.

Understanding DHCP Relay Agent

DHCP Relay Agent is a routing protocol that allows client computers to obtain an address from a DHCP server on a remote subnet. Typically, DHCP clients broadcast DHCPDiscover packets that are then received and answered by a DHCP server on the same subnet. Because routers block broadcasts, DHCP clients and servers must normally be located on the same physical subnet.

However, two methods can help you work around this limitation. First, if the routers separating the DHCP server and clients are RFC 1542–compliant, the routers can be configured for Boot Protocol (BOOTP) forwarding. Through BOOTP forwarding, routers forward DHCP broadcasts between clients and servers and inform servers of the originating subnet of the DHCP requests. This process allows DHCP servers to assign addresses to the remote clients from the appropriate scope.

The second way to allow remote communication between DHCP servers and clients is to configure a DHCP relay agent on the subnet containing the remote clients. DHCP relay agents intercept DHCP Discover packets and forward them to a remote DHCP server whose address has been preconfigured. Although DHCP Relay Agent is configured through Routing And Remote Access, the computer hosting the agent does not need to be functioning as an actual router between subnets.

Figure 9-35 shows a network topology with six subnets.

 Exam Tip   Expect to see a topology question about DHCP Relay Agent and RFC 1542–compliant routers on the exam.

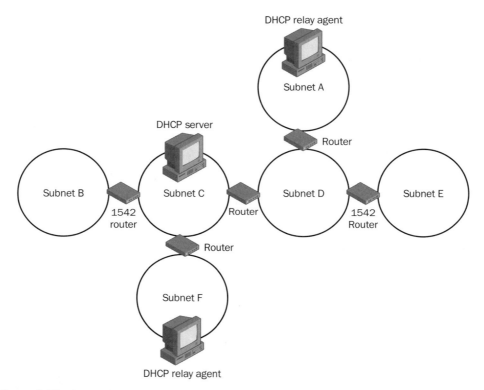

Figure 9-35   Network topology with DHCP Relay Agent

In the network, clients on all subnets except D and E will be able to obtain an IP address from the DHCP server on Subnet C:

■ Subnet A contains a DHCP relay agent. If we assume that the DHCP relay agent is configured to point toward the IP address of the DHCP server on Subnet C, DHCP clients on Subnet A will be able to obtain an address from this server.

■ Subnet B does not contain a DHCP server or a DHCP relay agent. However, the DHCP Discover broadcasts from clients on Subnet B are able to pass through the RFC 1542–compliant router (provided that BOOTP forwarding has been enabled). Therefore, the DHCP client requests on Subnet B are received by the DHCP server on Subnet C. This DHCP server can then answer these requests accordingly.

- Subnet C contains a DHCP server. Clients on this subnet will be able to receive an address from the DHCP server directly.

- Subnet D does not contain a DHCP server or a DHCP relay agent. Although one of its routers is 1542-compliant, this only helps pass DHCP request broadcasts to another subnet that does not have a DHCP server or a DHCP relay agent. As a result, clients on Subnet D will not be able to obtain an address from the DHCP server on Subnet C.

- Subnet E, like Subnet D, does not contain a DHCP server or a DHCP relay agent. The 1542-compliant router does not allow the clients on Subnet E to connect to a DHCP server.

- Subnet F is configured with a DHCP relay agent. If the relay agent is configured with the address of the DHCP server on Subnet C, the clients on Subnet F will have their DHCP requests intercepted by the DHCP relay agent and answered by the DHCP server.

> **Note**   You cannot use the DHCP Relay Agent component on a computer running any of the following: the DHCP service, the NAT routing protocol component with automatic addressing enabled, or ICS.

Configuring the DHCP Relay Agent

To configure the DHCP Relay Agent, first add the DHCP Relay Agent routing protocol to the Routing And Remote Access console. To add the DHCP Relay Agent, complete the following steps:

1. Open the Routing And Remote Access console.

2. In the console tree, right-click the General node, and then click New Routing Protocol.

3. In the New Routing Protocol dialog box, click DHCP Relay Agent, and then click OK.

Second, configure the DHCP Relay Agent to point to the address of at least one remote DHCP server. (More than one DHCP server can be used for fault tolerance.) This configuration is achieved through the DHCP Relay Agent Properties dialog box, shown in Figure 9-36. To configure global DHCP Relay Agent properties, complete the following steps:

1. Open the Routing And Remote Access console.

2. In the console tree, right-click the DHCP Relay Agent node within IP Routing, and then click Properties.

3. On the General tab, in the Server Address text box, type the IP address of your DHCP server, and then click Add.

4. Repeat step 3 for each DHCP server you need to add, and then click OK.

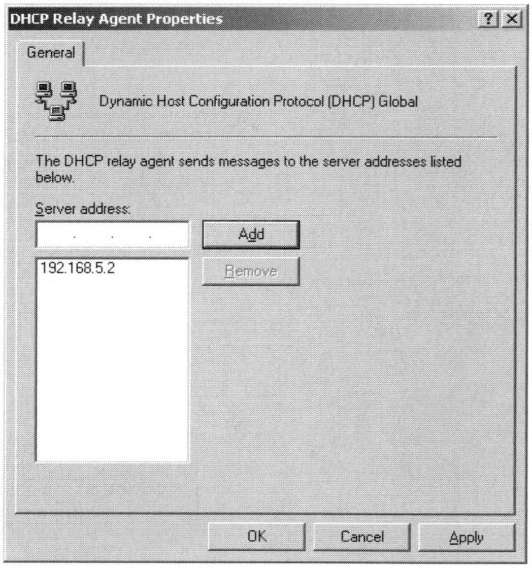

Figure 9-36   DHCP Relay Agent properties

Third, enable the protocol on the interface or interfaces pointing to the network segment containing the DHCP clients. To enable the DHCP Relay Agent on a router interface, complete the following steps:

1. Open the Routing And Remote Access console.

2. In the console tree, right-click the DHCP Relay Agent node, and then click New Interface.

3. Click the interface you want to add, and then click OK.

4. In the DHCP Relay Properties dialog box, on the General tab, verify that the Relay DHCP Packets check box is selected.

5. If needed, in Hop-Count Threshold and Boot Threshold (Seconds), click the arrows to modify the thresholds.

Verifying that DHCP Relay Agent Is Functioning

You can verify that the DHCP Relay Agent is functioning by using the Routing And Remote Access console. To do so, select the DHCP Relay Agent node and view the statistics in the details pane. The details pane compiles requests received, replies received, requests discarded, and replies discarded. If this data reveals that both requests and replies have been received, the DHCP Relay Agent is functioning.

Lesson Review

The following questions are intended to reinforce key information presented in this lesson. If you are unable to answer a question, review the lesson materials and try the question again. You can find answers to the questions in the "Questions and Answers" section at the end of this chapter.

1. What is a weakness of RIP authentication?

   _____

2. Besides using RIP authentication, how can you deter rogue routers from providing incorrect routes to your network routers through RIP?

   _____

3. Name five advantages of OSPF over RIP.

   _____

   _____

4. You want to deploy one DHCP server on your network that consists of two subnets. What are two methods that will enable you to achieve this task?

   _____

Lesson Summary

- RIP is a dynamic routing protocol that is easy to deploy but has a number of notable limitations. For example, RIP networks are limited to a diameter of 15 hops. In addition, RIP is relatively bandwidth-intensive.

- RIP has a number of configurable security features, including RIP authentication, peer filtering, route filtering, and neighbors.

- OSPF is a dynamic routing protocol designed for exchanging routing information within a large or very large internetwork. Although it is difficult to deploy, it has a number of advantages over RIP, including increased efficiency, accuracy, scalability, and configurability.

- If you want to provide automatic addressing to all subnets on your network, you must configure each subnet with a DHCP server or a DHCP relay agent pointing to a DHCP server. Alternatively, clients can be separated from DHCP servers or DHCP relay agents by routers able to perform BOOTP forwarding (in other words, RFC 1542–compatible routers).

Lesson 5: Configuring Packet Filters

When Basic Firewall is enabled on an external interface in the Routing And Remote Access console, that interface blocks all unsolicited traffic from entering your network. However, you might want to restrict all unsolicited requests except those intended for a specific internal service such a Web server. In this case, you can create packet filters that block all traffic from the external network except those requests destined for the specific service you choose.

After this lesson, you will be able to

- Configure packet filters to allow access to internal services

Estimated lesson time: 25 minutes

Understanding Packet Filters

Packet filters are rules defined for a particular interface that allow or restrict traffic by source address, destination address, direction, or protocol type. You can think of packet filters as holes you create in a firewall to allow external clients access to specific internal services. Without packet filters, a firewall would simply block all requests originating from the external network.

The packet filtering feature in Routing And Remote Access is based on exceptions. You can set packet filters per interface and configure them to do one of the following:

- Pass through all traffic except packets prohibited by filters.
- Discard all traffic except packets allowed by filters.

In Windows Server 2003, packet filters occur in two types: input filters and output filters. *Input filters* restrict traffic entering into an interface from the immediately attached network. *Output filters* restrict traffic being sent from an interface onto the immediately attached network. Figure 9-37 presents an example of an input filter denying all packets except those destined for TCP port 1723 and IP address 207.46.22.1.

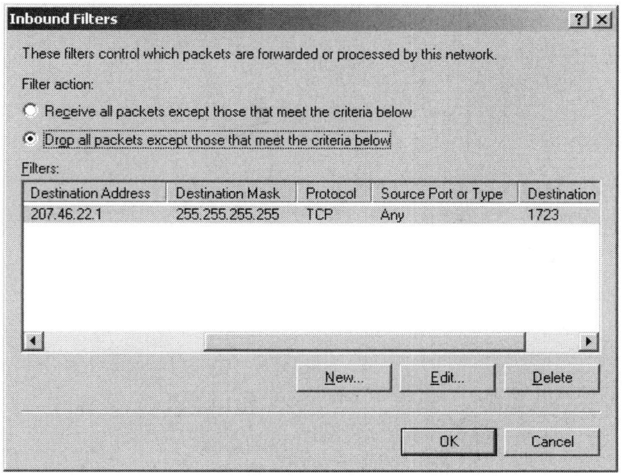

Inbound Filters   ? ×

These filters control which packets are forwarded or processed by this network.

Filter action:

○ Receive all packets except those that meet the criteria below

◉ Drop all packets except those that meet the criteria below

Filters:

Destination Address	Destination Mask	Protocol	Source Port or Type	Destination
207.46.22.1	255.255.255.255	TCP	Any	1723

New...   Edit...   Delete

OK   Cancel

Figure 9-37   Example packet filter

Exam Tip   Watch for questions in which all packet filters are defined correctly, but whose filter action is improperly configured.

Creating Packet Filters

You create packet filters in the Routing And Remote Access console through the IP Routing node. Within the IP Routing node, select either the General node or the NAT/Basic Firewall node. Packet filters are then configured through the properties dialog box of the appropriate interface, listed in the details pane. Note that the NAT/Basic Firewall node allows you to create packet filters only for external interfaces, whereas the General node allows you to create packet filters for any interface.

To add a packet filter, complete the following steps:

1. Open the Routing And Remote Access console.

2. In the console tree, expand IP Routing, and click the General node.

3. In the details pane, right-click the interface on which you want to add a filter, and then click Properties.

   The interface properties dialog box opens, shown in Figure 9-38.

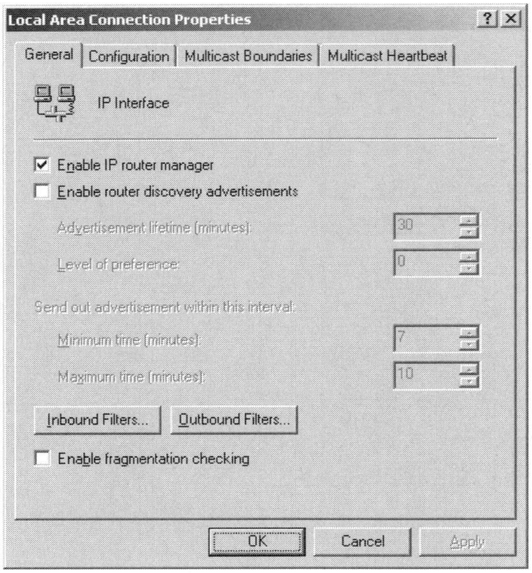

Figure 9-38   Configuring packet filters

4. On the General tab, click either Inbound Filters or Outbound Filters.

5. In the Inbound Filters dialog box or the Outbound Filters dialog box, click New.

6. In the Add IP Filter dialog box, type the settings for the filter, and then click OK.

7. In Filter Action, select the appropriate filter action, and then click OK.

> **Note**   You can also define packet filters in a remote access policy profile. Remote access policies, which are discussed in Chapter 10, allow you to apply rules and restrictions to specific remote access connections. By defining packet filters and the remote access policy level, you can apply different levels of access restrictions to different users.

Basic Packet Filtering Scenario

In a basic packet filtering scenario implemented on Windows Server 2003, two packet filters are configured on an external interface. These packet filters allow unsolicited connections to a Web server hosted on an internal network. Such a scenario, in which a Web server is hosted at the address 207.46.22.1, is illustrated in Figure 9-39.

Packet filter #1 is configured as an input filter and specifies a destination IP address of 207.46.22.1 with a mask of 255.255.255.255. This filter then specifies the protocol TCP and associated Web service port of 80. Once the filter is configured, the filter action in the Inbound Filters dialog box is set to Drop All Packets Except Those That Meet The Criteria Below.

Packet filter #2 is configured as an output filter and specifies a source IP address of 207.46.22.1 with a mask of 255.255.255.255. This filter then specifies the protocol TCP and associated Web service port of 80. Once the filter is configured, the filter action in the Outbound Filters dialog box is set to Drop All Packets Except Those That Meet The Criteria Below.

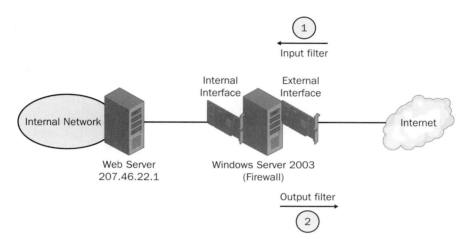

Figure 9-39   Basic packet filtering

Locked-Down Packet Filtering Scenario

In a packet filtering implementation designed for locked-down security, four filters are created for access to each service. As shown in Figure 9-40, one packet filter in this scenario is designed to match each of the four steps required for communication.

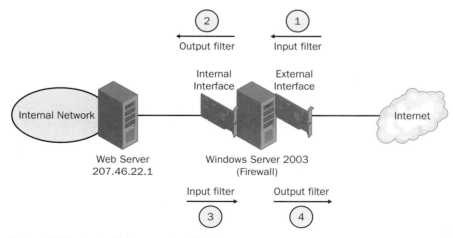

Figure 9-40   Locked-down packet filtering

In the case of an internal Web server, each packet filter indicates a protocol of TCP, an associated port of 80, and the IP address of the Web server (207.46.22.10) as either a source or destination, as appropriate:

1. External interface, input filter: Destination address—207.46.22.10/32, Protocol-TCP port 80

2. Internal interface, output filter: Destination address—207.46.22.10/32, Protocol-TCP port 80

3. Internal interface, input filter: Source address—207.46.22.10/32, Protocol-TCP port 80

4. External interface, output filter: Source address— 207.46.22.10/32, Protocol-TCP port 80

The set of packet filters is then configured to deny all other traffic.

> **Off the Record**   On the topic of packet filtering, exam reality definitely differs from real-world reality. In real-world reality, most administrators use a dedicated firewall product and simply define a single, bidirectional filter on the external interface of that firewall to provide access to a given internal service.
>
> But that scenario would just be too simple for the MCSE exam. On the exam, you're likely to see a question on packet filtering in which each answer choice lists a confusing array of four packet filters for each protocol session. Typically, at least two of the answer choices specify the correct port numbers, so it's up to you to determine which answer choice has correctly defined the filter directions on each interface. Such questions aren't easy, but if you can visualize the four steps in communication required through the external and internal interfaces, you should be in good shape.

Advanced Packet Filtering Scenarios

Unlike Web servers, many other services communicate over more than one channel. Point-to-Point Tunneling Protocol (PPTP) traffic, for example, uses TCP port 1723 to create and maintain a VPN connection and IP protocol 47 to send data over that connection. To support remote users connecting through PPTP to an internal VPN server, then, you must create one set of packet filters for TCP port 1723 and another set for protocol number 47. Each set of packet filters follows the input and output pattern shown in either Figure 9-39 or Figure 9-40.

> **Note**   A protocol number is typically used to define a stream of data associated with a specific service. To create a packet filter for a protocol number, in the Add IP Filter dialog box, select Other in the Protocol drop-down list box. Then type the appropriate value in the Protocol Number text box.

Another protocol used for VPN traffic, Layer2 Tunneling Protocol/Internet Protocol Security (L2TP/IPSec), requires three sets of packet filters. This type of VPN uses UDP ports 500 and 4500 to create and maintain the connection, and IP protocol 50 to send data.

VPNs, PPTP, and L2TP/IPSec are all discussed in more detail in Chapter 10. To learn of other port numbers associated with various TCP/IP services, see Lesson 1 of Chapter 2, "Understanding TCP/IP."

> **Exam Tip**   For the exam, know both the protocols numbers and ports required for PPTP and L2TP/IPSec.

Lesson Review

The following questions are intended to reinforce key information presented in this lesson. If you are unable to answer a question, review the lesson materials and try the question again. You can find answers to the questions in the "Questions and Answers" section at the end of this chapter.

1. Your organization uses a proprietary protocol named XCA that communicates over two separate TCP ports. You have been asked to allow external users to communicate with users on your internal network by means of XCA. What is the minimum number of packet filters you must create on your Windows Server 2003 remote access server that will enable XCA connections to and from your internal network?

2. You have deployed a Windows Server 2003 computer running the Routing And Remote Access service to function as a simple firewall. How many packet filters do you need to create to support remote access to a VPN server through L2TP/IPSec? Assume that you want to provide the strictest security standards.

3. Which ports and protocol numbers must you leave open to support access to a PPTP-type VPN server located behind a firewall? Which ports and protocol numbers must you leave open to support access to an L2TP/IPSec-type VPN server located behind a firewall?

_____

_____

Lesson Summary

- Packet filters are rules defined for a particular interface that allow or restrict traffic by source or destination address, direction, or protocol type. Without packet filters, a firewall would simply block all requests originating from the external network.

- To allow external users to connect to a server or service hosted on your internal network, you can create packet filters on a firewall that blocks all requests originating from the external network except those requests for the internal service you specify.

- In Windows Server 2003, each packet filter restricts traffic in only one direction. To allow external access to an internal service, you can configure one input filter and one output filter on the external interface of your firewall. For each filter, specify the service protocol and the address at which the service is hosted. To heighten security, you can configure an additional, similar set of filters on the internal interface of the firewall.

Case Scenario Exercise

You are consulting for a pharmaceutical company named Fabrikam, Inc. that specializes in the development of drugs that fight heart disease. Fabrikam is located in Ithaca, New York, and employs a staff of over 600 scientists and researchers, many of whom have worked for other companies in the pharmaceutical industry.

Within the past 18 months, Fabrikam's research teams have made some breakthrough discoveries that they believe might lead to revolutionary treatments for cardiovascular disease. Despite this optimism, company executives are also concerned about the potential for security leaks and corporate espionage. A history of such leaks exists in the industry, and even if they cannot always be proven, such breaches of security are potentially disastrous for a company's bottom line.

To address these concerns, company executives want to store all research data relating to the scientific breakthroughs in a new secure subnet. The corporate network consists of 12 subnets overall, four of which belong to Research and Development. The company has deployed RIP routing but is concerned about the potential for hackers to learn of routes to subnets.

Figure 9-41 shows the relevant portion of the network.

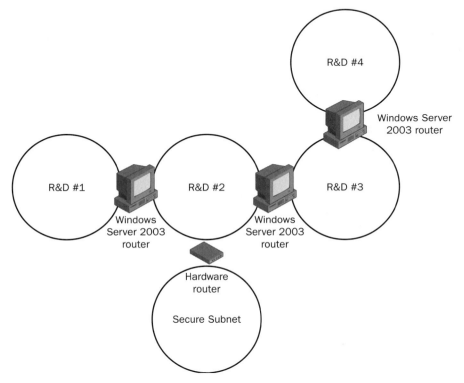

Figure 9-41   Fabrikam R&D network

For each of the following problems, answer the question by recommending the best course of action.

1. Company executives want to improve router security on the network and have made clear that they would not be satisfied with a solution that merely authenticates routers with a plaintext password. What other measures can you take to ensure that rogue routers are not deployed on the network and that network routes are not intercepted? (Choose all that apply.)

     a. Deploy Active Directory directory service.

     b. Configure RIP to use autostatic routes.

     c. Configure RIP neighbors.

     d. Configure peer filtering.

     e. Configure route filtering.

2. How can you ensure that only members of the R&D Subnet 2 can access the route to the new secure subnet?

     a. Deploy OSPF on the network and configure the router connected to the secure subnet as an area border router.

     b. Configure peer filtering on the router connected to the secure subnet.

     c. Encrypt the routes using MPPE.

     d. Do not deploy a routing protocol on the router connected to the secure subnet. Configure workstations in R&D Subnet 2 with static routes to the secure subnet.

3. A team of 20 of Fabrikam's scientists are conducting research for 10 months in Ottawa, Ontario. They have set up a computer network that they want to connect periodically to the main office in Ithaca. How can you ensure that the incoming calls you receive to the network router at the main office are in fact originating from the router at the temporary Ottawa office?

     a. Configure the answering router at the Ithaca office to authenticate all incoming calls.

     b. Configure callback on the answering router at the Ithaca office.

     c. Configure callback on the calling router at the Ottawa office.

     d. Disable autostatic routes on both routers.

Troubleshooting Lab

In this exercise, you troubleshoot an error in NAT. Before you begin, verify that you have not configured any additional demand-dial interfaces on Computer1 besides Remote Router.

1. From Computer2, log on to Domain1 as Administrator.

2. Open Internet Explorer and connect to any external Web site such as *http:// www.windowsupdate.com*.

If the demand-dial interface named Remote Router on Computer1 is not already connected, Internet Explorer might time out before the Web page appears. If you receive an error that the page cannot be displayed, click the Refresh button in Internet Explorer.

3. When you have connected to an external Web site from Computer2, from Computer1, log on to Domain1 as Administrator, and open a command prompt.

4. At the command prompt, type **netsh ro ip na se in "r" p**.

5. Switch back to Computer2 and attempt to connect to another external Web site.

No external Web sites can be reached.

6. On Computer1, review the NAT configuration in the Routing And Remote Access console. What is the error in the configuration? Write your answer in the space provided.

_____

_____

7. On Computer1, at the command prompt type **netsh routing ip nat set interface "Remote Router" fullfirewall**.

8. Verify that you can now connect to external Web sites from Computer2.

9. Log off Computer1 and Computer2.

Chapter Summary

- The Routing And Remote Access service can be configured to operate as a software router.

- The Routing And Remote Access console is the principal tool used for configuring and managing the Routing And Remote Access service.

- In Windows Server 2003, you can view the IP routing table through the Routing And Remote Access console or through the Route Print command.

- Without dynamic routing protocols, a router requires static routes to connect to non-neighboring subnets when those subnets do not lie in the same direction as its default route.

- You can add static routes through the Routing And Remote Access console or through the Route Add command. Adding the –p switch to the Route Add command makes the static route persistent, which means it remains in the routing table even after the router is rebooted.

- Demand-dial routing is the process of sending traffic from one router to another over a dial-up connection. This dial-up connection can be enabled as needed in a dial-on-demand scenario or remain connected as a persistent link.

- NAT is a service built into a router that modifies the source address of IP datagrams before sending them on to the public Internet. This functionality allows NAT clients to connect to the Internet by sharing one or more publicly registered IP addresses on the computer running the NAT service. NAT can be understood as a fully configurable version of ICS.

- RIP is a dynamic routing protocol that is easy to deploy but that is resource-intensive and unsuitable for very large networks. OSPF is a dynamic routing protocol that is difficult to deploy but that is scalable, smart, and efficient.

- DHCP Relay Agent is a routing protocol configured in Routing And Remote Access that allows DHCP clients to obtain an IP configuration from a DHCP server on a remote subnet.

- To allow external users to connect to a server or service hosted on your internal network, you can create packet filters on a firewall that block all requests originating from the external network except those requests for the internal service you specify.

Exam Highlights

Before taking the exam, review the key topics and terms that are presented in this chapter.

Key Topics

- Know when and how to create static routes.

- Be comfortable reading a routing table.

- Be familiar with all of the configuration options related to demand-dial interfaces.

- Be able to compare and contrast ICS and NAT. Know which is appropriate for given network scenarios.

- Be able to compare and contrast RIP and OSPF. Know which is appropriate for given network scenarios.

- When looking at a network topology, be able to determine which subnets require a DHCP relay agent.

- Know which packet filters you must define on a firewall to provide external users access to internal services such as a Web or VPN server.

Key Terms

callback   A feature in which an answering router drops a dial-up connection and calls back to a preconfigured phone number.

BAP/BACP   Bandwidth Allocation Protocol/Bandwidth Allocation Control Protocol. These protocols are used to allow Multilink connections to add or drop lines in response to a corresponding rise or fall in available network bandwidth.

autostatic routes   A feature in which RIP does not send its usual announcements over a given link. Instead, routes are updated semiautomatically: either when an administrator chooses, or by a scheduled script.

router discovery   A feature relying on ICMP messages in which hosts send out solicitations to discover network routers. These hosts then use periodic advertisements from routers to determine when discovered routers are down.

BOOTP forwarding   A process by which RFC 1542–compliant routers forward DHCP broadcasts from one subnet to another.

Questions and Answers

Page
9-26
Exercise: Running the Routing And Remote Access Server Setup Wizard

■ How many basic routing functions can be configured through this wizard?

5

Page
9-27
Lesson 1 Review

1. Your department connects to the Internet through a Digital Subscriber Line (DSL) that it shares with the rest of the organization. However, you have just obtained a faster T1 connection to the Internet that you want to reserve for the IT department's use. A DHCP server provides all of your users with an IP configuration, but IT staff computers are interspersed throughout the same subnets as those of other staff members. How can you allow only IT staff members to use the new T1 line to connect to the Internet? You want to configure this setup only once and make the changes permanent.

   Use the –p switch with the Route command at the IT staff's computers to add a static route to the T1 connection. The –p switch makes the route permanent.

2. You are unable to connect to any computers outside your local subnet. You run the Route Print command and note the line below. What is most likely the cause of the problem?

Network Destination	Netmask	Gateway	Interface
0.0.0.0	0.0.0.0	192.168.1.1	192.168.1.1

   The default gateway is set to the address of the local computer.

3. You attempt to add a persistent static route through the Route command, but it does not appear in the Route Print output of the local machine. You have assigned the route a metric of 1. Assuming that you have entered the command successfully, what could be the cause of the problem?

   Another route source has been assigned a higher preference level.

4. Which protocols are used to allow Multilink connections to add and drop dial-up lines as needed?

   BAP and BACP

Page
9-43
Lesson 2 Review

1. Using Routing And Remote Access, you have configured demand-dial routing to join a branch office to your corporate LAN. However, even though you are using the RIP protocol, routes are not being updated across the WAN link. Why is this happening, and how can you allow the routes to be updated?

RIP has been configured for autostatic updates over demand-dial connections. In the General node within IP Routing in Routing And Remote Access, right-click the demand-dial interface and select Update Routes.

2. You are connected to a branch office over a demand-dial connection. How can you best prevent your users from connecting to the branch office during lunch hours?

Configure dial-out hours to deny access during lunch hours.

3. You have a branch office connected to your main office through a dial-on-demand Integrated Services Digital Network (ISDN) connection. You want to stop Hypertext Transfer Protocol (HTTP) requests from initiating the connection. How can you achieve this goal?

Configure an IP demand-dial filter at both routers to initiate connections for all traffic except that destined for TCP port 80.

4. Your main office is connected to a branch office through demand-dial routing. Each router is configured to call or answer the call of the other router as needed. However, the Finance Department has asked you to ensure that telephone connection charges between demand-dial routers be predominantly incurred by the main office. How can you achieve this goal?

Configure callback on the main office router so that when this router is the answering router, it will drop the call and call back the branch office router.

Page 9-51

Exercise 1: Configuring NAT Through a Demand-Dial Interface

6. Answer the following question: Which NAT service can be configured on this tab?

DHCP allocator

8. Answer the following question: Which NAT function can be configured on this tab?

DNS Proxy

Page 9-52

Exercise 2: Viewing and Configuring NAT Features

8. Answer the following question: Which physical interface owns the public address that the NAT service has mapped to the private address of Computer2?

The modem on Computer1

5. Answer the following questions:

a. Do these configuration parameters require that the address pool you assign to the external interface be a contiguous address space?

Yes

      b. Using Calculator, determine which subnet mask you must assign to the address pool 207.46.200.0–207.46.207.255.

      255.255.248.0

      c. What is the maximum number of deployable addresses contained within a pool assigned a subnet mask of 255.255.255.248?

      6

  8. Answer the following question: When would you use the Reservations button in configuring NAT properties?

    You would use the Reservations button if you had a pool of external addresses and wanted to map one particular public address to a particular internal computer.

  14. Answer the following questions: By default, does your router block outsiders from pinging your external interface? By default, does your router block insiders from pinging your external interface?

    Yes; no

Page
9-55

Lesson 3 Review

  1. You add a new computer to provide Internet connectivity to your network, which consists of a single subnet of client computers with static addresses ranging between 192.168.0.1 through 192.168.0.65 and critical servers with static addresses ranging between 192.168.0.100 through 192.168.0.120. After configuring ICS on the new computer, still none of the computers can connect to the Internet. What is the simplest way to solve the problem?

    Configure the client computers to obtain an address automatically and the critical servers to specify a default gateway of 192.168.0.1.

  2. Your network has 11 critical servers assigned various static addresses in the range 192.168.0.1–192.168.0.20. After you configure ICS on your network, users can no longer log on to the network, and network computers can no longer locate domain controllers or connect to network objects specified by name. Assuming that you cannot change the addresses of the critical servers, how can you best solve the problem?

    Use NAT instead of ICS to provide Internet connectivity. Assign the NAT server an unused address in the range of the critical servers. Configure the critical servers to specify the NAT server as the default gateway.

  3. Your network has critical servers assigned static addresses in the range 10.0.0.1–10.0.0.20. Client computers have been assigned static addresses in the range 10.0.0.21–10.0.0.100. None of the currently assigned network addresses should be changed. You configure a NAT server to distribute IP addresses in the same IP subnet as the current computers and to provide Internet connectivity. However, the computers on your network still cannot connect to the Internet. What is the most likely cause of the problem?

You have to configure the network computers to use the NAT server as the default gateway. (Do not configure a default gateway on the NAT computer itself.)

4. Your NAT server uses a DSL connection. From your ISP, you have obtained a block of eight addresses to be mapped to the external interface of the NAT computer. How can you configure this?

Configure the public interface to use an address pool. Define the pool by specifying the range of addresses you have obtained from the ISP.

Page 9-67

Lesson 4 Review

1. What is a weakness of RIP authentication?

Passwords are sent over the network in plaintext.

2. Besides using RIP authentication, how can you deter rogue routers from providing incorrect routes to your network routers through RIP?

Configure peer filtering on your RIP routers.

3. Name five advantages of OSPF over RIP.

Scalability, lack of a 15-hop limit, faster convergence times, less use of network bandwith, and loopfree OSPF-calculated routes.

4. You want to deploy one DHCP server on your network that consists of two subnets. What are two methods that will enable you to achieve this task?

You can separate the two subnets with an RFC 1542–compatible router and enable BOOTP forwarding, or you can configure a DHCP relay agent on the subnet that does not have the DHCP server.

Page 9-73

Lesson 5 Review

1. Your organization uses a proprietary protocol named XCA that communicates over two separate TCP ports. You have been asked to allow external users to communicate with users on your internal network by means of XCA. What is the minimum number of packet filters you must create on your Windows Server 2003 remote access server that will enable XCA connections to and from your internal network?

Four

2. You have deployed a Windows Server 2003 computer running the Routing And router to function as a simple firewall. How many packet filters do you need to create to support remote access to a VPN server through L2TP/IPSec? Assume that you want to provide the strictest security standards.

Twelve

3. Which ports and protocol numbers must you leave open to support access to a PPTP-type VPN server located behind a firewall? Which ports and protocol numbers must you leave open to support access to an L2TP/IPSec-type VPN server located behind a firewall?

For PPTP, TCP port 1723 and protocol number 47. For L2TP/IPSec, UDP ports 4500 and 500 and protocol number 50.

Page
9-75

Case Scenario Exercise

1. Company executives want to improve router security on the network and have made clear that they would not be satisfied with a solution that merely authenticates routers with a plaintext password. What other measures can you take to ensure that rogue routers are not deployed on the network and that network routes are not intercepted? (Choose all that apply.)

   a. Deploy Active Directory directory service.

   b. Configure RIP to use autostatic routes.

   c. Configure RIP neighbors.

   d. Configure peer filtering.

   e. Configure route filtering.

   a, c, d, e

2. How can you ensure that only members of the R&D Subnet 2 can access the route to the new secure subnet?

   a. Deploy OSPF on the network and configure the router connected to the secure subnet as an area border router.

   b. Configure peer filtering on the router connected to the secure subnet.

   c. Encrypt the routes using MPPE.

   d. Do not deploy a routing protocol on the router connected to the secure subnet. Configure workstations in R&D Subnet 2 with static routes to the secure subnet.

   d

3. A team of 20 of Fabrikam's scientists are conducting research for 10 months in Ottawa, Ontario. They have set up a computer network that they want to connect periodically to the main office in Ithaca. How can you ensure that the incoming calls you receive to the network router at the main office are in fact originating from the router at the temporary Ottawa office?

   a. Configure the answering router at the Ithaca office to authenticate all incoming calls.

   b. Configure callback on the answering router at the Ithaca office.

   c. Configure callback on the calling router at the Ottawa office.

   d. Disable autostatic routes on both routers.

   b

Page
9-77

Troubleshooting Lab

6. On Computer1, review the NAT configuration in the Routing And Remote Access console. What is the error in the configuration? Write your answer in the space provided.

The demand-dial interface added to the NAT protocol, Remote Router, is incorrectly configured as the interface connected to the private network.

10 Configuring and Managing Remote Access

Exam Objectives in this Chapter:

- Configure Routing And Remote Access user authentication
  - ❏ Configure remote access authentication protocols
  - ❏ Configure Internet Authentication Service (IAS) to provide authentication for Routing And Remote Access clients
  - ❏ Configure Routing And Remote Access policies to permit or deny access
- Manage Remote Access
  - ❏ Manage Routing And Remote Access routing interfaces
  - ❏ Manage devices and ports
  - ❏ Manage routing protocols
  - ❏ Manage Routing And Remote Access clients
- Implement secure access between private networks
- Troubleshoot user access to remote access services
  - ❏ Diagnose and resolve issues related to remote access VPNs
  - ❏ Diagnose and resolve issues related to establishing a remote access connection
  - ❏ Diagnose and resolve user access to resources beyond the remote access server
- Troubleshoot Routing And Remote Access routing
  - ❏ Troubleshoot router-to-router VPNs

Why This Chapter Matters

This chapter describes, step-by-step, how to configure remote access to a network through dial-up and virtual private network (VPN) connections. Remote access to corporate networks is expected by employers and employees alike, but deploying this feature securely is no simple matter. By explaining the concepts and procedures behind remote access addressing, authentication, authorization, and troubleshooting, this chapter enables you to configure remote access connectivity in a secure and manageable fashion.

Lessons in this Chapter:

- Lesson 1: Configuring Remote Access Connections .10-3

- Lesson 2: Authorizing Remote Access Connections 10-24

- Lesson 3: Implementing VPNs 10-49

- Lesson 4: Deploying the Internet Authentication Service 10-69

Before You Begin

To complete this chapter, you must have

- Networked two computers, named Computer1 and Computer2, each running Microsoft Windows Server 2003. Computer1 should be assigned a static address of 192.168.0.1/24, and Computer2 should be configured to obtain an address automatically. Computer2 should also have an alternate configuration address of 192.168.0.2/24.

- A separate phone line available to each computer (Recommended).

- Two Internet service provider (ISP) accounts, or one account that can can legally be used to connect two separate computers to the Internet simultaneously. (Recommended).

- Installed a DNS server on Computer1, which hosts an Active Directory–integrated primary zone named domain1.local.

- Configured Computer1 as a domain controller in the domain1.local domain and Computer2 as a member of the domain. The domain functional level should be Windows 2000 mixed.

- Installed a DHCP server on Computer1. The DHCP server should be authorized in the domain and include the scope Test Scope whose IP address range is 192.168.0.11–192.168.0.254. Through DHCP options, the scope assigns a router (gateway) of 192.168.0.1, a DNS server of 192.168.0.1, and a DNS domain name of domain1.local. The scope should be activated. Computer2 should have received its current IP configuration from this DHCP server.

Lesson 1: Configuring Remote Access Connections

Enabling users to connect to a network through a remote access connection such as a dial-up line requires several steps of preparation. Included among these steps are implementing an addressing solution that allows the dial-up clients to communicate on the remote network and configuring user authentication by implementing an appropriate authentication protocol.

After this lesson, you will be able to

- Configure remote access addressing
- Configure a dial-up remote access server
- Configure a dial-up remote access client
- Configure Routing And Remote Access user authentication
- Configure remote access authentication protocols

Estimated lesson time: 75 minutes

Using Dial-Up Networking

Remote access typically occurs through either a dial-up or a VPN connection. In this lesson, the steps necessary to configure remote access addressing and authentication are presented in the context of dial-up networking. Figure 10-1 illustrates this type of scenario.

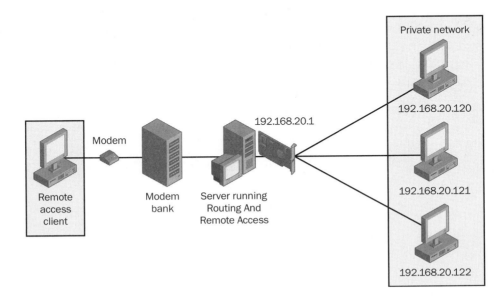

Figure 10-1   Dial-up networking scenario

In the scenario, the dial-up client is configured to connect through the Point-to-Point Protocol (PPP) to a Windows Server 2003 computer running Routing And Remote Access. This connection is typically established over a public switched telephone network (PSTN) telephone line, but it can also be established over an Integrated Services Digital Network (ISDN) or X.25 network.

The remote access server, also called the network access server (NAS), answers each simultaneous call from dial-up clients by means of a separate modem. You can install these modems in a modem bank, as shown in Figure 10-1, or you can install them in the remote access server itself.

Dial-up access requires configuration both at the client and at the server. On the client side, you must configure a dial-up connection to the remote access server through the New Connection Wizard. To configure remote access on the server side, you can use either the Routing And Remote Access Server Setup Wizard or the server properties dialog box in the Routing And Remote Access console.

> **Note**   The Routing And Remote Access Server Setup Wizard is available only when Routing And Remote Access has not yet been configured on your server. To open the Routing And Remote Access Server Setup Wizard, right-click the server icon in the Routing And Remote Access console and then click Configure And Enable Routing And Remote Access.

Using Remote Access Client Addressing

Each remote computer that connects to a remote access server is automatically provided with an Internet Protocol (IP) address during the PPP connection establishment process. The remote access server obtains the IP addresses allocated to remote access clients either from an existing DHCP server or from a static range of IP addresses.

You control how IP addresses are allocated in one of two places: the IP Address Assignment page of the Routing And Remote Access Server Setup Wizard, as shown in Figure 10-2, or the IP Address Assignment area of the server's IP properties in Routing And Remote Access, as shown in Figure 10-3.

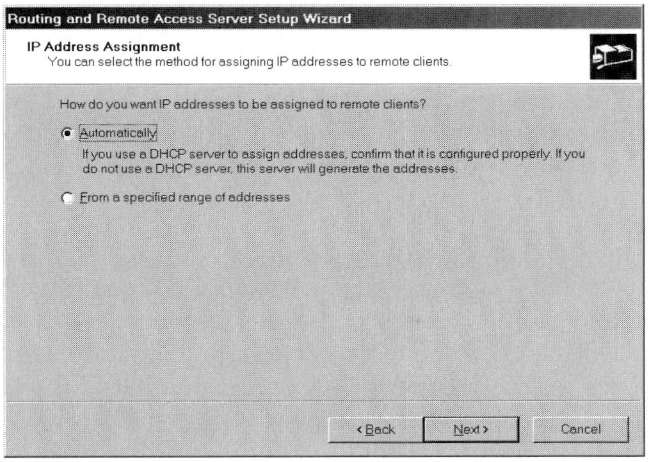

Figure 10-2   Configuring address assignment in the Routing And Remote Access Server Setup Wizard

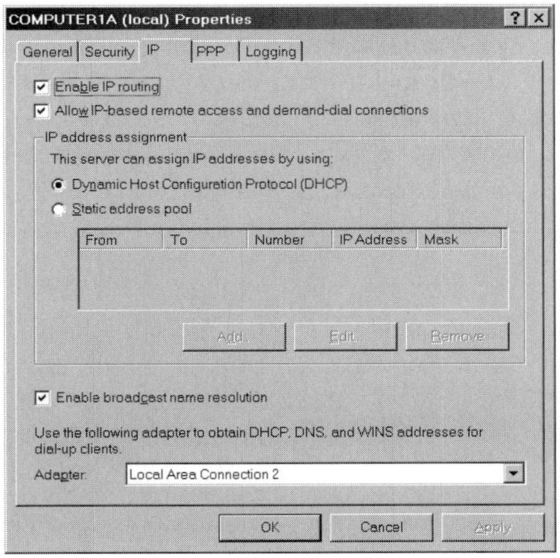

Figure 10-3   Configuring address assignment in server properties

DHCP

If DHCP is already deployed on your network, you should configure the remote access server to distribute addresses through the existing DHCP server. If the DHCP server does not lie within broadcast range of the remote access server, you must configure a DHCP relay agent on the remote access server, or on the same network segment as the remote access server.

When configured to obtain addresses for distribution from a DHCP server, the remote access server obtains a block of 10 addresses upon startup. The remote access server then uses the first of these addresses for itself and assigns subsequent addresses to TCP/IP-based remote access clients as they connect. When more than 10 IP addresses are needed at any given time, the remote access server obtains more blocks of 10 addresses as needed. If a DHCP server is not available when Routing And Remote Access is started, the remote access client instead assigns itself an address within the Automatic Private IP Addressing (APIPA) range from 169.254.0.1 through 169.254.255.254. This range normally does not allow connectivity to the remote access network.

> **Exam Tip**   For the exam, you need to be familiar with the way Routing And Remote Access obtains and distributes IP addresses. Know also that remote access malfunctions if Routing And Remote Access is unable to acquire 10 free leases from a DHCP server. A common sign of this malfunctioning is the presence of an APIPA address on the remote access client. Finally, remember that an APIPA address might also be a sign that you need to configure a DHCP server or DHCP relay agent on the remote access server's network segment.

Static Address Pool

When no DHCP server has been deployed on your network, you can configure the remote access server to assign addresses through a static address pool, as shown in Figure 10-4. Typically, the address pool is defined as a range that is logically connected but non-overlapping with the range of addresses beyond the remote access server. For example, if the internal address of the remote access server is 192.168.1.1/24, you could safely define your address pool as a section of the 192.168.1.0/24 range that does not include any addresses assigned to computers on the internal network.

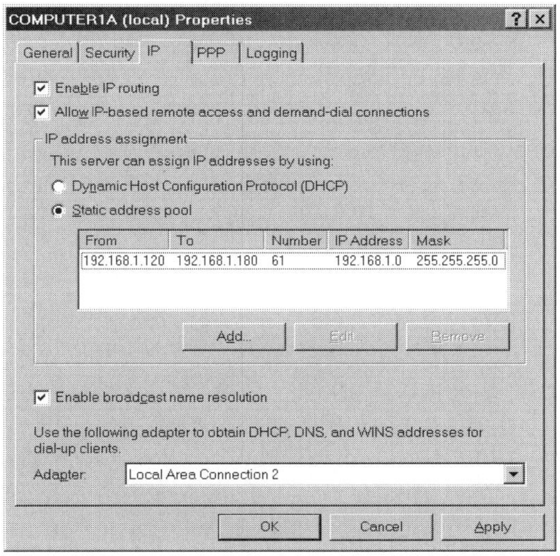

Figure 10-4   Configuring an address pool for remote access clients

If you define the static IP address pool as a distinct subnet (or set of subnets) logically separate from the subnets to which the remote access server is directly connected, you must configure the routers on your network with information about the new subnet. This configuration is identical to the configuration you would perform if you added a logical subnet to the remote access server's physical network segment. Specifically, the routers on your network must forward packets destined for the remote clients to the remote access server's network segment. For information on configuring routing protocols and static routes, see Chapter 9, "Routing with Windows Server 2003."

Configuring Remote Access Authentication

After the dial-up client calls the remote access server and the necessary IP addresses are assigned, the credentials submitted with the connection must be authenticated. *Authentication* is the process of validating—through verification of a password or of alternative credentials such as a certificate or smart card—that the user is in fact the person he or she claims to be. Remote access authentication precedes domain logon authentication; if a dial-up user is attempting to log on to a domain remotely, the dial-up connection must be authenticated, authorized, and established before normal domain logon occurs.

> **Note** Whereas *authentication* refers to the process of validating user credentials, *authorization* refers to the process of allowing users access to resources. After remote access authentication occurs, the remote access connection is authorized only if the proper permissions are configured both on the dial-up properties of the user account and in the remote access policy that applies to the connection. Lesson 2 of this chapter discusses remote access policy and authorization.

To log on to a domain through a dial-up connection, select the Log On Using Dial-Up Connection check box in the Log On To Windows dialog box. Then, after you type in your user name and password and click OK, a Network Connections dialog box appears. In the Choose A Network Connection drop-down list box, select the network connection you have configured for dial-up remote access, and then click Connect. The dial-up connection is then attempted; remote access authentication and authorization follow. Typically, the user name, domain, and password configured for the connection match those you submit for domain logon, but these two sets of credentials are configured and authenticated separately.

If the credentials of the dial-up connection are successfully authenticated, and if the remote access connection is authorized, a remote access connection is established. Normal domain logon follows; the credentials you enter in the Log On To Windows dialog box are submitted to a domain controller for domain authentication.

> **Note** If a user is dialing in to a stand-alone remote access server that is not a member of a domain, the user must first log on to his or her local computer or local domain before attempting to connect to the remote server. In this case, the remote computer's verification of the credentials sent with the dial-up connection is the only authentication that needs to occur before the connection is authorized and established. These credentials must be stored in the answering server's local Security Accounts Manager (SAM) before the user connects.

Performing Authentication Through RADIUS

You can configure remote access authentication to be performed through Windows authentication or through a Remote Authentication Dial-In User Service (RADIUS) server. Through Windows authentication, when the remote user attempts to dial up to a workgroup computer, the NAS authenticates the connection by verifying the user name and password in the server's own local security database. When the remote user attempts to dial in to a domain, the NAS forwards the authentication request to the domain controller. However, when you configure a RADIUS server to authenticate remote access connections, the NAS passes both the authentication and authorization responsibility to a central server running IAS. (Lesson 4 discusses RADIUS authentication in more detail.)

You choose this authentication method in one of two places: on the Managing Multiple Remote Access Servers page of the Routing And Remote Access Server Setup Wizard, as shown in Figure 10-5, or on the Security tab of the server properties dialog box in the Routing And Remote Access console, as shown in Figure 10-6. Note that in the wizard, if you want to use Windows authentication instead of a RADIUS server, you should select the option No, Use Routing And Remote Access To Authenticate Connection Requests.

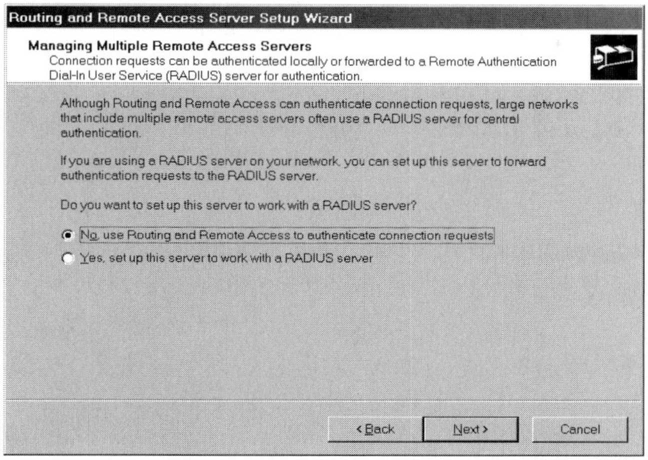

Figure 10-5   Choosing a remote access authentication method

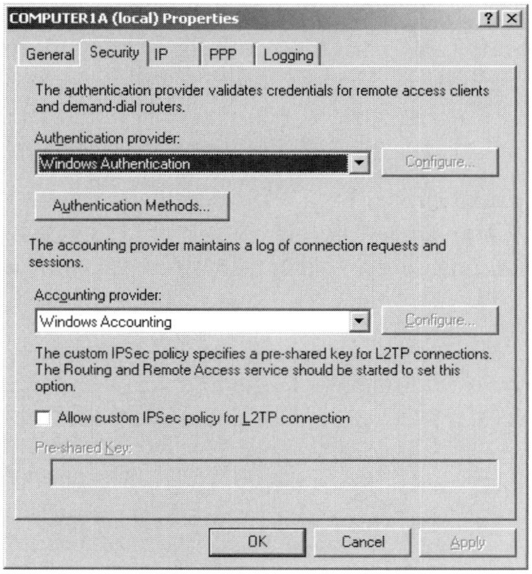

Figure 10-6   Choosing a remote access authentication method

Choosing Authentication Protocols

To authenticate the credentials submitted by the dial-up connection, the remote access server must first negotiate a common authentication protocol with the remote access client. Most authentication protocols offer some measure of security so that user credentials cannot be intercepted, and authentication protocols in Windows clients and servers are assigned a priority based on this security level.

The authentication protocol chosen for a remote access connection is always the most secure of those enabled in the client connection properties, the remote access server properties, and the remote access policy applied to the connection. For all remote access clients and servers running either Microsoft Windows 2000, Microsoft Windows XP, or the Microsoft Windows Server 2003 family, by default, that protocol is Microsoft Challenge Handshake Authentication Protocol version 2 (MS-CHAP v2).

The following is a complete list of the authentication protocols supported by Routing And Remote Access in Windows Server 2003 (listed in order from most secure to least secure):

- **Extensible Authentication Protocol-Transport Level Security (EAP-TLS)**   A certificate-based authentication based on *EAP*, an extensible framework that supports new authentication methods. Typically used in conjunction with smart cards. Supports encryption of both authentication data and connection data. Note that EAP-TLS is not supported on stand-alone servers; the remote access server running Windows Server 2003 must be a member of a domain.

- **MS-CHAP v2**   A mutual authentication method offering encryption of both authentication data and connection data. New cryptographic key is used for each connection and each direction of transmission. Enabled by default in Windows 2000, Windows XP, and Windows Server 2003.

- **MS-CHAP v1**   A one-way authentication method offering encryption of both authentication data and connection data. Same cryptographic key is used in all connections. Supports older Windows clients such as Microsoft Windows 95 and Microsoft Windows 98. (See Table 10-2 for a complete list of operating system compatibility.)

- **Extensible Authentication Protocol-Message Digest 5 Challenge Handshake Authentication Protocol (EAP-MD5 CHAP)**   A version of CHAP (see next bullet) ported to the EAP framework. Supports encryption of authentication data through the industry-standard MD5 hashing scheme. Provides compatibility with non-Microsoft clients, such as those running Mac OSX. Does not support encryption of connection data.

- **Challenge Handshake Authentication Protocol (CHAP)**   A generic authentication method offering encryption of authentication data through the MD5 hashing scheme. Provides compatibility with non-Microsoft clients. The group policy applied to accounts using this authentication method must be configured to store passwords using reversible encryption. (Passwords must be reset after this new policy is applied.) Does not support encryption of connection data.

- **Shiva Password Authentication Protocol (SPAP)** A weakly encrypted authentication protocol offering interoperability with Shiva remote networking products. Does not support encryption of connection data.

- **Password Authentication Protocol (PAP)** A generic authentication method that does not encrypt authentication data. User credentials are sent over the network in plaintext. Does not support encryption of connection data.

- **Unauthenticated access** Not an authentication protocol but a configuration option which—when set on the network access server and remote access policy applied to the connection—allows remote access connections to connect without submitting credentials. Can be used to troubleshoot or test remote access connectivity. Does not support encryption of connection data.

Table 10-1 provides information to help you map your requirements to the appropriate protocol.

Table 10-1   Authentication Protocol Features

Requirement	Select
Encrypted authentication support for Windows 95, Windows 98, Microsoft Windows Millennium Edition (Me), or Microsoft Windows NT 4 remote access clients (native support)	MS-CHAP v1
Encrypted authentication support for Windows 95, Windows 98, Windows Me, or Windows NT 4 remote access clients (with the latest Dial-Up Networking upgrade)	MS-CHAP v2 (VPN only for Windows 95)
Encrypted authentication support for certificate-based Public Key Infrastructure (PKI), such as those used with smart cards (when the remote access server is a member of a Windows 2000 Server or Windows Server 2003 domain)	EAP-TLS
Encrypted authentication support for other Windows 2000, Windows XP, and Windows Server 2003 remote access clients	MS-CHAP v2
Mutual authentication (client and server always authenticate each other)	EAP-TLS, MS-CHAP v2
Support for encryption of connection data	MS-CHAP v1, MS-CHAP v2, EAP-TLS

Table 10-1   Authentication Protocol Features

Requirement	Select
Encrypted authentication support for remote access clients that use other operating systems	CHAP, EAP-MD5 CHAP
Encrypted authentication support for remote access clients running Shiva LAN Rover software	SPAP
Unencrypted authentication when the remote access clients support no other protocol	PAP
Authentication credentials not supplied by the remote access client	Unauthenticated access

Exam Tip   Expect to see more than one exam question in which you need to know the features and limitations of various authentication protocols. At a minimum, you should be able to answer the following:

- Which protocol is required for smart cards?
- Which protocol requires the use of certificates?
- What are the special configuration requirements for CHAP?
- When is MS-CHAP v1 the best choice for authentication method?
- When is MS-CHAP v2 the best choice for authentication method?
- What is the difference between authentication encryption and data encryption?
- Which protocols support data encryption?
- Which protocol does not encrypt authentication data?
- Which protocols support mutual authentication?
- Which protocol must be used in conjunction with Active Directory directory service domains?

Authentication Protocols: Operating System Support   Table 10-2 summarizes the authentication protocols supported in various versions of Windows.

Table 10-2   Authentication Protocol Support

Dial-Up Networking Client	Supported Authentication Protocol	Unsupported Authentication Protocol
Windows Server 2003, Windows XP, Windows 2000	MS-CHAP, CHAP, SPAP, PAP, MS-CHAP v2, and EAP	
Windows NT version 4	MS-CHAP, CHAP, SPAP, PAP, and MS-CHAP v2 (with Windows NT 4.0 Service Pack 4 and later)	EAP

Table 10-2   Authentication Protocol Support

Dial-Up Networking Client	Supported Authentication Protocol	Unsupported Authentication Protocol
Windows NT version 3.5 and version 3.51	MS-CHAP, CHAP, SPAP, and PAP	MS-CHAP v2, and EAP
Windows Me, Windows 98	MS-CHAP, CHAP, SPAP, PAP, and MS-CHAP v2 (with Windows 98 Service Pack 1 and later)	EAP
Windows 95	MS-CHAP, CHAP, SPAP, and PAP (with the Windows Dial-Up Networking 1.3 Performance & Security Upgrade for Windows 95 and later)	MS-CHAP v2 and EAP

Exam Tip   For the exam, remember that Windows 95 does not support MS-CHAP v2 over dial-up connections. Also remember that EAP is supported only by Windows Server 2003, Windows XP, and Windows 2000.

Configuring Authentication Protocols: Client Side

To view or modify the authentication protocols enabled for a dial-up connection on the remote access client, open the properties dialog box of the dial-up connection on the client, and click the Security tab.

Figure 10-7 shows the default settings on the Security tab: the Typical (Recommended Settings) option is selected, and the Allow Unsecured Password setting is selected. If you click the Advanced (Custom Settings) option and then click the Settings button, the Advanced Security Settings dialog box opens. This dialog box, also shown in Figure 10-7, reveals the specific authentication protocols enabled by the current setting. Notice that the unencrypted authentication protocol PAP is enabled. The authentication protocol SPAP is also enabled. Although it encrypts authentication data, SPAP is not considered secure because it always sends each password over the network in the same reversibly encrypted form. Thus, the protocol is susceptible to replay attacks.

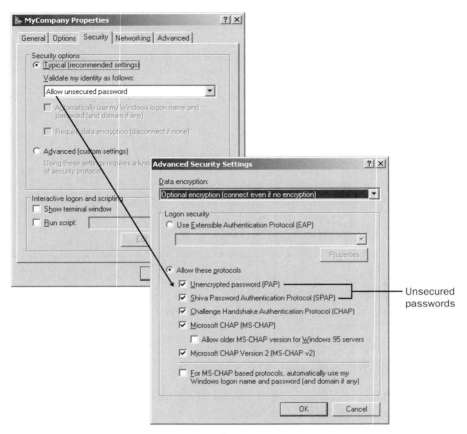

Figure 10-7 Default authentication protocols enabled on the dial-up client

When you select the Require Secured Password setting on the Security tab, as shown in Figure 10-8, the Advanced Security Settings dialog box reveals a different set of enabled authentication protocols. Specifically, only CHAP, MS-CHAP v1, and MS-CHAP v2 are enabled. The less secure PAP and SPAP are no longer available.

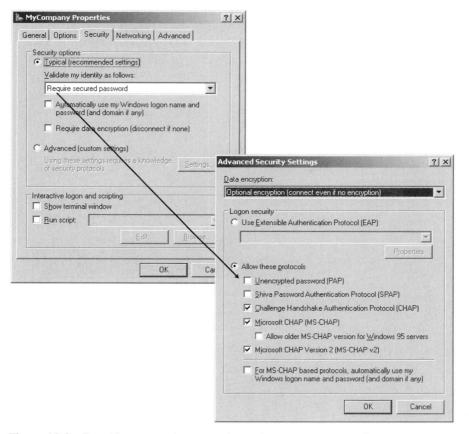

Figure 10-8   Requiring secured passwords on the remote access client

When you select the Require Data Encryption (Disconnect If None) check box, as shown in Figure 10-9, the list of enabled authentication protocols is further restricted. Specifically, only MS-CHAP v1 and MS-CHAP v2 are enabled, and CHAP is no longer available. For all authentication protocols except PAP, authentication data (user name and password) is encrypted. However, the MS-CHAP protocols also support encryption of PPP connection data through Microsoft Point-to-Point Encryption (MPPE). For the connection data to be successfully encrypted, the remote access policy applied to the connection must require data encryption. (Remote access policies do require data encryption by default.)

> **Note** The EAP-TLS authentication protocol also allows for encryption of PPP connection data. However, this protocol requires configuration and is not automatically enabled by the Require Data Encryption (Disconnect If None) setting on the Security tab of the connection.

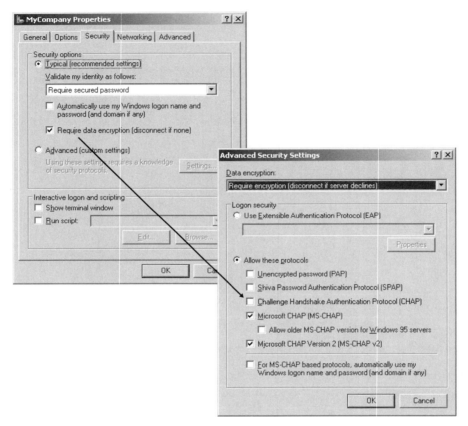

Figure 10-9 Requiring data encryption on the remote access client

Finally, when you select the Use Smart Card setting, as shown in Figure 10-10, only the EAP-TLS authentication protocol is enabled. On the client, the EAP-TLS protocol is designated by the Smart Card Or Other Certificate (Encryption Enabled) selection under the Use Extensible Authentication Protocol (EAP) option.

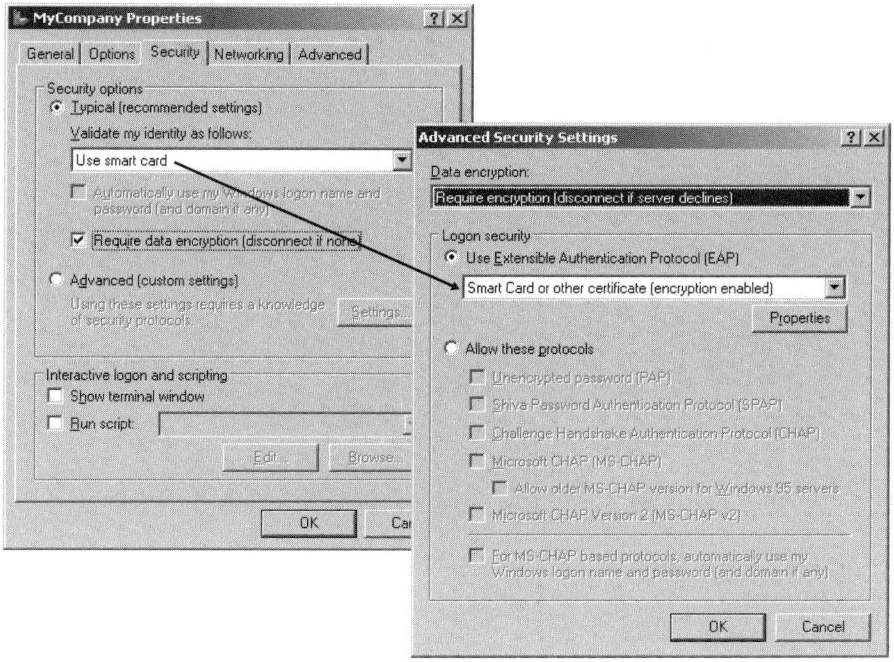

Figure 10-10 Requiring smart card authentication on the remote access client

Configuring Authentication Protocols: Server Side

To view or modify the authentication protocols enabled on the remote access server, right-click the server icon in the Routing And Remote Access console and then click Properties. In the server properties dialog box, select the Security tab. On the Security tab, click the Authentication Methods button to open the Authentication Methods dialog box, shown with its default settings in Figure 10-11.

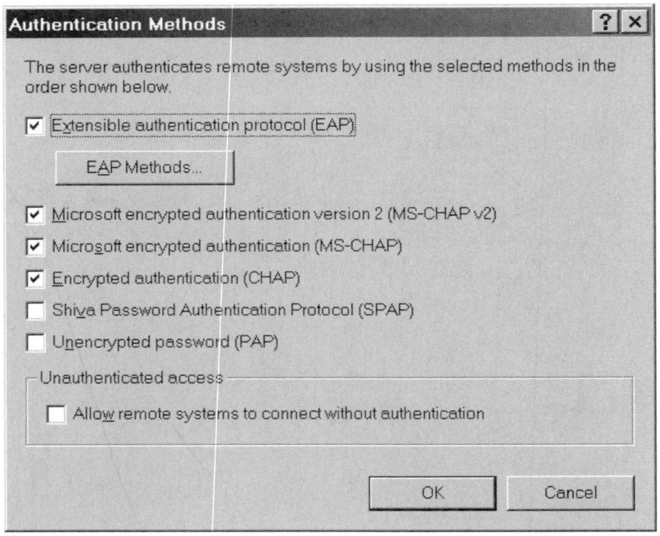

Figure 10-11 Authentication protocols in Routing And Remote Access

Finally, to view or modify the authentication protocols allowed by a remote access policy, select the Remote Access Policies node in the Routing And Remote Access console, double-click the appropriate policy, and then click the Edit Profile button in the policy properties dialog box. In the Edit Dial-In Profile dialog box, select the Authentication tab. Figure 10-12 shows the default settings of this tab. Note that by default, no EAP methods are enabled.

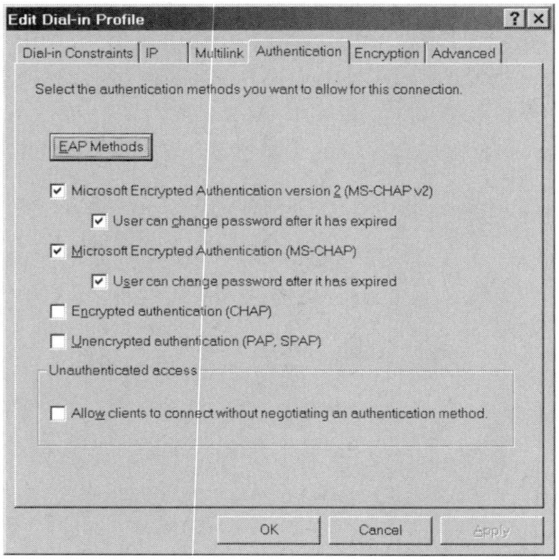

Figure 10-12 Authentication protocols in a remote access policy

Lesson 2 of this chapter covers remote access policies in more detail.

To configure authentication settings in a remote access policy, complete the following steps:

1. Perform one of the following tasks:

   ❑ Open the Routing And Remote Access console and, if necessary, double-click Routing And Remote Access and the server name.

   ❑ Open the Internet Authentication Service console and, if necessary, double-click Internet Authentication Service.

2. In the console tree, click Remote Access Policies.

3. In the details pane, double-click the policy that you want to configure.

4. Click Edit Profile.

5. On the Authentication tab, specify any required settings.

6. Click OK.

Practice: Creating a Dial-Up Access Server

In this practice, you use the Routing And Remote Access Server Setup Wizard to configure Computer1 as a dial-up remote access server.

Exercise 1: Creating a Dial-Up Server by Using the Routing And Remote Access Server Setup Wizard

In this exercise, you log on to Computer1 and remove any previous configuration from Routing And Remote Access. You then run the Routing And Remote Access Server Setup Wizard to begin configuring dial-up remote access to Computer1.

1. From Computer1, log on to Domain1 as Administrator.

2. Click Start, select Administrative Tools, and then click Routing And Remote Access. The Routing And Remote Access console opens.

3. In the console tree, right-click COMPUTER1 (Local), and then click Disable Routing And Remote Access. If this option is not available, go to step 5.

   A message box appears, informing you that you are disabling the router and asking whether you want to proceed.

4. Click Yes.

   A message indicates that the Routing And Remote Access service is stopping.

5. In the console tree, right-click COMPUTER1 (Local), and then click Configure And Enable Routing And Remote Access.

   The Routing And Remote Access Server Setup Wizard appears.

6. Click Next.

   The Configuration page appears.

7. Click Next to accept the default setting, Remote Access (Dial-Up Or VPN).

   The Remote Access page appears.

8. Select the Dial-Up check box, and then click Next.

   The Network Selection page appears.

9. Verify that Local Area Connection is selected (IP Address 192.168.0.1), and then click Next.

   The IP Address Assignment page appears.

10. Click Next to accept the default setting, Automatically.

    The Managing Multiple Remote Access Servers page appears.

11. Click Next to accept the default setting, No, Use Routing And Remote Access.

    The Completing The Routing And Remote Access Server Setup Wizard page appears.

12. Click Finish.

13. If a message appears indicating that you must configure the properties of DHCP Relay Agent, click OK.

    A message indicates that the Routing And Remote Access service is starting. After this, the Routing And Remote Access console shows a new configuration beneath the server icon.

14. Log off Computer1.

Exercise 2: Configuring a Connection to a Dial-Up Server

In this exercise, you configure a dial-up connection on Computer2. To complete this exercise, make sure Computer1 and Computer2 are physically connected to distinct phone lines. This exercise does not complete the configuration of dial-up remote access to Computer1. To finish this process, perform the practice in Lesson 2.

1. From Computer2, log on to Domain1 as Administrator.

2. Open the Network Connections window.

3. From the File menu, select New Connection.

   The New Connection Wizard opens.

4. Click Next.

   The Network Connection Type page appears.

5. Select the Connect To The Network At My Workplace option, and then click Next.

   The Network Connection page appears.

6. Click Next to accept the default selection, Dial-Up Connection.

   The Connection Name page appears.

7. In the Company Name text box, type **MyCompany**, and then click Next.

   The Phone Number To Dial page appears.

8. In the Phone Number text box, type the number of the phone line to which Computer1 is connected, and then click Next.

   The Connection Availability page appears.

9. Click Next to accept the default setting, Anyone's Use.

   The Completing The New Connection Wizard page appears.

10. Click Finish.

    The Connect MyCompany dialog box appears.

11. Click the Properties button.

    The MyCompany Properties dialog box appears.

12. Click the Options tab.

13. Select the Include Windows Logon Domain check box.

14. Click the Security tab.

    Note that Allow Unsecured Password is the default security setting.

15. Click the Advanced (Custom Settings) option, and then click the Settings button.

    The Advanced Security Settings dialog box appears. Note that PAP, SPAP, CHAP, MS-CHAP, and MS-CHAP v2 are enabled.

16. Click the Use Extensible Authentication Protocol (EAP) option.

    The following EAP setting appears: Smart Card Or Other Certificate (Encryption Enabled). This setting corresponds to the EAP-TLS protocol. The use of smart cards through EAP-TLS is the most secure form of authentication in Windows Server 2003 networks.

17. Expand the drop-down list box beneath the Use Extensible Authentication Protocol (EAP) option.

    Note that the only other EAP protocol listed is MD5-Challenge. This protocol is simply a version of CHAP that is performed through EAP messages. It is required in all EAP implementations but is not considered highly secure.

18. Close the list box, and then click Cancel to close the Advanced Security Settings dialog box.

19. On the Security tab, click the Typical (Recommended Settings) option. The Allow Unsecured Password option is selected.

20. Click OK to close the MyCompany Properties dialog box.

    In the Connect MyCompany dialog box, a new Domain text box appears with DOMAIN1 entered.

21. Click Cancel to close the Connect MyCompany dialog box.

22. Log off Computer2.

Lesson Review

The following questions are intended to reinforce key information presented in this lesson. If you are unable to answer a question, review the lesson materials and try the question again. You can find answers to the questions in the "Questions and Answers" section at the end of this chapter.

1. You have configured your remote access server to distribute addresses to remote access clients through a DHCP server. However, you find that your remote access clients assign themselves with only APIPA addresses. Name two possible causes of this scenario.

   _____

   _____

   _____

   _____

2. Which authentication protocol must you use to support the use of smart cards?

   _____

3. Which authentication protocols provide data encryption?

   _____

Lesson Summary

- The Routing And Remote Access server provides IP addressing for remote access clients either through a DHCP server or from a static range of IP addresses. Typically, the clients receive addresses that place them on the same logical subnet as computers immediately beyond the remote access server.

- Remote access authentication precedes domain logon authentication; if a dial-up user is attempting to log on to a domain remotely, the dial-up connection must be authenticated, authorized, and established before normal domain logon occurs.

- Authentication protocols are assigned priority based on security level. The authentication method used in any connection is the most secure protocol enabled on the remote access client, the remote access server, and the remote access policy applied to the connection.

Lesson 2: Authorizing Remote Access Connections

After the credentials submitted with the remote access connection are authenticated, the connection must be authorized. Remote access authorization consists of two steps: first, verification of the dial-in properties of the user account submitted by the dial-up connection, and second, application of the first matching remote access policy listed in the Routing And Remote Access console.

After this lesson, you will be able to

- Configure Routing And Remote Access policies to permit or deny access
- Manage Routing And Remote Access clients
- Diagnose and resolve issues related to establishing a remote access connection
- Diagnose and resolve client access to resources beyond the remote access server

Estimated lesson time: 90 minutes

Configuring Dial-In Properties of the User Account

Dial-in properties, which apply both to direct dial-up and VPN connections, are configured on the Dial-In tab of the user account properties dialog box. If a user is dialing in to a domain, a user account corresponding to the name sent through the dial-up connection must already exist in the domain. Dial-in properties for this account can thus be configured in the Active Directory Users And Computers console. If the user is dialing in to a stand-alone server, however, the account must already exist as a user account in the answering server's local SAM. Dial-in properties for this account can thus be configured in the Local Users And Groups console in Computer Management.

Figure 10-13 shows the Dial-In tab of the user account properties, which is described in the next section.

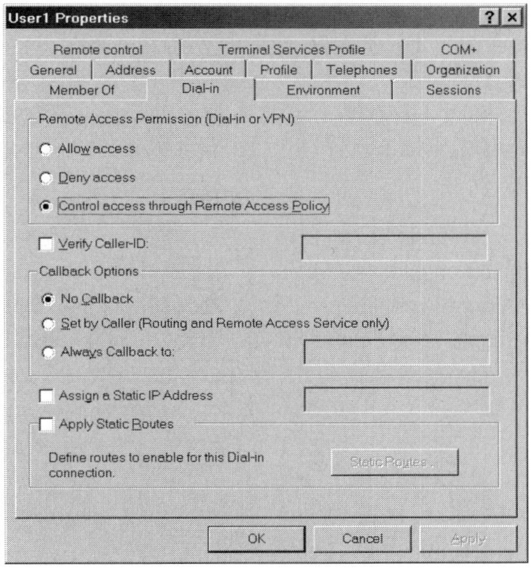

Figure 10-13   Configuring user dial-in properties

Remote Access Permission (Dial-Up or VPN)

You can set the remote access permission for user accounts to any one of the three following levels. In all server environments except Active Directory domains whose functional level is Windows 2000 mixed, the Control Access Through Remote Access Policy option is enabled by default.

Control Access Through Remote Access Policy   This particular option neither blocks nor allows dial-up access for the user. Instead, it specifies that access permissions for the user be determined by first matching the remote access policy applied to the connection. (By default, remote access policies block all remote access connections.)

Deny Access   When you select the Deny Access option, dial-up access for the user account is blocked regardless of other settings or policies applied to the account.

Allow Access   When you select the Allow Access option, dial-up remote access for the user account is permitted, overriding the remote access permission setting in remote access policies. Note that the Allow Access setting does not always prevent remote access policies from blocking remote access; a remote access policy can still restrict the account's remote access through the remote access policy profile. For example, dial-up hours specified in a remote access policy profile might prevent a user account from connecting in the evening hours even when the Allow Access option has been set for the dial-in properties of the user account. However, the Allow Access option specifies that the Deny Remote Access Permission setting in remote access policies is ignored.

> **Important**   By default, Active Directory domains in Windows Server 2003 are installed at the Windows 2000 mixed-mode domain functional level. In this server environment, only Allow Access and Deny Access remote access permissions are available for user accounts. In this case, the Allow Access setting is the default and is the equivalent of the Control Access Through Remote Access Policy setting in all other server environments. No setting at this functional level allows you to override user-level remote access permissions in remote access policies.

Verifying Caller ID

If the Caller ID check box is selected, the server verifies the caller's phone number. If the caller's phone number does not match the configured phone number, the connection attempt is denied.

Caller ID must be supported by the caller, the phone system between the caller and the remote access server, and the remote access server. On a computer running the Routing And Remote Access service, caller ID support consists of call answering equipment that provides caller ID information and the appropriate Windows driver to pass the information to the Routing And Remote Access service.

If you configure a caller ID phone number for a user and you do not have support for the passing of caller ID information from the caller to the Routing And Remote Access service, connection attempts will be denied.

Exploring Callback Options

By default, this setting is configured as No Callback. If the Set By Caller option is selected, the server calls the caller back at a number specified by the caller. If the Always Call Back To option is selected, an administrator must specify a number that the server will always use during the callback process.

> **Exam Tip**   The callback feature requires Link Control Protocol (LCP) extensions to be enabled in Routing And Remote Access server properties. (They are enabled by default.)

Assigning a Static IP Address

You can configure the Assign A Static IP Address setting to assign a specific IP address to a user when a connection is made.

> **Off the Record**   Internet service providers use the Assign A Static IP Address feature to provide customers with a reserved IP address at an extra cost. Now that you know how easy a reserved IP address is to configure, don't let your ISP charge you an exorbitant fee for one!

Applying Static Routes

You can use the Apply Static Routes setting to define a series of static IP routes that are added to the routing table of the server running the Routing And Remote Access service when a connection is made.

Understanding Remote Access Policies

A *remote access policy* is a set of permissions or restrictions, read by a remote access authenticating server, that applies to remote access connections. Many remote access policies can be stored on an authenticating server at any given time, but only one policy can be applied to a connection. To determine which policy is applied, the conditions of each remote access policy are compared individually to the current remote access connection. Only the first matching policy is applied to the remote access connection; if no policy matches the connection, the connection is blocked.

You can view currently configured remote access policies in the Routing And Remote Access console by selecting the Remote Access Policies node in the console tree, as shown in Figure 10-14.

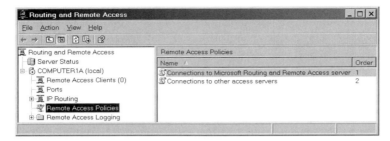

Figure 10-14   Viewing remote access policies

Remote access policies are unique to each local machine but not unique to Routing And Remote Access. Once created, they can be read either by Routing And Remote Access or by a RADIUS server configured on the local machine. Similarly, you cannot remove remote access policies simply by disabling Routing And Remote Access. They are written to the local hard disk and stored until they are specifically deleted either from the Routing And Remote Access console or from the Internet Authentication Service console (the administrative tool for RADIUS servers).

By default, two remote access policies are preconfigured in Windows Server 2003. The first default policy is Connections To Microsoft Routing And Remote Access Server. This policy is configured to match every remote access connection to the Routing And Remote Access service. When Routing And Remote Access is reading this policy, the policy naturally matches every incoming connection. However, when the policy is being read by a RADIUS server, network access might be provided by a non-Microsoft vendor; consequently, this policy will not match those connections.

The second default remote access policy is Connections To Other Access Servers. This policy is configured to match every incoming connection regardless of network access server type; however, because the first policy matches all connections to Routing And Remote Access, only connections to other remote access servers read and match the policy when the default policy order is not changed. Unless the first policy is deleted or the default policy order is rearranged, this second policy can be read only by RADIUS servers.

Policy Conditions

Each remote access policy is based on policy conditions that determine when the policy is applied. For example, a policy might include a condition that Windows-Groups matches DOMAIN1\Telecommuters; this policy would then match a connection whose user belongs to the Windows global security group Telecommuters. Figure 10-15 shows such a policy.

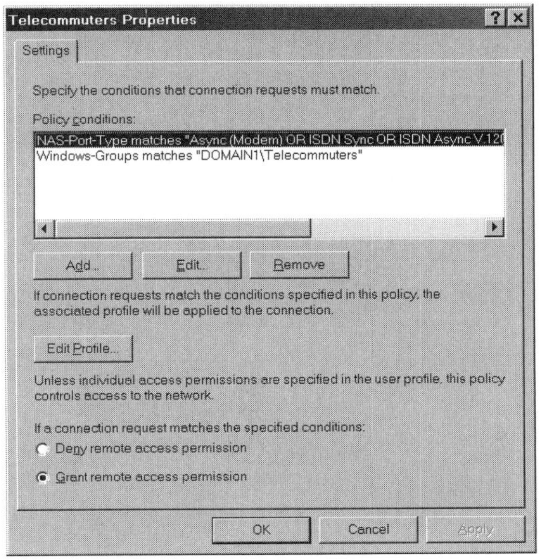

Figure 10-15   Conditions matching dial-up telecommuters

Clicking the Add button opens the Select Attribute dialog box, which allows you to add a new category for a remote access policy condition. For example, the NAS-IP-Address attribute allows a RADIUS server to distinguish remote access clients connecting through a particular remote access server (as distinguished by IP address). Figure 10-16 shows the Select Attribute dialog box and its associated set of configurable attributes.

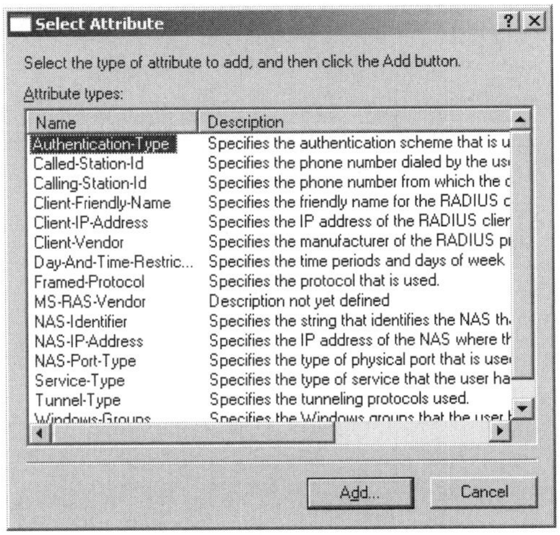

Figure 10-16   Policy condition attributes

By clicking the Add button in the Select Attribute dialog box, you can open a dialog box that allows you to configure the condition for a specific attribute. For example, if you click the Add button when the Authentication-Type attribute is selected, the Authentication-Type dialog box opens, as shown in Figure 10-17. This dialog box allows you to choose which remote access connections, as specified by authentication protocol, will match the policy. In the example given, the policy is configured to match unauthenticated connections. Similarly, you can specify the particular elements for any attribute you choose to serve as the conditions for a policy.

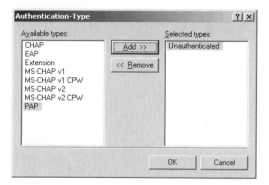

Figure 10-17 Examples of policy condition elements

 Note Only membership of global security groups can serve as a remote policy condition. You cannot specify membership of universal or domain local security groups as the condition for a remote access policy.

Remote Access Permission

Every remote access policy specifies whether the connection matching the policy is allowed or denied. These permission settings correspond to the Grant Remote Access Permission option and the Deny Remote Access Permission option, respectively, which can be seen in Figure 10-15. Remember that this setting is normally overridden by the Allow Access option (outside of Windows 2000 mixed-mode domains) or the Deny Access option in the dial-in properties for an individual user account.

Policy Profile

A remote access policy profile consists of a set of dial-up constraints and properties that can be applied to a connection. You can configure a remote access policy profile by clicking the Edit Profile button in the policy properties dialog box, shown in Figure 10-15. Clicking this button opens the Edit Dial-In Profile dialog box, shown in Figure 10-18. By default, the policy profile is not configured; consequently, no additional restrictions or properties are applied to the connection.

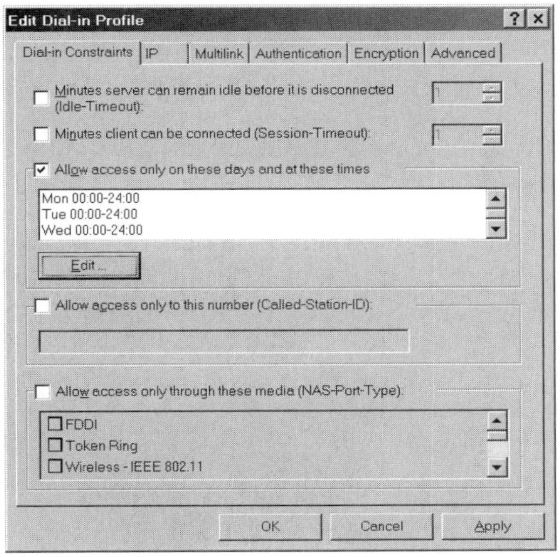

Figure 10-18   A configured dial-up remote access policy profile

The following sections describe the six tabs found in the policy profile.

Dial-In Constraints Tab   This tab allows you to set the following dial-up constraints:

- Minutes Server Can Remain Idle Before It Is Disconnected

- Minutes Client Can Be Connected

- Allow Access Only On These Days And At These Times

- Allow Access Only To This Number

- Allow Access Only Through These Media

IP Tab   You can set IP properties that specify IP address assignment behavior. You have the following options:

- Server Must Supply An IP Address.

- Client May Request An IP Address.

- Server Settings Determine IP Address Assignment (the default setting).

- Assign A Static IP Address. The IP address assigned is typically used to accommodate vendor-specific attributes for IP addresses.

You can also use the IP tab to define IP packet filters that apply to remote access connection traffic. Packet filters are discussed in more detail in Lesson 5 of Chapter 9, "Routing with Windows Server 2003."

Multilink Tab   You can set Multilink properties that both enable Multilink and determine the maximum number of ports (modems) that a Multilink connection can use. Additionally, you can set Bandwidth Allocation Protocol (BAP) policies that both determine BAP usage and specify when extra BAP lines are dropped. The Multilink and BAP properties are specific to the Routing And Remote Access service. By default, Multilink and BAP are disabled.

The Routing And Remote Access service must have Multilink and BAP enabled for the Multilink properties of the profile to be enforced.

Authentication Tab   You can set authentication properties to both enable the authentication types that are allowed for a connection and specify the EAP type that must be used. Additionally, you can configure the EAP type. By default, MS-CHAP and MS-CHAP v2 are enabled. In Windows Server 2003, you can specify whether users can change their expired passwords by using MS-CHAP and MS-CHAP v2 (enabled by default).

The Routing And Remote Access service must have the corresponding authentication types enabled for the authentication properties of the profile to be enforced.

Encryption Tab   Windows Server 2003 supports two general methods for the encryption of remote access connection data: Rivest-Shamir Adleman (RSA) RC4, and Data Encryption Standard (DES). *RSA RC4* is the family of algorithms used in MPPE, the encryption type used with the MS-CHAP or EAP-TLS authentication protocols in both dial-up and Point-to-Point Tunneling Protocol (PPTP)–based VPN connections. DES, meanwhile, is the general encryption scheme most commonly used with Internet Protocol Security (IPSec), the security standard used with the Layer 2 Tunneling Protocol (L2TP) authentication protocol in VPNs. (VPNs, PPTP, and L2TP/IPSec are discussed in Lesson 3 of this chapter.)

Both MPPE and IPSec support multiple levels of encryption, as shown in Table 10-3.

Table 10-3   Encryption Types

Encryption Type	Level of Encryption Supported
MPPE Standard	40-bit, 56-bit
MPPE Strong	128-bit
IPSec DES	56-bit
IPSec Triple DES	168-bit

The settings on the Encryption tab in a remote access policy profile, shown in Figure 10-19, enable you to specify allowable encryption levels in a manner independent of encryption type. However, the nature of each encryption level varies with the encryption scheme used, as explained after the figure.

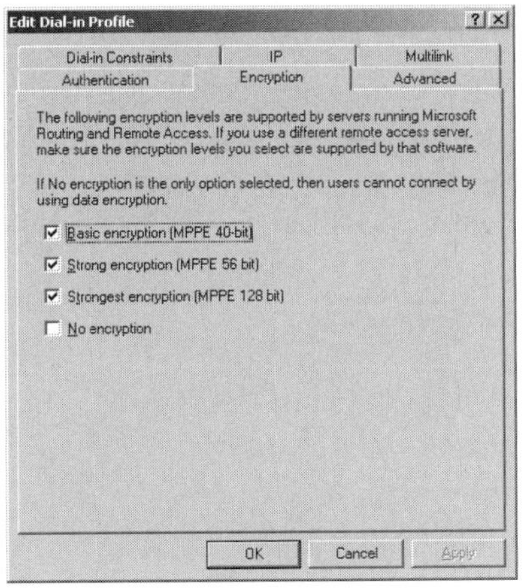

Figure 10-19   Remote access policy profile Encryption tab

- **Basic Encryption (MPPE 40-Bit)**   For dial-up and PPTP-based VPN connections, MPPE is used with a 40-bit key. For L2TP/IPSec VPN connections, 56-bit DES encryption is used.

- **Strong Encryption (MPPE 56-Bit)**   For dial-up and PPTP VPN connections, MPPE is used with a 56-bit key. For L2TP/IPSec VPN connections, 56-bit DES encryption is used.

- **Strongest Encryption (MPPE 128-Bit)**   For dial-up and PPTP VPN connections, MPPE is used with a 128-bit key. For L2TP/IPSec VPN connections, 168-bit triple DES encryption is used.

- **No Encryption**   This option allows unencrypted connections matching the remote access policy conditions. To require encryption, clear this option.

> **Exam Tip**   You need to be familiar with all of the encryption settings for the exam. For example, you should know that the Basic Encryption setting refers to 40-bit MPPE encryption with PPTP/dial-up and 56-bit DES encryption with L2TP/IPSec.

Advanced Tab   You can set advanced properties to specify the series of RADIUS attributes that are sent back by the IAS server to be evaluated by the NAS server/ RADIUS client. These settings are used only by RADIUS servers and are not read by Routing And Remote Access.

Exploring Remote Access Authorization Scenarios

The following selection presents a summary of the remote access authorization process. In each scenario, authorization settings at the remote access server differ when User1, a member of the Telecommuters group, attempts to connect through a dial-up line. Figure 10-20 shows the order of remote access policies defined at the server.

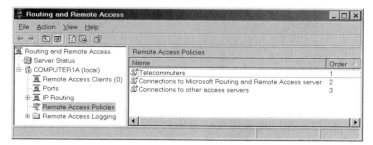

Figure 10-20   List of defined remote access policies

> **Note**   In each of the following scenarios, it is assumed that the domain functional level is not set to Windows 2000 mixed.

For each of User1's connection attempts, up to three sets of permissions and settings are applied, in the following order:

1. The dial-in properties of the user account provided with the connection

2. The access permission defined in the first matching remote access policy

3. The profile settings accompanying the first matching remote access policy

In scenario #1, shown in Figure 10-21, the remote access permission for User1's account has been left at the default setting: Control Access Through Remote Access Policy. Consequently, the remote access permission specified in the first matching remote access policy is applied to the connection. The first matching remote access policy, named Telecommuters, is configured to allow remote access for the Telecommuters security group.

Once the remote access permission of the Telecommuters policy is applied, the profile of the policy is verified. In this case, the Telecommuters policy profile permits access on all days except Sundays. The end result of these server settings is that User1 is permitted access unless the day is Sunday.

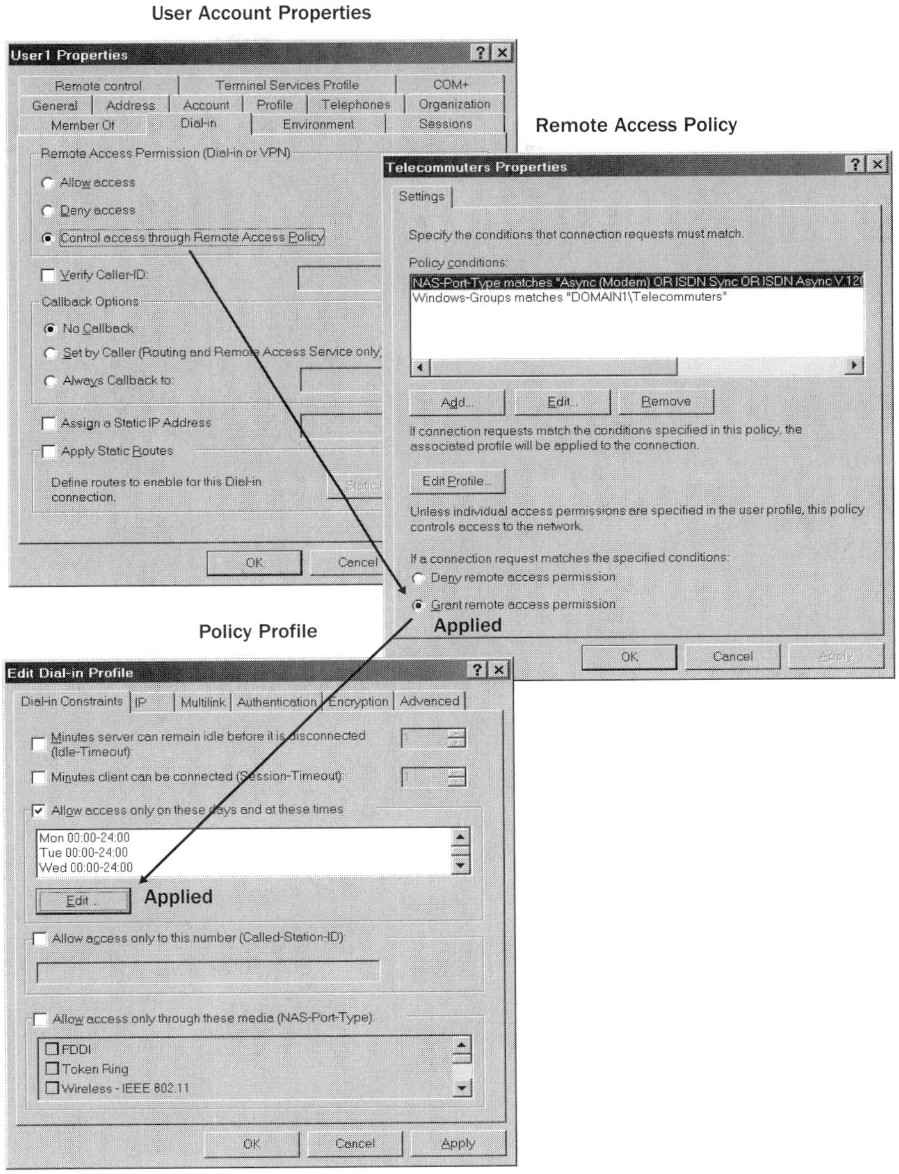

User Account Properties

Remote Access Policy

Policy Profile

Figure 10-21   Remote access authorization scenario #1

In scenario #2, shown in Figure 10-22, the remote access permission for User1's account is again left at the default setting. As a result, the remote access policy again determines the remote access permission. In this case, however, the Telecommuters policy has been configured to deny access to the Telecommuters group. As a result, User1's connection attempt is blocked, and the policy profile is not read.

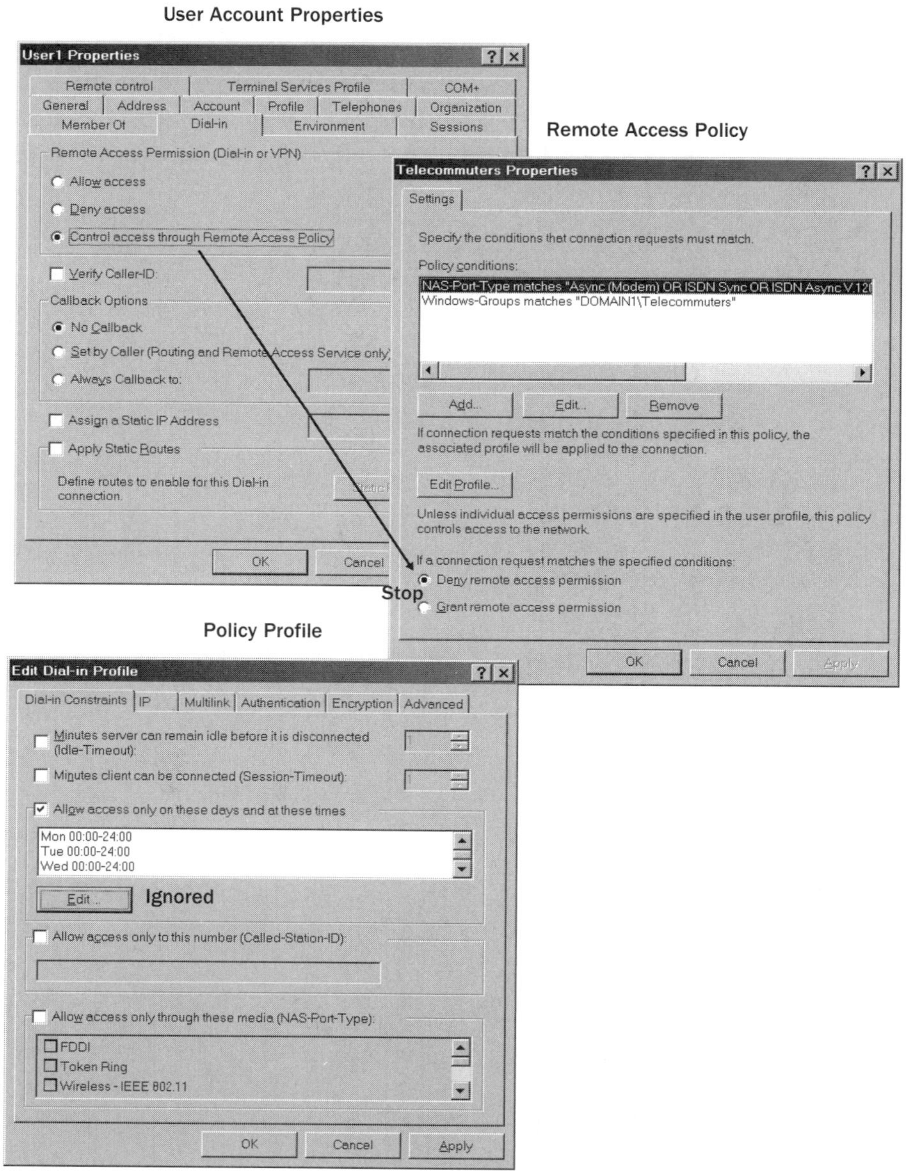

Figure 10-22 Remote access authorization scenario #2

Scenario #3 is illustrated in Figure 10-23. In this scenario, the remote access permission for User1's account has been modified from the default setting to Allow Access. In this case, the remote access permission setting is ignored in the Telecommuters remote access policy. However, the policy profile is still read and applied. As a result, User1 is permitted remote access unless the day is Sunday.

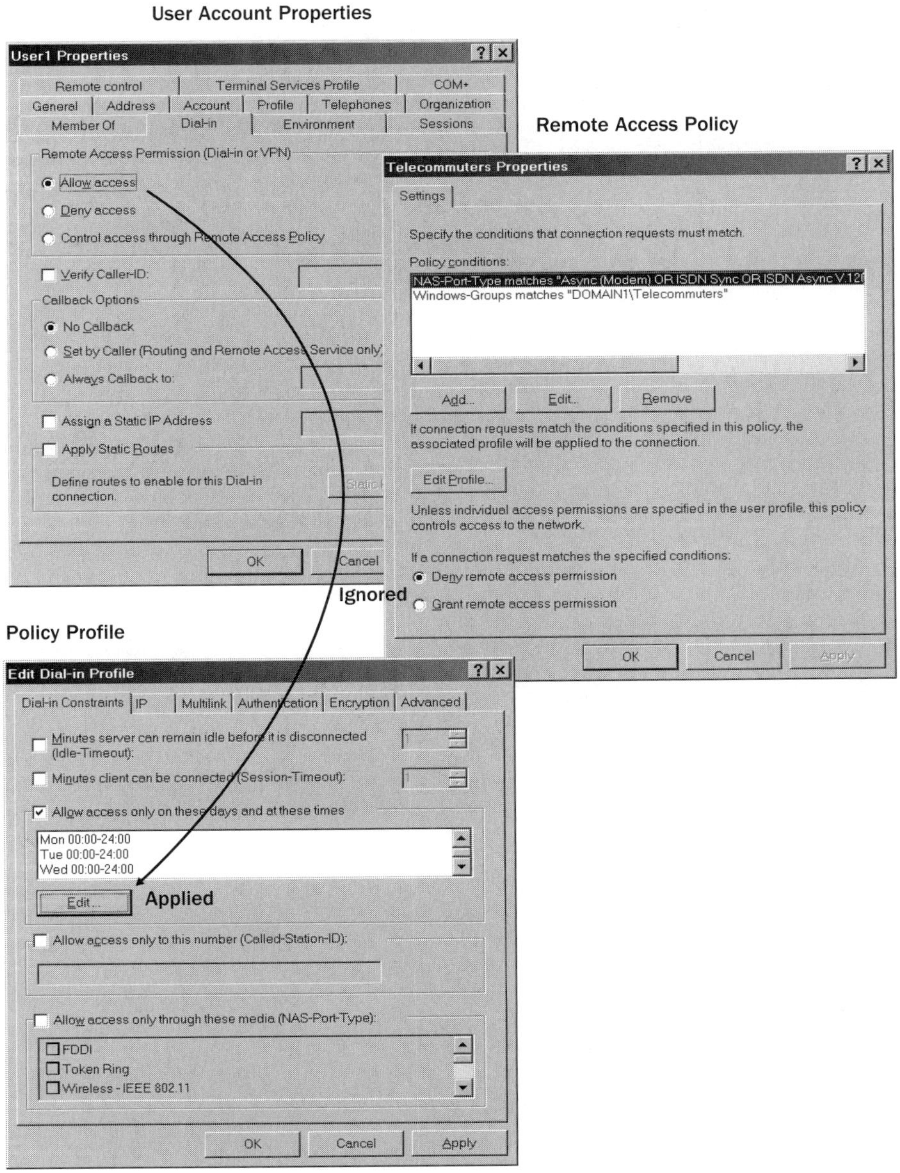

User Account Properties

Remote Access Policy

Policy Profile

Ignored

Applied

Figure 10-23   Remote access authorization scenario #3

In scenario #4, illustrated in Figure 10-24, the remote access permission for User1's account has been modified from the default setting to Deny Access. As a result of this server setting, the remote access connection is blocked, and no remote access policy or accompanying profile is read.

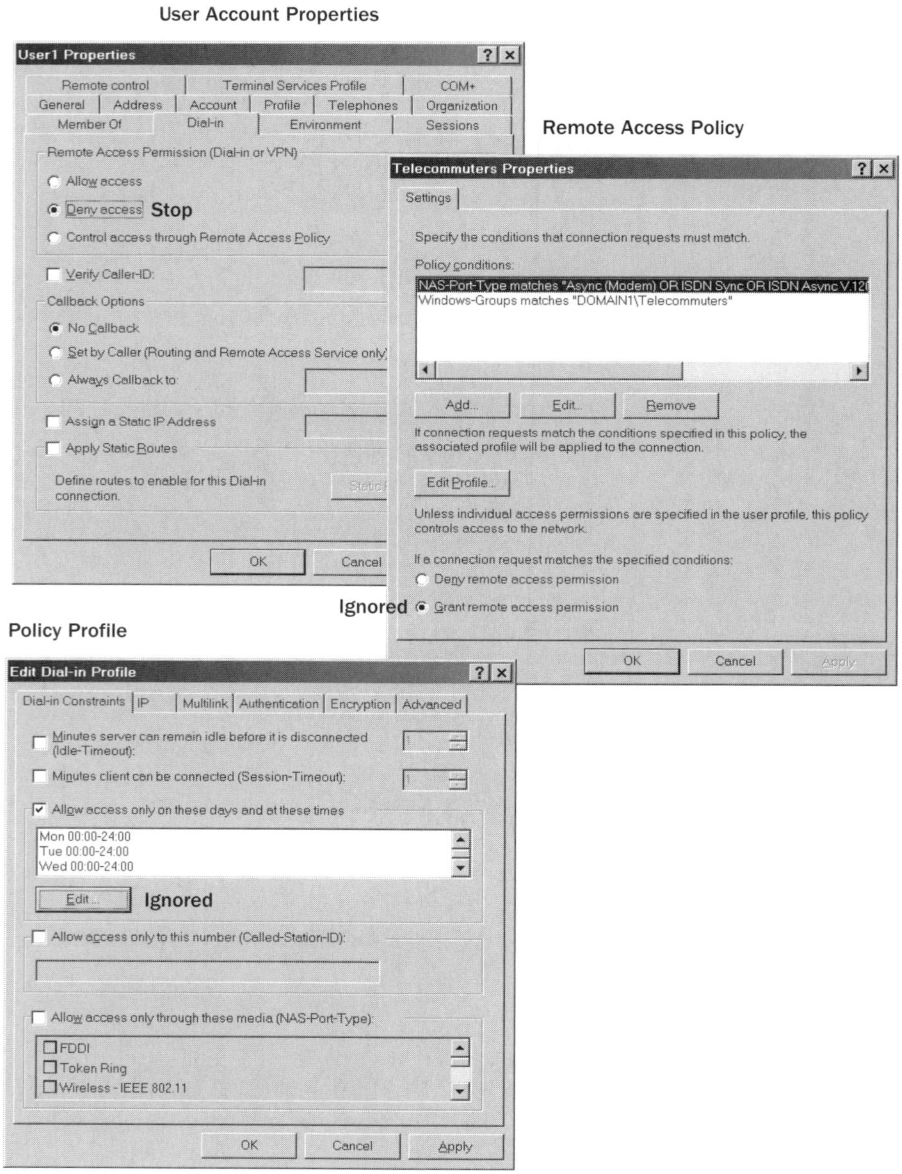

Figure 10-24   Remote access authorization scenario #4

In the final remote access authorization scenario, the remote access policies are deleted at the server. As a result, no matching policy can be applied to the inbound remote access connection. The connection request is thus denied regardless of the remote access permission for User1's account, which in this case is set to Allow Access. Scenario #5 is illustrated in Figure 10-25.

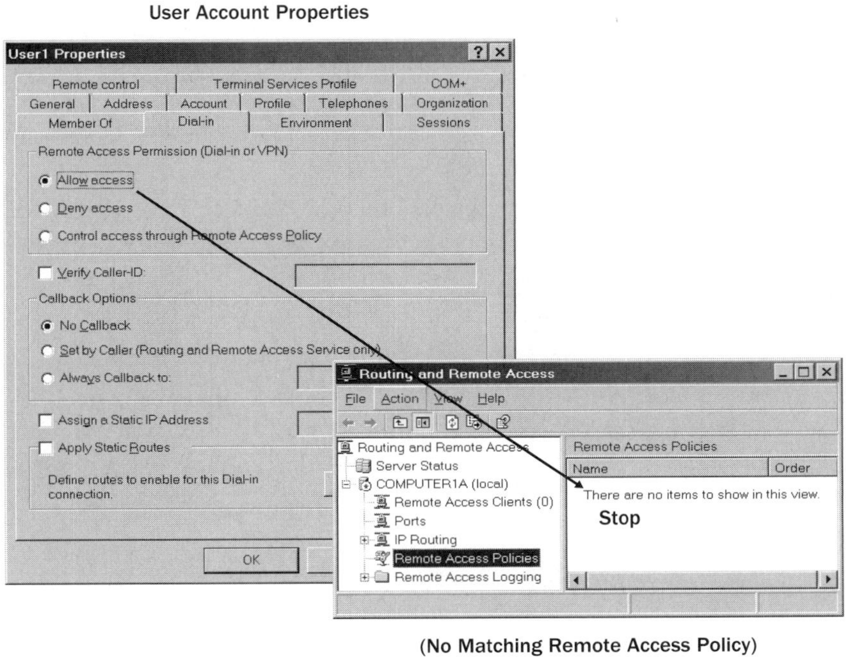

Figure 10-25   Remote access authorization scenario #5

Troubleshooting Dial-Up Remote Access Connections

Use the following checklist to troubleshoot dial-up remote access connections:

- Verify that the Remote Access Server option is enabled on the server properties General tab in the Routing And Remote Access console.

- If you have configured a static address pool, verify that the pool is large enough to accommodate the number of simultaneous client connections needed.

- If you have configured the remote access server to assign addresses through a DHCP server, verify that the address scope defined at the DHCP server is large enough to accommodate blocks of 10 addresses requested by the remote access server.

- Verify that enough modem devices are configured in the Ports node to accommodate the number of simultaneous client connections needed.

- Verify that the dial-up client, the remote access server, and the remote access policy are configured to use at least one common authentication protocol.

- Verify that the dial-up client, the remote access server, and the remote access policy are configured to use at least one common encryption strength.

- Verify that the dial-up remote access connection has the appropriate permissions through dial-in properties of the user account and remote access policies.

- Verify that the remote access server (or RADIUS server) computer is a member of the RAS And IAS Servers security group in the local domain.

- Verify that the settings of the remote access policy profile are not in conflict with properties of the remote access server.

- Verify that, if MS-CHAP v1 is being used as the authentication protocol, the user password does not exceed 14 characters.

Configuring Access Beyond the Remote Access Server

To configure a computer running Windows Server 2003 as a remote access server, you can simply run the Routing And Remote Access Server Setup Wizard and specify a Remote Access (Dial-Up Or VPN) configuration. However, even when properly configured, such a remote access server does not allow dial-up connections to see or use network resources beyond the remote access server.

To allow clients access to resources beyond the remote access server, you need to enable the remote access server as a router. To achieve this goal, select the Router check box on the General tab in the remote access server properties in the Routing And Remote Access console. This tab, and the required configuration, is shown in Figure 10-26.

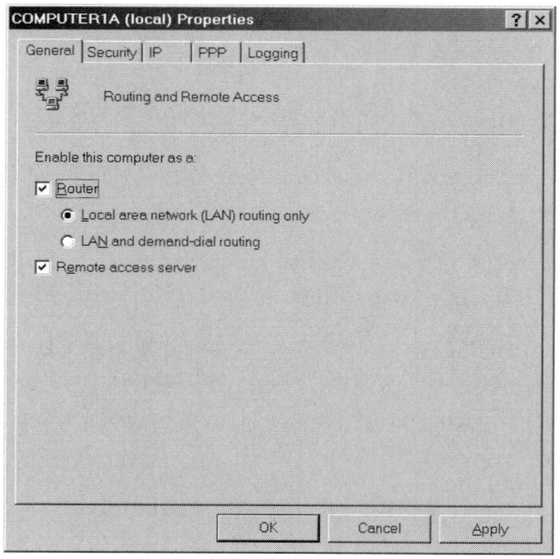

Figure 10-26   Configuring access beyond the remote access server

Access beyond the server depends on the proper configuration of other aspects of the remote access server as well. First, you need to make sure the remote access server assigns clients (through a DHCP server or static address pool) with an IP address configuration that places them on the same logical subnet as the computers immediately beyond the remote access server. If instead you assign remote access clients with an IP configuration that places them on a logical subnet distinct from the subnet beyond the answering modem, you must configure a routing protocol on the remote access server; or you can configure static routes on your network routers to identify the location of the remote access subnet.

> **Note**   When you deploy a routing protocol on the remote access server, you also need to configure neighboring routers to accept updates from that server.

Second, on the IP tab of the server properties dialog box in the Routing And Remote Access console, you need to verify that the Enable IP Routing check box is selected. (It is enabled by default.)

Third, for the use of network functions (such as a computer browsing through My Network Places) that require broadcast NetBIOS name resolution, and for conditions in which the remote access clients are not found on a distinct subnet, you must verify that the Enable Broadcast Name Resolution check box is selected. This check box is also found on the IP tab and is also selected by default. If this setting is not enabled, a WINS server must be configured on the network to provide NetBIOS name resolution, and the client must be configured with the address of the WINS server.

Troubleshooting Access Beyond the Remote Access Server

Use the following checklist to troubleshoot access to resources beyond the remote access server:

- Verify that the Router option is selected on the General tab of the server properties dialog box.

- Verify that the LAN And Demand-Dial Routing option is selected on the General tab of the server properties dialog box.

- Verify that the Enable IP Routing option is selected on the IP tab of the server properties dialog box.

- If your remote access clients are assigned an address range that places them on a subnet that is logically separate from the one immediately beyond the answering router, verify that the routers on your network have been configured with the location of the remote access subnet.

■ Verify that the Enable Broadcast Name Resolution option is selected on the IP tab of the server properties dialog box. This step is necessary only if your remote network uses NetBIOS name resolution, does not use WINS, and your remote access clients are located on the same logical subnet as the NetBIOS services to which they will connect.

Managing Remote Access Clients

Using the Routing And Remote Access console, you can view currently connected remote access clients in the details pane by selecting the Remote Access Clients node in the console tree. You can then manage these clients by viewing their status, disconnecting them, or sending a message to one or all of them. The following procedures describe how to perform each of these four functions.

To view connected remote access clients, complete the following steps:

1. Open the Routing And Remote Access console.
2. In the console tree, click the Remote Access Clients node.
3. In the details pane, right-click a user name, and then click Status.

To disconnect a remote access client, complete the following steps:

1. Open Routing And Remote Access.
2. In the console tree, click the Remote Access Clients node.
3. In the details pane, right-click a user name, and then click Disconnect.

To send a message to a single remote access client, complete the following steps:

1. Open Routing And Remote Access.
2. In the console tree, click the Remote Access Clients node.
3. In the details pane, right-click a user name, and then click Send message.
4. In Send Message, type your message, and then click OK.

To send a message to all remote access clients, complete the following steps:

1. Open Routing And Remote Access.
2. In the console tree, right-click the Remote Access Clients node.
3. Click Send To All.
4. In the Send Message dialog box, type your message, and then click OK.

Managing Clients Through Remote Access Policies

Besides being able to manage currently connected clients, you can also manage remote access clients in general by defining rules through remote access policies. For example, you can manage clients by restricting idle time, connection time, or access to specific parts of your internal network. You can configure these restrictions through a policy profile and apply them to any client type.

Practice: Deploying Remote Access

In this practice, you create a domain user account and a corresponding remote access policy. You then dial in with the user account to test the configuration.

Exercise 1: Creating a Telecommuter Group and User Account

In this exercise, you create a new user account named User1. You then make this account a member of a new global security group named Telecommuters.

1. From Computer1, log on to Domain1 as Administrator.

2. Click Start, select Administrative Tools, and then click Active Directory Users And Computers.

   The Active Directory Users And Computers console opens.

3. In the console tree, right-click the Users folder, select New, and then click User.

   The New Object – User dialog box appears.

4. In the Full Name text box, type **user1**.

5. In the User Logon Name text box, type **user1**.

6. Click Next.

   A new set of options appears in the New Object – User dialog box.

7. In the Password dialog box and the Confirm Password dialog box, enter a strong password for the User1 account.

8. Clear the User Must Change Password At Next Logon check box.

9. Click Next and then click Finish.

10. On Computer1, open a command prompt and enter **net group telecommuters /add/domain**.

    This command creates a new global security group named Telecommuters in the domain.

    At the command prompt, type **net group telecommuters user1/add/domain**.

    This command adds the User1 account to the Telecommuters group.

11. While the Users folder is selected in the Active Directory Users And Computers console tree, right-click empty space in the details pane, and then click Refresh.

   The new security group Telecommuters is now listed in the details pane.

12. In the Active Directory Users And Computers details pane, double-click User1.

   The User1 Properties dialog box opens.

13. Click the Dial-In tab.

14. Look at the options available on this tab. In the Remote Access Permissions area, only two options are available: Allow Access and Deny Access. Note that by default the Remote Access Permission is set to Deny Access.

15. Click OK.

16. In the Active Directory Users And Computers console tree, right-click the domain1.local icon, and then click Raise Domain Functional Level.

   The Raise Domain Functional Level dialog box appears.

17. From the Select An Available Domain Functional Level drop-down list box, select Windows Server 2003.

18. Click Raise.

   A message appears, indicating that the operation cannot be reversed.

19. Click OK.

   A message appears, indicating that the functional level was raised successfully.

20. Click OK.

21. Restart Computer1.

22. After Computer1 has finished restarting, log on to Domain1 again as Administrator.

23. Open the Active Directory Users And Computers console.

24. Open the User1 properties dialog box and select the Dial-In tab.

   In the Remote Access Permission area, a third option is now available: Control Access Through Remote Access Policy.

25. Note that the Control Access Through Remote Access Policy option is selected by default. Click OK.

26. Close the Active Directory Users And Computers console.

Exercise 2: Creating a Remote Access Policy for Telecommuters

In this exercise, you create a remote access policy named Telecommuters. You then browse the settings associated with this policy.

1. If you have not already done so, from Computer1, log on to Domain1 as Administrator.

2. Open the Routing And Remote Access console.

3. In the console tree, right-click the Remote Access Policies node, and then click New Remote Access Policy.

   The New Remote Access Policy Wizard appears.

4. Click Next.

   The Policy Configuration Method page appears.

5. In the Policy Name text box, type **telecommuters**, and then click Next.

   The Access Method page appears.

6. Click the Dial-Up option, and then click Next.

   The User Or Group Access page appears. The Group option is selected by default.

7. Click the Add button.

   The Select Groups page appears.

8. In the Enter Object Names To Select text box, type **telecommuters**, and then click OK.

   DOMAIN1\telecommuters is listed in the Group Name area.

9. Click Next.

   The Authentication Methods page appears.

10. Leave MS-CHAP v2 as the only selected authentication protocol, and click Next.

    The Policy Encryption Level page appears.

    These settings refer to connection data encryption, not password encryption. Basic, Strong, and Strongest are selected by default. Because MS-CHAP v2 supports data encryption through MPPE, these settings ensure that data sent over the MyCompany connection from Computer2 will be encrypted.

11. Click Next to accept the default settings.

    The Completing The New Remote Access Policy Wizard page appears.

12. Click Finish.

    In the details pane of the Routing And Remote Access console, you can now see that when the Remote Access Policies node is selected, the Telecommuters remote access policy is the first listed.

13. Double-click the Telecommuters policy in the details pane of the Routing And Remote Access console.

    The Telecommuters Properties dialog box appears.

14. Examine the settings configured in this dialog box. Notice that the first policy condition matches all dial-up connections, and the second policy condition matches the global security group DOMAIN1\telecommuters. Notice also that the setting assigned to the policy is Grant Remote Access Permission.

15. Click the Edit Profile button.

    The Edit Dial-In Profile dialog box appears.

16. Take a few minutes to browse the configuration options available on the six tabs of this dialog box. Do not change any settings.

17. Click Cancel to close the Edit Dial-In Profile dialog box.

18. Click Cancel to close the Telecommuters Properties dialog box.

19. Log off Computer1.

Exercise 3 (Optional): Testing the Remote Access Configuration

In this exercise, you use the User1 account to dial in to Computer1 from Computer2. Perform this exercise only if you have a separate phone line available for each computer. If you meet this requirement, connect each computer to one of the phone lines before beginning the exercise.

> **Note**   Disconnect the local cabling between the two computers for this exercise so you can see that the connection between the computers is occurring over the dial-up line.

1. On Computer2, press Ctrl+Alt+Del to open the Log On To Windows dialog box.

2. On the Log On To Windows screen, select the Log On Using Dial-Up Connection check box.

3. In the User Name text box, type **user1**.

4. In the Password text box, type the strong password you have assigned to the User1 account.

5. In the Log On To drop-down list box, select DOMAIN1.

6. Click OK.

    The Network Connections dialog box appears.

7. In the Choose A Network Connection drop-down list box, make sure MyCompany is selected, and then click Connect.

    The Connect MyCompany dialog box appears. The User Name text box already includes the name *user1*, the Password text box already includes a hidden password, and the Domain text box already includes the domain *DOMAIN1*.

8. Click the Dial button.

   The Connecting MyCompany message box displays the status of the connection. After the configured phone number is dialed, the telephone rings twice, and the Routing And Remote Access service on Computer1 answers. The user name and password are verified, and then the computer is registered on the network. Finally, the Connecting MyCompany message box closes, and domain logon proceeds using the supplied credentials.

9. Once domain logon of User1 has completed, open a Microsoft Internet Explorer window. Dismiss any messages or warnings that you receive.

10. In the Address text box, type **computer1.domain1.local**, and then press Enter.

    The shares available on Computer1 appear in the Internet Explorer window, which demonstrates that User1 has successfully connected to Computer1 over a dial-up connection.

11. Close Internet Explorer, and then log off Computer2.

Lesson Review

The following questions are intended to reinforce key information presented in this lesson. If you are unable to answer a question, review the lesson materials and try the question again. You can find answers to the questions in the "Questions and Answers" section at the end of this chapter.

1. When you create a new domain in a Windows Server 2003 network, the default domain functional level is Windows 2000 mixed. How is the Allow Access setting in the dial-in properties of a user account different in this environment from that in other server environments?

   _____

   _____

   _____

   _____

2. A remote access connection has been authenticated, the dial-in properties of the user account are set to Allow Access, and the first matching remote access policy is set to Grant Remote Access Permission. If the remote client still cannot successfully connect to the remote access server, what is the most likely explanation?

   _____

   _____

3. How can you enforce 128-bit encryption for dial-up connections at the remote access server?

_____

_____

Lesson Summary

- If a remote access connection is successfully authenticated, the connection must be authorized before remote access can occur. Remote access authorization occurs in two stages: first, the dial-in properties of the user account are verified, and then the first matching remote access policy is applied to the connection.

- The dial-in properties of the user account include a remote access permission setting that consists of three options: Allow Access, Deny Access, and Control Access Through Remote Access Policy.

- A remote access policy consists of a policy condition that describes the type of connection to which the policy is applied. Remote access policies are ordered, and only the first matching remote access policy is applied to a remote access connection. Remote access policies include a grant or deny access permission setting that can be overridden by user account settings. Remote access policies also include a policy profile that applies various attributes to the connection, such as authentication requirements, encryption requirements, or packet filters.

- To enable access for clients beyond the remote access server, the remote access server must be enabled as a router, and the IP routing option must be enabled in the Routing And Remote Access server properties.

- You can manage remote access client connections through the Remote Access Clients node in the Routing And Remote Access console.

Lesson 3: Implementing VPNs

A virtual private network allows users to securely connect through the Internet to a remote private network. In a remote access VPN scenario using Windows Server 2003, a single user connects across the Internet to a Windows Server 2003 computer running Routing And Remote Access. In an extranet scenario, private local area networks (LANs) are joined across the Internet by two Windows Server 2003 computers running Routing And Remote Access.

After this lesson, you will be able to

- Configure a remote access VPN
- Diagnose and resolve issues related to remote access VPNs
- Provide secure access between private networks through a router-to-router VPN
- Troubleshoot router-to-router VPNs
- Manage devices and ports
- Manage packet filters
- Troubleshoot client access to remote access services

Estimated lesson time: 75 minutes

Understanding Virtual Private Networks

Virtual private networks are logical networks that physically span the Internet. With a VPN, private packets are first encrypted and then encapsulated within a public packet addressed to the remote VPN server. This routing information allows the encrypted payload of private data to "tunnel through" the public network to reach its endpoint. Upon receiving the encapsulated data through a VPN tunnel, the VPN server then removes the public header and decrypts the private payload. Figure 10-27 illustrates this concept.

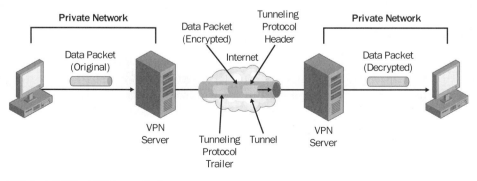

Figure 10-27   VPN tunneling

An important feature of VPNs is that the public physical network through which private data is sent becomes transparent to the two endpoints of communication, as illustrated in Figure 10-28. Two computers, Computer1 and Computer2, are physically connected only through the Internet. The transparency of this physical link is revealed in Figure 10-28 by the results of the Tracert command run at each computer. Although many hops separate the two computers, each appears to the other as only one hop away through the VPN connection. Communication occurs between the two private IP addresses, each within the 192.168.10.0 subnet, as if the computers were both located on an isolated network segment.

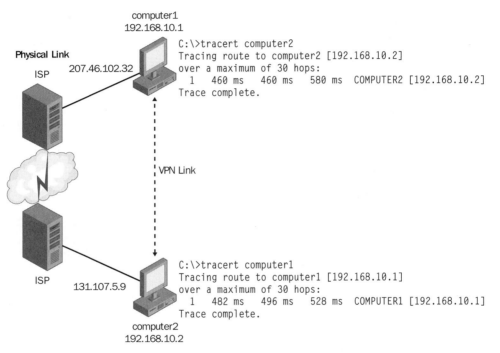

Figure 10-28   VPN example

Exploring VPN Deployment Scenarios

VPNs are typically deployed either to allow users remote access to a network or to connect two or more private networks. The following section describes the configuration requirements for these scenarios and for a third, mixed scenario in which the VPN server is located behind a firewall. Because all three scenarios involve network access beyond the VPN server, the VPN servers in all cases must be enabled for LAN and demand-dial routing (settings found on the General tab of the server properties dialog box in the Routing And Remote Access console). Furthermore, for all of the following scenarios, the dial-in properties for all user accounts are assumed to be left at the default setting of Control Access Through Remote Access Policy.

Remote Access VPN   In a basic remote access scenario, the VPN allows a telecommuter to connect to an office network through the Internet. To allow this type of VPN, an administrator typically defines a remote access policy granting access to connections matching a NAS-Port-Type condition of Virtual (VPN) and a Windows-Groups condition matching a group created specifically for the purpose of allowing VPN access. On the client side, the telecommuter uses the New Connection Wizard to create a VPN connection specifying his/her own user credentials and the IP address of the remote VPN server. The user then dials in to a local ISP and connects to the office intranet through the VPN connection. Alternatively, if the user is logging on to a domain over the VPN connection, he/she can specify both the VPN and ISP connections through the Log On To Windows dialog box.

Figure 10-29 illustrates this scenario.

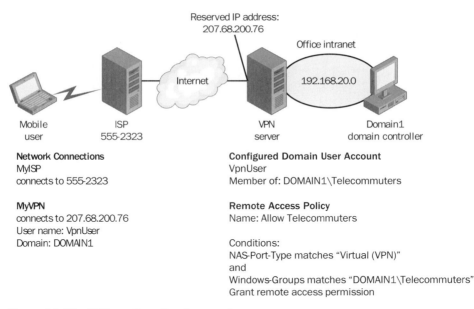

Figure 10-29   VPN configuration for remote access

Extranet/Router-To-Router VPN   In an extranet scenario, two office networks connect by means of VPN servers running Routing And Remote Access. On each server, demand-dial interfaces both initiate and answer VPN connections. VPN connectivity depends on the authorization of these demand-dial interfaces, not on the authorization of individual users.

> **Note**   Demand-dial interfaces do not necessarily describe dial-up connections. VPN interfaces in Routing And Remote Access are always considered a type of demand-dial interface, even when they initiate and respond to communication over a T1 line.

For each demand-dial VPN interface, you must configure a set of "dial-out" credentials including a user name, password, and domain; by default, the user name corresponds to the name of the demand-dial interface itself. However, this user name must also match the name of the demand-dial interface configured on the answering VPN server. To simplify configuration, you can assign opposing demand-dial interfaces the same name.

Figure 10-30 illustrates this scenario, in which both interfaces are given the name *Buf_Syr*, which is then used for dial-out credentials. Both VPN servers are members of a single domain named Domain1, and both subnets have local domain controllers. For connectivity to be authorized, a user account named Buf_Syr must already exist in the domain.

Remote access policies must also authorize the connection. In this example, the policy grants permission to VPN-type connections originating from user accounts in a global group named VPN-Routers. Because the user account Buf_Syr is a member of this global group, router-to-router VPN connections are authorized by the policy at both locations.

Finally, to allow full extranet connectivity, static routes must be deployed on each VPN server. The function of these static routes is to direct traffic destined for the opposite private network through the VPN demand-dial interface. These static routes are used for return traffic in addition to requests, so they must be configured on both servers even if all remote requests originate from the same network.

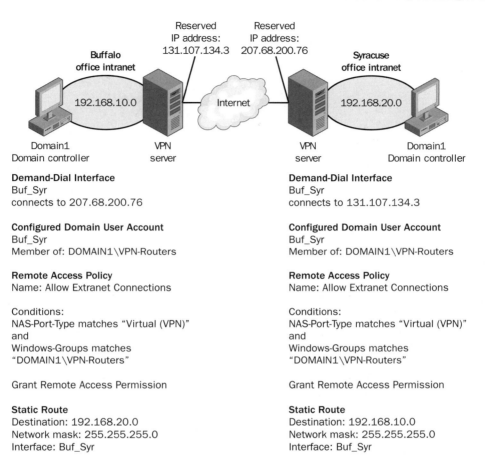

Reserved
IP address:
131.107.134.3

Reserved
IP address:
207.68.200.76

Buffalo
office intranet

Syracuse
office intranet

192.168.10.0

Internet

192.168.20.0

Domain1
Domain controller

VPN
server

VPN
server

Domain1
Domain controller

Demand-Dial Interface
Buf_Syr
connects to 207.68.200.76

Configured Domain User Account
Buf_Syr
Member of: DOMAIN1\VPN-Routers

Remote Access Policy
Name: Allow Extranet Connections

Conditions:
NAS-Port-Type matches "Virtual (VPN)"
and
Windows-Groups matches
"DOMAIN1\VPN-Routers"

Grant Remote Access Permission

Static Route
Destination: 192.168.20.0
Network mask: 255.255.255.0
Interface: Buf_Syr

Demand-Dial Interface
Buf_Syr
connects to 131.107.134.3

Configured Domain User Account
Buf_Syr
Member of: DOMAIN1\VPN-Routers

Remote Access Policy
Name: Allow Extranet Connections

Conditions:
NAS-Port-Type matches "Virtual (VPN)"
and
Windows-Groups matches
"DOMAIN1\VPN-Routers"

Grant Remote Access Permission

Static Route
Destination: 192.168.10.0
Network mask: 255.255.255.0
Interface: Buf_Syr

Figure 10-30   Router-to-router VPN scenario

Deploying Routing Protocols over VPNs   As an alternative to static routes, you can also deploy a routing protocol such as Routing Information Protocol (RIP) in an extranet scenario. To do so, first add the chosen routing protocol to the Routing And Remote Access console at each VPN server. Then add the VPN demand-dial interface to the protocol and configure as needed. For instance, in the case of RIP, you might choose to specify other VPN servers as RIP neighbors, to use peer filtering through password security, or to configure a much longer announcement interval than the default of 30 seconds. If you are deploying your VPN over dial-up lines, be sure to configure the routers for autostatic updates.

When deploying a routing protocol, verify that the protocol you choose is compatible with the other routers on your network. Finally, be sure to configure your network routers to accept updates from your VPN servers.

Mixed VPN with Firewall   Besides combining the remote access and extranet features described in the previous two scenarios, the network illustrated in Figure 10-31 adds a firewall to the network design. The VPN server, assigned a public address, is located behind this firewall in a perimeter network.

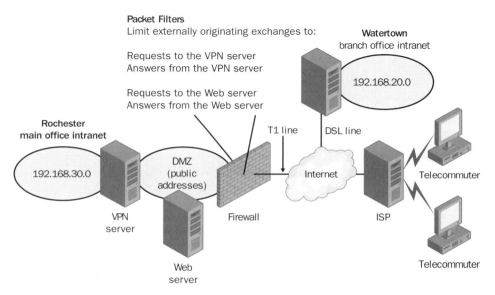

Figure 10-31   Complex VPN scenario

Firewalls typically allow all traffic exchanges originating from the internal network and block everything else. You then need to configure, where necessary, specific packet filters to allow traffic exchanges that originate from the external network to the VPN server.

In Figure 10-31, for example, packet filters are configured to allow request traffic to the VPN server and answer traffic from the same server. Because a Web server is also deployed in the perimeter network, packet filters have been defined to allow requests and answers to and from the Web server as well.

Packet filters are not necessary for access to services beyond the VPN server. Generally, firewalls cannot filter packets based on the information encapsulated within the VPN tunnel. Once these packets reach the VPN server, only then are they stripped of the VPN header and decrypted. At this point, they can be routed freely to any internal service.

Troubleshooting Remote Access VPNs

Use the following checklist to troubleshoot remote access VPN connections:

■ Verify that on the VPN server, enough ports have been configured in the Ports node for the relevant VPN type needed (PPTP or L2TP) and that not all available ports are currently being used.

■ Verify that the Remote Access Server option is enabled on the server properties General tab in the Routing And Remote Access console.

■ Verify that the VPN connection has the appropriate permissions through dial-in properties of the user account and remote access policies.

■ Verify that the VPN client, the remote access server, and the remote access policy are configured to use at least one common authentication protocol.

■ Verify that the VPN client, the remote access server, and the remote access policy are configured to use at least one common encryption strength.

■ Verify that the remote access server (or RADIUS server) computer is a member of the RAS And IAS Servers security group in the local domain.

■ Verify that the settings of the remote access policy profile are not in conflict with properties of the remote access server.

■ Verify that, if MS-CHAP v1 is being used as the authentication protocol, the user password does not exceed 14 characters.

Troubleshooting Router-to-Router VPNs

Use the following checklist to troubleshoot router-to-router VPNs:

■ Verify that at each end of the VPN connection, both the Router option and the LAN And Demand-Dial Routing option are selected on the General tab of server properties in the Routing And Remote Access console.

■ Verify that on each remote access server, the Enable IP Routing option is selected on the IP tab of server properties in the Routing And Remote Access console.

■ Verify that on each remote access server, enough ports have been configured in the Ports node for the relevant VPN type needed (PPTP or L2TP).

■ Verify that, for each demand-dial interface created for the VPN connection, you selected the option in the Demand-Dial Interface Wizard to route IP traffic over that demand-dial interface.

■ Verify that you have created static routes on each remote access server so that traffic destined for the opposite network is associated with the appropriate VPN interface.

- Verify that on each remote access server, the dial-out credentials of the locally configured demand-dial interface match the name of the remote answering interface and also match a user account name and password in the remote domain.

- Verify that each demand-dial (VPN) interface, answering remote access server, and answering remote access policy are configured to use at least one common authentication protocol and one common encryption strength.

- Verify that the remote access connection has the appropriate permissions through dial-in properties of the user account (corresponding to the name of the demand-dial interface) and through remote access policies.

- Verify that at each end of the VPN connection, the remote access server (or RADIUS server) computer is a member of the RAS And IAS Servers security group in the local domain.

- Verify that on each remote access server, the settings of the remote access policy profile are not in conflict with properties of the remote access server.

Configuring VPN Types

Windows Server 2003 includes support for two types of VPNs: PPTP and L2TP/IPSec. If you did not originally specify a VPN remote access server role when you ran the Routing And Remote Access Server Setup Wizard, Windows Server 2003 includes only five ports for each VPN type. Because each port enables a single remote access connection, a typical Routing And Remote Access installation by default allows only five simultaneous connections of each type. These ports appear in the Routing And Remote Access console when you select the Ports node, as shown in Figure 10-32.

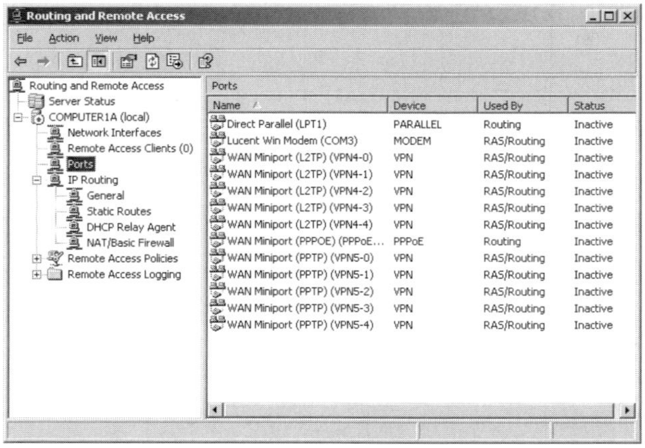

Figure 10-32   Viewing VPN ports

However, you can easily configure more ports for either type of VPN connection and allow more simultaneous connections. To perform this task, open the Ports Properties dialog box, select a port type, and click the Configure button. This procedure opens the Configure Device dialog box, shown in Figure 10-33. To modify the number of simultaneous connections your VPN server allows, enter an appropriate value into Maximum Ports.

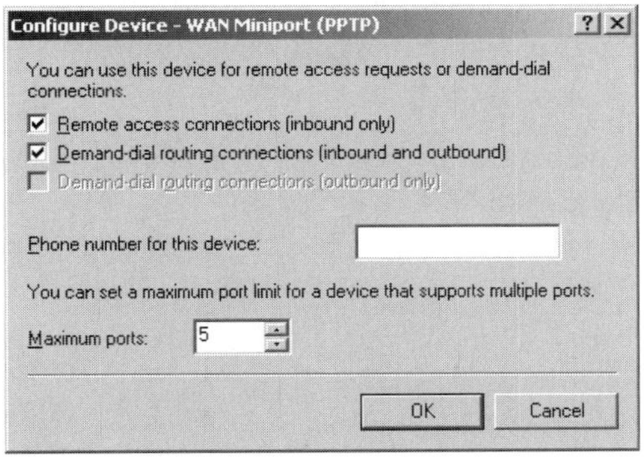

Configure Device - WAN Miniport (PPTP)   ? X

You can use this device for remote access requests or demand-dial connections.

☑ Remote access connections (inbound only)
☑ Demand-dial routing connections (inbound and outbound)
☐ Demand-dial routing connections (outbound only)

Phone number for this device:

You can set a maximum port limit for a device that supports multiple ports.

Maximum ports: 5

OK   Cancel

Figure 10-33   Adding more VPN ports

Windows Server 2003 can handle up to 1000 simultaneous VPN connections. You can configure a maximum of 1000 ports for PPTP connections and another 1000 ports for L2TP connections.

Note   If you originally specified a VPN remote access server role when you ran the Routing And Remote Access Server Setup Wizard, 128 ports of each VPN type will be configured by default.

Exam Tip   You need to understand VPN ports for the exam. Expect to see questions indicating that VPN access is blocked only because too few ports are configured. Other questions will test your knowledge of how many ports can be created and how many simultaneous connections Windows Server 2003 can handle.

Using PPTP

In general, PPTP-type VPN tunnels are easier to implement but less secure than those of the certificate-based L2TP/IPSec type. Although PPTP-based VPN connections do provide data confidentiality (captured packets cannot be interpreted without the encryption key), they do not provide data integrity (proof that the data was not modified in transit) or data origin authentication (proof that the data was sent by the authorized user).

For PPTP connections, encryption is provided by MPPE—which does not require you to configure a PKI or to assign certificates to users or computers at either end of the virtual private connection. However, you can use PPTP with a certificate infrastructure if you choose EAP-TLS as the authentication protocol.

Figure 10-34 illustrates PPTP-type encapsulation. The link between the two VPN end-points is treated as a PPP connection, which is encrypted through MPPE. The PPP frame is then wrapped with a Generic Routing Encapsulation (GRE) header and an IP header.

> **Exam Tip**   For the exam, if you see the protocol GRE mentioned in an answer choice, remember that it is merely an indirect reference to PPTP.

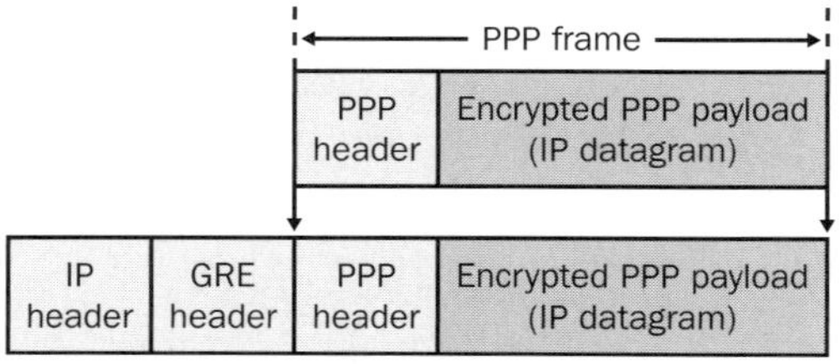

Figure 10-34   Sample PPTP packet

Configuring PPTP Connections on the VPN Server   To configure a remote access policy that permits VPN connections, you might need to create a policy condition that specifies VPN access through the NAS-Port-Type condition of Virtual (VPN). As long as a matching policy defined by Windows Group, NAS-Port-Type, or some other condition grants permission to the connection, VPN access is allowed. Aside from defining a remote access policy that matches the connection, you simply need to verify that enough PPTP ports exist to handle the number of simultaneous connections you want to support.

To deny PPTP connections to the VPN server, first open the Configure Device - WAN Miniport (PPTP) dialog box available by selecting Wan Miniport (PPTP) and clicking Configure in the Ports Properties dialog box. Then clear the Remote Access Connections (Inbound Only) check box and the Demand-Dial Routing Connections (Inbound And Outbound) check box.

> **Note**   The only way to distinguish VPN connections from other connections in remote access policies is through NAS-Port-Type. In remote access policies, the NAS-Port-Type for VPN connections is known as Virtual (VPN). Note also that there is no way to distinguish PPTP connections from L2TP/IPSec connections in remote access policies.

Configuring PPTP Connections on a VPN Client   To configure a PPTP-type VPN connection on a client, run the New Connection Wizard and specify a VPN connection. By default, VPN connection types are set to Automatic. In this mode, the VPN connection attempts communication first through L2TP over certificate-based IPSec, and then, if unsuccessful, through PPTP. Therefore, VPN connections default to the PPTP type when you have not deployed a certificate infrastructure to support IPSec. In addition, you can also configure a VPN connection to communicate only by means of the PPTP protocol by opening the properties dialog box for a VPN connection, clicking the Networking tab, and then selecting the PPTP VPN option in the Type Of VPN drop-down list box. Figure 10-35 shows this option.

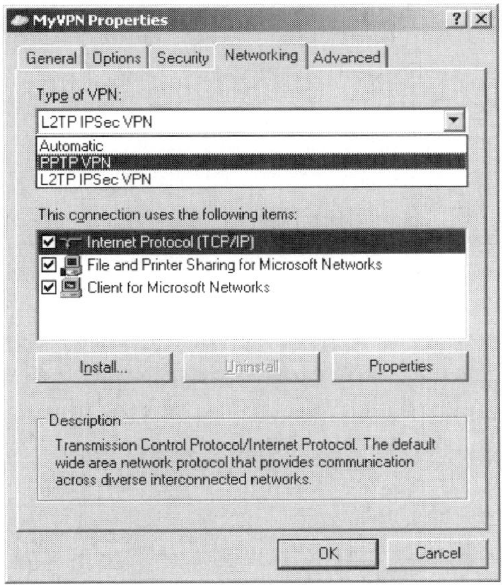

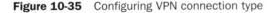

Figure 10-35   Configuring VPN connection type

Off the Record   PPTP-type VPNs have an undeservedly bad reputation for being insecure and, because they are also so easy to configure, tend to be frowned upon by would-be technical mavens as "VPNs for beginners." In reality, PPTP is not so much insecure as it is less secure than L2TP/IPSec, and PPTP is simply a better option than L2TP/IPSec in some networking scenarios. For example, if you need to support remote users who connect from public computers such as those found in a library, the unfeasibility of using computer certificates makes PPTP the only realistic VPN solution.

Using L2TP/IPSec

For L2TP/IPSec-type connections, the L2TP protocol provides VPN tunneling, and the Encapsulation Security Payload (ESP) protocol (itself a feature of IPSec) provides data encryption.

Figure 10-36 illustrates an L2TP/IPSec packet.

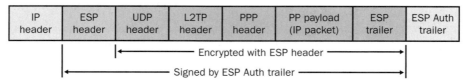

Figure 10-36 Sample L2TP packet

L2TP/IPSec connections, unlike those of PPTP, require computer authentication in addition to user authentication. Computer authentication is performed first; this process occurs during all L2TP/IPSec connection attempts between remote access clients and servers. After the tunnel endpoints are authenticated and a secure channel is established between the client and the server, user authentication follows. User authentication over L2TP/IPSec VPN connections occurs by means of any of the same set of authentication protocols that are used for PPTP and dial-up connections. Once user authentication is complete, computer authorization follows.

Computer Certificates and L2TP/IPSec   For most L2TP-based VPN connections, computer authentication is performed by means of a certificate infrastructure. To successfully implement this type of VPN, you must install computer certificates issued by the same certificate authority (CA) on each VPN client and VPN server. If you are using a Windows Server 2003 enterprise CA as an issuing CA, you should configure your Active Directory domain for autoenrollment of computer certificates by using the Computer Configuration group policy. Through this method, each computer that is a member of the domain automatically requests a computer certificate when the Computer Configuration group policy is updated.

> **Note**   Details related to certificate-based L2TP/IPSec deployment are beyond the scope of the 70-291 exam. However, you can learn more about this subject at the following address: *http://www.microsoft.com/technet/treeview/default.asp?url=/technet/prodtechnol /windowsserver2003/deploy/confeat/rmotevpn.asp.*

Certificates contain enhanced key usage (EKU) extensions that define the purpose of the certificate. The computer certificate that you assign to the L2TP/IPSec client must contain either the Client Authentication purpose or the IPSec purpose in the EKU extensions of the certificate. Meanwhile, the VPN server must contain the Server Authentication purpose if it is deployed as a remote access server, or it must contain both the Server Authentication purpose and the Client Authentication purpose if it is deployed in a router-to-router VPN. When two or more purposes are required, they must be included in the extensions of the same certificate.

> **Note** If you are using EAP-TLS for user authentication, you must install a user certificate on all VPN clients, and if the authenticating server is a RADIUS server, you must install a computer certificate on the RADIUS server. L2TP/IPSec VPNs do not require the use of EAP-TLS for user authentication.

Preshared Keys and L2TP/IPSec The only case in which certificates are not required for L2TP-based VPN connections is when both the VPN client and the VPN server are running Windows Server 2003. In this case, you have the option to configure computer authentication through the use of a *preshared key*: a shared string of plaintext that is used to encrypt and decrypt IPSec communication. Preshared keys are not considered a secure means of authentication and are therefore recommended only in test or temporary deployments.

Disabling L2TP/IPSec Connections To disable VPN access through L2TP connections, you merely need to set the maximum L2TP ports to 0 in the Routing And Remote Access console. (Note that this option is not available with PPTP.) To disable L2TP connections, open the Ports Properties dialog box, select WAN Miniport (L2TP), and then click the Configure button. In the Configure Device – WAN Miniport (L2TP) dialog box, type **0** into Maximum Ports. Click Yes when prompted.

Practice: Configuring a VPN

In this practice, you configure a PPTP-type and an L2TP/IPSec-type remote access VPN.

Exercise 1: Adding VPN Access as a Remote Access Policy Condition

> **Note** If you can only connect one computer at a time to the Internet, perform only Exercises 1, 2, and 4 below.

In this exercise, you modify the Telecommuters remote access policy so that the policy is applied to VPN connections as well as to dial-up connections.

1. On both Computer1 and Computer2, create a dial-up connection to your ISP named MyISP. This process is described in Chapter 4, "Configuring DNS Servers and Clients," Lesson 3, Exercise 2, steps 1-12. Do not modify any of the default properties of the dial-up connections.

> **Note** If desired, you can substitute a dedicated ISP connection for either or both of these dial-up connections. However, in order to deploy and test VPN connectivity, you will need to make minor adjustments to the instructions below.

2. From Computer1, while you are logged on to Domain1 as Administrator, open the Routing And Remote Access console.

3. In the console tree, select the Remote Access Policies node.

4. In the details pane, double-click the Telecommuters policy.

   The Telecommuters Properties dialog box opens.

5. In the Policy Conditions area, make sure the NAS-Port-Type Matches policy condition is selected.

6. Click the Edit button.

   The NAS-Port-Type dialog box opens.

7. In the Available Types area, select Virtual (VPN).

8. Click the Add button.

   Virtual (VPN) appears in the Selected Types area.

9. Click OK.

10. In the Telecommuters Properties dialog box, click OK.

11. From Computer1, log off Domain1.

Exercise 2: Creating a PPTP-Type VPN Connection

In this exercise, you create a VPN connection on Computer2 that connects to a current IP address on Computer1. The VPN connection defaults to a PPTP type because certificate-based IPSec is unavailable.

1. From Computer2, log on to Domain1 as Administrator.

2. Open Network Connections.

3. In the Network Connections window, select New Connection from the File menu.

   The New Connection Wizard launches.

4. Click Next.

   The Network Connection Type page appears.

5. Select the Connect To The Network At My Workplace option, and then click Next.

   The Network Connection page appears.

6. Select the Virtual Private Network Connection option, and then click Next.

   The Connection Name page appears.

7. In the Company Name text box, type **MyVPN**.

8. Click Next.

   The Public Network page appears.

9. In the Automatically Dial This Initial Connection drop-down list box, select MyISP.

10. Click Next.

   The VPN Server Selection page appears.

11. Leave Computer2 for the moment and move to Computer1. From Computer1, log on to Domain1 as Administrator. Use the MyISP connection to connect to the Internet. When you have connected, use the Ipconfig command to determine the public IP address currently assigned to Computer1.

12. Write the public IP address currently assigned to Computer1 in the space provided:

   _____

13. Return to Computer2.

14. On Computer2, on the VPN Server Selection page, type the public IP address currently assigned to Computer1 in the Host Name Or IP Address text box.

15. Click Next.

   The Connection Availability page appears.

16. Select the Anyone's Use option, and then click Next.

   The Completing the New Connection Wizard page appears.

17. Click Finish.

   The Initial Connection dialog box appears, asking whether you want to connect to MyISP now.

18. Click No.

19. Open Network Connections.

   In the window, a new heading named Virtual Private Network appears. Under this heading, you can see a new connection called MyVPN. Beneath its name, its status is described as Disconnected and its type is listed as WAN Miniport (PPTP).

20. Right-click MyVPN, and then click Properties.

   The MyVPN Properties dialog box opens.

21. Click the Options tab.

22. In the Dialing Options area, select the Include Windows Logon Domain check box.

23. Click the Networking tab.

   In the Type Of VPN drop-down list box, notice that Automatic is selected. With this setting, certificate-based L2TP/IPSec VPN connections with the VPN server are attempted first, and PPTP connections are attempted second.

24. Click OK.

25. From Computer2, log off Domain1.

26. Perform the following exercise before disconnecting Computer1 from the Internet to ensure that the address you entered in step 14 is still valid.

Exercise 3 (Optional): Logging on to a Domain Through a VPN Connection

In this exercise, you log on to Domain1 through a VPN connection. Before beginning the exercise, make sure both computers are connected to a separate phone line. You can also disconnect the local cabling between the two computers during the length of the exercise. Disconnecting the local cabling shows that the connection between the computers is occurring over the dial-up lines.

1. On Computer2, press Ctrl+Alt+Delete to open the Log On To Windows dialog box.

2. Select the Log On Using Dial-Up Connection check box.

3. In the User Name text box, type **user1**.

4. In the Password text box, type the password you have assigned to the User1 account.

5. In the Log On To drop-down list box, verify that DOMAIN1 is selected, and then click OK.

The Network Connections dialog box opens.

6. From the Choose A Network Connection drop-down list box, select MyVPN.

7. Click Connect.

The Initial Connection dialog box opens, asking you whether you want to connect to MyISP now.

8. Click Yes.

The Connect MyISP dialog box opens.

9. In the User Name text box and the Password text box, enter the user name and password of your ISP account.

10. Click Dial.

The Connecting MyISP message box displays the status of the connection. When the connection to your ISP has completed, the Connect MyVPN dialog box opens.

11. In the User Name text box, type **user1**.

12. In the Password text box, type the password you have assigned to the User1 account.

13. In the Domain text box, type **DOMAIN1**.

14. Click Connect.

The Connecting MyVPN message box shows the status of the connection. Once the connection is authenticated, authorized, and established, domain logon follows.

15. After logon from Computer2 is complete, open an Internet Explorer window. Dismiss any messages or warnings that appear.

16. In the Address text box, type **computer1.domain1.local**, and then press Enter.

After a moment, the connection to the address is established, and the shares available on Computer1 are shown in the Internet Explorer window.

17. Switch to Computer1 while you are still logged on as Administrator.

18. Open the Routing And Remote Access console.

19. In the console tree, click the Ports node.

In the details pane, you can see that only one WAN Miniport has an active status. The port name shows that this VPN connection is a PPTP connection.

20. Log off Computer1 and Computer2.

Exercise 4: Creating a VPN Connection Through L2TP/IPSec

In this exercise, you configure an L2TP/IPSec-type VPN connection between Computer2 and Computer1. To perform this task, you first configure a preshared key on the remote access client and server.

1. From Computer2, log on to Domain1 as Administrator.

2. Open Network Connections.

3. Right-click MyVPN, and then click Properties.

The MyVPN Properties dialog box opens.

4. Click the Security tab.

5. Click the IPSec Settings button.

The IPSec Settings dialog box appears.

6. Select the Use Pre-Shared Key For Authentication check box.

7. In the Key text box, type **test**.

> **Note**   Preshared keys are not secure because they are passed over the network in plaintext. However, they are a good way to test the functionality of an IPSec connection. You can also use preshared keys as a means to obtain computer certificates while your PKI is being deployed. When IPSec is based on a PKI using certificates instead of preshared keys, the encryption is considered more secure than that of PPTP-type VPN connections.

8. Click OK.

9. Leave the MyVPN Properties dialog box open, and switch to Computer1.

10. From Computer1, log on to Domain1 as Administrator.

11. Open the Routing And Remote Access console.

12. In the console tree, right-click COMPUTER1 (Local), and then click Properties. The COMPUTER1 (Local) Properties dialog box opens.

13. Click the Security tab.

14. Select the Allow Custom IPSec Policy For L2TP Connection check box.

15. In the Pre-Shared Key text box, type **test**.

    This preshared key must match the key configured at the client.

16. Click OK.

17. While you are still working on Computer1, use the MyISP connection to connect Computer1 to the Internet.

18. After the connection has been established, use the Ipconfig command to determine the currently assigned public IP address on Computer1.

19. Return to Computer2 and click the General tab in the MyVPN Properties dialog box.

20. In the Host Name Or IP Address Of Destination text box, type the public IP address currently assigned to Computer1.

21. Click the Networking tab.

22. In the Type Of VPN drop-down list box, select L2TP IPSec VPN.

23. Click OK.

24. From Computer2, log off Domain1.

25. Perform the next exercise before the MyISP connection disconnects on Computer1.

Exercise 5 (Optional): Testing the L2TP/IPSec Configuration

In this exercise, you test the connectivity of the new VPN.

1. From Computer2, log on to Domain1 as User1 through the MyVPN connection. Follow the same steps listed in Exercise 3, "Logging on to a Domain Through a VPN Connection."

2. Once the VPN connection is established, switch to Computer1.

3. On Computer1, open the Routing And Remote Access console.

4. In the console tree, click the Ports node.

In the details pane, you can now see that only one L2TP port has an active status. Notice that by default, only five PPTP ports, one PPP over Ethernet (PPPoE) port, and five L2TP ports are available. Thus, unless more ports are added, only these numbers of corresponding connections can be accepted by the server at once.

5. In the console tree, right-click the Ports node, and then click Properties.

   The Ports Properties dialog box opens.

6. In the list of devices, select WAN Miniport (L2TP), and then click the Configure button.

   The Configure Device – WAN Miniport (L2TP) dialog box opens.

> **Note**   The Demand-Dial Routing Connections check box is cleared by default. When enabled, this option allows this port to be used for demand-dial routing through VPNs.

7. In the Maximum Ports text box, type **1500**.

8. Click OK.

   A message box appears, indicating that the number of ports must be between 0 and 1000. In other words, you can configure the Routing And Remote Access service to accept up to 1000 simultaneous L2TP connections. In the same way, you can configure up to 1000 PPTP ports.

9. Click OK.

10. In the Configure Device – WAN Miniport (L2TP) dialog box, click Cancel.

11. In the Ports Properties dialog box, click Cancel.

12. Log off Computer1 and Computer2.

Lesson Review

The following questions are intended to reinforce key information presented in this lesson. If you are unable to answer a question, review the lesson materials and try the question again. You can find answers to the questions in the "Questions and Answers" section at the end of this chapter.

1. What is the difference between the certificates used for the EAP-TLS authentication protocol and those used for the L2TP/IPSec VPN protocol?

   _____

   _____

2. You have configured a VPN server, but users report that they sometimes cannot connect. You have noticed that the greatest number of complaints occur when network use is highest, and you have ruled out addressing as the cause. What is the most likely reason for the intermittent access problems?

_____

_____

3. Why are pre-shared keys in IPSec not considered secure?

_____

Lesson Summary

■ Virtual private networks are networks that logically emulate a local network but that physically span the Internet.

■ In a remote access VPN scenario using Windows Server 2003, a single user connects across the Internet to a Windows Server 2003 computer running Routing And Remote Access. In an extranet scenario, private LANs are joined across the Internet by two Windows Server 2003 computers running Routing And Remote Access.

■ In general, PPTP-type VPN tunnels are easier to implement but less secure than those of the certificate-based L2TP/IPSec type. For PPTP connections, MPPE provides encryption.

■ L2TP/IPSec connections, unlike those of PPTP, require computer authentication in addition to user authentication. When computer authentication is provided by the use of a certificate infrastructure, L2TP-type VPN connections are considered very secure. When computer authentication is provided by the use of preshared keys, L2TP-type VPN connections are not considered secure.

Lesson 4: Deploying the Internet Authentication Service

IAS is the Microsoft implementation of a RADIUS server and proxy. As a RADIUS server, IAS performs centralized connection authentication, authorization, and accounting for many types of network access, including wireless, authenticating switch, dial-up and VPN remote access, and router-to-router connections. As a RADIUS proxy, IAS forwards authentication and accounting messages to other RADIUS servers.

After this lesson, you will be able to

- Configure IAS to provide authentication for Routing And Remote Access clients

Estimated lesson time: 45 minutes

Exploring RADIUS Server Scenarios

The basic purpose of a RADIUS server is to centralize remote access authentication, authorization, and logging. RADIUS is useful, for example, in large organizations such as ISPs that need to manage many remote access connections to separate remote access servers.

Figure 10-40 illustrates such a scenario, in which dial-up users connect to an ISP in four different cities. The network access servers, running Routing And Remote Access, forward remote access requests to a RADIUS server by means of the RADIUS protocol. The RADIUS server then communicates with the domain controller for user authentication. After user authentication, remote access policies defined on the RADIUS server are applied to the connection. If the remote access connection is authorized, the RADIUS server communicates with the network access server to allow network access. If not, network access is denied.

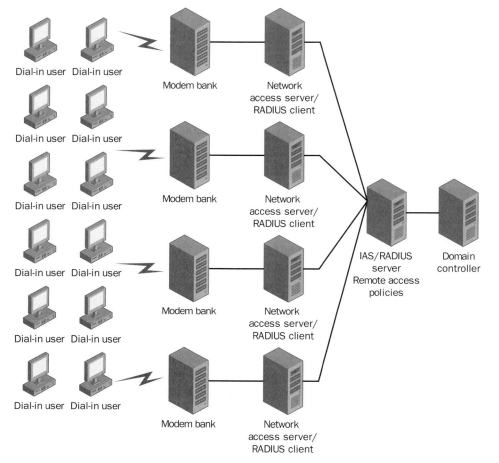

Figure 10-37 IAS deployed in an ISP

RADIUS servers also enable smaller organizations to centralize remote access management when a variety of remote access methods are supported, such as VPN, wireless, and dial-up. By deploying a central point of authorization, the organization can direct separate, medium-specific access requests toward a single set of remote access policies, as shown in Figure 10-38.

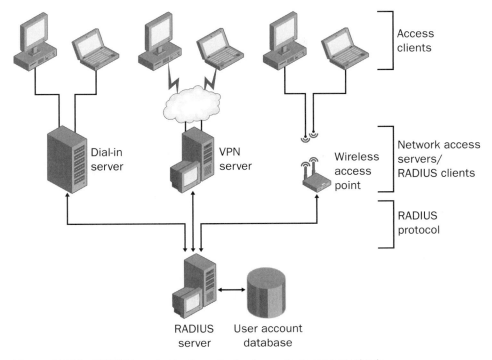

Figure 10-38 RADIUS centralization of mixed remote access methods

Finally, although in a traditional implementation the RADIUS server is deployed on a separate computer, the RADIUS server can also be deployed on a network access server. In this scenario, network access requests reaching the external interface of the server are handled by the Routing And Remote Access service. The Routing And Remote Access service then forwards these remote access requests to the IAS service, which is associated with the internal IP address of the same computer. This IAS service acts as a RADIUS server not only for RADIUS requests originating from the local machine, but also for RADIUS requests originating from other network access servers throughout the network. Figure 10-39 illustrates this scenario.

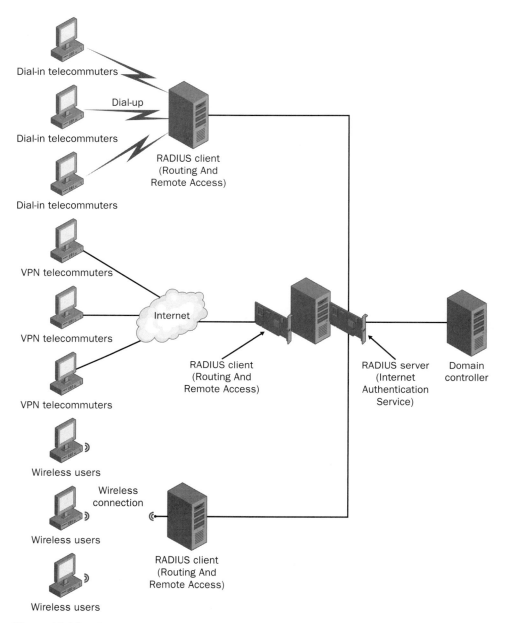

Figure 10-39   Computer deployed as both RADIUS client and server

Exploring RADIUS Proxy Scenarios

In Windows Server 2003, you can also deploy the IAS service as a RADIUS proxy. In this type of implementation, network access servers are configured to forward authentication and accounting to an IAS server, which is then configured as a RADIUS proxy to forward these messages to a RADIUS server group.

A *RADIUS server group* is a group of one or more RADIUS servers for which network access requests are load balanced dynamically by the RADIUS proxy. Each RADIUS server group represents a distinct set of remote access policies for a domain, forest, or organization. Separate RADIUS server groups can be defined for separate forests, Kerberos realms, or untrusted domains. *Connection request policies* can be defined at the RADIUS proxy to sort network access requests according to attribute-matching conditions (such as a specific user or realm name) and relay these requests to the appropriate RADIUS server group.

Figure 10-40 illustrates IAS deploying a RADIUS proxy between RADIUS clients (access servers) and a single RADIUS server group.

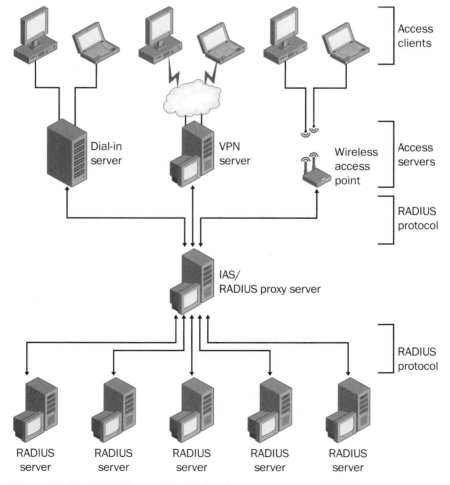

Figure 10-40   RADIUS proxy load balancing requests to a RADIUS server group

The following list describes a few of the scenarios in which RADIUS proxies are designed to be implemented:

■ You are a service provider that offers outsourced network access services to multiple customers. Through connection request policies, the RADIUS proxy can read the realm name attribute in various connection requests and route these requests to the appropriate customer's RADIUS server.

■ You want to provide authentication and authorization for user accounts that are not members of a domain trusted by the IAS server domain. Through connection request policies, the RADIUS proxy can read the realm name attribute in various connection requests and route these requests to the appropriate domain's RADIUS server.

■ You want to process a large number of connection requests as efficiently as possible. For this task, the RADIUS proxy dynamically balances the load of connection and accounting requests across multiple RADIUS servers and improves processing efficiency.

Deploying IAS as a RADIUS Server

For basic RADIUS scenarios in which no RADIUS proxy is implemented, deploying IAS as a RADIUS server requires configuration both at the client running Routing And Remote Access and at the server running IAS.

Configuring a RADIUS Client

To configure a computer running Routing And Remote Access as a RADIUS client, first open the server properties dialog box in the Routing And Remote Access console, and then select the Security tab. This tab allows you to select a RADIUS server for authentication, logging, or both. By default, both functions are handled by the local computer. To configure these functions to instead be passed to a RADIUS server, from the Authentication Provider drop-down list box, select RADIUS Authentication. From the Accounting Provider drop-down list box, select RADIUS Accounting. Figure 10-41 shows these options.

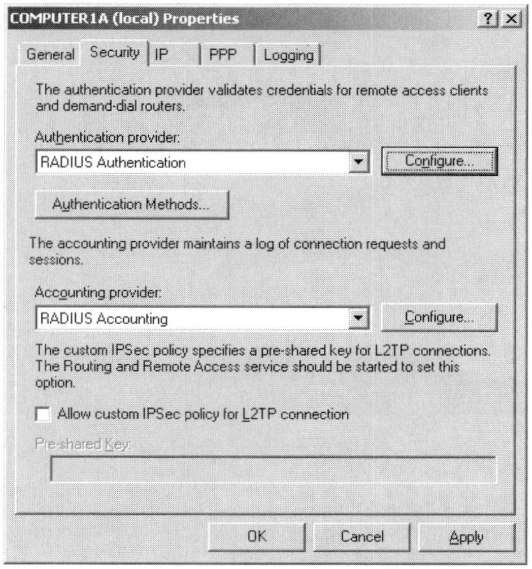

Figure 10-41   Configuring Routing And Remote Access to pass access requests to a RADIUS server

Specifying a RADIUS Server   After you select the options for RADIUS authentication and accounting in the Routing And Remote Access console, you need to specify the particular RADIUS server or servers you want to use. You must specify the RADIUS servers for authentication and accounting separately, but the configuration steps are identical for each. First, click the Configure button next to the Authentication Provider or the Accounting Provider drop-down list box. The RADIUS Authentication or RADIUS Accounting dialog box opens, which, when multiple RADIUS servers have been configured for fault tolerance, lists the query order of these servers. Then click the Add button to open the Add RADIUS Server dialog box. Figure 10-42 shows the dialog box that opens when you add a RADIUS authentication server.

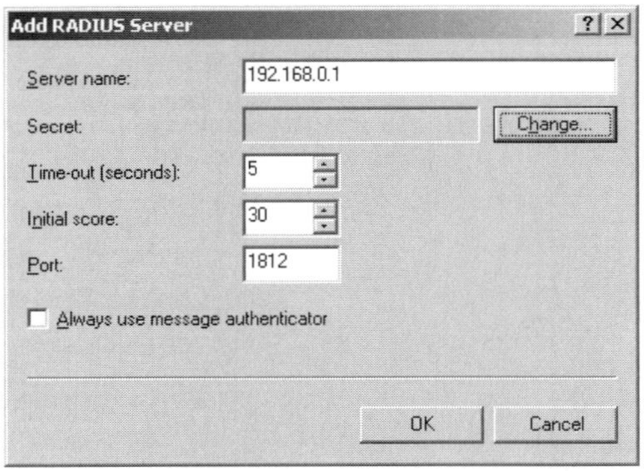

Figure 10-42   Adding a RADIUS authentication server

This dialog box allows you to specify a RADIUS server by resolvable name or IP address. In this box, you can also configure the following parameters:

- **Secret**   This field allows you to define a shared secret, which is a plaintext password used between a RADIUS client and server. You can also use shared secrets to encrypt certain message attributes, such as the user password. When defining a shared secret, be sure to use the same case-sensitive secret on the RADIUS client and RADIUS server; however, you should use a different shared secret for each RADIUS server-RADIUS client pair. For each shared secret, it is recommended that you use a random sequence of letters, numbers, and symbols at least 22 characters long.

- **Time-Out (Seconds)**   This parameter determines how many seconds a RADIUS client waits for a response from a RADIUS server before determining that the connection attempt is unsuccessful.

- **Initial Score**   When more than one RADIUS server is specified for a particular client, this value determines the querying order assigned to a particular RADIUS server.

- **Port**   This value allows you to specify the UDP port used for the RADIUS protocol. Standard ports used for RADIUS include UDP port 1812 for authentication and UDP port 1813 for accounting. However, many access servers use ports 1645 for authentication requests and 1646 for accounting requests by default. Whatever port numbers you decide to use, make sure IAS and your access server are configured to use the same ones.

- **Always Use Message Authenticator**   This option appears only when adding a RADIUS authentication server. The RADIUS Message Authenticator attribute is an MD5 hash of the entire RADIUS message. The shared secret is used as the key. If the Message Authenticator attribute is present, the hash is verified. If it fails verification, the RADIUS message is discarded. If the client settings require the Message Authenticator attribute and it is not present, the RADIUS message is discarded.

■ **Send RADIUS Accounting On And Accounting Off Messages**   This message appears only when adding a RADIUS accounting server. This option causes Routing And Remote Access to send Accounting-On and Accounting-Off messages to the RADIUS server when Routing And Remote Access starts and stop.

Configuring a RADIUS Server

To configure a RADIUS server, you first need to install the Internet Authentication Service Windows subcomponent of the Networking Services Windows component. After you install IAS, you can configure its features through the Internet Authentication Service console (Figure 10-43), available on the Administrative Tools menu.

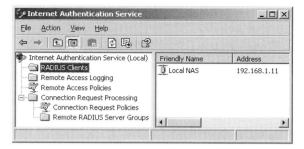

Figure 10-43   Internet Authentication Service console

Registering the IAS Server   The first step in deploying the IAS server is to register it in Active Directory. Through registration, the IAS computer joins the RAS And IAS Servers domain local security group in the domain of which the IAS server computer is a member. Members of the RAS And IAS Servers group are able to read remote access attributes of user accounts.

Specifying the RADIUS Clients   In the IAS console, you must specify each RADIUS client forwarding access requests to the local IAS server. To specify a new RADIUS client, right-click the RADIUS Clients folder in the console tree and then click New RADIUS Client. A wizard opens in which you must configure a friendly name for the connection, a resolvable name or IP address, the shared secret defined for the client/server pair, and (optionally) the Message Authenticator attribute.

> **Exam Tip**   You can back up, restore, or migrate a RADIUS server by using the Netsh command-line utility and the AAAA context. First, use the Netsh aaaa show config >*filename.txt* command to dump the complete IAS server configuration into a script file. Then you can install the configuration included in this script file onto a particular IAS server by running the Netsh exec [path]*filename.txt* command on the target server computer.

Practice: Deploying a RADIUS Server

In this practice, you configure IAS to handle remote access authentication and authorization from requests received by Routing And Remote Access.

Exercise 1: Configuring the RADIUS Client

In this exercise, you install IAS on Computer1 and configure Routing And Remote Access as a RADIUS client.

1. On Computer1, insert the Windows Server 2003 installation CD-ROM.

2. From Computer1, log on to Domain1 as Administrator.

3. By using Add Or Remove Programs in Control Panel and the Windows Components Wizard, install the Internet Authentication Service subcomponent of the Networking Services Windows component.

4. When the Windows Components Wizard has finished, close Control Panel.

5. Open the Routing And Remote Access console. In the console tree, right-click COMPUTER1 (Local), and then click Properties.

   The COMPUTER1 (Local) Properties dialog box opens.

6. Click the Security tab.

7. In the Authentication Provider drop-down list box, select RADIUS Authentication.

8. Click the associated Configure button.

   The RADIUS Authentication dialog box opens.

9. Click the Add button.

   The Add RADIUS Server dialog box opens.

10. In the Server Name text box, type **192.168.0.1**.

11. Click the Change button.

    The Change Secret dialog box opens.

> **Important**   This secret is used as a key to encrypt communication between a specific RADIUS client and RADIUS server. The same secret must be configured on the RADIUS server. In a production environment, you should configure the secret to be a random sequence of letters, numbers, and symbols at least 22 characters long. In this test environment, we will use a simple secret.

12. In the New Secret dialog box and the Confirm New Secret dialog box, type a strong password. Write this password in the space provided:

_____

13. In the Change Secret dialog box, click OK.

14. In the Add RADIUS Server dialog box, click OK.

15. In the RADIUS Authentication dialog box, click OK.

16. In the COMPUTER1 (Local) Properties dialog box, select RADIUS Accounting from the Accounting Provider drop-down list box.

    This setting moves remote access logging to the RADIUS server. Repeat steps 8-15 to configure the RADIUS Accounting server.

17. In the COMPUTER1 (Local) Properties dialog box, click OK.

    A message box indicates that to use the new authentication provider, you must restart Routing And Remote Access.

18. Click OK.

    A message box indicates that to use the new accounting provider, you must restart Routing And Remote Access.

19. Click OK.

20. At a command prompt, enter the following command: **net stop RemoteAccess**.

21. After a message appears indicating that the Routing And Remote Access service has stopped, enter the following command at the command prompt: **net start RemoteAccess**.

Exercise 2: Configuring the RADIUS Server

In this exercise, you configure the Internet Authentication Service on Computer1 to communicate with the RADIUS client you have already configured.

1. From Computer1, log on to Domain1 as Administrator if you have not already done so.

2. Click Start, select Administrative Tools, and then click Internet Authentication Service.

    The Internet Authentication Service console opens.

3. While the Internet Authentication Service (Local) icon is selected in the console tree, click the Action menu.

    Notice the Register Server In Active Directory command on the menu. In general, RADIUS servers performing authentication for a domain need to be registered in Active Directory. However, because this computer is also a domain controller, it has been registered in Active Directory automatically.

4. In the console tree, select the Remote Access Policies folder.

    Note that the policies listed in the details pane are the same as those configured for Routing And Remote Access on the local machine.

5. In the console tree, right-click RADIUS Clients, and then click New RADIUS Client.

   The Name And Address page of the New RADIUS Client Wizard appears.

6. In the Friendly Name text box, type **Local NAS**.

7. In the Client Address text box, type **192.168.0.1**.

8. Click Next.

   The Additional Information page appears.

9. In the Shared Secret text box and the Confirm Shared Secret text box, type the strong password you used in step 12 of Exercise 1, "Configuring the RADIUS Client."

10. Leave the default of RADIUS Standard as the Client-Vendor setting, and click Finish.

11. Close the Internet Authentication Service console, and log off Computer1.

Exercise 3 (Optional): Testing the RADIUS Configuration

In this exercise, you test the new RADIUS configuration by dialing in to Domain1 from Computer2. Perform this exercise only if you can connect Computer1 and Computer2 to separate phone lines.

1. On Computer2, press Ctrl+Alt+Delete to open the Log On To Windows screen.

   The Log On To Windows screen appears.

2. Select the Log On Using Dial-Up Connection check box.

3. In the User Name text box, type **user1**.

4. In the Password text box, type the password you have assigned to the User1 account.

5. In the Log On To drop-down list box, verify that DOMAIN1 is selected and click OK.

   The Network Connections dialog box appears.

6. From the Choose A Network Connection drop-down list box, select MyCompany.

7. Click Connect.

   The Connect MyCompany dialog box appears.

8. Verify that the credentials of User1 are specified in the appropriate boxes, and then click Dial.

   The Connecting MyCompany message box appears while the connection is being attempted. After two rings, Routing And Remote Access on Computer1 answers. The remote access connection is authenticated and authorized, and then the domain logon credentials are authenticated and authorized.

Logon completes. You have successfully logged on to a domain using a RADIUS server.

9. Log off Computer2.

Lesson Review

The following questions are intended to reinforce key information presented in this lesson. If you are unable to answer a question, review the lesson materials and try the question again. You can find answers to the questions in the "Questions and Answers" section at the end of this chapter.

1. What are the two basic types of RADIUS clients included with Windows Server 2003?

   _____

   _____

2. For a computer running IAS, what is the difference between remote access policies and connection request policies?

   _____

   _____

   _____

   _____

   _____

3. How can you migrate an IAS server?

   _____

   _____

   _____

   _____

Lesson Summary

- Internet Authentication Service is the Microsoft implementation of a RADIUS server. The basic purpose of a RADIUS server is to centralize remote access authentication, authorization, and logging.

- In a typical IAS/RADIUS server implementation, multiple network access servers running Routing And Remote Access forward access requests to the RADIUS server. The RADIUS server then queries the domain controller for authentication and applies remote access policies to the connection requests.

- IAS can also be deployed as a RADIUS proxy. In this type of implementation, network access servers are configured to forward authentication and accounting to an IAS server, which is then configured as a RADIUS proxy to forward these messages to a RADIUS server group. You can use this feature to provide load balancing for access requests or to enable an outsourced network access provider to relay access requests to appropriate organizations.

Case Scenario Exercise

You have been hired as a consultant by Lucerne Publishing to assist with the deployment of remote access services for company employees. For each of the following, explain how you would configure the required remote access feature.

1. Lucerne Publishing wants to provide special dial-up access for 10 employees. These 10 employees should be authenticated only by verifying that the phone numbers from which they are calling are in fact these employees' home phone numbers. The employees should not need to type in a user name and password. How can you implement this configuration?

   _____

   _____

   _____

   _____

   _____

   _____

   _____

2. Lucerne Publishing has already configured a PPTP-type VPN, but it wants to allow users who log on to the company domain to avoid having to type their user name and password twice. How can you allow users to avoid typing in their credentials in both the Log On To Windows screen and the VPN connection dialog box? Which authentication protocols can be used over this VPN connection?

   _____

   _____

   _____

   _____

3. Lucerne Publishing wants to allow certain employees to be able to connect to the company network over multiple phone lines, but it wants to restrict other employees from doing the same. For the employees who are permitted to connect over multiple phone lines, the company wants to ensure that these employees use only two phone lines maximum, and that when the connection falls below 40 percent bandwidth capacity for 2 minutes, one of the phone lines is dropped. How can you implement this configuration?

Troubleshooting Lab

In this lab, you recover from a faulty IAS installation.

1. From Computer1, log on to Domain1 as Administrator.

   Open a command prompt and type **netsh aaaa dump >iasconfig.txt**.

   This command dumps the current IAS configuration into a script file named Iasconfig.txt.

2. Open the IAS console, and select the Remote Access Policies node.

3. In the details pane, right-click the Telecommuters policy, and then click Delete.

   A message box appears, asking you to confirm the deletion.

4. Click Yes.

5. Close the IAS console.

6. At a command prompt, type **netsh exec iasconfig.txt**.

   This command executes the script stored in the file Iasconfig.txt.

7. Open the IAS console and select the Remote Access Policies node.

   The Telecommuters policy has been restored.

8. Log off Computer1.

Chapter Summary

- Remote access servers running Routing And Remote Access must provide IP addressing for remote access clients—either indirectly through a DHCP server or directly through a static address pool. Typically, the clients receive addresses that place them on the same logical subnet as computers immediately beyond the remote access server.

- Remote access connections must be authenticated before they can be authorized. Remote access authentication occurs by means of an authentication protocol, which usually encrypts the user name and password sent over the network. Some authentication protocols (EAP-TLS, MS-CHAP v2, and MS-CHAP v1) also encrypt the connection data.

- The authentication method used in any connection is the most secure authentication protocol enabled on the remote access client, the remote access server, and the remote access policy applied to the connection.

- Remote access authorization occurs first by means of verifying the dial-in properties of the user account and second by means of applying the first matching remote access policy to the connection.

- If a user is logging on to a domain remotely, domain logon occurs separately, and only after the remote access connection has been authenticated and authorized.

- To enable access beyond the remote access server, the remote access server must be enabled as a router, and the IP routing option must be enabled in the Routing And Remote Access server properties.

- Virtual private networks are networks that logically emulate a local network but that physically span the Internet. In remote access VPNs, the user account must be authenticated and authorized. In a router-to-router (extranet) VPN, the routers must be authenticated and authorized.

- In general, PPTP-type VPN tunnels are easier to implement but less secure than those of the certificate-based L2TP/IPSec type.

- The Internet Authentication Service is the Microsoft implementation of a RADIUS server. The basic purpose of a RADIUS server is to centralize remote access authentication, authorization, and logging.

Exam Highlights

Before taking the exam, review the key points and terms that are presented in this chapter to help you identify topics you need to review. Return to the lessons for additional practice, and review the "Further Reading" sections in Part 2 for pointers to more information about topics covering the exam objectives.

Key Topics

- Be able to describe the various features and limitations of all authentication protocols supported in Windows Server 2003.

- Be able to describe the various steps of remote access authentication and authorization. Know which conditions must be met for a remote access connection to be established.

- Be able to describe the configurable options on the dial-up properties of a user account.

- Be able to describe the configurable options in a remote access policy profile.

- Be able to describe the difference between PPTP and L2TP/IPSec-type VPNs.

- Be able to describe the functional differences between RADIUS clients, servers, and proxies. Describe the scenarios in which RADIUS servers and proxies are used.

Key Terms

3DES   Triple Data Encryption Standard. An algorithm used for strongest encryption of L2TP/IPSec connections.

DES   Data Encryption Standard. An algorithm used for strong (56-bit) encryption of L2TP/IPSec connections.

MPPE   Microsoft Point-to-Point Encryption. An implementation of the Rivest-Shamir Adleman (RSA) RC4 family of encryption algorithms. MPPE is used to encrypt connection data with the MS-CHAP (v1 and v2) and EAP-TLS authentication protocols. It is also used to encrypt connection data with PPTP-type VPNs.

RADIUS   Remote Authentication Dial-In User Service. A service that allows for centralized remote access authentication and authorization. The Microsoft implementation of RADIUS is the Internet Authentication Service.

Questions and Answers

Page
10-22

Lesson 1 Review

1. You have configured your remote access server to distribute addresses to remote access clients through a DHCP server. However, you find that your remote access clients assign themselves with only APIPA addresses. Name two possible causes of this scenario.

   There is not a DHCP server available on the network segment, and a DHCP relay agent has not been configured.

   The DHCP server did not have 10 free addresses in its scope when the Routing And Remote Access server started up.

2. Which authentication protocol must you use to support the use of smart cards?

   EAP-TLS

3. Which authentication protocols provide data encryption?

   EAP-TLS, MS-CHAP v2, and MS-CHAP v1

Lesson 2 Review

Page
10-47

1. When you create a new domain in a Windows Server 2003 network, the default domain functional level is Windows 2000 mixed. How is the Allow Access setting in the dial-in properties of a user account different in this environment from that in other server environments?

   In Windows 2000 mixed-mode domains, the Allow Access setting does not override the access permission set in the remote access policy. In other server environments, the Allow Access setting does override the access permission configured in the remote access policy.

2. A remote access connection has been authenticated, the dial-in properties of the user account are set to Allow Access, and the first matching remote access policy is set to Grant Remote Access Permission. If the remote client still cannot successfully connect to the remote access server, what is the most likely explanation?

   Constraints configured in the remote access policy profile, such as allowed dial-up hours, are preventing the connection from being established.

3. How can you enforce 128-bit encryption for dial-up connections at the remote access server?

In the policy profile for the applicable remote access policies, clear all encryption strength options except for Strongest Encryption (MPPE 128-Bit).

Lesson 3 Review

Page 10-67

1. What is the difference between the certificates used for the EAP-TLS authentication protocol and those used for the L2TP/IPSec VPN protocol?

EAP-TLS relies on user certificates for user authentication. Certificate-based L2TP/IPSec relies on computer (machine) certificates for computer authentication.

2. You have configured a VPN server, but users report that they sometimes cannot connect. You have noticed that the greatest number of complaints occur when network use is highest, and you have ruled out addressing as the cause. What is the most likely reason for the intermittent access problems?

You have not configured enough VPN ports to support the number of VPN users who want to connect at once during periods of high use.

3. Why are pre-shared keys in IPSec not considered secure?

They are passed over the network in plaintext.

Lesson 4 Review

Page 10-81

1. What are the two basic types of RADIUS clients included with Windows Server 2003?

The first type is a network access server running Routing And Remote Access. The second type is a RADIUS proxy running IAS.

2. For a computer running IAS, what is the difference between remote access policies and connection request policies?

Remote access policies are applied by IAS when it is functioning as a RADIUS server. In this case, policies apply permissions, constraints, or other attributes to these connections. Connection request policies are applied by IAS when it is functioning as a RADIUS proxy. In this case, the policies help sort connection requests so that these connections can be routed to an appropriate RADIUS server group.

3. How can you migrate an IAS server?

First, use the Netsh aaaa show config >*filename.txt* command to dump the complete IAS server configuration into a script file. Then you can install the configuration included in this script file onto a particular IAS server by running the Netsh exec *[path]\filename.txt* command on the target server computer.

Case Scenario Exercise

Page
10-82 You have been hired as a consultant by Lucerne Publishing to assist with the deployment of remote access services for company employees. For each of the following, explain how you would configure the required remote access feature.

1. Lucerne Publishing wants to provide special dial-up access for 10 employees. These 10 employees should be authenticated only by verifying that the phone numbers from which they are calling are in fact these employees' home phone numbers. The employees should not need to type in a user name and password. How can you implement this configuration?

   Create a new remote access policy. When you configure the policy condition, select Calling-Station-ID as the attribute. Type the home phone number of the first employee. In the same policy, add a similar condition for each of the nine remaining employees. Configure the policy to grant access to connections that match the policy conditions. Edit the policy profile to allow unauthenticated access. After the policy is configured, be sure to configure the server properties to allow unauthenticated access.

2. Lucerne Publishing has already configured a PPTP-type VPN, but it wants to allow users who log on to the company domain to avoid having to type their user name and password twice. How can you allow users to avoid typing in their credentials in both the Log On To Windows screen and the VPN connection dialog box? Which authentication protocols can be used over this VPN connection?

   Instruct the employees to modify the properties of the VPN connection so that on the Security tab, the Automatically Use My Windows Logon Name And Password (And Domain If Any) option is selected. Only MS-CHAP v1 and MS-CHAP v2 can be used.

3. Lucerne Publishing wants to allow certain employees to be able to connect to the company network over multiple phone lines, but it wants to restrict other employees from doing the same. For the employees who are permitted to connect over multiple phone lines, the company wants to ensure that these employees use only two phone lines maximum, and that when the connection falls below 40 percent bandwidth capacity for 2 minutes, one of the phone lines is dropped. How can you implement this configuration?

   Create two Windows security groups that correspond to the two groups of employees you want to accommodate. Create two remote access policies, one applied to each of the two Windows security groups. Edit the policy profile of the first policy so that Multilink connections are not allowed. Edit the policy profile of the second profile so that Multilink connections are allowed, the maximum number of ports allowed is 2, the percentage of capacity is 40, and the period of time is 2 minutes.

11 Managing Network Security

Exam Objectives in this Chapter:

- Implement secure network administration procedures.

  - Implement security baseline settings and audit security settings by using security templates.

  - Implement the principle of least privilege.

- Monitor network protocol security. Tools might include the IP Security Monitor Microsoft Management Console (MMC) snap-in and Kerberos support tools.

- Troubleshoot network protocol security. Tools might include the IP Security Monitor MMC snap-in, Event Viewer, and Network Monitor.

Why This Chapter Matters

Nothing you do matters if you do not have a strategy that considers your network's security. Your carefully conceived and implemented systems can be shut down or otherwise overwhelmed by Denial of Service attacks and malware. Your data can be stolen, modified, deleted, or corrupted because of viruses, accidents, or directed attack. A computer can be remotely controlled by a malicious attacker, your Web site modified, or your company's reputation sullied. Worse, unprotected systems and networks can become the source of attacks on other organizations' systems, on critical national infrastructures such as dams, electric power grids, and so on.

This chapter introduces you to some tools and techniques for increasing security on your network, fulfilling your organization's security policy, and monitoring and troubleshooting network security protocols. You learn how to protect the individual system, extend that control across the enterprise, and maintain control over data as it travels from one computer to another. In addition, an important security paradigm, the principle of least privilege, is introduced.

Lessons in this Chapter:

- Lesson 1: Implementing Secure Network Administration Procedures 11-3
- Lesson 2: Monitoring Network Protocol Security. 11-24
- Lesson 3: Troubleshooting Network Protocol Security. 11-71

Before You Begin

To complete this chapter, you must have

- A Microsoft Windows Server 2003 domain with a domain controller (Computer1) and member server (Computer2).

- Assigned a static address for the member server if you have been using a Dynamic Host Configuration Protocol (DHCP)–assigned address in previous exercises.

- Installed Network Monitor.

- A computer running Microsoft Windows 2000 Professional. It should not be a member of the domain. If you do not have a system running Windows 2000 Professional, you can remove the member server from the domain and use it instead; you will get the same results with Windows Server 2003.

Lesson 1: Implementing Secure Network Administration Procedures

Managing the Windows Server 2003 family couldn't be easier. Right. Well, the process is greatly simplified; you can manage most network security settings from two interfaces: the Local Security Policy console and the IP Security Policy Management snap-in. However, it is not necessary to configure security one computer at a time. You can develop a master security administration process by using security templates and the Security Configuration And Analysis snap-in. You can apply multiple security templates, one for each server role, by using batch files—or, in a Windows Server 2003 domain, by using Group Policy. In this manner, all computers in a domain will periodically receive security policy.

Furthermore, you can easily administer, monitor, and troubleshoot security policy using native tools. This section lays the groundwork for that type of enterprise-level plan by introducing the tools and processes involved and by emphasizing sound security axioms. However, this section is not a reference on using Group Policy to implement a security plan, nor does it fully explore every setting you must make to ensure sound, all-encompassing security.

After this lesson, you will be able to

- Implement baseline security for multiple security roles
- Use the Security Configuration And Analysis snap-in to test a server for compliance with security policy
- Select provided templates for use in administering security
- Recover default security settings
- Develop a new security template for a specific purpose
- Name and describe the uses for other native Windows Server 2003 security tools
- Implement the principle of least privilege using a security template

Estimated lesson time: 30 minutes

Introducing Network Security Protocols

Network security protocols are used to manage and secure authentication, authorization, confidentiality, integrity, and nonrepudiation. In a Windows Server 2003 network, the major protocols used are Kerberos, New Technology Local Area Network Manager (NTLM), Internet Protocol Security (IPSec), and their various subprotocols. Other network communication protocols support these protocols, and other security settings support and protect the use of these security protocols. Table 11-1 lists the security paradigms and the protocols that support them.

Table 11-1 Network Security Protocols

Paradigm	Purpose	Protocols
Authentication	To prove you are who you say you are	Kerberos and NTLM (The NT LAN Manager [LM] protocol is not available by default, but can be configured.)
Authorization	To determine what you can do on the network after you have authenticated	Kerberos and NTLM
Confidentiality	To keep data secret	Encryption components of Kerberos, NTLM, and IPSec (to secure communications other than authentication)
Integrity	To ensure that the data received is the same data that is sent	Components of Kerberos, NTLM, and IPSec
Nonrepudiation	To determine exactly who sent and received the message	Kerberos and IPSec

This section concentrates on the use of two snap-ins, Security Templates and Security Configuration And Analysis, to implement the protocols and settings for security. Additional sections of this chapter explore how to use other tools to administer, monitor, and secure network protocol security. (IP Security Monitor, Network Monitor, Netcap, Netsh, Kerbtray, and Klist are discussed in the section "Monitoring Network Protocol Security." Event logs, IP Security Monitor, and Network Monitor are discussed in the section "Troubleshooting Network Protocol Security.") Still other security tools are available in Windows Server 2003 but not discussed in this chapter.

Using Security Templates to Administer Network Security

The task of implementing server security configurations in a Windows network is threefold. First, you must understand what constitutes good security. Second, you must be able to implement security for the organization's information systems for the equipment you manage. Finally, you must make sure the tools and methodologies are available for quickly applying a security configuration, and you must understand how to use and maintain them.

Ultimately, management must determine the most appropriate security policies, but the discussion here gives you sound reasons for specific security settings. In the past, many tools and low-level Registry adjustments were necessary to fulfill a security policy. Today, however, security templates, and especially their global application through

Group Policy, can address the third task: quick enterprisewide application and maintenance. The first piece of that solution is knowing what to do with the templates.

Security Templates Snap-In

You load the Security Templates snap-in in an MMC. By default, several templates are available, you can add more templates, and you can modify settings or develop new templates. The recommended methods of using the templates include the following:

- Design a security baseline for each computer role. Computer roles include domain controllers, file and print servers, mail servers, database servers, network services servers (DHCP, Domain Name System [DNS], Windows Internet Name Service [WINS], and so on), Web servers, remote access servers, desktop systems, and so forth.

- Design security baselines for major server roles. Security configuration that is common to all baselines can be implemented as master baselines. Specifics for unique roles are implemented as supplemental baselines. In a typical Windows Server 2003 network, two master baselines are usually defined, one for domain controllers and one for all other computers.

- Implement master and additional baselines in security templates.

- Apply the master templates to all machines and supplemental templates to appropriate machines using deployment tools. You can deploy security templates in several ways, including using batch files that apply the templates directly and Group Policy.

Designing Master and Supplemental Security Baselines for Security Templates

The first step in designing the security baseline is to understand what the organization's security policy requires. After you have that information, the next step is to determine which security measures can be fulfilled by using the security templates. You should assign to the master template items that are common to all computer roles, and assign to individual supplemental templates those items that mark the difference between roles.

You will have to determine your organization's security policy, but this section describes the security settings that you can implement through security templates. You must implement additional security policy with other tools. Table 11-2 lists each section and subsection of the template and describes how you can use them to implement security policy. You should examine sample templates available in the Security Templates snap-in to see the hundreds of possible security settings. You should understand that you can add and manage additional elements in the templates and that you can apply additional security settings using other Windows Server 2003 tools.

> **Note**   Browsing the Security Templates snap-in, even changing settings on the templates, does not change the security policy of any computer. To change security, you must apply the template. The exercises that follow provide complete instructions for loading, browsing, modifying, creating, and applying security templates.

Table 11-2   Security Template Sections

Section	Subsection	Description
Account Policies	Password Policy	The configuration for passwords, including minimum length, history, complexity, and frequency of change.
	Account Lock-out Policy	The number of failed attempts before the account is locked out. How it is reset, and the amount of time between attempts that triggers the failed logon account to start over again.
	Kerberos Policy	The ticket lifetime, ticket renewal time, whether user logon restrictions are honored, and clock skew time.
Local Policies	Audit Policy	The types of audit events that are logged. Options include account logon, account management, object auditing, processing auditing, privilege use, and policy change.
	User Rights	What users can do on the system. Rights include logon rights, backup and restore, and so on.
	Security Options	The implementation of various security settings through Registry settings. A default listing includes items that affect authentication, narrow choices, prevent connection, and so on. The section "Understanding Security Template Settings That Affect Network Security" gives examples. Also, you can implement any Registry setting you make by adding it to a security template and applying the template.
Event Log		The ability to change size. Defines when logs are overwritten, how long records are retained, or both.
Restricted Groups		The ability to manage the memberships of any Windows group. Groups managed here can be added to and accounts removed in the normal manner, but if the template application is refreshed, the group membership is replaced by the membership listed here.
System Services		The ability to change the startup setting (Disabled, Automatic, or Manual) for individual services. Also, you can change security for services by determining who can stop, start, and modify startup settings for each service.

Table 11-2   Security Template Sections

Section	Subsection	Description
Registry		The security permissions for Registry keys. Settings in a template, if the template is applied, overwrite current permissions settings. Using the Registry Sections section of the security template is a good way to manage secured keys because the settings can be uniform throughout the domain and can be quickly reset should they be changed. Note that you cannot add new Registry keys here nor change their values. You can add management of security on existing Registry keys.
File System		The security permissions for files and folders.

The Security Templates snap-in links by default to the WINDOWS\Security\Templates folder where available templates are stored. You can add the default templates from the WINDOWS\Inf folder to the default template location so that they can be viewed. You can also create a folder and add templates from other sources.

See Also   The "Windows Server 2003 Security" white paper is an excellent source of security templates and describes how to use them to implement a strategy like the one defined here. (Go to *http://go.microsoft.com/fwlink/?LinkId=14846.*)

Table 11-3 describes the templates that come with Windows Server 2003.

Table 11-3   Security Templates

Template	Location	Description
Compatws	Security\Templates	Applies file and Registry permissions that might allow legacy applications to work. The Compatws template decreases security.
DC security	Security\Templates	Applies default security settings for a domain controller (DC).
Hisecdc	Security\Templates	Further secures a DC, includes increased security for NTLM, disables additional services, applies additional Registry and file security. Removes any members in the Power Users group. (Hisecdc is a stronger, more secure setting than Securedc.)

Table 11-3   Security Templates

Template	Location	Description
Hisecws	Security\Templates	Further secures a workstation, includes increased security for NTLM, removes any members in the Power Users group. Limits membership in the local Administrators group to Domain Admins and Administrator. Hisecws is a stronger, more secure setting than Securews.
Iesacls	Security\Templates	Applies Registry permissions on keys integral to Microsoft Internet Explorer. This template sets the Registry permissions to Everyone Full Control and Read.
Rootsec	Security\Templates	Applies root permission to the system drive.
Securedc	Security\Templates	Limits account policies. Applies LAN Manager restrictions.
Securews	Security\Templates	Enhances local account policies. Applies LAN Manager restrictions.
Setup security	Security\Templates	Represents the security applied to the current machine on installation.
Defltsv	WINDOW\Inf	Applies the default server template used during installation.
Defltdc	WINDOW\Inf	Applies the default DC template used during Dcpromo.

Using the Security Templates Snap-In to Define the Baselines

You can configure baseline templates using the Security Templates snap-in. To configure a baseline template, complete the following steps:

1. Create a Security Templates snap-in.

2. Add a folder for organization templates.

3. Copy a template to create a new organization baseline template.

4. Modify a template.

5. Save a template.

6. If necessary, modify a template by editing its Inf file.

> **Tip**   You should add most template settings using the Security Templates snap-in. The template file is a text file, but the required syntax might be confusing, and using the snap-in ensures that settings are changed using the proper syntax. However, the exception to this rule is adding Registry settings that are not already listed in the Security Option portion of the template. As new security settings become known, if they can be configured using a Registry key, you can add them to a security template. To do so, you add them to the [Registry Values] section of the template. The article "How to Add Custom Registry Settings to Security Configuration Editor" helps you understand how to perform this task. You can find it at *http://support.microsoft.com/?kbid=214752*.

Using the Security Configuration And Analysis Snap-In to Apply a Template and Monitor Security Policy Compliance

Creating and modifying templates does not improve security unless you apply the templates. You can use the Security Configuration And Analysis snap-in to apply a template to the local machine. You can also use the tool to compare the settings in any template with the settings that exist on the computer. This process is extremely useful. When an analysis is performed, the variations between the existing security implementation and those in the selected template are indicated in the interface by a red *x*. This type of comparison shows you the effect of applying a template.

However, even more useful is the ability to monitor security on a computer by periodically comparing the security configuration to the baseline template. Variations are evidence of policy noncompliance and need to be investigated and reset. (The exercises at the end of this section provide instructions for using the Security Configuration And Analysis snap-in to apply the template and to analyze security compliance.)

If you apply additional templates, you must decide whether to clear the database. If the database is cleared, only the settings in the new template will be applied. However, if the old template settings were previously applied to the machine, clearing the template from the database does not remove these settings. If the database is not cleared, adding an additional template means the following:

- If the new template setting is not defined and the old template setting is defined, the setting remains the way it is in the old template.

- If a setting in the new template is defined and the setting is not defined in the old template, the setting changes to the setting in the new template.

- If a setting is defined in both the old template and the new template, the new template setting is applied.

Using Secedit to Apply Security Templates

Secedit is a command-line version of the Security Configuration And Analysis snap-in and offers some additional functionality. The following statement indicates the Secedit syntax, and Table 11-4 defines each setting.

```
Secedit [\configure /db filename.sdb / [/areas,  area name, areaname][/cfg filename]
[/log filename][/quiet][ | \analyze db filename.sdb / [/cfg filename][/log filename]
[/quiet] | \import /db filename.sdb /mergedpolicy [/areas area name, areanname]
[/cfg filename][/log filename][/quiet]| \export db filename.sdb /overwrite
[/areas area name, areanname][/cfg filename][/log filename]|validate filename
[/quiet]|  | [\genereate rollback [/cfg] [/RBK ][/logfile][/quiet]]
```

Table 11-4   Secedit Syntax

Setting	Description	Comments
Configure	Applies security settings from a template.	Never use this setting without creating a rollback. A rollback can return most of the security configuration to the way it was, should you find that your template is not correct or causes problems.
Analyze	Compares settings in a database template to those set on the machine.	Use this setting to audit security settings for compliance.
Import	Imports a template into a database.	Use this setting to create the database to be used in a future configuration or analysis. You can also import and configure or analyze at the same time.
Export	Exports a template from a database.	Use this setting to build a new template by combining two or more templates. Simply add each template in the order you want into the database, and then use the Export command to produce an Inf template file.
Validate	Validates syntax of a template.	Use this setting if you have added settings directly to the Inf file.
Generate rollback	Makes a reverse template, that is, a template that removes most of the settings applied with a template.	Always make one rollback before applying a new template. However, be aware that it does not change access control lists (ACLs) on files and in the Registry that might have been set with the template.
Db	Specifies the name of the database file to create or to use.	You might need to enter the whole path.

Table 11-4   Secedit Syntax

Setting	Description	Comments
Cfg	Specifies the name of the template to use.	You might need to enter the whole path.
Overwrite	Overwrites any existing template in the file with another.	Use this setting if you do not want a combined effect when applying a template. If the old template in the file has already been applied, using this setting will not change security settings on the computer that are not overwritten by the new template.
Log	Specifies a log file to record errors.	This setting always records errors. By default, if no log file is specified, the system uses WINDOWS\Security\Logs\Scesrv.log.
Quiet	Specifies that no data should appear on the screen, and no comments on progress should be provided to the user.	When you use this setting in a script, the logged-on user does not need to know that the program is running.
Areas	Applies only the settings as listed in a specific area of the template. Other settings are ignored.	The areas are SECURITYPOLICY, GROUP_MGMT (restricted groups), USER_RIGHTS, REGKEYS, FILESTORE, and SERVICES.
Mergedpolicy	Merges and exports domain and local policy.	This setting captures all security settings.
RBK	Specifies the name of the security template to be created.	This setting is available only with the /generaterollback setting.

Following are some example Secedit commands:

- **To configure the machine using the XYZ template**   secedit /configure /db xyz.sdb /cfg xyz.inf /log xyz.log

- **To create a rollback template for the XYZ template**   secedit /generaterollback /cfg xyz.inf /rbk xyzrollback.inf /log xyzrollback.log

For more information about Secedit, refer to the Windows Server 2003 Help and Support Center.

Understanding Security Template Settings That Affect Network Security

Each security template can potentially have hundreds of settings that affect everything from password policy to group membership to permissions on files. All the settings can affect local and network security. Although all the settings and their importance cannot be listed here, you should be aware of the settings specific to network security access and protocols. Table 11-5 lists the settings and the area within the security template where they are located.

Table 11-5   Security Options for Improving Network Security

Setting	Template Location	Description
Access this computer from the network	User Rights	This setting determines which users and computers can access this computer.
Add workstations to a domain	User Rights	By default, all domain users have the right to add 10 computers to a domain.
Logon rights (multiple settings)	User Rights	This setting includes several logon rights, such as the right to log on locally, and the opposite, the right to deny logon locally, for example.
Digitally encrypt or sign secure channel data (multiple settings)	Security Options	This setting controls how secure channel data crosses the network. You want the most secure, but you must sometimes relax settings to get connectivity. For example, downlevel computers might not be able to communicate using the same security settings as Windows Server 2003.
Allow anonymous (multiple settings)	Security Options	This setting determines which types of anonymous connections and anonymous access are allowed.
Do not store LAN Manager hash value on next password change	Security Options	Because the new password hash for the change is not stored, a computer that can use only LM will not be able to authenticate.
LAN Manager authentication level	Security options	This setting determines which versions of the LM protocol are accepted. The insecure version, LM, is not allowed by default; instead, computers must use NTLM, NTLMv2, or Kerberos.
Minimum Sessions security (two settings)	Security Options	This setting determines whether message integrity, confidentiality, and encryption are required.

Applying the Principle of Least Privilege

One of the most important concepts that should guide your development and implementation of security policy is *the principle of least privilege*. Using this principle means that no employee and no user of information systems has more privileges or access to information and resources than they need to do their job. This principle includes removing privileges and access when employees change jobs within the organization or when they leave the company. The principle of least privilege also means that visitors to the organization or to any information resources—such as the public, contractors, temporary workers, partner representatives, and so on—should be treated in the same manner. No one, and that includes system administrators and IT workers, should have any more access or rights than they need to do their job.

There are many ways to implement and follow this maxim. The ways can be categorized according to those that are possible using security templates and those that require other mechanisms to implement. This subject is broad, and the following lists are by no means meant to be comprehensive. Instead, they are meant to teach the paradigm.

Security Template Least Privilege Opportunities

- Develop a strong password policy to keep unauthorized individuals off systems.
- Assign user rights sparingly. Reduce rights, especially access and logon rights, as much as possible. Set different rights on computers with different roles.
- Use security options to block access and restrict activity.
- Use file and Registry ACLs.
- Use the Restricted Groups section to force and limit membership in sensitive groups.
- Use the Services section to disable services and restrict who can manage them.
- Develop a baseline plan for every computer role and implement using templates that are imported into Group Policy Objects (GPOs) on representative organizational units (OUs).
- Apply a comprehensive auditing strategy.

Nonsecurity Template Least Privilege Opportunities

- Group users by role so that privileges and permissions can be granted by role.
- Configure ACLs for files, folders, Registry keys, directory objects, and printers to allow only the exact access any group of users needs.
- Physically protect servers. Allow access only to authorized personnel and screen this authorization.

- Review audit logs and other logs looking for needs to restrict further access.

- Use Web proxies to limit user access to external resources.

- Use firewalls to limit access to internal networks.

Practice: Creating and Using the Security Configuration And Analysis Console

Security templates are useful tools in network security management. An easy way to work with them is to create a console that includes access to them, as well as a way to apply them and analyze the resulting security policy. You can perform this task by creating a console and adding the Security Templates snap-in and the Security Configuration And Analysis snap-in.

Exercise 1: Create the Console: Apply Default Templates

In this exercise, you create a console within which you can view, configure, or copy security templates, add a new folder to hold a different location for templates, and apply a security template to a computer. Working with the templates in the console will not change security on the computer.

▶ **To create a Security Configuration And Analysis console**

1. From the Start menu select Run, type **MMC**, and click OK.

2. From the File menu, select Add/Remove Snap-In.

3. In the Add/Remove Snap-In dialog box, click the Add button, as shown in Figure 11-1.

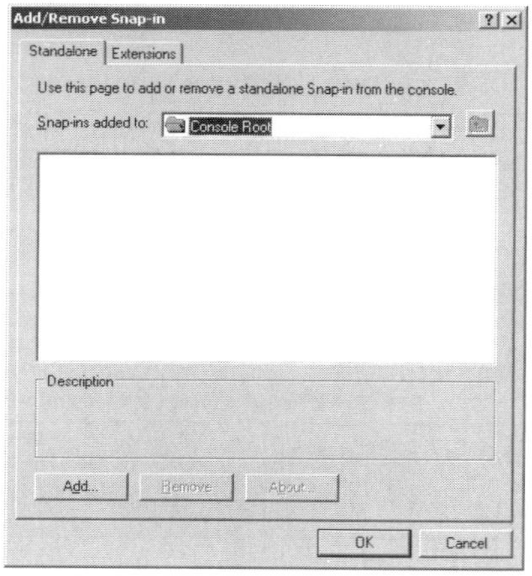

Figure 11-1   Adding the snap-in

4. From the Add Standalone Snap-In dialog box, select Security Templates. Then click Add, as shown in Figure 11-2.

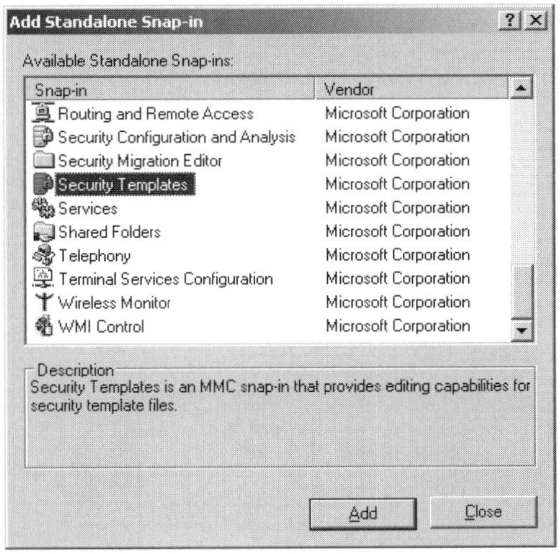

Add Standalone Snap-in

Available Standalone Snap-ins:

Snap-in	Vendor
Routing and Remote Access	Microsoft Corporation
Security Configuration and Analysis	Microsoft Corporation
Security Migration Editor	Microsoft Corporation
Security Templates	Microsoft Corporation
Services	Microsoft Corporation
Shared Folders	Microsoft Corporation
Telephony	Microsoft Corporation
Terminal Services Configuration	Microsoft Corporation
Wireless Monitor	Microsoft Corporation
WMI Control	Microsoft Corporation

Description
Security Templates is an MMC snap-in that provides editing capabilities for security template files.

[Add] [Close]

Figure 11-2   Selecting security templates

5. Select the Security Configuration And Analysis snap-in, click Add, and then click Close.

6. Click OK to add the snap-in to the console.

7. To save the console, from the File menu select Save As. Type **Security Configuration Management**. Then click Save.

▶ **To prepare a location for custom security templates and add it to the console**

1. In Windows Explorer, create a new folder named Custom Templates.

2. Open the Security Configuration Management console.

3. Right-click Security Templates, and from the shortcut menu select New Template Search Path.

4. Select the Custom Templates folder and click OK.

Note   Best practices recommend never modifying default templates. Instead, new templates or copies of current ones are placed in a separate location and then used to create custom templates. Consequently, you always have the default templates, and because custom templates are stored separately, it is easier to copy them and store originals in a safe place.

The new folder appears in the Security Configuration Management console, as shown in Figure 11-3.

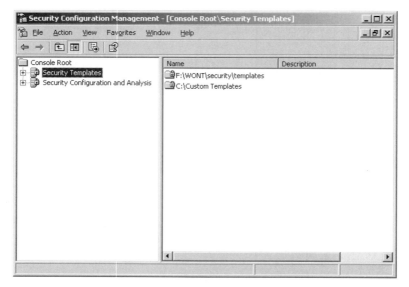

Figure 11-3 Additional template file locations

Exercise 2: Create Custom Templates

In this exercise, you develop your own custom templates. You select a default template that is close to the template you need, copy it, and then make adjustments to the copy. The Securews.inf template has some setting changes that strengthen network communication security.

1. In the Security Templates console, right-click the Securews.inf security template and select Save As.

2. Browse to the Custom Templates folder created previously.

3. Type **test1** for the new template name and click Save.

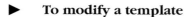 **To modify a template**

1. Expand the Custom Templates folder in the Security Configuration Management console. You might need to refresh the console to see the Test1 template.

2. Expand the Test1 template sections.

3. Expand the Local Policies node and select Security Options, as shown in Figure 11-4.

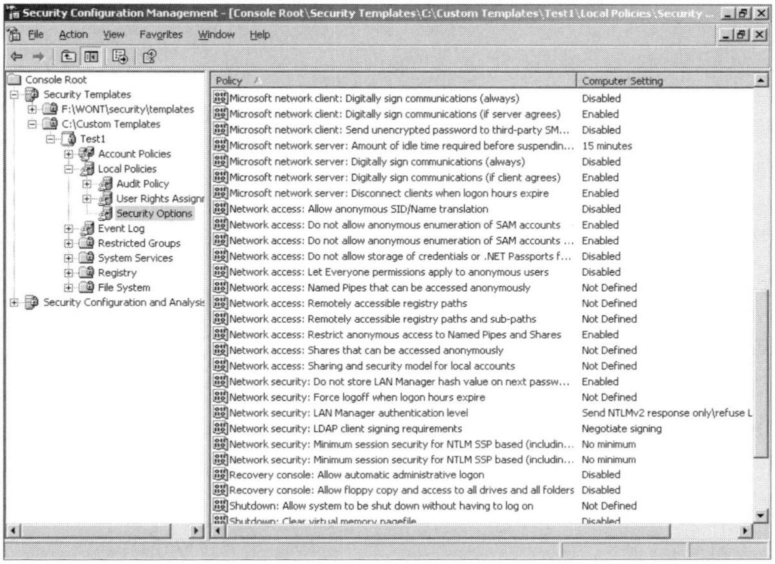

Figure 11-4   Examining Security Options

4. In the details pane, scroll to the Network Access and Network Security sections and note the settings.

   Note that the policy setting is Not Defined.

5. Double-click the policy, Shutdown: Allow System To Be Shut Down Without Having To Log On.

   The Shutdown: Allow System To Be Shut Down Without Having To Log On dialog box appears, as shown in Figure 11-5.

6. Select the Define This Policy Setting In The Template check box if it is not already selected, and then click Disabled.

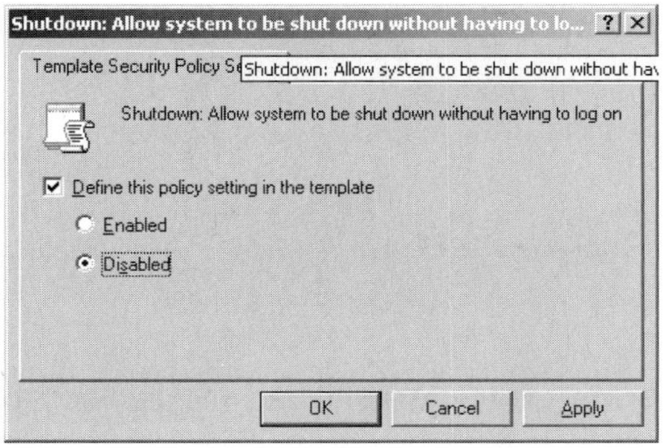

Figure 11-5   Modifying template settings

7. Click OK.

> **Note**   The settings and techniques that are available will vary depending on the setting. Many settings first require you to select Define This Policy Setting in the template before changing any specific settings using Add buttons, text boxes, drop-down lists, and option buttons.

8. Right-click the template name and click Save to save the changes to the template.

▶ **To modify a template by editing its Inf file**

1. In Windows Explorer, browse to the Custom Template folder.

2. Double-click the Test1 template to open it in Notepad.

3. Examine the [Registry Values] section, as shown in Figure 11-6.

   In this section, you can edit or add Registry values that will then be applied when the template is applied.

```
[Application Log]
RestrictGuestAccess = 1
[Registry Values]
machine\software\microsoft\windows\currentversion\polici
machine\system\currentcontrolset\control\lsa\disabledoma
machine\system\currentcontrolset\control\lsa\everyoneinc
machine\system\currentcontrolset\control\lsa\fipsalgorit
machine\system\currentcontrolset\control\lsa\forceguest=
machine\system\currentcontrolset\control\lsa\limitblankp
machine\system\currentcontrolset\control\lsa\lmcompatibi
machine\system\currentcontrolset\control\lsa\nodefaultac
machine\system\currentcontrolset\control\lsa\restrictanc
machine\system\currentcontrolset\control\securepipeserve
machine\system\currentcontrolset\control\securepipeserve
machine\system\currentcontrolset\control\session manager
machine\system\currentcontrolset\control\session manager
machine\system\currentcontrolset\services\lanmanserver\p
machine\system\currentcontrolset\services\ldap\ldapclier
machine\system\currentcontrolset\services\netlogon\param
[Privilege Rights]
seundockprivilege = *S-1-5-32-547,*S-1-5-32-544
sesystemtimeprivilege = *S-1-5-32-549,*S-1-5-32-544
```

Figure 11-6   Adding Registry settings to the Inf file to be applied when the template is applied

▶ **To apply the template**

1. Create a rollback template by using this command:

```
secedit /generaterollback /cfg test1.inf /rbk test1rollback.inf
/log test1rollback.log
```

   Using the Rollback command creates a template that can be used to roll back the security settings to the way they were before the Test1.inf template is applied. The Test1rollback.inf template is made first, then the Test1.inf template is applied.

Rollback is not supported for file and Registry security. That is, any permissions edited in these sections of the template file will not be reversible by applying the rollback template.

2. Open the Security Configuration Management console.

3. Right-click the Security Configuration And Analysis node in the console and select Open Database.

   A database is not created automatically, so the first step is to create one.

4. In the File Name text box, type the name for the new database and click Open.

   Since a rollback template has been made in step 1, the template designed to make changes we want is applied next. If later, it is found that this template is incorrect, the rollback template can be used to return things to the way they were before.

5. In the Import Template dialog box, select the Test1.inf template and click Open, as shown in Figure 11-7.

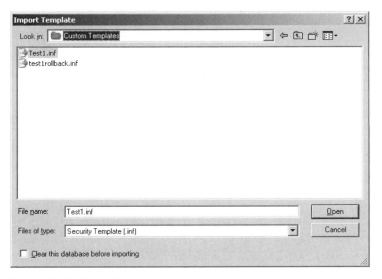

Figure 11-7   Importing a template

6. Right-click Security Configuration And Analysis and select Configure Computer Now.

7. Click OK when asked to confirm the location of the error log.

   The error log is also a good source of information about which templates were applied and when.

8. Wait for the configuration to complete, and close the console without saving it.

Exercise 4: Recover from the Application of a Bad Template

You could change the security settings and find that the computer has been rendered inaccessible on the network, or that security has been changed to make the computer less secure than is required. If a rollback template was made before the template was applied, you can roll the system back to a previous security state. If you need to recover Registry and file system permissions to an installation state, you can do so by applying one of the default installation templates. If this is not necessary, simply apply the rollback template.

In this exercise, you restore security configuration settings by applying a rollback template.

1. Open the Security Configuration Management console created in Exercise 1.

2. Right-click Security Configuration And Analysis and select Import Template.

3. In the Import Template dialog box, shown in Figure 11-8, select the Test1rollback.inf template.

4. Select the Clear This Database Before Importing check box, and click Open.

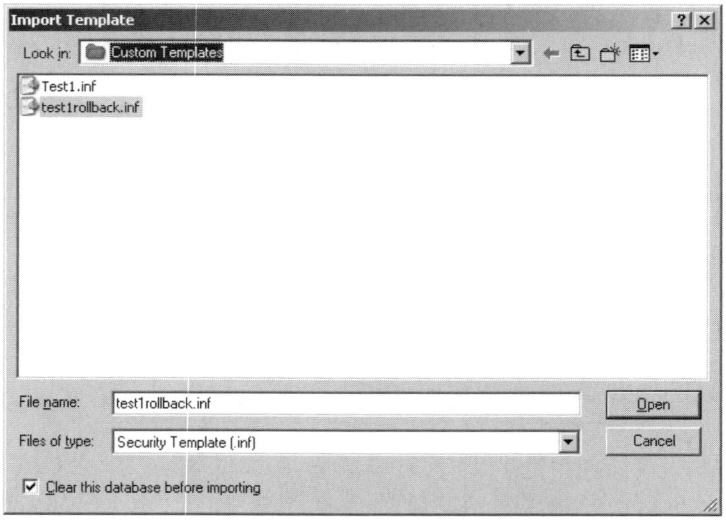

Figure 11-8   Clearing the database

If the check box is not cleared, the information in both templates is applied.

5. Right-click Security Configuration And Analysis and select Configure Computer Now.

6. Click OK to approve the error log file.

7. Close the console.

Exercise 5: Monitor Security Compliance

Security policies are often implemented by configuring security on systems and then they are ignored. When problems occur, security settings are often changed, and the changes are forgotten as well. To inspect systems for this type of change, in this exercise you use the Security Configuration And Analysis snap-in to compare the current settings to the template created to match security policy.

1. Open the Security Configuration Management console.

2. Right-click Security Configuration And Analysis and select Import Template.

3. Select the Test1.inf template, and then click Open.

4. Right-click Security Configuration And Analysis and select Analyze Computer Now.

5. Click OK to approve the error log path.

   When the analysis is complete, you can examine in the console the database settings and differences against policy.

6. Open each node and inspect the details pane, as shown in Figure 11-9, for changes.

   In the details pane, changes are marked with a red *x*. Note that the Database Setting column and the Computer Setting column are shown so that you can determine the exact differences, and also note where items are not analyzed and might have to be inspected manually.

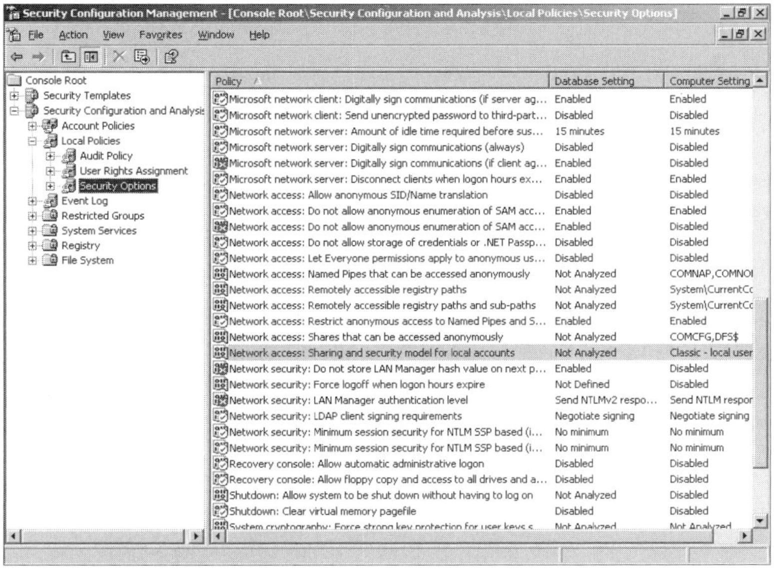

Figure 11-9   Inspecting for changes

7. Close the console.

Lesson Review

The following questions are intended to reinforce key information presented in this lesson. If you are unable to answer a question, review the lesson materials and try the question again. You can find answers to the questions in the "Questions and Answers" section at the end of this chapter.

1. You would like to apply a new Registry setting to all the servers on your network. What is an efficient way to perform that task?

_____

_____

_____

_____

_____

2. Which of the following settings can be applied using Security Configuration And Analysis and a security template? (Choose all that apply.)

    a. The password must be 15 characters long.

    b. The Accountants group is not allowed to access this computer over the network.

    c. IPSec must be used for all communications between Computer1 and Computer2.

    d. The root file permissions should be Everyone Full Control.

3. Which steps might be necessary to recover from the application of a security template to a file server that prevented all users from accessing the server over the network? Choose the most efficient way.

    a. Log on locally to the file server as Administrator and apply the root security template.

    b. Log on locally to the file server as Administrator and apply the rollback template produced from the bad security template.

    c. Log on remotely to the file server as Enterprise Admin and use the Local Security Policy console to change the user rights policies that might be incorrect.

    d. Log on remotely to the file server as Administrator and apply the rollback template produced from the security template.

Lesson Summary

- You can use security templates to define a large part of the computer baseline security policy approved by management.

- You can configure supplemental baseline templates to specifications for each computer role.

- You can use security templates to analyze computer security compliance. You can use security templates to apply security using the Security Configuration And Analysis snap-in.

- You can use the command-line tool Secedit to analyze and configure security as well as to export security templates from a security database.

- You can use Secedit to produce a rollback template, a template than can undo the harmful affects applied by a bad template.

Lesson 2: Monitoring Network Protocol Security

When the network appears to be running smoothly, you might be tempted to kick off your shoes, put your feet on the desk, lace your hands behind your neck, and breathe a deep sigh of relief. However, now is the time to monitor network security protocol activity—if you don't know what normal traffic looks like, how will you recognize the abnormal? How will you know when there are problems you must resolve and whether attacks are underway? How will you be able to use your diagnostic tools to find out why something is not happening correctly and what you must do to fix it? If some problems are masked by the resiliency of your network, it is far better to find them now, before they become downtime or disaster.

This is the perfect time to learn to use those utilities and tools that might help when your network goes down; when the VP of Marketing cannot log on to the domain; when no connection can be made to the Accounting database; when the boss is on line 2 and everyone else is standing around looking expectantly at you.

This lesson provides information on the tools available to monitor network security protocols. It tells you how to use them, and in doing so provides insight into the protocols themselves.

After this lesson, you will be able to

- Use Netsh to understand IPSec
- Use Netsh to manage IPSec
- Use IP Security Monitor to monitor IPSec traffic
- Use Netcap to capture network traffic
- Understand the basics of Kerberos
- Use Network Monitor to understand Kerberos
- Use the Kerberos tools Kerbtray and Klist to examine the Kerberos ticket cache

Estimated lesson time: 60 minutes

Understanding IPSec

IPSec is a complex protocol that you can use for the following tasks:

- Authenticate and encrypt traffic between two computers
- Block specific traffic from entering or leaving a computer
- Allow specific traffic to enter or leave a computer

The specifics of the protocol and how it works are defined in a large number of Internet Engineering Task Force (IETF) Requests for Comments (RFC). These RFCs detail the standards by which the protocol should be implemented, and, if published in book form, would fill hundreds of pages.

> **See Also**   To make an exhaustive study of IPSec, you can read these RFCs: 3457, 3456, 3281, 3193, 2857, 2709, 2451, and approximately 22 more; you can obtain copies at *http://www.ietf.org*.

However, you do not need to know the intimate details to understand the basics of how IPSec works, to implement an IPSec policy in Windows Server 2003, and to monitor its activity to ensure that it is protecting traffic. Several tools are available to help you do so, including these:

- The IP Security Monitor snap-in
- The graphical user interface (GUI)–based IP Security Policy Management tool available as a snap-in or in a GPO
- Netsh
- Netdiag
- Event logs

A brief overview of IPSec will assist your work.

Understanding How IPSec Works

You can think of *IPSec policies* as a collection of packet filters that enforce security policy on IP traffic. Each *filter* describes some network protocol action. If traffic leaving or arriving at the device (a computer or other IP network device) on which the policy is active matches one of the filters, the traffic is either blocked, allowed, or, before it can proceed, an IPSec connection is negotiated between the sending and receiving devices.

Filters can be the receipt or initialization of a specific protocol, a connection request from or to a specific device, or another action that can be determined by protocol, port, IP address, or range. These filters are defined in the IPSec policy in a rule. Example filters might include the following:

- All traffic from IP address 192.168.5.77
- All traffic to IP address 192.168.5.101
- All traffic on port 23, telnet's default port
- Traffic from 192.168.6.99 on port 23

Filters are combined into *filter lists*, which are, in turn, part of rules. Each *rule* also defines a *filter action* and potentially extensive configuration information that defines the specifics to be used for negotiating an IPSec connection. Filter actions are Block, Allow, or Negotiate Security. Each rule can have only one filter action, but a policy can be made up of many rules.

For example, if the result required is that only telnet sessions that originate from a specific computer will be accepted and must be encrypted, two rules should be written: one to block all telnet traffic and the other to negotiate telnet traffic from that specific computer. When an IPSec policy is evaluated, the more specific rule will take precedence. If the telnet traffic originates with the specified computer, the communication is negotiated, and, assuming the policy configuration matches where necessary, allowed to proceed. If the traffic originates from any other IP address, because no specific rule exists for the address, the more general rule is triggered and the communication will be blocked.

New IPSec Features for 2003

IPSec is natively available and can be used to protect network communications for Microsoft Windows 2000, Microsoft Windows XP Professional, and Windows Server 2003. A legacy client is available for Microsoft Windows NT 4, Microsoft Windows 98, and Microsoft Windows Millennium Edition (Me). You can download the legacy client from *http://www.microsoft.com/windows2000/server/evaluation /news/bulletins/l2tpclient.asp*. New features for IPSec include the following:

- The IP Security Monitor snap-in improves on the Ipsecmon.exe tool in Windows 2000. (New in Windows XP Professional and Windows Server 2003.)

- A stronger cryptographic master key is introduced, Diffie-Hellman 2048-bit.

- The Netsh command-line management tool provides convenience, plus many configuration possibilities that are not available from the IP Security Policy Management snap-in.

- Computer startup security (or stateful filter), if configured, is activated at startup and manages network traffic during startup. It allows only the outbound traffic that the computer initiates during startup, inbound traffic sent in response to the outbound traffic, and DHCP traffic.

- The persistent policy is applied if the local policy or the Active Directory directory service IPSec policy cannot be applied.

- Only Internet Key Exchange (IKE) traffic is exempt from traffic filters. This restriction is required in order to establish secured communication.

- Certain restrictions determine which computers are allowed to connect by domain, by certificate origin, or by computer group.

- The name of the certificate authority (CA) can be excluded from certificate requests to prevent exposure of information on computer trust relationships such as domain, CA, and company.

- Logical addressing is applied for local IP configuration—such as DHCP server, DNS, and WINS—to accommodate dynamic addressing.

- IPSec functionality over NAT lets Encapsulation Security Payload (ESP) packets pass through Network Address Translations (NATs) that allow User Datagram Protocol (UDP) traffic.

- Integration with Network Load Balancing has improved, which is good for load balancing IPSec-based virtual private network (VPN) services.

- Support is provided for the Resultant Set Of Policy (RSoP) snap-in to view existing IPSec policy assignments.

Negotiation Configuration

Negotiation is the process that determines which IPSec subprotocol will be used, and what specifics, such as key strength and cryptographic algorithms, will be used. Next is a list of the basic choices available to you when you configure an IPSec policy. You can make these choices by using the IPSec wizards, by editing a policy in the IP Security Policies snap-in or in Group Policy, or by using the Netsh command-line tool. Additional options are available when you configure policy using the Netsh command. The exercises at the end of this lesson show you how to use the provided wizards to write a policy, and you also learn how to find these elements in the GUI. In the exercises using Netsh, simply set them in the commands.

- **Authentication**   How the computers involved prove their identity.

- **Connection type**   Where the policy is active.

- **Diffie-Hellman group**   The size of the prime numbers used in the Diffie-Hellman master key calculation.

- **Filters**   Each filter list can contain many filters. Filters include Protocol, Source Port, Source IP Address, Source Mask, Source DNS Name, Destination Port, Destination DNS, Destination IP Address, and Destination Mask.

- **Filter Actions**   What happens when the filter is triggered.

- **IKE encryption protocol**   How IKE packets are encrypted.

- **IKE integrity protocols**   How IKE packets are protected to ensure data has not been changed during transport.

- **IKE security method**   How IKE is negotiated.

- **IP Security Rules**   Many rules can be defined.

- **IP Filter Lists**   Many filter lists can be defined.

- **Master Key Perfect Forward Security**   If selected, the master key will be recalculated for every sessions.

- **Tunnel Setting**   Whether the traffic uses a tunnel.

> **Note**   Many people have trouble understanding filter actions. They especially have trouble distinguishing between Request Security and Require Security. *Require Security,* if chosen, accepts unsecured communication but always responds using IPSec. If the client cannot speak IPSec, then the conversation ends there. It is as if you speak only English and another person speaks only Spanish. You ask a question and the other person responds, but you cannot understand. *Request Security* is different. Although the computer responds to a non-IPSec request by using IPSec, if the other computer does not answer using IPSec, the first one drops back and does not use IPSec. The communication can continue.

Negotiation Process

When an IPSec policy is Assigned (made active) and the IPSec service is running each network communication, both incoming and outgoing policies are evaluated to see whether they meet the conditions specified in the IPSec policy. If a condition match is made—for example, an outgoing Simple Mail Transfer Protocol (SMTP) communication that matches a filter—the filter is triggered and the filter action occurs. If the filter action is Block or Allow, that is what occurs, but if it is Negotiate, a number of processing steps must follow.

Processing can be divided into Phase I, or Main Mode negotiation, and Phase II, or Quick Mode negotiation. For purposes of this discussion, we'll use the computer names Red and Blue. Figure 11-10 illustrates a simplification of the process. A more detailed explanation follows.

1. A request has triggered the IPSec filter.

2. Main Mode (the master key and the IKE Security Association [SA] are established) negotiations begin and complete.

3. The negation of an SA pair (inbound and outbound) for application packet transfers completes.

4. The application packets are passed by the Transmission Control Protocol/Internet Protocol (TCP/IP) driver to the IPSec driver.

5. The IPSec driver formats and cryptographically processes the packets and sends them using the outbound SA.

6. Secure packets cross the network.

7. The IPSec driver on the receiving computer cryptographically processes the packets arriving on the inbound SA, formats them as normal IP packets, and then passes them to the TCP/IP driver.

8. The TCP/IP driver passes the packets to the application.

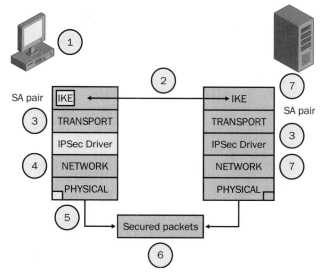

Figure 11-10   IPSec processing

See Also   IKE is the algorithm by which the first secure Security Association, or *SA* (a secure channel), is negotiated. It includes authentication, the calculation of the *master key* (the key from which all session keys are derived), and the establishment of the IKE SA. The most interesting part of IKE is that the master key is calculated separately on each computer. The same key is derived and is never transported across the network. A complex mathematical process is used. You can read more about IKE negotiation and this process at RFC 2409: *http://www.ietf.org/rfc/rfc2409.txt.*

The following steps explain the Main Mode process in detail:

1. A communication packet is sent from Computer Red to Computer Blue.

2. The IPSec driver on Computer Red checks its outbound IP filter lists and concludes that the packets match a filter and the filter action is Negotiate—the packets need to be secured.

3. The IPSec driver notifies IKE to begin negotiations.

4. Computer Red checks its policy for the Main Mode settings (authentication, Diffie-Hellman group, encryption, and integrity) to propose to Computer Blue.

5. Computer Red sends the first IKE message using UDP source port 500 and destination port 500.

6. Computer Blue receives the IKE Main Mode message that is requesting secure negotiation. It uses the source IP address and destination IP address of the packet to look up its own IKE filter. The IKE filter provides the security requirements for communications from Computer Red.

7. If the security settings proposed by Computer Red are acceptable to Computer Blue, negotiation of the Main Mode or IKE SA begins.

8. Both computers negotiate options, exchange identities and authenticate them, and generate a master key. The IKE SA is established.

> **Note**   Microsoft's implementation of IPSec supports offloading of encryption to network interface cards (NICs) that can perform encryption. Not every NIC can support offloaded encryption, but several are specifically designed to do so. Use of such cards can improve the performance on servers where many possible IPSec connections can be frequently used. You can read more about one of these special NICs at *http://www.3com.com/products/proddatasheet/datasheet /3c905b_fx.pdf.*

The following steps explain the Quick Mode process in detail:

1. Computer Red performs an IKE mode policy lookup to determine the full policy. (IKE negotiation does not factor in the port number, IP address, or other factors that might have triggered the negotiation.)

2. Computer Red proposes its options (cryptographic as well as frequency of key changes, and so on) and filters to Computer Blue.

3. Computer Blue does its own IKE mode policy lookup. If it finds a match with that proposed by Computer Red, it completes the Quick Mode negotiation to create a pair of IPSec SAs.

4. One SA is outbound, the other is inbound, each SA is identified by a Security Parameters Index (SPI), and the SPI is part of the header of each packet sent. Computer Red's IPSec driver uses the outbound SA and signs, and, if specified, encrypts the packets. If hardware offload of IPSec cryptographic functions is supported by the network card, the IPSec driver just formats the packets; otherwise, it formats and cryptographically processes the packets.

5. The IPSec driver passes the packets to the network adapter driver.

6. The network adapter driver puts the datagrams on the network.

7. The network adapter at Computer Blue receives the (encrypted) packets from the network.

8. The SPI is used to find the corresponding SA. (This SA has the associated crypto-graphic key necessary to decrypt and process the packets.)

9. If the network adapter is specifically designed to perform encryption and there-fore can decrypt the packets, it will do so. It passes the packets to the IPSec driver.

10. Computer Blue's IPSec driver uses the inbound SA to retrieve the keys and pro-cesses the packets if necessary.

11. The IPSec driver converts the packets back to normal IP packet format and passes them to the TCP/IP driver that passes them to the receiving application.

12. IPSec SAs continue processing packets. SAs are refreshed by IKE Quick Mode negotiation for as long as the application sends and receives data. When the SAs become idle, they are deleted.

13. IKE Main Mode is not deleted when idle. It has a lifetime of 8 hours, but this num-ber is configurable (5 minutes to a maximum of 48 hours). New traffic triggers a new Quick Mode negotiation. If IKE Main Mode expires, a new IKE mode is nego-tiated when needed.

> **Note**   Switches and routers between Computer Red and Computer Blue will simply forward the encrypted packets to their destination. However, a firewall or packet filtering router must be configured to allow IPSec traffic to pass.

Creating an IPSec Policy

Creating an IPSec Policy is easy. Creating one that does exactly what you want it to is not always so easy. This far, you have learned how policy works. Now you will use that knowledge to create a simple policy that you can use to block access to port 80 and another to ensure encryption of data between two computers. The two major tools used to create policy are IP Security and Netsh. The next section describes how to cre-ate a policy from the command line. The exercises at the end of this section teach you how to use the GUI tool and Netsh.

Using Netsh to Manage IPSec

Netsh is a native Windows Server 2003 command-line scripting tool that you can use to display or modify the local or remote network configuration of a computer running Windows Server 2003. You can run Netsh from a batch file or from the command prompt. The Netsh IPSec commands cannot be used on any other Windows computer.

See Also You can find a complete list of Netsh IPSec commands in the Windows Server 2003 Help And Support Center. You can locate them by clicking Tools, then Command Line Reference. Note that many of the commands look complex, but they can be simplified. If you use the same choices as the command uses for its defaults, the commands you must type in can be reduced. For example, you don't need to use the word "Kerberos" if that is the form of authentication you want to use. Enter nothing, and the command defaults to using Kerberos authentication.

To set the Netsh IPSec context, type the word **static** or **dynamic** while in the Netsh IPSec context. Our discussion is concerned only with Netsh commands that are useful to establish and monitor IPSec.

Once you have a context, you can use the Netsh commands to produce a policy or monitor IPSec activity. Two modes are possible. Static mode allows you to create, modify, and assign policies without affecting the active IPSec policy. Dynamic mode allows you to display the active state and immediately implement changes to the active IPSec policy. Dynamic Netsh commands affect the service only when it is running. If it is stopped, dynamic policy settings are discarded.

Caution Dynamic mode can be quite useful, for example, if you need to immediately initiate a change to IPSec processing. Although some IPSec commands require you to stop and start the IPSec service, others do not. However, Dynamic mode can also be a mixed blessing. Should you make a mistake in Dynamic mode, you will have no opportunity to discover it before implementing the change. You could end up creating an incorrect configuration without warning.

Using Netsh to Monitor IPSec You can use Netsh to monitor the current IPSec session. Monitoring consists of either displaying policy information, getting diagnostics and logging IPSec information, or both. Any information you can find by running the IP Security Monitor snap-in, you can find by running Netsh.

Displaying IPSec Policy Information First, of course, you might want to know what the current IPSec Policy is. To find out, you can use the Show command. If you choose to use the Show All command, a lot of information will be returned.

```
Netsh ipsec static show all
```

Sometimes it is useful to look at only a portion of the IPSec configuration information. A wide range of Show commands is available. Some are defined in Table 11-6. You can enter all commands from the Netsh IPSec Dynamic or the Netsh IPSec Static context, or, with modification, from the command line.

Table 11-6   Netsh IPSec (Dynamic|Static) Show Commands

Operation	Command
Displays a specific filter list	Show Filterlist Name=*filterlistname*
Displays the policy assigned to the specified GPO	Show Gpoassignedpolicy Name=*name*
Displays a specific policy	Show Policy Name=*policyname*
Displays a specific rule	Show Rule Name=*rulename*

Obtaining Diagnostic IPSec Information   One of the steps in diagnosing IPSec problems—or just establishing that the policy is working like you think it should—is to obtain information about the current policy. The Show commands described later in Table 11-7 provide that information. The information that each command reveals identifies the settings in the policy. For example, the Show Filterlist command lists the information in the policies filter list. Filter list options were listed in Table 11-6.

Some examples of the Show command syntax are illustrated next. In the commands, the equal sign is part of the command and the italicized words are replaced by some value as indicated below the command.

- **Show All Resolvedns=*value***   Resolves the DNS or NetBIOS computer name associated with an IP address. This command might assist you in determining whether the policy is affecting the right computer.

- **Show Mmsas**   Displays information on the IPSec Main Mode SA. You can see the source and destination addresses. When used with the Resolvedns=yes switch, the names of the computers are also displayed.

- **Show Qmsas**   Displays information about the IPSec Quick Mode SAs.

- **Show Stats**   Displays the IKE Main Mode statistics, IPSec Quick Mode statistics, or both. The statistics are the same ones described in Table 11-8, in the section "Understanding Main Mode and Quick Mode Statistics in IP Security Monitor" later in this chapter.

In addition to Show commands, you can use several Dynamic mode Netsh IPSec diagnostic commands to obtain diagnostic information, such as the following:

- **Set Config Property=Ipsecdiagnostics value=*value***   Can be set with a value of 0 through 7, indicating the level of IPSec diagnostic logging. The default is 0, which means logging is disabled. The level 7 causes all logging to be performed. The computer must be restarted for logging to begin.

- **Set Config Property=Ipsecloginterval value=*value***   Indicates how frequently in seconds the IPSec events are sent to the system event log. The range is 60 to 86,400 with a default of 3600.

- **Set Config Property=Ikelogging value=*value*** Can be set with a value of 0 or 1, determining whether IKE (Oakley) logging will occur. This command produces a log with a copious amount of information. You must be familiar with the RFCs at the expert level to completely understand the Oakley logs.

- **Set Config Property=Strongcrlcheck value=*value*** Determines whether certificate revocation list (CRL) checking is used. If 0, CRL checking is disabled. If 1 is the value, certificate validation fails only if the certificate is revoked. Level 2 fails if any CRL check error occurs. A CRL check fails if the CRL cannot be located on the network.

You can make other diagnostic efforts by modifying the current policy to reduce security. For example, if you change authentication to Shared Secret on both computers instead of Kerberos or Certificates, you eliminate the possibility that the problem is related to authentication. *Netdiag.exe* is a command-line tool that you can use to display IPSec information as well as to test and view network configuration. Netdiag is available for Windows Server 2003, Windows 2000, and Windows XP. However, it must be installed in a different way for each operating system. For Windows Server 2003, Netdiag is installed with the Windows Server 2003 Support Tools. For Windows 2000, Netdiag is included with the Windows 2000 Resource Kit tools that you can also download from the Internet. It is also available on the Windows XP Installation CD-ROM, and is installed by running Setup.exe from the Support\Tools folder.

You can obtain general network diagnostic information (not IPSec-specific) by using the Netdiag command. For example, the Netdiag /v /l command provides the IP configuration and routing configuration for a computer, tests WINS and DSN name resolution, reports the build version of the computer and the hotfixes that are installed, tests the validity of domain membership, verifies contacts by member computers with their domain controllers, and checks trust relationships. All of this information can be useful in eliminating general networking problems before attempting to diagnose IPSec issues.

However, although the Netdiag.exe tool is available for Windows Server 2003, the Netdiag /test:ipsec option is removed. Use the Netsh command instead. Because Netsh IPSec context commands will not work with downlevel Windows computers, use Netdiag for them. You might want to remotely examine the IPSec policy of a computer running Windows XP or Windows 2000 that is communicating, or attempting to communicate, with Windows Server 2003. In this case, use a remote desktop session and the Netdiag tool.

Using IP Security Monitor to Monitor IPSec Traffic

IP Security Monitor is a Windows XP and Windows Server 2003 snap-in used to monitor and troubleshoot IPSec. If an IPSec policy is active, you can use this console to examine the policy and its operations. You can use the IP Security Monitor console to monitor computers of only the same version as the one running the monitor. Information that you can obtain includes the following:

- Name of the active IPSec policy

- Details about the active IPSec policy

- Quick Mode statistics

- Main Mode statistics

- Information about active SAs

> **Note**   IPSec monitoring tools exist for Windows 2000 as well. To monitor IPSec on computers running Windows 2000, use the Netdiag Support Tool, the Ipsecmon.exe utility, or both.

Understanding Main Mode and Quick Mode Statistics in IP Security Monitor   Viewing IPSec statistics is simply a matter of expanding the server node, expanding the Main Mode node or the Quick Mode node, and then selecting the Statistics node. Understanding what each statistic means is more difficult. Table 11-7 describes the most common Main Mode statistics, and Table 11-8 describes the most common Quick Mode statistics. Within Table 11-7, several statistics appear to be related to Quick Mode. They are, but they are initialized by IKE during Main Mode, hence their inclusion as part of the Main Mode statistics table.

Table 11-7   IPSec Main Mode Statistics

Statistic	Description
Active Acquire	Number of pending requests for IKE negotiation for SA between IPSec peers.
Active Receive	Number of IKE messages queued for processing.
Acquire Failures	Number of failed outbound requests to establish SA since IPSec service started.
Receive Failures	Number of errors in receipt of IKE messages since IPSec service started.
Send Failures	Number of errors during sending of IKE.
Acquire Heap Size	Number of successive outbound requests to establish SAs.
Receive Heap Size	Number of IKE messages in IKE receive buffers.
Authentication Failures	Number of failed authentication failures since the IPSec service started. If you cannot make an IPSec connection, check to see whether authentication failures increase during an attempt. If so, authentication is the issue. Check to see that shared secrets match, peers are members of the domain, and certificates are correct.
Negotiation Failures	Number of Main Mode negotiation failures. Attempt to communicate and see whether negotiation failures increase. If so, check authentication and security method settings for unmatched or incorrect configuration.

Table 11-7   IPSec Main Mode Statistics

Statistic	Description
Invalid Cookies Received	Number of invalid cookies. A cookie is a value in an IKE message that is used to help identify the corresponding Main Mode SA.
Total Acquire	Number of requests submitted to IKE (including those resulting in soft SAs).
Total Get SPI	Number of requests to driver for SPI.
Key Additions	Number of outbound Quick Mode SA additions.
Key Updates	Number of inbound Quick Mode SAs added by IKE.
Get SPI Failures	Number of failed requests for a unique SPI.
Key Addition Failures	Number of failed outbound Quick Mode SA addition requests submitted by IKE.
Key Update Failures	Number of failed inbound Quick Mode SA addition requests.
ISADB List Size	Number of Main Mode state entries, successful Main Modes, Main Modes in negotiation, and those that fail or have expired but have not been deleted.
Connection List Size	Number of Quick Mode negotiations in process.
IKE Main Mode	Number of successful SAs in Main Mode.
IKE Quick Mode	Number of successful SAs that have been created during Quick Mode negotiations since the IPSec service was last started.
Soft Associations	Number of SAs formed with computers that have not responded to Main Mode negotiation attempts since the IPSec service was last started. Although these computers did not respond to Main Mode negotiation attempts, IPSec policy allowed communications with the computers. Soft SAs are not secured by IPSec.
Invalid Packets Received	Number of invalid IKE messages. Invalid header fields, payload lengths, and incorrect values. Check to see whether the preshared key is matched in the peer configuration. Invalid Packets Received statistics might also be the result of retransmitted IKE messages.

Table 11-8   IPSec Quick Mode Statistics

Statistic	Description
Active Security Association	Number of Quick Mode SAs.
Offloaded Security Associations	Number of Quick Mode SAs offloaded to hardware.
Pending Key Operations	Number of key exchange operations in progress.

Table 11-8   IPSec Quick Mode Statistics

Statistic	Description
Key Additions	Number of keys for Quick Mode SAs successfully added since computer started.
Key Deletions	Number of keys for Quick Mode SAs successfully deleted since computer started.
Rekeys	Number of successful rekey operations for Quick Mode.
Active Tunnels	Number of active tunnels.
Bad SPI Packets	Number of packets with incorrect SPI. Possibly the SPI has expired and an old packet just arrived. Likely to be larger if rekeying is frequent and there are a large number of SAs. Might indicate a spoofing attack.
Packets Not Decrypted	Number of packets that could not be decrypted since the computer was last started. A packet might not be decrypted if it fails a validation check.
Packets Not Authenticated	Number of packets for which data could not be verified (for which the integrity hash verification failed) since the computer was last started. Increases in this number might indicate an IPSec packet spoofing or modification attack or packet corruption by network devices.
Packets With Replay Detection	Number of packets containing an invalid sequence number. Increases might mean network problems or a replay attack.
Confidential Bytes Sent	Number of bytes sent using the ESP protocol.
Confidential Bytes Received	Number of bytes received using the ESP protocol (excluding nonencrypted ESP) since the computer was last started.
Authenticated Bytes Sent	Number of authenticated bytes sent using the Authentication Header (AH) protocol or the ESP protocol since the computer was last started.
Authenticated Bytes Received	Number of authenticated bytes received using the AH protocol or the ESP protocol since the computer was last started.
Transport Bytes Sent	Number of bytes sent using IPSec Transport mode.
Transport Bytes Received	Number of bytes received using IPSec Transport mode since the computer was last started.
Bytes Sent In Tunnels	Number of bytes sent using IPSec Tunnel mode.
Bytes Received In Tunnels	Number of bytes received using IPSec Tunnel mode.
Offloaded Bytes Sent	Number of bytes sent using hardware offload.
Offloaded Bytes Received	Number of bytes received using hardware offload.

Using Netcap to Capture Network Traffic

Netcap.exe is a command-line utility that you can use to capture network traffic to a capture file. You can then load the file in Network Monitor to view the captured traffic. The Network Monitor tool does not have to be installed on the computer running Windows Server 2003 to use Netcap. You can also use Netcap on computers running Windows XP, which makes it an extremely attractive way to capture traffic for later review. The tool is available after the Windows Server 2003 Support Tools have been installed. When you first run the command, the Network Monitor driver is automatically installed.

Table 11-9 describes the syntax used to obtain a capture.

Table 11-9   Netcap Syntax

Options	Description
/b:*Number*	Specifies buffer or capture size from 1 MB to 1000 MB with a default of 1 MB.
/t *Type Buffer HexOffset HexPattern*	Informs trigger when to stop the capture, when either the buffer or pattern is reached. The capture stops when the buffer is full if no trigger is defined. /t N can be used to cause the capture to continue when the buffer is full. New frames overwrite the oldest frames. Valid values for the Type parameter are B = buffer; P = pattern; BP = buffer then pattern; PB = pattern then buffer; N = no trigger. Valid values for the Buffer parameter are % Buffer size 25, 50, 75, and 100. This parameter is used with all *Type* values except P. Valid values for the HexOffset parameter are hex offset from start of frame used with P, BP, PB, but not B. Valid values for the HexPattern parameter are hex pattern to match. Used with P, BP, PB, but not B. The pattern needs to be an even number of digits.
/C:*CaptureFile*	Specifies a location where Netcap will move the temporary capture files. This location can be any valid local or remote path. If /C is not specified, the capture path remains in the default temporary capture folder.
/F:*FilterFile*.cf	Specifies a filter to use during the capture. A filter file has a .cf extension.
/L:*HH:MM:SS*	Captures for some amount of time.
/TCF:*FolderName*	Changes temporary capture folder. Path must be on a fixed local hard disk drive.
/Remove	Removes Netcap instance of the Network Monitor driver.
/N:*Number*	Provides the NIC index number for this computer. 0 = PPP/SLIP interface. 1 = Local Area Connection 2; 2 = Local Area Connection. Determine the NIC index number using the Netcap /? command. All adapters installed on the local computer will be listed.

The following are two example commands:

Capture the packets received on NIC 2 using a 20-MB buffer:

```
Netcap /n:2 /b:20
```

Capture for one hour:

```
Netcap /L:01:00:00
```

Understanding Kerberos

Kerberos is a complex authentication protocol described in RFC 1510. It is used as the preferred authentication protocol for Windows 2000 and Windows Server 2003 domains. Windows XP Professional, Windows 2000, and Windows Server 2003 computers that are domain members will preferably use Kerberos authentication. Knowledge of the authentication process allows you to determine the following:

- Whether Kerberos is being used. Kerberos is a more secure protocol than its predecessor, NTLM.

- Whether Kerberos errors represent normal functions, Kerberos problems that need to be corrected, or symptoms of attack.

- Whether Kerberos errors or issues mean problems with replication, Active Directory operation, DNS, or other critical network services.

Reading the RFC and even reading a shortened version of the algorithm is instructive, but it is much more fun to follow Kerberos logons using Network Monitor, the Security Event log, and Resource Kit utilities Kerbtray.exe and Klist.exe. The following sections introduce Kerberos by using these tools to monitor logon sessions. Be sure to complete the exercises so that you can observe Kerberos activity firsthand.

> **See Also**   To read the Kerberos RFC 1510, "The Kerberos Network Authentication Service," go to *http://www.ietf.org/rfc/rfc1510.txt?number=1510*. You can also find more information on how Kerberos is implemented in Windows in the Kerberos white paper at *http://www.microsoft.com/TechNet/prodtechnol/windows2000serv/deploy/kerberos.asp*.

Hands-On Kerberos Tracking

To track logon, you must first prepare and start the tools that will be used.

- Ensure that auditing of logon events and account logon events is turned on for domain controllers and domain computers. This should be done in the Default Domain Policy. Make sure the policy has been updated.

- Download and install the Resource Kit utilities Kerbtray.exe and Klist.exe. Make sure a copy is available on the logon client.

- Start Network Monitor and start a capture prior to logon.

- Optionally, make a folder on the domain controller to store network captures and a copy of the Security Event log. This folder can be temporarily shared to download these files to the server for examination. This way, you can study them while observing the details in the local Security Event log and looking at the tickets in the Kerberos cache. It is much easier than constantly moving between two computers or setting up a terminal session.

For the purposes of our example captures, from which screen shots for the figures were taken, a folder was created and named Captures. In addition, a small text file was created with the words "Hello World" in it. After the capture was started on the domain controller, the client server, a domain member server, was rebooted. Then the Administrator account was used for logon to the domain from the member server. After successful logon, the capture was stopped and saved to the folder. A copy of the Security Event log was also saved to the folder.

Kerberos at Computer Boot   When a domain member server running Windows 2003 Server starts, it must authenticate to the domain controller. The first step is a query to find a domain controller. Figure 11-11 shows the DNS query, looking for the Lightweight Directory Access Protocol (LDAP) service.

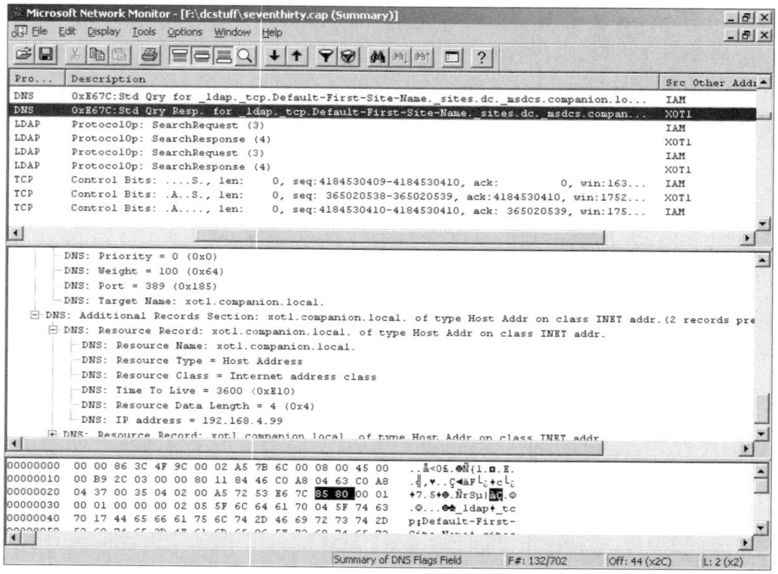

Figure 11-11   Client querying DNS, looking for the LDAP service

Figure 11-12 shows the LDAP query for the Netlogon service, and receiving the answer.

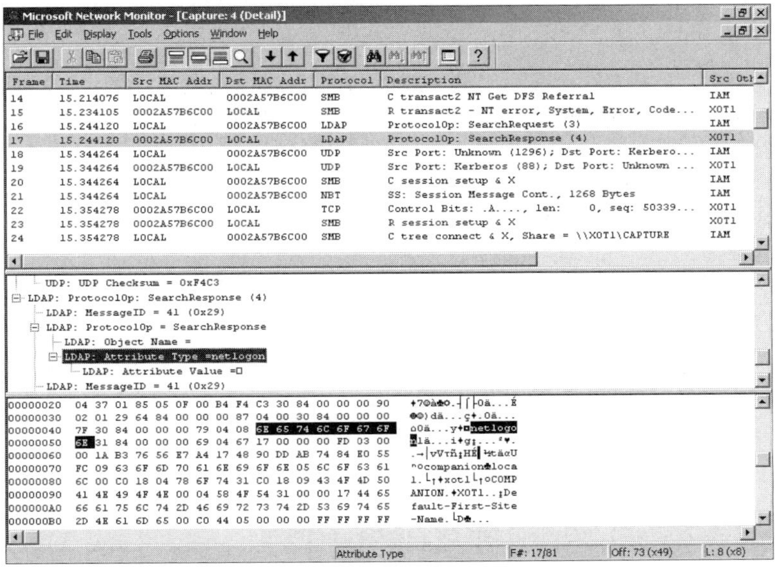

Figure 11-12   Client making an LDAP query

Next, the server sends a UDP query to the Kerberos port, 88, on the DC, and is answered by the DC. This is the server's request for a Ticket Granting Ticket (TGT). Figure 11-13 shows a portion of this packet. Of course, the TGT is necessary and must be presented before any resources can be accessed. The request is, in essence, the "Hey, here I am! Let me in the door!" speech and includes the server's credentials. The server's account password is used as the key in a cryptographic hash of a timestamp. A plaintext copy of the timestamp also accompanies the hash.

On the domain controller, the server time from the unencrypted timestamp is compared to the DC's time. By default, if the time is off by more than 5 minutes, the logon is rejected. (If Kerberos fails, NTLM might be attempted, for example, when mapping drives.) If the time is OK, the Kerberos Distribution Center (KDC) uses its copy of the server's password to create a cryptographic hash of the unencrypted timestamp. The two hashes, one made by the server, one by the KDC, are compared. If they match, the server is authenticated because only the server and the DC have a copy of the server's password.

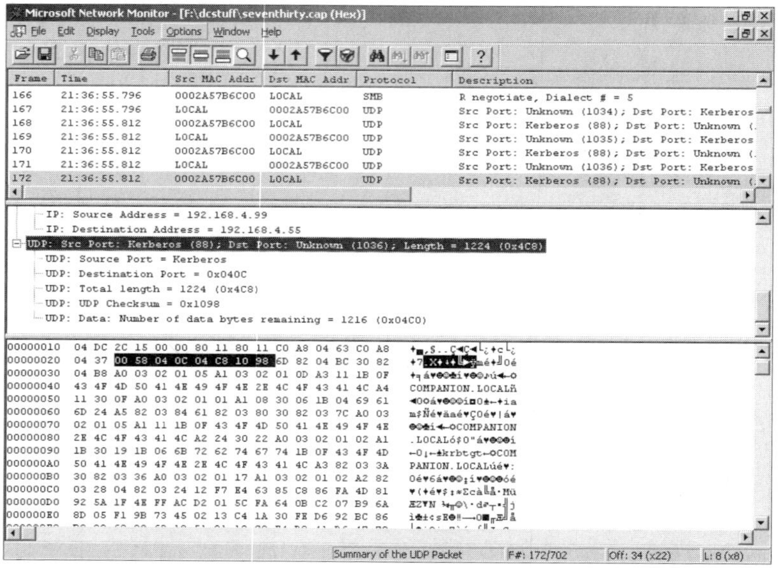

Figure 11-13   Requesting a TGT at the KDC at port 88, Kerberos

The KDC sends a TGT to the server in another UDP packet. Once again, the packet is unreadable in Network Monitor. This situation is appropriate, but how do you know the ticket request and ticket packets are truly being used for this purpose? Now the Security Event log can help. Figure 11-14 displays a successful logon event from the domain controller. Note the time on the event and compare it to the time of the Kerberos message displayed in Figure 11-13.

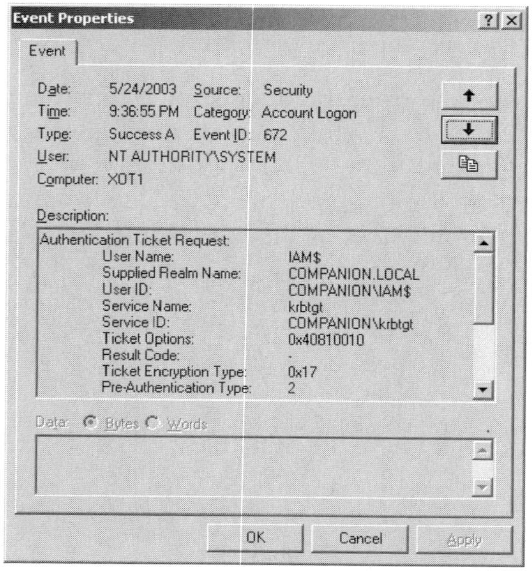

Figure 11-14   An event showing that a TGT was requested and the result was successful

The member server caches the TGT and can use it when necessary to request access to services. In fact, that is exactly what happens next. The server requests service tickets from the KDC. If you examine additional records in the security log near the TGT request, you will find that a request for a service ticket is successful as well.

At this point, the server uses the TGT to obtain a service ticket for access to its own resources. The Kerberos packets in the capture do not reveal any interesting information—the data is encrypted. You should also note the connection to download representative policy modules.

Kerberos at User Logon   Next, when a domain user—in this case, the Administrator—logs on, the process repeats. Credentials are presented and a TGT is requested. If the credentials are approved, the TGT is issued. In the Network Monitor log, more UDP frames are bound for port 88 on the domain controller, followed by a response. Check the time of these frames (Figure 11-15) and follow up with a look at the Security Event log for this time.

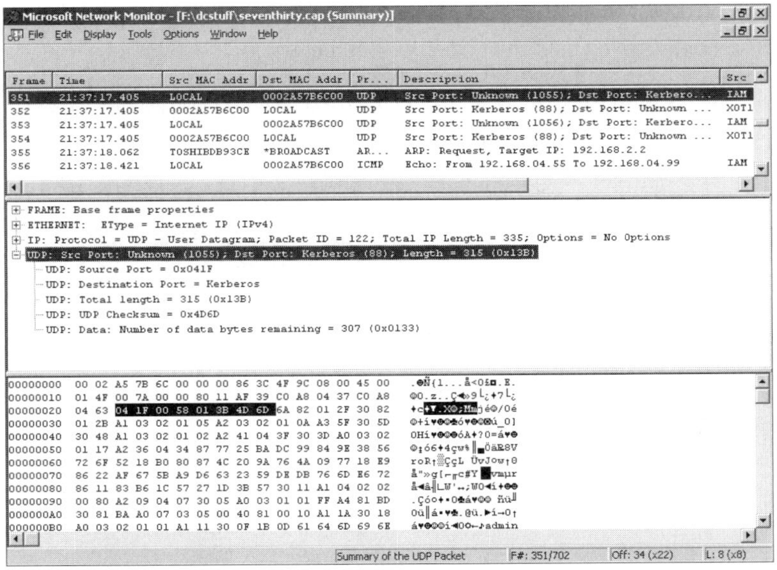

Figure 11-15   Security Event log showing a TGT request

Figure 11-16 shows the successful TGT request for the Administrator.

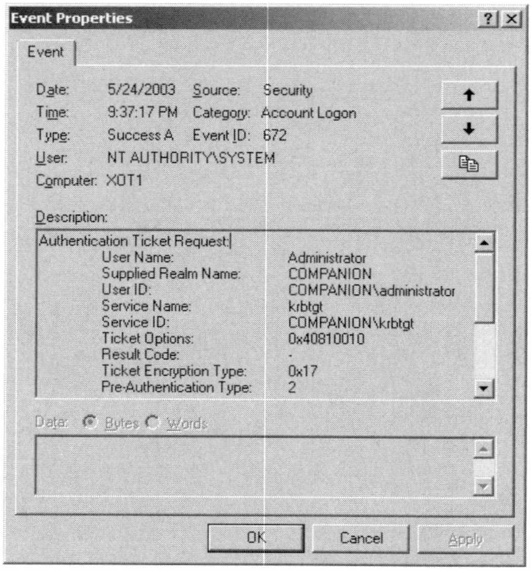

Figure 11-16   Security Event log confirming successful request

Now life gets interesting. The TGT for the Administrator account, like the TGT for the system, is stored in the Kerberos ticket cache. It is used when the Administrator account requests access to services. You can examine your ticket cache by using the Kerbtray.exe utility. To use Kerbtray.exe, you run the self-installing file by double-clicking it and then clicking the executable to run the tool. This procedure places an icon on the taskbar, which can then be opened by clicking it to reveal the tickets in the cache. Figure 11-17 shows the list of tickets in the cache and the Administrator account's TGT ticket.

Figure 11-17   Using the Kerbtray.exe utility to view Kerberos tickets in the ticket cache of the local machine

One of the first requests is for the services of the local computer. In Figure 11-17, notice that tickets are listed for several services: Host, IAM$, Common Internet File System (CIFS), and LDAP. All these services were requested at logon and represent the Administrator's ability to access the local computer (Host and IAM$), to access a share on the domain controller (CIFS), and to make LDAP queries to the directory service (LDAP).

Requests for service tickets include the TGT and another authenticator. Because the TGT is cached, you might wonder whether it could be captured and possibly used in a replay attack. The use of a new authenticator protects the KDC. Because the time on the server has changed, the authenticator message, the timestamp, will always be current, and the KDC can check that it is within the time skew policy of its domain. (*Time skew* is the difference between the KDC's time and the client's; if it is off by more than the policy skew time, the Kerberos request is rejected.)

Kerberos Role in Authorization   Kerberos is an authentication protocol, but it does play a role in authorization. If you map a drive to a share on a computer, the Kerberos TGT requests a session ticket for the CIFS Server service on the computer, implemented using the CIFS protocol. If a Network Monitor capture is made, you can trace the steps in accessing the share.

However, the service ticket does not give users access to the share. The ticket authenticates users only to the server. It says, in essence, that the users are who they say they are, and the server does not have to check in with the domain controller to verify this information. A portion of the service ticket is encrypted using the password hash for the server, so the server can decrypt it. Remember, the DC stores password hashes for computers as well as users. Because the server can decrypt the ticket, the server recognizes that it is valid and must come from a DC, because the DC is the only other entity that has the server's password.

Where does the authorization information come from? The service ticket, although it is only validation of user identity, does contain information useful for authorization. This information is the same as that collected by the KDC when the user first presented domain credentials, the user's security identifier (SID), and the SIDs of the groups of which the user is a member. The file server uses this information to create the access token, and then the file server can determine whether the user has the proper permission to access the share and the folders and files underneath.

You can use the Security Event log to determine whether access was allowed or denied, and Kerbtray.exe shows the CIFS service ticket in the cache. Note that the CIFS service ticket in the cache is issued for a specific server. If the user attempts access to a share on this server—or a reconnection if the connection has been broken—this service ticket can be used. If the user attempts access to another server, a new service ticket must be obtained. Once again, the service ticket requests are not viewable. However, Kerbtray.exe can be used to verify that a service ticket is issued. Figure 11-17 shows a CIFS service ticket.

Examine the properties of tickets in the cache. Note that both service tickets and TGT tickets are renewable. If a service ticket expires, a new one can be obtained transparently if a valid TGT is in the cache. If, however, there is no valid TGT, a new one must be obtained and the user will need to log on again. To determine the time frames, select the Times tab and check the Kerberos policy for the domain. This same process occurs on computers running Windows 2000 and Windows XP Professional that are joined in a domain.

You can use another Resource Kit utility, Klist.exe, to obtain a list of tickets in the cache. You can run Klist from the command line and thus can incorporate it in a script. You can place the records in a text file (use the command Klist.exe > Textfile.txt). Klist.exe does not show as much information as Kerbtray.exe, but it does have a unique advantage. You can use the Klist.exe Purge command to purge tickets, and you will be able to selectively retain or purge tickets one at a time.

Additional Uses for Kerberos Tools

Kerbtray.exe and Klist.exe provide a wealth of information. In addition, you can also use Netdiag to determine how Kerberos is functioning. These tools are all relatively simple to use.

Understanding Kerbtray   If the Kerbtray icon shows only question marks, you know that no Kerberos tickets are in the cache. This situation can occur if a computer is not connected to the network or if no domain controllers are available.

Double-click the Kerbtray icon to see a list of tickets obtained since logon. Right-clicking the tool presents two useful menu commands, List Tickets and Purge Tickets. Selecting List Tickets has the same effect as double-clicking the Kerbtray icon. If you select Purge Tickets, you will have to log on again to use Kerberos to access resources.

The Kerbtray display shows the name of the client principal (the user) who has obtained the tickets and shows a list of tickets for services. Selecting a ticket reveals its target: for which resource this ticket is used. The bottom of the screen provides information about the selected ticket, such as names, times, flags, and encryption types. Figure 11-17 shows the Names tab. Figures 11-18, 11-19, and 11-20 show examples of the other tabs.

The Names tab provides the following information:

- **Client Name**   Who requested the ticket.
- **Service Name**   The account principal for the service requested. The service name for the initial TGT is krbtgt.
- **Target Name**   The service name for which the ticket was requested, such as CIFS.

The Times tab provides the following information:

- **Start Time**   The time when the ticket becomes valid.

- **End Time**   The time when the ticket expires. An expired ticket cannot be used to authenticate to a service.

- **Renew Until**   If the ticket is renewable, the maximum lifetime of the ticket. Tickets can be renewed before the end time and renew until times expire. This functionality is transparent to the user.

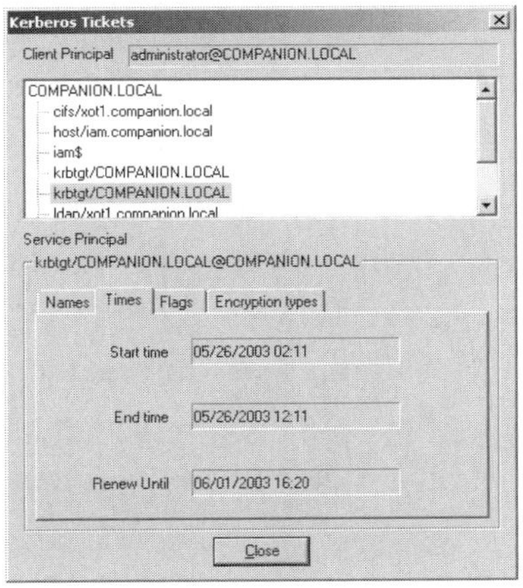

Figure 11-18   Times tab providing expiration dates

Kerberos flags indicate the status of a ticket, as well as define the uses the ticket might have. The Flags tab provides the following information:

- **Forwardable**   The authentication information can be forwarded and the user will not have to enter a password to use the ticket.

- **Forwarded**   The Ticket Granting Service (TGS) of the KDC sets this flag if a client presents a ticket with the FORWARDABLE flag set and requests that the FORWARDED flag be set.

- **Proxiable**   The information in this ticket can be passed on and a remote server can be given permission to perform a remote request on behalf of a client. The TGS issues a new service ticket with a different network address (a service ticket for another computer on behalf of a client).

- **Proxy**   If a ticket is issued to another computer on behalf of a client (a proxiable ticket was received), the new ticket is marked as a proxy ticket. An application server can be set to provide an audit trail based on this flag, and flags can be set to require additional authentication from any agent presenting the proxy.

- **May Postdate**   May Postdate is necessary in a TGT if a postdated ticket needs to be issued based on one presented. To clarify, a service ticket is normally requested for some service access that is required immediately. A postdated ticket is one that will not be usable for a while. Its start date is sometime in the future.

- **Postdated** A postdated ticket is one whose start date is sometime after its issuance date.

- **Invalid** The ticket is not valid. A postdated ticket is issued with this flag set. It must be returned to the KDC to be validated before it can be used. The KDC validates the ticket only after its start date has passed.

- **Initial** The ticket issued is not based on presentation of a TGT. An example is the first service ticket for the krbtgt. It is the TGT. No TGT is present when it is issued.

- **Renewable** A renewable ticket can be used for a longer period. A new authentication does not have to take place.

- **HW Authenticated** Authenticated provides more information about the initial authentication.

- **Preauthenticated** Shows the initial authentication request information.

- **OK As Delegate** The server (not client) listed in the ticket is a suitable recipient of delegation. The user's credentials are forwarded only to services that are marked OK As Delegate.

Figure 11-19 Flags tab providing information about what the ticket can be used for

The Encryption Types tab provides the following information:

- **Ticket Encryption Type** Shows the ticket encryption type used to encrypt the Kerberos ticket.

- **Key Encryption Type** Shows the key encryption type used with enclosed session key.

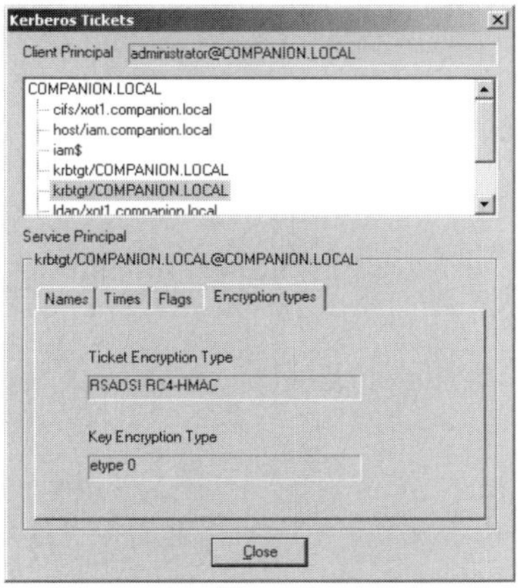

Figure 11-20   Encryption Types tab describing which encryption was used for the ticket

Understanding Klist   Klist is used at the command line to either display or purge tickets. There are a few choices:

- Klist Tgt displays the TGT tickets.

- Klist Tickets displays all tickets.

- Klist Purge deletes all tickets in the cache.

When the Klist Tickets command is used, the following information is displayed:

- Server and domain for the ticket (the service principal name).

- Kerbticket encryption type—the encryption type used to encrypt the Kerberos ticket.

- End time—after this time the ticket is no longer valid.

- Renew-time—if the ticket is renewable, this time shows the entire lifetime of the ticket.

You can obtain more information about the TGT tickets by using the Klist Tgt command.

- Servicename krbtgt—the name of the service the ticket can be used for. Since this is a TGT, krbtgt is the only service that will show.

- Targetname—the service for which it is requested.

- Fullservicename—the canonical name of the account principal for the service.

- DomainName—domain name of the service.

- Targetdomainname—if the ticket is cross-realm (meant for another domain for example, the TGT is for another domain in the forest, not the domain the user's account is in).

- AltTargetDomainName—the service principal name or SPN of the service that was given—the service context under which the ticket was generated.

- Ticket flags—a list of flags set on the ticket in hexadecimal. (Use the KerbTray tool to see them in English.)

- KeyExpirationTime—ticket expiration date.

- Starttime—time when the ticket is valid.

- EndTime—time when the ticket becomes not valid.

- RenewUntil—maximum lifetime of the ticket.

- TimeSkew—the reported time difference between the client computer and the server computer.

You can gather a wide range of troubleshooting information by using Klist.exe and Kerbtray.exe. For example, you can determine whether a ticket is valid, whether Kerberos was used, and if so, whether Kerberos was used to attempt to authenticate a domain.

Using Netdiag to Verify Kerberos Health   After you are familiar with Kerberos processing and the records in Network Monitor, the Security Event log, Kerbtray.exe, and Klist.exe, how can you best monitor Kerberos? You can't spend hours every day ensuring that all is in order. The trick, of course, is not to examine the thousands—perhaps millions—of records every day, but to look for warnings that might mean a Kerberos problem when viewing the logs and captures. You can use Netdiag to get a quick reading of Kerberos health on a server.

Netdiag runs a large number of tests, and one of them is the Kerberos test. If you run Netdiag from the command line, a minimal amount of information will provide the results of the Kerberos test. If something is wrong, it is reported. Running the specific test and using the /v switch for verbose, or /debug for more information, provides a list of tickets, an authentication test, domain information, and so on. Use the following statement to print this information to a file.

```
Netdiag /test:Kerberos /debug > ktest.txt
```

Figure 11-21 shows the results of a normal Kerberos test, and Figure 11-22 shows the results of a failed test.

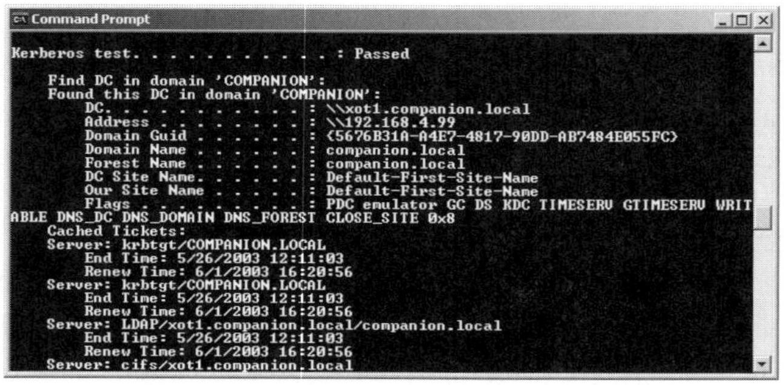

Figure 11-21   Normal Kerberos test

Figure 11-22   Failed Kerberos test

Practice: Using Network Security Protocols

In this practice, you use the IP Security Management snap-in and the Netsh command to manage IP security Policy.

Exercise 1: Use the IP Security Management Snap-In to Create a Blocking Policy

You can access IP security through a GPO, through the Local Security Policy console on Windows Server 2003, Windows 2000, and Windows XP Professional, and by loading IP Security Monitor snap-in in a console. To simplify monitoring of policy activity, in this exercise, you load the tool in the MMC and save the console for later use. The first policy you create is a *blocking policy*, which is useful in keeping unwanted traffic from being received on specific computers.

▶   **To create a blank console**

1. From the Start menu, select MMC to open an MMC.

2. From the File menu, select Add/Remove Snap-In.

3. Click the Add button.

4. In the Add Standalone Snap-In dialog box (Figure 11-23), select IP Security Policy Management, and then click Add.

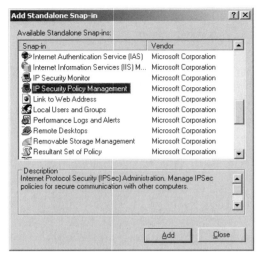

Figure 11-23   Selecting the IP Security Policy Management snap-in

5. In the Select Computer Of Domain dialog box, click Finish to accept the default selection, Local Computer. Then click Close.

In the Add/Remove Snap-In dialog box, shown in Figure 11-24, the IP Security Policies On Local Computer snap-in is listed. This tool is used for managing policies; the name is just different than the name displayed in Figure 11-23.

Figure 11-24   Verifying the IP Security Policy Management snap-in

6. Click OK.

7. From the File menu select Save As, type the filename **IP Security Policy Management**, and click Save.

▶   **To create a blocking policy**

1. Open the IP Security Policy Management console just created.

2. Right-click the IP Security Policies On Local Computer node and select Create IP Security Policy.

   The IP Security Policy Wizard launches.

3. Click Next on the wizard welcome page that appears.

4. In the Name text box, type **block web server access**.

5. In the Description text box, type a description, and click Next.

6. Clear Activate The Default Response Rule, and click Next.

   The default response rule allows insecure communication. In most cases, you will not want this so you will need to remove the rule. However, you can always reenable it from the interface later.

7. At the Default Response Rule Authentication Method, leave the default setting and click Next.

8. Click Finish.

9. In the new policy properties dialog box, shown in Figure 11-25, clear the Use Add Wizard check box and click Add.

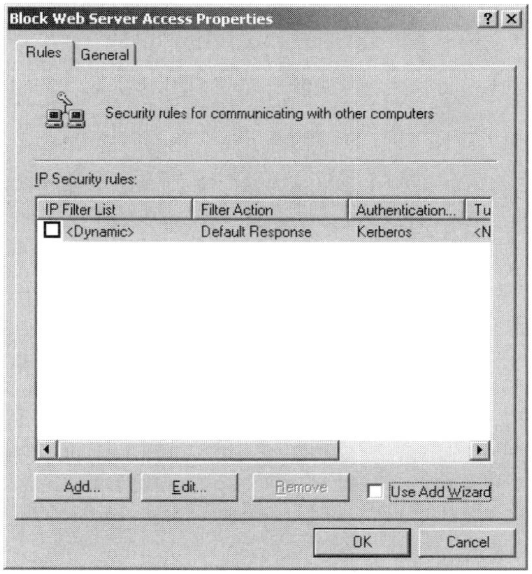

Figure 11-25   Clearing the Use Add Wizard check box

The wizard steps you through the creation of more complex policies and introduces confusion and extra work when a simple blocking policy is all you want. Instead of a wizard, you will get the policy properties dialog boxes after clicking Add.

10. On the IP Filter List tab, shown in Figure 11-26, click Add to create the filter list.

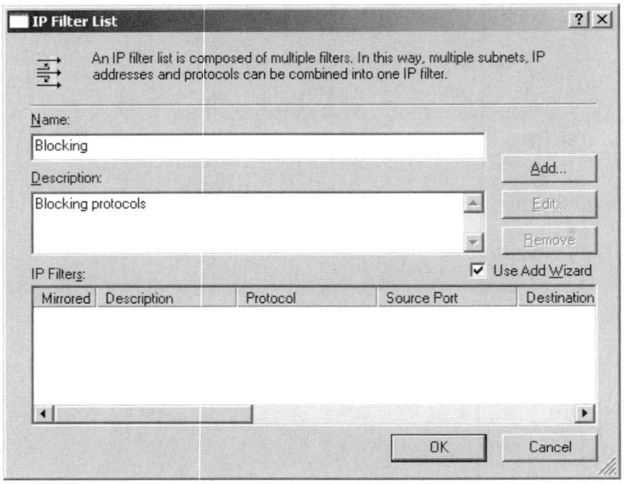

Figure 11-26   Adding a filter list

11. In the Name text box, type **blocking** as the name for the filter list.

12. In the Description text box, type **blocking protocols**.

13. Clear the Use Add Wizard check box and click Add to add a filter.

14. In the Source Address drop-down list, select Any IP Address.

15. In the Destination Address drop-down list, select My IP Address, as shown in Figure 11-27. Then click the Protocol tab.

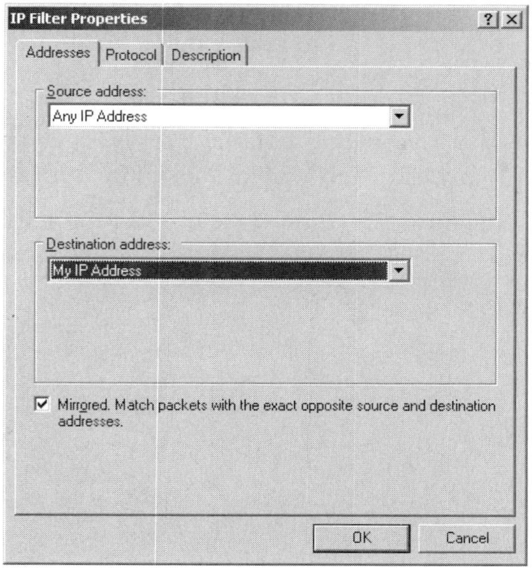

Figure 11-27   Creating the filter

16. In the Select A Protocol Type drop-down list, select TCP.

17. In the Set The IP Protocol Port box, shown in Figure 11-28, click To This Port, type **80**, and then click OK.

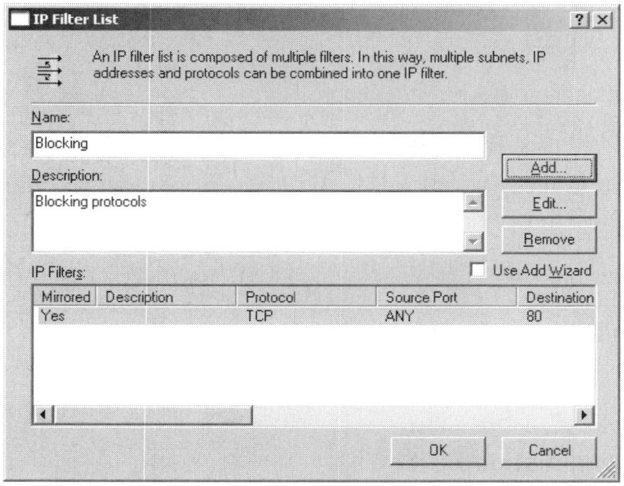

Figure 11-28   Defining filter ports

18. Select the Blocking entry in the IP Filter Lists box, and then click the Filter Action tab.

19. Clear the Use Add Wizard check box and click Add to add a filter action.

    The filter action determines what happens when the filter is triggered. In this case, the filter will be set to block any traffic arriving at this computer for port 80.

20. On the Security Methods tab, shown in Figure 11-29, select the Block option.

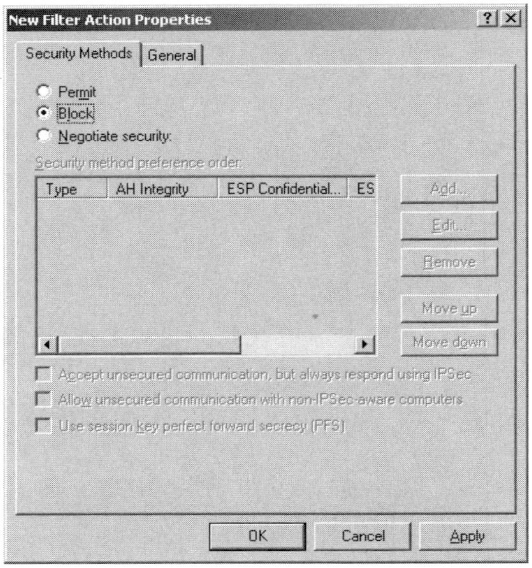

Figure 11-29   Creating the blocking filter action

21. Click the General tab and type **block** for the filter name. Then click OK.

22. Click the Filter Action tab. Select the Block filter action, click Close, and then click OK to finish creating the policy.

    Creating a policy does not change network activity on this machine. The policy must be activated before it will be used. You activate a policy by right-clicking it and selecting Assign from the context menu. Only one policy can be active per machine. In Exercises 2 through 5, you assign policies and monitor IPSec policy activity.

Exercise 2: Create a Negotiation Policy

A blocking policy requires that a rule be created on only one computer. A blocking rule keeps data from entering a computer. However, securing communications between two computers is a more complex task. In this exercise, you first create a more detailed policy, and then you ensure that a policy is present on each computer.

▶   **To create a policy to encrypt data between two computers**

A negotiation policy must find a match. For computers to communicate, the policy on each computer must have almost identical settings. The following policy needs to be exported and then imported on Computer1, and assigned on both computers before encrypted data can pass between them. In a Windows domain environment, if large numbers of computers can use the same policy, it can be created as part of a GPO.

1. Open the Security Configuration Management console created in Exercise 1.

2. Right-click IP Security Policies On Local Computer and select Create IP Security Policy.

   The IP Security Policy Wizard appears.

3. Click Next on the welcome page.

4. In the name text box, type **encrypt telnet traffic**. Type a description, and click Next.

5. Clear the Activate The Default Response Rule check box, click Next, and then click Finish.

6. In the policy properties dialog box, click the General tab (shown in Figure 11-30), and then click Settings to locate and adjust the key exchange settings.

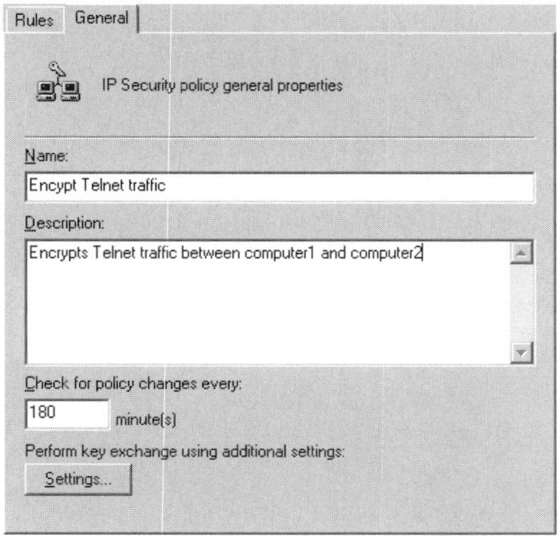

Figure 11-30   Locating the key exchange settings

7. In the Key Exchange Settings dialog box, shown in Figure 11-31, click Methods.

   The Key Exchange Settings dialog box is the location for changing master key generation particulars. Table 11-6 defines the parameters. Although frequent rekeying creates a more secure transport, it might also affect performance.

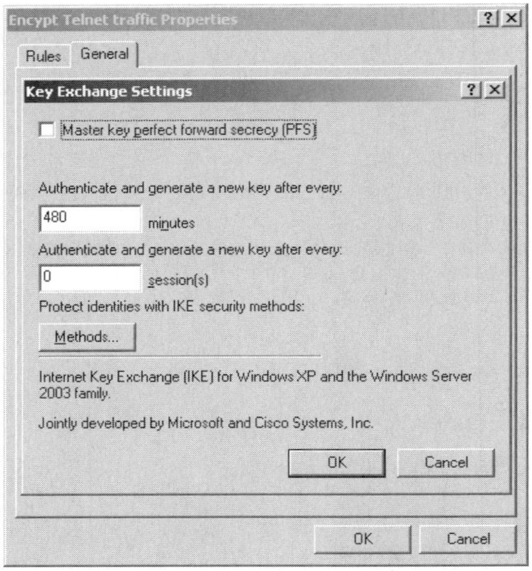

Figure 11-31 Inspecting security methods

8. In the Key Exchange Security Methods dialog box, select the fourth (last) default security method and click the Remove button. Then select the third security method and remove it as well. Two methods remain (Figure 11-32).

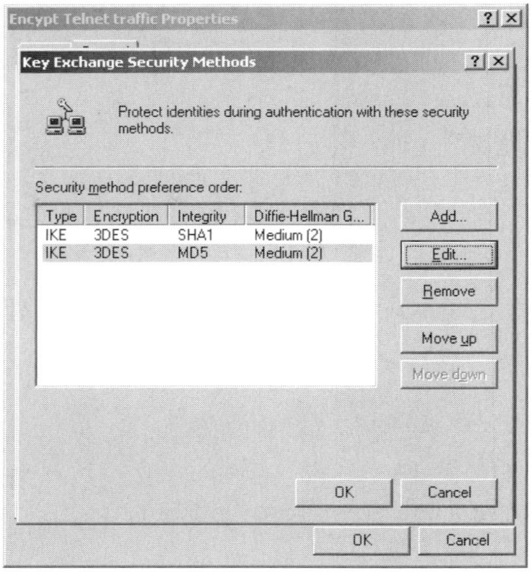

Figure 11-32 Reducing the number of security methods

Removing two of the security methods and changing the Diffie-Hellman group of the remaining security methods increases the security of the master key but might affect performance. A computer that attempts to negotiate a connection must be able to use at least one of the two remaining methods, or no connection will be made.

9. Select one of the security methods remaining and click Edit.

10. In the IKE Security Algorithms dialog box, in the Diffie-Hellman Group drop-down list, select High (2048), as shown in Figure 11-33. Then click OK. Repeat this process for the second security method.

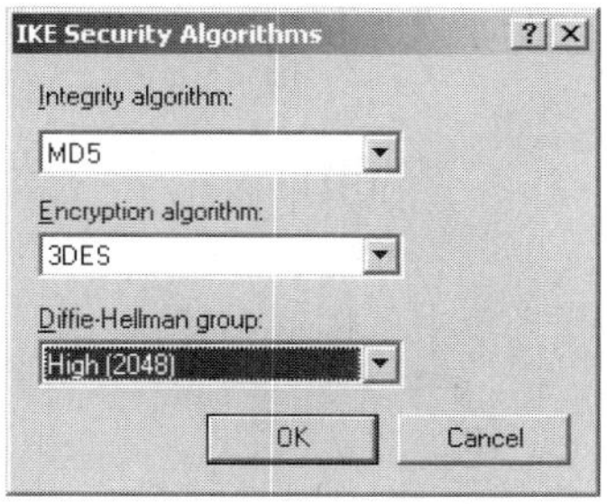

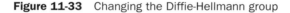

Figure 11-33   Changing the Diffie-Hellmann group

Changing the Diffie-Hellman group to high increases security in two ways. First, larger prime numbers are used in the calculation of the master key; second, communications can occur only with other computers running Windows Server 2003, because only they can use this parameter. Selecting the highest Diffie-Hellman group can cause problems because legitimate users might attempt connections using downlevel machines. It can also potentially affect performance, and the result is a larger key, and thus a longer time for encryption.

11. Click OK twice to return to the General tab. Then select the Rules tab.

12. Ensure that the Use Add Wizard box is selected and click Add to add a rule.

The Create IP Security Rule Wizard launches.

13. Click Next on the Welcome page.

14. Click Next on the Tunnel Endpoint page.

This policy will not use a tunnel.

15. On the Network type page, click Next to accept the default, All Network Connections.

This policy remains effective no matter where the connection is coming from.

16. On the IP Filter List page, click Add to add a filter list.

17. In the Name text box, type **negotiate**. In the Description text box, type a description.

18. Select the Use Add Wizard check box and click Add to add a filter.

    The IP Filter Wizard launches.

19. On the IP Filter Wizard welcome page, click Next.

20. In the Description text box, type a description for the filter and click Next.

21. For the IP traffic source, as shown in Figure 11-34, in the Source Address drop-down list, select A Specific IP Address.

22. In the IP Address text box, type the IP address of Computer1. Then click Next.

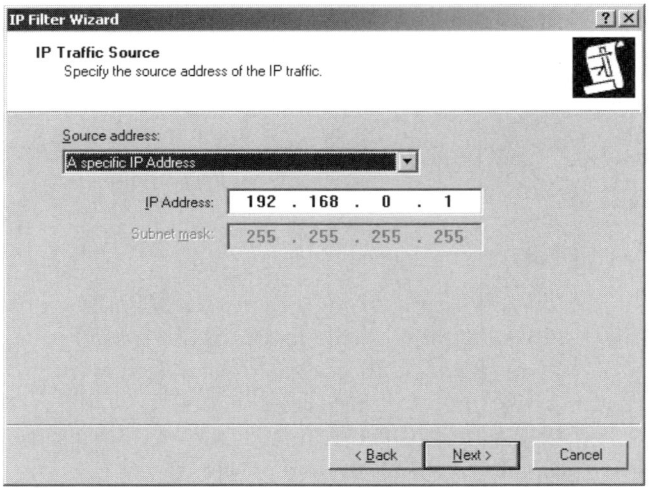

Figure 11-34 Entering a specific traffic source

23. On the IP Traffic Destination page, in the Destination Address drop-down list, select A Specific IP Address and type the IP address for Computer2. Then click Next.

24. On the IP Protocol Type page, select TCP. Then click Next.

25. Click To This Port, type **23**, click Next, and then click Finish.

26. Click OK to return to the IP Filter List page in the Security Rule Wizard.

27. Click Negotiate, and then click Next.

28. Click Require Security, and then click Next.

29. Select Kerberos for the authentication method, click Next, and then click Finish.

30. Click OK to complete the rule; then click OK again to finish the procedure.

▶   **To import and then export the policy to another computer**

Before activating a negotiation policy, you should make sure the other computer or computers have the same policy configuration. One way to perform this task is to create the policy by hand on the other computer. Another way is to export the policy and import it on the other computer, which you do in this exercise.

1. Open the IP Security Management console on Computer 2.

2. Right-click IP Security Policies On Local Computer, select All Tasks, and then click Export Policies.

    The trouble with exporting policy files is that you get all of the policies created on this computer. That result might not be what you want.

3. Browse to a shared folder on Computer1, type a name, and click Save.

4. On Computer1, create an IP Security Management console.

5. Right-click IP Security Policies On Local Computer, select All Tasks, and click Import Policies.

6. Select the policy file, and click Open.

    The security policy has been successfully copied between computers. Close all consoles and log off both systems.

Exercise 3: Use Netsh to Manage IPSec

Any task you can perform with the IP Security Policy snap-in and the IP Security Monitor snap-in, you can do with the Netsh command. You can also perform tasks with Netsh that you cannot do from a console, such as the following: instituting computer startup security, performing computer startup traffic exemptions, running diagnostics, performing default traffic exemptions, performing strong CRL checking, performing IKE (Oakley) logging, modifying logging intervals, and creating a persistent policy.

You create policies by configuring IKE parameters and adding rules that are composed of filter lists, filter actions, and other configuration parameters. In the following exercise, the commands create an IPSec policy to negotiate telnet security between Computer1 and Computer2 and to block telnet from any computer other than Computer2. You must create a policy at both Computer1 and Computer2. You can do so, as the exercise suggests, one command at a time. Alternatively, you could build a batch file and run it to implement the policy.

When using the Netsh command, this method, of course, would be the preferred way to do so in the real world. Each command in the step-by-step exercise is followed by pressing the Enter key. Figure 11-35 shows the commands to create the policy on Computer2 (steps 2 through 5), as entered at the Netsh IPSec Static command line. If you receive an error message, correct your syntax. If you need to start all over again, you can delete the policy with the command Delete Policy Name=Telnet.

Figure 11-35   Creating a policy with Netsh

1. Enter the Netsh IPSec Static context by entering the following commands:

```
Netsh
Netsh>ipsec static
```

2. Create a policy on Computer1 by entering the following command:

```
Add policy name="telnet"
description="only allow negotiated telnet from computer2 to computer1"
activatedefaultrule=no mmsecmethods="3DES-MD5-3"
```

This policy needs two rules. One blocks all telnet communications and the other negotiates telnet from Computer2 to Computer1. To add the rules, you must first add the filter list, its filters, and a filter action. If you create a filter for a filter list that doesn't exist, the filter list is created.

3. To create a filter list with one filter that triggers on telnet and a source IP address of 192.168.0.2 (Computer2), type the following command:

```
Add filter filterlist="telnet computer2"
srcaddr=192.168.0.2 dstaddr=Me description="computer2 telnet to computer1"
protocol=TCP mirrored=yes srcmask=32 dstmask=32 srcport=0 dstport=23
```

4. Type the following command to add a filter action to negotiate telnet from Computer2 to Computer1:

```
Add filteraction name="negotiate computer2 telnet"
qmpfs=no inpass=no soft=no action=negotiate qmsecmethods="ESP[3DES,MD5]"
```

5. Add the rule that will manage telnet negotiation by typing this command:

```
Add rule name="telnetN" policy="telnet" filterlist="telnet computer2"
filteraction="negotiate computer2 telnet"
Kerberos=yes description="this rule negotiates telnet if the source computer is
computer2"
```

Note that the rule ties the filter list and the filter action and selects the authentication method. If no authentication method is specified, Kerberos is used by default.

6. Prepare the filter list and filter action for the second rule. Create a filter list with one filter that triggers on telnet and blocks telnet from all computers:

```
Add filter filterlist="blocktelnet"
srcaddr=Any dstaddr=Me description="all telnet to computer1"
protocol=TCP mirrored=yes srcmask=24 dstmask=24 srcport=0 dstport=23
```

7. Add a filter action to block all telnet communications:

```
Add filteraction name="block all telnet" inpass=yes action=block
```

8. Add a rule that will manage this telnet negotiation:

```
Add rule name="telnetN" policy="telnet" filterlist="blocktelnet"
filteraction="block all telnet"
Kerberos=yes description="this rule negotiates telnet if the source computer is
computer2"
```

9. Assign the policy:

```
set policy name=telnet assign=yes
```

10. On Computer 2, log on as Administrator and open a command prompt.

11. Open Netsh.

   On Computer2, a single filter list, filter, and filter action are necessary. You are providing it the means to negotiate the telnet connection with Computer1. First, create the policy.

12. Type the following command:

```
Add policy name="telnet"
description="only allow negotiated telnet to computer1 from computer2"
activatedefaultrule=no mmsecmethods="3DES-MD5-3"
```

13. Next, create the filter list:

```
Add filter filterlist="telnet computer1"
srcaddr=Me dstaddr=192.168.0.2 description="computer2 telnet to computer1"
protocol=TCP mirrored=yes srcmask=32 dstmask=32 srcport=0 dstport=23
```

14. Next, create the filter action:

```
Add filteraction name="negotiate computer2 telnet"
qmpfs=no inpass=no soft=no action=negotiate
```

15. Then add the rule that will manage telnet negotiation:

```
Add rule name="telnetN" policy="telnet" filterlist = "telnet computer1"
filteraction="negotiate computer2 telnet"
Kerberos=yes description="this rule negotiates telnet to computer1"
```

16. Finally, assign the policy. Remember, only one policy can be active at a time. You must run this command at both computers.

```
set policy name=telnet assign=yes
```

17. Close Netsh.

Exercise 4: Use Netsh to Monitor IPSec

After you have created and assigned the IPSec policy using Netsh, use Netsh commands to monitor the session.

1. From either computer, start Netsh:

```
Netsh
Netsh>ipsec static
```

2. Use the Show command and review the active policy to see whether your policy application worked:

```
show policy name=telnet level=verbose
```

3. Enter Dynamic mode:

```
dynamic
```

4. Set the diagnostic value to log all events (the default is 0 or no logging) using this command:

```
set config property=ipsecdiagnostics value=7
```

5. Set the IPsecloginterval value to 60 seconds:

```
set config property=ipsecloginterval value=60
```

6. Display information about Main Mode and Quick Mode SAs using the Show Mmsas All (Figure 11-36) and Show Qmsas All (Figure 11-37) commands.

Figure 11-36   Viewing IKE Main Mode statistics

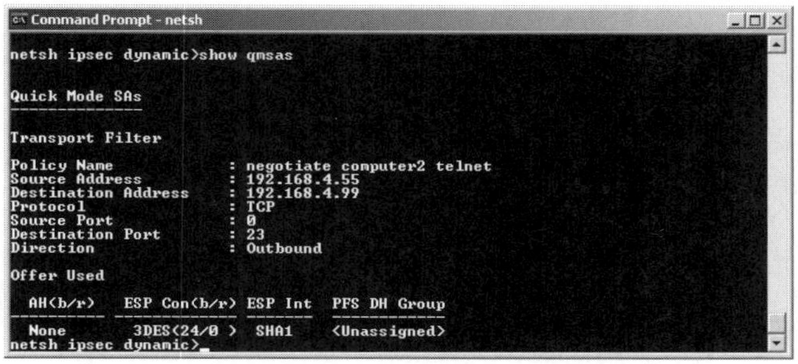

Figure 11-37   Viewing Quick Mode statistics

7. Type **quit** to exit Netsh.

Exercise 5: Use IP Security Monitor to Monitor an IPSec Connection

In this exercise, you monitor IPSec activity using the IP Security Monitor snap-in.

1. Open IP Security Monitor on both computers by adding the snap-in to an MMC.

2. Check that the active IPSec policy is the one you assigned.

3. Examine the details about the active policy. Are the details what you expected?

_____

4. Select the Main Mode (Figure 11-38) and Quick Mode (Figure 11-39) Security Associations nodes and double-click the SA in the details pane.

   This step tells you which encryption is being used.

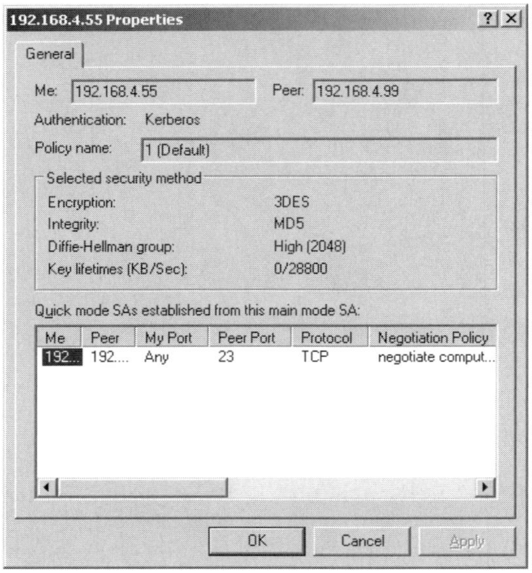

Figure 11-38 Main Mode SA showing information about encryption

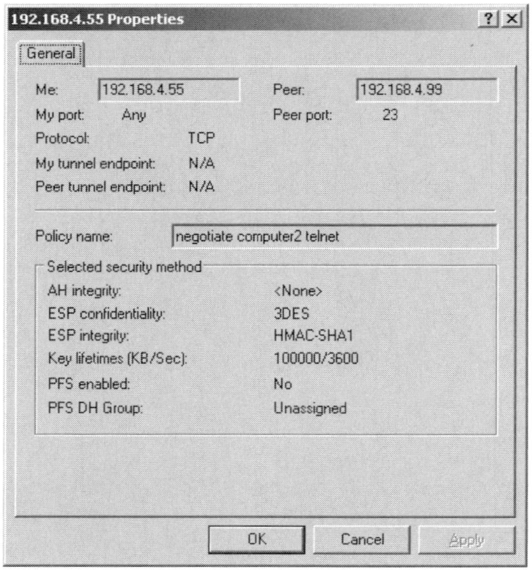

Figure 11-39 Quick Mode SA verifying connection and encryption

5. Examine the Quick Mode Statistics node.

6. Close the windows.

Exercise 6: Use Netcap to Capture Network Security Protocol Information

1. On Computer1, create a Test1.txt file by right-clicking the Shared Captures folder in Windows Explorer, selecting New, and clicking Text Document. Then type the name **test1.txt** and click OK.

2. On Computer2, Click Start, select All Programs, select Windows Support Tools, and click Command Prompt.

3. Run Netcap with a buffer size of 1 MB and save the capture file to C:\Authentication.cap (Figure 11-40). To do so, type this command:

```
netcap /c:c:\authentication.cap /n:0
```

Figure 11-40   Using Netcap to start and stop a capture without loading Network Monitor

4. While the capture is running, connect to the \\Computer1\My Captures share on the domain controller and double-click the Test1.txt file to open it in Notepad.

5. Make a change in the file and save it.

   An Access Denied error message appears because the default share permissions are Everyone Read.

6. From another command prompt, telnet to the domain controller using the following command:

```
telnet computer1
```

7. Return to the command prompt for Netcap and press the Spacebar to stop the capture.

   The name of the capture file is listed.

8. Open the capture file in Network Monitor and look for evidence of the file being read.

   The text in the file should be displayed in clear text.

9. Look for the ISAKMP negotiation and ESP frames. Answer the following question in the space provided.

   What do the frames tell you?

   _____

10. Close the capture files and close Network Monitor.

Exercise 7: Use Kerbtray to View the Kerberos Ticket Cache

To troubleshoot Kerberos issues, it is helpful to be able to view the ticket cache. It's a good idea to know how to do so, before it's necessary. This exercise shows that connecting to a file share results in the client computer obtaining a cifs service ticket. The ticket is used to authenticate to the remote computer, and the ticket remains in the cache and can be used later.

1. On Computer2, download and install the Windows Server 2003 Resource Kit tools from *http://www.microsoft.com/downloads/details.aspx?familyid=9d467a69-57ff-4ae7-96ee-b18c4790cffd&displaylang=en*.

2. Log off and log back on again.

3. Create a new connection to the My Captures share on Computer1.

4. From the C:\Program Files\Windows Resource Kits\Tools folder, run the Kerbtray.exe program.

5. In the status bar, double-click the Kerbtray icon.

6. Select the ticket used to authenticate to the share, and answer the following question in the space provided.

   Which service was used?

   _____

7. Examine the property tabs of each ticket in the cache in order to become familiar with the data that they hold.

8. Disconnect from the network share.

9. In the status bar, right-click the Kerbtray icon and click Exit Kerb Tray.

Exercise 8: Use Klist to Purge and View the Kerberos Ticket Cache

In this exercise, you use the Klist command to manage the Kerberos ticket cache.

1. Click Start, select All Programs, select Windows Resource Kit Tools, and then click Command Shell.

2. At the command prompt, type **klist tgt** to see information about the tickets on the computer.

3. At the command prompt, type **klist tickets** to see information about all the tickets on the computer.

4. At the command prompt, type **klist purge** to delete all the tickets. Then answer the following questions in the space provided.

   Can you connect to the file share? Why?

   _____

5. Log off and log back on again.

6. Use the Klist Tickets command to see the tickets in the ticket cache.

7. Close the command prompt, and log off the computer.

Lesson Review

The following questions are intended to reinforce key information presented in this lesson. If you are unable to answer a question, review the lesson materials and try the question again. You can find answers to the questions in the "Questions and Answers" section at the end of this chapter.

1. IPSec can be used to secure communications between two computers. What else can it do? (Choose all that apply.)

   a. Examine Kerberos tickets

   b. Block transfer of specific protocol packets

   c. Allow transfer of packets with a destination TCP port of 23 from any computer to the host computer

   d. Permit one user to use telnet to access the computer while denying another user

2. What is a good reason for assigning a policy by means of Netsh when Group Policy can be used to simply assign an IPSec policy across multiple computers?

   a. Using Netsh is the only way to apply a policy that can be used to permit a user's computer to be used for a telnet session with another computer while blocking all other telnet communications.

   b. Using Netsh is more easily implemented when multiple machines need to be configured.

   c. You can apply Netsh even if the computers are not joined in a domain, and Group Policy can work only in a domain.

   d. You can use Netsh to create a persistent policy that will be used if Group Policy cannot be used.

3. Netsh is used to create and assign an IPSec policy for a stand-alone server running Windows Server 2003. One of the commands used is the following, executed from the Netsh IPSec Static context:

```
Add rule name="SMTPBlock" policy="smtp" filterlist="smtp computerlist"
filteraction="negotiate smtp" description="this rule negotiates smtp"
```

Why is the policy not working?

    a. The policy is set with the wrong IP addresses.

    b. Each policy specifies a different encryption algorithm.

    c. No encryption is taking place. The evidence is revealed in the soft SAs.

    d. The policy is using Kerberos for authentication and the computer is not a member of a domain.

Lesson Summary

- You can use the Netsh IPSec Static mode to create and assign IPSec policies.

- You can use the Netsh IPSec Dynamic mode to add diagnostics, to add a persistent policy, and to change other configuration features.

- A persistent policy is one that will be in effect if a domain policy, or a policy created through the IP Security Policy Management snap-in, cannot be activated.

- You can use Kerbtray.exe to view information about the logged-on users' Kerberos tickets.

- You can use Klist.exe to view and purge tickets from the command line.

- You can use Netcap to create a network capture on a system that does not have Network Monitor installed. The capture can then be viewed on the computer running Network Monitor.

Lesson 3: Troubleshooting Network Protocol Security

This section begins by stating a problem and then shows you how to troubleshoot it using one or more of the tools.

> **Caution**   Adjust the guidelines given in this section when troubleshooting in the real world. You want to make sure you do not accidentally destroy data or interrupt critical transactions while troubleshooting. The recommendations here often include steps that need to be modified. For example:
>
> - Clearing logs gives you less data to pore over. In the real world, you might be able to use this technique by first saving the log. You want the Event logs intact. In addition, a good practice would be to save them, and then you can even evaluate them on a different computer.
>
> - You should not reboot unless you can ensure that the production system or the people using it will not be adversely affected.

> **Important**   When troubleshooting, keep in mind that the network's sole purpose is to support the business that runs it. That said, you must approach each troubleshooting effort as unique and make a decision about what you need to do and when. For example, if a critical system is offline, you might take a different approach than if you are just trying to fix a minor problem.

To follow the troubleshooting examples, or to complete the exercises that you will do on your own, you should perform the following tasks so that you will have less data to examine:

- Clear the Security, System, and Application Event logs.

- Unassign an IPSec policy you might have assigned. Even if you want to troubleshoot IPSec, you want to first ensure that no policy is in effect and then assign the policy you want to troubleshoot. For the tests in this section, it is best to unassign the policy and then reboot the server. To unassign a policy, simply right-click the assigned policy and select Unassign. This action ensures that you are troubleshooting the policy you think you are.

- If you have not rebooted, purge the Kerberos ticket cache and log on again. If you are going to troubleshoot Kerberos, shut down the server. Start the network capture on the DC and then reboot the server.

Do not perform these tasks when troubleshooting in the real world unless you know that you will not destroy data and you will not interrupt critical transactions by doing so. The recommendations here will, however, give you less data to pore through, and in the real world you might be able to use the techniques in some circumstances. You certainly want the Event logs intact. A good practice is to save them. Then you can even evaluate them on a different computer. So, save the Event logs, and then clear them if you want to reduce the amount of information to look at and if you can reproduce the activity. You will not want to reboot unless you can ensure it will not adversely affect the production system or the people using it. Whenever you are troubleshooting, keep in mind that the network's sole purpose is to support the business that runs it. That said, you must approach each troubleshooting effort as unique and make a decision about what to do and when. For example, if a system is not working, you might take a different approach than if you are just trying to fix a minor problem.

After this lesson, you will be able to

- Use tools such as Network Monitor, the Event Viewer, and the IP Security Monitor snap-in
- Use Kerberos tools such as Klist and Kerbtray to troubleshoot network protocol security

Estimated lesson time: 60 minutes

Problem 1: Making Your IPSec Policy Work

In the following exercise, you create and assign an IPSec policy, only to discover that the two computers cannot communicate at all. You can use a number of steps and tools to troubleshoot an IPSec policy, as described in the following list.

> **Note**   IKE auditing is turned on by default. If auditing of logon events is turned on, IKE posts negotiation results in the Security Event log. Once policies have been assigned and are working, you can turn this feature off by adding the DisableIKEAudits value and setting it to 1. You should then stop and start the IPSec service. The value should be created at HKEY_LOCAL_MACHINE\SYSTEM\CurrentControlSet\Control\Lsa\Audit.
>
> You can also increase the amount of information logged to the Security Event log by asking for per packet drop events. You perform this task by increasing the audit level to 7. You can either use Netsh or set the following Registry key to a value of 7: HKEY_LOCAL_MACHINE\SYSTEM\CurrentControlSet\Services\IPSec\EnableDiagnostics. Regardless of the method you use, you must restart the computer for the changes to take effect.

- Is the policy assigned? Use IPSec Monitor to tell you the currently active policy. Or use the Netsh Ipsec Static Show Gpoassignedpolicy command.

- If the policy is different from the one you were expecting, which GPO is responsible? To find out, you can use the Netsh Ipsec Static Show Gpoassignedpolicy command or the Resultant Set Of Policy snap-in.

- What are the details of the policy? Use the Netsh Ipsec Static Show All command. You are looking for confirmation that the policy is assigned and that its parameters are correct. You can also find this information by using the IP Security Policy Management snap-in to view the policies for the local machine.

- Is IKE negotiation succeeding? Check the Security Event log. If auditing is not turned on, use the Group Policy Object Editor snap-in to enable auditing. IKE negotiation uses the Logon Events category to report success or failure. If IKE negotiation is not succeeding, check IKE settings. Are authentication, encryption, and key change the same for both computers?

- If IKE is succeeding, is Quick Mode succeeding? Check the Security Event log. If Quick Mode is not succeeding, check to see that all Quick Mode encryption, integrity, key strength, key change, and so on are the same. Do filters make sense? For example, if you are entering from and to IP addresses, are they mirrors? If you are indicating on one computer from and to ports, is the other a mirror of this?

- Are packets reaching the correct computer? You can use Network Monitor to capture IPSec packets. You will not be able to see any encrypted text; however, you will know whether packets are reaching the computer. (You can view the source address.) Also, you will know whether IPSec is being applied. You can also modify your policy to use no encryption and then capture packets to learn more about them.

- Are packets being dropped? There is no IPSec performance counter. Dropped IPSec packets contribute to the Datagrams Received Discarded and Datagrams Outbound Discarded counters in the IPv4 performance object. However, the best way to determine whether packets are being dropped is to use the IP Security Monitor snap-in to see the packets dropped.

Problem 2: Determining Whether Your IPSec Blocking Rules Are Working

You can write blocking rules to prevent inbound and outbound packets. You can restrict packets from or to specific IP addresses or IP address ranges or restrict them by protocol or port. It is easy to test some of these instances: just use another computer and attempt to connect and communicate with the inbound ports or attempt to connect to the computer or use the protocol that is blocked outbound. Other problems are not as easy to isolate; furthermore, you need to ensure that some fluke is not preventing the connection rather than your policy, and you would like to know whether the policy is working overtime. You can use two tools to verify this information:

- You can use Netsh to set per packet drop logging.
- You can set diagnostics logging and view events.

Problem 3: Determining Whether Kerberos Is Being Used for Authentication

Windows Server 2003, Windows 2000, and Windows XP Professional all use Kerberos for authentication in a Windows Server 2003 or Windows 2000 domain. However, if Kerberos cannot be used, authentication might fall back to NTLM, or if the domain controller is not available, logon from cached credentials is used instead. Also, when drives are mapped using server IP address instead of computer name, NTLM is used for authentication. In a large enough domain, every day, somewhere, Kerberos is probably not being used.

You cannot "turn off" NTLM. You cannot somehow insist that only Kerberos be used in the domain. You can, however, make it easier for Kerberos to be used, and you can monitor and determine whether, in a specific instance, Kerberos was used for authentication. First, inspect the Event logs looking for Kerberos errors.

One common error has to do with computer clock skew time—that is, if the difference between the client computer's clock and the domain controller is off by more than 5 minutes, Kerberos fails and you will find Kerberos errors in the event log. Although the time service running on clients attempts to keep the client synchronized with the DC, if the time difference is over 30 minutes, synchronization will not occur. Other errors might indicate network problems.

Security Event log logon records indicate the protocol used. Examining logon events helps you determine which authentication protocol was used. You can also determine the authentication protocol from a Network Monitor capture.

Practice 1: Troubleshoot IPSec with IPSec Monitor

Perhaps one of the hardest aspects of networking to troubleshoot is IPSec. The best troubleshooting tool is your knowledge of how IPSec works, the specifics of your policies (what you are trying to accomplish and how the policy is configured), and the use of the IPSec Monitor.

Exercise 1: Preparing auditing to capture IPSec events

1. Verify that auditing is turned on for Logon Events, Account Logon Events, and Policy Change Events.

2. On Computer1, create a new MMC and use the Add/Remove snap-in to add two occurrences of the Group Policy Object Editor snap-in: the first for the Default Domain Policy, and the second for the Default Domain Controllers Policy.

3. Save this console with the name Domain GPOs.

4. Expand the Default Domain Controllers Policy, expand Computer Configuration, expand Windows Settings, expand Security Settings, expand Local Policies, and then click Audit Policy.

   Note that auditing is turned on for account logon events, account management, and object access.

5. Examine the Audit Policy for the Default Domain Policy. Then answer the following question.

6. Are these policies defined?

   _____

7. Define the Audit Logon Events, Audit Account Management, and Audit Object Access policies for success and failure.

   Setting audit policies in the Default Domain Policy sets them for all computers in the domain. This is all right in this case, but it might not be in your production network. Audit settings should be carefully designed to fulfill your security policy goals.

8. Open the IP Security Policy Management console created in Exercise 1 of Lesson 3.

9. Use the Add/Remove Snap-In menu to add another IP Security Policy Management snap-in, but point this one to the Local Computer.

10. View the details pane of each IP Security Policy to verify that no IPSec policy is assigned. If one is assigned, unassign it by right-clicking the policy and choosing Unassign.

11. Turn on additional auditing using the Netsh command by entering the following command:

    ```
    netsh Ipsec Dynamic Set Config Property=Ipsecdiagnostics value=7
    ```

Exercise 2: Modify the IPSec policy on Computer1

1. Select the IP Security Policies On Local Computer node in the IPSec Security Policy Management console.

2. In the details pane, double-click the policy made in Exercise 1 of Lesson 3.

3. Select the active (the one checked) IP Filter list.

4. Select the Filter Action tab.

5. Select the active action and click Edit.

6. On the Security Methods page, select a security method and click Edit.

7. Click Custom and click Edit; then click Settings.

8. Change the Encryption algorithm from 3DES to DES.

9. Click OK twice, and then select any remaining security methods (Figure 11-41) and change their encryption algorithms from 3DES to DES. Click OK twice.

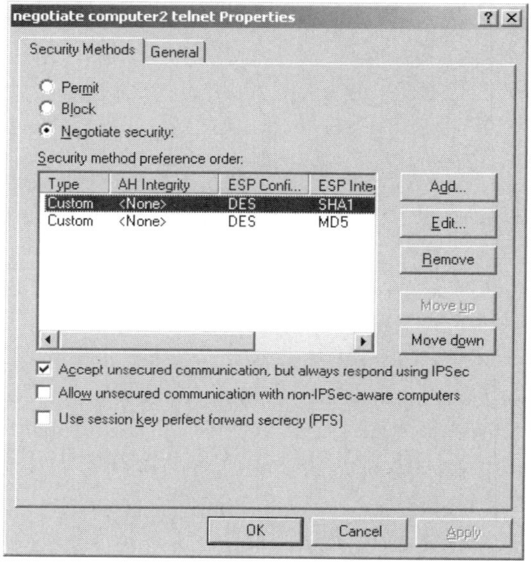

Figure 11-41 Setting Quick Mode session key changes

10. Click OK twice. Then click Close and then OK to save the policy changes.

11. Assign the telnet policy on both computers.

    This policy worked previously, but you have just made a change.

12. Attempt to telnet from Computer2 to Computer1.

    Does it work?

---

13. In the IP Security Management console, open the IP Security Monitor snap-in for Computer1 and select the Active Policy node. What is the Active Policy and when was it modified?

14. The Active Policy should be your telnet policy. If it is not, you might have already found the problem. Go back and review the previous part of this section of the exercise. Write down the time; in the production environment, you should always document when IPSec policies have changed. By comparing that date to the one

in the interface, you might discover an unauthorized change has been made. Although that might explain why a problem exists, it doesn't resolve it.

15. Examine the IP Security Monitor snap-in for Computer2 and select the Active Policy node. What is the active policy and when was it last changed?

_____

_____

_____

16. Open both monitors to the Main Mode, Statistics node and examine the details pane. Do you find any failures?

_____

17. Open both monitors to the Quick Mode, Statistics node and examine the parameters Key Additions, Key Deletions, and Rekeys.

What do you find?

_____

18. Unassign the changed policy and fix it. (Change the encryption type back to 3DES.)

19. Assign the policy and then stop and start the IPSec service.

What does IPSec Monitor show now?

_____

20. Unassign policies on both computers.

Practice 2: Troubleshoot Logon Issues with Network Monitor

You often want to determine which authentication protocol is in use so you can determine why some users are having trouble accessing resources. It is also an issue when you want to consider what visitors can access if they are allowed to plug into your network, or in order to plan security for the LAN Manager protocol. In this exercise, you troubleshoot these kinds of issues.

1. On Computer2, delete any mapped drives or other connections to Computer1.

2. Log off Computer2.

3. Unplug the network connection.

   If the computer is not plugged into the network, it cannot obtain Kerberos tickets; however, users who have previously authenticated to the domain will be able to log on. Even so, they will not be able to use Kerberos.

4. From Computer1, log on to the domain.

5. Start Kerbtray and note that there are no Kerberos tickets.

6. Reconnect the network connection.

7. Start a Network Monitor capture on Computer1.

8. Map to the capture share on Computer1. You should use the name of the computer in the path, in other words, \\Computer1\Capture.

9. From the Capture menu of Network Monitor, select Stop And View and answer the following questions.

   Were you successful?

   _____

   How can you tell?

   _____

10. For confirmation, check the network capture. You should be able to locate an SMB negotiate frame (Figure 11-42), which indicates NTLM was used. Record the time the frame was recorded. (In the test done for these exercises, the time was 8:24.)

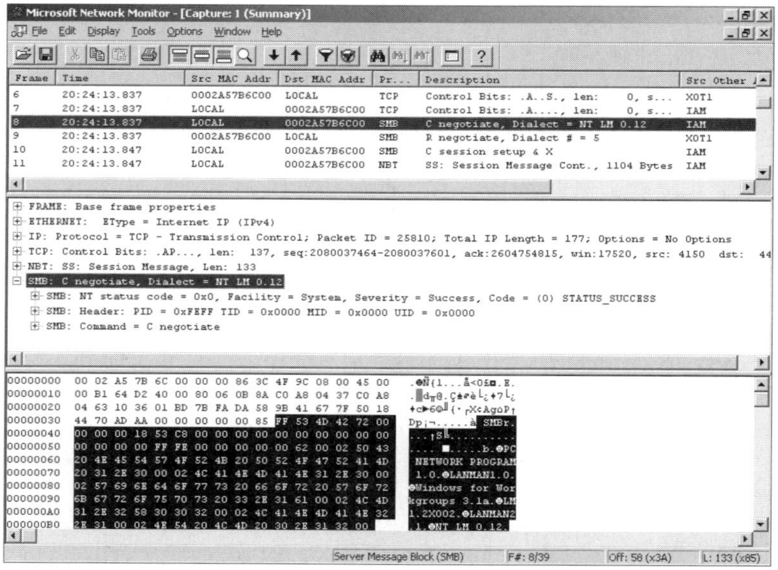

Figure 11-42   Finding NTLM negotiate in the Network Monitor capture

Practice 3: Use Event Logs for Troubleshooting

In the previous two exercises, you modified an IPSec policy and examined its behavior in IPSec Monitor. You also used Network Monitor to examine packets that indicated that Kerberos was not used for authentication. In this exercise, you examine the Event logs to find the events that correspond to those you saw in IPSec Monitor and in Network Monitor.

1. Use the time you recorded in Practice 1, "Troubleshoot IPSec with IPSec Monitor," and search the Computer1 Security Event log looking for IPSec events.

    You should find a record of IKE negotiation and ESP packets. You should also find some error messages indicating dropped packets.

2. Use the time you recorded in Practice 2, "Troubleshoot Logon Issues with Network Monitor," for logon. Search the Computer1 Security Event log to find the logon events for your account that occurred at the time recorded in Exercise 2. Examine these events and answer the following questions.

    Which event shows the NTLM logon success?

    _____

    _____

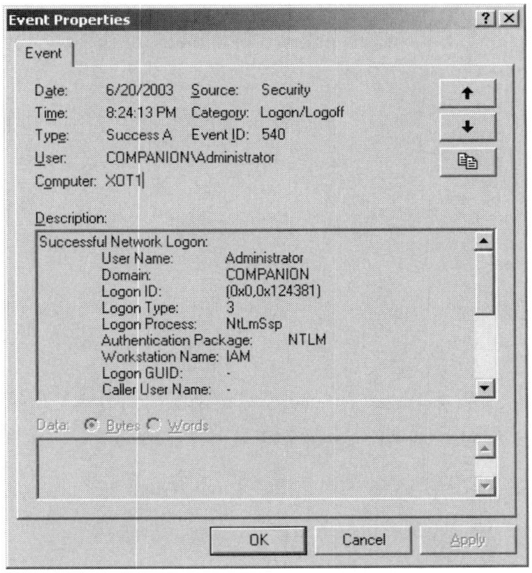

Figure 11-43   Finding NTLM negotiate in the success logon events

Lesson Review

The following questions are intended to reinforce key information presented in this lesson. If you are unable to answer a question, review the lesson materials and try the question again. You can find answers to the questions in the "Questions and Answers" section at the end of this chapter.

1. An IPSec policy has been assigned and communication is failing between two computers. The event shown in Figure 11-44 is found in the IP Security Monitor. Its timestamp indicates the event happened during the failure. What is the most likely reason for the failure?

   a. The failure is due to an authentication error.

   b. Main Mode negotiation is failing.

   c. Quick Mode negotiation is failing.

   d. The specific type of packets that the policy is supposed to be blocking are being blocked.

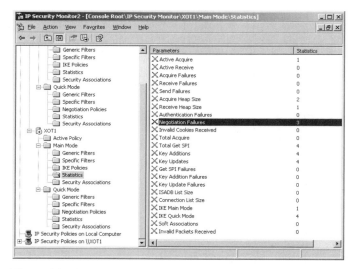

Figure 11-44   Viewing statistics

2. During a communication session between two computers, the IP Security Monitor snap-in shows the status in Figure 11-45. What does this status mean?

   a. The communication is not encrypted as expected.

   b. The communication is encrypted as expected.

   c. The communication is not occurring.

   d. The communication is not being received at this computer.

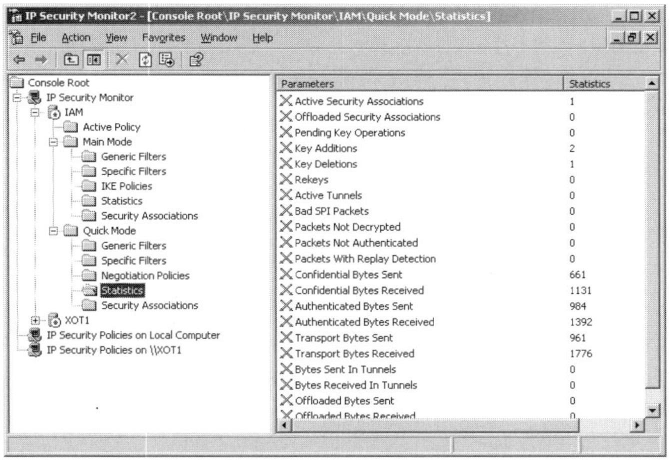

Figure 11-45   Troubleshooting by viewing statistics

3. You log on to the domain, map a drive to the share \\192.168.5.55\share, and then copy some files. You then use Kerbtray.exe to examine the Kerberos tickets. You find a ticket for your account and the service krgbt. You do not find a ticket for CIFS for this server. What is the most likely reason for this problem?

   a. The ticket with the service krgbt is the ticket for this type of connection.

   b. Using the IP address instead of server name means NTLM will be used.

   c. The Kerbtray.exe utility shows only TGT tickets, and the share ticket is a user or session ticket.

   d. The Kerbtray.exe utility shows only session tickets, and the share ticket is a TGT ticket.

Lesson Summary

- Several utilities exist for troubleshooting IPSec, including the IP Security Monitor snap-in, Netsh, the Security Event log, and Network Monitor.

- You can change the level of logging as needed to help troubleshooting. If logging this information is flooding the Event logs and no problems exist, you can reduce the logging by changing a Registry value.

- You can avoid many common errors with IPSec if you check the policies for completeness and matching elements.

- Kerberos is not always used in a domain environment for authentication.

Troubleshooting Lab

In this lab, you use your knowledge of the tools discussed in this chapter to trouble-shoot communication issues. The goal is to be able to telnet to Computer1 in a secure fashion using IPSec.

Setup

1. Log on as a member of Domain Admins.

2. Use the IPSec Security Management console created in this chapter to check the IP Security Policies on Computer1 and Computer2. If an IPSec policy is assigned, right-click the policy and select Unassign.

3. Start the telnet service on Computer1.

4. On Computer2, open a command prompt and telnet to Computer1.

5. After a connection is made, exit telnet.

6. On Computer2, copy the Ipsec2.bat file from the \70-291\Labs\Chapter11 folder on the supplemental CD-ROM to drive C.

7. Navigate from the command prompt to the root of C and run the batch file Ipsec2.bat by typing **ipsec2.bat** at the command prompt.

8. On Computer1, copy the Ipsec1.bat file from the \70-291\Labs\Chapter11 folder on the supplemental CD-ROM to drive C.

9. Open a command prompt, navigate to the root of C, and run the batch file Ipsec1.bat by typing **ipsec1.bat** at the command prompt.

10. Attempt to telnet to Computer1 from Computer2.

    Are you able to telnet to Computer1?

    _____

    _____

Find Out What the Problem Is

One day an ordinary task you perform works as usual. The next day it does not. What happened? Something has changed. Sometimes there are interpretable error messages, and sometimes things just don't work. As the administrator for these systems, your job is to fix them. The first step is to think of the reasons that might cause the problem.

1. What are some reasons why telnet would stop working?

   _____

   _____

_____

_____

_____

2. Take a minute to order your thoughts. This process sometimes allows you to eliminate some of the reasons and determine which tasks you should perform and in
   which order you should perform them.

   What tasks should you perform and in which order? Are there any tasks that you
   do not have to do?

   _____

   _____

   _____

   _____

   _____

   _____

   _____

   _____

   _____

   _____

3. Follow your list. At the command prompt on Computer2, ping Computer1 by typing **ping computer1**.

   Were you able to reach Computer1?

   _____

4. Open the Administrative Tools, Services console.

5. From the Action menu, select Connect To Another Computer.

6. On Computer1, scroll to the telnet service.

   Is the telnet service running?

   _____

7. Start the service.

8. Open the IP Security Management console and examine the IP Security Policies
   On Local Computer node and the IP Security Policies On \\Computer1 node.

   Is a new policy, one you have never seen before, assigned at both nodes?

   _____

9. Unassign the policies on both Computer1 and Computer2.

10. From the command prompt on Computer2, attempt to telnet to Computer1.

    Are you successful?

    _____

11. One or both of the policies must be the problem. Move on to the next exercise to troubleshoot the policies.

Troubleshoot IPSec

Troubleshooting IPSec is no different than troubleshooting anything else. You use your knowledge of which parameters are necessary and the available troubleshooting tools to resolve the issue.

1. Think about the order in which actions occur in a policy.

    What are the steps?

    _____
    _____
    _____
    _____
    _____
    _____
    _____
    _____
    _____
    _____
    _____
    _____
    _____

2. In the IP Security Management console, select IP Security Policies On The Local Computer, and double-click the assigned policy.

3. Click Edit to edit the IP filter list.

4. In the IP Filter List box, double-click the filter with its option selected, and then double-click the IP filter.

    Is the source address My IP Address?

    _____

Is the Destination address a specific IP address, and is it the IP address of Computer1?

_____

5. Change the IP address to Computer1's address. The subnet mask should be dimmed.

6. Click OK four times to close the policy.

7. Select the IP Security Policies On Computer1 node and double-click the Active policy.

   There are two rules to examine here.

8. Select the first rule and check its filter action by clicking the Filter Action tab and double-clicking the selected filter action.

   What is the filter action?

_____

9. Click OK, and then select the IP Filter List tab.

10. Double-click the selected filter action, and then double-click the filter.

    Is the source address a specific IP address, and is it correct? (Is it the address of Computer2?)

_____

    Is the destination address My Address?

_____

11. Change the source address to the address of Computer2. Then click OK four times to close the policy.

    Now that the IP addresses are correct, the best way to see whether any other problems are present and if so, where they are occurring, is to trigger the rule and examine the information produced in the IP Security Monitor snap-in.

12. Return to the IP Security Management console on Computer2. Assign each policy.

13. From the command prompt on Computer2, attempt to telnet to Computer1.

14. Return to the IP Security Management console, IP Security Monitor for Computer1 and select the Main Mode Statistics node.

    Are any authentication failures present?

_____

15. From the IP Security Management console, select the Main Mode Generic Filters node and double-click the filter in the details pane.

16. Select the Authentication Methods tab.

What is the authentication method?

_____

17. Select the Main Mode Generic Filters node for Computer2.

What is the authentication method?

_____

Therefore, the problem is that the authentication methods don't match. Because both computers are joined in the domain and Kerberos is a more secure authentication method, you need to change the authentication method to Kerberos in the policy on Computer2.

18. Select the IP Security Policies On Local Computer node and double-click the assigned policy.

19. Click Edit to open the rule properties.

20. Select the Authentication tab.

21. Click the Add button and select Active Directory default [Kerberos V5 Protocol]. Then click OK.

22. Select the Preshared Key authentication method and click the Remove button. Then click Yes when prompted.

23. Click OK twice to close the policy.

24. From a command prompt, attempt to telnet to Computer1.

Are you successful?

_____

Chapter Summary

- You can use IPSec monitoring tools to ensure that IPSec policies are working as expected. Netsh, IP Security Monitor, Network Monitor captures, and the Security Event log can all be used.

- You can monitor Kerberos activity to ensure this stronger authentication protocol is being used. Use Network Monitor and the Security Event log.

- When troubleshooting security protocols, remember that their failure means more than a simple inconvenience. If IPSec policies are failing and communications cannot occur that should be occurring, this is a major problem. However, if IPSec policies are failing and communications are occurring that shouldn't occur—or shouldn't occur unencrypted—this can be a security disaster.

- Problems with Kerberos can indicate problems with Active Directory, especially with replication.

- Kerberos errors can indicate normal Kerberos operation, failure, or evidence of attack. Knowledge of what behavior is normal and the ability to troubleshoot the problem can determine the difference.

- You can use security templates to configure security settings, and then apply them either by using the Security Configuration And Analysis snap-in on stand-alone machines or by importing the template into Group Policy in a domain.

- You can use the Security Configuration And Analysis snap-in to determine whether a computer complies with policy.

- You should follow the principle of least privilege—provide users with only the privileges and access they need to get the job done.

Exam Highlights

Before taking the exam, review the key points and terms that are presented in this chapter.

Key Points

- Understand what behavior is normal with security protocols so that you can troubleshoot them more easily when problems occur.

- Know that a Kerberos TGT is granted to a user after a successful Kerberos logon. A Kerberos service or user ticket is granted so that a user can use some service, such as accessing a share or making an LDAP query. A TGT is required in order to obtain a service ticket.

- Understand that Kerberos tickets are cached and can be reused and renewed. When they become unrenewable, new tickets can be acquired after a successful logon.

- Know how to use the IPSec monitoring tools Netsh, the Security Event log, and IP Security Monitor.

Key Terms

Netsh   The utility used to manage and troubleshoot IPSec in Windows Server 2003. Two modes exist—Static and Dynamic.

Main Mode   The first part of an IPSec connection. In Main Mode, each computer authenticates to the other and then IKE is used to calculate the master key. All other keys are generated from the master key. An IKE security association (SA) is created over which Quick Mode can be negotiated.

Quick Mode   The second phase of IPSec. In Quick Mode, agreement is reached for the encryption, integrity algorithms, and other policy settings. Two SAs are created, one incoming and one outgoing.

Ticket Granting Ticket (TGT)   A ticket that can be used to request tickets to access resources. The client must authenticate to the Kerberos Distribution Center (KDC) to receive the TGT. The first step in Kerberos authentication is obtaining a TGT.

session ticket   The ticket used to obtain access to resources. A TGT must be used to request a session ticket (also called a user ticket).

Questions and Answers

Lesson 1 Review

Page
11-22
1. You would like to apply a new Registry setting to all the servers on your network. What is an efficient way to perform that task?

Any Registry value can be added to a security template Inf file using Notepad. It should be added to the [Registry Values] section. The next time the template is applied, the Registry setting will be changed. You can write batch scripts to apply the template to multiple machines, or you can import the template into Group Policy.

2. Which of the following settings can be applied using Security Configuration And Analysis and a security template? (Choose all that apply.)

   a. The password must be 15 characters long.

   b. The Accountants group is not allowed to access this computer over the network.

   c. IPSec must be used for all communications between Computer1 and Computer2.

   d. The root file permissions should be Everyone Full Control.

a, b, d

3. Which steps might be necessary to recover from the application of a security template to a file server that prevented all users from accessing the server over the network? Choose the most efficient way.

   a. Log on locally to the file server as Administrator and apply the root security template.

   b. Log on locally to the file server as Administrator and apply the rollback template produced from the bad security template.

   c. Log on remotely to the file server as Enterprise Admin and use the Local Security Policy console to change the user rights policies that might be incorrect.

   d. Log on remotely to the file server as Administrator and apply the rollback template produced from the security template.

b

Lesson 2, Exercise 6

Page
11-67
9. Look for the ISAKMP negotiation and ESP frames.

What do the frames tell you?

Negotiation succeeded and the data is encrypted.

Lesson 2, Exercise 7

Page
11-68

6. Select the ticket used to authenticate to the share.

Which service was used?

The CIFS service

Lesson 2, Exercise 8

Page
11-68

4. At the command prompt, type **klist purge** to delete all the tickets.

Can you connect to the file share? Why?

Yes, because NTLM can be used.

Lesson 2 Review

Page
11-69

1. IPSec can be used to secure communications between two computers. What else can it do? (Choose all that apply.)

   a. Examine Kerberos tickets

   b. Block transfer of specific protocol packets

   c. Allow transfer of packets with a destination TCP port of 23 from any computer to the host computer

   d. Permit one user to use telnet to access the computer while denying another user

   b, c

2. What is a good reason for assigning a policy by means of Netsh when Group Policy can be used to simply assign an IPSec policy across multiple computers?

   a. Using Netsh is the only way to apply a policy that can be used to permit a user's computer to be used for a telnet session with another computer while blocking all other telnet communications.

   b. Using Netsh is more easily implemented when multiple machines need to be configured.

   c. You can apply Netsh even if the computers are not joined in a domain, and Group Policy can work only in a domain.

   d. You can use Netsh to create a persistent policy that will be used if Group Policy cannot be used.

   d

3. Netsh is used to create and assign an IPSec policy for a stand-alone server running Windows Server 2003. One of the commands used is the following, executed from the Netsh IPSec Static context:

```
Add rule name="SMTPBlock" policy="smtp" filterlist="smtp computerlist"
filteraction="negotiate smtp" description="this rule negotiates smtp"
```

Why is the policy not working?

    a. The policy is set with the wrong IP addresses.

    b. Each policy specifies a different encryption algorithm.

    c. No encryption is taking place. The evidence is revealed in the soft SAs.

    d. The policy is using Kerberos for authentication and the computer is not a member of a domain.

d

Lesson 3, Exercise 1

Page 11-75

6. Are these policies defined?

No

Lesson 3, Exercise 2

Page 11-76

12. Attempt to telnet from Computer2 to Computer1.

Does it work?

No

15. Examine the IP Security Monitor snap-in for Computer2 and select the Active Policy node. What is the active policy and when was it last changed?

The active policy should be your telnet policy. The time it changed might help you identify which policy was changed. However, if you inspected both policies, this might not be helpful.

16. Open both monitors to the Main Mode, Statistics node and examine the details pane. Do you find any failures?

A negotiation failure is present.

17. Open both monitors to the Quick Mode, Statistics node and examine the parameters Key Additions, Key Deletions, and Rekeys.

What do you find?

No activity

19. Assign the policy and then stop and start the IPSec service.

What does IPSec Monitor show now?

It should show that the policy is working.

Lesson 3, Practice 2

Page
11-78
9. From the Capture menu of Network Monitor, select Stop And View and answer the following questions.

Were you successful?

Yes

How can you tell?

Because NTLM was used

Lesson 3, Practice 3

Page
11-79
2. Use the time you recorded in Practice 2, "Troubleshoot Logon Issues with Network Monitor," for logon. Search the Computer1 Security Event log to find the logon events for your account that occurred at the time recorded in Exercise 2. Examine these events and answer the following questions.

Which event shows the NTLM logon success?

The event shown in figure 11-46 indicates a successful logon. It also indicates that the Authentication Package is NTLM.

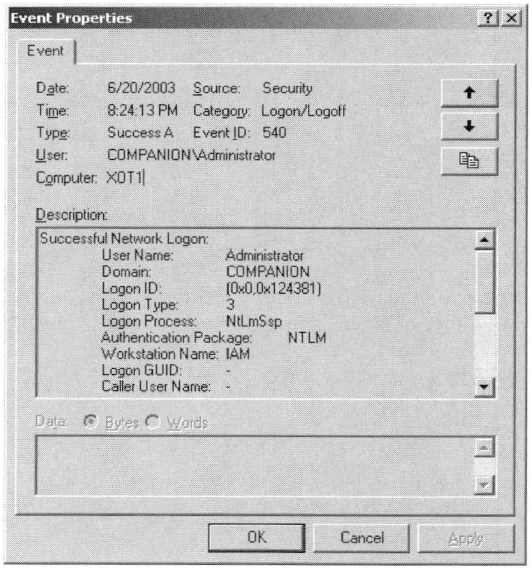

Figure 11-46   Finding NTLM negotiate in the success logon events

Lesson 3 Review

Page
11-80

1. An IPSec policy has been assigned and communication is failing between two computers. The event shown in Figure 11-47 is found in the IP Security Monitor. Its timestamp indicates the event happened during the failure. What is the most likely reason for the failure?

   a. The failure is due to an authentication error.

   b. Main Mode negotiation is failing.

   c. Quick Mode negotiation is failing.

   d. The specific type of packets that the policy is supposed to be blocking are being blocked.

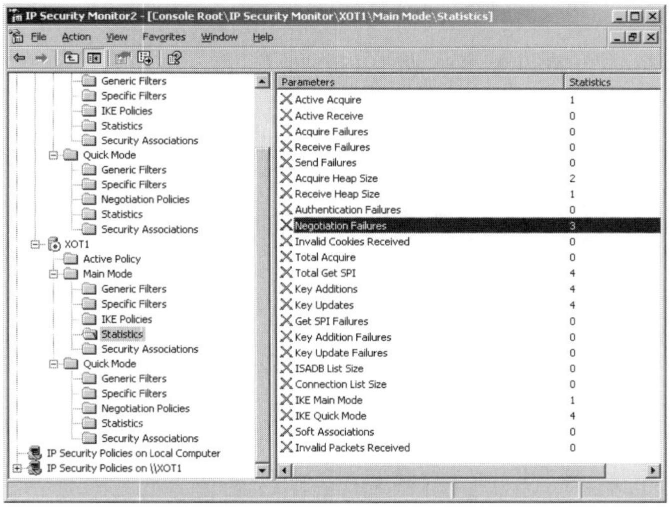

Figure 11-47   Viewing statistics

c

2. During a communication session between two computers, the IP Security Monitor snap-in shows the status in Figure 11-48. What does this status mean?

   a. The communication is not encrypted as expected.

   b. The communication is encrypted as expected.

   c. The communication is not occurring.

   d. The communication is not being received at this computer.

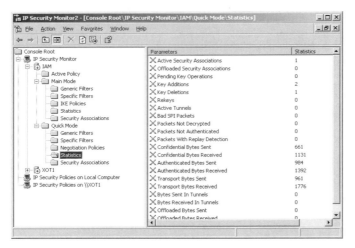

Figure 11-48   Troubleshooting by viewing statistics

b

3. You log on to the domain, map a drive to the share \\192.168.5.55\share, and then copy some files. You then use Kerbtray.exe to examine the Kerberos tickets. You find a ticket for your account and the service krgbt. You do not find a ticket for CIFS for this server. What is the most likely reason for this problem?

   a. The ticket with the service krgbt is the ticket for this type of connection.

   b. Using the IP address instead of server name means NTLM will be used.

   c. The Kerbtray.exe utility shows only TGT tickets, and the share ticket is a user or session ticket.

   d. The Kerbtray.exe utility shows only session tickets, and the share ticket is a TGT ticket.

b

Troubleshooting Lab, Setup

Page
11-82

10. Attempt to telnet to Computer1 from Computer2.

   Are you able to telnet to Computer1?

   No

Troubleshooting Lab, Find Out What the Problem Is

Page
11-82

One day an ordinary task you perform works as usual. The next day it does not. What happened? Something has changed. Sometimes there are interpretable error messages, and sometimes things just don't work. As the administrator for these systems, your job is to fix them. The first step is to think of the reasons that might cause the problem.

1. What are some reasons why telnet would stop working?

   Permissions have changed on one of the systems.

   Your administrative privileges have been taken away.

   Computer1 is not available on the network.

   The telnet service is not running on Computer1.

   An IPSec policy is in place on Computer1 and something is wrong with it.

2. Take a minute to order your thoughts. This process sometimes allows you to eliminate some of the reasons and determine which tasks you should perform and in which order you should perform them.

   What tasks should you perform and in which order? Are there any tasks that you do not have to do?

   The most obvious solution to check is the availability of Computer1 on the network. If it is not reachable, no other troubleshooting task will get anywhere.

   Next, remotely checking Computer1 to see whether the telnet service is running serves several purposes. Obviously, the telnet service needs to be running before you can access Computer1 using telnet. However, if you can use the Services console on Computer2 to access the list of services on Computer1, you have determined that you still have administrative privileges, that administrative tasks can be accomplished remotely, and if the telnet service is stopped, you can start it.

   Finally, look for evidence of an IPSec policy. If one is assigned, you can unassign it and test telnet. If telnet now works, you will need to troubleshoot the IPSec policy.

3. Follow your list. At the command prompt on Computer2, ping Computer1 by typing **ping computer1**.

   Were you able to reach Computer1?

   Yes

6. On Computer1, scroll to the telnet service.

   Is the telnet service running?

   No

8. Open the IP Security Management console and examine the IP Security Policies On Local Computer node and the IP Security Policies On \\Computer1 node.

   Is a new policy, one you have never seen before, assigned at both nodes?

   Yes

10. From the command prompt on Computer2, attempt to telnet to Computer1.

Are you successful?

Yes

Troubleshooting Lab, Troubleshoot IPSec

Page
11-84 Troubleshooting IPSec is no different than troubleshooting anything else. You use your knowledge of which parameters are necessary and the available troubleshooting tools to resolve the issue.

1. Think about the order in which actions occur in a policy.

What are the steps?

The policy is triggered.

The filter action is checked. Is it blocking? Allowing? Negotiating? A blocking rule simply stops communication and that is the end of it. An allow rule allows traffic.

A negotiation rule must be negotiated. Several steps include authentication, master key generation, SA establishment (Main Mode), session key generation, SAs for protocols, encryption, and communication.

The next step in troubleshooting IPSec is to see whether some of these steps can be eliminated. You must find out where the problem is. If authentication is occurring, for example, you do not need to see whether a problem is there. Or if restrictive IP addresses exist and they are incorrect, the policy won't work. Because it is usually easier to deal with the obvious issues first, a good practice in debugging IPSec policies is to check the IP address information.

4. In the IP Filter List box, double-click the filter with its option selected, and then double-click the IP filter.

Is the source address My IP Address?

Yes

Is the Destination address a specific IP address, and is it the IP address of Computer1?

No

8. Select the first rule and check its filter action by clicking the Filter Action tab and double-clicking the selected filter action.

What is the filter action?

Negotiate security

10. Double-click the selected filter action, and then double-click the filter.

Is the source address a specific IP address, and is it correct? (Is it the address of Computer2?)

No

Is the destination address My Address?

Yes

14. Return to the IP Security Management console, IP Security Monitor for Computer1 and select the Main Mode Statistics node.

Are any authentication failures present?

Yes

16. Select the Authentication Methods tab.

What is the authentication method?

Kerberos

17. Select the Main Mode Generic Filters node for Computer2.

What is the authentication method?

Shared Secret

24. From a command prompt, attempt to telnet to Computer1.

Are you successful?

Yes

12 Maintaining a Network Infrastructure

Exam Objectives in this Chapter:

- Monitor network traffic
- Troubleshoot connectivity to the Internet
- Troubleshoot server services
    - Diagnose and resolve issues related to service dependency
    - Use service recovery options to diagnose and resolve service-related issues

Why This Chapter Matters

Once you have gone through the motions of setting up your infrastructure, you don't want to simply leave it in that state. Indeed, to set up a network and leave it in a stagnant state could be quite hazardous. You should pay special attention to three areas.

First, you should ensure that the servers on your network are getting the resources they need to serve the population. You can leverage some of the built-in tools of the Microsoft Windows Server 2003 family to ensure that your servers are running optimally. You should also ensure that you are alerted if special activity occurs on the network that you should know about.

Second, you should ensure that users set up and maintain their connection to the Internet. After e-mail, access to the Internet is most critical for users. This chapter highlights some trouble spots to watch out for if users report they cannot access the Internet.

Finally, you should be able to adjust and maintain the services that your server runs. If users report an outage but the server is still up, one of the services to which the user was connected might have failed. To troubleshoot this sort of error, you need to catch it in the act and learn how to fix it under a variety of circumstances.

Overall, keeping on top of and maintaining your Windows Server 2003 network could be the most critical element in your day-to-day functions with the network. You don't just set it and forget it—rather, you set it, monitor it, and make sure your users are happy.

Lessons in this Chapter:

■ Lesson 1: Monitoring Network Performance 12-3

■ Lesson 2: Troubleshooting Internet Connectivity. .12-21

■ Lesson 3: Troubleshooting Server Services 12-31

Before You Begin

To complete this chapter, you must have

■ Networked two computers, named Computer1 and Computer2, each running Windows Server 2003. Computer1 should be assigned a static address of 192.168.0.1/24, and Computer2 should be configured to obtain an address automatically. Computer2 should also have an alternate configuration address of 192.168.0.2/24.

■ Two phone lines and cables connecting each of the computers (highly recommended).

■ Two dial-up accounts to an Internet service provider (ISP), or one dial-up account that can legally be used to connect two computers to the Internet simultaneously (highly recommended). (Although you can substitute a dedicated Internet connection for one or both of these Internet connections, you will have to make appropriate adjustments to lesson exercises.)

■ Installed a DNS server on Computer1, which hosts an Active Directory–integrated primary zone named domain1.local.

■ Configured Computer1 as a domain controller in the domain1.local domain and Computer2 as a member of the domain. The domain functional level should be Windows 2000 mixed.

■ Installed a DHCP server on Computer1. The DHCP server should be authorized in the domain and include the scope Test Scope whose IP address range is 192.168.0.11–192.168.0.254. Exclusions for the range should be 192.168.0.100 and 192.168.0.200–192.168.0.205. The scope should be activated.

Lesson 1: Monitoring Network Performance

Once your network is fully deployed, you must ensure that the nodes on your network have adequate bandwidth to handle the job. Like air is to humans, bandwidth is to applications—without it, they both suffocate. To that end, Windows Server 2003 provides several built-in tools that enable you to monitor your network performance.

Monitoring the network can help you isolate specific problems and discount others. Therefore, you will need to know specifically how to monitor the network using Windows Server 2003.

This section covers three tools that can help you when you encounter trouble areas. First, you explore the easy-to-use Network tab in Task Manager. Then you leverage what you learn there and move on to configuring triggers by using the Performance console. Finally, you explore some of the advanced capturing features found in Network Monitor.

After this lesson, you will be able to

- Find and use the Networking tab in Task Manager
- Find and set alerts using the Performance console
- Capture specific data using the version of Network Monitor included with Windows Server 2003

Estimated lesson time: 60 minutes

Using the Networking Tab in Task Manager

Sometimes, you just want to get quick information about what's going on. If you wanted a phone number for a local pizzeria, you could look in the phone book and find the one you wanted, or you could get on the Internet and do a search for pizzerias within 5 miles, or you could ask a friend. Or you could simply dial 411 and get the information immediately. The operator usually even connects your call for another 50 cents. The beauty here is in the speed of getting what you want.

If your users report that a specific server is not responding to their requests appropriately, you should take immediate steps to diagnose the problem. The problem might be *transient*; that is, it might go away on its own. For instance, a 20-GB file might be transferring to or from the server, and hence, other requests might not be getting through. Other network performance problems are *intermittent*: they come and go with or without a pattern. These problems can occur after someone sets up a job to communicate with a server on a schedule or changes the normal routine to something abnormal.

But no matter what the problem is, you will probably want to resolve it right away. That's what Windows Server 2003 Task Manager enables you to do.

Task Manager is a great tool for inspecting many areas of your server all at once. One area it can help you learn about your system is, in fact, networking performance. Although Task Manager might be less powerful than other tools (which you will explore later in this chapter in the section "Performance Console Differences"), it is quite simple to access and can tell you a lot about the activities on your network.

To access Task Manager, you press Ctl+Alt+Del and click the Task Manager button. Then select the Networking tab, as shown in Figure 12-1.

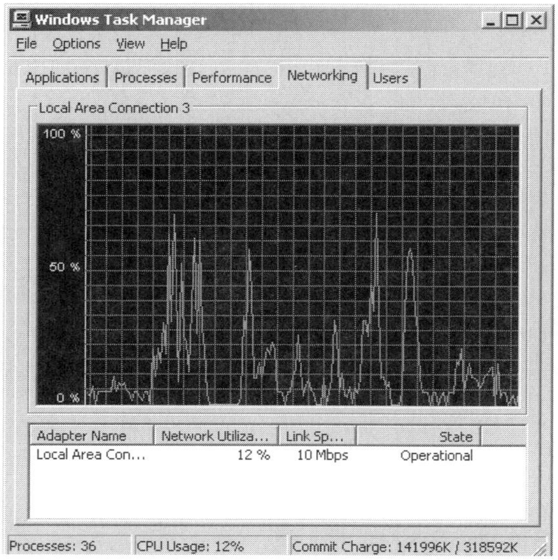

Figure 12-1 Networking tab in Task Manager

The Networking tab provides an overview of the use on your network card. The scale on the left is the percentage used, and it automatically changes scale depending on how much the link is used. You can also determine other miscellaneous data—such as whether the link is operational or unplugged—by looking at the State column. And in the Link Speed column, you can see what speed the link is.

Choosing What to See Within the History

If you are receiving reports that the server is not responding fast enough to reads or writes, you might want to isolate the view of the network traffic. Indeed, you can choose to show and highlight the total traffic (the default) or choose to show and highlight the bytes sent or bytes received, as shown in Figure 12-2.

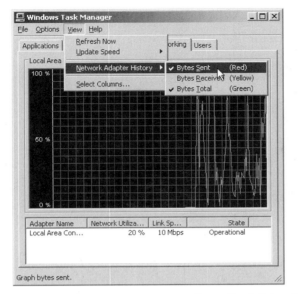

Figure 12-2   Filtering by selecting Bytes Total, Bytes Sent, or Bytes Received

Filtering allows you to ignore the other "direction" of the network flow. That is, if you are troubleshooting a server that is not responding quickly to writes, you can temporarily ignore the bytes sent. Conversely, if you are troubleshooting a server that is not responding quickly to reads, you can temporarily ignore the bytes received.

Choosing Columns

As you saw in Figure 12-1, you can obtain an overview of some important state data, such as link speed. However, Network Monitor can also be a useful tool to determine which types of traffic are coming across the interface. Your view of what's going on is greatly enhanced by means of a network *counter*: an exposed piece of information, sometimes called a data point, that you can access to see the current status. If you determine the value of an available data point over time, you are *sampling* the data.

You can choose to add more counters in the overview by opening the View menu and selecting Select Columns. Then you will expose all the available counters, as shown in Figure 12-3.

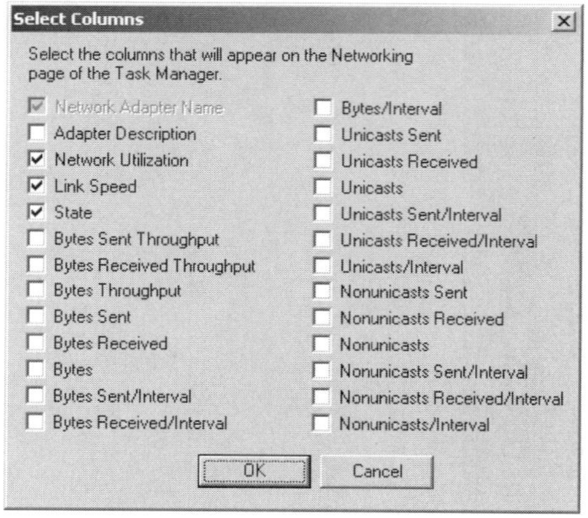

Figure 12-3   Choosing the counters you want to see

There are 26 counters for you to examine. However, not every counter will be important in your troubleshooting. Table 12-1 shows some of the most useful counters for troubleshooting network performance.

Table 12-1   Helpful Counters

Property	Description
Network Adapter Name	The name of the network adapter. This check box is always selected. If you have multiple network adapters, you will see multiple listings.
Link Speed	The speed of the network interface. If you suspect a bottleneck, verify that this number is the maximum speed of the network. Sometimes, the network card receives a signal from the router to fall back to a slower speed (typically 10 Mbps from 100 Mbps).
Bytes/Interval	The rate at which bytes are sent and received on the network adapter. You can best judge this counter after gaining a baseline of your operations when your network is running smoothly.
Unicasts/Interval	The number of unicast datagrams received during this interval. If this counter has data, you are likely dealing with real data and not broadcast traffic, which might be seen in the next counter, Nonunicasts/Interval.
Nonunicasts/Interval	The number of broadcast and multicast datagrams received during this interval. If this counter has data, your interface might be dealing with background or broadcast traffic. You might have problems on your network that aren't specifically related to this server if this counter is high.

Performance Console Differences

You will want to use the Performance console when you have big jobs to handle.

> **Note**   The Performance console was called Performance Monitor in earlier versions of Windows.

Although Task Manager is good for getting a snapshot of the local server's network performance, the Performance console provides detailed information necessary for in-depth analysis and an alerting feature useful for detecting problems before the symptoms become obvious. You will see that with triggers a bit later in the section entitled "Using Network Monitor Triggers."

Starting the Performance Console

You can start the Performance console in various ways. One of the simplest methods is to open the Start menu, select Run, type **perfmon.exe**, and click OK. Performance Monitor launches (see Figure 12-4) and automatically starts with three of the most used counters:

- Pages/Sec shows how often memory pages are being swapped in and out of random access memory (RAM) to disk. High sustained values here could indicate not having enough RAM.

- Avg. Disk Queue Length shows how many disk events are in queue by the disk subsystem. High sustained values could indicate not having a fast enough disk subsystem.

- % Processor Time shows how much processor is being used. High sustained values could indicate not having a fast enough processor.

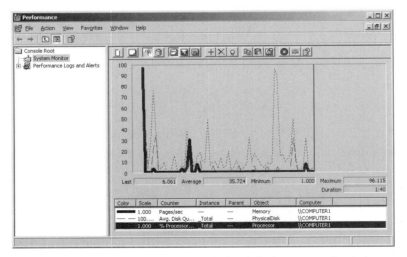

Figure 12-4   Performance console with the default counters loaded

Adding Network Counters

The Performance console is capable of sampling a huge range of performance counters—many more than Task Manager. Indeed, it can monitor many more networking and non-networking components that fall into several separate categories, as shown in Figure 12-5.

> **Note**   The categories available to you might vary based on installed server software.

Figure 12-5   Categories of counters for monitoring performance

However, our focus is on monitoring the networking items. The following list describes the key networking performance objects:

- **Network Interface**   This object contains some of the same counters that you find when using Task Manager. However, it also contains counters for monitoring specific details about packets on the network.

- **TCPv4**   This object contains counters related to Transmission Control Protocol (TCP) version 4 connections.

- **TCPv6**   This object contains counters related to TCPv6 connections.

- **NBT Connection**   This object contains counters that can help you determine the number of connections through Server Message Block (SMB); usually open shares.

- **RAS Port**   This category is helpful if you have virtual private network (VPN) or other Remote Access Service (RAS) connections set up. Then you can choose to troubleshoot your connection problems based on specific ports. You can check the errors on a port or other counters like the Percent Compression Out.

■ **RAS Total**   This object contains counters that show overall aggregate RAS performance, as opposed to the RAS Port object, which can help with a specific port.

Using the Performance Console to Create Alerts

So far in this chapter, you have seen that Task Manager is an easy-to-use tool, and you already know that the Performance console is a powerful tool. How do you know when it's best to use which tool? You might choose to use the Performance console over Task Manager for two main reasons:

■ Access to more performance counters

■ Ability to send alert triggers based on specific criteria

You have already seen that dozens of counters are available through the Performance console. Now let's take a look at the Performance console's second big strength—*triggered alerts*.

Although the Performance console works well when systems are actively performing poorly, when you can't wait around, you can set up triggers using the Performance console to catch bad systems in action. For instance, you might want to be alerted when a certain system is particularly busy handling network traffic or has generated errors on the network.

To start, you create alerts in the Performance Logs And Alerts snap-in in the Performance console. Right-click Alerts and select New Alert Settings, as shown in Figure 12-6.

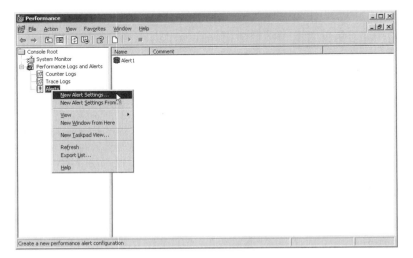

Figure 12-6   Setting up new alerts

You typically name the alert based on the type of counter or counters you want to monitor, and then you choose the counters. When you click the Add button, as shown in Figure 12-7, you can choose the different categories of counters and then pick a specific counter.

> **Tip**   Sometimes you might want to choose more than one counter to trigger an alert. For instance, you might choose to get a notification if both the network bandwidth is heavy *and* high amounts of errors are being generated.

Before choosing how you want the alert reported, on the General tab, you must specify several specifics about how you want to sample the counters.

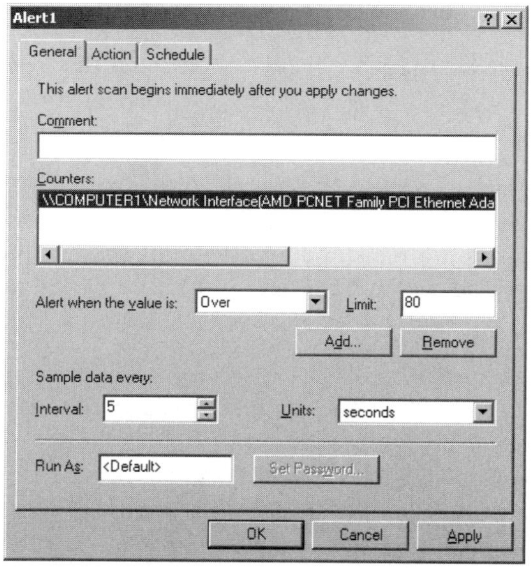

Figure 12-7   Configuring the counters to monitor before specifying how the alerts are handled

The following list describes some of the parameters you can configure on the General tab:

- **Comment**   Even though the alert has a name, you can also supply a comment to help you or others recall what the purpose of the alert is and to whom the alert goes.

- **Alert When The Value Is**   You can specify whether to trigger if the alert is under the Limit value or over the Limit value.

- **Limit**   You can specify the value of the counter to be monitored. When the value goes over or under this limit (based on the selection in Alert When The Value Is), the alert is triggered.

- **Interval**   You can set how often the Performance console queries the system for what you want to monitor. The system doesn't continuously monitor for the counters you want; rather, it performs samples over a certain amount of time. The longer the interval, the less accurate the sample is because it is being sampled less. The shorter the interval, the more accurate the sample is, but the more the processor is used when getting the sample.

- **Units**   You can specify the units in time to collect samples. For instance, you might not want to sample every 5 seconds; instead, you might want to sample every 30 seconds. Again, if you reduce the frequency of sampling, you'll use fewer processor cycles, but you will be less accurate.

- **Run As**   You can sample the counters by selecting either the System account or another account of your choice. Occasionally, counters can be user-specific, which is necessary. However, for monitoring network-related counters, the System account has access to what it needs to perform the work.

Tip   If two or more counters are being monitored, you must select each counter and set the Alert When The Value Is, Limit, Interval, and Units fields. The Comment field and Run As field will be used for all counters in an alert.

After you set these parameters, you select the Action tab, as shown in Figure 12-8.

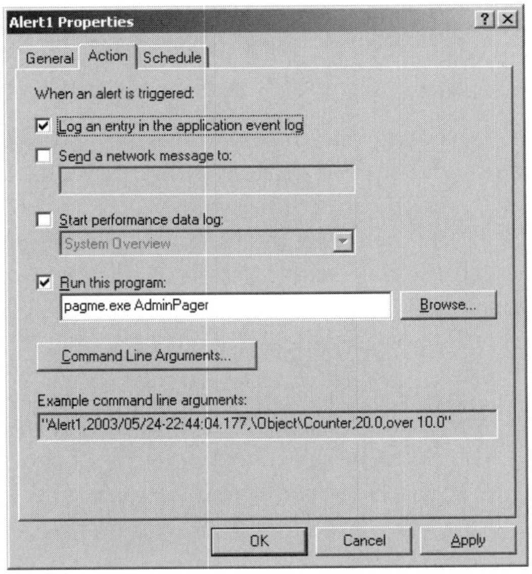

Figure 12-8   Using the Action tab to specify how you want to handle the notification of your trigger

The Action tab specifies what happens once an alert is triggered. A multitude of options let you know that your counter's criteria have been met. The various options are as follows:

- **Log An Entry In The Application Event Log** Selecting this option puts an event in the event log, which you can see using Event Viewer. A notice of the counter, value, and limit are part of the log entry, as shown in Figure 12-9.

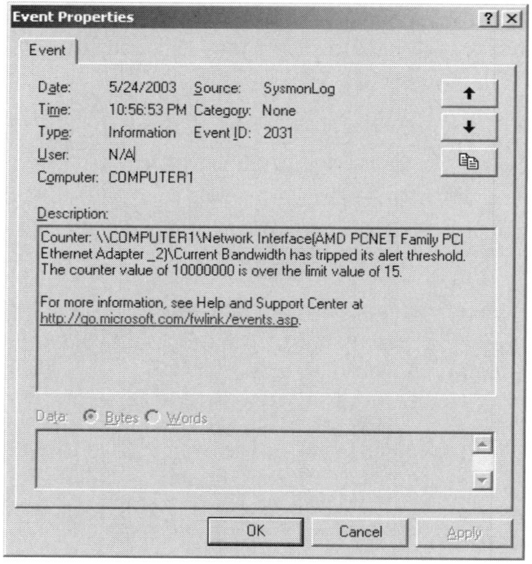

Figure 12-9 Example event based on triggers

- **Send A Network Message To** Selecting this option sends the equivalent of a Net Send command with the alert's message. You need to specify the name of a computer here, not a user. For messages to be sent out, the Alerter service must be started on the machine from which you are doing the monitoring. For messages to be received, the Messenger service must be started on the receiving computer. Neither of these services runs on a newly installed Windows Server 2003 server; you must manually change the state from Disabled to Automatic and ensure that the services are running.

- **Start Performance Data Log** You can configure the alert system to start by writing additional counters to a log file to be reviewed later. You need to preset the log file by using the Counter Logs node within the Performance Logs And Alerts node, as seen earlier in Figure 12-6.

- **Run This Program**   Once your trigger has gone off, you can execute an external program. You might have an external paging network or some other external alert system to help you find out when triggers go off. Or, in the most extreme case, you might choose to shut down the system when an alert is triggered. You would perform this task by running the built-in Shutdown.exe command found in Windows Server 2003.

Finally, you can configure the settings on the Schedule tab, which help you determine when to trigger. For instance, you might not want to get alerts at off-peak times or on weekends. Or maybe you do! It's your choice.

If you do not choose to run the alert within a schedule through the Schedule tab, you must manually start your alert. To do so, right-click the alert you just created and select Start, as shown in Figure 12-10.

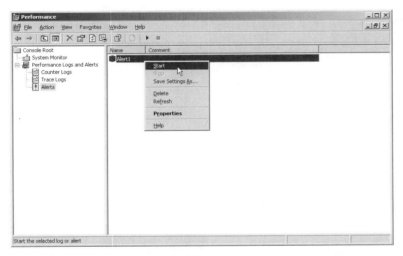

Figure 12-10   Starting your alerts manually

Once they are set up, your alerts can notify you of just about any network problem on your system.

Monitoring Network Traffic with Netstat

One tool you can use to help monitor your traffic is a command-line tool called *Netstat*. Netstat provides information about existing network connections and network activity statistics.

For instance, if you wanted to determine on which ports a system was listening for connections, you could execute the Netstat –a command. This would determine that the ports that you want closed are indeed closed.

However, just knowing which ports are open might not be enough data to close the hole. Indeed, you will want to know which application is using that port so you can further investigate the application and close the port. You can figure out the relationship between open ports and applications with the Netstat –o command. When you run the Netstat –o command, you can see the protocol, the local inbound port that is open, the connection from or to the other computer, and the port it is using, as shown in Figure 12-11.

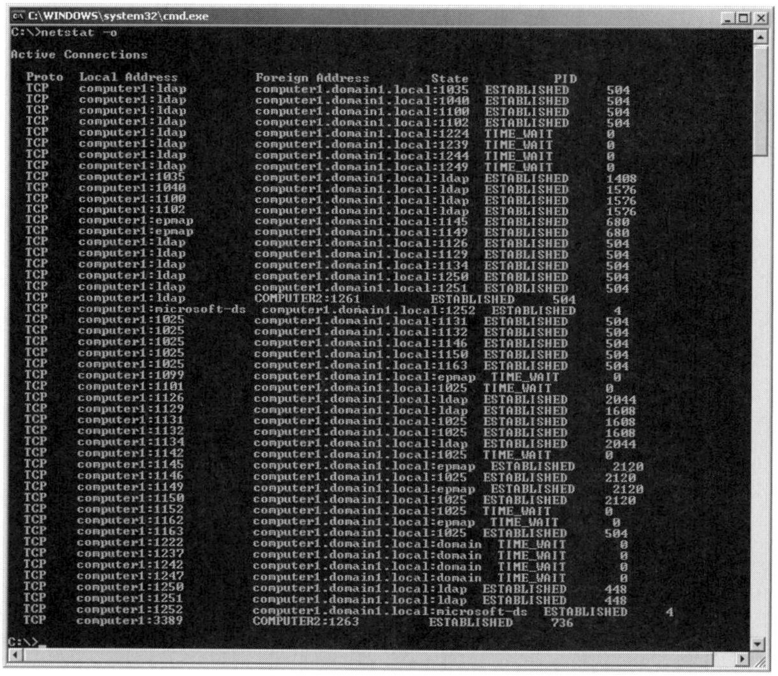

Figure 12-11   Using Netstat –o to show all the processes and ports used on a server

In this example, notice that the last entry shows that Computer1 and Computer2 are communicating over port 3389. In this specific instance, you can see that the Process Identifier (PID) is 736. If you then want to correlate that PID with the actual process that is using the port, you must return to Task Manager.

In Task Manager, you can select the Processes tab. However, by default the Processes tab does not display the PIDs of processes. You can choose to see the PIDs by opening the View menu, selecting Columns, and selecting PID (Process Identifier), as shown in Figure 12-12.

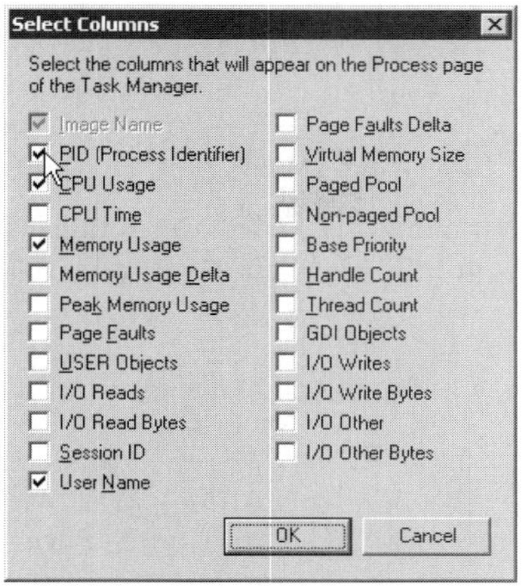

Figure 12-12 Using Task Manager to show the PID

Then you will obtain a listing of the processes on the machine that includes the PIDs, as shown in Figure 12-13.

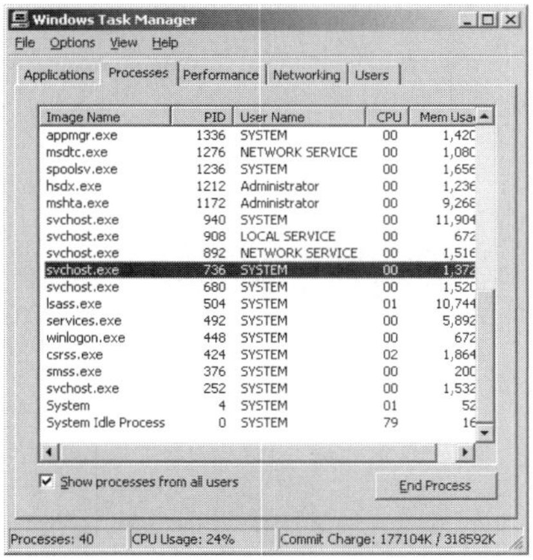

Figure 12-13 Using Task Manager to see which processes align with which PIDs

Simply match the PID and the process, and you will know which process or application has the port open. If your PID points to svchost, multiple services are probably running as a single process. To see which services they are, run Tasklist /svc. In this case, if you run Tasklist /svc, you will see that the svchost that equates to this computer's PID of 736 is for Terminal Services. Terminal Services uses port 3389 for communications.

In this way, you can find applications and services that open ports and close the door if you want.

Windows Server 2003 "Lite" and "Full" Network Monitor Tools

In Chapter 3, "Monitoring and Troubleshooting TCP/IP Connections," you installed the lite version of Network Monitor. This version comes with Windows Server 2003 and is pretty powerful for a free tool. However, remember that Microsoft has a more powerful full version of the Network Monitor tool. The full version of the tool, which is available only by purchasing Microsoft Systems Management Server, handles two tasks that the lite version cannot:

- It can run in promiscuous mode; in other words, it is able to capture 100 percent of the network traffic.

- It enables you to see where else Network Monitor is running. This information is useful when you are setting up multiple monitoring stations across your network and then using a central monitoring point to collect the data. You can also use it to monitor and prevent inside hack attempts by tracking down offenders, as shown in Figure 12-14.

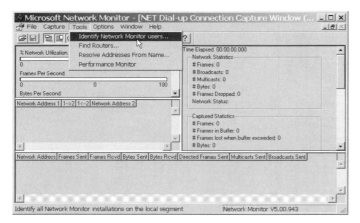

Figure 12-14   Tracking other Network Monitor instances

Using Network Monitor Triggers

Network Monitor's main function is to capture packets as they cross the network. So much occurs at once that trying to find the information you need is often nearly impossible. Therefore, one important skill to master with Network Monitor is the ability to quickly locate what you are looking for when the action happens.

Setting Triggers   Network Monitor provides a facility to alert you once certain conditions are met. This facility might be helpful under a variety of circumstances where you set up Network Monitor and then decide to move on to other tasks. You can set up this ability by using triggers. To configure a trigger, start Network Monitor, and from the Caption menu, select Trigger. The Capture Trigger dialog box opens, as shown in Figure 12-15.

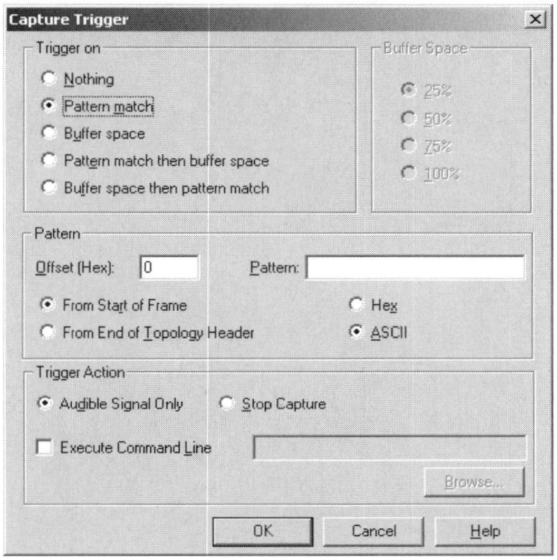

Figure 12-15   Configuring a trigger to alert you to specific conditions

Capturing Trigger Options   The default Trigger On option is set to Nothing, which means no triggers will be active. You can set up a trigger to alert you under certain key conditions. For instance, you can be notified when the buffer space is 25 percent, 50 percent, 75 percent, or 100 percent full. This might be your signal to take a look and clean it out before any packets are lost because of low buffer space.

You might also decide to use the handy Pattern Match feature (selected in the figure), which allows you to type in a hex or ASCII representation of what you want to find. For instance, you could look for any instance of a clear text string of characters, and then, by using the Execute Command Line option, have a message sent to you saying that your text string was found.

Practice: Sampling Performance

In this practice, you try out the advanced features of Task Manager and the Performance console.

Exercise 1: Monitor Network Traffic with Task Manager

In this exercise, you copy a large 75-MB file, called Driver.cab, from Computer1 to Computer2 and monitor the traffic using Network Monitor.

1. On Computer2, create a directory called C:\Temp and share it as Temp with Administrators: Full Control permissions.

2. Switch to Computer1 and while you are logged on as Administrator, press Ctl+Alt+Del and select Task Manager.

   Task Manager launches.

3. Select the Networking tab.

4. From the View menu, click Select Columns.

5. Choose to view the following counters:

   ❑ Network Utilization

   ❑ Link Speed

   ❑ State

   ❑ Unicasts/Interval

   ❑ Nonunicasts/Interval

6. Click OK.

7. From the Start menu, select Run, and type **cmd** to open a command prompt.

8. At the command prompt, type **net use T: \\computer2\temp**.

9. At the command prompt, type **copy "c:\windows\driver cache\i386\ driver.cab" T: /y**.

10. At the command prompt, type **net use T: /delete**.

    You will see the network utilization spike on the graph. Also note that the Unicasts/Interval will rise, but the Nonunicasts/Interval should stay flat. These counter values indicate that valid data is being transferred.

Exercise 2: Create a Network Alert Using the Performance Console

In this exercise, you create a network alert in the event log of Computer1 using the Performance console when the Packets Sent/Sec counter is more than 5.

1. From the Start menu, select Run, and type **perfmon.exe**.

2. Expand the Performance Logs And Alerts node, and then right-click Alerts and select New Alert Settings.

3. In the Name field, type **packets sent alert** and click OK.

4. On the General tab of the Packets Sent Alert window, click Add.

5. From the Performance Object list, select the Network Interface object, and choose Packets Sent/Sec from the counters in the list.

6. Select the instance of the network card you want to use, and click Add.

7. Click Close.

8. In the Packets Sent Alert window on the General tab, type **5** in the Limit box.

9. Select the Action tab. Ensure that Log An Entry In The Application Event Log is selected.

10. Select the Schedule tab.

11. Choose to start the scan at the current time (the default), and select OK.

12. From the Start menu, select Run and type **cmd** to start a command prompt.

13. At the command prompt, type **net use T: \\computer2\temp**.

14. Type **copy "c:\windows\driver cache\i386\driver.cab" T: /y**.

15. On Computer1, view the Application event log to see the event trigger.

Lesson Review

The following questions are intended to reinforce key information presented in this lesson. If you are unable to answer a question, review the lesson materials and try the question again. You can find answers to the questions in the "Questions and Answers" section at the end of this chapter.

1. You receive a report that Computer1 is responding slowly to user requests. You want a quick way to see which network traffic the server is using. You use Network Monitor. You want to see whether any general broadcast traffic is being sent to Computer1. Which counter should you enable?

   a. Nonunicasts/Interval

   b. Unicasts/Interval

   c. Bytes Sent/Interval

   d. Bytes Received/Interval

2. You set up Performance Logs And Alerts to send a message to Computer2 to notify an operator when the network use on Computer1 gets too high. However, Computer2 never receives the message sent from Computer1. What must you do to enable messages to be sent by Computer1 and received by Computer2? (Choose all that apply.)

   a. On Computer1, start the Messenger service.

   b. On Computer1, start the Alerter service.

   c. On Computer2, start the Messenger service.

   d. On Computer2, start the Alerter service.

3. You suspect that a virus has infected your computer running Windows Server 2003. You believe this virus is transmitting data from your server over the network using a specific port. You want to determine which process is using a specific port. Which command should you run?

   a. Nbtstat –RR

   b. Nbtstat –r

   c. Netstat –a

   d. Netstat –o

Lesson Summary

- Task Manager provides immediate results about how a system is performing.

- The Performance console delves deeper into a system through the use of counters, which find trouble spots. The Performance console alerts allow you to send a notification once a trigger has been set off.

- Network Monitor allows you to capture specific packets from your network to analyze network activity. Network Monitor triggers send you a message if the buffer becomes full or if the data you are looking for appears on the network.

Lesson 2: Troubleshooting Internet Connectivity

Sometimes an end user calls the help desk and boldly proclaims that the Internet is down. However, usually the user's *connection* to the Internet is down. In fact, quite often, just one missing link in a chain of events typically leads that user from his or her desktop out to the Internet.

This section explores several places that could be at fault should a user report that the Internet—or, more likely, that his or her connection to the Internet—is down.

Two approaches exist to troubleshooting Internet connectivity problems: from the top down or from the bottom up. That is, you can troubleshoot from the server connection and work your way closer to the client, or you can start at the client and see how far you can connect.

Neither approach is strictly better than the other. On one hand, starting from the client's machine and working up could be better and faster; but traveling to the desktop could be a hassle and be a slow start. On the other hand, starting from the server and working down could be quicker if you spot the problem right away; but if you can't find it right away, you could be potentially led down different network paths back to the client—none of which are really a problem.

Therefore, the best advice in troubleshooting these kinds of errors is to troubleshoot from the bottom up and travel to the client and work your way back through your network and out to the Internet.

Identifying the Specific Networking Issue

The first problem to gauge in troubleshooting connectivity to the Internet is to decide whether the problem is network related or name resolution related. The following sections take a look at each scenario.

Identifying Connectivity Issues

To verify whether it is a connectivity issue, you should start your journey with the Ping command. For instance, take a look at the example shown in Figure 12-16.

Figure 12-16 DNS responding, but packets not finding the destination

If you look closely, you can already get a clue about what might be wrong with this user's ability to connect to the Internet. Specifically, notice that Ping is returning the proper name of the target address (tailspintoys.com), but the Ping requests themselves are not making it through to the target. Therefore, name resolution to a DNS server is likely working properly, but the packets are probably not reaching their final destination.

The next most logical tool to use is PathPing, which shows you each route between the client and the target and helps you determine which link is not passing the packet on to the next destination.

Identifying Name Resolution Issues

Figure 12-17 shows another example that you might encounter.

Figure 12-17 DNS unable to resolve requested host name

Here, the result returns no sign that the name resolution is occurring. In this situation, the next logical step is to verify the user's DNS settings and server to ensure that both are returning the values expected from the Ping operation.

Check to see that the client's network adapter is using a DNS server that is part of your network. (Use the materials found in the next section, "Verifying the Computer's Network Settings.")

Important   In general, a client machine should be pointing at one of your internal DNS servers rather than using your ISP DNS server settings.

If you suspect DNS name resolution issues for your internal servers, you should next run the Nslookup command from the client system. Nslookup can help you determine whether your client is getting the right records returned from the DNS server you have told it to use.

See Also   An excellent primer article on Nslookup can be found at Microsoft Knowledge Base article 200525.

If you suspect DNS name resolution issues for names beyond the scope of this particular server, or if name resolution issues exist for names outside your company, you should next check the DNS server itself. First, make sure the DNS server is forwarding to the next logical place based on your network design. You perform this task by verifying the Forwarders tab, as shown in Figure 12-18.

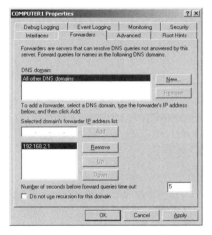

Figure 12-18   Ensuring that the forwarders are set up correctly

Typically, the DNS server forwards to a server with more knowledge of the network layout, or directly to the ISP itself. If this is not the case, you need to adjust the settings on the Forwarders tab.

Additionally, verify that the server itself is responding to requests and that it can also respond to tests on servers to which it forwards information. In the example shown in Figure 12-19, the server itself is responding to resolution requests; however, it is unable to get any resolution from servers to which it forwards.

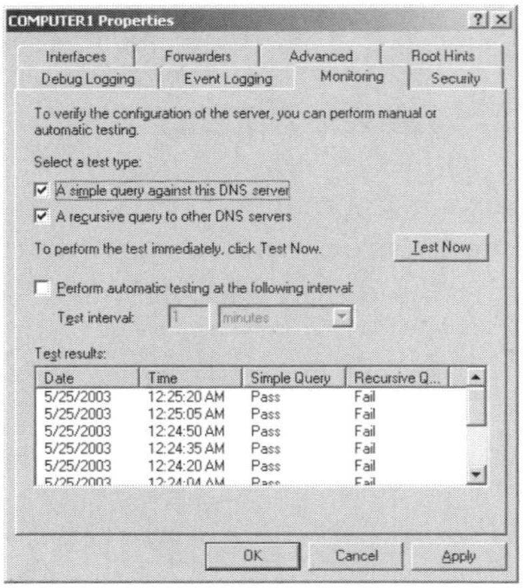

Figure 12-19   Failure of the recursive query, usually indicating a forwarding problem

This failure could indicate that the name resolution is not on your servers, but rather on servers on which your servers rely.

Verifying the Computer's Network Settings

If you inspect the client computer and you receive unexpected settings in the network adapter, there could be many possible causes. If the client is expected to use Dynamic Host Configuration Protocol (DHCP), you need to ensure that the network adapter is correctly receiving the DHCP information.

If you discover that the IP address of the client machine is in the range 169.254.0.0 through 169.254.255.255, you are using Automatic Private IP Addressing (APIPA). Therefore, your client is not receiving DHCP information from the DHCP server.

Using the Repair Feature

You can perform many steps in one step by using a new Windows Server 2003 feature inside the graphical user interface (GUI)—the network Repair feature. You can find this feature while inspecting the status of a network adapter, as shown in Figure 12-20.

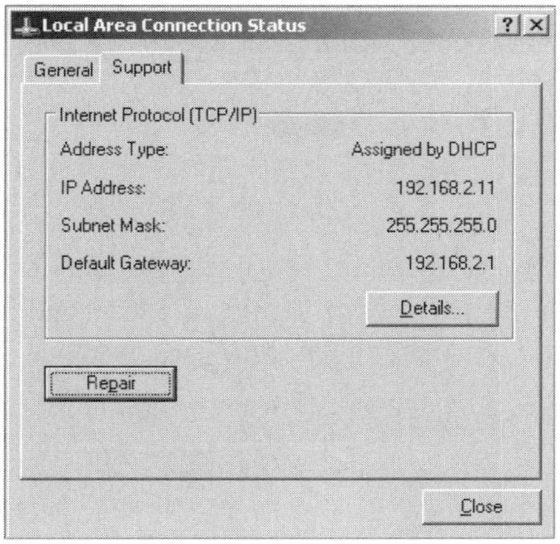

Figure 12-20   Using the Repair button to perform a multitude of configuration resets

Clicking the Repair button initiates many actions as if they were each typed on the command line. The commands are performed in the order listed in Table 12-2.

> **Tip**   The Repair feature is the same for Windows Server 2003 and Microsoft Windows XP Professional.

Table 12-2   Repair Actions

Action Performed by the Repair Function as if It Were Performed on the Command Line	Action
Ipconfig /renew	Attempts to renew the DHCP lease
Arp –d *	Flushes the Address Resolution Protocol (ARP) cache
Nbtstat –R	Reloads the NetBIOS cache
Nbtstat –RR	Sends the NetBIOS computer name to Windows Internet Name Service (WINS) for an update
Ipconfig /flushdns	Flushes the DNS cache
Ipconfig /registerdns	Registers the name with the DNS server

> **Tip**   The Repair button also initiates a wireless IEEE 802.11x Authentication Restart.

> **See Also**   You can learn more about the Repair button at Microsoft Knowledge Base article 289256.

Verifying the DHCP Server

If the client computer is not receiving an IP address and at least a primary DNS server address, the client will certainly not be able to find the Internet. The following are some reasons the DHCP information might not be delivered to the client:

- A router is blocking the Boot Protocol (BOOTP).
- No DHCP relay agent exists on segments without BOOTP relay.
- All addresses in the DHCP scope are used up.

Furthermore, while you are inspecting the DHCP server, you might also verify that the address range it is distributing is OK, that the gateway is valid, and that the DNS servers point to a location that makes sense for your organization.

You might also encounter a situation in which some clients can connect to the Internet and others cannot. After inspecting the clients' networking characteristics, you discover that some machines are configured differently from others. However, all client computers are configured for DHCP. In this case, you might have what is known as a *rogue* DHCP server—that is, a DHCP server that is set up in an ad-hoc fashion, perhaps for testing purposes. If this is the case, this server is likely providing the target clients with incorrect information—namely, the gateway, DNS server address, or both.

Microsoft Windows 2000 and Windows Server 2003 servers running DHCP must be authorized in the Active Directory directory service in order to serve as DHCP servers. If they are not, they automatically shut down. Use Dhcploc.exe, which is found in the Windows Server 2003 Support Tools, to discover DHCP servers that should not be authorized or other DHCP servers that do not need to be authorized, such as older Microsoft DHCP servers or non-Microsoft DHCP servers.

Bridging Multiple Networks

You might be asked to troubleshoot connections to the Internet that start from wireless machines. In some cases, you might want to share a single Wireless Access Point (WAP) with multiple and varying connection topologies, as shown in Figure 12-21.

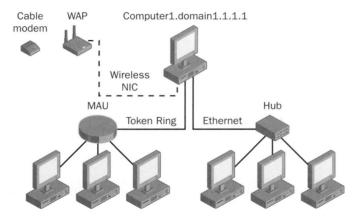

Figure 12-21   Example network that can leverage network bridging

In this example, an Internet connection is joined to a single WAP. The WAP then communicates with the wireless network interface card (NIC) in the server. Additionally, the server has an Ethernet connection and a token ring connection attached to other networks.

When you enable *network bridging* on this connection, all points entering the server (wireless, token ring, and Ethernet) appear on the same network. Hence, they can all share the wireless connection and get out to the Internet.

To bridge the networks, hold down Ctrl as you click the multiple connections on the server. Then right-click and select Bridge Networks, as shown in Figure 12-22.

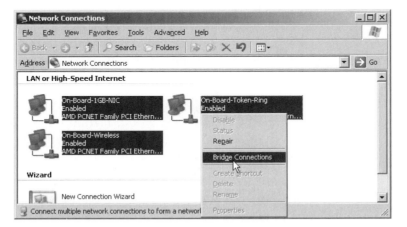

Figure 12-22   Selecting multiple networks, then right-clicking to bridge them

When you configure network bridging, you allow traffic from the wireless, Ethernet, and Token Ring NIC to share the same network space. Hence, a single wireless NIC can be the outbound gateway to disparate networks.

If asked to troubleshoot connectivity to the Internet, you should take several steps:

■ In the properties on the General tab of the bridged connection, verify that all networks are indeed being bridged.

■ The bridge itself should have its own IP address. Verify this by running Ipconfig /all. If the bridge does not have its own IP address, remove the bridge and recreate it.

■ Check the physical connectivity among all segments on the bridge.

Practice: Verifying the Configuration of DNS Forwarding

In this practice, you use the DNS console to determine whether DNS forwarding has been misconfigured.

Exercise 1: Verify DNS Forwarding Information

In this exercise, you use the Monitoring tab in DNS to verify that forwarding is working.

1. On Computer1, log on as Administrator.

2. On the Start menu, point to Administrative Tools, and then click DNS.

3. Right-click Computer1 and select Properties.

4. In the properties dialog box, select the Monitoring tab.

5. Select A Recursive Query To Other DNS Servers.

6. Select Test Now.

   If the test is successful, a Pass result appears in the Recursive Query column.

Lesson Review

The following questions are intended to reinforce key information presented in this lesson. If you are unable to answer a question, review the lesson materials and try the question again. You can find answers to the questions in the "Questions and Answers" section at the end of this chapter.

The following three questions relate to the network diagram of Tailspin Toys shown in Figure 12-23. You are the network administrator for Tailspin Toys.

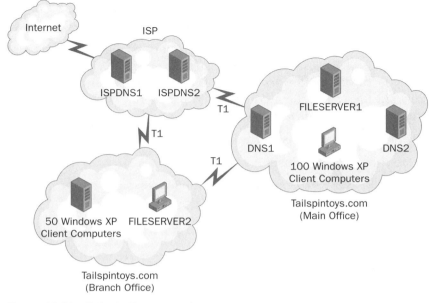

Figure 12-23   Tailspin Toys network

1. A user in the branch office reports that he cannot use Internet Explorer to open a commonly used Web site on the Internet. At your client computer in the main office, you are able to ping the target address. At the user's client computer, you cannot ping the target address. What should you do to troubleshoot? (Choose all that apply.)

    a. From the user's client computer, run **ping** destination address.

    b. From the user's client computer, select To Repair The Network Connection.

    c. From the DNS server, perform a simple query test.

    d. From the DNS server, perform a recursive query test.

2. You are setting up 50 new client machines in the branch office. Another administrator has already configured DHCP in the branch office. When you bring the first client computer online, you notice that DHCP is not providing Primary or Alternate DNS servers along with the IP address.

    You need to troubleshoot DHCP and configure it so the client computers can gain access to internal resources as well as browse the Internet. How should you configure the DHCP server? (Choose all that apply.)

    a. Set the DHCP server to provide clients the address to DNS1.

    b. Set the DHCP server to provide clients the address to ISPDNS1.

    c. Set the DHCP server to provide clients the address to DNS2.

    d. Set the DHCP server to provide clients the address to ISPDNS2.

3. A user in the branch office reports that he cannot use Internet Explorer to view a commonly used Web site on the Internet. At your client computer in the main office, you run Nslookup to verify the target address and receive the correct address. At the user's client computer, you also run Nslookup, but the address returned is incorrect. What should you do to troubleshoot? (Choose all that apply.)

    a. Verify that the client is using the correct DNS servers.

    b. Run Ipconfig /flushdns.

    c. Select the Network Connections icon in Accessories.

    d. Run Ipconfig /renew.

Lesson Summary

- To troubleshoot connectivity issues, you must determine whether the problems are related to networking or related to name resolution.

- If the connectivity issue is related to TCP/IP routing, you can use PathPing to determine at which point in the route the packets are stopped.

- If a problem is related to DNS, you must ensure that the client has the correct DNS server information. If so, first use the Nslookup command to verify that the server is correctly returning what you're expecting. Then verify the DNS server's forwarders.

Lesson 3: Troubleshooting Server Services

When a server is running you might think you can relax, when in fact, you must continue to be vigilant. This section explores how to troubleshoot services to keep the server running smoothly.

After this lesson, you will be able to

- Diagnose and resolve issues related to service dependency
- Use service recovery options to diagnose and resolve service-related issues

Estimated lesson time: 30 minutes

Diagnosing and Resolving Issues Related to Service Dependency

Your server running Windows Server 2003 is not just a black box that takes in raw data and produces more raw data again. Indeed, a server running Windows Server 2003 (or any other Microsoft server, for that matter) is made up of a collection of processes, which each perform a specific task. Sometimes, these tasks run as *services*. A service can run either in the foreground—requiring user interaction—or in the background—requiring no interaction. Often, services run in the background and require little to no user interaction to perform the specified job.

Depending on which Windows Server 2003 components you choose to load at installation, Windows Server 2003 can have upward of 100 services! If you choose to load other Microsoft products or third-party software on your server running Windows Server 2003, it too will likely load additional services.

To see the current services installed on a specific server, on the Start menu, right-click My Computer, and select Manage. Then select the Services node in the Computer Management console, as shown in Figure 12-24.

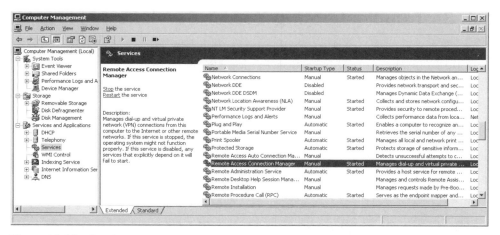

Figure 12-24   Services node showing the status of all the services

Services can be in one of three possible states: started, stopped, or paused. Three possible methods exist to configure a service for starting:

- **Automatic**   The service starts automatically when the system is restarted.

- **Manual**   The service does not start automatically when the system is restarted; however, if another process calls upon this service to start, the service will start.

- **Disabled**   The service will not start automatically when the system is restarted; the service will not start even if another process calls upon this service to start.

Some services depend on other services in order to start. It is like an automobile; there is no reason for the engine to turn over if the fuel pump is not working and will not give the engine any gas. Services are the same way: some are layered, and there is no reason to start unless the components "underneath" aren't already working properly.

This idea is called a *service dependency*. That is, some services depend on other services in order to start.

Therefore, if even only one service is not working properly, it could have a cascading effect throughout your entire server. If you take a closer look at the Remote Access Connection Manager by double-clicking it and selecting the Dependencies tab, you can see the services it depends on to start, as well as the services that depend on it to start, as shown in Figure 12-25.

Figure 12-25   Dependencies tab showing the dependency interaction

The implications of this one service are quite complex. In this case, you can see that this service relies on the Telephony service, which in turn relies on both the Plug And Play service and the Remote Procedure Call (RPC) service running. Conversely, if the Remote Access Connection Manager service is not running, neither the Internet Connection Firewall (ICF)/Internet Connection Sharing (ICS) service nor the Remote Access Auto Connection Manager service will start.

Using Service Recovery Options to Diagnose and Resolve Service-Related Issues

Most of the services that are installed by Windows Server 2003 run under the Local System context; that is, the special Local System account controls when the service should be started and stopped. However, additionally loaded services (usually by Microsoft or third-party applications) run under potentially different contexts. Often, when the service is being loaded, the administrator is asked for specific credentials under which the service is run. This way, instead of providing the service unobstructed access to the system by means of the special System account, the service is restricted to the context of the user the administrator provides. Sometimes this account is a local user to the computer (say, a local administrator account); other times, the account has even fewer privileges. The level of access required depends on the requirements of the application and the services it installs.

The best approach, however, is to provide to the account only the least amount of access that is required. For instance, if the service account could start with a local user account, you should not necessarily make the account a local administrator account simply because it is going to be used to control a service. Consult your installation documentation for specific rights required for each application you are planning to load.

Occasionally, after installing a new application that installs new services, the new application's services might not start. You can see whether the service is started by inspecting Computer Manager; however, diving into the System event log yields much more productive information, as shown in Figure 12-26 and Figure 12-27.

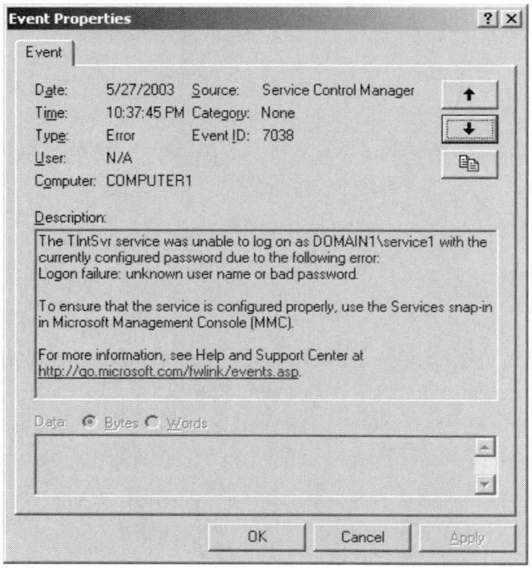

Figure 12-26   One possible error when account data is not valid

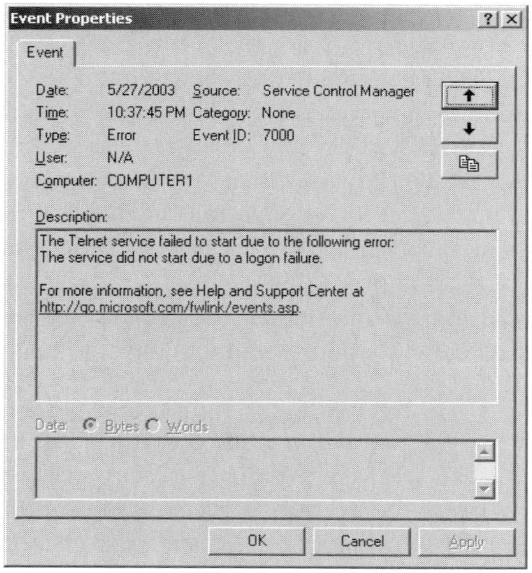

Figure 12-27   Another possible error when account data is not valid

> **Warning**   In real life, you would not actually change the logon account properties of the Telnet service. This figure showing the Telnet service is provided only as an example of what it looks like to change the account properties as if the service were a third-party installed service.

However, even the information in the event log needs to be reconciled. Just knowing that you have a logon failure is not enough. Indeed, there can be many possible reasons why the failure has occurred:

- The user name for the account has been renamed, deleted, disabled, or is otherwise invalid.
- The password for the account has expired and needs to be reset.
- The account specified to run the service has not been granted the Log On As A Service right.

To address any of these problems, first, in the service itself, inspect the Log On tab, as shown in Figure 12-28, to ensure that the account information provided is correct based on the application's specifications.

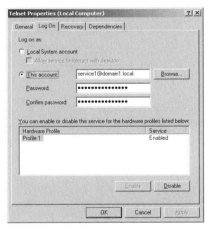

Figure 12-28   Using the Log On tab to ensure that the account information for the service is correct

After verifying the name of the account and the password, you should additionally ensure that the account has been granted the Log On As A Service right. If you are using a domain account to run the service, you should inspect the Default Domain Controller policy. To perform this task, from the Start menu, point to Administrative Tools, and then click Domain Controller Security Policy. In the left pane under the Local Policies node, double-click User Rights Assignment, and in the right pane, select Log On As A Service, as shown in Figure 12-29.

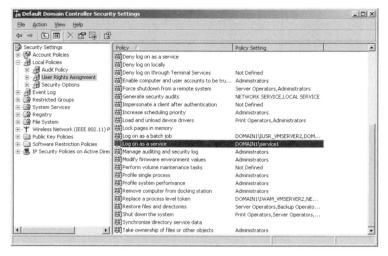

Figure 12-29   Ensuring that the service you want is granted the Log On As A Service right

Ensure that the domain account you want to use is specified in the Policy Setting and attempt to restart the service.

If the account you want to use is on a stand-alone machine running Windows Server 2003, run Gpedit.msc. Then expand Local Computer Policy, Computer Configuration, Windows Settings, Security Settings, Local Policies, and finally, select User Rights Assignment. Locate the Log On As A Service right and ensure that the account you want to use is listed.

Windows Server 2003 has many options about what it can do if a service fails to start because of any of the reasons described previously. If a service fails, events are logged to the server where the service is loaded. However, you can choose to take a more pro-active approach to service management.

If you select the Recovery tab of the service, a myriad of options allow you to specify behavior if a service fails, as shown in Figure 12-30.

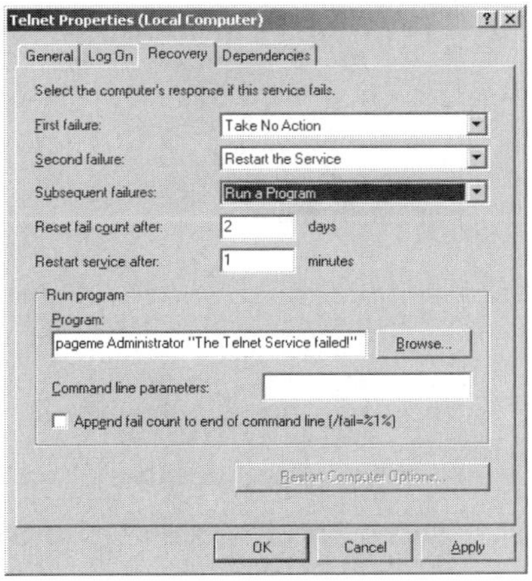

Figure 12-30 Setting behavior on the Recovery tab

If a service fails, you have four choices:

- Take No Action
- Restart The Service
- Run A Program
- Restart The Computer

A single service failure might be an anomaly. That is, the service could have failed to load initially because another service it depended on had not yet been started. This situation could occur for a number of reasons, including temporary slow disk access, or another service needing to finish writing to a log file before being fully started. Hence, because that other service was not fully started, this service could have requested to start, recognized that a service it depended on was not started, and simply missed the opportunity to start. Therefore, on the first failure, you are advised to restart the service.

However, if the service fails multiple times, you could try to restart it again, run a program to let you know that the service has not started, or restart the computer to see whether the timing dependency has disappeared.

Practice: Configuring Services

In this practice, you configure service dependency and recovery options on Computer1.

Exercise 1: Configure Service Dependency

In this exercise, you attempt to start the Clipbook service. Keep service dependency in mind.

1. On Computer1, click Start, right-click My Computer, and select Manage.

2. Expand Computer Management, Services And Applications, and then select Services.

3. Locate the Clipbook service in the list of services and double-click it to view its properties.

4. Change the Startup type from Disabled to Automatic and click Apply.

5. Click Start to attempt to start the service.

   An error states, "The dependency service or group failed to start."

6. Select the Dependencies tab to view the Clipbook service's dependencies.

7. Note that the Network DDE and Network DDE DSDM services must be started because the Clipbook service relies on them. Close the Clipbook Properties dialog box by clicking OK.

8. Locate the Network DDE DSDM service and double-click it to view its properties. Change the Startup Type from Disabled to Automatic, and click Apply.

9. Click Start to start the service. Click OK to close the Network DDE DSDM Properties dialog box.

10. Now locate the Network DDE service and double-click it to view its properties. Change the Startup Type from Disabled to Automatic, and click Apply.

11. Click Start to start the service. Click OK to close the Network DDE Properties dialog box.

12. Right-click the Clipbook service and click Start to start the Clipbook service.

    The Clipbook service starts.

Exercise 2: Configure Service Recovery Options

In this exercise, you deliberately break the Telnet service to see how a configured service responds to a failure.

1. On Computer1, click Start, right-click My Computer, and select Manage.

2. Expand Computer Management, Services, and Applications, and then select Services.

3. Double-click the Telnet service to view its properties.

4. Change the Startup type from Disabled to Automatic.

5. Select the Recovery tab. From the First Failure list, select Restart The Service.

6. Click OK to close the Telnet properties.

7. Right-click the Telnet service and select Start.

   The Telnet service launches.

8. Press Ctrl+Alt+Del and select Task Manager.

   The Task Manager opens.

9. Select the Processes tab.

10. Locate the Tlntsvr.exe process and click End Process.

    The Telnet service ends.

11. Wait about 1 minute and view the Processes tab listing again.

    Tlntsvr.exe should appear in the list of processes again after the service is automatically restarted.

Lesson Review

The following questions are intended to reinforce key information presented in this lesson. If you are unable to answer a question, review the lesson materials and try the question again. You can find answers to the questions in the "Questions and Answers" section at the end of this chapter.

1. You install a new application, which reports that it is installing a service on the computer. However, when you run the application for the first time, it is unable to start. You inspect the event log to determine the nature of the problem. You receive an error stating "The service did not start due to a logon failure." What should you do?

   a. Grant the account the Logon As A Service right.

   b. Change the password to the same name as the account.

   c. Verify the user name of the account being used to run the service.

   d. Grant the account administrative rights.

2. You install a new application, which reports that it is installing a service on the computer. However, when you run the application for the first time, it is unable to start. You inspect the service dependencies for the new service and notice that a service that is required is not started. However, your security policy states that services must remain stopped unless another application requires them to be on. How should you configure the dependent service to start?

    a. Automatic

    b. Automatic, but pause the service

    c. Manual

    d. Disabled

3. You install a new application on a member server. The application reports that it is installing a service on the computer. The installation for the service requests a user name and password for which to run the service. You provide the name DOMAIN1\Service1. However, when you run the application for the first time, it is unable to start. You suspect that the account has not been given enough rights to start. What do you do?

    a. On the member server, grant the Service1 account the Log On As A Service right.

    b. In the domain, grant the Service1 account the Log On As A Service right.

    c. On the member server, grant the Service1 account the Log On As A Batch Job right.

    d. In the domain, grant the Service1 account the Log On As A Batch Job right.

Lesson Summary

- Some services depend on other services in order to start. If a service is not starting, you should check to ensure that the services on which it depends are also started.

- When troubleshooting service failures, you should check the user name, password, and the Log On As a Service right.

- You can configure the recovery options to inform you when a service has failed to start.

Case Scenario Exercise

You work for Tailspin Toys. The main office is in Arkansas, and the branch office is in Delaware. Arkansas and Delaware are connected by a T1 line. The only connection to the Internet is through Arkansas. Tailspin Toys consists of one domain and employs 300 people. The IT department is located in Arkansas.

You are the network administrator for the company. Users and other administrators report issues on the network. You must decide which diagnostic tool is most appropriate to use in solving the problem.

Five different reports are described next. For each report, determine which tool is appropriate. Choose from the full version of Network Monitor, the Lite version of

Network Monitor, Netstat, Ping, the tests on the DNS Monitoring tab, the network Repair button, network bridging, and service configurations. Provide a reason to justify each of your choices. You might not need to use all the possible answer choices.

1. A user in Arkansas reports that he cannot browse the Internet. You ask him to ping the local gateway, and it is not available. Other users on the network are not having problems.

   _____

   _____

   _____

2. All users in the company report that they cannot browse the Internet. However, access to company resources is not affected.

   _____

   _____

3. A network administrator in Delaware wants to know the best way to implement a new segment on the network with a different physical topology. She doesn't want to buy a hardware router.

   _____

4. A network administrator in Delaware reports that a third-party service on a server refuses to start. He's restarted the service several times, but it doesn't start.

   _____

5. An administrator in Arkansas thinks her server might have been infected with a virus or Trojan horse program. This program seems to have a specific port open. How can this administrator determine which process uses which port?

   _____

   _____

Chapter Summary

- Maintaining your Windows Server 2003 network is one of your most critical daily functions.
- Getting quick status about the network interface on your server is easy with the Task Manager Networking tab.
- Use the Performance console to configure alerts. Alerts are added to the Application event log.

- Netstat helps monitor network traffic, and the Netstat –o command can be used to determine the PID of a process that has opened a port. Task Manager shows the PIDs of processes.

- The full version of the Network Monitor tool, which is found in SMS, can capture traffic between any computers on the local segment.

- Network Monitor triggers an alert when specific patterns are matched or a specific amount of buffer space is used.

- When troubleshooting Internet connectivity, you check the client's IP settings, DNS settings, and forwarder settings.

- The network adapter's Repair button performs a myriad of tests and functions that can resolve connectivity problems.

- Network bridging makes multiple networks appear as one network.

- Some services depend on each other in order to start. You can check their dependencies through a service's Dependencies tab.

- The service recovery options allow you to restart the service, run a program, or restart the computer after single or multiple service failures.

Exam Highlights

Before taking the exam, review the key points and terms that are presented in this chapter.

Key Points

- Know which tools are best for monitoring your network quickly versus which tools take time to set up and configure (but give you more data).

- Be able to use alerts to help you monitor items. However, know what must be configured for alerts to function properly.

- Understand that troubleshooting Internet connectivity is a multifaceted problem that can be partially client side and partially server side. Know where to start and how to finish.

- Know how to configure services that have trouble starting.

Key Terms

counter   A representation of an object found in the system. You monitor counters for performance reasons to help you determine whether processes are running smoothly.

sampling (or sample) rate   The frequency at which a counter is checked to see whether specific criteria are met. The faster a counter is sampled, the more accurate the response can be. However, the slower a counter is sampled, the less central processing unit (CPU) must be used.

Process Identifier (PID)   A unique value to a running process in the system.

trigger   An action taken when a sampled counter is set to go off. Triggers are typically set for when a counter rises above a certain value or drops below a certain value.

forwarder   The next server the DNS will query.

network bridging   A connection that makes two disparate networks act like one network.

service dependency   A relationship between services in which one service requires that other services are started before it can start.

Lesson 1 Review

Page
12-19

1. You receive a report that Computer1 is responding slowly to user requests. You want a quick way to see which network traffic the server is using. You use Network Monitor. You want to see whether any general broadcast traffic is being sent to Computer1. Which counter should you enable?

    a. Nonunicasts/Interval

    b. Unicasts/Interval

    c. Bytes Sent/Interval

    d. Bytes Received/Interval

    a

2. You set up Performance Logs And Alerts to send a message to Computer2 to notify an operator when the network use on Computer1 gets too high. However, Computer2 never receives the message sent from Computer1. What must you do to enable messages to be sent by Computer1 and received by Computer2? (Choose all that apply.)

    a. On Computer1, start the Messenger service.

    b. On Computer1, start the Alerter service.

    c. On Computer2, start the Messenger service.

    d. On Computer2, start the Alerter service.

    b, c

3. You suspect that a virus has infected your computer running Windows Server 2003. You believe this virus is transmitting data from your server over the network using a specific port. You want to determine which process is using a specific port. Which command should you run?

    a. Nbtstat –RR

    b. Nbtstat –r

    c. Netstat –a

    d. Netstat –o

    d

Lesson 2 Review

Page
12-28
The following three questions relate to the network diagram of Tailspin Toys shown in Figure 12-31. You are the network administrator for Tailspin Toys.

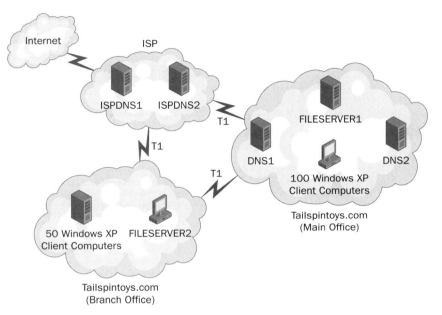

Figure 12-31   Tailspin Toys network

1. A user in the branch office reports that he cannot use Internet Explorer to open a commonly used Web site on the Internet. At your client computer in the main office, you are able to ping the target address. At the user's client computer, you cannot ping the target address. What should you do to troubleshoot? (Choose all that apply.)

   a. From the user's client computer, run **ping** destination address.

   b. From the user's client computer, select To Repair The Network Connection.

   c. From the DNS server, perform a simple query test.

   d. From the DNS server, perform a recursive query test.

   a, b

2. You are setting up 50 new client machines in the branch office. Another administrator has already configured DHCP in the branch office. When you bring the first client computer online, you notice that DHCP is not providing Primary or Alternate DNS servers along with the IP address.

You need to troubleshoot DHCP and configure it so the client computers can gain access to internal resources as well as browse the Internet. How should you configure the DHCP server? (Choose all that apply.)

   a. Set the DHCP server to provide clients the address to DNS1.

   b. Set the DHCP server to provide clients the address to ISPDNS1.

   c. Set the DHCP server to provide clients the address to DNS2.

   d. Set the DHCP server to provide clients the address to ISPDNS2.

a, c

3. A user in the branch office reports that he cannot use Internet Explorer to view a commonly used Web site on the Internet. At your client computer in the main office, you run Nslookup to verify the target address and receive the correct address. At the user's client computer, you also run Nslookup, but the address returned is incorrect. What should you do to troubleshoot? (Choose all that apply.)

   a. Verify that the client is using the correct DNS servers.

   b. Run Ipconfig /flushdns.

   c. Select the Network Connections icon in Accessories.

   d. Run Ipconfig /renew.

a, b

Lesson 3 Review

Page
12-39
1. You install a new application, which reports that it is installing a service on the computer. However, when you run the application for the first time, it is unable to start. You inspect the event log to determine the nature of the problem. You receive an error stating "The service did not start due to a logon failure." What should you do?

   a. Grant the account the Logon As A Service right.

   b. Change the password to the same name as the account.

   c. Verify the user name of the account being used to run the service.

   d. Grant the account administrative rights.

c

2. You install a new application, which reports that it is installing a service on the computer. However, when you run the application for the first time, it is unable to start. You inspect the service dependencies for the new service and notice that a service that is required is not started. However, your security policy states that services must remain stopped unless another application requires them to be on. How should you configure the dependent service to start?

   a. Automatic

   b. Automatic, but pause the service

   c. Manual

   d. Disabled

   c

3. You install a new application on a member server. The application reports that it is installing a service on the computer. The installation for the service requests a user name and password for which to run the service. You provide the name DOMAIN1\Service1. However, when you run the application for the first time, it is unable to start. You suspect that the account has not been given enough rights to start. What do you do?

   a. On the member server, grant the Service1 account the Log On As A Service right.

   b. In the domain, grant the Service1 account the Log On As A Service right.

   c. On the member server, grant the Service1 account the Log On As A Batch Job right.

   d. In the domain, grant the Service1 account the Log On As A Batch Job right.

   a

Case Scenario Exercise

Page 12-40

1. A user in Arkansas reports that he cannot browse the Internet. You ask him to ping the local gateway, and it is not available. Other users on the network are not having problems.

   The Repair button is best because this user probably lost connectivity to the network. Because other users are running fine, this problem is probably an isolated instance.

2. All users in the company report that they cannot browse the Internet. However, access to company resources is not affected.

   The DNS monitoring tests can verify whether the DNS server is getting proper responses from the server to which it forwards.

3. A network administrator in Delaware wants to know the best way to implement a new segment on the network with a different physical topology. She doesn't want to buy a hardware router.

   Network bridging is best used to connect two disparate networks together.

4. A network administrator in Delaware reports that a third-party service on a server refuses to start. He's restarted the service several times, but it doesn't start.

   Check the service configuration—especially dependencies and logon credentials.

5. An administrator in Arkansas thinks her server might have been infected with a virus or Trojan horse program. This program seems to have a specific port open. How can this administrator determine which process uses which port?

   Netstat –o shows all the ports in use. Then she can use the Task Manager PID to work backward and find the process.

Part 2
Prepare for the Exam

13 Implementing, Managing, and Maintaining IP Addressing (1.0)

IT professionals who work for **medium to large companies** as system or network administrators often have the worst of both worlds. You are stuck with a network structure designed by a consultant who took the money and ran. (I should know: I *was* that consultant.) At the same time, if you think your job won't involve some design, think again. Your organization wants to switch to **private Internet Protocol (IP) addressing**. You have to **summarize** the four (if you're lucky, try it with three) Class C subnets that your company leases. Internally, you need to **subnet** different sized subnets, so wipe the dust off the **Variable Length Subnet Masking (VLSM)** textbook.

Creating an effective **Transmission Control Protocol/Internet Protocol (TCP/IP) infrastructure** is one of the primary elements of network design and planning. A TCP/IP network infrastructure plan specifies how you are going to subnet your network and which **IP addresses** and **subnet masks** to use. Until recently, network administrators were given one or more Class C networks and either subnetted them or didn't. Now, with private networks, you can have 17 million IP addresses to play with if you want. Instead of nice, safe, understandable Class C networks, you will be allocated **classless interdomain routing (CIDR)** oddities like 131.16.64.0/19 or 200.234.14.128/25.

When your network design is implemented, you switch to your primary function, which is to manage and maintain the network. How will you allocate IP addresses? How will you ensure that IP address allocation is implemented for branch offices and remote users? **Static IP configuration** is error-prone, and it is now used mostly only for servers—in particular, domain controllers (DCs), infrastructure servers, Routing And Remote Access servers, and BackOffice servers. Client PCs that can be configured to receive their addresses automatically are typically configured using the **Dynamic Host Configuration Protocol (DHCP)**.

You need to know how to install and authorize a DHCP server; how to set up **scopes** to configure clients on a single network or on multiple subnets; how to set up **DHCP options**, and where it is appropriate to use server, scope, or client options; and how to set up a **superscope** and when it is appropriate to do so. You need to be able to exclude the IP addresses of hosts that either cannot or should not be configured automatically, and to create reservations for such hosts as network-enabled print devices that can be configured automatically but that must retain their IP configurations.

Microsoft Windows Server 2003 networks typically make use of **dynamic client registration** in the **Domain Name System (DNS)**. The DHCP service has a central role in this process, and you need to know how to configure the DNS properties dialog box of a DHCP server so that clients' resource records are registered in the most efficient manner.

DHCP, once installed and configured, might or might not work as planned. In the latter case, you need to know how to troubleshoot the new installation. If a DHCP server services several subnets, you need to know how to configure a DHCP relay agent, either on routers (including Routing And Remote Access servers) or on servers on remote subnets. You should be able to recognize the symptoms of DHCP failure by identifying an **Automatic Private IP Addressing (APIPA)** address.

Another scenario is when DHCP has worked in a satisfactory manner in a network, but problems arise later. Which troubleshooting tools are available? How do you verify DHCP database integrity and **reconcile** the database? How do you interpret entries in the DHCP audit log or in the system Event Log? How do you implement failover protection? How do you transfer a DHCP database to another server?

Finally, **multicasting** is being used more and more frequently for tasks such as Active Directory directory service replication and video conferencing. Microsoft Windows Server 2003 DHCP includes the **Multicast Address Dynamic Allocation Protocol (MADCAP)** and can allocate multicast addresses in the same way it can allocate unicast addresses. You need to be able to identify public and private multicast addresses and to set up a multicast scope.

Tested Skills and Suggested Practices

The skills that you need to successfully master the Implementing, Managing, and Maintaining IP Addressing objective domain on the 70-291 exam include the following:

- Configure TCP/IP addressing on a server computer.
  - ❑ Practice 1: A calculator is a useful tool, but it cannot help you understand the binary numbering system. Practice converting 8-bit binary numbers into their decimal equivalents and vice versa, without using a calculator or other electronic aid.
  - ❑ Practice 2: Choose both classful networks (Class B or Class C) and CIDR address ranges and subnet them so that you create a specified number of subnets with a specified number of hosts in each subnet. Calculate the IP address range and subnet mask for each of the subnets.
  - ❑ Practice 3: Take a reasonably large CIDR range (say with a /16 or /17 subnet mask). Using VLSM, create backbone subnets and further divide these into department-sized subnets. Study the **longest match algorithm**.
  - ❑ Practice 4: Learn the private address ranges, including the APIPA range.

■ Manage DHCP.

❑ Practice 1: Install DHCP on a Microsoft Windows Server 2003 member server (preferably Enterprise Edition). Create a scope, exclude any statically configured IP addresses, and specify a **lease period**. Authorize the server (if necessary) and activate the scope. Set up client PCs on your test network to receive their IP configurations and DNS server information automatically, and check that they have been configured. Access the DNS tab on the DHCP server properties page and note the current settings. If you have a Microsoft Windows NT 4.0 DHCP client on your network, set up DHCP to register that client's host A and PTR records in dynamic DNS (DDNS).

❑ Practice 2: Configure scope options 003 and 006 for your scope. Release and renew the DHCP leases on your clients, and check that they are configured with the correct **default gateway** and DNS server addresses.

❑ Practice 3: Configure a reservation for one of your clients. Set DHCP client options for this reservation to values different from those in your scope options. Release and renew the DHCP lease on this client, and check that it is configured with the same IP address as before but with the new default gateway and DNS server addresses.

❑ Practice 3: Configure a multihomed server as a router. Implement a second subnet. Set up DHCP Relay Agent on the router. Create a scope for the second subnet on your DHCP server, put both your scopes in a superscope, and activate the second scope. Check that you get the expected result. If you do not have a multihomed server, you can carry out this practice by assigning a second address to the router's **network interface card (NIC)** and creating two logical subnets on the same physical network.

■ Troubleshoot TCP/IP addressing.

❑ Practice 1: Deactivate a scope. Release and renew the lease on a client served by that scope. Note the IP address that has been leased to that client. Attempt to **ping** that client from other clients on the same subnet and on your other subnet. Reactivate the scope but do not attempt to renew the lease on the APIPA-configured client. Wait approximately 5 minutes. Confirm that the client now has a valid DHCP lease.

❑ Practice 2: Use **PathPing** and **Tracert** to trace the path between a client on your first subnet and one on your second subnet. Note the difference between the PathPing and Tracert outputs. Access help (use ?) to list all the switches available for the **Arp**, **Ipconfig**, Ping, Tracert, and PathPing commands.

❑ Practice 3: From the command line, issue a Netdiag command with the /fix switch. Examine the output.

■ Troubleshoot DHCP.

❑ Practice 1: Install a second DHCP server in the same subnet as the first. Define a scope so that it overlaps the scope for that subnet on the first server. Attempt to authorize the server. Delete and recreate the scope so there is no overlap. Attempt to authorize the server.

❑ Practice 2: Move the second DHCP server to the second subnet (reconfiguring it as necessary). Set up the DHCP servers so that each has a scope for both subnets and none of the scopes overlap. Configure the DHCP Relay Agent on the router so that both DHCP servers can service both networks. Stop the DHCP service on one server and examine the effect of releasing and renewing DHCP on a client on the same subnet.

❑ Practice 3: Examine the DHCP audit log and the system Event Log for DHCP errors. You will certainly have created a few by now!

❑ Practice 4: Examine the DNS tab of the properties dialog box of one of the DHCP servers. Ensure that you understand the function of each of the check boxes and options. (Note: It is hard to perform this task by experimentation because you will have difficulty determining whether a DNS resource record was created by a client or by the DHCP server.)

❑ Practice 5: Back up and restore the DHCP database using both the DHCP console and the Netsh utility.

❑ Practice 6: Verify the integrity of the DHCP database and reconcile it if necessary using both the DHCP console and the Netsh utility.

❑ Practice 7: Verify that reservations and reservation options have been set up correctly and that DHCP Relay Agent is working correctly. Repeat these procedures several times until you are fully familiar with them.

Further Reading

This section lists supplemental readings by objective. We recommend that you study these sources thoroughly before taking exam 70-291.

Objective 1.1   Review all Lessons of Chapter 2, "Understanding TCP/IP."

Microsoft Corporation. *Microsoft Encyclopedia of Networking, Second Edition.* Redmond, Washington: Microsoft Press, 2002. See entries for "subnet mask" and "subnetting."

Microsoft Corporation. *Microsoft Windows Server 2003 Deployment Guide.* Redmond, Washington. Review "Designing a TCP/IP Network," available on Microsoft's Web site at *http://www.microsoft.com/technet/treeview/default.asp?url=/technet/prodtechnol/windowsserver2003/evaluate/cpp/reskit/netsvc/rkdnstcp.asp.*

Objective 1.2   Review all of Chapter 7, "Configuring DHCP Servers and Clients."

Microsoft Corporation. *Microsoft Encyclopedia of Networking, Second Edition.* Redmond, Washington: Microsoft Press, 2002. See entry for "Dynamic Host Configuration Protocol (DHCP)."

Microsoft Corporation. *Microsoft Windows Server 2003 Deployment Guide.* Redmond, Washington. Review "DHCP—How To," available on Microsoft's Web site at *http://www.microsoft.com/technet/treeview/default.asp?url=/technet/prodtechnol/windowsserver2003/proddocs/entserver/sag_DHCP_NewWaysToDoFamiliarTasks.asp.*

Objective 1.3   Review Lesson 4 of Chapter 3, "Monitoring and Troubleshooting TCP/IP Connections."

Microsoft Corporation. *Microsoft Encyclopedia of Networking, Second Edition.* Redmond, Washington: Microsoft Press, 2002. See entry for "Automatic Private IP Addressing (APIPA)."

Microsoft Corporation. *Microsoft Windows Server 2003 Deployment Guide.* Redmond, Washington. Review "TCP/IP—Troubleshooting," available on Microsoft's Web site at *http://www.microsoft.com/technet/treeview/default.asp?url=/technet/prodtechnol/windowsserver2003/proddocs/entserver/sag_TCPIP_tro_topnode.asp.*

Objective 1.4   Review Lessons 2 and 3 of Chapter 8, "Monitoring and Troubleshooting DHCP."

Microsoft Corporation. *Microsoft Windows Server 2003 Deployment Guide.* Redmond, Washington. Review "DHCP—Troubleshooting," available on Microsoft's Web site at *http://www.microsoft.com/technet/treeview/default.asp?url=/technet/prodtechnol/windowsserver2003/proddocs/entserver/sag_TCPIP_tro_topnode.asp.*

Configure TCP/IP Addressing on a Server Computer

Assigning an appropriate and consistent IP addressing scheme is essential to the smooth running of your network. You might be designing a network from scratch, you might decide to subnet an existing network to reduce broadcast traffic collisions, or you might decide to implement a private addressing scheme and use **Network Address Translation (NAT)**. The last strategy has a number of advantages: use private IP addresses if you do not have sufficient public IP addresses to assign one to all your clients, or if you want to implement an additional layer of security on your intranet. The disadvantages of implementing a private address scheme are the following: you will have to redesign your network, possibly becoming involved in subnetting, super-netting, and VLSM, and you will have to ensure the appropriate level of Internet connectivity for both incoming and outgoing traffic.

Public or registered addresses are issued by the **Internet Assigned Numbers Authority (IANA)** or from an Internet service provider (ISP). These addresses are accessible from the Internet, and it is essential that computers that provide Internet services, such as Web servers, are allocated public addresses for this purpose, even if they are configured with private addresses on their intranets.

You can use whichever private addressing scheme you want without requiring authorization from the IANA or anyone else. You must, however, ensure that your private addresses are translated by a service such as NAT into registered public addresses in order to access the Internet. Private addresses fall within these ranges.

- 10.0.0.1 through 10.255.255.254 (the 10.0.0.0/8 network)
- 172.16.0.1 through 172.31.255.254 (the 172.16.0.0/12 network)
- 192.168.0.1 through 192.168.255.254 (the 192.168.0.0/16 network)

Another private network exists, but it is by default assigned automatically to Microsoft Windows Server 2003, Microsoft Windows 2000, and Microsoft Windows XP computers that are set up to receive their IP configurations automatically, but are unable to obtain DHCP leases. You should know this range because a computer configured with APIPA is often a symptom of DHCP problems on a network.

The APIPA range is 169.254.0.1 through 169.254.255.254 (the 169.254.0.0/16 network).

When you have selected or been allocated the address range with which you will be working, you might have to split it up into subnets, or if it consists of a number of contiguous networks, supernet it into a single network. You perform this task by manipulating the subnet mask, a number associated with the network that distinguishes between bits in the IP address that specify a network address and bits that specify a host on that network. Subnet masks consist of a number of binary ones followed by a number of binary zeros. They can be written in dotted decimal or slash notation. For example, 255.255.255.0 and /24 both represent a subnet mask of 24 ones followed by 8 zeros.

When you have defined your IP addressing scheme, you must implement it. Typically, client computers receive their IP address assignments (or leases) from a DHCP server, whereas servers are configured statically. This objective tests your ability to design a TCP/IP network and configure it on your servers.

Objective 1.1 Questions

1. Some time ago, your organization was allocated two Class C networks: 206.10.13.0 and 206.10.14.0. You now want to supernet these two networks so that your external router advertises only one network on the Internet. Which allowable configuration enables you to do this?

    A. Network address 206.10.13.0 and subnet mask 255.255.254.0

    B. Network address 206.10.12.0 and subnet mask 255.255.252.0

    C. Network address 206.10.13.0 and subnet mask 255.255.253.0

    D. It can't be done.

2. Your organization has leased the Class C network 199.205.15.0/24. You are subnetting this network using VLSM. Your routers support the zero subnet and the longest match algorithm. You ask one of your support staff to design a subnetting structure, but when she submits this you suspect that some of the network/subnet mask allocations are invalid. Which of the following are *not* valid networks? (Choose all that apply.)

    A. 199.205.15.64/25

    B. 199.205.15.192/26

    C. 199.205.15.130/26

    D. 199.205.15.96/26

    E. 199.205.15.8/27

    F. 199.205.15.40/28

3. Your company has leased the network 138.16.0.0/21. You want to subdivide this network into 10 evenly sized subnets. No single subnet will ever contain more than 100 users. You do not use NAT or private network addresses. The default gateway is always the lowest possible user address on a subnet. You use DHCP for your client PCs, but your servers are configured manually. The 10 lowest IP addresses on each subnet are excluded from the DHCP scope so they can be used for manual configuration. Which of the following configurations is a valid server?

    A. IP address: 138.16.1.5

        Subnet mask: 255.255.255.0

        Default gateway: 138.16.1.1

    B. IP address: 138.16.8.5

        Subnet mask: 255.255.255.128

        Default gateway: 138.16.8.1

    C. IP address: 138.16.3.133

          Subnet mask: 255.255.255.128

          Default gateway: 138.16.3.129

    D. IP address: 138.16.1.134

          Subnet mask: 255.255.255.128

          Default gateway: 138.16.1.128

4. You are designing a subnetting scheme for a company, which uses the 10.0.0.0/8 private network. Although you have an abundance of network addresses, you want to limit the maximum number of user addresses on any subnet to 126 to ensure that collisions because of broadcast traffic are kept at an acceptable level. Which of the following are both valid subnets on your internetwork and support a maximum of 126 user addresses? (Choose all that apply.)

    A. 10.1.0.64/25

    B. 10.1.0.128/24

    C. 10.1.0.0/25

    D. 10.1.0.64/26

    E. 10.1.0.128/25

    F. 10.1.0.0/24

5. Your organization has leased the Class C address of 199.16.24.0. You subnet using a 255.255.255.224 subnet mask. You are using Cisco routers. How many IP addresses are available to be allocated to PCs (clients and servers)?

    A. 62

    B. 29

    C. 0

    D. 13

6. You work for a large organization that has leased the Class B address 131.188.0.0. It uses VLSM. The network is divided into 6 backbone subnets, each with 8190 host addresses. These hosts are then subnetted as required. The 131.188.96.0/19 subnet is divided into 62 equal-sized subnets. On which subnet would you find host 131.188.97.140?

    A. 131.188.96.0/19

    B. 131.188.97.0/24

    C. 131.188.97.0/25

    D. 131.188.97.128/25

7. You work for an ISP with four customers who each require a specific number of IP addresses:

■ Datum Corporation: 7,000 addresses

■ Adventure Works: 900 addresses

■ Coho Vineyard: 400 addresses

■ Margie's Travel: 45 addresses

Currently, the ISP has a number of CIDR subnets that it can allocate.

■ Subnet A: 131.107.0.0/18

■ Subnet B: 157.54.0.0/19

■ Subnet C: 157.60.64.0/22

■ Subnet D: 157.60.128.0/23

■ Subnet E: 206.73.118.0/24

■ Subnet F: 207.209.68.128/25

■ Subnet G: 208.147.66.0/26

How should you allocate these networks to make the most efficient use of address space? (Choose all that apply. No subnet can be allocated twice.)

A. Datum Corporation, Subnet A

B. Datum Corporation, Subnet B

C. Datum Corporation, Subnet C

D. Adventure Works, Subnet C

E. Adventure Works, Subnet D

F. Coho Vineyard, Subnet C

G. Coho Vineyard, Subnet D

H. Margie's Travel, Subnet E

I. Margie's Travel, Subnet F

J. Margie's Travel, Subnet G

Objective 1.1 Answers

1. **Correct Answers: D**

   A. Incorrect: This configuration seems at first glance to be OK. The subnet mask has been reduced by a single 1 and the addresses are contiguous. However, let us look at the third octet:

   The subnet mask is 11111110

   ANDing with 13 00001101

   Gives 00001100

   The subnet mask is 11111110

   ANDing with 14 00001110

   Gives 00001110

   So the two networks would have different network addresses given a /23 (255.255.254.0) subnet mask.

   B. Incorrect: This supernetted network is valid: 206.10.12/22 with a host range 206.10.12.1 through 206.10.15.254. However, the networks allocated to your organization are 206.10.13.0/24 and 206.10.14.0/24, and an allowable configuration must not advertise addresses outside these networks.

   C. Incorrect: 225.225.253.0 is not a valid subnet mask.

   D. Correct: Two Class B subnets can be supernetted only if they are contiguous and the lower of the two values in the third octet is an even number. Note that this is not a "trick." It is a real-world situation that can have serious consequences. Before the need for summarization was fully understood, Class C networks were regularly allocated that were contiguous, yet could not be summarized as a single supernet. You must know how to recognize this situation if you come across it in your professional career.

2. **Correct Answers: A, C, and E**

   A. Correct: Mask = 255.255.255.128

   Increment = 256 − 128 = 128

   Because 128 is not a factor of 64 (64 is not divisible by 128), this network is not valid.

   B. Incorrect: Mask = 255.255.255.192

   Increment = 256 − 192 = 64

   64 is a factor of 192, so this network is valid.

C. **Correct:** The value in the fourth octet must be a power of 2, for example, 128, 64, 32, and so on. This network is not valid.

D. **Incorrect:** Mask = 255.255.255.224

Increment = 256 – 224 = 32

32 is a factor of 96, so this network is valid.

E. **Correct:** Mask = 255.255.255.240

Increment = 256 – 240 = 16

16 is not a factor of 8, so this network is not valid.

F. **Incorrect:** Mask = 255.255.255.248

Increment = 256 – 248 = 8

8 is a factor of 40, so this network is valid.

3.   Correct Answers: C

A. **Incorrect:** The 255.255.255.0 (/24) subnet mask supports 254 users. Because the maximum number of users for a /21 mask is 2,046, subnetting with a /24 mask will not support 10 networks.

B. **Incorrect:** The (/21) subnet mask supports up to 2,046 users. The valid IP address range is therefore 138.16.0.1 through 138.16.7.254.

C. **Correct:** The 138.16.3.128/25 network supports an address range of 138.16.3.129 through 138.16.3.255. The default gateway is therefore 138.16.3.129. The IP address 138.16.3.133 is one of the lowest 10 IP addresses in the subnet.

D. **Incorrect:** The default gateway address has all zeros in its host portion and is therefore a network address. It should be 138.16.1.129.

4.   Correct Answers: C and E

A. **Incorrect:** 10.1.0.64 is an invalid subnet address for a /25 subnet mask.

B. **Incorrect:** The /24 subnet mask supports 254 user addresses. Also, 10.1.0.128 is not a valid subnet address for the /24 subnet mask.

C. **Correct:** This address gives a user an IP address range of 10.1.0.1 through 10.1.0.1.126.

D. **Incorrect:** The /26 subnet mask supports only 62 user addresses, in this case, 10.1.0.65 through 10.1.0.126.

E. **Correct:** This address gives a user an IP address range of 10.1.0.129 through 10.1.0.1.254.

F. **Incorrect:** The /24 subnet mask supports 254 user addresses, in this case, 10.1.0.1 through 10.1.0.254.

5. Correct Answers: B

A. Incorrect: A 255.255.255.224 subnet mask gives five host address bits, so the maximum number of host addresses is $2^5 - 2 = 30$ host addresses. However, one address is needed for the router interface, so 29 is the correct answer.

B. Correct: A 255.255.255.224 subnet mask gives five host address bits, so the maximum number of host addresses is $2^5 - 2 = 30$ host addresses. However, one address is needed for the router interface, so 29 is the correct answer.

C. Incorrect: A 255.255.255.224 subnet mask gives five host address bits, so the maximum number of host addresses is $2^5 - 2 = 30$. However, one address is needed for the router interface, so the correct answer is 29.

D. Incorrect: A 255.255.255.224 subnet mask gives five host address bits, so the maximum number of host addresses is $2^5 - 2 = 30$. However, one address is needed for the router interface, so the correct answer is 29. If the subnet mask were 255.255.255.240, 13 would be the correct answer.

6. Correct Answers: D

A. Incorrect: Although the address 131.188.97.140 is in the 131.188.96.0/19 range, VLSM employs the longest match algorithm, which looks for the most specific (smallest) subnet for which the address is valid. If host 131.188.97.40 were placed by mistake on the backbone subnet and a more specific route existed to a different network segment, it could never be reached.

B. Incorrect: Splitting the backbone network 131.188.96.0/19 into 62 equal-sized subnets requires a /25 subnet mask. 131.188.97.0/24 does not meet this requirement.

C. Incorrect: The host address range for this subnet is 131.188.97.1 through 131.188.97.128.

D. Correct: The host address range for this subnet is 131.188.97.129 through 131.188.97.254. It is also the most specific subnet in the path. Host 131.188.97.140 is found on this subnet.

7. Correct Answers: B, D, G, and J

A. Incorrect: A /18 subnet mask provides a maximum of 16,382 host addresses. This number is surplus to requirements.

B. Correct: A /19 subnet mask provides a maximum of 8,190 host addresses. This number is adequate.

C. Incorrect: A /22 subnet mask provides a maximum of 1,022 host addresses. This number is inadequate.

D. Correct: A /22 subnet mask provides a maximum of 1,022 host addresses. This number is adequate.

E. Incorrect: A /23 subnet mask provides a maximum of 510 host addresses. This number is inadequate.

F. Incorrect: A /22 subnet mask provides a maximum of 1,022 host addresses. This number is surplus to requirements.

G. Correct: A /23 subnet mask provides a maximum of 510 host addresses. This number is adequate.

H. Incorrect: A /24 subnet mask provides a maximum of 254 host addresses. This number is surplus to requirements.

I. Incorrect: A /25 subnet mask provides a maximum of 126 host addresses. This number is surplus to requirements.

J. Correct: A /26 subnet mask provides a maximum of 62 host addresses. This number is adequate.

Manage DHCP

DHCP is typically configured on a member server in an **Active Directory** domain. This objective assumes that DHCP has been installed, configured, and authorized in Active Directory, and that it has given out leases to clients. However, this scenario is never the end of the story. You might be asked to set up an additional scope, possibly to support a second subnet or to support remote access clients. You create scopes from the DHCP console using the **New Scope Wizard**. The wizard prompts you for a start and end address and for an exclusion range, and it expedites the task of setting up scopes—provided you understand the significance of the information you are supplying.

A reservation ensures that a client always obtains the same IP address when it renews its lease. A client with a reservation receives a DHCP lease even if all the leases available for nonreserved clients have been allocated. Reservations are typically set up for such clients as network-enabled print devices that other clients access by specifying a fixed IP address. Politically, you would also be wise to create a reservation for your boss! You create a reservation by expanding the appropriate scope, right-clicking Reservations, and selecting New Reservation. You are then asked to supply a reservation name (usually the host name), the IP address to be allocated, and the **Media Access Control (MAC)** address of the client.

DHCP options allow you to configure a large number of settings on a client. Typically, however, you will configure options 003, 006, and 015: default gateway (router), DNS server, and domain name, respectively. You can define options at the server level for all scopes, at the scope level for all clients, and at the client level only for client reservations. Client options override scope options for a specific reserved client, and scope options override server options for a specific scope.

If your DHCP server services two network segments, you must set up a DHCP relay agent unless the router connecting the two subnets is RFC 2123–compliant and is already configured to pass DHCP broadcasts. Servers running the Microsoft Windows Server 2003 Routing And Remote Access service that are configured as routers do not pass DHCP broadcasts; therefore, you need to install DHCP Relay Agent on the router and configure it with the address of the DHCP server from the Routing And Remote Access console. Alternatively, you can install and configure DHCP Relay Agent on a server in the subnet that does not contain the DHCP server. You do not need to install and configure DHCP Relay Agent on a server in the same subnet as the DHCP server, and it will not run on the DHCP server itself. Another situation in which you need to install DHCP Relay Agent is when you have a server running the Routing And Remote

Access service that supports remote access clients, but does not have a DHCP server available on its network segment. Even when the Routing And Remote Access service allocates client addresses from a static pool, you should still install DHCP Relay Agent to enable the remote clients to receive DHCP options.

The Jetpack utility automatically backs up and regularly restores the DHCP database. A new feature in Microsoft Windows Server 2003 DHCP enables you to back up the database and restore it from the DHCP console. In previous Windows operating systems, moving a DHCP database from one server to another involved editing the Registry of the new server. The Network Shell (Netsh) utility now allows you to perform this task without needing either to edit the Registry edits or to recreate the scopes and superscopes.

Only one scope can be active (in other words, can issue leases) on a single physical subnet at any one time. Sometimes, you want to replace a scope with another: for example, if you are converting to a private addressing scheme. In this case, if you create a new scope and simply deactivate the old one, errors will occur and your clients will not obtain new leases. The solution is to put both the old and new scopes in a superscope. You can then deactivate the old scope or add its addresses to the exclusion range of the superscope. Clients are then leased IP addresses from the new scope. Another use of superscopes is when you have two or more logical subnets on the same physical network segment and want the DHCP server to issue leases for clients in both logical subnets.

You can implement DHCP failover protection by having two DHCP servers on the same network issue valid address leases from nonoverlapping scopes. This method is seldom satisfactory, however, and the recommended method is to cluster two DHCP servers. This configuration results in a virtual DHCP server with a single virtual host name and IP address. Which of the two servers is actually issuing leases is transparent to the client.

Paradoxically, failover protection is easier to implement when you have two network segments. You then configure a DHCP server on each segment and create two scopes: one for the local subnet and one for the remote subnet. Approximately 80 percent of the available leases should be contained in the local scope. If no scope overlap exists and the DHCP relay agent is configured to point to both DHCP servers, either server will service both subnets if the other goes down.

1. Fred is the administrator of a Microsoft Windows Server 2003 domain. Francesca, his assistant, also has a Domain Admin account. Fred and Francesca have ordinary user accounts in addition to their administrator accounts. Joe, Jim, Helge, and Anibal are technical support personnel. Active Directory–integrated DNS is used in the domain. Four infrastructure servers in the domain are running such network services as DHCP, Windows Internet Name Service (WINS), Internet Information Services (IIS), and the Routing And Remote Access service. A further six servers provide file and print services. DNS servers are domain controllers and are not considered to be infrastructure servers. Fred wants to achieve the following results:

- Only Fred and Francesca should carry out Active Directory and DNS administration in the context of their administrator accounts.

- Fred, Francesca, Joe, and Jim should be able to administer the organizational units (OUs) that contain the infrastructure servers and the file and print servers in the context of their user accounts.

- Helge and Anibal should be able to administer the OU that contains the file and print servers in the context of their user accounts.

- Helge and Anibal should not be able to administer the OU that contains the infrastructure servers.

Fred takes the following actions:

- He creates a global security group called Server Admins and adds to that group user accounts of Francesca, Joe, Jim, Helge, Anibal, and himself.

- He creates a global security group called Infrastructure Admins and adds to that group the user accounts of Francesca, Joe, and Jim, and himself.

- He creates a high-level OU called Member Servers and moves the computer accounts of the file and print servers into that OU.

- He creates an OU called Infrastructure Servers as a child of Member Servers and moves the computer accounts of the infrastructure servers into that OU.

- He runs the Delegation Of Control Wizard to give the Server Admins group full control of the Member Servers OU.

- He moves the Infrastructure Admins group into the Infrastructure Servers OU.

Which result or results do Fred's actions achieve? (Choose all that apply.)

A. Only Fred and Francesca can carry out Active Directory and DNS administration in the context of their administrator accounts.

    B. Fred, Francesca, Joe, and Jim can administer the OUs that contain the infrastructure servers and the file and print servers in the context of their user accounts.

    C. Helge and Anibal can administer the OU that contains the file and print servers in the context of their user accounts.

    D. Helge and Anibal cannot administer the OU that contains the infrastructure servers.

2. You work for a U.S.-based ISP that is using MADCAP (on a Microsoft Windows Server 2003 DHCP server) to specify public multicast addresses for use on the Internet. You have obtained an Autonomous System (AS) number and registered it with the IANA. Which one of the following configurations represents a valid scope and subnet mask?

    A. AS number: 8069

        Start address: 239.31.133.1

        End address: 239.31.133.254

        Subnet mask: 255.255.255.0

    B. AS number: 8069

        Start address: 233.128.105.1

        End address: 233.128.105.254

        Subnet mask: 255.255.255.0

    C. AS number: 8069

        Start address: 233.31.133.1

        End address: 233.31.133.254

        Subnet mask: 255.255.255.0

    D. AS number: 8069

        Start address: 239.31.133.1

        End address: 239.31.133.126

        Subnet mask: 255.255.255.128

3. You administer a Microsoft Windows Server 2003–based network. Client computers obtain their configuration automatically. The DHCP service is installed on a Microsoft Windows Server 2003, Enterprise Edition computer with a single hard disk. You are concerned about the number of hardware errors on this server and see that disk error messages are increasing in frequency. You decide to transfer the DHCP function to another computer and install Microsoft Windows Server 2003, Enterprise Edition and DHCP on that PC. Which is the most efficient way to transfer the DHCP database?

A. Use third-party disk imaging software such as Ghost.

B. Use the Windows Backup Wizard.

C. Use the Backup and Restore actions in the DHCP console.

D. Use the command-line utility netsh dhcp backup.

4. Your internetwork consists of three subnets, A, B, and C, linked by Routers 1 and 2. Router 1 has an interface 199.160.1.1 on Subnet B and links Subnet B to Subnet A. Router 2 has an interface 199.160.1.2 on Subnet B and links Subnet B to Subnet C. Client computers on Subnet B obtain their IP configurations from a single scope on a DHCP server in that subnet. Subnets A and C are used for resource servers. The following graphic illustrates the internetwork.

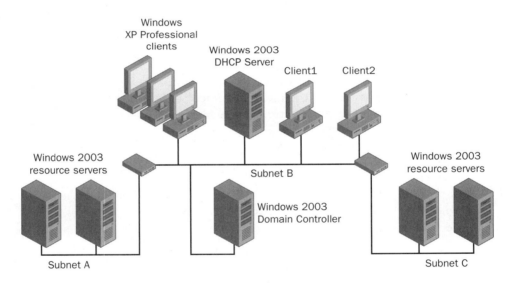

Most of the users on Subnet B access Subnet A regularly and seldom access Subnet C. However, two users mainly access Subnet C and rarely access Subnet A. These users are seated at PCs called Client1 and Client2. How do you set up the DHCP server to ensure fast and efficient access to resources? (Choose all that apply. Each answer forms part of the solution.)

A. Configure DHCP scope option 006, and give it a value of 199.160.1.2.

B. Configure DHCP scope option 003, and give it a value of 199.160.1.2.

C. Configure DHCP scope option 003, and give it a value of 199.160.1.1.

D. Configure DHCP reservations for Client1 and Client2.

E. Configure DHCP option 003 for Client1's reservation, and give it a value of 199.160.1.1.

F. Configure DHCP option 003 for Client2's reservation, and give it a value of 199.160.1.2.

G. Configure DHCP option 003 for Client1's reservation, and give it a value of 199.160.1.2.

H. Configure the Classless Static Route option on Client1 and Client2, and specify a route to Subnet C.

5. You administer a Microsoft Windows Server 2003 domain and have the Microsoft Windows Server 2003 Administration Tools Pack installed on your client PC. Your network does not use private addresses. You have set a long lease time on the DHCP server on your network so that clients normally retain the same configuration and so that broadcast traffic because of DHCP is minimized. As a result, you regularly delete leases issued to clients that are no longer on the network. Which of the following methods can you use to perform this task? (Choose all that apply.)

A. Use the Ipconfig /release utility while logged on at your client PC.

B. Open the DHCP console on your own PC. In the console tree, expand the server that holds the lease, expand the appropriate scope, and click Reservations. In the details pane, right-click the appropriate client and select Delete.

C. Open the DHCP console on your own PC. In the console tree, expand the server that holds the lease, expand the appropriate scope, and click Address Leases. In the details pane, right-click the appropriate lease and select Delete.

D. Open the DHCP console on the DHCP server that has issued the lease. In the console tree, expand that server, expand the appropriate scope, and click Address Leases. In the details pane, right-click the appropriate lease and select Delete.

E. Open a command prompt on the DHCP server that has issued the lease. At the Netsh prompt, switch to the appropriate scope using the dhcp server scope ScopeAddress command. Then, use the dump IPAddress command to remove the lease.

F. Open a command prompt on the DHCP server that has issued the lease and start the Netsh command. At the Netsh prompt, switch to the appropriate scope using the dhcp server scope ScopeAddress command. Then, use the delete lease IPAddress command to remove the lease.

6. You administer a subnet that includes a DHCP server. Currently, a single scope is on the DHCP server that contains the address range 208.147.66.20 through 208.147.66.254, with a 255.255.255.0 subnet mask. You want to migrate to a private addressing scheme and create a new scope that contains the address range 10.0.0.20 through 10.0.1.245, with a 255.255.254.0 subnet mask. You create and activate the new scope, but you discover that clients are still obtaining addresses from the original scope. What should you do next?

    A. Disable the original scope.

    B. Create a superscope. Put both the original and new scopes in the superscope.

    C. Exclude the original scope's range from the new scope's range.

    D. Create a superscope that includes only the original scope.

7.   Your organization's network is shown in the following graphic. Subnet C is a wide area network (WAN) connection. DNS is Active Directory–integrated. All client PCs are configured from scopes held on a superscope on the DHCP server on Subnet A. The routers are not RFC 2132–compliant. Which subnets require a DHCP relay agent? (Choose all that apply.)

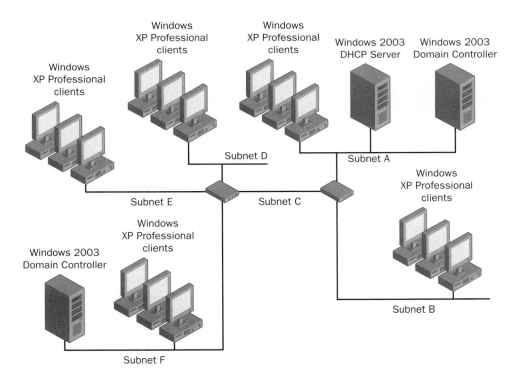

    A. Subnet A

    B. Subnet B

    C. Subnet C

    D. Subnet D

    E. Subnet E

    F. Subnet F

8.   You want to create four logical subnets (multinets) on the same physical network segment. You have a Microsoft Windows Server 2003 DHCP on the subnet. The first logical subnet uses the range 10.1.1.1 through 10.1.1.254, the second logical subnet uses the range 10.1.2.1 through 10.1.2.254, the third logical subnet uses the range 10.1.3.1 through 10.1.3.254, and the fourth logical subnet uses the range 10.1.4.1 through 10.1.4.254. How should you set up these ranges on the DHCP server?

  A. Set up a superscope that contains member scopes for all four ranges.

  B. Create four separate scopes and activate all of them.

  C. Put all four address ranges in a single scope.

  D. Place each scope in its own superscope.

9.   You install a new DNS server on the Microsoft Windows Server 2003 domain that you administer and configure it as the authoritative server for your standard primary DNS zone. On the DHCP server, you reconfigure scope option 006 to specify the new DNS server. You release and renew the leases on all client PCs, then check their configurations using Ipconfig /all. All the clients except two are configured to use the new DNS server. On the two clients that are still set up to use the old DNS server, you check the TCP/IP properties on the LAN interfaces, but both are configured to obtain a DHCP address automatically. What should you do next?

  A. Reconfigure server option 006.

  B. Issue the Ipconfig /flushdns command on the two misconfigured clients.

  C. Set up the two PCs for manual configuration of the DNS server address and enter the IP address of the new DNS server.

  D. Reconfigure reserved client option 006 on the two misconfigured clients, and then release and renew their DHCP leases.

Objective 1.2 Answers

1. **Correct Answers: A, B, and C**

   A. Correct: Fred has not delegated control of the domain controllers OU. Only Fred and Francesca have administrator accounts and can administer domain controllers. All DNS servers are domain controllers.

   B. Correct: Control of the Member Servers OU has been delegated to the Server Admins group, of which Fred, Francesca, Joe, and Jim are members. Because the Infrastructure Servers OU is a child of the Member Servers OU, control of that OU is delegated by default to the Server Admins group.

   C. Correct: As members of the Server Admins group, Helge and Anibal have full control of the Member Servers OU.

   D. Incorrect: By default, delegating control of the Member Servers OU to the Server Admins group also delegates control to all child OUs. Helge and Anibal therefore have full control of the Infrastructure Servers OU. Placing the Infrastructure Admins group in this OU makes no difference to the permissions set on it. Instead, Fred should have run the Delegation Of Control Wizard so that the Infrastructure Admins group has full control of the Infrastructure Servers OU rather than the Server Admins group.

2. **Correct Answers: C**

   A. Incorrect: Multicast addresses starting with 239 should be used on a private intranet (administrative scoping). In this case, an AS number is not required.

   B. Incorrect: The American Registry for Internet Numbers normally issues numbers in decimal form. Because there is no indication that the AS number given is hexadecimal, it must be assumed to be decimal.

   C. Correct: Multicast scopes are supported through the use of MADCAP. Creating a scope for use on the intranet is known as *global scoping*. The 233.0.0.0 range of the Class D address space is recommended for global scoping. When this range is used, the second and third octets are based on an assigned AS number. (In the US, for example, access *http://www.arin.net/intro.html*.) The AS number is recorded with the IANA registry for your region. The final octet is for local use, and a /24 (255.255.255.0) subnet mask should be applied.

   D. Incorrect: Multicast addresses starting with 239 should be used on a private intranet (administrative scoping). In this case, an AS number is not required.

3.   Correct Answers: C

A. Incorrect: Third-party imaging software is not the preferred method of transferring data from one Microsoft Windows Server 2003 computer to another.

B. Incorrect: You can back up data on one PC and restore it to another. This solution, however, is not particularly suitable for the DHCP database and would require additional administrative effort.

C. Correct: This feature is new in Microsoft Windows Server 2003. It is the recommended method of performing a manual DHCP database backup. The database can then be restored on the original computer or transferred to another computer.

D. Incorrect: You can use the Netsh utility to back up the DHCP database; however, the correct command is Netsh dhcp server dump.

4.   Correct Answers: D, F, and G

A. Incorrect: Option 006 specifies the IP address of the DNS server. The question does not specify any DNS settings.

B. Incorrect: Most of the users on Subnet B access Subnet A regularly, and they should therefore have their default gateways configured with the interface of Router 1, which is 199.160.1.1, not 199.160.1.2.

C. Correct: Most of the users on Subnet B access Subnet A regularly. This setting configures their default gateways with the interface of Router 1, 199.160.1.1.

D. Correct: Client1 and Client2 should have a default gateway that differs from that of the other client PCs on the subnet. You can give them reserved IP addresses and then set DHCP client options for these reservations.

E. Incorrect: Client1 accesses Subnet C regularly. Client1's default gateway should therefore be 199.160.1.2.

F. Correct: Client2 accesses Subnet C regularly. This setting correctly specifies Client2's default gateway as 199.160.1.2.

G. Correct: Client1 accesses Subnet C regularly. This setting correctly specifies Client1's default gateway as 199.160.1.2.

H. Incorrect: The Classless Static Route DHCP option is new to Microsoft Windows Server 2003. Virtual private network (VPN) clients can request this option so that they can perform split tunneling when connecting to remote networks. Local area network (LAN) clients can also request the Classless Static Route DHCP option to obtain additional routing information. However, in this scenario the requirement is to specify the correct default gateways for efficient resource access rather than to add additional routes.

5.   **Correct Answers: C, D, and F**

    A. Incorrect: The Ipconfig /release utility deletes the DHCP lease of the PC on which it is run. You do not want to delete the lease on your own client PC. You could use this method on the client whose lease you want to delete, except that this client is no longer on the network.

    B. Incorrect: You want to delete a lease, not a reservation. If a reservation exists for the client, you must delete it also, but that is not what the question asks.

    C. Correct: This method is the standard way of deleting a lease. It works for both Microsoft Windows Server 2000 and Microsoft Windows Server 2003 DHCP servers.

    D. Correct: Although from a security point of view it is preferable to carry out administration tasks from your client PC, this method is a valid way of deleting a lease. You might choose to use this method if (for example) you happen to be in the same room as the DHCP server and your client PC is on another floor of the building.

    E. Incorrect: The dump utility is used at server level to back up a DHCP database. It cannot be used to delete a lease.

    F. Correct: You can use the command Netsh dhcp server scope ScopeAddress delete lease to delete DHCP leases. You can access this utility from the command line, or you can create a script to facilitate this task.

6.   **Correct Answers: B**

    A. Incorrect: If the original scope is disabled, clients that attempt to renew their leases will not obtain the appropriate responses and will not be issued configurations from the new scope.

    B. Correct: When both scopes are in a superscope, you can then deactivate the original scope without generating an error condition. Alternatively, you can exclude the original scope's range from the superscope's range. Clients that attempt to renew their leases will now receive a DHCPNAK broadcast and will request new leases, which the DHCP server provides from the new scope.

    C. Incorrect: The original scope's range is not in the new scope's range and cannot therefore be excluded. You should instead exclude the original scope's range from the superscope's range.

    D. Incorrect: This action changes nothing. The original scope remains activated and continues to issue configuration information.

7.   **Correct Answers: B, D, E, and F**

   A.   **Incorrect:** The DHCP server is on Subnet A. Therefore, this subnet does not require a DHCP relay agent.

   B.   **Correct:** Client computers are on Subnet B and no DHCP server is on the subnet. Therefore, this subnet requires a DHCP relay agent.

   C.   **Incorrect:** No computers are on Subnet C. Therefore, this subnet does not require a DHCP relay agent.

   D.   **Correct:** Client computers are on Subnet D and no DHCP server is on the subnet. Therefore, this subnet requires a DHCP relay agent.

   E.   **Correct:** Client computers are on Subnet E and no DHCP server is on the subnet. Therefore, this subnet requires a DHCP relay agent.

   F.   **Correct:** Client computers are on Subnet F and no DHCP server is on the subnet. Therefore, this subnet requires a DHCP relay agent.

8.   **Correct Answers: A**

   A.   **Correct:** This configuration is a standard use for a superscope. Because all four ranges are in the same superscope, addresses can be leased from each of them.

   B.   **Incorrect:** Only one scope on a DHCP server can actively assign leases on a single physical subnet. To have all four scopes assigning leases, you need to put them in a superscope.

   C.   **Incorrect:** You cannot define multiple ranges on a standard DHCP scope.

   D.   **Incorrect:** This action will have no effect. Only one superscope can actively assign leases on a single physical subnet, so the situation is identical to having four separate scopes.

9.   **Correct Answers: D**

   A.   **Incorrect:** Server options allow you to set up configuration options for all the scopes on the DHCP server. Scope options override server options, and scope option 006 is already configured.

   B.   **Incorrect:** This action flushes the DNS cache. It has no effect on the primary DNS server address configured for the two PCs.

   C.   **Incorrect:** This action would solve the immediate problem, but it is bad practice. If the IP address of the DNS server were to change again, the two PCs would have to be reconfigured, creating unnecessary work.

   D.   **Correct:** This problem exists because the two clients have DHCP reservations, and option 006 is configured for the client reservations. Because client options override scope options, reconfiguring scope option 006 has no effect on these two clients.

Objective 1.3
Troubleshoot TCP/IP Addressing

Static IP addressing is an error-prone procedure, and the techniques for debugging errors such as duplicate IP addresses, mistyped IP addresses, incorrect subnet masks, and incorrect default gateways are well known. The Ipconfig command-line utility displays TCP/IP configuration information, whereas Tracert addresses the problem of packet loss in a large network. The Ping command-line utility determines whether a specified IP address is reachable. The PathPing utility, introduced in Microsoft Windows 2000, combines the functions of Ping and Tracert. The Netdiag utility, also introduced in Microsoft Windows 2000, is a powerful Support Tool that can locate a wide range of network configuration faults and sometimes automatically fix them.

The use of DHCP dramatically reduces the number of TCP/IP configuration faults that occur on a network. It is much easier to diagnose a bad configuration on a single DHCP server than on several hundred clients. However, the use of DHCP can introduce its own problems. A DHCP server might be set up perfectly, but bad configurations can occur because a scope has issued all its leases, because the server is offline, or because the DHCP service has been stopped. In this case, Microsoft Windows 2000, Microsoft Windows XP, and Microsoft Windows Server 2003 clients (by default) configure themselves with APIPA addresses. Microsoft Windows 98 and Microsoft Windows NT 4 clients disable TCP/IP networking.

If clients are on a network that cannot be or should not be configured automatically, the static addresses of these clients must be excluded from the DHCP scope. If this is not done, duplicate IP addresses can manifest on the network. A common scenario is that a client that has been in for repair or that has been sitting in a storeroom for a while is plugged back in to the network without the administrator's knowledge and has a nonexcluded static IP address. DHCP can be set up so that it tests for duplicate addresses and does not issue a lease if that address is detected on the network. However, this fix is only temporary. The long-term solution is to find the client that is causing the problem and reconfigure it.

Another problem occurs when a client is correctly configured with an IP address but it cannot access resources by host name. This problem happens when the client is configured statically with the wrong DNS server address, or when the client has a reservation and client option 006 is misconfigured.

Objective 1.3 Questions

1. You are the administrator of an internetwork that consists of two network segments, A and B, connected by a router. The network has been configured so that clients on both network segments obtain their IP configuration automatically from a DHCP server on Subnet B. A new client computer is installed on network segment A. You configure it in the same way as the others. The new client computer cannot communicate with any of the computers on either network. You use the Ipconfig command and determine that the client computer has no default gateway configured. All other computers are operating normally. You determine that the DHCP server is connected to network segment B and the DHCP service is running. What should you do next?

    A. Check the number of addresses currently leased on the DHCP server.

    B. Enable the router to pass Boot Protocol (BOOTP) broadcasts.

    C. Configure one of the servers on Subnet A as a DHCP relay agent.

    D. Check that scope option 003 is correctly configured on the DHCP server.

2. Your company employs a number of traveling salespersons who access your Microsoft Windows Server 2003 intranet through dial-up connections from their laptop computers running Microsoft Windows XP Professional, which are set up to obtain their IP configurations automatically. They report that although they can log in, they cannot access resources on the intranet by specifying names of servers. You test a laptop in the office by docking it directly into the intranet, and it works perfectly. What should you do to resolve this problem?

    A. Configure an Internet Protocol Security (IPSec) policy that requires IPSec encryption for all remote access communication.

    B. Enable dial-back security.

    C. Configure all the laptops statically.

    D. Set up the Routing And Remote Access service as a DHCP relay agent.

3. All client PCs on your network obtain their IP configurations from a DHCP server on the same subnet. A user reports that she rebooted her PC, which had been powered down while she was on vacation, and it is no longer working properly. You log on the PC as the local administrator and use the Ipconfig command-line utility. The PC has an IP address of 169.254.65.10 with a 255.255.0.0 subnet mask. Which of the following could have caused this problem? (Choose all that apply).

    A. The DHCP server is powered down.

    B. The cable has become disconnected from the client's NIC.

    C. All addresses in the DHCP scope have been leased to other clients.

    D. The cable has become disconnected from the DHCP server's NIC.

    E. APIPA has not been disabled on the client PC.

4. Your organization has a number of locations spread throughout the United States. You are the New York administrator. All client machines on your network obtain their configurations through DHCP and are operating correctly. An employee from Seattle visits your New York office and brings his laptop computer running Microsoft Windows XP Professional. He connects his internal NIC to a hub on the New York network. You have set up a user account for the visitor and he logs on successfully.

He can ping all the other computers on the network by IP address but not by host name, and he cannot access resources on your servers by specifying the server name. How should you reconfigure his computer?

    A. Install NetBEUI on his PC.

    B. Configure a DHCP reservation for his PC.

    C. Configure TCP/IP on his LAN interface to obtain the address of a DNS server automatically.

    D. Add the host names and IP addresses of the New York servers to the laptop's Hosts file.

5. You are a network administrator in a large international organization. Your company has a large intranet with many routers and WAN connections. Speed of communication is important in the organization, and the WAN links are over dedicated high-bandwidth lines. The routers are modern high-end devices, and all servers are either Microsoft Windows 2000 Advanced Server or Microsoft Windows Server 2003, Enterprise Edition. TCP/IP is the only protocol stack used in the company network. Employees report unacceptable delays in accessing resources on an internal Web server. The fully qualified domain name (FQDN) of the Web server is resources.chicago.worldtraders.corp. You are based in Los Angeles. How can you test the connection between Los Angeles and Chicago and determine where the delays are occurring?

    A. Open a command prompt and execute the command PathPing resources.chicago.worldtraders.corp.

    B. Open a command prompt and execute the command Ping –f resources.chicago.worldtraders.corp.

    C. Open a command prompt and execute the command Tracert –d resources.chicago.worldtraders.corp.

    D. Open a command prompt and execute the command Netstat –s –p ip.

6. You are the network administrator in a school. The school network is organized as a single Microsoft Windows Server 2003 Active Directory domain. Private IP addressing is used and all the classrooms are configured as separate subnets. All client PCs run Microsoft Windows XP Professional and are configured to obtain their IP addresses automatically. They are all powered down at night. On the Monday morning after spring break, you are informed that the PCs in one classroom cannot communicate with the rest of the school. You go to the classroom and find that the connection to the router has been pulled out. You plug it back in. Some of the classroom PCs still cannot communicate with the rest of the school network, whereas others can. You are extremely busy. Which action do you take to resolve the problem with the minimum of administrative effort?

    A. Issue Ipconfig /release and then Ipconfig /renew on the PCs that can't communicate with the rest of the network.

    B. Reboot all the PCs.

    C. Do nothing.

    D. Stop and restart the DHCP service.

7. You have inherited a network in a somewhat chaotic condition. IP addresses are statically configured and bear no relation to the physical topology of the network. PCs are scattered, seemingly at random, throughout an old and rambling building. You upgrade the Microsoft Windows NT 4 primary domain controller (PDC) and backup domain controllers (BDCs) to Microsoft Windows Server 2003 DCs, and also upgrade the member servers to Microsoft Windows Server 2003, Enterprise Edition. You set the clients (where possible) to obtain their IP configurations automatically, install DHCP on a member server, and configure a scope that excludes the addresses that are configured statically. The improvements are not as dramatic as you expected. You are still getting errors. What can you do immediately to significantly reduce the scale of the problem? (Choose all that apply.)

    A. Reconcile the DHCP database.

    B. Add client reservations for the clients that cannot be configured automatically.

    C. Enable address conflict resolution.

    D. Increase the lease duration.

Objective 1.3 Answers

1. **Correct Answers: A**

    A. Correct: Because no gateway exists and the new client cannot connect to any other computers on either subnet, it has likely been configured by APIPA. Because the DHCP server is on the network and the DHCP service is running, the new client probably cannot obtain a configuration through DHCP because all the addresses in the scope have been allocated. If a lease can be deleted because the computer to which it is assigned is no longer on the network, or if the size of the DHCP scope can be increased, the error will be resolved automatically in 5 minutes or less. If immediate reconfiguration is required, you can issue the Ipconfig /release and Ipconfig /renew commands on the new client.

    B. Incorrect: Either the router is already BOOTP-enabled or a server in Subnet A is configured as a DHCP relay agent. Otherwise, the other client computers on Subnet A would not have obtained configurations from the DHCP server.

    C. Incorrect: Either a server in Subnet A is already configured as a DHCP relay agent or the router is BOOTP-enabled. Otherwise, the other client computers on Subnet A would not have obtained configurations from the DHCP server.

    D. Incorrect: If this option were incorrectly configured, none of the clients on Subnet A would have been configured with the correct default gateway.

2. **Correct Answers: D**

    A. Incorrect: The ability to access resources by server name has nothing to do with encryption.

    B. Incorrect: Dial-back security requires that the Remote Access Service breaks the connection once the user has been authenticated and then dials back using a predefined telephone number. This arrangement will not solve the problem of accessing servers by name, and in any case, this solution is impractical when the users are traveling salespersons who might be dialing from one of a number of locations.

    C. Incorrect: The laptops are obtaining valid IP addresses, subnet masks, and default gateways; otherwise, the salespersons could not connect to the Routing And Remote Access service and access the intranet. The problem is that the laptops cannot resolve the names of the servers on the intranet IP addresses. Although static IP configuration, including configuration of the DNS server address, would solve this problem, it is usually impractical in this situation, is error prone, and would involve a great deal of administrative effort.

D. Correct: The laptops are obtaining IP address, subnet mask, and default gateway configuration from the Routing And Remote Access service. They are not, however, receiving other DHCP options, such as option 006, DNS Server. As a result, they cannot access DNS to resolve server host names to IP addresses. Configuring the Routing And Remote Access service as a DHCP relay agent solves this problem.

3.   Correct Answers: A, C, and D

A. Correct: The client has obtained an IP address through APIPA. This problem occurs when the DHCP server cannot provide a configuration: it is powered down, it is disconnected from the network, the DHCP service is stopped, or all IP addresses in its scope have been leased.

B. Incorrect: In this case, the Ipconfig utility returns the response Media State: Cable Disconnected.

C. Correct: The client has obtained an IP address through APIPA. This problem occurs when the DHCP server cannot provide a configuration: it is powered down, it is disconnected from the network, the DHCP service is stopped, or all IP addresses in its scope have been leased.

D. Correct: The client has obtained an IP address through APIPA. This problem occurs when the DHCP server cannot provide a configuration: it is powered down, it is disconnected from the network, the DHCP service is stopped, or all IP addresses in its scope have been leased.

E. Incorrect: If a client is set up to obtain an address automatically and its DHCP lease has expired (or it has never obtained one), it sends a DHCPDiscover broadcast to attempt to locate a DHCP server. If no server can be located, by default, it programs itself through APIPA. APIPA can be disabled, but then the PC would configure itself with the IP address of 0.0.0.0 rather than with an address from the APIPA range.

4.   Correct Answers: C

A. Incorrect: NetBEUI cannot be installed on a computer running Microsoft Windows XP Professional.

B. Incorrect: The laptop is already correctly configured with an IP address and subnet mask. Otherwise, it would not be possible to ping the other computers on the network.

C. Correct: The laptop is obtaining its IP address automatically but is not obtaining the correct address for the New York DNS server. It is thus unable to obtain hostname-to-IP-address resolution. This problem cannot be caused by incorrect configuration of the New York DHCP server because all your clients are operating correctly. The visitor's laptop must therefore be statically configured to point to the Seattle DNS server rather than to obtain the address of a DHCP server automatically.

D. Incorrect: This solution would enable your visitor to access servers by host name, but it would involve excessive administrative effort.

5. **Correct Answers: A and C**

   A. Correct: The PathPing utility traces the route taken through the network and returns time-delay statistics for each hop. Because several routes probably exist from Los Angeles to Chicago, multiple PathPings should be sent. PathPing is not infallible because it might indicate a nonexistent delay in a fast-track router. Nevertheless, if the same router is identified as a problem over several paths, a problem probably exists with that router.

   B. Incorrect: The Ping utility will test whether a route exists to resources.chicago.worldtraders.corp. It will not return time-delay statistics for each hop. The –f flag will prevent the ping packet from being fragmented, which is not relevant in this scenario.

   C. Correct: The Tracert utility traces the path through the network. It does not give as much detail as PathPing, but it is a valid method of solving the problem that is described in the scenario. The –d flag speeds up Tracert operation considerably, but at the cost of not resolving IP addresses to host names.

   D. Incorrect: This solution displays the number of IP packets received and the number of errors detected. Although it can indicate a packet delivery problem, it does not show where in the network this problem is happening.

6. **Correct Answers: C**

   A. Incorrect: This solution will work, but it will use up your valuable time.

   B. Incorrect: This solution will work, but there's an even easier option.

   C. Correct: The DHCP lease has expired on some of the PCs. Because the subnet was physically disconnected from the rest of the school network, these PCs have not been able to obtain a lease and have configured themselves through APIPA. Clients configured with APIPA broadcast for a DHCP server every 5 minutes. Now that the subnet is reconnected, they will find one.

   D. Incorrect: Not only will this solution not solve the problem, but it will also involve unnecessary administrative effort.

7. **Correct Answers: C and D**

   A. Incorrect: This solution identifies and repairs inconsistencies in the DHCP database. It does not solve IP configuration problems.

   B. Incorrect: A client reservation ensures that a specific client always obtains the same IP address from the DHCP server. Clients that cannot obtain their addresses automatically cannot be configured through DHCP, so you needn't create reservations for them.

C. **Correct:** In the DHCP console, access the server's properties, select the Advanced tab, and specify a value greater than 0 in the Conflict Detection Attempts box. Do not specify a number greater than 2 because this will adversely affect the DHCP server's performance. The most likely problem with the network described is that you have failed to locate statically configured clients and have not excluded their IP addresses from the scope. Conflict detection is not a perfect solution because the PC that is causing the problem could be powered down when the duplicate address is leased. However, enabling conflict detection reduces errors while you search for the statically configured client that you missed.

D. **Correct:** This solution reduces the frequency with which new leases are issued and, hence, the frequency of possible conflicts with undiscovered static addresses. It will not solve the problem but will lessen its effect while you search for the statically configured client that you missed.

Troubleshoot DHCP

Clients can have network connectivity problems for a variety of reasons. Sometimes these problems occur because of no particular configuration fault, for example, when a scope runs out of leases. Sometimes they occur because of misconfiguration in the client itself, such as an incorrect static DNS server address configuration. And sometimes they occur because of misconfiguration of a server other than the DHCP server, for example, an incorrectly configured DHCP relay agent on the router.

Sometimes, however, the fault is in the DHCP server itself. Options might be configured at the wrong level. A scope for a second subnet could be added, but option 003 is set at the server level and specifies the local default gateway. As a result, clients on the second subnet get a default gateway that isn't on their subnet and will not be able to ping clients on the first subnet.

When a DHCP server is installed and configured in an Active Directory domain, it needs to be authorized in Active Directory. This process usually happens automatically for the first server. Consequently, you are likely to forget to perform this task for the second server. Alternatively, the second server might not be authorized because of overlapping scopes, for example. An unauthorized (or rogue) server will not issue leases.

Options are sometimes set at incorrect levels. Where different options apply to different scopes, they should be set at the scope level. Where they apply to all the scopes in the server, they should be set at the server level. Sometimes, options are set at the client reservation level, and it is easy to forget to update them if, for example, the IP address of a primary DNS server changes.

DHCP databases sometimes need to be reconciled. The integrity of the database can become compromised, possibly by a hardware or system glitch. Fortunately, reconciling a database at either the server or scope level is a straightforward operation, and you can initiate it either from the DHCP console or by using the Netsh utility.

Sometimes errors in DHCP configuration result in DNS errors rather than DHCP errors. DHCP controls how DNS resource records are dynamically registered and deleted when leases expire. A DHCP server that has been removed from the DNSUpdateProxy group can cause problems when DNS clients are set up to register their own host A resource records. The DNS tab of the server properties dialog box in the DHCP console looks deceptively simple, but misconfiguration here can have serious effects. You must understand the exact effect each check box and option has.

Finally, tools are available for diagnosing DHCP server operation. Neither the DHCP server audit log nor the system error log can be described as intuitive or user-friendly, but they are exceptionally useful for diagnosing DHCP problems.

Objective 1.4 Questions

1. You have a Microsoft Windows Server 2003, Enterprise Edition computer running the DHCP service. It is configured to supply IP configurations from the scope 192.168.1.20 through 192.168.1.254 with no exclusions. The subnet mask is 255.255.255.0. Scope option 003 is set up as 192.168.1.1. Scope option 006 is set up as 192.169.1.10. Scope option 015 is set up as valeriesviolins.com. You are concerned about failover protection for your DHCP service. You install DHCP on a second Microsoft Windows Server 2003, Enterprise Edition computer. You configure the scope as 192.168.1.128 through 192.168.1.254. You configure the same scope options as on the original DHCP server.

When you have configured the second server, you notice a red arrow beside the server name in the DHCP console. You right-click the server name and select Authorize. The hourglass symbol appears, but the arrow does not turn green. What is the problem?

A. You cannot have two DHCP servers on the same network with the same scope option 003 setting.

B. The scopes overlap.

C. A superscope that contains both scopes is required on both DHCP servers.

D. You have two DHCP servers on the same network with the same scope option 006 setting.

2. You are the domain administrator for tailspintoys.com. Client computers on your main office subnet and your several branch office subnets all obtain their IP configuration from a Microsoft Windows Server 2003 DHCP server in your main office. You decide to install DHCP in a branch office that has 30 users on its own subnet. You exclude the range for that subnet in the superscope on your main office DHCP server. You install the DHCP service on a Microsoft Windows Server 2003 computer at the branch office and create a scope for the local computers. To ensure that you do not receive DHCP configuration information from your main office, you disable User Datagram Protocol (UDP) port 67 on the router in your branch office.

Users in your branch office report that they are no longer receiving DHCP leases. You inspect the DHCP audit log and obtain the following result:

ID, Date, Time, Description, IP Address, Host Name, MAC Address

00, 6/12/03, 11:10:40, Started,,,,

54, 6/12/03, 11:10:42, Authorization failure, stopped servicing,, tailspintoys.com,,

What should you do next?

    A. Disable TCP port 67 on the router instead of UDP port 67.

    B. Use the Jetpack utility.

    C. Issue the Ipconfig /release and Ipconfig /renew commands.

    D. Authorize the DHCP server in Active Directory.

3. You are the network administrator for a company whose intranet is organized as a single domain. Active Directory-integrated DNS is configured and you can ping any computer on the intranet by host name. The company has a main office and one branch office. Both offices are cabled as single subnets. DHCP is set up on a Microsoft Windows Server 2003, Enterprise Edition cluster in the main office, and all client computers in the main office and suboffices are configured from the appropriate scopes in a superscope. They all obtain valid IP addresses, subnet masks, default gateways, and DNS server information. All client PC operating systems are Microsoft Windows XP Professional.

The only problem in the network is that the supply of available leases sometimes becomes exhausted. This problem can happen in both the main office and branch office scopes. You have suggested using a private numbering scheme, but management has rejected this approach. A lot of work can be done offline, and management does not perceive the occasional client PC powering up offline to be a problem.

However, the client PCs used by senior management at the head office and by the branch manager must always be online when required. The managers do not care which IP addresses are configured on their PCs, but these addresses must allow them to access the intranet. You have a list of the host names of the PCs used by the managers. Currently, all of these PCs have valid leases.

You want to accomplish the following:

    ■ The senior managers' PCs will always be configured with IP addresses that allow them to access the Internet.

    ■ The branch manager's PC will always be configured with an IP address that will allow it to access the Internet.

    ■ All managers will be able to obtain a DHCP lease even when the supply of leases is exhausted.

    ■ DHCP leases issued to the managers' PCs will include the same DNS server and default gateway configurations that they do at present.

You carry out the following tasks for each PC on your list:

- You use the Arp –d command to clear the ARP cache on your own Microsoft Windows XP computer (on which the Microsoft Windows Server 2003 Administration Tools Pack is installed).

- You ping the PC by host name and note its IP address.

- You use the Arp –a command to determine the MAC address.

- You open the DHCP console, expand the virtual server name, expand the superscope, and expand the scope that contains the IP address you have noted.

- You right-click Reservations and create a reservation using the host name and the IP and MAC addresses you have noted.

Which of the following objectives have you accomplished? (Choose all that apply.)

A. The senior managers' PCs will always be configured with IP addresses that allow them to access the Internet.

B. The branch manager's PC will always be configured with an IP address that will allow it to access the Internet.

C. All managers can obtain a DHCP lease even when all available leases have been allocated.

D. DHCP leases issued to the managers' PCs include the same DNS server and default gateway configurations that they do at present.

4. The DHCP service in your network appears to be working correctly, but events 1010, 1014, and 1016 appear regularly on your DHCP server's System event log. What is the most appropriate tool for diagnosing these errors?

A. The DHCP Administration Tool

B. Netdiag

C. The Jetpack utility

D. Microsoft Network Monitor

5. You administer a Microsoft Windows Server 2003 domain. All client PCs run either Microsoft Windows 2000 Professional or Microsoft Windows XP Professional. DNS dynamic update is enabled for both forward and reverse lookup zones. All client computers are configured with their default dynamic update options. However, dynamic updates are not working as expected and you suspect that the DHCP server is incorrectly configured. You want to ensure that DHCP permits clients to use their default dynamic update options for DNS. In addition, you want DHCP to remove host A resource records from the DNS database when leases expire. You open the DHCP console, right-click the appropriate server, and click Properties. You want to enable only those options that are relevant to your requirements. How should you configure the DHCP server? (Choose all that apply. Each answer forms part of the solution.)

A. Access the Advanced tab in the server properties dialog box.

B. Access the DNS tab in the server properties dialog box.

C. Ensure that the Dynamically Update DNS A And PTR Records Only If Requested By The DHCP Clients check box is selected.

D. Ensure that the Enable Dynamic Updates According To The Settings Below check box is cleared.

E. Ensure that Always Dynamically Update DNS A And PTR Records is selected.

F. Ensure that the Discard Forward (Name To Address) Lookups When Leases Expire check box is selected.

G. Ensure that the Discard Forward (Name To Address) Lookups When Leases Expire check box is selected.

H. Ensure that the Enable DNS Dynamic Updates For DNS Clients That Do Not Request Updates (for example, clients running NT 4.0) check box is selected.

6. You suspect that the database has become inconsistent on one of the scopes in your DHCP database. Which tool or tools can you use to check database integrity and reconcile the database for that scope? (Choose all that apply.)

A. The DHCP Administration Tool

B. Netdiag

C. The Nbtstat command-line utility

D. The Netsh command-line tool

7. Your network consists of two subnets, Subnet A and Subnet B, which are connected by a multihomed Microsoft Windows Server 2003, Enterprise Edition computer configured as a router. All your domain controllers and resource servers are installed on Subnet A. Subnet A also contains a number of Microsoft Windows XP Professional client computers. Apart from the router connection, no servers are on Subnet B. This subnet contains a mixture of Microsoft Windows 98, Microsoft Windows NT 4 Workstation, Microsoft Windows 2000 Professional, and Microsoft Windows XP Professional clients.

You install the DHCP service on a Microsoft Windows Server 2003, Enterprise Edition computer on Subnet A. You create a scope for Subnet A and exclude the IP addresses of the statically configured servers. You create a scope for Subnet B and exclude the IP address of its router connection. You set up scope options 003 and 006 for both scopes as appropriate. You place both scopes in a superscope.

You set up all client computers to obtain their IP configurations and DNS server addresses automatically. You install and configure DHCP Relay Agent on the router. Finally, you ensure that the DHCP server is authorized and activate both scopes.

All the clients on Subnet A can connect to the servers and can ping each other by host name or IP address. They can ping Subnet B's router gateway. They cannot ping any of the clients on Subnet B by host name or by IP address.

On Subnet B, all the Microsoft Windows 2000 and Microsoft Windows XP clients have IP addresses and can ping each other using these addresses. They cannot ping each other by host name. They cannot ping either router gateway or access Subnet A. The Microsoft Windows 95 and Microsoft Windows NT 4 clients are all configured with an IP address of 0.0.0.0 and are off the network.

What is the most likely cause of the problem?

A. DHCP Relay Agent should be installed on the DHCP server.

B. The Microsoft Windows Server 2003 DHCP service cannot issue leases to a network that includes legacy clients.

C. The DHCP server is a rogue server.

D. DHCP Relay Agent is incorrectly configured.

8. You administer an Active Directory domain in which all servers are Microsoft Windows Server 2003, but some client computers use legacy operating systems such as Microsoft Windows 98 and Microsoft Windows NT 4 Workstation. To take advantage of dynamic DNS, you have configured your Microsoft Windows Server 2003 DHCP server to always update DNS. You apply for and obtain money to upgrade all the clients to Microsoft Windows XP Professional.

When all clients have been upgraded, you reconfigure DHCP to update DNS only if the DHCP client requests. You find that the clients' A resource records are not updated in DNS when they obtain new DHCP leases. What is the most likely cause of the problem?

A. DNS is not Active Directory–integrated.

B. The DHCP server is not authorized in Active Directory.

C. The DHCP server's computer account is not a member of the DNSUpdateProxy global security group.

D. The clients are not configured to update their own host A resource records.

9. Your Microsoft Windows Server 2003 DHCP server is on Subnet A (10.0.10.0/25), as are two Microsoft Windows Server 2003 domain controllers DC1 and DC2, and various resource servers. The same subnet also contains XP Professional clients. Subnet B (10.0.10.128/25) is connected to Subnet A by a server running the Microsoft Windows Server 2003 Routing And Remote Access service configured as a router. DHCP Relay Agent is set up correctly to point to the DHCP server address. Subnet B contains only XP Professional clients. DNS is Active Directory–integrated and DHCP option 006 is configured to point to DC1. Option 003 is set at scope level so that the clients on each subnet obtain the correct default gateway addresses.

Two clients, Client003 and Client016, on Subnet A have DHCP reservations. Because they access the servers frequently by host name, client option 006 on Client003's reservation specifies DC2, whereas Client016 is configured with a static DNS server address, which is also the address of DC2.

Clients on Subnet B report logon delays. To solve this problem, you move DC2 to Subnet 2 and reconfigure its IP address and default gateway. You ensure that DC2 specifies itself as its own primary DNS server, and you amend Client016's configuration so that the new IP address of DC2 is set as Client016's DNS server address. On Client003, you run the command-line utility Ipconfig /flushdns. You set scope option 006 for the Subnet B scope to point to the new address of DC2. What are the effects of these changes? (Choose all that apply.)

A. All clients on Subnet B access DC2 the next time they require name resolution.

B. All clients on Subnet A access DC1 for name resolution.

C. Client016 can ping Client003 by host name.

D. Client003 can ping Client016 by host name.

Objective 1.4 Answers

1. **Correct Answers: B**

   A. Incorrect: Scope option 003 specifies the default gateway. You can specify the same default gateway for two separate scopes on two separate servers.

   B. Correct: Two DHCP servers cannot provide the same IP address on the same subnet. Otherwise, two PCs on that subnet could be configured with the same IP address. The second DHCP server identifies the overlap and classifies itself as a rogue server. It will therefore not be authorized in Active Directory. Failover protection for DHCP is provided by clustering or by configuring DHCP servers (usually on different subnets) with nonoverlapping scopes.

   C. Incorrect: A superscope is not required in this situation. Also, a superscope cannot contain overlapping scopes.

   D. Incorrect: Scope option 006 specifies the DNS server address. You can specify the same DNS server address for two separate scopes on two separate servers.

2. **Correct Answers: D**

   A. Incorrect: UDP port 67 passes DHCP broadcast traffic.

   B. Incorrect: Jetpack is a Microsoft Windows Server 2003 utility that is used to manage database files such as the WINS and DHCP databases. The DHCP audit log does not indicate any database problems.

   C. Incorrect: Because the clients cannot obtain leases, releasing and renewing the leases on the clients will have no effect.

   D. Correct: New DHCP servers in a Microsoft Windows Server 2003 domain need to be authorized in Active Directory. This process ensures that rogue servers with scopes that overlap other DHCP servers in the domain will not be able to issue leases. The DHCP audit log indicates that this DHCP server has not been authorized.

3. **Correct Answers: A and D**

   A. Correct: Reservations have been set up correctly for senior managers' PCs, all of which are in the main office and therefore on the same subnet as your PC. As a result, senior managers' PCs will retain the IP addresses with which they are currently configured and will be able to access the Internet.

   B. Incorrect: The reservation has not been set up correctly for the branch manager's PC. Because the branch manager's PC is on another subnet, the MAC address you obtained from your ARP cache will be the address of the default gateway on the main office subnet. The branch manager's PC could therefore be configured with an IP address other than the one with which it is currently configured. If no leases are available, then the branch manager's PC will be configured through APIPA and will not be able to access the Internet.

C. **Incorrect:** The senior managers have reservations and will be able to obtain their reserved leases even when the available leases for nonreserved clients have all been allocated. However, the branch manager does not have a valid reservation and cannot obtain a lease if all leases in the branch office scope have been allocated.

D. **Correct:** You have not configured any client options for the reservations. Therefore, by default the reserved clients will be configured using the scope options, which have not been changed.

4.   Correct Answers: C

A. **Incorrect:** You can use the DHCP Administration Tool (or DHCP console) to reconcile the DHCP database, either for a single scope or for all scopes on a server. This tool identifies and repairs any inconsistencies. However, the errors recorded do not indicate unreconciled IP addresses, but rather buffer allocation or database identity problems.

B. **Incorrect:** Netdiag is a Microsoft Windows Server 2003 Support Tool. It can check a host computer's network configuration and fix simple DNS problems. It cannot, however, diagnose and repair DHCP database problems.

C. **Correct:** You can use the Jetpack utility to manage the DHCP database and identify problems. The error codes listed indicate the following:

1010: Invalid database ID

1014: Out of database page buffers

1016: Too many columns in an index

However, the fact that the errors are occurring regularly might indicate that the problem is related to the periodic automatic backup of the DHCP database. Jetpack can indicate the source of the errors.

D. **Incorrect:** This problem is a DHCP database issue that is internal to the DHCP server. Monitoring network traffic to and from the server will not detect the error.

5.   Correct Answers: B, C, F, and G

A. **Incorrect:** DHCP settings for managing dynamic DNS records are on the DNS tab.

B. **Correct:** DHCP settings for managing dynamic DNS records are on the DNS tab.

C. **Correct:** Selecting this check box enables DHCP to update the resource records of clients that are capable of sending DHCP option 81 to the DNS server—that is Microsoft Windows XP Professional and Microsoft Windows 2000 Professional clients—as requested by the client. This results in the DHCP service updating the client's PTR record and the client updating its own host A record. This check box is selected by default.

D. **Incorrect:** If this check box is cleared, DHCP will not supply dynamic update information, and the DHCP client attempts to update host and PTR resource records itself. The check box is selected by default.

E. **Incorrect:** Selecting this option causes the DHCP server to update both host and PTR resource records. This behavior is not the default, nor is it required by the question scenario. The option is cleared by default.

F. **Correct:** If this option is selected, DHCP will discard a client's host A record when the client's DHCP lease expires. This option is selected by default in Microsoft Windows 2003 DHCP.

G. **Correct:** By default, the entity that updates a record also deletes it when the lease expires. Because the DHCP server does not create host resource records for Microsoft Windows 2000 Professional and Microsoft Windows XP Professional clients by default, it will not delete them unless you select this check box. The check box is cleared by default.

H. **Incorrect:** This enables DHCP to update the records of clients that cannot update their own resource records in DNS. This check box is cleared by default. Selecting this check box is not necessary in this scenario, and the question requires that only options relevant to your requirements should be specified.

6. **Correct Answers: A and D**

A. **Correct:** You can use the DHCP Administration Tool (or DHCP console) to reconcile the DHCP database, either for a single scope or for all scopes on a server. In this case, right-click the appropriate scope, click Reconcile, and click Verify. If the database is inconsistent, select the displayed addresses that need to be reconciled and click Reconcile.

B. **Incorrect:** Netdiag is a Microsoft Windows Server 2003 Support Tool. It can check a host computer's network configuration and fix simple DNS problems. It cannot, however, reconcile a DHCP database.

C. **Incorrect:** The Nbtstat command-line utility displays NetBIOS statistics. It cannot reconcile a DHCP database.

D. **Correct:** When set to the proper DHCP scope, the Network shell command Initiate Reconcile checks and reconciles the database for the scope specified.

7. **Correct Answers: D**

  A. **Incorrect:** DHCP Relay Agent should be installed either on a router or on a server on a subnet that contains client PCs but no DHCP server. It should not be installed on a DHCP server.

  B. **Incorrect:** Microsoft Windows Server 2003 DHCP can issue leases to any client that can be set up to obtain its IP configuration automatically. This includes (among others) all the clients on Subnet B.

  C. **Incorrect:** The DHCP server has been authorized in Active Directory and is issuing valid leases to clients on Subnet A. It is not, therefore, a rogue server.

  D. **Correct:** Subnet B is not receiving DHCP leases. As a result, the Microsoft Windows 2000 and Microsoft Windows XP clients are configuring themselves with APIPA addresses while the Microsoft Windows 98 and Microsoft Windows NT 4 clients are configuring themselves with IP address 0.0.0.0. The most likely reason is that DHCP Relay Agent is not configured with the correct address of the DHCP server. In the Routing And Remote Access console on the router, right-click DHCP Relay Agent and click Properties. The IP address of the DHCP server should be specified on the General tab. If it is not, enter the correct address in the Server Address text box and click Add.

8. **Correct Answers: C**

  A. **Incorrect:** Both Active Directory–integrated zones and standard primary DNS zones on Microsoft Windows Server 2003 computers can be configured to update their records dynamically.

  B. **Incorrect:** A DHCP server on an Active Directory domain must be authorized in Active Directory before it can issue leases. In this scenario, the DHCP server has issued leases and must therefore be authorized.

  C. **Correct:** By default, the computer that updates a DNS record owns that record, and no other computer can update it. Because the DHCP server has been updating host A resource records, it owns these records. This problem was not apparent when the DHCP server was updating both A and PTR resource records, but now it has been reconfigured to allow clients to update their own host resource records. The clients cannot perform this task because the DHCP server owns the records.

    The DNSUpdateProxy group was created to solve this problem. Members of this group can update resource records but do not own them. The DHCP server would have become a member of this group automatically when it was configured to issue host resource records, but for some reason, it has been removed. You can reconfigure the DHCP server to update both host and PTR resource records, but a better solution is to add the server to the DNSUpdateProxy group, manually delete the clients' host records, and then either reboot the clients or use the Ipconfig /registerdns command-line utility on each client.

D. Incorrect: By default, Microsoft Windows XP Professional clients are configured to update their own host resource records. Although this default could have been changed on a single client, it has probably not been changed on all of them.

9. **Correct Answers: B and C**

  A. Incorrect: Clients on Subnet B retain their current leases and access DC1 for name resolution as before. Only when they obtain new leases will they access DC2. If you wanted them all to access DC2 the next time they required name resolution, you should have released and renewed their leases from the command line.

  B. Correct: Scope option 006 is not set for the Subnet A scope, which continues to apply server option 006 as before.

  C. Correct: Client016 has been statically configured to access the new IP address of DC2 for name resolution. Client003's host name will therefore be resolved to the correct IP address.

  D. Incorrect: You haven't changed Client003's client option 006, nor have you released and renewed the lease. Client003 therefore attempts to use the old address of DC2 to access a DNS server. Client003 might have been able to ping Client016 if Client016's IP address and host name were cached because of a previous ping, but you cleared Client003's DNS cache. Client003 would be able to ping Client016 if the Ipconfig /renew command had been executed instead.

14 Implementing, Managing, and Maintaining Name Resolution (2.0)

The **Domain Name System (DNS)** is a service that resolves (or translates) **host names** into **IP addresses**. The host names can be local such as ServerA, or remote **Fully Qualified Domain Names (FQDNs)** such as www.fabrican.com. Local names are typically (but not necessarily) resolved to **private IP addresses** such as 10.10.16.5. Remote FQDNs are resolved to **registered IP addresses** such as 206.73.118.10.

The significance of this last statement cannot be overemphasized. Any Web-based resource can be resolved to a registered IP address across the Internet. Resources internal to a large corporation, but not local to the **resolver**, can also be found by iterative queries across a large organization. You can sit at your PC and access resources on the other side of the world, and you don't need to know the IP addresses, or even the physical locations. The ubiquity of DNS makes it a security hazard for organizations that want to access Internet resources and want to make their presence known on the Internet, but need to protect their internal resources. DNS has come a long way from the 1980s, with more and more sophisticated tools becoming available to set up more and more complicated structures to manage DNS. One of the key tasks of the network administrator is to make access as easy as possible for the people who need to access resources and as difficult as possible for the others.

In its initial form, DNS was a static and uninspiring service consisting of some merged hosts files, and what was then known as the DNS cache (now **root hints**) that contained the IP addresses of a few **top-level (root) servers** in the DNS hierarchical structure. DNS is now dynamic, with clients registering their own **resource records**—including **reverse lookup (PTR) resource records**. The number of record types has increased beyond recognition from the simple **host (A)** resource records through **AAAA (QuadA)** IPv6 records, **start-of-authority (SOA)** resource records, and **SRV (service)** resource records.

Any Microsoft Network Infrastructure examination will focus heavily on DNS, and this book is no exception. You need to become familiar with components, concepts, and practices of using DNS in a Microsoft Windows Server 2003 environment. You need to know when it is appropriate to configure a DNS zone as **Active Directory–integrated primary**, **standard primary**, **secondary**, or **stub**. You should be familiar with the difference between a **forward** and a **reverse lookup zone**. You should be aware of the functions of **secondary servers**, **caching-only servers**, **stub servers**, and **forwarders**, and when it is appropriate to use each of them. You need to know how to allow dynamic updates, how to allow only secure dynamic updates, and when to use each of these functions. You should know how to disable recursion, and be familiar with resource record aging and the scavenging process.

DNS works closely with the **Dynamic Host Configuration Protocol (DHCP)**. The settings in the relevant DNS and DHCP properties dialog boxes look comparatively simple, but they combine in complex ways. You need to be able to configure settings that give the maximum possible support for **dynamic updates** of resource records for hosts with such legacy operating systems as Microsoft Windows 95, Microsoft Windows 98, and Microsoft NT 4, and such non-Microsoft operating systems as NetWare and UNIX, while still maintaining the security and integrity of your network.

Tested Skills and Suggested Practices

The skills that you need to successfully master the *Implementing, Managing, and Maintaining Name Resolution* objective domain on the 70-291 exam include the following:

- Install and configure the DNS Server service.

  - Practice 1: Create or obtain a configuration plan that defines primary, secondary, and stub zones. Identify a strategy for setting up an efficient DNS infrastructure that includes secondary, stub, and caching-only servers.

  - Practice 2: Install DNS on a stand-alone server, and configure standard primary forward lookup zones and reverse lookup zones.

  - Practice 3: Install DNS on a second server, and configure it as a secondary server for the zones created in Practice 2. Add some resource records manually on the primary server, and force **replication** from the secondary server.

  - Practice 4: Promote one of your servers to a domain controller (DC), and configure your zones as Active Directory–integrated. Allow only **secure dynamic updates**. Add hosts that can register their resource records to the domain, and check that their records are updated.

- Manage DNS.

  - Practice 1: Install DHCP on your second server. Experiment with the DNS tab in the DHCP server properties dialog box. It would be useful if you could add legacy or non-Microsoft operating system hosts to the network.

  - Practice 2: Use the DNS console to view the contents of the **server cache**. Based on the cache parameters, decide whether the cache needs to be cleared. Clear it anyway.

  - Practice 3: Modify the settings of a DNS zone. Settings include specifying the zone name and the zone type, specifying whether dynamic updates are allowed, specifying whether only secure dynamic updates are allowed

(Active Directory–integrated only), specifying other DNS servers as authoritative, setting **aging** and **scavenging** parameters, and modifying security (Active Directory–integrated only).

❑ Practice 4: In the DNS console, select a forward zone. From the Action menu, select Add Other Records. Scroll through the records, using the Explain button to find out what each one does. If you do not understand the function of any record, refer to the recommended reading or to the server help files.

❑ Practice 5: In the DNS console, access the Advanced tab of the DNS server properties dialog box. Right-click each of the server options in turn, and select What's This to access in-context help. If possible, test the effects of changing these options. (This task could be difficult on a small test network.)

■ Monitor DNS.

❑ Practice 1: At a command prompt, run **Nslookup** and then type **?** and press Enter to display the switches. Use the Set command with the Ls and query-type switches to display records of various types.

❑ Practice 2: Use the **Performance Logs And Alerts tool** to create a log file that defines a baseline for DNS performance. Use the Explain button to obtain explanations for all the counters, including the ones you decide not to use.

❑ Practice 3: Access the **DNS server log**, either from the DNS console or from Event Viewer. View the contents, particularly any warning or error messages.

❑ Practice 4: Open the **DNS console**. On the Debug Logging tab in the server properties dialog box, specify what you want to monitor. Generate some DNS traffic. (Reconfigure statically configured clients or release and renew leases for dynamically configured clients, and then issue Ipconfig /registerdns at the Command console.) View the resultant DNS debug log.

❑ Practice 5: Run a simple and a recursive test on a DNS server. If you do not know how to perform this task, find out.

Further Reading

This section lists supplemental readings by objective. We recommend that you study these sources thoroughly before taking exam 70-291.

Objective 2.1   Review Chapter 5, "Implementing a DNS Infrastructure."

Microsoft Corporation. *Microsoft Encyclopedia of Networking, Second Edition.* Redmond, Washington: Microsoft Press, 2002. See entries for "DNS," "Domain Name System (DNS)," and "Dynamic DNS (DDNS)."

Microsoft Corporation. *Microsoft Windows Server 2003 Deployment Guide*. Redmond, Washington. Review "DNS Overview," available on Microsoft's Web site at *http://www.microsoft.com/technet/treeview/default.asp?url=/technet/prodtechnol /windowsserver2003/proddocs/entserver/sag_DNS_und_Topnode.asp*.

Objective 2.2 Review Chapter 5, "Implementing a DNS Infrastructure."

Microsoft Corporation. *Microsoft Encyclopedia of Networking, Second Edition*. Redmond, Washington: Microsoft Press, 2002. See entries for "DNS Server."

Microsoft Corporation. *Microsoft Windows Server 2003 Deployment Guide*. Redmond, Washington. Review "DNS—How to," available on Microsoft's Web site at *http://www.microsoft.com/technet/treeview/default.asp?url=/technet/prodtechnol /windowsserver2003/proddocs/entserver/sag_DNS_pro_OptimizingServersNode.asp1.3*.

Objective 2.3 Review Chapter 6 "Monitoring and Troubleshooting DNS."

Microsoft Corporation. *Microsoft Encyclopedia of Networking, Second Edition*. Redmond, Washington: Microsoft Press, 2002. See entries for "Nslookup" and "NS record."

Microsoft Corporation. *Microsoft Windows Server 2003 Deployment Guide*. Redmond, Washington. Review "DNS—Troubleshooting," available on Microsoft's Web site at *http://www.microsoft.com/technet/treeview/default.asp?url=/technet /prodtechnol/windowsserver2003/proddocs/entserver/ sag_DNS_pro_OptimizingServersNode.asp*.

Install and Configure the DNS Server Service

A workable DNS infrastructure is the direct result of good planning and careful implementation during the installation phase. You must understand the basic guidelines for DNS installation and know how to identify individuals who have rights to **manage the DNS zones**. You need to understand how **one-to-one mapping** of domains in the Active Directory directory service corresponds to and integrates with DNS. You also need to know how to verify your DNS configuration.

You are required to understand the different zone types: standard primary, Active Directory–integrated primary, secondary, and stub. You need to know the functions of primary, secondary, stub, and caching-only servers; know when to configure forwarders; know when to disable **recursion**; and understand the function of root hints. You also need to know how to configure aging and scavenging properties, and **application directory partition settings**.

Objective 2.1 Questions

1. The Active Directory domain structure of the fourthcoffee.com forest is shown in the following illustration. DC1 is the first domain controller in domain accounts.denver.fourthcoffee.com. Client1 is a client in the same domain. No changes have been made to the primary or connection-specific DNS suffixes on either PC. What is the FQDN of Client1?

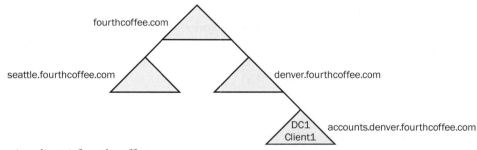

   A. client1.fourthcoffee.com

   B. client1.DC1.denver.accounts.fourthcoffee.com

   C. client1@denver.accounts.fourthcoffee.com

   D. client1.accounts.denver.fourthcoffee.com

2. Resource1 is a mutihomed Windows Server 2003 member server in the design.treyresearch.corp Active Directory domain. One of Resource1's network interface cards (NICs) is connected to a 10-MB Ethernet network, and it is configured with IP address 10.10.1.12. The second NIC is configured with IP address 10.10.2.200, and it is connected to a Gigabit Ethernet network. Active Directory–integrated DNS is implemented on the domain.

    Clients on the Gigabit network need fast access to large data files on Resource1. Clients on the 10-MB network require normal file server functions. Both sets of clients access Resource1 by FQDN.

    You configure a connection-specific DNS suffix of text.design.treyresearch.corp on the NIC configured with IP address 10.10.1.12. You configure a connection-specific DNS suffix of video.design.treyresearch.corp on the NIC configured with IP address 10.10.2.200. Which host A resource records are recorded for Resource1 in DNS? (Choose all that apply.)

   A. Resource1.text.design.treyresearch.corp: 10.10.2.200

   B. Resource1.text.design.treyresearch.corp: 10.10.1.12

   C. Resource1.video.design.treyresearch.corp: 10.10.2.200

   D. Resource1.video.design.treyresearch.corp: 10.10.1.12

   E. Resource1.design.treyresearch.corp: 10.10.2.200

   F. Resource1.design.treyresearch.corp: 10.10.1.12

3. You install DNS on a stand-alone server running Windows Server 2003, Enterprise Edition. During installation, an error message reports that the DNS service has not started in a timely fashion, but when you click OK, DNS installs. You configure a standard primary forward lookup zone. You do not allow dynamic updates.

When you open the DNS console, you notice an red *x* beside the server name. You access the DNS Event Log and discover a 414 warning entry that has the error message shown in the following figure.

You try to start the DNS service but cannot do so. You then realize that the server has become disconnected from the network. You plug the connector back in, and now you can restart the DNS service. However, the *x* is still showing beside the DNS server, and most of the entries on the Action menu are unavailable. What should you do next?

   A. Restart the DNS service.

   B. Allow dynamic updates.

   C. Delete and recreate the zone.

   D. From the Action menu, select Refresh.

4. The Active Directory domain structure of the fourthcoffee.com forest is shown in the following illustration.. DC1 through DC7 are domain controllers. The domain structure has been set up from scratch using default settings. DC1 is the first DC in the forest. DNS is Active Directory–integrated, and both forward and reverse zones have been created. The DNS Server service is installed on all DCs. All servers are Windows Server 2003, Enterprise Edition. All clients are Microsoft Windows XP Professional. Clients register their own host resource records in DNS, and DHCP registers their pointer (PTR) resource records. Which of the following statements is correct?

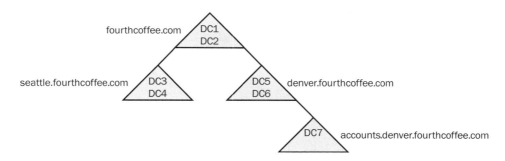

A. The zone file on DC7 contains the host resource records for all the clients in the fourthcoffee.com domain.

B. DC5 is authoritative for the denver.fourthcoffee.com DNS zone.

C. If you open the DNS console and access DC7 server properties, the SOA tab will be present but the parameters are unavailable.

D. DC1 is the only domain controller on which you can access the Security tab in the DNS server properties dialog box.

5. Litware, Inc. is a large, multinational corporation with its headquarters in Chicago and large offices all over the world. The Singapore office is experiencing rapid expansion. Singapore has considerable autonomy and users in Singapore seldom access resources in Chicago. Users in Chicago access resources in Singapore sporadically. However, when they do access these resources, they need to be able to do so without undue delay.

To reduce replication traffic over WAN links, the Delegation Of Control Wizard has been used to create the child DNS zone singapore.litwareinc.com, for which the Singapore domain controllers are authoritative. Both the singapore.litwareinc.com and the litwareinc.com zones are Active Directory–integrated.

Users in Chicago report that access to resources in Singapore is becoming increasingly slow as the Singapore operation expands. How can you improve access to Singapore without unduly increasing network traffic?

   A. Create a secondary DNS server for singapore.litwareinc.com in the Chicago office.

   B. Install a caching-only server in Chicago.

   C. Install a stub server for singapore.litwareinc.com in Chicago.

   D. Configure a forwarder in Chicago to forward queries to a DNS server in Singapore.

6. Your small business has a peer-to-peer network with Windows 98 and Microsoft Windows NT 4 Workstation clients and a single Windows NT 4 file and print server. You do not use DHCP. You upgrade the server to Windows Server 2003 and decide to take advantage of DDNS. You install DNS on the server, and you configure the standard primary forward zone to use dynamic updates. You configure all PCs (including the server) to use the server's IP address as the preferred DNS server. You reboot all the clients. You find that some clients fail to register resource records in DNS. What action should you take?

   A. Open the DNS console. On the Advanced tab of the server's properties dialog box, select the Always Update DNS option.

   B. Configure a reverse lookup zone.

   C. Manually create host A resource records for the Windows NT 4 Workstation clients.

   D. Manually create host A resource records for the Windows 98 clients.

7. You work for Margie's Travel, which has a main office in Detroit and small branch offices in Toledo and Cleveland. DNS is implemented on a standard primary server and a standard secondary server in Detroit. All client PCs in the organization are configured to access one of these servers as their preferred DNS server, and the other as their alternate DNS server. Clients in the branch office access resources in Detroit regularly. They report that access is often slow. You do not want to increase traffic on the WAN links. How should you improve resource access for branch office staff?

   A. Install a caching-only DNS server in the Cleveland and Toledo branches.

   B. Install a secondary DNS server in the Cleveland and Toledo branches.

   C. Install a stub DNS server in the Cleveland and Toledo branches.

   D. Install a domain controller in the Cleveland and Toledo branches.

8. Proseware, Inc. has sites in several different countries. Active Directory–integrated DNS has been installed for the forest root domain, proseware.com. The DNS Server service is installed on four Windows Server 2003 domain controllers in Proseware's main facility in the United States. The servers are named Pixie, Dixie, Tom, and Jerry. They do not host any DNS zones other than proseware.com.

You are a consultant tasked with implementing Proseware's network infrastructure in Europe. You install a domain controller called London and create the Active Directory child domain europe.proseware.com. The DNS service on London is Active Directory–integrated. Authority for the europe.proseware.com DNS zone is delegated to London. You configure the Preferred DNS Server field in the TCP/IP properties dialog box for London to point to London's IP address. How can you ensure that name resolution requests originating in the europe.proseware.com domain for resources in the proseware.com domain are dealt with efficiently?

A. Configure Pixie, Dixie, Tom, and Jerry as conditional forwarders on London.

B. Configure Jerry as a master name server for London.

C. Add Pixie, Dixie, Tom, and Jerry to the root hints on London.

D. Configure Pixie, Dixie, Tom, and Jerry as alternative DNS servers on London.

9. You administer an Active Directory domain that has 200 clients. DNS is set up as a standard primary zone on a stand-alone server. Your network uses registered IP addresses. You want your DNS server to perform recursive queries on behalf of DNS clients to resolve FQDNs of external Internet sites, while still continuing to resolve internal host names. How do you configure the DNS server?

A. Configure the DNS server as a caching-only server.

B. Configure the DNS server to use forwarders.

C. Configure the DNS server as a stub server.

D. Configure the primary zone to allow dynamic updates.

10. You administer a Windows Server 2003 Active Directory domain with 100 Windows NT 4 Workstation clients. The clients are statically configured, and they have static entries in the DNS zone domain1.local. DNS is Active Directory–integrated and allows only secure dynamic updates. You upgrade all your clients to Windows XP Professional. You install DHCP, and you configure your clients to obtain their IP configurations and their preferred DNS server addresses automatically. DHCP is configured to always update client records in DNS.

Clients report that they can no longer access other clients by host name. You examine the DNS database and find that A resource records are not being updated, but PTR resource records are. How should you solve this problem?

A. Reconcile the DHCP scope.

B. Manually delete all the static A resource records. Run Ipconfig /registerdns on each client PC.

C. Run Dnscmd /ageallrecords domain1.local.

D. Run Dnscmd /startscavenging.

11.   On the morning after your organization has been closed for a two-week vacation, several users report that they cannot access an intranet Web site on your Windows Server 2003 network from the browsers on their clients running Windows XP Professional. You ping the Web server's static IP address from your own PC and the ping times out. You check the Web server PC and discover that it has become disconnected from the network.

You plug it back in and run Ipconfig /registerdns followed by Net stop netlogon and Net start netlogon. You can now access the Web site by typing the URL into your browser. However, the clients that previously could not access the site using their browsers still cannot access them. How do you solve this problem? (Choose all that apply).

   A. Run Ipconfig /release and then Ipconfig /renew on the Web server.

   B. Run Ipconfig /registerdns on each client PC that cannot access the Web site.

   C. Run Ipconfig /flushdns on each client PC that cannot access the Web site.

   D. Tell the users to go and have an early lunch, and everything will be OK when they come back.

12.   You administer a single Windows Server 2003 Active Directory domain. DNS is installed on a domain controller and configured as a primary zone but the zone is not stored in the Active Directory. Because clients access servers and not each other, host A resource records for the servers have been added to the primary zone. The network is expanding and the installation of several new servers is planned. You plan to configure dynamic updates, but management is concerned that rogue PCs could register themselves in the organization's DNS. What is the first step you should take to help implement your plan while meeting management's concerns?

   A. In the zone properties dialog box on the General tab, select Nonsecure And Secure at the Dynamic Updates list.

   B. In the zone properties dialog box on the General tab, select Secure at the Dynamic Updates list.

   C. In the DHCP console, open the server properties dialog box. On the DNS tab, select the Always Dynamically Update DNS A And PTR Records option.

   D. Convert the DNS standard primary zone to an Active Directory–integrated zone.

Objective 2.1 Answers

1.   Correct Answers: D

    A. Incorrect: The FQDN consists of the client name followed by the DNS primary suffix. By default, the DNS primary suffix is the name of the domain that the client is in. Client1 is in the accounts.denver.fourthcoffee.com domain and therefore has the FQDN client1.accounts.denver.fourthcoffee.com.

    B. Incorrect: The FQDN does not include the name of the domain controller or controllers in that domain. Client1 is in the accounts.denver.fourthcoffee.com domain, not the DC1.accounts.denver.fourthcoffee.com domain.

    C. Incorrect: The at (@) symbol is used in Simple Mail Transfer Protocol (SMTP) e-mail addresses, not in FQDNs.

    D. Correct: Client1 is in the accounts.denver.fourthcoffee.com domain and therefore has the FQDN client1.accounts.denver.fourthcoffee.com. (Note that in Windows Server 2003 DNS, FQDNs are not case-sensitive.)

2.   Correct Answers: B, C, E, and F

    A. Incorrect: The connection-specific DNS suffix text.design.treyresearch.corp is specified for the 10.10.1.0 network.

    B. Correct: This FQDN is on the 10.10.1.0 network.

    C. Correct: This FQDN is on the 10.10.2.0 network.

    D. Incorrect: The connection-specific DNS suffix video.design.treyresearch.corp is specified for the 10.10.2.0 network.

    E. Correct: Specifying a connection-specific DNS suffix does not alter the default DNS suffix. Resource1 can still be accessed on either interface using its default FQDN.

    F. Correct: This answer is correct for the reason stated in the explanation for answer E.

3.   Correct Answers: D

    A. Incorrect: Starting the DNS service did not remove the x. Restarting it will not help.

    B. Incorrect: You cannot perform this task when the server is disabled, and it has nothing to do with enabling the server in any case.

C. **Incorrect:** Deleting and creating zones has no effect on server status.

D. **Correct:** Everything is in place for the DNS server to be activated. All you need to do is refresh it.

4. Correct Answers: A

A. **Correct:** DNS is Active Directory–integrated, all DCs have the DNS Server service installed, and clients register their host resource records dynamically. Therefore, the zone files on all DCs contain the host resource records for all clients.

B. **Incorrect:** The question does not mention that the Delegation Of Control Wizard has been run. Therefore, denver.fourthcoffee.com is not a DNS zone. It is important to distinguish between Active Directory domains, DNS domains, and DNS zones.

C. **Incorrect:** If you access this tab on a standard secondary zone, the parameters are unavailable. However, DC7 does not host a standard secondary zone—it hosts an Active Directory–integrated zone, for which it is authoritative.

D. **Incorrect:** In an Active Directory–integrated zone, you can access the Security tab from the DNS server properties dialog box of any participating DC.

5. Correct Answers: C

A. **Incorrect:** This approach would speed up access, but it would also increase network traffic due to zone transfers from the master in Singapore to the secondary in Chicago. This solution is overkill for sporadic resource access.

B. **Incorrect:** This idea might be good, but it would not solve this particular problem. A caching-only server speeds up name resolution if a server name has been resolved recently, and the results are cached. Because Chicago users access resources in Singapore only sporadically, the record of a previous query would likely time out before the query is repeated.

C. **Correct:** Access to Singapore resources is becoming slower because as the Singapore operation expands, more DNS servers are being installed. A stub server holds records for all the authoritative name servers in the singapore.litware-inc.com zone and therefore speeds access to resources. Because the stub server receives information only when a new name server is added, the additional network traffic that is generated will be minimal.

D. **Incorrect:** This approach would cause queries that cannot be resolved locally in Chicago to be forwarded to Singapore. Thus, traffic on the Singapore WAN link would increase and would delay the majority of resolution requests, which are not for Singapore servers. It would make sense to configure a conditional forwarder that would forward name resolution requests only for the singapore.litware-inc.com zone, but this is not what the question specifies.

6.   Correct Answers: C

A. **Incorrect:** This setting is available in the DHCP server properties dialog box, not in the DNS console.

B. **Incorrect:** This approach enables IP-address-to-host-name resolution. It has nothing to do with dynamic updates.

C. **Correct:** Windows NT 4 Workstation clients cannot register resource records in DNS. In the absence of DHCP, these records need to be created manually. Another solution is to install Windows Internet Name Service (WINS), but the question does not allow for this alternative.

D. **Incorrect:** Windows 98 clients can register resource records in DDNS.

7.   Correct Answers: A

A. **Correct:** You should install DNS on servers in Cleveland and Toledo, and configure their root hints to point to the DNS servers in Detroit. It is probably wise for one caching-only server to access the primary server first, and for the other to access the secondary server first. No further configuration is required. Caching-only servers are not authoritative for any zone, so no zone transfer traffic will be generated. Because users in the branch offices access resources in the main office regularly, most name resolution requests will be satisfied from cache. As a result, resource access should be quicker and host name resolution traffic should decrease.

B. **Incorrect:** This solution would reduce resource access delays, but at the cost of increasing zone transfer traffic over the WAN links. Because the branch offices are small, additional secondary DNS servers are not appropriate in this scenario.

C. **Incorrect:** Stub servers hold resource records only for the authoritative name servers in their zone. In this case, additional DNS servers are unlikely to be installed in the main office regularly. Stub servers can be useful in large multinational organizations with delegated zones, where it is necessary for one zone to keep track of all the servers that are authoritative for the others.

D. **Incorrect:** DNS is not Active Directory–integrated, so a DC would not assist in name resolution unless it were also configured as a secondary DNS server. (Refer to the explanation for answer B.) Installing DCs in Cleveland and Toledo would speed up login at the branch offices but would have no effect on name resolution, and would generate Active Directory replication traffic. Because the branch offices are small, this solution would be overkill. In any case, the question does not specify that Maggie's Travel has an Active Directory domain.

8.   Correct Answers: A

> **A. Correct:** This solution ensures that all requests with FQDNs ending in proseware.com (except for those ending in europe.proseware.com) are passed directly to a DNS server that is authoritative for the proseware.com zone. Note that a DNS server can be configured with a number of forwarders.
>
> **B. Incorrect:** Jerry and London host separate zones. You can use this configuration only if you set up London as a secondary server for the proseware.com DNS zone, which would increase replication traffic over the WAN link.
>
> **C. Incorrect:** Pixie, Dixie, Tom, and Jerry do not host a root zone.
>
> **D. Incorrect:** This configuration would result in London forwarding a query to one of the proseware.com servers only if it could not resolve the query. London would first attempt to resolve the query by accessing a server on its root hints file. This solution is not the most efficient way of resolving queries ending in proseware.com.

9.   Correct Answers: B

> **A. Incorrect:** A caching-only server is not authoritative for any zone and would hold address resolution information that it obtained only from the server it uses for name resolution. It could not resolve internal name resolution requests.
>
> **B. Correct:** The DNS server would then forward requests that it could not resolve from its zone file or cache to another DNS server, typically your ISP's DNS server.
>
> **C. Incorrect:** A stub server holds a list of authoritative name servers only for its master zone. It cannot resolve internal name resolution requests.
>
> **D. Incorrect:** This solution would allow clients to register their resource records dynamically. It would have no effect on external name resolution.

10.   Correct Answers: C

> **A. Incorrect:** This solution repairs inconsistencies in the DHCP scope. It does not delete static DNS resource records.
>
> **B. Incorrect:** This solution would work, but it involves excessive administrative effort.
>
> **C. Correct:** Unlike PTR resource records, static A resource records do not age and cannot be removed automatically. The Dnscmd /ageallrecords command causes all records to age, which in effect converts static records into dynamic records. Dnscmd is a Microsoft Windows Server 2003 support tools utility. To run it you need to install Support Tools from the sever CDROM and change to the \program files\support tools directory.

D. Incorrect: Scavenging removes all stale records from the DNS zone. Static records do not age, and consequently, are never identified as stale. You need to convert all records to dynamic.

11. **Correct Answers: C and D**

A. Incorrect: The Web server has a static IP address. There is no point in trying to renew its DHCP lease.

B. Incorrect: You have no reason to believe that the clients are not registered in DNS. No problems have been reported about clients not accessing each other.

C. Correct: Windows XP Professional DNS employs negative caching. The Web server has been disconnected for a length of time that is sufficient for its host resource record to have been removed from the DNS zone file. Thus, when the users tried to access the Web server's FQDN by typing in the URL, their client PCs cached that the FQDN could not be resolved. On the other hand, you pinged the Web server's IP address and did not, therefore, request name resolution. When the users tried to access the Web site again, the client PCs used cached information and discovered that the FQDN had been cached as invalid. Clearing the negative result from the clients' caches solves the problem.

D. Correct: Cache entries, including negative entries (refer to the explanation for answer C), typically time out in 45 minutes or less.

12. **Correct Answers: D**

A. Incorrect: This solution would expose the network to registration attempts by rogue PCs.

B. Incorrect: This configuration can only be done in an Active Directory–integrated primary zone.

C. Incorrect: This solution has no effect if DNS is not enabled to allow dynamic updates.

D. Correct: On the General tab of the zone properties dialog box for an Active Directory–integrated zone, you can allow only secure dynamics updates. This solution allows resource records to be updated automatically while preventing computers that do not have accounts in Active Directory from registering their details. However, you need to convert the zone to Active Directory–integrated first.

Manage DNS

This section of the exam requires that you understand how the DNS server answers queries. You should know how to ensure that DNS is working properly, and that legacy desktops are updating DNS through DHCP.

You need a mastery of DNS zone settings, record settings, and server options. You should know how to allow updates, how to allow only secure updates, and how to set the **Time to Live (TTL)** both for zones and for individual records. You also need to know how to display the DNS cache on both servers and clients, and understand the significance of **negative caching**. You should be aware of what server options such as **round robin** and **disable recursion** do, and when they should be enabled.

You should be familiar with (at least) all of the commonly used resource record types, such as A, PTR, name server (NS), SOA, and mail exchange (MX). You should know how to add records to a zone, how to monitor them, and how to delete them. You should be able to verify that both forward and reverse lookup zones are configured correctly.

Objective 2.2 Questions

1. Your DNS domain seattle.fourthcoffee.com has two mail servers, mail1 and mail2. You want mail1 to be the primary mail server and mail2 to be the secondary mail server. Which DNS resource records should you create? (Choose all that apply.)

   A. MX 10 mail1.seattle.fourthcoffee.com.

   B. MB 10 mail1.seattle.fourthcoffee.com.

   C. MX 200 mail1.seattle.fourthcoffee.com.

   D. MB 20 mail1.seattle.fourthcoffee.com.

   E. MX 20 mail2.seattle.fourthcoffee.com.

   F. MB 20 mail2.seattle.fourthcoffee.com.

   G. MX 10 mail2.seattle.fourthcoffee.com.

   H. MB 10 mail2.seattle.fourthcoffee.com.

2. You are the system administrator at Lucerne Publishing. You administer the books.lucernepublishing.com Windows Server 2003 Active Directory domain. Active Directory–integrated DNS is configured on all domain controllers in the domain. You configure a member server, ServerA, to host an internal Web site for the intranet. You want employees to access this Web site using the URL books.internal.lucernepublishing.com. What should you do?

   A. Create a canonical name (CNAME) resource record called books, and specify internal.lucernepublishing.com as the target host.

   B. Create a new zone called internal.lucernepublishing.com. Create a CNAME resource record called books in that new zone, and specify ServerA.books.lucernepublishing.com as the target host.

   C. Create a CNAME resource record called books.internal and specify ServerA.books.lucernepublishing.com as the target host.

   D. Create a CNAME resource record called internal and specify ServerA.books.lucernepublishing.com as the target host.

3. You administer a large mixed-mode Active Directory domain. All the domain controllers are servers running Windows Server 2003, Enterprise Edition, but the servers are a mixture of Windows Server 2003, Windows 2000 Server, and Windows NT 4 Server. Client PCs are Windows XP Professional, Windows 2000 Professional, or Windows NT 4 Workstation. DHCP is installed on two clustered servers running Windows Server 2003, Enterprise Edition. You have configured DNS to allow only secure dynamic updates.

Some hosts can be accessed by host name. Others cannot. All hosts can be accessed by IP address. What can you do to help ensure that all hosts can be accessed by host name?

A. Install NetBEUI on the hosts that cannot be accessed by host name.

B. Set DNS to allow all dynamic updates.

C. In the DNS console, on the Advanced tab of the zone properties dialog box, select the Always Update DNS option.

D. In the DHCP console, on the DNS tab of the server properties dialog box, select the Enable DNS Dynamic Updates According To The Settings Below option, and then select Always Dynamically Update DNS A And Pointer Records.

4. You have a technical support position at one of the major branch offices of Humongous Insurance. A Windows Server 2003 computer on the branch office network acts as a secondary DNS server for a master server (also Windows Server 2003) in Humongous Insurance's main office. The master server is authoritative for a single standard primary forward zone. Users in the branch office are having problems accessing resources in the main office. You suspect that some DNS resource records on the secondary server have become stale. What action should you take?

A. Open the DNS console on the secondary DNS server. Right-click the server name and select Launch Nslookup. Run the command Set msxfr.

B. Open the DNS console on the secondary DNS server. Right-click the server name and select Launch Nslookup. Run the command Set nomsxfr.

C. Open the DNS console on the primary DNS server. Access the Start of Authority (SOA) tab in the forward zone's properties dialog box, and increment the Serial Number setting.

D. Open the DNS console on the secondary DNS server. Right-click the applicable zone and select Reload From Master.

5. Your Windows Server 2003 Active Directory domain fabrikam.com contains three Web servers that are used to host a frequently accessed intranet Web site. All three Web servers have identical content. They have static IP addresses 10.12.1.10, 10.12.1.15, and 10.12.1.20, respectively. You want employees to be able to access the intranet Web site with the single URL internal.fabrikam.com. You create three host resource records in the fabricam.com forward lookup zone as follows:

internal:10.12.1.10

internal:10.12.1.15

internal:10.12.1.20

However, when you analyze network traffic, you find that only the first of these servers is receiving Hypertext Transfer Protocol (HTTP) requests. What is likely to be the problem?

   A. Round robin is disabled on the DNS server.

   B. CNAME resource records should have been used, not host resource records.

   C. PTR resource records should have been used, not host resource records.

   D. Only Active Directory–integrated DNS supports this option.

6. You want to inspect the DNS cache on a client computer to check for negative cache entries and TTL parameters. How do you perform this task?

   A. Use the Ipconfig /flushdns command-line utility while logged on to the client PC.

   B. Use the Ipconfig /displaydns command-line utility while logged on to the client PC.

   C. Open the DNS console. In the console tree, right-click the appropriate server, and select Clear Cache.

   D. Use the Ipconfig /registerdns command-line utility while logged on to the client PC.

7. You administer a network that consists of a number of subnets. For historical reasons, different subnets contain different types of operating systems. Some subnets contain UNIX servers, some contain Novell NetWare servers, and some contain Windows NT 4 servers. There are also UNIX, NetWare, Windows 95, Windows 98, NT 4 Workstation, Windows 2000 Professional, and Windows XP Professional clients. All PCs have static IP configurations.

You set up an Active Directory domain with Windows Server 2003 domain controllers. You implement DHCP and configure all workstations that can do so to obtain their IP configurations automatically. You set exclusions in the DHCP scopes for clients that require static configuration. You configure Active Directory–integrated DNS zones. You configure DHCP to update DNS records for all DHCP clients. You configure DNS to allow only secure dynamic updates. Legacy Berkeley Internet Name Domain (BIND) UNIX servers are configured as secondary servers for the Active Directory–integrated DNS primary zone.

Client workstations do not require access to each other, but all clients need to be able to access all severs by host name. You find that certain servers cannot be accessed by host name. What should you do?

   A. Install WINS.

   B. Create Hosts file entries on all clients for all the servers that cannot currently be accessed by host name.

C. Manually enter host (A) resource records for the NetWare, UNIX, and Windows NT 4 servers.

D. Install NetBEUI on all client PCs.

8. You want to clear the DNS cache on a DNS server. How can you perform this task? (Choose all that apply.)

A. Use the Ipconfig /displaydns command-line utility while logged on to the DNS server.

B. Open the DNS console and select the appropriate server. From the Action menu, select Clear Cache.

C. Use the Ipconfig /flushdns command-line utility while logged on to the DNS server.

D. Open the DNS console and select the appropriate server. From the Action menu, select Scavenge Stale Resource Records.

9. For security reasons, you want to configure DNS server DNS2 so that it does not forward name requests that it cannot resolve from its own zone file. You log on to DNS2 as the local administrator. What should you do to achieve the desired result? (Choose all that apply.)

A. In the DNS console, access the DNS2 server properties dialog box. On the Advanced tab, select the Disable Recursion check box. Click OK.

B. At a command prompt, run Dnscmd . /config /norecursion.

C. At a command prompt, type Dnscmd . /config /norecursion 1.

D. At a command prompt, run Dnscmd DNS2 /config /norecursion 1.

10. Trey Research is a dynamic organization in an environment where rapid change is the norm. New servers are added frequently, and the names of existing resource servers are often changed to reflect new organizational structures. Active Directory–integrated DNS is hosted on all of the company's Windows Server 2003 domain controllers. There is a single forward lookup zone and a corresponding reverse lookup zone. Reverse DNS lookup is heavily used to support the security of the company's e-mail system.

Users report that sometimes name resolution fails, and they are told that a server is unavailable. At other times, they are directed to the wrong server. What can you do to improve the situation?

A. Open the DNS console. In the properties dialog box for each zone, access the Start Of Authority (SOA) tab and specify a new minimum default TTL.

B. Open the DNS console. On the General tab of the properties dialog box for each zone, click the Aging button. Select the Scavenge Stale Resource Records check box.

C. Open the DNS console. In the properties dialog box for each server, access the Start Of Authority (SOA) tab, and specify a new minimum default TTL.

D. Open the DNS console. For each server, from the Action menu select Set Aging/ Scavenging For All Zones. Select the Scavenge Stale Resource Records check box.

11. You are a network administrator for Contoso, Inc. Contoso manufactures military equipment, and security is very important. You have converted the DNS zones on your Windows Server 2003 Active Directory domain to Active Directory–integrated zones. You suspect that Contoso is under attack from a malicious Internet user. In particular, you suspect that redirection is being used to feed incorrect data into the organization. How can you combat such an attack? (Choose all that apply.)

A. Disable recursion on all DNS servers.

B. Disable round robin on all DNS servers.

C. Ensure that all server caches are secured against pollution.

D. Allow only secure dynamic updates on all DNS zones.

12. The School of Fine Art has a standard primary DNS zone configured on a server running Windows Server 2003, Enterprise Edition. Previously, name resolution was carried out by a legacy UNIX server, and this server has been reconfigured to host a secondary zone that provides backup for the Windows server. The primary sever is powered down so that a second hard disk can be installed, and users report that they are having problems accessing resources. You bring the Windows server back online and the problem disappears.

You investigate and find that zone transfers are not occurring. What should you do next?

A. Disable recursion on the primary server.

B. Ensure that the BIND Secondaries check box on the primary server is selected.

C. Enable IXFR on the secondary server.

D. Enable AXFR on the primary server.

1. **Correct Answers: A and E**

A. **Correct:** MX resource records specify mail exchange servers. The fourth parameter specifies the priority. Here, 10 is the lower of the two numbers. The lower the number, the higher the priority, so mail1 is the primary mail server.

B. **Incorrect:** MX resource records specify mail exchange servers. Mailbox (MB) resource records indicate the DNS domain names of the hosts on which the records reside.

C. **Incorrect:** MX resource records specify mail exchange servers. The fourth parameter specifies the priority. Here, 10 is the lower of the two numbers. The lower the number, the higher the priority; thus, mail1 would be the secondary mail server.

D. **Incorrect:** This answer is incorrect for the reason stated in the explanation for answer B.

E. **Correct:** MX resource records specify mail exchange servers. The fourth parameter specifies the priority. Here, 20 is the higher of the two numbers. The lower the number, the higher the priority, so mail2 is the secondary mail server.

F. **Incorrect:** This answer is incorrect for the reason stated in the explanation for answer B.

G. **Incorrect:** This record would make mail2 the primary mail exchange server. Refer to the explanation for answer E.

H. **Incorrect:** This answer is incorrect for the reason stated in the explanation for answer B.

2. **Correct Answers: B**

A. **Incorrect:** No host exists called internal.lucernepublishing.com.

B. **Correct:** This zone would map books.internal.lucernepublishing.com to ServerA.books.lucernepublishing.com. The new zone can be either standard primary or Active Directory–integrated.

C. **Incorrect:** This approach would map books.internal.books.lucernepublishing.com to the Web server. However, you want the Web server to be accessed as books.internal.lucernepublishing.com.

D. **Incorrect:** This approach would map internal.books.lucernepublishing to the Web server. However, you want the Web server to be accessed as books.internal.lucernepublishing.com.

3. **Correct Answers: D**

    A. **Incorrect:** Windows Server 2003 Server does not support NetBEUI, and it cannot be installed on Windows XP Professional. Even if it were installed on the hosts that can support it, NetBEUI would not solve this problem. It cannot resolve Net-BIOS names across a router, and a large domain is likely to be subnetted.

    B. **Incorrect:** The problem is that some hosts cannot update resource records in DNS and need DHCP to perform this task for them. Allowing all dynamic updates would not solve this problem, plus it would compromise security in the domain.

    C. **Incorrect:** This setting is a DHCP setting, and it cannot be configured from the DNS console.

    D. **Correct:** DHCP updates resource records for Windows NT 4 clients that cannot register their own details in DNS, for example. Note that this solution might not be complete. Any Windows NT 4 server that has a static IP configuration needs to have its host A resource record entered manually. WINS would be a good solution in this scenario, but the question does not provide this alternative.

4. **Correct Answers: D**

    A. **Incorrect:** This action enables Microsoft fast zone transfer, which uses compression and can include multiple records in a single TCP message. It does not initiate a zone transfer, and cannot solve the problem described in this scenario.

    B. **Incorrect:** This action disables Microsoft fast zone transfer. This answer is incorrect for the reason stated in the explanation for answer A.

    C. **Incorrect:** When a zone transfer is initiated, either manually or as a scheduled operation, the master sever compares the serial numbers of the primary and secondary SOA records to determine whether the records on the secondary server need to be updated. Incrementing this number manually will not solve the problem outlined in this scenario.

    D. **Correct:** Resource records in the secondary zone have become stale either because regular zone transfers have not occurred, or because a lot of recent changes have been made to resource records on the DNS master. This procedure initiates zone transfer manually.

5. **Correct Answers: A**

    A. **Correct:** Round robin is a server option that implements load sharing. When the same host name in resource records is associated with several IP addresses, requests for resolution of the host name result in each IP address being supplied to resolvers in turn. Round robin is enabled by default in Windows Server 2003 (for several types of resource records). Round robin has probably been disabled in this scenario.

B. **Incorrect:** The CNAME record associates a number of host names (or aliases) with the same IP address, not vice versa.

C. **Incorrect:** The PTR resource record is used to resolve IP addresses to host names, which is not what this scenario requires.

D. **Incorrect:** You implement round robin by having several host records that all have the same host name or FQDN, but different IP addresses. It makes no difference whether these records are held in an Active Directory–integrated primary zone file, a standard primary zone file, or a secondary zone file.

6. Correct Answers: B

A. **Incorrect:** This solution flushes the DNS cache on the client. You want to inspect it.

B. **Correct:** This solution displays the DNS cache on the client.

C. **Incorrect:** The DNS console can be used to manage the cache on a DNS server. You cannot inspect client caches from the console.

D. **Incorrect:** This solution registers the client in DNS (assuming that DNS is set up to allow this to happen). It does not display the client's DNS cache.

7. Correct Answers: C

A. **Incorrect:** The legacy UNIX and Novell NetWare servers do not register with WINS, and they require static entries. Also, you would need to set up WINS proxies for the non-Windows workstations. This approach involves excessive administrative effort. (Note that non-legacy UNIX hosts can be WINS clients.)

B. **Incorrect:** This approach involves excessive administrative effort.

C. **Correct:** Statically configured legacy UNIX, NetWare, and Windows NT 4 servers cannot update their own records in DNS, and DHCP cannot update DNS records for statically configured clients. Host resource records for servers are easily added manually. If reverse lookup is required, PTR resource records can be created automatically when host records are added. (Note that non-legacy UNIX hosts can register their host and PTR records in DDNS.)

D. **Incorrect:** NetBEUI cannot resolve host names across a router. Also, Windows Server 2003 Server does not support NetBEUI, and it cannot be installed on Windows XP Professional.

8. Correct Answers: B and C

A. **Incorrect:** This approach displays cache entries. It does not flush the cache.

B. **Correct:** This method is for flushing the cache from the DNS console. You do not need to be logged on to the specific DNS server to use this method.

    C. Correct: This solution flushes the DNS cache of whatever PC you are logged on to: client or server.

    D. Incorrect: This approach does not flush the cache. It removes resource records that have timed out.

9.   **Correct Answers: A, C, and D**

    A. Correct: Recursion enables a DNS server to forward a request that it cannot resolve from its own zone file. Selecting the Disable Recursion check box ensures that the server resolves a host name only if that host name is in the zone for which the server is authoritative.

    B. Incorrect: This command needs one more parameter: 1 turns recursion off; 0 turns it on.

    C. Correct: This answer is correct for the reason stated in the explanation for answer B. Note that the full stop can be used in place of the server name only if you are logged on at that server.

    D. Correct: This answer is correct for the reason stated in the explanation for answer C.

10.   **Correct Answers: A**

    A. Correct: Stale resource records are being accessed. When a record's TTL has expired, it will not be used. In this scenario, the subsequent increase in name resolution traffic that results from a smaller TTL is acceptable if fewer stale records are accessed.

    B. Incorrect: The problem is that stale records are not timing out quickly enough in cache, not that stale records with zero TTL are failing to be removed from the zone. Although selecting this check box is probably a good idea in this scenario, this solution will not solve the immediate problem.

    C. Incorrect: You can set the default TTL for a zone, or you can set the TTL for individual records. You cannot set it at server level. There is no SOA tab in the server properties dialog box.

    D. Incorrect: This answer is incorrect for the reason stated in the explanation for answer B.

11.   **Correct Answers: C and D**

    A. Incorrect: Recursion can be disabled on DNS servers that do not respond directly to clients, but receive name resolution requests from other DNS servers. Forwarders are disabled automatically if recursion is disabled. Consequently, if such a DNS server receives a name resolution request that it cannot satisfy from the zones for which it is authoritative, it returns a negative result. If all of Contoso's

DNS servers had recursion disabled, no resolution of external names would be possible. This setup would certainly be secure, but it is not a good plan for a supplier of military equipment.

B. Incorrect: Round robin is a load-balancing mechanism that allows the same FQDN to be allocated to several hosts, each with a different IP, and balances access requests between these hosts. It has no effect on network security.

C. Correct: Redirection is when an attacker is able to redirect queries for DNS names to servers under the control of the attacker. One method of redirection is to pollute a DNS server cache with erroneous data. For example, if a query from Contoso requires resolution of the FQDN www.fabrikam.com, and a referral answer provides a resolution for fabrikam.com, the DNS server continues to use the cached data from crooks_r_us.com to resolve further queries for www.fabrikam.com. If all server caches are secured against pollution, such referrals are rejected. In Windows Server 2003 DNS, caches are secured against pollution by default, but in a high security environment, you should check that this setting has not been altered.

D. Correct: Redirection can be accomplished whenever an attacker has writable access to DNS data. Insecure dynamic updates allow computers that do not have computer accounts in Active Directory to register information in DNS.

12. **Correct Answers: B**

A. Incorrect: Recursion can be disabled on DNS servers that do not respond directly to clients, but receive name resolution requests from other DNS servers. Forwarders are disabled automatically if recursion is disabled. This action has no effect on zone transfer, and it is not appropriate in this scenario.

B. Correct: By default, DNS servers running Windows Server 2003 use a fast zone transfer format. This format uses compression and can include multiple records in a single TCP message. This format is incompatible with legacy (pre-version 4.9.4) BIND-based DNS running on UNIX servers. Enabling BIND secondaries disables fast zone transfer.

C. Incorrect: This is done by running Nslookup and using the command Set msxfr. However, this action is unnecessary in this scenario. By default, DNS servers running Windows Server 2003 use IXFR, which transfers only those records that have been changed or added since the previous transfer occurred. If the secondary server does not support IXFR, the primary server automatically uses AXFR instead. IXFR cannot be enabled on a legacy BIND server, and, in any case, it is the transfer format that is the problem, not the type of transfer.

D. Incorrect: This is done by running Nslookup and using the command Set nomsxfr. However, this action is unnecessary in this scenario for the reason stated in the explanation for answer C.

Objective 2.3
Monitor DNS

For the DNS troubleshooting portion of the exam, you should be familiar with the various **DNS troubleshooting tools**. You should know how to use Nslookup and Ipconfig to perform queries and view DNS settings. You should understand how to use **Event Viewer** to view the **DNS server log**. You should know how to analyze the **DNS debug log** and interpret the data.

You should understand how the **System Monitor** and the Performance Logs And Alerts tools are used to record **baselines** and monitor the DNS service. You need to know how to check that replication and zone transfer are working correctly. You also need to know how to perform **simple and recursive tests**, and the implications of failure of either or both.

1. You want to set up a baseline for DNS operation. DNS is set up on three stand-alone servers running Windows Server 2003 in your organization. Server DNS1 hosts a standard primary zone, and DNS2 and DNS3 are secondary DNS servers for that zone. Default zone properties settings are used. You open the Performance tool on DNS1, expand Performance Logs And Alerts, and click Counter Logs. From the Action menu, you select New Log Settings and save the log as Baseline. You click the Add Counters button and select the DNS Performance object. Which counters should you add? (Choose all that apply.)

   A. AXFR Request Sent

   B. AXFR Request Received

   C. Caching Memory

   D. Dynamic Update Written To Database

   E. IXFR Request Received

   F. IXFR Success Received

   G. IXFR Success Sent

   H. Recursive Queries

   I. Recursive Query Failure

   J. Conflict Check Queue Length

2. You are the administrator of a mixed-mode network that includes Windows NT 4 Server and Workstation computers. The DNS Server and Windows Internet Name Service (WINS) services are installed on Windows Server 2003, Enterprise Edition member servers. Each standard primary DNS zone is configured to use a WINS server to resolve NetBIOS names as needed. How do you tell whether a record that is returned by the Nslookup command-line utility is from a WINS server?

   A. Records that were obtained from a WINS server are marked as nonauthoritative, and the TTL value will have decreased when Nslookup is used again.

   B. Records that were obtained from a WINS server are marked as authoritative, and the TTL value will be unaltered when Nslookup is used again.

   C. Records that were obtained from a WINS server are marked as nonauthoritative, and the TTL value will be unaltered when Nslookup is used again.

   D. Records that were obtained from a WINS server are marked as authoritative, and the TTL value will have decreased when Nslookup is used again.

3. You are the network administrator at the branch office of a large company. The Windows Server 2003 DNS server in the branch office is a secondary server for the standard primary zone at the head office. However, for security reasons, you do not want the secondary DNS server to resolve external FQDNs over the Internet. You therefore specify as a forwarder the DNS server at the main office.

You test the setup and find that external FQDNs are not being resolved. You open the DNS console and access the Monitoring tab of the server's properties dialog box. You test the server's ability to perform simple and recursive queries. The server passes the simple test but fails the recursive test. What could be the problem? (Choose all that apply.)

    A. A firewall is blocking queries to the forwarder.

    B. The recursive time-out is too short.

    C. Replication from the master server is not occurring.

    D. The zones on your server are incorrectly configured.

4. You are an enterprise administrator based at the head office of the Wingtip Toys organization in New York. You administer the wingtiptoys.com Windows 2003 Active Directory domain, and the wingtiptoys.com Active Directory–integrated forward and reverse lookup DNS zones. Wingtip Toy's DNS zone structure mirrors its Active Directory structure, with control being delegated to the portland.wingtiptoys.com, seattle.wingtiptoys.com, and detroit.wingtiptoys.com DNS zones.

A domain administrator at Detroit has recently upgraded the DNS servers that service that zone. You suspect that this upgrade has resulted in incorrect configuration of the zone delegation. How do you verify that the zone delegation is properly configured?

    A. Run Nslookup –querytype=ns detroit.wingtiptoys.com server for each of the detroit.wingtiptoys.com servers. Use Nslookup to verify that the servers that are listed in the output of this command are functioning as name servers.

    B. Run Nslookup –ls –d detroit.wingtiptoys.com server for each of the detroit .wingtiptoys.com servers. Use Nslookup to verify that the servers that are listed in the output of this command are functioning as name servers.

    C. Use Replmon to check that replication is occurring between the wingtiptoys.com and detroit.wingtiptoys.com domains.

    D. Access the DNS object in System Monitor. Confirm that the Recursive Query Failures counter remains at zero.

5. You suspect that your DNS server operation has some bugs, and you want to record detailed information. You open the DNS console, access the Debug Logging tab of the server properties dialog box, select Log Packets For Debugging, and select the events that you want the DNS server to record for debug logging. Where, by default, will you find the information you need?

    A. In the DNS debug log file in %systemroot%\System32\Dns\Dns.log.

    B. In the DNS console, click DNS Events to view the DNS server system Event Log.

    C. In the DNS debug log file in %systemroot%\Dns\Dns.log.

    D. In the DNS server log in Event Viewer.

6. The DNS Server service is installed on all three Windows Server 2003 domain control-lers in your Active Directory domain, and all zones are Active Directory–integrated. You suspect problems exist in the replication of zone information. Which tool should you use to further isolate the problem?

    A. In System Monitor, check the IXFR Success Received counter.

    B. Use the Replmon utility.

    C. Check for errors in the DNS server Event Log.

    D. In the DNS console, access the Monitoring tab of the server properties dialog box for all three DNS servers. Enable automatic query testing.

7. You administer A. Datum Corporation's Windows Server 2003 Active Directory domain. The company's internal DNS server is located behind a firewall. The employ-ees report that they are having problems locating resources outside their own intranet. You use the Monitoring tab in the server's properties dialog box to run a simple and recursive test. The server passes the first test but fails the second. What can you do to solve this problem?

    A. Create a forward lookup zone and name it ".".

    B. Create a reverse lookup zone.

    C. Copy %systemroot%\System32\Dns\Samples\Cache.dns to %systemroot%\System32\Dns\Cache.dns.

    D. Move the DNS server outside the firewall.

8. You want to log User Datagram Protocol (UDP) and TCP DNS requests from host 10.2.2.100 to your DNS server. How can you perform this task with the least adminis-trative effort?

    A. Use Microsoft Network Monitor.

    B. Use Netdiag.

    C. Use the Monitoring tab in the server's properties dialog box.

    D. Use the Debug Logging tab in the server's properties dialog box.

Objective 2.3 Answers

1. **Correct Answers: C, E, G, H, and I**

   A. Incorrect: DNS1 hosts a primary zone. It does not make any transfer requests.

   B. Incorrect: All servers are Windows Server 2003. They are unlikely to use AXFR regularly.

   C. Correct: The Caching Memory counter indicates the total caching memory that is used by a DNS server. A significant increase over time might indicate the need for more random access memory (RAM) in the server.

   D. Incorrect: By default, a standard primary zone does not allow dynamic updates, so this counter remains at zero.

   E. Correct: This counter indicates the number of transfer requests received from the secondary servers.

   F. Incorrect: This counter indicates the total number of successful incremental zone transfers received by a secondary DNS server. It should be in the baseline logs of DNS2 and DNS3.

   G. Correct: This counter indicates the total number of successful incremental zone transfers from the master to the slave DNS server. If the number is significantly lower than the IXFR Request Received, a replication problem could exist.

   H. Correct: This counter indicates the total number of recursive queries received by DNS1. A significant change over time indicates a change in name resolution traffic.

   I. Correct: An increase in the number of recursive query failures over time could indicate a problem.

   J. Incorrect: This counter is a DHCP server counter.

2. **Correct Answers: D**

   A. Incorrect: Records obtained from a WINS server are marked as authoritative. Because these records are stored in the DNS server's cache rather than in a zone, their TTL values will decrease and will therefore be smaller the next time Nslookup is used to display them.

   B. Incorrect: This answer is incorrect for the reason stated in the explanation for answer A.

   C. Incorrect: This answer is incorrect for the reason stated in the explanation for answer A.

   D. Correct: This answer is correct for the reason stated in the explanation for answer A.

3. **Correct Answers: A and B**

    A. **Correct:** A server that passes the simple test but fails the recursive test is either unable to access its forwarder or is timing out before the query can be resolved. A common cause for this problem is that the chosen forwarder is a server in the main office intranet inside a secure firewall, rather than one in the perimeter zone.

    B. **Correct:** This problem would cause the name resolution request to time out before it can be satisfied. Refer to the explanation for answer A.

    C. **Incorrect:** The recursive test checks that external FQDNs can be resolved using a recursive query. Zone replication affects resolution of internal host names, not external FQDNs.

    D. **Incorrect:** If that were the case, the server would fail the simple test.

4. **Correct Answers: A**

    A. **Correct:** The Nslookup command-line utility is used to verify zone delegation, as specified in this answer.

    B. **Incorrect:** This command returns a full listing of the records in the detroit.wingtiptoys.com domain. It does not test DNS delegation.

    C. **Incorrect:** Wingtiptoys.com and detroit.wingtiptoys.com are separate Active Directory domains and separate DNS zones. Zone transfer does not occur. The Replmon utility is not appropriate in this scenario.

    D. **Incorrect:** System Monitor checks system performance. It cannot be used to check DNS delegation.

5. **Correct Answers: A**

    A. **Correct:** The DNS debug log file is located in %systemroot%\System32\ Dns\Dns.log.

    B. **Incorrect:** The DNS server system event log records system events such as failure of the DNS Server service to start. It does not record debug logging events.

    C. **Incorrect:** This answer is incorrect for the reason stated in the explanation for answer A.

    D. **Incorrect:** The dns.server log can be accessed from either Event Viewer or the DNS console. However, this log is not the one you want to access.

6. **Correct Answers: B**

    A. **Incorrect:** This counter indicates the total number of successful incremental zone transfers received by a secondary DNS server. In this scenario, the suspected replication problem is between domain controllers hosting Active Directory–integrated primary zones. The question does not mention secondary zones.

B. Correct: In Active Directory–integrated zones, resource record replication is part of Active Directory replication. Replication Monitor is a Windows Server 2003 support tool used to monitor and debug this process.

C. Incorrect: The DNS server event log records such system events as failure of the DNS Server service to start. This tool is not appropriate to use in this scenario.

D. Incorrect: Automatic query testing performs periodic simple and recursive tests on the server, which test name resolution. Although name resolution failures can occur because of faulty replication, this procedure does not specifically test Active Directory replication.

7.   Correct Answers: C

A. Incorrect: This approach creates an empty root zone and makes the internal server a root server. It would then never use forwarders and would resolve only internal queries. This approach is not a solution to this problem, although it could be a cause.

B. Incorrect: This approach enables IP-address-to-host-name resolution, but it does not solve the current problem.

C. Correct: The DNS server is either unable to access a forwarder, or it is not configured with forwarders. One possible cause is corruption or deletion of the root hints file. Copying the sample root hints file to the root hints file could fix this problem.

D. Incorrect: This approach exposes A. Datum Corporation's internal zone to attacks through the Internet.

8.   Correct Answers: D

A. Incorrect: You can set up an input or view filter in Network Monitor that specifies traffic from a particular IP address. You can also specify a filter based on pattern match. (Request packets are characterized by the QR bit being set to 0 in the DNS message header.) However, this task is not easy and requires excessive administrative effort.

B. Incorrect: The Netdiag utility helps to isolate networking and connectivity problems. It does not log packets on the network.

C. Incorrect: This tab lets you perform simple and recursive tests: either single tests or periodic tests. It does not monitor network traffic.

D. Correct: The Debug Logging tab lets you define the packets you want to log. You can specify packet direction, content, and type. You can enable filtering based on IP address. Server debug logging can be resource-intensive, and you should enable it only when you need detailed information about server traffic.

15 Implementing, Managing, and Maintaining Network Security (3.0)

Few, if any, aspects of **network design and implementation** have received more attention in the past few years—or seen more development—than **network security**. The danger of **external attacks** from the Internet is highly publicized, and you have probably heard of such attacks as Denial of Service, Distributed Denial of Service, and Redistribution. Sophisticated hacker tools are, unfortunately, readily available on the Internet, and as the tools get more user-friendly, the attackers become more numerous. Hacking is no longer a game for the highly knowledgeable prankster. The new tools have spawned a new breed of attacker who is less knowledgeable—and a lot more destructive.

Internal attacks get much less publicity. Few organizations are willing to admit that their intranets have been hacked by malicious insiders. Yet such attacks are, possibly, more common and more damaging than external attacks. They are also much more difficult to guard against.

Network security tools represent one of the fastest growing areas in the networking industry. Some remarkable tools are available. The levels of **encryption** currently used would have been almost unimaginable even five years ago, and the development of such protocols as **Internet Protocol Security (IPSec)** ensure that communications can be secured all the way from the source to the ultimate destination.

Kerberos is not a new authentication protocol, but it is a powerful one. Because it uses security certificates and timestamps, both ends of a connection can be **authenticated**, and there can be a good level of confidence that nobody is interfering in the middle. A few configuration parameters exist in Kerberos, but these are seldom changed from their default values, and this examination does not test Kerberos configuration.

You can configure many parameters in a Microsoft Windows Server 2003 Active Directory environment, or indeed on a Microsoft Windows Server 2003 stand-alone server. You can set up **security groups** and configure access control lists (ACLs) to protect your resources. You can determine the **level of privilege** of ordinary authenticated users, of various levels of administrators, and of anonymous users. You can determine how software is installed and updated, and how **security updates** are implemented. You can set up auditing and determine who is doing what on your network.

The complexity involved in configuring a large number of available **security settings** could make security administration impossibly complex. Fortunately, you do not have to start from scratch. **Security templates** are available that allow you to set up various standard levels of security. You can also **analyze** a custom security setting by comparing it against **standard templates**. Security is always a balance. There is no point in setting up policies on your servers so strict that many of your users, particularly those with legacy client operating systems, cannot access the resources or run the software that they require to do their jobs. However, if security settings do become too restrictive, tools such as **Resultant Set Of Policy** allow you to quickly identify the source of the problem.

The 70-291 examination does not require you to know how to design security systems. You do, however, need to know how to **audit** systems using security templates, and how to implement **predefined security settings** for software and security updates. You need to be able to check that security configurations are working correctly, and to troubleshoot them if they are not. You also need to be able to access and analyze **security statistics**.

Finally, you need to be aware that security must present a moving target. What is secure today might not be secure tomorrow, and breached security is usually worse than no security at all.

Tested Skills and Suggested Practices

The skills that you need to successfully master the *Implementing, Managing, and Maintaining Network Security* objective domain on the 70-291 exam include the following:

- Implement secure network administration procedures.

  ❑ Practice 1: Create a security management tool by adding the **Security Configuration And Analysis snap-in** and the **Security Templates snap-in** to the **Microsoft Management Console (MMC)**.

  ❑ Practice 2: Use the security management tool that you created in Practice 1 to create a new database. Import a security template and analyze security. Do not use the default log; instead, specify a log file. Analyze the system security against several security templates.

  ❑ Practice 3: Use the **Secedit** command-line utility to perform the same task for which you used the MMC in Practice 2.

  ❑ Practice 4: Carry out a security analysis using the MMC and Secedit as before, but use the **Runas** command while logged on with an ordinary user account.

  ❑ Practice 5: Define a new security template. **Export** the template and apply it to a PC other than the one on which you defined it.

■ Install and configure software update infrastructure.

❑ Practice 1: Access "Checklist: Securing Computers Using Security Configuration Manager" in the Windows Server 2003 Help And Support Center. Work through the "Preparing to Set Up Security" and the "Modifying Security Settings" procedures. Pay particular attention to the **Microsoft Windows Logo Program for Software**, and research this topic on the Microsoft Web site (*http://www.microsoft.com*).

❑ Practice 2: Install and configure **Windows Update** by accessing the Windows Update home page from the Microsoft Web site, and clicking Personalize Windows Update. Select the Display The Link To The Windows Update Catalog Under See Also check box, and click Save Settings. Ensure that you receive **security updates**.

❑ Practice 3: Install and configure Microsoft Software Update Services (SUS) on a server running a member of the Windows Server 2003 family on your network.

❑ Practice 4: Configure Windows Update (**SUS client**) on a client PC to receive Windows patches and updates from the **SUS server**.

■ Monitor network protocol security.

❑ Practice 1: Use the **IP Security Monitor snap-in** to view details about the active IPSec policy that is applied to your domain, or to a local host running Windows Server 2003 or Microsoft Windows XP Professional. View **Quick Mode** and **Main Mode statistics**, and active **IPSec Security Associations (SAs)**.

❑ Practice 2: Search TechNet and the Microsoft Web site for "**Kerberos Tools**." Do not download any third-party support tools.

■ Troubleshoot network protocol security.

❑ Practice 1: Use the Internet Protocol (IP) Security Monitor snap-in to search for specific Main Mode or Quick Mode filters. Search for all matches for filters of a specific traffic type.

❑ Practice 2: If you have on your network a server or client running Microsoft Windows 2000, use Ipsecmon on that computer to monitor IPSec statistics. (You can also use Remote Desktop Connection from a server running Windows Server 2003 to connect to a Windows 2000 Server system and remotely monitor IPSec using **Ipsecmon**, but that is not in the current examination specification.)

❑ Practice 3: Install **Network Monitor** on a server running Windows Server 2003. Capture and display encrypted traffic between two hosts on your network. Perform this task by capturing all traffic and setting up a **display filter**.

Further Reading

This section lists supplemental readings by objective. You should study these sources thoroughly before taking exam 70-291.

Objective 3.1   Review Lessons 1 and 2 of Chapter 11, "Managing Network Security."

Microsoft Corporation. *Windows Server 2003 online help.* Redmond, Washington. Review "Secedit," "Analyze and Configure Security," "For Administrative Tasks, Use the Principle of Least Privilege," and "Security Configuration Manager Tools."

Microsoft Corporation. *Microsoft Windows Server 2003 Deployment Guide.* Redmond, Washington. Review "Baseline Security Analysis," available on the Microsoft Web site at *http://www.microsoft.com/technet/treeview/default.asp?url=/technet/security/tools/tools /mbsawp.asp 2.2.*

Objective 3.2   Review all of Chapter 12, "Maintaining a Network Infrastructure."

Microsoft Corporation. *Windows Server 2003 online help.* Redmond, Washington. Review "Windows Update," "Windows Automatic Updates," and "Windows Logo Program for Software."

Microsoft Corporation. *Microsoft Windows Server 2003 Deployment Guide.* Redmond, Washington. Review "Best Practices for Security," available on the Microsoft Web site at *http://www.microsoft.com/technet/treeview/default.asp?url=/technet/prodtechnol /windowsserver2003/proddocs/standard/sag_seconceptsbp.asp.*

Objective 3.3   Review Lesson 3 of Chapter 11, "Managing Network Security."

Microsoft Corporation. *Windows Server 2003 online help.* Redmond, Washington. Review "Viewing Details About the Active IPSec Policy and IPSec Statistics in IP Security," "Kerberos Policy," and "Security Configuration Manager Tools."

Microsoft Corporation. *Microsoft Windows Server 2003 Deployment Guide.* Redmond, Washington. Review "Internet Protocol Security," available on the Microsoft Web site at *http://www.microsoft.com/technet/treeview/default.asp?url=/technet/prodtechnol /windowsserver2003/proddocs/standard/sag_IPSECtopnode.asp3.4.*

Objective 3.4   Review Lesson 3 of Chapter 11, "Managing Network Security."

Microsoft Corporation. *Windows Server 2003 online help.* Redmond, Washington. Review "Troubleshooting Tools: Internet Protocol Security (IPSec)" and "Troubleshooting: Internet Protocol Security (IPSec)."

Microsoft Corporation. *Microsoft Windows Server 2003 Deployment Guide.* Redmond, Washington. Review "Internet Protocol Security—Troubleshooting," available on the Microsoft Web site at *http://www.microsoft.com/technet/treeview/default.asp?url=/tech- net/prodtechnol/windowsserver2003/proddocs/standard/sag_IPSECtrouble.asp2.1.*

Implement Secure Network Administration Procedures

You can use **predefined security templates** to implement particular levels of security, or as a starting point for creating security policies that are customized to meet different organizational requirements. You can customize a template with the **Security Templates snap-in**, and then use the new template to customize other computers.

You can configure individual computers by using the **Security Configuration And Analysis snap-in**, by using the **Secedit** command-line tool, or by importing a template into Local Security Policy. You can configure multiple machines by importing a template into the **Security Settings extension of Group Policy**. You can also use the Security Configuration And Analysis snap-in, or Secedit /analyze, and choose a security template as a baseline for analyzing a system for potential security vulnerabilities, or for policy violations.

The predefined security template types are as follows:

- Default security (Setup security.inf)
- Domain controller default security (DC security.inf)
- Compatible (Compatws.inf)
- Secure (Secure*.inf)
- Highly secure (Hisec*.inf)
- System root security (Rootsec.inf)
- Auditing of Internet Explorer security (Iesacls.inf)

Where the wildcard (*) is used, you can apply the security template to a workstation, a server, or a domain controller (DC), with differing results. You might also receive different results by applying the same template, depending on whether the operating system was implemented by a **clean install** or by an **upgrade**.

Even if a security template is predefined, you should not assume it is safe to use on your network. Do not apply predefined security templates to your production network without testing them first. This principle applies even more to templates that you customize yourself.

Always save a modified security template with a filename that is different from the name of the template from which you created it. Do not alter and then save standard templates. In particular, never edit the Setup security.inf template, because it gives you the option to reapply the default security settings.

No user should ever be given more rights and privileges than he or she needs to do the job at hand. This principle applies particularly to the administrator. If you are using Word to write a report, you should be logged on with your ordinary user account, not your administrator account. If you need to perform a task that requires administrator rights, you do not need to log off; instead, you can use the Runas utility. Whenever possible, you should carry out administrative tasks while logged on at your client computer with your ordinary account. If you do have to log on to a server, then use an administrator level account. This standard is known as the **principle of least privilege**.

The examination requires that you know how to use security templates to implement baseline security, and how to import a standard template to audit security settings on systems on which a customized template has been either imported or created. You should also be familiar with the principle of least privilege.

Objective 3.1 Questions

1. You are the domain administrator for the Baldwin Museum of Science. The museum has 50 computers running Microsoft Windows NT 4 Workstation. A customized software package is installed on the clients that allows users to obtain illustrations and descriptions of the museum's exhibits. The domain's two domain controllers also act as file servers, and they have recently been upgraded to Windows Server 2003. Museum visitors who sign on for this service are given user names and passwords that allow them to log on and use this facility.

During a closure period, you upgrade all the clients to Windows XP Professional. Now users report that they cannot use the software. How should you solve the problem with the least administrative effort?

   A. Use the Security Configuration And Analysis snap-in to configure the domain controllers with the Compatible security template.

   B. Use Microsoft Windows 2003 group policy to configure the client PCs with the Compatible security template.

   C. Use the Security Configuration And Analysis snap-in to configure the clients with the Compatible security template.

   D. Put all user accounts into the Power Users group on the client PCs.

2. You administer a Windows Server 2003 Active Directory domain. Your manager has become concerned with password authentication security, and she has asked you to ensure that no password policy setting for the domain is any less restrictive than those specified by the account policy settings in the Securedc.inf template. Any setting that is as restrictive, or more restrictive, should be retained. All user accounts in your domain are in either the Accounts organizational unit (OU) or the Sales OU.

You use the Security Configuration And Analysis snap-in on a domain controller, and use Securedc.inf to analyze the computer settings. You find the following differences:

Policy	Database	Computer
Enforce Password History	24 passwords remembered	6 passwords remembered
Maximum Password Age	42 days	100 days
Store Password Using Reversible Encryption	Disabled	Enabled

What should you do?

  A. Create a new Group Policy Object (GPO) and link it to the Sales OU and the Accounts OU. Import the Securedc.inf template into the new GPO.

  B. Import the Securedc.inf template into the Domain Security Policy.

  C. Create a new security template. Set Enforce Password History to 24 passwords and Maximum Password Age to 42 days. Create a new GPO and link it to the Sales OU and the Accounts OU. Import the new template into the new GPO.

  D. Create a new security template. Set Enforce Password History to 24 passwords and Maximum Password Age to 42 days. Import the new template into the Domain Security Policy.

3. You are the administrator of a Windows Server 2003 Active Directory domain. Your Windows XP client PC has Windows Server 2003 Administration Tools Pack installed. You are currently logged on using your user account while using Microsoft Word to write a report. A user calls and tells you that she has forgotten her password. You want to access Active Directory Users And Computers with your Domain Admin account and change the user's password. What is the recommended procedure?

  A. Log off, and log back on again using your Administrator account.

  B. Use the Runas command at the command line.

  C. From the Start menu, select All Programs, point to Administrative Tools, right-click Active Directory Users And Computers, and select Runas.

  D. From the Start menu, select All Programs, point to Administrative Tools, hold down the Shift key, right-click Active Directory Users And Computers, and select Runas.

4. You are experimenting with security settings on a member server running Windows Server 2003 in your Active Directory domain. You want to be able to restore the settings on the computer when you have finished. What should you do before you start and after you have finished testing the new settings? (Choose all that apply.)

  A. Before you start changing the settings, you should use the Security Templates snap-in to create a template containing the current security settings. After experimenting, you should import and apply this template using the Security Configuration And Analysis snap-in, and selecting the Clear This Database Before Importing check box during the import operation.

  B. Before you start, use the Secedit /export command to export a template that contains the original security configuration. Then use Secedit /configure with the /overwrite switch to import the template into a database to restore the settings from this database.

C. You do not need to do anything before you start. You can use Secedit /configure with the /areas switch set to SECURITYPOLICY to import the Setup security.inf template into a database, and use this database to configure the original settings.

D. Before you start, you should use Secedit /generaterollback to create a rollback template. You can then use Secedit /refreshpolicy to apply this rollback template when you are finished.

5. You administer a Windows NT 4 domain. Most client computers are running Windows NT 4 Workstation with Service Pack 3 installed. However, some clients cannot support this operating system and have Microsoft Windows 98 installed instead. You upgrade your primary domain controller (PDC), backup domain controllers (BDCs), and servers to Windows Server 2003 domain controllers and member servers. You configure your domain controllers using the Hisecdc.inf template. None of the clients can access the domain controllers. You do not have a budget to upgrade client hardware or install new client operating systems at this time. You do not want to weaken the security on your domain controllers. What can you do to enable your clients to join the domain? (Select all that apply. Each answer forms part of the solution.)

A. Upgrade your clients running Windows 98 to Windows 98, Second Edition.

B. Create accounts in Active Directory for the client computers.

C. Log on to each client as a local administrator, and then join the domain.

D. Upgrade the computers running Windows NT 4 Workstation with the latest service pack.

E. Configure all clients to use Kerberos version 5 for authentication.

F. Install the Active Directory Client Extensions pack on the clients running Windows 98.

6. Company policy requires that all client machines in the Payroll department be secured using the Securews.inf template settings. You create a Payroll OU in your Microsoft Windows 2003 Active Directory domain, put all the relevant computer accounts into this OU, create a GPO linked to the OU, and import the Securews.inf template into that GPO. All computers in the Payroll department are clients running Windows XP Professional.

You find that some clients in the Payroll department are able to access an unsecure member server running Windows NT 4 that has no service packs installed. You have been intending to upgrade this server, but you welcome the indication that some clients are not as secure as they ought to be. What should you do to ensure that Securews.inf is applied to all the Payroll computers?

A. Run the Convert command-line utility on the unsecured clients.

B. Use the Security Configuration And Analysis snap-in to import the Securews.inf template on each of the unsecured clients, selecting the Clear This Database Before Importing check box during the import operation.

    C. Configure loopback policy so that clients in the Payroll OU are denied access to the unsecure server.

    D. Run the Gpupdate command-line utility on the unsecured clients.

7. You administer a Windows Server 2003 Active Directory domain that has 50 clients running Windows 2000 Professional, 20 clients running Windows NT 4 Workstation, and 25 clients running Windows 98, Second Edition. You want to convert all clients to Windows XP Professional. You upgrade the clients running Windows 2000 Professional but decide to do a clean install of Windows XP Professional on the clients running Windows NT 4 and Windows 98. You specify the NTFS disk filing system for all client hard disks.

You want all client computers to have the same security settings. You create an OU called Clients and move all client computer accounts into that OU. You create a GPO linked to the OU. How do you ensure that all client PCs are configured with the same security settings?

    A. Use Group Policy to apply the Compatws.inf security template to the OU.

    B. Use Secedit to apply the Compatws.inf security template to all the upgraded computers.

    C. Use Secedit to apply the Setup security.inf security template to all the upgraded computers.

    D. Use Group Policy to apply the Setup security.inf security template to the OU.

8. You administer a Windows Server 2003 Active Directory domain for a large manufacturing company. For security reasons, the client computers used by the various design departments are subject to more stringent settings than the client computers used in other parts of the operation. A security consultant has created a security template called Secure-Design.inf that you have to apply to the client computers in all design departments.

The client computers that the managers of the design department use are subject to the same restrictions as all other design department client computers. However, separate policies outside these security requirements can be applied to the managers' computers.

The domain contains a top-level OU called Design. The Managers OU is a child of Design. You move all the client computers used by design personnel into the Design OU. You create a GPO called DesignPolicy and link it to the Design OU. You import the SecureDesign.inf template to the DesignPolicy GPO.

When you test the system, you find that the design managers' computers do not have some of the security settings specified in the new template. The computers with accounts in the Design OU all have the correct security configurations. What should you do to solve the problem, and to make sure the settings are applied without delay? (Choose all that apply. Each answer forms part of the solution.)

A. Move all the design managers' user accounts into the Managers OU.

B. Move all the managers' computer accounts into the Design OU.

C. Select the No Override check box in the DesignPolicy GPO.

D. Run the Gpupdate command-line utility on all of the managers' computers.

E. Link the Managers OU to the DesignPolicy GPO.

F. Create a DesignManagers global security group and put all the managers' user accounts into that group. Grant the group Read and Execute permissions to the DesignPolicy GPO.

Objective 3.1 Answers

1. **Correct Answers: B**

    A. Incorrect: Domain controllers should never be configured with the Compatible security template. In any case, the software runs on the workstations, not the domain controllers.

    B. Correct: This solution allows the software to run as it did before on the machines running Windows NT 4. An added advantage is that only one configuration change is necessary. You do not have to reconfigure each client PC.

    C. Incorrect: This approach would work, but you would have configure each client individually—it could not be automated.

    D. Incorrect: This approach would work, but it would give the users too many rights. Also, this solution would take more administrative effort than using group policy.

2. **Correct Answers: D**

    A. Incorrect: Account policies are set at the domain level, not at the OU level.

    B. Incorrect: This solution enables the more restrictive settings for Enforce Password History and Maximum Password Age. However, it disables Store Password Using Reversible Encryption. This last setting is more restrictive and should be retained.

    C. Incorrect: This answer is incorrect for the reason given in the explanation for answer A.

    D. Correct: This solution enables the more restrictive settings for Enforce Password History and Maximum Password Age. Because the new template has no setting for Store Password Using Reversible Encryption, the current, more restrictive setting is retained.

3. **Correct Answers: D**

    A. Incorrect: This practice is inappropriate when you want to perform only one small administrative task. You could easily forget to log back on with your ordinary user account before continuing to type your report, which would violate the principle of least privilege. It also gives you extra work.

    B. Incorrect: You can use this command, but the syntax is complex (for example, Runas /env /profile /user:mydomain\administrator "mmc winnt\system32\filename.msc), and you would need to know the name of the file to run. If you had this command in a batch file, running that batch file would be a sensible option.

C. Incorrect: On Windows XP, Runas is not available on this menu without holding down the Shift key.

D. Correct: This procedure accesses Runas.

4. **Correct Answers: A and B**

A. Correct: If you choose a setting that is not specified in the computer's original configuration, that setting will by default remain at what you changed it to when you applied the template. However, you can achieve the result you want by selecting the Clear This Database Before Importing check box during the import operation.

B. Correct: The /overwrite switch clears all the security settings before applying a template, so the original settings will be restored.

C. Incorrect: The settings that are configured on the computer when you start to experiment will not necessarily be the original default settings.

D. Incorrect: You can create a rollback template as described, which is used when a new template is applied. Then you must roll back this operation and restore the original settings. However, Secedit /refreshpolicy does not perform the rollback operation and has, in any case, been replaced by Gpupdate.

5. **Correct Answers: D and F**

A. Incorrect: Clients running Windows 98, Second Edition do not support NT LAN Manager version 2 (NTLMv2). Highly secure Windows Server 2003 domain controllers require that clients use at least NTLMv2 authentication.

B. Incorrect: Computer accounts can be created either when the client joins the domain, or in advance. However, if the clients cannot access the domain controllers, they cannot join the domain regardless of how their accounts are created.

C. Incorrect: The clients cannot access the domain controllers. It makes no difference which account is used to log on.

D. Correct: Computers running Windows NT 4 Workstation with Service Pack 4 or later can use NTLMv2 authentication, and can therefore connect to a highly secure Windows Server 2003 domain controller.

E. Incorrect: The only Windows clients that can currently use Kerberos version 5 are clients running Windows 2000 Professional and Windows XP.

F. Correct: You can install the Active Directory Client Extensions pack enabling clients running Windows 98 to use NTLMv2 authentication, and to access Active Directory. At the time of this writing, it needs to be installed from a Microsoft Windows Server 2000 CD-ROM.

6.   Correct Answers: A

A. Correct: The clients are in the correct OU and the correct template is applied to the appropriate OU. However, security templates can be applied only to client PCs that use the NTFS disk filing system. Using Convert c: fs:ntfs on the unsecured (FAT-formatted) clients should solve the problem.

B. Incorrect: The template is already applied to the GPO that controls the Payroll OU settings. Importing the template on individual clients in the OU has no effect.

C. Incorrect: This solution treats the symptom, not the cause. The clients will no longer be able to access the insecure server, but the secure settings will not be applied to them.

D. Incorrect: Group Policy is automatically refreshed periodically, so the Gpupdate command is unlikely to solve the problem. You should run Gpupdate if template settings have been applied by a method other than Group Policy, or if you want to ensure that changes made through Group Policy apply immediately.

7.   Correct Answers: C

A. Incorrect: Clients that are upgraded to Windows XP Professional, rather than having a clean install, retain the security settings that they had before they were upgraded. The Compatible security template is incremental—that is to say, it alters a security setting on the computer only if that setting clashes with a setting in the template. Thus, the upgraded computers can retain security settings that are not implemented on the computers that were cleanly installed.

B. Incorrect: A clean install sets up and applies the Default security (Setup security.inf) template, not the Compatible template. Also, because the Compatible template is incremental, this procedure cannot guarantee consistency even among the upgraded computers. Finally, the question does not state that software outside the Windows Logo Program for Software needs to be run, so the Compatible template might not be appropriate.

C. Correct: The Default security template overrides any settings already on the computers. It is not incremental. It is also the template that is applied during a clean install. This procedure therefore ensures that the upgraded computers will have consistent security settings, and that these settings will match the security settings on the computers that had a clean install.

D. Incorrect: You should never apply Setup security.inf using Group Policy. This template contains a large amount of data, which would move through the domain when Group Policy is periodically refreshed. You should apply this template in parts because it is so large, and the /areas switch in Secedit /configure lets you perform this task.

8. **Correct Answers: C and D**

A. **Incorrect:** The Managers OU is set up to hold computer accounts so that they can be configured through Group Policy. Moving user accounts into this OU would not help, and it is bad practice.

B. **Incorrect:** This approach would ensure that the Group Policy settings applied to the design personnel's computers would also apply to the managers' computers. However, it would be difficult to assign additional policies to only the managers' computers.

C. **Correct:** Block inheritance is set on some of the policy settings in the Managers OU, which is why some settings are not being applied. Setting No Override prevents settings that should be inherited from being blocked.

D. **Correct:** Perform this task after you have specified No Override. This solution ensures that the changes are applied immediately, without having to wait until the next time Group Policy is refreshed.

E. **Incorrect:** Managers is a child of Design. It is inappropriate practice to link both child and parent OUs to the same GPO.

F. **Incorrect:** User permissions are not an issue here. This approach would not solve the problem.

Install and Configure Software Update Infrastructure

Windows Update is used to download such items as security fixes, critical updates, the latest help files, drivers, and Internet products. New content is added to the site regularly, so you can always get the most recent updates. You can configure Windows Update so that you can access the **Windows Update Catalog**. This strategy lets you select updates that you plan to deploy later, and is of particular use to someone who administers a number of machines.

Automatic Updates is built into Windows 2000, Windows XP, and Windows Server 2003. It enables the operating system to automatically download and install critical updates from the Windows Update site. Windows Update and Automatic Updates are two separate components designed to work together to keep Windows secure. You have full control over the level of this interaction. For example, you can choose to automatically download and install updates as they become available, or you can be notified when new updates become available.

Software Update Services (SUS) lets you download a limited version of the Windows Update site and distribute updates to clients through Automatic Updates. As a result, you can control how and when updates are deployed, and deliver updates to users through your intranet and inside your firewall.

Running **legacy programs** on Windows XP Professional, Windows Server 2003, or Windows 2000 Server or Professional typically requires that you modify the system settings that allow members of the **Power Users group** to run these programs. These same permissions also make it possible for Power Users to gain additional privileges on the system. Therefore, you should deploy applications that belong to the Windows Logo Program for Software. These programs can run successfully under the secure configuration that is provided by the Users group.

The other problem associated with legacy considerations occurs when clients with legacy operating systems need to have software installed and updated. If a client cannot access Active Directory, it cannot be updated through Group Policy. The Active Directory Client Extensions pack allows legacy systems to access Active Directory and make use of Group Policy.

You must be familiar with all of these facilities for the examination.

Objective 3.2 Questions

1. You want to obtain critical updates and security fixes for your PC running Windows XP Professional. You access the Windows Update site. However, you cannot find the Windows Update Catalog under See Also in the left pane. What is the problem?

    A. You have not installed and configured SUS.

    B. You have not installed and configured Automatic Updates.

    C. TCP port 80 is blocked for incoming traffic on the firewall at your Internet service provider (ISP).

    D. You need to configure the Windows Update site.

2. You administer your company's Windows Server 2003 Active Directory domain. All client PCs run Windows XP Professional. Company policy states that employees cannot download software or software updates from the Internet. Software must be installed or upgraded on client machines automatically through Group Policy. As the domain administrator, you have been exempted from this policy so that you can download operating system upgrades, security fixes, virus definitions, and Microsoft utilities from the Windows Update site. You then want these upgrades, fixes, and so forth, to be installed automatically on other users' PCs when these users log on to the domain. What do you need to do after you have downloaded the software?

    A. Install and configure SUS on your PC.

    B. Install Automatic Updates on the client computers.

    C. Create a Windows installer package.

    D. Configure Remote Installation Services (RIS) to distribute the software.

3. You want to install an application that runs on client computers running Windows XP Professional in your Active Directory domain. You do not want to add user accounts to the Power Users group on these machines, nor do you want to configure the client computers using the Compatible security template. How can you find out whether an application you have chosen will run under these constraints?

    A. Consult the Microsoft Windows Catalog and look for the Designed For Windows XP logo.

    B. Obtain a VeriSign Code Signing Identity.

    C. Create a Windows installer package.

    D. Consult the Windows Catalog and look for the Compatible With Windows XP logo.

Objective 3.2 Answers

1.   Correct Answers: D

A. Incorrect: You need to install SUS only if you are downloading updates to a server so that you can later install them to client machines from the server. This situation does not apply to this scenario.

B. Incorrect: Automatic Updates can be configured so that a client PC can receive updates from a server on its network. In this scenario, however, you are attempting to update your PC from the Internet. Automatic Updates is installed by default on a client running Windows XP Professional.

C. Incorrect: If this situation were the case, you could not have accessed the Windows Update site.

D. Correct: You should select Personalize Windows Update and select the Display The Link To The Windows Update Catalog Under See Also check box.

2.   Correct Answers: C

A. Incorrect: You would need SUS if users were permitted to access an internal Web server as if they were accessing the Internet, and download and install the relevant programs. However, they cannot perform this task. Software must be installed automatically through Group Policy.

B. Incorrect: Automatic Updates is installed by default on computers running Windows XP Professional. The Windows Update site can be configured to send updates automatically to a client. However, in this scenario, clients do not receive updates or fixes by this method, but instead through Group Policy.

C. Correct: You need to create an OU, and put all the accounts of the users that need to get the update in the OU (or computer accounts if you want to install on reboot). You then create a GPO linked to the OU, download the software you want to install, create a Windows installer package, and apply that package to the GPO.

D. Incorrect: RIS is typically used to automatically install operating systems and application software. It is not the appropriate tool in this scenario.

3.   Correct Answers: A

A. Correct: The Designed For Windows XP logo for software helps customers identify products that deliver a high-quality computing experience with the Windows XP operating system. Products that bear this logo can run on Windows XP without having to change any security or security group settings.

B. Incorrect: This step is one that third-party software developers should take if they want to submit applications for possible inclusion in the Windows Catalog, and validation through the Designed for Windows XP Logo Program for Software.

C. Incorrect: You can create a Windows installer package for many applications, not all of which will run on Windows XP under the conditions stated in the question.

D. Incorrect: No logo is associated with the Compatible With Windows XP designation, although the application is listed in the Windows Catalog. This designation is intended primarily for older applications, which the product vendor has determined will have basic functionality on Windows XP, and which will not interfere with operating system or application stability. There is no guarantee that the application will run in the context of an ordinary user.

Objective 3.3

Monitor Network Protocol Security

The IP Security Monitor is implemented as a Microsoft Management Console (MMC) snap-in on the Windows Server 2003 and Windows XP Professional operating systems. It includes enhancements that allow you to view details about an active IPSec policy, in addition to Quick Mode and Main Mode statistics, and active IPSec SAs. IP Security Monitor also enables you to search for specific **Main Mode** or **Quick Mode filters**.

The examination requires you to know how to use IP Security Monitor to verify that IPSec is being used to encrypt and secure communications. You are not expected to design and implement complex IPSec policies, for example, creating a virtual private network (VPN) IPSec over a **Layer2 Tunneling Protocol (L2TP) tunnel**. At the same time, if you do not understand IP settings, the results you obtain from IP Security Monitor will be meaningless. You should at least have seen, and preferably have used, the **Create IP Security Rule Wizard**. You should be familiar with **the IP Filter List, Filter Action, Authentication Methods, Tunnel Setting, and Connection Type settings**.

You need a working knowledge of Kerberos, although you will not be required to specify a Kerberos configuration or manage a **Kerberos trust**.

1. You are investigating the settings for an IPSec policy using IP Security Policies. Which of the following are valid authentication options? (Choose all that apply.)

   A. Active Directory default (Kerberos version 5 protocol)

   B. L2TP

   C. MPPE

   D. A certificate from a **certificate authority (CA)**

   E. **EFS**

   F. Use a **preshared key**

2. You administer an Active Directory domain. All domain controllers are running Windows Server 2003, Enterprise Edition. The domain contains servers running Windows Server 2003, servers running Windows 2000, clients running Windows 2000 Professional, and clients running Windows XP Professional. All internal traffic in the domain is encrypted using IPSec.

   To confirm that IPSec policies are operating correctly on the domain, you regularly check names of active IPSec policies against the name of the GPO to which the policy is assigned. You need to be able to perform this task from any host on the network. Which tools can you use from which hosts?

   A.

Host	View IPSec Policy Name	View GPO to Which Active IPSec Policy Is Assigned
Windows Server 2003	IP Security Monitor consoleNetsh ipsec static show gpoassigned-policy command	Resultant Set of Policy (RSoP) console Netsh ipsec static show gpoassignedpolicy command
Windows XP Professional	IP Security Policy Management console Netdiag /test:ipsec command	Netdiag /test:ipsec command
Windows 2000 Server	Netdiag /test:ipsec command TCP/IP Properties/ Advanced/ Options/IPSec Gpresult.exe	Netdiag /test:ipsec command Gpotool.exe
Windows 2000 Professional	Netdiag /test:ipsec command TCP/IP Properties/ Advanced/ Options/IPSec Gpresult.exe	Netdiag /test:ipsec command Gpotool.exe

B.

Host	View IPSec Policy Name	View GPO to Which Active IPSec Policy Is Assigned
Windows Server 2003	IP Security Monitor console Netsh ipsec static show gpoassignedpolicy command	Resultant Set of Policy (RSoP) console Netsh ipsec static show gpoassignedpolicy command
Windows XP Professional	Netdiag /test:ipsec command	Netdiag /test:ipsec command IP Security Policy Management console
Windows 2000 Server	Netdiag /test:ipsec command TCP/IP Properties/ Advanced/ Options/IPSec	Netdiag /test:ipsec command Gpresult.exe Gpotool.exe
Windows 2000 Professional	Netdiag /test:ipsec command TCP/IP Properties/ Advanced/ Options/IPSec	Netdiag /test:ipsec command Gpresult.exe Gpotool.exe

C.

Host	View IPSec Policy Name	View GPO to Which Active IPSec Policy Is Assigned
Windows Server 2003	IP Security Monitor console RSOP console Netsh ipsec static show gpoassignedpolicy command	Netsh ipsec static show gpoassignedpolicy command
Windows XP Professional	IP Security Policy Management console Netdiag /test:ipsec command	Netdiag /test:ipsec command
Windows 2000 Server	Netdiag /test:ipsec command TCP/IP Properties/ Advanced/ Options/IPSec	Netdiag /test:ipsec command Gpresult.exe Gpotool.exe
Windows 2000 Professional	Netdiag /test:ipsec command TCP/IP Properties/ Advanced/ Options/IPSec	Netdiag /test:ipsec command Gpresult.exe Gpotool.exe

D.

Host	View IPSec Policy Name	View GPO to Which Active IPSec Policy Is Assigned
Windows Server 2003	IP Security Monitor console Netsh ipsec static show gpo-assignedpolicy command	Resultant Set of Policy (RSoP) console Netsh ipsec static show gpoassignedpolicy command
Windows XP Professional	IP Security Policy Management console Netdiag /test:ipsec command	Netdiag /test:ipsec command
Windows 2000 Server	Netdiag /test:ipsec command TCP/IP Properties/Advanced/Options/IPSec	Netdiag /test:ipsec command Gpresult.exe Gpotool.exe
Windows 2000 Professional	Netdiag /test:ipsec command TCP/IP Properties/Advanced/Options/IPSec	Netdiag /test:ipsec command Gpresult.exe Gpotool.exe

3. A security consultant has configured and assigned an IP security policy for your Windows Server 2003 Active Directory domain. He logs on to a member server using a temporary administrator-level domain account and uses Network Monitor to demonstrate that traffic to and from the server is encrypted.

The next day, users report that they cannot log on at their hosts running Windows XP Professional. You use your Administrator account to log on at a server. You use the IP Security Monitor snap-in, and find that the assigned policy is Secure Server (Require Security). You use the IP Security Policies On Local Computer console and find that the IP Security rules for this policy are set as shown in the following figure.

You cannot log onto the domain while your client is running Windows XP Professional. You instead log on using the Local Administrator account. You access the IP Security Management snap-in and find that no IP security policy has been assigned. You need encrypted communication between clients and servers in your domain. You need to let users log on as soon as possible. All the member server computer accounts in your domain are in one top-level OU and all the client computer accounts are in another. What should you do?

A. Configure all servers to use the Server (Server Request) IPSec policy.

B. Configure all clients to use the Client (Respond Only) IPSec policy.

C. Include the Internet Control Message Protocol (ICMP) in the IP security rules for the policy on the servers.

D. Use a certificate from a CA for authentication, rather than Kerberos.

4. You want to analyze the Main Mode IPSec statistics on a member server running Windows Server 2003 in your domain. The server is accessed frequently by a large number of clients, and you know there will be a lot of statistical information. What procedure should you use to export this information for future analysis.?

A. Use the IP Security monitor snap-in to export the data to a text file.

B. At the command line, type **netsh ipsec dynamic show stats type=ike**.

C. At the command line, type **netsh ipsec dynamic show stats type=ike>***File-Name***.txt**.

D. At the command line, type **netsh ipsec dynamic show stats type=ipsec>***File-Name***.txt**.

5. You are a network administrator for Wingtip Toys. Wingtip has a single Active Directory domain that consists of a main site at its head office in New York, and a small branch office in Boston. The branch office connects to the main office by a dial-up connection through a VPN. The VPN uses the Point-to-Point Tunneling Protocol (PPTP) with MPPE encryption.

Wingtip has recently upgraded all its servers to Windows Server 2003. Client machines are either Windows 2000 Professional or Windows XP Professional hosts. The company wants to encrypt all internal traffic and intends to assign IPSec policies to all hosts. Traffic across the VPN should also use IPSec encryption. A consultant will configure customized IPSec policies that meet the company's security requirements.

The company also wants to migrate to a private IP addressing scheme and to install NAT-enabled routers at both the main and branch offices. You have been asked to compile a preliminary report. What should you tell management?

    A. This task can be achieved, but the VPN needs to be reconfigured to use L2TP and IPSec encryption.

    B. This task cannot be achieved. IPSec encrypts NAT headers; therefore, NAT will not work.

    C. This task can be achieved, but the VPN must use a persistent broadband connection rather than a dial-up connection.

    D. This task cannot be achieved. Kerberos authentication is required for IPSec, and Kerberos cannot be used to authenticate VPN traffic.

6. The Graphic Design Institute has commissioned a small research company, Trey Research, to investigate the marketing potential of a series of graphic images. The Institute has implemented a Windows Server 2003 Active Directory domain. All of the Institute's servers are running Windows Server 2003, Enterprise Edition, and its clients are a mixture of Windows 2000 Professional and Windows XP Professional hosts. Trey Research's small network consists of a workgroup with 3 stand-alone servers and 15 clients running Windows XP Professional. Trey Research and the Graphic Design Institute intend to share data over the Internet and agree to use IPSec to encrypt this data. Neither organization has previously implemented IPSec.

You are the network administrator for the Graphic Design Institute. You have not been tasked with designing and implementing an IPSec solution, but your IT manager considers that an out-of-box configuration could be implemented. She suggests implementing the Secure Server (Require Security) default IPSec policy on all servers and the Client (Respond Only) default policy on all clients.

She asks you whether this solution would work. What should you reply?

    A. Yes, but the policy on the clients could permit unsecure communication. You need a more secure client policy for use over the Internet.

    B. Yes, but it would be advisable to specify the triple DES (3DES) encryption algorithm.

    C. No, but it would work if the authentication method were changed to public key certificates, and certificates were obtained from a certificate authority.

    D. No, but it would work if a VPN were set up between the two organizations, and Trey Research staff were permitted to log on to the Graphic Design Institute's domain.

Objective 3.3 Answers

1.   Correct Answers: A, D, and F

    A.   Correct: The Kerberos version 5 security protocol can be used for authentication if a Windows 2000 or Windows Server 2003 Active Directory domain, or a trusted Active Directory domain, validates the source and destination computers.

    B.   Incorrect: L2TP is a tunneling encapsulation protocol. It is not used for authentication.

    C.   Incorrect: Microsoft Point-to-Point Encryption is used for encryption, not authentication.

    D.   Correct: This setting uses a public key certificate for authentication. If the name of the CA is not displayed, the Exclude The CA Name From The Certificate Request check box was selected when the policy was created.

    E.   Incorrect: The Encryption File System is used to protect confidential files on NTFS-formatted hard disks. It is not an IPSec policy option.

    F.   Correct: The same key is specified on the source and destination computers. This setting is valid, but it is a weak method of authentication and its use is not recommended.

2.   Correct Answers: D

    A.   Incorrect: The Gpresult.exe Windows 2000 Resource Kit tool shows the GPO name on both Windows 2000 Professional and Windows 2000 Server, not the IPSec policy name.

    B.   Incorrect: The IP Security Policy Management console on Windows XP Professional shows the IPSec policy name, not the GPO name.

    C.   Incorrect: The RSoP console on Windows Server 2003 shows the GPO name, not the active IPSec policy name.

    D.   Correct: These tools are correct. The RSoP console is used in Windows Server 2003 to determine which IPSec policies are assigned—but are not being applied—to IPSec clients. The Windows XP implementation of the RSoP console does not support the display of IPSec policies. Also, the Gpresult /scope computer command does not display the Group Policy object that contains an IPSec policy assignment. Therefore, you should use Netdiag to view IPSec policy assignment information on computers running Windows 2000 Professional or Server or Windows XP Professional. The Netdiag /test:ipsec command displays the Group Policy object that contains the IPSec policy assignment, and the OU to which the Group Policy object is assigned. Gpotool.exe monitors the health of GPOs on domain controllers. You can use this tool to check the consistency and replication of GPOs and to display GPO properties. The IPSec Security Management console in Windows XP Professional displays the active IPSec policy name only for local policies. TCP/IP Properties/Advanced/Options/IPSec displays a globally assigned IPSec policy that is not specific to the connection. Gpresult.exe and Gpotool.exe are not installed on Windows 2000 hosts by default, but are part of the Resource Kits.

3. **Correct Answers: B**

   A. **Incorrect:** This solution would enable the clients to communicate with the servers, and users could log on. However, communication between the clients and the servers would not be encrypted.

   B. **Correct:** The clients will use IPSec encryption when required by the servers to do so. You can assign this policy to a GPO, and link this to the client computer's OU. This solution is not ideal, however, because clients will be able to communicate unsecurely with each other, and Cryptographic, Hashing, and Session Key Regeneration settings might not be exactly what your company requires. Nevertheless, the solution meets the stated requirements of encrypting client-to-server traffic, and quickly allowing users to log on.

   C. **Incorrect:** This solution encrypts the payload of ICMP Echo messages. Encrypting pings, for example, is unnecessary, and does not enable users to log on at their client PCs.

   D. **Incorrect:** The problem is that the servers require IPSec and it is not enabled on the clients. Changing the authentication method will not solve this issue.

4. **Correct Answers: C**

   A. **Incorrect:** This snap-in can display statistics. It cannot, however, export them.

   B. **Incorrect:** This command results in a lengthy, rapidly scrolling output that is difficult to see, never mind analyze. It does not export its output to a text file.

   C. **Correct:** This command exports the statistical information to a text file. It can then be viewed, printed out, and analyzed.

   D. **Incorrect:** This solution exports the Quick mode statistics to a text file.

5. **Correct Answers: A**

   A. **Correct:** L2TP/IPSec VPN clients that are behind NAT routers can establish IPSec-secured connections over the Internet to their corporate network by using IPSec ESP Transport mode. In this scenario, this approach ensures that VPN traffic will be encrypted using IPSec.

B. Incorrect: IPSec ESP packets can pass through NAT routers that allow User Datagram Protocol (UDP) traffic. The Internet Key Exchange (IKE) protocol automatically detects the presence of a NAT router and uses UDP-ESP encapsulation to allow IPSec traffic to pass through it.

C. Incorrect: This solution would improve performance but is not essential to allow IPSec-encrypted traffic to use the VPN.

D. Incorrect: Kerberos is one of several authentication methods that can be used in IPSec policies. Kerberos is the default authentication protocol in Windows Server 2003 and can be used to authenticate VPN communications.

6.   Correct Answers: C and D

A. Incorrect: You do need a more secure policy for Internet use. However, the plan as stated would not work because the authentication method needs to be changed, or a VPN created.

B. Incorrect: The 3DES encryption algorithm is the default for both policies. Where IPSec-encrypted communication is initiated with a host that does not support 3DES (a Windows 2000 system that does not have Service Pack 2 or later installed), DES will be used. The authentication method, not the encryption algorithm, is the problem in this scenario.

C. Correct: No Active Directory trust exists between Trey Research and the Graphic Design Institute. Such a trust cannot be created because Trey Research does not have a domain. Kerberos cannot, therefore, be used for authentication. The choice is either to set up a VPN (see the explanation for answer D), or to change the authentication method. Public key certificate authentication is an appropriate method in this scenario. It is likely that certificates would be obtained from a third-party CA, such as Verisign.

D. Correct: This is a standard method of resolving this situation. A common technique is to create a single user account in one domain and perform a one-to-many mapping of this account to user certificates. Users in one organization then use a certificate-based authentication (for example, smart card authentication) to log on with that account.

Objective 3.4

Troubleshoot Network Protocol Security

You can use the version of Network Monitor provided on the Windows Server 2003 installation CD-ROM to view only the network traffic that is sent to or from the computer on which it is installed. To view network traffic that is sent to or from another computer and is routed through your computer, you need to use the Network Monitor component that is provided with **Microsoft Systems Management Server**.

By default, Network Monitor captures and displays all traffic sent to or from the host it is running on, which is often too much information. You can configure view and capture filters so that you can either view only the traffic that you are interested in, or capture only that traffic. Network packets can be filtered by source or destination IP address, for example, or by protocol. **Capture filters** can be triggered by a pattern match so that you can specify when the capture starts.

Typically, you use Network Monitor in conjunction with other tools such as IP Security Monitor (or **Ipsecmon** on computers running Windows 2000). Network Monitor could be used, for example, to identify the server to which unencrypted traffic is going. You could then use IP Security Monitor to determine which SAs are set up between that server and other hosts on the network. Alternatively, the **System log** in **Event Viewer** might indicate an unacceptable number of packet-related faults, and you can use Network Monitor to discover what is causing the problem.

The examination requires that you know how to install, configure, and use Network Monitor, and understand how it complements other troubleshooting tools.

1. You create a VPN through your company's intranet. You specify L2TP. Windows Server 2003 automatically creates an IPSec policy when L2TP is specified. However, after the VPN has been set up, you are unsure whether the IPSec policy has been configured correctly. Which tool can you use to verify IPSec policy assignments?

    A. Performance Monitor

    B. IP Security Monitor

    C. System Monitor

    D. Network Monitor

2. Your company does not use a domain structure but instead has a number of work-groups. The Research workgroup has six clients running Windows XP Professional, four clients running Windows 2000 Professional, and two stand-alone servers running Windows Server 2003. Communication between hosts in this workgroup must be secure. A member of your support staff configures and assigns an IPSec security policy on all hosts on the Research workgroup. All hosts can ping each other by IP address, but Research department staff cannot access files on the servers from their client PCs.

You log on to one of the servers using the Local Administrator account, access the security Settings node within Local Computer Policy, and enable success and failure auditing for logon events. You open Event Viewer and locate a failure audit event 547 in the security log. The failure reason given is "Failed to obtain Kerberos server credentials for ISAKMP/ERROR_IPSEC_IKE service." What is the most likely cause of the problem?

    A. The default response rule is not activated.

    B. Kerberos has been specified as the initial authentication method.

    C. The 3DES encryption algorithm has been specified, and it cannot be used on the clients running Windows 2000.

    D. The incorrect policy has been assigned.

3. You are using Network Monitor on a Windows Server 2003 domain controller named ServerA. You want Network Monitor to capture network traffic between ServerA and a client running Windows 2000 named ClientA. ClientA has been assigned the Client (Respond Only) default IPSec policy. ServerA has been assigned the Secure Server (Require Security) IPSec policy. You want to make sure encrypted data packets are being sent from ClientA to ServerA, and from ServerA to ClientA. When you stop and view the capture, you see that a large number of packets have been captured. You realize that you have forgotten to specify a capture filter. How should you set up your display filter to view encrypted packets?

A. AND

Protocol==ESP

ServerA(IP)?‡ClientA(IP)

B. AND

Protocol==AH

ServerA(IP)?‡ClientA(IP)

C. AND

Protocol==ESP

ServerA(IP)?‡ANY

D. AND

Protocol==AH

ServerA(IP)?‡ANY

4. You administer a Windows Server 2003 Active Directory domain. All client PCs are in a top-level OU called Clients, and all server PCs (apart from domain controllers) are in a top-level OU called Servers. The domain controllers are in their default OU. Secure Server (Require Security) default IPSec policy has been assigned to all servers (including DCs). Client (Respond Only) default IPSec policy has been assigned to all clients. All client PCs are Windows 2000 Professional hosts.

Management is concerned that the client computers in the Research department communicate unsecurely with each other and with other clients. Only four such machines exist. On one of them, you create a custom policy that requires secure communications. You export it to a file and import it into the other three client machines in the Research department. You assign the policy on all four machines.

Subsequently, you use the IP Security Monitor console on one of the machines and find that no SAs are set up between the Research department hosts, or between these machines and clients in other departments. You capture traffic using Network Monitor and discover that unencrypted traffic is passing between the Research clients. What is your first step to solve the problem?

A. Change the authentication method on the custom policy to use a preshared key.

B. Change the encryption algorithm from 3DES to DES.

C. Create an OU.

D. Move the Research department computer accounts into the Server OU.

5.   You want to set up a tool for maintenance and monitoring of IP policies on remote hosts in your domain. You add the IP Security Monitor and IP Security Policies snap-ins to an MMC. However, when you try to add the host ClientA to the IP Security Monitor, you get the error message shown in the following figure.

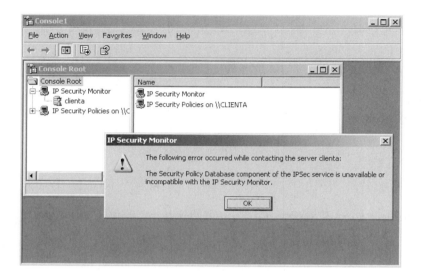

How can you manage and monitor IP Security on ClientA?

A.   You cannot do so. ClientA is a legacy host that does not support IPSec.

B.   ClientA is not part of the domain. You need to join the host to your domain if you want to use IP Security Monitor.

C.   Only IP Security policies that use your authentication can be managed and monitored using IP Security Monitor. You need to assign such a policy to ClientA.

D.   You should use legacy Ipsecmon.

Objective 3.4 Answers

1. **Correct Answers: B**

    A. Incorrect: Performance Monitor is a Windows NT 4 tool.

    B. Correct: IP Security Monitor is used to verify IPSec policy assignments and to display IPSec status.

    C. Incorrect: System Monitor displays system counters such as Memory:Pages/sec in real time. It cannot verify IPSec policy assignments.

    D. Incorrect: Network Monitor captures network traffic. You can use it to display and check IPSec packets, but you cannot use it to verify IPSec assignments.

2. **Correct Answers: D**

    A. Incorrect: This rule specifies that to communicate securely, the computer must respond to requests for secure communication. Clearing the check box that specifies this rule would make communication less secure, but would not prevent it altogether.

    B. Incorrect: Kerberos cannot be used for authentication in this scenario because the hosts are not in an Active Directory domain. The IP Security Policy Wizard would not create a policy if Kerberos were specified.

    C. Incorrect: A system running Windows 2000 that does not have Service Pack 2 or later installed does not support 3DES. If 3DES is specified, however, the rule defaults to the Data Encryption Standard (DES) for communication with that computer.

    D. Correct: The error detected occurs when Kerberos is specified as the authentication protocol in an environment that cannot support it (such as a workgroup). It is not possible to create a new policy in this environment, so one or more of the default policies must have been assigned. The most common mistake in this situation is to assign Secure Server (Require Security) on the servers.

3. **Correct Answers: A**

    A. Correct: ESP packets contain Frame, Ethernet, IP, and ESP header information. The rest of the frame is encrypted. This filter displays ESP network traffic between ServerA and ClientA.

    B. Incorrect: The Authentication Header (AH) provides authentication, integrity, and anti-replay for the entire packet. It does not affect encryption.

    C. Incorrect: ESP is the correct protocol, but this setup displays the ESP traffic between ServerA and all participating clients.

    D. Incorrect: This answer is incorrect for the reasons given in the explanations for both answer B and answer C.

4. **Correct Answers: C**

   A. **Incorrect:** The policy was exported from one client and exported to the others, so the same authentication method is specified in the policy on all four machines. The authentication method is unlikely to be the problem. In any case, the pre-shared key authentication method is weak authentication and is not appropriate in this scenario.

   B. **Incorrect:** A system running Windows 2000 that does not have Service Pack 2 or later installed does not support 3DES. If 3DES is specified, the rule defaults to DES for communication with that computer. The encryption algorithm is not, therefore, a factor in this scenario.

   C. **Correct:** In this scenario, assigning an IPSec policy locally has no effect. This situation happens when the hosts are in a domain and a policy has been assigned through Group Policy. In this case, the Client (Respond Only) policy has been assigned to a GPO that is linked to the Clients OU. You need to create an OU called Research, move the four client computer accounts into that OU, create a GPO linked to Research, and assign the custom IPSec policy to that GPO.

   D. **Incorrect:** This approach would ensure that communication between the Research department's computers, and between these computers and all other hosts in the domain, is encrypted. However, it is not the best solution. Servers are often put into one OU and clients into another for a number of reasons, not merely to assign IPSec policy. This solution would result in the Research department clients being configured with other settings (such as Log On Locally rights) that might be inappropriate.

5. **Correct Answers: D**

   A. **Incorrect:** The figure shows that the IP Security Policies snap-in has already been added to the MMC for ClientA. Therefore, ClientA supports IPSec.

   B. **Incorrect:** Hosts can be managed and monitored using the IP Security Monitor snap-in whether they are joined to a domain or not.

   C. **Incorrect:** The authentication method has no bearing on whether IP Security Monitor can be used.

   D. **Correct:** This error occurs when you try to add a Windows 2000 host to IP Security Monitor. Legacy Ipsecmon is the appropriate tool to use for such hosts. Unfortunately it is not possible to create a single-seat maintenance tool by this method if some of your client hosts run Microsoft Windows 2000 operating systems.

16 Implementing, Managing, and Maintaining Routing And Remote Access (4.0)

Microsoft Windows Server 2003 can be configured as a **router**, as a **dial-up server**, as a **virtual private network (VPN) server**, and as a **Network Address Translation (NAT) provider**. Two such servers can be configured to send data between two **private networks** securely over the Internet. The **Internet Authentication Service (IAS)** on Windows Server 2003 can be configured to provide the **Remote Authentication Dial-In User Service (RADIUS)** to RAS servers that are RADIUS clients.

Where Windows Server 2003 is configured as a RAS server, you need to know about its **security** and **authentication** methods, and how to configure **dial-up permissions** and **dial-up properties**. You also need to know how to administer policies and permissions for a particular scenario, how to mandate the use of the **Kerberos version 5** protocol for user authentication, and how to specify a strong password policy. You should have some knowledge of **smart card authentication**, although the examination is unlikely to ask for an in-depth knowledge of this last topic.

The **Routing And Remote Access service** uses **policies** to permit or deny user access. You can configure these policies at the server level, but in larger organizations, RAS servers are configured to use RADIUS. An IAS server is configured as a RADIUS server to provide centralized authentication policies, and it can also provide management statistics. You need to know how to configure authentication on an IAS server.

Multihomed servers running Windows Server 2003 are often used as routers. The computer is (arguably) easier to configure than a dedicated hardware router and can also be less expensive, especially when combing routing with other server roles. You need to know how to manage these servers, ensure their continued operation, and reconfigure them when the requirements of your organization change. In particular, you need to know how to manage **routing interfaces**, **devices**, **ports**, **packet filters**, and **clients**.

Routing is implemented using **routing tables**, which can be configured manually or automatically using such routing protocols as **Routing Information Protocol (RIP)**— usually RIP version 2, although version 1 is still supported—and **Open Shortest Path First (OSPF)**. Note that OSPF is not supported in 64-bit versions of Windows Server 2003. You need to know how to view and manage routing tables and ensure that they reflect the network structure of your organization. Currently, the examination does not require you to know how to configure RIP and OSPF.

You need know which routing protocols are applicable to a given scenario. Make sure you understand how Windows Server 2003 uses routing protocols to update routing tables dynamically. You should be able to administer the various routing protocols, and devise strategies to cope with the additional network traffic that such protocols might generate.

Extranets are becoming more and more popular. Privileged communication between co-operating organizations has many advantages but brings its own security problems. Confidential information is passed between private networks over public **wide area network (WAN)** links—often over the Internet—and you need to know how to secure both the data and the networks themselves from an attacker.

Finally, you need to know how to troubleshoot both routing and RAS. You need to be able to solve problems related to remote access dial-up clients and VPNs, including problems accessing resources beyond the RAS server. You also need to be able to troubleshoot demand-dial routing and router-to-router VPNs.

This domain is one of the largest in the examination specification, and it is specified in a highly detailed fashion. It is likely that the same weighting will be given to it in the exam itself.

Tested Skills and Suggested Practices

The skills that you need to successfully master the Implementing, Managing, and Maintaining Routing And Remote Access (4.0) objective domain on the *Managing and Maintaining a Microsoft Windows Server 2003 Network Infrastructure* exam include the following:

- Configure Routing And Remote Access user authentication.
  - ❑ Practice 1: Configure a server running Windows Server 2003 as a remote access dial-up server. Preferably, this computer should be multihomed, but you can configure a computer that has a single network interface card (NIC). Configure RAS policies to require Kerberos v5 and strong passwords.
  - ❑ Practice 2: Plan a security structure to meet the needs of remote access clients and users. This plan should involve the use of security groups and possibly the creation of at least one organizational unit (OU). Implement this plan using Active Directory.
  - ❑ Practice 3: Create at least one user account by accessing the Demand-Dial Wizard through the Routing And Remote Access snap-in.
  - ❑ Practice 4: Examine the various methods of allocating IP addresses to RAS clients. Choose a method. Then implement and test it.

❑ Practice 5: Configure a remote access client. Preferably, you should use a computer with either the Microsoft Windows XP Professional or the Microsoft Windows 2000 Professional operating system, which enables you to specify Internet Protocol Security (IPSec) encapsulation. If you cannot connect through a telephone line, use a null modem cable to connect to the server.

❑ Practice 6: Configure your network so that the RAS server is a RADIUS client, and IAS provides authentication policies.

■ Manage remote access.

❑ Practice 1: Configure as a router a computer running Windows Server 2003. Although you can configure the NIC with two IP addresses and create a logical subnet, you would be better off using a multihomed machine connected to at least two physical subnets.

❑ Practice 2: Configure a Transmission Control Protocol/Internet Protocol (TCP/IP) packet filter that restricts traffic between subnets. TCP/IP can filter IP packets based on the TCP port number, the User Datagram Protocol (UDP) port number, and the IP protocol number.

❑ Practice 3: Use the Routing And Remote Access snap-into view connected remote access clients, send a message to a single client, send a message to all clients, and disconnect a client.

❑ Practice 4: Use the Routing And Remote Access snap-in to add a routing interface. If you have not already done so, add a demand-dial interface. Configure demand-dial filters and dial-out hours.

❑ Practice 5: By default, Windows Server 2003 NAT translates a single public address to a range of private addresses. Reconfigure your sever to provide the NAT service. Configure NAT to use a range of public IP addresses. If your practice network consists of two isolated subnets, you can declare one of them public and the other private, and practice NAT configuration before you go on the Internet for real.

❑ Practice 6: If you can do so on your practice network, configure a second server as a router. Configure demand-dial interfaces on the first (calling) router and on the second (answering) router for certificate-based Extensible Authentication Protocol (EAP) authentication. If problems occur with this procedure, configure the routers to use preshared key authentication instead.

■ Manage TCP/IP routing.

❑ Practice 1: View an IP routing table. If you are unsure of the function of any of the columns (or "fields"), consult the references listed in the "Further Reading" section.

❑ Practice 2: Add a Layer2 Tunneling Protocol (L2TP) and a Point-to-Point Tunneling Protocol (PPTP) port. Configure a device on a port.

■ Provide secure access between private networks.

❑ Practice 1: Reconfigure your two routers, specifying a secure connection between two private networks in the Routing And Remote Access Server Setup Wizard on each server. The connection between the two servers can be persistent (always on) or on demand (demand-dial).

❑ Practice 2: Investigate how to set up a secure VPN between the two servers. (Note: The examination does not explicitly state that you need to know how to perform this task, but you'll gain a lot of valuable information through this investigation.)

■ Troubleshoot client access to remote access services.

❑ Practice 1: Use the Routing And Remote Access snap-in to check the port status of a particular port.

❑ Practice 2: Use the Logging function in the Routing And Remote Access snap-in to monitor error logging in the system Event Log. Investigate the various levels of event logging and decide which level is required for various types of monitoring tasks.

❑ Practice 3: Investigate "Troubleshooting Remote Access VPNs" in the *Windows Server 2003 online help* files.

■ Troubleshoot Routing And Remote Access routing.

❑ Practice 1: Determine how to gather demand-dial troubleshooting information. You should know how to check the following: the unreachability reason, the credentials being used by the calling router, the authentication provider being used by the answering router, the status of the port on the answering router, the status of the demand-dial interface, and the static route for a demand-dial interface.

❑ Practice 2: Examine "Troubleshooting Demand-Dial Routing" and "Troubleshooting Router-to-Router VPN Routing" in the *Windows Server 2003 online help* files.

Further Reading

This section lists supplemental readings by objective. We recommend that you study these sources thoroughly before taking exam 70-291.

Objective 4.1   Review Lessons 1, 2 and 3 in Chapter 10, "Configuring and Managing Remote Access."

Microsoft Corporation. *Windows Server 2003 online help*. Redmond, Washington. Review "Elements of a Remote Access Policy," "Deploying Demand-Dial Routing," "Security Information for Remote Access," and "Authentication Methods."

Microsoft Corporation. *Microsoft Windows Server 2003 Deployment Guide*. Redmond, Washington. Review "Checklist: Installing and Configuring the Remote Access Server," available on the Microsoft Web site at *http://www.microsoft.com /technet/prodtechnol/windowsserver2003/proddocs/entserver/sag_RASSchecklist.asp*.

Objective 4.2   Review Lesson 4 in Chapter 9, "Routing with Microsoft Windows Server 2003."

Microsoft Corporation. *Windows Server 2003 online help*. Redmond, Washington. Review "Checklist: Installing and Configuring the Router," "Manage Remote Access Clients," "Manage Routing Protocols," "Manage Devices and Ports," "Manage Routing Interfaces," and "Manage Packet Filters."

Microsoft Corporation. *Microsoft Windows Server 2003 Deployment Guide*. Redmond, Washington. Review "Checklist: Installing and Configuring the Router," available on the Microsoft Web site at *http://www.microsoft.com/technet/prodtechnol /windowsserver2003/proddocs/entserver/sag_rtrchecklist.asp*.

Objective 4.3   Review Lessons 1 and 4 in Chapter 9 "Routing with Microsoft Windows Server 2003."

Microsoft Corporation. *Windows Server 2003 online help*. Redmond, Washington. Review "Manage Routing Protocols," "Manage Routing Interfaces," "Understanding the IP Routing Table," "To View Routing Tables," and "Manage Devices and Ports."

Microsoft Corporation. *Microsoft Windows Server 2003 Deployment Guide*. Redmond, Washington. Review "Routing Tools and Utilities," available on the Microsoft Web site at *http://www.microsoft.com/technet/prodtechnol/windowsserver2003 /proddocs/entserver/sag_rras-ch5_20.asp*.

Objective 4.4   Review Lessons 2 and 4 in Chapter 10 "Configuring and Managing Remote Access."

Microsoft Corporation. *Windows Server 2003 online help*. Redmond, Washington: Review "Common Configurations for Remote Access Servers," "Common Configuration for the VPN Server," and "New Features for Virtual Private Networks."

Microsoft Corporation. *Virtual Private Networking with Microsoft Windows Server 2003: Overview* (white paper). Redmond, Washington. Available on the Microsoft Web site at *http://www.microsoft.com/windowsserver2003/techinfo /overview/vpnover.mspx*.

Objective 4.5   Review Lessons 3 and 4 in Chapter 10 "Configuring and Managing Remote Access."

Microsoft Corporation. *Windows Server 2003 online help.* Redmond, Washington: Review "Troubleshooting Remote Access VPNs," "Deploying Demand-Dial Routing," and "Troubleshooting IAS as a RADIUS Server."

Microsoft Corporation. *Microsoft Windows Server 2003 Deployment Guide.* Redmond, Washington. Review "Internet Protocol Security—Troubleshooting," available on the Microsoft Web site at *http://www.microsoft.com/technet/prodtechnol /windowsserver2003/proddocs/standard/sag_IPSECtrouble.asp.*

Objective 4.6   Review Lesson 2 in Chapter 9 "Routing with Microsoft Windows Server 2003," and Lesson 3 in Chapter 10 "Configuring and Managing Remote Access."

Microsoft Corporation. *Windows Server 2003 online help.* Redmond, Washington: Review "Troubleshooting Demand-Dial Routing" and "Troubleshooting Router-to-Router VPNs."

Microsoft Corporation. *Microsoft Windows Server 2003 Deployment Guide.* Redmond, Washington. Review "Troubleshooting," available on the Microsoft Web site at *http: //www.microsoft.com/technet/prodtechnol/windowsserver2003/proddocs/entserver /sag_rras-ch5.asp.*

Objective 4.1

Configure Routing And Remote Access User Authentication

This objective requires that you know how to configure RAS on a server running Windows Server 2003. You need to be able to configure user authentication to a preprepared specification. You need to know how to ensure that a secure authentication protocol (Kerberos v2) is used, and how to prevent the use of downlevel protocols such as **NTLM**.

You should know that with EAP, the mechanism that authenticates a remote access connection is negotiated by the remote access client and the authenticator (either the remote access server or the RADIUS server). Because EAP may not provide sufficient encryption in all circumstances, the protocol is seldom used in isolation; rather, it is combined with another protocol such as **Transport Layer Security (TLS)**. Windows Server 2003 RAS includes support for **EAP-TLS** and **Message Digest 5 (MD5)-Challenge**. EAP-TLS is used in smart card login and authentication. **EAP-RADIUS** is not an EAP type, but it is the passing of EAP messages of any EAP type by an authenticator to a RADIUS server for authentication.

You need to know the differences between **Microsoft Challenge Handshake Authentication Protocol (MS-CHAP) versions 1 and 2**, and that MS-CHAP is used with **Microsoft Point-to-Point Encryption (MPPE)** to encrypt the data sent over **Point-to-Point Protocol (PPP)** or **Point-to-Point Tunneling Protocol (PPTP)** connections.

Weaker protocols exist for compatibility with legacy or non-Microsoft operating systems. You should know that CHAP uses reversible password encryption and is therefore less secure than other protocols, and that **Password Authentication Protocol (PAP)** uses plaintext passwords and is the least secure authentication protocol. You are unlikely to be asked in-depth questions about **Shiva Password Authentication Protocol (SPAP)**, but you should be aware of its existence.

Windows Server 2003 also supports **unauthenticated access**, which means that user credentials are not required. In some situations unauthenticated access is useful, and you should be aware of them.

For a remote user to gain access to a network, a number of conditions must be satisfied. These conditions are applied in a sequential fashion using a remote access policy. You need to know how to configure such a policy, and be able to analyze its effects. You also need to know that the RAS server can apply such a policy, and that a consistent set of network policies can be centralized and maintained by an IAS server that is configured as a RADIUS server. In this case, the RAS server is a RADIUS client.

Finally, users will not be able to access a network remotely if their client computers are incorrectly configured. You need to know how to integrate RAS with **Dynamic Host Configuration Protocol (DHCP)**, how to set up a static address pool, and when it is necessary to configure **Microsoft DHCP Relay Agent** on an RAS server.

Objective 4.1 Questions

1. Your IAS server provides RADIUS authentication to RAS on a number of network access servers that support dial-up clients. A wireless access point is added to your network and is set up as a RADIUS client. You check that Protected EAP (PEAP) support is enabled in your remote access policy and that PEAP-EAP-MS-CHAPv2 is used to authenticate wireless clients. Users cannot access your network from their 802.11 wireless client computers. What is the most likely cause of the problem?

    A. Smart card user authentication is mandated for 802.11 wireless client computers.

    B. RADIUS cannot be used to provide remote access attributes to network access servers that service a wireless access point.

    C. The Ignore User Dial In Properties attribute has not been configured on the IAS server.

    D. EAP-TLS is the appropriate authentication mechanism for wireless connections, not PEAP-EAP-MS-CHAPv2.

2. You have configured IAS on your network to accept multiple authentication methods. You have also configured your network access servers to attempt to negotiate a connection by using the most secure protocol first. When a remote access client attempts to connect to your network, RAS on your servers running Windows Server 2003 therefore tries to negotiate a connection using EAP first. In this situation, which two entities attempt to negotiate the EAP authentication mechanism?

    A. The RAS server and the IAS server

    B. The IAS server and the remote access client

    C. The RAS server and the remote access client

    D. The RADIUS client and the remote access client

3. Your Windows Server 2003 Active Directory domain provides access to home workers, who establish dial-up connections to the Routing And Remote Access service on a server running Microsoft Windows Server 2003, Enterprise Edition. Your employees use a variety of client operating systems and telephone networks, and CHAP is used for authentication. Management is concerned about security and requires that you make access to the network more difficult for unauthorized dial-up users. You do not have a budget to buy additional equipment, and management requires that no changes be made to the client environment. How can you meet these requirements?

    A. Enable Caller ID.

    B. Audit failed account logon events.

    C. Implement Basic Firewall on your Routing And Remote Access service server.

    D. Enable Callback.

4. You administer a large Windows Server 2003 Active Directory domain. All servers in the domain are either running Windows Server 2003 or Microsoft Windows 2000 Server. All internal client PCs are running Windows XP Professional. Your company employs a large number of home workers who log on to your domain using dial-up connections. RAS runs on a number of servers, and remote access policies are centralized and applied by an IAS server configured as a RADIUS server. You want to ensure that remote users are authenticated using the Kerberos v5 authentication protocol. You want to ensure that such downlevel protocols as NTLM are not used. How do you implement this requirement?

    A. On the IAS server, configure the Authentication-Type remote access policy condition to specify a connection restriction that is based on the authentication protocol.

    B. Create an OU and move the remote client computer accounts into that OU. Create a Group Policy Object (GPO) and link it to that OU. Edit the GPO. In the Kerberos policy container, enable Enforce Logon Restrictions.

    C. Create an OU and move the remote client computer accounts into that OU. Create a GPO and link it to that OU. Edit the GPO. Expand Computer Configuration \Windows Settings\Security Settings\Local Policies\Security Options. Configure Network Security: LAN Manager Authentication Level to Send NTLMv2 Response Only\Refuse LM & NTLM.

    D. Specify an IPSec policy that requires encryption and uses the triple DES (3DES) encryption algorithm.

5. You use the Internet Authentication Service snap-in on a server running Windows Server 2003 to create a new remote access policy. The Authentication Methods page of the New Access Policy Wizard allows you to select only MS-CHAP, MS-CHAP version 2, and various methods of EAP authentication. You want to create a remote access policy that meets the following requirements:

- Dial-up users can authenticate with a user name and password.

- Certificate-based authentication methods (such as smart card authentication) can be used.

- All passwords are encrypted using a nonreversible encryption algorithm.

- All passwords are stored in encrypted form.

- Remote access users can use XP Professional, Windows 2000 Professional, Microsoft Windows NT 4 Workstation, or Microsoft Windows 98 hosts.

- Remote users cannot use password authentication to access the domain from hosts with non-Microsoft operating systems.

- Users can change their passwords after these passwords expire.

You select the Extensible Authentication Protocol (EAP) check box. In the Type drop-down box, you select Protected EAP (PEAP). You select the Microsoft Encrypted Authentication Version 2 check box. You ensure that the Microsoft Encrypted Authentication check box is cleared. You complete the wizard and do not edit the new policy's authentication properties. Which of the following will result from applying the policy? (Choose all that apply.)

A. Dial-up users can authenticate with a user name and password.

B. Certificate-based authentication methods (such as smart card authentication) can be used.

C. All passwords are encrypted using a nonreversible encryption algorithm.

D. All passwords are stored in encrypted form.

E. Remote access users can use Windows XP Professional, Windows 2000 Professional, Windows NT 4 Workstation, or Windows 98 hosts.

F. Remote users cannot use password authentication to access the domain from hosts with non-Microsoft operating systems.

G. Users are able to change their passwords after the passwords expire.

6. ServerA is a stand-alone server running Windows Server 2003, configured as a VPN server. Its internal interface is on a 10.10.1.0/24 private network, and it has the static IP address of 10.10.1.9. You install Windows Server 2003, Enterprise Edition as a fresh install on a new computer that you intend to use as a file server. You perform a default install on the new computer and name it ServerF. You configure its IP address statically as 10.10.1.12, with a 255.255.255.0 subnet mask.

VPN users report that they cannot gain access to files that you placed on ServerF. You check that file and folder permissions are set up correctly. You ping ServerF successfully by IP address from ServerA. You cannot, however, ping ServerA from ServerF. What is the likely cause of the problem?

A. A faulty network connection exists between ServerF and the network hub.

B. Packet filters are configured on ServerA.

C. ServerF has an incorrect subnet mask.

D. ServerF is part of a domain, whereas ServerA is a stand-alone server.

7. Litware, Inc. makes extensive use of home workers who access the corporate Windows Server 2003 Active Directory domain through dial-up connections. Several of the organization's administrators regularly work from home and perform remote monitoring and administration. These administrative tasks require a large amount of network bandwidth. You want administrators to be able to use multiple phone lines. You want the settings on the Routing And Remote Access service server to determine the ability of ordinary users to use multiple phone lines. (By default, the server settings do not permit Multilink.)

You want to configure multiple phone line connections to adapt to bandwidth conditions. When the phone line capacity of a multiple connection falls below 50 percent, you want to reduce the number of phone lines used for that connection. Currently, a single remote access policy with default settings allows all users to connect to the network by using the Routing And Remote Access service.

What steps do you take to achieve these goals? (Choose all that apply.)

A. Edit the current policy's dial-up profile settings.

B. Create a new remote access policy.

C. Edit the new policy's dial-in profile settings.

D. Enable Multilink for the current policy.

E. Enable Multilink for the new policy.

F. Select the Require BAP For Dynamic Multilink Requests check box.

G. Specify additional connection attributes to be returned to the remote access server.

8. Fabricam, Inc. has asked you to implement a dial-up remote access policy for its employees that is based on time and day restrictions. The company has the following requirements:

■ Administrators can access the network 24 hours a day, 7 days a week.

■ Managers cannot access the network after 6:00 P.M. and before 8:00 A.M. during the week. They can, however, access it at any time during the weekend.

■ All other employees can access the network only between 8:00 A.M. and 6:00 P.M. on weekdays.

You create five custom remote access policies based on security groups and time restrictions:

■ Policy A—managers: permit

■ Policy B—administrators: permit

■ Policy C—weekend: deny

- Policy D—weekday 8:00 A.M. to 6:00 P.M.: permit
- Policy E—weekday 6:00 P.M. to 8:00 A.M.: deny

In which order can you apply the policies to achieve the required results? (Choose all that apply.)

   A. DABCE

   B. DBEAC

   C. CABDE

   D. DECBA

   E. BDEAC

9. Blue Yonder Airlines has a large number of employees who connect to the company intranet through VPNs. Because of the number of users who try to connect at peak times, delays are experienced in clients receiving IP configurations. Blue Yonder's VPN server allocates IP address leases that it receives from the company's DHCP server in blocks of 10. You want the DHCP server to allocate blocks of 25 instead. Both the VPN and DHCP servers run Windows Server 2003. How do you change this setting?

   A. Right-click the server name in the DHCP console. Select Set Predefined Options.

   B. On the VPN server, edit the HKEY_LOCAL_MACHINE\SYSTEM\CurrentControl-Set\Services\RemoteAccess\Parameters\Ip Registry key. Set the InitialAddress-PoolSize value to 25.

   C. Right-click the VPN server in the Routing And Remote Access snap-in and select Properties. On the IP tab, click Dynamic Host Configuration Protocol (DHCP). Increase the pool allocation to 25.

   D. Use the Netsh Ras Set Dhcpallocate command.

Objective 4.1 Answers

1. **Correct Answers: C**

   A. **Incorrect:** User name and password authentication can be used whether client computers are wireless access or dial-up hosts.

   B. **Incorrect:** RADIUS can provide attributes to any network access server that is configured as a RADIUS client. How remote client PCs access the network does not affect this functionality.

   C. **Correct:** User dial-in properties include the following: caller ID, callback, static IP address, and static routes. These properties are designed for a client that is dialing in to a network access server, not for wireless access points. A wireless access point that receives these settings in a RADIUS message might not be able to process them, which could cause the wireless client to be disconnected. When IAS provides authentication and authorization for users who are both dialing up and accessing the organization network through wireless technology, support for wireless connections is provided by the Ignore User Dial In Properties attribute. You can create different remote access policies based on different types of connections for a single security group, or even for a single user.

   D. **Incorrect:** EAP-TLS is used mostly for smart card logon authentication.

2. **Correct Answers: B**

   A. **Incorrect:** The remote access client requires authentication and must therefore be a party in the negotiation. The RAS and IAS servers do not need to authenticate each other in this scenario.

   B. **Correct:** The remote access client requires authentication. Accepted authentication methods are configured on the IAS server. Authentication mechanisms are therefore negotiated between these two entities.

   C. **Incorrect:** This solution would be correct if the RAS server were not set up as a RADIUS client. In this scenario, however, remote access policies, including authentication methods, are configured centrally on the IAS RADIUS server.

   D. **Incorrect:** In this scenario, the RAS server is the RADIUS client. This answer is therefore incorrect for the reason given in the explanation for answer C.

3.   Correct Answers: D

A. Incorrect: Caller ID must be supported both by the caller and by the phone system between the caller and the remote access server. Caller ID support on the Routing And Remote Access service server requires call answering equipment that provides Caller ID information and the appropriate driver to pass the information to the Routing And Remote Access service. This solution, therefore, requires the appropriate hardware and could require changes to the users' environment. Note that the question does not state that the server's modems support Caller ID, and this cannot be assumed.

B. Incorrect: An excessive number of failed account logon events can indicate that your system is under attack from a malicious outsider. Auditing these events can alert you to a dictionary attack, for example. However, auditing cannot by itself prevent unauthorized network access. Auditing only gathers information and you then need to act upon this information. This answer is incorrect because it is incomplete.

C. Incorrect: Basic Firewall prevents traffic from a public network, such as the Internet, from gaining access to your intranet. This service is typically configured on a VPN sever or a NAT router. In this scenario, however, users are connecting through telephone lines, not via the Internet.

D. Correct: Callback causes the Routing And Remote Access service server to call back using a telephone number that is provided by the user or is specified by an administrator. In the latter case, the administrator configures the option to use the home workers_f home telephone numbers. This solution significantly increases security because an attacker needs to obtain access to a home worker_fs telephone. This option is appropriate in this scenario because the remote access users are home workers. It would be inappropriate if they were members of a traveling sales force.

4.   Correct Answers: A

A. Correct: You can configure a remote access account policy in Windows Server 2003 IAS that refuses a connection unless the Kerberos v5 authentication protocol is used.

B. Incorrect: The Enforce Logon Restrictions setting is enabled by default and applies to user accounts, not computer accounts. It determines whether the Kerberos Distribution Center (KDC) validates every request for a session ticket against the user rights policy of the user account. It does not mandate Kerberos v5 as the only authentication policy that can be used.

C. Incorrect: This restriction prevents the use of LM and NTLM authentication protocols. However, it does not mandate the use of Kerberos v5.

D. Incorrect: This solution affects encryption, not authentication.

5.   **Correct Answers: A, C, D, F, and G**

A. Correct: MS-CHAP v2 permits password authentication. By default, the policy applies the strongest authentication method (EAP), but if that cannot be used, it then applies the next strongest (MS-CHAP v2).

B. Incorrect: PEAP is used to authenticate wireless access. Certificate-based authentication requires EAP-TLS. You need to select Smart Card Or Other Certificate in the EAP drop-down box.

C. Correct: Both MS-CHAP and MS-CHAP v2 use nonreversible password encryption. CHAP encrypts passwords, but it is less secure because the encryption is reversible.

D. Correct: MS-CHAP v2 stores passwords in encrypted form. MS-CHAP does not, but it was not selected.

E. Incorrect: Windows NT 4 Workstation and Windows 98 hosts cannot use MS-CHAP v2. (Note: If MS-CHAP were also selected, these host operating systems could be used, but passwords entered on these computers would be stored in unencrypted form.)

F. Correct: Non-Microsoft operating systems cannot use MS-CHAP v2. Modern Linux systems can use MS-CHAP, but this is not specified.

G. Correct: This is the default for MS-CHAP v2. You did not edit the authentication properties after the policy was created, so the defaults apply.

6.   **Correct Answers: B**

A. Incorrect: ServerA could ping ServerF, so the network connection is OK.

B. Correct: When a ping works one way and not the other, packet filters are selectively filtering Internet Control Message Protocol (ICMP) packets. ServerF has been set up by a fresh install with default settings and does not therefore have the Routing And Remote Access service configured or any packet filters specified. ServerA is a VPN server and will have packet filters configured. These filters will need to be reconfigured to allow the communication between the two servers that the scenario requires.

C. Incorrect: The dotted decimal subnet mask 255.255.255.0 is equivalent to /24.

D. **Incorrect:** ServerF has been set up using the defaults and is a member of the default workgroup. Hosts on the same subnet can ping each other regardless of whether they are in the same domain or workgroup.

7. **Correct Answers: B, C, E, and F**

A. **Incorrect:** You need two policies: the current policy (unedited) for ordinary users, and an additional policy for administrators. The current policy has the default setting Server Settings Determine Multilink Usage. This configuration is what you require for ordinary users. (If you do not want ordinary users to use multiple connections whatever the server settings, you can disable Multilink for this policy. This solution is not, however, what the question specifies.)

B. **Correct:** You need a remote access policy that allows the administrators to use Multilink.

C. **Correct:** You need to alter settings on the Multilink tab of the Edit Dial-In Profile dialog box for the administrators' remote access policy.

D. **Incorrect:** You want to enable Multilink for the administrators, not the ordinary users.

E. **Correct:** Select the Allow Multilink Connections option. Specify the number of ports you want to use.

F. **Correct:** Bandwidth Allocation Protocol (BAP) drops a multiple connection if bandwidth falls below a specified percentage for a specified time. BAP needs to be enabled in this scenario. The default BAP settings do not need to be changed.

G. **Incorrect:** You configure these settings on the Advanced tab of the Edit Dial-In Profile dialog box. It is not relevant to this scenario.

8. **Correct Answers: B and F**

A. **Incorrect:** This order allows managers to access the network 24 hours a day, 7 days a week.

B. **Correct:** This order permits all users access on weekdays between 8:00 A.M. and 6:00 P.M. It permits access to administrators at any time. Anyone other than an administrator attempting to access on a weekday between 6:00 P.M. and 8:00 A.M. is denied access. If it is the weekend, managers are permitted access. Everyone other than managers and administrators are denied access at the weekend.

    C. **Incorrect:** This order permits nobody to access the network on the weekends. Managers can access the network at any time on weekdays.

    D. **Incorrect:** This order permits access to all users (including managers and administrators) only between 8:00 A.M. and 6:00 P.M. on weekdays.

    E. **Correct:** This order permits access to administrators at any time. It permits all users access on weekdays between 8:00 A.M. and 6:00 P.M. Anyone other than an administrator attempting to access on a weekday between 6:00 P.M. and 8:00 A.M. is denied access. If it is the weekend, managers are permitted access. Everyone other than managers and administrators is denied access on the weekend.

9.   Correct Answers: B

    A. **Incorrect:** This setting lets you set DHCP options that the DHCP server provides to DHCP clients. It does not affect the size of the address pool that is sent to a VPN server.

    B. **Correct:** The configuration needs to be set through the Registry. Where configurations can have a significant impact on performance, they are typically implemented through Registry edits. Take care not to set this value too high because it could result in exhaustion of your DHCP pool. InitialAddresPoolSize is not in the Registry by default, and it needs to be added as a new D_WORD value.

    C. **Incorrect:** The Dynamic Host Configuration Protocol (DHCP) setting is an option that lets you specify DHCP as the IP configuration provider. This setting cannot be used to increase the size of the DHCP block allocation.

    D. **Incorrect:** This setting cannot be altered by the Netsh utility. Netsh Ras Set commands let you specify user properties and authentication modes.

Manage Remote Access

For this objective, you need to be able to configure as a **router** a server running Windows Server 2003, and to know how to use several such routers to connect a **subnetted network infrastructure**. The **security** of such an infrastructure depends on, among other factors, correctly configured **packet filters** that determine the type of traffic that is allowed to pass both into and out of a router. You can configure packet filters per interface. You can also configure them either to pass all traffic except that specified by the filter conditions, or to pass only the traffic that the filter conditions specify. You must know the difference between **input** (or inbound) and **output** (or outbound) filters.

You need to know how to add, configure, modify, and delete a packet filter. You should know how to add **local host filters**, and know the various types of filters that can be added. You also need to know how to add **PPTP filters** and **L2TP over IPSec filters**.

The task of managing routers is largely concerned with configuring **interfaces**. You need to know how to add a **routing** and a **demand-dial interface**, how to configure **demand-dial filters** and set dial-out hours, and how to configure both the calling router and the answering router for certificate-based **EAP authentication** or **pre-shared key authentication**. You also need to know how to delete an interface.

In addition, you need to know how to enable routing on ports and configure devices, and how to add PPTP and L2TP devices. Both this domain and the next one require that you know how to add and delete a **routing protocol**, and how to configure **preference levels**.

More and more organizations are implementing **private IP addressing** schemes. Because of this trend, routers are frequently configured to provide the NAT service. The current examination syllabus does not specifically mention NAT, but questions on NAT configuration could be asked in this objective.

This objective leans toward the practical. Nevertheless, you should look into its aspects in more depth than is provided merely by the "How to" sections of the help file. Being able to perform a task is of no enduring worth unless you know why you are doing it.

1. ServerA is a server running Windows Server 2003, Enterprise Edition, configured as a router. InterfaceA has an IP address of 10.10.1.1. You want to specify that only Hypertext Transport Protocol (HTTP) traffic on TCP port 80, and Secure Hypertext Transport Protocol (HTTPS) traffic on TCP port 443 will be allowed into the router through that interface. You configure two inbound packet filters on Interface A, as shown in the following figure.

   You suspect that other network traffic is not being filtered and confirm this hunch by using Network Monitor. How do you ensure that only TCP port 80 and TCP port 443 traffic enters InterfaceA?

   A. Configure two outbound packet filters to permit traffic only from TCP ports 80 and 443 on the interface.

   B. Specify UDP ports 80 and 443.

   C. On the InterfaceA LAN interface on ServerA, configure TCP/IP properties, enable TCP/IP filtering, and permit only TCP ports 80 and 443.

   D. Select the Drop All Packets Except Those That Meet The Criteria Below option.

2. Adventure Works employs numerous traveling salespersons who connect using VPNs. The salespersons' computers run a variety of Microsoft client operating systems, including Windows 98, Second Edition, and PPTP is used as the tunneling protocol. A VPN server, AdventureVPN, is located outside the Adventure Works firewall. AdventureVPN is a stand-alone server running Windows Server 2003, configured as a VPN server and

a router. The firewall is configured to allow inbound access only from AdventureVPN. The firewall is connected directly to AdventureVPN's internal interface.

You configure PPTP ports on AdventureVPN. You need to configure packet filters that allow only VPN traffic on AdventureVPN's Internet (external) interface. You must prevent non-VPN users from accessing resources on the Adventure Works intranet. How do you configure these filters? (Choose all that apply. Each answer forms part of the solution.)

- **A.** Create an inbound packet filter on AdventureVPN. Use the PPTP ports as source ports. Use the IP address of AdventureVPN's external interface as the source IP address.

- **B.** Create an outbound packet filter on AdventureVPN. Use the PPTP ports as destination ports. Use the IP address of AdventureVPN's external interface as the destination IP address.

- **C.** Create an inbound packet filter on AdventureVPN. Use the PPTP ports as destination ports. Use the IP address of AdventureVPN's external interface as the destination IP address.

- **D.** Create an outbound packet filter on AdventureVPN. Use the PPTP ports as source ports. Use the IP address of AdventureVPN's external interface as the source address.

- **E.** Create an inbound packet filter on AdventureVPN. Use the PPTP ports as destination ports. Use the IP address of AdventureVPN's internal interface as the destination IP address.

- **F.** Create an outbound packet filter on AdventureVPN. Use the PPTP ports as source ports. Use the IP address of AdventureVPN's internal interface as the source address.

3. You administer a peer-to-peer Windows Server 2003 network that consists of 20 clients running Windows XP Professional, and two servers running Windows Server 2003, named ServerA and ServerB. ServerA has a dedicated cable modem connection to the Internet. No DHCP server exists. ServerA is multihomed and is configured to provide NAT and Basic Firewall services. ServerA is statically configured with an IP address of 10.10.10.1, and it allocates IP addresses to clients from the range 10.10.10.10 through 10.10.10.48.

ServerB is a Web server. It is configured with an IP address of 10.10.10.2 and a default gateway of 10.10.10.1. Your ISP has allocated two public IP addresses, 206.73.118.12 and 206.73.118.13. You want to allow external Internet users to use the IP address 206.73.118.13 to access the resources on ServerB through the NAT service on ServerA. How should you configure your network?

A. Configure the public NAT interface on ServerA to use an address pool with a starting address of 206.73.118.12 and a subnet mask of 255.255.255.254. Reserve the public address 206.73.118.13 for the private address 10.10.10.2.

B. Configure ServerB with a static route on the LAN interface. Use the destination address 10.10.10.2, the gateway address 206.73.118.13, and the subnet mask 255.255.255.255.

C. Configure ServerA with a static route on the NAT private interface. Use the destination address 206.73.118.13, the gateway address 10.10.10.2, and the subnet mask 255.255.255.255.

D. Configure the LAN interface on ServerB so that it uses multiple IP addresses and assign the additional IP address 206.73.118.13 to the interface.

4. Your Windows Server 2003 Active Directory domain has two servers running Windows Server 2003 that access the Internet. ServerA is configured as a router and provides Basic Firewall and NAT services. ServerB is a VPN server. Your client PC running Windows XP Professional has the Windows Server 2003 Administration Tools Pack installed.

ServerB has to come offline for maintenance. You want to send messages to this effect to all VPN clients. You open a blank console on your client PC and add the Routing And Remote Access snap-in. You expand the Routing And Remote Access container. What do you do next?

A. Right-click ServerA and select Messages. In the Message dialog box, select Send To All.

B. Expand ServerA. Right-click the Remote Access Clients container, and select Send To All.

C. Right-click ServerB and select Messages. In the Message dialog box, select Send To All.

D. Expand ServerB. Right-click the Remote Access Clients container, and select Send To All.

5. You are adding inbound filters to an interface on a server running Windows Server 2003, configured as a router. You expand the IP Routing node in the Routing And Remote Access snap-in and select the General container. In the details pane, you right-click the interface that you want to configure, and click Properties. On the General tab, you click Inbound Filters. You intend to add three local filters, and then select the Drop All Packets Except Those That Meet The Criteria Below option.

You want the interface to accept packets sent directly to the router, broadcast packets to the local subnet, and all IP multicast packets. The IP address of the router interface is 10.10.10.1, with a subnet mask of 255.255.255.0. Which of the filters listed should you configure? (Choose all that apply.)

A.

Destination IP address	Destination subnet mask	Protocol
10.10.10.1	255.255.255.255	Any

B.

Destination IP address	Destination subnet mask	Protocol
10.10.10.255	255.255.255.255	Any

C.

Destination IP address	Destination subnet mask	Protocol
10.255.255.255	255.255.255.255	Any

D.

Destination IP address	Destination subnet mask	Protocol
255.255.255.255	255.255.255.255	Any

E.

Destination IP address	Destination subnet mask	Protocol
224.0.0.0	240.0.0.0	Any

6. You are planning your TCP/IP filtering strategy for a router interface. Which of the following can you specify when configuring an inbound packet filter? (Choose all that apply.)

    A. Destination TCP port

    B. Destination UDP port

    C. ICMP type

    D. Protocol number

Objective 4.2 Answers

1.   Correct Answers: D

   A. Incorrect: You want to control traffic into the router. Therefore, you should configure inbound (or input) traffic filters.

   B. Incorrect: TCP ports 80 and 443 are used for HTTP and HTTPS traffic, respectively.

   C. Incorrect: This solution would block both inbound and outbound traffic on this interface other than through the specified ports. It is inappropriate practice to use this method of filtering traffic on a router; packet filters should be used instead. Finally, this solution takes more administrative effort than the correct solution.

   D. Correct: Selecting this option would permit this traffic and.block traffic through all other ports.

2.   Correct Answers: C and F

   A. Incorrect: Inbound filters use PPTP ports as destination ports.

   B. Incorrect: Outbound filters use PPTP ports as source ports.

   C. Correct: The only inbound traffic that is allowed is traffic to the external interface of AdventureVPN.

   D. Incorrect: The source of an outbound packet filter must be the IP address of AdventureVPN's internal interface.

   E. Incorrect: The only destination IP address that is allowed is the IP address of AdventureVPN's external interface.

   F. Correct: The only outbound traffic allowed is traffic originating from AdventureVPN's internal interface.

3.   Correct Answers: A

   A. Correct: ServerB can access resources on the Internet from the private network. Return traffic to ServerB can cross the NAT interface because the connection was initiated from the private network. To allow Internet users to access ServerB when ServerB has not initiated the connection, you must configure a static IP address on ServerB so that ServerB is on the private network. You must ensure that this static address is excluded from the range of addresses allocated by ServerA. ServerA's IP address must also be set up as ServerB's default gateway. You must configure a special port that is a static mapping of a public address and port number to a private address and port number. This port maps an inbound connection from an external Internet user to the private address of the Web server. To perform this task, you must configure ServerA's public NAT interface to correspond to the addresses provided by the ISP, and statically map one of these addresses (to be used for access from the Internet) to ServerB's private IP address.

B. Incorrect: The mapping is made on the NAT computer, not the Web server, and a special port is used, not a static route.

C. Incorrect: A special port is used, not a static route.

D. Incorrect: The Web server requires only one IP address. This private address must, however, be statically mapped to a public IP address by configuring a special port on the NAT server.

4. Correct Answers: D

A. Incorrect: The shortcut menu does not contain a Messages item. Also, messages are sent from the VPN server (ServerB), not from the router.

B. Incorrect: The Remote Access Clients container does not exist in ServerA. This container exists only on RAS and VPN servers.

C. Incorrect: The shortcut menu does not contain a Messages item.

D. Correct: You can right-click the container to send and select Send To All if you want to send the same messages to all clients. If you want to send a message to an individual client, you can select the container, right-click the client name in the details pane, and select Send Message.

5. Correct Answers: A, B, and E

A. Correct: This filter accepts packets sent directly to the local computer.

B. Correct: This filter accepts packets broadcast to the local subnet.

C. Incorrect: This filter accepts packets broadcast to all subnets of a class-based network (in this case, Class A).

D. Incorrect: This filter accepts packets broadcast to the limited broadcast (the all-ones) address.

E. Correct: This filter accepts all IP multicast packets.

6. Correct Answers: A, B, C, and D

A. Correct: Traffic can be permitted or denied based on its destination TCP port.

B. Correct: Traffic can be permitted or denied based on its destination UDP port.

C. Correct: Traffic can be permitted or denied based on its ICMP type, its ICMP code, or both.

D. Correct: If you select Other in the Protocol drop-down box when adding an IP filter, you can specify a protocol by its number—as specified in Request for Comments (RFC) 1700.

Manage TCP/IP Routing

A **routing table** is a straightforward concept. If a router must send a packet to a specified network, it references its routing table to determine which gateway should receive the packet. Routes can be added manually or by such **routing protocols** as **RIP** and **OSPF**. You need to be able to view and interpret routing tables, and understand how to add and remove **static routes**.

You need to be aware of the difference between a **static** and **dynamic** route, and know the difference between a link state routing protocol such as OSPF and a distance vector protocol such as RIP. You also need to be aware of the differences between RIP and **RIP v2**, and the significance of RIP v2's ability to carry **network mask information**. You need to know the implications of running two routing protocols on the same network, and how to configure **routing preference**. You also need to know the advantages and disadvantages of each protocol, and be able to determine when it is appropriate to use one or the other.

The examination will probably not test OSPF configuration in depth.

Objective 4.3 Questions

1. A. Datum Corporation is a consulting company that designs and tests networking solutions. The network test laboratory at A. Datum has four hosts running Windows Server 2003, Enterprise Edition, configured as routers. Each of these computers has four NICs. The test network is reconfigured regularly, and testing is performed regularly over multihop routes.

A. Datum has the following requirements:

- The network is reconfigurable with the minimum administrative effort.
- Every host on the network can access every other host.
- Testing can be performed over multihop routes.
- Broadcast traffic on the network is minimized.

You install RIP version 2 for Internet Protocol on all the routers and add all the router interfaces to the protocol. Which requirements have you met? (Choose all that apply.)

A. The network is reconfigurable with the minimum administrative effort.

B. Every host on the network can access every other host.

C. Testing can be performed over multihop routes.

D. Broadcast traffic on the network is minimized.

2. Northwind Traders' main office has a private intranetwork that consists of 20 subnets and 11 multihomed servers running Windows Server 2003, configured as routers. Multiple routes exist from any subnet to any other subnet. RIP version 2 for IP is installed on all the routers, and all router interfaces have been added to the protocol. Access between subnets is sometimes slow. Network analysis reveals a significant amount of UDP port 520 broadcast traffic. How can you reduce this traffic?

A. Increase the Periodic Announcement Interval setting to 300 seconds on all router interfaces.

B. Disable split horizon.

C. Configure the operation mode on all router interfaces to Autostatic Update.

D. Increase the Time Before Routes Expire setting to 1800 seconds.

3. Your network consists of two subnets connected by a server running Windows Server 2003, configured as a router. The router has two interfaces with IP addresses 10.10.10.1 on the 10.10.10.0/25 subnet, SubnetA, and 10.10.10.129 on the 10.10.10.128/25 subnet, SubnetB, respectively. A file server, ServerA, on SubnetA has the IP address of 10.10.10.100. A client PC, Client24, on SubnetB has the IP address of 10.10.10.222. All host IP settings are manually configured.

A user at Client24 reports that she cannot access resources on ServerA. From Client24, you ping ServerA's IP address but the ping times out. You are also unable to ping the remote router interface from Client24. You can ping the local router interface and all the other hosts on SubnetB.

The Route Print command on Client 24 gives the following output:

Destination	Netmask	Gateway	Interface	Metric
0.0.0.0	0.0.0.0	10.10.10.129	10.10.10.222	1
127.0.0.0	255.0.0.0	127.0.0.1	127.0.0.1	1
10.10.10.0	255.255.255.0	10.10.10.222	10.10.10.222	1
10.10.10.222	255.255.255.255	127.0.0.1	127.0.0.1	1
10.10.10.255	255.255.255.255	10.10.10.222	10.10.10.222	1
224.0.0.0	224.0.0.0	10.10.10.222	10.10.10.222	1
255.255.255.255	255.255.255.255	10.10.10.222	10.10.10.222	1

What is preventing Client24 from connecting to ServerA?

A. The route from Client24 to ServerA is configured with an incorrect interface.

B. Client24 is configured with an incorrect gateway.

C. The route from Client24 to ServerA is configured with an incorrect metric.

D. Client24 is configured with an incorrect subnet mask.

4. Litware, Inc. has a large international intranet linked by dedicated T1 and T3 lines. Currently, 60 subnets are linked by 35 routers running Windows Server 2003. The company requires that every host is able to communicate with every other host, and that network configuration changes are propagated to all routers. Litware wants to minimize the additional traffic that router announcements generate on the WAN links. What should you do?

    A. Create an additional subnet on all routers and designate this as the backbone subnet. On each router, install OSPF, and add all interfaces to the protocol.

    B. Reconfigure the routers and network segments as a backbone configuration. On each router, install OSPF and add all interfaces to the protocol.

    C. Install RIP v2 on all routers and add all router interfaces to the protocol. Configure the outgoing packet protocol as RIP version 2 multicast, and configure the incoming protocol as RIP version 2 only.

    D. Install RIP v2 on all routers, and add all router interfaces to the protocol. Configure RIP v2 to use neighbors instead of broadcast or multicast.

5. You administer a network that is part of a corporate WAN. All internal routers in your network are multihomed servers running Windows Server 2003, and they all have RIP v2 installed. Your network is allocated the 10.20.16.0/21 segment of the corporate private IP address scheme. Users in your network never communicate with users on the 10.21.0.0/16 segment, and you do not want any network addresses from that segment in your routing table. How do you exclude these addresses?

    A. Configure a RIP route filter.

    B. Configure a TCP/IP filter.

    C. Configure a packet filter.

    D. Configure a RIP peer filter.

6. Contoso, Ltd. has three offices, each with its own subnet. You want to configure a server running Windows Server 2003 as a router and RAS server at each office. You also want to connect the offices by Integrated Services Digital Network (ISDN) demand-dial links. You do not want routing table announcements to be broadcast on the network, but you want any changes on the network to be propagated to all the routers. How should you configure the routers?

    A. Use static routes.

    B. Use RIP v1.

    C. Use RIP v2.

    D. Use OSPF.

Objective 4.3 Answers

1.   Correct Answers: A, B, and C

   A. Correct: RIP is self-configuring. When the network is reconfigured, the routing tables will be regenerated automatically.

   B. Correct: RIP automatically reconfigures the routing tables on the network so that there are routes to all noncontiguous networks. Therefore, any host can contact any other host on any other network. The limitation is that the maximum number of hops is 15. However, in this scenario, with only four routers and split horizon enabled by default, the maximum number of hops between hosts will be less than 15, regardless of the configuration.

   C. Correct: RIP automatically generates routing tables that provide routes to non-contiguous subnets, so testing can be performed over multiple hops. The 15-hop limitation is not a problem in this scenario. Refer to the explanation for answer B.

   D. Incorrect: The default setting for the outgoing packet protocol is RIP Version 2 Broadcast. Changing this setting to RIP Version 2 Multicast reduces broadcast traffic. You can also increase the Periodic Announcement Interval setting on the router interfaces to reduce broadcast traffic. OSPF generates less broadcast traffic than RIP and can be used instead. Therefore, broadcast traffic is not minimized.

2.   Correct Answers: A

   A. Correct: By default, RIP keeps its routing tables up-to-date by broadcasting routing table information every 30 seconds. In this scenario, the network infrastructure is unlikely to change frequently, and it is safe to increase this interval to 300 seconds, which decreases broadcast traffic. In this scenario, in which all of your routers are servers running Windows Server 2003, you can also reduce broadcast traffic by selecting RIP version 2 multicast as the outgoing packet protocol. However, this option was not given in the question.

   B. Incorrect: Split horizon prevents the advertising of routes in the same direction in which they were learned. This solution helps prevent routing loops. Disabling split horizon does not reduce broadcast traffic, however.

   C. Incorrect: Autostatic Update is used only on demand-dial interfaces. It is not appropriate in this scenario.

   D. Incorrect: By default, routes expire after 180 seconds if they are not updated. You should increase this setting if you increase the Periodic Interval Announcement setting. However, increasing this setting does not, by itself, decrease broadcast traffic.

3. **Correct Answers: D**

A. **Incorrect:** The Interface column indicates the interface from which the local host will forward an IP packet. This is either Client24's IP address or the loopback address 127.0.0.1.

B. **Incorrect:** The Gateway column indicates the router interface to which an IP packet for a distant network should be forwarded. In this case, it is the IP address of the router interface on SubnetB, and it is correctly set at 10.10.10.129.

C. **Incorrect:** Metric determines the cost of a route. Here all metrics are the same because only one route exists from SubnetB to SubnetA. The metrics are correct.

D. **Correct:** The subnets are /25 networks, and hosts should have 255.255.255.128 subnet masks. Line 3 in the table shows that Client24 has been incorrectly configured with a 255.255.255.0 subnet mask. Client24 therefore attempts to connect to ServerA on its local subnet rather than the remote subnet.

4. **Correct Answers: B**

A. **Incorrect:** OSPF configuration requires that areas connect to each other through a backbone. Creating separate subnets on all routers is not an efficient way to do this.

B. **Correct:** OSPF is efficient and requires little overhead. It is a link state protocol and does not include all routing table entries in its announcements. It ensures that any host has a route to any other, and propagates network changes. No hop-count problems should arise. OSPF divides the internetwork into different areas. The areas are contiguous networks and are connected to each other through a backbone area.

C. **Incorrect:** The use of multicast ensures that routing announcements are not broadcast over the WAN links, and RIP ensures that a route exists from any host to any other host (provided the distance between them is 15 hops or less), and that network configuration changes are propagated to all routers. However, RIP v2 is a distance vector protocol and includes all routes in router announcements. Therefore, RIP v2 is not suitable for large networks with large routing tables.

D. **Incorrect:** RIP is a distance vector protocol, and it includes all routes in its announcement whether broadcast, multicast, or unicast is used. Also, the hop count between some networks might be greater than 15.

5. **Correct Answers: A**

   A. **Correct:** In the Routing And Remote Access snap-in, expand the console tree for each server. Expand IP Routing, and select the RIP node. In the details pane, right-click each interface in turn, and select Properties. Then, click the Security tab. In the Action box, ensure that For Incoming Routes is selected. Select the Ignore All Routes In The Ranges Listed option, and add the range of network addresses to be excluded. You can also create RIP route filters for outgoing routes, but that is not required in this scenario.

   B. **Incorrect:** TCP/IP filters can restrict traffic on any host (not just a router). Traffic is permitted or denied by IP protocol, destination UDP port, or destination TCP port. This is not what this scenario requires.

   C. **Incorrect:** IP traffic filters can be configured on router interfaces to restrict inbound and outbound traffic. They cannot, however, block routing table announcements based on network IDs.

   D. **Incorrect:** RIP peer filters can be configured to block routing table announcements from specified routers. They cannot, however, block routing table announcements based on network IDs.

6. **Correct Answers: C**

   A. **Incorrect:** If static routes are used, each change must be entered manually on all routers. Changes are not propagated to the routers.

   B. **Incorrect:** When RIP is installed in routers running Windows Server 2003, RIP v2 is configured by default. However, you can configure the interfaces to use RIP version 1 broadcast as the outgoing packet protocol, and RIP version 1 only as the incoming packet protocol. This configuration allows compatibility with older routers. However, this configuration does not meet the scenario requirements because routing table announcements would be broadcast on the network.

   C. **Correct:** By default, RIP v2 broadcasts routing announcements. However, because all routers are Microsoft Windows Server 2003 and can use multicast, RIP v2 can be configured to multicast RIP announcements to multicast address 224.0.0.8. RIP v2 will propagate all changes in the network to all routers, and will work over nonpersistent demand-dial connections.

   D. **Incorrect:** OSPF is used in large networks. It is not appropriate for a three-router network linked by nonpersistent demand-dial connections.

Provide Secure Access Between Private Networks

Two Windows Server 2003 servers running the Routing And Remote Access service can be configured to send private data securely across the Internet. You can specify this option when you run the **Routing And Remote Access Server Setup Wizard** on each server. The connection between the two servers can be **persistent** or **demand-dial**.

After the wizard finishes, you can configure each server with additional options. For example, you can configure which routing protocols each server accepts, and how each server routes traffic between the two networks. You need to know the principle of **mutual authentication** and how the two endpoints of the connection authenticate each other by exchanging **credentials**. You also need to know the conditions under which **mutual authentication** is required, and the various protocols used to achieve it.

You need to know about **data encryption**, **encryption keys**, and how to use **IPSec** to encrypt L2TP VPN connections. Almost all the **security** and **authentication** issues covered in previous domains also apply to this one. You will need to understand **Callback** and the **Caller ID** feature. You need a sound knowledge of **authentication protocols**.

Private networks typically implement secure communication by the use of VPNs. You need to know how these networks work, how **encapsulation** and **tunneling** are implemented, and how authentication and encryption are configured. Typically, private networks use private addressing schemes. Although this objective does not specifically mention NAT, NAT questions would be appropriate in this part of the examination.

Objective 4.4 Questions

1.   Coho Vineyard and Coho Winery are separate but closely linked organizations. They both use private networks with private addressing schemes. Coho Vineyard has implemented a Windows Server 2003 Active Directory domain. A server called VineyardRRAS that is running Windows Server 2003 provides a secure communications link with Coho Winery.

Coho Winery has a Windows 2000 Server Active Directory domain. However, a standalone server called WineryRRAS that is running Windows Server 2003, Enterprise Edition provides a secure communications link with Coho Vineyard. Both servers have the Routing And Remote Access service configured to provide secure access between private networks. They are connected by a demand-dial link. Confidential company data is transferred several times a day across this connection.

You want to accomplish the following goals:

■ VineyardRRAS and WineryRRAS can validate each other.

■ Data is transmitted securely across the WAN link.

■ Traffic over the demand-dial link is minimized during business hours.

■ VineyardRRAS and WineryRRAS maintain up-to date routing tables.

You take following steps:

■ You enable MS-CHAP v2 as the authentication protocol on both VineyardRRAS and WineryRRAS.

■ You enable OSPF on the demand-dial interfaces.

■ You ensure that both computers require encryption.

What are the results of your actions? (Choose all that apply.)

   A. VineyardRRAS and WineryRRAS can validate each other.

   B. Data is transmitted securely across the demand-dial link.

   C. Traffic over the demand-dial link is minimized during business hours.

   D. VineyardRRAS and WineryRRAS maintain up-to-date routing tables.

2.   Coho Vineyard and Coho Winery are separate but closely linked organizations. They both use private networks with private addressing schemes. Coho Vineyard has implemented a Windows Server 2003 Active Directory domain. A server called VineyardRRAS that is running Windows Server 2003 provides a secure communications link with Coho Winery.

Coho Winery has a Windows 2000 Server Active Directory domain. However, a stand-alone server called WineryRRAS that is running Windows Server 2003, Enterprise Edition provides a secure communications link with Coho Vineyard. Both servers are configured to provide secure access between private networks. They are also configured as VPN servers.

A VPN has been configured to connect the two organizations. It uses demand-dialing over an ISDN line. Sensitive data is sent over this link at random times, usually outside office hours. Both routers are calling routers and VPN connections are two way. The tunneling protocol is PPTP, and strong MPPE encryption is used. MS-CHAP v2 provides mutual encrypted authentication.

Management at both companies is concerned about security. They want a stronger authentication method based on EAP. They also want to use L2TP over IPSec. You are employed as a consultant. What is the first step you recommend?

A. Use a dedicated permanent connection between the two routers.

B. Reconfigure the remote access policies on each router to use EAP, and specify Smart Card Or Other Certificate.

C. Configure IPSec in the demand-dial interface properties dialog box.

D. Join WineryRRAS to the Coho Winery domain.

3.   Contoso, Ltd. and Contoso Pharmaceuticals communicate confidential information via a VPN through the Internet. Both companies have a permanent broadband connection to their local provider. This connection, however, does not support multicasting.

Both companies want to multicast audio and video presentations to each other. All client computers in both companies are running either Windows 2000 Professional or Windows XP Professional. All servers are running Windows Server 2003. Two servers configured to provide secure access between the networks are tunnel endpoints over the ISDN line. How should you configure these servers?

A. No further configuration is required. A VPN connection will transmit multicast datagrams through connections that do not support multicasting.

B. Configure the tunnel type as Automatic.

C. Configure Multicast Heartbeat on each server.

D. Configure multicast boundaries on each server.

Objective 4.4 Answers

1. **Correct Answers: A, B, and D**

    A. Correct: MS-CHAP v2 supports two-way authentication. VineyardRRAS and WineryRRAS can therefore validate each other.

    B. Correct: MS-CHAP v2 supports encryption and you have ensured that the default setting, which requires encryption, has not been changed. Data transmitted over the connection is secure.

    C. Incorrect: No steps have been taken to minimize traffic over the demand-dial link during business hours.

    D. Correct: OSPF has been enabled on the demand-dial link. The routers will maintain up-to-date routing tables.

2. **Correct Answers: D**

    A. Incorrect: You do not need a permanent connection to use either L2TP over IPSec or EAP-TLS. The scenario does not justify the expense of a permanent connection.

    B. Incorrect: WineryRRAS is a stand-alone server and does not have the required certificate.

    C. Incorrect: You can specify only preshared key authentication until a machine-based certificate is installed in WineryRRAS.

    D. Correct: You need a machine-based certificate infrastructure such as Kerberos v5 to implement EAP-TLS and L2TP over IPSec. A member server can obtain a computer certificate from an enterprise certificate authority. A stand-alone server cannot. EAP-TLS requires domain membership and cannot be implemented on a stand-alone server.

3. **Correct Answers: A**

A. **Correct:** By default, a VPN tunnel operates as an IP-in-IP tunnel. It encapsulates an IP datagram in an IP header that can be sent from one tunnel endpoint to the other. This functionality enables multicast datagrams, for example, to travel through networks that would not otherwise support them.

B. **Incorrect:** Remote access VPN clients running Windows XP or Windows Server 2003 routers configured as calling routers on router-to-router VPNs, use the Automatic tunnel option. They try to establish a PPTP-based VPN connection first, and then they try to establish an L2TP over IPSec VPN connection. This functionality does not, however, affect the transmission of multicast traffic.

C. **Incorrect:** Multicast Heartbeat enables an RRAS server to detect a regular multicast notification to a specified group address. This facility verifies that IP multicast connectivity is available on the network. It does not, however, affect the transmission of multicast datagrams.

D. **Incorrect:** Multicast boundaries are administrative barriers to the forwarding of IP multicast traffic. They do not affect the transmission of multicast datagrams.

Troubleshoot Client Access to Remote Access Services

Troubleshooting client access to a remote network is not only about solving problems. Good maintenance is **preemptive**. The process does not merely involve **diagnosing** and **resolving** issues related to client access to remote access VPNs and establishing connections to resources beyond the remote access server. The process involves **monitoring traffic and trends**, **predicting** when faults are likely to occur, and **taking corrective action** before the user is aware of the problem.

You need to know how to diagnose and resolve such issues, and how to use the tools that are provided to do so. You also need to know how to **audit remote logons** and recognize trends. You need to be able to deal with the problems of **slow access**, and you need to know how to guard against **external attacks**.

You also need to know how to resolve problems such as these: the remote access client's user account is locked out, expired, disabled, or has attempted a connection outside the configured logon hours. You need to resolve the situation that occurs when RAS or the VPN service have not started, or the required ports or protocols have not been enabled. You should know how to resolve the problem when a **VPN server** cannot access Active Directory, cannot authenticate users, or cannot access the **RADIUS server**.

Furthermore, you need to know how to gather troubleshooting information, and know which events you should **audit**—or **performance counters** you should log—to keep track of trends that might affect reliability. The examination will almost certainly present you with some **failure scenarios**. It might also ask you which procedures you could implement to foresee and prevent such failures.

Objective 4.5 Questions

1. You have configured a server running Windows Server 2003 as a VPN server and added 100 PPTP ports and 100 L2TP ports. L2TP tunnels use IPSec encryption. PPTP tunnels use built-in MPPE encryption. You have specified both MS-CHAP and MS-CHAP v2 authentication and strong encryption. Three hundred salespeople in your domestic sales force use laptops running Windows 98, Second Edition. Two hundred salespeople in your international sales force use laptops running Windows XP.

Sometimes your domestic salespeople can connect to your network, and sometimes they cannot. Your international salespeople can always connect. How do you solve the problem?

   A. Use only MS-CHAP for authentication.

   B. Specify basic encryption.

   C. Create more PPTP ports.

   D. Use Serial Line Internet Protocol (SLIP) as your transport protocol.

2. You have configured a server running Windows Server 2003 as a VPN server. The server is also a file server, and VPN clients access their home directories on that server. The VPN server issues addresses to VPN clients from a single static address pool. No problems are reported.

You move clients' home directories to a dedicated file server and set up appropriate share and NT file system (NTFS) permissions. You configure the VPN server to allow clients to access resources on the intranet. Clients report that they can log on successfully but cannot access their home directories. You check that the LAN protocols used by VPN clients allow access to the network on which the VPN server has an interface. The VPN server and the file server are on different subnets, but they can ping each other. How do you allow users to access their home directories on the file server? (Choose all that apply.)

   A. Add a static IP route to the routers on your intranet, including the VPN server. The route will specify the address range of your static IP address pool, as defined by its network IP address and a mask that specifies its range.

   B. Install RIP v2 on all the routers on your intranet, including the VPN server, and add all internal interfaces to the protocol.

   C. Move the clients_f Encrypting File System (EFS) certificates from the VPN server to the file server.

   D. Move the recovery agent EFS certificate from the VPN server to the file server.

3.   Northwind Traders employs home workers who connect to the corporate intranet through dial-up connections. A server running Windows Server 2003 is configured as an RAS server to implement this service. Users report no problems.

For security purposes, Northwind has decided to implement Callback. You access the properties dialog box for each remote user. On the Dial-In tab, you select the Always Callback To option and specify the user's home phone number. Users report that they can connect and log on, but that the connection is then dropped. How do you enable Callback?

    A. On the Dial-In tab of each user's properties box, select the Allow Access option.

    B. Create a global security group called RASusers. Grant that group Log On Locally rights to the RAS server.

    C. Install DHCP Relay Agent on the RAS server.

    D. Enable Link Control Protocol (LCP) Extensions on the PPP tab of the RAS server properties dialog box.

4.   You are the network administrator at Tailspin Toys. You have configured a server running Windows Server 2003 as a VPN server. This computer has four NICs and is also configured as a router. You have configured the VPN server to issue IP address leases that it obtains from a DHCP server on one of its local subnets. The IP addresses allocated to VPN clients are in a separate DHCP scope from those allocated to local clients. All VPN users report that they cannot access the Tailspin Toys network.

You access the VPN server through a dial-up connection and find that your client PC has been allocated an IP address of 169.254.223.10. This address is not in any scope on Tailspin Toys' DHCP server. You verify that the DHCP server has been configured correctly and is not offline. You can ping all the interfaces of the VPN server from the DHCP server. You verify that the VPN server is not using any protocols that are not understood by VPN clients. What do you check next?

    A. The number of available PPTP and L2TP ports.

    B. The routing table on the VPN server.

    C. The number of available leases in the DHCP server_fs scope.

    D. The VPN server has selected the proper LAN adapter from which it can obtain DHCP-allocated IP addresses.

5.   Contoso, Ltd. is a sales organization based in Boston, Massachusetts. Contoso sales representatives operate mainly in the eastern United States. They access the company network through the Internet, using voluntary VPNs. They mostly perform this task in the evening, to upload sales data and download product information. For security reasons, access is controlled by a number of access policies that are configured on a VPN server running Windows Server 2003.

Don Hall, a Contoso salesperson, has been asked to go to Perth, Australia, where there is the possibility of a large contract. Contoso checks that its ISP is part of a confederation, and that Don can dial in to a point of presence (POP) in Perth and establish a VPN to Boston. Don has been operating in eastern America for some time and has had no problems accessing Contoso through a VPN.

Don calls from Australia. He can log in to Contoso's domain, but the connection is then dropped. Don can access the ISP from his laptop and can browse the Internet.

You are Contoso's domain administrator. What do you do?

A. Specify that weaker encryption can be accepted because strong encryption cannot be used outside the United States.

B. Ask Don to dial in to a POP somewhere else in Australia.

C. Create an access policy specifically for Don. Do not set any time restriction on this policy.

D. Ask Don to use an Internet café rather than his hotel room because the hotel switchboard is interfering with communications.

Objective 4.5 Answers

1.   Correct Answers: C

   A. Incorrect: If a client cannot use the strongest authentication method, it will use the next strongest. Also, clients running Windows 98 can use MS-CHAP v2 for authentication over VPN links, but not over dial-up links.

   B. Incorrect: Both types of client can use strong encryption.

   C. Correct: Clients running Windows 98 create voluntary tunnels to PPTP ports. Typically one hundred and twenty-eight PPTP ports are created by default, and you have created one hundred more. You need to create at least another eighty-two.

   D. Incorrect: SLIP is a transport protocol that UNIX servers use. Windows clients can connect to remote UNIX servers using SLIP, but Windows servers do not support it.

2.   Correct Answers: A and B

   A. Correct: Currently, no route exists between VPN clients and hosts on your intranet. You can add this route manually.

   B. Correct: Currently, no route exists between VPN clients and hosts on your intranet. A routing protocol can propagate this route to your intranet.

   C. Incorrect: A user_fs EFS certificate is included in his or her profile and is typically stored in the client PC. This issue is not about encryption, and the question does not indicate that files in the clients_f home directories are encrypted.

   D. Incorrect: Windows Server 2003 (unlike Windows 2000 Server) does not mandate that a recovery agent be established before EFS is implemented. If a recovery agent certificate does exist, however, it should be stored on a floppy disk that is locked in a safe. It should not be stored on a computer. This issue is not about encryption, and the question does not indicate that files in the clients_f home directories are encrypted.

3.   Correct Answers: D

   A. Incorrect: Users could access the intranet before you enabled Callback. You have done nothing that would affect this access.

   B. Incorrect: RAS users have no need to log on locally to the RAS server.

   C. Incorrect: If DHCP provides IP address leases to the RAS clients, DHCP Relay Agent will already be installed and configured on the RAS server. If not, there is no need to install it.

    D. Correct: PPP requires LCP extensions to implement Callback. By default, this check box is selected, but it has been cleared in this scenario.

4.   **Correct Answers: D**

    A. Incorrect: If it were a ports issue, some users would be able to access the network.

    B. Incorrect: If no route were available to allow users access to the Tailspin Toys intranet, they would still be able to access the VPN server.

    C. Incorrect: The scope cannot have run out of available leases. None have been allocated to VPN clients. Addresses allocated to non-VPN clients are in different scopes, so local client allocations cannot consume the VPN clients_f scope.

    D. Correct: By default, the VPN server randomly chooses the adapter to use to obtain IP addresses from DHCP. If more than one LAN adapter exists, the Routing And Remote Access service can choose an adapter on a LAN on which no DHCP server is available.

5.   **Correct Answers: C**

    A. Incorrect: 128-bit (strongest) encryption can be used in Australia. In any case, Don is creating a private connection between his client computer and Contoso_fs VPN server. Encryption strength is not an issue in this scenario.

    B. Incorrect: Don can browse the Internet. There is no problem with the POP or with the ISP he is using.

    C. Correct: Don's user account, permissions, and password have not changed, nor have the access policies on the VPN. A tunnel can be created from anywhere in the world where a suitable POP can be accessed. The only variable that has changed is the time zone Don is in. When Don is exempt from the normal time restrictions, he will be able to log in from any time zone.

    D. Incorrect: Don can browse the Internet from his hotel room. The hotel switchboard is not a problem.

Objective 4.6

Troubleshoot Routing and Remote Access Routing

Routing faults are often difficult to diagnose because they can be **transitory**. If a user, even a remote access user, cannot access a resource on your network that he or she requires to do a job, that is a local problem capable of local resolution. If, on the other hand, the resource is on a remote subnet, was accessible two days ago, was not accessible yesterday, and has reappeared again today, that problem is usually more complex.

If **demand-dial access** is used, you need to know how to check the **unreachability reason**, ensure that the **calling router** is using the correct **credentials**, and ensure that the **answering router** is receiving appropriate **authentication** information. You need to know how to check the status of the port on the answering router, the status of the demand-dial interface, and the **static route** for that interface.

The problem could be that a **router-to-router VPN connection** cannot be established. You need to know how to determine whether LAN and WAN routing is enabled on the calling router and the answering router, whether PPTP or L2TP ports are enabled for inbound and outbound demand-dial routing connections, and if they are, whether they are already being used by currently connected remote access clients or demand-dial routers. You also need to know how to determine whether the answering router supports the **tunneling protocol** of the calling router.

You need to be able to determine whether the calling and answering routers use remote access policies with at least one **common authentication method** and one **common encryption method.**

As with all troubleshooting modules, the examination will test not only that you know how to go about solving a specific problem. It will also test that you can set up **monitoring** and **auditing** to detect when problems are likely, and identify the **underlying cause**.

1. Trey Research has a branch office in Boston, Massachusetts, and a head office in New York. The two offices are connected by means of a Windows Server 2003 two-way demand dial connection over an ISDN line. Company policy dictates that this connection must be used only once a day, outside office hours, to transfer data between the two offices. Management discovers that the line is being used several times a day, often at peak times. You are asked to investigate.

You find that an ISDN link is being initiated several times each day, but that the traffic consists of router announcements. How do you regulate this traffic, and how do you prevent the routers from accessing the ISDN line during business hours? (Choose all that apply. Each answer forms part of the solution.)

    A. Ensure that only the OSPF routing protocol is enabled on the routers that access the connection.

    B. Configure the demand-dial interface to accept inbound traffic only outside business hours.

    C. Configure the demand-dial interface to dial out only outside business hours.

    D. Create a remote access policy that prevents the ISDN line from being used for router-to-router traffic.

    E. Create a demand-dial filter on the demand-dial interface.

    F. Implement Basic Firewall at both ends of the connection.

2. Litware, Inc. has a branch office in El Paso, Texas, and a head office in Houston, Texas. Communication between the two offices is implemented by a router-to-router VPN over a demand-dial connection. Communication is always initiated by El Paso. The calling router in El Paso is a Windows Server 2003 router configured as a VPN client. The answering router in Houston is a Windows Server 2003 router configured as a VPN and a RAS server. Home workers in the Houston area access the corporate network remotely through this server.

The host name of the El Paso router is passrouter. The host name of the Houston router is housrouter. The routers are making a connection but are unable to send or receive data.

Both routers are configured to use an L2TP over IPSec tunnel. They both use MS-CHAP v2 for authentication and the strongest level of encryption. The demand-dial interface is configured to use RIP v2 autostatic updates. The calling router has a user account in the Houston domain that is correctly configured to enable network access. The user name of this account is passrouter.

In the RRAS snap-in, you check that the passrouter account appears under Dial-In Clients. What do you check next?

A. An L2TP port is available on housrouter for the connection.

B. The user name passrouter matches the name of a demand-dial interface on housrouter.

C. Packet filters on the demand-dial interfaces of the calling router and answering router are preventing the flow of traffic.

D. Packet filters on the remote access policy profile are preventing the flow of IP traffic.

3. The calling router in your branch office cannot connect to the answering router in your main office. The routers have connected previously and data has been sent and received successfully over the VPN connection. No changes have been made to tunnel type, encryption method, authentication method, or encryption strength. No machine certificates have been revoked. No changes have been made to access policies. WAN and LAN routing has not been disabled. The Routing And Remote Access service is started. No hardware failures have been detected in either router, or in the connection between them.

Both routers are running Windows Server 2003. Which of the following could be causing the problem? (Choose all that apply.)

A. The user account of the calling router has been locked out, has expired, or is disabled.

B. No port is available.

C. The answering router is interpreting the calling router as a remote access client.

D. The connection attempt was made outside the calling router account's logon hours.

Objective 4.6 Answers

1. **Correct Answers: C and E**

    A. **Incorrect:** This solution reduces router-to-router traffic but does not eliminate it. OSPF is designed for large internetworks and can be difficult to configure and maintain.

    B. **Incorrect:** A demand-dial interface is used for outbound traffic.

    C. **Correct:** This solution ensures that the ISDN line is not used during business hours.

    D. **Incorrect:** Router-to-router traffic ensures that routing tables are current. It is unwise to block all of this traffic. You want to regulate the traffic and ensure that it does not occur during business hours.

    E. **Correct:** A filter lets you control which traffic can initiate the demand-dial link. It can permit or deny specific source or destination IP addresses, ports, or protocols. You can therefore ensure that only essential traffic can initiate the link.

    F. **Incorrect:** Basic Firewall prevents traffic from a public network, such as the Internet, from gaining access to your intranet. It is typically configured on a VPN sever or a NAT router. In this scenario, however, connection is through an ISDN line, not via the Internet.

2. **Correct Answers: B**

    A. **Incorrect:** The connection has already been made. Another port is not required.

    B. **Correct:** The user name of the calling router appears under Dial-In Clients on the answering router. As a result, housrouter interpreted passrouter as a remote access client. The calling router is correctly identified if its name matches the name of a demand-dial interface. If the incoming caller is a router, the port on which the call was received shows a status of Active and the corresponding demand-dial interface is in a connected state.

    C. **Incorrect:** Packet filters can prevent traffic flow of preferred traffic if they are incorrectly configured. In this scenario, however, the problem is identified as the answering router interpreting the calling router as a remote access client.

    D. **Incorrect:** You can use remote access policies to configure TCP/IP input and output packet filters that control the exact nature of the TCP/IP traffic that is allowed on the VPN connection. If this is done incorrectly, essential traffic can be blocked. In this scenario, however, the problem is identified as the answering router interpreting the calling router as a remote access client.

3.   **Correct Answers: A, B, and D**

    A. Correct: The calling router is a VPN client and has a user account. This account is treated exactly the same as any other user account in an Active Directory domain. If the account is inactive for any reason, the connection will not be made.

    B. Correct: By default, 128 PPTP ports and 128 L2TP ports are (typically) installed on a router running Windows Server 2003. More can be added. If an insufficient number of ports is created, all ports could have been in use by remote access or VPN clients when the connection attempt was made.

    C. Incorrect: This solution would not prevent connection. It would prevent data transfer.

    D. Correct: Day and time restrictions for a number of remote access clients or VPN clients are normally implemented through access policies. However, for a client such as a calling router, configuring user account logon hours is a valid technique.

17 Maintaining a Network Infrastructure (5.0)

This examination domain requires that you know how to maintain and troubleshoot your network. You need to know how to monitor the health of your network and ensure that it can cope with the **bandwidth requirements** specified by the **network design plan**. You need to know when a network is operating normally, and how to produce a **baseline** showing normal traffic patterns. You need to know how to capture **network traffic statistics**, and how to compare these statistics with your baseline data in order to troubleshoot **network faults** and **track trends**.

You need to be able to use such tools as **Network Monitor**, **System Monitor**, and **Event Viewer**, and to analyze the data captured by these tools. You need to know how to generate **logs** and the **performance counters** that can be included in these logs. In this domain, the **network interface object** is of particular interest. You need to know what such counters as **Current Bandwidth**, **Output Queue Length**, **Bytes Total/sec**, and **Packets/sec** measure. You need to know the **acceptable value ranges** for the commonly used Network Interface counters.

The domain requires that you know how to troubleshoot **Internet connectivity** problems. The examination is mostly concerned with **user-side problems**—that is, why your network has lost connectivity. Therefore, you are unlikely to get a lot of questions on **supplier-side problems**—that is, why your **Internet Information Services (IIS)** server is not working properly.

The final domain objective covers **troubleshooting services** on a server running Microsoft Windows Server 2003. You need to know the effects of a service not starting at reboot, and the faults that would cause this problem. You need to know what problems **service dependencies** can cause, and which services depend on which other services. You need to know how to stop, start, pause, and restart a service, and what to do next if a service does not start.

Tested Skills and Suggested Practices

The skills that you need to successfully master the Maintaining a Network Infrastructure objective domain on the *Managing and Maintaining a Microsoft Windows Server 2003 Network Infrastructure* exam include the following:

- Monitor network traffic.

  - Practice 1: On a server running Windows Server 2003, install Network Monitor tools from the Windows Server 2003 CD-ROM. If the server is multihomed, specify the network on which you want to capture data.

  - Practice 2: Use Network Monitor to capture data frames sent to and from a network adapter on your server. Find the following information in a frame: the protocol in use, the IP address of the source computer, the destination IP address of the frame, the source Media Access Control (MAC) address, and the destination MAC address.

  - Practice 3: Configure a Network Monitor view filter to view captured frames by protocol and by communicating host.

  - Practice 4: Use System Monitor to view data generated by the Network Interface object counters. Use the Performance console to capture a baseline log for network traffic. Configure an alert that fires when the Network Interface: Bytes Total/sec counter exceeds a predefined value, and then trigger the alert by transferring a large file across your network.

- Troubleshoot connectivity to the Internet.

  - Practice 1: Install IIS on a server on your network. Create a simple internal Web site and File Transfer Protocol (FTP) site. Experiment by creating errors, such as disabling the Web site or the World Wide Web (WWW) service. Note the error messages that are caused by internal Web server problems and those that are caused by connection problems.

  - Practice 2: Configure a server running Windows Server 2003 as a router and Network Address Translation (NAT) provider. Implement Internet connectivity for a private network.

  - Practice 3: Configure your NAT provider as a Dynamic Host Configuration Protocol (DHCP) allocator.

- Troubleshoot server services.

  - Practice 1: Use the Microsoft Management Console (MMC) Services snap-in to create a single seat tool that can administer services on remote hosts on your network.

  - Practice 2: Stop key services, such as the Workstation service and the Server service. Find out how this affects other services. Access the System event log by using the Event Viewer and list the errors that are generated when key services are stopped.

Further Reading

This section lists supplemental readings by objective. We recommend that you study these sources thoroughly before taking exam 70-291.

Objective 5.1   Review Lesson 1 in Chapter 3, "Monitoring and Troubleshooting TCP/IP Connections," and Lesson 1 in Chapter 12, "Maintaining a Network Infrastructure."

Microsoft Corporation. *Microsoft Windows Server 2003 online help.* Redmond, Washington. Review "Troubleshooting: Monitoring Performance" and "System Monitor Overview: Monitoring Performance."

Microsoft Corporation. *Microsoft Network Monitor online help.* Redmond, Washington. Review "Concepts," "How To: Capture Network Data," and "How To: Display Network Data."

Microsoft Corporation. *Microsoft Windows Server 2003 Deployment Guide.* Redmond, Washington. Review "How To: Monitor Network Connections," available on Microsoft's Web site at *http://www.microsoft.com/technet/treeview/default.asp?url=/ technet/prodtechnol/windowsserver2003/proddocs/entserver/NetcfgMonitorn- ode.asp.*

Objective 5.2   Review Lesson 3 in Chapter 9, "Routing with Windows Server 2003."

Microsoft Corporation. *Microsoft Windows Server 2003 online help.* Redmond, Washington. Review "Repair a LAN or High-Speed Internet Connection," "Error Messages: Network Connections," and "Configuring a Translated Connection."

Microsoft Corporation. *Microsoft Windows Server 2003 Deployment Guide.* Redmond, Washington. Review "Network Connections," available on Microsoft's Web site at *http://www.microsoft.com/technet/treeview/default.asp?url=/technet/prodtech- nol/windowsserver2003/proddocs/entserver/NetCfgtopnode.asp.*

Objective 5.3   Review Lesson 2 in Chapter 12, "Maintaining a Network Infrastructure."

Microsoft Corporation. *Microsoft Windows Server 2003 Resource Kit.* Redmond, Washington. Review "Troubleshooting Startup for the Performance and Trouble- shooting guide."

Microsoft Corporation. *Microsoft Windows Server 2003 online help.* Redmond, Washington. Review "Troubleshooting: Services."

Microsoft Corporation. *Microsoft Windows Server 2003 Deployment Guide.* Redmond, Washington. Review "Managing Services," available on Microsoft's Web site at *http://www.microsoft.com/technet/treeview/default.asp?url=/technet/prodtechnol/ windowsserver2003/proddocs/entserver/ctasks016.asp.*

Monitor Network Traffic

For this objective, you need to know how to use key tools such as **Network Monitor, System Monitor**, **Performance Logs And Alerts**, and **Event Viewer**.

The version of Network Monitor that is provided on the Windows Server 2003 installation CD-ROM can be used to view only the network traffic that is sent to or from the computer on which it is installed. To view network traffic that is sent to or from another computer and that is routed through your computer, you need to use the Network Monitor component that is provided with **Microsoft Systems Management Server (SMS)**.

Network Monitor captures and displays **network packets** at **byte-level**. This is often too much information, and **view** and **capture filters** can be configured so that you can either view only the traffic that you are interested in, or capture only that traffic. You can create a view filter by specifying source or destination IP address, or protocol. Capture filters can be triggered by a **pattern match**, for example, so that you can specify when the capture starts.

The examination requires that you know how to install, configure, and use Network Monitor, and also know how it complements other troubleshooting tools such as System Monitor and Event Viewer.

System Monitor lets you view the values returned by the counters for various system objects. In this objective, you are mostly concerned with the Network Interface object, but valuable information can also be gathered by adding Protocol_layer_object counters. These exist for the TCPv4 and TCPv6 objects. It is unlikely that the TCPv6 objects will form part of the exam. Counters of particular interest include the following:

- Network Interface: Bytes Total/sec
- Network Interface: Bytes Sent/sec
- Network Interface: Bytes Received/sec
- Protocol_layer_object: Segments Received/sec
- Protocol_layer_object: Segments Sent/sec
- Protocol_layer_object: Frames Sent/sec
- Protocol_layer_object: Frames Received/sec

You need to know what these counters indicate and what their acceptable value ranges are. You need to know how to generate a baseline log and compare this with current performance. The Protocol_layer_object counters are found in the TCPv4 and TCPv6 objects. As stated previously, it is unlikely that the TCPv6 objects will form part of the exam.

Objective 5.1 Questions

1.   You are configuring a router-to-router virtual private network (VPN) connection on a router running Windows Server 2003 in your domain. You decide to install Network Monitor tools from the Windows Server 2003 CD-ROM to monitor the traffic on the VPN connection. The installation does not complete, but stops with the message shown below.

```
Windows Components Wizard                                          [X]

  Configuring Components                                          [CD icon]
      Setup is making the configuration changes you requested.

      [clock icon]  Please wait while Setup configures the components. This may take
                    several minutes, depending on the components selected.


      Status:  Completing configuration of Management and Monitoring Tools...

      [███████████████████████████                              ]


Optional Networking Components                                    [X]

  [!]   Installation or removal of Network Monitor Tools has been interrupted because Remote
        Router Properties is accessing the needed information.  Please close Remote Router
        Properties and then click Retry.

                    [  Retry  ]      Cancel


                    < Back      Next >                    Help
```

What is the problem?

A.   Network Monitor tools must be installed by running Suptools.msi from the \Support\Tools folder on the Windows Server 2003 CD-ROM.

B.   You have failed to close a dialog box in the Routing And Remote Access snap-in.

C.   You cannot install Network Monitor tools on a VPN server. It must be installed on a domain controller.

D.   You need to install Network Monitor tools on each network interface as a protocol.

2.   You are using Network Monitor on a Windows Server 2003 domain controller named Dom1. You have performed a capture of all inbound and outbound traffic at Dom1_fs local area network (LAN) interface. You want to view all Address Resolution Protocol (ARP) frames that Dom1 has sent to, and received from, a client running Microsoft Windows XP Professional named Client26. How do you specify your display filter?

A. AND

   Protocol==ARP

   Dom1(IP)←→Client26(IP)

B. AND

   Protocol==ARP_RARP

   Dom1(IP)←→ANY

C. AND

   Protocol==IP

   Dom1(IP)←→ANY

D. AND

   Protocol==ARP_RARP

   Dom1(IP)←→Client26(IP)

3. You are having a problem with excessive network traffic. You install Network Monitor on the server that seems most affected, a file server running Windows Server 2003. You want to obtain the source IP address, the destination IP address, and the destination port number of every inbound and outbound TCP/IP frame. You want to log the information for a period of six hours. What do you do?

   A. On the Capture Buffers Settings menu, increase the frame size.

   B. On the Capture Buffers Settings menu, increase the buffer size.

   C. On the Capture Buffers Settings menu, decrease the frame size.

   D. On the Capture Buffers Settings menu, decrease the buffer size.

4. You administer a Windows Server 2003 Active Directory domain at Blue Yonder Airlines. The domain is on a single network segment and contains 120 clients running Microsoft Windows 2000 Professional and Windows XP Professional, and five servers running Windows Server 2003. Two of the servers are domain controllers, one is a router and NAT provider, one is a file and print server, and the fourth is an application server named App1. App1 runs a line-of-business booking registration client/server application.

Users report long response times. You examine the client/server application and find that it is transmitting large amounts of data to one client on the network. The application cannot identify the client. You need to identify this client computer. What do you do?

   A. Add Network Monitor driver to the interface on your client computer and create a capture filter to capture traffic between any client computer and App1.

   B. Install Network Monitor tools on App1. Create a capture filter to capture traffic that is generated by the client/server application.

    C. Use the Performance Logs And Alerts tool on your client computer to create an alert that fires when network use exceeds 80 percent.

    D. Use the Performance Logs And Alerts tool on App1 to create an alert that fires when network use exceeds 80 percent.

5. Which System Monitor counter can help to detect an insufficient bandwidth problem?

    A. Network Interface: Current Bandwidth

    B. Network Interface: Output Queue length

    C. Network Interface: Bytes Total/sec

    D. Network Interface: Packets/sec

Objective 5.1 Answers

1.   Correct Answers: B

  A.   Incorrect: You install Network Monitor tools from Add Or Remove Programs in Control Panel.

  B.   Correct: In this case, the Remote Router Properties dialog box is open. You need to close the dialog box, and click Retry.

  C.   Incorrect: You can install Network Monitor tools on any server running Windows Server 2003.

  D.   Incorrect: Network Monitor Driver (not tools) is installed on a network interface as a protocol.

2.   Correct Answers: D

  A.   Incorrect: ARP frames contain either forward ARP or reverse ARP (RARP) traffic. The correct protocol specification is ARP_RARP.

  B.   Incorrect: ARP_RARP is the correct protocol, but this filter displays the ARP traffic between Dom1 and all participating clients.

  C.   Incorrect: This answer is incorrect for the reasons given in the explanations for both answer A and answer B.

  D.   Correct: This filter displays both forward and reverse ARP network traffic between Dom1 and Client26.

3.   Correct Answers: B and C

  A.   Incorrect: The frame size needs to be decreased, not increased.

  B.   Correct: The buffer size needs to be increased from its default of 1 MB. If this is done, the buffer is less likely to become full, and data will not be overwritten.

  C.   Correct: The frame size needs to be decreased from its default value of 65,472 bytes. More frames can then be stored before the buffer becomes full and data is overwritten.

  D.   Incorrect: The buffer size needs to be increased, not decreased.

4.   Correct Answers: B

  A.   Incorrect: You need Network Monitor tools, not driver. The version of Network Monitor tools that is supplied with Windows Server 2003 cannot capture traffic between any computers on a network. It can capture traffic only between itself and other computers.

B. Correct: This solution captures all the traffic between App1 and client computers that is generated by the client/server applications. You can use the source and destination addresses contained in this traffic to identify the client computer.

C. Incorrect: Performance Logs And Alerts indicates the volume of network traffic through an interface. It cannot analyze the content of this traffic.

D. Incorrect: This answer is incorrect for the reason given in the explanation for answer C.

5. Correct Answers: C

A. Incorrect: Current Bandwidth usually shows the theoretical bandwidth of the connection. It does not indicate how much of this bandwidth is being used.

B. Incorrect: Output Queue length should be zero. If it is consistently greater than two, the NIC should be upgraded. This counter indicates a problem with the NIC rather than with the network bandwidth.

C. Correct: Bytes Total/sec shows the data transfer rate on a given network interface. If the transfer rate is consistently close to the network's nominal capacity, the communication link should be upgraded to one with a higher bandwidth.

D. Incorrect: Packets/sec cannot provide an accurate estimate of the portion of bandwidth that is being used because packets can be of different lengths.

Objective 5.2

Troubleshoot Connectivity to the Internet

This objective requires that you know how to troubleshoot Internet connectivity problems. You need to know how to properly configure Internet connectivity and check for faults and misconfigurations. Many intranets use **private networks**, so you need to know how to configure NAT and **Internet Connection Sharing (ICS)**. You need to know how a **DHCP allocator** works and how TCP and UDP use port numbers. You need to know which protocols are used for Internet connectivity and how to filter traffic.

You are unlikely to be asked detailed questions about **Microsoft Proxy server** or about **firewall** configuration. However, you should be aware of the functionality of these devices and the part they play in Internet communications. You need to know how your intranet can be attacked from the Internet and the precautions you should take to secure your network.

Objective 5.2 Questions

1. Margie's Travel is a small office configured as a peer-to-peer network. The network contains one multihomed server running Windows Server 2003, Mag1, and 12 clients running Windows XP Professional. Mag1 connects to the Internet via a dial-up connection to an ISP. The internal interface address of Mag1 is 10.10.10.1.

Margie's Travel wants all client computers to be able to connect to the Internet. You are asked to set this up. You do the following:

- Install and enable the Routing And Remote Access service on Mag1.
- Ensure that Mag1 has no default gateway and a subnet mask of 255.255.255.0. Mag1 is already configured with the IP address of 10.10.10.1 on its private interface.
- Enable routing on Mag1's dial-up port.
- Create a demand-dial interface that connects to the ISP.
- Create a default static route that uses the public Internet interface.
- Add the NAT routing protocol.
- Add the private and public interfaces on Mag1 to NAT, choosing the appropriate setting for each on the NAT/Basic Firewall tab.
- Enable network address translation and name resolution.
- Configure the client computer default gateways with the public IP address that is supplied by the ISP.

The clients cannot connect to the Internet. You review your procedure. What do you need to change?

A. Create the demand-dial interface on the local area connection.

B. Configure the public NAT interface with an address pool of 10.10.10.1.

C. Change the default gateway IP address on the clients to 10.10.10.1.

D. Enable Basic Firewall on the public interface.

2. You administer a Windows Server 2003 domain for Litware, Inc. in Denver, Colorado. The network consists of 150 clients running Windows XP Professional, 2 domain controllers running Windows Server 2003, 1 DHCP server running Windows Server 2003, 2 file and print servers running Windows Server 2003, and 1 router running Windows Server 2003 called Denver6 that is connected to an ISP through a permanent broadband link. All the client computers are configured with private addresses through DHCP. All the servers are configured statically.

Litware's ISP has allocated the public IP addresses 208.147.66.16 through 208.147.66.23. You install NAT and add the public and private interfaces. Internet connectivity is achieved, but users report that it can be quite slow. You use Network Monitor on Denver1's public interface and discover that only two of the public IP addresses are being used.

How do you ensure that all eight addresses are used?

    A. Configure the LAN interface in the NAT routing protocol to use a starting address of 208.147.66.16 and a subnet mask of 255.255.255.248.

    B. Configure NAT to use a starting address of 208.147.66.16 and a subnet mask of 255.255.255.248 for the DHCP allocator.

    C. Configure the public interface in the NAT routing protocol to use a starting address of 208.147.66.16 and a subnet mask of 255.255.255.248.

    D. Use a special port to map public address 208.147.66.16 to the private address of Denver1's local interface.

3. Contoso, Ltd.'s company policy mandates that only e-mail and Hypertext Transport Protocol (HTTP) traffic can pass in or out of its intranet. As a result, only inbound and outbound TCP port 25 and TCP port 80 traffic is permitted. Contoso's employees frequently access the Web site of the company's main supplier at *http://www.northwindtraders.com* to download product information.

Northwind Traders announces that its site is going down over a weekend so that it can implement improvements. When Contoso employees access the site on the following Monday they get the message, "Web page requested is not available." You are Contoso's network manager. You note that https:// appears in the address bar. You confirm that the site is up and running by accessing it from your home computer.

What action should you take?

    A. Allow traffic on TCP port 443.

    B. Allow traffic on TCP port 53.

    C. Configure the default IPSec Client (Respond Only) policy on the client computers.

    D. An authentication problem exists. You need to get passwords from Northwind Traders.

Objective 5.2 Answers

1.   Correct Answers: C

    A. Incorrect: The ISP is dialed on demand, not Mag1.

    B. Incorrect: The public address pool consists of the public address provided by the ISP. The private address 10.10.10.1 should not be in the public address pool.

    C. Correct: The clients' default gateway has to be on the same network that the clients are on, in this case, the private network.

    D. Incorrect: This action is probably wise, but it will not solve the problem in this scenario.

2.   Correct Answers: C

    A. Incorrect: The LAN uses private addresses, not public addresses.

    B. Incorrect: Whether they get their addresses from DHCP or from the NAT DHCP allocator, the clients need to get private IP addresses.

    C. Correct: The most probable fault is that a subnet mask of 255.255.255.254 is configured on the public interface. The configuration in answer C ensures that all eight public addresses are used.

    D. Incorrect: Special ports allow external users to access resources on a private network through the Internet. Typically, a special port allocates a public address to the private address of a Web server that hosts the company's Web site. This setup is not needed in this scenario.

3. **Correct Answers: A**

A. **Correct:** The message "Web page requested is not available" indicates an encryption problem when https:// appears on the address bar. Web page encryption is implemented using the Secure Sockets Layer (SSL) protocol. This protocol uses TCP port 443. Northwind's improvements probably include onsite ordering or other facilities that require a secure site.

B. **Incorrect:** TCP port 53 is used for DNS transfers. The scenario does not state that Contoso has a DNS server that needs to receive zone information from an external source. DNS is not the problem. Clients are resolving http://www.northwind-traders.com to an IP address—otherwise, they would not be getting the message stated.

C. **Incorrect:** You have connected to the site from your home computer, and Contoso employees are connected to Northwind's Web server, although they cannot obtain the Web page. Internet Protocol Security (IPSec) is not the problem. In any case, IPSec is used to encrypt data through VPN tunnels, not to encrypt Web sites.

D. **Incorrect:** The message does not state that users do not have sufficient permissions to access the Web page. In any case, you can access the site from home without a password.

Troubleshoot Server Services

This objective requires you to know how to manage and troubleshoot the services that run on servers and clients running Windows Server 2003. The **principle of least privilege** mandates that you use the **Services snap-in** from your client machine to perform these functions because you should be logged on using your ordinary user account, and ordinary users cannot (typically) log on locally to a server. You need to know how to do this. You need to know about **service dependencies**, and what would happen if a core service failed on which many other services depend.

You need to know how to configure services to automatically recover after a failure. You need to know how to configure services to start **automatically** or **manually**, and how to **disable** a service. You need to know how to interpret messages in Event Viewer that indicate service failure.

Objective 5.3 Questions

1. Another administrator has been changing settings on a member server running Windows Server 2003 in your domain. When the computer is rebooted, you discover that the Net Logon service has failed to start. This problem does not happen if you reboot any other computer in your domain. The member server is connected to your network segment, and its IP settings are statically configured and have not been changed. What could be causing the problem? (Choose all that apply.)

    A. The startup type has been set to Manual or Disabled.

    B. The Remote Procedure Call (RPC) service is stopped.

    C. The Workstation service is stopped.

    D. The Allow Service To Interact With Desktop check box is cleared.

    E. A password has been set for the Local System account.

    F. The Server service is stopped.

2. A client on your network fails to restart, and you suspect that settings have been changed in one of the core services. How do you recover from this situation? (Choose all that apply. Each answer forms part of the solution.)

    A. Boot using the Last Known Good Configuration option.

    B. Boot into Safe mode.

    C. Boot using the Directory Service Restore Mode option.

    D. Restore to its default the account under which the service runs.

    E. Manually start the core service_fs dependent services.

3. You are remotely administering the services on a member server running Windows Server 2003, ServerA, in your domain. You start the MMC, add the Services snap-in, and specify the remote computer. The snap-in is added, but when you double-click Services (SERVERA) in the console tree, a dialog box appears with the message Error 1722: The RPC Server Is Unavailable. What is the most likely cause of the problem?

    A. You cannot connect to the remote computer.

    B. The Remote Registry service is not running.

    C. The RPC Locator service is not running.

    D. The Remote Access Connection Manager service is not running.

4.   You need to modify the configuration of a service from Safe Mode With Command Prompt to repair a system that will not start normally. Which command-line utility enables you to do this?

   A. Msconfig.exe

   B. Netsh.exe

   C. Netdiag.exe

   D. Sc.exe

Objective 5.3 Answers

1. **Correct Answers: A, C, and F**

  A. **Correct:** These settings can be changed in the Net Logon service properties dialog box.

  B. **Incorrect:** The Net Logon service does not depend on the RPC service.

  C. **Correct:** The Net Logon service is a dependent service of the Workstation service.

  D. **Incorrect:** This check box is cleared by default. This setting does not prevent the service from starting.

  E. **Incorrect:** This account does not have a password. Any password set on the account will be ignored.

  F. **Correct:** The Net Logon service is a dependent service of the Server service.

2. **Correct Answers: B and D**

  A. **Incorrect:** You use this option when a driver misconfiguration is preventing a reboot. It will not allow you to boot if a core service is disabled.

  B. **Correct:** In Safe mode, core services that are required to start the operating system are started in a default scheme, regardless of any changes that are made to the service settings. You can change the service configuration or restore the default configuration in Safe mode.

  C. **Incorrect:** This option is used only for restoring the SYSVOL directory and the Active Directory directory service on a domain controller.

  D. **Correct:** When a core service fails to start and the computer cannot boot into normal mode, it is usually because the user account under which the service runs (indicated on the Log On tab of the properties dialog box for the service) has been changed.

  E. **Incorrect:** The core service is not running, so you cannot start the dependent services. After you reconfigure the core service, you should reboot the computer. The dependent services that should be running will start on reboot.

3. **Correct Answers: A**

  A. **Correct:** Although the remote computer name appears in the snap-in, Error 1722 normally indicates that a connection cannot be made. This problem can be due to name resolution failure, or the remote computer could be powered down or disconnected from the network.

B. Incorrect: If this service is stopped or disabled, you receive a Connection Manager error message when you try to access the properties dialog box for a service. You can, however, connect to the remote computer and you do not get Error 1722.

C. Incorrect: This service is started manually and does not run by default. It allows certain types of application program interfaces (APIs) to locate RPC servers. These APIs are not used internally in Microsoft Windows.

D. Incorrect: This service is started manually and does not run by default. It detects unsuccessful attempts to connect to a remote computer or network and suggests alternative connection methods.

4.   Correct Answers: D

A. Incorrect: The System Configuration utility (Msconfig.exe) automates the routine troubleshooting steps that are used to diagnose Windows configuration issues. It is not the appropriate tool in this scenario.

B. Incorrect: The Network Shell utility (Netsh.exe) can perform a wide range of system configuration tasks. However, it is not the appropriate tool for configuring services.

C. Incorrect: The Network Diagnostic utility (Netdiag.exe) can diagnose and repair a wide range of faults. It is a diagnostic tool, and it is not used for automating the configuration of services.

D. Correct: The Service Controller utility (Sc.exe) can configure a specific service, retrieve the current status of a service, and stop and start a service. You can create batch files that automate the startup or shutdown sequence of services. The tool's capabilities are similar to those of the Services MMC snap-in.

Glossary

802.1X authentication   An Institute of Electrical and Electronics Engineers (IEEE) standard for port-based network access control that provides authenticated network access to Ethernet networks and wireless 802.11 local area networks (LANs).

ACK (acknowledgment)   A message transmitted to indicate that data has been received correctly. The Transmission Control Protocol (TCP) requires that the recipient acknowledge successful receipt of data. Such acknowledgments (ACKs) generate additional network traffic, decreasing the rate at which data passes but increasing reliability. To reduce the impact on performance, most hosts send an acknowledgment for every other segment or when a specified time interval has passed.

Active Directory directory service   The Windows-based directory service. Active Directory stores information about objects on a network and makes this information available to users and network administrators. Active Directory gives network users access to permitted resources anywhere on the network using a single logon process. It provides network administrators with an intuitive, hierarchical view of the network and a single point of administration for all network objects.

Active Directory replication   The synchronization of Active Directory partition replicas between domain controllers. Replication automatically copies the changes that originate on a writable directory partition replica to all other domain controllers that hold the same directory partition replica. More specifically, a destination domain controller pulls these changes from the source domain controller.

Active Directory–integrated zone   A primary DNS zone that is stored in Active Directory so that it can use multimaster replication and Active Directory security features.

address (A) resource record   A resource record (RR) used to map a DNS domain name to a host Internet Protocol version 4 (IPv4) address on the network.

address class   A predefined grouping of Internet addresses that defines a network of a certain size. The range of numbers that can be assigned for the first octet in the IP address is based on the address class. Class-based IP addressing has been superseded by classless interdomain routing (CIDR).

address pool   The addresses within a DHCP scope range of addresses that are available for leased distribution to clients.

Address Resolution Protocol (ARP)   In Transmission Control Protocol/Internet protocol (TCP/IP), a protocol that uses broadcast traffic on the local network to resolve a logically assigned Internet Protocol version 4 (IPv4) address to its physical hardware or Media Access Control (MAC) layer address.

administrative credentials   Logon information that is used to identify a member of an administrative group. Groups that use administrative credentials include Administrators, Domain Admins, and DNS Admins. Most systemwide or domainwide tasks require administrative credentials.

administrator   In the Microsoft Windows Server 2003 family, a person who is responsible for setting up and managing local computers, stand-alone servers, member servers, or domain controllers. An administrator sets up user and group accounts, assigns passwords and permissions, and helps users with networking problems. Administrators can be members of the Administrators group on local computers or servers. A person who is a member of the Administrators group on a local computer or server has full access to that computer or server and can assign access control rights to users as necessary.

Administrators can also be members of the Domain Admins group on domain controllers and have full control over user and computer accounts residing in that domain.

administrator account   On a local computer, the first account that is created when you install an operating system on a new workstation, stand-alone server, or member server. By default, this account has the highest level of administrative access to the local computer, and it is a member of the Administrators group.

In an Active Directory domain, the first account that is created when you set up a new domain by using the Active Directory Installation Wizard. By default, this account has the highest level of administrative access in a domain, and it is a member of the Administrators, Domain Admins, Domain Users, Enterprise Admins, Group Policy Creator Owners, and Schema Admins groups.

Administrators group   On a local computer, a group whose members have the highest level of administrative access to the local computer. Examples of administrative tasks that can be performed by members of this group include installing programs; accessing all files on the computer; auditing access control; and creating, modifying, and deleting local user accounts.

algorithm   In cryptography, a mathematical process that is used in cryptographic operations such as the encryption and digital signing of data. An algorithm is commonly used with a cryptographic key to enhance security.

application directory partition   An Active Directory partition that stores application-specific data that can be dynamic (subject to Time to Live [TTL] restrictions). Application directory partitions can store any type of object except security principles and are not replicated to the global catalog. The replication scope of an application directory partition can be configured to include any set of domain controllers in the forest.

application programming interface (API)   A set of routines made available to applications by another application, a service, or an operating system component.

area border router (ABR)   A router placed at the perimeter of an Open Shortest Path First (OSPF) area. ABRs publish a summary of the internal networks to ABRs at the perimeters of neighboring areas.

Asynchronous Transfer Mode (ATM)   A high-speed, connection-oriented Layer 2 protocol used to transport many different types of Layer 3 network traffic. ATM packages data in a 53-byte, fixed-length cell that can be switched quickly between physical connections on a network.

authentication   The process for verifying that an entity or object is who or what it claims to be. Examples include confirming the source and integrity of information, such as verifying a digital signature or verifying the identity of a user or computer.

Authentication Header (AH)   A header that provides authentication, integrity, and antireplay for the entire packet (the IP header and the data payload carried in the packet).

authentication protocol   The protocol by which an entity on a network proves its identity to a remote entity. Typically, identity is proved with the use of a secret key, such as a password, or with a stronger key, such as the key on a smart card. Some authentication protocols also implement mechanisms to share keys between client and server to provide message integrity or privacy.

authoritative   A DNS server that hosts a primary or secondary copy of a DNS zone.

authorization   The process that determines what a user is permitted to do on a computer system or network.

Automatic Private IP Addressing (APIPA)   A TCP/IP feature in Microsoft Windows XP, Windows 2000, and products in the Windows Server 2003 family that automatically configures an IP address from the range 169.254.0.1 through 169.254.255.254 when the TCP/IP protocol is configured for dynamic addressing and a DHCP server is not available. The APIPA range of IP addresses is reserved by the Internet Assigned Numbers Authority (IANA), and IP addresses within this range are not used on the Internet.

autostatic updates   The process of adding static routes to the routing table automatically. When you configure an interface to use autostatic update mode, the router sends a request to other routers and inherits routes. The routes are saved in the routing table as autostatic routes and are kept even if the router is restarted or the interface goes down. Autostatic updates are supported in Routing Information Protocol (RIP) for IP and in RIP for Internetwork Packet Exchange (IPX), but they are not available for use with Open Shortest Path First (OSPF).

backbone   In Open Shortest Path First (OSPF), an area common to all other OSPF areas that is used as the transit area for interarea traffic and for distributing routing information between areas. The backbone must be contiguous.

backbone router   In Open Shortest Path First (OSPF), a router that is connected to the backbone area. This includes routers that are connected to more than one area (area border routers [ABRs]). However, backbone routers do not have to be ABRs. Routers that have all networks connected to the backbone are internal routers.

Backup Operators group   A type of local or global group that contains the user rights you need to back up and restore files and folders. Members of the Backup Operators group can back up and restore files and folders regardless of ownership, permissions, encryption, or auditing settings.

Bandwidth Allocation Protocol (BAP)   A Point-to-Point Protocol (PPP) control protocol that is used on a multiprocessing connection to dynamically add and remove links.

batch program   An ASCII (unformatted text) file that contains one or more operating system commands. A batch program's filename has a .cmd or .bat extension. When you type the filename at the command prompt, or when the batch program is run from another program, its commands are processed sequentially. Also called *batch files.*

Berkeley Internet Name Domain (BIND)   An implementation of DNS written and ported to most available versions of the UNIX operating system. The Internet Software Consortium maintains the BIND software.

binding   A process by which software components and layers are linked together. When a network component is installed, the binding relationships and dependencies for the components are established. Binding allows components to communicate with each other.

broadcast   The transmission of packets to all interfaces on the local area network (LAN).

broadcast address   An address that is destined for all hosts on a particular network segment.

broadcast message   A network message sent from a single computer that is distributed to all other devices on the same segment of the network as the sending computer.

broadcast network   A network that supports more than two attached hosts and has the ability to address a single message to all the attached hosts. Ethernet is an example of a broadcast network.

browsing   The process of creating and maintaining an up-to-date list of computers and resources on a network or part of a network by one or more designated computers running the Computer Browser service.

built-in groups   The default security groups installed with the operating system. Built-in groups have been granted useful collections of rights and built-in abilities. For example, members of the built-in Backup Operators group can back up and restore files and folders. To provide a needed set of capabilities to a user account, assign it to the appropriate built-in group.

caching-only server   A DNS sever that does not host any DNS zones but that forwards name resolution requests and stores the results in its cache.

callback security   A form of network security in which a remote access server calls a user back at a preset number after the user has made an initial connection and has been authenticated.

certificate   A digital document that is commonly used for authentication and to secure information on open networks. A certificate securely binds a public key to the entity that holds the corresponding private key. Certificates are digitally signed by the issuing certificate authority (CA), and they can be issued for a user, a computer, or a service.

certificate authority (CA)   An entity responsible for establishing and vouching for the authenticity of public keys belonging to subjects (usually users or computers) or other certificate authorities. Activities of a certificate authority can include binding public keys to distinguished names through signed certificates, managing certificate serial numbers, and handling certificate revocation.

Certificate Services   A software service that issues certificates for a particular certificate authority (CA). It provides customizable services for issuing and managing certificates for the enterprise. Certificates can be used to provide authentication support, including secure e-mail, Web-based authentication, and smart card authentication.

Challenge Handshake Authentication Protocol (CHAP)   A challenge-response authentication protocol for Point-to-Point Protocol (PPP) connections described in Request for Comments (RFC) 1994. It uses the industry-standard Message Digest 5 (MD5) hashing algorithm to hash the combination of a challenge string issued by the authenticating server and the user's password in the response.

child domain   For DNS and Active Directory, a domain located in the namespace tree directly beneath another domain (the parent domain). For example, example.microsoft.com would be a child domain of the parent domain microsoft.com. Also known as a *subdomain*.

Class A IP address   A unicast IP address that ranges from 1.0.0.0 through 127.255.255.255. The first octet indicates the network, and the last three octets indicate the host on the network. Class-based IP addressing has been superceded by Classless Interdomain Routing (CIDR).

Class B IP address   A unicast IP address that ranges from 128.0.0.0 through 191.255.255.255. The first two octets indicate the network, and the last two octets indicate the host on the network. Class-based IP addressing has been superceded by Classless Interdomain Routing (CIDR).

Class C IP address   A unicast IP address that ranges from 192.0.0.0 through 223.255.255.255. The first three octets indicate the network, and the last octet indicates the host on the network. Network Load Balancing provides optional session support for Class C IP addresses (in addition to support for single IP addresses) to accommodate clients that make use of multiple proxy servers at the client site. Class-based IP addressing has been superceded by Classless Interdomain Routing (CIDR).

classless interdomain routing (CIDR)   An IP address and routing management method that allocates IP addresses in a way that reduces the number of routes stored on any individual router, while also increasing the number of available IP addresses. CIDR replaces class-based IP address allocation.

client   Any computer or program connecting to, or requesting the services of, another computer or program. Client can also refer to the software that enables the computer or program to establish the connection.
For a local area network (LAN) or the Internet, a computer that uses shared network resources provided by another computer (called a *server*).

Client Service for NetWare   A service included with recent versions of Windows that allows clients to make direct connections to resources on computers running legacy NetWare server software by using only the Internetwork Packet Exchange (IPX) protocol.

Computer Browser service   A service that maintains an up-to-date list of computers that share resources on your network and that supplies the list to programs that request it. The Computer Browser service is used to view a list of available network resources.

computer name   A unique name of up to 15 uppercase characters that identifies a computer to the network. The name cannot be the same as any other computer or domain name in the network.

conflict detection   For DHCP, an optional server-side mechanism for detecting whether a scope IP address is in use on the network. When enabled, the DHCP server pings an address first before offering that address to clients, and then it briefly awaits a response. If the pinged address responds, a conflict is registered and that address is not offered to clients obtaining a lease from the server.

connection request policy   A set of conditions and profile settings that network administrators use to specify how Internet Authentication Service (IAS) servers handle incoming authentication and accounting request messages.

connectionless   A network protocol in which a sender broadcasts traffic on the network to an intended receiver without first establishing a connection to the receiver.

connection-oriented   A type of network protocol that requires an end-to-end virtual connection between the sender and receiver before communicating across the network.

console   A framework for hosting administrative tools, such as Microsoft Management Console (MMC). A console is defined by the items in its console tree, which might include folders or other containers, World Wide Web pages, and other administrative items. A console has windows that can provide views of the console tree and the administrative properties, services, and events that are acted on by the items in the console tree.

console tree   The left pane in Microsoft Management Console (MMC) that displays the items contained in the console. The items in the console tree and their hierarchical organization determine the capabilities of a console.

credentials   A set of information that includes identification and proof of identification that is used to gain access to local and network resources. Examples of credentials are user names and passwords, smart cards, and certificates.

cryptography   The processes, art, and science of keeping messages and data secure. Cryptography is used to enable and ensure confidentiality, data integrity, authentication (entity and data origin), and nonrepudiation.

Data Encryption Standard (DES)   An encryption algorithm that uses a 56-bit key and maps a 64-bit input block to a 64-bit output block. The key appears to be a 64-bit key, but 1 bit in each of the 8 bytes is used for odd parity, resulting in 56 bits of usable key.

datagram   One packet, or unit, of information that includes relevant delivery information, such as the destination address, that is sent through a packet-switching network.

dedicated connection   A communications channel that connects two or more geographic locations. Dedicated connections are private or leased lines, rather than on-demand connections.

delegation   An assignment of administrative responsibility to a user, computer, group, or organization.
For Active Directory, an assignment of responsibility that allows users without administrative credentials to complete specific administrative tasks or to manage specific directory objects. Responsibility is assigned through membership in a security group, the Delegation Of Control Wizard, or Group Policy settings.
For DNS, an assignment of responsibility for a DNS zone. Delegation occurs when a name server (NS) resource record in a parent zone lists the DNS server that is authoritative for a child zone.

demand-dial connection   A connection, typically using a circuit-switched wide area network (WAN) link, that is initiated when data needs to be forwarded. The demand-dial connection is typically terminated when there is no traffic.

demand-dial routing   Routing that makes dial-up connections to connect networks based on need. For example, a branch office with a modem that dials and establishes a connection when there is network traffic only from one office to another.

Denial of Service attack   An attack in which an intruder exploits a weakness or a design limitation of a network service to overload or halt the service so that the service is not available for use. This type of attack is typically started to prevent other users from using a network service such as a Web server or a file server.

dependency tree   A diagram for visualizing the dependency relationships between resources.

details pane   The right pane in Microsoft Management Console (MMC) that displays details for the selected item in the console tree. The details can be a list of items or they can be administrative properties, services, and events that are acted on by a snap-in.

DHCP Acknowledgment message (DHCP ACK)   A message sent by the DHCP server to a client to acknowledge and complete a client's request for leased configuration. This message contains a committed IP address for the client to use for a stated period of time, along with other optional client parameters. The DHCP acknowledgment message name is *DHCPACK*.

DHCP class identifier   A special reserved option type used by DHCP clients to optionally identify membership in a specific DHCP option class, either a vendor or user class. For vendor class identification, hardware vendors can choose to pre-define specific identifier values: for example, to identify a client's hardware configuration. For user class identification, values can be defined administratively to identify a logical group of DHCP clients, such as all clients in a particular building and floor location.

DHCP client   Any network-enabled device that supports the ability to communicate with a DHCP server for the purpose of obtaining dynamic leased IP configuration and related optional parameters information.

DHCP client alternate configuration   An alternate static configuration option for TCP/IP network connections that provides simplified computer migration between networks.

DHCP Decline message (DHCP DECLINE)   A message sent by a DHCP client to the DHCP server to decline the offer of an IP address on the network. This message is used when the client detects a potential conflict because the IP address is found to be already in use on the network. The DHCP decline message name is *DHCP-DECLINE.*

DHCP Information message (DHCP INFORM)   A reserved DHCP message type used by computers on the network to request and obtain information from a DHCP server for use in their local configuration. When this message type is used, the sender is already externally configured for its IP address on the network, which might or might not have been obtained using DHCP. The DHCP information message name is DHCPINFORM.

DHCP Negative Acknowledgment message (DHCP NAK)   A message sent by a DHCP server to a client to indicate that the IP address that the client requested is not correct for the local IP network served by the DHCP server. This message is most often used when the client computer was moved to a new location, but it could also indicate that the client's lease with the server has expired. The DHCP Negative Acknowledgment message name is DHCPNAK.

DHCP Offer message (DHCP OFFER)   A message used by DHCP servers to offer the lease of an IP address to a DHCP client when it starts on the network. When this message is used, a client can receive more than one offer if multiple DHCP servers are contacted during the DHCP discovery phase, but the client typically selects the first address it is offered. The DHCP offer message name is *DHCPOFFER.*

DHCP option   Address configuration parameters that a DHCP service assigns to clients. Most DHCP options are predefined, based on optional parameters defined in Request for Comments (RFC) 1542, although extended options can be added by vendors or users.

DHCP Release message (DHCP RELEASE)   A message sent by clients to the DHCP server to indicate release of its leased IP address. The client uses this message to cancel its currently active lease. You can perform address release manually by using the Ipconfig /release command at a command prompt. The DHCP release message name is *DHCPRELEASE*.

DHCP Request message (DHCP REQUEST)   A message sent by clients to the DHCP server to request or renew lease of its IP address. The client uses this message under the following conditions:

- To select and request a lease from a specific DHCP server when lease offers were made simultaneously from several different servers
- To confirm a previously leased IP address after the client system is restarted
- To extend the current IP address lease for the client
- The DHCP request message name is *DHCP REQUEST*.

DHCP server   A computer running the Microsoft DHCP service that offers dynamic configuration of IP addresses and related information to DHCP-enabled clients.

DHCP service   A service that enables a computer to function as a DHCP server and configure DHCP-enabled clients on a network. DHCP runs on a server, enabling the automatic, centralized management of IP addresses and other TCP/IP configuration settings for network clients.

DHCP/BOOTP Relay Agent   The agent program or component responsible for relaying DHCP and Boot Protocol (BOOTP) broadcast messages between a DHCP server and a client across an IP router. A DHCP relay agent supports DHCP/BOOTP message relay as defined in Requests for Comments (RFCs) 1541 and 2131. The DHCP Relay Agent service is managed using the Routing And Remote Access service.

dial-in constraints   Settings in a remote access policy that permit or deny access to remote access clients.

dial-up connection   The connection to your network if you use a device that uses the telephone network. This includes modems with a standard telephone line, Integrated Services Digital Network (ISDN) cards with high-speed ISDN lines, or X.25 networks.

dial-up line   A standard dial-up connection, such as telephone and Integrated Services Digital Network (ISDN) lines. Also called *switched circuit*.

Diffie-Hellman key agreement protocol   A cryptographic mechanism that allows two parties to establish a shared secret key without having any preestablished secrets between them. Diffie-Hellman is frequently used to establish the shared secret keys that are used by common applications of cryptography, such as Internet Protocol Security (IPSec). It is not normally used for data protection.

direct hosting   For Microsoft networking, the sending of file and print sharing traffic using the Server Message Block (SMB) protocol (also known as the Common Internet File System [CIFS] protocol) without the use of Network Basic Input Output System (NetBIOS). Direct hosting for the Microsoft redirector (the Workstation service) and file server (the Server service) is supported over both TCP/IP and Internetwork Packet Exchange (IPX). Although direct hosting might be more efficient, a direct hosting client can connect only to a direct hosting server.

directory service   Both the directory information source and the service that makes the information available and usable. A directory service enables the user to find an object when given any one of its attributes.

Distributed File System (DFS)   A service that allows system administrators to organize distributed network shares into a logical namespace, enabling users to access files without specifying their physical location and providing load sharing across network shares.

DNS client   A client computer that queries DNS servers in an attempt to resolve DNS domain names. DNS clients maintain a temporary cache of resolved DNS domain names.

DNS server   A server that maintains information about a portion of the DNS database and that responds to and resolves DNS queries.

DNS suffix   For DNS, a character string that represents a domain name. The DNS suffix shows where a host is located relative to the DNS root, specifying a host's location in the DNS hierarchy. Usually, the DNS suffix describes the latter portion of a DNS name, following one or more of the first labels of a DNS name.

DNS zone   In a DNS database, a contiguous portion of the DNS tree that is administered as a single, separate entity by a DNS server. The zone contains resource records for all the names within the zone.

domain   In Active Directory, a collection of computer, user, and group objects defined by the administrator. These objects share a common directory database, security policies, and security relationships with other domains.
In DNS, any tree or subtree within the DNS namespace. Although the names for DNS domains often correspond to Active Directory domains, DNS domains should not be confused with Active Directory domains.

domain controller   In an Active Directory forest, a server that contains a writable copy of the Active Directory database, participates in Active Directory replication, and controls access to network resources. Administrators can manage user accounts, network access, shared resources, site topology, and other directory objects from any domain controller in the forest.

domain controller locator (Locator)   An algorithm running in the context of the Netlogon service that enables a client to locate a domain controller. Locator can find domain controllers by using DNS or Network Basic Input Output System (NetBIOS) names. The DNS service (SRV) resource records registered by Locator on behalf of domain controllers are also known as *domain controller locator (Locator)* resource records.

domain functionality   The functional level of an Active Directory domain that has one or more domain controllers running Windows Server 2003. The functional level of a domain can be raised to enable Active Directory features new to Windows Server 2003 that will apply only to that domain. Four domain functional levels exist: Windows 2000 mixed, Windows 2000 native, Windows Server 2003 interim, and Windows Server 2003. The default domain functional level is Windows 2000 mixed. When the domain functional level is raised to Windows 2000 native, Windows Server 2003 interim, or Windows Server 2003, advanced domainwide Active Directory features are available.

domain hierarchy   The parent/child tree structure of domains.

domain local group   A security or distribution group that can contain universal groups, global groups, other domain local groups from its own domain, and accounts from any domain in the forest. Domain local security groups can be granted rights and permissions on resources that reside only in the same domain where the domain local group is located.

domain name   The name given by an administrator to a collection of networked computers that share a common directory. Part of the DNS naming structure, domain names consist of a sequence of name labels separated by periods.

Domain Name System (DNS)   A hierarchical, distributed database that contains mappings of DNS domain names to various types of data, such as IP addresses. DNS enables the location of computers and services by user-friendly names, and it also enables the discovery of other information stored in the database.

domain suffix   For DNS, an optional parent domain name that can be appended to the end of a relative domain name used in a name query or host lookup. The domain suffix can be used to complete an alternate fully qualified DNS domain name to be searched when the first attempt to query a name fails.

domain tree   In DNS, the inverted hierarchical tree structure that is used to index domain names. Domain trees are similar in purpose and concept to the directory trees used by computer filing systems for disk storage. For example, when numerous files are stored on disk, directories can be used to organize the files into logical collections. When a domain tree has one or more branches, each branch can organize domain names used in the namespace into logical collections.

In Active Directory, a hierarchical structure of one or more domains, connected by transitive, bidirectional trusts, that forms a contiguous namespace. Multiple domain trees can belong to the same forest.

Dynamic Host Configuration Protocol (DHCP)   A TCP/IP service protocol that offers dynamic leased configuration of host IP addresses and distributes other configuration parameters to eligible network clients. DHCP provides safe, reliable, and simple TCP/IP network configuration, prevents address conflicts, and helps conserve the use of client IP addresses on the network.

DHCP uses a client/server model where the DHCP server maintains centralized management of IP addresses that are used on the network. DHCP-supporting clients can then request and obtain lease of an IP address from a DHCP server as part of their network boot process.

dynamic update   An update to the DNS standard that permits DNS clients to dynamically register and update their resource records in zones.

Encapsulating Security Payload (ESP)   An Internet Protocol Security (IPSec) protocol that provides confidentiality, in addition to authentication, integrity, and anti-replay. ESP can be used alone, in combination with Authentication Header (AH), or nested with the Layer2 Tunneling Protocol (L2TP). ESP does not normally sign the entire packet unless it is being tunneled. Ordinarily, just the data payload is protected, not the IP header.

encapsulation   The method used to pass data from one protocol over a network within a different protocol. Data from one protocol is wrapped with the header of a different protocol.

Encrypting File System (EFS)   A feature of NTFS that enables users to encrypt files and folders on an NTFS volume disk to keep them safe from access by intruders.

encryption   The process of disguising a message or data in such a way as to hide its substance.

enterprise certificate authority   A certificate authority (CA) that is fully integrated with Active Directory.

entire zone transfer (AXFR)   The standard query type supported by all DNS servers to update and synchronize zone data when the zone has been changed. When a DNS query is made using AXFR as the specified query type, the entire zone is transferred as the response.

event   Any significant occurrence in the system or an application that requires users to be notified or an entry to be added to a log.

Event Log service   A service that records events in the system, security, application, and other logs. Events recorded by the Event Log service can be viewed by using the Event Viewer.

Event Viewer   A component you can use to view and manage event logs, gather information about hardware and software problems, and monitor security events.

exclusion range   A small range of one or more IP addresses within a DHCP scope excluded from the DHCP service. Exclusion ranges ensure that these scope addresses will never be offered to clients by the DHCP server.

Extensible Authentication Protocol (EAP)   An extension to the Point-to-Point Protocol (PPP) that allows for arbitrary authentication mechanisms to be employed for the validation of a PPP connection.

extranet   A limited subset of computers or users on a public network, typically the Internet, that can access an organization's internal network. For example, the computers or users might belong to a partner organization.

fault tolerance   The ability of computer hardware or software to ensure data integrity when hardware failures occur. Fault-tolerant features appear in many server operating systems and include mirrored volumes, RAID-5 volumes, and server clusters.

File Transfer Protocol (FTP)   A member of the TCP/IP suite of protocols used to copy files between two computers on the Internet. Both computers must support their respective FTP roles: one must be an FTP client and the other an FTP server.

firewall   A combination of hardware and software that provides a security system, usually to prevent unauthorized access from outside to an internal network or intranet. A firewall prevents direct communication between network and external computers by routing communication through a proxy server outside the network. The proxy server determines whether it is safe to let a file pass through to the network.

forest   One or more Active Directory domains that share the same class and attribute definitions (schema), site and replication information (configuration), and forest-wide search capabilities (global catalog). Domains in the same forest are linked with two-way, transitive trust relationships.

forest root domain   The first domain created in a new forest. The forestwide administrative groups, Enterprise Admins and Schema Admins, are located in this domain. As a best practice, new domains are created as children of the forest root domain.

forward lookup   A DNS query for a DNS name.

forwarder   A DNS server designated by other internal DNS servers to be used to forward queries for resolving external or offsite DNS domain names.

frame   In synchronous communication, a package of information transmitted as a single unit from one device to another.

frame type   The way in which a network type, such as Ethernet, formats data to be sent over a network. When multiple frame types are allowed for a particular network type, the packets are structured differently and are, therefore, incompatible. All computers on a network must use the same frame type to communicate. Also called *frame format.*

full computer name   A fully qualified domain name (FQDN). The full computer name is a concatenation of the computer name (for example, client1) and the primary DNS suffix of the computer (for example, microsoft.com.). The same computer could be identified by more than one FQDN. However, it has only one full computer name.

fully qualified domain name (FQDN)   A DNS name that has been stated to indicate its absolute location in the domain namespace tree. In contrast to relative names, an FQDN has a trailing period (.) to qualify its position to the root of the namespace (host.example.microsoft.com.).

global account   In an Active Directory network, a normal user account in a user's domain. Most user accounts are global accounts. If multiple domains exist in the network, it is best if each user in the network has only one user account in only one domain, and each user's access to other domains is accomplished through the establishment of domain trust relationships.

global catalog   A directory database that applications and clients can query to locate any object in a forest. The global catalog is hosted on one or more domain controllers in the forest. It contains a partial replica of every domain directory partition in the forest. These partial replicas include replicas of every object in the forest, as follows: the attributes most frequently used in search operations and the attributes required to locate a full replica of the object.

global group   A security or distribution group that can contain users, groups, and computers from its own domain as members. Global security groups can be granted rights and permissions for resources in any domain in the forest.

globally unique identifier (GUID)   A 16-byte value generated from the unique identifier on a device, the current date and time, and a sequence number. A GUID is used to identify a particular device or component.

glue chasing   In DNS, queries to resolve delegation name server (NS) resource records that do not have corresponding glue address (A) resource records in the same zone.

glue record   In DNS, a delegation resource record used for locating the authoritative DNS servers for a delegated zone. These records are used to glue zones together and provide an effective delegation and referral path for other DNS servers to follow when resolving a name.

handshaking   A series of signals acknowledging that communication can take place between computers or other devices. A hardware handshake is an exchange of signals over specific wires (other than the data wires), in which each device indicates its readiness to send or receive data. A software handshake consists of signals transmitted over the same wires used to transfer data, as in modem-to-modem communications over telephone lines.

hash   A fixed-size result that is obtained by applying a one-way mathematical function (sometimes called a *hash algorithm*) to an arbitrary amount of data. If there is a change in the input data, the hash changes. The hash can be used in many operations, including authentication and digital signing. Also called a *message digest*.

hash algorithm   An algorithm that produces a hash value of some piece of data, such as a message or session key. With a good hash algorithm, changes in the input data can change every bit in the resulting hash value; for this reason, hashes are useful in detecting any modification in a data object, such as a message. Furthermore, a good hash algorithm makes it computationally infeasible to construct two independent inputs that have the same hash. Typical hash algorithms include MD2, MD4, MD5, and SHA-1. Also called a *hash function*.

hexadecimal   A base-16 number system represented by the digits 0 through 9 and the uppercase or lowercase letters A (equivalent to decimal 10) through F (equivalent to decimal 15).

host   Any device on a TCP/IP network that has an IP address. Examples of hosts include servers, workstations, network-interface print devices, and routers. Sometimes used to refer to a specific network computer that is running a service used by network or remote clients.
For Network Load Balancing, a cluster consists of multiple hosts connected over a local area network (LAN).

host ID   The portion of the IP address that identifies a computer within a particular network ID.

host name   The DNS name of a device on a network. These names are used to locate computers on the network. To find another computer, its host name must either appear in the Hosts file or be known by a DNS server. For Windows-based computers, the host name and the computer name are generally the same.

Hosts file   A local text file in the same format as the 4.3 Berkeley Software Distribution (BSD) UNIX /etc/hosts file. This file maps host names to IP addresses, and it is stored in the WINDOWS\System32\Drivers\Etc folder.

hub   A common connection point for devices in a network. Typically used to connect segments of a local area network (LAN), a hub contains multiple ports. When data arrives at one port, it is copied to the other ports so that all segments of the LAN can see the data.

IEEE   Institute of Electrical and Electronics Engineers, founded in 1963. IEEE is an organization composed of engineers, scientists, and students, best known for developing standards for the computer and electronics industry.

in-addr.arpa domain   A special top-level DNS domain reserved for reverse mapping of IP addresses to DNS host names.

incremental zone transfer (IXFR)   In DNS, a zone transfer request involving only incremental resource record changes between each version of the zone. An IXFR contrasts with an entire zone transfer (AXFR) request for all resource records.

.inf   The filename extension for files that contain device information, scripts to control hardware operations, or security template information.

International Telecommunication Union-Telecommunication Standardization Sector (ITU-T)   The sector of the International Telecommunication Union (ITU) responsible for telecommunication standards. ITU-T replaces the Comité Consultatif International Télégraphique et Téléphonique (CCITT). Its responsibilities include standardizing modem design and operations, and standardizing protocols for networks and facsimile transmission. ITU is an international organization within which governments and the private sector coordinate global telecom networks and services.

Internet Authentication Service (IAS)   The Microsoft implementation of a Remote Authentication Dial-In User Service (RADIUS) server and proxy, which provides authentication and accounting for network access.

Internet Control Message Protocol (ICMP)   A required maintenance protocol in the TCP/IP suite that reports errors and allows simple connectivity. ICMP is used by the Ping utility to perform TCP/IP troubleshooting.

Internet Engineering Task Force (IETF)   An open community of network designers, operators, vendors, and researchers concerned with the evolution of Internet architecture and the smooth operation of the Internet. Technical work is performed by working groups organized by topic areas (such as routing, transport, and security) and through mailing lists. Internet standards are developed in IETF Requests for Comments (RFCs), which are a series of notes that discuss many aspects of computing and computer communication, focusing on networking protocols, programs, and concepts.

Internet Group Management Protocol (IGMP)   A protocol used by Internet Protocol version 4 (IPv4) hosts to report their multicast group memberships to any immediately neighboring multicast routers.

Internet Information Services (IIS)   Software services that support Web site creation, configuration, and management, along with other Internet functions. Internet Information Services include Network News Transfer Protocol (NNTP), File Transfer Protocol (FTP), and Simple Mail Transfer Protocol (SMTP).

Internet Key Exchange (IKE)   A protocol that establishes the security association and shared keys necessary for two parties to communicate by using Internet Protocol Security (IPSec).

Internet Protocol (IP)   A routable protocol in the TCP/IP protocol suite that is responsible for IP addressing, routing, and the fragmentation and reassembly of IP packets.

Internet Protocol multicasting   The extension of local area network (LAN) multicasting technology to a TCP/IP network. Hosts send and receive multicast datagrams, the destination fields of which specify IP host group addresses rather than individual IP addresses. A host indicates that it is a member of a group by means of the Internet Group Management Protocol (IGMP).

Internet Protocol Security (IPSec)   A set of industry-standard, cryptography-based protection services and protocols. IPSec protects all protocols in the TCP/IP protocol suite and Internet communications by using Layer2 Tunneling Protocol (L2TP).

Internet service provider (ISP)   A company that provides individuals or companies access to the Internet and the World Wide Web. An ISP provides a telephone number, a user name, a password, and other connection information so users can connect their computers to the ISP's computers. An ISP typically charges a monthly or hourly connection fee.

Internetwork Packet Exchange (IPX)   A network protocol native to NetWare that controls addressing and routing of packets within and between local area networks (LANs). IPX does not guarantee that a message will be complete (no lost packets).

Internetwork Packet Exchange/Sequenced Packet Exchange (IPX/SPX) Transport protocols used in Novell NetWare networks, which together correspond to the combination of TCP and IP in the TCP/IP protocol suite. Windows implements IPX through NWLink.

IP address For Internet Protocol version 4 (IPv4), a 32-bit address used to identify a node on an IPv4 internetwork. Each node on the IP internetwork must be assigned a unique IPv4 address, which is made up of the network ID, plus a unique host ID. This address is typically represented with the decimal value of each octet separated by a period (for example, 192.168.7.27). You can configure the IP address statically or dynamically by using DHCP.
For Internet Protocol version 6 (IPv6), an identifier that is assigned at the IPv6 layer to an interface or set of interfaces and that can be used as the source or destination of IPv6 packets.

IPSec policy A configuration policy that defines which traffic Internet Protocol Security (IPSec) examines, how that traffic is secured and encrypted, and how IPSec peers are authenticated.

iterative query A query made to a DNS server for the best answer the server can provide without seeking further help from other DNS servers. Also called a *nonrecursive query.*

Kerberos V5 authentication protocol An authentication mechanism used to verify user or host identity. The Kerberos V5 authentication protocol is the default authentication service. Internet Protocol Security (IPSec) can use the Kerberos protocol for authentication.

key In Registry Editor, a folder that appears in the left pane of the Registry Editor window. A key can contain subkeys and entries. For example, Environment is a key of HKEY_CURRENT_USER.
In IP Security (IPSec), a value used in combination with an algorithm to encrypt or decrypt data. Key settings for IPSec are configurable to provide greater security.

Layer2 Tunneling Protocol (L2TP) An industry-standard Internet tunneling protocol that provides encapsulation for sending Point-to-Point Protocol (PPP) frames across packet-oriented media. For IP networks, L2TP traffic is sent as User Datagram Protocol (UDP) messages. In Microsoft operating systems, L2TP is used in conjunction with Internet Protocol Security (IPSec) as a virtual private network (VPN) technology to provide remote access or router-to-router VPN connections. L2TP is described in Request for Comments (RFC) 2661.

Layer2 Tunneling Protocol/Internet Protocol Security (L2TP/IPSec)   A virtual private network (VPN) connection method that provides session authentication, address encapsulation, and strong encryption of private data between remote access servers and clients. L2TP provides address encapsulation and user authentication, and Internet Protocol Security (IPSec) provides computer authentication and encryption of the L2TP session.

lease   The length of time for which a DHCP client can use a dynamically assigned IP address configuration. Before the lease time expires, the client must either renew or obtain a new lease with DHCP.

Lightweight Directory Access Protocol (LDAP)   The primary access protocol for Active Directory. LDAP is an industry-standard protocol, established by the Internet Engineering Task Force (IETF), that allows users to query and update information in a directory service. Active Directory supports both LDAP version 2 and LDAP version 3.

link state database   A map of an area maintained by Open Shortest Path First (OSPF) routers. It is updated after any change in the network topology. The link state database is used to compute IP routes, which must be computed again after any change in the topology.

Lmhosts file   A local text file that maps Network Basic Input Output System (NetBIOS) names (commonly used for computer names) to IP addresses for hosts that are not located on the local subnet. This file is stored in the WINDOWS\System32\ Drivers\Etc folder.

local area network (LAN)   A communications network connecting a group of computers, printers, and other devices located within a relatively limited area (for example, a building). A LAN enables any connected device to interact with any other on the network.

log file   A file that stores messages generated by an application, service, or operating system. These messages are used to track the operations performed. For example, Web servers maintain log files listing every request made to the server. Log files are usually plaintext (ASCII) files and often have a .log extension.
In Backup, a file that contains a record of the date the tapes were created and the names of files and directories successfully backed up and restored. The Performance Logs And Alerts service also creates log files.

Management and Monitoring Tools   Software components that include utilities for network management and monitoring, along with services that support client dialing and the updating of client phone books. Also included is the Simple Network Management Protocol (SNMP).

MD5   An industry-standard one-way, 128-bit hashing scheme, developed by RSA Data Security, Inc., and used by various Point-to-Point Protocol (PPP) vendors for encrypted authentication. A hashing scheme is a method for transforming data (for example, a password) in such a way that the result is unique and cannot be changed back to its original form. The Challenge Handshake Authentication Protocol (CHAP) uses challenge response with one-way MD5 hashing on the response. In this way, you can prove to the server that you know your password without actually sending the password over the network.

Media Access Control (MAC) address   The address that is used for communication between network adapters on the same subnet. Each network adapter has an associated MAC address.

metric   A number used to indicate the cost of a route in the IP routing table that enables the selection of the best route among possible multiple routes to the same destination.

Microsoft Point-to-Point Encryption (MPPE)   A 128-bit key or 40-bit key encryption algorithm using RSA RC4. MPPE provides for packet confidentiality between the remote access client and the remote access or tunnel server, and it is useful where Internet Protocol Security (IPSec) is not available. MPPE is compatible with Network Address Translation (NAT).

minimum TTL   In DNS, a default Time to Live (TTL) value that is set in seconds and used with all resource records in a zone. This value is set in the start-of-authority (SOA) resource record for each zone. By default, the DNS server includes this value in query responses. It is used to inform recipients how long they can store and use resource records, which are provided in the query answer, before they must expire the stored records' data. When TTL values are set for individual resource records, those values override the minimum TTL.

mixed mode   In a Windows 2000 domain, the default domain mode setting. Mixed mode enables Windows NT–based backup domain controllers to coexist with Windows 2000–based domain controllers. Mixed mode does not support universal groups or the nesting of groups. You can change the domain mode setting to native mode when all Windows NT–based domain controllers are removed from a domain.
In Windows Server 2003 domains, mixed mode is referred to as *Windows 2000 mixed*, and it is one of three domain functional levels available.

multibyte   A character set that can consist of both 1-byte and 2-byte characters. A multibyte-character string can contain a mixture of 1-byte and 2-byte characters. Windows Server 2003 DNS uses the Unicode Transformation Format 8 (UTF-8) encoding scheme described in Request for Comments (RFC) 2044 to interpret and transform multibyte characters into 1-byte characters of 8-bit length.

multicasting The process of sending a message simultaneously to more than one destination on a network.

multihomed computer A computer that has multiple network adapters or that has been configured with multiple IP addresses for a single network adapter.

multimaster replication A replication model in which any domain controller accepts and replicates directory changes. This model differs from single-master replication models, in which one domain controller stores the single modifiable copy of the directory and other domain controllers store backup copies.

name resolution The process of having software translate between names that are easy for users to work with and numerical IP addresses, which are difficult for users but necessary for TCP/IP communications. Name resolution can be provided by software components such as DNS or Windows Internet Name Service (WINS).

name resolution service A service, such as that provided by WINS or DNS, that allows friendly names to be resolved to an address, or other specially defined resource data used to locate network resources of various types and purposes.

name server (NS) resource record A resource record used in a zone to designate the DNS domain names for authoritative DNS servers for the zone.

namespace A naming convention that defines a set of unique names for resources in a network. For DNS, a hierarchical naming structure that identifies each network resource and its place in the hierarchy of the namespace. For WINS, a flat naming structure that identifies each network resource using a single, unique name.

native mode In Windows 2000 domains, the domain mode in which all domain controllers in a domain are running Windows 2000 and a domain administrator has switched the domain operation mode from mixed mode to native mode. Native mode supports universal groups and nesting of groups. In native mode, domain controllers running Windows NT 4 or earlier are not supported.
In Windows Server 2003 domains, native mode is referred to as *Windows 2000 native*, and it is one of three domain functional levels available.

negative caching In DNS, client caching of failed responses to a query. Negative caching improves the response time for successive queries for the same name.

Netlogon service A user-mode service that runs in the Windows security subsystem. The Netlogon service passes the user's credentials through a secure channel to the domain database and returns the domain security identifiers and user rights for the user. In addition, the Netlogon service performs a variety of other functions related to the user logon process, such as periodic password updates for computer accounts and domain controller discovery.

NetBIOS name   A 16-byte name of a process using Network Basic Input Output System (NetBIOS). The NetBIOS name is a name that is recognized by Windows Internet Name Service (WINS), which maps the name to an IP address.

netmask ordering   A method DNS uses to give ordering and preference to IP addresses on the same network when a requesting client queries for a host name that has multiple host address (A) type resource records. This is designed so that the client program will attempt to connect to a host using the closest (and fastest) IP address available.

network access server (NAS)   The device that accepts Point-to-Point Protocol (PPP) connections and places clients on the network that the NAS serves.

network adapter   A device that connects your computer to a network. Sometimes called an *adapter card* or *network interface card*.

Network Address Translation (NAT)   An IP translation process that allows a network with private addresses to access information on the Internet.

network administrator   A person responsible for planning, configuring, and managing the day-to-day operation of the network. Also called a *system administrator*.

Network Basic Input Output System (NetBIOS)   An application programming interface (API) that can be used by programs on a local area network (LAN). NetBIOS provides programs with a uniform set of commands for requesting the lower-level services required to manage names, conduct sessions, and send datagrams between nodes on a network.

network bridge   A device that connects networks by forwarding frames. A network bridge operates at the network interface layer.

Network Connections   A component you can use to gain access to network resources and functionality, whether you are physically at the network location or in a remote location. By using the Network Connections folder you can create, configure, store, and monitor connections. Formerly called *Network And Dial-Up Connections* or *Dial-Up Networking*.

notify list   A list maintained by the primary master for a zone of other DNS servers that should be notified when zone changes occur. The notify list is made up of IP addresses for DNS servers configured as secondary masters for the zone. When the listed servers are notified of a change to the zone, they initiate a zone transfer with another DNS server and update the zone.

Nslookup   A command-line tool used to diagnose DNS infrastructure.

NWLink IPX/SPX/NetBIOS Compatible Transport Protocol (NWLink)   The Microsoft implementation of the Internetwork Packet Exchange/Sequenced Packet Exchange (IPX/SPX) protocol used on NetWare networks. NWLink allows connectivity between Windows-based computers and NetWare networks running IPX/SPX. NWLink also provides Network Basic Input Output System (NetBIOS) functionality and the Routing Information Protocol (RIP).

Open Shortest Path First (OSPF)   A routing protocol used in medium-sized and large networks. This protocol is more complex than Routing Information Protocol (RIP), but it allows better control and is more efficient in propagation of routing information.

Open Systems Interconnection (OSI) reference model   A networking model introduced by the International Organization for Standardization (ISO) to promote multivendor interoperability. OSI is a seven-layered conceptual model consisting of the application, presentation, session, transport, network, datalink, and physical layers.

packet   An Internet layer transmission unit that consists of binary information representing both data and a header containing an identification number, source and destination addresses, and error-control data.

packet filtering   Prevents certain types of network packets from either being sent or received. This strategy can be employed for security reasons (to prevent access from unauthorized users) or to improve performance by preventing unnecessary packets from going over a slow connection.

parent domain   For DNS and Active Directory, domains that are located in the namespace tree directly above other derivative domain names (child domains). For example, microsoft.com would be the parent domain of example.microsoft.com, a child domain.

Password Authentication Protocol (PAP)   A simple plaintext authentication scheme for authenticating Point-to-Point Protocol (PPP) connections. The user name and password are requested by the remote access server and returned by the remote access client in plaintext.

performance counter   In System Monitor, a data item that is associated with a performance object. For each counter selected, System Monitor presents a value corresponding to a particular aspect of the performance that is defined for the performance object.

perimeter network   A network segment that contains resources, such as Web servers and virtual private network (VPN) servers, that are available to Internet users. Also known as *screened subnet* or *demilitarized zone.*

Ping   A utility that verifies connections to one or more remote hosts. The Ping command uses Internet Control Message Protocol (ICMP) echo request and echo reply packets to determine whether a particular IP system on a network is functional. Ping is useful for diagnosing IP network or router failures.

pointer (PTR) resource record   A DNS resource record used in a reverse lookup zone to map an IP address to a DNS name.

Point-to-Point Protocol (PPP)   An industry standard suite of protocols for the use of point-to-point links to transport multiprotocol datagrams. PPP is documented in Request for Comments (RFC) 1661.

Point-to-Point Tunneling Protocol (PPTP)   Networking technology that supports multiprotocol virtual private networks (VPNs), enabling remote users to access corporate networks securely across the Internet or other networks by dialing into an Internet service provider (ISP) or by connecting directly to the Internet. PPTP tunnels, or encapsulates, IP, Internetwork Packet Exchange (IPX), or NetBIOS Extended User Interface (NetBEUI) traffic inside IP packets. This means that users can remotely run applications that depend on particular network protocols.

port   See port ID.

port ID   The method that Transmission Control Protocol (TCP) and User Datagram Protocol (UDP) use to specify which program running on the system is sending or receiving the data. Also known as a port number.

Power Users group   A group whose members can manage accounts, resources, and applications that are installed on a workstation, stand-alone server, or member server. This group does not exist on domain controllers. Administrative tasks that can be performed by members of this group include creating local users and groups; modifying and deleting accounts that they have created; removing users from the Power Users, Users, and Guests groups; installing most applications; and creating and deleting file shares.

preshared key   An Internet Protocol Security (IPSec) technology in which a shared, secret key is used for authentication in IPSec policy.

primary zone   A copy of the zone that is administered locally.

principle of least privilege   The security guideline that a user should have the minimum privileges necessary to perform a specific task. This helps to ensure that, if a user is compromised, the impact is minimized by the limited privileges held by that user. In practice, a user runs within the security context of a normal user. When a task requires additional privileges, the user can use a tool such as Run As to start a specific process with those additional privileges or to log on as a user with the necessary privileges.

Print Server For Macintosh   A service that enables Macintosh clients to send and spool documents to printers attached to a computer running Windows NT Server; Windows 2000 Server; or an operating system in the Windows Server 2003 family, excluding 64-bit editions and Windows Server 2003 Web Edition, and that enables clients to send documents to printers anywhere on an AppleTalk network. Also known as *MacPrint*.

private key   The secret half of a cryptographic key pair that is used with a public key algorithm. Private keys are typically used to decrypt a symmetric session key, digitally sign data, or decrypt data that has been encrypted with the corresponding public key.

process   The virtual address space and the control information necessary for the execution of a program.

process identifier (PID)   A numerical identifier that uniquely distinguishes a process while it runs. Use Task Manager to view PIDs.

protocol   A set of rules and conventions for sending information over a network. These rules govern the content, format, timing, sequencing, and error control of messages exchanged among network devices.

protocol parser   A dynamic-link library (DLL) that enables Network Monitor to identify the protocols used to send a frame onto the network.

proxy server   A firewall component that manages Internet traffic to and from a local area network (LAN) and that can provide other features, such as document caching and access control. A proxy server can improve performance by supplying frequently requested data, such as a popular Web page, and it can filter and discard requests that the owner does not consider appropriate, such as requests for unauthorized access to proprietary files.

public key   The nonsecret half of a cryptographic key pair that is used with a public key algorithm. Public keys are typically used when encrypting a session key, verifying a digital signature, or encrypting data that can only be decrypted with the corresponding private key.

public key encryption   A method of encryption that uses two encryption keys that are mathematically related. One key is called the *private key* and is kept confidential. The other is called the *public key* and is freely given out to all potential correspondents. In a typical scenario, a sender uses the receiver's public key to encrypt a message. Only the receiver has the related private key to decrypt the message. The complexity of the relationship between the public key and the private key means that, provided the keys are long enough, it is computationally infeasible to determine one from the other. Also called *asymmetric encryption*.

public key infrastructure (PKI)   The laws, policies, standards, and software that regulate or manipulate certificates and public and private keys. In practice, it is a system of digital certificates, certificate authorities, and other registration authorities that verify and authenticate the validity of each party involved in an electronic transaction. Standards for PKI are still evolving, even though they are being widely implemented as a necessary element of electronic commerce.

Quality of Service (QoS)   A set of quality assurance standards and mechanisms for data transmission.

realm   A set of security principles, in a non-Windows networked environment, that are subject to Kerberos authentication.

realm name   An identifying prefix or suffix appended to a user name to enable appropriate routing and authentication during a remote logon process.

rebinding state   A state used by DHCP clients to extend and renew their address lease when the current lease is close to expiring. In this state, the client broadcasts to the network to locate any DHCP server that can either renew or replace its currently leased configuration. The rebinding state begins when 87.5 percent of the client's lease time has elapsed.

recursive query   A query made to a DNS server in which the requester asks the server to assume the full workload and responsibility for providing a complete answer to the query. The DNS server then uses separate iterative queries to other DNS servers on behalf of the requester to assist in completing an answer for the recursive query.

recursive resolution   One of the two process types (iterative and recursive) for DNS name resolution. In this process, a resolver (a DNS client) requests that a DNS server provide a complete answer to a query that does not include pointers to other DNS servers. When a client makes a query and requests that the server use recursive resolution to answer, it effectively shifts the workload of resolving the query from the client to the DNS server. If the DNS server supports and uses recursive resolution, it contacts other DNS servers as necessary (using iterative queries on behalf of the client) until it obtains a definitive answer to the query. This type of resolution allows the client resolver to be small and simple.

refresh interval   An interval of time used by secondary masters of a zone to determine how often to check whether their zone data needs to be refreshed. When the refresh interval expires, the secondary master checks with its source for the zone to see whether its zone data is still current or whether it needs to be updated using a zone transfer. This interval is set in the start-of-authority (SOA) resource record for each zone.

remote access   Part of the integrated Routing And Remote Access service that provides remote networking for telecommuters, mobile workers, and system administrators who monitor and manage servers at multiple branch offices. Users can use Network Connections to dial in to remotely access their networks for services such as file and printer sharing, electronic mail, scheduling, and SQL database access.

remote access policy   A set of conditions and connection parameters that define the characteristics of the incoming connection and the set of constraints imposed on it. Remote access policy determines whether a specific connection attempt is authorized to be accepted.

remote access server   A Windows-based computer running the Routing And Remote Access service and configured to provide remote access.

Remote Access Service (RAS)   A Windows NT 4 service that provides remote networking for telecommuters, mobile workers, and system administrators who monitor and manage servers at multiple offices.

Remote Authentication Dial-In User Service (RADIUS)   A security authentication protocol based on a client/server model and widely used by Internet service providers (ISPs). RADIUS is the most popular means of authenticating and authorizing dial-up and tunneled network users today. A RADIUS client is included in the Routing And Remote Access service that ships with the Windows Server 2003 family. A RADIUS server, named Internet Authentication Service (IAS), is included in Windows Server 2003, Standard Edition; Windows Server 2003, Enterprise Edition; and Windows Server 2003, Datacenter Edition.

remote procedure call (RPC)   A message-passing facility that allows a distributed application to call services that are available on various computers on a network. Used during remote administration of computers.

replica   In Active Directory replication, one instance of a logical Active Directory partition that is synchronized by means of replication between domain controllers that hold copies of the same directory partition. *Replica* can also refer to an instance of an object or attribute in a distributed directory.

In the File Replication service (FRS), a computer that has been included in the configuration of a specific replica set.

replication   The process of copying updated data from a data store or file system on a source computer to a matching data store or file system on one or more destination computers to synchronize the data.

In Active Directory, replication synchronizes schema, configuration, application, and domain directory partitions between domain controllers.

In Distributed File System (DFS), replication synchronizes files and folders between DFS roots and root targets.

Request for Comments (RFC)   An official document of the Internet Engineering Task Force (IETF) that specifies the details for protocols included in the TCP/IP family.

reservation   A specific IP address within a scope permanently reserved for leased use to a specific DHCP client. Client reservations are made in the DHCP database using DHCP Manager and based on a unique client device identifier for each reserved entry.

resolver   DNS client programs used to look up DNS name information. Resolvers can be either a small *stub* (a limited set of programming routines that provide basic query functionality) or larger programs that provide additional lookup DNS client functions, such as caching.

resource record (RR)   A standard DNS database structure containing information used to process DNS queries. For example, an address (A) resource record contains an IP address corresponding to a host name. Most of the basic resource record types are defined in RFC 1035, but additional RR types have been defined in other RFCs and approved for use with DNS.

retry interval   The time in seconds after the refresh interval expires, used by secondary masters of a zone to determine how often to try and retry contacting its source for zone data to see whether its replicated zone data needs to be refreshed. This interval is set in the start-of-authority (SOA) resource record for each zone.

reverse lookup   A DNS query for a hostname based on a known IP address.

reversible encryption   A mechanism that stores an encrypted password in such a way that the original password can be unencrypted and retrieved. Some applications require the unencrypted password so that they can perform certain tasks.

Rivest Shamir Adleman (RSA) cryptographic algorithms   A widely used set of public key algorithms that were published by RSA Data Security, Inc. The RSA cryptographic algorithms are supported by the Microsoft Base Cryptographic Service Provider and the Microsoft Enhanced Cryptographic Service Provider.

root certificate authority   The most trusted certificate authority (CA), which is at the top of a certification hierarchy. The root CA has a self-signed certificate. Also called the *root authority*.

root domain   The beginning of the DNS namespace. In Active Directory, the initial domain in an Active Directory tree. Also, the initial domain of a forest.

root hints   DNS data stored on a DNS server that identifies the authoritative DNS servers for the root zone of the DNS namespace. The root hints are stored in the file Cache.dns, located in the WINDOWS\System32\Dns folder.

root servers   DNS servers that are authoritative for the root of the namespace.

round robin   A simple mechanism used by DNS servers to share and distribute loads for network resources. Round robin is used to rotate the order of resource records (RRs) returned in a response to a query when multiple RRs of the same type exist for a queried DNS domain name.

router   Hardware that helps local area networks (LANs) and wide area networks (WANs) achieve interoperability and connectivity and that can link LANs that have different network topologies (such as Ethernet and Token Ring). Routers match packet headers to a LAN segment and choose the best path for the packet, optimizing network performance.

routing   The process of forwarding a packet through an internetwork from a source host to a destination host on different local area networks.

Routing Information Protocol (RIP)   An industry standard, distance vector routing protocol used in small-sized to medium-sized IP and Internetwork Packet Exchange (IPX) internetworks.

routing protocol   Any of several protocols that enable the exchange of routing table information between routers. Typically, medium-sized to large-sized TCP/IP internetworks implement routing protocols to simplify the administration of routing tables.

Run As   A feature that provides users with a secondary logon capability. By using Run As, users can run applications or commands in a different security context without having to log off. Run As prompts the user for different credentials before running the application or command.

scavenging   The process of cleaning and removing extinct or outdated names data from the Windows Internet Name Service (WINS) database.

schema   The set of definitions for the universe of objects that can be stored in a directory. For each object class, the schema defines which attributes an instance of the class must have, which additional attributes it can have, and which other object classes can be its parent object class.

scope   A range of IP addresses that are available to be leased or assigned to DHCP clients by the DHCP service.

secondary zone   A read-only copy of a DNS zone that is transferred from an authoritative DNS server to another DNS server to provide redundancy.

second-level domain   A DNS domain name that is rooted hierarchically at the second tier of the domain namespace, directly beneath the top-level domain names. Top-level domain names include .com and .org. When DNS is used on the Internet, second-level domains are usually names that are registered and delegated to individual organizations and businesses.

secure dynamic update   The process in which a DNS client submits a dynamic update request to a DNS server and the DNS server performs the update only if the client is authenticated.

Secure Hash Algorithm (SHA-1)   An algorithm that generates a 160-bit hash value from an arbitrary amount of input data. SHA-1 is used with the Digital Signature Algorithm (DSA) in the Digital Signature Standard (DSS), among other places.

secure zone   A DNS zone that is stored in Active Directory and to which access control list (ACL) security features are applied.

Security Association (SA)   A combination of identifiers, which together define Internet Protocol Security (IPSec) that protects communication between sender and receiver. An SA is identified by the combination of a Security Parameters Index (SPI), destination IP address, and security protocol (Authentication Header [AH] or Encapsulation Security Payload [ESP]). An SA must be negotiated before secured data can be sent.

security group   A group that can be listed in discretionary access control lists (DACLs) used to define permissions on resources and objects.

security template   A physical file representation of a security configuration that can be applied to a local computer or imported to a Group Policy Object (GPO) in Active Directory. When you import a security template to a GPO, Group Policy processes the template and makes the corresponding changes to the members of that GPO, which can be users or computers.

Server Message Block (SMB)   A file-sharing protocol designed to allow networked computers to transparently access files that reside on remote systems over a variety of networks. The SMB protocol defines a series of commands that pass information between computers. SMB uses four message types: session control, file, printer, and message.

service   A program, routine, or process that performs a specific system function to support other programs, particularly at a low (close to the hardware) level. When services are provided over a network, they can be published in Active Directory, facilitating service-centric administration and use. Some examples of services are the Security Accounts Manager service, File Replication Service, and Routing And Remote Access service.

service resource record (SRV)   A DNS resource record used to identify computers that host specific services, specified in Request for Comments (RFC) 2782. SRV resource records are used to locate domain controllers for Active Directory.

session key   In Internet Protocol Security (IPSec), a value that is used in combination with an algorithm to encrypt or decrypt data that is transferred between computers. A session key is created for every pair of computers to provide enhanced security on computers that have multiple simultaneous active sessions.

Simple Network Management Protocol (SNMP)   A network protocol used to manage TCP/IP networks. In Windows, the SNMP service is used to provide status information about a host on a TCP/IP network.

smart card   A credit card–sized device that is used with an access code to enable certificate-based authentication and single sign-on to the enterprise. Smart cards securely store certificates, public and private keys, passwords, and other types of personal information. A smart card reader attached to the computer reads the smart card.

sniffer   An application or device that can read, monitor, and capture network data exchanges and read network packets. If the packets are not encrypted, a sniffer provides a full view of the data inside the packet.

socket   An identifier for a particular service on a particular node on a network. The socket consists of a node address and a port number, which identifies the service. For example, port 80 on an Internet node indicates a Web server. Two kinds of sockets exist: streams (bidirectional) and datagrams.

stand-alone certificate authority   A certificate authority (CA) that is not integrated with Active Directory.

start-of-authority (SOA) resource record   A record that indicates the starting point or original point of authority for information stored in a zone. The SOA resource record (RR) is the first RR created when adding a new zone. It also contains several parameters used by other computers that use DNS to determine how long they will use information for the zone and how often updates are required.

static routes   Routes in a routing table that are permanent until changed by a network administrator or by an automatically scheduled autostatic update.

strict RFC checking   For DNS, a form of domain name checking that examines characters used in DNS names for compliance with DNS naming requirements and valid character usage as specified in Request for Comments (RFC) 1123. For strict RFC compliance, DNS domain names use name labels made up of only valid uppercase and lowercase letters (A through Z, a through z) number characters (0 through 9), and hyphens, (-), separated by periods.

strong password   A password that provides an effective defense against unauthorized access to a resource. A strong password is at least seven characters long, does not contain all or part of the user's account name, and contains at least three of the four following categories of characters: uppercase characters, lowercase characters, base 10 digits, and symbols found on the keyboard (such as !, @, #).

stub zone   A copy of a zone that contains only the resource records required to identify the authoritative DNS servers for that zone. A DNS server that hosts a parent zone and a stub zone for one of the parent zone's delegated child zones can receive updates from the authoritative DNS servers for the child zone.

subdomain   A DNS domain located directly beneath another domain name (the parent domain) in the namespace tree. For example, example.microsoft.com would be a subdomain of the domain microsoft.com. Also called *child domain*.

subnet   A subdivision of an IP network. Each subnet has its own unique subnetted network ID.

superscope   An administrative grouping feature that supports a DHCP server's ability to use more than one scope for each physical interface and subnet. Superscopes are useful under the following conditions: if more DHCP clients must be added to a network than were originally planned, if an IP network is renumbered, or if two or more DHCP servers are configured to provide scope redundancy and fault-tolerant design DHCP service for a single subnet. Each superscope can contain one or more member scopes (also known as *child scopes*).

switching hub   A central network device (multiport hub) that forwards packets to specific ports rather than, as in conventional hubs, broadcasting every packet to every port. In this way, the connections between ports deliver the full bandwidth available. Also known as a switch or a layer 2 switch.

symmetric encryption   An encryption algorithm that requires the same secret key to be used for both encryption and decryption. Because of its speed, symmetric encryption is typically used when a message sender needs to encrypt large amounts of data. Also called *secret key encryption*.

systemroot   The path and folder name where the Windows system files are located. Typically, this is C:\Windows, although you can designate a different drive or folder when you install Windows. You can use the value %systemroot% to replace the actual location of the folder that contains the Windows system files.

Systems Management Server (SMS)   A Microsoft product that includes inventory collection, software deployment, and diagnostic tools. SMS automates the task of upgrading software, allows remote problem solving, provides asset management information, and monitors software use, computers, and networks.

Task Manager   A tool that provides information about programs and processes running on the computer. Using Task Manager, you can end or run programs, end processes, and display a dynamic overview of your computer's performance.

taskbar   The bar that contains the Start button and appears by default at the bottom of the screen. You can click the taskbar buttons to switch between programs. You can also hide the taskbar, move it to the sides or top of the screen, and customize it in other ways.

Telnet   A protocol that enables an Internet user to log on to and enter commands on a remote computer linked to the Internet, as if the user were using a text-based terminal directly attached to that computer. Telnet is part of the TCP/IP suite of protocols. The term *telnet* also refers to the software (client or server component) that implements this protocol.

ticket   A set of identification data for a security principal, issued by a domain controller for purposes of user authentication. Two forms of tickets in Windows are Ticket Granting Tickets (TGTs) and service tickets.

Ticket Granting Service (TGS)   A Kerberos V5 service provided by the Kerberos V5 Key Distribution Center (KDC) service that issues service tickets that allow users to authenticate to services in a domain.

Ticket Granting Ticket (TGT)   A credential issued to a user by the Kerberos Distribution Center (KDC) when the user logs on. The user must present the TGT to the KDC when requesting session tickets for services. Because a TGT is normally valid for the life of the user's logon session, it is sometimes called a *user ticket*.

Time to Live (TTL)   A numeric value included in packets sent over TCP/IP-based networks that each router decrements before forwarding the packet. If TTL is decremented to zero, the router drops the packet. For DNS, TTL values are used in resource records within a zone to determine how long requesting clients should cache and use this information when it appears in a query response answered by a DNS server for the zone.

time-out error   A condition where a response is not received in the expected time. When this condition occurs, the software assumes that the data has been lost and requests that it be resent.

timestamp   A certification specifying that a particular message existed at a specific time and date. In a digital context, trusted third parties generate a trusted time-stamp for a particular message by having a timestamping service append a time value to a message and then digitally signing the result.

Token Ring   The Institute of Electrical and Electronics Engineers (IEEE) 802.5 standard that uses a token-passing technique for Media Access Control (MAC). Token Ring supports media of both shielded and unshielded twisted-pair wiring for data rates of 4 megabits per second (Mbps) and 16 Mbps.

tombstone   In Active Directory, an object that is removed from the directory but not yet deleted.

top-level domains   Domain names that are rooted hierarchically at the first tier of the domain namespace directly beneath the root (.) of the DNS namespace. On the Internet, top-level domain names such as .com and .org are used to classify and assign second-level domain names (such as microsoft.com) to individual organizations and businesses according to their organizational purpose.

topology   The physical layout of computers, cables, switches, routers, and other components of a network. *Topology* also refers to the underlying network architecture, such as Ethernet or Token Ring.
In Active Directory replication, the set of connections that domain controllers use to replicate information among themselves.

Transmission Control Protocol/Internet Protocol (TCP/IP)   A set of networking protocols widely used on the Internet that provides communications across interconnected networks of computers with diverse hardware architectures and various operating systems. TCP/IP includes standards for how computers communicate and conventions for connecting networks and routing traffic.

trap   In Simple Network Management Protocol (SNMP), a message sent by an agent to a management system indicating that an event has occurred on the host running the agent.

triple DES (3DES)   An implementation of Data Encryption Standard (DES) encryption that employs three iterations of cryptographic operations on each segment of data. Each iteration uses a 56-bit key for encryption, which yields 168-bit encryption for the data. Although 3DES is slower than DES because of the additional cryptographic calculations, its protection is far stronger than DES.

tunnel   A logical connection over which data is encapsulated. Typically, both encapsulation and encryption are performed, and the tunnel is a private, secure link between a remote user or host and a private network.

tunnel server   A server or router that terminates tunnels and forwards traffic to the hosts on the target network.

tunneling protocol   A communication standard used to manage tunnels and encapsulate private data. Data that is tunneled must also be encrypted to be a virtual private network (VPN) connection. Two commonly used tunneling protocols are the Point-to-Point Tunneling Protocol (PPTP) and Layer2 Tunneling Protocol (L2TP).

UCS Transformation Format 8 (UTF-8)   A character set for protocols evolving beyond the use of ASCII. The UTF-8 protocol provides for support of extended ASCII characters and translation of UCS-2, an international 16-bit Unicode character set. UTF-8 enables a far greater range of names than can be achieved using ASCII or extended ASCII encoding for character data.

UNC (Universal Naming Convention) name   The full name of a resource on a network. It conforms to the *servername**sharename* syntax, where *servername* is the name of the server and *sharename* is the name of the shared resource. UNC names of directories or files can also include the directory path under the share name, with the following syntax: *servername**sharename**directory**filename*.

unicast   An address that identifies a specific, globally unique host.

Unicode   A character encoding standard developed by the Unicode Consortium that represents almost all of the written languages of the world. The Unicode character repertoire has multiple representation forms, including UTF-8, UTF-16, and UTF-32. Most Windows interfaces use the UTF-16 form.

Universal Naming Convention (UNC)   A convention for naming files and other resources beginning with two backslashes (\\), indicating that the resource exists on a network computer. UNC names conform to the *servername**sharename* syntax, where *servername* is the server's name, and *sharename* is the name of the shared resource. The UNC name of a directory or file can also include the directory path after the share name, by using the following syntax: *servername**sharename**directory**filename*.

user class   An administrative feature that allows DHCP clients to be grouped logically according to a shared or common need. For example, a user class can be defined and used to allow similar DHCP leased configuration for all client computers in a specific building or site location.

User Datagram Protocol (UDP)   A Transmission Control Protocol (TCP) complement that offers a connectionless datagram service that guarantees neither delivery nor correct sequencing of delivered packets (much like IP).

user principal name (UPN)   A user account name (sometimes referred to as the *user logon name*) and a domain name identifying the domain in which the user account is located. This is the standard usage for logging on to a Windows domain. The format is as follows: someone@example.com (as for an e-mail address).

vendor class   An administrative feature that allows DHCP clients to be identified and leased according to their vendor and hardware configuration type. For example, assigning a vendor class of HP to a printer vendor such as Hewlett-Packard would allow all Hewlett-Packard printers to be managed as a single unit so they could all obtain a similar DHCP leased configuration.

virtual local area network (VLAN)   A logical grouping of hosts on one or more local area networks (LANs) that allows communication to occur between hosts as if they were on the same physical LAN.

virtual private network (VPN)   The extension of a private network that encompasses encapsulated, encrypted, and authenticated links across shared or public networks. VPN connections can provide remote access and routed connections to private networks over the Internet.

voluntary tunnel   A tunnel that is initiated by the client. A voluntary tunnel tunnels Point-to-Point Protocol (PPP) over IP from the client to the tunnel server, and then the data is forwarded to the target host by the tunnel server.

VPN server   A computer that accepts virtual private network (VPN) connections from VPN clients. A VPN server can provide a remote access VPN connection or a router-to-router VPN connection.

weak password   A password that does not provide an effective defense against unauthorized access to a resource. A weak password can be less than seven characters long, contain all or part of a user's account name, or contain less than three of the four following categories of characters: uppercase characters, lowercase characters, base 10 digits, and symbols found on the keyboard (such as !, @, #).

well-known services   Services that are so pervasive in the computer industry that standard bindings are universally recognized. These services often maintain a machine-centric status and are frequently legacy services such as those developed for use in TCP/IP networks, for example, Telnet and File Transfer Protocol (FTP). Well-known services can be published in Active Directory, but because their bindings are widely known, the information is superfluous.

Windows Internet Name Service (WINS)   A software service that dynamically maps IP addresses to computer names (Network Basic Input Output System [NetBIOS] names). This enables users to access resources by name instead of requiring them to use IP addresses that are difficult to recognize and remember.

Windows Support Tools   Tools that administrators, developers, or support personnel can use to diagnose and troubleshoot operating system configuration problems. Although Windows Support Tools are included on the operating system CD, they are not guaranteed or supported by Microsoft, and they must be installed separately from the operating system.

Winsock   Windows Sockets. An application programming interface (API) standard for software that provides a TCP/IP interface under Windows.

workgroup   A simple grouping of computers, intended only to help users find such things as printers and shared folders within that group. Workgroups in Windows do not offer the centralized user accounts and authentication offered by domains.

X.500   A set of standards defining a distributed directory service, developed by the International Standards Organization (ISO).

zone   In a DNS database, a manageable unit of the DNS database that is administered by a DNS server. A zone stores the domain names and data of the domain with a corresponding name, except for domain names stored in delegated subdomains.

zone transfer   The synchronization of authoritative DNS data between DNS servers. A DNS server configured with a secondary zone periodically queries the master DNS servers to synchronize its zone data.

Index

Symbols and Numbers

; (semicolon), 4-33
% Processor Time counter, 12-7
* (wildcard), 15-5
. (trailing dot), 4-13
@ (at symbol), 5-34
3DES (Triple Data Encryption Standard)
  defined, 10-85
  Q & A, 16-10, 16-16
80/20 rule, 7-9 to 7-10

A

A resource records. *see* Host (A) resource records
AAAA (QuadA) records, IPv6, 14-1
ABRs (area border routers), 9-62
access control
  Allow Access setting, 10-25 to 10-26, 10-30,
    10-86
  Control Access Through Remote Access Policy
    setting, 10-25, 10-26
  Deny Access setting, 10-25 to 10-26, 10-30
account policies, 11-6
ACK (acknowledgement) messages, 8-5, 8-11 to
  8-12
Action tab, Performance Logs and Alerts, 12-11 to
  12-12
Activate menu command, scopes, 7-13
Active Directory
  DHCP configuration, 13-15
  DHCP server authorization, 7-5
  installing, 1-28
  Load Zone Data On Startup option, 5-51
  overview of, 1-10
  RADIUS server configuration, 10-77
  SRV resource record verification, 5-14 to 5-18
Active Directory Client Extensions pack, 15-16
Active Directory-integrated zones
  defining, 4-30
  dynamic updates, 5-26 to 5-29
  overview of, 5-22 to 5-23
  replication, 5-23 to 5-24
  Replication Monitor, 6-20 to 6-24
active leases, 7-6
Add Or Remove Programs tool, 1-25, 4-26
Address (A) resource records, Host (A) resource
  records
address conflicts, 8-28
address pools
  defined, 7-9
  static, 10-5 to 10-6
Address Resolution Protocol. *see* ARP (Address
  Resolution Protocol)
addressing, 1-8 to 1-9. *see also* IP addresses
adjacency, OSPF, 9-61
administrators
  DHCP Administrators group, 7-52
  DHCP server installation, 7-4
  Enterprise Admins group, 7-5, 7-52
  network security. *see* security administration
  security alerts, 1-2
  TCP/IP configuration, 2-43
  TCP/IP installation, 2-42
advertisements, 9-35
aging, zones, 5-29 to 5-30
alerts. *see also* Performance Logs and Alerts
  Network Monitor, 12-16 to 12-17
  Performance console, 12-9 to 12-13, 12-18 to
    12-19
algorithms
  IKE security, 11-59
  RSA RC4 (Riveset-Shadmir Adleman), 10-32
  Shortest Path First (SPF) algorithm, 9-61
Alias (CNAME) resource records, 4-34 to 4-35
All Names name-checking method, 5-50 to 5-51
all zone transfer queries. *see* AXFR (all zone
  transfer) queries
Allow Access setting, remote access, 10-25 to
  10-26, 10-30, 10-86

alternate configuration, IP addresses, 2-9, 2-45 to 2-46

Always Use Message Authenticator, Add RADIUS Server dialog box, 10-76

American Registry for Internet Numbers (ARIN), 2-7

Analyze setting, Secedit, 11-10

AND function, Calculator, 2-39, 8-32

APIPA (Automatic Private IP Addressing), 1-17 to 1-20
  address ranges, 13-6
  alternate addresses, 2-45 to 2-46
  defining, 1-32
  DHCP client migration, 7-14
  DHCP leases and, 8-3
  disabling, 1-17 to 1-18
  overview of, 1-17
  remote access through DHCP, 10-5
  troubleshooting, 1-18 to 1-19

APNIC (Asia-Pacific Network Information Center), 2-7

AppleTalk routing, 9-4

application directory partitions, 5-25 to 5-26

application layer, TCP/IP
  Network Monitor and, 3-12
  overview of, 2-5
  Q & A, 2-56

application startup, Computer Management console, 12-34

area border routers (ABRs), 9-62

areas, OSPF, 9-62

Areas setting, Secedit, 11-11

ARIN (American Registry for Internet Numbers), 2-7

arp –a command, 2-3

ARP (Address Resolution Protocol)
  defined, 2-55
  overview of, 2-3
  Q & A, 2-56
  troubleshooting TCP/IP connections, 3-26

arp –d command, 2-3

Asia-Pacific Network Information Center (APNIC), 2-7

at (@), 5-34

attributeSchema, 6-33

audit logging, DHCP, 8-20 to 8-26
  event codes, 8-23
  exam highlights, 8-41 to 8-42
  lesson review, 8-25 to 8-26
  overview of, 8-20 to 8-22
  Q & A, 8-45 to 8-46, 16-9 to 16-10, 16-15
  server logs, 8-22 to 8-25, 13-36

auditing
  IKE, 11-72
  IPSec, 11-73

authentication. see also IAS (Internet Authentication Service)
  authorization vs., 10-8
  defined, 10-7
  demand-dial router-to-router, 9-36
  mutual authentication, 16-33 to 16-35
  network security and, 11-4
  remote access. see remote access, authentication
  RIP, 9-59

Authentication Methods dialog box, 10-17 to 10-19

authentication protocols
  CHAP, 10-10 to 10-13
  choosing, 10-10 to 10-11
  client-side, 10-13 to 10-16
  EAP, 16-9, 16-11, 16-14 to 16-18
  EAP-MD5 CHAP, 10-10 to 10-13
  EAP-TLS, 10-10 to 10-13, 10-16 to 10-17, 10-58, 10-87
  features of, 10-11 to 10-12
  lesson review, 10-22
  MS-CHAP v1, 10-10 to 10-13, 10-15
  MS-CHAP v2, 10-10 to 10-13, 10-15, 16-10 to 16-11, 16-16, 16-33 to 16-34, 16-36, 16-39, 16-42
  operating system support, 10-12 to 10-13
  PAP, 10-11 to 10-15
  practice exercises, 10-20 to 10-22
  Q & A, 10-86

RADIUS, 10-8 to 10-9, 10-28, 10-69 to 10-81, 10-85, 10-87, 16-9, 16-14
   server-side, 10-17 to 10-19
   SPAP, 10-11 to 10-14
Authentication tab, Edit Dial-In Profile dialog box, 10-32
Authentication-Type dialog box, 10-30
authoritative answer, 4-22
authorization
   authentication vs., 10-8
   demand-dial router-to-router, 9-36
   DHCP servers, 7-5
   Kerberos and, 11-45 to 11-46
   network security, 11-4
   troubleshooting DHCP, 13-35
automatic addressing, DHCP servers, 1-20, 7-3
Automatic Private IP Addressing. *see* APIPA (Automatic Private IP Addressing)
Automatic Updates, 15-16
autostatic routes, 9-34, 9-79
Autostatic Update, 16-27, 16-30
Average Disk Queue Length counter, Performance console, 12-7
AXFR (all zone transfer) queries
   DNS performance counters for, 6-25
   overview of, 5-36 to 5-37
   Q & A, 5-81

B

Backup command, DHCP console, 7-31 to 7-32
backups
   DHCP server database, 7-31 to 7-33, 7-37
   disabling NetBIOS, 4-7 to 4-8
BACP (Bandwidth Allocation Control Protocol), 9-11, 9-79
bandwidth, 17-1
BAP (Bandwidth Allocation Protocol)
   defined, 9-11
   port and device properties, 9-32
   remote access policies, 10-31 to 10-32
Basic Firewall
   NAT, 9-46
   Q & A, 16-10, 16-15, 16-45, 16-47

Batch mode, 7-24
binary notation
   converting manually, 2-10 to 2-13
   converting with calculator, 2-13
   defined, 2-9
   exercise converting, 2-18 to 2-19, 2-56 to 2-57
   lesson review, 2-19 to 2-20
   Q & A, 2-58
BIND Secondaries, Advanced tab of DNS server properties, 5-45 to 5-46
Bindings dialog box, 8-32
blocking policies
   creating, 11-51 to 11-56
   troubleshooting rules for, 11-73 to 11-74
BOOTP (Boot Protocol) forwarding
   defined, 9-79
   DHCP Relay Agent, 9-63
Bridge Networks setting, 12-27 to 12-28
bridges
   multiple network bridging, 12-26 to 12-28
   routers compared with, 9-3
broadcasts
   limited broadcast addresses, 9-16
   RRAS name resolution, 9-9 to 9-10
   subnetting and, 2-26
browsing, 4-7 to 4-8

C

cables, crossover, 1-19
Cached Lookups folder, 4-37 to 4-38
Cache.dns file, 5-9
caching
   caching-only servers, 4-31
   DNS client cache, 4-22 to 4-23, 4-54 to 4-55, 14-20 to 14-21, 14-25 to 14-26
   DNS resolver cache, 4-54 to 4-55
   DNS server cache, 4-37 to 4-38, 5-49
   forwarding and, 5-6
   Secure Cache Against Pollution option, 5-49
Caching Memory counter, DNS, 6-26

Calculators
  calculating host IDs per subnet, 2-29
  AND function, 8-32
  notation conversions and, 2-13
  Q & A, 2-56 to 2-59
callbacks
  defined, 9-79
  Q & A, 9-81, 16-10, 16-15, 16-40, 16-42 to 16-43
  remote access permissions and, 10-26
called router, 9-36
Called-Station-ID attribute, 9-32
Caller ID
  Q & A, 16-9, 16-15
  remote access permissions, 10-26
calling router, 9-36
canonical names (CNAME), 4-34 to 4-35
Capture Trigger dialog box, 12-17
Capture window, Network Monitor, 3-7 to 3-8
CAs (certificate authorities), 10-60 to 10-61
case-sensitivity, DNS names, 4-45
certificate authorities (CAs), 10-60 to 10-61
Certificate Services component, 1-27 to 1-28
certificates
  L2TP/IPSec and, 10-60 to 10-61
  overview of, 1-11
  Q & A, 1-33
Cfg setting, Secedit, 11-11
Chaddr (Client Ethernet Address) field
  DHCP ACK, 8-8 to 8-9
  DHCP Discover, 8-7 to 8-8
  DHCP Offer, 8-8
Challenge Handshake Authentication Protocol.
    see CHAP (Challenge Handshake
    Authentication Protocol)
Change Zone Replication Scope dialog box, 5-23
    to 5-26
Change Zone Type dialog box, 5-22 to 5-23
CHAP (Challenge Handshake Authentication
    Protocol)
  defined, 10-10 to 10-11
  features/exam tips, 10-11 to 10-12
  operating system support, 10-12 to 10-13
Ciaddr (Client IP Address) field, 8-11

CIDR (classless interdomain routing)
  applying, 2-32 to 2-33
  defined, 2-55
  Q & A, 13-10, 13-12 to 13-13
CIFS (Common Internet File System)
  defined, 1-32
  functions of, 1-23
  Kerberos and, 11-45
  NetBIOS and, 1-9
Class field, 4-33
classes
  IP address, 2-15 to 2-16
  user, 7-34 to 7-36
classless interdomain routing. see CIDR (classless
    interdomain routing)
classSchema, 6-33
clean install, 15-5
client configuration
  authentication protocols, 10-13 to 10-17
  demand-dial router-to-router, 9-36
  DHCP server, 7-13 to 7-14, 7-18 to 7-19
  network, 1-8, 1-14
  PPTP on VPN, 10-58 to 10-59
  RADIUS, 10-74 to 10-75, 10-77
  RADIUS proxy, 10-73
  remote access, 10-4 to 10-7, 10-42 to 10-43,
    16-38 to 16-43
  troubleshooting DHCP, 8-27 to 8-31
  troubleshooting IP addressing, 13-27
Client Ethernet Address field. see Chaddr (Client
    Ethernet Address) field
Client For Microsoft Networks, 1-14, 3-36
Client IP Address (Ciaddr) field, 8-11
Client Service For Netware
  defined, 1-14
  installing, 1-24 to 1-25
CNAME (Alias) resource records, 4-34 to 4-35
comments, resource records, 4-33
Common Internet File System protocol. see CIFS
    (Common Internet File System)
compaction, 7-33 to 7-34, 8-37
compatws security template, 11-7
Computer Browser service, 4-8

Computer Management console
  application startup and, 12-34
  Services node, 12-31 to 12-32
computer names
  DNS clients, 4-45
  Enable Netmask Ordering option, 5-46 to 5-48
  Enable Round Robin option, 5-48 to 5-49
  overview of, 4-4 to 4-5
computers
  APIPA addresses and, 1-17
  grouping into workgroups or domains, 1-9
  multihomed, 1-21
conditional forwarding, 5-4
conditions, remote access policy, 10-28 to 10-30
confidentiality, network security, 11-4
Configure A DNS Server Wizard, 4-27 to 4-28
Configure Device dialog box
  configuring VPN types, 10-57
  port and device properties, 9-32
Configure Option, DHCP servers, 7-12
Configure setting, Secedit, 11-10
Configure Your Server Wizard, 1-28
conflict detection
  DHCP servers, 7-31
  Q & A, 8-46, 13-30, 13-34
connection endpoint addressing, 9-36
connection request policies, 10-73, 10-87
connection-specific DNS suffixes
  configuring DNS client, 4-46 to 4-48
  overview of, 4-5
connectionless services, UDP, 2-5
connections
  New Connection wizard, 1-13, 10-58 to 10-59
  remote access policies, 10-28
connections, network. see network connections
connectivity. see Internet connectivity
constraints, 10-86
Control Access Through Remote Access Policy
  setting, 10-25, 10-26
Convert utility, 15-9, 15-14
counters. see performance counters
Create IP Security Rule Wizard, 11-59 to 11-60

credentials
  Q & A, 16-33, 16-36
  remote access authentication, 10-8
  Set Credentials command, 9-30
crossover cables, 1-19
cryptography. see encryption; public key cryptography
Custom Templates
  creating, 11-16 to 11-19
  default templates compared with, 11-15

D
data capture, 3-6
Data Encryption Standard (DES)
  defined, 10-85
  remote access and, 10-32
data integrity, 10-57
data stream, 3-6
data types, 6-7
database restore flag, 8-42
databases, DHCP. see DHCP database
Db setting, Secedit, 11-10
DC security template, 11-7
Debug Logging tab, DNS server
  configuring log file, 6-11 to 6-12
  overview of, 5-9 to 5-10
  Q & A, 14-30 to 14-31, 14-33 to 14-34
debugging
  DNS log, 6-3
  DNS log, 6-11 to 6-12, 6-16 to 6-18
  Nslookup, 6-5
decimal notation
  converting manually, 2-10 to 2-13
  converting with calculator, 2-13
  defined, 2-9
  exercise converting, 2-18 to 2-19
  lesson review, 2-19 to 2-20
  Q & A, 2-56 to 2-57
default gateways, 2-18
default routes, 9-15
default update behavior, 4-52
defltdc security template, 11-8

delegation. *see* zone delegation
Demand-Dial Interface Wizard, 9-28 to 9-29
demand-dial interfaces, 9-28 to 9-35
   defined, 9-6
   extranet/router-to-router VPNs, 10-51 to 10-53
   IP routing, 9-34 to 9-35
   NAT, 9-49 to 9-51, 9-81
   network interface properties, 9-30 to 9-32
   overview of, 9-28 to 9-29
   port and device properties, 9-31 to 9-32
   Routing and Remote Access, 9-7
   Set Credentials command, 9-30
   Set IP Demand-Dial Filters command, 9-30
   shortcut menu commands, 9-29 to 9-30
   Unreachability Reason command, 9-30
demand-dial routing, 9-28 to 9-42
   case scenario, 9-74 to 9-76, 9-84 to 9-85
   defined, 9-28
   exam highlights, 9-78 to 9-79
   IIS installation and, 9-39
   interfaces. *see* demand-dial interfaces
   lesson review, 9-43
   practice exercises, 9-38 to 9-42
   Q & A, 9-80 to 9-81, 16-34 to 16-37, 16-45 to
      16-48
   router-to-router, 9-36 to 9-37
   RRAS configuration, 9-39 to 9-41
   testing configuration, 9-42
   troubleshooting, 9-37 to 9-38, 16-44 to 16-46
   troubleshooting lab, 9-76 to 9-77, 9-85
Deny Access setting, 10-25 to 10-26, 10-30
Dependencies tab, Remote Access Connection
   Manager, 12-32 to 12-33
DES (Data Encryption Standard)
   defined, 10-85
   remote access data encryption, 10-32
Designed For Windows XP logo, 15-17 to 15-18
details pane, Frame Viewer window, 3-10, 3-11
device configuration
   port and device properties, 9-32
   VPNs, 10-57
DFS (distributed file system), 4-7

DHCP ACK (Acknowledgement) message
   DHCP leases and, 8-5
   overview of, 8-11 to 8-12
DHCP Administration Tool, 13-39 to 13-40, 13-
   to 13-45
DHCP: Client Identifier fields, 8-7 to 8-9
DHCP console
   creating DHCP scopes, 7-6 to 7-7
   disabling audit logging, 8-21
   migrating DHCP servers, 7-32
   reconciling DHCP databases, 8-35
   server status, 7-22 to 7-23
   verifying server installation, 7-4
DHCP databases
   backups, 7-31 to 7-33
   Q & A, 13-18 to 13-19, 13-24
   reconciling, 8-34 to 8-35
   troubleshooting, 13-35
DHCP Discover message
   defined, 8-42
   DHCP leases and, 8-3
   NACK messages and, 8-13
   overview of, 8-7 to 8-8
DHCP leases
   analyzing DHCP messages, 8-5 to 8-7
   exclusion ranges, 7-8 to 7-9
   initial processes, 8-3 to 8-4
   lesson review, 8-18
   overview of, 7-6 to 7-7, 13-16
   practice exercises, 8-14 to 8-17, 8-44
   Q & A, 8-44 to 8-46, 13-20, 13-25 to 13-26,
      13-28, 13-30 to 13-31, 13-34
   remote access and, 10-5
   renewal, 8-4 to 8-5
   reservations, 7-10
   Shutdown /i command, 8-29
   troubleshooting, 8-29
DHCP management, 7-22 to 7-40, 13-15 to 13-26
   audit logging, 8-20 to 8-26, 8-45 to 8-46
   case scenario, 7-46 to 7-47, 7-54 to 7-55
   command line, 7-24 to 7-25
   connecting clients to remote servers, 7-26
   database backups, 7-31 to 7-33

exam highlights, 7-49 to 7-50
further reading, 13-5
Host (A) resource records and, 4-34
lesson review, 7-39 to 7-40
manual compaction, 7-33 to 7-34
migrating, 7-32 to 7-33
options classes, 7-34 to 7-36
overview of, 13-15 to 13-16
practice exercises, 7-37 to 7-39
Q & A, 7-52 to 7-53, 13-17 to 13-26
servers, 7-22 to 7-24
subnet addresses, 7-30 to 7-31
superscopes, 7-26 to 7-30
tested skills/suggested practices, 13-3
troubleshooting lab, 7-48
DHCP messages
    analyzing, 8-5 to 8-7
    DHCP ACK, 8-11 to 8-12
    DHCP Discover, 8-7 to 8-8
    DHCP NACK, 8-12 to 8-14
    DHCP Offer, 8-8 to 8-9
    DHCP Request, 8-9 to 8-11
    lesson review, 8-18
    practice exercises, 8-14 to 8-17
    Q & A, 8-43 to 8-45
DHCP NACK (Negative Acknowledgement)
    message
    defined, 8-42
    initial lease process and, 8-5
    overview of, 8-12 to 8-13
DHCP Offer messages, 8-3 to 8-4
DHCP Option field, 8-8
DHCP options
    assigning, 7-11 to 7-12
    overview of, 13-15
    troubleshooting, 13-35
    user classes and, 7-34 to 7-36
DHCP Relay Agent
    configuring, 9-65 to 9-66, 13-15 to 13-16
    lesson review, 9-67
    overview of, 9-63 to 9-65
    Q & A, 13-21, 13-28 to 13-29, 13-32, 13-41,
        13-46
    verifying functioning of, 9-66

DHCP Request messages, 8-9 to 8-10, 8-31
DHCP scopes. see scopes
DHCP server logs
    event codes, 8-23
    lesson review, 8-25 to 8-26
    overview of, 8-22 to 8-23
    Q & A, 8-45 to 8-46
    sample excerpts from, 8-24 to 8-25
    server authorization events, 8-23 to 8-24
DHCP Server Properties dialog box, 7-23 to 7-24,
        7-31, 8-20 to 8-21
DHCP Server role, 7-4, 7-16 to 7-18
DHCP servers, 7-3 to 7-21
    audit logs, 13-36
    authorization, 7-5
    automatic addressing, 1-20, 7-3
    case scenario, 7-46 to 7-47, 7-54 to 7-55
    clients and, 7-13 to 7-14
    connectivity problems, 12-24 to 12-26
    DNS updates, 7-41 to 7-47, 7-53 to 7-54, 13-41,
        13-46 to 13-47, 17-41 to 17-43
    dynamic IP addressing, 2-8 to 2-9
    dynamic updates, 5-28
    exam highlights, 7-49 to 7-50
    finding location, address or name of, 8-31
    installing, 7-4
    IP addressing problems, 13-27
    lesson review, 7-20 to 7-21
    Manage Your Server window, 7-4
    options, 7-11 to 7-13
    practice exercises, 7-15 to 7-20
    Q & A, 7-51 to 7-52, 12-45 to 12-46, 13-37 to
        13-47
    Relay Agent configuration, 9-66
    remote access, 10-5
    scopes, 7-6 to 7-11, 7-13
    verifying configuration, 7-14 to 7-15, 8-32 to
        8-34
DHCP traffic, 8-1 to 8-19
    case scenario, 8-38 to 8-39, 8-46 to 8-47
    DHCP ACK, 8-11 to 8-12
    DHCP Discover, 8-7 to 8-8
    DHCP messages, 8-5 to 8-7
    DHCP NACK, 8-12 to 8-14

DHCP traffic, *continued*
    DHCP Offer, 8-8 to 8-9
    DHCP Request, 8-9 to 8-11
    exam highlights, 8-41 to 8-42
    initial lease process, 8-3 to 8-4
    lease renewal process, 8-4 to 8-5
    lesson review, 8-18
    practice exercises, 8-14 to 8-17
    Q & A, 8-43 to 8-45
DHCP, troubleshooting
    audit logging. *see* audit logging, DHCP
    case scenario, 8-38 to 8-39, 8-46 to 8-47
    client configuration, 8-27 to 8-31
    DHCP database, 8-34 to 8-35
    Event Viewer and, 8-35 to 8-37
    exam highlights, 8-41 to 8-42
    further reading, 13-5
    lab, 8-40, 8-48
    lesson review, 1-35 to 1-40, 8-37 to 8-38
    overview of, 13-35 to 13-36
    Q & A, 1-41 to 1-45, 8-43 to 8-46
    server configuration, 8-32 to 8-34
    tested skills/suggested practices, 13-4
    traffic analysis. *see* DHCP traffic
DHCP Discover packets, 9-63
Dhcploc.exe utility, 8-29, 12-26
DHCP Server events, 8-35 to 8-37
dial-back security, 13-28, 13-31
Dial-In Constraints tab, remote access policy,
    10-31
dial-in properties, user accounts
    authorization, 10-34 to 10-39
    practice exercises, 10-43 to 10-47
    Q & A, 10-86
    remote access authorization, 10-34 to 10-39
    remote access permissions, 10-24 to 10-26
Dial-Out Hours, demand-dial interface, 9-30
dial-up networking
    applying, 10-3 to 10-4
    authentication, 10-13 to 10-17
    client-side configuration, 10-13 to 10-17
    practice exercises, 10-19 to 10-22
    Q & A, 16-9 to 16-18, 16-40 to 16-43
    remote access authentication, 10-8
    troubleshooting, 10-39 to 10-40

Diffie-Hellman Group, 11-59
directory partitions, 6-21 to 6-22
Disable Recursion, Advanced tab of DNS server
    properties, 5-44 to 5-45
Disabled option, Services console, 7-24
distributed file system (DFS), 4-7
DNS client cache
    overview of, 4-23
    Q & A, 14-20 to 14-21, 14-25 to 14-26
    viewing/clearing, 4-54 to 4-55
DNS clients, 4-44 to 4-63
    case scenario, 4-60 to 4-61, 4-68
    computer names, 4-45
    connection-specific suffixes, 4-5, 4-46 to 4-48
    default update behavior, 4-52
    DHCP troubleshooting and, 13-35 to 13-36
    dynamic updates, 4-51 to 4-52
    exam highlights, 4-63 to 4-64
    lesson review, 4-59
    name resolution, 4-3 to 4-4
    NetBIOS names, 4-45
    overview of, 4-44 to 4-45
    practice exercises, 4-55 to 4-58
    primary suffixes, 4-45 to 4-46
    Q & A, 4-67 to 4-68
    queries, 4-17 to 4-18
    servers list, 4-48 to 4-50
    suffix searches, 4-50 to 4-51
    TCP/IP settings, 4-53 to 4-54
    troubleshooting lab, 4-61 to 4-62
    viewing/clearing resolver cache, 4-54 to 4-55
DNS console
    defined, 4-26
    forwarding, 12-28
    general properties, 6-9 to 6-10
    resource records, 4-32 to 4-33
    server configuration, 4-27
    zones, 4-28
DNS debug log
    defined, 6-3
    overview of, 6-11 to 6-12
    practice exercise, 6-16 to 6-18
DNS (Domain Name System)
    caching, 4-22 to 4-23
    capturing name resolution traffic, 4-8 to 4-9

case scenario, 4-60 to 4-61, 4-68
components, 4-14 to 4-15
DHCP client configuration, 7-13
DHCP server updates, 7-41 to 7-47
domain names, 4-12 to 4-13
exam highlights, 4-63 to 4-64
lesson review, 4-10, 4-24
namespace, 4-12
NetBIOS and, 4-3 to 4-8
private domain namespace, 4-14
Q & A, 4-65 to 4-66
resolver cache, 4-23, 4-54 to 4-55
roots, 4-13
DNS Events log
accessing, 5-10
defined, 6-3
Q & A, 6-35
troubleshooting, 6-9 to 6-10
DNS Events Properties dialog box, 6-9 to 6-10
DNS management, 14-17 to 14-27
further reading, 14-4
overview of, 14-17
Q & A, 14-18 to 14-27
tested skills/suggested practices, 14-2 to 14-3
DNS monitoring, 6-20 to 6-28
case scenario, 6-28 to 6-30, 6-36 to 6-37
exam highlights, 6-32 to 6-33
further reading, 14-3 to 14-4
lesson review, 6-27 to 6-28
overview of, 14-28
Q & A, 6-36, 14-29 to 14-34
Replication Monitor, 6-20 to 6-24
System Monitor, 6-24 to 6-27
tested skills/suggested practices, 14-3
troubleshooting lab, 6-30 to 6-32, 6-38
DNS queries, 4-16 to 4-22
example, 4-20 to 4-21
local resolver, 4-17 to 4-18
overview of, 4-16
Q & A, 5-79
querying DNS server, 4-18 to 4-19
recursion, 4-19
resolution methods, 4-16

response types, 4-22
root hints, 4-19 to 4-20
DNS Server log, 6-9 to 6-10
DNS server properties, 5-1 to 5-19
case scenario, 5-73 to 5-75, 5-87 to 5-88
Debug Logging, 5-9 to 5-10
Event Logging, 5-10
exam highlights, 5-78
Forwarders, 5-4 to 5-8
general properties, 5-3
Interfaces, 5-4, 5-79 to 5-80
lesson review, 5-18 to 5-19
Monitoring, 5-11, 12-28
practice exercises, 5-12 to 5-18
Q & A, 5-79 to 5-80
Root Hints, 5-8 to 5-9, 5-80
Security, 5-11 to 5-12
DNS server properties, advanced
BIND Secondaries, 5-45 to 5-46
case scenario, 5-73 to 5-75, 5-87 to 5-88
Disable Recursion, 5-44 to 5-45
Enable Automatic Scavenging Of Stale Records,
    5-52
Enable Netmask Ordering, 5-46 to 5-48
Enable Round Robin, 5-48 to 5-49
exam highlights, 5-78
Fail On Load If Bad Zone data, 5-46
lesson review, 5-52 to 5-54
Load Zone Data On Startup, 5-51
Name Checking, 5-49 to 5-51
overview of, 5-43 to 5-44
performing scavenging, 5-30 to 5-31
Q & A, 5-83 to 5-85
recursion and, 5-8
Secure Cache Against Pollution, 5-49
DNS servers, deploying, 4-26 to 4-43, 14-5 to
    14-16
cache, 4-23, 4-37 to 4-38
case scenario, 4-60 to 4-61, 4-68
configuring, 4-27 to 4-29
DNS client, 4-48 to 4-50
exam highlights, 4-63 to 4-64

DNS servers, deploying, *continued*
  further reading, 14-4
  installing, 4-26 to 4-27
  lesson review, 4-42 to 4-43
  overview of, 14-5
  practice exercises, 4-38 to 4-42
  Q & A, 4-66 to 4-67, 12-46, 14-6 to 14-16
  querying, 4-18 to 4-21
  recursion, 4-19, 4-56 to 4-58
  resource records, 4-31 to 4-36
  tested skills/suggested practices, 14-2
  troubleshooting, 4-61 to 4-62, 6-4, 12-23
  types of, 4-29 to 4-31
DNS servers, troubleshooting, 5-9 to 5-10, 6-11 to
  6-12, 14-30 to 14-31, 14-33 to 14-34
DNS Suffix And NetBIOS Computer Name dialog
  box, 4-45 to 4-46
DNS suffixes
  connection-specific, 4-46 to 4-48
  search lists, 4-50 to 4-51
DNS troubleshooting, 6-3 to 6-19
  case scenario, 6-28 to 6-30, 6-36 to 6-37
  DNS Debug log, 6-11 to 6-12
  DNS Events log, 6-9 to 6-10
  DNS infrastructure, 5-76
  exam highlights, 6-32 to 6-33
  Internet connectivity, 12-22 to 12-24
  lab, 4-61 to 4-62, 6-30 to 6-32, 6-38
  lesson review, 6-18 to 6-19
  Nslookup, 6-3 to 6-8
  overview of, 14-28
  practice exercises, 6-12 to 6-18
  Q & A, 6-34 to 6-35, 14-29 to 14-34
DNS updates, 7-41 to 7-47
  default settings, 17-41 to 17-43
  DnsUpdateProxy security group, 7-43 to 7-44
  lesson review, 7-45
  Q & A, 7-53 to 7-54, 13-41, 13-46 to 13-47
DNS zones. *see* zone transfers
Dnscmd utility, 5-48, 6-22
Dns.log file, 6-11 to 6-12, 6-16 to 6-18
DnsUpdateProxy security group, 13-35 to 13-36
  DHCP server and, 7-43 to 7-44
  Q & A, 13-41, 13-46 to 13-47
  secure dynamic updates and, 5-28 to 5-29

Domain Controller Security Policy setting, 12-35
  to 12-36
domain controllers
  adding to Replication Monitor console, 6-21
  DHCP server installation and, 7-5
Domain Name System. *see* DNS (Domain Name
  System)
domain names
  defined, 4-5
  Name Checking option, 5-49 to 5-50
  overview of, 4-12 to 4-13
DomainDnsZones, 5-25, 6-28, 6-36
domains
  Active Directory vs. DNS, 1-10
  geographical, 4-13
  grouping computers into, 1-9
  Internet, 4-13 to 4-14
  logging onto with VPN connection, 10-64 to
    10-65
  organizational, 4-13
  private, 4-14
  reverse, 4-13
  root, 4-66
dotted-decimal notation
  converting, 2-10 to 2-13, 2-19
  defined, 2-9
  lesson review, 2-19 to 2-20, 2-56 to 2-60
  Q & A, 2-57, 2-58 to 2-59, 2-61
drivers, Network Monitor, 3-5 to 3-6
Dynamic Bandwidth Control Using BAP Or
  BACP, RRAS PPP tab, 9-11
dynamic IP internetwork, 9-58
Dynamic mode, Netsh IPSec
  diagnostic commands, 11-33 to 11-34
  displaying IPSec Policy information, 11-32 to
    11-33
  overview of, 11-32
dynamic routes
  answers, 16-30 to 16-32
  questions, 16-26 to 16-29
  static routes compared with, 9-17 to 9-18
dynamic updates
  DNS clients, 4-51 to 4-52
  Kerberos and, 5-28
  None dynamic updates, 5-26 to 5-27

nonsecure dynamic updates, 5-26 to 5-27
performance counters and, 6-26
Q & A, 7-53
zone configuration, 5-26 to 5-29

E

EAP (Extensible Authentication Protocol)
  Protected EAP (PEAP), 16-11, 16-16
  Q & A, 16-9, 16-11, 16-14 to 16-18
EAP-MD5 CHAP (Extensible Authentication Protocol-Message Digest 5 Challenge Handshake Authentication Protocol), 10-10 to 10-13
EAP-RADIUS, 16-7
EAP-TLS (Extensible Authentication Protocol-Transport Level Security)
  defined, 10-10
  encryption, 10-16
  features/exam tips, 10-11 to 10-12
  operating system support, 10-12 to 10-13
  PPTP used with, 10-58
  Q & A, 10-87
  smart card authentication, 10-16 to 10-17
Edit Dial-In Profile dialog box
  remote access policy profiles, 10-30 to 10-33
  server side authentication protocols, 10-18
EKU (enhanced key usage) extensions, 10-60
Enable Automatic Scavenging Of Stale Records, DNS, 5-52
Enable Broadcast Name Resolution, RRAS, 9-9 to 9-10
Enable Fragmentation Checking check box, RRAS, 9-35
Enable IP Router Manager check box, RRAS, 9-35
Enable Netmask Ordering, DNS, 5-46 to 5-48
Enable Round Robin, DNS, 5-48 to 5-49
Enable Router Discovery Advertisements check box, 9-35
encapsulation, 16-35, 16-37
encryption
  3DES, 10-85, 16-10, 16-16
  authentication protocols and, 10-15

Basic Encryption setting, 10-33
DES, 10-32, 10-85
EAP-TLS (Extensible Authentication Protocol-Transport Level Security), 10-16
MPPE, 10-15, 10-32 to 10-33, 10-57 to 10-58, 10-85
MPPE 128-Bit, 10-33, 10-87
MS-CHAP v1, 10-15
MS-CHAP v2, 10-15
No Encryption setting, 10-33
PPP, 10-15 to 10-16
PPTP connections, 10-57 to 10-58
Q & A, 10-87, 16-39, 16-42, 17-13, 17-15
remote access policy profiles, 10-32 to 10-33
VPN, 10-49
Encryption tab, remote access policies, 10-32 to 10-33
endpoint addressing, 9-36
Enforce Logon Restrictions setting, 16-10, 16-15
enhanced key usage (EKU) extensions, 10-60
Enterprise Admins group, DHCP, 7-5, 7-52
event ID codes, DHCP server logs, 8-23 to 8-24
Event Logging tab, DNS server properties, 5-10
event logs
  DNS, 5-10, 6-9 to 6-10
  increasing information logged to, 11-72
  Kerberos at computer boot, 11-42
  Kerberos at user logon, 11-43 to 11-44
  Kerberos in use, 11-74
  Log On tab, 12-34 to 12-35
  security templates, 11-6
  troubleshooting IPSec policies, 11-73
  troubleshooting with, 11-78 to 11-79
Event Viewer
  address conflict warning, 8-28 to 8-29
  DHCP Jet data corruption, 8-37
  DNS event logging, 5-10, 6-9 to 6-10
  troubleshooting DHCP, 8-35 to 8-37
exclusion ranges, DHCP leases, 7-8 to 7-9
Expires After text box, SOA tab, 5-32
Export setting, Secedit, 11-10
Extensible Authentication Protocol. *see* EAP (Extensible Authentication Protocol)

Extensible Authentication Protocol-Message
  Digest 5 Challenge Handshake Authentication
  Protocol (EAP-MD5 CHAP), 10-10 to 10-13
Extensible Authentication Protocol-RADIUS, 16-7
Extensible Authentication Protocol-Transport
  Level Security. *see* EAP-TLS (Extensible
  Authentication Protocol-Transport Level
  Security)
extranets, 16-2

F

Fail On Load If Bad Zone data, DNS, 5-46
failover protection, DHCP, 13-16
fast transfer format, zones, 4-30 to 4-31
fault tolerance, 9-24
File and Printer Sharing For Microsoft Networks,
  1-14
file services, networks, 1-27
file system, security templates, 11-7
filenames, zones, 5-26
filter actions
  blocking, 11-56
  defined, 11-26
  overview of, 11-28
filter lists
  blocking, 11-54 to 11-55
  defined, 11-26
Filter tab, DNS Events Properties dialog box, 6-9
  to 6-10
filters. *see also* packet filters
  IP Filter Wizard, 11-60
  IPSec policies, 11-25 to 11-26
  peer filtering, RIP, 9-59, 16-29, 16-32
  Set IP Demand-Dial Filters command, 9-30
  Task Manager, 12-5
firewalls
  Basic Firewall, 9-46, 16-10, 16-15, 16-45, 16-47
  ICMP, 2-4
  VPNs and, 10-54
Flags tab, Kerbtray, 11-47 to 11-48
ForestDnsZones, 5-25
forwarders, DNS
  conditional, 5-4

delegations taking precedence over, 5-59
disabling recursion, 5-7 to 5-8
overview of, 5-4 to 5-5, 12-28
Q & A, 5-79, 14-31, 14-34
when to use, 5-5 to 5-6
Forwarders tab, DNS server properties, 5-4 to 5-8
FQDNs (fully qualified domain names)
  defined, 4-4, 4-5
  Disable Recursion server option and, 5-44 to
    5-45
  multihomed host, 4-48
  overview of, 4-12 to 4-13
  Q & A, 4-66, 14-6, 14-12, 14-30, 14-33
fragmentation checking, RRAS, 9-35
Frame Viewer window, Network Monitor
  details pane, 3-10, 3-11
  hexadecimal pane, 3-11
  overview of, 3-9
  summary pane, 3-10
frames
  data capture, 3-6
  defined, 3-3
  IPX (NWLink) protocol, 1-25
full computer name, 4-5
fully qualified domain names. *see* FQDNs (fully
  qualified domain names)

G

Gateway column, IP routing tables
  overview of, 9-16 to 9-17
  Q & A, 16-28, 16-31
gateways
  comparing gateway addresses, 9-17
  defaults, 2-18
  IP addresses and, 2-18
  IP routing tables and, 9-16 to 9-17, 16-28, 16-31
Generic Routing Encapsulation (GRE) header,
  10-58
geographical domains, 4-13
Getmac utility, 8-34
Giaddr field, 8-31, 8-42
Globally Unique Identifier (GUID), 3-35
glue chasing, 5-58

glue records, 5-58
Gpedit.msc, 12-36
Gpupdate command-line utility, 15-10, 15-14
Grant Remote Access Permission, 10-86
graphs, System Monitor, 6-24 to 6-25
GRE (Generic Routing Encapsulation) header, 10-58
GUID (Globally Unique Identifier), 3-35

H

Help And Support Center, 3-20, 11-32
hexadecimal pane, Frame Viewer window, 3-11
hisecdc security template, 11-7
hisecws security template, 11-8
hops, routing, 9-15
Host (A) resource records
    default client update behavior, 4-52
    dynamic updates, 4-51 to 4-52, 5-28 to 5-29
    netmask ordering, 5-46 to 5-48
    overview of, 4-33 to 4-34
    round robin, 5-48 to 5-49
    zone delegations, 5-57 to 5-59, 5-60 to 5-61
host IDs
    IP addresses and, 2-14 to 2-15
    per subnet, 2-29
    Q & A, 2-58
    subnetting and, 2-27
host names, 4-4, 14-1
host route, 9-14
hubs, 1-19

I

IANA (Internet Assigned Numbers Authority), 2-7 to 2-8, 13-6
IAS (Internet Authentication Service), 10-69 to 10-84
    console, 10-77
    deploying as RADIUS server, 10-74 to 10-77
    exam highlights, 10-84 to 10-85
    lesson review, 10-81
    overview of, 10-69
    practice exercises, 10-78 to 10-81

Q & A, 10-87
    RADIUS proxy scenarios, 10-72 to 10-74
    RADIUS server scenarios, 10-69 to 10-72
    troubleshooting lab, 10-83
ICANN (Internet Corporation for Assigned Names and Numbers), 4-13 to 4-14
ICMP (Internet Control Message Protocol)
    defined, 2-55
    overview of, 2-4
    Q & A, 2-56
ICS (Internet Connection Sharing)
    dynamic DNS updates, 4-52
    migrating clients for DHCP server, 7-14 to 7-16
    NAT and, 9-46 to 9-47
    private IP addresses and, 2-8
    Q & A, 9-82 to 9-83
ID strings, 7-35
iesacls security template, 11-8
IIS (Internet Information Services), 9-39
IKE negotiation
    overview of, 11-29 to 11-31
    SA (secure channel), 11-29 to 11-31
    statistics, 11-64
    troubleshooting IPSec policies, 11-73
    turning off auditing, 11-72
IKE security algorithms, 11-59
Import setting, Secedit, 11-10
importing security templates, 11-19 to 11-20
incremental (IXFR) queries
    overview of, 5-36 to 5-37
    performance counters, 6-25, 6-27
    Q & A, 5-81
infrastructure. *see also* network infrastructure
    logical infrastructure, 1-6 to 1-11
    physical, 2-25 to 2-26
    physical infrastructure, 1-3 to 1-4
input filters, packet filtering
    basic, 9-70 to 9-71
    creating, 9-69 to 9-70
    defined, 9-68
    RRAS, 9-35

Integrated Services Digital Network. *see* ISDN
    (Integrated Services Digital Network)
    demand-dial links
integrity, network security, 11-4
interactive mode, Nslookup
  data types, 6-7
  exploring options, 6-5 to 6-6
  overview of, 6-4 to 6-5
  practice exercise, 6-13 to 6-16
  querying other name servers, 6-8
Interface column, IP routing tables, 9-17
interfaces, demand-dial, 9-28 to 9-35
  defined, 9-6
  extranet/router-to-router VPNs, 10-51 to 10-53
  IP routing, 9-34 to 9-35
  NAT, 9-49 to 9-51, 9-81
  network interface properties, 9-30 to 9-32
  overview of, 9-28 to 9-29
  port and device properties, 9-31 to 9-32
  Routing and Remote Access, 9-7
  shortcut menu commands, 9-29 to 9-30
interfaces, DNS server, 5-4, 5-79 to 5-80
interfaces, router
  adding in RRAS console, 9-6 to 9-7
  enabling DHCP Relay Agent on, 9-66
  overview of, 16-19
  Q & A, 16-20 to 16-25
  Route command, 9-23
interfaces, RRAS
  adding, 9-6 to 9-7
  configuring, 9-30 to 9-32
  defined, 9-6
  enabling routing protocols, 9-58
  New Interface command, 9-58
  shortcut menus, 9-28
intermittent problems, 12-3
Internet Assigned Numbers Authority (IANA), 2-7
    to 2-8, 13-6
Internet Authentication Service. *see* IAS (Internet
    Authentication Service)
Internet Connection Sharing. *see* ICS (Internet
    Connection Sharing)

Internet connectivity, 12-21 to 12-30, 17-11 to
    17-15
  bridging multiple networks, 12-26 to 12-28
  case scenario, 12-40 to 12-41, 12-47 to 12-48
  exam highlights, 12-42 to 12-43
  further reading, 17-3
  identifying issues, 12-21 to 12-22
  lesson review, 12-28 to 12-29
  name resolution issues, 12-22 to 12-24
  network settings verification, 12-24 to 12-26
  overview of, 17-11
  practice exercise, 12-28
  Q & A, 12-45 to 12-46, 17-12 to 17-15
  tested skills/suggested practices, 17-2
Internet Control Message Protocol (ICMP)
  defined, 2-55
  overview of, 2-4
  Q & A, 2-56
Internet domain namespace, 4-13 to 4-14
Internet Information Services (IIS), 9-39
Internet layer, TCP/IP
  Network Monitor and, 3-12
  overview of, 2-3 to 2-4
  Q & A, 2-56
Internet Protocol (TCP/IP) Properties. *see* TCP/IP
    properties
Internet Service Providers (ISPs), 10-27
Intranets, 4-6
IP addresses, 13-1 to 13-48
  alternate configuration, 2-9
  APIPA and, 1-17 to 1-20, 2-9
  decimal/binary notation, 2-18 to 2-19, 2-56 to
    2-60
  DHCP advantages, 7-3
  DHCP server and, 2-8 to 2-9
  further reading, 13-4
  gateways, 2-18
  lesson review, 2-19 to 2-20
  manual, 2-8
  overview of, 13-6 to 13-7
  private, 2-7 to 2-8, 13-6, 14-1, 16-19 to 16-25
  public, 2-7
  Q & A, 2-56 to 2-60, 13-8 to 13-14

remote access, 9-9, 10-4 to 10-7
resolving to host names, 6-4
scope configuration for, 7-7 to 7-8
structure, 2-9 to 2-16
subnet masks, 2-16 to 2-19, 2-56 to 2-60
tested skills/suggested practices, 13-2
Windows Server 2003 deployment guide, 13-4
   to 13-5
IP addresses, configuring, 2-43 to 2-50
automatically, 2-44 to 2-46
case scenario, 2-51 to 2-53, 2-62
lesson review, 2-50
manually, 2-47
overview of, 2-43 to 2-44
practice exercises, 2-47 to 2-49
Q & A, 2-62
IP addresses, troubleshooting, 13-27 to 13-34
answers, 13-31 to 13-34
further reading, 13-5
lesson review, 13-28 to 13-30
overview of, 13-27
tested skills/suggested practices, 13-3
IP Filter Wizard, 11-60
IP (Internet Protocol)
overview of, 2-3
Q & A, 2-56
RRAS and, 9-9 to 9-10, 10-31
IP Router Manager, 9-35
IP routing
general properties, 9-12 to 9-14
interface, 9-34 to 9-35
management, 16-26 to 16-32
RRAS and, 9-13 to 9-14
tables. see routing tables
Time Before Routes Expire setting, 16-27, 16-30
IP Routing node, RRAS console
applying, 9-7
defined, 9-6
general properties, 9-12 to 9-14
packet filters, 9-69 to 9-70
IP Security Monitor (Ipsecmon)
IPSec connections and, 11-65 to 11-66
monitoring IPSec with, 11-34 to 11-37

Network Monitor and, 15-29
overview of, 15-20
practice exercises, 11-74 to 11-77, 11-91 to
   11-92
Q & A, 11-93, 15-21 to 15-28, 15-31 to 15-32,
   15-34
statistics, 11-35 to 11-37
troubleshooting IPSec policies, 11-72
Ipconfig, 3-19, 13-27
Ipconfig/ all
APIPA troubleshooting, 1-17 to 1-19
ARP and, 3-26
case scenario, 1-30
DHCP server configuration, 7-14 to 7-15, 7-19
   to 7-20
DHCP troubleshooting, 8-27, 8-30
overview of, 3-19 to 3-20
Q & A, 3-37
Ipconfig/ displaydns, 4-54
Ipconfig/ flushdns
flushing DNS client cache, 4-54 to 4-55
Q & A, 12-46, 14-11, 14-16
Ipconfig/ registerdns
default client update behavior, 4-52
Host (A) resource records and, 4-34
Q & A, 4-65, 14-11, 14-16
Ipconfig/ release, 7-31
Ipconfig/ renew
APIPA client migration, 7-14
APIPA troubleshooting, 1-18 to 1-19
DHCP addresses, 8-30
DHCP leases, 8-4 to 8-5, 8-16 to 8-17
Q & A, 8-44
subnet address changes, 7-31
Ipconfig/ setclassid, 7-34 to 7-36
IPSec (Internet Protocol Security), 11-24 to 11-39,
   15-29 to 15-34. see also L2TP/IPSec (Layer2
   Tunneling Protocol/IP Security)
encryption settings, 10-32 to 10-33
exam highlights, 11-24 to 11-70, 11-87 to 11-88
features for 2003, 11-26 to 11-27
IP Security Monitor, 11-34 to 11-37
Kerberos and. see Kerberos

IPSec (Internet Protocol Security), *continued*
  negotiation configuration, 11-27 to 11-28
  negotiation process, 11-28 to 11-31
  Netdiag, 11-34
  Netsh, 11-31 to 11-34
  overview of, 11-24 to 11-26
  practice exercises, 11-51 to 11-67, 11-90
  Q & A, 11-90 to 11-91
  security paradigms, 11-4
  troubleshooting lab, 11-82 to 11-86, 11-94 to
    11-97
IPSec policies
  blocking policy, 11-53 to 11-56
  creating, 11-31 to 11-34
  defined, 11-25
  management snap-in, 11-51 to 11-56
  negotiation policy, 11-56 to 11-61
  overview of, 11-31
  Q & A, 11-93 to 11-94, 15-21 to 15-24, 15-26 to
    15-27, 15-30, 15-33
  troubleshooting, 11-72 to 11-74
Ipsecmon. *see* IP Security Monitor (Ipsecmon)
IPX (NWLink) protocol
  automatic installation, 1-24
  defined, 1-32
  frame types, 1-25
  Windows support, 9-4
ISDN (Integrated Services Digital Network)
  demand-dial links
  overview of, 10-4
  Q & A, 9-81, 16-29, 16-32, 16-45, 16-47
ISPs (Internet Service Providers), 10-27
iteration (iterative queries), 4-19, 5-78
IXFR (incremental) queries
  overview of, 5-36 to 5-37
  performance counters, 6-25, 6-27
  Q & A, 5-81

J

Jetpack utility
  defined, 7-50
  manually compacting DHCP servers, 7-33 to
    7-34

  overview of, 13-16
  Q & A, 13-38 to 13-39, 13-43 to 13-44
  troubleshooting, 8-37

K

KDC (Kerberos Distribution Center), 11-41 to
    11-42
Kerberos, 11-39 to 11-50
  authorization and, 11-45 to 11-46
  boot up and, 11-40 to 11-43
  dynamic updates and, 5-28
  exam highlights, 11-87 to 11-88
  Kerbtray, 11-46 to 11-48
  Klist, 11-49 to 11-50
  monitoring network security, 15-20
  Netdiag and, 11-50
  overview of, 11-39
  practice exercises, 11-68 to 11-69, 11-90
  Q & A, 11-90 to 11-91, 15-21, 15-26, 16-10,
    16-15 to 16-16
  security paradigms, 11-4
  tracking logon, 11-39 to 11-40
  troubleshooting, 11-74
  user logon and, 11-43 to 11-45
Kerbtray.exe
  Kerberos at user logon, 11-44
  Kerberos authentication role, 11-45
  overview of, 11-46 to 11-49
  practice exercise, 11-68, 11-90
  Q & A, 11-94
  tracking logon, 11-40
key exchange
  security methods, 11-58
  settings, 11-57 to 11-58
keys
  master key, 11-29
  preshared keys, 10-61, 10-87
Klist.exe
  Kerberos' role in authentication, 11-46
  overview of, 11-49 to 11-50
  practice exercise, 11-68 to 11-69, 11-90
  tracking logon, 11-40

L

L2TP/IPSec (Layer2 Tunneling Protocol/IP
    Security)
  applying, 10-59 to 10-60
  computer certificates, 10-60 to 10-61
  disabling connections, 10-61
  lesson review, 9-73 to 9-74
  packet filtering, 9-73
  preshared keys and, 10-61
  Q & A, 9-83, 10-87
  testing configuration, 10-66 to 10-67
  VPN connections, 10-65 to 10-66
LAN routing
  case scenario, 9-74 to 9-76, 9-84 to 9-85
  exam highlights, 9-78 to 9-79
  lesson review, 9-26 to 9-27
  practice exercise, 9-25 to 9-26
  Q & A, 9-80
  routing tables, 9-14 to 9-18
  RRAS. *see* Routing and Remote Access
  scenarios, 9-18 to 9-19
  static routes, 9-20 to 9-25
  understanding, 9-3 to 9-4
"layer 2" devices, 9-3
"layer 3" devices, 9-3
Layer2 Tunneling Protocol/IP Security. *see*
    L2TP/IPSec (Layer2 Tunneling Protocol/IP
    Security)
layers, TCP/IP, 1-7, 2-3 to 2-6
LCP (Link Control Protocol) Extensions
  defined, 9-11
  enabling, 10-26
LDAP (Lightweight Directory Access Protocol)
  Kerberos at computer boot and, 11-40 to 11-41
  SRV resource records and, 4-36
leases. *see* DHCP leases
least privilege principle, 11-13 to 11-14, 15-6
legacy programs, running, 15-16
Lightweight Directory Access Protocol (LDAP)
  Kerberos at computer boot and, 11-40 to 11-41
  SRV resource records and, 4-36
limited broadcast addresses, 9-16

Link Control Protocol (LCP) Extensions
  defined, 9-11
  enabling, 10-26
link state database, 9-61
loading, DNS zones
  Fail On Load If Bad Zone data, 5-46
  Load Zone Data On Startup, 5-51
Local Area Connection Status dialog box, 8-34
local policies, security templates, 11-6
Local Security Policy, 15-5
Local System account, 12-33
LocalNetPriority setting, 5-48
locked-down packet filtering, 9-71 to 9-72
logging
  auditing. *see* audit logging, DHCP
  DNS servers, 5-9 to 5-10, 6-11 to 6-12, 6-35,
      14-30 to 14-31, 14-33 to 14-34
  event logs, 12-35 to 12-36
  RRAS (Routing and Remote Access), 9-12 to
      9-13
  Secedit, 11-11
logical infrastructure, 1-6 to 1-11
logon
  as service, 12-46 to 12-47
  restrictions, 16-10, 16-15
  rights, 12-35 to 12-36, 12-46 to 12-47
  tracking with Kerberos, 11-39 to 11-40
  troubleshooting with Network Monitor, 11-77 to
      11-78
  user authentication and, 11-43 to 11-45
  VPN connections and, 10-64 to 10-65
  to Windows, 10-8
loopback addresses, 9-16
Ls command, Nslookup, 6-8
Lserver command, Nslookup, 6-8

M

MAC (Media Access Control) addresses
  overview of, 13-15
  verifying for reservations, 8-34
Macintosh, 1-35
mail exchanger (MX) resource records, 4-35

Main Mode node, IPSec
  defined, 11-88, 15-20
  negotiation configuration, 11-28 to 11-31
  practice exercises, 11-64 to 11-66
  Q & A, 15-24, 15-27
  viewing IP statistics, 11-35 to 11-36
management
  DHCP. *see* DHCP management
  DNS. *see* DNS management
  IP Router Manager, 9-35
  IP routing, 16-26 to 16-32
  IP security policies, 11-51 to 11-56
  Netsh and, 10-77, 11-31 to 11-34
  remote access, 16-19 to 16-25
  remote access clients, 10-42 to 10-43
  Task Manager, 12-3 to 12-6, 12-9, 12-14 to
    12-15, 12-17
Management And Monitoring Tools component,
  1-26
master key, calculating, 11-29
masters, defined, 4-30
Maximum Ports setting, 10-57
Media Access Control (MAC) addresses
  overview of, 13-15
  verifying for reservations, 8-34
Mergedpolicy setting, Secedit, 11-11
Metric column, IP routing tables, 9-17
metrics, 16-28, 16-31
Microsoft
  Calculator. *see* Calculator
  Point-to-Point encryption. *see* MPPE (Microsoft
    Point-to-Point Encryption)
  SMS (Systems Management Server), 12-16
  Terminal Services, 1-15 to 1-16
  Web site information. *see* Web site information,
    Microsoft
  Windows Explorer, 4-7
*Microsoft Encyclopedia of Networking, Second
  Edition*
  IP addressing, 13-4 to 13-5
  name resolution, 14-3 to 14-4
Microsoft Network Monitor online help, 17-3
Microsoft Windows
  networking components, 1-25 to 1-28
  networks, 1-15 to 1-16

Microsoft Windows 2000
  DHCP leases, 8-3
  DNS and, 4-6
  replication, 5-25
  zone transfers, 5-35
Microsoft Windows Components Wizard
  DHCP server installation, 7-4
  DNS server installation, 4-26
  overview of, 1-25
Microsoft Windows NT 4 domains, 15-9, 15-13
Microsoft Windows Server 2003
  Help and Support Center, 11-32
  Resource Kit, 17-3
  security white paper, 11-7
  Web Edition, 1-3
Microsoft Windows Server 2003, deployment
  guide
  IP addressing, 13-4 to 13-5
  name resolution, 14-4
  network infrastructure, 17-3
  network security, 15-4
  Routing and Remote Access, 16-5 to 16-6
Microsoft Windows Server 2003, online help
  network infrastructure, 17-3
  network security, 15-4
  Routing and Remote Access, 16-5 to 16-6
Microsoft Windows Update
  accessing Catalog, 15-16
  overview of, 15-16
  Q & A, 15-17 to 15-18
Microsoft Windows XP, 15-17 to 15-18
modems, 9-32 to 9-33
monitoring, DNS server properties, 5-11, 12-28
monitoring, network traffic, 12-3 to 12-21, 17-4 to
  17-10
  case scenario, 12-40 to 12-41, 12-47 to 12-48
  DNS. *see* DNS monitoring
  exam highlights, 12-42 to 12-43
  further reading, 17-3
  lesson review, 12-19 to 12-20
  Netstat, 12-13 to 12-15
  Network Monitor. *see* Network Monitor
  Networking tab of Task Manager, 12-3 to 12-6
  overview of, 17-4 to 17-5
  Performance Console, 12-6 to 12-13

practice exercises, 12-17 to 12-19
Q & A, 17-6 to 17-10
tested skills/suggested practices, 17-2
MPPE (Microsoft Point-to-Point Encryption)
 defined, 10-85
 encryption settings, 10-32 to 10-33
 PPP connections, 10-15
 PPTP connections, 10-57 to 10-58
MS-CHAP v1 authentication protocol
 defined, 10-10
 encryption, 10-15
 features/exam tips, 10-11 to 10-12
 operating system support, 10-12 to 10-13
MS-CHAP v2 authentication protocol
 defined, 10-10
 encryption, 10-15
 features/exam tips, 10-11 to 10-12
 operating system support, 10-12 to 10-13
 Q & A, 16-10 to 16-11, 16-16, 16-33, 16-34,
  16-36, 16-39, 16-42
Msconfig.exe (System Configuration utility),
 17-18, 17-20
multihomed computers, 1-21
Multibyte (UTF-8), 5-49 to 5-51
Multilink connections
 overview of, 9-11
 Q & A, 9-80
 remote access policies, 10-31 to 10-32
multinets
 defined, 7-50
 overview of, 7-26
 superscope supporting, 7-27 to 7-28
multipath IP internetwork, 9-58
mutual authentication, 16-33 to 16-35
MX (mail exchanger) resource records, 4-35
My Network Places, 4-7

N

NACK (negative acknowledgement) messages
 DHCP leases, 8-5
 overview of, 8-12 to 8-14
 superscopes, 7-29
Name Checking, DNS server properties, 5-49 to
 5-51

name resolution. *see also* DNS (Domain Name
 System)
 computer names and, 4-4 to 4-5
 DNS vs. NetBIOS, 4-3 to 4-8
 further reading, 14-3 to 14-4
 lesson review, 4-10
 Microsoft Windows Server 2003, deployment
  guide, 14-4
 name suffixes and, 4-4 to 4-5
 overview of, 1-9, 14-1 to 14-2
 practice exercises, 4-8 to 4-9
 Q & A, 1-33, 1-35, 4-65
 tested skills/suggested practices, 14-2 to 14-3
 traffic, capturing with Nbstat, 4-9
 troubleshooting Internet connectivity, 12-22 to
  12-24
 troubleshooting lab, 4-61 to 4-62
name resolution, NetBIOS
 defined, 1-9
 disabling, 4-7 to 4-8
 DNS clients, 4-45
 DNS servers, 5-12 to 5-14
 DNS vs. NetBIOS, 4-3 to 4-8
 Q & A, 4-65
Name Server resource records. *see* NS (Name
 Server) resource records
name suffixes, 4-4 to 4-5
names, computer
 DNS clients, 4-45
 netmask ordering and, 5-46 to 5-48
 overview of, 4-4 to 4-5
 round robin and, 5-48 to 5-49
Names tab, Kerbtray, 11-46
namespace
 DNS, 4-12
 Internet domains, 4-13 to 4-14
 private domains, 4-14
NAT (Network Address Translation), 9-45 to 9-56
 advantages, 13-6
 case scenario, 9-74 to 9-76, 9-84 to 9-85
 exam highlights, 9-78 to 9-79
 ICS compared with, 9-46 to 9-47
 incoming calls and, 9-47
 lesson review, 9-54 to 9-55

NAT (Network Address Translation), *continued*
  overview of, 1-11
  Q & A, 9-81 to 9-82
  RRAS and, 9-69
  troubleshooting, 9-44 to 9-46
  troubleshooting lab, 9-76 to 9-77, 9-85
  understanding, 9-45 to 9-47
NAT (Network Address Translation), practice
    exercises, 9-48 to 9-54
  configuring through demand-dial interface,
    9-49 to 9-51, 9-81
  viewing/configuring NAT features, 9-51 to 9-54,
    9-81 to 9-82
Nbstat command-line utility
  capturing name resolution traffic, 4-9
  Q & A, 4-65, 13-40, 13-45
NBT Connection performance object, 12-8
negative acknowledgement messages. *see* NACK
    (negative acknowledgement) messages
negotiation, IPSec
  configuring, 11-27 to 11-28
  IKE negotiation, 11-29 to 11-31, 11-72, 11-73
  policies, 11-56 to 11-61
  process, 11-28 to 11-31
Neighbors tab, RIP Properties dialog box, 9-61
NetBIOS
  defined, 1-9
  disabling, 4-7 to 4-8
  DNS clients, 4-45
  DNS name resolution compared with, 4-3 to 4-7
  DNS servers, 5-12 to 5-14
  Q & A, 4-65
NetBT (NetBIOS over TCP/IP), 1-23, 1-32
Netcap.exe
  overview of, 11-38 to 11-39
  practice exercise, 11-67, 11-90
Netdiag utility
  defined, 3-35
  displaying IPSec information, 11-34
  overview of, 3-22 to 3-23
  practice exercise, 3-28 to 3-30
  Q & A, 13-39 to 13-40, 13-44 to 13-45, 17-18,
    17-20

reloading SRV records, 4-36
  troubleshooting TCP/IP addressing, 13-27
  verifying Kerberos with, 11-50
Netlogon.dns, 4-36
Netmask column, IP routing tables, 9-16
netmask ordering, DNS, 5-46 to 5-48
Netsh utility
  defined, 11-88
  dynamic mode, 11-32
  managing IPSec, 11-31 to 11-34
  managing RADIUS servers, 10-77
  overview of, 7-24 to 7-25
  practice exercises, 11-61 to 11-65
  Q & A, 11-90 to 11-91, 13-40, 13-45, 17-18,
    17-20
  Show command, 11-33
  Show Mmsas All command, 11-64
  Show Qmsas All command, 11-64
  static mode, 11-32 to 11-33, 11-91
  troubleshooting IPSec, 11-73
Netstat utility
  lesson review, 12-20
  monitoring network traffic, 12-13 to 12-15
  Q & A, 12-44
NetWare Network, 1-15, 1-35
Network Address Translation. *see* NAT (Network
    Address Translation)
network bridging, 12-26 to 12-28
network clients
  defined, 1-8
  overview of, 1-14
Network Connection Details dialog box, 8-34
network connections
  adding components to, 1-23 to 1-25
  advanced settings, 1-14 to 1-16
  APIPA, 1-17 to 1-20
  automatically configured, 1-23
  configuring, 1-13
  overview of, 1-6 to 1-7, 1-13 to 1-14
  provider order, 1-15 to 1-16
  TCP/IP installation, 2-42
  TCP/IP settings, 1-16
  viewing, 1-13

Network Connections menu, 1-13 to 1-15, 1-23 to
     1-24, 2-42
network counters
     Performance console, 12-8 to 12-9
     Task Manager, 12-5 to 12-6
Network Destination column, IP routing tables
     comparing gateway address with, 9-17
     overview of, 9-16
Network Diagnostics
     defined, 3-35
     overview of, 3-20 to 3-23
     practice exercise, 3-26
network IDs
     CIDR and, 2-34
     IP addresses and, 2-14 to 2-15
     Q & A, 2-58
     subnet masks and, 2-16 to 2-17
network infrastructure, 1-3 to 1-12
     Active Directory, 1-10
     addressing, 1-8 to 1-9
     case scenario, 1-30 to 1-31, 1-36
     certificates, 1-11
     defining, 1-3 to 1-5
     exam highlights, 1-31 to 1-32
     lesson review, 1-11 to 1-12
     Microsoft Windows Server 2003 and, 17-3
     name resolution, 1-9
     Network Address Translation, 1-11
     network clients, 1-8
     network computer groups, 1-9
     network connections, 1-6 to 1-7
     network protocols, 1-7 to 1-8
     network services, 1-8
     Q & A, 1-33
     remote access, 1-11
network infrastructure, extending, 1-23 to 1-36
     adding Active Directory, 1-28
     adding components to connections, 1-23 to
          1-25
     case scenario, 1-30 to 1-31, 1-36
     exam highlights, 1-31 to 1-32
     installing components, 1-25 to 1-28
     lesson review, 1-28 to 1-29
     Q & A, 1-35

network infrastructure, maintaining, 12-46 to
          12-47, 17-1 to 17-20
     case scenario, 12-40 to 12-41, 12-47 to 12-48
     exam highlights, 12-42 to 12-43
     further reading, 17-3
     monitoring network traffic, 12-3 to 12-21, 17-4
          to 17-10
     overview of, 17-1
     Q & A, 12-44 to 12-48
     tested skills/suggested practices, 17-1 to 17-2
     troubleshooting Internet connectivity, 12-21 to
          12-30, 17-11 to 17-15
     troubleshooting server services, 12-31 to 12-40,
          17-15 to 17-20
network interface layer, TCP/IP
     bridges, 9-3
     Network Monitor and, 3-12
     overview of, 2-5 to 2-6
     Q & A, 2-56
Network Interface performance object, 12-8, 17-1
network interfaces, RRAS
     adding, 9-6 to 9-7
     configuring, 9-30 to 9-32
     defined, 9-6
     enabling routing protocols, 9-58
     options, 9-31
     shortcut menus, 9-28
Network Monitor, 3-3 to 3-18
     analyzing captured data, 3-9 to 3-11
     analyzing DHCP messages, 8-5 to 8-7
     case scenario, 3-31 to 3-33, 3-38 to 3-39
     data capture, 3-8
     defined, 3-35
     DHCP Discover, 8-7 to 8-8
     driver installation, 3-5 to 3-6
     exam highlights, 3-34
     frames, 3-3, 3-11 to 3-12
     installing, 3-4 to 3-5
     interface, 3-6 to 3-8
     lesson review, 3-16 to 3-17, 12-19
     "lite" and "full", 12-16 to 12-17
     Netcap and, 11-67
     online help, 17-3
     parsers, adding to, 3-12 to 3-13

Network Monitor, *continued*
   practice exercises, 3-13 to 3-16
   Q & A, 3-36 to 3-37, 12-44, 16-20, 16-24, 17-6 to
      17-7, 17-9
   Select A Network window, 3-6 to 3-7
   troubleshooting IPSec policies, 11-73
   troubleshooting logon, 11-77 to 11-78
   troubleshooting network protocol security,
      15-29 to 15-34
   versions of, 3-3 to 3-4
network performance. *see* monitoring, network
   traffic
network prefix subnet masks
   converting between dotted-decimal and, 2-19
   overview of, 2-17
   Q & A, 2-57
network protocols
   IPSec. *see* IPSec (Internet Protocol Security)
   Kerberos. *see* Kerberos
   lesson review, 1-11 to 1-12
   monitoring with Network Monitor, 3-11
   overview of, 1-7 to 1-9
   Q & A, 1-33
   security, 11-3 to 11-4
   traffic capture, 11-38 to 11-39
   viewing connection components, 1-14
network protocols, troubleshooting, 11-71 to
      11-86, 15-29 to 15-34
   exam highlights, 11-71 to 11-86
   lab, 11-94 to 11-97
   practice exercises, 11-91 to 11-92
   Q & A, 11-93 to 11-94
   troubleshooting lab, 11-82 to 11-86, 11-94 to
      11-97
network providers
   Provider Order tab, 1-15 to 1-16
   Q & A, 1-33 to 1-34
network route, 9-14
network security. *see* security
network services, 1-8, 1-14
   Other Network File and Print Services
      component, 1-27

Network Shell utility (Netsh.exe). *see* Netsh utility
Network Solution, 4-14
networking components
   case scenario, 1-30, 1-36
   connections, 1-13 to 1-20
   exam highlights, 1-31 to 1-32
   lesson review, 1-21 to 1-22, 1-33 to 1-34
   Q & A, 1-33 to 1-34
   routing, 1-20 to 1-21
   workgroups, 1-20
Networking Services component, 1-26 to 1-27
New Technology Local Area Network Manager
      (NTLM)
   Kerberos and, 11-74
   protocol, 16-10, 16-16
   security paradigms, 11-4
no-refresh intervals, 5-30
Nodebug option, Nslookup, 6-5
Nominet, 4-14
Non RFC name-checking method, 5-50 to 5-51
None dynamic updates, 5-26 to 5-27
noninteractive mode, Nslookup, 6-3 to 6-4, 6-12
      to 6-13
nonrepudiation, 11-4
nonsecure dynamic updates, 5-26 to 5-27
nonsecurity templates, 11-13 to 11-14
notation
   binary. *see* binary notation
   decimal. *see* decimal notation
   dotted-decimal. *see* dotted-decimal notation
notification settings, zone transfers
   overview of, 5-35 to 5-37
   performance counters, 6-25, 6-27
   practice exercise, 5-39 to 5-40
NS (Name Server) resource records
   configuring, 5-33 to 5-34
   new zones containing, 4-31
   zone delegations and, 5-57 to 5-59
   zone properties and, 5-33 to 5-34
Nslookup utility, 6-3 to 6-8
   data types, 6-7
   defined, 6-3
   interactive mode, 6-4 to 6-5

noninteractive mode, 6-3 to 6-4
options, 6-5 to 6-6
overview of, 6-3
practice exercises, 6-12 to 6-16, 6-34
Q & A, 6-35, 12-46, 14-28, 14-32 to 14-33
querying other name server, 6-8
Set All command, 6-5 to 6-6
Set Querytype (set q) command, 6-7
Set Type command, 6-7
troubleshooting Internet connectivity, 12-23
viewing zone data, 6-8
NTLM (New Technology Local Area Network
    Manager)
    Kerberos and, 11-74
    protocol, 16-10, 16-16
    security paradigms, 11-4
NWLink protocol. *see* IPX (NWLink) protocol

O

online help
    network infrastructure, 17-3
    Network Monitor, 17-3
    network security, 15-4
    Routing and Remote Access, 16-5 to 16-6
Open Shortest Path First. *see* OSPF (Open
    Shortest Path First) routers
options classes, 7-34 to 7-36
organizational domains, 4-13
OSI model, 3-11 to 3-12
OSPF (Open Shortest Path First) routers
    lesson review, 9-67
    overview of, 9-61 to 9-62
    Q & A, 9-83, 16-26 to 16-29, 16-30 to 16-32
    RIP and, 9-62 to 9-63
    routing table configuration, 16-1
output filters, packet filtering
    basic, 9-70 to 9-71
    creating, 9-69 to 9-70
    defined, 9-68
    RRAS, 9-35
Overwrite setting, Secedit, 11-11
Owner field, resource records, 4-33

P

packet filters, 9-68 to 9-74
    advanced, 9-72 to 9-73
    basic, 9-70 to 9-71
    case scenario, 9-74 to 9-76, 9-84 to 9-85
    creating, 9-69 to 9-70
    defined, 9-68
    exam highlights, 9-78 to 9-79
    IP Routing properties, 9-35
    IPSec policies, 11-25
    lesson review, 9-73 to 9-74
    locked-down, 9-71 to 9-72
    mixed VPNs with firewall and, 10-54
    overview of, 9-68 to 9-69
    Q & A, 9-83 to 9-84, 16-18, 16-20 to 16-25,
        16-29, 16-32, 16-46 to 16-47
    review of, 16-19
Pages/Sec counter, Performance console, 12-7
PAP (Password Authentication Protocol)
    defined, 10-11
    features/exam tips, 10-11 to 10-12
    operating systems supported, 10-12 to 10-13
    security and, 10-14 to 10-15
parsers
    adding to Network Monitor, 3-12 to 3-13
    defined, 3-35
partitions, Active Directory-integrated zones, 6-21
    to 6-22
Password Authentication Protocol. *see* PAP
    (Password Authentication Protocol)
PathPing utility
    defined, 3-35
    overview of, 3-23 to 3-25
    Q & A, 13-29, 13-33
    troubleshooting Internet connectivity, 12-22
    troubleshooting TCP/IP addressing, 13-27,
        13-33
Pause button, zone status, 5-22
PEAP (Protected EAP), 16-11, 16-16
peer filtering, RIP
    overview of, 9-59
    Q & A, 16-29, 16-32
perfmon.exe command, 12-7

Performance console, 12-6 to 12-13. *see also*
    monitoring, network traffic
    alerts, 12-9 to 12-13, 12-18 to 12-19
    general properties, 12-10 to 12-11
    lesson review, 12-19
    NBT Connection object, 12-8
    network counters, 6-26, 12-8
    Network Interface object, 12-8, 17-1
    Pages/Sec counter, 12-7
    Q & A, 12-44
    RAS Port performance object, 12-8 to 12-9
    starting, 12-7
    System Monitor in, 6-25
    Task Manager and, 12-7, 12-9
performance counters
    % Processor Time, 12-7
    Average Disk Queue Length, 12-7
    AXFR (all zone transfer) queries, 6-25
    IXFR (incremental) queries, 6-25, 6-27
    Total Query Received, 6-26
    Total Response Sent, 6-26
Performance Logs and Alerts
    actions, 12-11 to 12-13
    alerts, 12-9 to 12-10
    general properties, 12-10 to 12-11
    lesson review, 12-19
    Q & A, 12-44, 14-28, 14-32, 17-7, 17-10
    schedules, 12-13
peripheral routers, 9-25
permissions
    DHCP server authorization, 7-5
    least privilege principle, 11-13 to 11-14, 15-6
    remote access, 10-25 to 10-26, 10-30
persistent connections
    NAT configuration, 9-46
    Q & A, 16-34 to 16-36
physical infrastructure, 1-3 to 1-4
physical topology, 2-25 to 2-26
PIDs (Process Identifiers), 12-14 to 12-15
Ping utility
    overview of, 3-23 to 3-25
    Q & A, 12-45, 13-29, 13-33, 16-11, 16-14 to
    16-18

troubleshooting Internet connectivity, 12-21 to
    12-22
troubleshooting TCP/IP addressing, 13-27,
    13-33
PKI (Public Key Infrastructure), 1-35
Point-to-Point Protocol (PPP). *see also* MPPE
    (Microsoft Point-to-Point Encryption)
    dial-up networking and, 10-4
    encryption, 10-15 to 10-16
    PPP tab, RRAS, 9-10 to 9-12
Point-to-Point Tunneling Protocol. *see* PPTP
    (Point-to-Point Tunneling Protocol)
Pointer (PTR) resource records
    configuring Dynamic DNS updates, 4-51 to 4-52
    default client update behavior, 4-52
    overview of, 4-35
policies. *see also* IPSec policies; remote access
    policies
    account policies, 11-6
    authorization scenarios, 10-34 to 10-39
    blocking policies, 11-51 to 11-56, 11-73 to 11-74
    connection request policies, 10-73, 10-87
    local policies, 11-6
    profiles, 10-30 to 10-33
ports
    configuring PPTP on VPN server, 10-58
    configuring VPN, 10-56 to 10-57
    demand-dial, 9-32 to 9-33
    L2TP/IPSec connections and, 10-61
    Maximum Ports setting, 10-57
    packet filtering, 9-71 to 9-73
    Port Status dialog box, 9-33
    RADIUS servers, 10-76
    RAS Port performance object, 12-8 to 12-9
    TCP, 2-4 to 2-5
    UDP, 2-4 to 2-5, 2-56
positive answer, 4-22
Power Users group, 15-16, 15-17 to 15-19
PPP (Point-to-Point Protocol). *see also* MPPE
    (Microsoft Point-to-Point Encryption)
    dial-up networking and, 10-4
    encryption, 10-15 to 10-16
    PPP tab, RRAS, 9-10 to 9-12

PPTP (Point-to-Point Tunneling Protocol)
  overview of, 10-57 to 10-58
  packet filtering and, 9-72 to 9-73
  PPTP-type VPN connections, 10-62 to 10-64
  Q & A, 9-84, 16-39, 16-42
  VPN clients, 10-58 to 10-59
  VPN servers, 10-58
  when to choose, 10-59
predefined security templates, 15-5
preferences, IP Routing, 9-13 to 9-14
preshared keys, 10-61, 10-87
primary DNS suffix
  configuring, 4-55 to 4-56
  DNS clients, 4-45 to 4-46
  domain names, 4-13
  overview of, 4-5
  Q & A, 4-68
primary domain name, 4-5
primary servers
  notification, 5-36 to 5-37
  overview of, 4-29 to 4-30
  Primary Server text box, SOA tab, 5-31
  Q & A, 5-83 to 5-84
  zone transfer initiation, 5-36 to 5-37
primary zones
  defined, 4-29
  reconfiguring zones as, 5-22
  standard, 4-30
  zone transfers and, 5-34 to 5-35
principle of least privilege, 11-13 to 11-14, 15-6
print services, networks, 1-27
printer sharing, 1-14
private domain namespace, 4-14
private IP addresses
  configuring TCP/IP addressing, 13-6
  local names resolved to, 14-1
  overview of, 2-7 to 2-8, 16-19
  Q & A, 16-20 to 16-25
private networks
  ICS. see ICS (Internet Connection Sharing)
  NAT. see NAT (Network Address Translation)
  overview of, 16-33
  Q & A, 16-33 to 16-37

Process Identifiers (PIDs), 12-14 to 12-15
Processes tab, Task Manager, 12-14 to 12-15
profiles, remote access policies, 10-30 to 10-33
properties
  demand-dial, 9-29
  devices, 9-32 to 9-33
  DHCP Relay Agent, 9-66
  IP addresses. see IP addresses, configuring
  IP routing, 9-12 to 9-14
  network interfaces, 9-30 to 9-32
  ports, 9-32 to 9-33
  user account dial-in, 10-24 to 10-26
  zone. see zone properties
properties, DNS server, 5-3 to 5-12
  advanced, 5-8
  debug logging, 5-9 to 5-10
  event logging, 5-10
  forwarders, 5-4 to 5-8
  interfaces, 5-4
  monitoring, 5-11
  root hints, 5-8 to 5-9
  security, 5-11 to 5-12
Protected EAP (PEAP), 16-11, 16-16
protocols
  authentication. see authentication protocols
  network. see network protocols
  routing. see routing protocols
provider order, network connections, 1-15 to 1-16
PSTN (Public Switched Telephone Network),
    10-4
PTR resource records. see Pointer (PTR) resource
    records
public IP addresses, 2-7
public key cryptography
  certificates and, 1-11
  lesson review, 1-12
  Q & A, 1-33
Public Key Infrastructure (PKI), 1-35
Public Switched Telephone Network (PSTN),
    10-4

Q

QuadA (AAAA) IPv6 records, 14-1
Quick Mode, IPSec
    defined, 11-88
    negotiation, 11-28 to 11-31, 11-64 to 11-66
    overview of, 15-20
    troubleshooting IPSec policies, 11-73
    viewing IP statistics, 11-36 to 11-37
Quiet setting, Secedit, 11-11

R

RADIUS (Remote Authentication Dial-In User
        Service)
    adding, 10-75 to 10-77
    clients, 10-74 to 10-75
    defined, 10-85
    practice exercises, 10-78 to 10-81
    proxies, 10-72 to 10-74
    Q & A, 10-87, 16-9, 16-14
    remote access authentication, 10-8 to 10-9
    remote access policies, 10-28
    scenarios, 10-69 to 10-72
    Send RADIUS Accounting On and Accounting
        Off Messages, 10-77
    server groups, 10-73
    servers, 10-76, 10-77
RAS Port performance object, 12-8 to 12-9
RAS (remote access servers)
    access beyond, 10-40 to 10-42
    authentication. see remote access,
        authentication
    configuring Windows Server 2003 as, 16-1
    RAS Total performance object, 12-9
RBK setting, Secedit, 11-11
RDATA field, 4-33
rebinding state, DHCP lease renewal, 8-5
Reconcile All Scopes dialog box, 8-35
Reconcile dialog box, 8-35
recovery options, 12-33 to 12-37, 12-38 to 12-39
recursion
    configuring DNS server, 4-56 to 4-58
    disabling, 5-7 to 5-8, 5-44 to 5-45
        overview of, 4-19
        Q & A, 4-66 to 4-67, 14-21 to 14-22, 14-26 to
            14-27
    redirection, 14-22, 14-27
    referral answer, 4-22
    referrals, 5-45
    refresh intervals
        modifying, 5-30
        no-refresh, 5-30
        Refresh Interval box, SOA tab, 5-32
    registered IP addresses, 14-1
    Registry
        APIPA and, 1-17 to 1-18
        Q & A, 11-89
        security templates, 11-7, 11-9
    Relay Agent. see DHCP Relay Agent
    remote access, authentication, 10-7 to 10-19
        case scenario, 10-82 to 10-83, 10-88
        client-side protocols, 10-13 to 10-17
        exam highlights, 10-84 to 10-85
        lesson review, 10-22, 16-7 to 16-8
        overview of, 10-7 to 10-8
        practice exercises, 10-19 to 10-22
        protocols, 10-10 to 10-13
        Q & A, 10-86, 16-9 to 16-14
        server-side protocols, 10-17 to 10-19
        through RADIUS, 10-8 to 10-9
    remote access, authorization, 10-24 to 10-48
        access beyond remote access server, 10-40 to
            10-42
        Allow Access setting, 10-25 to 10-26, 10-30,
            10-86
        case scenario, 10-82 to 10-83, 10-88
        exam highlights, 10-84 to 10-85
        lesson review, 10-47 to 10-48
        managing clients, 10-42 to 10-43
        practice exercises, 10-43 to 10-47
        Q & A, 10-86
        remote access policies, 10-27 to 10-33
        scenarios, 10-34 to 10-39
        troubleshooting, 10-39 to 10-40
        user dial-in properties, 10-24 to 10-27

remote access, configuring
  dial-up networking, 10-3 to 10-4
  IP address assignments, 10-4 to 10-5
  private networks, 16-33 to 16-37
  remote client addressing, 10-4 to 10-7
  troubleshooting client access to, 16-38 to 16-48
  troubleshooting RRAS routing, 16-44 to 16-48
Remote Access Connection Manager, 12-32 to
  12-33
remote access policies
  authorization scenarios, 10-34 to 10-39
  client management, 10-43
  conditions, 10-28 to 10-30
  configuring, 16-1
  creating, 10-44 to 10-47
  defined at server, 10-34
  extranet/router-to-router VPNs, 10-52 to 10-53
  overview of, 10-27 to 10-28
  permissions, 10-25
  PPTP configuration on VPN server, 10-58
  profiles, 10-30 to 10-39
  Q & A, 10-87, 16-10 to 16-18
  Remote Access Policies node, RRAS, 10-18
  removing, 10-28
  Select Attribute dialog box, 10-29 to 10-30
  VPNs, 10-51, 10-61 to 10-62
remote access servers (RAS)
  access beyond, 10-40 to 10-42
  authentication. see remote access,
    authentication
  configuring Windows Server 2003 as, 16-1
  RAS Total performance object, 12-9
Remote Authentication Dial-In User Service. see
    RADIUS (Remote Authentication Dial-In User
    Service)
renewal process, DHCP leases, 8-4 to 8-5, 8-29
Repair button, 8-30
Repair feature, DHCP servers, 12-24 to 12-26
replication
  directory partitions and, 5-25 to 5-26
  overview of, 5-23 to 5-26
  Q & A, 6-36
Replication Monitor (replmon.exe)

AD-integrated zones, 6-20 to 6-24
  lesson review, 6-36
  Q & A, 6-36, 14-31, 14-34
Request for Comments. see RFCs (Request for
    Comments)
Request Security, IPSec, 11-28
Require Security, IPSec, 11-28
Réseaux IP Européens (RIPE NCC), 2-7
reservations, DHCP
  creating, 7-10 to 7-11
  New Reservation dialog box, 7-10 to 7-11
  options for, 7-12 to 7-13
  overview of, 13-15
  Q & A, 13-30, 13-33 to 13-34
  verifying, 8-33 to 8-34
resolver, 4-66, 14-1
Resource Kit, Microsoft Windows Server 2003,
    17-3
resource records, 4-31 to 4-36
  adding to zones, 4-31 to 4-32
  dynamic zone updates in, 5-26 to 5-29
  formats, 4-32 to 4-33
  host (A), 4-33 to 4-34, 4-51 to 4-52, 5-28 to 5-29,
    5-46 to 5-49, 5-57 to 5-61
  mail exchanger (MX), 4-35
  name server (NS), 4-31, 5-33 to 5-34, 5-57 to
    5-59
  netmask ordering, enabling, 5-46 to 5-48
  Owner field, 4-33
  pointer (PTR), 4-35, 4-51 to 4-52
  Q & A, 4-67, 5-86, 7-53, 14-6, 14-12, 14-18 to
    14-20, 14-23 to 14-25
  scavenging stale, 5-30 to 5-31, 5-52
  service location (SRV), 4-36, 5-14 to 5-18
  start-of-authority (SOA), 4-31, 5-31 to 5-33
  TTLs for, 5-32
restricted groups, security templates, 11-6
Resultant Set of Policy (RSoP), 11-73
retry intervals, SOA, 5-32
reverse domains, 4-13
reverse lookups
  Nslookup, 6-4
  Q & A, 6-35, 14-31, 14-34

RFCs (Request for Comments)
  DNS names (RFC 1123), 4-45
  IPSec, 11-25
  Kerberos, 11-39
  Non RFC name-checking method, 5-50 to 5-51
  router compliance (RFC 1542), 7-26, 9-64
RIP (Routing Information Protocol), 9-56 to 9-69
  advantages/disadvantages, 9-58
  authentication, 9-59
  configuring neighbors, 9-61
  configuring routing tables, 16-1
  deploying over VPNs, 10-53 to 10-54
  environment, 9-58
  lesson review, 9-67
  metric for, 9-17
  OSPF vs., 9-62 to 9-63
  peer filtering, 9-59
  Q & A, 9-80, 9-83, 16-26 to 16-31
  route filtering in, 9-60
  security and, 9-58 to 9-59
  static routing and, 9-25
RIPE NCC (Réseaux IP Européens), 2-7
Riveset-Shadmir Adleman (RSA RC4), 10-32
rogue servers
  defined, 7-5, 7-50
  troubleshooting Internet connectivity, 12-26
rollback settings, Secedit, 11-10
root domains, 4-66
root hints
  DNS server properties, 5-8 to 5-9, 5-80
  overview of, 4-19
  Q & A, 14-31, 14-34
rootsec security template, 11-8
round robin, DNS, 5-48 to 5-49, 5-83 to 5-84
Route command, 9-23, 9-80
route filtering, RIP, 9-60
router discovery, 9-35, 9-79
router-to-router VPNs
  overview of, 10-51 to 10-53
  troubleshooting, 10-55 to 10-56
routers
  called router, 9-36
  calling router, 9-36

default gateways, 2-18
  overview of, 16-19
  peripheral routers, 9-25
  Q & A, 16-20 to 16-25
  solicitations, 9-35
routing
  demand-dial. *see* demand-dial routing
  LAN. *see* LAN routing
  loops, 9-25
  NAT. *see* NAT (Network Address Translation)
  network infrastructure and, 1-20 to 1-21
  overview of, 9-3 to 9-4
  packet filters. *see* packet filters
  preferences, 16-26 to 16-32
  protocols. *see* protocols, routing
  remote access, 16-19 to 16-25
  remote DHCP servers and, 7-26
  TCP/IP, 16-26 to 16-32
  troubleshooting RRAS, 16-44 to 16-48
Routing and Remote Access. *see* RRAS (Routing
    and Remote Access)
Routing Information Protocol. *see* RIP (Routing
    Information Protocol)
routing protocols, 9-57 to 9-67
  adding and configuring, 9-57 to 9-58
  case scenario, 9-74 to 9-76, 9-84 to 9-85
  defined, 9-57
  deploying over VPNs, 10-53 to 10-54
  DHCP Relay Agent, 9-63 to 9-66
  exam highlights, 9-78 to 9-79
  lesson review, 9-67
  multiple-routers and, 9-19
  New Routing Protocol command, 9-57
  New Routing Protocol dialog box, 9-65
  OSPF overview, 9-61 to 9-62
  overview of, 16-19
  Q & A, 9-83, 16-20 to 16-32
  RIP, 9-58 to 9-61
routing tables
  configuring, 16-1
  dynamic routing, 9-17 to 9-18
  Q & A, 16-26 to 16-32
  reading, 9-15 to 9-17

routes, 9-14 to 9-15
static routing, 9-17 to 9-18
understanding, 9-3
viewing, 9-15
RRAS (Routing and Remote Access)
authentication. *see* remote access,
    authentication
authorization. *see* remote access, authorization
broadcast name resolution, 9-9 to 9-10
clients vs. routers, 9-35
configuring. *see* remote access, configuring
defined, 9-3
demand-dial interfaces, 9-28 to 9-35
demand-dial routing and, 9-39 to 9-42
disabled state, 1-20
enabling, 9-5
further reading, 16-4 to 16-6
IAS deployment. *see* IAS (Internet
    Authentication Service)
IP addresses, 9-9, 10-4 to 10-5
IP (Internet Protocol) and, 9-9 to 9-10, 10-31
IP Routing, 9-13 to 9-14
IP routing properties, 9-12 to 9-14
lesson review, 16-1 to 16-2
logging, 9-12
managing, 16-19 to 16-25
Microsoft Windows Server 2003, 16-5 to 16-6
overview of, 9-4 to 9-5
PPP and, 9-10 to 9-12
practice exercise, 9-25 to 9-26
private networks and, 16-33 to 16-37
properties, 9-7 to 9-12
routing tables, 9-14 to 9-18
Static Address Pool option, 9-9
static routing, 9-22
TCP/IP routing, 16-26 to 16-32
tested skills/suggested practices, 16-2 to 16-4
troubleshooting, 16-38 to 16-48
VPNs. *see* VPNs (virtual private networks)
RRAS (Routing and Remote Access), console
adding network interfaces, 9-6 to 9-7
configuring access beyond remote access
    server, 10-40 to 10-41
demand-dial properties, 9-29
DHCP Relay Agents, 9-65 to 9-66
IP Routing interface properties, 9-35
IP Routing node, 9-69 to 9-70
Network Interfaces node, 9-30
overview of, 9-5 to 9-8
packet filters, 9-69 to 9-70
Q & A, 1-34
RADIUS authentication, 10-9
RADIUS clients, 10-74 to 10-75
RADIUS servers, 10-75 to 10-77
remote access clients, 10-42 to 10-43
remote access policies, 10-27 to 10-28
routing protocols, 9-57 to 9-58
routing protocols over VPNs, 10-53 to 10-54
server side authentication, 10-17 to 10-19
RSA RC4 (Riveset-Shadmir Adleman), 10-32
RSoP (Resultant Set of Policy), 11-73
rules
defined, 11-26
IPSec policies, 11-73 to 11-74
Run As shortcut menu, 1-2
Runas command, 1-2

S

SA (secure channel), IKE, 11-29 to 11-31
Safe Mode With Command Prompt, 17-18, 17-20
SAM (Security Accounts Manager), 10-8
Save To File feature, Network Diagnostics, 3-22
scavenging
defined, 5-29 to 5-30
performing, 5-30 to 5-31
stale records, 5-52
Sc.exe (Service Controller utility), 17-18, 17-20
schedules, Performance Logs and Alerts, 12-13
schema, 6-33
scopes, 7-6 to 7-11
80/20 rule, 7-9 to 7-10
activating, 7-13
deactivating, 7-13
DHCP options, 7-12
scopes, *continued*

exam highlights, 7-49 to 7-50
exclusion ranges, 7-8 to 7-9
IP address range, 7-7 to 7-8
lesson review, 7-20 to 7-21
New Scope Wizard, 7-6 to 7-7, 7-38, 7-52, 13-15
overview of, 7-6 to 7-7, 13-15 to 13-16
Q & A, 7-51 to 7-53, 13-20 to 13-22, 13-25 to 13-26
reconciling, 8-35
reservations, 7-10 to 7-11
Scope Options dialog box, 7-12
subnet addresses and, 7-30 to 7-31
troubleshooting DHCP client, 8-31
verifying, 8-32 to 8-34
Secedit
Import setting, 11-10
Mergedpolicy setting, 11-11
overview of, 11-10 to 11-11
Overwrite setting, 11-11
Q & A, 15-8 to 15-9, 15-13
Quiet setting, 11-11
RBK setting, 11-11
Rollback setting, 11-10
secure networks, 15-5
Validate setting, 11-10
secondary servers
deploying, 5-37 to 5-40
notification/zone transfer initiation, 5-36 to 5-37
overview of, 4-30
Q & A, 5-81, 5-83 to 5-84
secondary zones
defined, 4-29
Q & A, 5-87
reconfiguring zone as, 5-22
zone transfers and, 5-35
Secret field, RADIUS servers, 10-76
Secure Cache Against Pollution, DNS server properties, 5-49
secure channel (SA), IKE, 11-29 to 11-31
secure dynamic updates
overview of, 5-28 to 5-29
performance counters, 6-26
Q & A, 7-53
securedc, security templates, 11-8

security
advanced settings, 10-13 to 10-17
DHCP servers, 7-5
dial-back security, 13-28, 13-31
disabling NetBIOS and, 4-7 to 4-8
further reading, 15-3
Group Policy settings, 15-5
groups, 6-27
IKE algorithms, 11-59
key exchange, 11-58
locked-down packet filtering, 9-71 to 9-72
Microsoft Windows Server 2003, 15-4
Microsoft Windows Server 2003 white paper, 11-7
network interfaces, 9-31
network protocol. *see* network protocols
overview of, 15-1 to 15-2
RAS servers and, 16-1
RIP properties, 9-58 to 9-60
software updates, 15-16 to 15-19
tested skills/suggested practices, 15-2 to 15-3
Security Accounts Manager (SAM), 10-8
security administration
Administrator accounts and, 1-2
exam highlights, 11-87 to 11-88
lesson review, 11-22
network security protocols, 11-3 to 11-4
overview of, 15-5 to 15-6
practice exercises, 11-14 to 11-21
principle of least privilege, 11-13 to 11-14
Q & A, 11-89, 15-7 to 15-15
security templates, 11-4 to 11-12
Security Configuration and Analysis snap-in
overview of, 11-9
practice exercises, 11-14 to 11-21
Q & A, 11-89, 15-7 to 15-8, 15-12 to 15-13
secure networks, 15-5
security event logs
increasing information logged to, 11-72
Kerberos at computer boot, 11-42
Kerberos at user logon, 11-43 to 11-44
Kerberos in use, 11-74
troubleshooting IPSec policies, 11-73
security, RRAS

client side authentication protocols, 10-13 to
    10-17
DNS servers, 5-11 to 5-12
overview of, 9-8
RADIUS clients, 10-74 to 10-75
server side authentication protocols, 10-17 to
    10-19
security templates, 11-4 to 11-11
    baselines, 11-5 to 11-9
    default vs. custom, 11-15
    least privilege opportunities, 11-13
    network security settings, 11-12
    overview of, 15-5 to 15-6
    practice exercises, 11-14 to 11-21
    predefined, 15-5
    Q & A, 11-89, 15-7 to 15-15
    Secedit and, 11-10 to 11-11
    Security Configuration and Analysis snap-in
        and, 11-9
Security Templates snap-in
    baselines, 11-5 to 11-9
    browsing, 11-6
    overview of, 11-5
    templates, 15-5
Select Network Component Type dialog box,
    1-23 to 1-24
semicolon (;), 4-33
Serial Line Internet Protocol (SLIP), 16-39, 16-42
Serial Number text box, SOA tab, 5-31
Server command, Nslookup, 6-8
Server Message Block. see SMB (Server Message
    Block) protocol
server services, 12-31 to 12-40, 17-15 to 17-20
    case scenario, 12-40 to 12-41, 12-47 to 12-48
    dependency options, 12-31 to 12-33
    exam highlights, 12-42 to 12-43
    further reading, 17-3
    lesson review, 12-39 to 12-40
    overview of, 17-16
    practice exercises, 12-38 to 12-39
    Q & A, 12-46 to 12-47, 17-17 to 17-20
    recovery options, 12-33 to 12-37
    tested skills/suggested practices, 17-2
servers

Configure Your Server Wizard, 1-28
DHCP. see DHCP servers
DNS. see DNS servers
    primary, 4-29 to 4-30, 5-31, 5-36 to 5-37, 5-83 to
        5-84
    RADIUS, 10-76, 10-77
    RAS, 10-28, 10-40 to 10-42, 12-9, 16-1
    rogue, 7-5, 7-50, 12-26
    secondary, 4-30, 5-36 to 5-40, 5-81, 5-83 to 5-84
    slave, 5-7 to 5-8
    stub, 4-31, 14-8 to 14-9, 14-13
Service Controller utility (Sc.exe), 17-18, 17-20
service dependencies
    configuring, 12-38
    overview of, 12-32 to 12-33
    Q & A, 12-47
service location (SRV) resource records
    overview of, 4-36
    verifying for Active Directory in DNS, 5-14 to
        5-18
services. see network services
Services console
    DHCP server status, 7-23 to 7-24
    migrating DHCP server, 7-33
Services node, Computer Management console,
    12-31 to 12-32
session ticket, 11-88
Set All command, Nslookup, 6-5 to 6-6
Set Credentials command, demand-dial interface,
    9-30
Set IP Demand-Dial Filters command,
    demand-dial interface, 9-30
Set Querytype (set q) command, Nslookup, 6-7
Set Type command, Nslookup, 6-7
Shared Secret authentication, 11-34
Shiva Password Authentication Protocol. see SPAP
    (Shiva Password Authentication Protocol)
shortcut menu commands, demand-dial
    interfaces, 9-29 to 9-30
Shortest Path First (SPF) algorithm, 9-61
Show command, Netsh utility, 11-33
Show Mmsas All command, Netsh utility, 11-64
Show Qmsas All command, Netsh utility, 11-64
Shutdown /i command, DHCP leases, 8-29

Simple Network Management Protocol (SNMP), 1-35
slave servers, 5-7 to 5-8
slave zones, 5-8
SLIP (Serial Line Internet Protocol), 16-39, 16-42
smart cards
  EAP-TLS authentication protocol and, 10-16 to 10-17
  Q & A, 10-86
  Use Smart Card setting, 10-16 to 10-17
SMB (Server Message Block) protocol
  CIFS as extension of, 1-9, 1-32
  Network Monitor and, 3-12
SMS (Systems Management Server), 12-16
snap-ins
  Add/Remove Snap-In dialog box, 11-52
  Add Standalone Snap-Ins dialog box, 11-51 to 11-52
  IP security, 11-51 to 11-56
  Security Templates, 11-5 to 11-9, 15-5
SNMP (Simple Network Management Protocol), 1-35
SOA (start-of-authority) record
  configuring, 5-31 to 5-33
  defined, 4-31
Software Update Services (SUS), 15-16
software updates, 15-16 to 15-19
solicitations, router, 9-35
SPAP (Shiva Password Authentication Protocol)
  defined, 10-11
  features/exam tips, 10-11 to 10-12
  operating system support, 10-12 to 10-13
  security and, 10-13 to 10-14
SPF (Shortest Path First) algorithm, 9-61
split horizon, 16-27, 16-30
SRV (service location) resource records
  overview of, 4-36
  verifying for Active Directory in DNS, 5-14 to 5-18
stack, TCP/IP, 1-7
standard primary zones, 4-30

start-of-authority (SOA) record
  configuring, 5-31 to 5-33
  defined, 4-31
static IP addresses
  authorizing remote access connections, 10-27
  creating reservations, 7-11
  DHCP server installation, 7-4
  pools, 9-9, 10-5 to 10-6
  RRAS, 9-9
  troubleshooting, 13-27
Static mode, Netsh utility
  displaying IPSec Policy information, 11-32 to 11-33
  overview of, 11-32
  Q & A, 11-91
static routes
  adding, 9-22 to 9-24
  advantages/disadvantages, 9-24
  designing, 9-25
  dynamic routes compared with, 9-17 to 9-18
  extranet/router-to-router VPNs, 10-53
  guidelines, 9-20 to 9-21
  linking to dial-on-demand connections, 9-37
  multiple-routers using, 9-19
  Q & A, 16-26 to 16-32
  remote access connections, 10-27
  RIP vs., 9-25
  Update Routes command, 9-34
statistics
  IKE, 11-64
  IP Security Monitor, 11-35 to 11-37
Strict RFC name-checking method, 5-50 to 5-51
Strongest Encryption (MPPE 128-Bit)
  defined, 10-33
  Q & A, 10-87
stub areas, 9-62
stub servers
  overview of, 4-31
  Q & A, 14-8 to 14-9, 14-13
stub zones, 5-65 to 5-76
  benefits of, 5-66
  case scenario, 5-73 to 5-75, 5-87 to 5-88
  defined, 4-29

DNS servers hosting, 4-31
exam highlights, 5-78
lesson review, 5-72
overview of, 5-65 to 5-66
practice exercise, 5-71 to 5-72
Q & A, 5-87
reconfiguring zone as, 5-22
updating, 5-70
when to use, 5-66 to 5-70
subnet masks, 2-22 to 2-32
address changes, 7-30 to 7-31
address ranges, 2-32
advantages of, 2-26 to 2-27
case scenario, 2-51 to 2-53
defining, 2-24 to 2-25
exam highlights, 2-54 to 2-55
examples, 2-30 to 2-31
excluding all Os/1s host IDs, 2-27
host capacity, 2-27 to 2-29
lesson review, 2-19 to 2-20, 2-40 to 2-41
network prefixes and, 2-17, 2-19, 2-57
overview of, 1-9, 2-16 to 2-17, 2-22 to 2-23
practice exercises, 2-37 to 2-40
Q & A, 2-56 to 2-61, 13-8 to 13-14, 13-24 to
    13-26, 16-28, 16-31
remote access authorization and, 10-27
supernetting vs., 2-32 to 2-33
TCP/IP addressing, 13-7 to 13-13
variable-length, 2-34 to 2-37
suite, TCP/IP, 1-7
summary pane, Frame Viewer window, 3-10
supernetting
CIDR, 2-33 to 2-34
overview of, 2-32 to 2-33
Q & A, 13-8, 13-11
TCP/IP addressing, 13-7
superscopes, 7-26 to 7-30
creating, 7-26 to 7-27
local multinets and, 7-27 to 7-28
New Superscope menu command, 7-27
overview of, 7-26
practice exercise, 7-37 to 7-39
Q & A, 7-53

remote multinets, 7-28
for two local DHCP servers, 7-28 to 7-30
SUS (Software Update Services), 15-16
System Configuration utility (Msconfig.exe),
    17-18, 17-20
system error log, DHCP, 8-35 to 8-37, 13-36
System log, Event Viewer
Network Monitor and, 15-29
troubleshooting server services, 12-34 to 12-35
System Monitor
DNS performance monitoring, 6-24 to 6-27
Q & A, 17-7, 17-10
System Properties dialog box, 4-45 to 4-46
system services, security templates, 11-6
Systems Management Server (SMS), 12-16

T

Task Manager
networking options, 12-3 to 12-6
overview of, 12-3 to 12-6
Performance console and, 12-9
PIDs and, 12-14 to 12-15
practice exercise, 12-17
TCP/IP
addressing. *see* IP addresses
case scenario, 2-51 to 2-53, 2-62
CIDR and, 2-33 to 2-34
configuring, 2-44 to 2-46
configuring for DNS clients, 4-53 to 4-54
exam highlights, 2-54 to 2-55
installing, 2-42 to 2-43
layers, 1-7, 2-3 to 2-6
monitoring network traffic. *see* Network
  Monitor
overview of, 2-4 to 2-5
Q & A, 2-56 to 2-62
routing, 16-26 to 16-32
subnetting. *see* subnet masks
supernetting, 2-32 to 2-34
variable-length subnet masks, 2-34 to 2-37
viewing default settings, 1-16
viewing network connection components, 1-14

TCP/IP connections, 3-19 to 3-35
    ARP tool, 3-26
    case scenario, 3-31 to 3-33, 3-38 to 3-39
    exam highlights, 3-35
    faulty configuration, 3-19 to 3-20
    further reading, 13-5
    lesson review, 3-30 to 3-31
    monitoring. *see* Network Monitor
    Network Diagnostics, 3-20 to 3-23
    overview of, 13-27
    PathPing, 3-23 to 3-25
    Ping, 3-23 to 3-25
    practice exercises, 3-26 to 3-30
    Q & A, 3-37 to 3-38, 13-28 to 13-34
    tested skills/suggested practices, 13-3
    Tracert, 3-25 to 3-26
TCP/IP properties
    alternate configuration options, 2-45 to 2-46
    automatic configuration, 2-44
    connection-specific DNS suffixes, 4-46 to 4-48
    custom DNS suffix search lists, 4-51
    default client update behavior, 4-52
    DHCP clients, 7-13 to 7-14
    DNS servers, 4-48 to 4-49
    IP addressing, 2-43 to 2-44
    manual configuration, 2-47
TCP/IP reference model
    layers, 1-7, 2-3 to 2-6
    Q & A, 2-56
TCP/IP Statistics command, 9-34
TCP (Transmission Control Protocol)
    fast zone transfer and, 4-30
    Q & A, 2-56
TCPv4 performance object, 12-8
TCPv6 performance object, 12-8
telephone lines, PSTN, 10-4
templates, 11-13 to 11-14. *see also* security
    templates
Terminal Services, 1-15 to 1-16
TGT (Ticket Granting Ticket)
    defined, 11-88
    Kerberos at computer boot, 11-41 to 11-43
    Kerberos at user logon, 11-43 to 11-45
    Kerberos authentication, 11-45 to 11-46

Time Before Routes Expire setting, IP routing,
    16-27, 16-30
Time-Out (Second) field, RADIUS servers, 10-76
time skew, 11-45
Time to Live. *see* TTL (Time to Live) values
Times options, Kerbtray, 11-46 to 11-47
topology
    defined, 1-3
    physical, 2-25 to 2-26
Total Query Received, DNS performance counter,
    6-26
Total Query Received/Sec, DNS performance
    counter, 6-26
Total Response Sent, DNS performance counter,
    6-26
Total Response Sent/Sec, DNS performance
    counter, 6-26
Tracert utility
    overview of, 3-25 to 3-26
    Q & A, 13-29, 13-33
    troubleshooting TCP/IP addressing, 13-27,
        13-33
traffic, DHCP. *see* DHCP traffic
trailing dot (.), 4-13
transient problems, 12-3
transport layer, TCP/IP
    Network Monitor and, 3-12
    overview of, 2-4
    Q & A, 2-56
triggers
    dynamic update, 5-28
    Network Monitor, 12-16 to 12-17
    Performance console alerts, 12-9 to 12-13
Triple Data Encryption Standard (3DES)
    defined, 10-85
    Q & A, 16-10, 16-16
troubleshooting
    APIPA, 1-18 to 1-19
    demand-dial routing, 9-37 to 9-38
    DHCP. *see* DHCP, troubleshooting
    dial-up connections, 10-39 to 10-40
    DNS. *see* DNS troubleshooting
    DNS clients, 4-61 to 4-62
    intermittent problems, 12-3

Internet connectivity. *see* Internet connectivity
IP addresses, IP addressing, troubleshooting
NAT, 9-46
network protocols. *see* network protocols,
    troubleshooting
network traffic. *see* Network Monitor
RAS clients, 16-38 to 16-43
RAS servers, 10-41 to 10-42
server services. *see* server services
TCP/IP connections. *see* TCP/IP connections
VPNs, 10-55
troubleshooting labs
    demand-dial routing, 9-76 to 9-77, 9-85
    DHCP, 7-48, 8-40, 8-48
    DNS, 6-30 to 6-32, 6-38
    IAS, 10-83
    IPSec, 11-82 to 11-86, 11-94 to 11-97
    name resolution, 4-61 to 4-62
    NAT configuration, 9-76 to 9-77, 9-85
TTL (Time to Live) values
    Minimum (Default) TTL box, 5-32
    overview of, 4-23
    Q & A, 5-82, 14-28, 14-32 to 14-33
    resource record formats, 4-33
    resource records and, 5-32
    SOA resource record and, 5-33
    troubleshooting with Tracert, 3-25
tunneling, VPN, 16-35, 16-37
Type field, resource records, 4-33

U
UDP ports, 2-5, 2-56
Unauthenticated Access option, PAP, 10-11 to
    10-12
unicast messages, RIP, 9-61
Unicode, 5-49
unnumbered connections, 9-24
Unreachability Reason command, demand-dial
    interface, 9-30
Update Routes command, IP routing, 9-34
updates
    default client, 4-52
    DNS. *see* DNS updates

Dynamic DNS, 4-51 to 4-52
    software, 15-16 to 15-19
upgrades, predefined security templates, 15-5
user accounts, dial-in properties
    authorization, 10-34 to 10-39
    practice exercises, 10-43 to 10-47
    remote access permissions, 10-24 to 10-26
user classes, 7-34 to 7-36
UTF-8 (Multibyte), 5-49 to 5-51

V
Validate setting, Secedit, 11-10
variable-length subnet masks. *see* VLSMs
    (variable-length subnet masks)
vendor classes, 7-34
*Virtual Private Networking with Microsoft
    Windows Server 2003: Overview*, 16-5
virtual private networks. *see* VPNs (virtual private
    networks)
VLSMs (variable-length subnet masks)
    defined, 2-55
    lesson review, 2-40 to 2-41
    overview of, 2-34 to 2-37
VPNs (virtual private networks), 10-49 to 10-68
    case scenario, 10-82 to 10-83, 10-88
    configuring, 10-56 to 10-61
    defined, 10-58
    deploying routing protocols over, 10-53 to
        10-54
    deployment scenarios, 10-50 to 10-51
    exam highlights, 10-84 to 10-85
    extranet/router-to-router, 10-51 to 10-53
    lesson review, 10-67 to 10-68
    mixed, 10-54
    overview of, 10-49 to 10-50
    Q & A, 10-87, 15-24 to 15-28, 16-11, 16-13,
        16-16 to 16-25, 16-35 to 16-43
    remote access permissions, 10-25
    troubleshooting, 10-55 to 10-56
VPNs (virtual private networks), practice
    exercises
    adding VPN access as remote policy condition,
        10-61 to 10-62

VPNs (virtual private networks), practice exercises, *continued*
  creating connection through L2TP/IPSec, 10-65 to 10-66
  creating PPTP-type VPN connection, 10-62 to 10-64
  logging onto domain through, 10-64 to 10-65

W

WANs (wide area networks)
  managing DHCP with Netsh, 7-24
  security, 16-2
  static routing and, 9-24
WAP (Wireless Access Point), 12-26 to 12-28
Web Edition, Microsoft Windows Server 2003, 1-3
Web site information
  IKE negotiation, 11-29
  IPSec, 11-25
  root hints updates, 5-9
Web site information, Microsoft
  certificate-based L2TP/IPSec deployment, 10-60
  IP addressing, 13-4 to 13-5
  IPSec features for 2003, 11-26 to 11-27
  Kerberos, 11-39
  name resolution, 14-4
  network infrastructure, 17-3
  Registry settings, adding to security templates, 11-9
  RRAS, 16-5 to 16-6
  security templates, 11-7
wide area networks. *see* WANs (wide area networks)
wildcard (*), 15-5
Windows. *see* Microsoft
Windows Explorer, 4-7
Windows Update
  catalog, 15-16
  overview of, 15-16
  Q & A, 15-17 to 15-18
WINS tab, zone properties, 5-34
WINS (Windows Internet Name Service)
  configuring with WINS tab, 5-34
  lookup counters, 6-25
Wireless Access Point (WAP), 12-26 to 12-28

wireless networks, 12-26 to 12-28
workgroups
  default networking and, 1-20
  grouping computers into, 1-9

Y

Yiaddr (Your IP Address) field, 8-8 to 8-9

Z

Zone Aging/Scavenging Properties dialog box, 5-29 to 5-30
zone delegation, 5-56 to 5-65
  case scenario, 5-73 to 5-75, 5-87 to 5-88
  creating, 5-59 to 5-62
  exam highlights, 5-78
  example of, 5-56
  lesson review, 5-62 to 5-64
  New Delegation Wizard, 5-59, 5-61
  overview of, 5-57 to 5-59
  Q & A, 5-85 to 5-87, 14-30, 14-33
  records, 5-58
  when to use, 5-57
zone properties, 5-20 to 5-42
  aging, 5-29 to 5-30
  case scenario, 5-73 to 5-75, 5-87 to 5-88
  dynamic updates, 5-26 to 5-29
  exam highlights, 5-78
  filenames, 5-26
  lesson review, 5-40 to 5-41
  name server (NS) options, 5-33 to 5-34
  no-refresh intervals, 5-30
  opening dialog box, 5-20 to 5-21
  practice exercises, 5-37 to 5-40
  Q & A, 5-80 to 5-82
  refresh intervals, 5-30
  replication, 5-23 to 5-26
  scavenging, 5-30 to 5-31
  start-of-authority (SOA) options, 5-31 to 5-33
  transfer options, 5-34 to 5-37
  WINS options, 5-34
  zone status, 5-22
  zone type, 5-22 to 5-23

zone transfers
  BIND compatibility and, 5-45 to 5-46
  configuring, 5-34 to 5-37
  DNS performance counters for, 6-25, 6-27
  Fail On Load If Bad Zone data, 5-46
  Microsoft Windows 2000, 5-35
  notification settings, 5-35 to 5-37, 5-39 to 5-40,
    6-25, 6-27
  Nslookup and, 6-8
  Q & A, 5-81 to 5-84, 14-22, 14-27
zones
  Active Directory-integrated, 4-30, 5-22 to 5-24,
    6-20 to 6-24
  creating, 4-28
  DomainDnsZones, 5-25, 6-28, 6-36
  fast zone transfer and, 4-30
  filenames, 5-26
  ForestDnsZones, 5-25
  loading on startup, 5-51
  New Zone Wizard, 4-28 to 4-29
  primary zones, 4-29, 5-22, 5-34 to 5-35
  Q & A, 5-82
  secondary zones, 4-29, 5-22, 5-35, 5-87
  slave zones, 5-8
  standard primary, 4-30
  status of, 5-22
  stub zones, 4-29, 4-31, 5-22, 5-65 to 5-76, 5-78,
    5-87 to 5-88

how to:

Make sure your training doesn't end here.

Want to help your Windows Server™ 2003 knowledge stay sharp? Subscribe to TechNet, the definitive resource IT professionals rely on to plan, deploy, manage, and support Microsoft® products. Enhance your career development with monthly technology updates direct from the source — all in a portable package of CDs or DVDs that goes wherever the job takes you.

Subscribe now and get 20% off our yearly rate.*

www.microsoft.com/technet/buynow/keeplearning or call 1-800-344-2121
Use promotion code: T20001

 **know how.**

Microsoft

CONFIDENT.
INTELLIGENT.
SECURE.

She must be a Microsoft Certified Professional.
She must have just tested with Pearson VUE.

Use the valuable Microsoft voucher included in this book at any Pearson VUE™ Authorized Center worldwide!

MCSA/MCSE certification on Microsoft Windows Server 2003 validates your technical expertise and enhances your credibility in the marketplace. Simply put, it helps position you as a strategic asset to employers.

At Pearson VUE, scheduling your exam is easy and convenient. Your exam results are securely and accurately merged with the Microsoft database — and your exam will be ready when you are.

Test with Pearson VUE

Visit www.PearsonVUE.com or call 1-800-TEST-REG
(North America only) **to schedule your exam.**

Pearson VUE has 3400+ test centers in 130 countries. For a toll-free phone number in your area or the location of a test center near you, visit www.PearsonVUE.com.

Focused on your future

Microsoft®
C E R T I F I E D
Exam Provider

MEASUREUP
Know what you know™
Official practice exam provider
of Pearson VUE

Microsoft® Windows® Server 2003 Enterprise Edition 180-Day Evaluation

The software included in this kit is intended for evaluation and deployment planning purposes only. If you plan to install the software on your primary machine, it is recommended that you back up your existing data prior to installation.

System requirements

To use Microsoft Windows Server 2003 Enterprise Edition, you need:

- Computer with 550 MHz or higher processor clock speed recommended; 133 MHz minimum required; Intel Pentium/Celeron family, or AMD K6/Athlon/Duron family, or compatible processor (Windows Server 2003 Enterprise Edition supports up to eight CPUs on one server)
- 256 MB of RAM or higher recommended; 128 MB minimum required (maximum 32 GB of RAM)
- 1.25 to 2 GB of available hard-disk space*
- CD-ROM or DVD-ROM drive
- Super VGA (800 × 600) or higher-resolution monitor recommended; VGA or hardware that supports console redirection required
- Keyboard and Microsoft Mouse or compatible pointing device, or hardware that supports console redirection

Additional items or services required to use certain Windows Server 2003 Enterprise Edition features:

- For Internet access:
  - Some Internet functionality may require Internet access, a Microsoft Passport account, and payment of a separate fee to a service provider; local and/or long-distance telephone toll charges may apply
  - High-speed modem or broadband Internet connection
- For networking:
  - Network adapter appropriate for the type of local-area, wide-area, wireless, or home network to which you wish to connect, and access to an appropriate network infrastructure; access to third-party networks may require additional charges

Note: To ensure that your applications and hardware are Windows Server 2003–ready, be sure to visit **www.microsoft.com/windowsserver2003**.

* Actual requirements will vary based on your system configuration and the applications and features you choose to install. Additional available hard-disk space may be required if you are installing over a network. For more information, please see **www.microsoft.com/windowsserver2003**.

Uninstall instructions

This time-limited release of Microsoft Windows Server 2003 Enterprise Edition will expire 180 days after installation. If you decide to discontinue the use of this software, you will need to reinstall your original operating system. You may need to reformat your drive.

System Requirements

Hardware Requirements

To complete the exercises in Part 1, you need to meet the following minimum system requirements:

- Microsoft Windows Server 2003, Enterprise Edition (A 180-day evaluation edition of Windows Server 2003, Enterprise Edition, is included on the CD-ROM).

- Microsoft Windows XP Professional—Optional (Not included on the CD-ROM. This software is required in optional hands-on exercises only).

- Minimum CPU: 133 MHz for *x*86-based computers and 733 MHz for Itanium-based computers (733 MHz is recommended).

- Display monitor capable of 800 x 600 resolution or higher.

- Minimum RAM: 128 MB (256 MB is recommended).

- Disk space for setup: 1.5 GB for *x*86-based computers and 2.0 GB for Itanium-based computers.

- CD-ROM or DVD-ROM drive.

- Microsoft Mouse or compatible pointing device.

To read the eBooks on a Pocket PC, the Pocket PC must meet the following minimum system requirements:

- Microsoft Pocket PC 2002 or later.

- Adobe Acrobat Reader 1.0 or later. (Visit the Adobe Web site for system requirements for running Acrobat Reader on a Pocket PC.)

- ActiveSync 3.1 or later.

- 16 MB or RAM (32 MB recommended).

- A built-in or add-on Flash Card adapter and CompactFlash or Secure Digital Media Card recommended.

Uninstall Instructions

The time-limited release of Microsoft Windows Server 2003, Enterprise Edition, will expire 180 days after installation. If you decide to discontinue the use of this software, you will need to reinstall your original operating system. You may need to reformat your drive.